# Studies in the Scriptures 1926-27

Volume 3
of
17 Volume Set

# Studies in the Scriptures
# 1926-27

## Volume 3
## of
## 17 Volume Set

### Arthur W. Pink

Sovereign Grace Publishers, Inc.
P.O. Box 4998
Lafayette, IN 47903
2001

*A. W. Pink's Studies in the Scriptures,*
**Volume 3 of 17 Vols - 1926-27 - Paperback Edition**
*Copyright © 2001
By Jay P. Green, Sr.
All Rights Reserved*

*Volume 1 = ISBN 1-58960-232-3*

# Studies in the Scriptures -- 1926
# Index

| | | |
|---|---|---|
| The Gospel of John | John 14:12-20 | 2 |
| Gleanings of Exodus | Exodus 17 | 9 |
| The Sovereignty of God | | 13 |
| The Power of God | Job 26:14 | 19 |
| A Perverted Gospel | | 22 |
| Gone Astray--Now Returned | 1 Peter 2:25 | 23 |
| The Gospel of John | John 14:21-31 | 26 |
| Gleanings in Exodus | Exodus 18 | 34 |
| Election | | 39 |
| God Securing His Inheritance | Deut 32:10 | 45 |
| The Gospel of John | John 15:1-6 | 50 |
| Gleanings from Exodus | Exodus 19 | 58 |
| Progressive Sanctification | | 63 |
| Divine Preservation | | 64 |
| Election | | 65 |
| The Gospel of John | John 15:7-16 | 74 |
| Gleanings in Exodus | Exodus 20 | 82 |
| Election | | 86 |
| "Accepted in the Beloved." | Eph. 1:5-6 | 94 |
| Sorrowful yet Always Rejoicing | 2 Cor. 6:10 | 95 |
| The Gospel of John | John 15:17, 27 | 98 |
| Gleanings in Exodus | Exodus 20 | 105 |
| Election | | 109 |
| In Regions Beyond | | 116 |
| The Pleasure of God | | 118 |
| The Gospel of John | John 16:1-11 | 122 |
| Gleanings in Exodus | Exodus 20 | 130 |
| Election | | 134 |
| Beholding | Psa. 34:5 | 141 |
| Repentance | | 143 |
| The Gospel of John | John 16:12-22 | 146 |
| Gleanings in Exodus | Exodus 21:1-6 | 154 |
| Human Responsibility | | 159 |
| Times of Trouble | | 164 |
| Divine Chastisement | Heb. 12:5 | 166 |
| Missionary Tidings | | 167 |
| The Gospel of John | John 16:23-33 | 170 |
| Gleanings in Exodus | Exodus 24 | 177 |
| Truth and Error | Jer. 33:3 | 181 |
| A Message of Comfort | Rom 8:32 | 187 |

| | | |
|---|---|---|
| Encouraging News | | 190 |
| The Gospel of John | John 17:1-5 | 194 |
| Gleanings in Exodus | Exodus 25-40 | 202 |
| Truth and Error | Luke 24:45 | 207 |
| Divine Chastisement | Heb. 13:5 | 212 |
| Good News | | 215 |
| The Gospel of John | John 17:6-12 | 218 |
| Gleanings in Exodus | Exodus 25:1-9 | 226 |
| Truth and Error | Luke 24:45 | 230 |
| Waiting | | 235 |
| Divine Chastisement | Heb. 12:5 | 237 |
| Unanswered Prayer | | 238 |
| The Gospel of John | John 17:13-19 | 242 |
| Gleanings in Exodus | Exodus 25:10-16 | 249 |
| Truth and Error | | 254 |
| Headship | | 257 |
| The Gospel of John | John 17:20-26 | 266 |
| Gleanings in Exodus | | 273 |
| Truth and Error | Jude 12 | 277 |
| The Sin of Unbelief | 1 John 5:10 | 281 |
| A Missionary Address | | 284 |

# Studies in the Scriptures -- 1927
# Index

| | | |
|---|---|---|
| The Gospel of John | John 18:1-11 | 2 |
| Gleanings in Exodus | Exodus 25:17-22 | 10 |
| The Jew in History | Hosea 3:4 | 21 |
| Expecting too Much of Fellow-Saints | | 23 |
| The Justification of God's Elect | Rom. 8:33 | 24 |
| The Gospel of John | John 18:12-27 | 26 |
| Gleanings in Exdous | Exodus 25:23-30 | 34 |
| The Home-Going of a Saint | Phil. 1:21 | 39 |
| Divine Chastisement | Heb. 12:7, 8 | 44 |
| The Gospel of John | John 18:2-40 | 50 |
| Gleanings in Exodus | Exodus 25:31-40 | 57 |
| The Greatest Miracle | | 62 |
| Abiding in Christ | | 66 |
| The Jew in Prophecy | Hosea 3:4, 5 | 69 |
| Jude 11 | | 71 |
| The Gospel of John | John 19:1-11 | 74 |
| Gleanings in Exodus | Exodus 26:1-14 | 81 |
| Acceptable Gifts | 1 Peter 2:5 | 86 |
| Tithing (No. 1) | | 90 |
| The Gospel of John | John 19:12-24 | 98 |
| Gleanings in Exodus | Exodus 26:7-14 | 105 |
| Tithing (No. 2) | Malachi 3:10 | 109 |
| Experimental Salvation | | 114 |
| Perfected for Ever | | 118 |
| The Gospel of John | John 19:25-42 | 122 |
| Gleanings in Exodus | Exodus 26:15-30 | 130 |
| Midnight at Midday | Matt 27:45 | 135 |
| Assurance | Rom. 8:16 | 139 |
| The Gospel of John | John 20:1-10 | 146 |
| Gleanings in Exodus | Exodus 25:31-33 | 153 |
| Cross-Bearing | Matt 16:24 | 158 |
| Blind Bartimaeus | | 162 |
| Financial Fellowship | | 167 |
| The Gospel of John | John 20:11-23 | 170 |
| Gleanings in Exodus | Exodus 26:36-37 | 180 |
| Songs in the Night | | 185 |
| Distinguishing Grace | 2 Tim 1:9 | 186 |
| Security | John 3:16 | 191 |
| The Gospel of John | John 20:24-31 | 194 |
| Gleanings in Exodus | Exodus 27:1-8 | 200 |

| | | |
|---|---|---|
| The Prophetic Parables of Matthew 13 | Matt. 13 | 205 |
| The Lawgiver | Psa. 119:4 | 209 |
| Forbidden Mixtures | Deut. 22:9-11 | 211 |
| Triumphant Faith | | 214 |
| The Gospel of John | John 21:1-14 | 218 |
| Gleanings in Exodus | Ex. 27:9-19 | 225 |
| The Prophetic Parables of Matthew 13 | Matt. 13 | 229 |
| A Live Coal | Isaiah 6:6, 7 | 232 |
| Testimony of Leland Wang | Psa. 66:16; Gal. 2:20; 1 Tim 1:15 | 235 |
| The Path of Faith | | 237 |
| Things to Come | | 238 |
| The Gospel of John | John 21:15-25 | 242 |
| Gleanings in Exodus | Ex. 27:20-28:2 | 249 |
| The Prophetic Parables of Matthew 13 | Matt. 13 | 253 |
| Gospel Responsibility | 2 Thess. 1:8 | 256 |
| On Glorifying God | Isa. 55:8 | 262 |
| John's Gospel | | 266 |
| Gleanings in Exodus | Ex. 28 | 269 |
| The Prophetic Parables of Matthew 13 | Matt. 13 | 273 |
| The Churches of God | 1 Thess. 2:14 | 277 |
| Divine Chastisement | Heb. 11:11 | 281 |
| Rejoicing Over Election | Luke 10:20 | 284 |
| Cloven Tongues | Acts 2:1-11 | 286 |

# STUDIES IN THE SCRIPTURES

"Search the Scriptures" John 5:39.

Copyright in all English-speaking Countries.

Arthur W. Pink, Publisher and Editor,
5 Norton Street, Ashfield, N.S.W., Australia.

Price: 10 cents per copy; $1.00 or 5/- per year.

## A New Year's Message.

Another year has passed away—gone into eternity with all its sad and glad records. Sad, because of our sins and failures, all of which have been observed and recorded by the All-seeing One. Sad, because of the increasing "falling away" which we now see on every side. Sad, because numbers who "did run well" do so no longer. Glad, because of the "goodness and mercy" which have surely followed us day by day. Glad, because some have been plucked as brands from the burning. Glad, because weak ones have been strengthened, sorrowing ones comforted, hungry ones fed. How has it been with you—progression or retrogression?

One thing is certain: January, 1926, finds you one year nearer to Heaven or nearer to Hell, whose denizens are forever separated from God. Reader, you have entered this New Year either accepted in God's Beloved or under God's holy wrath. How unspeakably solemn the alternative! To any unsaved reader who scans these lines we would say, this year commenced on earth may end for you in Hell, where never a ray of hope enters! O heed the Divine admonition: "Acquaint now thyself with God, and be at peace, thereby good shall come unto thee" (Job 22:21).

To the Christian—not to the professing one, but to the **real** believer—we would say, What a bright hope is ours! How precious the thought that ere 1926 ends we may be "forever with the Lord"! The bud of promise may have burst into the full fruit of bliss unspeakable. The springtime of faith and hope may have given place to the unending summertime of blessedness and glorious consummation. Since this be the case, let us be reminded of our solemn responsibility at the dawn of another year to yield ourselves afresh to God, to seek His face with full purpose of heart, to supplicate Him for new supplies of grace, that we may serve Him and witness for Him as never before. "Knowing the time, that now it is high time to awake out of sleep: for now is our salvation nearer than when we believed. The night is far spent, the day is at hand: let us therefore cast off the works of darkness, and let us put on the armour of light" (Rom. 13:11, 12).

"O God, Thou art my God, early will I seek Thee: my soul thirsteth for Thee, my flesh longeth for Thee in a dry and thirsty land, where no water is" (Psa. 63:1). These are the words which have been brought home in power to the heart of the writer: may it please the Spirit of Grace to apply them in blessing to each Christian reader. Surely they form a suitable motto for the New Year.

In this verse we have first a personal relationship avowed: "O God, Thou art **my** God." Fellow-Christian, who can begin to grasp what these words signify! You know something of the difference between looking upon a woman that is almost a stranger and saying, "She is Mrs. So-and-So, and looking upon another and saying, "This is **my** mother, or **my** wife," but this is nothing in comparison with the difference between one who is a stranger to His grace speaking about "God," and one who has passed from death unto life looking

(Continued on page 24)

## IMPORTANT NOTICES

Set of twelve issues for **1922**, unbound, **$1.00** or **5/-**. Bound **$1.50** or **7/-**.

Set of twelve issues for **1923**, unbound, **$1.00** or **5/-**. Bound **$1.50** or **7/-**.

Set of twelve issues for **1924**, unbound, **$1.00** or **5/-**. Bound **$1.50** or **7/-**.

Set of twelve issues for **1925**, unbound, **$1.00** or **5/-**. Bound **$1.50** or **7/-**.

Note: We cannot break a set or now supply any single 1925 issues.

Subscription—price: **$1.00** or **5/-** per year to any address in the world.

Change of Address: Please notify me promptly of any change of address, and be certain to give both old and new address.

Non-subscribers receiving this Magazine regularly will understand their subscription has been entered by a friend.

Copies lost in the mail duplicated only if we are notified promptly.

## CONTENTS

| | |
|---|---|
| The Gospel of John (John 14: 12-20) | 2 |
| Gleanings in Exodus | 9 |
| The Sovereignty of God | 13 |
| The Power of God | 19 |
| A Perverted Gospel | 22 |

## THE GOSPEL OF JOHN

**49. Christ Comforting His Disciples, continued: John 14: 12-20.**

Below is an analysis of the passage which is to be before us:—

1. Christ's cause furthered by His return to the Father v. 12.
2. Praying in the Name of Christ vv. 13, 14.
3. Love evidenced by obedience v. 15.
4. The coming of the Comforter vv. 16, 17.
5. Christians not left orphans v. 8.
6. Our life secured by Christ's v. 19.
7. Knowledge of Divine life in believers v. 20.

At first reading there does not appear to be much direct connection between the several verses of our present passage. This second section of John 14 seems to lack a central unity. Yet, as we read it more attentively, we notice that both v. 13 and v. 16 open with the word "And," which at once makes us suspect that our first hasty impression needs correcting. The fact is that the more closely this Pascal Discourse of Christ be studied, the more shall we perceive the close connection which one part of it sustains to another, and many important lessons will be learned by noting the relation which verse has to verse.

The first verse of our passage opens with the remarkable promise that the apostles of Christ should do even greater works than their Master had done. Then, in the next two verses reference is made to **prayer**, and the fact that these are prefaced with the word "And" at once indicates that there is an intimate relation between the doing of these works and the supplicating of God. This is the more striking if we recall the central thing in the former section. The opening verse of John 14 is a Call to Faith in Christ, and the closing verse (11) repeats it. Following the word upon prayer, the Lord next said, "If you love Me, keep My commandments" (v 15). Here we seem to lose the thread again, for apparently a new subject is most abruptly introduced. But only seemingly so, for, in truth, it is just here that we discover the **progress** of thought. The **faith** and the **praying** (the two essential pre-requisites for the doing of the "greater works") have their root in an already existing **love**, which is now to be evidenced by pleasing its object. What comes next next? The promise of "another Comforter." Surely this is most suggestive. It was only by the coming of the Holy Spirit that the apostles' faith in Christ was established, that power was communicated for the performing of mighty works, and that their love was purified and deepened. Thus we have a most striking example of the importance and value of studying closely the connection of a passage and noting the relation of one verse to another.

Having remarked upon the relation between the verses of our present passage, let a brief word be said upon the connection which exists between it as a **whole** and the first section of John 14. The Lord began by saying, "Let not your heart be troubled." All that followed was the assigning of various reasons why the apostles should not be so excessively perturbed at the prospect of His approaching departure. He began by setting before them three chief grounds of comfort: **He** was going to the Father's House of many mansions.

He was going there to prepare a place for them. When His preparations were complete, He would come for them in person to conduct them to Heaven, so that His place might be theirs forever. Then He had been interrupted by the question of Thomas and the request of Philip, and in response He had stated with great plainness the truth concerning both His person and His mission. Now, in the section before us, the Lord brings forward further reasons why the sorrowing disciples should not let their hearts be troubled. These additional grounds of consolation will come before us in the course of our exposition.

Though the Lord continues in this second section of His Discourse what He began in the first, yet there is a striking **advance** to be noted. At the beginning of John 14, Christ had referred to what the apostles **should** have known, namely, that the Son on earth had perfectly declared the Father, and this ought to have been the means of their apprehending **whither** He was going. This they knew (v 4), however dull they might be in perceiving the consequences. But now the Lord discloses to them that which they **could not** understand till the Holy Spirit was given. It was by the descent of the Comforter that they would be guided into **all** truth. It was by the Holy Spirit that Christ would come to them (v 18). And it was by the Spirit they would know that Christ was in the Father, and they in Him and He in them. The Lord did not say that they ought to have understood, even then, **these** things: the apprehension of them would not be until the day of Pentecost.

"Verily, verily, I say unto you, He that believeth on Me, the works that I do shall he do also" (v. 12). The "works" of which Christ here spake were His **miraculous** works, the same as those spoken of in the two preceding verses, works to which He appealed as proofs of His Divine person and mission. The one to whom Christ promised this was "He that believeth on Me." Some have understood this to refer to all the genuine followers of Christ. But this is manifestly wrong, for there is **no** Christian on earth to-day who can do the miracles which Christ did—cleanse the leper, give sight to the blind, raise the dead. To meet this difficulty it has been replied. This is due to a deficiency in the Christian's faith. But this is simply a begging of the question. Our Lord did not say, "He that believeth on Me **may** do the works that I do," but **shall** do!" But of whom, then, was Christ speaking?

We submit that "He that believeth on Me," like the expression "Them that believe" in Mark 16 : 17, of whom it was said certain miraculous signs should follow them, refers to a **particular** class of persons, and that these expressions must be modified by their reference and setting. In each case the promise was limited to those whom our Lord was addressing. "The only safe way of interpretating the whole of this Discourse, and many other passages in the Gospels, is to remember that it was addressed to **the apostles**—that everything in it has a **direct** reference to them—that much that is said of them, and to them, may be said of, and to, all Christian ministers, all Christian men—but that much that is said of them and to them, cannot be truly said either of the one or the other of those classes, and that the propriety of applying what is applicable to them, must be grounded on some other foundation than its being found in this Discourse.

"It is plain from the New Testament that there was a faith which was specially connected with miraculous powers. This faith was that Christ is possessed of omnipotence, and that He intends, through my instrumentality, to manifest His omnipotence in the performance of a miracle. But this faith, like all faith, **must rest on a Divine revelation made to the individual;** where this is not the case, there can be no faith—there may be fancy, there may be presumption, but there can be no faith. Such a revelation Christ made to the apostles and to the seventy disciples, when He said "Behold, I give unto **you** power to tread on serpents and scorpions, and over all the power of the enemy; and nothing shall by any means hurt **you**"(Luke 10 : 19). No man, to whom such a revelation **has not** been made, can work such miracles, and it would seem that even in the case of those to whom such a revelation was made, a firm belief of the revelation and reliance on the power and faithfulness of Him who made it, was necessary to the miracles being effectively produced in any particular instance.

"Keeping these undoubted facts in view, there is little difficulty in interpreting Christ's words here. The disciples had derived great advantage of various kinds from the exercise of their Master's power to work miracles. They were quite aware that if He should **leave them**, not only would they be deprived of the advantage of His superior powers, but that their own, which were entirely dependent on Him, would be withdrawn also. Now our Lord assures them in the most emphatic manner, by a repetition of the formula of affirmation, 'Verily, verily, I say unto you,' that His miraculous power was to **continue** to be exercised through them as a medium, and that, to its being exercised henceforth, as hitherto, faith on Him, on their part, would be at once necessary and effectual. Such a statement was obviously calculated to re-assure their shaken minds, and comfort their sorrowing hearts. And we find the declaration was filled to the letter. They, believing on Him, **did** the works which He did. We find them, like Him, instantaneously healing the sick, casting out demons, and raising the dead" (Dr. J. Brown). Hebrews 2:4 records the fulfilment of Christ's promise: "God also bearing them witness, both with signs and wonders, and with divers miracles, and gifts of the Holy Spirit."

"And greater than these shall he do" (v. 12). It is important to note that the word "works" in the second clause is **not** found in the original. We do not think Christ was now referring to miracles in the technical sense of that term, but to something else which, in magnitude and importance, would exceed the miracle done by Himself and the apostles. "Greater **things** would be better. What these greater things were it is not difficult to determine. The preaching of a risen and exalted Saviour, the proclaiming of the Gospel to "every creature," the turning of souls from darkness to light, and the power of Satan to the service of the living God, the causing of heathen to demolish with their own hands the temples of idolatry, the building of that Temple of living stones of which Christ is both the foundation and the chief-corner, and which far surpassed the temple at Jerusalem—these things were far greater than any interferences with the course of nature's laws. Thus did the Father honour His Son, owning the perfect work which He had done, by the greater wonders which the Holy Spirit effected through the disciples.

"Because I go unto My Father" (v 12). It is important to note how that in this "because" the Lord Jesus has Himself given us a partial explanation here of how His promise would be made good, though it is largely lost by placing a full stop at the end of v. 12. If we read straight on through v. 13 the Saviour's explanation is the more apparent: "Greater things than these shall he do, **because** I go unto My Father, **And** whatsoever ye shall ask in My name, that will I do." Christ would henceforth give to their prayers power from on high, so that what **they** did, **He** would do in and through them. Thus, in His "seed" was the pleasure of the Lord to prosper (Isa. 53:10). If the full stop be insisted on and its force rigidly pressed, v 12 would then teach that the disciples must now continue to work in the place of their Lord the still greater things **because He himself was no longer there.** But this is obviously wrong. He left them it is true; but He also returned to indwell them (v 18), and in this way came the **harvest** of His own seed-sowing. "And herein is that saying true, One soweth, and another reapeth. I sent you to reap that whereon ye bestowed no labour" (4:37, 38). Link v. 13 with v. 12 and all is plain and simple: thus connected we are taught that the greater things done by the apostles were, in reality, done by Christ Himself! as Mark 16:20 tells us, "And they went forth, and preached everywhere, the Lord working with them." But what He did was in answer to their believing prayers!

"And whatsoever ye shall ask in My name, that will I do, that the Father may be glorified in the Son" (v. 13). The connection of this with the whole context is very precious. Let it be kept steadily in mind that Christ was here **comforting** His disciples, who were troubled at the prospect of His leaving them, and that He was calling them to an **increased confidence** in Himself. In the previous verse He had just assured them that **His cause** would not suffer by His return to the Father, for even greater things should be done through and by them as a testimony of His glory. Now He reminds them that His **corporeal** absence would only unite these apostles to Him more intimately and more effectually in a spiritual way. True, He would be in Heaven, and they on earth, but **prayer** could remove all sense of distance, prayer could bring them into His very presence at any time, yea, prayer was all-essential if they were to do these "greater" things. And had he not already given them a perfect example? Had He not **shown** them that there was an intimate connection between the great works which He had done and the prayers which He had offered to the Father. Had they not heard Him repeatedly, "ask" the Father (see 6:11; 11:41; 12:28, etc)? Then let them do likewise. He was here **interpreting** His own words at the beginning of this Discourse: "Believe also in Me." Faith **in His person** was now to be manifested by prayer **in His name!**

"If ye shall ask any thing in My name, I will do it" (v. 14). Very blessed is this. The disciples were invited to count upon a power that could not fail, if sought aright. Christ was no mere man whose departure must necessarily bring to an end what He was wont to do upon earth. Though absent, He would manifest His Deity by granting their petitions: whatsoever they asked He would do. All power in heaven is His. The Father hath committed **all** judgment unto the Son (5:22) and in the exercise of this power He gives His own whatsoever they need.

"If ye shall ask any thing in My name, I will do it." What is meant by asking **in the name of Christ?** Certainly it is much more than the mere putting of His name at the end of our prayers, or simply saying, "Hear me for Jesus' sake." First, it means that we pray **in His person,** that is, as standing in His place, as fully identified with Him, asking by virtue of our very union with Himself. When we truly ask in the name of Christ, He is the real petitioner. Second, it means, therefore, that we plead before God the merits of His blessed Son. When men use another's name as the authority of their approach or the ground of their appeal to some one, the one of whom the request is made looks beyond him who presented the petition to the one for whose sake he grants the request. So, in all reverence, we may say, when we truly ask in the name of Christ, the Father looks past us, and sees the Son as the real suppliant. Third, it means that we pray only for that which is according to His perfections and what will be for His glory. When we do anything in another's name, it is **for** Him we do it. When we take possession of a property in the name of some society, it is not for our private advantage, but for the society's good. When an officer collects taxes in the name of the government, it is not in order to fill his own pockets. Yet how constantly do we overlook this principle as an obvious condition of acceptible prayer! To pray in Christ's name is to seek what He seeks, to promote what He has at heart!

"If ye shall ask any thing in My name, I will do it." From what has been said above it will be seen that Christ was very far from handing His disciples a 'blank check' (as some have expressed it), leaving **them to** fill it in and assuring them that God would honor it because it bore His Son's signature. Equally so is it a carnal delusion to suppose that a Christian has only to work himself up to an expectation to suppose that God will hear his prayer, in order to obtain what he asks for. To apply to God for any thing in the name of Christ the petition must be **in keeping with** what Christ is. We can only rightly ask God for that which will magnify His Son. To ask in the name of Christ is, therefore, to set aside our own will, and bow to the perfect will of God. If only we realised this more what a check it would be on our ofttimes rash and ill-considered requests! How many of our prayers would never be offered did we but pause to ask, Can I present **this** in that Name which is above every name?

"Not what I wish, but what I want,
O let Thy grace supply;
The good unasked, in mercy grant,
The ill, though asked, deny."
—Cowper.

"If ye love Me, keep My commandments" (v. 15). There seems to be a most abrupt change of subject here, and many have been puzzled in finding the connection. Let us first go back to the opening verse of our chapter. The apostles were troubled at heart at the prospect of their Master's departure, and this evidenced, unmistakably, their deep affection for Him. Here, with tender faithfulness, He **directs** their affection. Your love for Me is to be manifested not by inconsolable regrets, but by a glad and prompt compliance with My commandments. So much is clear; but what of the link with the more immediate context? In seeking the answer to this, let us ask? **"What is the leading subject** of the context?" This, as we have seen, is a call to **faith** in an ascended Christ: in the previous verse, a faith evidenced by praying in His name. Now He says, "If ye love Me, keep My commandments." Surely then the answer is plain: **love** is the **spring** of true **faith** and the **goal** of real **prayer.** "If ye shall ask any thing in My name, I will do it" He had just said, and this that the Father might be glorified in the Son. **For what,** then, shall we ask? is the natural inquiry which is now suggested? Here then is our Lord's response: an increase of **love** (in myself and in all who are Christ's) which will evidence itself by **doing** His will. Unless this be the first and foremost desire of our hearts, all other petitions will remain unanswered. "And whatsoever we ask, we receive of Him, **because** we keep His commandments, and do those things that are pleasing in His sight" (1 John 3:22).

"All sentimental talking and singing about love are vain. Unless, by grace, we show a truthful obedience, the profession of affection is worse than affectation. There is more hypocrisy than we suppose. Love is practical, or it is not love at all." (Mr. P. W. Heward.)

"If ye love Me, keep My commandments." How this verse rebukes the increasing Antinomianism of our day! In some circles one cannot use the word "Commandments" without being frowned upon as a "Legalist." Multitudes are now being taught that Law is the enemy of Grace, and that the God of Sinai is a stern and forbidding Deity laying upon His creatures a yoke grievious to be borne. Terrible travesty of the truth is this. The One who wrote upon the tables of stone is none other than Him who died on Calvary's cross; and He who here says "If ye **love Me**, KEEP MY COMMANDMENTS" also said at Sinai that He would show mercy unto thousands of them "that **love Me** and KEEP MY COMMANDMENTS!" It is indeed striking to note that this tender Saviour who was here comforting His sorrowing disciples, also maintained His Divine majesty and insisted upon the recognition of His Divine authority. Mark how His Deity appears here: "Keep **My** commandments": we never read of Moses or any of the prophets speaking of **their** commandments.

"If ye love Me, keep My commandments." What are Christ's commandments? We will let another answer: "The whole revelation of the Divine will, respecting what I am to believe and feel and do and suffer, contained in the Holy Scriptures is the law of Christ. Both volumes of Christ are the work of the Spirit of Christ. His first and great commandment is: 'Thou shalt love the Lord thy God with all thy heart, and soul, and strength'; and the second great commandment is like unto the first: 'Thou shalt love thy neighbour as thyself.' The commandments of Christ include whatever is good and whatever God hath required of us" (Dr. J. Brown). That the One who brought Israel out of Egypt, led them across the wilderness, and gave them the Law, was Christ Himself, is clear from 1 Cor. 10:9: "Neither let us tempt **Christ**, as some of them **also** tempted, and were destroyed by serpents" (cf. 1 Cor. 10:4).

"Obedience to the commandments of Christ is the test of love to Him, and there will be no difficulty in applying the test, if there be only an honest desire to have the question fairly settled; for there are certain qualities of obedience, which are to be found in every lover of Christ, and which are never found in any one else, and it is to these we must attend, if we would know what is our character. Every lover of Christ keeps His commandments **implicitly**: that is, he does what he does because Christ bids him. The doing what Christ commands may be agreeable to my inclinations or conducive to my interest; and if it is on **these** grounds I do it, I serve myself, not the Lord Jesus Christ. What Christ commands may be commanded by those whose authority I acknowledge and whose favour I wish to secure; if I do it on these grounds, I keep man's commandments, not Christ's. I keep Christ's commandments only when I do what He bids me **because** He bids me. If I love Christ, I shall keep His commandments **impartially**. If I do anything **because** Christ commands me to do it, I shall do **whatever** He commands. I shall not 'pick and choose.' If I love Christ, I shall keep His commandments **cheerfully**. I shall esteem it a privilege to obey His law. The thought that they are the commandments of Him whom I love, because of His excellency and kindness, make me love His law, for it must be excellent because it is His, and it must be fitted to promote my happiness for the same reason. If I love Christ I shall keep His commandments **perseveringly**. If I really love Him I can never cease to love Him, and if I never cease to love Him, I shall never cease to obey Him" (Condensed from Dr. J. Brown).

"And I will pray the Father, and He shall give you another Comforter, that He may abide with you forever" (v. 16). Note that this verse begins with "And." In the previous one the Lord had been speaking to the disciples' love for Him, marked by an obedient walk. Here He reveals His love for them, evidenced by Him asking for One who should shed abroad the love of God in their hearts (Rom. 5:5) and thus empower them to keep His commandments! Until now Christ had been their Comforter, but He was going to leave them; therefore does He ask the Father that another Comforter should be given to them. Here, again, we behold the Saviour loving them "unto the end!" There is also a blesssed link of connection between this verse and vv. 13, 14. There the Lord had taught them to "ask in His name," and in Luke 11:13, He had told them that the Father would give the Holy

Spirit if they "asked for Him." But here Christ is before them: His prayer precedes theirs—He would "ask" the Father for the Comforter to be sent unto them.

There has been a great deal of learned jargon written on the precise meaning of the Greek word here rendered "Comforter." Personally, we believe that no better term can be found, providing the original meaning of our English word be kept in mind. Comforter means more than Consoler. It is derived from two Latin words, **com** "along side of" and **fortis** "strong." A comforter is one who stands alongside of one in need, to strengthen. The reference here is, of course, to the Holy Spirit, and the fact that He is termed "**another Comforter**" signifies that He was to fill the place of Christ, doing for his disciples all that He had done for them while He was with them on earth, only that the Holy Spirit would minister from within as Christ had from without. The Holy Spirit would comfort, or strengthen, in a variety of respects: consolation when they were cast down, grace when they were weak or timid, guidance when they were perplexed, etc. The fact that the Lord here called the Holy Spirit "**another Comforter**" also proves Him to be a person, and a **Divine** person. It is striking to observe that in this verse we have mentioned each of the three Persons of the Blessed Trinity: "I will pray **the Father**, and He shall give you **another** Comforter!" One other thought suggested by the "**another Comforter**." The believer has **two** Comforters, Helpers or Strengtheners: the Holy Spirit on earth, and Christ in Heaven, for the same Greek word here rendered "Comforter" is translated "Advocate" in 1 John 2:1,—an "advocate" is one who aids, pleads the cause of his client. Christ "maketh intercession" for us on High (Heb. 7:25), the Holy Spirit within us (Rom. 8:26)! And this other "Comforter," be it noted, was to abide with them not just so long as they grieved Him not, but "for ever." Thus is the eternal preservation of every believer Divinely assured.

"Even the Spirit of truth: whom the world cannot receive, because it seeth Him not, neither knoweth Him" (v. 17). The Lord had just promised the apostles "another Comforter," that is, One like unto Himself and in addition to Himself. Here He warns them against expecting a **visible** Person. The One who should come is "The Spirit." Two thoughts are suggested by the title here given Him: "The Spirit of truth," or more literally, "The Spirit of the truth." The "Truth" is used both of the incarnate and the written Word. Christ had said to the disciples, "**I am** the Way, the **Truth,** and the Life;" a little later He would say to the Father, in their hearing, "**Thy Word** is Truth" (17:17). The Spirit, then, is the Spirit **of Christ**, because sent by Him (16:7), and because He is here to glorify Christ (16:14). The Spirit is also the Spirit **of the written Word**, because He moved men to write it (2 Peter 1:21), and because He now interprets it (16:13). Hitherto Christ had been their Teacher; henceforth the Holy Spirit should take His place. (14:26). The Holy Spirit works not independently of the written Word, but through and by means of it. "Whom the world cannot receive." Very solemn is this. It is not "will not," but **cannot** receive. Unable to receive the Spirit "the world" demonstrates its real character—opposed to the Father (1 John 2:16). The whole world lieth in the Wicked One (1 John 5:19), and he is a Liar from the beginning: how then could the world receive "The Spirit **of Truth**?" Our Lord adds another reason, "because it seeth Him not, neither knoweth Him." But what did the Lord mean? How can the invisible Spirit be seen? 1 Cor. 2:14 tells us: "The natural man receiveth not the things of the Spirit of God: for they are foolishness unto him; neither can he know them, because they are **spiritually** discerned." It is **spiritual** "seeing" which is in view, as in 6:40. And **why** cannot those who are of the "world" see Him? Because they have never been born again: "Except a man be born again, he **cannot** see the kingdom of God." And **why** should the Lord have made this statement here? Surely for the **comfort** of the disciples. "Another Comforter" had been promised them; One who should abide with them for ever; even the Spirit of Truth. What glorious conquests might they now expect to make for Christ! Ah, the Lord warns them of what would really take place: "the world" would not, could not, receive Him.

"But ye know Him: for He dwelleth with you, and shall be in you" (v. 17). "But" points a contrast: indicating at once that the work of the Spirit would be to separate the people of Christ from the world. "He dwelleth **with you**": He did, even then, for Christ was full of the Spirit (Luke 4:1; John 3:34). "And shall be **in you**" was future. The Lord Jesus here promised that the Third Person of the Holy Trinity should take up His abode within believers, making their bodies His temple. Marvellous grace was this. But, on **what ground** does the Holy Spirit enter and indwell the Christian? Not because of any personal fitness which He discovers there, for the old evil nature still remains in the believer. How, then, is it possible for the **Holy Spirit** to dwell where sin is still present. It is of the first moment that we obtain the correct answer to this, for multitudes are confused thereon: yet there is no excuse for this: the teaching of Scripture is abundantly clear. Jehovah of old, dwelt in the midst of Israel, even when they were stiff-necked and uncircumcised in heart. He did so **on the ground of atoning blood** (see Lev. 16:16). In like manner, the Holy Spirit indwells the believer now, as the witness to the excellency and sufficiency of that one offering of Christ's which has "perfected for ever them that are set apart (Heb. 10:14). Strikingly was this foreshadowed in the types. The "oil" (emblem of the Holy Spirit) was placed upon the blood—see Lev. 8:24, 30; 14:14, 17, etc.

"I will not leave you comfortless, I will come to you" (v. 18). The marginal rendering here is to be preferred: "I will not leave you **orphans**." It looks back to 13:33 where the Lord had addressed them as "little children." They were not to be like sheep without a Shepherd, helpless believers in a hostile world, without a Defender, forsaken orphans incapable of providing for themselves, left to the mercy of strangers. "I will come to you": how precious is this! Before we go to His place, to be with Him (vv. 2, 3), He comes to be with us! But what is meant by "I will come to you?" We believe that these words are to be understood in their widest latitude. He came to them **corporeately,** immediately after His resurrection. He came to them **in spirit** after His ascension. He will come to them **in glory** at His second advent. The present application of this promise to believers finds its fulfilment in the gift of the Holy Spirit—indwelling us individually, present in the midst of the assembly collectively. And yet we must not limit the coming of Christ to His children to the presence of the Holy Spirit. The mystery of the Holy Trinity is altogether beyond the grasp of our finite minds. Yet the New Testament makes it clear that in the unity of the Godhead, the advent of the Holy Spirit was also Christ coming, invisibly, to be really present with his own. "Lo, I am with you always, even unto the end of the age" (Matt. 28:20). "**Christ** liveth in me," said the apostle Paul (Gal. 2:20). "**Christ** among you, the hope of glory" (Col. 1:27). How unspeakably blessed is this? Friends, relatives, yea, professing Christians may turn against us, but he has promised "**I will never** leave thee nor forsake thee" (Heb. 13:5).

"Yet a little while, and the world seeth Me no more" (v. 19). The last time "the world" saw the Lord of glory was as He hung upon the Cross of shame. After His resurrection He appeared unto none but His own. "The world seeth Me no more" is not an accurate translation, nor is it true. "The world" **shall** see Him again. "Yet a little while and the world Me **no longer** sees" is what the original says. "**Every** eye shall see Him" (Rev. 1:7). When? When He is seated upon the Great White Throne to judge the wicked. Then shall they be punished with everlasting destruction from the presence of the Lord, and from the glory of His power" (2 Thess. 1:9).

"But ye see Me" (v. 19). They saw Him then, while He was speaking to them. They saw Him, again and again, after He had risen from the dead. They saw Him, as He went up to Heaven, till a cloud received Him out of their sight. They saw Him, by faith, after He had taken His seat at the right hand of God, for it is written "We see Jesus, who was made a little lower than the angels for the suffering and death, crowned with glory and honor" (Heb. 2:9). They see Him now, for they are **present with the Lord.** They shall see Him at His second coming. "When He shall appear, we shall be like Him; for we shall see Him as He is" (1 John, 3:2). They shall see Him for ever and ever throughout the **Perfect Day.** For it is written, "And they shall **see** His face; and His name shall be in their foreheads" (Rev. 22:4).

"Because I live, ye shall live also" (v. 19). "Your spiritual life now, and your eternal life hereafter, are both secured by **My** life. I live, have life in Myself, can never die, can never have My life destroyed by My enemies, and live on to all eternity. Therefore: ye shall live also—your life is secured forever, and can never be destroyed; you have everlasting life now, and shall have everlasting glory hereafter" (Bishop Ryle). The blessed truth here expressed by Christ is developed at length in the Epistles: there the Holy Spirit shows us believers are so absolutely one with Christ that they partake with Him of that holy happy life into which, in the complete enjoyment of it, Christ entered, when He rose again and sat down on the Father's Throne.

"At that day ye shall know that I am in My Father, and ye in Me, and I in you" (v. 20). The first reference in "that day" is to Pentecost, when Christ came, spiritually, to His disciples; came not merely to visit, but to abide with and in them. Then were they brought into the consciousness of their oneness of life with Him. The ultimate reference no doubt, is to the Day of His glorious manifestation: then shall we know even as we are known.

The following questions are on the closing section of John 14:—
1. How does Christ "manifest" Himself to us v. 21?
2. What is the difference between "commandments" in v. 21 and "words" in v. 23?
3. What is the double "peace" of v. 27?
4. How is the Father "greater" than Christ v. 28?
5. "Believe" what v. 29?
6. What is the meaning of v. 30?
7. What is the spiritual significance of the last clause in v. 31?

—Arthur W. Pink.

## GLEANINGS IN EXODUS
### 25. Amalek: Ex. 17.

One thing that impresses the writer more and more in his studies in and meditations upon the contents of this book of Exodus is the wonderful variety and the comprehensive range of truth covered by its typical teachings. Not only do its leading events and prominent characters foreshadow that which is spiritual and Divine, but even the smallest details have a profound significance. Moses is a type of Christ, Pharoah of Satan, Egypt of the world. Israel groaning in bondage pictures the sinner in his native misery. Israel delivered from their cruel task-masters speaks of our our redemption. Their journey across the wilderness points to the path of faith and trial which we are called on to walk. And now we are to see that the history of Israel also adumbrated the conflict between the two natures in the believer.

Our previous studies have already shown us that the experiences of Israel in the wilderness were a series of trials, real testings of faith. Now we are to see another aspect of the Christian's life strikingly set forth: Israel were called upon to do some fighting. It is very striking indeed to note the occasion of this, the stage at which it occurred in Israel's history. Not only is there a wondrous variety and comprehensiveness about the typical teachings of this second book of scripture, but the order in which they are given equally displays the Divine hand of their Author.

*Compare our comments on this striking feature about the types in the first book of Scripture: "Gleanings in Genesis," Vol. 2, pages 45 and 139.

*God is the God of order; Satan of confusion. The thoughless reader of the Scriptures loses much by failing to observe the perfect arrangement of everything in them.

In our last article we contemplated the smiting of the rock, from which flowed the stream of water and of which all the people drank. This, as we saw, typified the smiting of our blessed Saviour by the hand of Divine justice, and the consequent gift of the Holy Spirit to those who are His. But after the Holy Spirit comes to take up His abode within the believer, after a new and holy nature of His creating has been implanted, a strange conflict is experienced, something hitherto unknown. As we read in Gal. 5:17, "The flesh lusteth against the spirit, and the spirit against the flesh; and these are contrary the one to the other." It is this which the scripture to be before us so accurately depicts.

The typical scene which we are about to study is of great practical importance. Ignorance of what it sets forth, the truth which it illustrates, has resulted in great loss and has been responsible for untold distress in many souls. How many a one has thought, and how many have been taught, that when a sinner really receives Christ as his Saviour, that God will change his heart, and that henceforth he will be complete victor over sin. But "a change of heart" is nowhere spoken of in Scripture. God never changes anything. The old is set aside or destroyed, and something altogether new is created or introduced by Him. It is thus with the Christian. The Christian is one who has been "born again," and the new birth is neither the removal of anything from a man, nor the changing of anything within; but the impartation of something new to him. The new birth is the reception of a new nature: "that which is **born** of the Spirit, is Spirit" (John 3:6).

At the new birth a spiritual, Divine nature is communicated to us. This new nature is created by the Holy Spirit; the "seed" (1 John 3:9) used is the Word of God. (I Pet. 1:23). This explains John 3:5: "Born of **water** and of the Spirit." The "water" is the emblem of the pure and refreshing Word of God (cf. Eph. 5:26). This is what is in view, typically, in the first half of Ex. 17. But when the new nature is communicated by God to the one born again, the old sinful nature remains, and remains **unchanged** till death or the coming of Christ, when it will be destroyed, for then "this corruptible shall put on incorruption" (I Cor. 15:53). In the Christian, then, in **every** Christian, there are two natures: one sinful, the other sinless; one born of the flesh, the other born of God. These two natures differ from each other in origin, in character, in disposition and in the activities they produce. They have nothing in common. They are opposed to each other. This is what is in view, typically in the second half of Ex. 17.

The two natures in the Christian are illustrated in the life of Abraham. He had two sons: Ishmael and Isaac. The former represents that which is "born of the flesh;" the latter, that which is "born of the Spirit." Ishmael was born according to the common order of nature. Isaac was not. Isaac was born as the result of a miracle. God supernaturally quickened both Abraham and Sarah, when the one had passed the age of begetting and the other was too old to bear children. Ishmael, born first, was of "the bond-woman"; Isaac of the "freewoman" (Gal. 4:22). But after Isaac entered the household of Abraham, there was a conflict: "And Sarah saw the son of Hagar the Egyptian which she had born unto Abraham, **mocking.**" (Gen. 21:9). That what we have just heard said about the two sons of Abraham is no fanciful or strained interpretation of ours, will be seen by a reference to Gal. 4:29, where the Spirit of God has told us, "But as then he that was born after the flesh **persecuted** him that was born after the Spirit even so it is **now.**"

The two natures in the Christian are also illustrated in the life of Isaac's son, Jacob. Jacob had two names: one which he received from his earthly parents, ane one which he received from God. The Lord called him "Israel" (Gen. 32:28). From that point onwards the history of Jacob-Israel presents a series of strange paradoxes. His life exhibited a **dual** personality. At one moment we see him trusting God with implicit confidence, at another we behold him giving way to an evil heart of unbelief. If the student will read carefully through chapters 33 to 49 of Genesis he will notice how that sometimes the Holy Spirit refers to the patriarch as "Jacob," at other times as "Israel." When "Jacob" is referred to it is the activities of the old nature which are in view, when "Israel" is mentioned it is the fruits of the new nature which are evidenced. For example: when Joseph's brethren returned to their father from Egypt and told him that his favorite son was yet alive and was now governor over all the land of Egypt, we are told, "And **Jacob's** heart fainted **for** he believed them not" (45:26). But "They told him all the words of Joseph, which he had said unto them; and when he saw the wagons which Joseph had sent to carry him, the spirit of Jacob their father revived: And **Israel** said, It is enough; Joseph my son is yet alive" (45:48)! It is blessed to note the closing words concerning him: "When **Jacob** had made an end of commanding his sons, he gathered up his feet into the bed, and yielded up the spirit . . . and the physicians embalmed **Israel**" (49:33; 50:2)! "Jacob" died; "Israel" was embalmed. At death only the new nature will be preserved!

But that which we particularly emphasise here is, that during the Christian's life on earth there is **a conflict** between the two natures. Just as Ishmael "persecuted" Isaac, and just as the Jacob-nature frequently set aside the Isaac-nature, so it is in the Christian: "the flesh **lusteth against** the spirit, and the spirit against the flesh; and these are contrary the one to the other; so that ye cannot do the things that ye would." (Gal. 5:17). What, then, is the remedy? Is there no way by which the flesh may be subdued? Has God made no provision for the believer to walk in the spirit so that he may not fulfill the lusts of the flesh? Certainly He has; and absence of victory is due entirely to our failure to use the means of grace which God has put in our hands. What these are, and how the victory should be gained are clearly set forth in our type.

"Then came Amalek, and fought with Israel in Rephidim" (17:8). In the light of Gen. 21:25; 26:19, 20; Ex. 2:17; Num. 20:19; Judges 5:11, where we learn that the possession of water (wells, etc.) was frequently a bone of contention among the ancients, it is evident that the spread of the news that a river of water was now gushing from the rock in Rephidim, caused the Amalekites to attempt to gain possession. To do this meant they must first dispossess Israel; hence their attack.

The first thing to note here is the **identity** of Israel's enemy. It was Amalek. "Amalek" signifies "Warlike," apt name for that whose lusts ever **war** against the soul'" (1 Peter 2:11). Amalek was the grandson of Esau (Gen. 36:12): 'Who for one morsel of meat sold his birthright, and when he would have inherited the blessing was rejected,' is thus surely a representative of the 'old man'"(F.W.G.). Very striking in this connection is the prophetic word of Balaam: "And when he looked for Amalek, he took up his parable, and said, Amalek was the first of the nations that warred against Israel; but his **latter end** shall be that he perish forever" (Num. 24:20). The **character** of Amalek comes out plainly in the words of Moses concerning him at a later date—"He feared not God" (Deut. 25:17, 18)—such is "the flesh."

The second thing to be noted is the **time** when Amalek made his assault upon Israel: "**then** came Amalek and fought with Israel." The Holy Spirit has called our attention to the **time** when this occurred. It was when Moses smote the rock and the waters were given. Then, for the first time, Israel was called upon to do some fighting—contrast 13:17. They had done no fighting in the house of bondage, nor had the Lord called upon them to fight the Egyptians at the Red Sea. But now that that which typified the Holy Spirit had been given, their warfare commenced; yea, it was that which typified the Holy Spirit that **caused** the Amalekites to attack Israel! Wonderfully accurate is the type.

It is not until the Christian has been made partaker of the Divine nature (2 Peter 1:4) that the inward conflict begins. Previous to the new birth, he was dead in trespasses and sins; and therefore quite insensible to the claims of God's holiness. Until the Holy Spirit begins to shed abroad His light upon our wicked hearts, we do not realise the depths and power of the evil within us. Ofttimes the believer is astounded by the discovery of the tendencies and desires within him, which he never knew before were there. The religious professor knows nothing of the conflict between the two natures nor of the abiding sense of inward corruption which this experience conveys. The unregenerate man is entirely **under the dominion** of the flesh, he serves its lusts, he does its will. The "flesh" does not fight its subjects; it **rules** over them. But as soon as we receive the new nature the conflict begins.

It is striking to note that it was not Israel who attacked Amalek, but Amalek that attacked Israel. The new nature in the believer delights to feed upon the Word, to commune with God, and be engaged with spiritual things. But the flesh will not let him live in peace. The Devil delights to rob the believer of his joy, and works upon the flesh to accomplish his fiendish designs. The antitype is in perfect accord. Note how that in Gal. 5:17 it is first said that "The flesh lusteth against the spirit," and not vice versa.

Next, let us note carefully the record of **how** Israel engaged Amalek in fight: "And Moses said unto Joshua, Choose us out men, and go out, fight with Amalek; to-morrow I will stand on the top of the hill with the rod of God in mine hand. So Joshua did as Moses had said to him, and fought with Amalek; and Moses, Aaron, and Hur went up to the top of the hill. And it came to pass, when Moses held up his hand that Israel prevailed; and when he let down his hand, Amalek prevailed. But Moses' hands were heavy; and they took a stone and put it under him, and he sat thereon; and Aaron and Hur stayed up his hands, the one on one side and the other on the other side; and his hands were steady until the going down of the sun. And Joshua discomfited Amalek and his people with the edge of his sword" (vv. 9-13).

There is considerable difference of opinion among the commentators concerning the typical application of the above scripture. Some regard Moses at the top of the hill with hands uplifted toward heaven as the figure of Christ interceding for us on High. But that cannot be. And this for two reasons: Moses was **accompanied** by Aaron and Hur; furthermore, his hands grew heavy. It is grossly dishonoring to the perfect Word of God to say that the type is imperfect at this point—far better to confess our ignorance than to cast such reflections upon the Scriptures. Others regard Joshua as the type of Christ in this incident, but that cannot be, because Israel did not gain a complete victory over Amalek. Rather is it evident that the respective actions of Moses and Joshua point out **the provi-**

sions which God has made for us to combat the flesh.

The first thing to note here is that Israel's success against Amalek was determined by the uplifted hand of Moses: "And it came to pass, when Moses held up his hand, that Israel prevailed; and when he let down his hand Amalek prevailed" (v. 11). The significance of Moses' attitude is clearly defined in several scriptures. The uplifted hand was emblematic of **prayer**, the supplicating of God: "Hear the voice of my supplications, when I cry unto Thee, when I lift up my hands toward Thy holy oracle" (Psl. 28:2); "I will therefore that men **pray** everywhere, **lifting up holy hands**, without wrath and doubting" (1 Tim. 2:8).

Second, observe that "Moses' hands grew heavy." Here is where the real and beautiful accuracy of our type is to be seen. How soon we grow weary of supplicating God! "Men ought always to pray and **not to faint**" (Luke 18:1), said our Lord. But how sadly we fail. How quickly our **hearts** get "heavy"! And as soon as we lose the spirit of dependency upon God **the flesh prevails**.

Third, but Moses was not left to himself. Blessed it is to mark this. Aaron and Hur were with him, and "Stayed up his hands, the one on one side and the other on the other side." Here again we discover the beautiful accuracy of our type. Surely there is no difficulty in interpreting this detail. Aaron was the head of Israel's priesthood, and so speaks plainly of our great High Priest. "Hur" means "light"—the emblem of Divine holiness, and so points to the Holy Spirit of God. Thus God in His grace has fully provided for us. Supported on **either side**, both the earthly and the heavenly. "Likewise the Spirit also helpeth our infirmities. For we know not what we should pray for as we ought: but the Spirit Himself maketh intercession for us with groanings which cannot be uttered" (Rom. 8:26); this is on the earthly side. "And another angel (Christ as "the Messenger of the Covenant") came and stood at the altar having a golden censer; and there was given unto Him much incense, that He should offer it with the prayers of all saints upon the golden altar which was before the throne" (Rev. 8:3): this is on the heavenly side—Christ receiving our supplications and offering them to God, as accompanied by the sweet fragrance of His own perfections.

Fourth, the typical picture is completed for us by what is said in v. 13: "And Joshua discomfited Amalek and his people with the edge of the sword." The "sword" here points to the Holy Scriptures (see Heb. 4:12). It is not by prayer alone that we can fight the flesh. The Word, too, is needed. Said the Psalmist, "Thy Word have I hid in mine heart that **I might not** sin against Thee" (Psl. 119:11).

Some may object to what we have just said above about the Christian fighting the flesh. We are not unmindful of Rom. 6:11 and 2 Tim. 2:22 and much that has been written thereon. But there are scriptures which present **other phases** of our responsibility. There is a fight to be fought (see 1 Tim. 6:12; 2 Tim. 4:7 etc.). And this fight has to do with **the flesh**. Said the Apostle, "So fight I, not as one that beateth the air; but I keep under my body, and bring it into subjection" (I Cor. 9:26; 27).

Another thing which is important to note here is the fact that Amalek was not destroyed or completely vanquished on this occasion. We only read that "Joshua **discomfited** Amalek." Here too, the type is in perfect accord with the antitype. There is no way of **destroying** or eradicating the evil nature within us. Though discomforted it still survives. Why, it may be asked, does God permit the evil nature to remain in us? Many answers may be given, among them these: That we may obtain a deeper and personal realisation of the awful havoc which sin has wrought in man, the total depravity of our beings, and thereby appreciate the more the marvellous grace which has saved such Hell-deserving wretches. That we may be humbled before God and made more dependent upon Him. That we may appropriate to ourselves His all-sufficient grace and learn that His strength is made perfect in our weakness. That we may appreciate the more His keeping-power, for left to ourselves, with such a sink of iniquity within, we should surely perish.

A very helpful word and one which we do well to take to heart, is found in Deut. 25:17, 18: "Remember what Amalek did unto thee by the way, when ye were come forth out of Egypt; How he met thee by the way and smote the **hindmost** of thee, even all that were feeble behind thee, **when thou wast faint** and weary; and he feared not God." How this should stir us up to watchfulness! It was the "hindmost"—those farthest away from their leader—that were smitten. The flesh cannot smite us while we are walking in close communion with God! And note that it was when Israel were "faint and weary" that Amalek came down upon them. This too is a warning word. What is the remedy against faintness? This: "He giveth power to the faint; and to them that have no might He increaseth strength. Even the youths shall faint and be weary, and the young men shall utterly fail; But **they that wait upon the Lord** shall renew their strengtn, they shall mount up with wings as eagles; they shall run and not be weary; they shall walk, and not faint" (Isa. 40 30, 31).

Very blessed are the closing words of Ex. 17: "And the Lord said unto Moses, Write this for a memorial in a book, and rehearse it in the ears of Joshua; for I will utterly put out the remembrance of Amalek from under heaven. And Moses built an altar, and called the name of it Jehovah-Nissi: For he said, Because the Lord hath sworn that the Lord will have war with Amalek from generation to generation" (vv. 14-16). God here promised that in the end He would utterly annihilate Amalek. In the confident assurance of faith Moses anticipated God's final victory by erecting an altar and calling it "The Lord, our Banner." How blessed to know that at the end the Saviour shall "change our vile body, that it may be fashioned like unto His glorious body according to the working whereby He is able even to subdue all things unto Himself." (Phil. 3 : 21).

Arthur W. Pink.

## THE SOVEREIGNTY OF GOD.

### Address No. 3 by Dr. A. W. Pink, at the Ashfield Baptist Church, Monday, 22/6/25.

In the 26th chapter of Isaiah, we have a statement which we may take as our starting-point to-night. Isaiah 26 : 12. "Lord, Thou wilt ordain peace for us: for Thou also hast wrought all our works in us." "Thou also hast wrought all our works in us!"

Now in the last two addresses, on Thursday and Friday nights of last week, we endeavoured to show from Scripture that God is absolutely Sovereign, high above all, and that He exercises that sovereignty in His government of and His control over all creatures, both rational and irrational. To-night, I want to show from Scripture that God's government over us extends to every department of our lives, that we are not the creatures of chance nor of blind fate, but that our **lives are ordered** by our Creator.

Before I take up that truth in detail, let me just warn you that whenever we are considering any aspect of God's sovereignty we are dealing with the **Divine** side of things. There is another side, the human side, the side of human accountability, and those of you who have been attending these meetings for some time past, know quite well that the present speaker believes in and teaches regularly the responsibility of man, but that is **not** our subject to-night, and we are not going to deal with that aspect of truth: we are dealing with the Divine side, the neglected side, and the almost universally denied side; so to-night I want to show from Scripture that God's soveignty is exercised in every department of our lives.

First of all, in connection with our temporal affairs. 1. God determined **when we should be born.** That was fixed by Him, before any of us came into this world at all. God the Creator ordered when we should be born. Now in proof of that turn first of all to the Book of Ecclesiastes, the third chapter and the first two verses:—"To **everything** there is a season, and a time to every purpose under heaven: **a time to be born."** Now you have a striking illustration of that in connection with the birth of Isaac. Almost every truth and precept of scripture is also illustrated in scripture. If you will turn to the 21st chapter of Genesis, verse 2 (I am going to keep you pretty close to the Word to-night, I am not going to comment very much. I want the Word to speak for itself). The 21st chapter of Genesis and the 2nd verse. I will read the first verse to give the setting :—"And the Lord visited Sarah as He had said, and the Lord did unto Sarah as He had spoken. For Sarah conceived and bare Abraham a son in his old age, at **the set time** of which God had spoken to him." Now here we learn that Isaac was born at "a set time"—at an appointed time, for that is what the word "set" here signifies. He was born at God's appointed time, as He had previously announced. If you go back to chapter 18 you will find there that God had made a specific announcement. Genesis 18 : 13 : "And the Lord said unto Abraham, Wherefore did Sarah laugh, saying, Shall I of a surety bear a child, which am old? Is anything too hard for the Lord? At **the time appointed** I will return unto thee, according to the time of life, and Sarah shall have a son." "At the time appointed!" Now in like manner God appointed the time when **each of us** should be born.

2. If God appointed **the time** when we should be born we may logically expect that He has also appointed the place where we should be born. Now turn to Acts 17:26 (a part of Paul's address on Mars' Hill): "And hath made of one blood all nations of men for to dwell on all the face of the earth, and hath determined the times before appointed, and **the bounds of their habitation.**" God has not only determined "the times" beforehand, but also the very "bounds" of our habitation, where we live. Now you have a striking illustration of that in connection with the birth of Christ. God had made it known through Micah the prophet (you will find it in Micah 5:2) that the Saviour was to be born in **Bethlehem,** and when the time of Christ's birth drew nigh, Mary and Joseph were **not** living in Bethlehem, and so God caused the Roman Emperor to issue an edict. He set in operation the whole machinery of the Roman Empire to bring about His purpose! Christ could not be born at Nazareth, for God had purposed that He should be born at Bethlehem, and therefore He caused the Roman Emperor to issue an edict which obliged Joseph to take a journey yonder to Bethlehem in order that Christ might there be born!

3. Now not only has God determined the time of our birth and the place of our birth, but He has also determined **the time of our death,** should we die before the Lord returns. Now I know that is questioned by many to-day as to whether or not God has fixed the hour of our death. Turn to the 14th chapter of Job, the first verse. "Man that is born of a woman is of few days and full of trouble." Verse 5: "Seeing his days are **determined,** the number of his months are with Thee, Thou hast **appointed his bounds** that he **cannot** pass." You could not have anything plainer and more positive and dogmatic than that. "His days are determined." The "number of his months are with Thee." "Thou has appointed his bounds that he cannot pass." Now that is by no means the only Scripture. You turn back now to the first book of Samuel, chapter 2 and the sixth verse: "The Lord killeth, and maketh alive: **He** bringeth down to the grave, and bringeth up." No one doubts the latter. Everyone who believes in resurrection at all, believes that God Himself must do the resurrecting. In the same verse and in the same sentence we are told, **He bringeth down to the grave.** God does, and **He** bringeth up." Now you have a striking illustration of that. I want you to see that each one of these statements is illustrated. In the 47th chapter of Genesis and the 29th verse: "And the time drew nigh that Israel" should die?" No, it does not read that way, it is much stronger than that; look at it for yourselves. "The time drew night that Israel **must** die." He "must" because his appointed time had come, and all the physicians in Egypt could not have prolonged his life one minute! Now turn to the 68th Psalm and the 20th verse:—"He that is our God is the God of salvation; and unto the Lord belong the issues from death"—not unto the nurses and doctors, but unto God the Lord belong the issues from death.

Now simply to show that I am not trying to palm off on you to-night something that was "made in America," I am just going to read you a few lines from a sermon that was preached by Mr. C. H. Spurgeon, fifty years ago, on this very text, Psalm 68:20, "Unto God the Lord belong the issues from death" and I heartily say Amen to everything he here says:—

"Let us speak then with reverence upon this sovereign perogative of God. 'Unto God the Lord belong the issues from death.' Kings have been accustomed to keep the power of life and death in their own hands, but the great King of kings, the sovereign Ruler and absolute Lord of all worlds reserves this to Himself, that He shall permit men to die or shall give them an issue from death at His own good will and pleasure. He alike can create and destroy. He sendeth forth His Spirit, and they are created, and at His own pleasure He saith, Return ye children of men, and, Lo, they fall before Him as autumn's faded leaves. The prerogative of life or death belongs to God alone. We shall not die until the time which He appoints, for our death-time like all our time is in His hands. Our skirts may brush against the portals of the sepulchre and yet we shall pass the iron gate unharmed if the Lord be our guard. The wolves of disease will hunt us in vain until God shall permit them to overtake us. The most desperate enemies may waylay us, but no bullet shall find its billet in any heart unless the Lord allows it. Our life does not even depend upon the care of angels, nor can our death be compassed by the malice of devils. We are immortal till our work is done; immortal till the Immortal King shall call us home to the land where we shall be immortal in a still higher sense. When we are most sickly and most ready to faint into the grave we need not despair of recovery since the issues from death are in Almighty hands. 'The Lord killeth and maketh alive: He bringeth down to the grave and bringeth up.' When we have passed beyond the skill of the physician we have not passed beyond the succor of our God to whom belong the issues from death."

Ah, my friends, what a comforting truth that is, that the life of our loved ones, in the time of sickness, is not, in the final analysis, dependent on what the doctor does, but is dependent on what God has appointed; therefore, when death does come to our loved ones we can say, "The Lord gave and the Lord hath taken away": therefore we can add, "Blessed be the name of the Lord!"

Now, in the fourth place, God has determined just how far we shall **prosper in temporal things.** You turn back now to Deuteronomy 8 and the 18th verse: "But thou shalt remember" (Ah, we need this word because we are always in danger of forgetting). "But thou shalt remember the Lord thy God: for it is He that **giveth thee power** to get wealth." And those of you who have accumulated a little money and have it in the bank to-night, perhaps you thought that it is there because you have worked hard. My friends, there's lots of other men have worked just as hard as you have, and they have got nothing in the bank! Well, you say, it was because I was thrifty and saved. Yes, and there has been many another man who has been just as thrifty as you have and has been just as careful in saving, and a long sickness came upon him and his money melted, or the bank in which his money was deposited, failed! O, my friends, give God the glory, to whom alone it belongs. Why, my friends, you cannot even work one day unless God Himself gives you the health to work, and **that** is His gift! Now turn back for an **illustration** of this to the 24th chapter of Genesis, verse 35. These were the words of Abraham's servant:—"And the Lord hath blessed my master greatly; and he is become great: and He hath given him **flocks, and herds, and silver, and gold,"** "He hath given him." Abraham's servant ascribed the glory to God alone and put the praise and honour where it belonged.

Now, in the fifth place, God has appointed **our life's partner.** Oh there is nothing left to chance: We are just going to tighten it up to-night at every point and just encircle you with God's predestinating will. You turn now to the book of Proverbs, chapter 19, verse 14:—"House and riches are the inheritance of fathers: and a prudent wife is from the Lord." I know it is qualified here—a **prudent** wife. I will not turn aside now and speak about those men who have imprudent wives. If you have a prudent wife, a true helpmate, then you have to **thank God** for it—not your own wisdom in making your selection; but a prudent wife is "from the Lord," therefore **thanks** are due **to Him!** Oh, how we rob God of His glory, don't we? How anxious we are to take the credit to ourselves and impute it to our own wisdom, or our own something, instead of only to God Himself.

6. Now God has also determined whether we should have children and, if any, how many. The subject is too delicate for me to enter into, but if you want to find many proofs of that you will find them in the book of Genesis: You can read it through for yourselves.

7. God has determined **every** detail of our lives. Let me give you now three or four passages in proof of that. Acts 17: 28. I will read you the 27th:—"That they should seek the Lord, if haply they might feel after Him, and find Him, though He be not far from every one of us: for in Him **(in Him)** we **live,** and **move,** and have our being," and those words were not addressed to a company of saints, but were spoken to a heathen audience! In **God** we live and move. Our every action is circumscribed by His will. Now you turn back to Daniel 5: 23 which is strictly parallel. These were the words of Daniel to Belshazzar. I will read you verse 22:—"And thou his son, O Belshazzar, hast not humbled thine heart, though thou knewest all this; but hast lifted up thyself against the Lord of heaven; and they have brought the vessels of His house before thee, and thou, and thy lords, thy wives, and thy concubines, have drunk wine in them; and thou hast praised the gods of silver, and gold, of brass, iron, wood and stone, which see not, nor hear, nor know: and the God in whose hand thy breath is and **whose are all thy ways,** hast thou not glorified." "And the God in whose hand thy breath is and whose are all thy ways." What a sweeping statement to a heathen, corrupt rebel! "In whose hand thy breath is, and whose are all

thy ways." No qualification, no limitation! Now turn back to Jeremiah 10 and the 23rd verse:—"O Lord, I know (and I wonder how many of us 'know' it!) "O Lord, I know that the way of man is not in himself: it is **not** in man that walketh to direct his steps." There's mighty few **know** that to-day, and fewer still **believe** it! "O Lord, I know that the way of man is not in himself: It is not in man that walketh to direct his steps." Now turn back to Proverbs 16: 9:—"A man's heart deviseth his way: but **the Lord** directeth his steps."

Now then, what is the practical application of this truth to our lives? If God has determined when we should be born, and where we should be born, and when we should die, and who our life's partner should be, and whether we should prosper in temporal things, and has determined **all** our ways, what is the practical value of it to our hearts? I answer in the first place, it ought to teach us to **hold all our plans in subserviency to God.** You turn now to the 4th chapter of James, verse 13. Now may God impress this passage on every heart here to-night: It is most urgently needed to-day. James 4: v 3: "Go to now, ye that say, to-day or to-morrow **we will** go into such a city, and continue there a year, and buy and sell, and get gain: whereas ye know not **what** shall be on the morrow. For what is your life. It is even a vapor, that appeareth for a little time, and then vanisheth away. For that ye ought to say, If the **Lord** will, we shall live, and do this, or that." **Our** plans must be held in absolute subjection to God's plan, and instead of boasting what we will do and what **we** will not do, we ought always to say, "If the Lord will" I hope to do so-and-so.

I remember very well a forcible illustration that no doubt you will recall very readily. I think it was in the month of April, 1901 or 1902—I am not positive of the year. One morning coming down to breakfast in England, my father had the newspaper open in front of him, and in the middle of breakfast he turned to our mother and said, "Oh, I am sorry to see this worded like that." And she said, "What is it?" "Why," he said, "here is a proclamation that on a certain date Prince Edward will be crowned King at Westminster and, he said, there is **no D.V.**, no deo volente, God willing." Everything has been fixed all the princes and potentates from India and the other countries have been invited, and the programme has been made out, and on a certain hour of a certain day he **will be** crowned Edward VII. And my friends, three months later when that day came, Prince Edward was at the point of death, on his back with appendicitis." God will not allow even kings to say what they "will do," unless they submit their plans to His will! There is a solemn warning there for us. Just as surely as we make up our minds and say positively that we **will** do so and so, the probability is that God will blow on our plans! We ought to say, "If the Lord will."

Now, in the second place, if God has fixed and controls all the details of our lives, what ought to follow? This: we ought to **refrain from all murmuring.** No matter how our plans may be upset, no matter how we may be disappointed, no matter how unpleasant our circumstances or how trying they may be, God Himself having directed them, we ought to have a godly resignation to Him. Murmuring at our circumstances or our lot is rebellion and treason against the King of kings! I want you to turn back to 1 Samuel, 3rd chapter and the 18th verse: "And Samuel told him every whit, and hid nothing from him." That was Eli. God had made known to Samuel, and he now acquainted Eli the high priest, of the fact, that his two sons were to be slain, and they were wicked reprobates—sons of Belial. They were lost sinners, and God told their aged father that on this day they should die. How did he receive those awful tidings? What was his response to that terrible news that his two wicked sons should die that day? Look at it in 1 Samuel 3:18: "And he said, It is the Lord: let Him do **what seemeth Him good."** There is godly resignation. There is a bowing to the sovereign will of God! O what an example for us! No matter how unpleasant our circumstances may be, or how painful the trial, we ought always to say, It is the Lord, let Him do what seemeth Him good.

Third, If God orders every detail of my life, what ought my response to be? I ought to **praise Him for all things,** sin excepted, of course. I ought to praise Him for all things because He doeth all things well. That is what Job did when all his possessions and all his family were removed from him in a day. His response was, "The Lord gave and the Lord hath taken away." A pastor once called on a godly old woman whose money had been deposited in a bank which had failed, and he went round to comfort her, and in the course of his conversation he said, This must be a great disappointment to you. And she looked at the pastor and she said, Pastor, God has shown me a new way of spelling the word 'disappointment.' I change the first letter and instead of spelling it d-i-s I spell it H-i-s. Instead of spelling 'disappointment' I now spell it as 'His appointment.'" It is a grand thing, brother and sister, when you learn to spell disappointment in that godly manner: It takes all the bitterness out of the cup. It takes all the murmuring away from our rebellious hearts. It makes us bow in godly resignation once we recognise that God Himself is directing all things in our lives. Ah, my friends, this doctrine of the sovereignty of God is a practical one. It is of inestimable value to our daily lives once the heart lays hold of it—I said the **heart** —not the head!

Now in the second place, I just want to mention a few things in connection with the sovereignty of God as it concerns **our salvation.** We have seen the sovereignty of God in our temporal affairs, now let us see it in our spiritual affairs, and once more let me read you from this same sermon of Spurgeon's. I just want you to see how strongly he preached this doctrine—a man who was more widely used of God perhaps than any other man since the days of the Apostle Paul. Now here is one thing that he says in this sermon:—

". . . 'To God the Lord belong the issues from death.' Spiritually too this prerogative is with God. We are by nature under the condemnation of the law on account of our sins, and we are like criminals tried, convicted, sentenced and left for dead, and it is for God the Great Judge to see the sentence executed or to issue a free pardon according as He pleases, and He will have us know that it is upon His supreme pleasure that this matter depends. Over the universe of a world of sinners I hear this sentence thundering, 'I will have mercy on whom I will have mercy and I will have compassion on whom I will have compassion.' Shut up for death as men are by reason of their sins, it rests with God to pardon whom He may reserve. None have any claim to His favour, and it must be exercised upon mere prerogative. He has an absolute right to do with us as He pleases seeing He made us and not we ourselves. Men forget what they are and boast great things, but they are just as truly clay on the Potter's wheel and He can fashion them or break them as He pleases. They think not so, but He knoweth their thoughts that they are vain. O the dignity of man, what a theme for a sarcastic discourse. Just as the frog in the fable swelled itself until it burst asunder, so does man in his pride and envy against his Maker who nevertheless sitteth upon the circle of the heavens and reckoneth men as though they were grasshoppers and regardeth whole nations of them as the small dust of the balance! Our fall has involved forfeiture of the creature's claims, whatever they may have been. we are attainted of high treason and have each one been guilty of personal rebellion, and therefore we have not the rights of citizens but lie under condemnation of death. 'Unto God the Lord belong the issues from death.' It is a doctrine which is very unpalatable in these days." Ah, it was so fifty years ago and the world has not improved any since then. "It is a doctrine which is very unpalatable" (and yet he went on preaching it and that is why God honoured him) "but one nevertheless which is to be held and taught, that God is absolute Sovereign and doeth as He pleases." Yes, my friends, God exercises His sovereignty in the matter of salvation.

First of all, He exercises His sovereignty in **whom** He saves (Romans 9: 15). He has mercy on whom He wills to have mercy.

Second, He exercises His sovereignty when we are saved. Some are saved in childhood like Samuel was, and Timothy was. Others are saved in their dying hour, like the thief on the cross was. **That** is according to the sovereign will of God.

Third, God exercises His sovereignty in **where** we are saved. Some are saved inside of a church building under the sound of the gospel. Some are saved like the speaker was, in the privacy of his own room, when no human being was present (and profoundly thankful I am that it pleased God to save me in that way). I am such a frightful sceptic by nature, that if **man** had had anything to do with my salvation I would be very much afraid I had **not been** genuinely saved; but God in His mercy shut out man in my own case. That is not His general way. As a general rule God is pleased to use human instrumentality. Most people are saved under the preaching of His Word, but in His sovereign grace He permitted me to be saved without any human instrument, so I know that I have got the real thing. God saved me!

Then, in the fourth place, God exercises His sovereignty in the **texts applied.** I had a very striking demonstration of that some years ago in the City of Oakland, California. One Sunday night a man of some fifty years of age met me at the door of the tent where I had been for eighteen weeks for six nights a week, and he asked if he might be allowed to give his testimony on the platform, and I said, No. But, he said, I have got a real testimony that I want to give. Well, I said, I don't believe in testimonies. Well, he said, won't you give me a chance to let the people know that God saved me. Oh, I said, that is a different matter, Yes. So that night before I began preaching, he stood up and he said, Men and women I am a Roman Catholic. I was private secretary to the Cardinal in San Francisco and I had never read a chapter of the Bible and I had never once heard the gospel preached until two weeks ago last Thursday. I was passing down the street and I saw the tent, and I thought it was a circus, and so I made for it; and just as I got in the tent door I saw Dr. Pink on the platform and something gripped me and just shoved me in, and I sat down, and, he said, that night for the first time I heard the Gospel preached, and right on the spot God saved me. I said, Will you just mention again brother, the night? He said, It was two weeks ago last Thursday. And I thought to myself, Well the man has got that wrong. I said, Are you sure? He said, Yes, of course I am. And after the meeting was over (it only showed my own scepticism and how man wants to limit God) I said to him, What on earth was there in that sermon that could save you? Why, that particular night was a thanksgiving service and I preached for a whole hour on praising God and there wasn't a word of the gospel in it, there was'nt a word about hell in it, there wasn't anything about sin in it, there wasn't anything about the cross in it. I said, What on earth was there in that sermon to save you? You see I wanted to limit God. I was silly enough to think that God could not save a man who had never heard the Gospel, except by a Gospel sermon, and I was preaching from Heb. 13:15: "By Him therefore let us offer the sacrifice of praise to God continually, that is the fruit of our lips giving thanks to His name" and all through I was exhorting Christians to be praising God. Wny, he said, Dr. Pink, I will tell you. As I listened to that sermon, the Spirit of God just struck conviction into my heart by reminding me that I had never praised God and what a terrible sinner I must be! Ah, there is the sovereignty of God. God is sovereign in the very texts that He uses.

Mr. Spurgeon vouches for the statement that he knew a man 88 years of age who had lived as a hardened sinner, and one night he was reading through part of the 5th chapter of Genesis, which is one of the driest chapters in the Bible to most people. It just says So-and-so was the son of So-and-so and he lived so many years before he died, and the next verse is just a repetition right on to the end of the chapter. And Mr. Spurgeon says as this man read "And he died," and "Methuselah lived 969 years and he died" the old man said to himself, "Yes, and I am a sinner and I must die." Ah, my friends, God can use any verse of Scripture He pleases: we are not all of us saved under John 3:16.

Fifth, God is sovereign in **the experiences which accompany salvation.** A great many people have endured all kinds of trouble and anxiety because they failed to recognise that. Some of God's people have had a long season of deep conviction of sin and they have been months and months before peace came. Others have just been stricken down in a moment like Saul of Tarsus, and saved on the spot. Listen, dear friends, God is sovereign in the very experience of salvation. Don't you worry because your experience is not identical with somebody else's. Some Christians enter into full assurance of salvation within a few days or a few hours after they have been born again. There are other Christians—and I believe real Christians—who sometimes go for years before they have the full assurance of faith. God is sovereign there. Faith is God's gift and to some He gives little faith and to others large faith. If any of you doubt that read Bunyan's "Pilgrim's Progress."

Well now the time has almost gone. I just want to add one word in connection with the sovereignty of God in regard to **healing.** How many of God's children have been brought into bondage and have had their feelings harrowed because of their failure to recognise the **sovereignty** of God in connection with the healing of sickness. God is sovereign even there as in everything else. God heals some Christians and He allows others to continue sick. God does not heal all. Paul prayed three times that the thorn in the flesh might be removed but it was not, and he tells us in II Timothy 4, verse 20, "Trophimus have I left at Miletum sick."

Even the Apostle Paul with the miraculous powers that God had given him had to leave a beloved saint at Miletum sick. It was not God's will that he should be healed. God heals some but He doesn't others.

Again, God heals some Christian without the use of any means: they are healed without any medicines or doctors. That is illustrated in the miracles of Christ. There are other sick Christians who are just as truly healed by God but they are healed with the use of means. Hezekiah was. When he was sick God sent one of His servants to tell him to use means—a fig poultice. And if I had a boil, that is exactly what I would use. I believe God is wiser than man any time. God told Timothy through Paul to take a little wine for his stomach's sake.

Now in the third place, God heals some of His children in response to the believing prayers of the saints. That is taught in the 5th chapter of James. But God does not heal all. The very same people can pray for another sick one and that sick one won't get well. The great thing to recognise is that God does not act according to law. God is under no law. God is above all law. God does not act uniformly, but God always acts according to His own sovereign pleasure, and the practical lesson for us is to leave all our affairs in His hands and bow to His sovereign will.

Now to-morrow night, God willing, and the night following, we shall speak on the Sovereignty of God as it is manifested in the doctrine of Election, and I hope that there will be much prayer made that God will prepare both speaker and hearer for these services in order that He may be glorified and that we may be edified.

## THE POWER OF GOD.

"Lo! these are parts of His ways: but how little portion is heard of Him, but the thunder of His power, who can understand?" (Job 26:14).

Bildad, had, in the foregoing chapter, entertained Job with a discourse of the dominion and power of God, and the purity of His righteousness, whence he argues an impossibility of the justification of man in His presence, who is no better than a worm. Job, in this chapter, acknowledges the greatness of God's power, and descants more largely upon it than Bildad had done; but both preface it with a kind of ironical speech, as if He had not acted a friendly part, or spake little of the purpose, or the matter in hand: the subject of Job's discourse was the worldly happiness of the wicked, and the calamities of the godly: and Bildad reads him a lecture, of the extent of God's dominion, the number of His armies, and the unspotted rectitude of His nature, in comparison of which the purest creatures are foul and crooked. Job, therefore, from v. 1 to 4, taxed him in a kind of scoffing manner, that he had not touched the point, but rambled from the subject in hand, and had not applied a salve proper to this sore (v. 2): "How hast thou helped him that is without power? How savest thou the arm of him that hath no strength?" etc.; your discourse is so impertinent, that it will never strengthen a weak person, or instruct a simple one. But since Bildad would take up the argument of God's power, and discourse so short of it, Job would show that he wanted not his instruction in that kind, and that he had more distinct conceptions of it than his antagonist had uttered: and therefore from v. 5 to the end of the chapter, he doth magnificently treat of the power of God in several branches; and (v. 5) he begins with the lowest. "Dead things are formed under the waters, and the habitants thereof:" You read me a lecture of the power of God in the heavenly host: indeed, it is visible there, yet of a larger extent; and monuments of it are found in the lower parts. What do you think of those dead things under the earth and waters, of the corn that dies and by the moistening influences of the clouds spring up again with a numerous progeny and increase for the nourishment of mankind? What do you think of those varieties of metals and minerals conceived in the bowels of the earth; those pearls and riches in the depths of the waters, midwifed by this power of God? Add to these those more prodigious creatures in the sea, the inhabitants of the waters, with their vastness and variety, which are all the births of God's power, both in their first creation by His mighty voice, and their propagation by His cherishing providence. Stop not here, but consider that also His power extends to hell; either the graves the repositories of all the crumbled dust that had yet been in the world (for so hell is sometimes taken in Scripture: v. 6, "Hell is naked before Him, and destruction hath no covering."). The several lodgings of deceased men are known to Him: no screen can obscure them from His sight, nor their dissolution be any bar to His power, when the time is come to compact these moulded bodies to entertain again their departed souls, either for weal or woe. The grave, or hell, the place of punishment, is naked before Him; as distinctly discerned by Him, as a naked body in all its lineaments by us, or a dissected body is in all its parts to the skilful eye.

Destruction hath no covering; none can free himself from the power of His hand. Every person in the bowels of hell; every person punished there is known to Him, and feels the power of His wrath. From the lower parts of the world he ascends to the consideration of the power of God in the creation of heaven and earth; "He stretches out the North over the empty places" (v. 7). The north, or the north pole, over the air, which, by the Greeks, was elements; and He mentions here the north, or the north pole, for the whole heaven, because it is more known and apparent than the southern pole. "And hangs the earth upon nothing;" the massy and weighty earth hangs like a thick globe in the midst of a thin air, that there is as much air on the one side as on the other. The heavens have no prop to sustain them in their height, and the earth hath no basis to support it in its place. The heavens are as if you saw a curtain stretched smooth in the air without any hand to hold it; and the earth as if you saw a ball hanging in the air without any solid body to under-prop it, or any line to hinder it from falling; both standing monuments of the omnipotence of God. He then takes notice of His daily power in the clouds; "He binds up the waters in His thick clouds, and the cloud is not rent under them" (v. 8). He compacts the waters together into the clouds, and keeps them by His power in the air against the force of their natural gravity and heaviness, till they are fit to flow down upon the earth, and perform His pleasure in the places for which He designs them. "The cloud is rent under them;" the thin air is not spilt asunder by the weight of the waters contained in the cloud above it. He causes them to distil by drops, and strains them, as it were, through a thin lawn, for the refreshment of the earth; and suffers them not to fall in the whole lump, with a violent torrent, to waste the industry of man, and bring famine upon the world by destroying the fruits of the earth. What a wonder it would be to see but one entire drop of water hang itself by one inch above the ground, unless it be a bubble which is preserved by the air enclosed within it! What a wonder would it be to see a gallon of water contained in a thin cobweb as strongly as in a vessel of brass! Greater is the wonder of Divine power in these thin bottles of heaven, as they are called (Job 38:37); and therefore called His clouds here as being daily instances of His omnipotence: that the air should sustain these rolling vessels, as it should seem, weightier than itself; that the force of this mass of waters should not break so thin a prison, and hasten to its proper place, which is below the air: that they should be daily confined against their natural inclination, and held by so slight a chain; that there should be such a gradual and successive falling of them, as if the air were pierced by holes like a gardener's watering-pot, and not fall in one entire body to drown or drench some parts of the earth. These are hourly miracles of Divine power, as little regarded as clearly visible. He proceeds (v. 9), "He holds back the face of His throne, and spreads the clouds upon it." The clouds are designed as curtains to cover the heavens, as well as vessels to water the earth (Psa. 147:8). As a tapestry curtain between the heavens, the throne of God (Isa. 46:1), and the earth His footstool: the heavens are called His throne because His power doth most shine forth from there, and magnificently declare the glory of God; and the clouds are as a screen between the scorching heat of the sun, and the tender plants of the earth, and the weak bodies of men. From hence he descends to the sea, and considers the Divine power apparent in the abounding of it (v. 10). "He hath compassed the waters with bounds, till the day and night come to an end." This is several times mentioned in Scripture as a signal mark of Divine strength (Job 38:8; Prov. 8:27). He hath measured a place for the sea, and struck the limits of it as with a compass, that it might not mount above the surface of the land, and ruin the ends of the earth's creation; and this, while day and night have their mutual turns, till He shall make an end of time by removing the measures of it. The bounds of the tumultuous sea are, in many places as weak as the bottles of the upper waters; the one is contained in thin air, and the other restrained by weak sands, in many places, as well as stubborn rock in others; that, though it swells, foams, roars, and the waves, encouraged and egged on by strong winds, come like mountains against the shore; they overflow it not, but humble themselves when they come near to those sands, which are set as their lists and limits, and retire back to the womb that brought them forth, as if they were ashamed and repented of their proud invasion; or else it may be meant of the tides of the sea, and the stated time God hath set it for its ebbing and flowing, till night and day come to and end; both that the fluid waters should contain themselves within due bounds, and keep their perpetually orderly motion, are amazing arguments of Divine power. He passes on to the consideration of the commotions in the air and earth, raised and stilled by the power of God;" The pillars of heaven tremble, and are astonished at His reproof." By pillars of heaven are not meant angels, as some think, but either the air, called pillars of heaven in regard of place, as it continues and knits together the parts of the world, as pillars do the upper and nether parts of a building; as the lowest parts of the earth are called the foundations of the earth, so the lowest part of heaven may be called the pillars of heaven: or else by the phrase may be meant mountains, which seem, at a distance, to touch the sky, as pillars do the top of a structure; and so it may be spoken, according to vulgar capacity, which imagines the heavens to be sustained by the two extreme parts of the earth, as a convex body, or to be arched by pillars; whence Scripture, according to common apprehensions, mentions the ends of the earth, and the utmost parts of heaven, though they have properly no end, as being round. The power of God is seen in those commotions in the air and earth by thunders lightnings, storms, earthquakes, which rack the air and make the mountains and hills tremble as servants before a frowning and rebuking master. And as He makes motions in the earth and in the air, so is His power seen in their influences upon the sea; "He judges the sea with His power, and by His understanding He smites through the proud" (v. 12). At the creation He put the waters into several channels, and caused the dry land to appear barefaced for a habitation for man and beasts; or rather He split the sea by storms, as though He would make the bottom of the deep visible, and rakes up the sands to the surface of the waters, and marshals the waves into mountains and valleys. After that "He smites through the proud," that is, humbles the proud waves, and, by allaying the storm, reduceth them to their level; the power of God is visible, as well in rebuking, as in awakening winds; He makes them sensible of His voice, and according to His pleasure, exasperates or calms them. The "striking through the proud" here, is not probably meant of the destruction of the Egyptian army, for some guess that Job died that year, or about the time of the Israelites coming out of Egypt; so that this discourse here, being in the time of his affliction, could not point at that which was done, after his restoration to his temporal posterity. And now, at last, he sums up the power of God, in the chiefest of His works above, and the greatest wonder of His work below (v. 13); "By His Spirit He hath garnished the heavens; His hand hath formed the crooked serpent;" etc. The greater and lesser lights, sun, moon, and stars, the ornaments and furniture of heaven; and the whale, a prodigious monument of God's power, often mentioned in Scripture to this purpose, and, in particular, in this book of Job (ch. 41); and called by the same name of the crooked serpent (Isa. 27:1), where it is applied, by way of metaphor, to the king of Assyria or Egypt or all oppressors of the church. Various interpretations there are of this crooked serpent; some understanding that constellation in heaven which astronomers call the dragon; some that combination of weaker stars, which they call the galaxia, which winds about the heavens; but it is most probable that Job, drawing near to a conclusion of his discourse, joins the two greatest testimonies of God's power in the world, the highest heavens, and the lowest leviathan, which is here called a bar serpent, in regard of his strength and hardness, as mighty men are called bars in Scripture (Jer. 51:30); "Her bars are broken things." And in regard of this power of God in the creation of this creature, it is particularly mentioned in the catalogue of God's works (Gen. 1:21); "And God created great whales;" all the other creatures being put into one sum and not particularly expressed. And now he makes use of this lecture in the text, "Lo, these are parts of His ways; but how little a portion is heard of Him, but the thunder of His power who can understand?" This is but a small landscape of some of His works of power; the outsides and extremities of it; more glorious things are within His palaces: though those things argue a stupendous power of the Creator, in His works of creation and providence, yet they are nothing to what may be declared of His power. And what may be declared, is nothing to what may be conceived; and what may be conceived, is nothing to what is above the conceptions of any creature. These are but little crumbs and fragments of that Infinite Power, which is, in His nature, like a drop in comparison of the mighty ocean: a hiss or whisper in comparison of a mighty voice of thunder. This, which I have spoken, is but like a spark to the fiery region, a few lines, by the way, a drop of speech.

—Dr. S. Charnock, 1670.

## A PERVERTED GOSPEL.

I have been preaching about the New Covenant, I have been insisting upon it that what is preached around us for the Gospel is not the Gospel at all, but the conditional covenant of works, unto which the preachers pin Jesus and His death as those preachers did who bewitched the churches in Galatia, about whose wicked dogmas the churches desired the Apostles to hold a council to pronounce upon the same, which they did, Acts 15. There are seven charges laid against these preachers. 1. The Apostles charge them with lying—v. 24. 2. They charged them with tempting God—v. 10. 3. They charged them with preaching the law—v. 5. 4. They charged with yoking disciples in bondage —v. 13. 5. They charged them with troubling the churches—v. 24. 6. They charged them with subverting souls—v. 24. 7. Paul charged them with bewitching the churches—Gal. 3:1.

I affirm calmly and most considerately, after fifty years attention to our Protestant preachers in England and the Colonies, that nineteen out of every twenty of them are guilty of the same seven sins, and that their preaching is as foreign to the Gospel as was theirs.

What was the sum and substance of the preaching of these men against whom these seven charges were laid? Was it not that if the people would fulfil certain conditions they should be saved? And what is the preaching of these preachers around us? Is it not if their hearers will now perform certain conditions which they propound to them they shall be saved? The sum of their witchcraft is set forth in their often repeated lie," God the Father hath done all He can, God the Son has done all He can, God the Holy Spirit has done all he can for you, and now it is for you to perform your part, and you will be saved. Oh, sinner, do it, and you will be saved now." This is the covenant of works. "Do and live: He that doeth these things shall live in them. Why will ye die O house of Israel?" God again and again declares in His most Holy Word that this is not the covenant by which He saves poor sinners of His people—Jer. 31:33; Heb. 8:10, 13; Gal. 4:27; Isa. 59:21; Psa. 89. Preaching up a conditional salvation in the face of these testimonies of God is nothing less than attempting to make God a liar.

God says, "This covenant, by which I save sinners, is not according to that covenant that I made with the house of Israel when I brought them out of Egypt." These men say in effect affirm, "O, yes, it is the same conditional covenant." God says," It is more excellent ministry." These men say, "It is the same; do and be saved." God says, "It is built upon better promises." These men say, "O, we must fulfil the conditions." Now, so far as men can do it, these preachers do attempt to make God a liar, under the pretence of preaching the Gospel. I affirm that they neither preach the law nor the Gospel in their distinctive character, but a kind of conglomeration of them both. It is a hydra-headed bastard, with Pagan feet Papal eyes, Mosaic hands, a Nazarene mouth, a fox's nose, an Esau's head, a Popish belly, Nimrod's legs, a Jezebel neck, an Egyptian face, a Pelagian back, an Arminian breast, and it is robed in the old dress of Saul of Tarsus, which he wore when they stoned Stephen, but which he cast away when he saw Jesus. This is the horrid figure they now present to the people for what they call the Gospel, as violently opposed to the unconditional character and promises of the new covenant which God has made with His Son on behalf of His people, and Which He has sent His servants to proclaim to guilty men, who are destitute of any ability to perform one good deed until they receive grace, so that if they were left to a conditional salvation they must be eternally lost.

As opposed to these lying delusions of men, God proclaims in His unconditional covenant to guilty sinners, these seven things: 1. I will put My laws in their mind. 2. I will write them in their hearts. 3. I will be their God. 4. They shall be My people. 5. They shall all know Me. 6. I will be merciful to their unrighteousness. 7. Their sins and iniquities will I remember no more, Heb. 8:8, 12. These are the seven notes of the joyful sound of an unconditional salvation to guilty men.

What a sevenfold lie to say that God has done all He can do and they must now do their part, when here are seven things which He says He Himself will do for these poor, helpless sinners.

Thus we find the proclamation of a conditional salvation is a lying delusion, opposed to God's Word, and destruction to the souls of men. Also, we find God's testimony in the Gospel is what He will do in and for guilty men, without money and without price.

O, how divinely suited is this blessed Gospel of the Lord to my guilty and helpless soul. I can do, when God works in me, that which is pleasing to Him, but without that work of His in me I cannot do anything. I am shut up to the Lord entirely, to have all my works wrought in me by Him, and blessed be His name forever and ever, He tells me in this Gospel, this covenant, that He will do it. I must be eternally lost if this is not true; I cannot hope if this is not so for one moment. But it is so; it is true. He will do it; He does do it in you, and in me, and in all His own.

—The Late Pastor Allen of Sydney, 1884.

## GONE ASTRAY—NOW RETURNED.

"For ye were as sheep going astray, but are now returned unto the Shepherd and Bishop of your souls" (1 Peter 2:25.)

"Ye were as sheep going astray"; how distinctly this shows that those sinners that trust in the Lord Jesus for salvation were already His sheep, when as yet they had not been brought to know their need of the great salvation accomplished for them by their "good shepherd."

"Ye are now returned unto the Shepherd and Bishop of your souls;" how distinctly this shows the sure results of grace, through the quickening work of the Holy Spirit. As the result of that work, the Lord Jesus possesses the chiefest attraction for them. "My sheep hear My voice" ... and they follow Me." They now seek no other place of refuge, no other guide but Himself. They may possess but little comfort. They may have but a very faint assurance of their interest in His love. Great may be the depths of inbred evil over which they have to mourn, yet withal they can truly say, that their eyes are towards Him, and the desire of their hearts is after Him. The sure evidence this, that His eyes were previously toward them, and His desire first after them, and that His voice has effectually called them to Himself. "Them also I must bring, and they shall hear My voice." How emphatic! How certain is the Shepherd's language! "I must bring," "they shall hear."

How complete are the arrangements of the everlasting covenant! How irresistible are the workings of sovereign electing grace! So it is always. He begins the work in the soul of His beloved; and it is He who carries on that work unto the end. Both the beginning and the end shall ever more be to the glory of His matchless, free, and unmerited grace.

—Things to Come, 1902.

"When thou hearest of Christ do not think Him God only or man only, but both together; for I know Christ was hungry, and I know that with five loaves He fed five thousand men, besides women and children. I know Christ was thirsty, and I know Christ turned water into wine. I know Christ was carried in a ship, and I know Christ walked upon the waters. I know Christ died, and I know Christ raised the dead. I know Christ was set before Pilate, and I know Christ sits with the Father. I know Christ was worshipped by the angels, and I know Christ was stoned by the Jews. And truly some of these I ascribe to the human, the other to the Divine nature; for by reason of this is He said to be both together.

—Chrysostom, 390 A.D.

*(Continued from page 1.)*

up into His face and saying, "**my God**"! O, the marvel of it—the infinite, eternal, all-mighty God, mine! Ah, and cannot we say this with a depth of meaning which David never could? Has not the coming of Christ into this world, His taking upon Him human form, His atoning-death at Calvary, instituted a relationship which if David knew anything about he surely never fully entered into? God is my God and Father because He is Christ's God and Father (see John 20:17). How blessed to say with the Apostle "**My God** shall supply all your need" (Phil. 4:19).

Second, there is a **purpose of heart expressed**: "early will I seek Thee." Here we have deliberation, decision and singleness of aim. This calls to mind a passage in the Old Testament and another in the New, which are similar in substance and scope. "**One thing** have I desired of the Lord, that will I seek after; that I may dwell in the house of the Lord (the place of communion) all the days of my life, to behold the beauty of the Lord and to inquire in His Temple" (Psa. 27:4). "**This one thing** I do, forgetting those things which are behind, and reaching forth unto those things which are before, I press toward the mark for the prize of the high calling of God in Christ Jesus" (Phil. 3:13, 14).

"Early will I seek Thee." What abundant cause has He given us to seek Him! He sought us when we were dead in trespasses and sins, shall we not then seek Him now that He has imparted to us His own life! He desires to be sought, for He delights in our fellowship: that is one reason why He has appointed prayer as one of the principal means of grace. And **how** is He to be sought? **Early**: at the beginning of the day, before the things of the world engage our thoughts and strength. **Early** this New Year, remembering His promise "those that seek Me early shall find Me" (Prov. 8:17). He is also to be sought **diligently**: "He that cometh to God must believe that He is, and that He is a rewarder of them that diligently seek Him" (Heb. 11:6). He is also to be sought **whole-heartedly**: "Ye shall seek Me, and find Me, when ye shall search for Me with all your heart" (Jer. 29:13).

Third, there is a **thirsting of soul**: "My soul thirsteth for Thee." This is not the language of a man who has no acquaintance with God, but the yearning of a heart that already knows Him yet longs for a deeper knowledge of and closer walk with Him. Just as God only can **save**, so He alone can **sustain**. It is only as He is kept steadily before the soul and the eye of faith gazes upon His perfections that succor and strength is obtained for our daily pilgrimage and warfare. And just as God only can sustain, so He alone can **satisfy**. All our springs are in Him. From Him only cometh our help. The more we know Him the deeper will be our thirst for Him.

Fourth, there is a **felt desolation**: My flesh longeth for Thee in a dry and thirsty land, where no water is." There is good reason to conclude that this Psalm was written by David while he was dwelling in the wilderness of Judah. It was an arid tract of land stretching along the western shore of the Dead Sea. The dreariness of his surroundings symbolised the spiritual state of this world. As David looked on the burnt-up barren country around him, with great cracks in the soil, gaping for the rain which came not, he perceived that this was all a picture of the utter insufficiency of material things to minister to the life of a child of God. This world is nought but a "dry and thirsty land, where no water is" to the one walking in communion with the Lord. But this only makes him appreciate more deeply His gracious invitation, "If any man thirst, let him come unto Me and drink" (John 7:37). He alone can quench our thirst.

The verses that follow (in this sixty-third Psalm) are very precious. That which David longed for was "to see Thy power and Thy glory" (v 2). These Divine excellencies are unveiled to us in the four Gospels in a way that (most probably) the Psalmist was never permitted to gaze upon. "Because Thy loving kindness is better than life, my lips shall praise Thee" (v. 3): this should be our daily occupation, "My soul shall be satisfied as with marrow and with fatness; and my mouth shall praise Thee with joyful lips" (v. 5): but this is only the experience of one who can truly say, "O God, Thou art my God; early will I seek Thee: my soul thirsteth for Thee, my flesh longeth for Thee in a dry and thirsty land, where no water is." May the Lord add His own blessing to this little meditation.

Yours by His Grace,

Arthur W. Pink.

# STUDIES IN THE SCRIPTURES

"Search the Scriptures" John 5:39.

Copyright in all English-speaking Countries.

Arthur W. Pink, Publisher and Editor,
5 Norton Street, Ashfield, N.S.W., Australia.

Price: 10 cents per copy; $1.00 or 5/- per year.

## GOD'S INHERITANCE.

"For the Lord's portion is His people; Jacob is the lot of His inheritance" (Deut. 32:9).

This verse brings before us a most blessed and wonderful line of truth, so wonderful that no human mind could possibly have invented it. It speaks of the mighty God having an "inheritance," and it tells us that this inheritance is in His own people! God refused to take this world for His inheritance—it will yet be burnt up. Nor did Heaven, peopled with angels, satisfy His heart. In eternity past Jehovah said, by way of anticipation, "My delights were with the sons of men" (Prov. 8:31).

This is by no means the only scripture which teaches that God's inheritance is in His saints. In Psalm 135:4 we read, "For the Lord hath chosen Jacob unto Himself, and Israel for His peculiar treasure." In Mal. 3:17 the Lord speaks of His people as His "special treasure" (see margin)—so "special" that the highest manifestations of His love are made to **them,** the richest gifts of His hand are bestowed on **them,** the mansions on High are prepared and reserved for **them!**

The same wondrous truth is taught in the New Testament. In Eph. 1, we behold the apostle Paul praying that God would give unto His people the spirit of wisdom and revelation in the knowledge of Him: the eyes of their understanding being enlightened that they might know "what is the hope of His calling, and what the riches of the glory of His inheritance in the saints" (v. 18). This is a truly amazing expression; not only do the saints obtain an inheritance in God, but He also secures an inheritance in them! How overwhelming the thought that the great God should deem Himself the richer because of **our** faith, our love and worship! Surely this is one of the most marvellous truths revealed in Holy Writ—that God should pick up poor sinners and make them His "inheritance!" Yet so it is.

But what need has God of us? How can we possibly enrich Him? Does He not have everything—wisdom, power, grace and glory? All true, yet there is something that He needs, yes, needs, namely, vessels. Just as the sun needs the earth to shine upon, so God needs vessels to fill, vessels through which His glory may be reflected, vessels on which the riches of His grace may be lavished.

Mark that God's people are not only called His "portion," His "special treasure," but also His "inheritance." This suggests three things. First, an "inheritance" is obtained **through death:** so God's inheritance is secured to Him through the death of His beloved Son. Second, an "inheritance" denotes **perpetuity**—"to a man and his heirs forever" are the terms often used. Third, an "inheritance" is for **possession,** it is something which is entered into, lived upon, enjoyed. Let us now consider five things about God's inheritance:

*(Continued on page 24)*

## IMPORTANT NOTICES

Set of twelve issues for **1922**, unbound, $1.00 or 5/-. Bound $1.50 or 7/-.
Ditto 1923, 1924, 1925.

Note: We cannot break a set or now supply any single 1925 issues.

Subscription—price: $1.00 or 5/- per year to any address in the world.

Change of Address: Please notify me promptly of any change of address, and be certain to give both old and new address.

Non-subscribers receiving this Magazine regularly will understand their subscription has been entered by a friend.

Copies lost in the mail duplicated only if we are notified promptly.

## CONTENTS

| | |
|---|---|
| The Gospel of John (John 14: 21-31) ... | 26 |
| Gleanings in Exodus | 34 |
| Election | 39 |
| God Securing His Inheritance... | 45 |

## THE GOSPEL OF JOHN

**50. Christ Comforting His Disciples (concluded): John 14: 21-31.**

The following is an analysis of the closing section of John 14:

1. Christ manifested to the believer v. 21.
2. The quandary of Judas v. 22.
3. Christ's explanation vv. 23-25.
4. The ministry of the Spirit v. 26.
5. The gift of Christ's peace v. 27.
6. The failure in the disciples' love vv. 28-29.
7. The coming conflict vv. 30-31.

That the central design of Christ in the first main section of this Paschal discourse was to comfort His sorrowing disciples, and that this section does not close until we reach the end of John 14 is clear from v. 27: "Let not your heart be troubled." The Lord here repeats what He had said in the first verse, and then adds, "neither let it be afraid." That the first section of the discourse does terminate at the close of the chapter, is obvious from its final words: "Arise, let us go hence."

Many and varied were the grounds of comfort which the Lord had laid before the apostles. First, He assured them that He was going to the Father's House. Second, that He would make provision for their coming there. Third, that when the necessary preparations were completed, He would come and conduct them thither. Fourth, that He had opened the way for them, had made them acquainted with the way, and would give them the energy necessary to go along that way. Fifth, that He would not withdraw from them the miraculous powers which He had conferred upon them, but would enable them to do still greater things. Sixth, that whatever they needed for the discharge of the work to which He had called them, on asking in His name, they should assuredly obtain. Seventh, that a Divine Person should be sent to supply His place, acting as their instructor, guide, protector and consoler. Eighth, that they should not be "left orphans," but He would return to them in possession of an endless life, of which they should be partakers. Ninth, that in a soon-coming day they should apprehend the oneness of life, shared by the Father and the Son and the sons.

In the passage which is to be before us we find the Lord adding to these grounds of comfort. Tenth, He would manifest Himself to those who kept His commandments. Eleventh, those who kept His Word should be loved by the Father. Twelfth, the Holy Spirit would bring back to their remembrance all things Christ had said unto them. Thirteenth, Peace He left with them. Fourteenth, His own peace He bequeathed unto them. No wonder that He said, **"Let not** your heart be troubled, neither let it be afraid!"

"He that hath My commandments, and keepeth them, he it is that loveth Me, and he that loveth Me shall be loved of My Father, and I will love him, and will manifest Myself to him" (v. 21). In this instance we shall depart from our customary method of expounding the different clauses of a verse in the order in which they occur; instead, we shall treat this verse more or less topically. That in it which is of such vital importance is the final clause, where the Saviour promised to manifest Himself to the obedient believer. Now there is nothing the real Christian desires so much as a personal manifestation of the Lord Jesus. In comparison with this all other blessings are quite secondary. In order to simplify, let us ask and attempt to answer three questions: How does the Saviour now "manifest" Himself? What are the effects of such manifestation? What are the conditions which I have to meet.

In what way does the Lord Jesus now manifest Himself? It is hardly necessary to say, not corporeately. No longer is the Word, made flesh, tabernacling among men. No more does He say, as He said to Thomas, "Reach hither thy finger, and behold My hands, and reach hither thy hand, and thrust it into My side." (John 20:27). No longer may He be seen by our physical eyes (1 John 1:1). Nor is the promise of Christ which we are now considering made good through visions. We recall the vision which Jacob had at Bethel, when a ladder was set upon earth, whose top reached unto heaven, upon which the angels of God ascended and descended. We think of that wondrous vision given to Isaiah, when he saw the Lord sitting upon a Throne, before which the seraphim cried, "Holy, holy, holy." No, it is not in visions or in dreams that the Lord promises to come to His people. What then? It is a spiritual revelation of Himself to the soul! It is a vivid realisation of the Saviour's being and nearness, in a deep and abiding sense of His favour and love. "By the power of the Spirit, He makes His Word so luminous, that as we read it, He Himself seems to draw near. The whole biography of Jesus becomes in this way a precious reality. We see His form. We hear His words." It is through the written Word that the incarnate Word "manifests" Himself to the heart!

And what are the effects upon the soul of such a manifestation of Christ. First and foremost He Himself is made a blessed and glorious reality to us. The one who has been granted such an experience can say with Job, "I have heard of Thee by the hearing of the ear, but now mine eye (the eye of the heart) seeth Thee" (42:5). Such a one now discerns the surpassing beauty and glory of His person and exclaims, "Thou art fairer than the children of men." Again: such a manifestation of Christ to the soul assures us of His favour. Now we hear Him saying (through the Scriptures) "As the Father hath loved Me, so I have loved you." And now I can respond, "My beloved is mine, and I am His." Another consequence of this manifestation of Christ is "comfort and support in trials, especially in those trials, which, on account of their personal nature, are beyond the reach of human sympathy and love—the trials of desertion and loneliness, from which Jesus Himself suffered so keenly; heart trials, domestic trials, secret griefs, too sacred to be breathed in the ear of men—all these trials in which nothing can sustain us but the sympathy which His own presence gives." Just as the Son of God appeared to the three faithful Hebrews in the fiery furnace, so does He now come, to those in the place of trial and anguish. So too in the last great trial, should we be called upon to pass through it ere the Saviour comes. Then to earthly friends we can turn no longer. But we may say with the Psalmist, "Though I walk through the valley of the shadow of death, I will fear no evil; for Thou art with me."

Now, let us inquire, What are the terms on which the Saviour thus draws near? Surely every Christian reader is is most anxious to secure the key to an experience so elevating, so blessed. Listen now to the Saviour's words, "He that hath My commandments, and keepeth them, he it is that loveth Me: and he that loveth Me shall be loved of My Father, and I will love him, and will manifest Myself to him." The faith by which we are saved does not destroy the necessity for an obedient walk. "Faith is the root of which obedience is the beautiful flower and fruit. And it is only when faith has issued in obedience, in an obedience which stumbles not at sacrifices, and halts not when the way is rough and dark; in an obedience that cheerfully bears the cross and shame—it is only then that this highest promise of the Gospel is fulfilled ... When love for the Saviour shall lead us to keep His holy Word—lead us to an immediate, unreserved, unhesitating obedience—lead us to say, in the Spirit of entire self-surrender and sacrifice, 'Thy will, not mine, be done,' then, farewell to doubt and darkness, to loneliness and sorrow! Then shall we mourn no more an absent Lord. Then shall, we walk as seeing Him who is invisible, triumphant over every fear, victorious over every foe."*

---

*The above quotations are from an article by the late Mr. Ingliss, which appeared in the October 1922 issue of this Magazine.

This manifestation of Christ is made only to the one who really loves Him, and the proof of love to Him is not by emotional displays but by submission to His will. There is a vast difference between sentiment and practical reality. The Lord will give no direct and special revelation of Himself to those who are in the path of **disobedience**. "He that **hath** My commandments," means, hath them at heart. "And **keepeth them**," that is the real test. We **hear**, but do **we heed**? We **know**, but are we **doing** His will? My little children, let us not love in words, neither in tongue; but in **deed** and in **truth**" (1 John 3:18)!

"And he that loveth Me, shall be loved of My Father." There are three different senses in which Christians may be considered as objects of the loving favour of the Father and of the Son: as persons elected in sovereign grace to eternal life; as persons actually **united** to Christ by believing; and as persons **transformed** by the sanctifying work of the Spirit. It is in this last sense that Christ here speaks. Just as the Father is said to love the Son because of His obedience (John 10:17, 18), so is He said to love the believer for the same reason. It is the love of complacency, as distinguished from the love of compassion. The Father was well-pleased with His incarnate Son, and He is well-pleased with us when we honour and glorify His Son by obeying His commandments.

"Judas saith unto Him, not Iscariot, Lord, how is it that Thou wilt manifest Thyself unto us, and not unto the world?" (v.22). This question had in view the Lord's words when He had just said, "The world seeth Me no more" (v. 19), and that he would "manifest" Himself to him who kept His commandments. This conflicted sharply with the Jewish ideas of the Messiah and His kingdom. As yet Judas had failed to perceive that the **truth** of God must **sever** between those who receive it and those who reject it, and that therefore **His** kingdom was **"not of this world"** (18:36). And why was it that Judas understood this not? 1 Cor. 2:10,11 tells us—the Spirit had not yet been given.

"Judas saith unto Him, not Iscariot." "There is something very affecting in this brief parenthesis; the short, sad sentence which our Evangelist throws in—'Judas, not Iscariot.' The one is not for a moment to be confounded with the other; the true apostle with the traitor. How widely different may men be who yet bear the same name! How many have but the name in common!" (Dr. G. Brown.) The Judas who asked this question was the brother of James, the son of Alphaeus, see Luke 6:16.

"Lord how is it that Thou wilt manifest Thyself unto us and not unto the world?" How many there are to-day who, by means of legislation and social amelioration, wish to press on the world those teachings of Christ which are only for His own! Judas did not go quite so far as the unbelieving brethren of Christ according to the flesh—"Go show Thyself to the world" (7:4); but he was sorely puzzled at this breach between the world and them. Dull indeed was Judas, for the Lord had just said, "Even the Spirit of truth, whom the world **cannot** receive, because it seeth Him not, neither knoweth Him" (v. 17). But equally dull, most of the time, are all of us.

"Jesus answered and said unto Him, If a man love Me, he will keep My words: and My Father will love him, and We will come unto Him, and make Our abode with him." (v. 23). "If Judas had known what the world is, and what every human heart is by nature, instead of being puzzled at our Lord's withdrawal from the world, he would have wondered how Jesus could reveal Himself to any man" (Stier). The Lord here repeats that God has fellowship only with those whose hearts **welcome** Him, who love Him, and whose love is manifested by submission to His Word. **Then** He loves in return. The Old Testament taught precisely the same thing. "I love them that love Me" (Prov. 8:17). "If a man love Me **he will keep** My Word." Let not renewed souls torture themselves by attempting to define too nicely the extent of their "keeping." Let those who are tempted to do so meditate upon John 17:6—"I have manifested Thy name unto the men which Thou gavest Me out of the world: Thine they were, and Thou gavest them Me; and they **have kept** Thy Word." Mark it well that this was said by the Saviour in full view of all the infirmities and failures of the disciples, and said prior to the day of Pentecost!

To "keep" God's commandments is to obey them, and the primary, the fundamental thing in obedience, is the **desire** of the **heart,** and it is on the heart that God ever looks. Two things are true of every Christian: deep down in his heart there is an intense, steady longing and yearning to please God, to do His will, to walk in full accord with His Word. This yearning **may be** stronger in some than in others, and in each of us **it is** stronger at some times than at others; nevertheless, it is there! But in the second place, no real Christian **fully** realises this desire. Every genuine Christian has to say with the apostle Paul? "Not as though I had already attained, either were already perfect: but I follow after if that I may lay hold of that for which I am laid hold of by Christ Jesus" (Phil. 3:12).

Now we believe that it is this heart—obedience, this inward longing to be fully conformed to His will, this burning desire of the renewed soul, of which Christ here speaks. "If a man love Me, he will keep My word." Every true believer loves Christ; therefore every true believer "keeps" His Word, keeps it in the sense thus defined. Let it be repeated, God looks at the heart; whereas we are constantly occupied with the outward appearance. As we scrutinise our deeds, if we are honest, we have to acknowledge that we have "kept His word" very imperfectly; yea, it seems to us, that we are not entitled to say that we have "kept" it at all. But the Lord looks behind the deeds, and knows the longings within us. The case of Peter in John 21 is a pertinent illustration. When Christ asked him a third time, "Lovest Thou Me?" His disciple answered, "Lord, Thou knowest all things; THOU knowest that I love Thee (v. 17). My disgraceful actions contradicted my love; my fellow-disciples have good reason to doubt it, but Thou who who searchest the heart knowest better. In one sense it is an intensely solemn and searching thing to remember that nothing can be hidden from Him before whom all things are open and naked; but in another sense it is most blessed and comforting to realise that He can see in my heart what I cannot often discover in my ways, and what my fellow-believers cannot—a real love for Him, a genuine longing to please and glorify Him.

Let not the conclusion be drawn that we are here lapsing into Antinomian laxity, or making it a matter of no moment what our outward lives are like. To borrow words which treat of another subject, "As there was a readiness to will so there should be a performance also" (2 Cor. 8:11). Though the apostle acknowledged that he had not "already attained," yet he continued to "follow after." Where there is love for Christ, there cannot but be bitter sorrow (as with Peter) when we know that we have grieved Him. And more; there will be a sincere confession of our sins, and confession will be followed by earnest supplication for grace to enable us to do what He has bidden. Nevertheless, it is blessed to know that He who is the Truth declares, positively and without qualification, "if a man love Me, he will keep My Word;" and in the light of John 17:6, this must mean: first and absolutely, in the desire of his heart; secondly and relatively, in his walk.

It is to be noted that the Lord here makes a change of terms from what He had said in v. 21; a slight change, but an important one. There He had said, "He that hath My commandments, keepeth them;" here, "If a man love Me, he will keep My word"—in the Greek the singular number is used. "This is a beautiful difference, and of great practical value, being bound up with the measure of our attentiveness of heart. Where obedience lies comparatively on the surface, and self-will or worldliness, is not judged, a 'commandment' is always necessary to enforce it. People ask, 'Must I do this? Is there any harm in that?' To such the Lord's will is solely a question of commandment. Now there are commandments, the expression of His authority, and they are not grievous. But, besides, where the heart loves Him deeply, His 'word' will give enough expression of His will. Even in nature a parent's look will do it. As we well know, an obedient child catches the mother's desire before the mother has uttered a word. So, whatever might be the word of Jesus, it would be heeded, and thus the heart and life be formed in obedience" (Mr. W. Kelly).

"True also it is that something of both characters of love, as Christ affirms them, will be found in all true Christians—overborne by so much contrary influence that, like Peter in the high priest's palace, only He who knoweth all things can detect the true disciple beneath the false. There is the false within us all, as well as the true. Alas, in many, so often uppermost. The results cannot fail to follow: the blessing of which the Lord speaks attaches to that with which He here connects it. We find it in proportion as we answer to the character.

"Looked at in this way, there is no difficulty in seeing the deeper nature of a love that keeps Christ's 'word,' as compared with that which keeps 'commandments' only. Not to keep a positive command is simple, rank rebellion, nothing less. His 'word' is wider, while it addresses itself with less positiveness of authority to the one whose heart and conscience is less prompt to the appeal of love" (Numerical Bible). I do not "command" a **friend**: my mind is made known to him by my words, and he acts accordingly. One word has greater weight with Him than a hundred commands have on one at a distance! A **servant** receives my commands and obeys them, but he knows not my heart; but my **friend** walks with me in the intelligence of my deepest thoughts. Ah, is this so with us? Are we really walking with Him who calls us not servants, but **friends**—see John 15:15!

"And My Father will love him, and We will come unto him, and make Our abode with Him." Just as there is a marked advance from His 'commandments' in v. 21 to His 'word' in v. 23, so there is in the blessings respectively attached to the keeping of the one and the other. In the former He promises to **manifest** Himself to the heart, in the latter He speaks of both the Father and Himself coming to make Their **abode** with such a soul. "Abiding" speaks of **fellowship** all through John's writings. Not only is **our** fellowship with the Father and His Son (1 John 1:3), but to the one who truly heeds the Word, **They** will come and have fellowship with him. This is the reward of loving obedience: note the same order with Israel in the Millennium—Ezek. 36:27 first, 37:37 afterwards! The "result will be to manifest the competency of Scripture for the 'man of God' to whom alone it is pledged as competent,—'able to furnish thoroughly unto all good works.' Who is the man of God, but he who is out and out for God, and who else can expect to be furnished in this way, but he who is honestly intentioned to use his knowledge as before Him who gave it? The very passage which we are quoting here reminds us of where the profit is to be found: 'All Scripture is profitable for doctrine, for reproof, for correction, for instrucion in righteousness.' If we do not mean to accept the reproof and the correction, where is the use of talking about the rest?" (Numerical Bible).

"He that loveth Me not, keepeth not My sayings" (v. 24). Here was the final word to Judas: the line between "the world" and "His own" is clearly drawn by the "whoso loveth Me, whoso loveth Me not." Not to love the loveliest is because of **hatred**. There is no other alternative. Of old Jehovah had declared that He would visit the iniquities of the fathers upon the children unto the third and fourth generation of them that hated Him, but that He would show mercy unto thousands of them that loved Him and kept His commandments (Exodus 26:5, 6). What seems to be **indifference** is really **enmity**. All who are not with Christ are **against** Him (Luke 11:23).

"He that loveth Me not, keepeth not My sayings." Observe the change. In the previous verse the one who loves Christ keeps His **Word**; here the one who who lovest Him not, His **sayings** or words. Why this variation? Because unbelief does not combine in their **unity** the individual sayings, but dismisses them as they are isolated. The true believer hears in all God's words one Word—Him, the unbeliever heeds not! An unbeliever may observe **some** of Christ's words as a matter of policy and prudence, because they commend themselves to His reason; but others, which to him are distasteful, which appear impracticable or severe, he esteems not. If he loved Christ he would value His Word as a whole; but he does not; therefore he keeps not his words.

"And the Word which ye hear is not Mine, but the Father's which sent Me" (v. 24). Thus the Lord concludes this point by magnifying the **Word**. Here we say again, was the final answer to the question, "How is it that Thou wilt manifest Thyself unto us, and **not** unto the world?" Does the world believe on Me? Does it love Me? Does it keep my commandments? How, then, can I manifest Myself to it? "Thus did the Lord dispose of the three main stumbling blocks which hindered these disciples: the offence of Thomas, who would know all with his natural understanding; the offence of Philip, who was eager for visible manifestations to the outward senses; the offence of Judas, who would too readily receive the whole world into the kingdom of God" (Lange).

"These things have I spoken unto you, being yet present with you" (v.25). In the light of the verse which immediately follows we understand this to mean: I have said what I have in view of My near departure. Because I am yet with you, these things make little impression upon your hearts, but when the Holy Spirit has come you will be able to enter the better into their meaning and blessedness.

"But the Comforter, which is the Holy Spirit, whom the Father will send in My name, He shall teach you all things" (v. 26). This is one of many verses which contain clear proof of the Divine personality of the Holy Spirit. A mere abstract influence could not teach. Moreover, **"He shall teach you,"** being a masculine pronoun, could not be applied to any but a real **person.** The Comforter would be sent by the Father, but **in the name of Christ.** The significance of this can best be ascertained by a reference to John 5 : 43 : just as the Saviour had come in the **Father's name,** so the Holy Spirit would be sent in the Son's name : that is to say, in His stead, for His interests, with His authority. Just as the Son had made **known the Father,** so the Spirit would take of the things of Christ and show them to His people. Just **as** the Son had **glorified** the Father, so the Spirit would glorify Christ. Just as, hitherto, the Saviour had supplied all the needs of His own, henceforth the Comforter should fully provide for them.

"He shall teach you all things." Here is another instance where the words of Scripture are **not** to be taken in their absolute sense. If the apostles were to be taught all things, without any qualification, they would be omniscient. Nor did Christ mean that the Holy Spirit would teach them all that it was **possible** for finite creatures to know : He would not make known to them the secrets of futurity, or the occult workings of nature. Rather would He teach them all that it was necessary for them to know for their spiritual well-being, and this, particularly, in connection with what Christ had taught them, either full or in germ form. He would make clear to them that which, as yet, was mysterious in their Master's sayings.

"He shall teach you all things, and bring all things to your remembrance, whatsoever I have said unto you" (v. 26). Two striking examples of that are recorded in this very Gospel. In 2 : 22 we are told, "When therefore He was risen from the dead, His disciples re**membered** that He had said this unto them." Again, in 12 : 16 we read, "These things understood not His disciples at the first ; but when Jesus was glorified, then **remembered** they that these things were written of Him." No doubt this promise of Christ applies in a general way to all real Christians. Hundreds of times has the writer prayed to God, just before entering the pulpit, that He would be pleased to strengthen his memory and enable him to recall the exact words of Scripture as he quoted them ; and graciously has He answered us. We would confidently urge our fellow-believers to plead this verse before God on sleepless nights, or when on a bed of sickness, as well as before going to teach a Sunday School class, asking Him to bring back to your remembrance the comforting promises of His Word ; or, when tempted, that His precepts might flash upon you.

"Peace I leave with you, My peace I give unto you" (v. 27). Without being dogmatic, we believe that there is a double "peace" spoken of here : a peace **left** and a peace **given.** In the New Testament "peace" is spoken of in a twofold sense : as signifying reconciliation, contrasted from alienation : and a state of tranquillity as contrasted from a state of tumult. The one is objective, the other subjective. The former is referred to Rom. 5 : 1 : "Being justified by faith we have peace **with** God." His holy wrath against us and our vile opposition against Him are ended forever. The latter is mentioned in Phil 4 : 7 : "The peace of God, which passeth all understanding shall keep your hearts and minds through Christ Jesus." The one who fully unbosoms himself before the Throne of Grace enjoys rest within. The one then is judicial, the other, experimental. "Peace I leave with you" would be the result of the Atonement. "My peace I give unto you," would be enjoyed through the indwelling Spirit. The one was for the conscience ; the other for the heart.

"My peace I give unto you." This was the personal peace which He had enjoyed here on earth. He was never ruffled by circumstances, and never resisted the will of the Father. He was ever in a state of most perfect amity with God. The peace He here promised His disciples was the peace which filled His own heart, as the result of His unbroken communion with the Father. "For us it is restlessness of will which disturbs this—the strife with His will which this means, and the dissatisfaction of soul which follows every gain that may seem to make in that direction. Doing only **His** will, there can be no proper doubt as to the issue" (Numerical Bible).

"Not as the world giveth, give I unto

you" (v. 27). The peace which the worldling has is shallow, unstable, unsatisfying, false. It talks much about peace, but knows little of the thing itself. We have Peace-societies, Peace-programmes, a Peace-palace, and a League of Nations to promote peace; yet all the great powers are armed to the teeth! "When they shall say, Peace, peace, sudden destruction cometh upon them. (1 Thess. 5:4). The world's peace is a chimera: it fails under trial. When the world gives, it is to the ungodly, not to the godly, whom they hate. When the world gives, it gives away, and has no longer. But Christ gives by bringing us into what is eternally His own. When Christ gives He gives forever, and never takes away.

"Let not your heart be troubled, neither let it be afraid" (v. 27). Here the Lord concludes that section of His discourse which had been devoted to the comforting of His sorrowing disciples. Abundant had been the consolation He had proffered them. Their hearts ought now to have been at perfect peace, their minds being stayed upon God. And yet while this verse terminated the first section of the address, it is closely connected with the verses which follow where the Lord proceeded to make application of what He had been saying.

"Ye have heard how I said unto you, I go away, and come to you. If ye loved Me, ye would rejoice, because I said I go unto the Father: for My Father is greater than I" (v.28). Connecting this verse with the one immediately preceding, the force of our Lord's words is this: If you only believed what I have been saying to you, your cares and fears would vanish, and joy would take the place of sorrow. But what did the Lord mean by "If ye loved Me?" Was He not instructing and directing their love, in order to purify it. He knew that they loved Him, and what He had said in vv. 15, 21, 23, assumed it. But their love was not yet sufficiently dis-interested they were occupied too much with the thought of their own bereavement, instead of the heavenly joy into which the Redeemer was about to enter. If they had loved Him with a pure love, they would have been happy at His exaltation and forgotten themselves.

"My Father is greater than I." This is the favourite verse with Unitarians, who deny the absolute Deity of Christ and His perfect equality with the Father—a truth which is clearly taught in many scriptures. Those who use these words of our Lord in support of their blasphemous heresy, wrest them from their context, ignoring altogether the connection in which they are found. The Saviour had just told the apostles that they ought to rejoice because He was going to the Father, and then advances this reason, "For My Father is greater than I." Let this be kept definitely before us and all difficulty vanishes. The Father's being greater than Christ was the reason assigned why the disciples should rejoice at their Master's going to the Father. This at once fixes the meaning of the disputed "greater," and shows us the sense in which it was here used. The contrast which the Saviour drew between the Father and Himself was not concerning nature, but official character and position.

Christ was not speaking of Himself in His essential Being. The One who thought it not robbery to be "equal with God" had taken the servant form, and not only so, had been made in the likeness of man. In both these senses, namely, in His official status (as Mediator) and in His assumption of human nature, He was inferior to the Father. Throughout this discourse and in the Prayer which follows in chapter 17, the Lord Jesus is represented as the Father's Servant, from whom He had received commission, and to whom He was to render an account; for whose glory He acted, and under whose authority He spake. But there is another sense, more pertinent, in which the Son was inferior to the Father. In becoming incarnate and tabernacling among men, He had greatly humiliated Himself, by choosing to descend into shame and suffering in their acutest forms. He was now the Son of man that had not where to lay His head. He who was rich had for our sakes become poor. He was the Man of sorrows, and acquainted with grief. In view of this, Christ, was now contrasting His situation with that of the Father in the Heavenly Sanctuary. The Father was seated upon the Throne of highest majesty; the brightness of His glory was uneclipsed; He was surrounded by hosts of holy beings, who worshipped Him with uninterrupted praise. Far different was it with His incarnate Son—despised and rejected of men, surrounded by implacable enemies, soon to be nailed to a criminal's cross. In this sense too, He was inferior to the Father. Now in going to the Father, the Son would enjoy a vast improvement of situation. It would be a gain unspeakable. The contrast then was between His present state of humiliation and His coming state of exaltation to the Father! Therefore, those who really loved Him should have rejoiced at the tidings that He would go to the Father, because the Father was greater than He —greater both in official status and in surrounding circumstances. It was Christ owning His place as Servant, and magnifying the One Who had sent Him.

"And now I have told you before it came to pass, that, when it is come to pass, ye might believe?" (v. 29). "The question naturally occurs, Believe what? That question is answered by referring to the parallel statement in reference to the treachery of Judas: 'Now I tell you, that when it is come to pass, ye might believe that I am' (13:19)—that I am the Messiah, the Divinely appointed, qualified, promised, accredited Saviour: and of course, that all I have taught you is indubitably true; and all I have promised, absolutely certain. The disciples did believe this, but their faith was feeble; it required confirmation. It was to be exposed to severe trials, and needed support: and the declaration by Him of these events before they took place was of all things the best fitted for giving their faith that required confirmation and support" (Dr. J. Brown).

"Hereafter I will not talk much with you" (v. 30). In a very short time He would be cut off from them, while He undertook His greatest work of all. In reminding them that it would be impossible for Him to say much more to them. He hinted at the deep importance of them pondering over and over what He had just said, and what He was on the point of saying to them. This was to be His last address in His humbled state, and during the next few hours they would sorely need the sustaining and comforting power of these precious promises if they were not to faint.

"For the Prince of this world cometh, and hath nothing in Me" (v. 30). The awful enmity of the Serpent was now to be fully vented upon the woman's Seed: he was to be allowed to bruise the Saviour's heel. All that this meant we are incapable of entering into. It would seem that Satan began his assault in the Garden, and ceased not till he had moved Pilate to seal the sepulchre and place a guard about it. The words "and hath nothing in Me" refer to His inherent holiness. As the sinless One there was nothing within to which the Devil could appeal. How completely different is it with us! Throw a lighted match into a barrel of gunpowder, and there is a fearful explosion; cast it into a barrel of water and it is quenched!

"For the Prince of this world cometh, and hath nothing in Me." This too was said for the consolation of the apostles: the Saviour would assure them beforehand that the issue of the approaching conflict was not left in any doubt. There was no weak point in Him for Satan to find; therefore He must come forth more than Conqueror. Satan could find something in Noah, Abraham, David, Peter, but Christ was the Lamb "without blemish."

"But that the world may know that I love the Father; and as the Father gave Me commandment, even so I do. Arise, let us go hence" (v. 31). Most blessed is this. The last words of this sentence look back to the end of the previous verse. The Prince of this world cometh—but, nevertheless, I suffer him to come against Me, and I go to meet Him. Christ's love to the Father was thus evidenced by His willingness to allow the Dragon to lay hold upon Him. He went forth to meet Satan because He had received "commandment" from the Father to do so. It is remarkable that this is the only time that Christ ever spoke of His love to the Father; it was now that He was to give the supreme proof of it. How this rebukes those who are ever talking and singing of their love for the Lord? In the words "Arise let us go hence," the Lord must have got up from the supper-table, and apparently was followed by His apostles into the outer room, where they remained until they left for Gethsemane. cf. 18:1.

The following questions are to help the student on the first section of John 15 :—

1. What is meant by "the true Vine" v. 1?
2. In what sense is the Father the Husbandman v. 1?
3. What is meant by "He taketh away" v. 2?
4. What is meant by "purgeth" v. 2?
5. What is meant by "Abide in Me" v. 4?
6. What is meant by the last clause of v. 5?
7. Who is in view in v. 6?

ARTHUR W. PINK.

# GLEANINGS IN EXODUS

### 26. Moses' Wife: Ex. 18.

The chapter before us contains two distinct sections: the first, covering verses 1 to 12, presents to us a beautiful typical picture; the second, verses 13 to 27 contains important moral lessons. Ex. 18 is a parenthesis, interrupting the chronological order of the book. In Ex. 17 Israel is seen at Rephidim; in chapter 19 they are viewed at Sinai. The incident recorded in Ex. 18 occured just as Israel were about to leave Sinai and enter the wilderness of Paran. It was in the third month after leaving Egypt that Israel reached the Mount of the Law; it was eleven months later that Jethro came to Moses bringing his wife and children. The proof for this is conclusive.

In Num. 10:11, 12 we read "And it came to pass on the twentieth day of the **second month, in the second year,** that the cloud was taken up from off the tabernacle of the testimony. And the children of Israel took their journeys out of the wilderness of Sinai, and the cloud rested in the wilderness of Paran." Following this we are told "And Moses said unto Hobab, the son of Raguel, the Midianite, Moses' father-in-law, We are journeying unto the place of which the Lord said I will give it you; come thou with us, and we will do thee good; for the Lord hath spoken good concerning Israel. And he said unto him, I will not go; but I will depart to my own land, and to my kindred" (vv. 29, 30)—compare with this the last verse of Ex. 18. Now it was **after** the departure of Jethro (18:24, 25) that Moses carried out the suggestion of his father-in-law to select men to assist him in the work of governing Israel—see Num. 11:11-17. Further confirmation of this is supplied in Deut. 1. Note "in Horeb" (v. 6) and then Moses' words to Israel, "I spake unto you at that time, saying, I am not able to bear you myself alone . . . Take you wise men and understanding, and known among your tribes, and I will make them rulers over you" (vv. 9, 13). Finally; if Ex. 18 be read attentively there will also be found evidences therein that God had **already** given Israel the law when Jethro came to Moses. For instance, note the mention of "The Mount of God" in v. 5; Moses' statement that the people now came unto him "to inquire of God" (v. 15); his declaration that he "made them know the statutes of God and His laws" (v. 16).

"When Jethro, the priest of Midian, Moses' father-in-law, heard of all that God had done for Moses, and for Israel his people, and that the Lord had brought Israel out of Egypt; then Jethro, Moses' father-in-law, took Zipporah, Moses' wife, after he had sent her back, and her two sons; of which the name of the one was Gershom, for he said I have been an alien in a strange land; and the name of the other was Eliezer; for the God of my father, said he, was mine help, and delivered me from the sword of Pharaoh; And Jethro, Moses' father-in-law, came with his sons and his wife unto Moses into the wilderness, where he encamped at the Mount of God; and he said unto Moses, I thy father-in-law Jethro, am come unto thee, and thy wife, and her two sons with her." (vv. 1-6). The dispensational scene which is here foreshadowed is very beautiful, and the place which this one has in the series of typical pictures, in which the book of Exodus abounds, evidences once more the hand of God, not only in their production, but also in arranging their order. In Ex. 16 the manna speaks of the incarnate Son, come down from heaven to earth. In the first part of Ex. 17, the smiting of the rock views the Lord Jesus stricken of God. In the issuing forth of the water, we get a lovely emblem of the Holy Spirit ministering to the people of God. In the second half of Ex. 17, where we find Amalek attacking Israel, and the defeat of the former through the supplications of Moses—upheld by Aaron and Hur—we have adumbrated the believer's conflict with the flesh, and him sustained in that conflict by the joint intercession of Christ and the Holy Spirit. This goes on to the close of the Church age. Here in Ex. 18 we are carried forward to the next dispensation and are furnished with a blessed foreshadowment of **millennial** conditions.

Zipporah restored to Moses is a perfect type of Israel brought back to the Lord. Some see in Zipporah a type of the Church, but **nowhere in the Old Testament** is the Church (as such—a corporate whole) ever seen—Col. 1:26, 27, etc., makes this very plain. Moreover, the details of our type here should forbid such an interpretation.

In the first place, Zipporah had been **separated** from her husband. Now if

Zipporah figures the Church, and the Church is the prospective wife of Christ, the type fails us here completely. Those who believe that the Church is the Bride of the Lamb acknowledge that the "marriage" is yet future, occurring after the Rapture. If this be so, when, following the Rapture, will the Church ever be separated from Christ? When, indeed! But the type does not fail. It is perfectly accurate. Zipporah is the figure of Israel, the wife of Jehovah (see Isa. 54:6; Jer. 31:32, etc.), now alienated from Him (Hosea 2:2, etc.), Yet to be restored to His favour (Isa. 54:4-8, etc.).

In the second place, mark carefully the cause and occasion of Zipporah's separation from her husband. This is found recorded near the close of Ex. 4. When Moses started for Egypt to bring God's people out of the house of bondage his wife accompanied him. The Lord met him and sought to kill him. The reason for this was his failure in not having circumcised his son. The sequel suggests that the cause of this failure lay in his wife. At once Zipporah herself performed the operation on her son, and then, in hot anger, reproached Moses in the words: "A bloody husband thou art" (4:25), which is repeated in the very next verse. How plain, how accurate the type! The disobedience of Zipporah in the matter of circumcising her son points unmistakably to the failure of Israel under the Law. The separation of Zipporah from Moses, because he was a "bloody husband," or literally, "a husband of bloods," tells of Israel's alienation from God through the offence of the Cross. "We preach Christ crucified; unto the Jews a stumbling-block" (1. Cor. 1:23). It was blood-shedding which was the "stumbling-block" to Zipporah!

In the third place, note the fruit of her marriage. She bore Moses "two sons" (18:3). Those who regard Zipporah as a type of the Church ignore this detail, and conveniently so, for they can make nothing of it. But that is no way to treat the Word of God. Whenever we come across anything in it which fails to fit in with any of our views either of doctrine, prophecy or the types, that should show us that something is wrong with our views, that they need to be revised or enlarged. This line in our present picture is also found in several of its companions. Joseph's wife also bore him two sons. So did Isaac's. What then was typified thereby? The wife contemplated Israel when first espoused to Jehovah—at Sinai. The fruit of the marriage points to a later period in their history. What that period is we are not left in doubt. The outstanding point in Israel's later history was in the days of Rehoboam, when the kingdom was rent asunder and divided into two—the kingdom of Israel and the kingdom of Judah. Thus the "wife" was succeeded by her "two sons."

In the fourth place, the names of Zipporahs' sons are profoundly significant. The firstborn was "Gershom," which means "a stranger there." The reason for Moses giving him this name was, "I have been a stranger in a strange land" (2:22). Appropriately does this speak of Israel in their dispersion, away from their land. The second son was named "Eliezer," which means, "God is my helper." Though scattered throughout the world, Israel has been marvellously helped of God—He has preserved them all through the centuries, preventing them from being either annihilated or assimilated by the Gentiles. Many of the Jews fail to recognise how God is helping them, and it is most significant that the name of this second son of Zipporah is not given until Ex. 18, where we have the Millennium in view. Gershom is referred to in Ex. 2, not so Eliezer; not until Israel has been restored to God will they recognise how marvellously He has helped them!

Fifth, notice the time when Zipporah and her sons were restored to Moses. It was "When Jethro, the priest of Midian, Moses' father-in-law, heard of all that God had done for Moses, and for Israel His people, that the Lord had brought Israel out of Egypt; Then Jethro . . . took Zipporah . . . and her two sons . . . and came unto Moses." It was not while Moses was presenting Jehovah's demands before Pharoah, nor in the morning following the Passover-night; but it was when Moses had become Israel's leader and law-giver! In like manner, Israel will not be restored to God until their rejected Messiah is manifested on earth as their King and Lord.

Sixth, in striking accord with what we have just noted is the place where Moses was when the reconciliation took place: "he encamped at the Mount of God, (v. 5). Here, as always, the "mount" speaks of the kingdom, of governmental authority (Psl. 2:6; Isa. 2:

3 etc.) It was from the summit of this same Mount that Jehovah gave the Ten Commandments to Moses. It was while seated upon a Mount that the Lord Jesus gave the laws of His Kingdom (Matt. 5.). It was on the Mount that He was transfigured, which was a miniature of His Kingdom-glory. It is to the Mount that He shall return (Zech. 14:4). The "Mount of God" (v. 5) speaks, then, of the governmental glory of God. And it is when the governmental glory of God shall be displayed in the person of His Son on earth that Israel shall be restored to Him!

Seventh, let us now observe that Zipporah and her sons were brought to Moses **by a Gentile**, for Jethro was a Midianite. There are many types of Israel as Jehovah's wife—espoused, divorced and restored—but each one has its own distinctive features. Here we have that which, so far as the writer is aware, is not found elsewhere in the types, though it is the direct subject of prophecy. In Isa. 18 there is a remarkable prediction. A Divine call goes forth to some land "beyond the rivers of Ethiopia," a maritime power, most probably Great Britain. This land is bidden to send forth her ships as swift messengers to "A nation scattered and peeled. To a people terrible from their beginning hitherto; a nation meted out and trodden down." Clearly this oppressed people is Israel. In a coming day the maritime Gentile power shall carry the dispersed Hebrews back to the land of their fathers: "In that time shall the present be **brought unto** the Lord of hosts of a people scattered and peeled . . . to the place of the name of the Lord of hosts, the **mount Zion**" (Isa. 18:7). Note the words we have placed in black and compare the language of Ex. 18.

That which followed the reconciliation of Zipporah to her husband is equally interesting and meaningfull. First, we are told that "Moses told his father-in-law **all that the Lord had done** unto Pharoah and the the Egyptians for Israel's sake, and all the travail that had come upon them by the way, and how the Lord delivered them" (v. 8). Jethro, the Midianite, represents the Gentiles in the Millennium, who will then learn fully, how wondrously the Lord had preserved Israel not only through the vicissitudes of the centuries, but also through the birth-pangs of the Tribulation.

Next we are told that, "Jethro rejoiced for all the goodness which the Lord had done to Israel, whom He had delivered out of the hand of the Egyptians" (v. 9). In the millennium the jealousy and hatred of the Gentiles against the Jews will be removed. The confession of Jethro on this occasion is most noteworthy: "Now I know that the Lord is greater than all gods: for in the thing wherein they dealt proudly He was above them" (v. 11). Such will be the confession of the Gentiles when they learn of what the Lord has done for His ancient people.

Finally, in verse 12 we are told, "And Jethro, Moses' father-in-law took a burnt offering and sacrifices for God: and Aaron came, and all the elders of Israel, to **eat bread with** Moses' father-in-law before God." Very blessed is this. Here is a plain foreshadowing of what we read of in Isa. 2:2, 3 and other Scriptures: "And it shall come to pass in the last days, that the mountain of the Lord's house shall be established in the top of the mountains, and shall be exalted above the hills; and **all nations shall flow unto it.** And many people shall go and say, Come ye, and let us go up to the mountain of the Lord, to the house of the God of Jacob."

The second half of Ex. 18, though being mainly of a practical rather than a typical nature (so far as the writer is able to discern), adds one beautiful line to this picture of the millennium: "And Moses chose able men out of all Israel, and made them heads over the people, **rulers** of thousands, rulers of hundreds, rulers of fifties, and rulers of tens," (v. 25). Does not this plainly foreshadow what is promised to us in Rev. 3:21, "To him that overcometh will I grant to sit with me **in My throne.**"

The passage is too lengthy for us to quote in full, but let each reader turn to and read carefully Ex. 18:13-27. These verses record the failure of Moses and are written for our admonition. Several most important lesson are here plainly inculcated.

Moses had been appointed **by the Lord** as the leader and head of His people. As Jethro witnessed the exacting duties of his son-in-law, advising the people from morn to eve, he felt that Moses was undertaking too much. Jethro feared for his health, and suggested that his son-in-law appoint some assistants. In listening to Jethro, Moses did wrong. From a natural standpoint Jethro's counsel was kindly and well-meant. It was the amiability of the flesh. It presented a subtle temptation, no doubt. But the man of God is not to be guided by **natural** principles; only that which is spiritual should have any weight with him. Nor should he heed any human counsel when he is engaged in the service of the Lord; he is to take his orders **only** from the One who appointed him.

One thing that this passage does is to warn God's servant's against following the advise of their relatives according to the flesh. Jethro's eye was not upon God, but upon Moses. It was not the eternal glory of Jehovah which was before him, but the temporal welfare of his son-in-law—"**Thou** wilt surely wear away, both thou and this people that is with thee; for this thing is too heavy for **thee**; thou art not able to perform it thyself alone" (v. 18). A parallel case is found in connection with our Saviour. In Mark 3:20 we read, "And the multitude cometh together again, so that they **could not so much as eat bread.**" The Lord Jesus knew what it was to "spend and be spent." But those related to Him by fleshly ties did not appreciate this; for we are told in the very next verse that, "When His friends heard of it, they went out to lay hold on Him; for they said, **He is beside Himself.**" Very solemn is this and very necessary for the servant of God to heed. The flesh (in us) must be mortified in connection with our service just as much as in our daily walk.

When the Lord Jesus announced to His disciples for the first time that "He must go unto Jerusalem, and suffer many things of the elders and chief priests and scribes to be killed," we are told "then Peter took Him and began to rebuke Him, saying, Pity Thyself, Lord: this shall not be unto thee." (Matt. 16: 21, 22). Here again we behold the amiability of the flesh. It was what men would call 'the milk of human kindness.' But it ignored the will and glory of God. The answer of our Lord on this occasion is very solemn: "He turned, and said unto Peter, Get thee behind Me, Satan; thou art **an offence** unto Me: for thou **perceivest not** the things that be of God, but those that be of men." That was the severest thing that Christ ever said to one of His own. What a solemn warning against being influenced by the natural affections of our friends!

Subtle as was the temptation presented to Moses, if he had remembered the **Source** of his strength, as well as his office, he would not have yielded to it. "Hearken now unto **my** counsel" said Jethro (v. 19). But that was the very thing which Moses had no business to do. "So shall it be **easier for thyself**" (v. 22) pleaded the tempter. But was not God's grace sufficient! It is sad to see the effect which this specious suggestion had upon Moses. In Num. 11 we find that Moses complained to the Lord—"I am not able to bear all this people alone, because it is too heavy for me" (v. 14). Does some servant of God reading these lines feel much the same to-day? Then let him remember that he is not called upon to bear any people **alone.** Has not God said, "Fear thou not; for I am with thee, be not dismayed; for I am thy God, **I will** strengthen thee; yea, I will help thee; yea, I will uphold thee with the right hand of My righteousness" (Isa. 41:10)! And if the burden is "too heavy" for thee, remember that it is written, "Cast thy burden **upon the Lord,** and He shall sustain thee" (Psl. 55:22).

"It is here the servant of Christ constantly fails; and the failure is all the more dangerous because it wears the appearance of humility. It seems like distrust of one's self, and deep lowliness of spirit, to shrink from heavy responsibility; but all we need to enquire is, Has God imposed that responsibility? If so, He will assuredly be with me in sustaining it; and having Him with me, I can sustain anything. With Him, the weight of a mountain is nothing; without Him, the weight of a feather is overwhelming. It is a totally different thing if a man, in the vanity of his mind, thrust himself forward and take a burden upon his shoulder which God never intended him to bear, and therefore never fitted him to bear it; we may then surely expect to see him crushed beneath the weight, but if God lays it upon him, He will qualify and strengthen him to carry it.

"It is never the fruit of humility to depart from a 'Divinely-appointed' post. On the contrary, the deepest humility will express itself by remaining there in simple dependence upon God. It is a sure evidence of being occupied about self when we shrink from service on the ground of inability. God does not call us unto service on the ground of **our** ability, but of His own: hence, unless, I am filled with thoughts about myself, or with positive distrust of Him, I need not relinquish any position of service or testimony because of the heavy responsibilities attaching thereto. All power belongs to God, and it is quite the same whether that power acts through one agent or through seventy—the power is still the same; but if one agent refuse the dignity, it is only so much the worse for him. God will not force people to abide in a place of honor if they cannot trust Him to sustain them there" (C.H.M.).

Strikingly was this seen in the sequel. Moses complained to God of the burden, and the Lord removed it; but in the removal went the high honour of being called to carry it alone. "And the Lord said unto Moses, Gather unto Me seventy men of the elders of Israel, whom thou knowest to be the elders of the people, and officers over them; and bring them unto the tabernacle of the congregation, that they may stand there with thee. And I will come down and talk with thee there; and I will take of the spirit which is upon thee, and will put it upon them; and they shall bear the burden of the people with thee, that thou bear it not thyself alone" (Num. 11: 16, 17). Nothing was really gained. No fresh power was introduced; it was simply a **distribution** of the "spirit" which had rested on one now being placed on seventy! Man cannot improve upon God's appointments. If he persists in acting according to the dictates of 'common sense' **nothing** will be gained, and **much** will be lost.

A word should be said upon the closing verse of our chapter: "And Moses let his father-in-law depart; and he went his way into his own land" (v. 27). This receives amplification in Num. 10: "And Moses said unto Hobab, the son of Raguel the Midianite, Moses' father-in-law, We are journeying unto the place of which the Lord said, I will give it you; come thou with us and we will do thee good: for the Lord had spoken good concerning Israel. And he said unto him, I will not go; but I will depart to mine own land, and to my kindred" (vv. 29-30). How this revealed the heart of Jethro (here called Hobab). The ties of nature counted more with him than the blessings of Jehovah. He preferred his "own land" to the wilderness, and his own "kindred" to the people of God. He walked by sight, not faith; he had no respect unto "the recompense of the reward" of the future, but preferred the things of time and earth. How ill-fitted was such a one to counsel the servant of God!

In concluding this article we would point out how that Jethro's departure from Moses in no wise mars the typical picture presented in the earlier part of this chapter; rather does it give completeness to it. Jethro returned to his own land and kindred because he had no heart for the Lord and his people. A similar tragedy will be witnessed at the **end** of the Millennium. In Psl. 18 we read, "Thou hast delivered me from the strivings of the people; and Thou hast made me the head of the heathen (Gentiles); a people whom I have not known shall serve Me. As soon as they hear of Me they shall obey Me; the strangers shall yield **feigned** obedience unto Me. The strangers (Gentiles) shall **fade away**" (vv. 43-45). This will find its fulfillment in the Millennium. Many Gentiles will turn to the Lord, but their hearts are not won by Him. At the end, when Satan is released, they will quickly flock to his banner (see Rev. 20: 7-9).

May the Lord grant us stedfastness of heart, and keep us from being drawn away by the things of time and sense.

ARTHUR W. PINK.

---

*Will subscribers in the British Isles and in the U.S.A. kindly note that this Magazine will be mailed them two issues at a time, bi-monthly. Postage here is more than double there. Renewals are coming in very slowly. We shall value prayer for an increased circulation.*

## ELECTION.

*An Address delivered by Dr. Pink on Tuesday, June 23rd, 1925, in Ashfield N.S.W.*

**(No. 1.)**

I am going to speak to-night on one of the most hated doctrines of the Bible, namely:—that of God's sovereign Election. There are those who have dared to call it a terrible and horrible doctrine, which is surely a fearful way to speak of any truth in God's Word. There are others who speak of it with bated breath, as though it is something to be kept in the background. There are others who profess to believe in it and who say it is a most blessed truth, but for Christians only. And yet I have always found that such people have such a slight conception of the blessedness of this truth that they rarely if ever speak of it even among themselves, and I have never yet met a single preacher who argued that this truth was for Christians only, who actually preached it. Now the reason for man's antipathy against this truth is not far to seek. It is a truth that is too deeply humbling, in fact humiliating, for it makes nothing of man. It puts him into the dust where he belongs.

Now, my friends, I do not only believe in election, but I believe that election ought to be publicly preached, and there are hundreds of God's servants in the past, that have been used by Him, who have shared that conviction. I just want to read to you briefly, from a sermon that was preached by C. H. Spurgeon on 1 Thessalonians 1:4: "Knowing brethren beloved your election of God." He began his sermon with these words: "At the very announcement of the text, some will be ready to say, 'Why preach upon so profound a doctrine as election? I answer, because it is in God's Word and whatever is in God's Word is to be preached.' But, says the objector, "some truths ought to be kept back from the people lest they should make an ill use thereof". Mr. Spurgeon answers and says, "That is popish doctrine" and it is. "It was upon that very theory that priests kept back the Bible from the people. They did not give it to them lest they should mis-use it. But, says the objector, are not some doctrines dangerous. Answer: Not if they are true and rightly handled. Truth is never dangerous, it is error and reticence that are fraught with peril! But, says the objector, Do not men abuse the doctrines of grace? Answer: I grant you that they do, but if we destroyed everything that men mis-use, we should have nothing left. What, are there to be no ropes because some fools hang themselves, and must knives be discarded and pronounced dangerous, because some use them as weapons for the destruction of their adversaries? Decidedly not. And besides all this, remember that men do read the Scriptures and think about these doctrines and therefore often make mistakes about them. Who then shall set them right if we who preach the Word hold our tongues about the matter?"

Oh, that God would raise up some man to-day who could get the hearing that Mr. Spurgeon had, and who would preach with like plainness and faithfulness, fearing not the frown of man, and courting not his favours. Of course, the preacher who is seeking the favour of the world, and who is looking for his support from worldlings, must necessarily be silent on this subject, but any preacher who is silent upon it, I mean entirely silent, is so for one of two reasons, and it proves one of two things: Either he is an incompetent servant of Christ, incompetent because he is ignorant of one of the cardinal truths of Scripture; or he is an unfaithful servant of Christ, because he shuns to declare all the counsel of God. Now I do not mean by that that the preacher ought to be preaching on this subject all the time, far from it; but I mean that any true servant of God will believe that all Scripture is given by inspiration of God, and is profitable for doctrine, and therefore he will ignore no part of it.

Now in the second place, this doctrine of election ought always to be preached and spoken about, not in a spirit of controversy, but in the spirit of reverence and devotion. It is not a subject to be speculated upon; it is not one to be reasoned about; it is not for me to ask, Can I harmonise it with other truths? Still less is it for me to ask, Is it popular throughout Christendom? The first and foremost question to ask is, Does God teach it in the Holy Scriptures? If He does, whether I can understand it or not, whether other men believe it or not, whether I can see its value or not, it is my duty to receive it on the bare Word of the living God.

Now I said that this subject needs to be approached in the spirit of reverence and devotion. That is how the Lord Jesus Himself dealt with it. You will find it recorded in Matthew, 11 : 25, 26 : "At that time Jesus answered and said, I thank Thee, O Father, Lord of heaven and earth, because Thou hast hid these things from the wise and prudent, and hast revealed them unto babes. Even so Father, for it seemed good in Thy sight." That is how the apostle Paul dealt with it. You turn to 2 Thessalonians 2 : 13. It is very striking indeed to notice how the apostle Paul under the Holy Spirit begins this verse: "But we are bound to give thanks always to God, for you brehren, beloved of the Lord." (Give thanks for what ?) "because God hath from the beginning chosen you to salvation through sanctification of the Spirit and belief of the truth." The apostle Paul was there speaking of the subject of eternal election. "God hath from the beginning chosen you," and yet he begins the verse by saying, "We are bound to give thanks always to God because" etc. The doctrine of election was the cause of thanksgiving and praise to the apostle Paul, and it will be to us, once we receive it from God's Word, unquestioningly, as little children!

Now before I proceed any further, I want to mention two or three facts, simple facts, in connection with this doctrine, significant facts. The first fact is this and it is unassailable and unanswerable. All heretics to God's truth come from those who do not believe, or who deny the doctrine of election! You cannot find a single "Higher Critic" (I am measuring my words, and I know whereof I speak), you cannot find a single "Higher Critic" that has written, or a single Spiritualist, or a single Evolutionist, or a single Sinless-Perfectionist, who believes in the absolute sovereignty of God, and in the Divine doctrine of election. Without an exception you will find that heretics are Arminians to a man. That is a significant fact. Higher Critics and New Thought men, Evolutionists and Sinless-Perfectionists are not drawn from the ranks of Calvinism, they come from the ranks of the Arminians every time.

In the second place. Anyone who has been a student of the history of the Church for the last five hundred years knows full well that the weakest Protestants have always been found among those who did not believe in the doctrine of election, and the strongest Protestants all through the last five centuries, have been, to a man, sovereign-grace men. I was reading with interest, only this week, how that Augustus Toplady, the venerated author of that hymn "Rock of Ages," one hundred and seventy years ago issued a twofold challenge which was never accepted in his day. He challenged the whole Christian world to find one person who had ever really held the sovereignty of God, and who had gone over to Rome; and he challenged the whole Christian world to find the name of one person on the pages of history, who was an Arminian and who had died as a martyr. None of these Free-Willers ever died at the stake for God's truth. Those who have stood firm as a rock and have been faithful unto death (if any of you doubt it, read Foxes' book of Martyrs, and see what the men mentioned there believed) were without an exception, men and women who believed in the absolute sovereignty of God and in the doctrne of Divine election.

In the third place, you will find that the men who have been most widely used of God in the past have been men who believed in the sovereignty of God and the doctrine of election. Every one of the Reformers, Martin Luther, John Wycliffe, at an earlier date, Calvin, John Knox, each one of them has left it on record, clearly and emphatically, that they held and taught the absolute sovereignty of God and the doctrine of election. That was true of the Puritans, and God's Church was never purer thar in those days. That was true of the great "Revivalists," Jonathan Edwards, Whitefield, Toplady, and in more recent times, Spurgeon. That also is a significant fact, that the men who have held and taught these doctrines are the men who have been most used of God. Why? Because God has said: "Them that honor Me, I will honor," and these doctrines honor God in a superlative way.

My friends, one of the strongest proofs that this Book is the Word of God is what it teaches on the subject of election. If this Book were a counterfeit, if this Book were the invention of men, the doctrine of election would have found no place in it, for it is far too unpalatable, it is far too unpopular, it is far too contrary to the thoughts and desires of man's heart; and the only reason why anybody believes in election is because he finds it in this book. The doctrine of election, my friends, is one that all of us at first oppose, for we are all of us Arminians by nature.

Now not only does the Bible teach election, but the Bible makes election prominent, so prominent that you cannot get rid of election until you get rid of the Bible. It is the iBble part of it that is the great difficulty. No propositions that are ever laid down in the pulpit are so difficult to receive as the inspired language itself. And friends, that explains the great dislike which there is in the hearts of men against certain passages in this Book. During the last fifteen years, again and again. I have stood in the pulpit and just read certain passages from God's Word, without a single comment, and the simple reading of those passages made people uneasy, and their faces began to flush with anger, and you could see their very antipathy to it. My friends, there is something wrong with us when any truth of God's Word causes us to act thus!

Now without any further preliminaries let us define our terms. What do we mean by "election?" What does the term itself signify? It means that God has made a choice: the word "election" means a selection. It means to single out; it means to take one and to leave another. The doctrine of election means that, before the foundation of the world, God chose certain men and women out of Adam's fallen race to be conformed to the image of His Son, and that He passed by the others, leaving them to suffer the due reward of their sins. The doctrine of election means that before salvation entered this world God marked out the very ones to whom it should come. The doctrine of election means that God has not left it to chance as to whether or not the sacrifice of His Son shall be in vain. God has not left the cross-work of Christ to be contingent upon anything in us, but before Christ died God the Father gave to His Son a people as the reward of His suffering and as the travail of His soul.

Now in connection with **the truth of** election, before we consider election in the human realm, I want to call your attention, to what is to me the most striking case of all, and that is, that before the human race was created, God made a choice even among the angels! There was election in Heaven long before election was applied to those on earth! Now will you turn to the first Epistle to Timothy, 5:21. "I charge thee before God and the Lord Jesus Christ and the **elect angels.**" If there are elect angels, then necessarily, there must be non-elect angels, you cannot have one without the other; and in eternity past, God made an election among the angels in Heaven, and those whom He had elected stood fast, and those whom He had not elected fell when Satan rebelled; for when Satan rebelled he dragged down with him one third of the angels, and all those non-elect angels when they sinned, what did God do with them? When those angels sinned, what did God do **for** them? He provided no Saviour, He preached unto them no Gospel, He manifested unto them no mercy, He "spared them not," but consigned them in everlasting chains unto the judgment of the great day. 2 Peter 2:4. You look at that. "For if God spared not the angels that sinned, but cast them down to hell, and delivered them into chains of darkness to be reserved unto judgment." Ah, how unspeakably solemn that is; God spared not the angels that sinned.

Now listen. There is a truly marvellous thing. God determined to have a people for Himself (follow me closely): a people who should be nearer and dearer to Him than any other creatures; a people who should be conformed to the very image of His Son; and God chose that people out of the fallen human race. Why? Why did He Why should He? Why not have reserved that high honour for the angels? There was one race, the fallen angels and God passed them by. There was another race, the race of fallen men, and God had mercy on it. God never caused His Son to take upon Him the likeness of the angels; Christ was not made in the likeness of angelic flesh; there was no Saviour for them! O, the awe-inspiring sovereingty of God!

The angels were a higher order of beings than we, they were created before us. They were heavenly creatures, we are earthly creatures; but God passed them by. He chose us. Why? Just to manifest His sovereignty, passing by the greater and choosing the less! If there are any here to-night who hate the truth of God's absolute sovereignty, and who deny the doctrine of God's election, tell me this, Why was it that God passed by the angels that sinned, and spared them not, but cast them down to Hell? Why should He spare the human race, and provide for us a Saviour to take us to Heaven? Ah, my friends, Arminians are very carefull to ignore this first instance of election! Those who boast so much about free-will, you will never find them saying anything at all about God "passing by" the angels! They say that it is unjust for God to choose one man, and leave another; how can it be, when God chose one race, the fallen human race, and passed by another race, the fallen angelic race? They neither of them deserved any mercy, they each of them deserved judgment, and God gave mercy to one and judgment to the other. Why? And the only possible answer to it is, because God so willed it, and all that we can say is, "Even so Father for so it seemed good in Thy sight."

Now in the second place, the next great illustration and demonstration that we have of sovereign election is seen in God's choice of the nation of Israel. The nation of Israel began when God called out Abraham. Suddenly Jehovah appeared unto Abraham in the heathen city of Ur, in the heathen land of Chaldea. Why did He? Why did God single out Abraham to be the father of His chosen people? Scripture tells us that Abraham himself came from an idolatrous family. You will find that in Joshua 24. If you want to look it up sometime, I won't give you the verse—I am not here to encourage idleness, I am here to try and stimulate searching— If you want to find out something about the spiritual ancestry of Abraham, you will find it there in the last chapter of Joshua. Scripture tells us that Abraham's ancestors were idolaters, and Scripture indicates that there was no good thing in Abraham when God called him.

Turn now to the 51st chapter of Isaiah, the first two verses. It is very striking and I want you to notice this carefully. "Hearken to Me, ye that follow after righteousness." This of course, was addressed to the nation of Israel. "Ye that seek the Lord; look unto the rock whence ye are hewn, and unto the hole of the pit whence ye are digged. Look unto Abraham your father and unto Sarah that bore you:" Now notice that carefully: God there is humbling Israel and the method that He pursues, is to remind them of their lowly origin. He says, "Look unto the rock from whence ye are hewn, and to the hole of the pit whence ye are digged." That is what God likens Abraham to—"the hole of the pit!" "Look unto Abraham your father and unto Sarah that bore you, for I called him alone and blessed him and increased him."

There is sovereign election! "I called him alone." Out of all that great city, which modern excavation has shown was a city of hundreds of thousands of people, a city perhaps half as large as Sydney with all its suburbs included. Out of that vast people God called Abraham "alone." Why did He? Just because it was His sovereign pleasure to do so; for no other reason. Now then, out of Abraham developed the nation of Israel, and if you will turn to the 7th chapter of Deuteronomy you will find what God says there concerning this nation. Verse 6. "For thou art a holy people (the word holy means 'separated') unto the Lord thy God: the Lord thy God hath chosen thee to be a special people unto Himself, above all people that are upon the face of the earth." But why should He? Why did He? "The Lord did not set His love upon you nor choose you because ye were more in number than any people: for ye were fewest of all people. But because the Lord loved you, and because He would keep the oath which He had sworn unto your fathers.

"Now turn to the book of Amos. 3:2. Let me read you the previous verse to get the context. Verse 1. "Hear this word that the Lord hath spoken against you, O children of Israel, against the whole family which I brought up from Egypt saying, **You only** have I known of all the families of the earth." "You only," **you only** have I known of all the families of the earth. From the days of Moses until the days of Christ, a period of fifteen hundred years, God suffered all the heathen nations to walk in their own ways, and left them to the darkness and corruption of their own hearts. No other nation had God's Word, no other nation had a divinely-appointed priesthood. Israel alone was favoured with a written revelation from God.

Why did God choose Israel to be His special favourites? The Chaldeans were more ancient, the Egyptians were far wiser. Why did God call Israel? Certainly not because of any excellency in Israel, as the whole of their history shows. From the very starting point of their national history they were a stiffnecked and a hard-hearted and a rebellious people. It could not have been bceause of any good thing in them. Why was it that God chose Israel? Because it so pleased Him to exercise His sovereign will.

Now my friends, the same truth is taught plainly all through the New Testament as well. It is a very striking thing, but in connection with the very first event that is recorded in the New Testament you have the truth of election illustrated. What is the first event in the New Testament? It is the birth of Christ and you will find in connection with the birth of Christ, God's sovereignty and the truth of election were illustrated in two diffeernt ways. First, in the very place where He was born. Turn back to the prophet Micah 5 verse 2. Notice how God Himself puts it. "But thou Bethlehem Ephratah, though thou be little among the thousands of Judah, yet out of thee shall He come forth unto Me that is to be the ruler in Israel." That was one of the great Messianic prophecies, and the point that the Holy Spirit emphasised there is this, that Bethlehem, which was one of the least towns, one of the smallest and most insignificant places in the province of Judah, was the one that God had selected as the birth-place of our Saviour! God manifested His sovereignty in the fact that Christ was not born in the city of Jerusalem. He was not born in any of the principal towns of Palestine like Capernaum or Nazareth or any of the others; but He was born in the little despised, insignificant place of Bethlehem. There is the sovereignty of God on the very first page of the New Testament!

And in the second place, when Christ was born, to whom did God reveal the fact? To whom did God send His angels to announce the truth that the Saviour was born? Why, of course God sent the angels to the Temple at Jerusalem; of course, God announced it to the priests and the leaders in Israel, the rulers. Did He? Was that God's way? No, it never has been God's way; it is not now. God's way is always the opposite of man's. God chooses the weak things and the despised things and He passes by the strong and the mighty and the noble. God did not reveal the truth of the Saviour's birth to those in eminence in Israel, but He revealed it to the poor shepherds out yonder in the field; And how significant is the remainder of the statement: He revealed it to the Shepherds who were **"watching their flocks by night."** And God is doing exactly the same thing to-day. The men to whom God gives light on this Book, the men who receive communications from Heaven, are the Pastors, the Shepherds who are **faithful** to their "flocks!" It still remains true that it is the Shepherds who watch heir flocks that God the Holy Spirit teaches!

Now not only is the truth of election revealed in connection with the birth of Christ, but we find it prominently taught in His public ministry. Turn now to the 4th chapter of Luke, beginning at the 16th verse. Let me just read a verse here and there. Verse 16: "And He came to Nazareth, where He had here brought up, and as His custom was, He went into the synagogue on the Sabbath day and stood up for to read." Now here you have the first public message that Christ gave. It was the commencement of His public ministry. Verse 17: "And there was delivered unto Him the book of the prophet Esaias. And when He had opened the book, He found the place where it was written, The spirit of the Lord is upon Me, because He hath annointed Me to preach the gospel to the poor: (not the rich!) He hath sent Me to heal the broken-hearted; (not the stout-hearted) to preach deliverance to the captives (not those who boast in their "freedom"!) and recovery of sight to the blind (not those who **think** they **can** see!) and to set at liberty them that are bruised, (not those who think they are already "free"!); to preach the acceptable year of the Lord, and He closed the book." Verse 21: "And He began to say unto them, this day is the scripture fulfilled in your ears. And all bore Him witness and wondered at the gracious words which proceeded out of His mouth." Ah, so far so good. They wondered at the "gracious words" that proceeded out of His mouth. They enjoyed the first part of the sermon immensely, and now he began to test them. They believed in **grace**, for they wondered at the gracious words that proceeded out of His mouth; but did they believe in **sovereign** grace? All right, let us see. Verse 25: "But I tell you of a truth, many widows were in Israel in the days of Elias, when the heaven was shut up three years and six months, when great famine was throughout the land. But unto none of them was Elias sent, save unto Sarepta, a city of Sidon, unto a woman that was a widow." Now Christ is pressing upon these people the truth of God's **sovereignty**! There were **many** widows in that time of famine, and God sent His servant to just **one** of them, and ignored the others! Verse 27: "And many lepers were in Israel in the time of Eliseus the prophet, and none of them was cleansed saving Naaman the Syrian." Ah, you Jews, who profess to believe in election, I am going to test you! Do you really believe in **sovereign** election? Do you believe that God has the right to make a choice among the Gentiles if He so pleases? Verse 27: "There were **many** lepers in

Israel in the time of Eliseus the prophet, and **none** of them was cleansed **saving Naaman the Syrian.**" Now notice carefully verse 28: "And all they in the synagogue, when they heard these things, were filled with wrath." They did not like the second part of the sermon! If they had been outspoken like some people are to-day, they would have said, "The preacher was very good for a time but at the finish he spoilt it all!" Christ was testing them. Ah, how solemn that 28th verse is!. "And all they in the synagogue," not the unbelievers on the outside, not the irreligious I mean, but the religious people on the inside; and not a few of them, but all of them: "All they in the synagogue when they heard these things were filled with wrath, and rose up and thrust Him out of the city, and led Him unto the brow of the hill whereon their city was built, that they might cast Him down headlong." That is how the people received the truth of sovereign election when Christ preached it! And the only reason why the servant of God does not receive the same treatment to-day is because God in His grace has subdued the enmity in your hearts, and if you people here to-night do not feel like taking hold of this preacher and throwing him out of the city at the close of this service, it is because God has put into your hearts a love for the truth. I say **God** has, for every man by nature hates this doctrine; every last one of us is born an Arminian, and only God the Holy Spirit can overcome our enmity against it.

Now the time has almost gone, but I want to read a few more passages without commenting upon them. Let the Word just speak for itself. John 15:16. "Ye have not chosen Me, but I have chosen you, and ordained you, that ye should go and bring forth fruit." John 17:2. "As Thou hast given Him power over all flesh that He should give eternal life to as many as Thou hast given Him." Verse 6: "I have manifested Thy name unto the men which Thou gavest Me out of the world." Verse 9: "I pray for them; I pray not for the world, but for them which Thou hast given Me, for they are Thine" Acts 2:39. "For the promise is unto you and to your children and to all that are afar off even as **many as** the Lord our God shall call." Acts 13:48: "And when the Gentiles heard this, they were glad and glorified the Word of the Lord, and as many as were **ordained to** eternal life believed." Acts 15:14. "Simeon hath declared how God at the first did visit the Gentiles, (not to save them, but) **to take out of them** a people for His name." Romans 8:33: "Who shall lay anything to the charge of God's elect." 1 Corinthians 1:26: "For ye see your calling, brethren, how that not many wise men after the flesh, not many mighty, not many noble are called. But God hath chosen (not we choose, but **God** hath chosen), the foolish things of the world to confound the wise and God hath chosen the weak things of the world to confound the things which are mighty. And base things of the world, and things which are despised hath God chosen, yea, and things which are not, to bring to nought things that are. That no flesh should glory in His presence." Ephesians 1:4, 5. "According as He hath **chosen** us in Him, before the foundation of the world, that we should be Holy and without blame before Him. In love having predestinated us unto the adoption of children by Jesus Christ to Himself, according to (not **our** willingness, but according to) the good pleasure of **His** will." Titus 1:1: "Paul, a servant of God, and an apostle of Jesus Christ, according to the faith of God's **elect**." James 2:5: "Hearken, my beloved brethren, hath not God **chosen** the poor of this world." Revelation 13:8: "And all that dwell upon the earth shall worship him." (That is the anti-Christ the Beast of the previous verse.) "All that dwell upon the earth shall worship him, whose names are not **written in** the book of life of the Lamb slain from the foundation of the world." Revelation 17:14: "These shall make war with the Lamb, and the Lamb shall overcome them: for He is Lord of lords and King of kings: and they that are with Him are called, and **chosen and faithful**." Now dear friends, I have merely introduced the subject to-night. I have simply endeavoured to show you that the New Testament is **full** of this doctrine.

I just want to finish with this last word. Election does not mean that it prevents any sinner from being saved. Election does not mean that God **turns away** any sinner if his heart truly seeks Christ. Election does not mean that there is no mercy if a penitent sinner cries from his heart to God, "God be merciful to me." This book teaches, and I can say without any hesitation, (perhaps some of you do not want me to say it, but that does not matter), I can say without hesitation, there is a Saviour for any person in this room to-night who will receive Him by faith. There is a Saviour for any sinner outside of Hell that will believe on Him. "God now commandeth all men everywhere to repent," and if you refuse to repent, your blood will be on your own head!

ARTHUR W. PINK.

## GOD SECURING HIS INHERITANCE.

"He found him in a desert land, and in the waste howling wilderness; He led him about. He instructed him, He kept him as the apple of His eye" (Deut. 32:10).

In the previous verse we have the amazing statement that the Lord's "portion" is His people, and that there may be no misunderstanding, the same truth is expressed in another form: "Jacob is the lot of His inheritance." Here in our text we learn something of the pains which God takes to secure His heritage. There are four things to be noted and feasted upon.

1. Jehovah finding His people.
"He found him in a desert land." It needs hardly to be said that the word "found" necessarily implies a "search." Here then we have presented to our view the amazing spectacle of a seeking God! Sin came in between the creature and the Creator, causing alienation and separation. Not only so, but, as the result of the Fall, every human being enters this world with a mind that is "enmity against God." Consequently, there is none that seeketh after God. Therefore, God, in Him marvellous condescension and grace, becomes the Seeker.

The word "found" not only implies a search but, when we consider the sinful character and unworthiness of the objects of His search, it also tells of the love of the Seeker. The great God becomes the Seeker because He set His heart upon those whom He marked out to be the recipients of His sovereign favours. God had set His heart upon Abraham, and therefore did He seek and find Him amid the heathen idolators in Ur of Chaldea. God set His heart upon Jacob, and therefore did He seek out and find him as, a fugitive from his brother's vengeance, he lay asleep on the bare earth. So too it was because He had loved Moses with an everlasting love that the Lord sought out and found Him in Midian, at "the backside of the desert." Equally true is this with every true Christian living in the world to-day: "I was found of them that sought Me not; I was manifest unto them that asked not after Me" (Rom. 10:20).

Has God "found" you? To help you answer this question, ponder the remainder of the first clause of our text: "He found him in a desert land, and in the **waste howling wilderness.**" Is **that** how this world appears unto you? Do you find everything under the sun only "vanity and vexation of spirit?" Are you made to groan daily at what you witness on every hand? Do you find that the world furnishes nothing to satisfy the heart, yea nothing to even **minister** to it? Is the world, really, a "waste howling wilderness" to you?

Let a second test be applied: when God truly "finds" one of His own He **reveals Himself.** He imparts to the soul a realisation of His sovereign majesty, His awesome power, His ineffable holiness, His wondrous mercy. Has He thus made Himself known unto you? Has He given you, in any measure, a vision of His divine glory, His sovereign grace His wondrous love? Has He? "This is life eternal, that they might **know** Thee, the only true God, and Jesus Christ, whom Thou hast sent" (John 17:3).

Here is a third test: If God has revealed Himself He has given you **a sight of yourself,** for in His light we "see light." A most humbling, painful, and never-to-be-forgotten experience this is. When God was revealed to Abraham, he said "I am but dust and ashes" (Gen. 18:27). When He was revealed to Isaiah, the prophet said, "Woe is me for I am undone, because I am a man of unclean lips" (Isa. 6:5). When God revealed Himself to Job, he said, "I abhor myself, and repent in dust and ashes" (Job 42:6)—note, not merely I abhor my wicked ways, but my vile self. Is this **your** experience, my reader? Have you discovered your depravity and lost condition? Have you found there is not a single good thing in you? Have you seen yourself to be fit for and deserving only of hell? Have you, truly? Then that is good evidence, yea, it is proof positive that the Lord God has "found" you.

2. Jehovah leading His people.

"He led him about." The "finding" is not the end, but only the beginning of God's dealings with His own. Having found him, He remains never more to leave him. Now that He has found His wandering child He teaches him to walk in the Narrow Way. There is a beautiful word on God "leading" in Hosea 11:3 "I taught Ephriam also to go, taking them by their arms." Just as a fond mother takes her little one, whose feet are yet too weak and untrained to walk alone, so the Lord takes His people by their arms and leads them in the paths of righteousness for His name's sake. Such is His promise: "He will keep the feet of His saints (1 Sam. 2:9). There is a threefold "leading" of the Lord:

**Evangelical.**—The Lord Jesus declared, "I am the way, the truth, and the life: no man cometh unto the Father but by Me" (John 14:6). But again He said. "No man can come to Me, except the Father which hath sent Me draw him" (John 6:44). Here then is how God leads: He leads the poor sinner to Christ. Have you, my reader, been brought to the Saviour? Is Christ your only hope? Are you trusting in the sufficiency of His precious blood? If so, what cause have you to praise God for having led you to His blessed Son!

**Doctrinally.** The Lord Jesus declared, "When He the Spirit of truth is come, He will guide you into all the truth" (John 16:13). We are not capable of discovering or entering into the Truth of ourselves, therefore do we have to be guided into it. "As many as are led by the Spirit of God, they are the sons of God." (Rom. 8:14). It is He who makes us to lie down in the "green pastures" of Scripture and who leads us beside the "still waters" of His promises. How thankful we ought to be for every ray of light which has been granted us from the lamp of God's Word.

**Providentially.** "Thou in Thy manifold mercies forsookest them not in the wilderness: the pillar of the cloud departed not from them by day, to lead them in the way; neither the pillar of fire by night, to show the light, and the way wherein they should go" (Neh. 9:19). Just as Jehovah led Israel of old, so to-day He leads us step by step through this wilderness-world. What a mercy this is. "The steps of a good man are ordered by the Lord and He delighteth in His way" (Psa. 37:23). Yes, every detail of our lives is regulated by the Most High.

"All my times are in Thy hand,
All events at Thy command,
All must come and last and end,
As doth please our Heavenly Friend."

3. God instructing His people.

"He instructed Him." So He does us. It was to instruct us that God, in His great mercy gave us the Scriptures. He has not left us to grope our way in darkness, but has provided us with a lamp unto our feet and a light unto our path. Nor are we left to our own unaided powers in the study of the Word. We are supplied with an infallible Instructor. The Holy Spirit is our teacher. "Ye have an unction from the Holy One, and ye know all things . . . the anointing ye have received of Him abideth in you, and ye need not that any man teach you." (1 John 2:20, 27).

Right views of God's truth is not an intellectual attainment, but a blessing bestowed upon us by God. It is written, "a man can receive nothing, except it be given him from heaven" (John 3:27). No matter how legibly a letter may be written, if the recipient be blind he cannot read it. So we are told, "the natural man receiveth not the things of the Spirit of God: for they are foolishness unto him: neither can he know them because they are spiritually discerned" (1 Cor. 2:14). And spiritual discernment is imparted only by the Holy Spirit.

"He instructed him." How patiently God bears with our dullness! How graciously He repeats "line upon line and precept upon precept"! Yet slow as we are, He persevers with us, for He has promised to perfect that which concerns us (Psa. 128:8). Has He "instructed" you, my reader? Has He taught you the total depravity of man and the utter inability of the sinner to deliver himself? Has He taught you the humbling truth "Ye must be born again," and that regeneration is the sole work of God—man having no part or hand in it (John 1:13). Has He revealed to you the infinite value and sufficiency of the atoning sacrifice of Christ, that His blood cleanses "from all sin?" Then what cause you have to be thankful for such Divine instruction.

4. God Preserving His people.

"He kept him as the apple of His eye." A religion of conditions, contingencies, and uncertainties is not Christianity—its technical name is Arminianism, and Arminianism is a daughter of Rome. It is that God dishonouring, Scripture-repudiating, soul-destroying system of Popery—whose father is the Devil—which prates about human merit, creature-ability, freewill, works of supererogation and a lot more blasphemous rubbish, and which leaves its blinded dupes in the fogs and bogs of uncertainty. Christianity deals with certainties which originated in the purpose and love of an unchanging God, who when He begins a good work always completes it.

"For the Lord loveth judgment, and forsaketh not His saints; they are preserved forever" (Psa. 37:28). How blessed is this! Did Jehovah "forsake" Noah when he got drunk? No, indeed. Did He "forsake" Abraham when he lied to Abimelech? No, indeed. Did he "forsake" Moses for smiting the rock in anger? No, indeed as his appearance on the Mount of Transfiguration abundantly proves. Did He "forsake" David when he committed those sins which ever since have given occasion for the enemies of the Lord to blaspheme? No, indeed. He led him to repentence, caused him to confess his awful wickedness, and then sent one of His servants to say, "The Lord hath put away thy sin."

"The Lord is thy Keeper: the Lord is thy shade upon thy right hand. The sun shall not smite thee by day, nor the moon by night. The Lord shall preserve thee from all evil: He shall preserve thy soul. The Lord shall preserve thy going out and thy coming in from this time forth and even forevermore" (Psa. 121:5-8). Here are the covenant verities of our faithful God: here are the infalliable "shall's" of the triune Jehovah: here are the sure promises of Him who cannot lie. Note there were no "if's" or peradventure's, but the unconditional and unqualified declarations of the Most High. No circumstances can ever place the believer beyond the reach of Divine preservation. No change can alter or affect this Divine certainty. Wealth may ensnare, poverty may strip, Satan may tempt, inward corruptions may annoy, but nothing can ever destroy or lead to the destruction of a single sheep of Christ; nay, all these things only serve to display more manifestly and more gloriously the preserving Hand of our God.

We "are kept by the power of God through faith unto salvation ready to be revealed in the last time" (1 Peter 1:5). The rage of heathen monarchs, with their den of lions and fiery furnace, may be employed to try the faith of God's elect, but destroy them, harm them, they cannot. O brethren, in Christ what cause we have to praise the finding, leading, instructing, and preserving, Triune Jehovah!

ARTHUR W. PINK.

The above is a digest of a sermon preached in the Strict and Particular Baptist Church, Sydney, October 18th, 1925. May the God of all grace be pleased to bless it to others of His dear people.

*(Continued from page 1.)*

1. **God purposed** to have such an inheritance: "Blessed is the nation whose God is the Lord; and the people whom He hath chosen for His own inheritance." (Psa. 33:12). The "nation" here is identical with the "holy nation" the "chosen generation, royal priesthood, peculiar people" of 1 Peter 2:9. This favoured people was chosen by God to be His inheritance: it was not an afterthought with Him, but decreed by Him in eternity past. Ere the foundation of the world God fixed His heart upon having them for Himself.

2. God has **purchased** His people for an inheritance? In Eph. 1:14, we are told that the Holy Spirit is the earnest of our inheritance until the redemption of the **purchased possession**, unto the praise of His glory." So again in Acts 20:28 we read of "the Church of God which He hath **purchased** with His own blood." God has not only redeemed His people from bondage and death but for Himself..

3. God comes and **dwells** in the midst of His Inheritance: "For the Lord will not cast off His people, neither will He forsake His inheritance" (Psa. 94:14)—a clear proof that these scriptures are not referring to the nation of Israel after the flesh. Just as Jehovah tabernacled in the midst of the redeemed Hebrews, so He now indwells His church, both collectively and individually. "Know ye not that ye (plural) are the temple of God, and that the Spirit of God dwelleth in you?" (1 Cor. 3:16) "Know ye not that your body (singular) is the temple of the Holy Spirit?" (1 Cor. 6:19).

4. God **beautifies** His Inheritance: Just as a man who has inherited a house or an estate takes possession of it and then makes improvements, so God is now fitting His people for Himself. He who has begun a good work within His own is now performing it until the day of Jesus Christ (Phil. 1:6). He is now conforming us to the image of His son: each Christian can say with the Psalmist "the Lord will perfect that which concerneth me" (Psa. 138:8). Nor will God be satisfied until we have been glorified. The Lord Jesus Christ "shall change our vile body, that it may be fashioned like unto His glorious body, according to the working whereby He is able even to subdue all things unto Himself" (Phil. 3:21). "When He shall appear, we shall be like Him" (1 John 3:2).

5. And what of the **future**? God will yet possess, live upon, enjoy His inheritance. In the unending ages yet to be, God will make known the "riches of His **glory**" on the vessels of His mercy (Rom. 9:23). The glory which God shall ever live upon—as upon an inheritance—shall rise out of His people. What a marvellous statement is that which is found at the close of Eph. 2, where the saints are likened unto a building "fitly framed together (which) groweth unto an holy temple in the Lord," of whom it is said, "in whom ye also are builded together for an **habitation of God** through the Spirit."

Wonderful and glorious is the picture presented before us in Rev. 21: "And I saw a new heaven and a new earth: for the first heaven and the first earth were passed away; and there was no more sea. And I, John, saw the holy city, the new Jerusalem, coming down from God out of heaven, prepared as a bride adorned for her husband. And I heard a great voice out of heaven saying, Behold, the tabernacle of God is with men, and He will **dwell with them,** and they shall be His people, and God Himself shall be with them, and be their God" (vv. 1-3).

What a marvellous statement is that in Zephaniah 3:17: "The Lord thy God in the midst of thee is mighty; He will save, **He will rejoice** over thee with joy; **He will rest in His love,** He will joy over thee with singing." The great God will yet say, "I am satisfied: here will I rest. This is Mine inheritance that I will live upon forever, even the glory which I have bestowed on redeemed sinners." Surely we have to say with the Psalmist, "Such knowledge is too wonderful for me; it is high, I cannot attain unto it" (139:6). May Divine grace enable us to walk worthy of the vocation wherewith we are called.

Yours in Christ,

Arthur W. Pink.

P.S.—The above is a digest of a sermon preached at the Strict and Particular Baptist Church, Sydney, on Sabbath morning, October 18th, 1925, which the Lord blessed to numbers of His people.

# STUDIES IN THE SCRIPTURES

"Search the Scriptures" John 5:39.

Copyright in all English-speaking Countries.

Arthur W. Pink, Publisher and Editor,
5 Norton Street, Ashfield, N.S.W., Australia.

Price: 10 cents per copy; $1.00 or 5/- per year.

## The Beatitudes.

"Blessed are the poor in spirit: for theirs is the kingdom of heaven." (Matt. 5:3). Opinion has been much divided concerning design, scope, and application of the Sermon on the Mount. The majority of the commentators have seen in it an exposition of Christian ethics. Men like the late Count Tolstoi regard it as setting forth a "golden rule" for all men to live by. Others have dwelt upon its dispensational bearings and insist that it belongs not to the saints of the present dispensation, but is solely Jewish.

Now two statements indicate its scope: in 5:1-2, we learn that Christ here taught His "disciples;" in 7:28-29 "the people." Thus it is evident this Address of our Lord's contains instruction both for believers and unbelievers.

It needs to be borne in mind that this "Sermon" was Christ's first utterance to the general public, who had been reared in a defective Judaism; and probably, his first word to the disciples too. His chief design was not to teach Christian ethics—that we have in the Epistles—but to expose the errors of Phariseeism and to awaken the conscience of His legalistic hearers. In 5:20 He said, "Except your righteousness shall exceed that of the Scribes and Pharisees, ye shall in no case enter into the kingdom of heaven." Then, to the end of the chapter, He expounded the spirituality of the Law so as to arouse His hearers to see their need of His perfect righteousness. It was their ignorance of the spirituality of the Law which was the real source of Phariseeism, for its leaders claimed to fulfil it in the **outward** letter, therefore would the Lord awaken conscience by enforcing its true inner import and requirement.

It is to be noted that this Sermon on the Mount is recorded only in Matthew's Gospel: the differences between it and the Sermon on the Plain in Luke 6 are pronounced and numerous. Now while it is true that Matthew is by far the most Jewish of the four Gospels, yet we believe it is a serious mistake to limit its interpretation to godly Jews, either of the past or the future. The opening verse of the Gospel should warn us against such a restriction. There, Christ is presented in a twofold way: as Son of David and also as Son of Abraham, who is "the father of all them that believe" (Rom. 4:11). Therefore, we are fully assured that this Sermon enunciates spiritual principles which obtain in every dispensation, and on this basis we shall proceed.

"Christ's first preaching seems to have been comprised in one very short but very important sentence, like that of John the Baptist before Him, 'Repent, for the kingdom of heaven is at hand' (Matt. 3:2; 4:17). It is not perhaps best now to discuss that most interesting topic, the 'kingdom of heaven,' what it means and what are the various periods of its development, but these Beatitudes teach us something of those who **belong to that kingdom**, and upon whom Christ pronounced its highest forms of benediction.

Christ came once in the flesh, and He is coming yet again; and each advent has a special object as connected with the kingdom of heaven. The first coming was to make possible an empire in men and over men, by laying the found-

*(Continued on page 72)*

## IMPORTANT NOTICES

Set of twelve issues for 1922, unbound, $1.00 or 5/-. Bound $1.50 or 7/-.
Set of twelve issues for 1923, unbound, $1.00 or 5/-. Bound $1.50 or 7/-.
Set of twelve issues for 1924, unbound, $1.00 or 5/-. Bound $1.50 or 7/-.
Set of twelve issues for 1925, unbound, $1.00 or 5/-. Bound $1.50 or 7/-.
Note: We cannot break a set or now supply any single 1925 issues.
Subscription—price: $1.00 or 5/- per year to any address in the world.
Change of Address: Please notify me promptly of any change of address, and be certain to give both old and new address.
Non-subscribers receiving this Magazine regularly will understand their subscription has been entered by a friend.
Copies lost in the mail duplicated only if we are notified promptly.

## CONTENTS

| | |
|---|---|
| The Gospel of John (John 15:1-6) | 50 |
| Gleanings in Exodus | 58 |
| Progressive Santification | 63 |
| Divine Preservation | 64 |
| Election | 65 |

## THE GOSPEL OF JOHN

**51. Christ the true Vine: John 15: 1-6.**

The following is an Analysis of the passage which is to be before us:—

1. The Vine and the Husbandman v. 1.
2. The fruitless branch cared for v. 2.
3. The purging of fruitful branches v. 2.
4. Clean through the Word v. 3.
5. Conditions of fruit-bearing v. 4.
6. The absolute dependency of Christians v. 5.
7. The consequences of severed fellowship v. 6.

The passage which is to engage our attention is one that is, most probably, familiar to all of our readers. It is read as frequently, perhaps, as any chapter in the New Testament. Yet how far do we really understand its teachings? Why does Christ here liken Himself to a "vine"? What are the leading thoughts suggested by the figure? What does He mean when He says, "Every branch in Me that beareth not fruit He taketh away?" What is the "fruit" here referred to? And what is the force of "If a man abide not in Me, he is cast forth as a branch and is withered; and men gather them, and cast into the fire, and they are burned?" Now as we approach any portion of Scripture for the purpose of studying it, it is essential to keep in mind several elementary but important principles: Who are the persons addressed? In what connection are they addressed? What is the central topic of address? We are not ready to take up the details of any passage until we have first settled these preparatory questions.

The persons addressed in John 15 were the eleven apostles. It was not to unsaved people, not to a mixed audience that Christ was speaking; but to believers only. The remote context takes us back to 13:1. In chapters 13 and 14 we are taught what Christ is doing for us while He is away—maintaining us in communion with Himself, preparing a place for us, manifesting Himself to us, supplying our every need through the Holy Spirit. In John 15, it is the other side of the truth which is before us. Here we learn what we are to be and do for Him during the interval of His absence. In 13 and 14 it is the freeness and fulness of Divine grace; in 15 it is our responsibility to bear fruit.

The immediate context is the closing sentence of chapter 14: "Arise, let us go hence." Christ had just said, "Peace I leave with you, My peace I give unto you." He had said this while seated at the supper-table, where the emblems of His death—the basis of our peace—were spread. Now He gets up from the table, which prefigured His resurrection from the dead. Right afterwards He says, "I am the True Vine." Christ's symbolic action at the close of 14, views Him on resurrection-ground, and what we have here in 15 is in perfect accord with this. There must be resurrection-life before there can be resurrection-fruit. The central theme, then is not salvation, how it is to be obtained or the danger of losing it. Instead, the great theme here is fruit-bearing, and the conditions of fertility. The word "fruit" occurs eight times in the chapter, and in Scripture eight is the **resurrection**-number. It is associated with **a new beginning**. It is the number of **the new creation.** If these facts be kept in mind, there should be little difficulty in arriving at the general meaning of our passage.

The figure used by our Saviour on this occasion was one with which the apostles must have been quite familiar. Israel had been likened unto a "vine" again and again in the Old Testament. The chief value of the vine lies in its fruit. It really serves no other purpose. The vine is a thing of the earth, and in John 15, it is used to set forth the relation which exists between Christ and His people **while they are on earth.** A vine whose branches bear fruit is a **living** thing, therefore the Saviour here had in view those who had a living connection with Himself. The Vine and its branches in John 15 does not represent what men term "the visible Church," nor does it embrace the whole sphere of Christian profession, as so many have contended. Only **true** believers are contemplated, those who have passed from death unto **life.** What we have in vv. 2 and 6 in nowise conflicts with this statement, as we shall seek to show in the course of our exposition.

The word which occurs most frequently in John 15 is "Abide," being found no less than fifteen times in the first ten verses. Now "abiding" always has reference to fellowship, and only those who have been born again are capable of having fellowship with the Father and His Son. The Vine and its branches express **oneness,** a common life, shared by all, with the complete dependency of the branches upon the Vine, resulting in fruit-bearing. The relationship portrayed is that of which **this world** is the sphere and **this life** the period. It is here and now that we are to glorify the Father by bearing much fruit. Our salvation our essential oneness with Christ, our standing before God, our heavenly calling, are neither brought into view nor called into question by anything that it said here. It is by **dragging in** these truths that some expositiors have created their own difficulties in the passage.

A few words should now be said concerning the place which our present section occupies in this Paschal discourse of our Lord. In the previous chapter we have seen the apostles troubled at the prospect of their Master's departure. In ministering to their fearful and sorrowing hearts, He had assured them that His cause in this world would not suffer by His going away: He had promised that, ultimately, He would return for them; in the meantime, He would manifest Himself to them, and He and the Father would abide in them. Now He further assures them that their **connection** with Him and their connection with each other, should not be dissolved. The **outward** bond which had united them **was** to be severed; the Shepherd was to be smitten, and the sheep scattered (Zech. 13:7). But there was a deeper, a more intimate bond, between them and Him, and between themselves, a **spiritual** bond, and while this remained, increasing fruitfulness would be the result.

The link of connection between the first two main sections of the discourse, where Christ is first comforting and then instructing and warning His disciples, is found in the closing verses of chapter 14. There He had said, "Hereafter, I will not talk much with you; for the Prince of this world cometh, and hath nothing in Me. But that the world may know that I love the Father; and as the Father gave me commandment, even so I do." In the light of this, chapter 15 intimates: Let My Father now (when the Prince of this world cometh, but only as an instrument in the hands of His Government) do with Me as He will, It will only issue in the bringing forth of much fruit—if the Corn of wheat died it would bring forth "much fruit" 12:24. Fruit was the end in view of the Father's "commandment" and the Son's obedience. Thus the **transcission** is natural and logical.

"I am the True Vine" (v. 1). This word "true" is found in several other designations and descriptions of the Lord Jesus. He is the **"True** Light" (1:9). He is the **"True Bread"** (6:32). He is "a Minister of the Sanctuary, and of the **true** Tabernacle" (Heb. 8:2). The usage of this adjective in the verses just quoted help to determine its force. It is not true in opposition to that which is false; but Christ was the perfect, essential, and enduring reality, of which other lights were but faint reflections other bread and another tabernacle were but the types and shadows. More specifically, Christ was "the **True Light"** in contrast from His forerunner, John, who was but a "lamp" (John 5:35 R.V.), or light-bearer. Christ was "the **True** Bread" as contrasted from the "manna," which the fathers did eat in the wilderness and died. He was a Minister of "the true Tabernacle" in contrast from the one Moses made, which was "the example and shadow of heavenly things" (Heb. 8:5).

But in addition to these instituted types of the Old Testament, there are types in Nature. When our Lord used this figure of the "vine," He did not arbitrarily select it out of the multitude of objects from which an ordinary teacher might have drawn illustrations for his subject. Rather was the vine created and constituted as it is, that it might be a fit representation of Christ and His people bringing forth fruit to God. "There is a double type here. just as we find a double type in the 'bread,' a reference to the manna in the wilderness, and behind that, a reference to bread in general, as the staff of human life. The vine itself is indeed constituted to be an earthly type of a spiritual truth, but we find a previous appropriation of it to that which is itself a type of the perfect reality which the Lord at length presents to us. We refer to the passages in psalm and prophets where Israel is thus spoken of" (Waymarks in the Wilderness).

In Psalm 80:8-9 we read, "Thou hast brought a vine out of Egypt:Thou hast cast out the heathen, and planted it. Thou preparedst room before it, and didst cause it to take deep root, and it filled the land." Again, in Isaiah we are told "Now will I sing to My well-beloved a song of My beloved touching His vineyard. My well-beloved hath a vineyard in a very fruitful hill: And He fenced it, and gathered out the stones thereof, and planted it with the choicest vine, and built a tower in the midst of it, and also made a winepress therein: and He looked that it should bring forth grapes and it brought forth wild grapes . . . For the vineyard of the Lord of hosts is **the house of Israel,** and the men of Judah His pleasant plant" 5:1-2-7). These passages in the Old Testament throw further light on the declaration of Christ that He was "the True Vine." Israel, as the type, had proved to be a failure. "I had planted thee a **noble vine,** wholly a right seed: how then art thou turned into the degenerate plant of a strange vine unto Me?" (Jer. 2:21): "Israel is an empty vine, he bringeth forth fruit unto himself" (Hosea 10:1). In contrast from this failure and degeneracy of the typical people, Christ says "I am the **True Vine**"—the antitype which fulfills all the expectations of the Heavenly Husbandman. Many are the thoughts suggested by this figure: to barely mention them must suffice. The beauty of the vine; its exuberant fertility; its dependency —clinging for support to that on which and around which it grows; its spreading branches; its lovely fruit: the juice from which maketh glad the heart of God and man (Judges 19:13; Psa. 104:15), were each perfectly exemplified in the incarnate Son of God.

"And My Father is the Husbandman' (v. 1). In the Old Testament the Father is represented as the **Proprietor** of the vine, but here He is called the Husbandman, that is the **Cultivator,** the One who cares for it. The figure speaks of His love for Christ and His people: Christ as the One who was made in the form of a servant and took the place of **dependency.** How jealously did He watch over Him who "grew up before Him as **a tender plant,** and as a root out of a dry ground" (Isa. 53:2)! Before His birth, the Father prevented Joseph from putting away his wife (Matt. 1:18-20). Soon after His birth the Father bade Joseph to flee into Egypt for Herod would seek the young Child to destroy Him (Matt. 2:13). What proofs were these of the Husbandman's **care** for the True Vine!

"And My Father is the Husbandman." The Father has the same loving solicitude for **"the branches"** of the Vine. Three principal thoughts are suggested. His **protecting care:** His eye is upon and His hand tends to the weakest tendril and tenderest shoot. Then it suggests His **watchfulness.** Nothing escapes His eye. Just as the gardener notices daily the condition of each branch of the vine, watering, training, pruning as occasion arises; so the Divine Husbandman is constantly occupied with the need and welfare of those who are joined to Christ. It also denoted His **faithfulness.** No branch is allowed to run to waste. He spares neither the spray nor the pruning knife. When a branch is fruitless, He tends to it; if it is bearing fruit, He purgeth it. that it may bring forth more fruit. "My **Father** is the Husbandman." This is very blessed. He does not allot to others the task of caring for the Vine and its branches, and this assures us of the wisest, most tender, and most faithful care of it. But though this verse has a comforting and assuring voice, it also has a searching one, as has just been pointed out.

"Every branch in Me that beareth not fruit He taketh away" (v. 2). This has been appealed to by Arminians in proof of their view that it is possible for a true Christian to perish, for they argue that the words "taketh away" signify eternal destruction. But this is manifestly erroneous, for such an interpretation would flatly contradict such explicit and positive declarations as are to be found in John 4:14; 10:28; 18:9; Rom. 5:9-10; 8:35-39, etc., etc. Let us repeat what we said in the opening paragraph: Christ was not here addressing a mixed audience, in which were true believers and those who were merely professors. Nor was He speaking to the twelve—Judas had already gone out! Had Judas been present when Christ spoke these words there might be reason to suppose that He had him in mind. But what the Lord here said was addressed to the eleven, that is to believers only! This is the first key to its significance. Very frequently the true interpretation of a passage is discovered by attending to the character of those addressed. A striking example of this is found in Luke 15—where a case the very opposite of what we have here is in view. There the Lord speaks of the lost sheep and the lost coin being found, and the wayward son coming to the Father. Many have supposed that the Lord was speaking (in a parable) of the restoration of a backslidden believer. But the Lord was not addressing His disciples and warning them of the danger of getting out of communion with God. Instead He was speaking to His enemies (Luke 15:2) who criticised Him because He received sinners. Therefore, in what follows He proceeded to describe how a sinner is saved; first from the Divine side and then from the human.\* Here the case is otherwise. The Lord was not speaking to professors, and warning them that God requires truth in the inward parts; but He is talking to genuine believers, instructing, admonishing and warning them.

"Every branch in Me that bareth not fruit He taketh away." Many Calvinists have swung to the other extreme, erring in the opposite direction. We greatly fear that their principal aim was to overthrow the reasoning of their theological opponents, rather than to carefully study this verse in the light of its setting. They have argued that Christ was not speaking of a real believer at all. They insist that the words "beareth not fruit" described one who is within the "visible Church" but who has not vital union with Christ. But we are quite satisfied that this too is a mistake. The fact is, that we are so accustomed to concentrate everything on our own salvation and so little accustomed to dwell upon God's glory in the saved, that there is a lamentable tendency in all of us to apply many of the most pointed rebukes and warnings found in the Scriptures (which are declared to be "profitable for reproof and correction," as well as "for instruction in righteousness") to those who are not saved, thus losing their salutary effects on ourselves.

The words of our Lord leave us no choice in our application of this passage —as a whole and in its details—no matter what the conclusions be to which it leads us. Surely none will deny that they are believers to whom He says "Ye are the branches" (v. 5). Very well then; observe that Christ employs the same term in this needed word in v. 2: "Every branch in Me, that beareth not fruit." To make it doubly clear as to whom He was referring, He added, "Every branch in Me that beareth not fruit." Now if there is one form of expression, which, by invariable and unexceptionable use, indicates a believer more emphatically and explicitly than another, it is this:—"in Me," "in Him," "In Christ," Never are these expressions used loosely; never are they applied to any but the children of God: "If any one be in Christ (he is) a new creation" (2 Cor. 5:17).

"Every branch in Me that beareth not fruit He taketh away." If then, it is a real believer who is in view here, and if the "taketh away" does not refer to perishing, then what is the force and meaning of our Lord's words? First of all, notice the tense of the first verb: "Every branch in Me not bearing fruit He taketh away" is the literal translation. It is not of a branch which never bore fruit that the Lord is here speaking, but of one who is no longer "bearing fruit." Now there are three things which cause the branches of the natural vine to become fruitless: either through running to leaf, or through disease (a blight), or through old age, when they wither and die. The same holds good in the spiritual application. In 2

---
\*See the Author's 44 page booklet on "The Prodigal Son," 10 Cents (6d.) each.

Peter 1:8, we read: "For if these things be in you, and abound, they make you that ye shall neither be barren nor unfruitful in the knowledge of our Lord Jesus Christ." The unescapable inference from this is that if the "these things" (mentioned in 2 Peter 1:5-7) do not abound in us, we shall be "barren and unfruitful"—compare Titus 3:14. In such a case we bring forth nothing but leaves—the works of the flesh. Unspeakably solemn is this: one who has been bought at such infinite cost, saved by such wondrous grace, may yet, in this world, fall into a barren and unprofitable life, and thus fail to glorify God.

"He taketh away." Who does? The "Husbandman," the Father. This is conclusive proof that an unregenerate sinner is not in view. "The Father judgeth no man, but hath committed all judgment unto the Son" (John 5:22). It is Christ who will say, "Depart from Me" (Matt. 25). It is Christ who shall sit upon the Great White Throne to judge the wicked (Rev. 20). Therefore it cannot be a mere professor who is here in view—taken away unto judgment. Again a difficulty has been needlessly created here by the English rendering of the Greek verb. "Airo" is frequently translated in the A.V. "lifted up." For example: "And they lifted up their voices" (Luke 17:13, so also in Acts 4:24). "And Jesus lifted up His eyes" (John 11:41). "Lifted up His hand" (Rev.10:5) etc. In none of these places could the verb be rendered "taken away." Therefore, we are satisfied that it would be more accurate and more in accord with 'the analogy of faith' to translate, "Every branch in Me that beareth not fruit He **lifteth up**"—from trailing on the ground. Compare with this Dan. 7:4: "I beheld till the wings thereof were plucked, and it was **lifted** up from the earth, and made to stand upon the feet like a man."

"And every branch that beareth fruit' He purgeth it, that it may bring forth more fruit" (v. 2). The words "branch in Me," though clearly understood, are not expressed in the Greek. Literally, it is "And every one that fruit bears," that is, every one of the class of persons mentioned in the previous clause. How this conforms the conclusion that if **believers** are intended in the one case they must be in the other also! The care and method used by the Husbandman are told out in the words: "He purgeth it." The majority of people imagine that "purgeth" here is the equivalent of "pruning," and understand the reference is to affliction, chastisement, and painful discipline. But the word "purgeth" here does not mean "pruning," it would be better rendered, "cleanseth," as it is in the very next verse. It may strike some of us as rather incongruous to speak of cleansing a branch of a vine. It would not be so if we were familiar with the Palestine vineyards. The reference is to the washing off of the deposits of insects, of moss, and other parasites which infest the plant. Now the "water" which the Husbandman uses in cleansing the branches is **the Word**, as v. 3 tells us. The thought, then, is the removal by the Word of what would obstruct the flow of the life and fatness of the Vine through the branches. Let it be clearly understood that this "purging' **is not** to fit the believer for Heaven (that was accomplished, once for all, the first moment that faith rested upon the atoning sacrifice of the Lord Jesus Christ), but is designed to make us more fruitful, while he is here in this world.

"And every branch that beareth fruit, He purgeth it, that it may bring forth more fruit." "It is that action of the Father by which He brings the believer more fully under the operation of the 'quick and powerful' word. The Word is that by which the believer is born, with that new birth to which no uncleanness attaches (1 Peter 1:23). But while by second birth he is 'clean,' and in relation to his former condition is 'cleansed,' he is ever viewed as exposed to defilement, and consequently as needing to be 'cleansed.' And as the Word was, through the energy of the Spirit, effectual in the complete cleansing, so in regard to defilement by the way and in regard to the husbandman's purging to obtain more fruit, the purging is ever to be traced up to the operation of the Word (Psa. 119:9; 2 Cor. 7:1). Whatever other means may be employed, and there are many, they must be viewed as subordinate to the action of the 'truth,' or as making room for its purging process. Thus when affliction as a part of the process is brought into view, it is only as a means to the end of the soul's subjection and obedience to the Word. So the Psalmist said, "Before I was afflicted, I went astray: but now have I kept Thy Word ... It is good for me that I have been afflicted; that I might learn Thy statutes" (119:67, 71). It will, we think, be apparent, that all means which Divine wisdom employs to bring to real subjection to the Word, must be regarded as belonging to the process of 'purging' that we may bring forth more fruit.

"It would be interesting to pursue our inquiry into the course of our purging but our present limits forbids this. We may just remark that much that may be learned on this point from such passages as those of which, without any extended remark, we cite one or two. Here is one which suggests a loving rebuke of all **impatience** under the operations of the Husbandman's hand: 'For a season **if need be**, ye are in heaviness through manifold trials' (I Peter 1:7). Then we have a text in James, which calls for **joy** under the Father's faithful purging: 'My brethren, count it all joy when ye fall into divers trials; knowing this, that the trying of your faith worketh patience. But let patience have her perfect work, that ye may be perfect and entire, wanting nothing' (1:2-4). Once more, we take the words of Christian exultation which declare our fellowship with God in the whole process and fruit of our purging: 'And not only so, but we **glory** in tribulations also: knowing that tribulation worketh patience; and patience experience; and experience, hope. And hope maketh not ashamed; because the love of God is shed abroad in our hearts by the Holy Spirit which is given unto us' (Rom. 5:3-5). O that we might learn from these revelations of the Father's work, upon us and in us, quietly and joyfully to endure; and rightly to interpret all that befalls us only desiring that He may fulfill in us all the good pleasure of His will, that we may be fruitful in every good work" (Mr. C. Campbell).

"Now (better "already") ye are clean through the Word which I have spoken unto you," (v. 3). The purging or cleansing of the previous verse refers to the believer's **state;** the cleanness here describes his **standing** before God. The one is progressive, the other absolute. The two things are carefully distinguished all through. We **have** purified our souls in obeying the truth through the Spirit (1 Peter 1:22), yet we need **to be purifying** ourselves, even as Christ is pure (1 John 3:3). We "are washed" (1 Cor. 6:11), yet there is constant need that He who washed us from our sins at first should daily wash our feet (John 13:10). The Lord, having had occasion to speak here of a purging which is constantly in process, graciously stopped to assure the disciples that they were **already** clean. Note He makes **no** exception—"Ye": the branches spoken of in the previous verses. If the Lord had had in mind two entirely different classes (as almost all of the best commentators argue), namely, formal professors in the former part of the verse and genuine believers in the latter He would necessarily have qualified His statement here. This is the more conclusive if we contrast His words in 13:10: "Ye are clean, but **not all!"** Let the reader refer back to our remarks upon John 13:10 for a fuller treatment of this cleanness.

"Abide in Me" (v. 4). The force of this cannot be appreciated till faith has laid firm hold of the previous verse: "Already ye are clean." "Brethren in Christ what a testimony is this: He who speaks what He knows and testifies what He has seen, declares us 'clean every whit.' Yea, and He thus testifies in the very same moment as when He asserts that we had need to have our feet washed; in the very same breath in which He reveals our need of cleansing in order to further fruit-bearing. He would thus assure us that the defilement which we contract in our walk as pilgrims, and the impurity which we contract as branches do in nowise, nor in the least degree, affect the absolute spotless purity which is ours in Him.

"Now in all study of the Word this should be a starting-point, the acknowledgement of our real oneness with Christ, and our cleanness in Him by His Word. It may be observed that He cannot 'wash our feet' till we **know that** we are cleansed 'every whit;' and we cannot go on to learn of Him what is needful for fruit-bearing unless we first drink in the word, 'Ye are already clean.' We can only receive His further instruction when we have well learned and are holding fast the first lesson of His love—our completeness in Him" (Mr. C. Campbell).

"'Clean every whit,' Thou saidst it, Lord!
Shall one suspicion lurk?
Thine surely is a faithful Word,
And Thine a finished Work."

"Abide in Me." "To be" **in Christ** and **"to abide"** in Him are two different things which must not be confounded. One must first be **"in Him"** before he can **"abide in Him."** The former respects a union effected by the creating-power of God, and which can neither be dissolved nor suspended. Believers are never exhorted to be "in Christ"—they are in Him by new creation (2 Cor. 5:7; Eph. 2:10). But Christians are frequently exhorted to **abide** in Christ, because this privilege and experience may be interrupted. "To 'abide,' 'continue,' 'dwell,' 'remain' in Christ—by all these terms is this one word translated —has always reference to the maintainance of fellowship with God in Christ. The word 'abide' calls us to vigilance lest at any time the **experimental** realisation of our union with Christ should be interrupted. To abide in Him, then, is to have sustained conscious communion with Him" (Mr. Campbell). To abide in Christ signifies the constant occupation of the heart with Him—a daily active faith in Him which, so to speak maintains the dependency of the branch upon the Vine, and the circulation of life and fatness of the Vine in the branch. What we have here is parallel to that other figurative expression used by our Lord in John 6:56: "He that eateth My flesh, and drinketh My blood, dwelleth (**abideth**) in Me, and I in him." This is but another way of insisting upon the continuous exercise of faith in a crucified and living Saviour, deriving life and the sustenance of life from Him. As the initial act of believing in Him is described as "coming" to Him, ("He that cometh to Me shall never hunger, and he that **believeth** on Me shall never thirst: 6:35), so the **continued** activity of faith is described as "**abiding** in Him."

"Abide in Me, and **I in you**" (v. 4). The two things are quite distinct, though closely connected. Just as it is one thing to be "**in Christ**," and another to "**abide** in Him," so there is a real difference between His being in us, and His **abiding** in us. The one is a matter of His grace; the other of our responsibility. The one is perpetual, the other may be interrupted. By our **abiding** in Him is meant the happy conscious fellowship of our union with Him, in the discernment of what He is for us; so by His abiding in us is meant the happy conscious recognition of His presence, the assurance of his goodness, grace and power—Himself the **recourse** of our soul in everything.

As the branch cannot bear fruit of itself, except it abides in the vine no more can ye, except ye abide in Me" (v. 4). "Thus our Lord enforces the necessity of maintaining fellowship. He is not only the source of all fruit, but He also puts forth His power while there is personal appropriation of what He is for us, and in us. And this, if we receive it, will lead us to a right judgment of ourselves and our service. In the eyes of our own brethren, and in our own esteem, we may maintain a goodly appearance as fruit-bearing branches. But whatever our own judgment or that of others, the **apparent** springs from 'innermost fellowship and communion' the true Vine will never own it as His fruit.

"Moreover, all this may, by His blessing, bring us to see the **cause** of our imperfect or sparse fruit bearing. Thousands of Christians are complaining of barrenness; but they fail to trace their barrenness to its right source—the meagreness of their communion with Christ. Consequently, they seek fruitfulness in activities, often right in themselves, but which, while He is unrecognised, can never yield any fruit. In such condition, they ought rather to cry, 'Our leanness! Our leanness;' and they ought to know that leanness can only be remedied by that **abiding** in Christ, and He in them, which 'fills the soul with marrow and its fatness.' 'Those that be planted in the house of the Lord (an Old Testament form for 'abiding in Him') shall flourish in the courts of our God. They shall bring forth fruit in old age; they shall be fat and flourishing" (Psa. 92:13. 14). We are surely warranted to say, Take heed to the fellowship, and the fruit will spring forth" (Mr. C. Campbell).

"I am the Vine, ye are the branches: He that abideth in Me, and I in him, the same bringeth forth much fruit" (v. 5). This is very blessed, coming in just here. It is a word of assurance. As we contemplate the failure of Israel as God's vine of old, and as we review our own past resolutions and attempts, we are discouraged and despondent. This is met by the announcement, "**I am the Vine**, ye are the branches." It is not a question of **your** sufficiency; yea, let your insufficiency be admitted, as settled once for all. In your self you are no better than a branch **severed** from the vine —dry, dead. But "he that abideth in Me, and I in him, the same bringeth forth much fruit." "No figure could more forcibly express the complete dependence of the believer on Christ for all fruit-bearing than this. A branch cannot bear fruit of itself, except it abide in the vine. In itself it has no resources though in union with the vine it is provided with life. This is precisely the believer's condition: 'Christ liveth in me.' The branch **bears** the clusters, but it does not **produce** them. It bears what the vine produces; and so the result is expressed by the Apostle, 'to me to live is Christ.' It is important that in this respect, as well as with reference to righteousness before God, we should be brought to the end of self with all its vain efforts and strivings. And then there comes to us the assurance of unfailing resources in Another" (Waymarked in the Wilderness).

"For without Me (better **"severed from Me"**) ye can do nothing" (v. 5). Clearly this refers not to the vital union existing between Christ and the believer, which shall never be broken, either by his own volition or the will of God through all eternity (Rom. 8:38-39): but to the interruption of fellowship and dependency upon Him, mentioned in the immediate context. This searching word is introduced here to **enforce** our need of heeding what had just been said in the previous verse and repeated at the beginning of this.

"Severed from Me ye can do nothing." There are many who believe this in a general way, but who fail to apply it in detail. They know that they cannot do the important things without Christ's aid, but how many of the little things we attempt in **our own** strength! No wonder we fail so often. "Without Me ye can do **nothing**" 'Nothing that is spiritually good; no, not any thing at all, be it little or great, easy or difficult to be performed; cannot think a good thought, speak a good word, or do a good action: can neither begin one, nor when it is begun, perfect it" (Dr. J. Gill). But mark it well, the Lord did not say, "Without you I can do nothing." In gathering out His elect, and in building up His Church, He employs human instrumentality; but that is not a matter of necessity, but of choice, with Him; **He could** "do" without them, just as well as with them.

"Severed from Me ye can do nothing." Urgently do we need this warning. Not only will the allowance of any known sin break our fellowship with Him, but concentration on any thing but **Himself** will also surely do it. Satan is very subtle. If only he can get us occupied with ourselves, our fruit-bearing, or our fruit, his purpose is accomplished. Faith is nothing apart from its object, and is no longer in operation when it becomes occupied with itself. Love, too, is in exercise only while it is occupied with its Beloved. "There is a disastrous delusion in this matter when, under the plea of witnessing for Christ and relating their experience, men are tempted to parade their own attainments: their love, joy and peace, their zeal in service, their victory in conflict. And Satan has no more effectual method of severing the soul from Christ, and arresting the bringing forth of fruit to the glory of God, than when he can persuade Christians to feast upon their own fruit, instead of eating the flesh and drinking the blood of the Son of man. But shall we not bear witness for Christ? Yes, verily, but let your testimony be **of Him**, not of yourself." (Waymarks in the Wilderness).

"If a man abide not in Me, he is cast forth as a branch, and is withered; and men gather them, and cast into the fire, and they are burned" (v. 6). This is another verse which has been much misunderstood, and it is really surprising to discover how many able commentators have entirely missed its meaning. With scarcely an exception, Calvinistic expositors suppose that Christ here referred to a different class from what had been before Him in the three previous verses. Attention is called to the fact that Christ did not say, "If a **branch** abide not in Me he is cast forth," but "If a **man** abide not in Me." But really this is inexcusable in those who are able, in any measure, to consult the Greek. The word "man" is not found in the original at all! Literally rendered it is, "unless any one abide in Me he is cast out as the branch" (Bagster's Interlinear). The simple and obvious meaning of these words of Christ is this: If any one of the **branches**, any believer, continues out of fellowship with Me, he is "cast forth." It could not be said of any one that had **never** "come" to Christ that He does not abide in Him. This is made the more apparent by the limitation in this very verse: "he is cast forth as a branch." Let it be remembered that the central figure here employed by the Lord has reference to our sojourn **in this world**, and the bringing forth of fruit to the glory of the Father. The "casting forth" is done by the Husbandman, and evidently had in view the stripping of the believer of the gifts and opportunities which he failed to improve. It is similar to the salt "losing its savour" (Matt. 5:13). It is parallel with Luke 8:18: "And whosoever hath not, **from him** shall be taken even that which he seemeth to have.\*" It is analogous to that admoni-

---
\*See our comments on this verse under John 9:17.

tion in 2 John 8: "Look to yourselves, that we lose not those things which we have wrought, but that we receive a full reward."

But what is meant by, "Men gather them, and cast into the fire, and they are burned?" Observe, first, the plural pronouns. It is not "men gather him and cast into the fire, and he is burned," as it would most certainly have been had an unbeliever, a mere professor, been in view. The change of number here is very striking, and evidences, once more, the minute accuracy of Scripture. "Unless any one abide in Me, he is cast forth, and men gather them and cast into the fire and they are burned. The "them" and the "they" are what issues from the one who has been cast forth "as a branch." And what is it that issues from such a one—what but dead works: "wood, hay stubble!" and what is to become of his "dead works." 1 Cor. 3:15 tells us: "If any man's work shall be burned (the very word used in John 15:16!), he shall suffer loss: but he himself shall be saved: yet so as by fire." Lot is a pertinent example: he was out of fellowship with the Lord, he ceased to bear fruit to His glory, and his dead works were all burned up in Sodom, yet he himself was saved!

One other detail should be noticed. In the original it is not "men gather them," but "they gather them." Light is thrown on this by Matt.13:41, 42: "The Son of man shall send forth His angels and they shall gather out of His kingdom all things that offend, and them which do iniquity: And shall cast them into a furnace of fire: There shall be wailing and gnashing of teeth." Note the two distinct items here: the angels gather "all things that offend" and "them which do iniquity." In the light of John 15:6 the first of these actions will be fulfilled at the session of the judgment-seat of Christ (2 Cor. 5:10), the second when He returns to the earth.

Here then is a most solemn warning and heart-searching prospect for every Christian. Either your life and my life is, as the result of continuous fellowship with Christ, bringing forth fruit to the glory of the Father, fruit which will remain; or, because of neglect of communion with Him, we are in immense danger of being set aside as His witnesses on earth, to bring forth only that which the fire will consume in a coming Day. May the Holy Spirit apply the words of the Lord Jesus to each conscience and heart.

Studying the following questions will prepare for our next lesson:
1. What is the connection between v. 7 and the context?
2. How is "ye shall ask what ye will in v. 7 to be qualified?
3. What is meant by "so shall ye be My Disciples" v. 8?
4. What is the relation between vv. 9-12 and the subject of fruit-bearing?
5. What constituted Christ's "joy" v. 11?
6. What is suggested by "friends" vv. 13-15?
7. Why does Christ bring in election in v. 16?

Arthur W. Pink.

## GLEANINGS FROM EXODUS

### 27. Israel at Sinai. Ex. 19.

"In the third month, when the children of Israel were gone forth out of the land of Egypt, the same day came they into the wilderness of Sinai. For they were departed from Rephidim, and were come to the desert of Sinai, and had pitched in the wilderness; and there Israel camped before the mount." (vv. 1, 2). Thus was fulfilled God's promise to Moses. When he appeared to him at the burning bush He had declared, "Certainly I will be with thee; and this shall be a token unto thee, that I have sent thee: When thou hast brought forth the people out of Egypt, ye shall serve God upon this mountain." (3:12).

Many difficulties had stood in the way, but they had disappeared before the irresistible execution of God's counsels like the dew before the morning sun. Israel had been made willing to depart from Egypt, and their masters had been glad to let them go. The waters of the Red Sea had parted asunder so that the covenant-people went through dryshod. The wilderness of Etham had been crossed so too had the Wilderness of Sin, and though two whole months had passed since they left the land of Pharaoh, not an Israelite had perished with hunger or died through sickness. "Ye shall serve God upon this mountain" (3:12), and they did. No word of God can fail. No matter how the enemy may rage, "the counsel of the Lord shall stand" (Prov. 19:21).

"In the third month... the selfsame day.... Israel camped before the mount." The time-mark here is important. It supplies a key to what follows. Three is ever the number of manifestation. Jehovah was now to give His people a wondrous manifestation of Himself. Previously, they had seen His judgments upon Egypt; they had beheld His power displayed at the Red Sea; they had witnessed His guiding-hand in the pillar of Cloud and Fire; they had experienced His mercies in the providing of the manna and the giving of water from the smitten rock; but they were now to behold His exalted majesty —suitably was this displayd from the mount.

"And Moses went up unto God, and the Lord called unto Him out of the mountain, saying, Thus shalt thou say to the house of Jacob, and tell the children of Israel; Ye have seen what I did unto the Egyptians and how I bore you on eagles' wings and brought you unto Myself. Now, therefore, if ye will obey My voice indeed, and keep My covenant, then ye shall be a peculiar treasure unto Me above all people, for all the earth is Mine" (vv. 3-5). These verses have suffered much from the hands of certain commentators. Most erroneous conclusions have been drawn from them. Men well versed in the Scriptures have strangely overlooked other passages in the previous chapters which plainly contradict their assertions. One respected expositor begins his remarks on Ex. 19 and 20 as follows:—"A new dispensation is inaugurated in these chapters. Up to the close of chapter 18, as before indicated, grace reigned, and hence characterised all God's dealing with His people, but from this point they were put, with their own consent, under the rigid requirements of law." In this he is followed by others of the school to which he belongs. A wide influence has been exerted by this school, and to-day thousands blindly accept the dicta of its leaders as though they were infallible. Indeed, one will at once court suspicion of his orthodoxy if he dares to challenge their ex cathedra utterances. Nevertheless, it is our bounden duty to test by the Word all that men have to say upon it.

So far as our own light goes, we know of nothing in Scripture which warrants the assertion that "a new dispensation" began when the children of Israel reached Sinai. John 1:17 is often appealed to in proof:—"The law was given by Moses, but grace and truth came by Jesus Christ." But this verse is far from proving what is assumed. The Lord does not here say that a "new dispensation began" with the giving of the law: that is what men have read into it. If "the law was given by Moses" signifies that the Jewish dispensation began at that point, then the second clause—"but grace and truth came by Jesus Christ"—must mean that the Christian dispensation began with the coming of Jesus Christ. But it did not. The Christian dispensation did not begin, and could not, till after the death of our Saviour. John 1:17 contrasts the ministries of Moses and Jesus Christ.

When, then, did the Mosaic dispensation begin? If not when Israel reached Sinai, at what other point in their history? Without any hesitation we answer, on the Passover night; it was from that night their national history is to be dated, and that the Mosaic dispensation commenced. Previous to that night they had no existence as a nation, no corporate existence; they were a disorganised crowd of slaves. But that night everything was changed for them. Then, for the first time, were they termed an "assembly" (Ex. 12:6). That the Passover marked not only the beginning of their national existence but also the commencement of the Mosaic dispensation, is abundantly clear from the fact that their calendar was then changed by Divine order (Ex. 12:2)!

The new dispensation (the Mosaic) began by the establishment of a new relationship between Jehovah and His people. They were now His redeemed. As we have shown in a previous paper, redemption is two-fold—by purchase and by power. Israel were purchased to God by the blood of the "lamb," they were delivered from their enemies by His power at the Red Sea. If, as some able expositors contend, the crossing of the Red Sea was three days after the Passover night, then the analogy between the beginning of the Mosaic dispensation and the beginning of the Christian dispensation is perfect. In one sense the Christ-dispensation began at the death of Christ, with the "rending of the veil"; in another sense, it began three days later, at His resurrection from the dead.

The leaders of the "school" referred to above teach that, prior to Sinai, God dealt with Israel in pure grace, but that at Sinai they, for the first time, came under law. Such a mistake is even more excuseless than the statement that a "new dispensation" began then. Israel were under law before they reached the

Mount of God. Listen to the testimony of Ex. 15:25-26, "And he cried unto the Lord; and the Lord showed him a tree, which when he had cast into the waters, the waters were made sweet; there He made for them a statute and an ordinance and there He proved them. And He said, If thou wilt diligently hearken to the voice of the Lord thy God, and wilt do that which is right in His sight, and wilt give ear to **His commandments**, and keep all **His statutes**, I will put none of these diseases upon thee, which I have brought upon the Egyptians." Surely this is plain enough; reference is made to both God's "commandments" and His "statutes." But lest the quibble be raised that this was prospective, i.e., in view of the Law which He was shortly to give them, we beg the reader to weigh carefully our next reference. In Ex. 16:4 we read that God said, "Behold, I will rain bread from heaven for you; and the people shall go out and gather a certain rate every day, that I may prove them, whether they will walk in **My law**, or no." The meaning of this is explained in v. 23, "This is that which the Lord had said, Tomorrow is the rest of the Holy Sabbath unto the Lord; bake that which ye will bake to-day and seethe that ye will seethe; and that which remaineth over lay up for you to be kept until the morning." Israel's response to this is given in v. 27 "And it came to pass, that there went out some of the people on the seventh day for to gather, and they found none." Now mark attentively the next verse, "And the Lord said unto Moses, How long refuse ye to **keep My commandments** and **My laws?**" Certainly this was not "prospective." It was retrospective. It furnishes indubitable proof that Israel were **under law** before they reached Sinai.

That there was a marked change in Jehovah's dealings with Israel after Sinai cannot be denied, and we suppose it is from this premise that the erroneous conclusion has been drawn that a new dispensation then began. Before Sinai was reached, when Israel "murmured," God bore with them in greatest long-sufferance, but after Sinai their murmurings were visited with summary chastisements. How then, is this to be explained? If it was not the giving of commandments and statutes which introduced the change in God's dealings with His people, what was it? We answer, it was because of the **covenant** which Israel there solemnly entered into. Prior to Sinai, God dealt with Israel on the ground of the Abrahamic covenant; but from Sinai onwards, He dealt with them, nationally, according to the terms of the Sinaiatic covenant. As this is of vital importance to the understanding of the later Scriptures we must dwell upon it in a little more detail.

Gen. 15 records the covenant which God made with Abraham, confirmed later to Isaac and Jacob. We cannot now attempt an exposition of the second half of Gen. 15, though it is of deep importance. Briefly the facts are these: In verse 6 we read for the first time of Abraham's · justification. Following this, the Lord bids Abraham prepare Him a sacrifice. This Abraham does, dividing each animal "in the midst." Then a deep sleep fell upon Abraham, and while asleep, God promised to bring His descendants, of the fourth generation, into Canaan. Then we read of the Shekinah-glory passing between the pieces of Abraham's sacrifices—an action which symbolically signified the **making of a covenant**, see Jer. 34:18, 19. Following which, we are told, "In the same day the Lord made a **covenant** with Abraham saying, Unto thy seed have I given this land" (Gen. 15:18).

Three things should be carefully noted. First, there was only one party to this covenant—Jehovah himself. Abraham was asleep. Its fulfilment therefore, turned alone on the **Divine** faithfulness. There were no conditions attached to it which man had to meet. Second, it was based upon a sacrifice. Third, it was a covenant of pure grace. Mark "unto thy seed **have I given** this land." Contrast from this Gen. 13:15. "For all the land which thou seest to thee **will I** give it!" But now a sacrifice had been offered, blood had been shed, the purchase-price had been paid, a solemn covenant had been made; hence the change from "I will" to "I have."

Now it is of the very first moment to observe that God's deliverance of Israel from Egypt was on the ground of His covenant with Abraham. Proof of this is furnished in Ex. 2:24 where we read "And God heard their groaning, and God remembered **His covenant with Abraham**, with Isaac and with Jacob." Again, in 6:3, 4, we find God reminding Moses of this: "And I appeared unto Abraham, unto Isaac and unto Jacob, by the name of God Almighty, but by My name Jehovah was I not known to them. And I have also established **My** covenant with them to give them the land of Canaan, the land of their pilgrimage wherein they were strangers." It was on the ground of this covenant that the Lord dealt with Israel up to the time they reached Sinai! The last thing recorded before Israel reached Sinai was the giving of water from the smitten rock, and mark how the Psalmist refers to this, "He opened the rock, and the waters gushed out: they ran in the dry places like a river. For He remembered His holy promise to Abraham His servant" (Psl. 105:41,42). But at Sinai Jehovah's relationship to Israel was placed upon a different basis.

In Ex. 19:5 we find God, from the Mount, bidding Moses say unto His people, "Now therefore, if ye will obey My voice indeed, and keep My covenant, then ye shall be a peculiar treasure unto Me above all people; for all the earth is Mine; and ye shall be unto Me a kingdom of priests, and an holy nation." There has been much confusion upon this and much consequent error. The Lord was not here referring to His covenant with Abraham (that patriarch is not mentioned at all in the chapter). This is made unmistakably clear from His words, "If ye will obey My voice indeed and keep My covenant." There was nothing about God's covenant with Abraham that Israel could "keep." There were no conditions attached to it, no stipulations, no provisos. It was unconditional so far as Abraham and his descendants were concerned. But here at Sinai, God proposed to make another covenant, a covenant, to which there should be two parties—Himself and Israel; a covenant of works, a covenant whch Israel must "keep" if they were to enjoy the conditional blessings attached to it.

What were the terms of the Siniatic covenant, and what were the conditions and blessings attached to it? The answer to these questions is plainly stated in the Scriptures. In Ex. 34:27, 28, we read, "And the Lord said unto Moses, Write thou these words: for after the tenor of these words I have made a covenant with thee and with Israel. And he was there (on the Mount) with the Lord forty days and forty nights; he did neither eat bread, nor drink water. And he wrote upon the tables the words of the covenant, THE TEN COMMANDMENTS." Forty years later, Moses reminded Israel, "And He declared unto you His covenant, which He commanded you to perform, ten commandments; and He wrote them upon two tables of stone" (Deut. 4:13).

Returning to Ex. 19, we learn there that in response to Jehovah's proposal to enter into a legal covenant with them, Israel unanimously and heartily accepted the same: "All the people answered together, and said, All that the Lord hath spoken we will do" (v. 8). These words were repeated by the people after Moses had made known to them the details of the covenant, "And Moses came and told the people all the words of the Lord, and all the judgments; and all the people answered with one voice, and said, All the words which the Lord hath said will we do" (24:3). Then the covenant was solemnly ratified by blood. See Ex. 24:4-8.

Now it was on the ground of this Siniatic covenant, not on the ground of the Abrahamic, that Israel entered Canaan in the days of Joshua; and it was on the ground of this Siniatic covenant that God dealt with Israel during their occupancy of the land. This was made apparent right from the beginning. As soon as it became evident that there was an Israelite who had broken the eighth commandment, the Lord declared, "Israel hath sinned, and they have also transgressed My covenant which I commanded them; for they have even taken of the accursed thing, and have also stolen, and dissembled also, and they have put it even among their own stuff.... And it shall be that he that is taken with the accursed thing shall be burnt with fire, he and all that he hath; because he hath transgressed the covenant of the Lord, and because he hath wrought wickedness in Israel" (Josh. 7:11, 15). Accordingly we find that Achan and all his family were stoned to death. At a later date, we read, "And it came to pass, when the judge was dead, that they returned and corrupted themselves more than their fathers, in following other gods to serve them, and to bow down unto them; they ceased not from their own doings, nor from their stubborn ways. And the anger of the Lord was hot against Israel; and He said, Because that this people hath transgressed My covenant which I commanded their fathers, and have not hearkened unto My voice; I also will not henceforth drive out any from before them of the nations which Joshua left when he died" (Judges 2:19, 21). The rending of the kingdom was because Solomon failed to keep this covenant

(1 Kings 11:11). Throughout Israel's occupation of Canaan, God dealt with them on the ground of the Siniatic covenant. See Jer. 11.

A few words upon the **circumstances** attending the Siniatic covenant must suffice. In verses 10 and 11 we read, "And the Lord said unto Moses, "Go unto the people, and sanctify them today and to-morrow, and let them wash their clothes, and be ready against the third day; for the third day the Lord will come down in the sight of all the people upon Mount Sinai." Here we have emphasised what was noted upon the opening verse of the chapter. It was in the **third** month when the children of Israel were gone forth out of the land of Egypt that they arrived at Sinai; and it was on the **third** day of this month (twice repeated) that the Lord declared He would "come down in the sight of His people." Clearly, then, what we have here is a **manifestation** of the Lord Himself, cf. Deut. 5:24. And everything that followed was in perfect keeping with that fact bearing in mind the typical character of that Dispensation.

The people were to "sanctify" themselves, even to the point of washing their clothes. How plainly this intimated that God would draw nigh only to a people who were clean—that it is sin which separates the Creator from His creatures.

"And thou shalt set bounds unto the people round about, saying, Take heed to yourselves, that ye go not up into the mount or touch the border of it; whosoever toucheth the mount shall be surely put to death" (v. 12). Much has been made of this in the endeavour to prove that a "new dispensation" had begun, that God was no longer dealing with Israel in grace. But it is only another example of men reading their own pre-conceived ideas into Scripture. Moreover, it is, in this instance, to ignore what has gone before. Months earlier when Jehovah had appeared to Moses at the burning bush and Moses had said, "I will now turn aside, and see this great sight," God at once called to him and said, "draw **not nigh** hither put off thy shoes from off thy feet, for the place whereon thou standest is holy ground" (3:5)!

"And it came to pass on the third day in the morning that there were thunders and lightnings, and a thick cloud settled upon the mount, and the voice of the trumphet exceeding loud; so that all the people that was in the camp trembled" (v. 16). This, too, has been twisted to mean something quite different from its obvious import. These were the awe-spiring attendants of the awful majesty of Jehovah, upon whose face none could look and live. Were these phenomena intended to show that Israel had done wrong in entering into this covenant? Or were they designed to manifest the dignity, the holiness, the greatness of the One with whom they were making the covenant? Surely the latter. If proof of this be required it is furnished in 20:20. "And Moses said unto the people, "Fear not, for God has come to prove you, and that **His fear may be before your faces that ye sin not**" and cf. Deut. 5:24. Let it not be forgotten that in heaven itself the apocalytic seer is given to behold a Throne out of which "proceeded lightnings and thunderings and voices" (Rev. 4:5)—the identical things witnessed on Sinai!

There is a passage in Deuteronomy which should forever settle the question as to whether or not Israel acted wisely in entering into the Siniatic covenant, as to whether they did right or wrong in promising to do all that the Lord had said, and as to whether God was pleased or displeased with them. This passage is found in the fifth chapter of that book. Moses is there reviewing what took place at Sinai. He declares, "These words, the Lord spake unto all your assembly in the mount out of the midst of the fire of the cloud, and of the thick darkness, with a great voice and He added no more. And He wrote them on two tables of stone, and delivered them unto me." (v. 22). He then reminds Israel of the response which they made, "And it came to pass, when ye heard the voice out of the midst of the darkness, (for the mountain did burn with fire), that ye came near unto me, even all the heads of your tribes, and your elders; and ye said, Behold, the Lord our God hath showed us **His glory** and **His greatness**, and we have heard His voice out of the midst of the fire; we have seen this day that God doth talk with man, and he liveth. Now therefore, why should we die? For this great fire will consume us; if we hear the voice of the Lord our God any more, then shall we die. For who is there of all flesh, that hath heard the voice of the living God speaking out of the midst of the fire as we have, and live? Go thou near, and hear all that the Lord our God shall say; and speak thou unto us all that the

Lord our God shall speak unto thee; and we will hear it and do it" (vv. 23, 27). And then in v. 28 we are told, "And the Lord heard the voice of your words, when ye spake unto me; and the Lord said unto me, I have heard the voice of the words of this people, which they have spoken unto you; they have well said all that they have spoken." Nothing could be plainer than this. God was **not displeased** with Israel for their avowal of allegiance, any more than he was displeased with Joshua when he said, "But as for me and my house, we will serve the Lord" (Josh. 24:15).

Finally, it must not be forgotten that Ex. 24 completes what is before us in Ex. 19. There we read of the ratification of the covenant. There we are told, "And he took **the book of the covenant**, and read in the audience of the people, and they said, All that the Lord hath said will we do, and be obedient" (24:7). Now what is of special importance to note is the words which immediately follow, "And Moses took the blood and sprinkled it on the people, and said, 'Behold **the blood of the covenant**, which the Lord hath made with you concerning all these words." The application of the blood to the people plainly signified that God would deal **graciously** with them. What, then, was the outstanding lesson which Jehovah taught Israel at Sinai? This, that His grace towards them would henceforth **"reign through righteousness"** (Rom. 5:21).

In closing, let us make practical application of what has been before us. Such a view of God's majesty as Israel were favoured with at Sinai is the crying need of our day. The eye of faith needs to see Him not only as our "Father," as "The God of all grace," but also as the "High and Lofty One that inhabiteth eternity" (Isa. 57:15), as the "Great and Dreadful God" (Dan. 9:4), as the One who has said, "Behold, the nations are as a drop in a bucket, and are counted as the small dust of the balance; behold, He taketh up the isles as a very little thing . . . . all nations before Him are as nothing; and they are counted to Him less than nothing, and vanity" (Isa. 40:15, 17), read the whole of Isa. 40. If we beheld Him thus, then should we work out our own salvation with "fear and trembling." Let it not be forgotten that the God of the Old Testament and the God of the New Testament is one and the same; He is a God into whose hands it is a fearful thing to fall. May His Holy Spirit so reveal Him to us, as the One to be reverenced, obeyed and worshipped.

Arthur W. Pink.

# PROGRESSIVE SANCTIFICATION

Progressive sanctification are the words used by some to express the very chief of Satan's wiles—the greater and greater holiness of **"the vile body."** "The flesh in which dwelleth no good thing," No, not even in holy Paul. We have nothing to do with this meaning of these words, only to denounce it as the most God-insulting, Bible-denying, saint-distressing dogma that ever Satan infused into the minds of Christless, graceless Pharisees. Others, again, mean, by the same words, the progressive work of the Holy Spirit in the elect of God, who are said to be "begotten," "quickened," "brought to the birth," "born again," "new born babes," "little children," "young men," and "fathers." They mean that this work of the Holy Spirit in God's people will give rise to more and more rectitiude of character and conduct in the recipients of this wondrous grace. They mean that the holy, blessed Spirit will carry on the work of grace in their souls, until they shall at death be without the least taint or stain of sin; and, after that, bring their vile bodies from the bondage of corruption into the glorious liberty of the sons of God, and fashion them like unto the glorious body of the Lord Jesus. To this meaning of the words, "Progressive Sanctification," we have no objections to urge. We can only say, if we know anything of this growth of grace in our own souls, it has produced four things in us in a most unmistakeable way.

1. It has made our vile flesh **appear** in our own eyes a thousand times more vile than it did, when the light of God first dawned upon our spirit. The more the sun's rays have shone into the chamber of our heart, the more the terrible dust of sin has been discovered in our mind. We grow in this way— the very opposite way to the fleshly perfectionist—more and more vile. The pious child of Satan, in his satanic conceit, gets more and more holy in his own eyes, as the Lord has said, "There is a generation who are pure in their

own eyes, yet are not washed from their filthiness." As opposed to these, the more the Holy Spirit sanctifies the soul of a child of God, the more will such see that "in their flesh dwelleth no good thing," and cry out, relative to their "vile body"—"O wretched man that I am, who shall deliver me from the body of this death?"

2. This growth in grace has made the mercy of the Lord very great in our eyes. The more sin is discovered, the more mercy we need. Mercy providing for such ruin, mercy atoning for such sin, mercy pardoning such sin, mercy bearing with such sin, mercy sustaining us under such sin, mercy cleaving to us notwithstanding such sin, is wonderful mercy indeed. Sin is a thousand times more sinful, and mercy is a million times greater than when grace first entered our souls 50 years ago. Hence we feel:

"Without God's free mercy we could not live here;
Sin soon would reduce us to utter despair;
But through Thy free goodness our spirits revive,
And He who first made us still keeps us alive."

3. This growth in grace has brought about more prayer: prayerful dependence upon the Lord in the hourly apprehensions of danger of falling by these sins thus discovered to our souls by the Holy Spirit of God. We used to think at first of standing by manly dignity, moral excellency, and high-toned respectability. When we went abroad, we used to say to ourselves, in the words of Solomon—"Now, play the man." Ah, yes, play the man, indeed! The world, the flesh, and the devil soon made a slaughter of the man. Pretty figure the man cut in the awful field of battle. The man became the laughing-stock of hell; the shame of Israel, and the terror of himself. Then we said, **"Come, be pious."** So we met the foe again—we fell, and lay down in shame. The Man of Bethlehem, the Lord of Calvary once more raised us up, and cheered our saddened hearts by His atoning blood;

so that we lifted our once downcast eyes up to Him and said most imploringly:—

"Dear Refuge of our weary souls,
On Thee when sorrows rise;
On Thee, when waves of trouble roll,
Our fainting hopes relies."

Thus we were brought from the playing of the man and sheltering in piety, to put our trust, by daily and hourly dependence, in the Lord and the riches of His grace.

4. The growth of grace has led us to aim at more rectitude of character and godliness of conduct. When violent passions and fiery tempers have stung us with dark days and dismal nights, in which the displeasure of God, the condemnation of conscience, the accusations of Satan, the grief of brethren, the sadness of home, the complaints of the world, and the shame of Zion has been felt, we have implored the Lord to give us **more grace** unto **rectitude of character** and **conduct** in **spirit and life,** worthy of the dear and glorious name we espouse, and by which we are named before men, devils and angels. Knowing how shamefully unlovely we are by nature, in the dispositions of our flesh, we do feel thankful in our hearts that grace must have been more and more enlarged in our hearts in its powers of restraint upon our sins, and in its forces of constraints upon our souls; thus to have formed anything like Christian character and conduct in our lives and conversation, in the world and in the Church of God. If improprieties have been laid aside; if we have exemplified more of the meek and lowly spirit of Christ, this is not because our flesh is better than it was, or that it has less power to sin: no, it is because the Lord has given us more grace; because the Holy Spirit has put upon us more restraint and constraint in the growth of grace, from the first germ of its holy seed unto its full corn in the ear. Thus there is a progressive growth in the life of grace in the souls of God's people.

Pastor Allen, Sydney, Aus., 1886.

## DIVINE PRESERVATION.

A touching little story of an incident in a Belgian town is told by the United Free Church of Scotland, (1915).

"There had been a sharp engagement, and the British troops holding a village had been hurriedly forced to retire. In the confusion three Scottish privates and a corporal were cut off in the streets, so they backed into the first open door they came to. The occupants had fled, and they made their way up a long staircase, intending to find the roof and watch events from there. But it ended in an empty loft, where there was only a skylight beyond their reach.

"Better lie low for a while," suggested the corporal, as they stood listening to the terrible sounds outside. The Germans were evidently burning, looting, and killing. Now and again they heard screams and the discharge of rifles; sometimes an explosion would shake the building; while the smell of burning wood penetrated to their retreat. This went on for hours. The soldiers knew they would be discovered sooner or later and expected no mercy.

Suddenly the corporal said "Lads, its time for church parade; lets hae a wee bit service here; it may be oor last." The soldiers looked a little astonished, but they piled their rifles in a corner and came and stood at attention. The corporal took out a small Testament from his breast pocket and turned over the pages. "Canna we sing something first. Try ye're hand at the 23rd psalm. Quiet noo—very quiet."

"Yea, though I walk death's dark vale,
Yet will I fear no ill;
For Thou art with me; and Thy rod
And staff ma comfort still."

There was not much melody about the tune, but the words came from the heart.

Then the corporal began:—

"Fear not them which kill the body, but are not able to kill the soul; but rather fear Him which is able to destroy both soul and body in hell. Are not two sparrows sold for a farthing? And one of them shall not fall on the ground without your Father. But the very hairs of your head are all numbered. Fear not, therefore, ye are of more value than many sparrows."

As he read there were loud shouts below; doors banged, and glass was smashed. But he went on:—

"He that findeth his life shall lose it; and he that loseth his life for My sake shall find it."

He ended reading and said, "Let us pray."

The corporal stood, with his book in his hand, and the others knelt and bowed their heads. A little haltingly, but very simply, he committed their way to God, and asked for strength to meet their coming fate like men.

While he prayed the door was thrust open and they heard an exultant exclamation and then a gasp of surprise. Not a man moved, and the corporal went calmly on, then he began, with great reverence to repeat the Lord's Prayer. That a German officer or private was standing there they realised; they did not see, but they felt, what was taking place. They heard the click of his heels, and they knew that he was also standing at attention. For a moment the suspense lasted, and then came the soft closing of the door and his footsteps dying away. The tumult in the house gradually ceased, and soon afterwards the storm of war retreated like the ebb of tide. At dusk the four men ventured forth, and by making a wide detour worked round the flank of the enemy and reached the British outposts in safety."

—From the Christian's Pathway, April, 1915.

## ELECTION.

An Address delivered by Dr. Pink, June, 1925 in the Baptist Tabernacle, Ashfield, N.S.W.

### No. 2.

The question of election or no election is really the Word of God on the one side and human reason on the other. The moment a servant of God begins to present the Scriptural doctrine of Divine election, men at once begin to tell us what they think and how they feel about it, and of course human opinions differ. One man thinks that if he is a respectable citizen and leads a moral life that God will take him to heaven when he dies. Another man's opinion is that something more is needed, that we ought to bring in the Bible, that we must have some doctrine, that we must believe that God is a Trinity and that Christ is God's Son, and that His death is an atoning one; and that if we do not believe those things we cannot be saved. But my friends, the man who says that, the man who brings in the Bible at all, gives up the whole contention and argument so far as his opposition to election is concerned, because if you bring in God's Word you cannot pick and choose. You cannot take heaven and leave out hell. You cannot take salvation by grace and then insist on salvation by works. You cannot take the doctrine of the new birth and leave out sovereign elecion.

If we take the Bible at all we must take it as the Word of God and that all

Scripture is inspired of God and is profitable for doctrine, and when God speaks on any subject that is the end of the matter. Of course, this Book being the Word of God, we shall expect to find in it things that are strange to us, things which mere human reason could never have discovered. What were the use of God giving to us a revelation about things that we already knew? God has been pleased to make known in this book things which we could never have found out for ourselves, and my friends if this is the Word of God we must expect to find in it things which are contrary to our reason, things which are mysterious and strange to us. God Himself is a mystery and none can find Him out by searching. His own Word tells us that clouds and darkness are round about Him and that He dwelleth in light inaccessible. His own Word tells us that His thoughts are not as our thoughts and that His ways are not as our ways, therefore we expect to find in it things which are contrary to our ideas and to our preconceptions.

If someone were to step up and stand out here to-night and say, Dr. Pink, the things which you are teaching do not sound right to me, they do not ring true, I would answer at once, These things are not my thoughts, I am not presenting my views or any other man's views, I am here, by the Holy Spirit's enablement, to present to you what God says. Supposing He replied, Well but it doesn't seem so to me. I would at once answer, No, perhaps not, and these things did not once seem so to me, nor do they to any unregenerate man in the darkness of his natural state. God tells us in 1 Corinthians, 2:14, "The natural man receiveth not the things of the Spirit of God: for they are foolishness unto him: neither can he know them," therefore we must not be surprised if the great majority of our fellow men fail to understand this doctrine of election; yea, who look upon it with contempt and ridicule. God says the natural man cannot receive: He says they are foolishness unto Him. My friends, we do not come to the House of God to talk about what we think and what seems right to us: we come here (or ought to) to find out what God has said, and you take issue with God at your peril! My friends, you cannot handle God, but He can handle you and it is the part of wisdom for each one of us to bow before this Book by which each one of us shall yet be judged, and though the doctrine of election be contrary to reason, proud reason must bow to it either now or later on.

Now last night I developed the subject of the fact of election, the fact that it is a truth taught all through God's Word in the Old and in the New Testaments alike, and before I go any further I just want to read briefly to show you that this doctrine of God's sovereign election is no new invention of mine, is no heresy of the twentieth century, but has been taught in the leading confessions of faith of evangelical Christendom. Now listen if you please closely to this brief quotation: "Predestination to life is the everlasting purpose of God whereby before the foundations of the world were laid He hath constantly decreed by His secret counsel to us to deliver from curse and condemnation those whom He hath chosen in Christ out of mankind and to bring them by Christ to everlasting salvation as vessels made to honour."

I wonder how many of you know what I have just read from. (A voice, The 39 articles.) The Thirty-nine Articles of the Anglican Church, to which every one of their ministers have to conform and sign before they are ordained. That is according to the Thirty-nine Articles of the Church of England—their ultimate standard and confession of faith.

Now in the second place, listen to another brief quotation, "What are the decrees of God? God's decrees are the wise, free and holy acts of the counsel of His will whereby for all eternity He hath for His own glory unchangeably fore-ordained whatsoever comes to pass in time. God by an eternal and immutable decree out of His mere love, for the praise of His glorious grace to be manifested in due time, hath elected some angels to glory and in Christ hath chosen some men to eternal life and the means thereof." I have read just now out of the Presbyterian Larger Catechism, otherwise known as the Westminster Confession of Faith to which every Presbyterian preacher has to subscribe before he is ordained.

Now I am going to read you another brief quotation from the Baptist Confession of Faith, which is the standard throughout the Northern States in America, and which was appealed to two years ago in the great controversy at St. Louis in the public convention between the fundamentalists and the modernists: "God hath decreed in Himself from all eternity by the most wise and holy counsel of His own will, freely and unchangeably, all things whatsoever comes to pass, yet so as thereby God is neither the author of sin nor hath any fellowship therein. By the decree of God for the manifestation of His glory some men and angels are predesinated or foreordained to eternal life through Jesus Christ. These angels and men thus predestinated and foreordained are particularly and unchangeably designed, and their number is so certain and definite that it cannot be either increased or diminished." Again, in this same confessions of faith, "Man by his fall into a state of sin has wholly lost all ability of will to any spiritual good accompanying salvation, so that as a natural man being altogether averse from that which is good and dead in sin is not able by his own strength to convert himself or even to prepare himself thereunto."

Now I have read from those three confessions of faith to-night, not because they are of any authority, and not because the Word of God needs any human buttressing, but solely for the purpose of showing that, two hundred years ago the truths of God's sovereignty, of predestination and election, and the bondage of the human will, were held and taught by the leading denominations in Christendom, and the very fact that these truths are no longer taught to any extent is a sign of the times. God has said in II Thessalonians 2, that the day of the Lord shall not come except there come a "falling away" first, and that "falling away" is evidenced on every side by the very fact that these doctrines which once held a prominent place in the leading denominations of evangelical Christendom are no longer being taught - God prophesied through the Apostle Paul to Timothy that the time would come when they would not endure—what? Sound doctrine. God did not say the time will come when they will not endure the gospel. God not say the time will come, when they will not endure prophecy. There are thousands in our churches to-day who will endure the gospel and who will endure prophecy, but won't endure sound doctrine, and that is exactly as God said it would be.

Now in the next place, I want to develop in detail, the truth of election, and the first point that I wish to make is this: God's election is unto salvation. There are those who say that the Bible does teach election, but election is only to service or to some office in the church:
God elected, or rather Christ elected the apostles and God has elected pastors and deacons, but election is not unto salvation. What saith the Scriptures? You turn with me now, if you please, to Acts 13 : 48 :—"And when the Gentiles heard this, they were glad, and glorified the word of the Lord : and as many as believed were ordained to eternal life." Now that is the idea which many have to-day. Man always gets the things of God upside down. This verse emphatically says that, "as many as were ordained to eternal life believed." They were not ordained unto some service or to some office, but they were ordained unto eternal life! You could not have anything plainer than that, so that if any man tells you that election is not unto salvation he contradicts God's Word.

Now turn to 2 Thessalonians 2:13: "But we are bound to give thanks alway to God for you, brethren beloved of the Lord, because God hath from the beginning chosen you to (service ?—Not at all) God hath from the beginning chosen you to salvation." There you have a plain and a pointed statement, that election, or God's choice, does have to do with the salvation of the soul. Now before I pass on from this verse, let me just make a brief comment in regard to the second half of it. Listen! "God hath from the beginning chosen you unto salvation." Now there are some people when they hear that say, Well, if that is true, we can just sit down and fold our arms : if God has chosen us unto salvation, well, that is an end of the matter; we are going to be saved anyhow, we don't need to read the Bible, we don't need to go to church, we don't need to be worried or concerned about our souls : if God has chosen us to salvation, well, we can just sit down and fold our arms we will be saved anyhow. Now God knew that some silly people would say that. God knows the end from the beginning, and so God purposely anticipated this by telling us at the end of this very verse that that is a wrong conclusion to draw. Now look at it. "God hath chosen you to salvation through (and the Greek word for "through" is sometimes translated "by means of") "God hath chosen you to salvation through or by means of sanctification of the Spirit and belief of the truth." So my friends, that verse teaches us plainly that no man ever will be saved until he believes the truth.

There is no such thing as my sitting

down and folding my arms and being saved anyhow. There is only one way of being saved. There never has been any other from the days of Abel until now, and that is by **believing God's truth**; and if you have not believed God's truth then you are still in your sins, even though you may be a church-member and a Sunday-school teacher. And my friends, if you never believe God's truth then you never will be saved. Well, but, you say, supposing that God has chosen me unto salvation, what then? Why, if God has chosen you unto salvation God will give you some commonsense and He won't allow you to act like a fool. What would you think of a farmer who at the beginning of Spring said, Well, I believe God is the One who gives us our daily bread, I believe we can do nothing apart from God, so I am not going to plow my fields this Spring at all, I am not going to sow any seed at all: God has promised in His Word that as long as the earth remaineth there shall be seed-time and harvest, so therefore I am just going to sit down and fold my arms. Well, any man who talked thus would be ready for the lunatic asylum! Now you can see that when it belongs to the natural realm, why is there any difficulty when it belongs to the spiritual realm? God has promised there shall be a harvest, but God has so ordered it that that harvest shall only be brought into existence through man performing his duty. And in like manner, God has chosen His people unto salvation, but it is only through sanctification of the Spirit and belief of the truth; so, if there is anyone here to-night who is unsaved and who says, Well I heard a man talking about God choosing some to salvation and therefore if He has not chosen me, well, there is no hope for me and if He has chosen me, well, I need not worry myself, God will look after it anyhow—my friend you are just quibbling and trying to shelter behind an empty excuse. God has said if ever you are to be saved it will be through and by means of **believing the truth**, and if you do not believe the truth you will be damned, and your blood will be on your own head.

Now one other Scripture in 2 Timothy 1:9:—"Who hath saved us, and called us with an holy calling, not according to our works, but according to his own purpose and grace, which was given us in Christ Jesus before the world began." Now that is plain enough, so there is no need for me to develop that point any further. God's election is unto salvation.

Now secondly, God's election is according to His own **sovereign choice** and not because of anything in us. The 20th chapter of Matthew and the 15th verse. I thing I will begin at the 9th verse to give you the context. "And when they came that were hired about the eleventh hour (it is a part of the parable of the vineyard), they received every man a penny. But when the first came, they supposed that they should have received more; and they likewise received every man a penny. And when they had received it, they murmured against the goodman of the house, saying, These last have wrought but one hour, and thou hast made them equal unto us, which have borne the burden and heat of the day." Now in this parable Christ gives us a picture of the human heart and how ready it is to rebel and murmur against the ways of God. In this parable Christ shows us that **God does not act uniformly**. God does not act unjustly, but does according as He pleases. To those who have laboured the whole day he gave a penny, and then those who had laboured just one hour, the last hour of the day, he gave them the same penny, and of course, the first ones began to grumble. "Oh," they said, "that is very unjust, that is not at all fair. Now you are showing partiality, that is not right"—the very things that men say when you affirm that God hath chosen one and not chosen another, that God has elected one unto salvation and has passed by another. Oh, they say, that is unjust, that is not fair, God must not be partial.

Now how does Christ answer that objection? The 15th verse. Here is the answer of the Lord to that very objection: "Is it not lawful for Me to do what I will with Mine own?" There is no answer to that. That is a silencer. Suppose I went out of this church at the close of the service and met three beggars on the street, three blind men, all of them total strangers to me; and suppose I put my hand into my pocket and gave the first man a penny, and then suppose I went to the second beggar and gave him a shilling, and then suppose I passed by the third man and gave him nothing, and you were walking along with me, and you said, Dr. Pink, I think that is very unjust. Do you know what I would tell you to do?—Why should I? Because I have a perfect right to dispense charity as I please. I am not under any obligation to any of the three. I am not indebted to any of them. Have I not a perfect right to give charity just as I please? Why, of course I have. Well, has not God got the same right, Salvation is a gift. Now if salvation is a gift, does not God have the right to give it to whom He pleases? If He gives it to one and not to another, that is His business, and you mind your own! Who art thou O man that repliest against God? That is what the Scripture says. That is the very question it asks the one who is murmuring against the ways of the Almighty. Now then God's election is a sovereign one according to His own choice and pleasure and not because of anything in man.

3. Now God's election is irreversible. That is to say, God's purpose before the foundation of the world cannot be overthrown in time: it is immutable. Turn for a moment to Acts 9, verse 5. Now some of you perhaps may not agree with my exposition, or rather interpretation of this. Well if you do not, nothing hinges on it, I am not building anything on it, but I just want to submit it to you. The 9th chapter of Acts and the 3rd verse:—"And as he journeyed (that is Saul of Tarsus) he came near Damascus" and you know what he was going to do in Damascus, don't you? Saul of Tarsus was on his way to Damascus to persecute and to imprison the people of God. He was opposing Christ. "And as he journeyed, he came near Damascus: and suddenly there shined around him a light from heaven: and he fell to the earth." That was Almighty power subduing that proud rebel. That was Divine Omnipotency bringing him into the dust. "And he fell to the earth, and heard a voice saying unto him, Saul, Saul, why persecutest thou Me? And he said, Who art thou, Lord? And the Lord said, I am Jesus whom thou persecutest: it is hard for thee to kick against the pricks." What pricks had he been kicking against? "It is hard for thee to kick against the pricks." I suppose you all know what the reference there is to. In Palestine they did not use horses when they plowed or when they had a burden to be borne: they used oxen and those oxen were in pairs yoked together, and the driver did not use a whip but he used a prick, a stick with a sharp point to it, a goad. That is what the word here means. It is hard for thee to kick against the "goad." When the ox did not want to go where he intended it to, when it stood in its tracks, he just pricked it; and the Lord here says, It is hard for thee to kick. That is what the oxen did when the man who was driving them prodded them with the goad. Why, of course, the oxen resisted and kicked backwards. Now the Lord uses that very figure, that well-known figure, and applies it to Saul. He says Saul it is hard for thee to kick against the pricks: you have been resisting Me up to now, but I have marked you out for salvation before the foundation of the world. You are one of Mine elect. No matter how hard you fight and how sternly you oppose, it is a mighty hard thing for you to kick against the pricks. You see it now, don't you. Now that you are helpless on the ground? God's election is irreversible. Man cannot resist it.

Now in the fourth place, God's election is by grace. Turn to Romans 11, verse 5:—"Even so then at this present time also there is a remnant according to the election of grace." I presume that most of us, if not all of us, believe that salvation is "by grace," and I presume that most of us, if not all of us understand what the word "grace" signifies. Grace is the opposite of justice. Justice demands that each man shall receive that which is his due, that which he deserves; but grace is giving to a man something he does not deserve. Grace is charity shown to the undeserving. Grace is the favour of God to one who has no merit at all. Very well then, that is true of salvation. But Romans 11:5 says that election is according to grace, it is not because of something from me or in me. If God's election is of grace it is not because I am repentant, and it is not because I believe. It is not because of anything in me, or otherwise it would not be by "grace." It is not "according to the election of repentance" but "the election of grace!"

Now that brings me to the 5th point God's election is not because of something good which He foresaw in us. There are lots of people to-day who claim to believe in election, but they say God elected the ones that He did because He foreknew that they would believe in Christ; that is the reason why He elected them, because He foreknew that they would receive Christ as their Saviour. Now listen, if that is the reason why God elected us, then He elected us because of something in us, something from us—our willingness, our receptiveness, our behaviour, our believing. Very well then, if God elected us because of something **in us** it could not be by **grace.** Now let me give you two or three Scriptures on that point.

Turn back to John 10:26: "But ye are not My sheep because ye believe not." Sounds right, doesn't it? That sounds very logical, doesn't it? "Ye are not My sheep because ye believe not." Why, of course, we all understand that! Yes, we do—it is very easy to "understand" things when man turns them upside down. That is what man does every time. You will always find that man reverses the order of God. Man talks about body, soul and spirit. God does not. God says spirit and soul and body. You turn to man's hymn books and what do you find? You will always find (I do not know an exception, I have never seen an exception: some of you perhaps may) whenever man writes a hymn he always says, so far as I know, "pilgrims and strangers." It is the very opposite in God's Word: "strangers and pilgrims." Man reverses God's order. He does so here with this verse. Now look at that: John 10: 26: they are the words of Christ Himself:—"But ye believe not, because ye are not of My sheep." Believing does not make us the sheep of Christ. If we have believed that is one of the **proofs** that we were the sheep of Christ!

You have to be a "sheep" before you can believe; not you have to believe before you become a sheep. You know it's a funny thing to me there's a whole lot of orthodox people to-day who say they do not believe in evolution. No, they say, I have no patience with this doctrine of evolution. (Well I haven't either: I believe it was born in hell), but the strange thing is, they say they do not believe in **evolution,** and then a few minutes later on they contradict themselves because they say that they believe this: That we are born "goats," and then we "believe" and we become "sheep!" If **that is not** "evolution" what is it? That is the transmutation of species with a vengeance isn't it? No, my friends, if you **are** one of the "sheep" of Christ, you were so from **eternity!** You do not become so, you were made so by **God;** and if you are His sheep you will **manifest** that fact by following the Shepherd! That is how I know that I am a sheep of Christ. I know that I am one of God's sheep because by His blessed grace I am following the Shepherd. I am not following nearly as closely as I wish I were. Often times, like Peter, I am following "afar off," but thank God I **am** following, and that is how I know that I am one of the "sheep."

Now turn to Ephesians, 1:4:—"According as He hath chosen us in Him before the foundation of the world because we were holy." No, that is not the reason why at all. That is a very unscriptural "because." "According as He hath chosen us in Christ before the foundation of the world, that we **should** be holy;" not because we were. not because of any **good thing in us,** either actual or foreseen, but in order that we should become holy. Well now someone says, Don't you believe that God did "foreknow" that we would believe? Why, of course God foreknew · He foreknows everything, but God's "foreknowledge" was not the **reason** why He chose us. Let me give you an illustration. Suppose I were to meet ten beggars and I gave to five of them a shilling and I did not give anything to the remaining five, and someone said to me, Well, why was it that you gave a shilling to the first five? What would you think of me if I gave you this answer? I gave a shilling to the first five because I **foresaw** that they would accept it: I gave a shilling to each one of those five because I **foreknew** that they would receive it? What an absurdity! **How** could I foreknow that they would receive it **apart from the fact that I gave it to them?** No, my friends, I say it in all reverence: God Himself could not foreknow that I would receive His salvation apart from the fact that He **purposed to give** it to **me.** Salvation is God's gift, and the fact that He **purposed** to give salvation to me certainly was the **reason why** He gave it to me. You cannot have a cause and an effect at the same time. **Why was it that God did** purpose to give salvation to you? And the only possible answer is, Because He so pleased, because it was His own sovereign will!

Now then, in the sixth place, God election is of **persons,** individuals. There are some who say, Yes I believe in election, but election has to do with nations: God does not elect persons: He chooses nations like He chose the nation of Israel. Well, what is a nation made of individuals. A nation is simply the totality of units, that is all. If God chose the nation of Israel then He necessarily chose the individuals in it. He chose Abraham, Isaac, Jacob, Moses, David, and so on all the way down the line, and my friends, it is the same to-day. God's choice is of individuals. What does Christ say in John 10? "He calleth His own sheep by name." That is personal enough, isn't it?

Now in the last place, God's election is eternal. Did any of you see a stick that had only got one end? Why, of course not. Now listen, I believe the majority of you present to-night believe that now that God has saved you, you are safe forever, don't you? You believe in a salvation that is eternal at one end? Now if your salvation is eternal at this end, it has got to be eternal at the other end too! You cannot have a stick with only one end to it. No, I am not reasoning, I am just presenting to you an axiom:—Only that which came out of eternity can last for eternity, and if your salvation is eternal for the future it must have been eternal in the past, and my friends. the most inconsistent and illogical theologian on the face of this earth to-night is the man who believes in the final preservation of God's people and does not believe in eternal election, for he is trying to believe in a stick that has only got one end to it? Now then, what saith the Scriptures? The first chapter of Ephesians and the fourth verse:—We looked at that a a moment ago:—"According as he hath chosen us in Him" —when? When we believed? No. "Before the foundation of the world." Now turn again to Thessalonians 2:13. We looked at this verse in another connection, now let us look at it in this light. II Thessalonians 2:13: "But we are bound to give thanks always to God for you, brethren beloved of the Lord, because God hath from the beginning," What is that? "God hath from the beginning chosen you unto salvation." Then God's salvation is like Himself, it is eternal, it had no beginning, it will have no end.

Now let me sum it up in these few words (If any of you are preachers I will give you an outline for a sermon): God the Father purposed our salvation. God the Son purchased our salvation. God the Holy Spirit applied salvation. "Salvation is of the Lord" (Jonah 2:9). The Father purposed it, the Son purchased it, the Holy Spirit applied it. Well then you say, Where does "faith" come in? Why, faith enjoys it, that is where faith comes in. The whole thing is done for us. Now then faith believes it and enjoys it. Salvation is of the Lord. God hath from the beginning chosen you unto salvation. Now my friends, that is the strongest argument there is in the Bible for the absolute security of God's people. Because God loved me in eternity past, God is going to love me for eternity future! What does it say in Jeremiah 31:3:—"The Lord hath appeared of old unto me, saying. Yea, I have loved thee with an everlasting love." O that our hearts might grasp that. If God loved me with an everlasting love then it cannot be because of anything in me, it cannot be because of anything from me, it cannot be because of anything by me. God does not love me because of what I do. How can that be, if He loved me before I came into existence? If God loved me with an with an everlasting love then His love cannot be based upon anything in me. Then His love can never change, and therefore His love can never end! Consequently, no object of God's eternal love shall ever perish.

Now the sequel to that is in John 13, verse 1, and with that we must close. John 13, verse 1: "Now before the feast of the passover, when Jesus knew that His hour was come that He should depart out of this world unto the Father, having loved His own which were in the world. He loved them unto the end." Now listen, the immediate context there is speaking of the eleven apostles and that word is recorded in connection with Christ less than twelve hours before the crucifixion:—"Having loved His own which were in the world He loved them unto the end." What did they do inside of these twelve hours? They all forsook Him and fled! Did He cease to love them? "Having loved His own which were in the world He loved them unto the end." What happened during those twelve hours? One of them denied Him, and denied Him with a curse, and deliberately repeated his denial. Did Christ cease to love him? "Having loved His own which were in the world He loved them unto the end!" The end of what? The end of all their failures, the end of all their back-slidings, the end of all their sins, the end of time itself. He loves them unto the end. Why does He? Why does He? His love can have no end because it had no beginning: It is eternal, like Himself, and therefore we can only say with the Apostle himself, such love passeth knowledge!

*Arthur W. Pink*

*(Continued from page 49.)*

dations of that empire in individual souls. His second coming will be for the purpose of setting up that empire in glory; so that it is of vast importance that we should understand what is the character of the subjects in that kingdom, so that we may know whether we belong to the kingdom ourselves, and whether its privileges, immunities and future rewards are a part of our present and future inheritance. Hence, the importance of a devout and careful study of these Beatitudes. We must examine them as a whole; we cannot take one alone, without losing a part of the lesson they jointly teach. These outlines pertain to one portrait. When an artist draws a picture, each line may be graceful and masterful, but it is the union of the lines that reveals their mutual relation; it is the combination of the various artistic delineations and even minutest touches that give us the completest portrait. So here, though the separate outlines have each their own peculiar beauty and grace, and show the hand of a master, it is only when we take all the lines in their combinations that we get the full portrait of a true subject and citizen in the kingdom of God" (Dr. A. T. Pierson).

It is indeed blessed to mark how this "Sermon" opens. Christ began not by pronouncing maledictions on the wicked, but benedictions on His people. How like Him was this to whom "judgment" is a strange work. Compare John 1:17. But how strange is the next word: "blessed" or "happy" are the poor—"the poor in spirit" who, previously, had ever regarded them as the blessed ones of earth? And who, outside believers, do so to-day? And how this opening word strikes the keynote of all Christ's subsequent teaching: not what a man does, but what he is.

"Blessed are the poor in spirit." What is poverty of spirit? It is the opposite of that haughty, self-assertive and self-sufficient disposition which the world so much admires and praises. It is the very reverse of that independent and defiant attitude which refuses to bow to God, which determines to brave things out, and which says with Pharaoh, "Who is the Lord that I should obey His voice?" To be "poor in spirit" is to realise that I have nothing, am nothing, and can do nothing, and have need of all things. Poverty of spirit evidences itself by its bringing the individual into the dust before God acknowledging his utter helplessness. It is the first experimental evidence of a Divine work of grace in the soul and corresponds to the initial awakening of the prodigal in the far country, when he "began to be in want."

God's great salvation is free, "without money and without price." This is a most merciful provision of Divine grace, for were God to offer salvation for sale no poor sinner could secure it, seeing that he has nothing with which to purchase it. But the vast majority are insensible of this, yea all of us are until the Holy Spirit opens our sin-blinded eyes. It is only those who have passed from death unto life that become conscious of their poverty, take the place of beggars, are glad to receive Divine charity, and begin to seek the true riches. Thus "the poor have the Gospel preached to them" (Matt. 11:5) preached not only to their ears, but to their hearts!

Poverty of spirit, a consciousness of my emptiness and need, results then from the work of the Spirit within. It issues from the painful discovery that all my righteousnesses are as filthy rags. It follows the awakening that my very best performances are unacceptable, yea an abomination, to the thrice Holy One. Thus one who is "poor in spirit" realises himself to be a Hell-deserving sinner.

Poverty of spirit may be termed the negative side of faith. It is that realisation of my utter worthlessness which precedes the laying hold of Christ, the eating of His flesh and drinking of His blood. It is, the Spirit emptying the heart of self that Christ may fill it: it is a sense of need and destitution. This first Beatitude then is foundational describing a fundamental trait which is found in every regenerated soul. The one who is poor in spirit is nothing in his own eyes and feels that his proper place is in the dust before God. He may, through false teaching or worldliness, leave this place, but God knows how to bring him back; and in His faithfulness and love He will do so, for it is the place of blessing for His children. How to cultivate this God-honouring spirit is revealed in Matt. 11:29.

He who is in possession of this poverty of spirit is pronounced "blessed" because he now has a disposition the very reverse of what was his by nature; because he possesses the first sure evidence that a Divine work of grace has been wrought within him; because such a spirit causes him to look outside of himself for true enrichment; because he is an heir of the kingdom of heaven.

Arthur W. Pink.

# STUDIES IN THE SCRIPTURES

### VOL. V — APRIL, 1926 — NO. 4

"Search the Scriptures" John 5:39.

Copyright in all English-speaking Countries.

Arthur W. Pink, Publisher and Editor,
5 Norton Street, Ashfield, N.S.W., Australia.

Price: 10 cents per copy; $1.00 or 5/- per year.

"Blessed are they that mourn" Matt. 5:4. Mourning is hateful and irksome to poor human nature. From suffering and sadness our spirits instinctively shrink. By nature we seek the society of the cheerful and joyous. Our text presents an anomaly to the unregenerate, yet is it sweet music to the ears of God's elect. If "blessed" why do they "mourn?" if they "mourn" how can they be "blessed?" Only the child of God has the key to this paradox. The more we ponder our text the more we are constrained to exclaim, "Never man spake like this Man!" "Blessed (happy) are they that mourn" is at complete variance with the world's logic. Men have in all places and in all ages, deemed the the prosperous and the gay the happy ones, but Christ pronounces happy those who are poor in spirit and who mourn.

Now it is obvious that it is not every species of mourning that is here referred to. There is a "sorrow of the world which worketh death." The mourning to which Christ promises comfort must be restricted to that which is spiritual. The mourning which is blessed is the result of a realisation of God's holiness and goodness which issues in a sense of our own wickedness—the depravity of our natures, the enormity and guilt of our conduct and the sorrowing over our sins with a godly sorrow.

We intimated in our last that the eight Beatitudes are arranged in four pairs; proof of this will be furnished as we proceed. The first of the series is the blessing which Christ pronounced upon those who are poor in spirit, which we took to mean, they who have been awakened to a sense of their own nothingness and emptiness. Now the transcision from such poverty to mourning is easy to follow, in fact it follows so closely that it is rather its companion.

The mourning which is here referred to is manifestly more than that of bereavement, affliction or loss. It is mourning for sin. "It is mourning over the felt destitution of our spiritual state, and over the iniquities that have separated between us and God; mourning over the very morality in which we have boasted, and the self-righteousness in which we have trusted; sorrow for rebellion against God, and hostility to His will; and such mourning always goes side by side with conscious poverty of spirit" (Dr. Pierson).

A striking illustration and exemplification of the spirit upon which the Saviour here pronounced His benediction is to be found in Luke 18. There a vivid contrast is presented to our view. First, we are shown a self-righteous Pharisee looking up toward God and saying, "God, I thank Thee that I am not as other men are, extortioners, unjust, adulterers, or even as this publican. I fast twice in the week; I give tithes of all that I possess." This may have been all true as he looked at it, yet this man went down to his house in a state of of condemnation. His fine garments were rags, his white robes were filthy, though he knew it not. Then we are shown the publican, standing afar off, who, in the language of the Psalmist was so troubled by his iniquities, that he was not able to look up (Psa. 40:12). He dared not so much as lift up His eyes to Heaven, but smote upon his breast, conscious of the fountain of corruption within, and cried, "God be merciful to me a sinner," and that man went down to his house justified, because he was poor in spirit and mourned for sin.

*(Continued on page 96)*

## IMPORTANT NOTICES

Set of twelve issues for **1922**, unbound, **$1.00** or **5/-**.  Bound **$1.50** or **7/-**.

Set of twelve issues for **1923**, unbound, **$1.00** or **5/-**.  Bound **$1.50** or **7/-**.

Set of twelve issues for **1924**, unbound, **$1.00** or **5/-**.  Bound **$1.50** or **7/-**.

Set of twelve issues for **1925**, unbound, **$1.00** or **5/-**.  Bound **$1.50** or **7/-**.

Note: We cannot break a set or now supply any **single** 1925 issues.

Subscription—price: **$1.00** or **5/-** per year to any address in the world.

Change of Address: Please notify me promptly of any change of address, and be certain to give both old and new address.

Non-subscribers receiving this Magazine regularly will understand their subscription has been entered by a friend.

Copies lost in the mail duplicated only if we are notified promptly.

## CONTENTS

| | |
|---|---|
| The Gospel of John (John 15: 7-16) | 74 |
| Gleanings in Exodus | 82 |
| Election | 86 |
| Accepted in the Beloved | 94 |
| Sorrowful, yet always Rejoicing | 95 |

## THE GOSPEL OF JOHN

**52. Christ the True Vine Concluded: John 15: 7-16.**

Below is an Analysis of the second section of John 15:—

1. Fellowship and prayer v. 7.
2. The Father glorified by much fruit v. 8.
3. Fruit found in love vv. 9-10.
4. Fruit found in joy v. 11.
5. Fruit found in peace v. 12.
6. The proofs of Christ's love vv. 13-15.
7. The purpose of Christ's choice v. 16.

That the theme of this second section of John 15 is the same as was before us in its opening portion is clear from vv 8 and 16: in both of these verses the word "fruit" is found, and as we shall see, all that lies between is intimately connected with them. Before taking up the study of our present passage let us summarise what was before in our last lesson.

The Vine and its branches, unlike the "body" and its Head, does not set forth the vital and indissoluable union between Christ and His people—though that is manifestly presupposed; instead, it treats of that relationship which exists between Him and them while they were upon earth, a relationship which may be interrupted. The prominent thing is fruit-bearing and the conditions of fertility. Three conditions have already been before us. First, to be a fruit-bearing branch of the Vine, one must be **in Christ**. Second, to be a fruit-bearing branch of the Vine, the Father must purge him by the cleansing action of the Word. Third, to be a fruit-bearing branch of the Vine, he must **abide** in Christ. The first two are solely of God's grace: they are Divine actions. But the third is a matter of Christian responsibility, and this is what is enforced throughout John 15.

As pointed out in the introduction to our last article, the broad distinction between John 14 and 15 is that in the former we have the **grace** of God unfolded; in the latter Christian **responsibility** is pressed. Further evidence of this will be found in the frequent repetition of two pronouns. In John 14 the emphasis is upon the "Me;" in John 15 upon the "ye." In John 14 it is: "Believe on **Me**" (v. 1); "No man cometh unto the Father but by **Me**" (v. 6); "If ye had known **ME** ye should have known My Father also" (v. 7); "Have I been so long time with you, and yet hast thou not known **Me**, Philip?" **(v.** 9); and so on. Whereas in John 15 it is **"Ye are clean"**(v. 3); "Herein is My Father glorified that ye bear much fruit" (v. 8); **"Continue ye in My love"** (v.9); **"Ye are My friends if"** etc. (v. 14). The word "ye" occurs no less than twenty-two times in John 15!

That which is of such deep importance for the Christian is the **third condition** noted above; hence our Lord's repeated emphasis upon it. Mark how in v. 4 the word "abide" occurs no less than three times, Note how the same truth is reiterated in v. 5. Observe how v. 6 is devoted to a solemn statement of the consequences of **failure to** "abide" in Christ. Observe also how this same word "abide" is found again in vv. 7, 9, 10, 11, and 16. Just as necessary and imperative as Christ's command "Come unto Me" is to the sinner, so absolutely essential is His "Abide in Me" to the saint. As then this subject of **abiding in Christ** is of such moment, we will now supplement our previous remarks upon it.

First, to abide in Christ is to continue in the joyful recognition of the value of His perfect sacrifice and the efficacy of His precious blood. There can be no fellowship with the Lord Jesus, in the full sense of the word, while we harbor doubts of our personal salvation and acceptance with God. Should some soul troubled on this very point be reading these lines, we would earnestly press upon him or her the fact that the only way to be rid of torturing uncertainty is to turn the eye away from self, **unto the Saviour.** Here are His own blessed words: "he that eateth My flesh, and drinketh My blood dwelleth **(abideth)** in Me and I in him" (John 6:56). That means that I feed upon, am satisfied with, that Sacrifice of sweet savour which has fully satisfied God.

Second, to abide in Christ is to maintain a spirit and an attitude of entire **dependency** on Him. It is the consciousness of my helplessness; it is the realisation that "severed from Him, I can do nothing." The figure which the Lord here employed strongly emphasised this. What are the branches of a vine but helpless, creeping, clinging, things? They cannot stand alone; they need to be supported, held up. Now there can be no abiding in Christ while we entertain a spirit of self-sufficiency. To have **no** confidence in the flesh, to renounce our own might, to lean not unto our own understanding, precedes our turning unto Christ: there must be a recognition of my own emptiness before I shall turn to and draw from His fulness. "As the branch cannot bear fruit of itself, except it abide in the vine; **no more can ye except ye abide in Me.**" In itself a branch has absolutely no resources: in union with the vine it is pervaded with life.

Third, to abide in Christ is to **draw from His fulness.** It is not enough that I turn from myself in disgust, I must turn to Christ with delight. I must seek His presence; I must be occupied with His excellency; I must commune with Him. It is no longer a question of my sufficiency, my strength, or my anything. It is solely a matter of **His** sufficiency. The branch is simply a conduit through which flows the fruit-producing juices, which result in the lovely clusters of grapes. Remember that the branch **does not produce,** but **simply bears** them! It is the **vine which produces,** but produces through the branch, by the branch being in the vine. It is not that the believer finds in Christ a place of rest and support, whither he may go in order to produce his own fruit. This is the sad mistake made by those who are ever speaking of their own self-complacency, self-glorifying experiences, which shows that their souls are occupied with themselves rather than with Christ. It is of the greatest practical importance to know that Christ is "all and in all"—not only as our standing before God and our ultimate perfection, but also as to our **present life** to the glory of the Father.

"If ye abide in Me, and My words abide in you, ye shall ask what ye will, and it shall be done unto you" (v. 7). The connection between this verse and the ones preceding is as follows. In vv. 4 and 5 the Lord had exhorted His disciples to abide in Him. In v. 6 He had warned them what would be the consequences if they did not. Now He turns, or rather returns, to the consolatory and blessed effects which would follow their compliance with His admonition. Three results are here stated. First, the answer of whatever prayers they presented to God; the glorification of the Father; the clear witness to themselves and to others that **they were** His disciples. Thus would Christ most graciously encourage us.

"If ye abide in Me, and My words abide in you, ye shall ask what ye will, and it shall be done unto you." What erroneous conclusions have been drawn from these words! How often they have been appealed to in order to justify the most unworthy views of prayer! The popular interpretation of them is that if the Christian will only work himself up to an importunate pleading of this promise before the Throne of Grace, he may then ask God for what he pleases, and the Almighty will not—some go so far as to say He cannot—deny him. We are told that Christ has here given us a blank check, signed it, and left us to fill it in for what we will. But 1 John 5:14 plainly repudiates such a carnal conception—"And this is the confidence that we have in Him, that, if we ask any thing **according to** His will, He heareth us." Therefore, what we ask shall not be done unto us unless **our** will is subordinated to and is in accord with the will of **God.**

What then is the meaning of our Lord's promise? Certainly it does not give praying souls **carte blanche.** For God to gratify us in everything we required, would not only be dishonouring to Himself, but, ofttimes, highly injurious to ourselves. Moreover, the experience of many of those who frequent the Throne of Grace dissipates such a delusion. All of us have asked for many things which have not been "done unto" us. Some have asked in great earnestness, with full expectation, and they have been very importunate and yet their petitions have been denied them. Does this falsify our Lord's promise? A thousand times no! Every word He uttered was God's infallible truth. What then? Shall we fall back upon the hope that's God's time to answer has not yet come; but that shortly He will give us the desire of our hearts? Such a hope may be realised, or it may not. It all depends upon whether the **conditions** governing the promise in John 15:7 are being met. If they are not, it will be said of us? "Ye ask, and have not, because ye ask amiss" (James 4:3).

Two conditions here qualify the promise: **"If ye abide in Me."** Abiding in Christ signifies the **maintaining** of heart communion with Christ. **"And** My words abide in you": not only must the heart be occupied with Christ, but the life must be regulated by the Scriptures. Note it is not here "My Word," but "My words." It is not the Word as a whole, but the Word, as it were, broken up. It is the precepts and promises of Scripture personally appropriated, fed upon by faith, hidden in the heart. It is the practical heeding of that injunction, "Man shall not **live** (his daily life) by bread alone, but by every word that proceedeth out of the mouth of God." And mark that it is Christ's words **abiding** in us. It is no fitful, spasmodic, occasional exercise and experience, but constant and habitual communion with God through the Word, until its contents become the substance of our innermost beings.

"Ye shall ask what ye will." But for what **would** such a one ask? If he continues in fellowship with Christ, if His **"words"** remain in him, then his **thoughts** will be **regulated** by and his desires **formed** by that Word. Such an one will be raised above the lusts of the flesh. Such an one will "bring into captivity every thought to the obedience of Christ" (2 Cor. 10:5), proving "what is that good, and acceptable, and perfect will of God" (Rom. 12:2). Consequently, such an one will ask **only** for that **which is** "according to **His** will" (1 John 5:14); and **thereby** will he verify the Lord's promise "it shall be done unto you."

Such a view of prayer is glorifying to God and satisfying to the soul. For one who communes with the Saviour, and in whom His words dwells "richly," supplication is simply the pulsation of a heart that has been won to God. While the believer is in fellowship with the Lord and is governed from within by His Word, he will **not** ask for things "amiss." Instead of praying in the energy of the flesh (which, alas, all of us so often do), he will pray "in the Spirit" (Jude 20). "Why is there so little power of prayer like this in our own times? Simply because there is so little close communion with Christ, and so little strict conformity to His words. Men do not 'abide in Christ,' and therefore pray in vain. Christ's words do not abide in them, as their standard of practice, and therefore their prayers are not answered. Let this lesson sink down into our hearts. He that would have answers to his prayers, must carefully remember Christ's directions. We must keep up intimate friendship with the great advocate in Heaven, if our petitions are to be granted" (Bishop Ryle).

"Herein is My Father glorified, that ye bear much fruit" (v. 8). This is an appeal to our hearts. The "glory" of the Father was that which Christ ever kept before Him, and here He presses it upon us. He would have us concerned as to whether our lives honour and magnify the Father, or whether they are a reproach to Him. An unfruitful branch is a **dishonour** to God. What an inducement is this to "Abide in Christ!"

It is time that we now inquire as to the **nature** or **character** of the "fruit" of which Christ here speaks. **What is** the "fruit," the much fruit, by which the Father is glorified? Fruit is not something which is attached to the branch and fastened on from without, but is the organic product and evidence of the inner life. Too often attention is directed to **outward** services and actions, or to the **results** of these services, as the "fruit" here intended. We do not deny that this fruit is frequently manifested externally, and that it also finds expression in outward works is clear from v. 6: "Severed from Me we can do nothing." But there is a twofold evil in **confining** our attention to these. First, it often becomes a **source of deception** in those who may do many things in the will and energy of the flesh, but these are dead works, often found on corrupt trees. Second, it often becomes a **source of discouragement** to children of God who, by reason of sickness, old age, or unfavourable circumstances, cannot engage in such actions, and hence are made to believe that they are barren and useless.

"We may say, in brief, that the fruit borne by the branches is precisely that which is produced by the Vine; and what that is, may be best understood by looking at what He was as God's witness in the world. The fruit is **Christlike** affections, dispositions, graces, as well as the works in which they are displayed. We cannot undervalue the work of faith and labour of love; but we would remember that 'the fruit of the Spirit is love, poy, peace, longsuffering, gentleness, goodness, faith, meekness, temperance;' and those who are prevented from engaging in the activities of Christian service, may often be in circumstances most favourable to the production of the fruit of the Spirit" (Waymarks in the Wilderness).

It is deeply important for us to recognise that the "fruit is the outflow of our union with Christ; only thus will it be traced to its true origin and source. Then will it be seen that our fruit is produced not merely by Christ's power acting upon us, but, as it truly is, is the fruit of the Vine. Thus, in every branch, is His word literally verified: From **Me** is Thy fruit found (Hoseah 14:8), and therefore should every branch say, "Not I, but the grace of God." This is all one as to say that **our fruit is Christ's** fruit; for God's operations of grace are only wrought in and by Christ Jesus. Thus saints are "filled with the fruits of righteousness which are **by Jesus Christ** to the praise and glory of God" (Phil. 1:11). If there be any love, it is "**the love of Christ**" (2 Cor. 5:14); if there be any joy, it is **Christ's** joy (John 15:11); if there be any peace, it is **His** peace, given unto us (John 14: 27); if there be any meekness and gentleness it is "the meekness and gentleness **of Christ**" (2 Cor. 10:1)! How thoroughly this was realised by the apostle, to whom it was given to be the most signal example of the Vine sending forth fruit by His branches, may be gathered from such expressions: "I will not dare to speak of any of those things which **Christ** hath not wrought by me" (Rom. 15:); "**Christ** speaking in me" (2 Cor. 13:3); "**He** that wrought effectually **in** Peter . . . was mighty **in me**"(Gal. 2:8); "**Christ liveth in me**" (Gal. 2:20); "I can do all things through **Christ** who strengtheneth me" (Phil. 4:13). Thus, and thus only as this is recognised, all depencency upon and all glorying in self is excluded, and Christ becomes all in all.

"Herein is My Father glorified, that ye bear much fruit." There are four relationships which need to be distinquished. Life **in** Christ is salvation. Life **with** Christ is fellowship. Life **by** Christ is fruit-bearing. Life **for** Christ is service. The "fruit" is Christ manifested through us. But note the gradation: in v. 2 it is first "fruit," then "**more** fruit," here "**much** fruit." This reminds us of the "some thirty-fold, some sixty, and some a hundred fold" (Mark 4:20).

"So shall ye be My disciples" (v. 8). With this should be compared 8:31: "**If ye continue** in My Word, then are ye My disciples **indeed.**" Continuance in the Word is not a **condition** of discipleship, but an **evidence** of it. So here, to bear much fruit will make it **manifest** that we are His disciples. Just as good fruit on a tree does not **make** the tree a good one, but marks it out as such, so we prove ourselves to be Christ's disciples by displaying Christlike qualities.

"As the Father hath loved Me, so I have loved you" (v. 9). There is no change of theme, only another aspect of it. In the two previous verses the Lord had described three of the **consequences** of abiding in Him in order to fruitfulness, here, and in the three verses that follow, He names three of the **varieties** of the fruit borne, and it is very striking to note that they are identical with the first three and are given in the same order as those enumerated in Gal. 5:22, where the "fruit of the Spirit" is defined. Here in v. 9, it is love; in v. 11, it is **joy,** while in v. 12 it is peace—the happy issue of brethren loving one another.

"As the Father hath loved Me, so have I loved you." "As the Father loved Him from everlasting, so did He love them; as His Father loved Him with a love of complacency and delight, so did He love them; as the Father loved Him with a special and peculiar affection, with an unchanging, invariable, constant love, which would last forever, in like manner does Christ love His people; and with this He enforces the exhortation which. follows" (Dr. John Gill).

"As the Father hath loved Me, so have I loved you; continue ye in My love." (v. 9). Christ's love to us is unaffected by our changeableness, but our **enjoyment** of His love depends upon our **continuance** in it. By this continuance in His love, or abiding in it, as it should be (the Greek word is the same), is meant our actual assurance of it, our reposing in it. No matter how mysterious His dispensations be, no matter how severe the trials through which He causes us to pass, we must never doubt His immeasurable love for us and to us. The measure of His love for us was told out at the Cross, and as He is, the same to-day as yesterday, therefore He loves us just as dearly now, every moment, as when He laid down His life for us. To "abide" in His love, then, is to be occupied with it, to count upon it, to be persuaded that nothing shall ever be able to separate us from it. Dwelling upon our poor, fluctuating love for Him will make us miserable; but having the heart fixed upon His wondrous love, that love which "passeth knowledge," will fill us with praise and thanksgiving. Very blessed but very searching is this. To "abide" in Christ is to abide in His love. Our growth proceeds from love to love.

"If ye keep My commandments, ye shall abide in My love." (v. 10). Even still more searching is this. There can be no fruit for the Father, no abiding in Christ's love, unless there be real subjection of will. It is only in the path of obedience that He will have fellowship with us. Alas, how many err on this point. We are living in an age wherein lawlessness abounds. Insubordination is rife on every hand. In many a place even professing Christians will no longer tolerate the word "Commandments." Those who would urge the duty of obedience to the Lord, are regarded as enemies of the faith, seeking to bring Christians into bondage. Satan is very subtle, but we are not ignorant of his devices. He seeks to persuade sinners that they must keep God's commandments in order to be saved. He tries to make saints believe that they must not keep God's commandment, otherwise they will be putting themselves "under law," beneath a yoke grievous to be borne. But let these specious lies of the Devil be tested by Scripture, and their falsity will soon appear. 1 Cor. 9:21 tells us that we are "under the law to Christ." Romans 13:10 assures us that "love is the fulfilling of the law:" the fulfilling mark, not the abrogating of it, nor a substitution for it. The apostle Paul declared that he "delighted in the law of God after the inward man," and that he "served the law of God" (Rom. 7:22-25). And here in John 15 the Lord Himself said to His disciples, "If ye keep My commandments, ye shall abide in My love." O fellow Christians, let no sophistry of man (no matter how able a Bible teacher you may deem him), and no deceptive art of Satan, rob you of this word of the Saviour; a word which we all need, never more than now, when all authority, Divine and human, is more and more flouted. Note that this was not the only time that Christ made mention of His commandment and pressed upon His people their obligations to keep them. See John 13:34; 14:15; 15:10; Matt. 28:20, etc.

"Even as I have kept My Father's commandments, and abide in His love" (v. 10). Here is the final word against those who decry godly obedience as "legalism." The incarnate Son walked according to His Father's commandments. He "pleased not Himself" (Rom. 15:3). His meat was to do the will of the One who had sent Him. And He has left us an example that we should follow His steps. "He that saith he abideth in Him ought to himself so to walk even as He walked" (I John 2:6). The one who disregards God's "commandments" is not walking as Christ walked: instead, he is walking as the world walks. Let no one heed the idle quibble that the "commandments" of Christ are opposed to or even different from the commandments of the Father. Christ and the Father are one—one in nature, one in character, one in authority. "The commandments of Christ include the whole of the preceptive part of the inspired volume, with the exception of those ritual and political statutes which refer to the introductory dispensations which have passed away" (Dr. J. Brown). And let it be said again, that no Christian can abide in Christ's love unless he is keeping Christ's commandments!

"Even as I have kept My Father's commandments, and abide in His love." The "even as" refers to the character of Christ's obedience to the Father. "His obedience was the obedience of love, and so must ours be. His obedience was but the expression of His love. External obedience to Christ's commandments, if not the expression of love, is, in His estimation, of less than no value, for He sees it to be what it is—vile hypocrisy or mere selfishness. No man will continue in His love by such obedience. His obedience was, in consequence of its being the result of love, cheerful obedience. He delighted to do the will of His Father. It was His meat to do the Father's will, and so must be our obedience to Him. We must run in the way of His commandments with enlarged hearts. We are to keep them, not so much because we must keep them as because we choose to keep them, or, if a necessity is felt to be laid upon us, it should be the sweet necessity resulting from perfect approbation of the law, and supreme love to the Law-giver. Christ's obedience to the Father was **universal** —it extended to every requisition of the law. There was no omission, no violation; and in our obedience to the Saviour, there must be no reserves—we must count His commandments to be in all things, what they are—right; and we must abhor every wicked way. Christ's obedience to the Father was **persevering.** He was faithful unto death; and so must we be. This is His promise: "To him that overcometh will I give to sit with Me on My throne, even as I have overcome, and am set down with My Father on His throne" (Rev. 3:21). It is thus, then—only thus—by keeping the commandments of our Lord as He kept the commandments of His Father, that we shall continue in His love, as He continued in His Father's love" (Dr. John Brown).

"These things have I spoken unto you, that My Joy might remain in you" (v. 11). The "these things" covers the whole of the ten preceding verses. The fruit of the Spirit (Gal. 5:22) is "love, joy, peace." Having mentioned love in the previous verse, Christ now goes on ot speak of joy. Just as in 14:27 there is a double "peace," so here there is a twofold joy. First, there is the joy of Christ Himself, that joy which had been His during His sojourn on earth, He mentions this in His prayer in John 17: "These things I speak in the world, that they might have **My joy** fulfilled in themselves" (v. 13). How this reveals to us the inner life of the Saviour! Abiding in His Father's love. He had a joy which certainly not His enemies and perhaps not His friends would have credited the "Man of Sorrows." His joy was in pleasing the Father, in doing His will and glorifying His name. Then, too, He rejoiced in the prospect before Him: "Looking unto Jesus the Author and Finisher of faith; who for **the joy** that was set **before Him** endured the cross" (Heb. 12:2). This double joy of the incarnate Son, is mentioned in Psalm 16, where the Spirit of prophecy recorded the Saviour's words long beforehand: "I have set the Lord always before Me: because He is at My right hand, I shall not be moved. Therefore My heart is **glad,** and My glory **rejoiceth**" (vv. 8-9). This was the joy of communion and obedience. "Thou wilt show Me the path of life: in Thy presence is fullness of joy; at Thy right hand there are pleasures forever more" (v. 11): this was the joy "set before Him."

"These things have I spoken unto you, that My joy might remain in you." The "these things" refers, more specifically, to the maintenance of communion with Christ, and the conditions upon which this may be realised. When fellowship with the Lord Jesus is broken, joy disappears. This was illustrated in the experience of the Psalmist. David had sinned; sinned grievously against the Lord, and in consequence, he no longer enjoyed a comforting sence of His presence. David was wretched in soul, and after making earnest confession of his sin he cried, Restore unto me the **joy** of Thy salvation" (51:12): salvation he had not lost, but the joy of it he had. It was the same with Peter: he went out and **wept bitterly"** (Luke 22:62). A child of God can only be miserable when he is away from Christ. It is important for us to recognise and realise that we need Christ just as much for **our every-day-life,** as we do for eternity; just as really for the fruit which the Father expects from us, as for our title to Heaven.

"And that your joy might be full"' (v. 11). The grounds of the Christian joy are not in himself, but in Christ: "rejoice in the Lord" (Phil. 4:4). But the measure in which we enter into this is determined by our daily communion with the Lord. "Our fellowship is with the Father, and with His Son Jesus Christ, **and** these things write we unto you that your **joy** may be full" (I John 1:3-4)! Our **joy** ought to be steady and constant, not fitful and occasional: "Rejoice in the Lord **alway:** and again I say, Rejoice" (Phil. 4:4). Joy is not "happiness" as the world uses the term; it is much deeper. The worldling finds his happiness in circumstances and surroundings; but the Christian is quite independent of these. Paul and Silas, in the Philippian dungeon, with backs bleeding, "sang praises unto God" (Acts 16:25). What a blessed triumphing over circumstances was that! Prison-walls could not cut them off **from Christ!** But how this puts us to shame! The reason why we are so often dull and despondent, the cause of our restlessness and discontent, is because we walk so little in the light of the Lord's countenance. May we earnestly seek grace to heed the things which He has "spoken unto us" that our joy **may be** "full."

"This is My commandment, that ye love one another, as I have loved you" (v. 12). "Love is benignant affection, and the appropriate display of it. In this most general meaning of the term, 'love is the fulfilling of the law.' The exercise of this principle in supremacy in a well-informed intelligent being, secures the performance of all duty. It cannot co-exist with selfishness and malignity, the great causes of sin. In the degree it prevails, they are destroyed. 'Love does'— love can do—'no evil' (Rom. 13:10). Love does—love must do—all practical good. If evil is done—if good is not done—it is just because love is not there in sufficient force" (Dr. John Brown).

It is important that we distinguish between love and benevolence. The benevolence of Christ knows no limits to any of His people. Just as the Father maketh His sun to rise on the evil and on the good, and sendeth the rain on the just and on the unjust, so Christ ever ministers to and supplies the every need of each of His people, whether they are abiding in Him or no. But just as He abides only in the one who is abiding in Him, just as he finds complacency only in him who keeps His commandments 14:21), so the Christian is to regulate his actions, manifest his love. "As a Christian I am to cherish and exercise love toward every one who give evidence that he is a brother in Christ. It is only in this character that he has any claim upon my brotherly affection, and the degree not of my good will, for that should in every case be boundless: yet my esteem of, and complacency in a christian brother, should be proportioned to the manifestation which he makes of the various excellencies of the Christian character. The better he is, and shows himself to be, I should love him the better. My love should be regulated on the same principle as Christ's, whose benevolence knows no limit in reference to any of His people, but whose esteem and complacency are always proportioned to holy principles and conduct on the part of His people" (Dr. John Brown).

"Greater love hath no man than this, that a man lay down his life for his friends." It is to be observed that these words follow right on after Christ saying "love one another as I have loved you." In view of this, we believe that vv. 13 to 16 set forth a number of proofs of Christ's love, each of which manifested some distinctive feature of it, and that these are here advanced in order to teach us how we should love one another. The Lord places first the highest evidence of His love: He laid down His life for His people. It is to be observed that in the Greek the word "man" is not found in this verse. Literally rendered it reads, "Greater than this love no one has, that one his life lay down for friends his." Christ emphasises once more the great fact that His death, imminent at the time He spoke, was purely voluntary. He "laid down" His life; none took His life from Him. This life was laid down for His friends, and in thus dying on their behalf, in their stead, He furnished the supreme demonstration of His love to and for them. Romans: 5:6-10 emphasises the same truth, only from a different standpoint. There, the objects of Christ's atoning sacrifice are described as Divine justice saw them, they are viewed as they were in themselves, by nature and practice—ungodly, sinners, enemies. But here in John 15 the Saviour speaks of them in the terms of Divine love, and as they were by election and regeneration, His "friends."

"Greater love hath no man than this, that a man lay down his life for his friends." Now in this verse the Lord not only speaks of His own unselfish sacrificial, illimitable love, but He does so for the express purpose of supplying both a motive and an example for us. He has given us a commandment that we "love one another," and that we love our brethren as He loved them.

There is to be no limitation in our love: if occasion requires it we are to be ready to lay down our life one for another. The same truth is found in John's first Epistle: "Hereby perceive we the love of God, because He laid down His life for us; and we ought to lay down our lives for the brethren" (3:16). "Herein is love, not that we loved God, but that He loved us, and sent His Son to be the propitation for our sins. Beloved, if God so loved us, we ought also to love one another." How these scriptures rebuke us! What is it worth if we hold the theory that we are ready, in obedience to God's Word, to lay down our lives for our brethren, when we fail so sadly in ministering to the common and daily needs and sufferings of God's children? "My little children, let us not love in word, neither in tongue; but in deed and in truth" (1 John 3:18)!

"Ye are My friends, if ye do whatsover I command you" (v. 14). Here is the second proof of Christ's love for His own. He had treated them with unreserved intimacy. He had brought them into close fellowship with Himself. He had dealt with them not as strangers, nor had He acted as men do toward casual acquaintances. Instead, He had, in infinite condescension, given them the unspeakable privilege of being His friends. And such they would continue, so long as they did whatsoever He had commanded them, for the Lord will not be on intimate terms with any who are out of the path of obedience. This was something far higher than the attitude which the Rabbis maintained toward their disciples, and higher still than the feeling which a master entertained for his servants. The Lord of glory deigned to treat his disciples and servants as **friends**!

"Ye are My friends, if ye do whatsoever I command you." It is to be carefully noted that Christ did not here say, "**I am** your friend!" "Just now there is a great deal in the more popular hymnbooks about Jesus as **our** friend. How few seem to appreciate the desire of our Lord to make us **His** friends! The difference is very real. When a man who has attained the highest position in the nation notices a man of the labouring class and calls him his friend, it is a condescension, for he hereby exalts that unknown man to his own level. But for the insignificant man to say of the famous one, 'He's my friend,' by no means exalts that one; indeed, it might be considered a presumption, a piece of impudence. This familiarity, this calling Jesus **our Friend**, is dimming in people's hearts the consciousness that He is something more than that: He is our Saviour! He is our Lord! He is really, in His own essential nature, our God" (Mr. C. H. Bright). The same rebuke is called for by those who term the incarnate Son of God our Elder Brother! It is true that He, in marvellous grace, is "not ashamed to call **us** brethren," but it ill requites that grace for us to term Him **our** 'Elder Brother.' Let us ever remember His own Word "Ye call Me **Master** and **Lord**: and ye say **well**; for so I am" (13:13).

"Henceforth I call you not servants; for the servant knoweth not what his Lord doeth: but I have called you friends, for all things that I have heard of My Father I have made known unto you" (v. 15). Here is the third proof of the love of Christ for His own. He not only **treated** the disciples as friends, but **He owned** them as such, and took them fully into His confidence. Our thoughts at once revert to Abraham, who is expressly called "the **friend** of God" (James 2:23). The reference no doubt is to what we read of in Gen. 18:17, God was about to destroy Sodom. Lot knew nothing of this, for he was at too great a moral distance from God. But the Lord said, "Shall I hide from Abraham that thing which I do?" In Abraham God found delight, and therefore did He make him the confident of His counsels. It it is striking that Abraham is the **only** Old Testament saint directly termed the **friend** of God (see Isa. 41:8). But Abraham is "the father of all them that believe," and here the Lord calls his believing children His "friends." The term speaks both of confidence and intimacy —not our confidence in and intimacy with Him, but He in and with us. He would no longer call them "servants," though they were such; but he makes them His companions. He reveals to them the Father's thoughts, bringing them into that holy nearness and freedom which He had with the Father. What a place to put them into! If they were not fit to receive these intimacies, He would be betraying the confidence of the Father! It is the **new nature** which gives us the needed fitness.

"I have called you friends." This is not to be restricted to the Eleven, but applies equally to all His blood-bought people. The King of kings and Lord of Lords not only pities and saves all them that believe in Him, but actually calls them His **friends**! In view of such language, we need not wonder that the apostle said, "The love of Christ passeth knowledge." What **encouragement** this should give us to pour our hearts to His in prayer! Why should we hesitate to unbosom ourselves to One who calls us His "friends!" What **comfort** this should give us in trouble. Will He not minister of His own mercy and grace to his "friends!" And what **assurance** is here for the one who doubts the final issue. Weak and unworthy, we all are in ourselves, but Christ will never forsake His "friends!"

"For all things that I heard of My Father I have made known unto you." The "all things" here were those which pertained to His Mediatorship. Mark 4 supplies us with a striking illustration of how the Lord made His disciples His special confidants: "And He said unto them, **Unto you** it is given to know the mystery of the kingdom of God: but unto them that are without, all these things are done in parables . . . Without a parable spake He not unto them (the multitudes) : and when they were alone, He expounded all things to His disciples" (vv. 11, 34). And again in the Gospel records we find the Saviour distinguishing His disciples by similiar marks of His love. To them only did He confide His approaching betrayal into the hands of wicked men. To them only did He declare that His place in the Father's House. should be theirs. To them only did He announce the coming of the Comforter.

In like manner Christ has revealed many things to us in His Word which the wise of this world know nothing about. "For yourselves know perfectly that the Day of the Lord so cometh as a thief in the night. For when they shall say Peace and safety; then sudden destruction cometh upon them as travail upon a woman with child; and they shall not escape. But ye, brethren, are **not in darkness**, that that Day should overtake you as a thief" (1 Thess. 5 : 2-4). How highly we should value such confidences. How much **would** He reveal to us, now hidden, if only we gave more diligent heed to His commandments! Ever remember that "the secret of the Lord is with **them that fear Him!**" Ere passing to the next verse let it be pointed out again that the Lord was not only here refering to the evidences of **His own** love for us, but was also making known how our love should be manifested one toward another. "He that hath friends will **show himself friendly**" (Prov. 18 : 24). Then let us abstain from encroaching on a brother's spiritual liberty ; let us not usurp dominion over a brother's faith : let us treat our brother not as a servant,, still less as a stranger, but as a **friend**!

"Ye have not chosen Me, but I have chosen you, and ordained you, that ye should go and bring forth fruit, and that your fruit should remain ; that whatsoever ye shall ask of the Father in **My** name He may give it you" (v. 16). "This love was at the **foundation** of all for them : and to it they owed, and we owe, that choice was on His side, not ours. 'Ye have not chosen Me,' He says, 'but I have chosen you.' Thus in conscious weakness the power of God is with us : and as He sought us when lost, when there was nothing but our misery to awaken His compassion—so we may count assuredly upon Him, whatever our helplessness, to perfect the work He has begun. What comfort lies for us in the royal word, 'I have chosen you !'

"But grace enables us to fulfill the conditions necessarily imposed by the holiness of the Divine nature, and cannot set these aside: therefore the closing words. They are in the same line with others that we have lately heard : which they emphasise only in a somewhat different way. Fruit that abides is that which alone satisfies God. How much that looks well has not that quality in it which ensures permanence. How much that seems truly of God reveals its character by its decay ! This 'abiding' connects itself, in the Gospel of John, with the Divine side of things which is see all through" (Numerical Bible).

The following questions are to help the student prepare for our next lesson :

1. What is the link between vv. 17 to 27 with the context ?
2. What is our Lord's central design in this passage ?
3. Wherein is the depravity of man exhibited ?
4. Why does Christ repeat v. 12 in v. 17 ?
5. What is the meaning of v. 19 ?
6. What is the force of "had not had sin" vv. 22, 24 ?
7. Of what does the testimony of vv. 26-27 consist ?

ARTHUR W. PINK.

## GLEANINGS IN EXODUS

### 28. The Law of God: Ex. 20.

In His Olivet discourse the Lord Jesus prophesied that "Because iniquity (Greek, lawlessness) shall abound, the love of many shall wax cold." (Matt. 24:12). Surely no anointed eye can fail to see that this prediction is now being fulfilled. Lawlessness **abounds** on every side. Men are bent on pleasing themselves. Authority is openly flouted. Discipline is becoming a thing of the past. Parental control is rarely exercised. Marriage has, for the most part, degenerated into a thing of convenience. Nations regard their solemn treaties as 'scraps of paper.' In the U.S.A. the 18th Amendment is despised on every side. Yes, "lawlessness" **is** abounding. And God's own people have not escaped the chilling effects of this; the love of **many** of them has waxed cold.

The supreme test of love is the desire and effort to please the one loved, and this measured by conformity to his known wishes. Love to God is expressed by **obedience** to His will. Only One has perfectly exemplified this, and of Him it is written, "I will delight to do Thy will, O My God: yea, Thy law is within My heart," (Psa. 40:8). But we ought so to walk even as He walked (1 John 2:6). Simple but searching is that word of His, "He that hath My **commandments** and **keepeth** them he it is that loveth Me"( John 14:21). And again it is written, "By this we know that we love the children of God, when we love God, and keep **His commandments**. For this is the love of God, that we **keep** His commandments: and His commandments **are not grievous."** (1 John 5:2-3). The "waning" of love, then, means departing from, failing to keep, God's commandments!

The prophecy of Christ in Matt. 24: 12 does not stand alone. In the book of Jude, that treats of conditions which are to obtain in the closing days of the history of Christendom, apostates are described as those who **"despise dominion,** and spake evil of dignities" (v. 8). The despising of dominion is the essence of lawlessness. Those latter-day apostates are also referred to in the second Epistle of Peter: "While they promise them liberty they themselves are the slaves of corruption" (2:19). Their slogan is, emancipation from authority, deliverance from all law.

While we cannot but deplore the lawlessness which abounds in the world and the effect which it is having on many who bear the name of Christ, far more sad and solemn is it to hear their teachers giving out that which can only foster and further this evil spirit. Reputable Bible teachers are declaring that the Law of God is not binding on men to-day least of all on Christians. They say that the Law was only for Israel. They insist that this is the Dispensation of Grace, and that Law is the enemy of Grace. They affirm that when we become members of the new creation, all the responsibilities attaching to the old creation automatically cease. They argue that because a Christian is indwelt by the Holy Spirit, he needs no law. They brand as legalists the few who press the claims of God's Law upon the consciences of men. They regard with scornful pity men mightily used of God in the past who taught that the Law of God is a rule of life, a standard for moral conduct.

Now it is of first importance that we obtain a Scriptural view of the **nature** of the Law. The very fact that it is the law **of God** should at once show us that it cannot contain anything inimical to man's welfare. Like every thing else that God has given, the Law is an expression of His love, a manifestation of His mercy, a provision of His grace. The Law of the Lord was **Christ's** delight (Psa. 1:2); so also was it the apostle Paul's (Rom. 7:22). In Rom. 7, the Holy Spirit has expressly affirmed, "Wherefore the Law is holy, and the commandment holy, and just, and **good"** (v. 12); yea more, He has declared "The Law is **spiritual"** (v. 15). How terrible then for men to despise that Law and speak evil of it! What state of soul must they be in who **wish** to be delivered **from it!**

Above, we have said that the Law expressed God's **love.** This comes out clearly in Deut: 33: "The Lord came from Sinai, and rose up from Seir unto them; He shined forth from Mount Paran, and He came with ten thousands of saints: from His right hand went a fiery law for them. **Yea, He LOVED the people."** (vv. 2-3). Love is the **fulfilling** of the law from the human side and love **provided** the Law from the Divine side. What, then, ought to be our response to such a Law? Surely that of David: "O **how love I Thy Law;** it is my meditation all the day" (Psa. 119:97).

While Divine love provided the Law, the prime purpose of God in giving it was that His **authority** should be maintained. Israel must be brought to see that they were under His **government.** And this of necessity. The creature must be made to recognise the rights of his Creator. No sooner did the Lord God place man in the Garden which He had planted for him, than He com**manded** him—note how in Gen. 3 God pressed this both upon Eve and Adam (vv. 11, 17). The very ground of the sentence passed upon them was that they had repudiated His creatorial claims.

Now what we have in Ex. 19 and 20 is the enforcement of God's claims upon **double** one. They belonged to Him not Israel. His claim upon them was a only because He had made them, but also because He had purchased them: they were not only His creatures, but they were also His redeemed people. It was this second relationship which is now pressed upon them both in Ex. 19 and 20. In the former He says, "Ye have seen what I did unto the

Egyptians, and how I bare you on eagles' wings, and brought you unto Myself. Now **therefore**, if ye will obey My voice indeed, and keep My covenant, then ye shall be a peculiar treasure unto Me above all people: for all the earth is Mine" (vv. 4-5). In the latter, **He** prefaces the Ten Commandments with the statement, "I am the Lord thy God, which have brought thee out of the land of Egypt, out of the house of bondage" (v. 2). But it should be carefully noted that in Ex. 20 He presses both of His claims upon Israel. In the first verse it is, "And God (the Creator) spake all these words"; while in v. 2, He reminds them, that as **the Lord** their God He had brought them out of the land of Egypt.

Now what we would particularly emphasise here, is the fact that redemption does not cancel the claims which God has upon men **as His creatures.** Instead, these claims are still enforced, but, the new relationship into which redemption introduces, imposes **additional** responsibilities, or, more accurately speaking, supplies an additional **motive** for recognising and meeting God's claims upon us. In the previous chapters we have witnessed God dealing in marvellous grace with Israel, bearing with them in tender patience, supplying their every need. But now the point has been reached when they must be taught that God has righteous claims upon them, that His Throne must be established over them, that His authority must be owned, that His will is supreme and must be made the regulator of their lives, and that as His redeemed they were under the deepest possible obligations to fear, obey, and serve Him. Notice how Moses pressed this upon Israel near the close of his life: "The Lord thy God **redeemed** thee, **therefore I command** thee this thing to-day" (Deut. 15:15).

"The laws which God gave unto Israel fall into three classes: the moral, the ceremonial and the civil. The people of Israel may be considered three ways. First, as **rational creatures**, depending upon God, as the Supreme Cause, both in a moral and natural sense. And thus the **law of the decalogue** was given them; which, as to its substance is one and the same with the law of nature (the work of which is written on man's heart. A.W.P.) binding man as such. Second, as **the Church of the Old Testament,** who expected the promised Messiah, and happy times when He should make every thing perfect. And in that character they received the **ceremonial** law, which really showed the Messiah was not yet come, and had not perfected all things by His satisfaction (sacrifice), but that He would come and make all things new. Third, as a **peculiar people**, who had a policy of government suited to their genius and disposition in the land of Canaan: a republic constituted not so much according to those forms which philosophers have delineated, but which was in a peculiar manner, a **theocracy** as Josephus significantly calls it, God Himself holding the reins of government therein—Judges 8:23. Under this view God prescribed their political laws" (Dr. Herman Witsius, 1680—a deeply-taught theologian from whom our moderns might learn **much**).

We heartily concur with the remarks of the late Mr. D. L. Moody in "Weighed and Wanting"—"The commandments of God given to Moses in the mount at Horeb are as binding to-day as ever they have been since the time when they were proclaimed in the hearing of the people. The Jews said the Law was not given in Palestine (which belonged to Israel), but in the wilderness, because the Law was for all nations." We believe that the Ten Commandments are binding on all men, and especially upon Christians, and that for the following reasons:—

First, because it is both right and meet that the great Creator's **authority** should be proclaimed by Him and acknowledged by His creatures. This was the demand which He made upon Adam, and every sober mind will acknowledge it was a righteous one. Even the unfallen angels are beneath a regime of law: of them it is said, "Bless the Lord ye His angels that excel in strength, that do His **commandments,** hearkening unto the voice of His word" (Psa. 103:20). Only a spirit of lawlessness can inveigh against the statement that every human creature is responsible to keep the law of God.

Second, because the Ten Comamndments have never been repealed. The very fact that they were written by the finger of God Himself, written not upon parchment, but on tables of **stone,** argues conclusively their permanent nature. If it was contrary to the mind of God that those living during the Christian dispensation should regard the Ten Commandments as binding upon them, then surely He would have said so in plain language. But the New

Testament will be searched in vain for a single word which announces their cancellation.

Third, because we need them. Has human nature so improved, is man so much better than he was three thousand years ago, that he no longer stands in need of the Divine Law? If the covenant people of old required to have such statutes are the Gentiles to-day any less self-sufficient? Are men now so little prone to idolatry that they need not the Divine command "Thou shalt have no other gods before Me? Has the enmity of the carnal mind been so refined that it is no longer timely to say "Thou shalt not take the name of the Lord thy God in vain?" Are the children of this twentieth century A.D. so devoted to their parents and so marked by the spirit of obedience that it is superfluous to say to them "Honour thy father and thy mother?" Is human life now held in such reverence that it is idle to say "Thou shalt not kill?" Has the marriage-relationship come to be so sacredly regarded that "Thou shall not commit adultery" is an impertinance? And is there now so much honesty in the world that it is a waste of breath to remind our fellows that God says "Thou shalt not steal?" Rather is it not true that in the light of present-day conditions the Ten commandments need to be thundered forth from every pulpit in the land?

Fourth, because the Lord Jesus Christ Himself respected them. Gal. 4:4 tells us that He was, "made under the Law." On entering this world He declared "I delight to do Thy will, O My God: yea, Thy Law is within My heart." (Psa. 40:8), and the record of His earthly life fully bears this out. When the ruler asked Him, "What shall I do to inherit eternal life?" He answered, "Thou knowest the commandments—'Do not commit adultery,'" etc. Whatever may have been our Lord's reason for returning such a reply, one thing is clear—He honored the holy Law of God! When the lawyer tempted Him by asking, "Which is the greatest commandment in the Law?" (Matt. 22:36), His answer once more shows Him maintaining the authority of God's Law.

Fifth, because of our Lord's teaching on the subject. In the Sermon on the Mount we find Him saying, "Think not that I am come to destroy the Law, or the Prophets: I am not come to destroy, but to fulfil. For verily I say unto you till heaven and earth pass, one jot or one tittle shall in nowise pass from the Law, till all be fulfilled. Whosoever therefore shall break one of these least commandments, and shall teach men so, he shall be called the least in the kingdom of heaven: but whosoever shall do and teach them, the same shall be called great in the kingdom of heaven" (Matt. 5:17-19). What could be clearer than this? So far from affirming that He had come to cancel the Law, He declared that He would fulfil it. Yea, more, He insisted that the Law shall remain, and remain intact so long as the earth remained. His words that not "one jot or tittle of the Law should pass away (become obsolete) proves conclusively that the fourth commandment (on the Sabbath) would remain in force equally with the other nine! Finally, He solemnly warns us that the one who should teach men to break one of these commandments, shall suffer loss in a coming day.

Sixth, because of the teaching of the New Testament Epistles. In them we find the Ten Commandments recorded and enforced. At the close of Romans 3, where the apostle treats of Justification, he raises the question, "Do we then make void the Law through faith?" and the emphatic answer is "God forbid: yea, we establish the Law." In the same Epistle he declares again after quoting five of the Commandments, "Love is the fulfilling of the Law" (13:10), and love could not "fulfil" the Law if it had been abrogated. Once more, in I Cor. 9:21, Paul says, "Being not without Law to God, but under the Law to Christ."

Seventh, because God has threatened to chastise those Christians who disregard His Law. In the 89th Psa. there is a striking prophetic passage which brings this out plainly. In vv. 27-29 God declares of Christ, "I will make Him My Firstborn, higher than the kings of the earth. My mercy will I keep for Him for evermore, and My covenant shall stand fast with Him. His seed also will I make to endure for ever, and His throne as the days of heaven." And then God solemnly adds, "If His children forsake My Law, and walk not in My judgments; If they break My statutes, and keep not My commandments: then will I visit their transgression with the rod, and their iniquity with stripes." The writer often wonders how much of the afflictions that so many Christians are now groaning under are explained by this scripture!

The Ten Commandments have been rightly designated **the moral law**, inasmuch as they enunciate a rule or standard for human conduct. Their application is race wide. Even Mr. Darby admitted in his Synopsis (Vol. 1, p. 86), "such is the character of the Law, a rule sent out to **man**, taken in its **largest** character." (italics ours). While dissenting from the expression "moral law," and while denying that the Law was a "rule of life," for the believer, nevertheless Mr. Darby did not go to the lengths of Antinomianism to which some of his followers have gone in their teachings. In Vol. 10 of his "Collected writings" he said," If I make of the law a moral law (including therein the principle of the New Testament and all morality in heart and life), to say a Christian is delivered from it **is nonsense, or utter monstrous wickedness:** certainly it is not Christianity. Conformity to the Divine will, and that as **obedience to commandments** is alike the **duty of the renewed mind.** I say obedience to commandments. Some are afraid of the word, as if it would weaken love, and the idea of a new creation; Scripture is not. Obedience, and keeping the commandments of one we love, is the proof of that love, and the delight of the new nature." As to Mr. Darby's **consistency** in arguing that the believer nevertheless is not under the Law in any sense, we leave the reader to judge.

It is not our intention to refute the objections which have been made against the truth that the Ten Commandments are not binding on men to-day, and that believers especially are in no sense under the Law. We have dealt with these, and expounded the scriptures which are supposed to support the objections, in our booklet on "The Saint and the Law." Suffice it now to point out that in the Word a sharp distinction is drawn between "the law of **Moses**" and "The Law of **God**:" the former was for Israel only: the latter is for all men. The Lord grant that writer and reader may be able to truthfully say with the Apostle Paul. "**I delight** in the Law of God after the inward man" (Rom. 7:22); and again, "So then with the mind I myself **serve** the Law of God; but with the flesh the law of sin" (Rom. 7:25).

ARTHUR W. PINK.

## ELECTION.

An Address delivered by Dr. Pink, June 1925, in the Tabernacle, Ashfield, N.S.W.

### (No. 3).

I have been asked to say a few words to-night upon the difference between Arminianism and Calvinism. The theological world in Christendom is divided into two antagonistic forces known as Calvinists and Arminians, and the issue between them is the issue between truth and error. Calvinism, of course, takes its name from John Calvin, the great Reformer, who was raised up by God in the early part of the 16th century and was so wondrously used of Him in Europe.

Arminianism is named after James Arminius who was born in Southern Holland in the year 1560. His parents were killed during his childhood and he, as a boy and as a young man, served in a public house. In his youth, a clergyman took a liking to him and decided to have him educated for the ministry. He was sent to Geneva and studied under Beza, the successor of Calvin, and while in Geneva Arminius betrayed a strong tendency to call into question a number of the great fundamentals of the faith. He did it in a very subtle way and ultimately he was expelled from Geneva in disgrace. After he left Geneva he journeyed to Rome and it is on record that in Rome he kissed the Pope's toe.

I am mentioning these facts that you might know a little of the originator of this system. Water will not rise above its own level, and I want you to know where Arminianism originated. It originated in one whose boyhood was spent in a publichouse as a bar-tender, who in early manhood was expelled from Geneva in disgrace, and who then went to Rome and after he had made obeisance to the Pope, entered into a secret compact with Cardinal Bellamine, the great Romish theologian, and was induced to return to Holland, his native country, and pose as an orthodox preacher in order to gain the confidence of the people and, after he had done so, to then instil poison into them. He became Professor of Theology in Leyden University, and after a time it was discovered that he was teaching error to the theological students there, and a council was called by which he was to be examined, when death snatched him away. Some of his disciples then made an effort to popularise his system of theology and succeeded because there was a falling away, a decline, a growing cold in the love of God's people in these days, and Arminianism became popular and increased vastly in its influence and territory.

Now Arminianism teaches that man is a free will agent, and that because God has endowed him with free-will God must not and will not interfere with him. If that be true, then man is a creature who is not under the governmental control of God. If God leaves man free to himself, then he is not subject to God's will. Therefore Arminians teach that because man has a free will, that he is the architect of his own fortunes and the determiner of his own destiny, and that no matter what God may want, no matter what God may desire, man having a freewill has the power to thwart Him. Arminians teach that we become saved by an act of our own free will, and therefore they consistently teach that we can become lost again by an act of our own free will. If I am saved to-day by an act of mine, then it necessarily follows that I can unsave myself to-morrow by an act of mine. There is no getting away from that. A rule that does not work both ways is not a rule. You cannot have a negative without a positive. If I have been saved by my act, then I may be unsaved to-morrow by my act, and therefore Arminians consistently teach that because I am endowed with free will, therefore I can lose my salvation. That is Arminianism in a bald outline.

Now Calvinism teaches that when man became a sinner he fell, that he is a fallen creature, that he is depraved, and not only is he depraved, but he is totally depraved. Not only is his heart depraved, but his will is depraved as well. Not only has his body become subject to death, not only has his mind been darkened, not only have his affections been alienated, but his will has been brought into bondage; and therefore Calvinists teach that man is **no longer** a free will agent, but rather that he is the slave of sin and the captive of the devil, and that the poor sinner never does become free until Christ opens the prison and liberates the prisoner. Christ says in John 8:36, "If the Son shall make you free, ye shall be free indeed." But a man does not need to be "made free" if he is free already; he has to be "made free" before he becomes free. Therefore Calvinists teach that man in his fallen condition is so totally depraved that he cannot do one single thing for himself, and that if ever he is to be saved God must save him.

Now I am quite sure that the great majority who are present to-night believe that last statement. You believe that if a sinner is to be saved God has to save him, and the proof that you believe that is seen in the fact that you very often ask God to save certain people. You have loved ones who are unsaved, and every Christian here to-night is constantly asking God to save them. Well that proves that you believe that salvation is God's work. Don't be so inconsistent as to say man has a part in it. Salvation is of the Lord, and no man can come to Christ except the Father which hath sent Him draw him.

Now then, the great difference between Arminianism and Calvinism is this. The whole centre of Arminianism is m-a-n. The great centre of Calvinism is G-o-d. Calvinism makes nothing of man, but it makes everything of God. Arminianism reduces God to a helpless being, who wants to do many things but man won't let Him: who is trying to do lots of things but the devil is prevening Him: who is filled with amiable intentions but unable to carry them out. If Arminianism were true there would be a defeated Father, a disappointed Christ and a disgraced Holy Spirit. If God the Father wants everybody to be saved, and Christ died in order to save everybody, and the Holy Spirit is now trying to save everybody, and everybody is **not** saved, then you **must** have a disappointed Father, a defeated Christ, and a disgraced Holy Spirit.

Now then Calvinism says, man (every man the world over) is so sinful and so corrupt and so depraved and so dead in sins, that if God were to leave us to ourselves nobody ever would be saved, and therefore God, knowing that, elected certain people to be saved. If there had been no election no one here to-night ever would have been saved. So instead of being afraid of election you ought to be mighty thankful for it. I repeat that. If there had been no election by God before the foundation of the world, no sinner ever would have been saved, and the death of Christ would have been in vain. Scripture says in Isaiah 53:11 that Christ shall "see of the travail of His soul and be **satisfied**" There is going to be no dissatisfied and defeated Christ when this world's history is wound up!

Now I just want to mention one other point before I start my address for to-night, and I want you to listen very closely to this for I believe it will be news to most of you. I am sorry it will be. It ought not to be, but I am afraid it will be new to the great majority of you—possibly to all. In the year 1563, or rather a few years before that, the Roman Catholic Church was shaken to its very foundations. God had so mightily used Martin Luther and John Calvin and others and so many people had left the Roman Catholic Church and had received the truth of Scripture, that Rome began to tremble for its own future, and many of its theologians began to waver—even those who remained inside of Rome were influenced to some extent by the writings of the Reformers. Some of them believed one thing and some another. In the year 1563, by the order of the Pope, there was a Council held at Trent, and Rome then and there defined her theological position on the points that had been raised by the reformers, and one of their decrees read thus. (Now the decrees of the Council of Trent are their standard to-day on controverted points):—"If anyone shall affirm that since the fall of Adam, man's free will is lost, let him be accursed." I want to read that again. What I am reading now is Roman Catholic doctrine according to their own standards, the decrees of the Council of Trent in the year 1563. One of those decrees read thus:—"If anyone shall affirm that since the fall of Adam, man's free will is lost, let him be accursed." So that those who insist on man's free will place themselves side by side with Rome on that doctrine! **That is Romanism,** and it only goes to show how terribly Protestantism is honeycombed by Rome. It only goes to show how the leven of Romanism has been working in the meal of Protestantism.

There is nothing that Rome hates so much as the doctrines of Calvinism—that makes nothing of man and everything of God's grace, nothing. The sad, sad, sad thing is to-day that a generation has grown up in Protestantism that is as ignorant as Hottentots are concerning the original controversy between Rome and the Protestants. And I would like to say this in passing. I just commend this to your serious thought. I make so bold as to say that every Sunday-school that is represented here to-night either by a pastor or a superintendent, or a teacher, ought to make it their business to see that they have a small library (if you do not have one) in your Sunday-school, and in that library you ought to have Foxe's Book of Marytrs and other books which give the history of what Rome did in the dark ages and what she would do now if she were in power. The young people of this generation ought to be instructed and not allowed to remain in the ignorance they are in to-day. I want to commend this to your serious thought—the importance of having books in a circulating library in your Sunday-school—and if there are any of you brethren here to-night who have a few pounds in the bank that you want to us in the Lord's work and you do not know how best to use it, I do not believe you could put that money to better use than starting a small circulating library in your Sunday-school of sound Scriptural literature and teach our young people to read, and read something that is worth reading.

Now then let me give you a brief summary of the ground we have already covered. There is far more Romanism in Protestantism to-day than most of us are aware of. There is far more Romanistic doctrine being preached from Protestant pulpits than most of us are aware of. In the last two addresses we have shown, first, that Scripture teaches God does have an elect people, a people whom He has chosen to be His own, and chose them before the foundation of the world, and chose them because it so pleased **Him** In the second place, I have sought to show that these chosen people of God are the ones who are now being saved, and the reason why any of us have been saved is because God chose us to salvation from the beginning.

As to why God should have singled out certain one's from Adam's fallen race to be redeemed by Christ and to be conformed to His image, and pass by the others is a profound mystery. As to why God should have singled out the ones that He has and left the others in their sins is something that is beyond the finite mind of man to fully grasp. That is freely admitted, but the fact that the doctrine of election is mysterious is no reason why it should be rejected. My friends we are surrounded by mystery on every side, even in the natural world. Let me put a few things before you. Why is it that this globe on which we are living—this earth—why is it that two-thirds of its surface is covered by water and therefore uninhabitable to man? Why is it that of the remaining third, the land portion, vast tracts of it, millions of acres, are unfit for human habitation or human cultivation? Why is it that there are great deserts, rocky wastes, north and south poles, and vast fields of millions of acres of ice? Why is it that God causes the fruit trees to be filled with blossoms and then sends a strong wind or a frost to destroy them? Why has God created rats and mice and cats and dogs to kill them? Ah, you smile, but there is not one of you can answer them! The only reason is because it so pleased Him.

I am just now trying to show that even in the natural world we are surrounded by mystery on every side, therefore we must not be surprised at mystery in the spiritual world. That God's ways are mysterious He tells us Himself in His own Word. In Isaiah 55, 8 and 9 He says, "My thoughts are not your thoughts, neither are your ways My ways, for as the heavens are higher than the earth, so are My ways higher than your ways, and My thoughts than your thoughts." He says again in Rom. 11:33: "How unsearchable are His judgments, and His ways (His **ways**) past finding out." How humbling that is! How that bears witness to the limitations of our intellect! God's ways are "past finding out!"

Turn for a moment to II Peter 3:16. I will begin at verse 15: "And account that the longsuffering of our Lord is salvation; even as our beloved brother Paul according to the wisdom given unto him hath written unto you; as also in all his epistles, speaking in them of these things; (Now notice!) in which (that is, in the Epistles of Paul) are some things hard to be understood." The Holy Spirit tells us so. God says there are some things that are **hard to be understood** That is in the Epistles of Paul, and the Apostle Paul deals with God's sovereignty and election more fully than any other writer in the New Testament. You read Romans 9 and Romans 11 and you will find that out. Now then, because they are hard to understand are we to ignore them? Some good people have said to me more than once in the past, Why, Dr. Pink, if these things are hard to understand, then why do you preach on them? Why my dear friends that is the very reason I do preach on them. There is not much use my preaching to you something that you already understand, is there? You have come here to learn something haven't you, or have you? If you think you know it all already, you are just wasting your time here to-night, and mine as well. It is a waste of time for any of you people to go to church if you are satisfied you know it all now—might as well stay at home. The very fact that these things are "hard to be understood" is all the more reason why the pulpit should preach on them, that God may be pleased to use His servants to lead His people to understand them. Of course, if the preacher does not understand them he had better shut up or he will only darken counsel by words. The best thing for the preacher, if he does not understand these things, is to get down on his knees and cry to God for light, and then turn to the only source from which he can get light: study diligently the Book of books.

Now then, man has made a very special effort to try and get rid of the great mystery in connection with election. Man says that God's choice is based upon His foreknowledge. I raised that point last night—mentioned one or two things on it—and I wish to follow this up tonight and go into it a little more deeply. Man says the reason why God elected the ones that He did was because He foreknew that they would believe. Well, if that is true, there is nothing hard to understand about it, a child can understand that. The very fact that that explanation is so simple, is evidence that it is not the true one, for God says these things are hard to understand.

In the second place. Nothing can be foreknown unless it is absolutely **certain** that it will be, and nothing is absolutely certain to be, except what God has predestinated. Now let me repeat that. Nothing can be foreknown unless it is absolutely certain that it shall be, and nothing is certain to be except what God has foreordained shall be. Therefore God knows what will be because He has predestinated what shall be.

In the third place. God could not foresee anything good in me except what He purposed to put in me. There is nothing good in me by nature. "In me, that is in my flesh, dwelleth no good thing," and whatever good thing there is in me now, by grace, God has put there. Now listen! There are those who say that God has elected certain ones because He foreknew that they would believe. No man can believe until God gives him faith. Well, but you say, faith and believing are the same thing. No, you need to go back to school again and learn how to parse, if you say that. "Faith" is a noun and "believing" is a verb, and which is it that expresses action? Do nouns express action, or do verbs? Why, verbs of course. Now listen! Sight, is God's gift: seeing is my use of the gift. Breath, the noun, is God's gift: breathing, the verb, is my use of the gift. The moment God takes my breath away from me I cannot breathe. The moment God takes my sight away from me I can no longer see. Sight is God's gift: seeing is my use of the gift. Breath is God's gift: breathing is my use of the gift. Faith is God's gift: believing is my use of the gift.

No man can believe until God has given him faith. Where is your proof text for that, preacher? All right, that is good; I don't want you to accept anything from me unless I can prove it by God's Word. Do not accept anything from any preacher, no matter who he is, unless he gives you a "Thus saith the Lord" to back it up with. Now turn to Ephesians 2, verses 8 and 9:—"For by grace are ye saved through faith; and that not of yourselves:" Faith is not of yourselves: "believing" is, just as seeing is. "By grace are ye saved through faith; and that not of yourselves: it is **the gift of God.**" Now turn to II Thessalonians, 3:2. I will read you the first verse. II Thessalonians 3, 1 and 2, and brothers and sisters in Christ, this is what I wish that you would pray for this preacher: "Finally, brethren, pray for us, that the Word of the Lord may have free course and be glorified, even as it is with you: and that we may be delivered from unreasonable and wicked men for **all** have not faith." The word "men" is in italics. It is correct here, because he is speaking of men in the first part of the verse: "That we may be delivered from unreasonable and wicked men for all men have not faith." Why do not all men have faith? Because God does not give it to all, that is the reason why all men do not believe. Well, you say, why does not God give it to all? You must ask Him! II Peter, 1:-1, and then I must pass on to something else: "Simon Peter, a servant and an apostle of Jesus Christ, to them that have **exercised** like precious faith." No, sir, it does not say that: "to them that have **obtained** like precious faith." From whom did they obtain it? The third verse tells us:—"According as His Divine power hath given unto us all things that pertain unto life and godliness." It was His divine power that gave us all things that pertain unto life and godliness.

God foresaw and God foreknew that not a single member of the human race ever would believe if He left them to themselves. Consequently, in His own sovereign grace He purposed to **give** faith to His own "elect." Well, you say, where is your proof of that? First verse of Titus—I am going to keep you close to the Scriptures to-night. "Paul, a servant of God, and an apostle of Jesus Christ, according to **the faith of God's elect."** There you have it staring you right in the face! It is coming at you like a cannon ball, and you had better duck your head if you want to escape it. You had better bow before it! God in His Word says, "the faith of God's elect," "**all** men have not faith." Who do have? Those to whom God gives it. To whom does He give it? His elect. Why does He give it to them and to nobody else? That is His business, and **that** is one of the things that is "hard to be understood."

All right now, let us pass on to the second point. I am still speaking of God's foreknowledge. My second point is this. Now listen to me closely. Never once in this Book anywhere do we read of faith foreknown. That expression is foreign to Scripture. We never read in Scripture of God foreknowing that we should believe. That is not how Scripture puts it. Scripture never speaks of God foreknowing our **actions.** Of course God **did,** but that is not **how** it is put in Scripture. Scripture always speaks of **persons** that were foreknown, not something in those persons—not their faith foreknown, but the people themselves. Turn to Romans 11:2: "God hath not cast away His **people** which He foreknew." It is His people that He foreknew not their faith—That is a theory of man, but it is not in Scripture at all.

Now in the third place, Scripture plainly teaches that God's "foreknowledge" is based on His previous "purpose." Turn to Romans 8, verse 29: "For **what** He did foreknow." No, it does not say so. Scripture never speaks about what God foreknew, but it says. **"Whom** He did foreknow"—people, individuals, "whom"—pronoun—**"Whom** He did foreknow, He also did predestinate." Well, you say, "that is the very thing that I believe, and that is the very opposite of what **you** said a moment ago. I believe that God predestinated us because He first foreknew us." Go back one verse more. Go back to the next verse, the 28th and put your glasses on this time. "And we know that all things work together for good to them that love God, to them who are the called according to **His purpose. For** whom He did foreknow, He also did predestinate." Now there you have the **Divine** order. Now if you forget everything else to night I want you to remember this God's order is this:—First, His purpose second, His foreknowledge; and third, His predestination. Now that is God's order. There is something that goes behind His foreknowledge. God's foreknowledge is not the foundation of His workings. Behind His foreknowledge is His purpose. All things work together for good to them that love God, to them who are—first, the called according to His purpose (not according to their faith, not according to their repentance, but according to His purpose). Second, for whom He did foreknow comes second. Them also He did predestinate to be conformed to the image of His Son comes third.

Now turn back to the second chapter of Acts and I will show you the same thing there. Acts 2:23: "Him, being delivered by the determinate counsel and foreknowledge of God." Now I want you to notice that in that verse God's foreknowledge comes second and not first. "Him being delivered by the determinate counsel." That is His purpose, "and foreknowledge." God's foreknowledge rests upon His determinate counsel. God first purposes what shall be and then He foreknows what will be. What has God told us in the 20th chapter of Revelation? God has told us that at the end of Millennium Satan is going to be released out of his prison for a little season. How does God "know" that? How does God know that at the end of Millennium the devil is going to come up out of his pit to deceive the world again? Why, the simple answer is, Because He has so decreed. God has so purposed it, and therefore He knows it, and consequently He has made it known to us. Now then, God has chosen us, not because of anything good which He foresaw in us, but solely according to His own sovereign will. In other words, the reason for our election was in God Himself and not in us.

Now before I pass on to the next point, let me just interpose this remark. I want you to be clear upon it. There are those who misrepresent the doctrine of election in this way. Here I am sitting down at my table to-night with my family to tea. It is a cold winter's night, and outside on the street are some hungry starving tramps and children, and they come and knock on my door and they say, "We are so hungry, Sir, Oh, we are so hungry and cold, and we are starving: won't you give us something to eat?" "Give you something to eat? No, you do not belong here, get off with you." Now people say that is what election means, that God has spread the gospel feast and some poor sinners conscious of their deep need come to the Lord and say, Have mercy upon me, and the Lord says, No, you are not among My elect. Now, my friends, that is not the teaching of this Book, nor anything like that. That is absolutely a false representation of God's truth. I do not believe anything like that my friends, and I would not insult you by asking you to come here night by night and listen to anything like that.

Now, then, here is the truth. God has spread the feast, but the fact is that nobody is hungry, and nobody wants to come to the feast, and everybody makes an excuse to keep away from the feast, and when they are bidden to come they say, No, we do not want to, or We are not ready yet. Now God knew that from the beginning, and if God had done nothing more than spread the feast every seat at His table would have been vacant for all eternity! I have no hesitation in saying there is not one man or woman in this church to-night, but who made excuses time after time before you first came to Christ. You are just like the rest. You made excuses, so did I, and if God had done nothing more than just spread the feast every chair would have been vacant, therefore what do you read in that parable in Luke 14? Because the feast was not furnished with guests God sent forth His "servants." Oh, put your glasses on. It does not say "servants," it says God sent forth His "servant" and told Him to "compel" hem to come in that His feast might be furnished with guests. And there is not a man or a woman in this church to-night or in any other church that would ever sit down at the marriage-supper of the Lamb unless you had been compelled to come in, and compelled by God.

Well, you say, what do you mean by "compelled?" I mean this, that God had to overcome the resistance of your will, God had to overcome the reluctance of your heart, God had to overcome your loving of pleasure more than loving of God, your love of the things of this world more than Christ. I mean that God had to put forth His power and draw you, and if any of you know anything of the Greek or have a Strong's Concordance, look up that Greek verb for 'draw' in John 6, verse 44, "No man can come to me, except the Father which hath sent me draw him." It means 'use violence.' It mean to drag by force. There is not a Greek scholar on earth that can challenge that statement—I mean and back it up with proof. It is the same Greek word that is used in John 21 when they drew the net to the land full of fishes. They had to **pull** with all their might for it was full of fishes. They had to **drag** it. Yes, my friend, and **that** is how you were brought to Christ. You may not have been conscious of it, you may not have known inside yourself what was taking place, but every last one of us was a rebel against God, fighting against Christ, resisting His Holy Spirit, and God had to put forth almighty power and overcome that resistance and bring us to our knees, and if any of you object to that strong language, then I am here to tell you, you do not believe in the teaching of this Book on the absolute **depravity** of man.

Man is lost, and man is dead in trespasses and sins by nature. Listen, it is not simply that man is sick and needs a little medicine: it is not simply that man is ignorant and needs a little teaching: it is not simply that man is weak and needs a little help: man is **dead**, dead in trespasses and sins, and only almighty power from heaven can ever resurrect him and bring him from death unto life. **That** is the gospel I believe in and I do not preach the gospel because I believe the sinner has power in himself to respond to it. Well, you say, then what is the use of preaching the gospel if men are dead? What is the use of preaching it? I will tell you. Listen! Here was a man with a withered hand, paralysed, and Christ says, "Stretch forth thine hand." It was the one thing that he **could not** do! Christ told him to do a thing that was impossible in himself. Well then you say why did Christ tell him to stretch forth his hand? Because Divine power went with the very word that commanded him to do it! Divine power **enabled** him to. The man could not do it of himself. If you think that he could you are ready for the lunatic asylum, I do not care who you are. Any man or woman here who thinks that that man was able to stretch forth his paralysed arm by an effort of his own will is ready for the lunatic asylum! How can paralysis move?

Well, I will give you something stronger than that. You need something strong to-day, you need something more than skim-milk, you need strong meat if ever you are going to be built up and grow and become strong in the Lord and the power of His might. Here is a man who is dead and buried and his body has already begun to corrupt so that it stank. There he was in the grave and someone came to that graveside and said, Lazarus, come forth. And if that someone had been anyone less than God Himself manifest in flesh, he might have stood there till now calling, Come forth. What on earth was the use of telling a dead man to come forth? None at all, unless the One Who spoke that word had the power **to make that word good.**

Now then my friends, I preach the gospel to sinners, not because I believe the sinner has any power at all in himself to **respond** to it: I do not believe that any sinner has any capacity in himself whatever. But Christ said, "the words that I speak unto you, **they are** spirit and they are life," and by God's grace I go forth preaching this Word because **it** is a word of power, a word of spirit, a word of life. The power is not in the sinner, it is in the Word when God the Holy Spirit is pleased to use it. And, my friends, I say it in all reverence: if God told me in this Book to go out and preach to the **trees**, I would go! Yes sir. God once told one of His servants to go and preach to **bones** and he went. I wonder if **you** would have gone! Yes, that has a local application as well as a future interpretation prophetically.

Now the question arises again, why are we to preach the gospel to every creature?—if God has only elected a certain number to be saved? The first reason is, because God **commands** us to do so. Well, but, you say, it does not seem **reasonable** to me. That has got nothing to do with it; your business is to **obey** God and **not** to argue with Him. God commands us to preach the gospel to every creature, and it means what it says—**every** creature—and it is a solemn thing. Every Christian in this room to-night has yet **to answer to Christ** why he has not done everything in his power to send that gospel to every creature! Yes, I believe in missions—probably stronger than most of you do, and if I preached to you on missions perhaps I would hit you harder than you have been hit yet. The great majority of God's people who profess to believe in **missions**, are just playing at them. I make so bold as to say of our evangelical denominations to-day that we are just **playing** at missions and that is all. Why my friends, there is almost half of the human race—think of it—in this 20th century—travel so easy and cheap, Bibles printed in almost every language under heaven, and as we sit here to-night there is almost half of the human race that never yet heard of Christ, and we have got to answer to Christ for that yet! **You** have and **I** have. Oh, yes, I believe in man's responsibility. I do not believe in man's "freedom" but I **do** in man's responsibility, and I believe in the Christian's responsibility in a double way, and everyone of us here to-night has yet got to face Christ and look into those eyes as a flame of fire, and He is going to say to us, I entrusted to **you** My gospel. It was committed as a "trust" to you. (See 1 Thess. 2:4). It is required of stewards that a man be found **faithful.**

Oh, my friends, we are playing at things. We have not begun to take religion seriously, any of us. We profess to believe in the pre-millennial coming of Christ, and we profess to believe that the one reason why Christ has not come back yet is because His Church, His Body, is not yet complete. We believe that when His body is complete He **will** come back. And my friends, His "body" never, never, will be complete until the last of His elect people will be called out, and His elect people are called out **under the preaching of the gospel** by the power of the Holy Spirit, and if you are really anxious for Christ to come back soon, then you had better be more wide awake to your responsibility in connection with taking or sending the gospel to the heathen!

Christ's word, and it is Christ's word to us, is "Go ye into all the world and preach the gospel." He does not say **"Send** ye." He says **"Go** ye." He does not say "Pay for someone else to go, He says "Go **ye,"** and **you** have to answer to Christ yet because you **have not** gone! Well, you say, do you mean by that that everyone of us here to-night ought to go out to the mission field? I have not said that. I am not any man's judge. Many of you here to-night have a good reason which will satisfy Christ why you have not gone. He gave you work to do here. He put you in a position here. He has given you responsibilities to discharge here, but every Christian who **is** free to go, and **does not** go, has got to answer to Christ for it yet.

"Go ye into all the world." Well then you say, **Where am** I to go to? Oh, that is very easy. You say, easy? Yes, I mean it: it is **very** easy. There is nothing easier in the world than to know **where** you ought to begin missionary work. You have it in the first chapter of Acts and the 8th verse: "Ye shall receive power after that the Holy Ghost is come upon you: and ye shall be witnesses unto Me both in Jerusalem (that is the city in which they were) and in all Judaea (that is the State in which their city was), and in Samaria (that is the adjoining State), and unto the uttermost part of the earth." If you want to begin missionary work, you have to begin it in your home-town, and my friends if you are not interested in the salvation of the Chinese in Sydney, then you are not really interested in the salvation of the Chinese in China, and you are only fooling yourselves if you **think** you are! Oh, I am calling a spade a spade to-night. If you are anxious about the souls of the Chinese in China, then you will be equally anxious about the souls of the Chinese here in Sydney, and I wonder how many in this building to-night have ever made any serious effort to reach the Chinese in Sydney with the gospel! I wonder? I wonder how many here to-night have been round to the Bible House in Sydney and have said to the Manager there, Do you have any New Testaments in the Chinese language, or do you have any Gospels of John in the Chinese language? How much are they per hundred? or per dozen? And I wonder how many of you have bought a thousand or a hundred, and then have gone round to the houses in the Chinese quarter and have said, My friend, this is a little gift that will do your soul good if you will read it.

Ah, my friends, we are **playing** at missions, it is just a farce, that is all! Everyone here to-night has got to answer to God, to Christ at the Judgment-seat. "Go ye" is the first command. Go where? Those around me first. Go what with? The gospel! Well, you say, **Why** should I go? Because God has **commanded** you to! Well, you say, what is the use of doing it if He has just elected certain ones? Because that gospel is the means that God uses to **call out** His own elect, **that** is why! You do not know, and I, do not know, and nobody here on earth knows, **who are** God's elect and who are not. They are scattered over the world, and therefore we are to preach the gospel to every creature, that it may reach the ones that God has marked out among those creatures.

Now my next point is, Is God's election just? There are those who say that it is **unjust** for God to single out one and to pass by another. Now listen, **salvation is not a matter of justice.** What is

Justice? Justice, strict justice, is that every man shall receive his just due. Strict justice is simply each man getting what he deserves. Men and women, do you want God to give you what you deserve? Now be honest with yourself. Dare you look up into the face of heaven to-night and say, God, I want you to give me exactly what I deserve. Do you? Dare you say that? No, you dare not say that? No, you dare not. If I had received what I deserved I would be in the flames of hell right now. I won't speak for you. I know that it is true of myself. If God were to give me what I deserved, even since I became a Christian, if God dealt with me to-night on the ground of justice, because of my life this last month, I would be in hell right now. O, thank God we can say in the language of Psalm 103, "He hath not dealt with us after our sins nor rewarded us according to our iniquities." My friends, salvation is not a matter of justice. Salvation is not a wage that we earn. Salvation is not a prize that we win. Salvation is not a crown that we merit. Salvation is God's **free gift**. Then if it is God's "gift" God gives it **to whom HE pleases**. That is His business. No man has any claim on Him: every man forfeited that claim when he became a sinner: and what God does to-day is in grace and in grace only.

Now my last word is this. You say that it is unjust of God to chose one and to pass by another. Listen, it is not. It is not unjust, because God never yet refused salvation to any man who really asked Him for salvaion, and asked from his heart. God never yet turned away one single sinner that sought Him in true penitence. Oh, if there is a sinner here to-night, prove it for yourself. If there is a sinner here to-night, **test it out for yourself**. Christ has said, "Come unto Me all ye that labor and are heavy laden, and I will give you rest," and if you will **come to Him** there is rest for you! Try Him right now and see! Put Him to the proof right now. Well but, you say, that contradicts what you have been saying all night. No, it doesn't, for no sinner will come to Him unless he is drawn by God **to come**. It is his responsibility to come and he will be damned if he does not come. And listen, get this plainly, the sinner will be damned, not because God created him for that purpose, he will be damned because of his own sins. He will receive the just reward of his iniquities, but nevertheless it is the responsiblity of the sinner to come, and if he **will** come there is salvation for him.

ARTHUR W. PINK.

---

## "ACCEPTED IN THE BELOVED."

"**According to the good pleasure of His will, to the praise of the glory of His grace, wherein He hath made us accepted in the beloved**" (Eph. 1:5-6).

It is a great comfort to know that our standing in Christ, and acceptance in Him, are not according to the measure of our spiritual experience, but "according to the good pleasure of His will, to the praise of the glory of His grace, wherein He hath made us accepted in the Beloved." "Hath made us"—it is of the Father's own doing, and it is already done, and so done, that no want of experience, or weakness of faith, or failure of testimony, or slowness of progress, or want of realisation, or consciousness of evil within, can possibly alter it in the least.

This is an unchangeable acceptance. We stand in Christ; and as He stands. This, then, is a sure foundation for our hope, and a sure foundation for our joy, notwithstanding the fact that everything of our own is marred and worthless. We rejoice in the Lord Jesus always, as our ground of acceptance, though often sorrowful because of increasing consciousness of our ill-desert. We rejoice also in the love and grace of our Father who has, because of that love and grace, "made us accepted in the Beloved."

—Things to Come, 1900.

## SORROWFUL YET ALWAYS REJOICING.

"Sorrowful yet always rejoicing" (2 Cor. 6:10).

"Sorrowful," because there is so much power for evil in the world. "Sorrowful," because error increases, and spiritual truth is less and less relished. "Sorrowful," because of so little fellowship among true believers. "Sorrowful," because Christ is so little known, so little loved, so little honoured. And sorrowful, Oh! how sorrowful, because of a heart prone to wander, because of an evil nature within, that so constantly wars against the new and better.

"Yet always rejoicing," for the Lord Jesus giveth grace, and giveth victory, and in Him the believer is evermore complete and changelessly perfect before God. "Alway rejoicing," because the Lord Jesus liveth and reigneth, and His purposes are sure of accomplishment. "Alway rejoicing," because greater is He that is with His people, than all they that can be against them. "Alway rejoicing," because the Lord's love for His people is ever the same, and His presence ever abides with them. "Alway rejoicing," because the Lord is coming "to be glorified in His saints, and to be admired in all them that believe." "Alway rejoicing" for the Lord is near, and full redemption draweth nigh. "Alway rejoicing" because of a glorious future in a bright and happy home with Jesus. Let this "alway rejoicing" be ours; for 'tis the earnest of the joys of heaven, the forecaste of that home experience, in which the "sorrowful" no more doth mingle, for there it is everlasting joy, and sorrow and sighing have forever fled away.

—Things to Come, 1900.

"The more excellent a mere natural man is, the less of evil is he conscious of possessing. Not so the child of God; for the more spiritually-minded he becomes, the more conscious he is of his imperfections, and of his utter inability of himself for anything good before God. This is the only feature in the child of God which has no natural imitation. There may be a natural faith in Christ, a natural love for Christ, a natural following of Christ, and even a natural conviction of sin, all without salvation; but never is there a continued natural conviction of utter inability for anything good before God. This is entirely and always the result of a spiritual nature previously given. The more a mere natural man has of natural religious regard for the Lord Jesus, the more satisfied he is with himself, whereas the more there is of spiritual regard for the Lord Jesus, the more is there of increased dissatisfaction with self. The natural man has no new spiritual nature, with its spiritual principles, whereby to judge the natural, and therefore the natural judging the natural, he is right well pleased. The child of God, however, possesses a new spiritual nature whereby, with its spiritual principles, he can judge the natural that is within him. He only is able to have a right understanding of the natural and the more healthy the manifestation of the spiritual nature, the more deep and vivid is the consciousness of the evil of the mere natural.

—Things to Come, 1899.

*(Continued from page 73.)*

Here then are the first birth-marks of the children of God, and he who has never come to be poor in spirit, and has never known what it is to really mourn for sin, though he belong to a church and be a office-bearer in it, has neither entered nor seen the kingdom of God. How thankful the Christian reader ought to be that the great God condescends to dwell in the humble and contrite heart! Where can we find anything in all the Old Testament more precious than that?—that He, in whose sight the heavens are not clean, who cannot find in any temple that man ever builded for Him, however magnificent, a proper dwelling-place, has said Isa. 66:2 and Isa. 57:15!

"Blessed are they that mourn." Though the primary reference be to that initial mourning, usually termed "conviction of sin," it is by no means to be limited to this. Mourning is ever a characteristic of the normal Christian state. There is much that the believer has to mourn over—the plague of his own heart makes him cry, "O wretched man that I am;" the unbelief which "doth so easily beset us" and sins which we commit that are more in number than the hairs of our head, are a continual grief; the barrenness and unprofitableness of our lives make us sigh and cry; our propensity to wander from Christ, our lack of communion with Him, the shallowness of our love for Him, cause us to hang our harps upon the willows.. But this is not all. The hypocritical religion prevailing on every hand, having a form of godliness but denying the power thereof; the awful dishonour done to the truth of God by the false doctrines taught in countless pulpits; the divisions among the Lord's people, the strife between brethren, occasion continual sorrow of heart. The awful wickedness in the world, men despising Christ, the untold sufferings around, make us groan within ourselves. The closer the Christian lives to God, the more will he mourn over all that dishonours Him. With the Psalmist he will say: 119:53; with Jeremiah, 13:17; 14:17; with Ezekiel 9:4.

"They shall be comforted." This refers first of all to the removal of the conscience guilt which burdens the conscience. It finds its fulfilment in the Spirit's application of the Gospel of God's grace to the one whom He has convicted of his dire need of a Saviour. It issues in a sense of free and full forgiveness through the merits of the atoning blood of Christ. This Divine comfort is the peace of God which passeth all understanding filling the heart of the one who is now assured that he is "accepted in the Beloved." God wounds before healing, abases before He exalts. First there is a revelation of His justice and holiness, then the making known of His mercy and grace.

"They shall be comforted" also receives a constant fulfilment in the experience of the Christian. Though he mourns his excuseless failures and confesses them to God, yet he is comforted by the assurance that the blood of Jesus Christ His Son cleanses him from all sin. Though he groans over the dishonour done to God on every side, yet is he comforted by the knowledge that the day is rapidly approaching when Satan shall be removed from these scenes and when the Lord Jesus shall sit upon the throne of His glory and rule in righteousness and peace Though the chastening hand of the Lord is often laid upon him and though "no chastening for the present seemeth to be joyous, but grievous," nevertheless, he is consoled by the realisation that this is all working out for him "a far more exceeding and eternal weight of glory." Like the Apostle, the believer who is in communion with his Lord can say, "As sorrowful yet always rejoicing." He may often be called upon to drink of the bitter waters of Marah, but God has planted near by a tree to sweeten them. Yes "mourning" Christians are comforted even now by the Divine Comforter, by the ministrations of His servants, by encouraging words from fellow Christians, and when these are not to hand by the precious promises of the Word being brought home in power to his memory and heart.

"They shall be comforted." The best wine is reserved for the last. Sorrow may endure for a night, but joy cometh in the morning. During the long night of His absence, the saints of God have been called to fellowship with Him who was the Man of Sorrows. But, blessed by God, it is written, "If we suffer with Him we shall also be glorified together." What comfort and joy will be ours when shall dawn the morning without clouds! Then shall "sorrow and sighing flee away" Isa. 35:10). Then shall be fulfilled the saying— Rev. 21:3-4.

ARTHUR W. PINK.

# STUDIES IN THE SCRIPTURES

"Search the Scriptures" John 5:39.

Copyright in all English-speaking Countries.

Arthur W. Pink, Publisher and Editor,
5 Norton Street, Ashfield, N.S.W., Australia.

Price: 10 cents per copy; $1.00 or 5/- per year.

---

"Blessed are the meek: for they shall inherit the earth" (Matt. 5:5).

There has been considerable difference of opinion as to the precise significance of the word "meek." Some regard its meaning as patience, a spirit of resignation; some as unselfishness, a spirit of self-abnegation; others as gentleness, a spirit of non-retaliation, bearing quietly the afflictions of God and our fellow-men. Doubtless, there is a measure of truth in each of these definitions, yet it appears to the writer that they hardly go deep enough, and they fail to take note of the order of this third Beatitude. Personally, we would define meekness as humility. "Blessed are the meek"—the humble, the lowly. Let us see if other passages bear this out.

The first time the word occurs in Scripture is in Numbers 12:3. Here the Spirit of God has pointed a contrast from what is recorded in the previous verses. There we read of Miriam and Aaron speaking against Moses: "Hath the Lord indeed spoken only by Moses? Hath He not spoken also by us?" Such language betrays the pride and haughtiness of their hearts, their self-seeking and craving for honour. As the antithesis of this we read, "Now the man Moses was very meek." This must mean that he was actuated by a spirit the very reverse of his brother's and sister's.

Moses was humble, lowly and self-renouncing. Beautifully does this come out in Heb. 11:24, 26. Moses turned his back on worldly honours and earthly riches, deliberately choosing a life of a pilgrim rather than that of a courtier, the wilderness in preference to the palace. The humbleness of Moses is seen again when Jehovah first appeared unto him in Midian and commissioned him to lead His people out of Egypt: "Who am I," he said, "that I, should go unto Pharaoh, and that I should bring forth the children of Israel out of Egypt?" (Ex. 3:11). What lowliness do these words breathe! Yes, Moses was "very meek."

Other scriptures bear out and seem to necessitate the definition suggested above. "The meek will He guide in judgment: and the meek will He teach His way" (Psa. 25:9). What can this mean but that the humble and lowly-hearted are the ones whom God promises to counsel and instruct? "Behold thy King cometh unto thee, meek, and sitting upon an ass" (Matt. 21:5): Here is meekness or lowliness incarnate. "If a man be overtaken in a fault, ye which are spiritual, restore such an one in the spirit of meekness; considering thyself, lest thou also be tempted (Gal. 6:1). Is it not plain that this means a spirit of humility is required in him who would be used of God in restoring an erring brother? We are to learn of Christ who was "meek and lowly in heart," the latter explaining the former term: note they are linked together again in Eph. 4:2: "lowliness and meekness:" the order here being designedly reversed from Matt. 11:29 to show us that they are synonymous terms.

(*Continued on page 119*)

## IMPORTANT NOTICES

Set of twelve issues for 1922, unbound, $1.00 or 5/-. Bound $1.50 or 7/-.

Set of twelve issues for 1923, unbound, $1.00 or 5/-. Bound $1.50 or 7/-.

Set of twelve issues for 1924, unbound, $1.00 or 5/-. Bound $1.50 or 7/-.

Set of twelve issues for 1925, unbound, $1.00 or 5/-. Bound $1.50 or 7/-.

Note: We cannot break a set or now supply any single 1925 issues.

Subscription—price: $1.00 or 5/- per year to any address in the world.

Change of Address: Please notify me promptly of any change of address, and be certain to give both old and new address.

Non-subscribers receiving this Magazine regularly will understand their subscription has been entered by a friend.

Copies lost in the mail duplicated only if we are notified promptly.

## CONTENTS

| | |
|---|---|
| The Gospel of John (John 15:17-27) ... | 98 |
| Gleanings in Exodus ... ... ... | 105 |
| Election ... ... ... ... | 109 |
| In Regions Beyond ... ... ... | 116 |
| The Pleasure of God ... ... ... | 118 |

## THE GOSPEL OF JOHN

### 53. Christ Fortifying His Disciples: John 15:17,27.

The following is an Analysis of the closing section of John 15:—

1. Christians commanded to love one another v. 17.
2. Christians warned of the world's hatred v. 18.
3. Causes of the world's hatred vv. 19-21.
4. The greatness of the world's guilt vv. 22-24.
5. The fulfilment of God's Word v. 25.
6. The witness of the Spirit v. 26.
7. The witness of Christians v. 27.

The principal subject in the passage which is to be before us is the world's hostility against Christ and His people. Its hatred is mentiotned seven times—solemn witness to its awful entirety and inveteracy. The transition from the preceding section is quite natural and easy. The Lord had been speaking to and of "His own;" now He contemplates "the world." He had just declared that His disciples are His friends; now He turns to describe His and their enemies. He had set before the apostles the proofs of His love for them; now He warns them of the world's hatred. The connection between the last verse of the previous section and the opening one of our present portion is most significant. "These things I command you, that ye love one another." Various motives had been presented for them loving one another, chief among them being the example of His own wondrous love. Now an entirely new and different reason is advanced: Christians need to be united together by the bonds of brotherly affection because the world, their common enemy, hated them.

A loving heart would feign discover or induce love everywhere. To be ungratified in that desire and more than that, to be hated, is a hard and bitter lot, the bitterest ingredient in all affliction. Therefore does the Lord here faithfully prepare His disciples for such an experience, that they might not marvel at the world's hostility nor be stumbled by it—"Marvel not, My brethren, if the world hate you" (1 John 3:13). Graciously did the Saviour proceed to fortify His disciples against the storm of persecution which He knew full well would burst upon them shortly after His departure. Charged with such a mission as they were, proclaiming such a message, invested with miraculous powers of benevolence, the apostles might fondly imagine that the world would soon be won to Christ. But they must be prepared for disappointment. Therefore, did Christ arm them beforehand, that their spirits might not be overwhelmed by the bitter malice and opposition which they would surely encounter.

There is little or nothing in the Gospel records to intimate that the apostles had been subjected to persecution while their Master was with them. After the Seventy were sent forth we read that they "returned again with joy, saying, Lord, even the demons are subject unto us through Thy name" (Luke 10:17). When the Scribes and Pharisees were offended because the disciples transgressed the tradition of the elders, eating with unwashen hands, instead of assailing them directly, the complaint was laid before the Lord Jesus (Matt. 15:2). When the Saviour was arrested in the Garden, He said to the officers, "Let these (the apostles) go their way" (John 18:8). Even after His crucifixion, they were allowed to go, unmolested, back to their fishing (John 21:23). But after His return to the Father, they too would experience the world's malignity. Therefore did the Lord forewarn them of the treatment which they must expect and would certainly receive at the hands of the ungodly.

The warning which the Lord Jesus here gave the apostles is much needed by young believers to-day. The inexperienced Christian supposes that the hatred of the world against him is a reproach. He thinks that he is to blame for it. He imagines that if only he were kinder, more gentle, more humble, more Christlike, the enmity of unbelievers would be overcome. This is a great mistake. The truth is, the more Christlike we are, the more shall we be antagonised and shunned. The most conclusive proof of this is found in the treatment which our blessed Saviour received when He was in the world. He was "despised and rejected of men." If then the purest love which was ever manifested on earth, if goodness incarnate was hated by men in general, if the brighter His love shone, the fiercer was the enmity which it met with in response, then how can we expect to be admired and esteemed by the world? Surely none will entertain the horrible thought that any of us can surpass the prudence of the Son of God!

And how all of this rebukes the popularity which so many professing Christians, yea, and many of the profest servants of Christ now enjoy! Have we forgotten that severe rebuke, "Ye adulterers and adulteresses, know ye not that the friendship of the world is enmity with God? Whosoever therefore will be a friend of the world is the enemy of God" (James 4:4). Solemn indeed are the terms used here. Adulterers and adultereresses are they who seek and enjoy illicit love. In like manner, for a professing Christian—one who claims to love Christ—to seek His delight in the world, to company with the ungodly, is to be guilty of spiritual adultery. "Love not the world, neither the things that are in the world. If any man love the world, the love of the Father is not in him" (1 John 2:15). "Be not conformed to this world: but be ye transformed by the renewing of your mind" (Rom. 12:2).

"These things I command you, that ye love one another" (v. 17). There is something peculiarly searching and heart-rebuking in this. How humbling to find that Christ had to command us to love one another! How humbling to hear Him repeating this command, for He had already given this same commandment to His disciples in 13:34! And how humbling to find Him here repeating it again, for He had only just said, "This is My commandment, That ye love one another, as I have loved you" (v. 12)! Was it because He foreknew how little Christian love would be exercised among His people? Was it because He knew how much there is in each of us that is so unlovely? Was it because He foresaw that the Devil would stir up bitterness and strife among His followers, seeking to make them bite and devour one another? Whatever may or may not have been before Him, one thing cannot be denied—Christ has expressly commanded His people to love one another.

"These things I command you, that ye love one another." Not only does the insistent emphasis of our Lord upon this word indicate that here is something which every Christian needs to seriously take to heart, but the large place given to it in the Epistles adds strong confirmation. The following commandments of the Holy Spirit through the apostles are but repetitions and expansions of the precept now before us: "Be kindly affectioned one to another" (Rom. 12:10). "Forbearing one another in love" (Eph. 4:2). "Endeavouring to keep the unity of the Spirit in the bond of peace" (Eph. 4:3). "Be ye kind one to another, tender-hearted, forgiving one another" (Eph. 4:32). "If any man have a quarrel against any: even as Christ forgave you, so also do ye" (Col. 3:13). "See that ye love one another with a pure heart fervently" (1 Peter 1:22). Love the brotherhood" (1 Peter 2:17). "And above all things have fervent charity among yourselves" (1 Peter 4:8). "Finally, be ye all of one mind, having compassion one of another, love as brethren, be pitiful, be courteous" (1 Peter 3:8). Envy, malice, ill-feeling, evil-speaking among brethren are a sure proof of the lack of this brotherly love!

"If the world hate you, ye know that it hated Me before it hated you" (v. 18). Here the Lord introduces the subject of the world's enmity, and He begins by pointing out to His apostles that what they would suffer was only what He had suffered before them; they must not be surprised then at finding themselves in the midst of a hostile people. For their part they must be meek and gentle, living peaceably with all men so far as they would allow them to. They must do nothing maliciously to provoke or warrant the hatred of the world; but if they were faithful to the Lord, they must be prepared for the same evil treatment which He met with.

"Ye know that it hated Me before it hated you." The word "before" here refers not so much to time as it does to experience. Christ was assuring them that He trode the very same path which they would be called on to follow. He had preceded them in it: "When He putteth forth his own sheep He goeth before them" (John 10:4). How this should comfort us! It was Christ identifying the disciples with Himself. If we belong to the Lord Jesus that is sufficient to arouse the world's rancour. But it is blessed to know that it hates us because of Him, not because of ourselves! It is the repulsion of human nature for what is of God. And nowhere is the awful depravity of fallen man more evidenced than in his hatred of that which is pure, lovely, good, holy.

"If ye were of the world, the world would love his own; but because ye are not of the world, but I have chosen you out of the world, therefore the world hateth you" (v. 19). Here the Lord proceeds to state the various causes of the world's hatred. Two are given in this verse: first, His people are no longer "of the world;" second, Christ, had "chosen them out of the world." The two are really resolvable into one: it is because Christ has chosen us out of the world that we no more belong to it. We no longer share its spirit, are no more actuated by its aims, are not now governed by its principles. Note the Lord's emphatic emphasis here: five times in this one verse does the Lord mention "the world"! Do you, He seems to ask, desire the smiles of men, are you anxious to stand high in their favour? That would be tragic indeed; that would prove you also belonged to the world. In 8:23, Christ had declared of Himself, "Ye are from beneath; I am from above; ye are of this world; I am not of this world." Now, for the first time, He predicates the same thing of His disciples. It is striking to note that this was not until after 14:31 and Christ had (figuratively) taken His place—identifying the disciples with Himself in that place—on **resurrection** ground. It is only as united to a risen Christ that we are taken (positionally) **out of** "the world."

"I have chosen you out of the world, therefore the world hateth you." It is remarkable that the first reason Christ here gives as to **why** the world hates believers, is because of their **election.** "The world cannot endure the thought of God's sovereignty and electing love" (Mr. F. W. Grant). The world is enraged at the very idea of Christians being the singled-out favourites of God. Strikingly was this demonstrated almost at the beginning of our Lord's public ministry. After announcing that the prophecy of Isa. 61:1, 2 found its fulfilment in His mission, He went on to say how that while the heaven was shut up for three years and a half, during the subsequent famine, though there were many widows in Israel, God, in His sovereign grace, sent Elijah unto **none** but the widow of Zarephath; and though there were **many** lepers in Israel in the time of Elisha, **none of them** were cleansed, though God in His sovereign mercy healed Naaman, the Syrian. The response to our Lord's words was very shocking. "And all they in the synagogue, when they heard **these things,** were filled with wrath, and rose up and thrust Him out of the city, and led Him unto the brow of the hill whereon their city was built, that they might cast Him down headlong" (Luke 4:28, 29).

It is just the same to-day. Nothing so stirs up the enmity of the carnal mind as to hear of God's absolute sovereignty: choosing some, passing by others. Then how much **worldliness** there must now be in many professing Christians! It should be noted in the example cited above that it was the **religious world** which was so enraged against Christ: it was the synagogue-worshippers that sought to murder the Saviour, because He pressed upon them the fact that God had compassion on whom He pleases. Nor have things changed for the better. Let any servant of God to-day expound the truths of Divine election and foreordination, and he will be assailed the most fiercely by those who claim to be the people of God. So, too, with believers in general. Let their lives attest their calling, let their walk make it manifest that they **are not** "of the world" because "chosen out of it" and the bitter enmity of the ungodly will indeed be excited. But let us not be cast down at this, rather let us see in the hostility of unbelievers a precious evidence that we are one with Him whom the world cast out.

"Therefore the world hateth you." It will not hate mere professors. The man who is conformed to this world, who takes part in its politics, who shares its pleasures, who acts according to its principles, even though he bears the name of Christ, will not be ostracised or persecuted. The woman who is conformed to this world, who follows its fashions, who enjoys its society, who works for its reformation, will not be shunned by it. The world loves its own. But those who walk in separation from the world (and they are few in number), those who follow a rejected Christ, will know something of what it means to enter into "the fellowship of His sufferings" (Phil. 3:10). God has said, "Yea, and all that will live godly in Christ Jesus shall suffer persecution" (2 Timothy 3:12). But let such recall and be cheered by those words of our Saviour, "Blessed are they which are persecuted for righteousness' sake: for theirs is the kingdom of heaven. Blessed are ye, when men shall revile you, and persecute you and shall say all manner of evil against you falsely, for My sake. Rejoice, and be exceedingly glad, for great is your reward in heaven: for so persecuted they the prophets which were before you" (Matt. 5:10, 12).

"Remember the word that I said unto you, the servant is not greater than his Lord" (v. 20). How touching is this! Christ would have us forget no words spoken by Him! He here reminds the apostles of what He had said to them a little previously, though in another connection—showing how full His utterances are, designed for various applications. His purpose here is to press upon us that it is a mark of genuine discipleship if we share the experiences of our Master, encountering the hatred of the world. "If they have persecuted Me, they will also persecute you; if they have kept My sayings, they will keep yours also" (v. 20). The "if" looks back to the same word at the beginning of vv. 18 and 19. If you are My followers, My friends, then must you have fellowship in My sufferings. They have persecuted the Lord, and just so far as they live and act accordingly, they will also persecute His servants. The world may boast of its liberal principles; it may for a time tolerate a lukewarm Christianity; but, let the people of God be out and out for Him, and the secret hatred of the heart will soon manifest itself. When the "I have chosen you out of the world" becomes a practical reality, then the world's rage and ban will be displayed. But after all, what is the world's hatred in comparison with Christ's love! And yet, as has been said, "If there is anything that true Christians seem incessantly forgetting, and seem to need incessantly reminding of, it is the real feeling of unconverted people towards them, and the treatment they must expect to meet with" (Bishop Ryle).

"If they have persecuted Me, they will also persecute you; if they have kept My saying, they will keep yours also." There seems to be a note of irony here. The Lord had spoken nought, but the unadulterated truth of God, yet the world had not kept His sayings. And why? Because His sayings condemned them. "For every one that doeth evil hateth the light, neither cometh to the light, lest his deeds should be reproved" (7:20). "The world cannot hate you (His unbelieving brethren); but Me it hateth, because I testify of it, that the works therefore are evil" (7:7). And just so far as we proclaim the truth of God, so will men (in general) reject our message! "They are of the world: therefore speak they of the world, and the world heareth them. We are of God: he that knoweth God heareth us; he that is not of God heareth not us" (1 John 4:5, 6).

"But all these things will they do unto you for My name's sake, because they know not Him that sent Me" (v. 21). Here the Lord gives the deepest reason why His disciples would be hated by the world. "For My name's sake" means, of course, on account of it. It was because they would represent Him, acting as His ambassadors that men would persecute them. Christ would grant His people the high privilege of sharing His sufferings: "If ye be reproached for the name of Christ, happy are ye; for the spirit of glory and of God resteth upon you" (1 Peter 4:14). It is the confession of Christ's name which arouses the rancour of depraved hearts. May we, like Moses, "esteem the reproach of Christ greater riches than the treasures of Egypt"—the world (Heb. 11:26)). "Because they know not Him that sent Me": for from this ignorance affording an excuse, it was inexcusable, because wilful.

"If He had not come and spoken unto them, they had not had sin: but now they have no cloke for their sin" (v. 22). Here is an example of where the words of Scripture cannot be taken in their absolute sense. When our Lord declared of the Jews that if He had not become incarnate and spoken unto them "they had not had sin," He does not mean that they would have been without sin in every sense. The chief design of the first three chapters of Romans is to establish the fact that all the world, Jew and Gentile alike, were "guilty before God." Christ was speaking in a comparative sense. Compared with their immeasurable guilt of rejecting the Lord of glory, their personal sins were as nothing. Similar instances where things are represented absolutely, though intended in a comparative sense, are found frequently in Scripture. For example: "All nations before Him are as nothing; and they are counted to Him less than nothing" (Isa. 40:17). "So then neither is he that planteth any thing, neither he that watereth; but God that giveth the increase" (1 Cor. 3:7).

There had been sin all along, and the governmental dealings of God with men clearly evidenced that He took account of it. But evil as man had shown himself all through his history, the coming of Christ to the earth brought sin to such a head, that all that had gone before was relatively speaking, a trifling thing when compared with the monstrous evil that was done against incarnate Love. It is a question of the standard of measurement. There are a number of passages which clearly teach that there will be degrees of punishment meted out to those who are lost: Matt. 11:22; Heb. 10:28, 29, etc. The degree of punishment will be determined by the heinousness of the sins committed, and that will be decided by the degree of light sinned against. When One who was more than man came into the world, the Divine dignity of His person, the love and light which He manifested, brought in a new standard of measurement. Christ was here speaking according to the glory of His person. It will be more tolerable for Sodom and Gomorroah in the Day of Judgment than for Capernaum. And why? Because the latter turned its back upon the King of kings and Lord of Lords.

The principle here enunciated by the Saviour is very solemn in its application, and one which we all do well to take to heart Spiritual privileges carry with them heavy responsibilities: "For unto whomsoever much is given, of him shall be much required." (Luke 12:48)! To dwell in a land of open Bibles and preached Gospel, places men on a very different footing before God than the heathen who have never heard of Christ. Judgment will be according to the light enjoyed! The mere fact that men knew the way of truth, and walked not therein, will only increase their condemnation. To receive Divine instruction and not improve it is, as Christ here plainly declares, to leave men without any cloke (or "excuse") for their sin.

"He that hateth Me hateth My Father also" (v. 23). The Lord here furnished proof that the sin of despising Him involved guilt of unparalled magnitude. Christ's words were not only His own words, but the Father's also. He and the Father were one. The idea of some that they can acceptably worship the Father while rejecting His Son is a deceit of man's depraved heart and a lie of the Devil. "The Jews professed that they loved God, and that on the ground of that love they hated Christ; the God however, whom they loved was not the true God, but a phantom which they named God. The fact that they rejected Christ, in spite of all His words of spirit and truth, showed them to be the enemies of the Father" (Hengstenberg).

"He that hateth Me hateth My Father also." Very solemn is this. In the previous verses the Lord had shown that the principal reason why the world would hate His disciples was because of their oneness with Himself. Now He shows that the reason why the world hated Him was because of His oneness with the Father. Christ revealed the Father. He was the express image of His person. In Him dwelt all the fullness of the Godhead bodily. He that saw Him, saw the Father also. His doctrine was the truth of God. His life revealed the perfections of God. His laws expressed the will of God. To dislike Him, then, was proof positive that they hated God. It is a most fearful fact, but one most clearly revealed in Scripture, that men in their natural state are "haters of God" (Rom. 1:30); their minds being "enmity against God" (Rom. 8:7). It is this hatred of God which causes people to reject Christ and dislike Christians. Conversely their rejection of Christ demonstrates their hatred of God. Christ is the test of the state of every human heart! "What think ye of Christ?" honestly answered, reveals whether we are His friends or His enemies. There is no God in the universe except the God and Father of our Lord Jesus Christ, and if men do not believe in, love, worship and serve the Son, they hate the Father. Just as faith begets love, so unbelief begets hatred.

"If I had not done among them the works which none other man did, they had not had sin: but now have they both seen and hated both Me and My Father" (v. 24). How decidedly does the Lord Jesus place Himself above all the other messengers of God that had preceded Him! The words "they had not had sin" have the same force here as in v. 22. If Israel had not enjoyed such **privileges, they had not contracted such guilt.** If they had not heard Him who spake as never man spake, and if they had not witnessed works such as never men performed, their criminality in the sight of God would have been so much less that, in comparison with their culpability now that they had heard and seen and believed not, had been as nothing. It is to be noted that Christ first mentioned what He had **spoken** unto them (v. 22), and they referred to the works which He had **done** among them.

"If I had not done among them the works which none other man did, they had not had sin, but now have they both seen and hated both Me and My Father" "The presence and testimony of the Son of God had the gravest possible results. It was not only an infinite blessing in itself and for God's glory, but it left men, and Israel especially, reprobate. Law had proved man's weakness and sin, as it put under the curse all who took their stand on the legal principle. There was none righteous, none that sought after God, none that did good, no, not one. The heathen were manifestly wicked, the Jews proved so by the incontestable sentence of the law. Thus every mouth was stopped, and all the world obnoxious to God's judgment. But the presence of Christ brought out, not merely failure to meet obligations as under law, but **hatred of Divine goodness** come down to men in perfect grace.... Sin before or otherwise was swallowed up in the surpassing sin of rejecting the Son of God come in love and speaking not merely as man never spoke, but as God had never spoken."

"But this cometh to pass, that the word might be fulfilled that is written in their law. They hated Me without a cause" (v. 25). Terrible indictment of Israel was this. "There was nothing in Christ to provoke hatred in any but morally disordered, depraved minds. Nothing in His character, it was faultless; nothing in His doctrines, they were all true; nothing in His laws, they were holy, just and good. He never had done the world any harm: He had spent His life in bestowing favors on men. Why, then, did they hate Him, why did they persecute Him, why did they put Him to death? They hated Him, because they hated His Father" (Dr. John Brown).

"But this cometh to pass, that the word might be fulfilled that is written in their law, They hated Me without a cause." Here the Lord was tracing the world's enmity back to its true source. He had given no cause for it; it must therefore, be attributed to their desperately-wicked hearts. The Lord was further fortifying His disciples. They must not be surprised nor offended at the bitterness and malice of the ungodly. **His** conduct had been mild and benevolent; yet they hated Him. Let us see to it that **we** give men no "cause" to hate us. Let their enmity against us be provoked only by fellowship with Christ: "It is enough for the disciples that he be as his Master, and the servant as his Lord. If they have called the Master of the house Beelzebub, how much more shall they call them of His household" (Matt. 10:25).

"But this cometh to pass, that the word might be fulfilled that is written in their law, They hated Me without a cause." No doubt Christ was also anticipating an objection here. How is such hatred possible? Why does God permit it? The Lord answers by saying, This hatred of the world is but the fulfillment of God's Word, and therefore of His inscrutable counsels. So little do the wicked affect by their malice, they only fulfil the Scriptures—while they draw down upon themselves the judgments which other passages therein announce. In quoting here from **"their Law,"** Christ showed that the written Word testified **against** Israel!

"But when the Comforter is come, whom I will send unto you from the Father, even the Spirit of truth, which proceedeth from the Father, He shall testify of Me" (v. 26). The connection here is apparent. The Lord had been warning the disciples of the opposition they would meet with from that kingdom over which Satan is "the Prince.' But that only distresses the more their already saddened hearts, therefore did their tender Master revert again to His original promise—the one promise repeated most frequently in this Paschal Discourse—that the Divine Comforter would come to their relief. It was presupposed in vv. 20, 21 that His disciples would be hated, like Himself, on account of their word. He predicted their fate to them as His witnesses. It was obvious that they should think, But how shall we poor, weak men persist in our testimony, yea, even bear it in the face of such predicted hatred? He therefore confirms to them their vocation, and predicts to them with equal clearness that they shall bear Him testimony in the future (v. 27). "Not of themselves, however, and in their own human persons: the Paraclete (the Comforter) will conduct the cause. He then, however, returns to the former again, and consoles them by the emphatic assurance that they might not stumble at this: I have now (more clearly than ever before) foretold to you both the coming of the Spirit as a Witness against the hatred of the world, and at the same time the continuance of that hatred in spite of His testimony" (Sier).

"But when the Comforter is come, whom I will send unto you from the Father, even the Spirit of truth, which proceedeth from the Father, He shall testify of Me." That the Spirit is here said to "proceed from the Father" (a statement which has split the Greek from the Roman "Church," into whose differences we shall not here enter) is **supplementary** to what the Lord had said in 14: 26. There the Comforter was to be sent in Christ's name: here He proceeds from the Father. The two statements placed side by side, bring out the Unity of the Godhead. This additional word also shows that the Spirit was not exclusively subordinate to Christ, as some have argued from 14: 26. "He shall testify of Me" amplifies His former word in 14: 16 **"another** Comforter." The Spirit would further Christ's interests, and be unto the disciples (only in another way) all that Christ would have been unto them had He remained on earth.

"But when the Comforter is come, whom I will send unto you from the Father, even the Spirit of truth, which proceedeth from the Father, He shall testify of Me." "Here the Comforter is viewed as **sent** by the ascended Christ from the Father, and consequently as witness of His **heavenly** glory. This is an advance on what we saw in the previous chapter where Christ **asks** and the Father gives the Paraclete to be with them forever, sending Him in His Son's name. Here the Son Himself **sends**, though of course, from the Father. The Spirit of truth is thus the suited Witness of Christ as He is above" (The Bible Treasury). "Whom I will send" brings out the glory of the exalted Saviour in a most striking way.

"And ye also shall bear witness, because ye have been with Me from the beginning" (v. 27). Here the Lord explains to the disciples **how** the Spirit would testify and of **what** it would consist. He would not make any corporeal manifestation of Himself as had the Son, but He would bear witness in and through the disciples. He would testify that which they had already seen in Him, and that which they had already heard from Him—nothing besides, essentially different or new. Thus it will be seen that the two "testimonies" of vv. 26 and 27 are not separate and independent, but natural and harmonious.

"And ye also shall bear witness." Marvellous grace was this. Neither hostility nor hatred had quenched the compassion of Christ. The world might cast Him out, yet still would His mercy linger over it. Before **Judgment** ultimately descended on the world, a further witness to **Himself** should be given it, a witness which has already continued for over eighteen centuries! May Divine power enable every real Christian to witness faithfully and constantly for our absent Lord. May we by lip and life bear testimony, in season and out of season, to His excellency, and to Him as our sufficiency.

The following questions are to aid the student on the opening portion of John 16:—

1. What is the central theme of vv. 1-11?
2. What is the meaning of v. 1?
3. What does the last clause of v. 2 go to prove?
4. What blessings would "remembrance" bring the apostles v. 4?
5. Why did the apostles ask "whither goest thou?" v. 5?
6. Why "expedient" for Christ to go v. 7?
7. In what way does the Spirit "reprove the world?" v. 8.

ARTHUR W. PINK.

## GLEANINGS IN EXODUS
### 29. The Ten Commandments: Ex. 20.

Much confusion prevails to-day among those who speak of "The law." This is a term which needs to be carefully defined. In the New Testament there are three expressions used which require to be definitely distinguished. First, there is "The law of God" (Rom. 7:22, 25, etc.). Second, there is "The law of Moses" (John 7:2-, Acts 13:39, 15:5, etc.). Third, there is "the law of Christ" (Gal. 6:2). Now these three expressions are by no means synonymous, and it is not until we learn to distinguish between them, that we can hope to arrive at any clear understanding on the subject of "The law."

The "law of God" expresses the mind of the Creator, and is binding upon all rational creatures. It is God's unchanging moral standard for regulating the conduct of all men. In some places the "law of God" may refer to the whole revealed will of God, but usually it has reference to the Ten Commandments, and it is in this restricted sense we shall here use the term. The Law was impressed on man's moral nature from the beginning, and though now fallen, he still shows the work of it written on his heart. This Law has never been repealed, and, in the very nature of things, cannot be. For God to abrogate the moral law would be to plunge the whole universe into anarchy. Obedience to the law of God is man's first duty. This is why the first complaint that Jehovah made against Israel after they left Egypt was "How long refuse ye to keep My commandments and My laws?" (Ex. 16:2, 27). That is why the first statutes which God gave to Israel after their redemption were the Ten Commandments, i.e., the moral law. That is why in the first discourse of Christ recorded in the New Testament, He declared, "Think not that I am come to destroy the Law, of the Prophets: I am not come to destroy, but to fulfil" (Matt. 5:17), and then proceeded to expound and enforce the moral law. And that is why in the first of the Epistles, the Holy Spirit has taught us at length the relation of the Law to sinners and saints, in connection with salvation and the subsequent walk of the saved: the word "law" occurs in Romans no less than seventy-five times, though, of course, not every reference is to the law of God. And that is why sinners (Rom. 3:19), and saints (Jas. 2:12), shall be judged by this law.

The "law of Moses" is the entire system of legislation, judicial and ceremonial, which Jehovah gave to Israel during the time they were in the wilderness. The "law of Moses, as such, is binding upon none but Israelites. The "law of Moses" has not been repealed, for it will be enforced by Christ during the Millennium "Out of Jerusalem shall go forth the Law, and the Word of the Lord from Jerusalem" (Isa. 2:3). That the "law of Moses" is not binding on Gentiles is clear from Acts 15.

The "law of Christ" is God's moral law in the hands of a Mediator. It is the law that Christ Himself was "made under (Gal. 4:4). It is the law which was "in His heart" (Psa. 40:8). It is the law which He came "fulfil" (Matt. 5:17). The "law of God" is now termed "the law of Christ" as it relates to Christians. As creatures we are under bonds to "serve the law of God" (Rom. 7:25): as redeemed sinners we are "bondslaves of Christ" (Eph. 6:6); and as such it is our bounden duty to "serve the Lord Christ" (Col. 3:2b). The relation between these two appellations, "the law of God" and "the law of Christ," is clearly intimated in 1 Cor. 9:21, where the apostle states that he was not "without law to God," for he was "under the law to Christ." The meaning of this is very simple. As a human creature, the Apostle was still under obligations to obey the Moral Law of God, his Creator; but as a saved man, he now belongs to Christ, the Mediator, by redemption. Christ had purchased him: he was His, therefore was he under the "law of Christ." The "law of Christ," then, is just the moral of law of God now in the hands of the Mediator—cf. Ex. 34:1 and what follows!

Should any one object against our definition of the distinction drawn between God's moral law and "The law of Moses" we request them to attend closely to what follows. God took special pains to show us the clear line of demarcation which He Himself has drawn between the two. The Moral Law became incorporated in the Mosaic law, yet was it sharply distinguished from it:—

In the first place, the Ten Commandments, and they alone, of all the laws which God gave unto Israel, were promulgated by the voice of God, amid the most solemn manifestations and tokens of the Divine presence. Second, the Ten Commandments and they alone of all Jehovah's statutes to Israel, were written directly by the finger of God, written upon tables of stone, and written thus to denote their lasting and imperishable nature. Third, the Ten Commandments were distinguished from all the other laws which had merely a local application to Israel by the fact that **they alone were laid up in the ark**. A tabernacle was prepared by the special direction of God, and within it an ark was placed, in which the two tables of stone were deposited. The ark, formed of the most durable wood, was overlaid with gold within and without. Over it was placed the mercy seat, which became the throne of Jehovah in the midst of His redeemed people. Not until the tabernacle had been erected and the Law placed in the ark, did Jehovah take up His abode in Israel's midst. Thus did the Lord signify to Israel that the Moral Law was the basis of all His governmental dealings with them!

It is therefore clear beyond room for doubt that the Ten Commandments are to be sharply distinguished from the "law of Moses." The "law of Moses," excepting the Moral Law incorporated therein, was binding upon none but Israelites or Gentile proselytes. But the "Law of God," unlike the Mosaic, is binding upon **all men**. Once this distinction is perceived, many minor difficulties are cleared up. For example: someone says, If we are to keep the Sabbath-day holy, as Israel did, why must we not observe the other "sabbaths"—the Sabbatic year, for instance? The answer is, Because the Moral Law alone is binding upon Gentiles and Christians. But why, it may be asked, does not the death-penalty attached to the desecration of the Sabbath day (Ex. 31:14, etc.) still obtain? The answer is, Because though that was a part of the **Mosaic** law, it was not a part of the Moral Law, i.e., it was not inscribed on the tables of stone: therefore it concerned none but Israelites. Let us now consider separately, but briefly, each of the Ten Commandments.

The **order** of the Commandments is most significant. The first four concern human responsibility **Godwards**; the last five our obligations **manwards**: while the fifth suitably bridges the two, for in a certain sense parents occupy to their children the place of God. We may also add that the substance of each commandment is in perfect keeping with its numerical place in the Decalogue. One stands for **unity** and **supremacy** so in the first commandment the absolute sovereignty and pre-eminency of the Creator is insisted upon. Since God is who He is, He will tolerate no competitor or rival: **His** claims upon us are paramount.

1. "Thou shalt have no other gods before Me" (Ex. 20:3). If this first Commandment received the respect it demands, obedience to the other nine would follow as a matter of course. "Thou shalt have no other gods before Me" means, Thou shalt have no other object of worship: thou shalt own no other authority as absolute: thou shalt make Me supreme in your hearts and lives. How much this first commandment contains! There are other "gods" besides idols of wood and stone. Money, pleasure, fashion, fame, gluttony, and a score of other things which make self supreme, usurp the rightful place of God in the affections and thoughts of many. It is not without reason that even to the saints the exhortation is given, "Little children keep yourselves from idols" (1 John 5:21).

2. "Thou shalt not make unto thee any graven image, or any likeness of any thing that is in heaven above, or that is in the earth beneath, or that is in the water under the earth: Thou shalt not bow down thyself to them, nor serve them for I the Lord thy God am a jealous God, visiting the iniquity of the fathers upon the children unto the third and fourth generation of them that hate Me; and showing mercy unto thousands of them that love Me, and keep My commandments" (vv. 4-6). Two is the number of **witness**, and in this second commandment man is forbidden to attempt any visible representation of Deity, whether furnished by the skill of the artist or the sculptor. The first commandment points out the one only object of worship; the second tells us how He is to be worshipped—in spirit and in truth, by faith and not by images which appeal to the senses. The design of this commandment is to draw us away from carnal conceptions of God, and to prevent His worship being profaned by superstitious rites. A most fearful threat and a most gracious promise are attached. Those who break this commandment shall bring down on their children the righteous judgment of God; those who keep it shall cause mercy to be extended to thousands of those who love God. How this shows us the vital and solemn importance of parents teaching their children the unadulterated truth concerning the Being and Character of God!

3. "Thou shalt not take the name of the Lord thy God in vain; for the Lord

will not hold him guiltless that taketh His name in vain" (v. 7). God requires that the majesty of His holy name be held inviolably sacred by us. His name must be used neither with contempt, irreverently, or needlessly. It is striking to observe that the first petition in the prayer the Lord taught His disciples is. "Hallowed be Thy name!" The name of God is to be held profoundly sacred. In our ordinary speech and in our religious devotions nothing must enter that in anywise lowers the sublime dignity and the high holiness of that Name. The greatest sobriety and reverence is called for. It needs to be pointed out that the only time the word "reverend" is found in the Bible is in Psa. 111:9 where we read, "Holy and reverend is His name." How irreverent then for preachers to style themselves "reverend"!

4. "Remember the Sabbath day to keep it holy. Six days shalt thou labour and do all thy work, but the seventh day is the sabbath of the Lord thy God: in it thou shalt not do any work, thou, nor thy son nor thy daughter, thy manservant, nor thy maidservant, nor thy cattle, nor the stranger, that is within thy gates; For in six days the Lord made heaven and earth, the sea, and all that in them is, and rested the seventh day : wherefore the Lord blessed the Sabbath day and hallowed it" (vv. 8-11). There are two things enjoined here: First, that man should work six days of the week. The same rule is plainly enforced in the New Testament: "And that ye study to be quiet, and to do your own business, and to work with your own hands, as we commanded you" (1 Thess. 4:11). "For even when we were with you this we commanded you, that if any would not WORK, neither should he eat" (2 Thess. 3:10)! The second thing commanded is, that on the seventh day all work must cease. The Sabbath is to be a day of rest. Six days work; one day for rest. The two must not be separated: work calls for rest; rest for work.

The next thing we would observe is that the Sabbath is not here termed "the seventh day of the week." Nor is it ever so styled in Scripture! So far as the Old Testament is concerned any day which was used for rest, and which was followed by six days of work was a Sabbath! It is not correct, then, to say that the "Sabbath" can only be observed on a Saturday. There is not a word of Scripture to support such a statement.

In the next place, we emphatically deny that this Sabbath law has ever been repealed. Those who teach it has, are guilty of the very thing which the Saviour so pointedly condemns in Matt. 5:19. There are those who allow that it is right and proper for us to keep the other nine Commandments, but they insist that the Sabbath has passed away. We fully believe that this very error was anticipated by Christ in Matt. 5:19: "Whosoever shall break one (not "any one") of these least commandments, and shall teach men so, he shall be called the least in the kingdom of heaven." Heb. 4:9 tells us that Sabbath-keeping remains: it has not become obsolete.

The Sabbath (like all the other Commandments) was not simply for Israel but for all men. The Lord Jesus distinctly declared "the Sabbath was made for MAN" (Mark 2:27) and no amount of quibbling can ever make this mean Jews only. The Sabbath was made for man : for man to observe and obey ; also for man's well-being, because his constitution needed it. One day of rest each week is requisite for man's physical, mental, and spiritual good.

"But we must not mistake the means for the end. We must not think that the Sabbath is just for the sake of being able to attend meetings. There are some people who think they must spend the whole day at meetings or private devotions. The result is that at nightfall they are tired out and the day has brought them no rest. The number of church services attended ought to be measured by the person's ability to enjoy them, and get good from them, without being wearied. Attending meetings is not the only way to observe the Sabbath. The Israelites were commanded to keep it in their dwellings as well as in holy convocation. The home, that centre of so great influence over the life and character of the people, ought to be made the scene of true Sabbath observance" (The late Mr. D. L. Moody).

5. "Honour thy father and thy mother: that thy days may be long upon the land which the Lord thy God giveth thee" (v. 12). The word "honor" means more than obey, though obedience is necessarily included in it. To "honor" a parent is to give him the place of superiority, to hold him or her in high esteem, to reverence him. The Scriptures abound with illustrations of Divine blessing coming upon those who honored their parents, and the Divine curse descending on those who honoured them not. The supreme example is that of the Lord Jesus. In Luke 2:52, we read

"And He went down with them and came to Nazareth, and was **subject unto** them." On the Cross we see the Saviour honoring His mother by providing a home for her with His beloved disciple John.

It is indeed sad to see the almost universal disregard of this fifth Commandment in our own day. It is one of the most arresting of the many "signs of the times." Eighteen hundred years ago it was foretold, "In the last days perilous times shall come. For men shall be lovers of their own selves, covetous, boasters, proud, blasphemous, disobedient to parents, unthankful, unholy, **without natural affection**" (2 Tim. 3:1, 3). Unquestionably, the blame for most of this lies upon the parents, who have so neglected the moral and spiritual training of their children that (in themselves) they are worthy of neither respect nor honor. It is to be noted that the promise attached to the fulfilment of this Commandment as well as the command itself is repeated in the New Testament—see Eph. 6:1, 3.

6. "Thou shalt not kill" (v. 13). The simple force of this is, Thou shalt not murder. God Himself has attached the death-penalty to murder. This comes out plainly in Gen. 9:5, 6, "And surely your blood of your lives will I require; at the hand of every beast will I require it, and at the hand of man; at the hand of every man's brother will I require the life of man. Whoso sheddeth man's blood, by man shall his blood be shed, for in the image of God made He man." This statute which God gave to Noah has **never been rescinded**. In Matt. 5: 21, 22, we have Christ's exposition of this sixth commandment: He goes deeper than the letter of the words and gives the spirit of them. He shows that murder is not limited to the overt act, but also pertains to the state of mind and the angry passion which prompts the act —cf., 1 John 3:15.

In this sixth Commandment, God emphasises the sacredness of human life and His own sovereignty over it—He alone has the right to say when it shall end. The force of this was taught Israel in connection with the cities of refuge. These provided an asylum from the avenger of blood. But they were not to shelter murderers, but only those who had killed "unwittingly" (R.V.). It was only those who had unintentionally taken the life of a fellow-creature who could take refuge therein! And this, be it observed, was not regarded as a light affair: even the man who had taken life "unawares" was deprived of his liberty till the death of the high priest!

7. "Thou shalt not commit adultery" (v. 14). This respects the marriage relationship which was instituted in Eden—"Therefore shall a man leave his father and his mother, and shall cleave unto his wife: and they shall be one flesh" (Gen. 2:24). The marriage-relationship is paramount over every other human obligation. A man is more responsible to love and care for his wife than he is to remain in the home of his childhood and take care of his father and mother. It is the highest and most sacred of human relations. It is in view of this relationship that the seventh Commandment is given. "Thou shalt not commit adultery" means, Thou shal not be unfaithful to the marriage obligations.

Now in Christ's exposition of this Commandment we find Him filling it out and giving us its deeper meaning: "I say unto you, That whosoever looketh on a woman to lust after her hath committed adultery with her already in his heart" (Matt. 5 : 28). Unfaithfulness is not limited to the overt act, but reaches to the passions behind the act. In Christ's interpretation of the law of divorce He shows that one thing only can dissolve the marriage relationship, and that is unfaithfulness on the part of the husband or the wife. "I say unto you, Whosoever shall put away his wife, **except for fornication**, and shall marry another, committeth adultery: and whoso marrieth her which is put away doth commit adultery" (Matt. 19:9). Fornication is the general term; adultery the specific: the former includes the latter. 1 Cor. 7:15 supplies no exception: if one **depart** from the other, except it be on the ground of **unfaithfulness**, neither is free to marry again. Separation **is not divorce** in the **scriptural** sense. "If she depart, let her remain unmarried" (1 Cor. 7:11).

8. "Thou shalt not steal" (v. 15). The design of this Commandment is to inculcate honesty in all our dealings with men. Stealing covers more than pilfering. "Owe no man anything" (Rom. 13:8), "Providing for honest things, not only in the sight of the Lord, but also in the sight of men" (2 Cor. 8:21). I may steal from another by fraudulent means, without using any violence. If I borrow a book and fail to return it, that is **theft**—it is keeping what is not my own. How many are guilty here! If I misrepresent an article for sale, the price which I receive over and above its fair market-value is **stolen**! The man who

obtains money by gambling, receives money for which he has done no honest work, and is therefore a thief! "Parents are woefully lax in their condemnation and punishment of the sin of stealing. The child begins by taking sugar, it may be. The mother makes light of it at first and the child's conscience is violated without any sense of wrong. By and by it is not an easy matter to check tne habit, because it grows and multiplies with every new commission" (Mr. D. L. Moody).

9. "Thou shalt not bear false witness against thy neighbour" (v. 16). The scope of these words is much wider than is generally supposed. The most flagrant form of this sin is to slander our neighbours—a lie invented and circulated with malicious intentions. Few forms of injury done by one man to another is more despicable than this. But equally reprehensible is tale-bearing where there has been no careful investigation to verify the evil report. False witness may be borne by leaving a false impression upon the minds of people by a mere hint or suggestion. "Have you heard about Mr. ——?" "No." "Ah! Well, the least said the soonest mended." Again, when one makes an unjust criticism or charge against another in the hearing of a third party, and that third party remains silent, his very silence is a breach of this ninth Commandment. The flattering of another, exaggerated eulogy, is a false witness. Rightly has it been said, "There is no word of the Decalogue more often and more unconsciously broken than this ninth Commandment, and men need perpetually and persistently to pray 'Set a watch, O Lord, before my mouth; keep the door of my lips.'"

10. "Thou shalt not covet thy neighbour's house, thou shalt not covet thy neighbour's wife, nor his manservant, nor his maidservant, nor his ox, nor his ass, nor any thing that is thy neighbour's" (v. 17). This Commandment differs from all the others in that while they prohibit the overt act, this condemns the very desire to act. The word "covet" means **desire**, and the Commandment forbids us to covet **any thing** that is our neighbour's. Clear proof is this that these Commandments are not of **human** origin. The tenth Commandment has never been placed on any human statute book! It would be useless to do so, for men could not enforce it. More than any other, perhaps, does **this** Commandment reveal to us **what we are**, the hidden depths of evil within. It is **natural** to **desire** things, even though they belong to others. True; and that only shows the fallen and depraved state of our nature. The last Commandment is especially designed to show men their sinfulness and their need of a Saviour. Believers, too, are exhorted to "beware of coveteousness" (Luke 12:15). There is only one exception, and that is stated in 1 Cor. 12:31: "Covet earnestly **the best gifts.**"

May the Holy Spirit of God fasten these Commandments upon the memory of both writer and reader, and may the fear of God make us tremble before them.

ARTHUR W. PINK.

## ELECTION.

Address by Dr. A. W. Pink, at Ashfield Baptist Church, 26/6/'25.

### No. 4.

Let me first give a brief review of the ground already covered in these addresses on the doctrine of election as revealed in the Holy Scriptures. First of all, we have seen that the word "elect" means to choose, to select, to pick out one and pass by another. Second, we have seen that election is a fact illustrated even among the angels. God has elect angels and therefore there are non-elect angels. We have seen that this fact was illustrated in Old Testament times, when God chose the nation of Israel to be His special favourites, giving to them a revelation which was given to no other nation. Third, we have seen that the ground of election lies upon nothing in ourselves. God did not elect us because He foresaw that we would believe, for no man or woman has any faith at all until God gives it to him or to her. The truth is that God knew that nobody ever would believe if He were to leave us to ourselves, and therefore in His sovereign grace He chose out a people to whom He has given faith with which to believe.

Turn now to Romans 11:2: "God hath not cast away His people which he foreknew (that is the nation of Israel). Wot ye not (or know ye not) what the scripture saith of Elias? How he maketh intercession to God against Israel, saying, Lord, they have killed Thy prophets, and digged down Thine altars;

and I am left alone, and they seek my life. But what saith the answer of God unto him? I have **reserved to Myself seven thousand men,** who have not bowed the knee to Baal."And if God had not made that reservation, every last one of the nation of Israel **would** have bowed their knees. Those seven thousand men did not bow their knees because God had "reserved" them. "I have reserved to Myself seven thousand men who have not bowed the knee unto Baal." God made a choice, a reservation: if He had not done so every last one of them would have apostatised from Him.

Notice now in Romans 9:29:—"And as Esais said before, Except the Lord of Sabbath (that means the Lord of Hosts)—Except the Lord of Hosts had left us a seed, we had been as Sodoma, and been made like unto Gomorrha." "Except **the Lord** had left us a seed we had been as Sodoma." There is the proof. If God had not made an election no one would ever have been saved. Every saved person in this room to-night owes his salvation to the **electing grace** of God. You say, I thought I owed my salvation to the blood of Christ? So you do, One in Three, and Three in One. The Three Persons in the Godhead are united. Every saved person here to-night owes his salvation, first to the electing grace of the Father; second, to the atoning death of the Son; and third, to the regenerating power of the Holy Spirit. I wonder how many of you know this, that if the Holy Spirit of God had never come into this world Christ's death would never have saved anybody? If Christ had died and gone back to heaven and the Holy Spirit had not come down, then nobody would ever have reaped the benefits of Christ's death so far as salvation is concerned. The Holy Spirit of God had to be sent down if the benefits of that Death Divine were to be applied to the sons of men. So you owe your salvation first to the electing grace of the Father, second to the atoning death of the Son, and third to the regenerating power of the Holy Spirit. Then if that is true, **all** the glory belongs to **God!**

Now listen again. If God were to offer heaven to everybody no one would accept that offer unless God put forth His drawing-power to bring us to the feet of Christ. I want to show you a very striking illustration of that in the book of Ezra. First chapter of Ezra and the first verse:—"Now in the first year of Cyrus, king of Persia, that the word of the Lord by the mouth of Jeremiah might be fulfilled, **the Lord stirred up** the spirit of Cyrus, king of Persia, that he made a proclamation throughout all his kingdom, and put it also in writing, saying, Thus saith Cyrus, king of Persia, The Lord God of heaven hath given me all the kingdoms of the earth; and He hath charged me to build Him an house at Jerusalem, which is in Judah. Who is there among you of all His people? His God be with him, and let him go up to Jerusalem, which is in Judah, and build the house of the Lord God of Israel, (He is the God), which is in Jerusalem." Now then, the Children of Israel were in captivity. They had been in Babylon for seventy years. The Babylonish kings were dead, and the Persians had conquered Babylon, and Cyrus was the king of Babylon at this time. There were the Israelites in captivity, and God stirred up the spirit of Cyrus to issue this proclamation or, if you prefer it, an invitation. The proclamation was, that every Israelite who desired was now free to leave the land of bondage and go back again to Palestine. They were given permission to leave the place of captivity and go back again to their own country. Now then they didn't need anything more did they? There was the offer: Anybody who wants to is now free to leave Babylon and go back again to Palestine.

The king himself made the offer. What happened? Why, of course, every Israelite gladly availed himself of it. Every Israelite in the whole land of Babylon started off the next day as hard as he could go to the land of Israel. Nothing of the sort! The offer was made to them, and if there had been nothing more than that offer no one of them would have accepted that! The vast majority **did not** accept it. They would not leave the place of captivity even when there was an offer made for them to do so. They preferred rather to stay in the land of captivity, Babylon, than go back again to the land of God (Palestine). Now notice the fifth verse: "Then rose up the chief of the fathers of Judah and Benjamin, and the priests, and the Levites, with all them whose **spirit God has raised** to go up to build the house of the Lord which is in Jerusalem." Some of them **did** accept the offer. **Some** of them rose up at once to go back again to Jerusalem. **Who** were they? Who was that "some"? Now let me read it again: "Then rose up the chief of the fathers of Judah and Benjamin, and the priests, and the Levites, with all them whose spirit God had raised." The Hebrew word here for "raised" is the same word that you have in the first verse "stirred up." God had to "stir up" their hearts before any of them were ready to accept the offer that King Cyrus had made to them!

Now you could not have a clearer case than that. Israel was in the place of bondage. An offer was made to the whole nation to leave that place of bondage and go back to their own land, and if there had been nothing more than that offer none would have accepted. God had to stir up the hearts of a small company who did accept it—less than 50,000 all told. Now that illustrates this fact, that though the gospel comes to all men, that is, the 'all men' who hear it—half of the human race has not heard it—that if there were nothing more than the gospel not one of them would be saved. Every man if he were left free to himself would reject the gospel. God has to "stir up" our hearts and overcome the enmity and resistance of our wills before we are ready to believe in the Lord Jesus Christ!

Now that brings me to the next point. I did not complete last night what I wanted to say on this question, Why should we preach the gospel to every creature? If God has elected a definite number, and that number cannot be either decreased or increased, then why ought we to preach the gospel to every creature under heaven? The first reason is, because God has commanded us to do so. Well, but, you say, it is not reasonable: if God does not mean to save any more than His own elect people it is not reasonable to preach the gospel to the others. My friends, it is not a question of reason, it is a question of doing what God has told us to do. What did God tell Noah to do? God told Noah to build an ark: and if some of us had been Noah, well, I am afraid that perhaps we would have said, Lord, that is most unreasonable. Here am I hundreds of miles away from the sea, far inland—and there had never been a shower of rain before the flood: the flood was the first time it rained on earth. There had been no rain and God told Noah to build an ark, because a flood was coming.

Why, Noah might have said, That is most unreasonable, Lord: and if he had acted according to his own reason he would have been drowned! The first thing God requires of you and me is obedience to His commandment: whether they strike you as reasonable or no, therefore the first answer to the question why the gospel ought to be preached to every creature is because God has commanded it.

The second reason is (and I want you to get hold of this) why the gospel is to be preached to every creature is because God has designed that a universal testimony shall be borne to His Son. Now turn to the first chapter of Romans, "Paul, a servant of Jesus Christ, called to be an apostle, separated unto the gospel of God." Notice that carefully, "separated unto the gospel of God, (which He had promised afore by His prophets in the holy scriptures)." Now you will notice the second verse is in brackets: that means it is a parenthesis, a secondary subordinate clause, that interrupts the order of thought. Now if you read the third verse right after the first, leaving out the second, you will get the complete thought. Verse 1: "Paul, a servant of Jesus Christ, called to be an apostle, separated unto the gospel of God concerning sinners." Now that is what most people believe it is. Most people in this twentieth century are so ignorant they imagine that the gospel concerns sinners. It does not, and the gospel is not about sinners. The gospel is the gospel of Christ! It is about the person and the work of God's Son! Now listen, I want you to get this very clearly. The gospel is not an "offer," the gospel is a proclamation, not an "invitation." The gospel is a proclamation about Christ, and the gospel, is true even if not one man on earth to-night believed it! My believing the gospel does not make the gospel true. The gospel is true whether I believe it or no, because the gospel is not about me, the gospel is about Christ.

Now listen to my next statement, and let this sink in. We are not responsible to bring sinners to Christ. No preacher is responsible to do that No open-air worker is responsible to bring any sinner to Christ, for there is none of us can do it; we have not got the power. Our responsibility is to bring Christ to the sinner. Did you get that? Our responsibility is to preach Christ to the sinner! How man turns God's things upside down doesn't he, every time, and the awful thing to-day is, and it is true almost everywhere, that we are far more concerned about the results of the gospel than we are about the purity of it! We are more concerned in the blessing of man than we are about the glory of Christ! Is not that true? Is it not true that the first great question asked everywhere to-day is, What are the "results"? What is the fruitage? How many people have been saved in your church the last year? I am not saying that the question has no importance, but I do say, that if that is the first question that is asked, it only shows what a low level we are living on! The first question we ought to ask is, How **scripturally** is the gospel being preached in your church? Is the preacher magnifying **Christ**? Is the preacher emphasising the absolute sufficiency of **His** finished work? Does the preacher make it plain that God does not ask the sinner to do anything, that **Christ** has done it all for him? Ah, my friends, when the preachers to-day are tested by **that** there is mighty few of them that will survive the test. How many there are to-day who tell the poor sinner that he has got to give his heart to God. Well, you say, isn't that right? Isn't that true? **Must not** the sinner give his heart to the Lord if he is going to be saved? Oh the tragedy that such a question has to be asked! We talk about progress and advancing, why my friends we need indoctrinating in the ABC of Christianity, and the ABC of Christianity is **the gospel.** No, my friends, no sinner was ever saved by giving his heart to God. We are not saved by **our** giving, we are saved by **God's** giving. "God so loved the world that **He** gave." **That** is the gospel. I am not saved by my giving something to God, I am saved by **receiving His gift!** Well, but doesn't it say in Scripture, "Son, give Me thine heart?" Yes, it does, but that is not addressed to an unconverted sinner, that is addressed to **a son! After God has** saved you by grace alone, then your first duty is to **dedicate** yourself to His service, to give your heart to Him, to be used by Him as He wills and where He wills and when He wills, and to realise that you are no more your own but the purchased property of another.

Will you turn now to Matthew 13:25. I just want to call your attention to a little part in this verse that possibly may have escaped the attention of most of you. Matthew 13:25. I will read you the 24th verse: "Another parable put He forth unto them, saying, The kingdom of heaven is likened unto a man which sowed good seed in His field and while men slept, His enemy came and sowed tares among the wheat and then **sat down to see what the results would be."** Is that how it reads? Look at it closely! "While men slept, his enemy came and sowed tares among the wheat, and **went his way."** After he had sowed the tares what did the enemy do? He "went his way." **Why** did he? Why did he go on his way after he had sowed the tares? Because he had **confidence in the seed** that he had sown: he had confidence to believe that the seed **would** produce a harvest, and he did not just sit down to see what the results were but he went his way to go and do some more sowing!

Now, my friends, a whole lot of our so-called Christian work to-day reminds me of little children when they first witness father or mother doing some gardening. The ground is prepared and then the seed is sown, and every day the child goes into the garden it looks around to see if the seed is beginning to sprout, and it doesn't show any signs and it wants to make sure that the seed **is** beginning to sprout, it just scratches around amongst the soil. It wants to **see** something. My friends, that is what a lot of us are doing in connection with so-called Christian work to-day! O we have so little confidence in **the** power and in **the sufficiency of** the Divine "seed" to bring about the harvest that God has ordained it shall do! When the devil sowed his seed he went his way to sow some more—didn't stop to wait for results. O that God would give us like faith to just rest on His promise, "My word . . . shall not return unto Me void, but it **shall** accomplish that which I please, and it shall prosper in the thing whereto I sent it." It may not perform what **you** please, it may not prosper in the way you want it to, but it **shall** prosper in the thing whereunto God hath sent it, it **shall accomplish** that which He pleases! O brethren in Christ, we have nothing to do with "results," that is God's business. Our business is to sow the Seed and go on sowing and continue sowing and leave results **to Him:** He is "the Lord of the harvest." He alone "giveth the increase."

Now come back to the question, Why we should preach the gospel. We should preach the gospel to every creature because God so loved His Son that He would have **a universal testimony borne to Him.** The gospel is about Christ, and God is so concerned about the glory of His Son that He would have Christ preached throughout the whole world. Listen. The salvation of sinners is quite a secondary matter with God. **The glory of His Son** comes first! O that it might with us. O that God by His grace would so teach us by His Spirit that we might learn to put the glory of Christ even before the success of our service. And my friends, you need not be afraid about results if you have an eye single to the glory of that. One whose Name is above every name. You need not bother about results then, it is the devil that would get us occupied with results and get our eyes upon man instead of Christ. O how subtle our enemy is. That is how he deceived us when we were unconverted: He got us occupied with ourselves instead of with God's Lamb, and now that we are seeking to serve Him. He gets us occupied with sinners instead of with Christ. Yes, my friends, we need to be instructed even in the ABC, God alone knows how terribly ignorant all of us are, and I freely include myself with you: what I know of this Word is just a fragment only, and it is only the Holy Spirit in His sovereign grace that can increase that knowledge. We none of us know anything yet as we ought to know—not even the Gospel. O we need to learn what "service" is! Service is not deserving of the name of service unless it is done for the glory of Christ: If it is done simply for the blessing of men that is nothing more than the mere sentiment of the flesh.

In the third place, the gospel ought to be preached to every creature because it is God's appointed means for gathering out His own people.

Now I will pass on from that question to another. I have no doubt that some of you have been thinking in your minds during these addresses on election, What about that text which says "God is no respecter of persons?" Doesn't the Bible say God is no respecter of persons? Yes, my friends, it does, and election gives one of the clearest proofs that God is no respecter of persons. When the angels sinned and fell He provided no Saviour for them: when the human race sinned and fell He did provide a Saviour for them. If God had been a respecter of persons, He would have honored the angels and passed by men! The very fact that God is no respecter of persons is seen in the character of the people whom He chooses. What was the nation that God chose—His elect people—in the Old Testament? The Israelitish nation. And what sort of a people were they? A stiff-necked, hard-hearted, rebellious people from the beginning of their history to the end. And my friends, what kind of a man is the Jew to-day? I mean from the human standpoint: I mean according to nature. He is the most unlovable and unlovely man there is on this earth. Yes, my friends, God is no respecter of persons or He would never have chosen the Jew.

But listen again. It is equally true in New Testament times. What does it say in James 2:5? God hath chosen the poor of this world. Thank God He has. If God had chosen the rich of this world it would fare ill with most of us, wouldn't it? Oh, no, God is no respecter of persons. God did not pick out millionaires and princes and kings and peers and dukes. God hath chosen the poor of this world. God hath chosen (1 Cor. 1: 26, 27) the despised, the weak, the vile, the things that are not, nonentities. These are the ones that God has chosen. My friends, if God were a respecter of persons He would never have chosen you! "Jacob have I loved" and what on earth was there in Jacob to love? And echo still says, What was there? Ah, my friends, God's sovereign election demonstrates the fact that He is no respecter of persons—the respectable Pharisees passed by and publicans and harlots drawn into the gospel feast. If God had been a respecter of persons none of us would have been saved!

Now then, in the next place, someone says, Does not this doctrine reduce man to a mere machine? Well, in the first place, suppose it does, which is the worse, to reduce man to a machine or to reduce the Almighty to an impotent Being?—a God who is filled with benevolent designs and unable to carry them out? Which is the more serious, to reduce man to a machine or to reduce God to a helpless Being? But my friends, the scriptural doctrine of election does not reduce man to a machine; it does far more than that. My friends, the sinner in his natural condition is far worse than a machine. I have seen many machines, and so have you, that will respond to the will of those who made them, that will do the work that they ought to do, that are very orderly and systematic: they will move, they will run. But, my friends, fallen man will not do the revealed will of the One who made him; he will not produce the works that he ought to do, and instead of running he cannot even walk. He is dead! Man is far worse than a machine unless you refer to a machine, on the scrap pile. That is a more appropriate figure for fallen man.

Well, you say, does not Scripture insist upon the responsibility of man? Certainly it does, and so ought we. Well, but, you say, I do not see how the two things harmonise: if God is sovereign and doing His will, if God has elected, and that election is being made good, I cannot see how man is a responsible creature. There are lots of things you cannot see. Some things perhaps you never will see, I do not know. I very much doubt if any of us in eternity will fully understand the doctrine of the Holy Trinity. I very much question if, even in eternity, we will be able to comprehend God, in fact I am sure we won't for the finite will never be able to grasp the Infinite. The only question is, is it true? God is sovereign, man is responsible. The two things are true. Whether you can harmonise them or not is not your business. Believe them both because they are both in this Word.

Now then, passing on to the next point. Some say, Why preach this doctrine of election? Answer first of all, because the Bible is full of it and the preacher is not free to pick and choose. God's servant is not free to alter or to adulterate, or to trim down, still less to leave out: his duty is to preach the **whole counsel of God**. Second, the doctrine of election ought to be preached because it gives God all the glory. It does so in three different ways. If I have "believed," it was because God **predestinated** that I should, and therefore there is no credit to me: all the glory belongs alone to Him. My friends, the doctrine of election gives God the first place. The doctrine of election says that salvation began not with an act of my will, salvation began in the mind of God before the foundation of the world. This doctrine gives God all the glory because it magnifies His **power**. It magnifies His power because it shows us that though man is a rebel, that though his heart is corrupt, his mind depraved, and his will steeled against God, God in His invincible power comes and, like it was with Saul of Tarsus of old, it strikes him to the ground, and the victory is God's. This doctrine honors God because it magnifies His **grace**. The doctrine of election says that salvation is a gift that God gratuitously bestows on whom He pleases; it is not a wage that we earn: it is not a prize that we win.

Listen, this doctrine is to be preached because it **humbles man**, and anything that humbles man must be a blessing: anything that abases our proud hearts must be of God. Now I want to put it in a very simple way. Let me put it to you in this form. Is there any difference between you, the Christian, and the unbelieving man of the world? Why, you say, of course, there is. Is there any difference between what you are to-night and what you once were? You say, Yes, there is. **Who** made that difference, you or God? Now that is the very essence of the doctrine of election. My friends, I am not asking you to subscribe to a creed, and I am not asking you to believe in my way of stating this doctrine: what I want you to do is to believe in a doctrine that gives God all the glory for your salvation and does not take one particle of it to yourself. I am not asking you to believe my way of stating this doctrine; it is a very poor way, a very halting, a very imperfect way; what I want you to believe is a doctrine that gives God all the glory for your salvation. This doctrine, once it is blessed by God, will drive the sinner to despair—I mean despair of doing anything for himself—and whilever the sinner is hoping for anything from himself he is the enemy of the cross of Christ. It is not until we are brought to the place where like a drowning man in the water clutching at a straw that we will be ready to cast ourselves at the feet of Christ and to say,

"A helpless, guilty, worthless worm
  On Thy strong arms I fall.
Be Thou my strength and righteousness,
  My Saviour and my All."

This doctrine is to be preached, not only because it gives God all the glory, not only because it humbles man, but because it is **an enobling** one: it puts iron into our spiritual blood: it gives a strength and a stability to character that nothing else does. Listen, who was it that carved out the liberties of England? Who was it, under God, that delivered England from the yoke of Rome? Who was it? It was Oliver Cromwell and his Ironsides. And **what was it** that made Cromwell and his men invincible? It was an unshaken assurance that they were the chosen of God, and they rushed forth into battle with the conviction that the Lord was with them **and therefore none could withstand them.** Oh, I wish that the life, the biography, of Oliver Cromwell was in the homes of everyone here. These doctrines of the Sovereignty of God and Predestination and Election have given a strength to character that nothing else ever has. History does not record a single case of one Arminian that has even died as a martyr. My friends, freewillers fall from grace when they are faced with the stake, to resume it again when the fires are out! But the men who have believed, by God's grace, in the absolute sovereignty of the Lord, have stood firm, and have died rather than deny Him. History records the fact that there are thousands of men who have been burned at the stake for **these very doctrines** that I have been preaching here by the Lord's help these last two weeks and, my friends, what we need to-day is more backbone—we are too flabby, we are too anaemic, we need something that will fill our spiritual veins with blood, and I know of nothing that will do it but a firmer confidence in the **throne** of God and the absolute **sovereignty** of the Lord.

As I said last night, the sad thing is that in this twentieth century a generation has arisen that is as ignorant as the Hottentots are of the great issue and the great controversy between Rome and Protestantism. We call ourselves Protestants. Why, do you know what a "Protestant" is? Do you know what the word"Protestant" means? A Protestant is one who **protests**, and a man or a woman who will just sit still and allow Rome to take away our spiritual liberties is not a Protestant at all. He is not worthy of the name! Now do not misunderstand me. I do not hate any Roman Catholic—God forbid—but I hate with every drop of blood in me the Roman Catholic system, and the soul-destroying and God-dishonouring and Scripture-denying dogmas that she stands for, and I hope that many of you who were here last night will follow up the suggestion that I made, and see to it that every Sunday-school that is represented here will start a circulating library of sound literature that will instruct the rising generation. My friends, Rome begins with the child in the cradle Rome does not wait till the boy or girl is in its teens, Rome begins to instruct from the cradle up. Rome is not asleep, if we are! And to anyone here to-night who is desirous of following up that suggestion, I made it my business to go into Sydney to see Mr. Ardill to find out what supply of books was obtainable —Foxe's Book of Marytrs, and other books which reveal the real character of Rome and the issue at stake,and I am glad to say he has a good supply and you can get the books if you go to him. And I just want to mention here, I have obtained 200 copies of "Roman Catholic Doctrine examined in the light of Scripture" which may be had for 3d. each. The booklet just mentions in a few lines one by one the various dogmas of Rome and then shows the texts of Scripture that refute them. It will be an eye-opener to some of you.

Now then I must draw to a close. In the last place—I wish the clock would stand still for about a couple of hours, I really do. Someone said to me this afternoon, Well, if Pastor Harrison wants you to come back here for another month, what are you going to do? You have preached to them fifty times already: isn't the barrel beginning to run dry? Ah, my friends, listen, the preacher who relies on anecdotes and clippings from the newspaper, his barrel will soon run dry; of course, it will; but the man who preaches the Word of God has an inexhaustible supply to draw from. My dear friends, the trouble is I hardly know what to bring in and what to leave out. I would like to speak to you by the Lord's help every night for ten years, and then perhaps we would all of us know something of the Word— not much then, but a little.

Now the last point I want to bring in is this, How may I know whether or not I am among the elect? If the Lord spares us till Monday night I will take up that question at greater length. Let me just give you one word on it now. I Thessalonians 1:4: "Knowing, brethren beloved, your election of God." There are some who say it is **not** possible to know whether we are elected, that we shall never find out until we come to die, But the Apostle Paul here writing to the saints at Thessalonica said, **"Knowing** brethren beloved, your election of God." It is possible to know it. It is possible to know it here and now— not to **hope** it, but to **know** it. Now God has told us no less than five different ways by which we may know whether or not we are among the elect of God. I will just mention one only to-night, the other four, the Lord willing, on Monday night, The first way in which God reveals to us our election— His election—is **by regenerating us.** Everybody is not a child of God. All mankind are not inside God's family. The "Universal Fatherhood of God" is a lie. All men are not God's spiritual children. **Who are?** Only those are God's spiritual children who have been born again, born into God's family, born of God. And my friends, those who are born of God do nothing more of themselves to be born than they did to be born into the human family. I was not born into my father's household by any act of my will, nor any act of my heart, nor any act of my mind. I was not consulted in the matter. I had nothing to do with it. And that is equally true of the new birth! We are born of God, not partly of God and partly of the preacher. We are born of God, **not by our** wills but by **His** will. The first chapter of John and the 13th verse emphatically says, "Which were born, not of blood, nor of the will of the flesh, nor of the will of man, but of God." Now then, have you been born again? Do you know that by sovereign grace you are a child of God? Is there One within your soul that causes you to look up to heaven to-night and say, Abba, Father? Then you are a child of God: you have one of the marks of His election, for the only ones that God regenerates are His Own elect people.

Now I just want to close with this statement. It is getting late, but just follow me closely for a few more moments. Regeneration is the work of God alone. The preacher does not bring it about. The sinner's will does not bring it about. God only can regenerate. Now listen! It is not until we really believe **that** we are ever going to do any real earnest praying for lost sinners. It is not until we realise that the condition of the sinner is so desperate, that the sinner is **unable** to do one thing for himself, that we will get down on our faces and earnestly beseech God to do for sinners what we are unable to do and what **the sinner** is unable to do for himself! My friends, if we only saw the truth of man's depravity, that the sinner is **lost**—not that there is something wrong with him, but that he is lost: not that he is sick, but that he is **dead**, and that **if** ever he is to be regenerated only **God** can regenerate him: once we really believe that, we will get down on our knees and we will pray as we never prayed before. Oh, I want to say earnestly to the members of this church, that no matter how faithfully your pastor preaches, no matter how simply he presents the truth of God, unless the almighty power of the Holy Spirit accompanies the Word through him it will all be in vain. No matter how earnest he is, no matter though he weeps and breaks his heart over sinners, sinners will not be saved in this place unless God the Holy Spirit saves them. That is not only true of this church, it is true of every church and assembly represented here to-night. O that God would show us and make us realise that **He only can save**, that man is unable to save himself, then we will feel as never before the importance of getting down on our knees and saying, O God for Christ's sake, not for the sake of my earnestness, not for the sake of my prayers, not for the sake of my love for my lost relative, but **for Christ's sake**, have mercy on them. May the Lord teach you and teach me **how** to pray!

ARTHUR W. PINK.

## IN REGIONS BEYOND.

By the time our friends read this we shall have been in Australia over twelve months. It has been a year crowned with the Lord's goodness. Abundant have been His mercies, sufficient His grace, and great His faithfulness. Our expectation has been in Him and He has not disappointed.

Long before we came to this Continent the Lord moved numbers of His starved and scattered sheep to cry earnestly unto Him that He would be pleased to send them a teacher. Many had listened to preaching for years, but it fed not their souls and failed to open to them the precious contents of the Scriptures. Numbers had gone from Church to Church hoping to find a place where there would be something really edifying, but in vain. Some had tired the Plymouth Brethren's meetings but found them no more spiritual than those they condemned: "Ichabod" was long since written over the system founded by Mr. Darby. But the Lord heard the cries of His needy people and is now ministering to the hunger His own grace created.

For the first six months God took us from place to place, thus giving access to different companies, in each of which were a few longing for something better than the chaff which almost all the preachers were giving them. These eagerly followed wherever we went—some considerable distances—for the sheep will go where the green pastures are to be found! Of course, this aggravated their pastors (?), but they have only themselves to blame, for had they done the work to which they professed to have been called, they would not have lost some of their most spiritual members.

At the end of September we were invited to preach in the Strict and Particular Baptist Church, in Sydney, a Church which by Divine grace has faithfully stood for all the counsel of God for over sixty years, but which had been pastorless for twelve months. During that time, rather than invite the preachers who were not thoroughly sound in the faith, different "lay" brethren of their own number supplied the pulpit. When we arrived in this country we had no knowledge at all of this Church, but the Lord, who doeth all things well, brought us to it, though "by a way that we knew not." The name of this Church defines its creed. They are "strict" in insisting upon a regenerated church-membership and in guarding the Lord's table, and they hold fast to Particular Redemption rather than the General-Atonement-theory of the Arminians.

For the past six months we have ministered God's Word in this Church every Sabbath and each Wednesday evening, and there has been a joyous response in the souls of its members. Hating all "strange doctrines," having no patience with the compromising spirit of these degenerate times, they have fervently praised the Triune Jehovah as He has graciously enabled His unworthy servant to proclaim the truth which is so honouring to Him and so dear to their hearts. Numbers have been revived and refreshed, and we have reason to believe that some of their children are now under conviction and seeking the Saviour.

Being situated in Sydney this Church proved of most convenient location, the interested ones in the various suburbs (where we first ministered from May to September) making it their gathering centre. Goodly numbers of those whom we reached in the earlier meetings have continued to attend regularly and new ones are gradually being added. Never before, during our sixteen years ministry, have we experienced such blessing and joy in our own souls, such liberty of utterance, and such an encouraging response as we have in this highly favoured portion of Christ's Vineyard.

And how all of this has stirred up the malice of the Enemy! But we "are not ignorant of his devices" (2 Cor. 2:11).

In our Lord's day it was the religious leaders (with a form of godliness, but denying the power thereof) who took the lead in persecuting the faithful and true Witness. So it is now, but it is written, "It is enough for the disciple that he be as his Master, and the servant as his Lord. If they have called the Master of the house Beelzebub, how much more them of His household?" (Matt. 10: 25).

During our stay here we have been taught afresh the need of heeding our Lord's example as set before us in John 2:24: "Jesus did not commit Himself unto them." Most of those who were loudest in our praise at the beginning have proven the most fickle: those who were the most effusive in their avowals of friendship were but wolves in sheep's clothing. Not without cause are we warned "Meddle not with him that flattereth with his lips" (Prov. 20:19). The tactics employed against us by some of the leaders here only show how thoroughly they are under the dominion of that old Serpent, the devil.

The last few years in America we were members of no denomination or sect, for we could not fellowship much of what was going on among them. But on the first Sabbath in March the Editor and his wife were received into the membership and fellowship of the Strict and Paricular Baptist Church in Sydney. Having carefully examined their Articles of Faith and found them in thorough accord with the Word of Truth, having personally seen that the Lord was pleased to manifest Himself in their midst, having the scriptural example of the Apostle Paul who "assayed to join himself to the disciples" (Acts 9: 26), desiring their more intimate fellowship for our spiritual welfare, hoping to strengthen their hands and desiring to encouraging others to do likewise, we felt clear before God that it was both our privilege and duty to apply for membership and belong to a church which is patterned after the New Testament Churches in its order, teaching and discipline.

We have no plans for the future. Our times are in God's hands. How long He will keep us here we know not. We believe that the Lord has opened for us a great and effectual door, and if so, none can shut it. The need here is great. So far as we can discover, there is not another preacher in all

Sydney (with its million souls) who is proclaiming the Sovereignty of God, eternal election, particular and efficacious redemption, and unconditional salvation. The vast majority of the ministers here are preaching "another Jesus" (2 Cor. 11:4): a Jesus who wants to save everybody, but cannot because so many will not let Him—rather than the Jesus Who "shall save His people from their sins" (Matt. 1:21); and are preaching another Gospel" (Gal. 1:6)—a man-devised scheme with its terms and conditions, which the poor sinner must fulfil —rather than the "Gospel of Christ which is the power of God unto salvation to every one that believeth" (Rom. 1:16).

In addition to our ministry in Sydney, we are conducting Bible classes two nights each week in the suburbs, which are splendidly attended. We need, then, the prayers of God's saints that we may be kept faithful and humble and thoroughly furnished unto all good works. We still think and speak of our many dear friends in the U.S.A. with happy remembrances and supplicate the Throne of Grace on their behalf.

With every good wish to all.

Yours by Sovereign Grace,

ARTHUR W. PINK.

## THE PLEASURE OF GOD.

There are some persons and things in which God has no pleasure. "He has no pleasure in wickedness" (Psa. 2:4). He had no pleasure in Coniah (Jer. 22:28). "Some are pleasureless vessels" (Jer. 48:38; Hos. 8:8; Matt. 1:10; Rom. 9:21). "He has no pleasure in their damnation (Ezek. 18:23). He has no pleasure in their life or death, in their time or eternity, being or punishment, on earth or in hell.

This awful fact is no evidence that He ever loved them, chose them, wished to save them, gave His Son for them, and sent His Spirit to them. These facts prove that He did not do any of these things for them, in them or to them. If it had been His pleasure to do these things for them, it would have been done, for He says, "My counsel shall stand, and I will do all My pleasure" (Isa. 46:10). The blasphemy of the age is that "He cannot do His pleasure; man will not allow Him. Man, mighty man, hinders half the pleasures of the Almighty God would enjoy if He could." Thus they form a god like themselves. But our God says "I will do all My pleasure."

Has our Queen any pleasure in those who have been hung for their vile crimes in vindication of her laws? No, yet it was necessary to hang them to vindicate the honour of her laws. Those poor wretches have been less vile towards our Queen than the blasphemous professors I refer to are towards God. Not one of these hanged men have said, "Oh, Queen don't hang me; it is cruel and unjust to do so. You ought to be ashamed to do so, for if you had elected me to be your husband, and made me one of your children, and put me in your palace, and kept me, I should not have done the vile deed; it is your fault. Besides, even now you ought not to hang me; you should be merciful. Never mind your law or justice mind mercy and save me. Don't make yourself a cruel monster by hanging me." This is the way the clergy preach about our sovereign God if He dares to leave some men out of His election, out of His love, out of His body the Church, out of His family, and out of His Son, Spirit and Covenant. If He leaves them to themselves in sin, and then punishes them for their sins, in vindication of His law, and in honour of His justice, as the Queen executes her criminals, then, oh then, He must be a very dreadful God. Thus the professors of the age are more blasphemous of God, relating to the lost, than the criminals of our nation are towards our Queen.

In the subjects of God's Empire there are vessels of wrath in whom He has no pleasure. Now, as the Queen has loyal subjects, court friends, and a Royal family, in these she has pleased, as distinct from her criminals, in whom she has no pleasure, even so our God has loyal subjects, court friends, and Royal family in whom He has eternal pleasure as distinct from His criminals who have violated His laws and in whom He has no pleasure.

—The late Pastor Allen of Sydney, 1883.

*(Continued from page 97.)*

Having thus sought to establish that "Blessed are the meek" signifies "Blessed are the **humble** and **lowly**," let us now note how this is further borne out by the context and then endeavour to determine the manner in which such meekness finds expression. It must be steadily kept in mind that in these Beatitudes our Lord is describing the orderly developement of God's work of grace as it is experimentally realised in the soul. First, there is poverty of spirit—a sense of my insufficiency and nothingness, a realisation of my unworthiness and unprofitableness, next; there is mourning over my lost condition, sorrowing over the awfulness of my sins against God. Following this, in order of spiritual experience, is humbleness of soul.

The one in whom the Spirit of God has wrought, producing a sense of nothingness and of need, is now brought into the dust before God. Speaking as one whom God used in the ministry of the gospel, the apostle Paul said, "The weapons of our warfare are not carnal, but mighty through God to the pulling down of strongholds; casting down imaginations, and every high thing that exalteth itself against the knowledge of God, and bringing into captivity every thought to the obedience of Christ" (2 Cor. 10:4, 5). The "weapons" which the apostles used were the searching, condemning, humbling truths of Scripture. These, as applied effectually by the Spirit, were mighty to the pulling down of strongholds—powerful prejudices, and self-righteous devises in which they took refuge. The result was that proud "imaginations" or "reasonings"—the enmity of the carnal mind, the opposition of the human will—are all subdued, "cast down," and every thought concerning salvation is now brought into captivity to the obedience of Christ.

By nature every sinner is pharisaical, desiring to be justified by the works of the law. By nature we all inherit from our first parents the tendency to manufacture for ourselves a covering to hide our shame. By nature every member of the human race walks in "the way of Cain," who sought to find acceptance with God on the ground of an offering produced by his own labours. In a word, we desire to gain a standing before God on the basis of personal merits, we wish to purchase salvation by our good deeds, we are anxious to win Heaven by our own doings. God's way of salvation is too humbling to suit the carnal mind, for it removes all ground for **boasting,** therefore is it unacceptable to the proud heart of the unregenerate.

Man wants to have a hand in his salvation. To be told that God will receive nought from him, that salvation is solely a matter of divine mercy, that eternal life is only for those who come empty-handed to receive it solely as a matter of **charity,** is offensive to the self-righteous religionist. But not so to the one who is poor in spirit and who mourns over his vile and wretched state. The very word "mercy" is music in his ears: eternal life as God's free gift just suits his poverty-stricken condition: grace—the sovereign favour of God to the hell-deserving—is just what he feels most in need of. Such an one no longer has any thought of justifying himself in his own eyes: all his haughty objections against God's benevolence are now silenced. He is glad to own himself a beggar and bow in the dust before God. Once, like Naaman, he rebelled against the humbling terms announced by God's servant; but now, like Naaman at the end, he is glad to dismount from his chariot of pride and take his place in the dust before the Lord.

It was when Naaman bowed before the humbling word of God's servant that he was healed from his leprosy: so when the sinner owns his worthlessness Divine favour is shown to him. Such an one receives the Divine benediction for **"Blessed are the meek."** Speaking anticipatively through Isaiah, the Saviour said, "the Lord hath anointed Me to preach good tidings unto the meek" (61:1). And again it is written, "For the Lord taketh pleasure in His people: He will beautify the meek with salvation" (Psa. 149:4).

While humility of soul in bowing to God's way of salvation is the primary reference in the third Beatitude, it is not to be limited to this. "Meekness" is also an intrinsical part of that "fruit of the Spirit" which is wrought in and produced through the Christian (Gal. 5:22). It is that spirit which has been schooled to mildness by discipline and suffering and brought into sweet resignation to the will of God. When in exercise, it is that grace in the believer which causes him to bear patiently insults and injuries, which makes him ready to be instructed and admonished by the meanest of saints, which leads him to esteem others more highly than himself, which teaches him to ascribe all that is good in himself to the sovereign grace of God.

On the other hand, true "meekness" is not weakness. A striking proof of this is furnished in Acts 16:35, 37. The apostles had been wrongfully beaten and cast into prison. Next day the magistrates gave orders for their release, but Paul said to their agents "Let them come themselves and fetch us out." God-given meekness can stand up for God-given rights. When one of the officers smote our Lord, He answered, "If I have spoken evil, bear witness of the evil: but if well, why smitest thou Me?" (John 18:23).

The spirit of meekness was perfectly exemplified only by the Lord Jesus Christ, who was "meek and lowly in heart." In His people it fluctuates, oftentimes being beclouded by the risings up of the flesh. Of Moses it is said, "They provoked his spirit, so that he spake unadvisedly with his lips" (Psa. 136:33). Of Ezekiel it is recorded, "I went in bitterness in the heat of my spirit; but the hand of the Lord was strong upon me" (3:14). Of Jonah, after his miraculous deliverance, we read "It displeased Jonah exceedingly and he was very angry" ((4:1). So of the humble Barnabas, he parted from Paul in a bitter temper (Acts 15:37, 39). What warnings are these! How much we need to learn of Christ!

"Blessed are the meek for they shall inherit the earth." This was a quotation from Psalm 37:11. The promise seems to have both a literal and spiritual meaning: the meek shall inherit the earth and shall delight themselves in the abundance of peace." The "meek" are they who have the greatest enjoyment of the good things of the present life. Delivered from a greedy and grasping spirit, they are content with such things as they have. "A little that a righteous man hath is better than the riches of many wicked" (Psa. 37:16). Contentment of mind is one of the fruits of meekness of spirit. The proud and restless do not "inherit the earth," though they may own many acres of it. The humble Christian has far more enjoyment in a cottage than the wicked in a palace. "Better is little with the fear of the Lord than great treasure and trouble therewith" (Prov. 15:16).

"The meek shall inherit the earth." As we have said, this is a quotation from Psalm 37:11 and most probably the Lord Jesus was using Old Testament language to express new covenant truth. The 'flesh and blood" of John 6, the "water" of John 3:5 have, to the regenerate, a **spiritual** meaning; so here with the word "earth" or "land."Both in the Hebrew and in the Greek there is only one term for our English words earth and land, the context usually deciding which is preferable. "His words, literally understood, are, 'they shall inherit the land,' i.e., Canaan, 'the land of promise.' He speaks of the blessings of the new economy in the language of Old Testament prophecy. Israel, according to the flesh,—the external people of God, under the former economy were a figure of Israel according to the spirit—the spiritual people of God under the new economy; and Canaan, the world's inheritance of the former, is the type of that aggregate of heavenly and spiritual blessings which form the inheritance of the latter. To 'inherit the land' is to enjoy the peculiar blessings of the people of God under the new economy; it is to become heirs of the world; heirs of God and joint heirs with Christ. It is to be 'blessed with all spiritual blessings in the heavenlies in Christ,' to enjoy that true peace and rest of which Israel's in Caanan was a figure" (Dr. J. Brown). No doubt there is also an ultimate reference to the "new earth."

ARTHUR W. PINK.

# STUDIES IN THE SCRIPTURES

"Search the Scriptures" John 5:39.

Copyright in all English-speaking Countries.

Arthur W. Pink, Publisher and Editor,
5 Norton Street, Ashfield, N.S.W., Australia.

Price: 10 cents per copy; $1.00 or 5/- per year.

---

"Blessed are the merciful: for they shall obtain mercy" (Matt. 5:7).

In the first four Beatitudes which we have already considered there is a decided advance to be observed. First, there is a discovery of the fact that I am nothing, have nothing, and can do nothing;—poverty of spirit. Second, there is conviction of sin, a consciousness of guilt, producing godly sorrow—mourning. Third, there is a renouncing of self-dependence and a taking of my place in the dust before God—meekness. Fourth, this is followed by an intense longing after Christ and His salvation—hungering and thirsting after righteousness. But all of this is simply negative, a perception of what is defective and a yearning for what is desirable. In the next four Beatitudes we come to the manifestation of positive good, the fruits of a new creation, the blessings of a transformed character. How this shows us, once more, the importance of noting the order in which God's truth is presented to us!

"Blessed are the merciful: for they shall obtain mercy." Grossly has this been perverted by merit-mongers. They who insist that the Bible teaches salvation by works appeal to this verse in support of their pernicious error. But nothing could be less to their purpose. Our Lord was not here explaining the foundation on which rests the sinner's hope of mercy from God, but is describing the character of His genuine disciples. Mercifulness is a prominent trait in this character, and the meaning of our Lord's words evidently is: Mercy is an essential feature of that holy character which God has inseparably connected with the enjoyment of that happiness which is the result of His sovereign kindness. Thus, there is nothing whatever in this verse which favours the erroneous teachings of Romanism.

The place occupied by this Beatitude is another key to its interpretation. The first four describe the initial exercises of heart in one who has been awakened by the Holy Spirit. In the preceding verse, the soul is seen hungering and thirsting after Christ, and then filled by Him. Here we are shown the first effects and evidences of this. Having obtained mercy of the Lord, the saved sinner now exercises mercy. It is not that God requires us to be merciful in order to entitle us to His mercy—that would be to overthrow the whole scheme of Divine grace—but having been the recipient of His wondrous mercy I cannot but now act mercifully to others.

What is mercifulness? It is a gracious disposition toward my fellow-creatures and fellow-Christians. It is that kindness and benevolence which feels the miseries of others. It is a spirit which compassionates the sufferings of the afflicted. It is that grace which deals leniently with an offender and scorns the taking of revenge. "It is the forgiving spirit; it is the non-retaliating spirit; it is the spirit that gives up all attempt at self-vindication; and would not return an injury for an injury, but rather good in the place of evil, and love in the place of hatred. That is mercifulness. Mercy being received by the forgiven soul, that soul comes to appreciate the beauty of mercy, and yearns to exercise toward other offenders similar grace to that which is exercised towards one's self" (Dr. A. T. Pierson).

(Continued on page 144)

## IMPORTANT NOTICES

Set of twelve issues for **1922**, unbound, $1.00 or 5/-. Bound $1.50 or 7/-.
Set of twelve issues for **1923**, unbound, $1.00 or 5/-. Bound $1.50 or 7/-.
Set of twelve issues for **1924**, unbound, $1.00 or 5/-. Bound $1.50 or 7/-.
Set of twelve issues for **1925**, unbound, $1.00 or 5/-. Bound $1.50 or 7/-.
Note: We cannot break a set or now supply any **single** 1925 issues.
Subscription—price: $1.00 or 5/- per year to any address in the world.
Change of Address: Please notify me promptly of any change of address, and be certain to give both old and new address.
Non-subscribers receiving this Magazine regularly will understand their subscription has been entered by a friend.
Copies lost in the mail duplicated only if we are notified promptly.

## CONTENTS

The Gospel of John (John 15: 17-27) ... 122
Gleanings in Exodus ... ... ... 130
Election ... ... ... ... ... 134
Beholding ... ... ... ... ... 141
Repentance ... ... ... ... 143

## THE GOSPEL OF JOHN

### 54. Christ Vindicated by the Spirit: John 16: 1—11.

The following is an Analysis of the passage which is to be before us:—

1. Reason why Christ warned His disciples v. 1.
2. Details of what they would suffer v. 2.
3. Cause of the world's hostility v. 3.
4. Christ's tender solicitude v. 4.
5. The disciples' self-occupation vv. 5, 6.
6. The promise of the Spirit v. 7.
7. The Spirit vindicating Christ vv. 8, 11.

The chapter division between John 15 and 16 is scarcely a happy one, though perhaps it is not an easy matter to indicate a better: 16:12 would probably have been a more suitable point for the break, for v. 12 obviously begins a new sub-section. In the passage which is to be before us we find the Lord continuing the subject which had engaged Him at the close of chapter 15. There He had been speaking of the hatred of the world—against the Father, against Himself, and against His disciples. Then He had assured them that He would send the Holy Spirit to conduct His cause. The **character** in which Christ mentioned the Third Person of the Godhead—"the Comforter"—should have quietened the fears and sorrows of the apostles. Now Christ returns to the world's hatred, entering more into detail. Previously, He had spoken in general terms of the world's enmity; now He proceeds to speak more particularly, sketching as He does the future fortunes of Christianity, describing the first chapter of its history.

Most faithfully did the Saviour proceed to warn His disciples of the treatment which would be meted out to them by their enemies. Strikingly has Dr. John Brown commented upon our Lord's conduct on this occasion. "The founders of false religions have always endeavoured to make it appear to be the **present** interest of those whom they addressed to acquiesce in their pretentions and submit to their guidance. To His countrymen the Arabian imposter held out the lure of present sensual indulgence; and when he at their head, made war in support of his imposture, the terms proffered to the conquered were proselytism, with a full share in the advantages of their victors, or continued unbelief with slavery or death. It has, indeed been the policy of all deceivers, of whatever kind, to conceal from the dupes of their artifice, whatever might **prejudice** against their schemes, and skillfully to work on their hopes and fears by placing in a prominent point of view all the **advantages** which might result from them embracing their schemes, and all the **disadvantages** which might result from their rejecting them. An exaggerated view is given both of the probabilities of success, and of the value of the benefits to be secured by it, while great care is taken to throw into the shade the privations that must be submitted to, the labour that must be sustained, the sacrifices that must be made, the sufferings that must be endured, and the ruin that may be incurred, in joining in the proposed enterprise.

"How different the conduct of Jesus Christ! He had no doubt promised His followers a happiness, ample and varied as their capacities of enjoyment, and as enduring as their immortal souls; but He distinctly intimated that this happiness was **spiritual** in its nature, and to be fully enjoyed only in a **future** world! He assured them that, following Him, they should all become inheritors of a kingdom; but He with equal plainness stated that that kingdom was not of this world, and that he who would enter into it must 'forsake all,' and 'take up his cross.' Himself poor and despised, 'a Man of Sorrows and acquainted with grief,' He plainly intimated that His followers must be 'in the world, as He was in the world.'"

The disciples of Christ were to be hated by the world! But it is highly important that we do not form too narrow a view of what is meant by "the world." Satan has tried hard to obliterate the line which separates between those who are **"of the world"** and those who are **"not of the world."** And to a large extent he has succeeded. The professing "Church" has boasted that it would convert the world. To accomplish this aim, it has sought to popularise "religion." Innumerable devices have been employed—many of which even a sense of propriety should have suppressed —to attract the ungodly. The result has been the world has converted the "professing Church." But notwithstanding this it still remains true that "the world" **hates** the true followers of the Lamb. And nowhere is this more plainly evident than in those who belong to what we may term the **religious** world. This will come before us in the course of our exposition.

The closing verses of our present portion announce the relationship of the **Holy Spirit** to "the world" and it is this which **distinguishes** the first division of John 16 from the closing section of John 15. In the concluding verses of John 15 the Lord had spoken of the world's hatred, and this still engages Him in the first few verses of chapter 16. But in v. 7 He refers once more to the Holy Spirit, and in vv. 8-11 presents Him as His Vindicator. It is this which has guided us in selecting the title of our present chapter: its suitability must be determined by the interpretation which follows.

"These things have I spoken unto you, that ye should not be offended" (v. 1). Before the Lord describes in detail the forms in which the world's hostility would be manifested, He paused to acquaint the disciples with His **reasons** for announcing these things. First, it was in order that they should not be "offended" or "stumbled" or "scandalised" as the word means. To be forewarned is to be forearmed. Christ would prepare His people beforehand by telling them plainly what they might expect. Instead of contending among themselves which should be the greatest. He bids them prepare to drink of the cup He drank of and to be baptised with the baptism wherewith He was to be baptised. It was not that He would discourage them, far from it; He would fortify them against what lay ahead. And how this evidenced the tender concern of their Master! How it demonstrates once more that He "loved them unto the end"! And how gracious of the Lord to thus warn us! Should we not often have **stumbled** had not He not told us beforehand what to expect?

"These things have I spoken unto you, that ye should not be offended." That there was **need** for this warning is very evident. Already the question had been asked, "Behold, we have forsaken all, and followed Thee **what shall we have** therefore?" (Matt. 19:27). Moreover, that very night all **would be** "offended" because of Him: "Then saith Jesus unto them, All ye shall be offended because of Me this night; for it is written, I will smite the Shepherd, and the sheep of the flock shall be scattered abroad" (Matt. 26:31). But, it may be asked, why should Christ here forewarn the disciples when He knew positively that they **would be** offended? Ah, why tell Peter to "watch and pray lest he enter into temptation" (Mark 14:38), when the Lord had already foretold that he **would** deny Him thrice! Why command that the Gospel should be preached to every creature when He foreknows that the great majority **will not** believe it! The answer to each of these questions is: to **enforce** human responsibility.

"They shall put you out of the synagogues: yea, the time cometh, that whosoever killeth you will think that he doeth God service" (v. 2). Out of the catalogue of sufferings to which the disciples should be subjected, the Lord selects for mention two samples of all the rest: an extreme torture of the mind and the final infliction upon the body. It is indeed solemn to observe that this persecution of Christ's people comes from the **religious** world. The first fulfilment of this prophecy was from the Jews, who professed to be the people of God. But Christ identifies them with **the world** Their sharing in and display of its spirit showed plainly where they belonged. And the same is true to-day. Where profession is not real, even those who bear the name of Christ are part of "the world," and they are the first to persecute those who do follow Christ When the walk of the Christian condemns that of the worldly professor, when faithfulness to his Lord prevents him from doing many things which the the world does, and when obedience to the Word obliges him to do many things which the world dislikes, then enmity is at once aroused and persecution follows—persecution just as bitter and real to-day, though its forms be changed.

"To be 'put out of the synagogue' was more than simply to be excluded from the place of public worship. It cut a man off from the privileges of his own people, and from the society of his former associates. It was a sort of moral outlawry, and the physical disabilities followed the sufferer even after death. To be under this ban was almost more than flesh and blood could bear. All men shunned him on whom such a mark was set. He was literally an outcast; in lasting disgrace and perpetual danger. Those familiar with the history of the dark ages, or who are acquainted with the effects of losing caste among the Hindoos, will be able to realise the terrors of such a system" (Dr. Geo. Brown).

Sometimes the degradation of excommunication was the prelude to death. Cases of this are recorded in the book of Acts. We find there mention made of a class called "zealots." They were a desperate and fanatical faction who thirsted for the blood of Christians. "And when it was day, certain of the Jews banded together, and bound themselves under a curse, saying that they would neither eat nor drink, till they had killed Paul. And they were more than forty which had made this conspiracy" (Acts 23:12, 13). That such men were not restricted to the lower classes is evident from the case of Saul of Tarsus, who tells us that in his unregenerate days, "I verily thought with myself, that I ought do many things contrary to the name of Jesus of Nazareth. Which thing I also did in Jerusalem: and many of the saints did I shut up in prison, having received authority from the chief priests; and when they were put to death, I gave my voice against them." (Acts 26:9, 10).

How fearfully do such things manifest the awful depravity of the human heart! It has been the same in every age: godliness has always met with hatred and hostility. "Cain, who was of the Wicked one, and slew his brother. And wherefore slew he him? Because his own works were evil, and his brother's righteous" (1 John 3:12). "He that is upright in the way is abomination to the wicked" (Prov. 29:27). "They hate him that rebuketh in the gate, and they abhor him that speaketh uprightly" (Amos 5:10). It is the same now. Faithfulness to Christ will stir up religious rancour. In spite of the boasted liberalism of the day, men are still intolerant, and manifest their enmity just so far as they dare.

"And these things will they do unto you, because they have not known the Father, nor Me" (v. 3). Here the Lord traces, once more, the world's undying ill-will to its true source: it is because they are not acquainted with the Father and the Son. Hatred and persecution of God's children are both the consequence and the proof of the spiritual ignorance of their enemies. Had the Jews really known the Father in whom they vainly boasted, they would have acknowledged the One whom He had sent unto them, and acknowledging Him, they would not have mistreated His followers. Thus it is to-day! "Whosoever believeth that Jesus is the Christ born of God. And every one that loveth Him that begat loveth him also that is begotten of Him" (1 John 5:1).

"But these things have I told you, that when the time shall come, ye may remember that I told you of them" (v. 4). The Lord had already given one reason (v. 1), why He had spoken these things to the disciples, now He gives them another: He made these revelations that their faith in Him might be increased when the events should confirm His prophecy. The fulfilment of this prediction would deepen their assurance in Him as the omniscient God, and this would encourage them to depend upon the veracity of His promises. If the evil things which He foretold came to pass, then the good things of which He had assured them must be equally dependable.

"And these things I said not unto you at the beginning, because I was with you" (v. 4). "The Lord also tells them why He had not told them at the first. The full revelation was more than their weak hearts could bear. They would be staggered at the prospect. They must be gradually trained to this. Not all at once, but by little and little, as they were able to bear it, He unfolds the scheme of His cross, and of their duties and dangers. The Lord has milk for His babes, and meat for His strong men.

And there was as yet no need for this. For He Himself was with them, and by the less could prepare for the greater. He was with them, as a nurse her children; to lead them on from strength to strength, from one degree of grace and Christian virtue to another. But now that He was about to depart from them, and leave them, as it were, to themselves; to see how they will acquit themselves in that contest for which He has been training them all the while; it is necessary that all the more plainly and fully He should lay before them their future—at first this was not needed. 'Sufficient unto the day is the evil thereof.' And He was yet with them and could gradually unfold it to them. And there was yet time. But as time goes on, we see Him and hear Him opening page after page of the volume of His secret Providence to their opening minds; till finally, as here, He tells them plainly and fully even of the extremest trials that are coming upon them" (Dr. Geo. Brown).

"And these things I **said not** unto you at the beginning, because I was with you." But how are we to reconcile this with such passages as Matt. 5: 10, 12, 10: 21, 28, etc.? In addition to the solution offered above, namely, that Christ **gradually** unfolded these things to the apostles, we may point out: First, He had not previously said that **the world** would do these things unto them, that is, He had not hitherto intimated that they would be hated by **all** men. Second, previously He had not declared that the reason for this hatred was because of men's **ignorance** of the Father and the Son. Third, He had not previously predicted that such persecution would proceed from the delusion that the perpetrators would imagine that they were doing God a service!

"But now I go My way to Him that sent Me" (v. 5). There are some who would connect this first clause of the verse with the end of v. 4, thus: "And these things I said not unto you at the beginning, because I was with you; but now I go My way to Him that sent Me." And then after a brief pause, the Lord asked, "And does no one of you ask whither I go; but because I have thus spoken to you, your heart is filled with sorrow." This is quite likely, and seems a natural and beautiful connection.

"And none of you asketh Me, whither goest Thou?" (v. 5). In 13:36, we find Peter asking Christ. "Whither goest Thou?" But this was an unintelligent forwardness for he evidently thought that the Lord was going on an earthly journey (cf. 7: v5). In 14:5: Thomas said, "We know not whither Thou goest," but this was more by way of objection. What the Lord wanted was an intelligent, sympathetic, affectionate response to what He had been saying. But the apostles were so absorbed in grief that they looked not beyond the cloud which seemed to overshadow them; they were so occupied with the present calamity as not to think of the blessing, which would issue from it. They were depressed at the prospect of their Master's departure. Had they only asked themselves whither He was going, they would have felt glad for Him; for though it was their loss, it was certainly His gain—the joy of being with His Father, the rest of sitting down on high, the blessedness of entering again into the glory which He had before the foundation of the world. It was therefore a rebuke for their self-occupation, but how tenderly given!

"But because I have said these things unto you, sorrow hath filled your heart" (v. 6) How often it is thus with us! We magnify our afflictions, and fail to dwell upon the blessings which they bear. We mourn and are in heaviness in the "cloudy and dark day," when the heavens are black with clouds and the wind brings a heavy rain, forgetting the beneficial effects upon the parched earth, which only thus can bring forth its fruits for our enjoyment. We wish it to be always spring, and consider not that without winter first, spring cannot be. It was so with the disciples. Instead of making the most of the little time left them with their Master, in asking Him more about His place and work in Heaven, they could think of nothing but His departure. What a warning is this against being swallowed up by overmuch sorrow! We need to seek grace to enable us to keep it under control.

"But because I have said these things unto you, sorrow hath filled your heart." It is blessed to learn that the disciples did not continue for long in this disconsolate mood. A very different spirit was theirs after the Saviour's resurrection. Strikingly is this brought out in the concluding verses of Luke's Gospel: "And He led them out as far as to Bethany, and He lifted up His hands, and blessed them. And it came to pass, while he blessed them, He was parted from them, and carried up into heaven. And they worshipped Him, and returned to Jerusalem **with great joy:** And were continually in the temple, praising and blessing God." Forty days of fellowship with Him after He had come forth Victor of the grave, had removed their doubts, dispelled their fears, and filled their souls with joy unspeakable.

"Nevertheless I tell you the truth; it is expedient for you that I go away: for if I go not away, the Comforter will not come unto you" (v. 7). Blessed contrast! The disciples, at the moment, had no thought for Him, but He was thinking of them, and assured them that though they lost Him for a while, it would be their gain. Though they had failed to ask, their compassionate Master did not fail to answer. Ever more ready to hear than we are to pray, and wont to give more than we desire; ready to make allowance for them in their present distress, and thinking always more of the sufferings of others than His own; thinking more now of those He is leaving behind, than of the agony He is going forth to meet—before they call He answers, answers what should have been their request, declaring unto them the expediency of His departure.

"Nevertheless" is adversative: I know you are saddened, at the prospect of My departure, **but** My going is needful for you. **"I** tell you the truth": the personal pronoun is emphatic in the Greek —I who love you, I who am about to lay down My life for you: therefore you must believe what I am saying. I tell you **the truth.** Your misgivings of heart have beclouded your understandings, you misapprehend things. You think that if I remain with you, all the evils which I have mentioned would be prevented. Alas, you know not what is best for you. "It is **expedient** for you that I go away:" It is for your profit your advantage. It is striking to note the **contrast** between our Lord's use here of "expedient" from the same words on the lips of Caiaphas in 11:50!

"But what did the Lord mean? How was His going away their **gain?** We believe that there is a **double** answer to this question according as we understand Christ's declaration here to have a double reference. Notice that He did not say "It is expedient for you that I go My way **to Him** that sent Me?" as He **had** said in v. 4. He simply said, "It is expedient for you that **I go away."** We believe that Christ designedly left it abstract. **Whither was** He "going" when He spake these words? Ultimately, to the Father; but **before** that He must go to the **cross.** Was not His first reference then to His impending death? And was it not highly **expedient** for the disciples and for us, that the Lord Jesus should go to and through the sufferings of Calvary!

"For if I go not away, the Comforter will not come unto you." The atoning death of Christ was necessary to make it consistent with the Divine government to bestow on men these spiritual blessings which are necessarily connected with the saving influence of the Holy Spirit. All such blessings from the beginning had been bestowed with a reference to that atonement; and it was fitting that these blessings, in their richest abundance, should not be bestowed till that atonement was made (Dr. John Brown). " 'Unless I go away,' that is, unless I die, nothing will be done—you will continue as you are and everything will remain in its old state: the Jews under the law of Moses, the heathen in their blindness—all under sin and death. No scripture would then be fulfilled, and I should have come in vain" (Dr. Martin Luther).

But while we understand our Lord's first reference in His words "If I go not away" to be to His death, we would by no means limit them to this. Doubtless He also looked forward to His return to the Father. This also was expedient for His disciples. "So fond had they grown of His fleshly presence, they could not endure that He should be out of their sight. Nothing but His corporeate presence could quiet them. We know who said, If Thou hadst been here, Lord, as if absent, He had not been able to do it by His Spirit, as present by His body. And a tabernacle they would needs build Him to keep Him on earth still; and ever and anon they were still dreaming of an earthly kingdom, and of the chief seats there, as if their consummation should have been in the flesh. The corporeate presence therefore is to be removed, that the spiritual might take place" (Bishop Andrews).

In other ways, too, was it "expedient" for His disciples that the Saviour should take His place on High. It is of a **glorified** Christ that the Spirit testifies, and for **that** the Saviour had to "go away." Moreover, had Christ remained on earth He had been **localised,** His bodily presence confined to one place: whereas by the Spirit He is now omnipresent—where two or three disciples are gathered together in His name, there is He in the midst. Again; had the Lord Jesus remained on earth there had been far less room and opportunity for His people to exercise faith. Furthermore, this cannot be gainsaid: after Christ had ascended and the Spirit descended, the apostles were new men. They did far more for an absent Lord, than they ever did while He was with them in the flesh.

"But if I depart, I will send Him unto you" (v. 7). "Every rendering of this verse ought to keep the distinction between apeltho and poreutho, which is not sufficiently done in the English Version, by 'going away' and 'depart.' 'Depart' and 'go' would be better! The first expressing merely the leaving them, the second, the going up to tne Father" (Dean Alford). We believe our Lord's fine discrimination here confirms our interpretation above of the double reference in His "if I go not away," though we know of no commentator who takes this view.

"And when He is come, He will reprove the world of sin, and of righteousness, and of judgment" (v. 8). There are few verses in this Gospel which has been more generally misunderstood than the one just quoted. With rare exceptions this verse is understood to refer to the benign activities of the Holy Spirit among those who hear the Gospel. It is supposed to define His work in the conscience prior to conversion. It is regarded as a description of His gracious operations in bringthe sinner to see his need of a Saviour. So firmly has this idea taken root in the minds even of the Lord's people it is difficult to induce them to study this verse for themselves—study it in the light of what precedes, study it in the light of the amplification which follows, study the terms employed, comparing their usage in other passages. If this be done carefully and dispassionately, we feel confident that many will discover how untenable is the popular view of it.

In the context, as far back as 15:19 the Lord Jesus had been speaking of the hatred of the world; surely, then, this would be a strange place to introduce a mention of the initial work of the Spirit in bringing men to a saving knowledge of the truth! But if the word "reprove" signifies "to condemn" to "bring in guilty" then this would announce God's response to the world's enmity! Again; in 16:7, Christ had said, "I will send Him (The Spirit) unto you" (the disciples), while in v. 13 He adds, "Howbeit when He, the Spirit of truth is come, He will guide you (believers) into all truth." Between these two statements the Lord Jesus declared that the Spirit would "reprove the world." Obviously then an altogether different class is here in view. Again, it is very evident that something must be wrong if this verse is interpreted so as to clash with Christ's explicit statement in 14:17: "the Spirit of truth whom the world cannot receive!" Once more; if Christ had been referring to that work of the Spirit within men which is designed to bring them out of darkness into God's marvellous light, how is it possible to explain the order of the three things which the Spirit "reproves"—sin, righteousness and judgment? If reproof of sin means, convicting the sinner of his lost condition, and if reproving of righteousness means, convicting him of Christ's righteousness to supply his own unrighteousness, wherein would then lie the need of still further convicting him of "judgment"? We have never seen any real attempt made to grapple with this difficulty.

Now the first thing to note in seeking to ascertain the meaning of our verse is the character in which the Holy Spirit is here said to "reprove the world." He shall reprove. Who shall? The previous verse tells us: "the Comforter." Not the Holy Spirit," nor "the Spirit of truth,"but the Paraclete. Now this same word is translated "Advocate," and righly so, in 1 John 2:1; and it is as "Advocate," as Christ's Advocate, the Spirit of God is here viewed. The office and duty of an "advocate" is to vindicate His client when his cause permits of it; to do so by adducing evidence which will silence his adversary. Now it is in this character that the Holy Spirit is related to "the world." He is here not to improve the world, and make it a better place to live in, but He is here to establish its consummate sin, to furnish proof of its guilt, and thus does He vindicate that blessed One whom the world cast out.

"And when He is come, He will reprove the world of sin, and of righteousness, and of judgment." The word "reprove" is rendered "convince" in the margin, and is translated "convict" in the Revised Version. It is found in John 3:20: "For every one that doeth evil hateth the light, neither cometh to the light, lest his deeds should be reproved." It is found again in 8:46: "Which of you **convinceth** Me of sin?" It occurs in James 2:9: "But if ye have respect to persons, ye commit sin, and are **convicted** of the law as transgressors." In its substantive form it is found in Heb. 11:1: "Now faith is the substance of things hoped for, the **evidence** of things not seen." Now in all of these passages it is **not** a subjective but an **objective** "reproof" which is in view; and it is in **this** sense that the word is here used in 16:8: "Inward conviction is certainly not the meaning of the word rendered 'reproof.' It is rather refutation by proofs, convicting by unanswerable arguments as an advocate, that is meant" (Bishop Ryle).

"And when He is come, He will reprove the world of sin, and of righteousness, and of judgment." How does the Holy Spirit do this? By the preaching of the Word? By working on the consciences of men, by striking terror into their hearts? No, that is not the **subject of this** verse. It is the **fact** of the Spirit's **presence** in the world which **demonstrates its guilt**. To illustrate: Suppose I saw a man hanging on the gallows, **of what** would that "convince" me? Why, that he was a **murderer**. How would I be thus convinced? By reading the record of the trial? By hearing a confession from his own lips? No; but by the **fact** that he was hanging there. So John 16:8-11 is not describing the activities of the Spirit. His subjective work in men's hearts; but announces **the consequences of** His **presence** on earth. The fact that He is now here demonstrates, furnishes proof, establishes conviction, that the world is guilty. How this is so the verses which follow explain.

The Holy Spirit ought not to be here at all. That is a startling statement to make, but we say it thoughtfully. **Christ** is the One who **ought** to be here —speaking, of course, from the human side of things. He was sent here by the Father, but the world did not want Him, would not have Him, hated Him and cast Him out. The presence of the Holy Spirit in the world to-day, therefore **demonstrates its guilt**. He is here to take the place of an absent Christ: here to vindicate Him. The very fact of Him **being** here "reproves the world"—objectively, not subjectively.

"Of sin, because they believe not on Me." Under three indictments does the Holy Spirit bring the world in guilty.

First, His presence here furnished proof of its "sin" or **guilt**, for that is the force of the word here—as in Rom. 3:9, 1 John 1:7, etc. The evidence of their guilt is that they "believed not" on Christ. "Here the Holy Ghost is not spoken of as dealing with individuals when He regenerates them and they believe, but as bringing conviction to the world because of sin. The Holy Ghost being here, convicts the world, i.e., what is outside where He is. Were there faith, He would be in their midst; but the world does not believe. Hence Christ is, as everywhere in John, the standard for judging the condition of men" (Mr. W. Kelly).

"Christ has been in the world: He has been rejected and cast out of it: it is only too plain to be denied that He died a malefactor's death. Men may say for themselves, that individually they had no hand in it. This they do say: how is it possible that they can be guilty of what was done by men of another race and of another time? Well, look at the Jew in the centuries that have elapsed since then; has not His blood been upon them, and on their children? If Christ was not what He claimed, was He not worthy of the sentence under which He suffered? If you do not **believe** in Him, do **you** not affirm that sentence to be righteous? Who were these Jews who put Him to death? Were they not a people carefully prepared for centuries to receive the One they rejected? If you had been among them, would not **you** have rejected Him too?

"The unbelief for which the world is condemned is naturally characteristic of us all: and those who are brought to receive Him are just those who will most fully own this; the language of the prophet will be theirs: 'He was despised and rejected of men a Man of Sorrows and acquainted with grief; and we hid, as it were, our faces from Him; He was despised, and we esteemed Him not.' If there be any difference as to any, it is the mercy of God that has made the difference" (Numerical Bible).

"Of righteousness, because I go to My Father and ye see Me no more" (v. 10). If it were the dealing of the Holy Spirit with individuals in regenerating souls this would have read, "of **un**-righteousness because **they** are destitute of it." But this is not the thought here at all! It is the presence here of the Holy Spirit which establishes Christ's "righteousness," and the evidence is, that He has gone to the Father. Had Christ been an Imposter, as the religious world insisted when they cast Him out, the Father had not received Him. But the fact that the Father did exalt Him to His own right hand, demonstrates that He was completely innocent of the charges laid against Him; and the proof that the Father has received Him, is the presence now of the Holy Spirit on earth for Christ has sent Him from the Father! The world was **unrighteous** in casting Him out; the Father **righteous** in glorifying Him, and this is what the Holy Spirit's presence here establishes. "So perfectly did Christ glorify God in death, as he always did in life the things that pleased His Father, that nothing short of putting Him **as Man** at His own right hand could meet the case. Wondrous fact! A Man now in glory at the right hand of God, above all angels, principalities, and powers. **This is the proof of** righteousness. It is what God the Father owed to Christ, who has so perfectly pleased and so morally glorified Him, even in respect of sin. All the world, yea, all worlds, would be too little to mark His sense of value for Christ and His work—nothing less than setting Him as Man at His right hand in heaven." (Mr. W. Kelly). Thus the Paraclete "reproves the world," supplies "evidence," that Christ's doctrine was true, His claims just, His conduct unblamable. The last clause of our verse "and ye shall see Me **no more**" is another example of words being used in Scripture in a **relative** sense: the disciples were no more to see Him in a state of humilation.

"Of judgment, because the Prince of this world is judged" (v. 11). This is the logical climax. The world stands guilty for refusing to believe in Christ: its condemnation is attested by the righteousness of Christ, exhibited in His going to the Father; therefore nothing awaits it but judgment. The Spirit's presence here is the evidence that the Prince of this world has been judged—when He departs sentence is executed, both on the world and on Satan! That will be God's answer to the unjust sentence of the world in condemning to death His Beloved. Moreover, proof has already been furnished in the partial overthrow of Satan's power, by delivering portions of the world from his dominion, and a multitude of his subjects from his service. The accumulating evidence of Christ's victory over the Devil demonstrates that he is a conquered foe, only awaiting the doom already passed upon him.

Thus we do not understand John 16:8 to 11 to refer to the **mission** of the Spirit **in** the world, but to His **condemnation of** the world, and in condemning (that is what "reproving" is) the world He has **vindicated** Christ. The world cast out the Lord Jesus as a blasphemer and an insurrectionist: the Advocate is here to show the falsity of the world's charges. It is to this we believe that 1 Tim. 3:16: "Justified (pronounced righteous) **by the Spirit**" speaks. Not that we would limit the reference to this, but certainly as including it. Christ was "justified by the Spirit"—**vindicated**—at His baptism (Matt. 3:16; at His resurrection (Rom. 1:4); and here, after His ascension. Note how in 1 John 2:1, the Holy Spirit speaks of Him as "Jesus Christ the **Righteous!**"

The following questions are to aid the student for our next lesson:

1. What did Christ mean by "Ye cannot bear them now" v. 12?
2. Have the "many things" been said v. 12?
3. What is implied by the word "guide" v. 13? Meditate on it.
4. What is meant by "He shall not speak of Himself" v. 13?
5. Where has the Spirit shown us "things to come" v. 13?
6. To whom was Christ referring in v. 16?
7. Find the verse which records the disciples "rejoicing" v. 22.

ARTHUR W. PINK.

---

*We shall be glad if our readers will join us in earnest daily prayer that the Lord will enlarge the present circulation of this magazine. This year there has been quite a falling-off in the number of subscribers. Do you tell other Christians about this publication.*

# GLEANINGS IN EXODUS

**30. The Decalogue and its Sequel: Ex. 20.**

The Ten Commandments expressed the obligations of man in his original state, while enjoying free and open communion with God. But the state of innocence was quickly departed from, and as the offspring of fallen Adam, the children of Israel were sinners, unable to comply with the righteous requirements of God. Fear and shame therefore made God's approach terrible, as He appeared in His holiness, as a consuming fire. The effects upon Israel of the manifestation of Jehovah's majesty at Sinai are next given: "And all the people saw the thunderings, and the lightnings, and the noise of the trumpet, and the mountain smoking: and when the people saw it, they removed, and stood afar off. And they said unto Moses, Speak thou with us, and we will hear; but let not God speak with us, lest we die" (20:18, 19).

Here was a plain acknowledgment from Israel that they were **unable** to deal with God directly on the ground of the Decalogue. They felt at once that some provision needed to be made for them. A **mediator** was necessary: Moses must treat with God on their behalf. This was alright so far as it went, but it failed to meet fully the requirements of the situation. It met the need from **their** side, but not from God's. The Lawgiver was holy, and His righteous requirements must be met. The transgressor of His Law could not be dealt with simply through a mediator as such. **Satisfaction** must be made: sin must be expiated: only thus could the inexorable demands of Divine justice be met. Accordingly this is what is brought before us in the sequel. The very next thing which is here mentioned in Exodus 20 is an ALTAR!

The "altar" at once tells of the provision of Divine **grace**, a provision which fully met the requirements of God's governmental claims, and which made it possible for sinners to approach Him without shame, fear, or death; a provision which secured an agreement of peace. On such a basis was the Siniatic covenant ratified. Not that this rendered null and void what Jehovah had said in Ex. 19:5, "Now therefore, if ye will obey My voice indeed, and keep My covenant, then ye shall be a peculiar treasure unto Me above all people." The Siniatic covenant was an agreement wherein God proposed to deal with Israel in blessing on the ground of **their obedience.** Governmentally this was never set aside. **But provision was made for their failure,** and this, right from the beginning! Israel's failure to appropriate God's gracious provision only rendered the more inexcusable their subsequent wickedness.

We read of no "altar" in Eden. Man in his innocence, created in the image and likeness of God, needed **none.** He had no sin to be expiated upon an altar: he had no sense of shame, and no fear of God in coming into his Maker's presence and communing with Him directly. It was man's **sin** which made necessary an "altar," and it was Divine **grace** which provided one. There are two things to bear in mind here in Ex. 20: Jehovah was not dealing with Israel on the **alone** ground of His righteousness, but also according to His rich mercy!

It is vitally important to see the relation between the two great subjects of our chapter: God giving **the Law** and God furnishing instructions concerning **the altar.** If it was impossible for Israel to enter **directly** into the Siniatic covenent (a mediator being necessary), and if they (as sinners) were unable to keep the Decalogue, why propose the one and give the other? Three answers may be returned First, **to show to Israel** (and the race) **that man is a sinner.** A fixed standard which definitely defined man's fundamental relations both with God and his fellows, a standard holy and just and good in all its parts, revealed to man his want of conformity to God's Law". I had not known sin (its inner workings as lust) but by the Law . . . that sin by the commandment might become exceeding sinful" (Rom. 7:7, 13). Second, **to bring to light man's moral inability.** The Law with its purity and its penalty, disclosed the fact that on the one hand, man was **unable** (because of his corrupted nature) to keep the Law; and on the other hand, unable to atone for his transgressions of it— "Sin taking occasion by the commandment wrought in me all manner of concupiscence . . . For I was alive without the Law once; but when the commandment came, sin revived and I died.

And the commandment, which was ordained to life, I found to be unto death" (Rom. 7:8, 10). Third, **to show man his need of the Saviour.** "Wherefore then serveth the Law? It was added because of transgressions, till the Seed should come to whom the promise was made . . . But before faith came, we were kept under the law, shut up unto the faith which should afterwards be revealed. Wherefore the Law was our schoolmaster unto Christ, that we might be justified by faith" (Gal. 3:19, 23 24).

It is therefore abundantly clear that the Ten Commandments were never given to men or to Israel as a means of salvation, i.e., being saved through obeying them. They were not given in **statutory form** till after man had become a sinner, and his nature so corrupted that he had neither ability nor desire to keep them. The Law was not a way of life, but a rule of conduct. The writing of the Ten Commandments on tables of stone long after man had become a fallen being, was to show that God's claims upon His creatures had not been cancelled, any more than has the **right** of a creditor to collect though the debtor be **unable** to pay. Whether unfallen, or fallen, or saved, or glorified, it ever remains true that man **ought** to love God with all his heart and his neighbour as himself. Whilever the distinction between right and wrong holds good, man is under obligation to keep God's Law. This is what God was enforcing at Siani—His righteous claims upon Israel, first as His creatures, then as His redeemed. It is true that Israel were unable to meet those claims, therefore did God, in His marvellous grace, make provision both for **their** failure and the upholding of **His** claims. This we see in the "altar."

Before we examine the typical significance of the "altar" we would call attention to a most lovely thing not found here in Exodus 20, but given in a later scripture. As Israel beheld the fearful phenomena which manifested the presence of Jehovah upon the Holy Mount, they said unto Moses, "Speak thou with us, and we will hear: but let not God speak with us lest we die" (20:19). Now it is exceedingly blessed to mark God's **response** to this. But not to the careless reader is this discovered. It is only by prayerfully and diligently comapring scripture with scripture that its exquisite perfections are revealed, and only thus are we able to obtain **a complete** view of many a scene. In Deut. 5:22, 27 Moses reviews the giving of the Law at Sinai and the effects which that had upon the people. Then he says, "And the Lord heard the voice of your words, when ye spake unto me, and the Lord said unto me, I have heard the voice of the words of this people, which they have spoken unto thee: **they have well said ALL that they have spoken."** Now if we compare with this Deut. 18:17, 18, we discover the full response which the Lord made to Israel's request: "And the Lord said unto me, They have well spoken that which they have spoken. **I will raise them up a Prophet** from among their brethren, like unto thee, and I will put My words in His mouth; and **He** shall speak unto them all that I shall command Him." The desire of Israel for a **mediator,** for one of their own number to act as God's mouthpiece unto them was to be realised, eventually, in the great Mediator, the chief Prophet or Spokesman of God. How blessedly does this reveal to us the thoughts of **grace** which Jehovah had unto Israel even at Sinai! How refreshing to turn away from the miserable perversions of many of the modern commentators and learn what the Scriptures have to say concerning that memorable day at Sinai!

"And the people stood afar off, and Moses drew near unto the thick darkness where God was" (v. 21). In the above paragraph we have sought to point out a part, at least, of the precious revelation which Jehovah made to Moses in the "thick darkness." Following this, Moses returned to the people with this message from the Lord: "Ye have seen that I have talked with you from heaven. Ye shall not make with Me gods of silver, neither shall ye make unto you gods of gold" (vv. 22, 23). Idolatry was expressly forbidden. It was God, once more, insisting upon His unrivalled supremacy. And then immediately after this, instructions are given concerning the "altar."

"An altar of earth shall thou make unto Me, and shalt sacrifice thereon thy burnt offerings, and they peace offerings, thy sheep and thine oxen" (v. 24). The Tabernacle had not yet been erected. Clearly then, what we have here were Divine instructions for Israel's immediate compliance: an altar was to be built **at the foot of Sinai!** It was not the future which was in view, but the present. All doubt as to the correctness of this conclusion is forever removed by what we read of in Exodus 24:4—what intervenes being a connected account of what Jehovah made known unto Moses on the Mount to be communicated unto the people. Here we are told, "And Moses wrote all the words of the Lord, and rose up early in the morning, and builded an altar under the hill, and twelve pillars, according to the twelve tribes of Israel." That there may be no possibility of failure to identify this "altar," it is immediately added, "And he sent young men of the children of Israel, which offered **burnt offerings** and sacrificed **peace offerings** of oxen unto the Lord. Here then was the "altar" (of earth), and here were the "burnt offerings" and the "peace of offerings." And why has the Holy Spirit been so careful to record these details here in Exodus 24? Why, if not to show us the fulfilment of Jehovah's word unto Pharoah: "Thus saith the Lord God of Israel, Let My people go, that they may hold **a feast** unto Me in the wilderness" (5:1)! The "peace-offering" is the one offering of all others specially connected with **feasting**: "And Solomon awoke; and, behold it was a dream. And he came to Jerusalem, and stood before the ark of the covenant of the Lord, and offered up burnt offerings and offered **peace** offerings, and made **a feast** to all his servants (1 Kings 3:15, cf. 8:64, 65, etc).

"In all places where I record My name I will come unto thee, and I will bless thee" (v. 24). Plainly this begins a **new** sentence and is connected with what follows, as the first words of v. 25 clearly show. Jeremiah 7:12 affords an illustration of what is meant by God recording His name in a place: "But go ye now unto My **place** which was in Shiloh, where **I set My name** at the first." Let the interested reader look up the various references to "Shiloh." Compare also "Bethel" and "Zion" where God's name was also recorded.

"And if thou wilt make Me an altar of stone, thou shalt not build it of hewn stone: for if thou lift up thy tool upon it thou hast pollutted it" (v. 25). The connection between this and the last clause of v. 24 is most significant and important. God had promised to "come unto" Israel and "bless" them in all places where His name was recorded. But if Israel were to **come unto** Jehovah an "altar" must be erected, an altar where blood should flow and fire consume: blood to propitiate God; fire to signify His acceptance of the sacrifice.

The first thing to notice about this altar (like the one in the previous verse) is its extreme simplicity and plainness. This was in marked contrast from the "gods of silver" and "gods of gold" (v. 23) of the heathen. The altar which Israel was to erect unto God must not be made of that which man had manufactured, nor beautified by his skill: there should be in it no excellence which human hand had imparted. Man would naturally suppose that an altar to be used for **Divine** sacrifices should be of gold, artistically designed and richly ornamented. Yes, but that would only allow man to glorify **himself** in his handiwork. The great God will allow **"no"** flesh to glory in **His** presence" (1 Cor. 1:29). Solemn indeed are the words "If thou liftest up thy tool upon it, thou hast **polluted** it." "Not by works of righeousness which we have done" (Titus 3:5) is the New Testament equivalent. Sinfulness cannot approach the thrice holy God with any thing in hand which his own labours have produced. That is why the Lord had not respect unto the offering which Cain brought to Him: Cain presented the fruits of the ground, the product of his own labours; and God rejected them. And God **still rejects** all the efforts of the natural man to propitiate Him. All the attempts of the sinner to win the notice and merit the respect of God by his efforts at self-improvement are worse than vain. What God demands of His fallen creatures is that they should take the place of **lost sinners** before Him, coming empty-handed to receive **undeserved** mercy.

"Neither shalt thou go up by steps unto Mine altar" (v. 26). The meaning of this is not difficult to perceive. It is parallel in principle to what was before us in the previous verse. "Steps" are a human contrivance to avoid the strain of rising from a lower level to a higher. Man cannot climb up to God by any steps of his own making. What God requires from the sinner is, that he shall take his true place before Him —in the dust. **There** God will meet with him. It is true that morally and spiritually man is separated from God by a distance, a distance far too great for man to ever bridge. But though man cannot climb up to God, God, in the person of His Son, has come down all the way to the poor sinner. The second chapter of Philippians describes that marvellous and gracious descent of the Lord of glory. Five distinct "steps" are there marked—the number of **grace.** He who was in the form of God, and thought it not robbery to be equal with God (1) "made Himself of no reputation," (2) "took upon Him the form of a servant," (3) "and was made in the likeness of men." (4) "Being found in fashion as a man He humbled Himself," (5) "and became obedient unto death, even the death of the cross." Self-evident is it then that there are no "steps" for man to climb!

"Neither shalt thou go up by steps unto Mine altar, that thy nakedness be not discovered thereon" (v. 26). The very efforts of men to climb up to God only expose their own shame. Remarkably is this brought out in the very chapter which records the entrance of of sin into this world. As soon as Adam and Eve had eaten of the prescribed fruit we are told, "And the eyes of them both were opened, and they knew that they were naked; and they sewed fig leaves together, and made themselves aprons" (Gen. 3:7). But of what avail were these aprons before Him who can read the innermost secrets of the heart? The very next thing we read is "And they heard the voice of the Lord God walking in the garden in the cool of the day, and Adam and his wife **hid themselves** from the presence of the Lord God amongst the trees of the garden." Their fig-leaf "aprons" did not now even satisfy themselves! But that is not all: "and the Lord God called unto Adam, and said unto him, Where art thou?" And what was our guilty forefather's response? This: "And he said I heard Thy voice in the garden, and I was afraid, because I was naked; and I hid myself." The apron of fig-leaves only served to make manifest and emphasise the fact that he **was** naked—naked even with the "apron" on! How true, then, that man's very efforts to climb up to God do but expose his shame!

It should be pointed out, in conclusion, that the two "altars," the one of "earth" and the other of "stone," both point to the person of the Lord Jesus, bringing out His varied perfections. On this we cannot do better than let Mr. Grant interpret for us:—

"The material which God accepts for His altar, then, is either earth or stone, —things which are in contrast with one another; 'earth' deriving its name from its crumbling character (**eratz, from ratz,** to crumble away, says Parkhurst, of the Hebrew word); and 'stone,' which resists pressure, and is characterised by its hardness and durability. Of the dust of the earth man is made, and as this is fertile as it **yields** to the hand that dressed it, so is man to God, as he yields himself to the Divine hand. Earth seems thus naturally to stand for the creature in its frailty,—conscious of it, and accepting the place of weakness and subjection, thus to the bringing forth of fruit to God. While 'stone' stands for the strength that is found in another, linked with and growing out of the consciousness of weakness: 'When I am weak, then am I strong.'

"Now in both respects He who was perfect, who came down to all the reality of manhood, to know both its weakness and the wondrous strength which is wrought out of weakness, thus waiting upon and subject to God. It was thus in endurance He yielded Himself up, and endured by yielding Himself to His Father's will."

The "earth" then, corresponds in thought to the "fine flour" of the meal offering (Lev. 2), speaking of the perfect **yieldedness** of Christ's to the Father's will. Most blessedly was this evidenced in Gethsemane, where we hear Him saying, "Nevertheless, not My will, but Thine be done." The "stone" points to the same thing as the "brass" in the Tabernacle altar. It showed there was that in Christ (and in Him alone) capable of **enduring** the fearful fires of God's wrath. The fact that the stones of this altar must not be "hewn," shaped by human chisel, shows once more how jealously God guarded the accuracy of these types. The stones must be left just as the Creator had made them—man must not change their form. The antitype of this would be that Christ, as it were, **retained** the "form" which God had given Him. And all the pressure of circumstances and all the efforts of men and Satan could not alter it. When the Lord announced the Cross (the "altar" on which the great Sacrifice was to be offered), Peter said, Spare Thyself": that was Satan, through man, attempting to "hew" the "stone'"; but the Lord suffered it not.

May God stir up writer and reader to a more diligent and prayerful **searching of the Scriptures.**

ARTHUR W. PINK.

# ELECTION.

**Address by Dr. A. W. Pink, at Ashfield Tabernacle, 29/6/'25.**

## No. 5.

Now to-night I want to complete the last division but one of our subjects, which I was unable to finish on Friday night, namely, the value of this doctrine and the reasons why it ought to be preached. Let me just review, briefly, the ground that I have already covered. First, the doctrines of God's Sovereignty and Divine Election ought to be preached because the Bible is full of them. "Preach the Word" is the marching orders of every servant of Christ—not preach **part** of it: we are not free to pick and choose, to single out those portions that we like and to ignore the portions we do not like. Our marching orders are to preach the Word, all the counsel of God, and the doctrines of God's Sovereignty and Election hold such a prominent place in Scripture, therefore they ought to be taught.

In the second place, they ought to be taught because these are the doctrines which most exalt God: they give God the first place. If I have believed in Christ to the saving of my soul it is because God predestinated that I should do so and gave me the enabling power to do so, therefore I have absolutely no ground for boasting, and consequently all the glory for my salvation belongs alone to God. That is why this doctrine should be preached —it most exalts God. This doctrine magnifies the **grace** of God as none other does. It magnifies God's grace by showing that eternal life is His gift: it is not something that He sells: it is not something that we earn: it is something which He gives: and He gratuitously bestows it on whom He pleases, and the proof of that is this, that those who have received the gift of eternal life are no better in themselves than others who have not received it, therefore they have the more cause to praise God. I have the additional reason to praise God because He has done more for me and done more in me than He has in those who believed not, and the more He has done in me the more reason I have to praise Him, therefore when we see what we owe **everything** to God it magnifies His grace and it deepens our thanksgiving to Him.

Third, this doctrine should be preached because it humbles man, and anything that **humbles** man is necessarily a blessing. Now let me put it to you this way. If I have any hand in my own salvation that inevitably leads to self-consciousness, and self-consciousness begets self-righteousness, and self-righteousness ends in Pharisasm. Now let me repeat that. If I have a hand in my own salvation it leads to self-consciousness. Necessarily I think about the part I did, and self-conscious ness leads to self-righteousness, and self-righteousness ends in Pharisaism. If I have a part in salvation, then my litany will be, "I thank Thee O God that I am not as other men are"; my heart must be softer than theirs, my will could not have been quite so rebellious as theirs, because I submitted to Thee and they did not, therefore I can pat myself on the back. But once we see that the very faith that we believe with was given to us by God, that He has wrought all our works in us, there is no cause for boasting, and we are humbled into the dust before God. In other words the doctrine of election strips us of the last shred of human merit by showing us that the very faith which we had to believe in the Saviour with was given us by God.

In the fourth place, this doctrine ought to be preached because it is ennobling. That is to say, this doctrine gives a strength and a stability to character that nothing else does. I grant you freely that the real Calvinist may seem stern, stern like Moses was, stern like Elijah was, stern like John the Baptist was. We need more stern men to-day. I do not say harsh. I do not say cruel. I do not say unfeeling: but I say that we need men of more stamina, more backbone, men with unflinching courage, men who will not compromise, men who will stand firm in the face of any opposition and the history of the last thousand years show, without an exception, that the men who have stood firm in the time of storm, the men who refused to compromise or bend or trim-down have been men, one and all, whose hearts have been gripped by the truths of sovereign grace.

Again, this doctrine ought to be preached because it is of great comfort to the people of God. It is comforting because it shows me that God's love for me is not based upon anything in me. Now I want you to get hold of this clearly. God does not love me because of my earnestness, or because of my sincerity, or because of my faithfulness. The only reason why God loves me is because He looks at me in Christ—in the Person of His Beloved Son. The only reason why God loves me is because I have been accepted in the Beloved. Very well then, if God's love for me is not based upon anything in me, then nothing can change His love. His love is like Himself—everlasting: it is invariable: for you must remember dear friends, that love is not an attribute of God, love is the very nature of God, and to say that God's love could change means that God Himself would change, and if God Himself were to change He would cease to be God; therefore, because love is His very nature His love cannot change, and because His love for me is not determined by anything in me, thereHis love will never vary toward me In other words, it is as we are told in Jeremiah 31:3, "I have loved thee with an everlasting love, therefore with loving-kindness have I drawn thee."

In the sixth place, this doctrine ought to be preached because it fills the believer with deepest gratitude. It fills the true Christian with deepest gratitude because it shows that the God who chose me might have justly passed me by, for in myself I am not a particle better than thousands whom He has passed by. Once we realise in our souls this truth we shall be constrained to say,

" 'Twas not that I did choose Thee
For Lord that could not be;
This heart would still refuse Thee,
But Thou hast chosen me."

" 'Twas sovereign mercy called me
And taught my opening mind;
The world had else enthralled me
To heavenly glories blind."

Yes, my friends, once we see this truth, and it grips our hearts, we shall be constrained to say without hesitation or limitation:

"A monument of grace I stand
A sinner saved by blood;
The streams of love I trace
Up to their fountain God;
And in His mighty breast I see
Eternal thoughts of love for me."

Now in the seventh place, this very doctrine of election provides the evangelist with a stimulus and an assurance that nothing else can give him. Now follow me closely. I am sure there must be some who have thought that even if this doctrine be true, and while it may be a blessing to preach to Christians, it will probably be injurious to the evangelist—it will make him less zealous in his work, and the more the evangelist believes election the more it will handicap him. Now listen: The evangelist who believes in the docrine of divine election will go forth fully assured that his success is absolutely certain before he begins, because he knows that if he preaches God's Word that Word cannot return to Him void, that that Word of God shall accomplish what He pleases and it shall prosper in the thing whereunto He sent it. Now listen, so many evangelists and Christian workers get discouraged because they expect what God has never promised. I had a missionary magazine handed me this very week, or rather last week, published by one of the leading evangelical Christian Missionary Societies, and on the front page was a picture and around the picture were these words: "The world for Jesus." My friends, God has not promised to save the world in this age at all, that is not God's purpose. God has told us plainly in Acts 15:14 that He is now taking out of the world, out of the Gentiles, **taking out of** them—there is election—a people for His name. And my friends, the gospel is not being preached to suit our wishes, the gospel is being preached to fulfill God's purpose.

Now turn for a moment to John 6:37. You are all very familiar with the latter half of the verse, but I want you to notice carefully the first half. They were the words of the Lord Jesus Christ, John 6:37: "All that the Father giveth Me shall come to Me." "All that the Father giveth Me." That is, all that the Father chose before the foundation of the world shall come to Me; that is, come to Him for salvation. **"All that the Father giveth Me shall** come to Me." There is no perhaps, there is no maybe, there are no 'ifs', it is a positive, unqualified, unequivocal declaration. "All that the Father giveth Me shall come to Me." Now then, suppose I go out as a missionary to China, and I begin to preach the gospel, and there are hundreds and thousands of the heathen all around me and they are worshipping their idols, and I preach the gospel to them and there is no response; and I go on preaching the gospel, and there is no response, and I get discouraged and say, Well, perhaps I do not understand the psychology of the Chinese, perhaps the methods that I used in Australia are not suitable to use in China, so we will try and attract them with something else. We will give them some moving pictures and see if they will draw them. We will have a brass band and see if that will attract them: or perhaps they want amusing; I must send back to Sydney for a book of jokes and translate them into Chinese and give them one or two of those in each sermon: perhaps I am too stern and too dry for them. Now that is always the temptation to every servant of Christ when he has preached and there are no seeming results. He gets discouraged at the lack of results and so he thinks he must change his methods, and perhaps the change is effected. But if he rested in faith on the doctrine of election, if he believed this verse here in John 6:37: "All that the Father giveth to Christ shall come to Him," then he will say, No, I will not change my method, God has sent me out here to preach His Word, not to save China but to gather out from the Chinese a people for His name; and therefore I will go on preaching, knowing that in God's time the ones that He has marked out for salvation will be saved, for Christ has said, "All that the Father giveth Me shall come to Me." Now the man who knows that, the man who believes that, knows that his work in the Lord cannot be in vain.

Let me give you an illustration nearer home. Here we have these texts, texts of Scripture in the tramcars —Thank God we do: we all of us here to-night ought to be praying that God will use them. We ought to be thankful, deeply thankful, that God's Word is getting before the public in that way. Now let me suppose those texts have been there for five years and those who were responsible for putting them there have never heard of anybody being saved by them, and have never heard of anyone being blessed by them, they could not see any results. Well, what shall we do? Why, of course quit putting them there! It all depends whether you are walking by sight or walking by faith. If you are walking by sight you are always going to be guided by the evident results, the results that you can see; but if you are walking by faith, you know if it is **God's** Word that is there in the trams, God has promised that His Word shall not return to Him void, therefore faith rests on it. Faith knows that whatever God has put that Word there for it shall accomplish and it will accomplish without any preacher to interpret it or explain it either. I for one have absolute confidence that the Word of God under the power of the Holy Spirit will do its own work. That does not mean that God never uses preachers, but God is not tied up and limited to preachers. My friends, God's work would go on in this world if every preacher died to-night, make no mistake about that. If every evangelist and preacher and Bible teacher died to-night God's work would still go on: don't you be so silly as to think that God is limited to any one method of working. Why, the Lord Jesus said that if those disciples did not cry out His hosannas, that the very stones would cry out, and I believe He meant what He said: I am just simple enough to believe that. God is able to make stones cry out if He wants to: of course He is.

Now then turn to John 10:16, "And other sheep I have, which are not of this fold": The speaker again was Christ, in the day of His earthly ministry in the land of Palestine. "This fold" was the Jewish fold that then existed. "Other sheep I have, which are not of this fold: them also I must bring. (Listen!) and they **shall** hear my voice." Every one of those sheep **shall** hear His voice when His own time comes, therefore when I go out as an evangelist in the work of the Lord my success is absolutely certain before I begin! My success will be determined by what God has purposed before He sent me forth. Now one other point. Inasmuch as no evangelist has any means of knowing which are God's elect and which are not God's elect, his business is to preach the gospel with equal faithfulness and with equal earnestness to every soul that he can reach. My business is to preach God's Word to every man, woman and child that I can reach, knowing that God will bless that Word in His own way, according to His own eternal purpose: so my friends to sum it up it means this. When the servant of God goes out in his evangelistic work he is not going out at random: the success of his work is not left to chance: the fruitage of his ministry is not left to the uncertain and fickle will of men, but the success of his ministry is assured beforehand, because it is bound to accomplish what God has purposed: therefore I say that the truth of election is a powerful impetus and a soul-assuring doctrine for every evangelist.

Now then in the next place I want to speak of how I may know that I am one of God's elect. It is true that we do not have access to the Lamb's Book of Life. We have not yet got to heaven and seen our names written there, but it is possible for God's elect on earth to know and to be sure that they are among that favoured number. How? How may we be sure? First, by God creating us anew in Christ. All men are not God's spiritual children. It is regeneration which makes anyone a child of God experimentally. "Of His own will begat He us with the word of truth." Now then, have I been born again? If so, if I have, then I have one of the marks of election.

Second, How may I know if I am among God's elect? By the Lord calling me to Himself. Now turn to the 10th chapter of John, verse 3:—"To Him the porter openeth; and the sheep hear His voice: and He calleth His own sheep by name, and leadeth them out. And when He putteth forth His own sheep, He goeth before them, and the sheep follow Him: for they know His voice." Fourteenth verse:—"I am the Good Shepherd; and know My sheep, and am known of Mine." What I want you to notice particularly is in the third verse. "To Him the porter openeth; and the sheep hear His voice: and He calleth His own sheep by name." Now turn over to Romans 8:29:— "For whom He did foreknow, He also did predestinate to be conformed to the image of His Son, that He might be the firstborn among many brethren. Moreover whom He did predestinate, them He also called." Now listen, God gives to each one of His own elect a call, an effectual call, an irresistible call, which calls us out of death into life, just as He gave dead Lazarus a call; a call which brings us out of darkness into God's marvellous light, as He did in the first day in Genesis 1. God said, Let there be light, and the darkness disappeared: there was light. Now then, has a Divine call come to your soul? Have you heard God calling to you? Was there a time in your life when you heard, in an unmistakable manner, Christ saying to you, "Come unto Me" and you came? He called you: He called His own sheep: have you received such a call? That is one of the proofs that you are one of God's elect people, for "whom He did predestinate, them He also called." Now it is simple, isn't it? God's truth is simple. Thank God it is, for we are simple people.

Now then, in the third place, How may I know that I am among the elect? By God's Word coming home to my soul in power. Turn to the first Epistle to Thessalonians, 1st chapter and the 4th and 5th verses:—"Knowing, brethren beloved, your election of God." Now notice how that 4th verse reads: not guessing, not imagining, not concluding, but "knowing, brethren beloved, your election of God." It can be known. Now how is it known? "For (that means 'because') our gospel came not unto you in word only, but also in power." Now listen, the gospel does not come in power to all who hear it. Wherein does the power lie? Not in the eloquence of the preacher: If it did, then men would be the converters of souls. Not in the learning of the preacher if it did, regeneration would lie in the wisdom of men. Not in the pathos or moving power of the preacher. Why, my friends, there are actors on the stage who play their parts so cleverly that they can move an audience to tears: the mere fact that a preacher can make you cry does not prove anything: the power of the gospel does not lie in the pathos of the preacher, it lies in the quickening, convicting and drawing power of God the Holy Spirit. Now let me read that verse again: "Knowing, brethren beloved, your election of God." How do we know it? "Because our gospel came not unto you in word only, but also in power." Now let me ask you these questions:—Has the gospel come home to you in power? Has it convicted your conscience? Has it melted your heart? Has it subdued your pride? Has it overcome the rebellion of your will? Has the gospel ever come home to your heart in power so that it has made Christ a living reality to you? Has it? Has the gospel come home to your heart in such power that you have seen His sufficiency, His excellency, so that tonight He is the fairest of ten thousand to your soul? If the gospel has come home in such power to your heart then you have one of the marks of election. That is another of the proofs whereby we may discover whether or not we are among the chosen favoured people of God.

Fourth, how may we know whether or not we are among God's elect? By God working in us both **to will and to do of His good pleasure.** Turn to Philippians 2:13: "For it is God which worketh in you both to will and to do of His good pleasure." Now listen! The will of the natural man, the will of the unregenerate man is opposed to God: he is unwilling. That is how you were once. But the will of the regenerate man, the will of the saved man or woman is in harmony with Christ. Now listen! Can you truthfully say that what I want in my life is God's will to be done? I want God's will to be wrought out in me and through me? If you can, then that is another mark of your election. No unregenerate, non-elect man does; he wants his own will, he wants his own way. If to-night you prefer God's way to your own and His will to yours, then that proves that God has worked in you both to will and to do of His good pleasure. Now, of course, the question arises, Why does not God work that in everybody? And the only answer that we can give is because it does not so please Him; why, we do not know, and probably never shall. God giveth no account of His matters. Why did God pick me out and pass by someone else? I do not know, but I am profoundly thankful that He did. Instead of worrying my poor little brain with questions that no human intelligence can answer, I am going to occupy myself in thanking and praising Him because He did elect me.

Now, in the fifth place, How may I know whether I am one of God's elect? By His working in and through me or producing in and through me **the fruit of the Spirit.** Turn to Galatians 5, verse 22:—"But the fruit of the Spirit is love, joy, peace, long-suffering, gentleness, goodness, faith." Now, mark you, that is the fruit **of the Spirit,** not the fruit of my willingness, not the fruit of my consecration, not the fruit of my earnestness, not the fruit of my anything; it is the fruit of the Spirit. The fruit of the Spirit is "love," do you have any love for God? Do you really love Him? The fruit of the Spirit is "joy"—do you have any joy in the things of God? The fruit of the Spirit is "peace"—is there any peace in your conscience? is there peace in your soul? If there is, then there is present in your heart the fruit of the Spirit, and if that fruit is there you have another mark of your election.

So in those five ways God reveals to us His election—by creating us anew in Christ, by regenerating us, by calling us to Himself, by the Word coming home to us in power, by working in us both to will and to do of His good pleasure, and by producing in us the fruit of the Spirit.

Now again. The elect prove their own election **to themselves.** Not only does God reveal it in those five ways but the elect prove it unto themselves. Now you turn to II Peter 1:10, I have no doubt that this is a verse which has been running in many of your minds this last week. "Wherefore the rather, brethren, give diligence to make your calling and election sure." Now that is something that we are exhorted to do for ourselves. We are exhorted to make our election sure. Well, you say, how on earth can we do that? Not that we are to make it sure unto God—it cannot be any surer there than it was before the foundation of the world, but we are to make it sure to ourselves. How are we going to do that? In four ways. There are at least four ways in which every Christian must make his calling and election sure to himself.

First, by abandoning himself to Christ. Now go back again to John 6:37:—"All that the Father giveth Me shall come to Me: and him that cometh to Me I will in no wise cast out." Now notice the two statements linked together and the order of them. In the first half of the verse you have election —God's side. In the second half of the verse you have human responsibility—man's side: both linked together in the same verse. "All that the Father giveth Me (that is election) shall come to Me" (that is the Divine side), "and him that cometh to Me (that is the human side), I will in no wise cast out." Now that is the first way in which you can find out whether or not you were one of those that the Father gave to Christ. If you were among the number that the Father gave to Christ you will prove it for yourself by coming to Christ. That is simple. Now if there is an unsaved person in this building to-night and you are saying within yourself, Well, this doctrine of election has troubled me very much—thank God if it has; I am always thankful for anything that will trouble a sinner: I am very worried when I see a sinner untroubled, it shows he is sound asleep, or, worse still, he is dead. When a sinner is troubled there are signs of life, an awakening has begun. But suppose there is a sinner here to-night who is troubled, and is troubled about this very question of election, and he is saying to himself. Well, if God has elected me to be saved I shall be, and if He has not elected me to be saved then I won't be, no matter what I do: how am I to find out whether or not I am among the elect, that is what is bothering me? If I knew that I were one of the elect I would believe, but until I do, well, I don't see any reason in believing now. My friends, you are trying to get things upside-down, you cannot know that you are one of the elect until you have come to Christ. That is the first thing you have to do to prove that you are one of the elect. "All that the Father giveth Me shall come to Me; and him that cometh to Me I will in no wise cast out." Very well then, if you come to Christ to-night, just as you are, right in your seat—you do not have to come forward into any inquiry-room or mourners' bench, or raise your hand or do anything, you may come to Christ right at this moment, just where you are sitting, just as you are, empty-handed, a beggar, in all your sins, and Christ has promised and He cannot lie, that if you come to Him He will in no wise cast you out. If you will come to Him then you will have the first proof that you are one of God's elect, and you never will know that you are one of His elect until you have come to Christ. So then, the first way in which we make our calling and election sure is by abandoning ourselves to Christ.

The second way is by an obedient walk. Turn to the first Epistle of Peter and the second verse:—"Elect according to the foreknowledge of God the Father, through sanctification of the Spirit, unto obedience." That is what we are elected unto. "Elect according to the foreknowledge of God the Father, through sanctification of the Spirit, unto obedience." Now listen: if you are walking contrary to the precepts of God's Word, if you are living in disobedience to God's commandments, then you have no reason whatever to regard yourself as one of God's elect. If you are living a life of self-pleasing, a life of self-will, a life of self-gratification, a life that is not regulated by God's Word, then you have no cause at all to regard yourself as one of God's elect; but if, by God's grace, you are anxious to be a doer of the Word as well as a hearer; if by God's grace you are daily asking God to enable you to be more obedient, and if you confess to Him your failures and cry unto Him for increased grace to obey His precepts, then by an obedient walk you will prove to yourself and make sure your own election. You all remember the 23rd Psalm, "The Lord is my Shepherd, He leadeth me in the paths": He, the Shepherd, leadeth me, the sheep, in the paths of what? Do you remember?—Righteousness!—that is whither He leads, those are the paths into which He directs us. "He leadeth me in the paths of righteousness." Is that the path you are walking in? Are you seeking strength from God to tread the narrow way and walk in the paths of righteousness? If you are, you have one of the proofs that you are one of His sheep and that the Shepherd is leading you.

Third, we can prove our own election unto ourselves by separating from all that is contrary to God. Ephesians 1:4, "According as he hath chosen us in him before the foundation of the world, that we should be holy"—not because we were, for we were not, but He hath chosen us in Him before the foundation of the world, that we should be holy. The word "holy" does not mean sinless, the word "holy" means separated, and God has chosen us in Him (that is, in Christ) that we should be separated, listen, that we should be separated from everything that is contrary to the Holy Name of Him whose name we bear. That means we are separated from every known sin, from everything that is sinful in the sight of God. If I know a thing is wrong, forbidden by God, sinful in His sight, then I am to separate myself from it. That means of course, that I have to get down on my knees and earnestly seek grace from God to do so. Again, I must not only separate myself from all that is sinful but I must separate myself from all that is dishonoring to Christ and that means, my friends, in plain language, that if you are the Lord's people you are doing wrong if you support a preacher who is not honoring Christ. If the preacher sets his denomination above the honour and glory of our Saviour, if he teaches any doctrines which dishonour our Saviour, if he denies the deity of Christ or the virgin birth of Christ, or the atoning death of Christ, or the literal resurrection of Christ, or the coming again in glory of Christ then my duty is plain: no matter how many friends I may have in that place, no matter how dear that church may be to me, if the man in that pulpit is dishonouring Christ, then I dishonour Christ if I remain there. God has chosen us in Christ that we should be holy: that means separated from all that is dishonoring and contrary to Christ. And my friends, that is a searching test to-day. I have not been in Australia very long I know, but unless Australia is very different from every other country I have lived in—and I have lived in several—unless Australia is very different from what other countries in Christendom are, it is becoming a difficult matter, it is becoming a rare thing to find a preacher who is really and truly exalting Christ, magnifying Him above everything else. Oh, I know that they all mention Christ: they have to do that as a matter of respectability, but are they constantly magnifying Christ and holding Him up as the only Saviour for sinners and as the only hope of the believer, for He is our all in all. .

Now in the fourth place, we prove our own election and make it sure by a steady perseverance in the faith, and **there** is where false professors may be distinguished from the elect of God. Turn now to John 8 : 31 :—"Then said Jesus to those Jews which believed on Him. If ye continue in My word, then are ye My disciples indeed." "If ye continue." Now turn over to I John 2 : 19 :—"They went out from us, but they were not of us (the apostle now is referring to some who had been in this assembly or church: they had posed as real Christians and they were nothing more than empty professors). "They went out from us, but they were not of us; for if they had been of us, they would have **continued** with us; but they went out, that they might be made manifest that they were not all of us." If they were of us they would have continued with us. Now that is the point. God's elect manifest their election and make their own election sure by **continuing** in the faith and by **persevering** to the end. False professors may make a good start seemingly but they do not last. It is just like the fruit trees: they are covered with blossoms in the Spring, but all the blossoms do not come to fruit—just the same in nature as it is in grace. There are lots of blossoms when God sends a revival and sinners are getting saved: there are lots of blossoms as well as real fruit. The blossoms come to nothing, but the real people of God, His elect, when they are saved by Him, manifest their election by continuing in God's Word and persevering to the end.

My last word is in Colossians 3. Now the passage that I am going to read to you shows us how the elect of God ought to live . Beginning at the 12th verse : "Put on therefore, as the elect of God, holy and beloved, bowels of mercies, kindness, humbleness of mind, meekness, long-suffering; forbearing one another, if any man have a quarrel against any: even as Christ forgave you, so also do ye." Now notice the 12th verse :—"Put on therefore, as the elect of God"— Verse 14 : "And above all these things put on charity, which is the bond of perfectness. And let the peace of God rule in your hearts, to the which also ye are called in one body ; and be thankful. Let the Word of Christ dwell in you richly in all wisdom ; teaching and admonishing one another in psalms and hymns and spiritual songs, singing with grace in your hearts to the Lord. And whatsoever ye do in word or deed, do all in the name of the Lord Jesus, giving thanks to God and the Father by him."

Oh dear friends, as I draw this last address on Election to a close I want to remind you and I want to remind myself, that this doctrine of election is one that is everywhere spoken against and one of the most effective ways of silencing objectors is by lives that will bear witness to the fact that we are the elect of God. The best way of silencing the critics against this doctrine is that we shall live lives that will adorn it, that our ways and our walk will show that God **has** done more for us than He has for them. So I press upon you in this closing word our personal responsibility in connection with this truth. Read and re-read that passage in Colossians 3 : 12, 17. It is God's Word telling us how His elect ought to live.

ARTHUR W. PINK.

---

*TO NEW READERS.—The back issues of this Magazine are obtainable in bound form. Vol. I contains the first twelve expositions of John's Gospel, eight articles on "The Anti-Christ," and many other shorter ones. Price 7/- post paid. Send for one. Our supply is strictly limited, and will not be re-issued.—A.W.P.*

## BEHOLDING.

"They looked unto Him and were lightened" (Psa. 34:5).

In these words we have the secret of peace and happiness and real progress in the Christian life. All looking else where, whether at ourselves or at others, ends in darkness and trouble. Hence the danger of reading biographies to the neglect of the Word of God. Our great Enemy knows, better than thousands seem to know, that our strength, light, peace and joy come from "looking off unto Jesus," and occupation of heart with Him. Hence his one great aim is to keep us from doing this.

The **sinner** he will occupy with his **sins** as long as he can; with the pursuit of sin, and the pleasures of sin. When quickening comes, then:

The **penitent** he will occupy with his **repentance,** and his sorrow for sin; until he is concerned as to whether he has repented enough or aright.

The **believer** he will occupy with his **faith,** in the same way.

The **servant** he will occupy with his **service** till he becomes so absorbed in it that he has no time to be occupied with Him to whom the service is supposed to be rendered. And finally:

The **saint** he will occupy with his **holiness**; and so absorb him with his walv, and his life, and his state, before God, that he fails to learn the **standing** which God has given him in Christ, and loses the very power which alone can secure for him the walk which he strives to attain.

Now it is clear that, in each of these cases, the enemy succeeds in this one great object. Anything, however good and true and even right in itself, the enemy will use, provided it engage the heart and prevent it from locking unto Him who is the only true source of light and peace. Our temptation is to seek the blessing, instead of the Blesser, who has already blessed us with all spiritual blessings in Christ (Eph. 1:3).

What we need is the spirit that breathes in this Psalm (34):

"I will bless Jehovah at all times:
His praise shall continually be in my mouth.
My soul shall make her boast in Jehovah:
The humble shall hear thereof and be glad.
O magnify Jehovah with me,
And let us exalt His name together."

This is occupation of heart with Him, which will do more to make our walk what we would have it then all our efforts and attentions bestowed on the walk itself. Occupied with Him we are saved from the snare which ever besets the Christian. We are prone to believe that we **are** just what we **feel** we **are**: that we are just as good as we feel we are; or just as bad as we feel we are. But this is not the case, not is it the standard by which we are to be tried.

We find it difficult to understand how we can be different in God's sight from what we are in our own. Yet so it is. We are different in His sight from what we are in our own. We see ourselves in the light which He shreds abroad in our hearts: and, which reveals to us more and more the awful corruptions of our old nature. Whereas God sees us in Christ, and as what He has made us to be in Him. He can look upon the humblest and weakest believer, and say as He said of Christ: "This—this is My beloved son!"

This seems too good to be true! and so thousands of real Christians think it presumption to take such high ground; and yet it is nothing but disobedience not to take it. When we are told that to "walk worthy," it means that we are to walk, "giving thanks unto the Father which hath made us meet to be partakers of the inheritance of the saints in light" (Coloss. 1:10, 12).

This brings us back to the secret of a holy life. It is summed up in one word:

### "BEHOLDING."

This is the English word; but in the Greek there are four important words, which all bear on this great subject. We want our readers to see them and learn their lessons.

1. Kat-op-tri-'zom-e-noi. This occurs only once, in 2 Cor. 3:18, and it means beholding-as-in-a-mirror. Moses had been with God, and the Divine glory was reflected in his face. He had begun to be changed! And we shall be like Him altogether when we shall see Him as He is (1 John 3:2). Beholding Him now, as in a mirror, we get more and more like Him: but when we shall see Him as He is, we shall be changed, in a moment, in the twinkling of an eye, and these bodies of our humiliation shall become like His own glorious body (Phil. 3:21).

In looking at himself in an Eastern mirror, which was made, not of glass, but of polished metal, the person saw himself in the mirror but those around saw the reflection of the mirror on his face. And this would be white or yellow, etc., according to the metal of which the mirror was made; he would not see this reflection or **change** on his face at all, but **others** would see it Just so it is with those who are thus as in a mirror "beholding" Christ in the glory of His person and the perfection of His work. They become changed, and Christ—the mirror—whom they behold is reflected on and in them, and thus, without an effort, they are more and more "conformed to His image." **They** may not be conscious of it, but **others** will see it, and take knowledge of them that they have been with Jesus.

2. **The-a'-o-mai.** It means **to behold-as-in-a-theatre.** In fact our word **theatre** is a Greek word from this very root. So the verb means—to behold as persons behold in a theatre, i.e., with interest, eagerness and delight. This is the word used of Christ, when He tabernacled among men. (John 1:14). Here was occupation with Christ. "We have seen with our eyes" (I John 1:1), the enraptured apostle exclaims. This is the word used of those who saw Him go into heaven (Acts 1:11). They beheld, as persons entranced: and we shall thus behold when He comes again to be glorified in His saints.

3. **The-o'-re-o.** This is a kindred word, relating rather to the Oyympic games (which we must remember were **sacred occasions** to the Greeks); or, as we should say to-day, athletic sports. The the-o-res was the **official** State representative at these great festivals. As we should put it in English, he would have the **Royal Box**, or chief and best seat, in the best position for beholding what is going on. Hence we may say that it means to **behold as from the Royal Box**, the place of privilege. It is used by Christ of us in His prayer to His Father in John 17:24. "Father I will that they also, whom Thou hast given me, be with Me where I am; that they may behold My glory, which Thou hast given Me." That is how the saints are to behold His glory. They are to be "with Him": in the highest, chiefest position: and are to behold, as at a mighty festival, the display of that glory before their eyes.

4. **Ep.-op-teu'-o.** This means **to-behold-as-an-initiate.** It is the verb used of initiating into all the secrets connected with heathen mysterious or religions. The **ep-op'-tees was** the one who had been thus initiated and admitted to the full communion with those with those who possessed the knowledge of the religious secrets of the Eleusinian and other so-called "mysteries." This word is used by the Holy Spirit only in the Epistles of Peter. In 2 Peter 1:16, Peter says, "We were made or admitted to be eye-witnesses of His majesty" on the Mount of Transfiguration. It was indeed an initiation to the three apostles when they thus beheld His glory. In Peter 2:12, we have another initiation, viz., that which the heathen had when they beheld the good works of Christians ("your good works which they shall behold"), and 3:2, "on beholding your chaste conduct." That is to say, the life of a true Christian was to the heathen as great a revelation as when they first beheld the mysteries of their religion.

Here, then, we have a complete view of these four words, and the lessons they teach:

1. Beholding as in a mirror.
2. Beholding as in a theatre.
3. Beholding as from a privileged position at a high and sacred festival.
4. Beholding as an initiate.

Thus is the secret of a holy life set before us. It is all summed up in the verse with which we commenced from Psalm 34. "They looked unto HIM and were lightened." The word in this verse is, of course, Hebrew, and has no connection with the four Greeks words we have enlarged upon. It means **to direct the eye to, to look with deep interest, regard, respect, affecion, etc.** It first occurs in Gen. 25:5, in connection with the Covenant which God was about to make with Abram, and He says to him "Look now toward heaven!" Yes, that is it. Look now toward heaven. Look unto Him. Behold the overlasting Covenant. "To Abraham, and his seed were the promises made": and **beholding** and directing the eye to these promises we shall indeed be enlightened. We shall behold the Promiser, and not merely the promises; the Blesser, and not merely the blessing; "Him" and not "It." Herein lies the secret of getting true light. Light in the heart; light in the understanding; light on the walk; light for time; light in the valley of the shadow of death; light for eternity.

—Things to Come, 1900.

## REPENTANCE.

The words of Christ are perfect. "One sinner that repenteth" (Luke 15 : 7, 10). How often to-day we hear man's way of describing a human change, "He has made a profession." If that is all in your life, or mine, there is no real work for eternity. Not a few speak of themselves, with earnestness, and use the following expressions: "I gave my heart to God," "I have accepted Christ," "I came out last evening." Such may "mean right," and in some cases, may have experienced the work of God, but their description is painfully defective.

Thanks be unto God, His salvation is infinitely greater, and resting upon a firm foundation, and abiding eternity. Head-knowledge of the way of salvation does not save a man, nor does ignorance of much of God's truth "unsave" him—although it may indicate he is unsaved, and all lack of knowledge should grieve us. It is true that a child lives before he understands what his life is. But if we have been saved, dear reader, it is that we may "know Him that is true." (1 John 5 : 20). And it is so important to know what the grace of God is—First, that we may test ourselves by God's touchstone as to whether we have really passed out of death into life (John 5 : 24). Second, that if we are His blood-bought people, we may not mislead others by a wrong explanation of the riches of His love.

There is joy in heaven "over one sinner that repenteth." Repentance is so definitely marked by Christ, "Except ye repent, ye shall all likewise perish" (Luke 13 : 3, 5). This includes sorrow for sin, because it is sin, and not only sorrow for its punishment. Ah, dear reader, there is not enough true anguish for sin to-day. Men have rebelled against God, but they treat their crimes so lightly. They do not feel for His honour. God called Israel to be ashamed of their iniquities" (Ezek. 43 : 10), and are you not ashamed of sin?

Your heart was not good enough to "give" to God, but salvation is infinitely beyond this :—God gives a new life, yea, eternal life. It is God's gift, not yours : God's glory, not yours. What a joy to a truly troubled sinner. And there is joy in heaven when such brokenness of heart is experienced. God will not despise a broken and contrite heart (Psa. 51 : 17), for that is His work. Mere profession, without heart-humbling, is not in accord with the gospel of the grace of God.

The blood of Christ makes an anxious sinner **loath** himself in his own sight (Ezek. 20 : 43 ; 36 : 31). That is **repentance**, and repentance unto life (Acts 11 : 18) takes God's standpoint, and the sinner who thus repents does not dare to trust to his repentance, but by the very repentance, is ashamed of everything in himself—except that which God's grace has humblingly brought about. Reader, have you ever known such a precious and mighty work of God? Or is there no joy in heaven over you? Or have you been brought up in "Christian surroundings," attended many missions, "decided for Christ" in your own way, and yet never, never, NEVER been brought down to **loath yourself before Him,** to know the love of One who is forgiven! Till you cast away your best things, as well as your worst things, and see that the Spirit of God blows even on the goodliness of the flesh, there is only your short-lived joy (Matt. 13 : 20), the joy of a selfish rocky heart that has never been broken. You have never felt, for God's glory? But when your works are all set aside, then there is joy in heaven. (Luke 15 : 6, 7, 10, "with Me") and God Himself rests in His love and joys with singing (Zeph. 3 : 17) over the burdened sinner whom He has set free by the blood of His beloved Son. Thanks be unto God for a real salvation to the praise of the glory of His grace (Eph. 1 : 6).

Mr. P. W. HEWARD

---

*(Continued from Page 144)*

wilt show Thyself merciful" (Psa. 37 : 25). On the other hand, the Saviour warned His disciples, "But if ye forgive men not their trespasses, neither will your Father forgive your trespasses" (Matt. 6 : 15).

"For they shall obtain mercy." Like the promises attached to the previous Beatitudes, this one also looks forward to the future for its final fulfilment. In 2 Tim. 1 : 16, 18 we find the apostle writing, "The Lord give mercy unto the house of Onesiphorus . . . The Lord grant unto him that he may find mercy of the Lord **in that day."** In Jude 21, the saints are also exhorted to be "looking for the **mercy of** our Lord Jesus Christ," which refers to His Second Advent.

ARTHUR W. PINK.

*(Continued from page 121.)*

The source of this merciful temper is not to be found in anything in the flesh. It is true that there are some who make no profession of being Christians in whom we often see not a little of kindliness of disposition, sympathy for the suffering, and a readiness to forgive those who have wronged them. Yet admirable as this may be from a purely human viewpoint, it falls far below that upon which Christ here pronounces His benediction. The amiability of the flesh has no spiritual value, for its movements are not regulated by the Scriptures and are not exercised in reference to the Divine authority. The mercifulness of this fifth Beatitude is that spontaneous outflow of a heart that is occupied with the mercy of God.

The mercifulness of our text is the product of the new nature in the child of God, and it is called into exercise by contemplating the wondrous grace, pity and longsufferance of God toward such an unworthy wretch as I am. The more I ponder God's sovereign mercy to me, the more I think of the unquenchable fire from which I have been delivered through the sufferings of the Lord Jesus, the more conscious of what a debtor I am to Divine grace, then the more mercifully shall I act toward those who wrong me, injure me, hate me.

This mercifulness is one of the attributes of that spiritual nature which I received at the new birth. Mercifulness in the child of God is but a reflection of the abundant mercy which is found in his Heavenly Parent. Mercifulness is one of the natural and necessary consequences of a merciful Christ indwelling me. It may not always be in exercise, it may through indulging the flesh be checked and for a time choked, but, taking the general tenor of a Christian's character and the main trend of his life, it is an unmistakable trait of the new man. "The wicked borroweth, and payeth not again; but the righteous showeth mercy, and giveth" (Psa. 37:21). It was "mercy" in Abraham, after he had been wronged by his nephew, which caused him to go after and secure the deliverance of Lot. It was "mercy" on the part of Joseph after his brethren had so grievously mistreated him, which caused him to freely forgive them. It was "mercy" in Moses, after Miriam had rebelled against him, and the Lord had smitten her with leprosy, which caused him to cry," "Heal her now, O God, I beseech Thee" (Num. 12:13). It was "mercy" which caused David to spare the life of his enemy Saul when that wicked king was in his hands. In sad and striking contrast, of Judas, it is said he "remembered not to show mercy but persecuted the poor and needy Man" (Psa. 109:16).

In Romans 12:8 there is an important word on the spirit in which mercy is to be exercised: "he that showeth mercy, with cheerfulness." The reference here is to the giving of money for the support of poor brethren, but in its wider application relates to all compassion which is shown to the afflicted. Mercy is to be exercised cheerfully so as to evidence that it is not only voluntary but also a pleasure: this spares the feelings of the one helped and soothes the sorrows of the sufferer. It is this quality of "cheerfulness" which gives most value to the service rendered. The Greek word is most expressive, denoting joyful eagerness, gladsome affability, which makes the visitor a sunbeam, warming the heart of the afflicted. If Scripture tells us that God loveth a cheerful giver, also true is it that the Lord taketh note of the Spirit in which we respond to His admonitions.

"For they shall obtain mercy." These words enunciate a principle or law in the government of God over our lives here on earth. It is summarised in that well-known word "Whatsoever a man soweth that shall he also reap." The Chrstian who is merciful in his dealings with others will receive merciful treatment at the hands of his fellows"—With what measure ye mete, it shall be measured to you again" (Matt. 7:2). Therefore it is written, "He that followeth after righteousness and mercy findeth life, righteousness and honour" (Prov. 21:21). The one who shows mercy to others is the personal gainer thereby: "the merciful man doeth good to his own soul" (Prov. 11:17).. There is an inward satisfaction in the exercise of benevolence and pity to which the highest gratification of the selfish man is not to be compared: "He that hath mercy on the poor, happy is he" (Prov. 14:21). The exercise of mercy is a source of satisfacion to God Himself: "He delighteth in mercy" (Micah 7:18)—equally so must it be to us.

"For they shall obtain mercy." Not only does the merciful Christian gain in his own soul by the happiness resulting, not only will the Lord in His overruling providence make his mercifulness return again to him at the hands of his fellow-men, but he will also obtain mercy from God: "With the merciful Thou

*(Continued on Page 143)*

# STUDIES IN THE SCRIPTURES

"Search the Scriptures" John 5:39.

Copyright in all English-speaking Countries.

Editor: Arthur W. Pink, 22 Parramatta Road, Summer Hill, N.S.W., Australia.
Hon. Agent in U.S.A.: Mr. C. S. Pressel, 559 Dupont Ave., York, Penna.

Price: 10 cents per copy; $1.00 or 5/- per year.

"Blessed are they which do hunger and thirst after righteousness: for they shall be filled" (Matt. 5:6).

In the first three Beatitudes we are called upon to witness the heart exercises of one who has been awakened by the Spirit of God. First, there is a sense of need, a realisation of my nothingness and emptiness. Second, there is a judging of self, a consciousness of my guilt and sorrowing over my lost condition. Third, there is an end of seeking to justify myself before God, an abandonment of all pretences to personal merit, a taking of my place in the dust, before God. Here, in the fourth, the eye of the soul is turned away from self to Another: there is a longing after that which I know I have not got and which I am conscious I urgently need.

There has been much needless quibbling as to the precise import of the word "righteousness" in our present text. The best way to ascertain its significance is to go back to the Old Testament scriptures where this term is used, and then turn on these the fuller light furnished by the New Testament Epistles.

"Drop down, ye heavens, from above, and let the skies pour down **righteousness**: let the earth open, and let them bring forth **salvation**, and let righteousness spring up together; I, the Lord have created it" (Isa. 45:8). The first half of this verse refers, in figurative language, to the advent of Christ to this earth; the second half to His resurrection, when He was "raised again for our justification." "Hearken unto Me, ye stout-hearted, that are far from righteousness: I bring near My righteousness; it shall not be far off, and **My salvation** shall not tarry: and I will place salvation in Zion for Israel My glory" (Isa. 46:12-14). "**My righteousness** is near; **My salvation** is gone forth, and Mine arms shall judge the people; the isles shall wait upon Me, and on Mine arms shall they trust" (Isa. 51:5). "Thus saith the Lord, Keep ye judgment, and do justice: for **My salvation** is near to come, and **My righteousness** to be revealed" (Isa. 56:1). "I will greatly rejoice in the Lord, my soul shall be joyful in my God; for He hath clothed me with the garments of **salvation**, He hath covered me with the robe of **righteousness**" (Isa. 61:10). These passages make it clear that God's "righteousness" is synonymous with God's "salvation."

The above scriptures are unfolded in the Epistle to the Romans where the 'Gospel" receives its fullest exposition, see 1:1. In 1:16, 17, we are told "I am not ashamed of the Gospel of Christ, for it is the power of God unto **salvation** to every one that believeth; to the Jew first, and also to the Greek. For therein is the **righteousness** of God revealed from faith to faith." In 3:22, 24, we read, "Even the righteousness of God which is by faith of Jesus Christ unto all and upon all them that believe. for there is no difference: For all have sinned, and come short of the glory of God; Being justified freely by His grace through the redemption that is in Christ Jesus." In 5:19, the blessed declaration is made "for as by one man's disobedience many were made (legally constituted)

(Continued on page 144)

## IMPORTANT NOTICES

Set of twelve issues for 1922, unbound, $1.00 or 5/-. Bound $1.65 or 7/-.

1923, 1924, 1925 same as 1922.

Note: We cannot break a set or now supply any **single** 1925 issues.

Subscription—price: **$1.00** or **5/-** per year to any address in the world.

Change of Address: Please notify me promptly of any change of address, and be certain to give both old and new address.

Non-subscribers receiving this Magazine regularly will understand their subscription has been entered by a friend.

Copies lost in the mail duplicated only if we are notified promptly.

## CONTENTS

| | |
|---|---|
| The Gospel of John (John 16: 12-22) ... | 146 |
| Gleanings in Exodus ... ... ... | 154 |
| Human Responsibility ... ... ... | 159 |
| Times of Trouble ... ... ... ... | 164 |
| Divine Chastisement ... ... ... | 166 |
| Missionary Tidings ... ... ... | 167 |

## THE GOSPEL OF JOHN

**55. Christ Glorified by the Spirit: John 16: 12-22.**

Below is an Analysis of the passage which is to be before us:—

1. The need for the Spirit's coming v. 12.
2. The purpose of the Spirit's coming v. 13.
3. The end accomplished by the Spirit's coming v. 14.
4. The subordination of the Spirit v. 15.
5. The effect of the Spirit's coming v. 16.
6. The disciples' mystification vv. 17-19.
7. The Lord's profound prediction vv. 20-22.

That which is central in this second section of John 16 is the Holy Spirit glorifying the Lord Jesus. The more closely our present passage be studied, the more will it be found that this is the keynote of it. At first sight there does not seem to be any **unity** about this portion of Scripture. In v. 12, the Lord declares that He had yet many things to say unto the apostles, but they were unable to bear them. In vv. 13-15, Christ made direct reference to the Holy Spirit, and what He would do for and in believers. In v. 16 the Saviour uttered an allegorical proverb (see v. 25), which mystified the disciples, causing them to ask one another what He meant by it. While in the last three verses He made mention of their sorrow and of the joy which would follow His departure. Yet, varied as these subjects appear to be, closer study will show that they are intimately connected and logically grow out of what is found in the opening verses.

Nowhere else did our Lord give so full a word concerning the blessed person and work of the Holy Spirit. Seven things are here postulated of Him. He would act as "the Spirit of Truth;" He would guide believers into all Truth; He would not speak of Himself; He would speak what He heard; He would show believers things to come; He would glorify Christ; He would take of the things of Christ and show them unto His people. Why, then, it may be asked, have we not entitled this chapter, The Work of the Spirit with and in Christians? Because what is here predicated of Him is in special and direct relation to Christ. It is the Holy Spirit **glorifying** the Lord Jesus, glorifying Him by **magnifying** Him before believers. Not only is this expressly affirmed in v. 14, but the **character** in which He acts throughout affords further proof.

In v. 7 the Saviour declared, "But I **the Truth** say to you, It is profitable for you that I should go away; for if I go not away the Paraclete will not come" (Bagster's Interlinear). Now in v. 13, He says, "But when He, the Spirit of the Truth (the Greek has the article) has come, He will guide you into all the truth." It is, then, as the Spirit of **Christ** that He is here viewed. This is further emphasised in v. 14: "He shall glorify Me, for He shall receive of Mine, and shall show it unto you"—words which are repeated in v. 15. It is therefore plain that the central and distinguishing subject of our present section is **Christ glorified by the Spirit.** How this applies to the closing verses will be indicated in the course of our exposition.

"It has been repeatedly shown, and in this chapter most expressly, that the presence of the Spirit depended on the departure of Christ to heaven consequently fitting the saints for the new truths, work, character, and hopes of Christianity. The disciples were not ignorant of the promise that the Spirit should be given to inaugurate the reign of the Messiah. They knew the judgment under which the chosen people abide, 'until the Spirit be poured upon us from on high, and the wilderness be a fruitful field, and the fruitful field be counted for a forest,' so vast outwardly, no less than inwardly, the change when God puts forth His power for the kingdom of His Son. They know that He will pour out His Spirit upon all flesh; not only the sons and daughters, the old and young of Israel enjoying a blessing far beyond all temporal favours, but the servants and the handmaidens, in short, all flesh, and not the Jews alone sharing it.

"But here it is the sound heard when the great High Priest goes in into the sanctuary before Jehovah (Ex. 28:25), and not only when He comes out for the deliverance and joy of repentant Israel in the last days. It is the Spirit given when the Lord Jesus went on high, and by Him thus gone. For this they were wholly unprepared, as indeed it is one of the most essential characteristics, of God's testimony between the rejection and the reception of the Jews; and the Spirit, when given, was to supply what the then state of the disciples could not bear." (Bible Treasury.)

Never can we be sufficiently thankful for the gift of the Holy Spirit. Though our blessed Saviour is in heaven, we have a **Divine Person** with us on earth: a person who quickens us (John 3:5), who indwells us (1 Cor. 6:9), who loves us (Rom. 15:13), who leads us (Rom. 8:14), who gives us assurance of our sonship (Rom. 8:16), who helpeth our infirmities by making intercession for us (Rom. 8:26), and who has sealed us unto the Day of Redemption (Eph. 4:30). O that we may not grieve Him. O that we may recognise His indwelling presence and act accordingly. O that we may avail ourselves of His Divine fullness and power.

"I have yet many things to say unto you, but ye cannot bear them now" (v. 12). The contents of vv. 8 to 11 are parenthetical in their character, in that in vv. 1 to 7, Christ had been speaking of and to His disciples, digressing for a moment to complete what He said previously about "the world." Now He turns to consider His own again, and they in connection with the sending of the Holy Spirit to them. The Lord had yet many things to say unto those who had followed Him in the day of His rejection, things which it was deeply important for them to know, but things which they were then in no condition to receive—"ye cannot bear them now." The Greek word here for "bear" is used in a double sense in the New Testament, literally and figuratively. In John 10:31 it is rendered, "Then the Jews took **up** stones again to stone Him;" they **laid hold of** these stones. In Luke 10:4 it is translated, **"Carry** neither purse nor scrip." In Matt. 20:12, the word is employed figuratively: "Thou hast made them equal with us which have **borne** the burden and heat of the day." So in Rev. 2:2: "I know thy works, and thy labour, and thy patience, and how thou canst not bear them which are evil." From these references it would appear that our Lord signified that the apostles were then incapable of laying hold of or retaining what He, otherwise, would have said to them; incapable because they could not endure such revelations.

"I have yet many things to say unto you, but ye cannot bear them now." The fact that the Eleven were in no condition to receive, unable to endure these further revelations from the Saviour, demonstrated their **need** for the Holy Spirit to come and guide them into all the truth: suitable introduction, then, was that for this new section! Moreover, it hints strongly of the **nature** of the "many things" which Christ then had in mind. The apostles were prejudiced. Their hearts were set on the establishment of the Messianiac kingdom. They could not tolerate the thought of Christ leaving them and returning to the Father. But the Lord Jesus could not at that time ascend the throne of David. Israel had **rejected Him**, and bitter would be the results for them, though most merciful would be the consequences for the Gentiles. Hence, we take it, that what our Lord here had in view was God's rejection of Israel, and His turning unto the Gentiles: the abolishing of the old covenant, and the introduction of the new: the abrogation of the ceremonial law and the bringing in of another order of priesthood: instructions for the government of His churches: prophecies concerning the future.

"I have yet many things to say unto

you, but ye cannot bear them now." This is both blessed and searching. Blessed, because it shows our Lord's tender considerateness: He would not press upon them what they were in no condition to receive. Few things are more irritating than to hear without understanding. What an example for teachers now to follow! Much discernment and wisdom is needed if we are to minister the Word "in season," a word suited to the spiritual condition of our hearers, and such wisdom can only be obtained by earnest waiting upon God. But there is also a searching and solemn force to this utterance of Christ's. How many a communication would He not make to us, could we "bear" it! Paul had to have a thorn in the flesh sent him, lest he be exalted above measure through "the abundance of the revelations" which he received when he was caught up into Paradise; and in view of this, we are strongly inclined to believe that the "many things" which Christ had in mind also included revelations about Paradise and Heaven, the more so in view of v. 5: "But now I go My way to Him that sent Me; and none of you asketh Me, Whither goest Thou?!" But "sorrow" had filled their hearts (v. 6), and this unfitted them for fuller disclosures about the Higher World.

"Howbeit when He, the Spirit of truth is come, He will guide you into all truth" (v. 13). Here is the answer to a question which must have occurred to many in meditating upon the previous verse: Did these apostles ever after bewail a lost opportunity? No; graciously did the Lord provide against that. "Howbeit," even so, though they could not bear these things then, when the Paraclete had come, He should guide them into all the truth! The One who would thus undertake for them is called "The Spirit of the Truth." In addition to affirming that He was the Spirit of "The Truth" (of Christ), this title also emphasised His suitability for such a task, His competency as the Saviour's Witness. The Spirit was fully qualified because He is "The Spirit of the Truth": because of His perfect knowledge of the Truth, because of His infinite love for the Truth, and because of His absolute incapacity for falsehood. Scripture speaks of "The Spirit of error" (I John 4: 6). There is a lying spirit who controls the blind that lead the blind, and in consequence they "both fall into the ditch."

Another thing suggested by this title of the Third Person of the Godhead is His relation to and connection with the **written Word**, which, like the incarnate Word is also called "the Truth": "Sanctify them through Thy truth: Thy Word **is truth**" (John 17:17). The inspiration of the Holy Scriptures is in an unique sense the work of the Holy Spirit: "holy (separated) men of God spake moved by **the Holy Spirit**" (2 Peter 1:21). So too the Interpretation of Scripture is the special work of the Spirit: "Eye hath not seen, nor ear heard, neither have entered into the heart of man, the things which God hath prepared for them that love Him. But God **hath** revealed unto us **by His Spirit**: for the Spirit searcheth **all** things, yea, the deep things of God. For what man knoweth the things of a man, save (by) the spirit of man which is in him? Even so the things of God knoweth no man, but (by) the **Spirit of God**" (I Cor. 2:9-11). Before He can see, man must have both sight and light. Eyes cannot see in the darkness, and light shows nothing to the blind. So with regard to the Truth: there must be the seeing eye **and** illuminating light. For an interpreter we need a trustworthy guide, an infallible Teacher; and He is to be found not in the "Church," the "voice of tradition," the "intuitive faculty," or in reason, but in the Spirit of God. He it is who quickens, illumines, interprets, and the **only** instrument which He uses is the **written** Word. Therefore is He called "The Spirit **of the Truth**."

"He will **guide** you." There are three classes of people who need to be "guided": those who are blind, those who are too weak to walk alone, or those journeying through an unknown country. In each of these senses does the Holy Spirit guide God's elect. By nature, we are spiritually blind, and He guided us into the way of Truth" (2 Peter 2:2). Then as "babes" in Christ, He has to teach us how to walk (Rom. 8: 14). Then as travellers through this wilderness scene, as we journey to the Heavenly Country, He points out the Narrow Way which leadeth unto life. Note carefully, "He will **guide** you into all the truth," **not** "bring you into": there must be a **yieldedness** on our part, a corresponding **obedience**! If the Spirit "guides" our steps, the necessary implication is that we are walking **with Him**, that we are closely **following** His directions. This term also suggests an orderly, gradual and progressive advancing: we **grow** in "knowledge" as well as in "grace" (2 Peter 3:18).

"He will guide you into all the Truth."

not all **truths,** but "all the truth." God's truth is one connected, harmonious, indivisible whole (compare our remarks on 7:16). "All the Truth" here means all **revealed** truth, which is recorded in the written Word. That we have in our hands **"all the Truth"** is clearly implied by one of the closing verses in the last book of the Bible: "If any man shall **add** unto these things, God shall add unto him the plagues that are written in this Book" (Rev. 22:18).

"For He shall not speak of Himself." This does not mean, as some suppose, that He should not speak **about** Himself He has told us much about Himself in every section of the Scriptures. But He would not speak **from** Himself, **independently** of the Father and the Son. As the Son came not to act independently of the Father, but to serve His Father, so the Spirit is here to serve the Son. The reference is to His administrative position.

"I can of Mine own self do nothing: as I hear, I judge: and My judgment is just: because I seek not Mine own will, but the will of the Father which hath sent Me" (5:30). "I have many things to say and to judge of you: but He that sent Me is true; and I speak to the world these things which I have heard of Him" (8:26). "These declarations respecting both the Son and the Spirit must appear inconsistent with Their supreme Divinity, to every one who does not know the doctrine of the economical subordination of the Son and Spirit in the great plan of human redemption. **Essentially** the Spirit and the Son are equal to, for they are one with, the Father. **Economically,** the Father is greater than the Son and the Spirit, for he **sends** Them; the Son is greater than the Spirit, for He sends Him. Without apprehending this distinction, we cannot interpret the sacred Scriptures, nor form any clear notion of the way of salvation. The Spirit like the Son, would be faithful to Him who appointed Him. In speaking to the apostles, in conveying information to their minds, He would communicate just what He was sent to communicate, without excess, without defect, without variation" (Dr. Brown).

But whatsoever He shall hear, that shall He speak" (v. 13). This is parallel with 15:15, "For all things that I have **heard** of My Father, I have made known unto you." What a searching word is this for every teacher! "If the Spirit may not speak of Himself, if He speaks only what He has heard of the Father and the Son—O preacher! how canst thou draw thy preaching out of thyself, out of my head, or even thy heart?"

"And He will show you things to come" (v. 13). Mark the progressive order in these several statements concerning the work of the Spirit. In 14:26 the Lord declared that the Spirit would recall to the apostles the **past:** "But the Comforter, the Holy Spirit, whom the Father will send in My name, He shall teach you all things and **bring all things to your remembrance,** whatsoever I **have said** unto you." In 15:26, we learn that the Spirit would testify of the **present** glory of Christ. But here, in 16:13, it is promised that He would show them things concerning the **future!** There are many prophecies scattered throughout the Epistles—far more than most people imagine—which the Spirit has given. But the main reference, no doubt, in this word of Christ, was to the book of the Revelation, the opening sentence of which reads, "The Revelation of Jesus Christ, which God gave unto Him, to show unto His servants things which must shortly **come to pass."** It is the Revelation **of Jesus Christ,** for He is its chief subject and object; yet it was **given** by the Holy Spirit, hence the seven times repeated, "He that hath an ear to hear, let him hear what **the Spirit saith** unto the churches!" Thus whether it be things past, things present, or things to come, Christ is the grand Center of the Spirit's testimony!

"He shall glorify Me: for He shall receive of Mine, and shall show it unto you" (v. 14). This is the prime object before the Spirit: whether it be revealing the truth, speaking what He hears, or showing things to come, the **glorification of Christ** is the grand end in view. The light of the knowledge of the glory of God in the face of Jesus Christ (2 Cor. 4:6) is both the center and capstone of Divine ruth. **This** is the vital test for every lying spirit which would obtrude itself into the place of the Spirit: rationalism, ritualism, fanaticism, philosophy, science falsely so-called, all **dishonour** Christ, but the Spirit always **magnifies** Him. It is a notable fact that (so far as the writer is aware) nowhere in the Epistles has the Holy Spirit told us anything about the **Father** which had not previously been revealed in and by the Lord Jesus; but He **has** told us many things about the **Son,** which Jesus uttered not in the days of His humiliation.

"He shall glorify Me: for He shall receive of Mine, and shall show it unto you." The blessed work of the Spirit in revealing to believers the precious things of God is strikingly brought out in 1 Cor. 2: "Eye hath not seen, nor ear heard, neither have entered into the heart of man the thing which God hath prepared for them that love Him" (v. 10). This is a reference to Isaiah 64, and most Christians when quoting it stop at this point, but the very next verse goes on to say, "But God hath revealed them unto us by His Spirit: for the Spirit searcheth all things, yea, the deep things of God."

"All things that the Father hath are Mine" (v. 15). Very blessed is this: the Lord Jesus would not speak of His own glory apart from that of the Father. It is very similar to His words in 17:10: "And all Mine are Thine, and Thine are Mine." "Thus there is opened for us a glimpse into the living blessed bond of love in receiving and giving in the eternal ground of the triune essence of the Godhead. The Father hath from eternity given to the Son to have life and all things in Himself, yet always He is the Son who revealeth the Father, only as the Fatherhood remains with the Father. But all things the Son bringeth and giveth to the Father again, honoreth and glorifieth Him in His being glorified in His people. And this through the Spirit, who with equal rights in this unity taketh from the sole fullness of the Father and the Son, all that He livingly offers in His announcement" (Stier). "Take of Mine" should be **"receive of Mine"** as in the previous verse, otherwise the force of "therefore" here would be lost—in the Greek the word is the same in both verses.

"A little while, and ye shall not see Me: and again, a little while and ye shall see Me, because I go to the Father" (v. 16). In the previous verses Christ had touched upon lofty things, now He comes down to the level of His apostles' needs. He condescends to stoop to their weakness, by addressing Himself to their anguished hearts. From the awful heights of the triune essence of the Godhead, He descends to the sorrows and joys of His disciples. "A little while, and ye shall not see Me: and again, a little while, and ye shall see Me." But what did the Saviour mean? This cryptic utterance of His sorely puzzled those to whom it was first addressed, as is clear from the verses which follow. Chirst Himself termed it a **proverbial form of speech**" (v. 25), and this must be kept in mind as we seek its interpretation. Before inquiring into the meaning of our Lord's words here, let us first ask as to His purpose in thus speaking so enigmatically.

The Lord had previously said to the disciples, "Now is the Son of man glorified, and God is glorified in Him. Little children yet **a little while** I am with you. Ye shall see Me: and as I said unto the Jews, Whither I go, ye cannot come; so now I say unto you" (13:31, 33). But it is plain that they understood Him not: "Simon Peter said unto Him, Lord, **whither** goest Thou?" (13:36). He had said, "I go to prepare a place for you . . . and whither I go ye know, and the way ye know" (14:2, 4). But Thomas had responded, "Lord, we **know not** whither thou goest; and how can we know the way?" (v. 5). He had said, "Yet a little while, and the world seeth Me no more." (14:19). But they were unresponsive: "Now I go My way to Him that sent Me; and none of you asketh Me, **Whither** goest Thou?" (16:4). Now the Lord repeats in parabolic form what He had previously announced, in order to arouse them from their stupor of sorrow and to make a deeper impression upon their minds. That His end was gained is evident from the next verse. But we believe that He had a still deeper reason: He was also supplying them with material for comfort in future days of trial. Later, when they recalled these words, they would recognise that the **first part** of them had received fulfilment—a "little while" after He had spoken and they saw Him not; and this would cheer them with the sure hope that in another "little while" they **would** see Him again.

"A little while, and ye shall not see Me: and again, a little while, and ye shall see Me." In less than two hours, most likely, He was arrested in the Garden, and there the apostles lost sight of their Master—even Peter and John saw Him but for a very little while longer. But He not only disappeared from their bodily vision, but **spiritually** too they lost sight of Him. Their faith was eclipsed. The words of the two disciples on the way to Emmaus no doubt expressed the common sentiment among His followers at that time: "But we trusted that it **had** been He which should have redeemed Israel" (Luke 24:21). The fact that they believed not (Mark 16:11, 13) when they first heard of His resurrection, revealed their state of heart. They were in the darkness of doubt, and therefore could not see Christ with the eye of faith. But their seeing Him not, physically and spiritually, was of short continuance. After "a little while"—only three days—He reappeared to them, and then He disappeared again for another "little while" from their bodily vision, though never more would they spiritually lose sight of their Lord and their God.

Now while the above is probably the primary reference in our Lord's words, we have no doubt but that they contain a much deeper meaning, and an application to the whole company of Christians. "There is, as for Christ Himself, the breaking through death into life, so for the disciples a deeply penetrating, fundamental **change from sorrow to joy.** By no means merely their sorrow at His death, and their joy on His living again, after the analogy of the sorrow and joy of the children of men in their changing experience; but as the mediating expression of an essential internal process which the Holy Spirit completed in their case, but which is still going on to the the end of all. Thus as **the way of the disciples through sorrow to joy** between the crucifixion and resurrection of our Lord was already for them something preparatory and typical, it becomes to us a **type** of the way which **all His future disciples** have also to pass through that godly sorrow which distinguishes them fully from the world into the joy of faith and life in Christ Jesus" (Stier).

"A little while, and ye shall not see Me: and again, a little while, and ye shall see Me." We believe that it is misleading to place a comma after the word "again," because there are two distinct periods here in view, two "little while's": "a little while and ye shall not see Me" referred, first, to the interval between His death and resurrection; **"and again a little while and ye shall see Me,"** which first found its fulfilment after His resurrection, but in its deeper meaning signifies ye shall see Me in a more intimate and **spiritual** sense. Only ten days after His ascension, by the aid of the Spirit, they saw Him in a new, a deeper, a fuller way than ever before. But there is still a further meaning, with a wider application: "And again a little while": compare with this Heb. 10:37: "For yet a little while, and He that shall come will come, and will not tarry"! After this present interval of Christ's session at God's right hand believers will **"see Him as He is"** and be forever with Him.

"Because I go to the Father." This is assigned as the reason why the disciples should "see" Him after a "little while." It must be remembered that He was going to the Father in a **special** character, namely; as the One who had gloriously finished the Work which had been given Him to do. He was therefore going to the Father as One entitled to a rich reward. This reward would be bestowed upon Him personally, but also upon the people whom He had purchased for Himself. Hence, His going to the Father thus guaranteed the sending of the Holy Spirit to that people (Acts 2:33), and it was by the Spirit they were enabled to "see" Him (Heb. 2:9). Thus it was His glorification which afforded the means for Him to now reveal Himself unto us **spiritually.** Moreover, **because** He has gone to the Father in this character, He will yet come again and receive us unto Himself (John 14:2-3) when we shall see Him, no longer through a glass darkly. His going to the Father thus manifested His title and fitness to introduce us to the Father's House!

"Then said some of His disciples among themselves, What is this that He saith unto us, A little while, and ye shall not see Me: and again, a little while, and ye shall see Me; and, Because I go to the Father?" (v. 17). The Lord's words sounded strangely in the ears of the disciples, and some of them began to discuss the seeming paradox. That they should see Him, and that they should not see Him!—it sounded like a contradicton in terms. And even His expression of going to the Father was by no means plain to them. They thought that the Messiah would **remain** on the earth (12:34). There was no place in their theology for His leaving them and returning to the Father. And yet there **ought** to have been: see Psalm 68:18; 110:1. They erred through not knowing the Scriptures; hence their bewilderment here. How forcibly this illustrates the fact that the **difficulties** we find in the words of Scripture are **self-created**—due to our preconceptions and prejudices.

"They said therefore, What is this that He saith, A little while? We cannot tell what He saith" (v. 18). This refers, apparently, to the answer which others among the Eleven made to those of their number (mentioned in the previous verse) who were quietly discussing what the Lord had just said. The first group were completely bewildered; the second puzzled mainly by the "little while." They "desired" to ask Christ, as is clear from v. 19, yet they refrained from doing so. And how slow, oftentimes, are we to seek for light! "Ye have not, because ye ask not" (James 4:2)! God has designedly put many things in His Word in such a way that their meaning cannot be obtained by a rapid and careless reading. He has done so in order to exercise us, and to drive us to our knees; to make us cry, "Open Thou mine eyes, that I may behold wondrous things out of Thy law" (Psa. 119:18); and to pray, "That which I see not, teach Thou me" (Job 34:22).

"Now Jesus knew that they were desirous to ask Him, and said unto them "Do ye inquire among yourselves of that I said, A little while, and ye shall not see Me: and again a little while, and ye shall see Me?" (v. 19). "It may seem strange that the desire did not at once find expression in direct inquiry; for surely they had been long enough with Him, and had known Him sufficiently well to induce the conviction that He was 'meek and lowly in heart,' and always more ready to give, than they were to receive, instruction. The truth seems to be, that on this occasion they were both ashamed and afraid to seek the information which they were anxious to obtain—ashamed to acknowledge their ignorance on a subject on which their Master had so often addressed them; and afraid, it may be equally, that they should draw down on themselves a faithful, though kindly rebuke. What is said of a former declaration, seems to have been true of that which now perplexed them, 'they understood not the saying, and they were afraid to ask Him'; Mark 9:22"(Dr. John Brown).

"It is to be noted that the Lord did not reply directly to their intended question. He does not give them further information on the subject concerning which they were curious. The point which perplexed them was His promised speedy return. They had half made up their minds to lose Him. They had a kind of vague, undefined suspicion that their worst fears regarding Him were about to be realised; but if so, what could He mean by speaking of this quick return? If He must die, how can it be only for 'a little while?' As yet they knew not the Scriptures what the rising from the dead should mean. Their minds were confused, and their hearts filled with sorrow. So the Lord dwells upon this point of time, though He does not directly answer the desired question. He prefers now rather to give them some general prospect of brighter days to come: their sorrow shall give place to joy: that should be short, this should be lasting; **that** for a time only, **this** forever." (Dr. George Brown).

The Lord knows what things we have need of before we ask : all things are open before Him, even our hearts! He would not leave His disciples in uncertainty : "Before they call I will answer; and while they are yet speaking, I will hear" (Isa. 65:24). There is something very impressive in the way in which the Lord Jesus here **repeats** what He had said just before: evidently with the intention of fixing these words in their minds. Seven times in these four verses occurs this expression "a little while." How the Spirit would impress upon us the **brevity** of our earthly pilgrimage! How the Lord here emphasises the blessed truth that we should be daily, hourly, **expecting** His return!

"Verily, verily, I say unto you, That ye shall weep and lament, but the world shall rejoice; and ye shall be sorrowful, but your sorrow shall be turned into joy" (v. 20). There is no change of subject here as some have strangely thought. Instead, the Lord mentions, the **effects** of not seeing Him **and** seeing Him again. The **double** meaning of His words in v. 16 must be borne in mind—their **immediate** reference to the apostles, and their wider application to all Christians. As they concerned the Eleven, Christ made it known that they would first mourn for Him as one dead, and not only would the decease of their unfailing Comforter result in deep lamentation, but the rejoicing of the world over its seeming victory and His defeat would intensify their sorrows. But after a short season their grief would be turned into rejoicing.

Strikingly was this prediction fulfilled. When Mary Magdalene came to the apostles to announce the Saviour's triumph over the grave, she found them mourning and weeping (Mark 16:10). When Christ approached the two disciples walking to Emmaus, He asked "What manner of communications are these that ye have one to another? as ye walk, and are sad" (Luke 24:17). How often during those three days must they have remembered His words "Ye shall weep and lament." And while the beloved disciples were sunk in sorrow, their enemies were rejoicing. Solemnly does this come out in the prophetic plaint of the Messiah : "Let not them that are Mine enemies wrongfully rejoice over

Me: neither let them wink with the eye that hate Me without a cause" (Psa. 35:19). But these words of Christ also have a direct application to all His people on earth: "Sorrow" is their portion too—how could it be otherwise as **identified with** the Man of Sorrows during the time of His rejection! The awful enmity of men against God; the way in which the world still treats His beloved Son; the many false prophets who dishonour the Lord; the absence of the Saviour Himself; and the sight of our fellow-creatures rushing heedlessly to destruction, these are enough to make Christians "weep and lament." Add to these our own sad failures, and the failures of our brethren—often more apparent to us than our own—and we can at once perceive the force of the apostle's words, "Even we ourselves **groan** within ourselves waiting for the adoption, the redemption of our body" (Rom. 8:23)

"But your sorrow shall be turned into joy" (v. 20). The women who saw the risen Saviour as they returned from the sepulchre "with fear **and great joy**" (Matt. 28:8) ran to announce the glad tidings to the disciples. When He Himself appeared to them we read, "Then were the disciples **glad,** when they saw the Lord" (John 20:20). And when He ascended on high "they worshipped Him and returned to Jerusalem with **great joy**" (Luke 24:22). But mark here the minute discrimination of our Lord's language. It was not only that their sorrow should **give place** to joy, but be "turned into joy." Their sorrowing became joy! The very **cause** of their sorrow—the death of Christ—now became the ground and **subject** of their joy! Grief would not only be replaced by joy, but be transmuted into joy, even as the water was turned into wine! The cross of Christ is glorified into an eternal consolation. And **what** was it, or rather **Who** was it that brought this about? None other than the Holy Spirit He has so interpreted for us the death of the Saviour that we now cry, "God forbid that I should glory save in the cross of our Lord Jesus Christ." So our title for this chapter still holds good here: it is **Christ glorified by the Spirit.**

The final meaning of this profound and full word of Christ's "your sorrow shall be turned into joy" will find its ultimate realisation in all His people when He comes to receive us unto Himself. Weeping may endure for a night, but joy cometh in the morning. And even here the exactitude of our Lord's language is to be seen: **our** "sorrow" shall be **"turned into** joy": our present groanings are but creating within us a larger capacity for joy in the grand hereafter: "Our light affliction, which is but for a moment, **worketh for us** a far more exceeding and eternal weight of glory" (2 Cor. 4:17). But how fearful the contrast in the case of unbelievers: "Woe unto you that **laugh** now: for ye sha'l mourn and weep" (Luke 6:25)!

"A woman when she is in travail hath sorrow, because her hour is come: but as soon as she is delivered of the child she remembereth no more the anguish, for joy that a man is born into the world" (v. 21). Plain and simple though this verse appears to be, yet we believe, there is a depth and fullness in it which has never been fully apprehended. First of all it is evident that we have a double parallelism: "a little while and ye shall not see Me" (v. 16), "ye shall weep and lament, but the world shall rejoice, and ye shall be sorrowful" (v. 20) "a woman when she is in travail hath sorrow, because her hour is come (v. 21), all refer to the same thing—the same period of time, the same experience. So too "again a little while and ye shall see Me" (v. 16), "your sorrow shall be turned into joy" (v. 20), and "as soon as she is delivered of the child, she remembereth no more the anguish, for joy that a man is born into the world" (v. 21), also correspond. What we have here in verse 21 **repeats,** but in **figurative** language, what Christ had said in the previous verses. The Lord now **illustrates** by a reference to the most familiar of all examples of joy issuing from sorrow. The force of the figure used to portray our sufferings intimates the necessity of them, their severity, their brief duration, and the fact that they are antecedent to and productive of joy. So much is clear on the surface. But in its deeper meaning the figure which the Saviour here employed went beyond His literal language in the previous verse.

The symbolical domain of nature has much to teach us if we have eyes to see and hearts to receive. God has wisely and graciously ordered it that the pangs of the mother are compensated in her joy over the fruit of her anguish. And this is a symbolical prophecy, written in nature by the Creator's finger, of the birth of the new man. That, too, is preceded by travail, both on the part of the Spirit and of the one He brings forth: but here travail gives place to joy. The same process is also repeated in the Christian life. The travail-pangs of "mortification" are the precursors of resurrection-joys. There must be, for us too, the cross before the crown. There must be **fellowship** with the sufferings of Christ, before we share His glory (Rom. 8:17). Plain intimation of this is given in His words here: "her **hour** is come"—the same expression used by Him so often in conjunction with **His own** "travail"! The Holy Spirit has also used this same figure of a travailing woman to set forth the relation in which this present life stands to the future life: see Rom. 8:12, 19, 22, 23.

Marvellously full is this word of Christ's. Fulfilled not only in the experience of the apostles, fulfilled in our regeneration, still further fulfilled in our Christian life, it also looks forward to a yet future fulfilment, a **dispensational** fulfilment in connection with Israel. The Greek has the definite article —"**The** Woman." Her travail is the "sorrows" (literally **"birth-pangs"**) of Matt. 24:8. The period of these is the time of Jacob's Trouble (Jer. 30:7). It is the "woman" of Rev. 12, the Jewish remnant. It is of her the following Scriptures speak: "Therefore will He give them up, until the time that she which **travaileth** hath brought forth" (Micah, 5:3). See also Hosea 13:13. Micah, 4:9, 10. The "child" that she bears is the **new** Israel, millennial Israel, the Nation "born at once" (Isa. 66:8). Her joy is described in many Old Testament passages: see Isa. 66:10, 11. e.g.

"And ye now therefore have sorrow. But I will see you again, and your heart shall rejoice, and your joy no man taketh from you" (v. 22). There is little need for us to enter into a lengthy exposition of this verse. In it the Lord gathers up into a brief summary all that He had said from v. 15 onwards. There is the same fullness of reference as before. Directly, it applied, to the case of the apostles. For a short season they sorrowed over their Master's death and absence. This gave place to rejoicing at His resurrection and ascension But the **permanency** of their joy—"none taketh from you"—was secured by the coming of the Spirit. But our Lord's words were also addressed to the entire body of His people, therefore, as has been said, "The way of the first disciples between the Passion and Pentecost is a type of the whole interval of the Lord's Church between His departure to the Father and His final return" (Stier).

The following questions are to aid the student on the closing portion of John 16:—

1. In what "day" v. 23?
2. What is meant by "ask Me nothing" v. 23?
3. What is the meaning of "the first part of v. 24?
4. When did Christ show them "plainly" v. 25?
5. What is the meaning of v. 26?
6. Did the disciples really understand Christ now v. 29?
7. In what sense did Christ "overcome the world" v. 33?

ARTHUR W. PINK.

## GLEANINGS IN EXODUS

### 31. The Perfect Servant: Exodus 21:1-6.

The law of Moses had three grand divisions: the moral the civil, and the ceremonial. The first is to be found in the Ten Commandments; the second (mainly) in Ex. 21-23; the third (prinpally) in the book of Leviticus. The first defined God's claims upon Israel as human creatures; the second was for the social regulation of the Hebrew commonwealth; the third respected Israel's religious life. In the first we may see the governmental authority of God the Father; in the second, the sphere and activities of God the Holy Spirit—maintaining order among God's people; in the third, we have a series of types concerning God the Son.

"Now these are the judgments which thou shalt set before them. If thou buy an Hebrew servant, six years he shall serve: and in the seventh he shall go out free for nothing. If he came in by himself, he shall go out by himself: if he were married, then his wife shall go out with him. If his master has given him a wife, and she have borne him sons or daughters; the wife and her children shall be her master's, and he shall go out by himself. And if the servant shall plainly say, I love my master, my wife, and my children, I will not go out free: Then his master shall bring him unto the judges; he shall also bring him to the door, or unto the doorpost; and his master shall bore his ear through with an aul; and he shall serve him forever"

Ex. 21:1-6). This passage begins the series of "judgments" or statutes which God gave unto Israel for the regulation of their social and civil life. Its chief value for us to-day lies in its spiritual application to the Lord Jesus Christ. We have here a most beautiful and blessed foreshadowment of His person and work: Psalm 40 : 6 compared with Ex. 21 : 6 proves this conclusively. In that great Messianic Psalm the Lord Jesus, speaking in the spirit of prophecy, said, "Sacrifice and offering Thou didst not desire; Mine ears hast Thou digged."

The passage before us pertained to the servant or slave. It brings out, in type, the Perfect Servant. Messianic prophecy frequently viewed Him in this character: "Behold, My Servant, whom I uphold" (Isa. 42:1). "Behold, I will bring forth My Servant, the Branch" (Zech. 3:8). "Behold, My Servant shall deal prudently, He shall be exalted and extolled, and be very high" (Isa. 52 : 13). "By His knowledge shall My righteous Servant justify many for He shall bear their iniquities" (Isa. 53: 11).

In Phil. 2 we are exhorted, "Let this mind be in you which was also in Christ Jesus" (v. 5). This is enforced as follows: "Who, being in the form of God thought it not robbery to be equal with God: But made Himself of no reputation, and took upon Him the form of a Servant, and was made in the likeness of man: And being found in fashion as a man He humbled Himself, and became obedient unto death, even the death of the cross." Marvellous stoop was this: from the place of highest authority, to that of utmost dependency; from honor and glory, to suffering and shame. The Maker of heaven and earth entering the place of subjection. The One before whom the seraphim veiled their faces being made lower than the angels. May we never lose our sense of wonderment at such amazing condescension; rather may we delight in reverently contemplating it with ever-deepening awe and adoration.

One whole book in the New Testament is devoted exclusively to setting before us the service of the perfect Servant. The design of Mark's Gospel is to show us how He served: the spirit which actuated Him, the motives and principles which regulated Him, the excellency of all that He did.*

---
*This has been treated of in our book. "Why Four Gospels": $1.00 or 4/6 from the Editor.

"Lo, I come, to do Thy will, O God" (Heb. 10:9), was His utterance when He took the Servant form. "Wist ye not, that I must be about My Father's business" (Luke 2:49) are His first recorded words after He came here. "I came down from heaven, not to do Mine own will, but the will of Him that sent Me" (John 6:38) summed up the whole of His perfect life while He tabernacled among men. As the perfect Servant, He was dependent upon the pleasure of His Master. He "pleased not Himself" (Rom. 15:3). "I am among you as He that serveth" (Luke 22:27) were His words to the apostles.

The servanthood of Christ was perfectly voluntary. The passages cited above prove that. And herein we behold the uniqueness of it. Who naturally chooses to be a servant? How different from the first Adam! He was given the place of a servant, but he forsook it. He was required to be in subjection to his Maker, but he revolted. And what was it that lured him from the place of submission? "Ye shall be as God" was the appealing lie which caused his downfall. With the Lord Jesus it was the very reverse. He was "as God," yea, He was God; yet did He make Himself of **"No** reputation." He voluntarily laid aside His eternal glory, divested Himself of all the insignia of Divine majesty, and took the servent form. And when the Tempter approached Him and sought to induce Him to repudiate His dependency on God, "make these stones bread," He announced His unfaltering purpose to live in subjection to the Father of spirits. Never for a moment did He deviate from the path of complete submission to the Father's will.

"If thou buy an Hebrew servant, six years he shall serve" (v. 2). The first thing to be noted here is the service of the servant. His master had a certain definitely defined claim upon him: "six years he shall serve him." Six is the number of man (Rev. 13:18), therefore what is in view here is the measure of **human responsibility** what man owes to his lawful Owner. The Owner of man is God, what, then, does man owe to his Maker? We answer, unqualified submission, complete subjection, implicit obedience to His known will. Now the will of God for man is expressed in the Law, conformity to which is all summed up in the words "Thou shalt love the Lord thy God with all thy heart . . . . and thy neighbour as thyself." This, every descendent of fallen Adam has failed to do. The Law has brought in all the world guilty before God (Rom. 3:19).

Now the Lord Jesus came down to this world to honour God in the very place where He had been universally dishonoured. He came here to "magnify the Law and make it honourable." Therefore was He "made under the Law" (Gal. 4:4). Therefore did He formally announce, "Think not that I am come to destroy the law, or the prophets: I am not come to destroy but to fulfill" (Matt. 5:17). God's Law was within His heart (Psa. 40:8). In it He meditated day and night (Psa. 1:2). From beginning to end, in thought, word, and deed, He kept the Law. Every demand of God upon man was fully met by the Perfect Man: every claim of God completely upheld. Christ is the only man who ever fully discharged human responsibility Godwards and manwards.

"And in the seventh he shall go out free for nothing" (v. 2). After the Hebrew servant had served for six years, his master had no further claim upon him. When the seventh year arrived (which tells of **service completed**) he was at liberty to go out, and serve no more. This was also true of the Lord Jesus, the anti-type. The time came in His life when, as Man, He had fulfilled every jot and tittle of human responsibility, and when the Law had, therefore no further claim upon Him. We believe that this point was reached when He stood upon the "holy mount," when in the presence of His disciples He was transfigured, and when there came a voice from the excellent glory proclaiming Him to be the One in whom the Father delighted. This, we believe, was the Father bearing witness to the fact that Christ was the faithful "Hebrew Servant." Right then He could (so far as the Law was concerned) have stepped from that mount to the Throne of Glory. He had perfectly fulfilled every righteous claim that God had upon man: He had loved the Lord with all His heart and His neighbour as Himself.

"If he came in by himself, he shall go out by himself: if he were married, then his wife shall go out with him. If his master has given him a wife, and she have borne him sons and daughters; the wife and her children shall be her master's and he shall go out by himself" (vv. 3, 4). We shall confine our remarks on these verses to the antitype. The Lord Jesus had no wife when He entered upon "His service," for Israel had been divorced (Isa. 50:1). Now although He was entitled by the Law to "go out free," the same Law required that He should go out alone—"by himself." This points us to something about which there has been much confusion. There was no **union** possible with the Lord Jesus in the perfections of His human life: "Verily, verily, I say unto you, Except a corn a wheat fall into the ground and die, it abideth **alone**" (John 12:24). Nothing could be plainer than this. The very perfections of the Servant of God only served to emphasise the more the distinction between Him and sinful man. It is only on **resurrection**-ground that **union** with Christ is possible, and for that, death must intervene. It was on the resurrection-morning that He, for the first time, called His disciples "**brethren.**" Does, then, our type fail us here? No, indeed. These typical pictures were drawn by the Divine Artist, and like Him, they are perfect. The next two verses bring this out beautifully.

"And if the servant shall plainly say, I love my master, my wife, and my children, I will not go free: Then his master shall bring him unto the judges; he shall also bring him to the door, or unto the door posts; and his master shall bore his ear through with an aul; and he shall serve him for ever" (vv. 5, 6). Most blessed is this. It was love which impelled him to forego the freedom to which He was fully entitled by the Law—a threefold love: for His Master, his wife, and his children. But mark it well: "if the servant **shall plainly say,** I love my master," etc. When was it that the perfect Servant said this? Clearly it must have been just after the Transfiguration, for as we have seen, it was then that He had fulfilled every requirement of the Law, and so could have gone out free. Equally plain is it that we must turn to the **fourth** Gospel for the avowal of His love, for it is there, as nowhere else, His love is told forth by the apostle of love. Now in John's Gospel there is no account of the Transfiguration, but there is that which closely corresponds to it: John 12 gives us the parallel and the sequel to Matthew 17. It is here that we find Him saying, "The hour is come that the Son of Man should be glorified. Verily, verily; I say unto you, Except a corn of wheat fall into the ground and die, it abideth alone" (John 12:23, 24), and then He added "But if it die, it bringeth forth much fruit." Mark carefully what follows: "**Now** is My soul troubled; and what shall I say? Father save Me from this hour?" Ah,

He answered His own question: "But for this cause came I unto this hour: Father, glorify Thy name" (vv. 27, 28). "What led Him to say that? Love! Love, that thinks not of self at all; love that places itself entirely at the disposal of the loved ones. No matter what that terrible 'hour' contained, and He knew it all, He would go through it in His love to His Father and to us" (J. T. Mawson). Love led Him to undertake a service that the Law did not lay upon Him, a service that involved suffering (as the "bored" ear intimates) a service which was to last forever.

Every detail in this truly wondrous type calls for separate consideration. "If the servant shall plainly say, I love my master." This, be it noted, comes before the avowal of his love for his wife and children. This, of itself, is sufficient to establish the fact that what we have here must be of more than local application, for when and where was there ever a servant who put the love of his "master" before that of his wife and children? Clearly we are obliged to look for someone who is "Fairer than the children of men." And how perfectly the type answers to the antitype! There is no difficulty here when we see that the Holy Spirit had the Lord Jesus in view. Love to His Father, His "Master;" was ever the controlling motive in the life of the perfect Servant. His first recorded utterance demonstrated this. Subject to Mary and Joseph He was as a child, yet even then the claims of His Father's "business" were paramount. So too, in John 11, where we read of the sisters of Lazarus (whom He loved) sending Him a message that their brother was sick. Instead of hastening at once to their side, He "abode two days still in the same place where He was!" And why, "For the glory of God" (v. 4). It was not the affection of His human heart, but the will of His Father that moved Him. So, once more, in John 12, when He contemplated that awful 'hour' which troubled His soul, He said, "Father, glorify Thy name." The Father's glory was His first concern, At once, the answer came, "I have both glorified (Thee) and will glorify (Thee) again" (v. 28). What is meant by the "again"? The Father's name had already been glorified through the perfect fulfilment of His Law in the life of the Lord Jesus, as well as in that which was infinitely greater—the revelation of Himself to men. But He would also glorify Himself in the death and resurrection of His Son, and in the fruits thereof.

"I love . . . my wife." In the type, this was said prospectively. The Lord Jesus is to have a Bride. The "wife" is here carefully distinguished from His "children." The "wife," we believe, is redeemed millennial Israel. Both the "wife" and the "children" are the fruit of His death. The two are carefully distinguished again in John 11: "But being high priest that year, he (Caiaphas) prophesied that Jesus should die for (1) that nation; and not for that nation only, but that (2) also He should gather together in one the children of God that were scattered abroad" (vv. 51 : 52). Looking forward to the time when Christ shall see of the travail of His soul and be satisfied, the Holy Spirit says to Israel, "Fear not, for thou shalt not be ashamed: neither be thou confounded: for thou shalt not be put to shame: for thou shalt forget the shame of thy youth, and shalt not remember the reproach of thy widowhood any more. For thy Maker is thine Husband: the Lord of hosts is His name; and thy Redeemer the Holy One of Israel; the God of the whole earth shall He be called. For the Lord hath called thee as a woman forsaken and grieved in spirit, and a wife of youth, when thou wast refused, saith thy God. For a small moment, have I forsaken thee; but with great mercies will I gather thee. In a little wrath I hid My face from thee for a moment: but with everlasting kindness will I have mercy on thee, saith the Lord, thy Redeemer" (Isa. 54: 4-8).

"I love . . . My children." Christ's love was not limited to Israel, even though here, as ever, it is the Jew first. No; not only was He to die for "that Nation" not "this Nation," the then present nation of Israel, but "that" future Nation, which shall be born "at once," (Isa. 66:8), but also He should "gather together in one (family) the children of God that were scattered abroad." "Children of God" is never applied in Scripture to Israel. These "children" were to be the fruit of His dying travail. Blessed is it to hear Him say, "Behold I and the children which God hath given Me" (Heb. 2:13).

"Then his master shall bring him unto the judges; he shall also bring him to the door, or unto the door post, and his master shall bore his ear through with an aul" (v. 6). The boring of the ear marked the entire devotedness of the servant to do His Master's will. "The door-post was the sign of personal limits: by it the family entered, and none else had the right. It was not therefore a thing that might pertain to a stranger, but pre-eminently that which belonged to that household. This too was the reason why it was on the door-post that the blood of the paschal lamb was sprinkled; it was staying the hand of God, so far as that house was concerned, on the first-born there, but on no one else. So here" (Mr. W. Kelly). Important truth is this. Christ died not for the human race—why should He when half of it was already in Hell! He died for the Household of God, His "wife" and "children," and for none else: John 11:51, 52 proves that cf., also Matt 1:21; John 10:11; Heb. 2:17, 9:28, etc. Significant too is this: when his master took his servant and bored his ear, so long as he lived that servant carried about in his body the mark of his servitude. So, too, the Lord Jesus wears forever in His body the marks of the Cross! After He had risen from the dead, He said to doubting Thomas, "Reach hither thy finger, and behold My hands; and reach hither thy hand, and thrust it into My side" (John 20:27). So, too, in Rev. 5 the Lamb is seen, "as it had been slain" (v. 6).

"And his master shall bore his ear through with an aul, and he shall serve him **forever**" (v. 6). Very wonderful is this in its application to the Antitype. The service of the Lord Jesus did not terminate when He left this earth. Though He has ascended on high, He is still ministering to His own. A beautiful picture of this is found in John 13, though we cannot now discuss it at any length. What is there in view is a parabolic sample of His work for His people since He returned to the Father. The opening verse of that chapter supplies the key to what follows: "When Jesus knew that His hour was come that He should depart out of this world unto the Father." So, too, in the fourth verse: "He riseth from supper (which spoke of His death) and laid aside His garments," which is literally what He did when He left the sepulchre. In John 13, then, from v. 4 onwards, we are on this side of the resurrection.

The washing of the disciples feet tells of Christ's present work of maintaining the walk of His own as they pass through this defiling scene. The towel and the basin speak of the love of the Servant-Saviour in ministering to the needs of His own. Even now that He has returned to the glory He is still serving us.

"But "he shall serve him **forever**." Will this be true of the Lord Jesus? It certainly will. There is a remarkable passage in Luke 12 which brings this out: "Blessed are those servants, whom the Lord when He cometh shall find watching: verily I say unto you that He shall **gird** Himself, and make them to sit down to meat, and will come forth and **serve** them" (v. 37). Even in the Kingdom He will still serve us. But how can that be? Our feet will not require washing; we shall no longer have any need to be met. True, gloriously true. But if there is no need on our part, there is love on His, and love ever delights to minister unto its beloved. Surpassingly wonderful is this: "He will come forth and serve them." How great the condescension! In the kingdom He will be seated upon the Throne of His Glory, holding the reigns of government: acknowledged as the King of kings and Lord of lords; and yet He will delight to minister unto our enjoyment. And too, He will serve "forever": it will be the eternal activity of Divine love delighting to minister to others.

Thus in this wondrous type we have shown forth the love of God's faithful Servant ministering to His Master, His wife, and His children, in His life, His death, His resurrection, and in His kingdom. The **character** of His service was perfect, denoted by the six years and **seventh** "go out free." The **spring** of His service was love, seen in His declining to go out free. The **duration** of His service, is "for ever"! The Lord enable us to heed that searching and needful word, "Let this mind be in you, which was also in Christ Jesus" (Phil. 2:5).

ARTHUR W. PINK.

---

*The Editor has written a work, "Gleanings in Genesis," the price of which is $2.75 or 12/6 for the two volumes. Like "Gleanings in Exodus" it deals mainly with the TYPES. In it we have shown that the life of Joseph foreshadowed our Saviour in one hundred points. If you like these articles on Exodus, we are sure you will enjoy the series on Genesis.*

# HUMAN RESPONSIBILITY.

A Paper by the Editor, read at Monthly Meeting of the N.S.W. Baptist Ministers' Fraternal, on August 4th, 1925.

That man, though a fallen and depraved being, is a responsible creature I firmly believe: Scripture affirms it and human consciousness confirms it. That the truth of man's responsibility is of fundamental importance and needs to be continually pressed upon the people, I have not a shadow of doubt. But I contend that in maintaining human responsibility we need to be careful lest we repudiate an equally vital and scriptural truth, namely, that of man's total depravity. Such care has not always been exercised. Yea, human responsibility is frequently presented in such terms that man's depravity is virtually, if not explicitly, denied. For example: many suppose that in order to maintain man's full responsibility it is necessary to insist that he is a "free moral agent." But great pains must be taken in defining this expression lest we are found taking issue with Scripture regarding the effects of the Fall.

Here is a man on a bed of sickness, both his hands and feet are paralysed. Would you say that he was a "free agent"? In one sense, yes, for there are no handcuffs on his wrists and no fetters on his feet. In another sense, no, for he is unable to get out of his bed and move around. So we read in Romans 5:6, "For when we were yet without strength in due time Christ died for the ungodly." And again, Christ declared, "No man can come to Me, except the Father which hath sent Me draw him" (John 6:44). Once more: here is a man in prison, securely shut in his cell: the door is locked, the window barred. Would you say that he was a "free agent"? Yet this is precisely how Scripture represents the case of the sinner: "The Spirit of the Lord God is upon Me; because the Lord hath anointed Me to preach good tidings unto the meek; He hath sent Me to bind up the broken-hearted, to proclaim liberty to the captives, and the opening of the prison to them that are bound" (Isa. 61:1). The well-known words of our Lord in John 8:36 are most pertinent just here: "If the Son therefore shall make you free, ye shall be free indeed."

But, it may be asked, Does not human responsibility rest upon the fact that man has the power to do what God bids him? Would not human accountability go by the board if man were not a "free agent"? Is not the very term "responsibility" emptied of all meaning if man is devoid of capacity to render to God what He justly requires? Instead of answering these questions explicitly, let me point out that the premise "Power equals obligation," or "Capacity to perform my duty is the essence of responsibility," proves too much. God says, "Be ye holy, for I am holy" (1 Peter 1:16). This is God's command, and therefore my duty. Now if obligation presupposes power to perform, if responsibility be measured by capacity to obey, then it necessarily follows that therefore I can be holy, and hence, sinless perfection in this life is possible. Obligation and power, then, are not commensurate! This brings me to outline.

### 1. The Problem of Human Responsibility.

How can man be held accountable for doing, what he has not the power to perform? Or, to put it in other words, How can God righteously hold man responsible to do that which he cannot do? I have no desire to dodge the difficulty, therefore have I stated it in its strongest form. Nor shall I do what many have done—seek to get rid of the difficulty by denying its existence. The difficulty does exist and I shall seek to emphasise rather than minimise it, before presenting what I believe to be the Scriptural solution of the problem.

1. Let me first call attention to a number of Scriptures which plainly and positively affirm man's inability to perform that which God requires of him:

I begin with the well-known words of John 3:3, "Except a man be born again, he cannot see the kingdom of God." If words have any meaning, this affirms the fearful fact that an unregenerate person is totally incapable of discerning spiritual things.

"Why do ye not understand My speech? Even because ye cannot hear My Word" (John 8:43. Christ was here speaking to men who failed to grasp His simplest statements and continued to pervert His utterances. He then proceeded to tell them why they understood not His speech, and it was, because they could not hear His Word.

"And I will pray the Father, and He shall give you another Comforter, that He may abide with you forever; even the Spirit of Truth, whom the world cannot receive, because it seeth Him not, neither knoweth Him" (John 14:16, 17). How solemn is this utterance of Christ's! He did not simply say that the world would not receive the Holy Spirit when He was given, but that the world could not!

"The carnal mind is enmity against God; for it is not subject to the law of God, neither indeed can be" (Rom. 8:7). Not only is it a fact that the carnal mind is not subject to the law of God, but such subjection is impossible. Sin cannot be in subjection to God's Law: to say it could, is a contradiction in terms, for to be subject to the Law of God, it would be holy. If, then, sin is essentially and in direct terms contrary to holiness, the sinful nature can never yield subjection to the holy Law. Men may speculate all they please about metaphysical "possibilities," but the decision of the inspired apostle is here final: the thing is impossible.

"So then they that are in the flesh cannot please God." (Rom. 8:8). They that are "in the flesh," in contrast from those who are "in Christ," are totally incompetent to perform that which is acceptable unto the Most High. They "cannot" because they are completely incapacitated until all-mighty power and sovereign grace bring them from death unto life.

"The natural man receiveth not the things of the Spirit of God for they are foolishness unto him: neither can he know them, because they are spiritually discerned" (1 Cor. 2:14). Before spiritual things can be spiritually discerned, there must be spiritual discernment; before there can be spiritual discernment, there must be a spiritual faculty of discernment; before there can be a faculty of spiritual discernment there must be a spiritual man, and for this there must be the new birth. Therefore, the unregenerate cannot discern spiritual things.

"Having eyes full of adultery, and that cannot cease from sin" (2 Peter 2:14). Here again it is not "will not" but "cannot." Personally, I would not dare to make the assertion that there are those who "cannot cease from sin" unless God Himself had done so. As God has so said, I bow to His Word.

Now here are seven passages, and I could easily give you seven more, which affirm in the most unequivocal language the inability of the natural man. I pause not to define now the nature of this inability except to say that it is innate, total, and ineradicable by any self-help, or self-motion. The natural man can no more turn to God than the dead can sit up in their coffins. The sinner can no more originate a good desire than he can create a universe. And whoever denies this, repudiates the total depravity of fallen man.

2. Now let me affirm in the second place that, every man ought to do the very things which the above scriptures insist men are incapable of doing. Ought not men to "hear" the Word of Christ? Has He not spoken as never man spake! Are not His words vested with supreme authority! Men have ears for the lies of Satan, why, then, should they not heed the sayings of Him who is Truth incarnate?

Again; ought not the carnal mind "to be in subjection to the Law of God"? That Law is holy, just, and good! God's commandments are not grievous! If sinners respect human laws, on what legitimate ground may they disregard the Divine statutes?

Once more; certain men "cannot cease from sin." But ought they not to do so? It is never right to do wrong. If men are so degraded and so besotted that they have become the helpless slaves of sin, does that in anywise excuse them? What would be thought of a murderer whose only defence was that he hated his victim so bitterly that he could not but slay him!

3. Nothing is clearer in Scripture than the fact that God does require of man that which is beyond his power to perform. God gave the law to Israel at Sinai and demanded a full compliance with it, and solemnly pointed out what would be the consequences of their disobedience (See Deut. 28). There was nothing in that law which was either unrighteous or unreasonable. It was designed to promote the good of man as well as the glory of God. Therefore were the Israelites fully responsible to keep it. But they did not. They ought to have done so, they promised to do so: they confidently declared "All that the Lord hath spoken we will do" (Ex. 19:8). But they did not, and what is more, they could not. If any one is inclined to challenge the statement that Israel was unable to keep the law, I would promptly refer him to Rom. 8:3: "For what the law could not do, in that it was weak through the flesh." That which the law "could not do" was to bring forth the peaceable fruit of righteousness:" it commanded, but was un-

able to produce that obedience which is due the Creator. The reason why the law could not do this was not because of any imperfection, undue severity, or unreasonable exactions in it; but solely because of the weakness of the flesh. Man, because of the infirmities and corruptions which are the entail of sin, is **unable** to fully keep the very law which he **ought** to obey.

Should it be answered, God gave the Law which man was unable to keep, in order to demonstrate the need of a Saviour; that is readily granted. I am not now inquiring as to God's reasons for His actions, but simply emphasising the bare fact that He **has** demanded from men that which they could not render. If it be further said, But God is making no such demand since Christ came, we answer that such an assertion is quite erroneous.

Leaving out the sinner for a moment, let us point out how that God has set before **Christians** a standard to which **they cannot** now attain. God requires of us that which it lies **not** within our power to give. Take such passages as the following: "Be ye therefore perfect even as your Father in heaven is perfect" (Matt. 5:48). There is no need to whittle this down in the effort to make it signify less than what is actually affirmed. These words of Christ mean precisely what they say. Nothing less than spiritual perfection, Divine perfection, is the standard set before us. Again, in Phil. 4:6 we are exhorted, "In nothing be anxious." Where is the Christian who has fully complied with this admonition? Is there one here this morning who can truthfully say that **he** has ever lived a single day **entirely** free from anxiety? I am far from offering any excuse: anxiety is just as sinful as selfishness, pride, or ingratitude. Yet the fact remains that no far as our own unaided powers are concerned we could just as easily fly to heaven as live here on earth free from all anxiety. Again, take this exhortation: "Let each esteem others better than themselves" (Phil. 2:3) Do we act thus? No, indeed. Every last one of us believe that we are just as good as any one else, probably a little better. We might not be honest enough to say no with our lips, but in our hearts—which are deceitful above all things and desperately wicked —that is precisely how we feel. Once more: in 1 Cor. 15:34, God says to us, "Awake to righteousness and sin not." There is no modification: **all** sin is prohibited; absolute sinlessness is the Divine standard set before us. But none, save the God-man, ever measured up to it!

Here then is a truth which cannot be gainsaid: God sets before us a standard which we **cannot** attain; God makes demands of us which we are **unable** to meet; God requires of us that which we are altogether **incapable** of rendering. This is true both in Old Testament and New Testament times. It is true of saint and sinner alike. In Isa. 42:18, we find the Lord saying, "Hear ye deaf; and look ye blind, that ye may see." It is scarcely possible to state it more strongly than that: God asks the "deaf" to **hear,** and calls upon the "blind" to see, which is the very thing that they are **unable** to do! This leads us to consider now:—

## II. The Solution to the Problem.

Why has God demanded of man that which he is incapable of performing? The first answer must be, Because God will not lower His standard to the level of our sinful infirmities. Being perfect, God must set a perfect standard before us. Therefore mark the folly, as well as the impiety, of reasoning from human analogies: I would not demand of my child that which I knew it was impossible for him to perform, therefore God will not! God tells us that His ways are different from ours; and denies that we have any right to call them in question. I repeat it: being perfect, God refuses to set before us any other than a perfect standard.

But now this important question confronts us, If man be incapable of measuring up to God's standard, **wherein** lies his responsibility? Difficult as the problem may appear, it is, nevertheless, capable of a simple and satisfactory solution. The answer, in a word, is this: Man is responsible to acknowledge before God his inability, and to cry unto Him for enabling grace. Surely this will be admitted by every true Christian. It is my bounden duty to **own** before God my ignorance, my weakness, my sinfulness, my impotency, o comply with His holy and just requirements. It is also my bounden duty, as well as blessed privilege to earnestly beseech God to give me the wisdom, grace, and strength which will enable me to do that which is pleasing in His sight; to ask Him to **"work in me"** both to will and to do of His good pleasure.

In like manner, the sinner, is responsible to call upon the Lord. Of himself, he can neither repent nor believe: he can neither turn to Christ nor from his sins, God tells him so, and his first duty is to "set to his that He is true." His second duty is to cry unto God for His enabling grace; to ask God in mercy to overcome his enmity, and "draw" him to Christ; to beg from Him the gifts of repentance and faith. It he will do so, sincerely from the heart, then most surely God will respond to his appeal.

If it be asked, where is the Scripture which presents it thus? The answer is, the Bible contains many such passages, "If thou criest after knowledge, and liftest up thy voice for understanding; if thou seekest her as silver, and searchest for her as for hid treasures, then shalt thou understand the fear of the Lord, and find the knowledge of God." (Prov. 2:3-5). "Seek ye the Lord while He may be found, call ye upon Him while He is near" (Isa. 55:6). If the sinner, any sinner, will seek the Lord, penitently and sincerely, if he will "call" from the heart, then most surely God will respond to his cry, for it is written: "Whosoever shall call upon the name of the Lord shall be saved" (Rom. 10:13). And I believe that, without any reservation or qualification, There is a Saviour for every sinner out of Hell who will truly repent before God and by faith receive His Son.

Let me sum up this section by an illustration. Here is a man who has slipped on the icy pavement, late at night, and has broken his hip. He is unable to rise; if he remains on the ground, he will freeze to death. What, then, ought he to do? If he is determined to perish, he will lie there silent; but the blame will be his own. If he is anxious to be rescued, and knows that relief is available, he will cry for help! So, the sinner, though unable to rise and take the first step to Christ, is responsible to cry unto God; and if he does, from the heart, there is a Divine Deliverer to hand, for God is "not far from any one of us" (Acts 17:27). But if the sinner refuses to cry unto the Lord, if he is determined to perish, then his blood is on his own head, and his "damnation is just" (Rom. 3:8). A few words now upon,

### III. The Extent of Human Responsibility.

It is obvious that the measure of human responsibility varies in different cases and is greater or less with particular individuals. The standard of measurement was given in the Saviour's words, "For unto whomsoever much is given, of him shall much be required" (Luke 12:48). Surely God did not require as much from those living in Old Testament times as He does from those who have been born during the Christian dispensation. Surely God will not require as much from those who lived during the "dark ages," when the Scriptures were accessible to but a few, as He will from those of this generation, when practically every family in the land owns a copy of His Word for themselves. In the same way, God will not demand from the heathen what He will from those in christendom. The heathen will not perish because they have not believed in Christ, but because they failed to live up to the light which they did have—the testimony of God in nature and conscience.

A word now upon our responsibility in connection with the use of means. It is our responsibility to use the Divinely-appointed means: the results of their usage are to be committed unto God. Our business is to plant and to water, and to leave the "increase" unto the Lord of the harvest. It is not true that the elect will be saved whether the Gospel be proclaimed or no. The same God who has predestinated the end, has also predestinated that the end shall be attained through the means which He has appointed. A striking proof of this is furnished in the case of Hezekiah. God was absolutely determined to add fifteen years to that king's life, yet He sent one of His servants instructing him to use a fig-poultice; thereby enforcing the fact that it is man's responsibility to use means.

My friends, instead of denying man's responsibility (as I am accused of doing), I insist upon it, and probably believe in it to a greater degree and further extent than do some of my detractors. I have heard some men say, "I do not believe in the perseverance of the saints, but I do believe in the preservation of saints." I hope none of you have said anything so silly. Brethren, I believe in both. I believe that we are preserved by means of our perseverance. "We are kept by the power of God through faith" (1 Peter 1:5). There you have both the Divine and the human sides. It is just as foolish to say that there is no need or no room for my "perseverance" if God "preserves" me, as it be to affirm that there is no need for me to breathe, because God has given me breath.

There is a striking illustration of this

in Acts 27. The apostle Paul was being conveyed by ship to Italy. A fearful storm arose. Its force was so fierce and its continuance so long that "all hope that we should be saved was then taken away" (v. 20). In the midst of their fears, the angel of God appeared to the apostle and said, "Fear not, Paul; thou must be brought before Caesar: and, lo, God hath given thee all them that sail with thee" (v. 24). That was definite enough and positive enough. Was then all human effort now rendered unnecessary? Might they simply fold their arms and be utterly indifferent? Read the sequel. A little later, as they neared the coast, they cast anchor, and fearng that the ship would go to pieces on the rocks, began to take to the boats. But the apostle said, "Except these abide in the ship, ye annot be saved" (v. 31). And mark you, this was said by Paul after he had been assured by God that "all" would be saved. But their preservation was secured only by their perseverance, that is, by using the means to hand. Nothing could be more pertinent, and nothing could more conclusively expose the folly of those who deny the need for the saints to "persevere" by insisting on a mechanical "preservation," which, in fact, amounts to a flat denial of the Christian's responsibility. Scripture says, "We are made partakers of Christ, if we hold the beginning of our confidence steadfast unto the end" (Heb. 3:14). And therefore are believers exhorted, "Cast not away therefore your confidence, which hath great recompense of reward." There is equal danger on either side: danger, lest in our zeal to maintain the sovereignty of God we fail to enforce the responsibility of man: danger, lest we are so occupied with the human side of things that we ignore the Divine, and thus fail to ascribe to God the glory which is His due. We are in constant need of wisdom from on High to enable us to preserve "the balance of Truth."

And now to sum up. The fact of man's responsibility is witnessed to by conscience, and is insisted on throughout the Scriptures. The ground of man's responsibility is that he is a rational creature, capable of weighing eternal issues, and that he possesses a revelation from God in which his duty toward the Creator is plainly defined. The measure of responsibility varies in different individuals, being determined by the degree of light each one has enjoyed from God. The problem of human responsibility receives at least a partial solution in the Holy Scriptures, and it is our solemn obligation as well as privilege to search them prayerfully and carefully for further light, looking to the Holy Spirit to guide us "into all truth." It is written "The meek will He guide in judgment and the meek will He teach His way" (Psa. 25:9).

ARTHUR W. PINK.

---

A full column in "The Australian Baptist" of Aug. 11th, 1925, was devoted to commenting upon this paper and what followed it. The reviewer stated:

"Opportunity was taken at the lunch table to express the thanks of the Fraternity to the visitor for his address, the vote of thanks being very heartily carried on the motion of the Rev. Sharp, seconded by Dr. Waldock . . . At the close of the meal, an adjournment was made to the committee room where, for upwards of an hour, the doctor was submitted to a further series of questions, all of which he answered with unfailing courtesy. It was a fairly searching test, and one calculated to reveal any weak spots in his theological armor, supposing such to have existed and whether in full agreement with him or otherwise, there was a concensus of opinion that a more profitable and thougt-provoking session of the Fraternal had not been held."

At the next meeting of this Fraternal, the following resolution was passed and inserted in the Australian Baptist of Sept. 29th, 1925:

"Having heard conflicting statements concerning the doctrinal position of Dr. A. W. Pink, at the invitation of the Baptist Ministerial Fraternal of New South Wales, he stated his views in a paper at a meeting held on Tuesday, 8th September. (Note their care for accuracy!—A.W.P.) As a result of this paper and the questions and discussion which followed, the Minister's Fraternal unanimously resolved that they could not endorse Dr. Pink. Yours in Christian service. Signed by the Chairman and Hon. Sec."

We refrain from any other comment on the above except to point out what a solemn and vivid illustration it furnishes of that declaration of Holy Writ: "The legs of the lame are not equal" (Prov. 26:7)!

## TIMES OF TROUBLE.

The tenth Psalm is the latter of a pair of Psalms that refer to the days of Anti-Christ, which are called "times of trouble" (9:9; 10:1): i.e., the great Tribulation. The interpretation, therefore, belongs to those times when "the enemy" (9:6), "the wicked" one (10:13), "the man of the earth" (10:18) shall be oppressing and terrifying God's people (10:18) and God shall be preparing His Throne for judgment (9:7).

The two Psalms are united by an irregular and incomplete Acrostic running through them, commencing with 9:1, and ending with 10:17. The Acrostic is broken and troubled, as those times will be. But there are expressions in these Psalms of which the application is true for all time and all times. The words of 10:17, for example, express an eternal truth, "Lord, Thou hast heard the desire of the humble: Thou wilt prepare their heart, Thou wilt cause Thine ear to hear." If this be true of Israel in the day of "Jacob's trouble," how much more true is it of the Church in this day of grace.

Here we have the characters and desires and encouragement of those who will stand out in opposition to the "man of the earth," and in contrast with all who receive his mark. They are called "humble," from the root (anah), afflicted in soul, wretched, and always with the idea of meekness, i.e., "the humble and the meek," who prefer to suffer wrong rather than do wrong. The word stands out in contrast with the word used of "the man of the earth" in 10:10. "He humbled himself that the poor may fall by his strong ones." The word here is (shachacn), to bow down, to crouch, and refers merely to the act of the body. The word in verse 7 refers to the act of the soul.

Ah, the truly humbled are over those whom God has humbled. God finds none thus naturally. Pride is the one great characteristic of human nature. Nothing is too mean for man not to be proud of it. Family, attainments, possessions (of course); and, above all, morality and righteousness. But the really humbled are those who have seen themselves in the light of the glory of God, which has tarnished all earthly glories, and revealed the real worthlessness and and vileness of all else. The glory of God is the refiner's fire which purges us of our dross; and there is no dross so great as the high thoughts we have of ourselves. Hence the daily conflict, if we are beholding as in a mirror the glory of God in Christ (2 Cor. 3:18).

Peter had been in this furnace. Pride and self-confidence characterised him before; but mark how, afterwards, he is the one selected by the Holy Spirit to exhort the elders to be humble, and not to lord it over God's heritage (1 Peter 5:1-3); how he counsels the younger to submit themselves to the elder (v. 5); how he exhorts all to be "clothed with humility;" how he encourages them with the promise that God "giveth grace to the humble."

Oh, how humiliating to have to learn that not one of our "good works" is really good, perfectly good; that our very prayers and praises are so full of infirmity, that they are sufficient to condemn us eternally, were it not for the infinite precious merits of Him through whom they are offered. There is even enough pride left in our very humility to ruin us forever, were it not for the infinite merits of atoning blood, and for the perfect righteousness which is ours in Christ.

But there is "desire" spoken of. All are full of desires. All are seeking for something they cannot find. The new nature, too, has desires imparted to it, which none but God can satisfy. They come from above, and are always reaching forth thither. They are ever longing for the presence of God, leaning on His Word, looking for His glory, waiting for His Son from heaven.

There are also "encouragements" which all humble ones have. Three are mentioned here in this verse 17.

(1) "Thou hast heard the desire of the humble."

Yes, our "desire;" not our eloquent or beautiful prayers—the prayer of our intellect or our lips; but our "desire" the desire of our heart: because these spiritual desires come from God, and return to Him. All the sweetness of these words lie in the word "THOU." Thou hast heard for Thou didst give. Hence the humble one can sing "the new song" which has been put in his mouth, "HE inclined unto me, and heard me, HE brought me up also out of an horrible pit, out of the miry clay, and set my feet upon a rock, and established my goings" (Psa. 40:1, 2).

Yes, HE did it all. He implanted this "desire." Hence it returns to Him. "O God, THOU art my God; Early will I seek THEE, My soul thirsteth for

THEE, my flesh longeth for THEE. In a dry and thirsty land where no water is, To see THY power and THY glory, so as I have seen THEE in the Sanctuary, Because THY loving kindness is better than life, my lips shall praise THEE. Thus will I bless THEE while I live: I will lift up my hands in THY name." (Psa. 63:1-4).

Yes, He is the One who inclined unto us: who bore with us through all our wanderings, even when we inclined not unto Him. He put within us the spark of heavenly fire, when we were cold and lifeless. He preserved it, and has preserved it until now. He it was who said, "Let there be light; and there was light." This is the same GOD of whom it is here said "THOU hast heard the desire of the humble."

There is another work of grace here.

**(2) "THOU wilt prepare their heart."**

The word "prepare" is interesting. It is koon, and in the Hipil conjugation (as it is here) it means to **cause to be ready, to make ready, to prepare.** It is used in Gen. 43:25, where Joseph's brethren **"got ready"** their present against his coming. It is used in Gen. 43:16, "Bring these men home, and slay and **make ready,** for these men shall dine with me at noon." This is just what God does for the heart., HE **prepares** it. It is not prepared by nature. It is not ready to love and serve and worship Him. It has to be made ready. A heart thus prepared is then like "good ground" which (unlike the way-side, the thorny, and stony ground) was **prepared** ground.

How wonderful it is that the very disposition of the heart for spiritual things is God's own preparation and providing. HE it is who first makes us dissatisfied with ourselves; and then excites new desires within us; and then, blessed be His name, satisfies those desires which He has Himself created. But there is a third mercy:

**(3) "Thou wilt cause Thine ear to hear."**

Then it is not my prayer that causes Him to hear. I always thought it was! I thought it was my earnestness, my importunity that did it. No! HE Himself is the cause. Could there be anything, dear readers, more precious to our souls, than thus to trace all our blessings up to their fountain-head—the living God Himself: with Christ as the channel of them; and the Spirit the power of them, making them real in our experience? If we are among those whom God has made humble, then this is our distinguishing mark. This it is which stamps us as HIS. We trace, and love to trace, all our blessings up to Him, and to give Him all the glory and all the praise.

Nothing will so secure holiness of life as never thinking of ourselves, or our own "blessing" but, instead of such self-occupation, being **always occupied with God:** using every trial as a message bidding us think of His mercy; using our weakness as reminding us of His strength; using our every necessity as telling us of His fullness. Thus daily, hourly, and almost unconsciously, acquiring the habit of occupation of the heart with God, and with His Christ. Oh, to look backward and upward, at the long unbroken chain of God's "goodness and mercy." Nothing will revive our drooping hearts like this; nothing will increase our faith like this; nothing will encourage our hope like this; nothing will inflame our love like this; and enable us to go forward in loving, diligent service.

**"THOU wilt cause Thine ear to hear."** This is the language of faith. THOU hast given the promise, and I believe it. Oh that we might, with childlike simplicity, thus speak and thus act with God. The moment we look at ourselves **it is fatal to all our peace.** That is the beginning of our troubles. For we see no cause in ourselves why He should hear; and then we set to work to procure a cause. When we are occupied with ourselves, we see so much of our unworthiness that our temptation is to try and make ourselves more worthy and more meet. Thus it is we get into the horrible pit, and plunge about in the miry clay, until He again brings us "up" and "out" of it, and sets our feet again upon Himself, the Rock, and puts the new song in our mouths, and prepares our hearts to sing it. Then, and not till then, can we go on our way again, "giving thanks unto the Father which **hath made us meet** to be partakers of the inheritance in light" (Col. 1:12). As long as we look at ourselves it seems impossible that such grace should be bestowed upon us. But, when we look at His Word, at His truth, at His faithfulness, at His love, then we learn that it is **impossible** it could be otherwise.

—Things To Come, 1900.

# DIVINE CHASTISEMENT.

"Despise not thou the chastening of the Lord, nor faint when thou are rebuked of Him" (Heb. 12:5).

It is of first importance that we learn to draw a sharp distinction between Divine punishment and Divine chastisement—important for maintaining the honour and glory of God, and for the peace of mind of the Christian. The distinction is very simple, yet is it often lost sight of. God's people can never by any possibility be **punished** for their sins, for God has already punished them at the Cross. The Lord Jesus, our Blessed Substitute, suffered the full penalty of all our guilt, hence it is written "The blood of Jesus Christ His Son cleanseth us from all sin." Neither the justice nor the love of God will permit Him to again exact payment of what Christ discharged to the full.

The difference between punishment and chastisement lies not in the **nature** of the sufferings of the afflicted: it is most important to bear this in mind. There is a threefold distinction between the two. First, the **character** in which God acts. In the former God acts as **Judge**, in the latter as **Father**. Sentence of punishment is the act of a judge, a penal sentence passed on those charged with guilt. Punishment can never fall upon the child of God in this judicial sense, because his guilt was all transferred to Christ: "Who His own self bear our sins in His own body on the tree."

But while the believer's sins cannot be punished, while the Christian cannot be condemned (Rom. 8:33), yet he may be **chastised**. The Christian occupies an entirely different position from the non-Christian: he is a member of the Family of God. The relationship which now exists between him and God is that of Parent and child; and as a son he must be disciplined for wrongdoing. Folly is bound up in the hearts of all God's children, and the rod is necessary to rebuke, to subdue; to humble.

The second distinction between Divine punishment and Divine chastisement lies in the recipients of each. The objects of the former are His enemies. The subjects of the latter His children. As the Judge of all the earth God will yet take vengeance on all His foes. As the Father of His family God maintains discipline over all His children. The one is judicial, the other parental.

A third distinction is seen in the **design** of each: the one is retributive, the other remedial. The one flows from His anger, the other from His love. Divine punishment is never sent for the good of sinners, but for the honouring of God's law and the vindicating of His government. But Divine chastisement is sent for the well-being of His children: "We have had fathers of our flesh which corrected us, and we gave them reverence: shall we not much rather be in subjection unto the Father of spirits, and live? For they verily for a few days chastened us after their own pleasure; but He **for our profit**, that we might be partakers of His holiness" (Heb. 12:9-10).

The above distinction should at once rebuke the thoughts which are so generally entertained among Christians. When the believer is smarting under the rod let him not say, God is now punishing me for my sins. That can never be.? That is most dishonouring to the blood of Christ. God is **correcting** thee in love, not smiting in wrath. Nor should the Christian regard the chastening of the Lord as a sort of necessary evil to which he must bow as submissively as possible. No, it proceeds from God's goodness and faithfulness, and is one of the greatest blessings for which we have to thank Him. Chastisement evidences our Divine sonship: the father of a family does not concern himself with those on the outside: but those within he guides and disciplines to make them conform to his will. Chastisement is designed for our good, to promote our highest interests. Look beyond the rod to the All-wise hand and that wields it!

ARTHUR W. PINK.

## MISSIONARY TIDINGS.

We have recently received a most cheering letter from a Missionary in China, who has just returned from a furlough, to whom Studies in the Scriptures has been sent for several years. We are inserting it here as an encouragement to those who have had fellowship with us in this blessed work of sending out the magazine free to many isolated laborers in Christ's vineyard; and also because we hope that others of our readers will follow their good example. To quote:—

"So many thanks for continuing to send me "Studies in the Scriptures," while I was in England. As you see, the Lord has now brought me back to China.

"You will be interested to hear what I have done with the papers. I had had some bound while in China, and took them with me; we read them on the steamer. Other copies were lent around in England as they came. Then I found a dear Christian woman, not rich in this world's goods, but filled with love to the Lord. Last Autumn I sent her two years' numbers—the first you sent me: I cannot tell you her delight. She has been drinking in the messages. Now I hear that some in this little out-of-the-way village, where they only hear the **truth** preached once in a long time, that she turns the furniture (there's not much) out of her wee cottage and puts in tiny chairs so as to hold more, and invites a preacher out who is true to God. When there is no preacher this little group of Christians meet together and read the messages from those papers.

"The last two years, 1924 and 1925, I gave to a dear old saint of God—one also not rich in this world's goods, in fact, she is now entirely dependent on the gifts of the Lord's children. She is over seventy and has lately had to have her foot removed, so is now more than ever "shut in." She used to be an earnest worker for the Lord, so I gave her the magazines because she was unable to get out and they will be a mine of wealth to her.

"A few days ago I was visiting one of our stations in China and found that they daily read together at morning prayers their copies of "Studies in the Scriptures." So, dear friend, you will see how the Lord uses the printed message. May He bless you richly and use you more and more. Should the Lord enable you to continue sending the magazine to me I should be very grateful. I trust He will use you mightily in Australia.

"Pray for us out in China. The problems are stupendous—but God!" Thank God for that: without it we dare not come "our sufficiency is of God."

We trust that many of our readers will be much in prayer for those of the Lord's servants who are on the firing line.

If our readers know of any Missionaries whom they feel sure would value and read "Studies" (so many are too busy!), we shall be glad to have their names and addresses, so that they may be added to our Free List.

Many letters have recently come to hand, from all parts of the world; thank us and our friends for the magazine. Pray that the Lord will enable us to continue and enlarge this blessed work for Him and those dear to His heart.

ARTHUR W. PINK.

---

To U.S.A. Subscribers:— Please note this Magazine is now mailed directly to you by us once every two months. Mr. Pressel has no copies of this year's issues, so it is useless writing him if your's gets lost in the mail. We are doing out utmost at this end. Ask the Lord to **protect** your copies through the mail. When your address is changed, notify us in Australia with a five cent stamp on the envelope, and enquire at old address for magazines till you begin receiving at new address.

*(Continued from page 121.)*

sinners, so by the obedience of One shall many be made (legally constituted) righteous." While in 10:4, we learn "Christ is the end of the law **for righteousness** to every one that believeth."

The sinner is destitute of righteousness, for "there is none righteous, no not one." God has therefore provided in Christ a perfect righteousness for each and all of His people. This righteousness, this satisfying of all the demands of God's holy law against us, was wrought out by our Substitute and Surety. This righteousness is now **imputed**—legally placed to the account of the believing sinner. Just as the sins of God's people were all transferred to Christ, so His righteousness is placed upon them, see 2 Cor. 5:21. Such is a brief summary of the teaching of Scripture on this vital and blessed subject of "Righteousness."

"Blessed are they which do hunger and thirst after righteousness." Hungering and thirsting express vehement desire, of which the soul is acutely conscious. First, the Holy Spirit brings before the heart the holy requirements of God. He reveals to us His perfect standard, which He can never lower. He reminds us that "Except your righteousness exceed the righteousness of the scribes and Pharisees, ye shall in no case enter the kingdom of heaven. Second, the trembling soul, conscious of its own abject poverty, realising his utter inability to measure up to God's requirements, sees no help in self. This is a painful discovery, which causes him to mourn and groan. Have you done so? Third, the Holy Spirit now creates in the heart a deep "hunger and thirst," which causes the convicted sinner to look for relief and seek a supply **outside** of himself. The eye is now directed to Christ, "The Lord our Righteousness" (Jer. 23:6).

Like the previous ones, this fourth Beatitude describes a dual experience: an initial and a continuous, that which begins in the unconverted, but is perpetuated in the saved sinner. There is a repeated exercise of this grace, felt at varying intervals. The one who longed to be saved by Christ, now yearns to be made like Him. Looked at in its widest aspect, this hungering and thirsting refers to that panting of the renewed heart after God (Psa. 42:1), that yearning for a closer walk with Him, that longing for more perfect conformity to the image of His Son. It tells of those aspirations of the new nature for divine blessing which alone can strengthen, sustain and satisfy.

Our text presents such a paradox that it is evident no carnal mind ever invented it. Can one who has been brought into vital union with Him who is the Bread of Life, and in whom all fullness dwells, be found **still** hungering and thirsting? Yes, such is the experience of the renewed heart. Mark carefully the tense of the verb: it is not "Blessed are they **which have**" but "Blessed are they **which do** hunger and thirst." Do you, dear reader? Or are you **content** with your attainments and satisfied with your condition? Hungering and thirsting after righteousness has ever been the experience of God's saints: see Psalm 82:4; Phil. 3:8, 14, etc.

"They shall be filled." Like the first part of our text, this also has a double fulfilment—an initial and a continuous. When God creates a hunger and a thirst in the soul it is that He may satisfy them. When the poor sinner is made to feel his need for Christ, it is that he may be drawn to and led to embrace Him. Like the prodigal, who came to the Father as a penitent, the believing sinner now feeds on the One figured by the "fatted calf." He is made to exclaim "surely **in the Lord** have I righteousness."

"They shall be filled." Not with wine wherein is excess, but "filled with the Spirit." "Filled" with the peace of God that passeth all understanding." "Filled" with divine blessing to which no sorrow is added. "Filled" with praise and thanksgiving unto Him who has wrought all our works in us. "Filled" with that which this poor world can neither give nor take away. "Filled" by the goodness and mercy of God, till their cup runneth over. And yet, all that is enjoyed now is but a little foretaste of what God has prepared for them that love Him. In the Day to come we shall be "filled" with divine holiness, for we shall be "like Him" (1 John 3:2). Then shall we be done with sin forever; then shall we "hunger no more, neither thirst anymore" (Rev. 7:16).

ARTHUR W. PINK.

# VOL. V     AUG., 1926     NO. 8
# STUDIES IN THE SCRIPTURES

"Search the Scriptures" John 5:39.

Copyright in all English-speaking Countries.

Editor: Arthur W. Pink, 22 Parramatta Road, Summer Hill, N.S.W., Australia.
Hon. Agent in U.S.A.: Mr. C. S. Pressel, 559 Dupont Ave., York, Penna.

Price: 10 cents per copy; $1.00 or 5/- per year.

---

**"Blessed are the pure in heart; for they shall see God"** (Matt. 5: 8)

"This is another of the Beatitudes which has been grossly perverted by the enemies of the Lord; enemies who have, like their predecessors the Pharisees, posed as the champions of the truth and boasted of a superior sanctity to that confessed by the true people of God. All through this Christian era there have been poor deluded souls who have claimed an entire purification of the old man, or who have insisted that God has so completely renewed them that the carnal nature has been eradicated, and in consequence that they not only commit no sins but have no sinful desires or thoughts. But God tells us: "If we say we have no sin, we deceive ourselves, and the truth is not in us" (1 John, 1: 8). Of course such people appeal to the Scriptures in support of their vain delusion, applying to experience verses which describe the legal benefits of the Atonement. "The blood of Jesus Christ His Son cleanseth us from all sin" does not mean that our hearts have been washed from the corrupting defilements of evil, but that the sacrifice of Christ has availed for the judicial blotting out of sins. "Old things are passed away; behold, all things are become new (2 Cor. 5: 17) refers not to our state in this world, but to the Christian's standing before God.

That purity of heart does not mean sinlessness of life is clear from the inspired record of the history of all of God's saints. Noah got drunk; Abraham equivocated; Moses disobeyed God; Job cursed the day of his birth; Elijah fled in terror from Jezebel; Peter denied Christ. Yes, perhaps someone will exclaim, but all these were before Christianity was established. True, but it has also been the same since then. Where shall we go to find a Christian of superior attainments to those of the Apostle Paul? And what was his experience? Read Romans 7 and see. When he would do good evil was present with him (v. 21); there was a law in his members warring against the law of his mind, and bringing him into captivity to the law of sin (v. 23). He did, with the mind, serve the law of God, nevertheless; with the flesh he served the law of sin (v. 25). Ah, Christian reader, the truth is that one of the most conclusive evidences that we do possess a pure heart is the discovery and consciousness of the impurity of the old heart dwelling side by side within. But let us come closer to our text.

"Blessed are the pure in heart." In seeking an interpretation to any part of this Sermon on the Mount the first thing to bear in mind is that those whom our Lord was addressing had been reared in Judaism. As said one who was deeply taught of the Spirit: "I cannot help thinking that our Lord, in using the terms before us, had a tacit reference to that character of external sanctity or purity which belonged to the Jewish people, and to that privilege of intercourse with God which was connected with that character. They were a people separated from the nations polluted with idolatry; set apart as holy to Jehovah; and, as a holy people, they were permitted to draw near to their God, the only living and true God, in the ordinances of His worship. On the possession of this character, and on the enjoyment of this privilege, the Jewish people plumed themselves.

(Continued on page 192)

## IMPORTANT NOTICES

Set of twelve issues for **1922**, unbound, **$1.00** or **5/-**. Bound **$1.65** or **7/-**.

1923, 1924, 1925 same as 1922.

Note: We cannot break a set or now supply any **single** 1925 issues.

Subscription—price: **$1.00** or **5/-** per year to any address in the world.

Change of Address: Please notify me promptly of any change of address, and be certain to give both old and new address.

Non-subscribers receiving this Magazine regularly will understand their subscription has been entered by a friend.

Copies lost in the mail duplicated only if we are notified promptly.

## CONTENTS

The Gospel of John (John 16: 23-33) ... 170
Gleanings in Exodus ... ... ... 177
Truth and Error ... ... ... 181
A Message of Comfort ... ... 187
Encouraging News ... ... ... 190

## THE GOSPEL OF JOHN

**56. Christ's Concluding Consolations: John 16:23-33.**

The following is an Analysis of the closing section of John 16:—
1. Asking the Father in the name of Christ vv. 23, 24.
2. Christ's promise to show the Father plainly v. 25.
3. The Father's love made known, vv. 26, 28.
4. The confession of the apostles vv. 29, 30.
5. Christ's challenge of their faith v. 31.
6. Christ's solemn prediction v. 32.
7. Christ's comforting assurance, v. 33.

Our present section contains the closing words of our Lord's Paschal Discourse. We trust that many readers have shared the writer's sense of wonderment as we have passed from chapter to chapter and verse to verse. A truly wondrous one was this Address of Christ. It stands quite by itself, for there is nothing else like it in the four Gospels. Here the Saviour is alone with His own, and most blessedly does He reveal His tender affections for them. Here He speaks no longer to those whose hopes were to be realized in Judaism. Here He anticipates what is treated of in fuller detail in the Epistles, speaking as He does of the Christian's position, portion, privileges and responsibilites. There is a fullness in His words which it is impossible for us to exhaust, a depth we can never completely fathom in this life. Every verse will richly repay the most diligent and prolonged study.

In the closing verses of John 16 the Lord Jesus proceeds to set forth even more fully the blessings and privileges which were to issue from His going to heaven, declaring, too, the Father's love for those whom He had given to the Son. First, He assures believers of the readiness of the Father to grant unto them whatsoever they asked Him in the Son's worthy name. Next, He tells them that in thus asking, their joy should be made full. Then He announces that the time would come when He should no more speak in dark sayings, but He would show plainly of the Father. This is followed by the declaration that the Father loveth them because they loved the Son. Then He reminds them again that, having come forth from the Father into the world, He would leave the world and return to the Father. After this there is a break made by the disciples affirming their faith in Him. This is met by the solemn warning that, nevertheless, they would forsake Him. Then He closes by His never-to-be-forgotten words, "Be of good cheer, I have overcome the world." May the Spirit of the Truth grant us His sorely needed guidance as we ponder this passage together.

"In that day ye shall ask Me nothing." (v. 23). This short sentence has proven a sore puzzle to many of the commentators. There is wide difference of opinion both as to what "day" is in view here, and as to what is signified by "ye shall ask Me nothing." That Christ was here looking forward needs not to be argued; but how far forward is what many have not found it easy to decide. Did He mean that day, after the brief interval of separation when they should meet again, of His resurrection? Did He mean the Day of Pentecost, when the Spirit was to descend upon them, enduing them with power? Did He mean the whole period of Christianity, the "Day of Salvation?" Or, did He employ this term in the sense that it has in so many O.T.

prophecies (see Isa. 2:11; 5:2; 11:10, etc.), the Day of His public manifestation? Or, did He look beyond the bounds of earth's history to the unending perfect "day," the Day of Glory? Each of these meanings has been severally contended for by able expositors, and in view of the profound fullness of our Lord's words we would hesitate to limit them to any one of these possible alternatives: probably several of them are to be combined.

"And in that day ye shall ask Me nothing." This is not the first time that this expression was used by Christ. In 14:20 we find that He said, "At (in) that day ye shall know that I am in My Father and ye in Me, and I in you." But even there this expression can hardly be limited to one specific reference. If the reader will turn back to our comments on that verse he will find that we have explained it to signify: first, the Day when the Holy Spirit was given to guide believers into all the truth; second, and ultimately, to the Day of Glory, when we shall know even as we are known. It is thus that we understand "In that day" here in 16:23; having both a narrower and wider meaning, a nearer and a remoter application.

"When in immediate connection with what has just been said, we find the greatest promise connected with the strikingly prominent 'in that day' it becomes needful to mark carefully the meaning of this formula. It is obvious that it cannot mean any individual day; and we cannot avoid seeing that the time signified by it begins with the day of the resurrection, if we rightly understood the great turning point of the Future, which our Lord since 14:3 has had always before His eyes, has its commencement in the resurrection-morning after the night of suffering and death. But as certain as we have seen embraced in vv. 20-22, a comprehensive glance at all the future of the Church, must we in this connected but heightened conclusion of all, give the words their furtherest reach of signification. The Lord, as we think at least, intends this 'in that day' to include first of all, the whole period of the dispensation of the Spirit, which already typically commenced in His first return and seeing them again:—and then, pre-eminently, the end of this time, the consummation of the fullness of the Spirit in His own, when He shall have unfolded and imparted all that is Christ's to His people. This is plain from the greatness of the promise connected with it, which can never have its full realisation till that goal is reached. 'And in that day ye shall ask Me nothing. Great and unfathomable word.' " (Stier.)

But what is meant by "Ye shall ask Me nothing?" Strangely and deplorably has this been perverted by some. There have been a few who have argued from this verse that we are here forbidden to address Christ, directly, in prayer. But Acts 1:24; 7:59, to say nothing of many passages in the Epistle, clearly refutes such an error.

"Ye shall ask Me nothing." The first key to this is found in the particular term our Lord here employed. In the Greek another word is used in the latter part of this same verse where He says, "Whatsoever ye shall ask the Father in My name, He will give it you." While it is true that these two words are used, in some passages, almost interchangeably, yet that they have a distinct meaning is clear from several considerations. If the usage of each word be carefully traced through the New Testament it will be found that the former (erotao) is expressive of familiar entreaty, whereas the second (aiteo) signifies a lowly petition. Hence, whilst the Lord Jesus is found employing the former in His asking the Father on behalf of His disciples, never once does He use the latter term. Even more significant is it to find that Martha—who had not sat at His feet and learned of Him as had her more spiritual sister—used the latter word when she said, "I know that even now, whatsoever Thou wilt ask of God, God will give it Thee" (John 11:22); failing to discern the Divine glory of His person, she supposed that He would have to appeal to God as a suppliant.

According to its classical usage, "erotao" signifies "to ask questions, to make inquiry in order to obtain information." It is employed in this sense in a number of passages: to seek no further, we find it bearing this meaning in 16:19. "Now Jesus knew that they were desirous to ask Him, and said unto them, 'Do you inquire among yourselves?" But like the words "in that day," so "ye shall ask Me nothing" seem to have a double significance here—a relative and an absolute, an immediate and remote, a primary and an ultimate.

"Verily, verily, I say unto you. Whatsoever ye shall ask the Father in My name, He will give it you" (v. 23). Here is the second key to the first part of this verse, so far as its primary meaning and immediate application is concerned: asking the Father everything, is contrasted from asking the Son nothing. "In that day" refers primarily to the time when the Holy Spirit was given to them, in which "day" we are now living. But when the Holy Spirit came, Christ would be absent; then, instead of asking the Saviour questions (as they did constantly while He was with them), they would petition the Father. "The Lord is really signifying the great change from recourse to Him as their Messiah on earth for every difficulty, not for questions only, but for all they might want day by day, to that access to the Father into which He would introduce them as the accepted Man and glorified Saviour on high" (Mr. W. Kelly). This accounts for the "Verily, verily" with which Christ introduced this second statement: it emphasised the certainty and sufficiency of the new Recourse of the disciples which He now made known unto them. And how this emphasised His "it is expedient for you that I go away" (v. 7)! Petitions in Christ's all-prevailing name the apostles would be permitted to present to the Father, which was something no saint before the Cross had ever been instructed to urge. As the God of Israel He had been known: but now believers were to approach Him in the conscious relationship of children addressing their Father!

But if we look forward to the ultimate fulfilment of Christ's words "in that day ye shall ask Me nothing," they signify that in the Glory we shall know even as we are known, and there will no longer be any need to interrogate Him about any of the problems which now so sorely perplex us. Then we shall — to speak in the language of the context—understand the meaning of our present "sorrows" and "rejoice" forever, for the wise Love that appointed them. Having thus pointed us forward to the Final Goal, the Lord provides encouragement for us as we journey toward it—"Whatsoever ye shall ask the Father in My name He will give it you." The "whatsoever" must be qualified by whatever is for the Father's glory, will promote His Son's interests, and is for our good.

"Hitherto have ye asked nothing in My Name" (v. 24). The Lord was not reproving His disciples for a failure in their prayer-life, but was announcing one of the consequences of the great change then at hand. If the reader will note carefully what we said on 14:13, 14, he will see how impossible it was for saints to pray in the name of the Lord Jesus before His ascension. In the previous verses we have learned what the results of the coming of the Spirit would be saintwards, here we are shown the effects Godwards. Consequent on Christ's exaltation, the Spirit in and with believers would draw out their hearts in prayer, teaching them to present their petitions to the Father in the all-prevailing name of the Son.

"Ask, and ye shall receive, that your joy may be full" (v. 24). "I enjoin you thus to pray, that not only may you be delivered from all despondency and heart-trouble, but that in the enjoyment of all heavenly and spiritual blessings, and in the possession of all that is necessary and sufficient to secure the success of the great enterprise on which you are about to enter, you may be filled with holy happiness, heavenly joy—joy in the Holy Spirit. There is a close connection between the two advices given by an apostle under the influence of the Spirit of His Master: 'Rejoice evermore: pray without ceasing' (1 Thess. 5:16, 17). The second is the means of securing the first. If we cease to pray, we are likely to cease to rejoice—we must 'pray without ceasing' that we may 'rejoice evermore': and were we, instead of being anxious, careful, and troubled about many things, to 'be anxious about nothing, but in everything by prayer and supplication, make our requests known unto God, with thanksgiving' (Phil. 4:6), assuredly the 'peace of God would keep our hearts and minds through Christ Jesus'; and, amid external troubles, our joy would be full" (Dr. John Brown).

"These things have I spoken unto you in proverbs: but the time cometh when I shall no more speak unto you in proverbs, but I shall show you plainly of the Father" (v. 25). It will be noted that the margin gives "parables" as an alternative for "proverbs." In this word of Christ there is, again, a fullness of meaning which no brief definition can comprehend. In the Greek there are two words used (for the one Hebrew word "mashal")—"parabole" and "paroimia": the former is never used in John's Gospel: the latter occurs in 10:6 and here. Possibly it had been better to render it "dark saying" in the present instance, as the Lord sets it in antithesis from "showing plainly of the Father." And yet the thoughts connected with "proverbs" is not to be excluded. The wisdom of Solomon is recorded in his "Proverbs." So the Lord here intimates that He, the Truth, the "greater than Solomon," would not do otherwise than speak in sentences with a fullness of meaning which no mere mental acumen can penetrate. But again, the Greek word here may properly be rendered "parables," and the distinctive idea connected with this term is probably to be included as well.

"Parables are truths given and yet concealed from those who cannot or will not receive them; but to the ready heart that can take them in, they can be made known, as we see in Matt. 13:13-16. The parables there were not understood by His enemies and would not have been by the disciples, but He opened them. A parable is not a story to illustrate a truth; it is the truth itself. As though He would say, 'It will not be received, but I will speak it nevertheless.' It is like a nut, needing to be cracked open, but the kernel is there; and rich too. Now He had spoken to them in that way. Many of the incidents that occur have truth in them that would be open only to the ear and eye of the new man, enlightened and exercised by the Holy Spirit.

"He had said these things, whether they understood them or not; but the hour was coming when He would no more speak unto them in parables, but would show them plainly of the Father. That is now by the Holy Spirit. There is no book in the Scripture that is more full of teaching that requires fellowship with the subject, and the mind of the writer—the Spirit—than the Gospel of John. Wherein we fail, it is that we are so little in fellowship with Him. The deeper the fellowship, the more thoroughly we would understand all that has been told. That is, then, the reason for speaking in parables, but not doing it when the Holy Spirit comes (there are no parables in the Epistles, and note 2 Cor. 3:12: A. W. P.). The Holy Spirit's business is to take of the things of Christ and tell them out and make them actually ours." (Mr. Malachi Taylor).

The Lord went on to say that the time (hour) was at hand when He would speak no more obscurely to the disciples, but would plainly "show them of the Father." This promise began to be accomplished even before Pentecost. On the very day of His resurrection, "beginning at Moses and all the prophets, He expounded" to the two disciples on the way to Emmaus, "the things concerning Himself" (Luke 24:27). To Mary Magdalene He made known that His Father was His brethren's Father (John 20:17). So in Luke 24:45 we are also told, "Then opened He their understanding, that they might understand the Scriptures." But the complete fulfilment was given in the coming of the Spirit to guide them into all the Truth: then the veil was completely taken off their hearts, and with open face they contemplated the glory of God in the face of Jesus Christ. In v. 14 the Lord had said the Spirit would "show," here He says "I will show"; there He had spoken of the Spirit showing the things "of Mine," here "I will show of the Father." This interchange strikingly attests the unity of the Three Persons in the Godhead.

"At that day ye shall ask in My name" (v. 26). In the Day of the Spirit believers would ask the Father in the name of Christ, not only plead His name as a motive, but come to God in the value of His person. What an incentive is this for each Christian reader to engage in this holy exercise! "The benefit of prayer is so great that it cannot be expressed. Prayer is the dove which, when sent out, returns again, bringing with it the olive-leaf, namely, peace of heart. Prayer is the golden chain which God holds fast, and lets not go until He blesses. Prayer 'is the Moses' rod which brings forth the water of consolation out of the Rock of Salvation. Prayer is Samson's jawbone, which smites down our enemies. Prayer is David's harp, before which the evil spirit flies. Prayer is the key to heaven's treasures" (John Gerhard).

"And I say not unto you, that I will pray the Father for you." The first design of Christ in these words was to repel a false notion which many have entertained, namely that the Father must be besought by Christ before He will notice us. It is not that Christ here denies that He would intercede for us, but He would assure us that such intercession on His part is not needed to induce the Father to love us—the next verse makes it very clear It was Christ assuring His disciples that, following His exaltation ("in that day"), the way would be open for them to come into the Father's presence "I say not unto you, that I will pray the Father for you." "This no more denies Christ's intercession for us, than v. 23 forbids the servant praying to his Lord about His work or His house. It is not an absolute statement, but it is simply an ellipse, which the words following explain." (Mr. W. Kelly.)

"For the Father Himself loveth you, because ye have loved Me, and have believed that I came out from God." (v. 27.) This at once indicates the line of thought in the Saviour's mind at the close of the previous verse. It was not that He had to coerce the Father either to hear our prayers or to love us. The favours which we receive from the Father are not extorted from Him by the importunate pleading of the Saviour. So far from the Father having no regard for our hapipness He loves us, loves us with a special love of approbation because we love His Son: therefore is He ever ready to minister to our welfare, watching over us with paternal affection and care. The Father does not love us because Christ intercedes for us; but Christ intercedes for us because we are the objects of the Father's special love. What a blessed word is this! Spoken for our assurance and comfort as we journey Homewards. "Whatsoever they ask in Christ's name shall be given them, is secured by the love of the Father, no less than by the intercession of Christ; nay, even more so, inasmuch as the only fountain is more than the only channel, though both are equally necessary in their own places." (Dr. John Brown.)

"For the Father Himself loveth you, because ye have loved Me, and have believed that I came out from God." (v. 27.) It is to be noted that "love" is here placed before "believing." One reason for this was because Christ had just been speaking of love in the previous verse; now He proceeds to speak of faith so as to prepare the way for that profession of faith which the disciples at once made. But no doubt the word "believe" here is used as in 14:1. It was not the initial act of faith in the Lord Jesus, but the confiding in and on Him after His return to the Father.

"I came forth from the Father, and am come into the world; again, I leave the world, and go to the Father." (v. 28.) "Having been led to mention His coming forth from God, our Lord concludes His explicatory remarks by stating in the fewest words the truths which, above all others, it was of importance that the disciples should hold fast in the hour of temptation, which was just coming on them to try them." (Dr. John Brown.) These are the vital facts for faith to lay hold of. First, Christ came forth from the Father. He is the Heavenly One come down to earth; not only "sent" officially, but "come" by voluntary consent. Second, He came into the world; and why? That He might be the Saviour of sinners. Third, He has gone back to the Father. How? Through death and resurrection. With what intent? To diffuse from on high the benefits of His redeeming work. Christ's design here was to show the apostles how fully warranted was their confidence in Himself.

"His disciples said unto Him, Lo, now speakest Thou plainly, and speakest no proverb. Now are we sure that Thou knowest all things, and needest not that any man should ask Thee; by this we believe that Thou camest forth from God." (vv. 29, 30.) This confession of the apostles looks back to what Christ had just said in vv. 27, 28. The assurance that the Father Himself loved them had comforted their hearts: the declaration from their Master's own lips that they "loved and believed" in Him gave them new confidence. As Calvin beautifully puts it: "The disciples did not fully understand the meaning of Christ's discourse; but though they were not capable of this, the mere odor of it refreshed them." All was no longer dark to them; their faith was confirmed. When they declared, "Now speakest Thou plainly, and speakest no proverb" (obscure saying), they were looking back to what He had said in v. 25. It seems clear that the apostles imagined the "day" the Lord mentioned had already arrived, and that their Master was now making good His promise to them. This is the more evident from their statement, "Now are we sure that Thou knowest all things, and needest not that any man should ask Thee," which looks back to v. 23: "And in that day ye shall ask Me nothing."

"Now are we sure that Thou knowest all things, and needest not that any man should ask Thee: by this we believe that Thou camest forth from God." The disciples perceived that the Lord had accurately discerned their thoughts, and, unasked, had solved their difficulties. Yet it is clear that they failed to take in the fulness of what He had just said. They believed that He had come forth from "God" (v. 27). So far, so good. But He had spoken of coming forth from "the Father" and of returning to Him (v. 28). Upon this they were silent, and for a very good reason: at that time they neither believed nor understood that deeper point of view. The "Father" is God truly. But God speaks of the one

Divine Being who is over all—Creator, Governor, Sustainer, Judge. **Father** speaks of relationship, the relationship of God to His children. Of this the disciples, as yet, understood little, perhaps nothing.

"We believe that Thou camest forth from God." Really this went no further than a confession that He was the promised Messiah. Nicodemus said, "Rabbi, we know Thou art a Teacher come from God" (John 3:2). The woman of Samaria exclaimed, "Come, see a man who told me all things that ever I did: is not this the Christ?" (4:29). Those who witnessed the miracle of the loaves avowed, "This is of a truth that Prophet that should come into the world." (6:14). Peter testified, "We believe, and are sure that Thou are that Christ, the Son of the living God"—not "Father"! (6:69). Martha said, "Yea, Lord, I believe that Thou art the Christ, the Son of God, which should come into the world." (11:27). The words of the apostles here in 16:30 went no farther than these other confessions. "We believe that Thou camest forth from God." In truth they had apprehended nothing that raised them above the effect of Christ's rejection; only the realisation that He came forth from the Father and was returning to Him, could give this.

"They had no conception of the mighty change from all that they had gathered of the Kingdom as revealed in the Old Testament, to the new state of things that would follow His absence with the Father on high and the presence of the Holy Spirit here below. It sounded plain to their ears; but even up to the ascension they feebly, if at all, caught a glimpse of it. They to the last clung to the hopes of Israel, and these surely remain to be fulfilled another day. But they understood not this 'Day,' during which, if the Jews are treated as reprobate, even as He was rejected of them, those born of God should in virtue of Christ and His work be placed in immediate relationship with the Father. His return to the Father was a parable still, though the Lord does not correct their error, as indeed it was useless: they would soon enough learn how little they knew. But at least even then, they had the inward consciousness that He knew all, and, as He penetrated their thoughts had no need that any should ask Him. 'Herein we believe that Thou camest out from God.' Undoubtedly—yet how far below the truth He had uttered (in v. 28), is that which they were thus confessing! The Spirit of His Son sent into their hearts would give them in due time to know the Father; as redemption accomplished and accepted could alone provide the needful ground for this" (The Bible Treasury). No wonder the Lord had just previously announced to the apostles: "I have yet many things to say unto you, but ye cannot bear them now"!

"Jesus answered then. Do ye now believe?" (v. 31). It seems to us that the Lord was here challenging their faith. In a real sense they did believe that He was the promised Messiah—"come out from God." But their faith was on the eve of being severely tested, and under that testing it would be shaken to its very foundations; though fail it would not. He with His own omniscient foresight, knew what lay ahead of them. The indignity, the sufferings, the crucifixion of their Master would indeed cause them to be "offended." Their faith was genuine; but it was not strong as they supposed. This explains, we think, the "now"—"Jesus answered them, Do ye now believe?"; ye believe Me while I am with you and things are going according to your minds, but what will you do when I shall be taken from you, delivered into the hands of the Gentiles, die, and be buried! The Lord, then was warning them against their self-confidence.

"We need not doubt that the profession of the Eleven was real and sincere. They honestly meant what they said. But they did not know themselves. They did not know what they were capable of doing under the pressure of the fear of men and strong temptation. They had not rightly estimated the weakness of the flesh, the power of the Devil, the feebleness of their own resolutions, the shallowness of their own faith. All this they had yet to learn by painful experience. Like young recruits, they had yet to learn that it is one thing to know the soldier's drill and wear the uniform, and quite another to be steadfast in the day of battle. Let us mark these things and learn wisdom. The true secret of spiritual strength is self-distrust and deep humility. 'When I am weak, then am I strong" (2 Cor. 12:10). None of us, perhaps, have the least idea how much we might fall if placed suddenly under the influence of strong temptation. Happy is he who never forgets the words, 'Let him that thinketh he standeth take heed lest he fall,' and, remembering our Lord's disciples, pray daily, 'Hold Thou me up and then I shall be safe.'" (Bishop Ryle).

"Behold, the hour cometh, yea, is now come, that ye shall be scattered, every man to his own, and shall leave Me alone" (v. 32). This was spoken for the disciples' sakes, that His prediction of the heavy hour of pressure might prepare them for it. It was said to humble them, to destroy their present self-confidence. Note the opening, "Behold" to arrest their attention! "Ye shall be scatttered!" Without the Shepherd, they would be dispersed abroad. "Every man to his own"—his own shelter or hiding-place. Each of them would provide for his own safety. When the storm burst there was shelter for all but Christ. He performed his Work of Atonement alone, because He alone was qualified to do it.

"And yet I am not alone, because the Father is with Me." (v. 32). How gracious of the Saviour to address this word for the comfort of their hearts! Moreover, the consciousness of the Father's presence was the stay of His own heart. This is clear from Isa. 50:7, "For the Lord God will help Me; therefore shall I not be confounded; therefore have I set My face like a flint, and I know that I shall not be ashamed." "Let us here, in transcision to the following verse mark how all this is a type for the entire future of the Church. Often is this scattering of the disciples from His presence repeated, in various degrees and with various manifestations, but He is not alone. And even if in this day all men were to leave Him, He abides what He is, and the Father is with Him. His holy cause can never be forsaken or lost" (Stier). Similarly Calvin remarks: "Whosoever well ponders this will hold firm his faith though the world shake, nor will the defection of all others overturn his confidence; we do not render God full honour unless He alone is felt to be sufficient to us."

"These things have I spoken unto you, that in Me ye might have peace" (v. 33). Having made a final reference to the awful "hour" then at hand, the Lord winds up His matchless discourse with a parting word of encouragement and victory. He here condenses into a single sentence the instruction which he had given them in the upper room. The "Peace" of His own was what His tender heart was concerned about. "Ever thinking more of others than of Himself, even in this near prospect of the bitter cross, He forgets His own grief in the grief of His disciples. He is occupied in comforting those who ought to have been His comforters" (Dr. G. Brown). The "peace" of which He spake can be enjoyed only by communion with Himself. In the previous verse He had mentioned their forsaking His; but He had not forsaken them. Three days later He would return with His "peace be unto you" (20: 19), then did they learn, once for all, that in Him alone was peace to be found. But He does not hide from them the fact that "in the world" they should have "tribulation," but He first assures them that, notwithstanding this, there was peace for them in Him.

"In the world ye shall have tribulation (v. 33). This is not to be restricted to the violent enmity of the ungodly. It is a general term for distress of any kind. The Latin word from which our "tribulation" is taken, was used of the flail which separated the wheat from the chaff. There are temptations, trials, troubles in the world as well as from it. "In the world" is to be in place of testing. While the Christian is left down here he suffers from the weakness and weariness of the body, from temporal losses and disappointments, from the severing of cherished ties, as well as from the sneers and taunts, the hatred and persecution of the world. But though "in the world" is tribulation, " in Christ there is peace." The world cannot rob us of that, nor can its evil "prince" destroy it. But let us never forget that this "peace" is only enjoyed by faith. It is only as we abide in conscious communion with the Saviour that we can anticipate the unclouded and unending joys of the future. The peace which is for us in Christ is appropriated just so far as faith lays hold of our perfect acceptance, our eternal security, and our wondrous portion in Him.

"But be of good cheer; I have overcome the world" (v. 33). The influence and power of "the world" is powerful, but not all-powerful. It has been fought and overcome. One greater than it, mightier than its "prince," has been here, and vanquished it. The world did its utmost in the battle, but the Son of God prevailed. Noah condemned the world (Heb. 11:7, but Christ conquered it. It has no longer any power left but what He permits. It was in the way of temptation, suffering and obedience that He fought and won. Therefore let us "Be of good cheer." The world is a conquered world; it has been conquered for us by Christ. Then let us take courage. The storms of trial and persecution may sometimes beat fiercely upon us; but let them only drive us closer to Christ.

"But be of good cheer; I have overcome the world." What a glorious close for this Discourse! The foundation of peace is our Saviour's personal victory, here anticipated by Him before the conflict! How this should stimulate us. The world is still essentially the same; but so is Christ! And our Lord is still saying, 'Be of good cheer; I have overcome the world.' There must be no surrender, no compromise, no fellowship with the world. Here is our Lord's warcry: "To him that overcometh will I grant to sit with Me in My throne, even as I also overcame, and am set down with My Father in His throne" (Rev. 3: 21). Ere long the conflict will cease by the victory gained, for "Whatsoever is born of God overcometh the world; and this is the victory that overcometh the world our faith" (1 John 5: 4). The day is nigh at hand when Christ shall come to reward His servants. Then shall the victor be crowned. "And oh, the delight of casting these crowns at His feet, and ascribing forever and ever, glory, and honour, and dominion and blessing to the Great Overcomer, to Him who conquered for us, who conquered in us, who made us more than conquerors! It is sweet to anticipate this glorious result of all our tribulations and struggles; and in the enjoyment of peace in Him amidst these struggles and tribulations, to raise, though in broken accents, and with a tremulous voice, the song which, like the sound of great waters, shall unceasingly, everlastingly, echo through heaven, 'Worthy is the Lamb that was slain'" (Dr. John Brown).

Let the student work on the following questions as preparation for our next lesson:—

1. What does the "lifting up of His eyes" teach us, v. 1?
2. What did Christ refer to in "glorify Thy Son" v. 1?
3. How is v. 2 related to Christ's petition?
4. Does v. 3 give a definition of "eternal life" or—?
5. Why did Christ refer to the Father as "the only true God" v. 3?
6. What was Christ's "glory" before the world v. 5?
7. By how many different pleas (in vv. 1, 4) does Christ support His petition in v. 5?

ARTHUR W. PINK.

## GLEANINGS IN EXODUS

### 32. The Covenant Ratified: Ex. 24.

The twenty-fourth chapter of Exodus introduces us to a scene for which there is nothing approaching a parallel on all the pages of inspired history prior to the Divine Incarnation and the tabernacling of God among men. It might suitably be designated the Old Testament Mount of Transfiguration, for here Jehovah manifested His glory as never before or after during the whole of the Mosaic economy. Here we witness Moses and Aaron, Nadab and Abihu, and seventy of the elders of Israel in the very presence of God, and not only are we told that "He laid not His hand on them," but they were thoroughly at ease in His presence, for they did "eat and drink" before Him! Before endeavouring to contemplate such a glorious scene let us offer a brief remark on its occasion and setting.

In Exodus 19 we behold Jehovah proposing to enter into a covenant of works with Israel, making their national blessing contingent upon their obedience to His commandments (vv. 5,6). To the terms of this covenant the chosen people unanimously and heartily agreed (v. 8). Following their purification of themselves, three days later God came down to the summit of Sinai and spake to Moses, charging him to go and again warn the people assembled at its base not to break the barrier which had been erected. After which God spake all that is recorded in Exodus 20 to 23. Concerning the Ten Words in chapter 20 and the typical significance of the "judgment" regarding slaves at the beginning of 21, we have already commented; the remainder of those chapters we now pass over as not falling within the scope of our present work, which is to concentrate upon that which is more obvious in the typical teachings of Exodus. That there is much spiritual teaching as well as moral instruction in Exodus 22 and 23 we doubt not, but so far as we are aware

God has not yet been pleased to enlighten any of His servants thereon. Let the student, however, read carefully through them, noting how just, comprehensive and perfect were the laws which the Lord gave unto Israel.

"And He said unto Moses, Come up unto the Lord, thou and Aaron, Nadab and Abihu, and seventy of the elders of Israel and worship ye afar off" (v. 1). In the light of what precedes, this is most significant and solemn. It tells us in language too plain to be misunderstood that man cannot approach unto God on the ground of his own works. Mark that this was said by the Lord before the legal covenant had been confirmed, and therefore before a single failure had been recorded against Israel under that economy. Even had there been no failure, no disobedience, yet the keeping of God's commandments cannot secure access into the Divine presence as the "afar off" plainly denoted. For any man to come unto the Father, the work of Christ was indispensable.

"And Moses alone shall come near the Lord; but they shall not come nigh, neither shall the people go up with him" (v. 2). An exception was made in the case of Moses, not because he possessed any superior claim upon God, nor because he was personally entitled to such a privilege, but only because he was the appointed mediator between God and His people, and therefore the type of the Lord Jesus Christ. It is this which gives meaning to and opens for us the typical significance of so much that is recorded about Moses. The repeated prohibition in this verse emphasises what is said in the previous one and confirms our comments thereon; Christ had to suffer for sins, "The Just for the unjust, that He might bring us to God" (Peter 3: 18).

"And Moses came and told the people all the words of the Lord, and all the judgments; and all the people answered with one voice, and said, All the words which the Lord hath said will we do" (v. 3). The "words" refer to the ten commandments recorded in Exodus 20, the "judgments" to what is found in chapters 21 to 23, as the first verse of 21 intimates. It is most important to observe that the Ten Words are here again definitely distinguished from the other "judgments," affording additional confirmation of what we have said thereon in previous articles. Once more the people unanimously registered their acceptance of the covenant of works.

"And Moses wrote all the words of the Lord, and rose up early in the morning, and builded an altar under the hill, and twelve pillars, according to the twelve tribes of Israel. And he sent young men of the children of Israel, which offered burnt offerings, and sacrificed peace offerings of oxen unto the Lord" (vv. 4, 5). That was in obedience to what the Lord had said unto Moses as recorded in 20: 24. The "young men" (probably the "first born" who had been sanctified unto the Lord, 13: 2, etc.) performed this priestly work because the Levites had not yet been set apart to that office. Much confusion has been caused through failing to note the specific character of these sacrifices. It was not the blood of atonement which was here shed, for wherever that is in view it is always for the averting of God's holy wrath against sin. But nothing like that is seen here. What we have before us is that which speaks of thanksgiving and dedication unto God (the "burnt" offering) and that which tells of happy fellowship (the "peace" offering).

"And Moses took half of the blood, and put in basons; and half of the blood he sprinkled on the altar. And he took the blood of the covenant, and read in the audience of the people; and they said All that the Lord hath said will we do, and be obedient" (vv. 6, 7). For a full exposition of the meaning of Moses' act we must refer the reader to Hebrews 9, regretting very much that we cannot here give a detailed interpretation of that most important chapter; it will be noted that vv. 18-20 refer specifically to what is here before us in Exodus 24. Suffice it now to say that, so far as the historical significance of this sprinkling of the blood was concerned, it denoted a solemn ratification of the covenant into which Israel entered with Jehovah at Sinai. Note how the covenant God made with Noah was also preceded by a sacrifice offered to Him: Gen. 8: 20 to 9; so too in connection with the Abrahamic covenant (Gen. 15: 9, 10, 17).

"Then went up Moses and Aaron, Nadab and Abihu, and seventy of the elders of Israel; and they saw the God of Israel" (vv. 9, 10). Precious beyond words is this, showing us the inestimable value of the blood, and the wondrous privileges it procures for those who are sprinkled by it. Note the connecting "then," i.e., when the blood had been applied. A similar example, equally forceful and blessed, is found in Rev.

7: 14, 15, where we read, "And He said to me, These are they which came out of great tribulation, and have washed their robes, and made them white in the blood of the Lamb. Therefore are they before the throne of God, and serve Him day and night in His temple." The "elders" of Exodus 24 were representatives of the Nation. Here then was a blood-sprinkled people, who had not yet broken the covenant, in communion with God. The eating and drinking told of the fulness of their welcome and of the peace which ruled their hearts in the Divine Presence.

"And they saw the God of Israel; and there was under His feet as it were a paved work of a sapphire stone, and as it were the body of heaven in his clearness" (v. 10). The "sapphire stone" speaks of Divine government—the throne of God—as a reference to Ezekiel 1:26 will show; that government which will yet rest upon the shoulders of "the Man" Christ Jesus. But why the "paved work"? May not the reference be to the finished work of the Saviour which forms the basis of His Millennial reign? Christ came here to finish the Father's work (John 5: 17, 17: 4), piecing it all together, that it might be a pavement of glory as the place of His feet. The "body of heaven in his clearness" may speak of the Divine counsels. If we look up to heaven on a clear day all is blue; it is the intensity of the depths of space, infinite—like Jehovah's counsels. But in Christ God has brought His counsels so near that we may contemplate them as the body of heaven in its clearness.

"And upon the nobles of the children He laid not His hand; also they saw God, and did eat and drink" (v. 11). "But yesterday it would have been death to them to 'break through to gaze' but now 'they saw God'! And such was their 'boldness,' due to the blood of the covenant, that 'they did eat and drink' in the Divine presence. The man of the world will ask, How could 'the blood of calves and goats' make any difference in their fitness to approach God? And the answer is, Just in the same way that a few pieces of paper may raise a pauper from poverty to wealth. The bank-note paper is intrinsically worthless, but it represents gold in the coffers of the Bank of England. Just as valueless was that 'blood of slain beasts,' but it represented 'the precious blood of Christ.' And just as in a single day the bank-notes may raise the recipient from pauperism to affluence, so that blood availed to constitute the Israelites a holy people in covenant with God" (Sir Robert Anderson).

There is one thing here that is very solemn, namely, the repeated mention of Nadab and Abihu; vv. 1, 9. "They were both sons of Aaron, and with their father were selected for this singular privilege. But neither light nor privilege can ensure salvation, nor, if believers, a holy and obedient walk. Both afterwards met with a terrible end. They 'offered strange fire before the Lord, which He commanded them not. And there went out fire from the Lord, and devoured them; and they died before the Lord' (Lev. 10: 1, 2). After this scene in our chapter, they were consecrated to the priesthood and it was while in the performance of their duty in this office, or rather because of their failure in it, that they fell under the judgment of God. Let the warning sink deep into our hearts, that office and special privileges are alike powerless to save" (Mr. Dennett).

Israel's history continued for almost fifteen hundred years after this memorable occasion, but never again did their elders "see God," and never again did they eat and drink in His presence. Sin came in; their very next act was to break the holy Law by making and worshipping a golden calf, and the next time we see them drinking, it is of the waters of judgment (32: 20). How unspeakably blessed to remember that what Israel (through their official heads) enjoyed for a brief season, is now ours for ever! A way has been opened for us into the very presence of God, and there, within the vail, we may commune with Him.

In the remainder of our chapter Moses is once again separated from Aaron, Nadab and Abihu and the seventy elders, resuming his mediatorial position, to receive from God the two tables of stone which He had written. For this purpose he is called up to meet the Lord in the Mount—apparently at the summit—where he remained forty days and nights alone with God. During this time the glory of the Lord was displayed before the eyes of Israel for seven days—a glory "like devouring fire" (vv. 15 to 18). "This was not the glory of His grace but the glory of His holiness, as is seen by the symbol of devouring fire—the glory of the Lord in His relationship with Israel on the basis of the law (compare 2 Cor. 3). It was a glory therefore that no sinner could dare approach, for holiness and sin cannot be brought together; but now, through the grace of God, on the ground of accomplished atonement, believers can not only draw near, and be at home in the glory, but with unveiled face beholding the glory of the Lord are changed into the same image from glory to glory, as by the Spirit of the Lord (2 Cor. 3: 18). We approach boldly, and with delight gaze upon the glory, because every ray we behold in the face of Christ glorified is a proof of the fact that our sins are put away, and that redemption is accomplished" (Mr. E. Dennett).

"And Moses went into the midst of the cloud, and gat him up into the mount; and Moses was in the Mount forty days and forty nights" (v. 18). Those forty days, what happened in them, and the typical significance of those happenings, together with the sequel, form one of the most wondrous of the many wonderful types in all the Old Testament. The Holy Spirit now focusses attention on Moses, type of our Lord Jesus Christ. First, he is seen entering the glory, consequent upon his having erected the altar and sprinkled the blood. "And the glory of the Lord abode upon Mount Sinai, and the cloud covered it six days; and the seventh day He called unto Moses out of the midst of the cloud. . . And Moses went into the midst of the Cloud" (vv. 16, 18). How beautiful and how perfect the type! After "six days," which speaks of work and toil, on the seventh day, which tells of rest, Moses, the mediator, is called by God to enter the glory. So of Him of whom Moses was the type it is written, "He that is entered into His rest, He also hath ceased from His own works (Heb. 4: 10). And what is the character of the "rest" into which He has entered? Does not His own request in John 17: 4, 5, furnish us with the answer: "I have finished the work which Thou gavest Me to do. And now, O Father, glorify Thou Me with Thine own self with the glory which I had with Thee before the world was." Yes, He has entered into the Glory. Moses going up the Mount and entering the cloud to commune with Jehovah is a type of the Ascension of Christ, following the triumphant completion of the work which had been given Him to do.

We are not left in ignorance as to what formed the subject of communion between the Lord and Moses during the forty days in the Mount; the next six chapters of Exodus tell us that it was about the marvellous and mysterious Tabernacle, the pattern of which Moses was shown while there on Sinai. As we shall yet see, the Tabernacle and all its parts prefigure the manifold perfections of the Lord Jesus, making known the full provisions of God's grace stored up in His beloved Son—provisions which meet every need of His favoured people. The tabernacle is what meets our eye in Exodus while Moses is up the Mount, for it is not until after it has been fully described that we behold him descending. Thus has the Holy Spirit supplied us with an important key to open the spiritual treasures of this portion of the Word, by intimating that the Tabernacle speaks of what God's grace has furnished for us during the interval of the Mediator's absence from the earth.

And what is the next thing recorded in this book so rich in typical pictures of the Redeemer? Why, the descent of Moses, which we have in chapters 32, 33, 34. Moses did not end His days there upon Sinai, but returned unto his people. So also the Lord Jesus who has gone on High is not to remain absent from the earth for ever; the words of the angels to His disciples at His ascension make this indelibly clear—"Ye men of Galilee, why stand ye gazing up into heaven? This same Jesus, which is taken up from you into heaven, shall so come in like manner as ye have seen Him go into heaven" (Acts 1: 11). Yes, shall return to this same earth from which He went to heaven, return in person just as literally and truly as He left it.

But, now, students of prophecy have discovered that the Holy Scriptures divide the second advent of Christ into two distinct stages; the first, when He descends into the air for His saints, to receive them unto Himself (1 Thess. 4; 16, etc.); the second, when He descends to the earth with His saints (Col. 3: 4, etc.). These two stages of His second advent each have a most important bearing upon the Jews; the first will be followed by judgment, the second by blessing. After the Church has been removed from this world, there follows the time of "Jacob's trouble" (Jer. 30: 7), when God deals with His earthly people and punishes them for their sins, this period also being known as the Great Tribulation. After this period has run its course, the Lord Jesus descends in blessing, purges Israel, and in full manifested glory dwells in their midst—this will be during the Millennium.

What is so striking in the type which we are now engaged with is that these two stages in the second advent of the great Mediator are here vividly foreshadowed. Mark how complete the type is: Moses came down twice from Sinai after he had entered the glory! But let us observe first how Israel were conducting themselves during the time of his absence in the Mount: "And when the people saw that Moses delayed to come down out of the Mount, the people gathered themselves together unto Aaron, and said unto him, Up, make us gods which shall go before us out of the land of Egypt, we wot not what is become of him" (32: 1). Is not this the very condition of the Jews to-day during the Messiah's absence? They are all at sea, knowing not what to think. But that is not all. During Moses' absence they made a calf of gold and worshipped it—and are we not now witnessing the very same thing over again? If there is one thing which characterises the Jew to-day above everything else it is not the love of conquest or of pleasure, as with the Gentiles, but the lust for gold.

Now just as Moses at his first descent from the Mount found Israel worshipping the golden calf, so at the first stage at the second coming of Christ the Jews will be wholly occupied with their greed for riches. And what was Moses' response? Read Exodus 32: 19-28. He acted in judgment. He made them drink a bitter cup of their own providing and gave orders for the sword to do its fearful work among them. Thus will it be right after the first stage of the Descent of Christ—they shall be made to drink of the vials of God's wrath. But though sore will be their desolations the Jews will not be completely destroyed. Blessed is it to mark the sequel here. Moses returned unto the Lord and interceded on Israel's behalf (32: 30, 32). So also will the Lord Jesus yet intercede before God on behalf of the Jews: See Zech. 3.

In Exodus 33 and 34 we have the second descent of Moses from the Glory. He came down from the Mount with shining face, so that the people were afraid to come near him. But he quickly reassured them. This time he descended not in judgment, but in mercy, and therefore did he place them at ease by talking with them—so that "all the children of Israel came nigh" (vv. 30-32). Thus will it be when the Sun of Righteousness rises upon Israel with healing in His wings. Moses now "gave them in commandment all the Lord had spoken with him in Mount Sinai" (v. 32), which was a beautiful type of Millennial conditions; "out of Zion shall go forth the Law and the Word of the Lord from Jerusalem" (Isa. 2: 3).

And what is the remainder of Exodus occupied with? Nothing but the erection of the Tabernacle. Chapters 35 to 39 give us God's habitation in the midst of Israel. In the closing chapters we read, "And he reared up the court round about the tabernacle and the altar, and set up the hanging of the court gate. So Moses finished the work. Then a cloud covered the tent of the congregation and the glory of the Lord filled the tabernacle" (vv. 33-34), a lovely type of Christ in the Millenium in the midst of Israel! And there the book of Exodus ends. May the Lord give us eyes to see and hearts to enjoy the wonders fo His own workmanship.

ARTHUR W. PINK.

## TRUTH AND ERROR

or

### Letters to a Friend.
#### 9. Man's Inability.
"Can the Ethiopian change his skin or the leopard his spots?"—Jer. 33:3.

You ask me what I think of the distinction commonly made between moral and physical inability. I answer that to a certain extent it is a right one. For clearing off certain difficulties and objections it is excellent; for bringing out man's responsibility, and man's real guilt, it is often useful. For many speak of their helplessness as a mere misfortune which has somehow or other befallen them, but for which they are not responsible, and which infers no guilt on their part. But it must not be abused or misunderstood.

The distinction, we say, is a good one, and ought never to be lost sight of. There is, for instance, a great difference between my being determined not to go to church and my being held from it by force. In the one case I am guilty, in the other I am not. The former is called moral, and the latter physical inability.

But I fear we cannot carry this distinction so far as some would have it carried.

You say, why not? I answer, because if we make every thing to turn upon this distinction, we must maintain that wherever there is guilt there can be nothing **physically** wrong with the guilty person; nothing so thoroughly wrong with him as to paralyze his moral powers, so that their free play in the direction of what is good is impeded. Anything like physical infirmity or inability of any kind would render him irresponsible.

The question is often asked, "Is moral depravity possible if there be any physical (or if you like to call it constitutional or organic) incapacity?" Now, in answering this, allow me to put another which must be previously answered, "Is moral depravity possible if there can be nothing **physically** wrong with the soul?" I apprehend not. In moral depravity the mind or soul is diseased; that is to say, some physical change has passed upon them; some change which has acted upon the **soul** in the same way as palsy or fever acts upon the **body** and its organs. Sin has brought on a real alteration of their nature. For how can a thing be diseased and its members be not altered? Can the limb be palsied, and yet remain physically the same? Can the tree rot and yet remain unchanged? Can the soul be corrupted, and yet be physically unaltered? Impossible! One depraved act might not necessarily infer a physical change, but a depraved nature must. "The people's heart is waxed gross, and their ears are dull of hearing, and their eyes have they closed" (Matt. 13: 14; Acts 28: 26).

If then this be true, the distinction alluded to will not suffice to carry us through all the intricacies of this controversy. If we admit sin, we must admit a change in the constitution of the soul. You may call that change a moral one. And no doubt it is. But it is also a physical one; that is, a change in our very nature, just as really as leprosy is a change in the nature of the body. Hence, while you may say that the sinner's inability is a moral one, you cannot help admitting that there is **something more** involved in it. Nor have I any doubt that it was this something more that the prophet alluded to, when he said, "Can the Ethiopian change his skin, or the leopard his spots"; and that Christ alluded to when He said, "No man can come to Me except the Father which hath sent Me draw him"; or again, "No man can come unto Me except it were given him from above" (John 6: 44, 65).

Is then this physical change or deterioration or inability, or by whatever name it is called, consistent with **responsibility**? This is the question. Let us examine it calmly, and see how it stands.

Men are depraved. "The heart is deceitful above all things and desperately wicked." "The wicked are estranged from the womb; they go astray as soon as they are born, speaking lies." "Behold I was shapen in iniquity, and in sin did my mother conceive me."

This depravity is thorough and total. Every imagination of the thoughts of his heart is only evil continually. It has deteriorated the soul in all its powers. It has not certainly taken away any powers or faculties from the soul, but it has most materially affected our power of **using** them aright. If you admit depravity in any degree, you must admit deterioration, and consequently less physical power for willing and acting aright. Does, then, this enfeebled capability infer diminished responsibility and guilt? We have already, so far, answered this question. We answer again, that it does not, and cannot do so unless this inability has been forced upon us by another mightier than ourselves. If it is a **voluntary inability**—voluntary at its commencement, and voluntary throughout all its progress, then the guilt remains. Whatever name we may give to it, still if it be an inability in which we acquiesce, nay rejoice, then it is sinful, and we are responsible. And this is the answer to the objection sometimes adduced, "We were born in this state; it was the fall that did this." Allowing it to be so, and granting what extenuation you please on this account—still is it not a **fact** that you are of your own will an enemy of God? Is it not a **fact**, there is nothing compelling you to hate God? Is it not a **fact**, that every step you take is voluntary, and that every feeling you cherish towards God is entirely unconstrained and unforced from without? If so, then there is still an awful mass of guilt for which you are accountable, even though you could prove that the origin of it may be urged as an extenuation or excuse. Whatever the fall did, it never forced you to admit a single sin. Whatever may be your original corruption, you cannot say that it ever compelled you to sin against your will. And is it not folly as well as profanity for a sinner to be casting the blame of the evil he does upon some foreign cause, when he is all the while conscious that he is doing it of his own will. It is vain, and worse than vain, to attempt to unfasten our guilt from ourselves, and fix it on our birth, or our education or our circumstances. These may account for our sin, but they cannot annul it. They may in part explain our conduct, but they cannot prove our innocence or secure our acquittal.

The question does not turn solely upon the kind or amount of inability, but upon this—is it or is it not inability produced or perpetuated by our own deliberate choice? Did not God give you ability, and you threw it away? You could not, indeed, throw away the powers themselves, love, judgment, memory, and such like; but you did what was far worse— you disabled and besotted them, so as to make them only capable of acting wrong. You changed the physical organisation of these powers from good to evil; and will you, after all this, venture to say, that you are not responsible for the change? You have done the evil, and you cannot undo it. But we are responsible for many things which we cannot undo. If we wilfully do them we are guilty. If a pilot undertakes to steer your vessel into port and then deliberately besots himself so that he cannot, is he not responsible? Rather, is he not doubly responsible, doubly guilty; guilty for not doing the thing contracted for, and guilty for rendering himself unable to do it? Is not the fact that he himself has rendered the doing of what he undertook a physical impossibility, an aggravation of his guilt?

On any other supposition there would be no such thing as right and wrong, nor any such thing as responsibility at all. If a man is not responsible for that which he is now unable to do, when he himself is the real cause of the inability, then nothing can be more easy than to evade responsibility altogether. If I have a disagreeable duty to perform, I have only to induce disease or maim my limbs, and then I am no longer responsible for it!

The real question is not simply, Am I unable? but, How did this inability come to pass? Have I destroyed and disabled myself, or did God do it? It is in vain to plead inability, so long as it is true that I produced it myself, in direct opposition to the will of Him that made me; and so long as I am daily perpetuating and strengthening it, willingly and deliberately. We may in many cases measure a man's guilt by reference to his present resources and capacities; but God measures it by reference to the original powers conferred upon him, and which he has deliberately thrown away. To measure it by any other standard would be to give man the entire power to fix the amount of his own guilt and estimate its penalty.

It is vain to say, Oh, yes, man is responsible for the act of throwing away his powers, but not for everything that has happened to him, or been done by him in consequence of these being disabled. I answer, if a man is responsible for the first act, then he is so for all the others; for what are the others but a repetition of the first? And even though they were not, yet in every act the measure of responsibility must be the power which God gave him to perform the act.

I do not maintain that the Holy Spirit creates new faculties or powers in us. No. He renews all our faculties, but He creates no new ones. Faith is not a new faculty, neither is love, neither is trust. What is faith but the soul believing; what is love but the soul loving; what is trust but the soul trusting? The work of the Spirit is to renew the soul, not to annihilate it; and being renewed, it believes and loves and trusts, when that which is true and lovable and trustworthy is presented to it. In its unrenewed state it rejects all that is true and lovable and trustworthy in God. Not till the Holy Spirit's renewing hand is laid on it will it receive these. But in all this there is no creating new faculties in the soul; there is simply the "renewing in the spirit of our minds."

I am willing to admit that we have all the powers that man ever had. We need no more. We require no new powers to be created in us. But then the right action of our powers—their action in the direction of what is good, is totally suspended, palsied, prostrate. The power of using these things aright is gone. These powers we still possess, the power we have cast away. I have all the bodily limbs that Adam had; but the power to use them is not like his. I have all the mental or moral powers which he possessed, but the power to use them I have sinned away. Now, it is the possession of the powers that makes me responsible not simply the possession of the power. If I came into the world bereft of intellect, then I could not be expected to understand the truth nor commanded to believe it. But if my understanding remains, however paralysed and darkened by sin, I am responsible. If I came into the world with out a conscience I could not be commanded to keep the holy law of God; but if I have a conscience, however depraved by sin, I am responsible for keeping it. If I came into the world without a heart to love, any more than the worm beneath my feet, I could not be enjoined to love. But if I have a heart still, however changed in regard to its tastes, then I am responsible up to the extent of my original powers of loving. If I came into the world without a will, like a stone, I could not be guilty; but if I have a will, though utterly set against God, utterly in bondage to sin, then I am responsible up to the full measure for which that will was given.

Man is truly a more depraved being than many seem to suppose. The seat of his disease lies far deeper than they imagine. They would make it a very superficial thing, easily cured, by a mere act of his own will. God makes it very different—deep-seated, awfully malignant, utterly incurable, save by the direct forthputting of the will and power of God.

Grant that the seat of the disease is the will, still the case remains unaltered. The will must have undergone a change, so that it is not now what once it was. The will has become depraved, and that depravity can only be removed by the mighty power of God. Let the seat of the malady be where you like, still it is a malady of such a nature as to require interposition of Omnipotence for its cure. The question then comes to be, not what is the disease, or what is the seat of it, but is it capable of removal by any but God?

Make then the inability small or great, make it natural or moral, make it of whatever kind you will, still this fact comes prominently out that man cannot remove it. God alone can do this. Man is utterly helpless. God must interpose; in whatever way He interposes there is a testimony of man's helplessness. If God must interpose, either directly or indirectly, then up to the amount of power put forth in that interposition, I am counted by Him as helpless. With this question the mode of operation has nothing to do. At another stage of the question this point will be discussed; but here we speak not of the necessity for a particular kind of operation but for any operation at all, mediate or immediate. Without the Spirit working in some way or other, it is admitted by all, that man would remain an unbeliever. Is he not then responsible for this unbelief—an unbelief which it requires the Spirit to remove? If it is confessed that he is responsible in such circumstances, then I answer the whole question is conceded; for it is granted that he is responsible for that which without the Spirit never will be done.

A favourite argument with many is, "How can a man be called on to believe if he is not able of himself to do so? and how can the gospel be free if a man be unable of himself to receive it?" On this I would make the following remarks.

1. This is a wrong way of settling the matter. The true question is as to what Scripture says and not as to what we think. Now, Scripture does call upon us, and command us to believe, yet declares also our entire helplessness. Both of these things are true, whether we can reconcile them or not. The truth of either of them does not depend upon our being able to adjust and explain them, but simply upon God's declaration concerning them. He has revealed both and it is not for us to ask how can both of these be true, or to refuse to admit one of them, because it appears to our reason inconsistent with the other. We know so little of the things of God, and are so utterly unable to reconcile many things much plainer than these that it becomes us to be silent. God commands men everywhere to believe and repent, yet He says, "No man can come to Christ unless it be given him of the Father." Let us receive both of these statements, for both are of God. It is sad indeed when men will not believe what God tells them, unless their own reason can approve of it. There can be little reverence for God when men will not receive His revelation unless borne out by the demonstrations of their own erring reasons. There can be little reverence for the Bible when men will not admit one of its plainest statements because they cannot see how it accords with another to which they happen to be particularly attached. There may be perfect harmony, thought we do not see it.

How foolish, then, and unreasonable to dwell upon such apparent contradictions, as if these could settle the question. Christ commanded Lazarus to come forth. Did that prove that Lazarus could do it of himself? How profane, as well as foolish, would it be to say Lazarus could not be entirely dead; he must have had some life and power remaining, else Christ would never have commanded him to come forth.

But, some will say, there is a mighty difference between this instance and the matter before us. I grant there is; but the difference is all against such an objection. It does not matter what you call the kind of death or the kind of inability, it may be moral or it may be physical, still it is death and it is inability. It is such a death and such an inability as require to be removed by the power of another.

And this is enough. Even where the power of another must go forth in order to enable the person to comply with the command, the command is quite consistent with man's responsibility. It is needless then to discuss the question of moral and physical inability. All I contend for here is an inability which the power of another is required to remove.

It is remarkable also that it is from resurrection that many of the expressions are taken regarding the power required to convert the soul. "You hath He quickened who were dead in trespasses and sins." "What is the exceeding greatness of His power toward us, who believe according to the working of His mighty power which He wrought in Christ, when He raised Him from the dead." It is then the exceeding greatness of His power that is required to raise us. It is the same mighty power which raised Christ—nothing less than this. It is more than creation-power. It is resurrection-power.

2. Upon any theory regarding the Spirit's work the same difficulty occurs, and the same question may be put regarding man's responsibility for believing the Gospel. If I entirely deny both the being and the work of the Spirit I can consistently put the question, how can you ask a man to believe and yet say that he needs the Spirit's aid in order to do this? But if I admit the Spirit's aid is necessary in any sense, then I admit that but for that help the sinner would not or could not have believed. And what is this but confessing the great truth that man is in himself helpless, but still responsible, that man cannot, or at least will not, believe without the Spirit—yet still that he may be called upon to do so, and condemned for not believing. Let us grant the Spirit does not operate directly, let me admit this to the fullest extent—still it remains true that His indirect operation is absolutely necessary and that without it the sinner's unbelief would remain immovable? If then there is an admission of the necessity of the Spirit's agency in any degree or mode, then there is confession that man in himself is helpless and yet responsible. You must either deny the Spirit and His work totally, or else admit the sinner's responsibility even in the midst of his helplessness.

3. Let me grant that the inability is wholly in the will and nowhere else; that the sinner can, if he will, do everything in believing, etc. Does this get clear of the difficulty? By no means. For still the will being wholly set against God presents the grand obstacle. God sees that man never will turn of his own accord, and yet he invites, entreats and commands him to do so. Is not this as great a difficulty as ever? Allowing that it places the question of the sinner's responsibility in a truer light, does it throw any light upon God's reasons for entreating sinners to do what He knows they never will? I might still ask the question, and insist upon a solution of the difficulty, "Why does God call on us to turn, when He knows we never will do so until He turns us? Is it not mockery in God to plead with us and ply us with arguments and motives, when He knows quite well that we never will comply with these of our own accord?" Here is the great difficulty—a difficulty which exists in our opponents' system as well as ours—a difficulty which, even upon their principles, would lead to the conclusion that God is insincere in what He says—giving us invitations which He knows will never be complied with.

4. God commands the sinner to keep the whole law, in every jot and tittle. The command is a just one. Man is responsible for obeying it. But does this prove that unrenewed man is able to keep the whole law? A man's being unrenewed does not free him from his obligation to keep the law. He is still bound to do so even in his unrenewed state. But does this prove that in that state he is also able to keep it? According to some, it does; otherwise God would not be just in enjoining him to keep it. But further, a man has the same power to keep the law as he has to believe the Gospel. His powers for both are of necessity the same, unless a new faculty be required in order to his keeping the law. If, then, he can believe of himself he can keep the law of himself. He is equally responsible for both.

5. God commands us to "make ourselves new hearts," Ezek. 18: 31. Are we able to do this? Not even the advocates of free-will maintain this. They admit that a man cannot convert himself, and give himself a new heart. Yet God commands us to do this, and tells us that if we do not do this iniquity will be our ruin. We are responsible for making our hearts good, for we made them evil. It is no excuse to say we have made them so evil that we cannot renew them; it is beyond our power. We are responsible for all the evil that we have done, whether we can undo it or not; and God is righteous in saying to us, Do this good or undo this evil.

These considerations may help to show us that man's utter helplessness is not at all inconsistent with God's authority over him, and that it is quite possible to hold the doctrine of man's inability, and yet to press upon him the command, to say, "Ye will not come unto Me, that ye might have life."

It is not surely very difficult to see the consistency between man's helplessness and his responsibility to obey the calls to believe, to turn, to repent. For these calls are not to anything save what the sinner feels he is bound to do, whether he be assisted or not in the doing of them. Those feelings which the Holy Spirit works are just what every man ought at all times to have, and which he is guilty for not having. If that which He wrought was something alien to our being, something so entirely new, that we could form no conception of it, then the inconsistency would exist. But since He only does for us, and in us, that which we ought always to possess, and for which we are responsible, the consistency is plain and indisputable.

As to freedom of the will, I must be content with a few remarks. Philosophers and Pelagians say that man's will is free; Scripture says that it is in bondage. I admit that God does not force it, that the devil cannot force, that nothing outward can force it. I admit that man is a free agent in what he does, in so far as anything outward is concerned. But still his will is a captive. Christ says, "Whosoever committeth sin is the servant of sin"; and He adds, "If the Son makes you free, ye shall be free indeed." Does not this mean that till Christ made us free we were not free? Paul also speaks of our being "servants of sin," of our being "carnal, sold under sin"; and Peter says, "They promise liberty, while they themselves are the servants of corruption; for of whom a man is overcome, of the same is he brought in bondage" (2 Peter 2: 19). Let these passages suffice for those who boast of the freedom of the will. But indeed, if they have not learned, in their own bitter experience, the miserable bondage of their own will, and the sad dominion which sin has over them, I despair of convincing them either by reason or Scripture

But you, my dear friend, know something of the struggles of the soul in bondage . Even when rejoicing in forgiveness, and walking in the liberty which the Son hath given, we are continually made to feel the remains of our former bondage, and to cry out because of it. Our chains no longer bind us, but their fragments still remain upon our limbs. And if even now we feel the traces of our bondage, how heavy and sore must it have been in other days! Our wills, our faculties, our entire nature were in bondage. We were not free till Christ made us so. And it is in this that we rejoice; we once were the slaves of sin, now we are set free; once it had dominion over us, now we are delivered from its yoke! And instead of being less free, because filled and moved by the indwelling Spirit, we are all the more free. It is His omnitotent interposition that gives us liberty. We were helpless bond-slaves before. Blessed be the name of Him who sent from above, and took us and drew us out of many waters! Blessed be His glorious name forever, who hath opened our prison-gates, and brought us forth out of the low dungeon to breathe in gladness the fresh air of a heavenly day! Those who say that the whole disease lies in the will, and nowhere else, must have some difficulty in sympathising with Paul, when he said, "To will is present with me, but **HOW TO PERFORM** that which is good I find not." I would earnestly recommend the careful study of the seventh chapter of the Romans in connection with this letter.

## WHAT SAITH THE LORD:

"God saw that the wickedness of man was great in the earth, and every imagination of the thoughts of his heart was only evil continually." Gen. 6: 5.

"Who can bring a clean thing out of an unclean? Not one." Job. 14: 4.

"Behold I was shapen in iniquity; and in sin did my mother conceive me." Psa. 51: 5.

"The heart is deceitful above all things and desperately wicked." Jer. 17: 9.

"No man can come to Me except the

Father, which hath sent Me, draw him." John 6: 44.

"No man can come unto Me, except it were given him of My Father." John 6: 65.

"I am carnal sold under sin. For that which I do I allow not; for what I would that I do not; but what I hate, that I do. . . . To will is present with me; but how to perform that which is good, I find not. . . . The good that I would I do not; but the evil which I would not, that I do. . . . I see another law in my members warring against the law of my mind, and bringing me into captivity to the law of sin." Rom. 6: 14-18, 19-23.

H. Bonar, (1851).

## A MESSAGE OF COMFORT.

"He that spared not His own Son, but delivered Him up for us all, how shall He not with Him also freely give us all things?" Rom. 8: 32.

The above verse supplies us with an instance of Divine logic. It contains a conclusion drawn from a premise: the premise is that God delivered up Christ for all His people, therefore everything else that is needed by them is sure to be given. There are many examples in Holy Writ of such Divine logic. "If God so clothe the grass of the field, which to-day is and to-morrow is cast into the oven, shall He not much more clothe you?" (Matt. 6: 30). "If when we were enemies we were reconciled to God by the death of His Son, much more being reconciled, we shall be saved by His life" (Rom. 5: 10). "If ye then being evil, know how to give good gifts unto your children, how much more shall your Father which is in heaven give good things to them that ask Him?" (Matt. 7: 11). So here in our text the reasoning is irresistable and goes straight to the understanding and heart.

Our text tells of the gracious character of our loving God as interpreted by the gift of His Son. And this, not merely for the instruction of our minds, but for the comfort and assurance of our hearts. The gift of His own Son is God's guarantee to His people of all needed blessings. The greater includes the less; His unspeakable spiritual gift is the pledge of all needed temporal mercies. Note in our text four things:—

### 1. The Father's Costly Sacrifice.

This brings before us a side of the truth upon which I fear we rarely meditate. We delight to think of the wondrous love of Christ, whose love was stronger than death, and who deemed no suffering too great for His people. But what must it have meant to the heart of the Father when His Beloved left His Heavenly Home! God is love, and nothing is so sensitive as love. I do not believe that Deity is emotionless, the Stoic as represented by the Schoolmen of the middle ages. I believe the sending forth of the Son was something which the heart of the Father felt, that it was a real sacrifice on His part.

Weigh well then the solemn fact which premises the sure promise that follows: God "spared not His own Son!" Expressive, profound, melting words! Knowing full well, as He only could, all that redemption involved—the Law rigid and unbending, insisting upon perfect obedience and demanding death for its transgressors. Justice, stern and inexorable, requiring full satisfaction, refusing to "clear the guilty." Yet God withheld not the only Sacrifice which could meet the case.

God "spared not His own Son," though knowing full well the humiliation and ignominy of Bethlehem's manger, the ingratitude of men, the not having where to lay His head, the hatred and opposition of the ungodly, the enmity and bruising of Satan—yet He did not hesitate. God did not relax ought of the holy requirements of His throne, nor abate one whit of the awful curse. No, He "spared not His own Son." The utmost farthing was exacted; the last dregs in the cup of wrath must be drained. Even when His Beloved cried from the Garden "if it be possible, let this cup pass from Me," God "spared" Him not. Even when vile hands had nailed Him to the tree, God cried "Awake, O sword, against My Shepherd, and against the man that is My Fellow, saith the Lord of Hosts; smite the Shepherd" (Zech. 13: 7).

### 2. The Father's Gracious Design.

"But delivered Him up for us all." Here we are told why the Father made such a costly sacrifice; He spared not Christ, that He might spare us! It was not want of love to the Saviour, but wondrous, meritless, fathomless love for us! O marvel anew at the wondrous design of the Most High. "God so loved the world that He gave His only begotten Son." Verily, such love passeth knowledge. Moreover, He made this costly sacrifice not grudgingly or reluctantly, but freely—out of love.

Once God had said to rebellious Israel, "How shall I give thee up, Ephraim?" (Hosea 11: 8), infinitely more cause had He to say this of the Holy One, His well-beloved, the One in whom His soul daily delighted. Yet, He "delivered Him up"—to shame and spitting, to hatred and persecution, to suffering and death itself. And He delivered His up for us—descendants of rebellious Adam, depraved and defiled, corrupt and sinful, vile and worthless! For us who had gone into the "far country" of alienation from Him, and there spent our substance in riotous living. Yes, "for us" who had gone astray like sheep, each one turning to "his own way." For us "who were by nature the children of wrath, even as others," in whom there dwelt no good thing. For us who were filled with all that is abominable and vile, with no soundness in us. For us who had rebelled against our Creator, hated His holiness, despised His Word, broken His commandments, resisted His Spirit. For us who richly deserved to be cast into the everlasting burnings and receive those wages which our sins so fully earned.

Yes, for thee fellow Christian, who art sometimes tempted to interpret your afflictions as tokens of God's hardness; who regard your poverty as a mark of His neglect, and your seasons of darkness as evidences of His desertion. O, confess to Him now the wickedness of such dishonouring doubtings, and never again question the love of Him who spared not His own Son, but delivered Him up for us all.

Faithfulness demands that I should point out the qualifying pronoun in our text. It is not God "delivered Him up for all," but "for us all." This is definitely defined in the verses which immediately precede. In v. 31 the question is asked, "If God be for us, who can be against us?" In v. 30 this "us" is defined as those whom God did predestinate and has "called" and "justified." The "us" are the high favorites of heaven, the objects of sovereign grace, God's elect. And yet in themselves they are, by nature and practice, deserving of nothing but wrath. But yet, thank God, it is "us all"—the worst as well as the best, the five-hundred-pounds-debtor equally as much as the fifty-pence-debtor.

### 3. The Spirit's Blessed Inference.

Ponder well the glorious "conclusion" which the Spirit of God here draws from the wondrous fact stated in the first part of our text, "He that spared not his own .n, but delivered Him up for us all, how shall He not with Him also freely give us all things." How conclusive and how comforting is the inspired reasoning of the apostle. Arguing from the greater to the less, He proceeds to assure the believer of God's readiness to also freely bestow all needed blessings. The gift of His own Son, so ungrudgingly and unreservedly bestowed, is the pledge of every other needed mercy.

Here is the unfailing guaranty and talisman of perpetual reassurance to the drooping spirit of the tried believer. If God has done the greater, will He leave the less undone? Infinite love can never change. The love that spared not Christ cannot fail its objects nor begrudge any needed blessings. The sad thing is that our hearts dwell upon what we have not, instead of upon what we do have. Therefore the Spirit of God would here still our restless self-communings and quiet the repinings of ignorance with a soul-satisfying knowledge of the truth, by reminding us not only of the reality of our interest in the love of God, but also of the extent of that blessing which flows therefrom.

Weigh well what is involved in the logic of this verse. First, the great Gift was given unasked; will He not bestow others for the asking? None of us supplicated God to send forth His Beloved; yet He send Him! Now, we may come to the throne of grace and there present our requests in the virtuous and all-efficacious name of Christ.

Second, the one great Gift cost Him much; will He not then bestow the lesser gifts which cost Him nothing save the delight of giving! If a friend were to give me a valuable picture, would he begrudge the necessary paper and string to wrap it in? Of if a loved one made me a present of a precious jewel, would he refuse a little box to carry it in? How much less will He who spared not His own Son, withhold any good thing from them that walk uprightly.

Third, the one Gift was bestowed when we were enemies; will not then God be gracious to us now that we have been reconciled and are His friends? If He had designs of mercy for us while we were yet in our sins, how much more will He regard us favourably now that we have been cleansed from all sin by the precious blood of His Son!

### 4. The Comforting Promise.

Observe the tense that is used here. It is not "how has He not with Him also freely given us all things," though this is also true, for even now are we "heirs of God (Rom. 8: 17). But our text goes further than this: "'How shall He not with Him also freely give us all things?" The second half of this wondrous verse contains something more than a record of the past; it supplies reassuring confidence both for the present and for the future. No time-limits are to be set upon this "shall." Both now in the present and forever and ever in the future God shall manifest Himself as the great Giver. Nothing for His glory and for our good will He withhold. The same God who delivered up Christ for us all is "without variableness or shadow of turning."

Mark the manner in which God gives: "How shall He not with Him also freely give us all things?" God does not have to be coaxed; there is no reluctance in Him for us to overcome. He is ever more willing to give than we are to receive. Again; He is under no obligations to any; if He were, He would bestow of necessity, instead of giving "freely." Ever remember that He has a perfect right to do with His own as He pleases. He is free to give to whom He wills.

The word "freely" not only signifies that God is under no constraint, but also means that He makes no charge for His gifts, He places no price on His blessings. God is no retainer of mercies or barterer of good things; if He were, justice would require Him to charge exactly what each blessing was worth, and then who among the children of Adam could find the wherewithal? No, blessed be His name, God's gifts are "without money and without price"—unmerited and unearned.

Finally, rejoice over the comprehensiveness of this promise: "How shall He not with Him also, freely give us all things?" The Holy Spirit would here regale us with the extent of God's wondrous grant. What is it you need, fellow Christian? Is it pardon? Then has He not said, "If we confess our sins, He is faithful and just to forgive us our sins, and to cleanse us from all unrighteousness" (1 John 1: 9). Is it grace? Then has He not said, "God is able to make all grace abound toward you; that ye, always having all sufficiency in all things, may abound to every good work" (2 Cor. 9: 8). Is it a "thorn in the flesh?" this too will be given—"there was given to me a thorn in the flesh" (2 Cor. 12: 7). Is it rest? Then heed the Saviour's invitation, "Come unto Me. . . and I will give you rest" (Matt. 11: 28). Is it comfort? Is He not the God of all comfort (2 Cor. 1: 3).

"How shall He not with Him also freely give us all things?" Is it temporal mercies that the reader is in need of? Are your circumstances adverse so that you are filled with dismal forebodings? Does your cruse of oil and barrel of meal look as though they will soon be quite empty? Then spread your need before God, and do it in simple childlike faith. Think you that He will bestow the greater blessings of grace and deny the lesser ones of Providence? No, "My God shall supply all your need" (Phil. 4: 19). True, He has not promised to give all you ask, for we often ask "amiss." Mark the qualifying clause: "How shall He not with Him also freely give us all things?" We often desire things which would come in between us and Christ if they were granted, therefore does God in His faithfulness withhold them.

Here then are four things which should bring comfort to every renewed heart. The Father's costly sacrifice. Our God is a giving God and no good thing does He withhold from them that walk uprightly. The Father's gracious design. It was for us that Christ was delivered up; it was our highest and eternal interests that He had at heart. The Spirit's infallible inference. The greater includes the less: the unspeakable Gift guarantees the bestowment of all other needed favours. The comforting promise. Its sure foundation, its present and future scope, its blessed extent, are for the assuring of our hearts and the peace of our minds. May the Lord add His blessing to this little meditation.

ARTHUR W. PINK.

The above is the substance of a sermon 1926, in the Strict and Particular Baptist Church, Sydney. Being most graciously preached on Sabbath evening, May 2nd, owned of God in its oral form, we thought our readers would value it in print. May it bring peace and comfort to many a heavy heart.

## ENCOURAGING NEWS.

Studies in the Scriptures is now being sent out free to three hundred missionaries scattered through forty foreign countries. Several of our readers have had fellowship with us in this sending forth of the magazine into distant lands, and we feel sure that others would do so if they would definitely look to the Lord about it. Let not this be construed as an indirect appeal for ourselves. It is not. If our friends sent in gifts to enable us to send out the magazine to another hundred missionaries we should reap no financial gain. It is for the sake of those who are now cut off from all oral ministry, and who are hungering for soul food, that this suggestion is submitted to our readers.

For the encouragement of those who are interested in this work and in the hope of stimulating others we give below a number of extracts from letters received from different ones far away.

"Greetings in Jesus' holy name. May grace be multiplied and peace from God our Father and from the Lord Jesus Christ. The Studies in the Scriptures is such a great light to me through the friend who send it. And I also thank the good Lord for the wisdom He gives to mortal men that they can understand His ways, for your revelations of the Scriptures, through Him, is mighty. May He ever keep you abounding in His truth more and more is the prayer of my heart." This is from a native Christian in the British West Indies.

"The monthly visits of Studies in the Scriptures are very welcome. I enjoy reading your interpretations and I find much useful material that I can use in my classes in the Seminary." This is from a brother in Mexico, who is teaching native Christians for evangelistic and pastoral work.

"I have to thank you once again for sending me Studies in the Scriptures for 1926. I had been praying the Lord to cause His servant to continue sending them to me. Yesterday I was the happy recipient of the material answer to my prayer when the Jan. and Feb. numbers arrived. I cannot tell you how helpful the different articles are. I am especially interested in the Addresses on the Sovereignty of God. So far as I know I am alone in the belief of this great doctrinal truth. In South Africa I have come into contact with but one person who has ever even mentioned the subject. Such doctrinal truths as God's electing grace and man's total depravity since Adam's fall, are not only not believed, but hated by almost all teachers and preachers of this present day. We can but magnify the distinguishing grace and discriminating mercy of God for having chosen us in Christ and given us to love those truths to which so many are strangers."

"I want to append a word of thanks to you for the Studies of the Scriptures, and to say that God has given me much blessing in the reading and study of them, and that there are truths I have learned and praise God for which I never knew of." This is from a brother in the Australian bush, who is working among the Aborigines.

"I really cannot tell you how much we appreciate and value Scripture Studies. We look forward to the copies month by month and never fail to find strength, encouragement and help." From a brother and sister in Egypt.

"Greetings in Him. I have never met you, but for some time have been the recipient of your invaluable magazine. I write now to thank you heartily for the same, and rejoice to know that I am to get it again during 1926." From a brother in India.

"Mr. P. of Kanshow has sent me word that through the kindness of a friend a copy of your monthly magazine is being sent to me. I have already had several copies and I would like to thank you for this kindness. I have had considerable pleasure and profit in going through "Christ Washing His Disciples' Feet." It is sometimes humiliating to us to see how often we miss the obvious, or what ought to be. So I am glad of such a stimulus to real study." From a brother in China.

If you are finding this magazine helpful to your soul, why not recommend it to other Christians, that they too may share in the blessing! It is thus the present very restricted circulation in Australia, England and the U.S.A. might be increased.

"If we are looking after the well-watered plains, as Lot did, we might be suffered to get them, but then we shall have sorrow, as Lot had. And we see cases like his now. Indeed for one Abram, we see fifty Lots".

Bible Treasury.

Prayer respects particular occasions, or special places of Scripture, whose exposition or interpretation we inquire after. This is the great duty of a **faithful interpreter**, that which in, with, and after, the use of all means, he betakes himself unto. An experience of divine guidance and assistance herein is that which unto some is invaluable, however to others it is despised. But shall we think it strange for a Christian, when it may be after the use of all the other means, he finds himself at a loss about the true meaning and intention of the Holy Spirit in any place or text of Scripture, to betake himself in a more ordinary manner unto God by **prayer**, that He would by His Spirit enlighten, guide, teach and so reveal the truth unto him? Or should we think it strange that God should hear such prayers, and instruct such persons in the secrets of His covenant? God forbid there should be such **atheistical** thoughts in the minds of any who would be esteemed Christians! Yea, I must say, that for a man to undertake the interpretation of any part or portion of Scripture in a solemn manner, without **invocation of God** to be taught and instructed by His Spirit, is a high provocation of Him; nor shall I expect thee discovery of truth from any one who so proudly and ignorantly engageth in a work so much above his ability to manage. I speak this of solemn and stated interpretations; for otherwise a "scribe ready furnished for the kingdom of God" may, as he hath occasion, from the spiritual light and understanding wherewith he is endued, and the stores he hath already received, declare the mind of God unto the edification of others. But this is the first means to render our **studying of the Scripture** useful and effectual unto the end aimed at.

This, as was said, is the **sheet-anchor** of a faithful expositor of the Scripture, which he betakes himself unto in all difficulties; nor can he without it be led into a comfortable satisfaction that he hath attained the mind of the Holy Spirit in any divine revelation. When all other helps fail as he shall in most places find them to do, if he be really intent on the disquistion of truth, this will yield him his best relief. And so long as this is attended unto, we need no fear farther useful interpretation of the Scriptures or the several parts of it, than as yet have been attained unto by the endeavours of others; for the stores of truth laid up in it are inexhaustible, and hereby will they be opened unto those that inquire into them with humility and diligence. The labours of those who have gone before us are of excellent use herein; but they are yet very far from having discovered the **depths** of this vein of wisdom; not will the best of our endeavours prescribe limits and bounds to them that shall come after us. And the reason **generality of expositors** go in the same track one after another, seldom passing beyond the beaten path of former endeavours, unless it be in some excursion of curiosity, is the want of giving up themselves unto the conduct of the Holy Spirit in the diligent performance of this duty.

(Dr. John Owen, 1650).

---

*(Continued from page 192)*

"They who are pure in heart 'see God' in this way, even in the present world; and in the future state their knowledge of God will become far more extensive and their fellowship with Him far more intimate; for though, when compared with the privileges of a former dispensation, even now 'as with open face we behold the glory of the Lord,' yet, in reference to the privileges of a higher economy, we yet see but 'through a glass darkly'—we 'know but in part'—we understand but in part, we enjoy but in part. But 'that which is in part shall be done away,' and 'that which is perfect shall come.' We shall yet see face to face and know even as we are known (1 Cor. 13: 9-12); or to borrow the words of the Psalmist, we 'shall behold His face in righteousness, and shall be satisfied when we awake in His likeness' (Psa. 17:15). Then, and not till then, will the full meaning of these words be understood 'the pure in heart shall see God.'" (Dr. John Brown).

ARTHUR W. PINK.

*(Continued from page 169.)*

"A higher character, however, and a higher privilege, belonged to those who should be the subjects of the Messiah's reign. They should not only be externally holy, but, 'pure in heart'; and they should not merely be allowed to approach towards the holy place, where God's honour dwelt, but they should 'see God,' be introduced into the most intimate intercourse with Him. Thus viewed, as a description of the spiritual character and privileges of the subjects of the Messiah, in contrast with the external character and privileges of the Jewish people, the passage before us is full of the most important and interesting truth." (Dr. John Brown).

"Blessed are the pure in heart." Opinion is divided as to whether these words of Christ are to be understood literally or figuratively, whether the reference be to the new heart itself received at regeneration, or to the moral transformation of character which results from a Divine work of grace being wrought in the soul. Probably both aspects of the truth are combined here. In view of the late place which this Beatitude occupies in the series it would appear that the purity of heart upon which our Saviour pronounced His blessing, is that internal cleansing which accompanies and follows the new birth. Yet, inasmuch as no heart purity exists in the natural man, what is here affirmed by Christ must be traced back to regeneration itself.

The Psalmist said, "Behold Thou desirest truth in the inward parts; and in the hidden part Thou shalt make me to know wisdom" (Psa. 51: 6). How far this goes beneath the outward renovation and reformation which comprises such a large part of the efforts now being put forth in Christendom! Much that we see around us is a hand religion—seeking salvation by works—or a head religion, which rests satisfied with an orthodox creed. But God looketh on the heart—an expression which appears to include the understanding, the affections and the will. It is because God looketh within that He gives a "new heart" (Ezek. 36: 26) to His own people, and "blessed" indeed are they who have received such, for it is a "pure heart."

As intimated above, we believe this sixth Beatitude contemplates both the new heart received at regeneration and the transformation of character which follows God's work of grace in the soul. First, there is a "washing of regeneration" (Titus 3:5) by which we understand a cleansing of the affections, which are now set upon things above, instead of things below; this is parallel with "purifying their hearts by faith" (Acts 15: 9). Accompanying this is the cleansing of the conscience"—having our hearts sprinkled from an evil conscience" (Heb. 10: 22), which refers to the removal of the burden of conscious guilt, the inward realisation that being justified by faith we "have peace with God."

But the purity of heart commended here by Christ goes further than this. What is purity? Freedom from defilement, undivided affections, sincerity and genuineness. As a quality of Christian character, we would define it as godly simplicity. It is the opposite of subtlety and duplicity. Genuine Christianity lays aside not only malice, but guile and hypocrisy. It is not enough to be pure in words and in outward deportment; purity of desires, motives, intents, are what should, and do in the main, characterise the child of God. Here then is a most important test for every professing Christian to apply to himself: are my affections set upon things above? Are my motives pure; why do I assemble with the Lord's people—to be seen of men, or to meet with the Lord and enjoy sweet communion with Him?

"For they shall see God." Once more we would point out how that the promises attached to these Beatitudes have both a present and a future fulfilment. The pure in heart possess spiritual discernment and with the eyes of their understanding they obtain clear views of the Divine character and perceive the excellency of His attributes. When the eye is single the whole body is full of light. "In the truth, the faith of which purifies the heart, they 'see God'; for what is that truth but a manifestation of the glory of God in the face of Jesus Christ—an illustrious display of the combined radiance of Divine holiness and Divine benignity! . . . And he not only obtains clear and satisfactory views of the Divine character, but he enjoys intimate and delightful communion with God. He is brought very near God, God's mind becomes his mind; God's will becomes his will; and his fellowship is truly with the Father and with His Son Jesus Christ.

*(Continued on page 191)*

# STUDIES IN THE SCRIPTURES

"Search the Scriptures" John 5:39.

Copyright in all English-speaking Countries.

Editor: Arthur W. Pink, 22 Parramatta Road, Summer Hill, N.S.W., Australia.
Hon. Agent in U.S.A.: Mr. C. S. Pressel, 559 Dupont Ave., York, Penna.

Price: 10 cents per copy; $1.00 or 5/- per year.

"Blessed are the peacemakers: for they shall be called the children of God" (Matt. 5:9).

This is the hardest of all the Beatitudes to expound. The difficulty is to determine the precise significance and scope of the word "peacemakers." It is not, Blessed are the peace-lovers, or the peace-keepers, but blessed are the peacemakers. Now it is apparent on the surface that what we have here is something more excellent than that love of concord and harmony, that hatred of strife and turmoil, which is sometimes to be met with in the natural man; evident because the peacemakers which are here in view shall be called "the children of God." Three things must guide us in seeking the true interpretation: the character of those to whom our Lord was speaking, the place occupied by our text in the series of Beatitudes, its connection with the one that follows.

"The Jews, in general, regarded the Gentile nations with bitter contempt and hatred, and they expected that, under the Messiah, there should be an uninterrupted series of warlike attacks made on these nations, till they were completely destroyed or subjugated to the chosen people of God (an idea based, no doubt, on what they read in the book of Joshua concerning the experiences of their forefathers.—A.W.P.). In their estimation, those emphatically deserved the appellation of 'happy' who should be employed under Messiah the Prince to avenge on the heathen nations all the wrongs these had done to Israel. How different is the spirit of the new economy! How beautifully does it accord with the angelic anthem which celebrated the nativity of its Founder: glory to God in the highest, and on earth peace, good-will toward men'!" (Dr. John Brown).

This seventh Beatitude has to do more with conduct than character, though, of necessity, there must first be a peaceable spirit before there will be active efforts put forth to make peace. Let it be remembered that in this first section of the Sermon on the Mount, the Lord Jesus is defining the character of those who should be subjects and citizens in His Kingdom. First, He described them according to the initial experiences of those in whom a Divine work is wrought. The first four may be grouped together as setting forth the negative graces of their hearts. They are not self-sufficient, but consciously poor in spirit: they are not self-satisfied, but mourning because of their spiritual state: they are not self-important, but lowly or meek: they are not self-righteous, but hungering and thirsting for the righteousness of Another. In the next three, the Lord names their positive graces, having tasted of the mercy of God, they are merciful in their dealing with others; having received of the Spirit a spiritual nature, their eye is single to the glory of God; having entered into the peace which Christ made by the blood of His cross, they are now anxious to be used by Him in bringing others to the enjoyment of such peace.

That which helps us, perhaps as much as anything else, to fix the meaning of this seventh Beatitude, is the link which exists between it and the one that immediately follows. In our previous meditations we have called attention to the fact that the Beatitudes are obviously grouped together in pairs. Poverty

(Continued on page 216)

## IMPORTANT NOTICES

Set of twelve issues for 1922, unbound, $1.00 or 5/-. Bound $1.65 or 7/-.

1923, 1924, 1925 same as 1922.

Note: We cannot break a set or now supply any single 1925 issues.

Subscription—price: $1.00 or 5/- per year to any address in the world.

Change of Address: Please notify me promptly of any change of address, and be certain to give both old and new address.

Non-subscribers receiving this Magazine regularly will understand their subscription has been entered by a friend.

Copies lost in the mail duplicated only if we are notified promptly.

## CONTENTS

| | |
|---|---|
| The Gospel of John (John 17: 1-5) | 194 |
| Gleanings in Exodus | 202 |
| Truth and Error | 207 |
| Divine Chastisement | 212 |
| Unanswered Prayer | 214 |
| Good News | 215 |

## THE GOSPEL OF JOHN

### 57. Christ Interceding: John 17: 1-5.

The following is an Analysis of the first section of John 17:

1. The Son praying v. 1.
2. His desire for the Father's glory v. 1.
3. His own glory subsidiary v. 1.
4. The consequences of His glorification v. 2.
5. The way to and means of eternal life v. 3.
6. The Son rendering an account of His stewardship v. 4.
7. His reward v. 5.

The seventeenth of John contains the longest recorded prayer which our Lord offered during His public ministry on earth, and has been justly designated **His Highly Priestly Prayer.** It was offered in the presence of His apostles, after the institution and celebration of the Lord's Supper, and immediately following the Paschal discourse recorded in 14 to 16. It has been appropriately said, "The most remarkable prayer followed the most full and consoling discourse ever uttered on earth" (Matt. Henry). It differs from the prayer which Christ "taught His disciples," for in that there are petitions which the Saviour could not offer for Himself, while in this there are petitions which none else but Christ could present. In this wonderful prayer there are a solemnity and elevation of thought, a condensed power of expression, and a comprehensiveness of meaning, which have affected the minds and drawn out the hearts of the most devoted of God's children to a degree that few portions of Scripture have done.

In John 17 the veil is drawn aside, and we are admitted with our great High Priest into "the holiest of all." Here we approach the secret place of the tabernacle of the Most High, therefore it behoves us to put off our shoes from off our feet, listening with humble, reverent and prepared hearts, for the place whereon we now stand is indeed holy ground. We give below a few brief impressions of other writers.

"This is truly, beyond measure, a warm and hearty prayer. He opens the depths of His heart, both in reference to us and to His Father, and He pours them all out. It sounds so honest, so simple; it is so deep, so rich, so wide, no one can fathom it" (Martin Luther).

Melanchthon, another of the Reformers, when giving his last lecture before his death, said on John 17: "There is no voice which has ever been heard, either in heaven or in earth, more exalted, more holy, more fruitful, more sublime, than the prayer offered up by the Son to God Himself."

The eminent Scottish Reformer, John Knox, had this chapter read to him every day during his last illness, and in the closing scene, the verses that were read from it consoled and animated him in the final conflict.

"The seventeenth chapter of the Gospel by John, is, without doubt, the most remarkable portion of the most remarkable book in the world. The Scripture of truth, given by inspiration of God, contains many wonderful passages, but none more wonderful than this—none so wonderful. It is the utterance of the mind and heart of the God-man, in the very crisis of His great undertaking, in the immediate prospect of completing, by the sacrifice of Himself, the work which had been given Him to do, and for the accomplishment of which He had become incarnate. It is the utterance of these to the Father who had sent Him. What a concentration of thought and affection is there in these few sentences! How 'full of grace,' how 'full of truth.' How condensed, and yet how clear the thoughts,—how deep, yet how calm, the feelings which are here, so far as the capabilities of human language permit, worthily expressed! All is natural and simple in thought and expression—nothing intricate or elaborate, but there is a width in the conceptions which the human understanding cannot measure—a depth which it cannot fathom. There is no bringing out of these plain words all that is seen and felt to be in them" (Dr. J. Brown).

"The chapter we have now begun is the most remarkable in the Bible. It stands alone, and there is nothing like it" (Bishop Ryle).

Even Mr. W. Kelly with his caution and conservatism writes, "Next follows a chapter which one may perhaps characterise truly as unequalled for depth and scope in all the Scriptures."

This prayer of our Lord is wonderful as a specimen of the communications which constantly passed between the Son and His Father while He was here on earth. Vocal prayer seems to have been habitual with our Saviour. While being baptized He was engaged in prayer (Luke 3:21). Immediately on the commencement of His public minstry we find that, after a short repose, following a day of unremitting labour, "He rose up a great while before day, and went out, and departed into a solitary place, and there prayed" (Mark 1:35). On the eve of selecting the twelve apostles He "went out into a mountain to pray, and continued all night in prayer to God" (Luke 6:12). It was while engaged in the act of prayer that He was transfigured (Luke 9:29). And it was while praying that He ceased to breathe (Luke 23:46). Only the briefest mention is made as to the substance of these prayers —in most instances none at all. But here in John 17, the Holy Spirit has been pleased to record at length His prayer in the upper room. How thankful we should be for this!

Perhaps the most interesting way to view this prayer is as a **model** of His High Priestly intercession for us, which He continually makes in the immediate presence of God, on the ground of His completed and accepted sacrifice. The first intimation of this is found in the fact that the Lord Jesus here prayed audibly in the presence of His disciples. He prayed that their interests might be secured, but He prayed audibly that they should be aware of this, that they might know what a wondrous place they had in His affections, that they might be assured that all His influence with the Father would be employed for their advantage. More plainly still is this intimated in v. 13: "And now come I to Thee and these things I speak in the world, that they might have My joy fulfilled in themselves"—q.d. 'These are intercessions which in heaven I will never cease to make before God; but I make them now in the world, in your hearing, that you may more distinctly understand how I am there to be employed in promoting your welfare, so that you may be made, in large measure, partakers of **My** happiness.' "The petitions for Himself are much briefer than those which He presents for His people —the former being only two, or, rather, but one, variously expressed; while the latter are quite a number, earnestly urged, with a variety of pleas. This arrangement and division of the matter of the prayer justifies the view which has not unfrequently been taken of it: that it was throughout **intercessory** and the substance and model of that intercession which He constantly makes in heaven as our great High Priest" (Dr. T. Houston).

It is in His **mediatorial** character that the Saviour here prays: as the eternal Son, now in the form of a Servant. The office of a mediator or day's-man is "to lay his hand upon both" (Job 9:33); to treat with each party. In the previous chapters we have beheld Christ dealing with believers in the name of the Father, opening His counsels to them; now we find Him dealing with the Father on behalf of believers, presenting their cause to Him, just as Moses, the typical mediator, spoke to God (Exodus 19:19) and from God (Exodus 20:19), do did our blessed Saviour speak from God and to God. And He is still performing the same office and work: speaking to us in the Word, speaking for us in His intercession on High.

The prayer that we are now about to meditate upon is a standing monument of Christ's affection for the Church. In it we are permitted to hear the desires of His heart as He spreads them before the Father, seeking the temporal, spiritual and eternal welfare of those who are His own. This prayer did not pass away as soon as its words were uttered, or when Christ ascended to heaven, but retains a perpetual efficacy. "Just as the words of creation hath retained their vigor these six thousand years: 'Increase and multiply: Let the earth bring forth after its kind.' So this prayer of Christ's retains its force, as if but newly spoken" (Dr. T. Manton). Let us remember our Lord's words, "Father, I thank Thee that Thou hast heard Me. And I knew that Thou hearest Me always" (John 11:41, 24) as we ponder this prayer together.

"These words spake Jesus, and lifted up His eyes to heaven" (v. 1). The first four words look backwards and their meaning is fixed by the opening clause in 16:33. They refer to the whole consolatary discourse recorded in the three preceding chapters. Having completed His address to the disciples, He now lifted up His eyes and heart to the Father. The connection is emphasised by the Spirit: "These words spake Jesus, and lifted up His eyes to heaven, and said." What an example for all of His servants! He had said everything to the apostles which a wise kindness could dictate in order to sustain them in the the supremely trying circumstances in which they were about to be placed, and as the hour was at hand when they were to be separated from Him. He employs the few moments now remaining in commending them to the care of the Father—His Father and their Father. From preaching He passed to prayer! Thereby He teaches us that after we have done all we can to promote the holiness and comfort of those with whom we are connected, we should in prayer and supplication beseech Him, who is the author of all good, to bless the objects of our care and the means which we have employed for their welfare. "Doctrine has no power, unless efficacy is imparted to it from above. Christ holds out an example to teach us, not to employ themselves only in sowing the Word, but by mingling prayers with it, to implore the assistance of God, that His blessing may render their labours fruitful" (John Calvin).

"And lifted up His eyes to heaven." While delivering the discourse recorded in the previous chapters His eyes, no doubt, had been fixed with tender solicitude upon His disciples. But now as a token that He was about to engage in prayer, He lifts up His eyes toward heaven. "This shows that bodily gestures in prayer and worship of God are not altogether to be overlooked as unmeaning" (Bishop Ryle). The gesture naturally expresses withdrawl of the thoughts and the affections from earthly things, deep veneration, and holy confidence. It denoted the elevation of His heart to God. Said David, "Unto Thee O Lord, do I lift up my soul" (Psa. 25:1). In true prayer the affections go out to God. Our Lord's action also teaches us the spiritual reverence which is due God: the heaven of heavens is His dwelling-place, and the turning of the eyes toward His Throne expresses a recognition of God's majesty and excellence. "Unto Thee lift I up mine eyes, O Thou that dwellest in the heavens" (Psa. 123:1). Again, such a posture signifies confidence in God. There can be no real prayer until there is a turning away from all creature dependencies: "I will lift up mine eyes unto the hills. From whence cometh my help? My help cometh from the Lord, which made heaven and earth" (Psa. 121:1-2). The believer looks around, and finds no ground for help; his relief must must come from God above.

"And said, Father." The Mediator here addresses God as Father. He was His "Father" in a threehold sense. First, by virtue of His human nature, miraculously produced. His body was "prepared" for Him by God (Heb. 10:5). Just as in the human realm the begetter of the child is its father, so the One who made the body of Christ, became the Father of His human nature: "And the angel answered and said unto her (Mary), The Holy Spirit shall come upon thee, and the power of the Highest shall overshadow thee: therefore also that Holy Thing which shall be born of thee shall be called the Son of God." (Luke 1:35). The man Christ Jesus is thus in a peculiar sense, the Son of God. In like manner, Adam, who was created by God in His own image and likeness, is called "the son of God" Luke 3:38). Second, God stands in the relation of "Father" to our Lord as the Head and Representative of the holy family redeemed from among men. He is thus "The First born among many brethren" (Rom. 8:29). To this the apostle seems to refer when he applies to the Lord Jesus that Old Testament word "I will be to Him a Father, and he shall be to Me a Son" (Heb. 1:5). Third, the appellation "Father" given to the first person of the Trinity by our Saviour, primarily, and usually refers to that essential relation which subsisted between the first and second persons of the Godhead from all eternity. Identity of nature is the chief idea suggested by the term. In Rom. 8:32, Christ is spoken of as God's "own Son," intimating that He is a Son in a sense absolutely peculiar to Himself.

"And said, Father." Two things were expressed. First, relationship: the relationship of sonship. This was His claim to be heard. It was as though He had said 'O Thou with whom I have existed in unity of essence, perfection, and enjoyment from the unbegun eternity, and by whose will and operation I have been clothed miraculously with human nature and constituted the Head of all appointed unto salvation—I now come to Thy throne of grace.' Second, it indicated affection. It expressed love, veneration, confidence, submission. In whom should a son trust if not in his father? It was as though He had said, 'I trust Thy power, Thy wisdom, Thy benignity, Thy faithfulness. Into Thy hands I commend Myself. I know that Thou wilt hear My prayer for Thou art My Father!' Previously Christ had commanded prayer: here, by His own blessed example He commends to us this holy exercise.

"The hour is come." This is the seventh and last time that the Lord Jesus refers to this most momentous "hour"—see our remarks on 2:4. This was the greatest "hour" of all—because most critical and pregnant with eternal issues—since hours began to be numbered. It was the hour when the Son of God was to terminate the labours of His important life by a death still more important and illustrious. It was the hour when the Lord of glory was to be made sin for His people, and bear the holy wrath of a sin-hating God. It was the hour for fulfilling and accomplishing many prophecies, types and symbols which for hundreds and thousands of years had pointed forward to it. It was the hour when events took place which the history of the entire universe can supply no parallel: when the Serpent was permitted to bruise the heel of the woman's Seed; when the sword of Divine justice smote Jehovah's Fellow; when the sun refused to shine; when the earth rocked on its axis; but when the elect company were redeemed, when Heaven was gladdened, and which brought, and shall bring to all eternity, "glory to God in the highest"

But why did the Saviour 'begin His prayer by referring to this "hour?" As a plea to support the petitions that He was about to present. "In our Lord's prayer for Himself there is pleading as well as petition, Prayer is the expression of desire for benefit by one who needs it, to one who, in his estimation, is able and disposed to confer it. Request or petition is therefore its leading element; but in the expression of desire by one intelligent being to another, it is natural that the reasons why the desire is cherished, and the request presented, should be stated, and the grounds unfolded, on which the hope is founded, that the desire should be granted. Petitions and pleading are thus connected in prayer from man to man; and they are so, likewise, in prayer from men to God. Whoever reads carefully the prayers uttered by holy men, influenced and guided by the Spirit of God, recorded in Scripture, will be struck with the union of petition and pleading, by which they are distinguished. When they are brought 'near to God'—when they, as Job says, 'find Him and come even to His seat,' how do 'they order their cause before Him, and fill their mouths with arguments' (Job 23:3-4). They 'plead' with Him, as Jeremiah expresses it" (12:1). (Dr. J. Brown).

Christ's first plea was the intimate and endearing relation in which He stood to the object of worship: "Father . . . glorify Thy Son." There is a powerful plea in each of these words. His second plea was "the hour is come"— the time appointed for granting this petition had arrived. Like so many of His words in these closing chapters, "the hour" here seems to have a double significance: referring not only to His sufferings, but also looking forward to the resurrection-side of the cross—compare our remarks on 13:31. "This is the appointed period for the remarkable glorification of the Son by the Father in His sufferings, by His sufferings, for His sufferings—under them, after them, 'The time, yea, the set time, is come,' and if the time be come shall not the event take place? It is a matter of Divine purpose, and when was a Divine purpose falsified! It is a matter of Divine promise, and when was a Diven promise falsified!" (Dr. J. Brown).

"Glorify Thy Son, that Thy Son also may glorify Thee" (v. 1). This is so closely connected with what follows in the next two verses that it is difficult to treat of it separately. In vv. 2 and 3 Christ describes the particular mode of glorifying the Father on which His heart was set, and the aspect of the glorification of Himself which He here prays for, namely to have power over all flesh and to give eternal life to as many as the Father had given Him. There was a double object of desire, a double subject of prayer; the glorification of the Father in the bestowal of eternal life upon the elect, and the glorification of the Son as subsidiary to this as the necessary and effectual means of accomplishing it. Thus we see the perfect dis-

**interestedness** of Christ. He prayed to be "glorified" not for His **own** sake, but that **the Father** might be glorified in **our** salvation! Here again we see Him loving us "unto the end!"

"Glorify Thy Son." This was the Saviour requesting the Father to support Him on the cross, afterwards to bring Him out of the grave and set Him at His own right hand, so as to bring to a triumphant completion the work given Him to do; and this in order that the glorious attributes of the Father—His justice, holiness, mercy and faithfulness —might be exhibited and magnified, for God is most "glorified" when the excellencies of His character are manifested to and acknowledged by His creatures. The glorification of the Son, in accord with the double meaning of the "hour" here, would mean, glorify Me **in My** sufferings, and glorify Me **after** My sufferings. In both of these respects was His prayer answered. The angel sent to strengthen Him in the Garden, the testimony of Pilate —"I find no fault in Him," the drawing of the dying thief to the Saviour while He hung upon the cross, the rending of the temple veil, the confession of the Centurion: "Truly, this was the Son of God," were all so many responses of the Father to this petition. His resurrection and exaltation to the highest seat in Heaven, was His glorification following His sufferings.

There is much for us to learn here. First mark the connection: "the hour is come, glorify Thy Son." "The true remedy of tribulation is to look to the succeeding glory, and to counterbalance future dangers with present hopes. **This** was comfort against **that** sad hour. So it must be our course: not to look at things which are seen, but to things which are not seen (2 Cor. 4:17); to defeat sense by faith. When the mind is in heaven it is fortified against the pains which the body feeleth on earth" (Dr. Manton—Puritan). Second, observe **what** Christ sought: to be "glorified" by the Father—not to be enriched by men, not to be honoured by the world. This should be our desire too. Christ rebuked those who received honour one from another instead of **seeking** the honor that cometh from God (John 5:44), and because they loved the **praise** of men, more than the **praise of God** (12:43). We should not only seek for grace, but glory. Third, note that Christ asked for **what** He knew would be given Him. The Father had said "I have both glorified, and will glorify again" (12:28). Neither promises nor providence render prayer meaningless or useless. Fourth,

Christ prayed for this glory in order that He might glorify **the Father.** Here too, He has left us an example. Whatsoever we do is to be done to the glory of God, and nothing should be asked from Him save for **His** glory.

"As Thou hast given Him power over all flesh, that He should give eternal life to as many as Thou hast given Him" (v. 2). "The Father is first of all to be glorified in the humanity of the Godman, who presents Himself to that end: then, through Him in His disciples, so that in this first word concerning the mutual glorification, that is already involved and included which follows in v. 10. In v. 2 we have a more specific development and explanation of the sense in which this glorification of the Father to and in fallen humanity is meant" (Stier). We regard the connecting "as" or "according as" as having a double force, supplying a **reason** for and describing **the manner of** the Father's glorification. Let us examine the verse in this order of thought.

Verse 2 contains the third plea which the Saviour presented to the Father: to glorify the Son was in accord with the place which the Father had destined Him to fill, and the work which He had appointed Him to perform: the glorification of the Son was neccessary to Him filling that place and executing that work. The place which God had destined Him to occupy was that of rightful authority over the whole human race, with complete control of all events in connection with them (see John 5:22: Eph. 1:19-21, etc.). The work appointed Him was to give eternal life to all the elect. But in order to the **accomplishment** of this purpose the Son must be glorified in and by and for His sufferings. He must be glorified by expiating sin upon the cross, by being raised from the dead, and by being set at God's right hand so as to be put into actual possession of this authority and power. How cogent then was His plea! Unless the Father glorified Him, He could not accomplish the ends of His mediatorial office.

The Father, in His eternal counsels, had appointed the Son to save a portion of the human race: to conduct to glory many sons, who, like their brethren in the flesh, were going to destruction These had been given Christ to save. By nature they were "dead in trespasses and sins": guilty, depraved, destitute of spiritual life, incapable of thinking, feeling, choosing, acting, or enjoying communion with the all-holy, ever-blessed One. If ever they were to be saved they must have eternal life bestowed upon them by the Saviour, and for Him to impart this inestimable boon, He must be exalted to the place of supreme dominion. This, then, was the Saviour's "argument" or plea here: the Father's glory being the end in view.

Verse 2 also describes the manner of the Father's glorification in and by the Son: let Thy Son glorify Thee by saving souls "according as" Thou hast appointed Him so to do. "As Thou hast given" obviously means promised to give—see such scriptures as Psa. 89:27; Dan. 7:14, etc. The fact that this "power" or authority over all flesh is given to Christ, at once shows the character in which He here appears, namely, as Mediator. That Christ receives this "gift" shows us that free grace is no dishonourable tenure. Why should haughty sinners disdain Divine charity, when the God-man was willing to accept a gift from the Father! "Power over all flesh" means, first, dominion over the whole human race. But it also means, most probably, authority over all creatures, for Christ "is gone into heaven, and is on the right hand of God; angels and authorities and powers being made subject unto Him" (1 Peter 3:22). "All power in heaven and earth" has been given to Him (Matt. 28:18). Not only is He the "Head of every man" (1 Cor. 11:3), but the "Head of all principality and power" (Col. 2:10). In the Millennium His universal dominion will be publicly manifested.

"As Thou hast given Him power over all flesh, that He should give eternal life to as many as Thou hast given Him." We must distinguish between Christ's universal authority and His narrower charge. Authority has been given Him over all; but out of this "all" is an elect company, committed to Him as a charge. This was typified by Joseph of old; authority over all Egypt was conveyed to him by the king, but his brethren had a special claim upon his affections. "The keys of heaven are in the hands of Christ; the salvation of every human soul is at His disposal" (Bishop Ryle). How blessed to rest upon this double truth—the universal dominion of Christ, His affection for His own. All has been put into the hands of our Saviour, therefore the Devil himself cannot move except so far as Christ allows. This universal dominion has been bestowed upon Christ "that," in order that, He may give eternal life to God's elect. The elect were given to Christ by way of reward (Isa. 53:10-12), and by way of charge (John 6:37; 18:9).

"And this is life eternal that they might know Thee the only true God, and Jesus Christ, whom Thou hast sent" (v. 3). There has been considerable difference of opinion as to what is meant by "This is eternal life." We shall not canvass the various interpretations that have been given, rather shall we seek to indicate what we believe was our Lord's meaning here. "This is life eternal," more literally, "this is the eternal life—that", etc. A parallel form of speech is found in 3:19: "And this is the condemnation—that," etc. In the words that follow in . 3:19 the ground and way of condemnation are stated—"light is come into the world, and men love darkness rather than light, because their deeds were evil." This helps us to arrive at the first meaning here: "This is the eternal life—that they might know Thee," etc.—this is the way to it. Again, in 12:50 we read, "His commandment is—life everlasting" that is, the outward means of it. Once more, in 1 John 5:20, we read, "This is the true God and eternal life"—Christ is the Author of it. Taken by themselves the words of this verse might be understood as speaking of the characteristics and manifestations of "eternal life," but the context would forbid this. Christ is here amplifying the plea of the previous verse. Thus: unless I am glorified, I cannot bestow eternal life; without My ascension the Holy Spirit will not come, and without Him there can be no knowledge of the Father and His Son, and so by consequence, no eternal life, for "knowing God" and "eternal life" are inseparable. Therefore "this is eternal life—that they might know Thee" etc., obviously signifies. This is the way to, the means of eternal life, namely, by the knowledge of God imparted by Jesus Christ.

"This is the eternal life, that they know Thee" (literal rendering). The knowledge spoken of here is not speculative but practical, not theoretical but experimental, not intellectual but spiritual, not inactive but saving. That it is a saving knowledge, which is here in view is clear from the double object—God and Christ. He that knoweth God in Christ knoweth Him as His reconciled Father, and so resteth on and in Him. "And they that know Thy name will put their trust in Thee" (Psa. 9:10). The knowledge here spoken of presupposes a walk in harmony with it, produced by it: "Hereby we do know that we know Him, if we keep His commandments" (1 John 2:3). How this strengthened the plea of the Saviour here scarcely needs pointing out. What would bring more "glory" to the Father than that He should be known (trusted, loved, served) by those to whom the Son gave eternal life!

"Know Thee, the **only** true God." Appeal is made to this by Unitarians in their horrible efforts to disprove the Godhead of the second and third persons of the Trinity. That Christ cannot be here denying the Deity of Himself and of the Spirit we well know from many other passages, but what did He mean by affirming that the Father is "the only true God"? We believe the answer is twofold:—

First, Christ was here excluding the idols of the Gentiles—false gods, cf., 1 Thess. 1:9:—to denote that that Godhead is only true that is in the Father. The Son and the Spirit are not excluded because they are of the same essence with the Father. The Son and the Spirit are "true God," not without, but in the Father. "I and the Father are one" (10:30); "the Father is in Me, and I in Him" (10:38): not divided in essence, but distinguished in personality. In I John 5:20 the Son Himself is called "the only true God!" Which no more excludes the Father than 17:3 excludes the Son. Many such exclusive statements are to be found in Scripture, that must be expounded by the analogy of faith. For example: "No one knoweth the Father, but the Son, and none knoweth the Son, but the Father" (Matt. 11:27); but this excludes not the Spirit, for He "searcheth the depths of God" (1 Cor. 2:10). One person of the Trinity does not exclude the others. When Scripture insists there is no God, but one, it simply denies that all others who are **"called gods" are** such.

Second, Christ was here speaking in view of the **order** and **economy** of salvation, for He had just mentioned the giving of "eternal life." In the economy of salvation the Father is ever represented as **Supreme,** the One in whom the sovereign majesty of Deity resideth. The Son sustains the office of **Mediator,** and in this character He could rightly say, "My Father is greater than I" (14:.8). In like manner, during the present dispensation, the Holy Spirit is the **Servant** of the Godhead (see Luke 14:17-23 and cf. John 16:13 and our remarks thereon). In the order of redemption the Father is the principal party representing the whole Godhead, because He is the Originator and Fountain of it.

"And Jesus Christ whom Thou hast sent." The connecting **"and"** gives plain warning that the Father, "the only true God" cannot be "known" **apart from** "Jesus Christ"! Just as the "only true God" is opposed to the vanities of the Gentiles, so is "Jesus Christ whom Thou hast sent" to the blindness of the Jews! "Sent" has a threefold intimation and signification. It points to His Deity: "We believe that Thou **camest forth from God"** (16:30). It refers to His incarnation: "When the fullness of time was come, God sent forth His Son made of a woman" (Gal. 4:4). It also signified His office of Mediator and Redeemer. For this reason He is called "The Apostle and High Priest of our profession" (Heb. 3:1), and "apostle" means the **sent** one. Jesus Christ is the great Ambassador to treat with us from God.

It is worthy of note that this is the **only** place in the New Testament where our Lord called Himself "Jesus Christ." In so doing He affirmed that He, **Jesus,** the Son of man, and Son of God was the only true **Christ** (Messiah): thereby He repudiated every false notion of the Messiah, as in the previous clause He had excluded every false god. It is very striking to observe how that in 1 John 5:1 we are told, "Whosoever believeth that **Jesus is the Christ** is born of God" while in 5:5 we read, "Who is He that overcometh the world; but he that believ- that **Jesus is the Son of God** ?" Do you, dear reader, **know** the Father and the Son—the Father as revealed in and by Jesus Christ! If you do not, you have not eternal life.

"I have glorified Thee on the earth:" (v. 4). Here is the next plea of the Saviour: I have glorified Thee, do Thou now glorify Me. God had been glorified in creation (Psa. 14:1) and by His providences (Ex. 15:6-7, etc.); but to a superlative degree, in an altogether unique way, He had been glorified by the Son. Christ has glorified the Father in His person (Heb. 1:3). He glorified Him by His miracles (Matt. 9:8, etc.). He glorified Him by His words, constantly ascribing all praise to Him (Matt. 11:25, etc.). But above all He had glorified Him by his holy life. The Saviour was sent into the world as the Representative of His people, to render obedience to that law which they had violated (Gal. 4:4); and perfectly had He in thought and word and deed discharged this duty. In Him—full of grace and truth—the disciples had beheld a moral glory possessed by none save Him who abode in the bosom of the Father. "I have glorified Thee **on the earth"**—in in the place where He had been so grievously dishonored.

In view of having glorified the Father on earth, the Son said "glorify Thou Me." "The more we examine the Gospel of John, the more we shall see One who speaks and acts as a Divine Person— one with the Father—alone could do, but yet always as One who has taken the place of a servant, and takes nothing to Himself but receives all from His Father. 'I have glorified Thee': 'now glorify Me.' What language of equality of nature and love! But He does not say. And now I will glorify Myself. He has taken the place of man to receive all, though it be a glory He had with the Father before the world was. This is of exquisite beauty. I add, it was out of this the enemy sought to seduce Him, in vain, in the wilderness" (Mr. Darby).

"I have finished the work which Thou gavest Me to do" (v. 4). Here is the final plea of the Saviour for His glorification. When He entered this world, He affirmed, "Lo, I come to do Thy will, O God" (Heb. 10:7). At the age of twelve, He said, "Wist ye not that I must be about My Father's business?" (Luke 2:49). In John 4:34 He declared, "My meat is to do the will of Him that sent Me, and to finish His work." Now He says "I have finished the work which Thou gavest Me to do." He anticipated by a few hours His cry from the cross, "It is finished" (19:30). The Saviour referred to His work on earth as though He had been already exalted to heaven. How evident it is all through His prayer that His heavenly mediation is in view—"Now I am no more in the world" (v. 11)!

"I have finished the work which Thou gavest Me to do." As the eternal Son He had, in the character of the faithful Servant, done what none other could do. He had performed the Father's will: He had delivered His message: He had not only taught but perfectly exemplified the truth. He had "finished transgression and brought in everlasting righteousness" (Dan. 9:24). He had put away sin by the sacrifice of Himself. He had "restored that which He took not away" (Psa. 69:4). Thus had He glorified the Father upon earth and finished the work given Him to do. There was every reason then why He should be "glorified." Every moral attribute of Deity required it. Having endured the cross, He was fully entitled to enter "the joy set before Him." Having poured out His soul unto death, it was but meet that the Father should "divide Him a portion with the great" (Isa. 53:12). Having glorified Him on earth, it was fittingly that the Saviour should be glorified in heaven.

"And now, O Father, glorify Thou Me with Thine own self, with the glory which I had with Thee before the world was" (v. 5). Having presented the various pleas suited to His glorification, the Son now returns to His petition. The verse before us conducts us to a height which we have no means of scaling. All that we can do is to humbly ponder its words in the light of the context and parallel scriptures. When the Saviour says, "glorify Thou Me" He speaks as the Mediator, as "Jesus Christ" (v. 3). As Jesus Christ He had been humiliated now, as Jesus Christ, He was to be glorified. The Father's answer to this is seen in Acts 2: "This Jesus hath God raised up . . . let all the house of Israel know assuredly,' that God hath made that same Jesus, whom ye have crucified, both Lord and Christ" (vv. 32, 36)—compare also Phil. 2:9-11. But the glorification here must not be confined to His humanity, as the remainder of the verse shows. As the eternal Son He has humbled Himself (Phil. 2:6) and as the Son He has been exalted and magnified—see Psa. 21:1-6; 110:1; Eph. 1:17-23; Rev. 5; 22:1.

That Christ asked to be "glorified," demonstrated His perfections: not even as risen did He glorify Himself. In addition to the fact that His glorification had been promised and earned by Him, three reasons may be given why He asked for it. First, for the comfort of His apostles who were troubled over His humiliation. Second, for our instruction: to teach us that suffering for God is the highway to glory. Third, for the benefit of His Church: Christ must be glorified before it could prosper. The example of the Saviour here teaches that we should pray that the Father may be pleased to honour us by fitting and using us to lead men to a knowledge of the only true God through Jesus Christ, and to enable us, in our creature measure, to glorify Him on earth and to finish the work which He has given us to do.

The following questions are to help the student on the next section:—

1. How many pleas does Christ here present on behalf of His own vv. 6-12?
2. Of whom is Christ speaking in v. 6?
3. In what senses were the elect "given" to Christ v. 6?
4. What important truth is pointed in the "and's" of v. 8?
5. How harmonise v. 9 with Luke 23:34?
6. Why "Holy" Father v. 11?
7. What is the unity of v. 12?

ARTHUR W. PINK.

# GLEANINGS IN EXODUS.
## 33. The Tabernacle: Exodus 25-40.

We have now arrived at the longest, most blessed, but least read and understood section of this precious book of Exodus. From the beginning of chapter 25 to the end of 40—excepting the important parenthesis in 32 to 34—the Holy Spirit has given us a detailed description of the Tabernacle, its structure, furniture, and priesthood. It is a fact worthy of our closest and fullest consideration that more space is devoted to an account of the Tabernacle than to any other single object or subject treated of in Holy Writ. Its courts, its furniture, and its ritual are described with a surprising particularity of detail. Two chapters suffice for a record of God's work in creating and fitting this earth for human habitation, whereas ten chapters are needed to tell us about the Tabernacle. Truly God's thoughts and ways are different from ours!

How sadly many of God's own people have dishonoured Him and His Word by their studied neglect of these chapters! Too many have seen in the Tabernacle, with its Divinely-appointed arrangements and services, only a ritual of the past—a record of Jewish manners and customs which have long since passed away and which have no meaning for or value to us. But **"all Scripture is given by inspiration of God and is profitable"** (2 Tim. 3:16). The Christian cannot neglect any portion of the Word without suffering loss: "whatsoever things were written aforetime (in the Old Testament) were written for our learning" (Rom. 15:4). Again and again in the New Testament the Holy Spirit makes figurative reference to the Tabernacle and its furniture, and much in the Epistle to the Hebrews cannot be understood without reference to the contents of Exodus and Leviticus.

"The tabernacle is one of the most important and instructive types. Here is such a variety of truths, here is such a fulness and manifoldness of spiritual teaching, that our great difficulty is to combine all the various lessons and aspects which it presents. The tabernacle has no fewer than three meanings. In the first place, the tabernacle is a type, a visible illustration, of that heavenly place in which God has His dwelling. In the second place, the tabernacle is a type of Jesus Christ, who is the meeting-place between God and man. And, in the third place, the tabernacle is a type of Christ in the Church—of the communion of Jesus with all believers" (Adolph Saphir).

The first of these meanings is clearly stated in Hebrews 9:23-24: "It was, therefore necessary that the **patterns of things in the heavens** should be purified with these (i.e. sprinklings of blood see Heb. 9:21-22); but the heavenly things themselves with better sacrifices than these. For Christ is not entered into the holy places made with hands, which are **the figures of the true;** but into Heaven itself, now to appear in the presence of God for us." "The tabernacle was a symbol of God's dwelling. There is a Sanctuary, wherein is the especial residence and manifestation of the glorious presence of God. Solomon, although he confesses that the heaven of heavens cannot contain God, yet prays that the Lord may hear in heaven His dwelling-place (2 Chron. 6). Jeremiah testifies, 'A glorious high throne from the beginning is the place of our sanctuary' (17:12). The visions of Ezekiel also bring before us the heavens opened and the likeness of a throne, and the appearance of the likeness of the glory of the Lord; the likeness as the appearance of a man above upon the throne (1:26). Of this heavenly locality David speaks, when he asks, 'Who shall abide in Thy tabernacle? Who shall dwell in Thy holy hill?' (Psa. 24:3). In the book of Revelation we receive still further confirmation of this truth: 'And after that I looked, and, behold, the temple of the tabernacle of testimony in Heaven was opened' (15:5) .... Almost all expressions which are employed in describing the significance of the tabernacle are also used in reference to Heaven" (A. Saphir).

Secondly, the Tabernacle is a type of the Lord Jesus Himself, particularly of Him here on earth during the days of His flesh. Just as the Tabernacle was Jehovah's dwelling-place in the midst of Israel so are we told that "God was in Christ reconciling a world unto Himself" (2 Cor. 5:19); and again, "In Him dwelleth all the fulness of the Godhead bodily" (Col. 2:9). Beautifully was this application of our type manifested at the Incarnation. The Tabernacle was not something which originated in the minds of Israel, or even of Moses, but was designed by God Himself. So the Manhood of Christ, which enshrined His Deity, was not begotten by man—"A body hast Thou prepared Me" (Heb. 10:5). He said. This second aspect of the type will be developed more fully below

But the tabernacle has yet a third aspect. "There God and His people met. The ark of the covenant was not merely the throne where God manifested Himself in His holiness, but it was also the throne of relationship with His people. In all the offerings and sacrifices God was manifested; just as regards sin, merciful as regards the sinner; there also God and the sinner met. So throughout the tabernacle there was the manifestation of God in order to bring Israel into communion with Himself. In the Tabernacle man's fellowship with God was symbolised through manifold mediations, sacrifices, offerings. But in Jesus we have the perfect and eternal fulfilment" (A. Saphir). This third aspect of our type is more than hinted at in Rev. 21: 3: "Behold, the **tabernacle** of God is with men, and He will **dwell** with them, and thy shall be His people, and God Himself shall be with them, and be their God."

The key to the Tabernacle, then, is **Christ.** In the volume of the Book it is written of Him. As a whole and in each of its parts the Tabernacle foreshadowed the person and work of the Lord Jesus. Each detail in it typified some aspect of His ministry or some excellency in His person. Proof of this is furnished in John 1:14: "And the Word became flesh and **tabernacled** among us." (R. V. margin). The reference here is to the Divine incarnation and first advent of God's Son to this earth, and its language takes us back to the book of Exodus. Many and varied are the correspondences between the type and the antitype. We take leave to quote from our comments on John 1:14.

1. The Tabernacle was **a temporary** appointment. In this it differed from the temple of Solomon, which was a permanent structure. The Tabernacle was simply a tent, a temporary convenience, something that was suited to be moved about from place to place during the journeyings of the children of Israel. So it was when our blessed Lord tabernacled here among men. His stay was but a brief one—less than forty years; and, like the type, He abode not long in any one place, but was constantly on the move, unwearied in the activity of His love.

2. The Tabernacle was **for use in the wilderness.** After Israel settled in Canaan, the Tabernacle was superceded by the temple. But during the time of the pilgrimage from Egypt to the promised land, the Tabernacle was God's appointed provision for them. The **wilderness** strikingly foreshadowed the conditions amid which the eternal Word tabernacled among men at His first advent. The wilderness-home of the Tabernacle unmistakeably foreshadowed the manger-cradle, the Nazareth-carpenter's bench, the "nowhere for the Son of man to lay His head," the borrowed tomb for His sepulchre. A careful study of the chronology of the Pentateuch seems to indicate that Israel used the Tabernacle in the wilderness rather less than thirty-five years!

3. The Tabernacle was **mean, humble, and unattractive in outward appearance.** Altogether unlike the costly and magnificent temple of Solomon there was nothing in the externals of the Tabernacle to please the carnal eye. Nothing but plain boards and skins. So it was at the Incarnation. The Divine majesty of our Lord was hidden beneath a veil of flesh. He came, unattended by any imposing retinues of angels. To the unbelieving gaze of Israel He had no form or comeliness; and when they beheld Him their unanointed eyes saw in Him no beauty that they should desire Him.

4. The Tabernacle was **God's dwelling place.** It was there, in the midst of Israel's camp, that He took up His abode. There, between the Cherubim, upon the mercy-seat He made His throne. In the holy of holies He manifested His presence by means of the Shekinah glory. And during the thirty-three years that the Word tabernacled among men, God had His dwelling-place in Palestine. The holy of holies received its anti-typical fulfilment in the person of the Holy One of God. Just as the Shekinah dwelt between the two Cherubim, so on the mount of transfiguration the glory of the God-man flashed forth from between two men—Moses and Elijah. "We beheld his glory "is the language of the tabernacle-type.

5. The Tabernacle was, therefore, the **place where God met with man.** It was termed "the Tent of Meeting." If an Israelite desired to draw near unto Jehovah he had to come to the door of the Tabernacle. When giving instruction to Moses concerning the making of the Tabernacle and its furnishings, God said, "And thou shalt put the mercy-seat above upon the ark, and in the ark thou shalt

put the testimony that I shall give thee. And there I will meet with thee, and I will commune with thee" (Exodus 25: 21-22). How perfect is this lovely type! Christ is the **meeting-place** between God and man. No man cometh unto the Father but by Him (John 14: 6). There is but one Mediator between God and men—the Man Christ Jesus (1 Tim. 2: 5). He is the One who spans the gulf between Deity and humanity, because Himself both God and Man.

6. The Tabernacle was **the centre of Israel's camp.** In the immediate vicinity of the Tabernacle dwelt the Levites the priestly tribe: "But thou shalt appoint the Levites over the tabernacle of testimony, and over all the vessels thereof; and over all things that belong to it; they shall bear the tabernacle and all the vessels thereof; and they shall minister unto it, and shall **encamp round about** the tabernacle" (Num. 1: 50); and around the Levites were grouped the twelve tribes, three on either side—see Num. 2. Again; we read that when Israel's camp was to be moved from one place to another, "then the tabernacle of the congregation shall set forward with the camp of the Levites **in the midst** of the camp" (Num. 2: 17). Once more, "And Moses went out, and told the people the words of the Lord and gathered the seventy men of the elders of the people, and set them **round about** the tabernacle. And the Lord came down in a cloud and spake unto him" (Num. 11: 24-25). How striking is this! The Tabernacle was the great gathering-centre. As such it was a beautiful foreshadowing of the Lord Jesus. He is our great gathering-centre, and His precious promise is that "where two or three are gathered together in My name there am I **in the midst** of them" (Matt. 18: 20).

7. The Tabernacle was **the place where the Law was preserved.** The first two tables of stone, on which Jehovah had inscribed the ten commandments, were broken (Exodus 32: 19); but the second set were deposited in the ark in the tabernacle for safe keeping (Deut. 10: 2-5). It was only there, within the holy of holies, that the tablets of the Law were preserved intact. How this, again, speaks to us of Christ! He it was that said, "Lo, I come: in the volume of the book it is written of Me; I delight to do Thy will, O My God: Yea, **Thy Law is within** My heart" (Psa. 40: 8). Throughout His perfect life He preserved in thought, word, and deed the Divine Decalogue, honouring and magnifying God's Law.

8. The Tabernacle was **the place where sacrifice was made.** In its outer court stood the brazen altar, to which the animals were brought, and on which they were slain. There it was the blood was shed and atonement was made for sin. So it was with the Lord Jesus. He fulfilled in His own person the typical significance of the brazen altar, as of every piece of the tabernacle furniture. The body in which He tabernacled on earth was nailed to the cruel Tree. The Cross was the altar upon which God's Lamb was slain, where His precious blood was shed, and where complete atonement was made for sin.

9. The Tabernacle was **the place where the priestly family was fed.** "And the remainder thereof shall Aaron and his sons eat: with unleavened bread shall it be eaten **in the holy place;** in the court of the tabernacle of the congregation they shall eat it . . . The priest that offereth it for sin shall eat it: **in the holy place** shall 't be eaten" (Lev. 6: 16-26). How deeply significant are these scriptures in their typical import! And how they should speak to us of Christ as the Food of God's priestly family to-day, i.e., all believers (1 Peter 2: 5). He is the Bread of life. He is the One upon whom our souls delight to feed.

10. The Tabernacle was the **place of worship.** To it the pious Israelite brought his offerings. To it he turned when he desired to worship Jehovah. From its door the voice of the Lord was heard. Within its courts the priests ministered in their sacred service. And so it was with the antitype. It is **by Him** we are to offer unto God a sacrifice of praise. (Heb. 13: 15). It is in Him, and by Him, **alone,** that we can worship the Father. It is through Him we have access to the throne of grace.

11. The Tabernacle **had but one door.** Think of such a large building with but a single entrance! The outer court, with its solid walls of white curtains, was pierced by one gate only; telling us there is but one way into the presence of the holy God. How this reminds us of the words of that One who said, "I am the way, the truth, and the life, no man cometh unto the Father but by Me!" Access can be obtained only

through Him who declared "I am the Door" (John 10:9).

12. **The Tabernacle was approached through the tribe of Judah.** This is a most striking detail not obvious at first sight, but which is clearly established by a comparison of scripture with scripture. Num. 2, records the ordering of the twelve tribes of Israel as they were grouped around the four sides of the Tabernacle, and verse 3 tells us that **Judah** was to pitch on the east side. Now Exodus 27:12-17 makes it clear that **the door** of the Tabernacle was also on the east side. Thus, entrance into the Divine sanctuary was obtained through Judah. The significance of this is easily discerned. It was **through Judah** that the true Tabernacle obtained entrance into this world. Therefore is our Lord designated "the Lion of the tribe of Judah." (Rev. 5:5).

13. **The Tabernacle hints at the universal Lordship of Christ.** This may be seen from the fact that every kingdom in nature contributed its share toward buiding and enriching the Tabernacle. The mineral kingdom supplied the metals and the precious stones; the vegetable gave the wood, linen, oil and spices; the animal furnished the skins and goats hair curtains, in addition to the multitude of sacrifices which were constantly required. How this reminds us of the words of Him whom the Tabernacle foreshadowed, "The silver is Mine, and the gold is Mine" (Hag. 2:8); and again, "The cattle upon a thousand hills are Mine" (Psa. 50:10).

14. **The Tabernacle was ministered unto by the Women.** Their part was to provide the beautiful curtains and hangings: "And all the women that were wise-hearted did spin with their hands, and brought that which they had spun, both of blue, and of purple, and of scarlet, and of fine linen. And all the women whose hearts stirred them up in wisdom, spun goats' hair" (Exodus 35:26). How beautifully this foreshadowed the loving devotion of those women mentioned in the Gospels who ministered to Christ of their substance: see Luke 7:37; 8:2-3; John 12:3; Luke 23:55-56.

Thus we see how fully and how perfectly the tabernacle of old foreshadowed the person of our blessed Lord, and why the Holy Spirit, when announcing the Incarnation, said, "And the Word became flesh, and **tabernacled** among us."

It should be pointed out that there is a series of striking contrasts between the wilderness tabernacle and Solomon's temple in their respective foreshadowings of Christ.

(1) The tabernacle foreshadowed Christ in His first advent; the temple looks forward to Christ at His second advent.

(2) The tabernacle was first historically; the temple was not built until long afterwards.

(3) The tabernacle was but a temporary erection; the temple was a permanent structure.

(4) The tabernacle was erected by Moses the **prophet** (which was the office Christ filled during His first advent); the temple was built by Solomon the **king** (which is the office Christ will fill at His second advent).

(5) The tabernacle was used in the **wilderness**—speaking of Christ's humiliation; the temple was built in Jerusalem, the "city of the great King" (Matt. 5:35)—speaking of Christ's future glorification.

(6) The numeral which figured most prominently in the tabernacle was five, which speaks of **grace**, and grace was what characterised the earthly ministry of Christ at His first advent; but the leading numeral in the temple was twelve, which speaks of **government**, for at His second advent Christ shall rule and reign as King of kings and Lord of lords.

(7) The tabernacle was unattractive in its externals—so when Christ was here before, He was as "a root out of a dry ground": but the temple was renowned for its outward magnificence—so Christ when He returns shall come in power and great glory.

The careful reader will have noticed that there are two full accounts given in Exodus of the construction of the Tabernacle. This is indeed noteworthy, and evidences once more the accuracy and fulness of the type. First we have a description of the Tabernacle and its furniture as it was given to Moses in the Mount directly by Jehovah Himself. Then, as a parenthesis, in chapters 32, 33, we have the record of Israel's transgressing the holy covenant in the sin of idolatry. Finally, from chapters 35 to the end of the book we have the actual erection of the Tabernacle. What was foreshadowed by this we shall now endeavour to indicate.

First, there is the tabernacle as it was **originally planned** in Heaven and then shown as a pattern to Moses on the Mount. What did this adumbrate but Christ set forth from eternity in the counsels of the Godhead? The great Sacrifice was no afterthought on the part of God. He was not taken by surprise, nor was His eternal purpose interfered with when Adam transgressed His commandment. The Lamb was "foreordained before the foundation of the world" (1 Peter 1:20)! Then, in Jehovah **showing to Moses** the pattern of the Tabernacle which **was to be** erected, we have prefigured the successive types and prophecies which God gave to His people before His Son became incarnate. Just as Moses later **built** the Tabernacle according to the actual model which God had shown him during the forty days on the Mount, so Christ was born, lived and died, in exact accord with the prophetic plan which God gave during the forty centuries that preceded.

Second, in chapters 32 and 33 we are introduced to a dark interval of rebellion, when Israel sinned grievously against their Divine Benefactor. How accurately this depicts the fall and failure of man during the whole of the Old Testament period, and how it witnessed to the need of that redemption which God, in His marvellous grace, had prepared! "Christ had been already provided, but man must feel the need of the Divine salvation by the actual experience of sin. It is touching beyond degree to know that all the time that man was rebelling against God, God's remedy was waiting in that mount of grace" (Christ in the Tabernacle, by A. B. Simpson). Despite Israel's fearful transgression in the interval, the Tabernacle was erected; even so the fearful wickedness of men and all their countless abominations did not turn God from His purpose of mercy. When the fulness of time was come, God sent forth His Son. Where sin abounded, grace did much more abound.

Third, in the last six chapters we have the inspired record of **the actual erection** of the Tabernacle. Here we see the counsels of God perfectly executed, and most striking is it to note the provision He made for carrying out His design of a sanctuary. In 35:30-31, we read, "And Moses said unto the children of Israel, See, the Lord hath called by name Bezeleel the son of Uri, the son of Hur, of the tribe of **Judah**; and he hath filled him with the Spirit of God, in wisdom, in understanding, and in knowledge, and in all manner of workmanship." Thus we learn that it was by the gracious agency of **the Spirit of God** that the Tabernacle was brought into existence! What anointed eye can fail to see here that which made possible and actual the Divine incarnation, namely, the supernatural operations of the Spirit of God—see Luke 1:34-35! And how remarkable (and yet not remarkable) that the instrument used belonged to the tribe of Judah: so Mary was of the royal stock! Thus, in type and Antitype, the Divine plan was secured through the operations of the Spirit of God. Thus, also, do we see all the three persons of the Godhead in connection with the Tabernacle.

How unspeakably blessed is the word recorded in 40:34: "Then a cloud covered the tent of the congregation and the glory of the Lord filled the Tabernacle." Mean as was the outward appearance of that Tent, yet within, abode the Divine glory. So it was with the Antitype. When He appeared before men, He had "no form nor comeliness" (Isa. 5.:2), yet in Him dwelt all the fulness of the Godhead bodily.

What has been said above in no wise conflicts with the closing paragraphs of the preceding article. David was inspired to write "Thy commandment is exceeding **broad**" (Psalm 119:96). Well, had it been if expositors and commentators had borne this more in mind. There is not only a depth, but also a fulness to the Scriptures which are worthy of their Divine Author. God's Word is many-sided in its application. Some times a single parable (that of the Sower, for example) contains important practical lessons, doctrinal instruction, a prophetic forecast and a dispensational picture. How many of the prophecies, perhaps all of them, have a double—a minor and a major, a germinal and a terminal—and sometimes a threefold fulfilment. Thus it is also with the types. Some Old Testament characters are equally types of Christ, of Israel, and of the Christian. So with the Tabernacle: many of its details have more than one typical significance. May the Holy Spirit be our Teacher as we endeavour to take them up.

ARTHUR W. PINK.

## TRUTH AND ERROR

or

### LETTERS TO A FRIEND.

**10. The Spirit and the Word:**

"Then opened He their understanding that they might understand the Scriptures"—Luke 24:45.

"When He the Spirit of truth is come, He will guide you into all truth" John 16:13.

You hear it often said by the holders of the new theology, "we do not deny the Spirit's work, but we maintain that He works only through the Word, nay, that He is in the Word, so that whenever the Word is read or preached, there is the Spirit." Let us examine this statement.

1. If the Spirit is the Word, how is it that we are never told so in the Scripture? There is not one passage in which this is stated, or even hinted at. The language used throughout the whole Bible is such as continually to impress upon us the idea of His direct, personal, and special agency. It is to Scripture that I appeal; let our opponents produce their proofs from the Word of God. Mere human inferences are not enough. It is vain to say, it must be so. It is worse than vain to rest upon the reasonings of man. In a matter like this, it is to God alone that we can listen. He always speaks of His work in the new creation as being equally direct and special with His work in the old. If there be nothing but indirect agency in the former, then we must maintain that was the same in the latter, which is precisely the conclusion at which modern infidelity has arrived.

2. If the Spirit is in the Word, how is He said to be in the hand of Christ, and at His disposal? If He is in the Word, then He is out of the hands of Christ, and it will not be true that He gives eternal life to as many as the Father hath given Him; it will not be true that "the Son quickeneth whom He will." The Spirit then will be at our disposal, and wherever we choose to send the Bible or the Gospel, thither we send the Spirit. Christ is not at liberty to "quicken whom He will," for the Spirit is to be dispensed according to our pleasure! If He is in the Word, then wherever the Word is, there is the Spirit in all His energy and power. How is this consistent with His being given to Christ, in order that He may pour Him out according to His will?

3. If He is in the Word, it is needless for us to pray so that He would teach us to understand that Word. If God has already put all the Spirit into the Word that He means us to have, it is sinful in us to ask, and foolish to expect more. Yet has not God put into our Lips more than a thousand prayers for the understanding of His Holy Word? When, therefore, we pray to be instructed therein, we ask God to do something for us inwardly, in addition to what He has already done for us outwardly, to the end that we may learn His truth. We may have read the Word many times beyond number, but still we know that when God touches the springs of the soul, renewing it and imparting relish for the truth in place of our natural disrelish, every word seems full of sweetness and beauty. Outwardly it is the same word; but the inward touch of the divine finger upon the soul operates with such wondrous efficacy, that all seems fresh and new. This is utterly inconceivable upon a scheme which admits of nothing but mere outward influence. If the same verse of the Bible appears sweeter at one time than another, the cause of this difference must be a change in the state of the soul. If the soul remains unchanged, the verse will appear the same. But if the soul undergo any alteration, the verse will be felt quite different. And if, in order to relish the things of Christ, which by nature I abhor, my soul must undergo a change, how can this be accomplished but by the Holy Spirit working in me and upon me, "to will and to do, of His good pleasure?" When I sit down in my closet alone, with my Bible in my hand, I life up my soul to God, and ask Him to bless the word I am to read. Of what use is this if there be no inworking Spirit? If He has no access at all to me save through the outward word, then what can He do for me which the Word alone cannot do? If He be precluded from direct contact with my soul, then He can afford me no better help than any human friend. Nay, not so much. For the friend, can converse with me, reason with me, place the matter before me in different aspects; but the Spirit has no living voice to reach the external ear. What He has written, He has written; and there it re-

mains, He has no means, therefore of explaining it to me if He has no direct access to my soul. If I hate the truth, then how can He change hatred into love? How can He make me cease to hate it, if He can only deal with me through outward means, if He can only approach me through that very thing which I hate and repel? If my heart be by nature enmity to God, then how foolish to speak of removing that enmity by merely teaching me more regarding that very thing which I hate.

4. His being in the word, and thus working equally on all that hear the word, is given as the reason why sinners are so responsible for believing, and so guilty in not believing. Our opponents take credit for holding the necessity of the Spirit's work in conversion, but maintain that He works equally in every man, and that were it not for this they could not call on sinners to believe the Gospel. Now, is not this an admission that there is in sinners an inability which it requires the power of another to remove? It does not matter in what way power operates, they are obliged to confess that there is an ability—which the sinner cannot remove of himself—an inability which needs the Spirit's power to overcome. But further, it is just saying that man is not responsible in himself—that it is the universal gift of the Spirit, that constitutes his responsibility, and that, but for this, it would be unjust in God to call on him to believe. This of course, is just the old Arminian theory of universal grace. In it all obligation and responsibility are founded on this grace which is said to be given to every man. So that if there was no grace, there could be no duty. Thus man's guilt is denied, and thrown over upon God. His accountability is represented not as rising out of the nature which God had originally given him, but out of this universal grace which God had superadded, since the fall, without which God could not in common justice call on the sinner to keep His law or to believe His gospel. Thus, man is not only in himself helpless, which they are thus obliged to admit, but his helplessness is **not sinful!** It is a helplessness which God is either bound to remove by some universal operation of the Spirit, or else to treat as innocent! It is confessed that his depravity is such as to need the Spirit's power for its removal; but it is thus maintained that, were that not given, he would not be accountable for it, or called on to abandon it. It is this universal gift of the Spirit that is the origin, the ground, the measure of man's responsibility!

A favorite and frequent illustration of these views is taken from the eleventh chapter of Matthew, in which they say that the Lord declares that an influence was exerted upon Chorazin and Bethsaida, sufficient to convert Tyre and Sidon. From this they infer two things: that God is using with all sinners an influence sufficient to convert them, and that this influence is merely outward, not inward; the words and deeds of Jesus being all the influence made use of.

Now, arguing in their own way, it would appear from this passage, that Jesus says, that an influence was at work, sufficient to have converted Tyre, but not sufficient to have converted Chorazin. How can this prove that God is using with all sinners an influence sufficient to convert them? One would naturally suppose it proved **precisely the reverse.** The influence, it is said, would have converted Tyre. But Chorazin was far worse than Tyre, more hardened, more unbelieving. It would require then a much greater influence than that which the Lord was putting forth; for what He was putting forth was only enough to have converted Tyre!

Again, we ask, who made the difference between Tyre and Chorazin? Was it not Jehovah in His sovereignty? Who dispensed to Tyre the lesser blessing and to Chorazin the greater? Jehovah in His sovereignty. Why did He withhold it? It seemed good in His sight.

We know of no passage which more distinctly and more solemnly declares God's absolute sovereignty. He did far more for Chorazin than for Tyre, yet we are told by some that "He has done the utmost that He can do for every sinner." Had He done for Chorazin what He did for Tyre, repentence would have followed; yet He did not do it. What would have converted Tyre, was withheld from Tyre. What would have converted Sodom, was not given to Sodom. What would have converted Chorazin, was not given to Chorazin. Is not all this manifest sovereignty?

These remarks will obviate the difficulty that has been raised, without imposing on us the necessity of entering at length into the meaning of the passage.

5. Let us take another instance. The Word is likened by our Lord to seed. "The good seed of the word," is that which is sown. But this is sown in various soils; and however good the seed may be, if the soil is bad it will bear no fruit. Until the soil be made good, the seed will not spring up. The seed may be the very best; it may be sown by the most skilful sower, and in the most skilful way; it may be shone upon by a genial sun; it may be watered by refreshing showers; but all this will not make it grow. Why? Because the soil is bad; it is sown in sand. No skill on the sower, no excellence in the seed, will convert sand into good soil. No showers nor sunshine will make sand fertile. There must be a direct process altering the character of the soil, before the seed will spring up. To make the soil fertile through means of the seed is an impossibility. What husbandman would speak in such a way? Would he speak of putting power into the seed to fertilise the soil? Would he speak of getting at the soil through the seed alone? Would he think of rectifying the soil through means of the seed alone? Would he not at once set about the direct process of manuring in order to change the soil and make it fruitful? And what would you think of a man who would say to you, "Oh, I do not deny the necessity of a power being put forth to change the soil; all I say is, that it must be put forth through the seed alone: the soil must not be touched directly, that would be an interference with the laws of nature; the power is in the seed; let the seed be well lodged in the ground, and it will soon show its power to change the soil." Would you not say that, whatever his professions might be, he did not really believe in any external or separate power at all, but that the soil and the seed contained all the power that was needed, and that the idea of a power operating independent of both was equally unnatural and absurd? In like manner, when men say, "Oh, we do not deny the Spirit's work and power, we merely say, that his power is in the word," I must say that I find it hard to understand how these men believe in a Holy Spirit at all.

The only way of getting over this difficulty is, by supposing some small remaining goodness about the soil, into which the seed may strike its roots. If this be admitted, then I understand the matter. But if the soil be totally and utterly barren, then nothing can be more unintelligible than to speak of a power in the seed, by which it is able to spring up, without any direct process being applied to the soil.

Or let me take another example. David's prayer was, "open Thou mine eyes that I may behold wondrous things out of Thy law." These are plain words. David asks God to open his eyes, in order that, being opened, he may behold these wondrous things. He knew something about the law; he knew that there were wondrous things in it. These he longed to see, but his eyes were closed and dim. In God directly, not through the medium of anything else—God's touch alone, direct and immediate, could open David's eyes. Had he lived in our day, and complained of dim and closed eyes, he would have been told, "Now you must not pray, you must not go to God, to tell Him your disease, and say open mine eyes; you must just set the object before you; there is power in the object to open your eye; but to go to God Himself and seek the direct forthputting of His power upon your eye, is nothing but unbelief of His Word." But David knew better than these miserable comforters. He knew himself and his disease better than they did; he knew the real seat of the disease, and the real nature of the cure required, better than they; he knew his gracious God, his healer, his enlightener, better than they; and therefore He went directly to Him, imploring the direct touch of His hand.

He felt exactly as blind Bartimeus felt. He knew that he was blind, and he wanted to see. Jesus of Nazareth was passing by. He was said to be able to open the eyes of the blind by His touch. Accordingly he went and was cured. And how? Did Jesus say, 'Don't come to Me and cry for the opening of your eyes, but just look before you at these objects of light; they have power in them to make you see; I only work through them; I do not put forth My power directly upon the eye, I only put it forth indirectly through these objects, and in no other way?" No, He touched his eyes, and said, Receive thy sight. Thus the eye of the body was cured; and thus the eye of the soul is also cured.

But is it not said, "The commandment of the Lord is pure, enlightening the eyes" Psa. 19:8? Yes, it is. But what of this? Does this contradict the other. No. In the first place it is not said here, that the Word opens, but merely that it enlightens the eyes. In the second place, I admit most fully the efficacy of the Word: "It is a lamp to our feet, and a light to our path." I do not in the very least depreciate the word of the living God. I wish merely to assign to it the place which God does. I see men superseding the Spirit, and setting aside His work, under pretence of honoring the Word. And it is this that I refuse to do. I admit the blessed efficacy of the word; but **I maintain also the direct agency of the Holy Spirit upon the soul in order to reception of that word.** The word is our light, but there must be an "opening of the eye" by the Spirit, ere, there can be a "beholding of the wondrous things out of the law."

I confess I do not see of what use the Holy Spirit is in such a system. Man has all the requisite power; he needs no foreign aid; the truth is presented to him, with all suitable motives and persuasives—what more is needed? In such a case it would be but mocking Him to tell him of the Holy Spirit. There is no need for any help in the matter, far less of Divine help. For **omnipotence** to interpose when no strength is needed beyond what the man possesses, is superfluous expenditure of power, a mere mockery of help. If the new theorists be correct, there is no necessity for the work of the Spirit in any sense. If man can do all, why call in the aid of the Spirit? To say that man needs the Spirit, is just to say that, without the Spirit, he could not perform what he is called on to do. If, however, to be really able to do all himself, it is absurd to speak of any work of the Spirit in him.

We believe that this point is often stated in the following manner—"man is equally and in the same sense able to believe God's truth as the devil's lie." This, I think is the strongest as well as the simplest way the matter can be put. Well. It will be admitted that, in no sense whatever, is the Spirit's aid needed or given in order to believe the lie; therefore, **in no sense whatever and in no way whatever**, either in the word or with the word, is the Spirit needed or given to enable men to believe the truth. Surely this is the honest and plain conclusion from a statement which, from the triumphant way in which it is generally put, seems to be reckoned irresistible. To speak of any work of the Spirit whatsoever, either in or out of the word, is to say that man is **not** equally and in the same sense able to believe the truth of God, as he is to believe the lie of the devil. Therefore, we infer that either this noted proverb must be abandoned, or else the Holy Spirit and His work, in every sense and in every way, must be denied. If a man no more needs the Spirit in order to his believing a lie, than in order to his believing the truth, it is plain that he needs no Holy Spirit at all. Why then is the Spirit and His work not totally denied? Men are not yet prepared for that. The **name** must in the meantime be retained. In a short time this may be unnecessary.

It has been sometimes said, "Is it not just as easy to believe as not to believe, as easy to turn to God as to turn away from God?" If this merely meant that the same facilities are required for both, there would be no harm in the expression. But if it means that our souls are so well balanced, so entirely free, so little injured by the fall, that they can move with the same facility towards God as from God, we deny and condemn the statement. On account of our bondage to sin and bias to evil, it is not as easy for us to be holy as to be unholy. The corrupt state of our souls has made the difference. But then, "we are not free agents," it will be said. What, is God not free because He cannot lie?" Must we not say it is as easy for the elect angels to blaspheme as to praise, to rebel as to obey? Their perfect holiness has made disobedience as impossible to them as our corruption has made obedience impossible to us. Is it not their highest glory as well as their completest liberty that they cannot disobey? And is it not our deepest shame and guilt and bondage that sin has such dominion over us, that even when to will is present with us, how to perform that which is good, we find not?

And as to this "power in the word," of which so much is spoken, I confess it is a mystery to me. That there is power in the Word—that the Word of God is a powerful word, I cordially admit. In no other words is there such a power and majesty. There are no words like the words of God for excellency and strength. Words so weighty, so fit, so full, so big with meaning, are nowhere else to be found. Though in themselves they be but the language of the creature the poor speech of man, yet it is the Almighty voice that speaks them; it is the thoughts of God Himself which they contain. If this is all that is meant by power being in the word, then no one will dispute the matter. But this is not all.

Nay this is not the point at all. No one denies that the words are the Word of God, and that they contain the thoughts of God. But the question is, Do these words contain some **mysterious power** of making those thoughts to be known and felt by the sinner? Do they contain a power, **independent of their meaning**, to make the sinner feel these thoughts which they contain? If it is said, "Oh no, they contain no such power apart from their meaning; but these **thoughts** conveyed by means of the Word, have power;" then we must say that this is hardly intelligible, or, at least, does not touch the point. For thoughts, and words, and ideas, are **passive** things; whereas, according to this idea, they are active things, a living agency capable of operating upon the mind by means of a mysterious power with which they are impregnated. But even granting that they do possess some such active power, still the difficulty is not explained. For the state of the sinner's soul is such as to repel and resist power. And how is this repelling and resisting attitude of the sinner to be removed? Take an illustration. Suppose the window of my house is darkened by a wall which excludes the sun. The sunbeams beat upon the wall, but still it remains, nay, it grows harder and more impenetrable under their influence. Had it been a wall of ice, it would have melted away, but its nature is such as to harden, not to soften, under these beams. And how then is the evil to be remedied? By putting greater power into the sunbeams? That is an absurdity. Besides, it is the nature of the wall to resist the sunbeam, and to harden under it; and to put additional power into the sunbeam would be only to call forth additional resistance, and produce more induration. The remedy is plainly the removing of the wall by a power fitted for that purpose—a power (if you like) going along with the sunbeams, and operating simultaneously, but still a **direct** power put forth upon the fabric for its overthrow.

I know that this illustration is an imperfect one. It fails in many points of resemblance. But still it does not make the case of the sinner worse than it really is. Nay, it does not bring out the worst features of the case. It does not show the **active and positive resistance** to the light which the sinner puts forth, and which is far worse and far harder to overcome than the resistance of mere inanimate matter. If then, it be said, that I have misrepresented and misstated the case, all I shall say is, that I have **understated** the case; but I have not **mis-stated** it. The difficulty is far greater than such an illustration can give us the least idea of.

I do hold, then, **a power along with the Word, and in connection with the Word**; but to say, that that power is in the Word, is either a mere figure of speech, or it is an absurdity. When God said, "Let there be light," there went out a power **along with** the Word, and the light came into being. Who would say that the power was **in** the word? When Jesus stood at the grave of Lazarus, and said, "Lazarus come forth," there went out a power **along with** he word; yet how absurd to say that it was **in** the word.

It is most needful to maintain the instrumentality of the word in conviction, conversation and sanctification. The whole process from first to last which the Spirit accomplishes, is in connection with the Word. The reverse of this might be shown to be scripturally untrue, and philosophically absurd. This is the principle on which God is acting in giving us His Bible. It is the principle on which the minister acts in proclaiming the Gospel. We cannot hold this too strenuously! for the denial of it would land us into darkness and mysticism; nay, it would be grieving to the Spirit of truth. But this is totally diverse from saying, that the Spirit is in the word, or that there is a mystic power in the word apart from its meaning or that the Spirit only works through the truth. There is no question as to its being truth by which the soul is impressed; the only question is whether it is possible for a depraved being (the very essence of whose depravity consists in his being "past feeling," or **unimpressible** by the truth) to be impressed by it until a power has been at work making him **impressible**. In his fallen state he utterly repels the truth —he is not suscepible until he is made susceptible of receiving its influence.

The truth is, that the sinner is most reluctant to admit that he is entirely in the hands and at the disposal of God, in regard to salvation. He wants to have salvation completely at his disposal. He sees, that if he can succeed in proving that there is no power apart from the word, nothing but what is contained in the word, he becomes the disposer of his own destiny. But if he admit a power not in the word, a power coming direct from God, then he is at the disposal of God. This is the secret of the modern idea of the Spirit being in the word. Man wants to be his own Saviour, and therefore, he tries to prove that God has made him so by giving him the word, and putting enough of power into it to save him. This shows us clearly man's dislike to the sovereign will of God, and his reluctance to admit that he is entirely at the mercy of God. But it reveals something more. It shows us that, after all, he does not feel himself safe in God's hands, and, therefore, he wishes to take salvation into his own. And what is this but a clear proof that these very men who speak so loudly of a free Gospel, and of the love of God, do not believe that Gospel and do not give credit to that love. If they did, they would not be so anxious to take salvation out of God's hands. They would feel far safer in His hands than in their own. And these ideas of theirs, instead of clearing up and enforcing the Gospel, plainly prove that the Gospel of the grace of God is not understood at all. These men have yet to learn what the Gospel is. It is from the dark suspicions of their own hearts as to the character of God that this attempt to wrest salvation out of his hands, and to place it in their own, proceeds.

Let me illustrate the point before us a little further. I shall state the following case. It is no imaginary one. A dull, stupid scholar once sat beside an intelligent teacher, who sought to instruct him in the things of God. The Bible lay upon the knees of both. But it was in vain. The boy could not be got to even understand the truth regarding the way of life. The teacher explained and simplified, and illustrated, but with no effect. Often did he wish that he had direct access to the boy's soul, that he might touch its secret springs, and rectify his understanding. He felt that nothing save this could be of any avail. But he could only dwell upon the truth, endeavour to open it up more fully, and press it clearly home. Thus, day after day, sat the teacher in his helplessness, and the scholar in his dullness. Meanwhile the former failed not to commend the boy to God, asking Him who had access to its hidden springs to touch them, asking that Spirit, who alone could renew, and enlighten, and enable, to do His work upon the soul, that the truth might at length find entrance. Thus he prayed, and the teaching was given up as hopeless. One day his pupil came eagerly to him, exclaiming, "Now I understand it all." "Who taught you?" "No one." How did you come to see it?" "Oh! In a moment I saw it; and it is just the very thing you have been telling me so long, but I never saw it till now: God has opened my eyes." And so it was. That the Holy Spirit, who alone has access to the soul of man, had put forth His power, and the boy's dullness had given way. But the work had not been through the truth alone upon his soul, in order to His understanding the truth. It had been exactly what David sought for in his own case, "give me understanding that I may learn Thy commandments" (Psa. 119 : 73).

(H. Bonar, 1851.)

(To be continued, D.V.)

---

## DIVINE CHASTISEMENT.

### Heb. 12 : 5.

The Hebrew Christians to whom this Epistle was first addressed were passing through a great fight of afflictions, and miserably were they quitting themselves. They were the little remnant out of the Jewish nation who had believed on their Messiah during the days of His public ministry, plus those Jews who had been converted under the preaching of the apostles. It is highly probable that they had expected the Messianic Kingdom would at once be set up on earth, and that they would be allotted the chief places of honour in it. But the Millenium had not begun, and their own lot became increasingly bitter. They were not only hated by the Gentiles, but ostracised by their unbelieving brethren, and it became a hard matter for them to make even a bare living. Providence held a frowning face. Many who had made a profession of Christianity had gone back to Judaism and were prospering temporally. As the afflictions of the believing Jews increased they too were sorely tempted to turn their back upon the new Faith. Had they been wrong in embracing Christianity? Was high Heaven displeased because they had idenfied themselves with Jesus of Nazareth? Did not their suffering go to show that God no longer regarded them with favour?

Now it is most instructive and blessed to see how the Apostle met the unbelieving reasoning of their hearts. He appealed to **their own Scriptures**! He reminded them of an exhortation found in Proverbs 3 : 11-12, and applied it to their case. Notice, first, the words we place in italics: "Ye have forgotten the exhortation which speaketh **unto you.**" This shows that the exhortations of the Old Testament were not restricted to those who lived under the old covenant: they apply with equal force and directness to those of us living under the new covenant. Let us not forget that "all Scripture is given by inspiration of God and is profitable" (2 Tim. 3 . 16). The Old Testament equally as much as the New Testament was written for **our** learning and admonition.

Second, mark the tense of the verb in our opening text: "Ye have forgotten the exhortation which **speaketh.**" The Apostle quoted a sentence of the Word written one thousand years previously, yet he does not say "which **hath** spoken," but "which speaketh." The same principle is illustrated in that sevenfold "He that hath an ear, let him hear what the Spirit saith (not "said"!) unto the churches" of Rev. 2 and 3. The Holy Scriptures are a **living** Word in which God is speaking to-day!

Consider now the words "Ye have forgotten." It was not that these Hebrew Christians were unacquainted with Prov. 3 : 11 and 12, but they had let them slip. They had forgotten the Fatherhood of God and their relation of Him as His dear children. In consequence they misinterpreted both the manner and design of God's present dealings with them, they viewed his dispensation not in the light of His Love, but regarded them as signs of His displeasure or as proofs of His forgetfulness. Consequently, instead of cheerful submission, there was despondency and despair. Here is a most important lesson for us: we must interpret the mysterious providences of God **not** by reason or observation, but by **the Word.** How often we "forget" the exhortation which speaketh unto us as unto children—"My son, despise not thou the chastening of the Lord, nor faint when thou art rebuked of Him."

Unhappily there is no word in the English language which is capable of doing justice to the Greek term here. "paideia" which is rendered "chastening" is only another form of "paidion" which signifies "young children," being the tender word that was employed by the Saviour in John 21 : 5 and Hebrews 2 : 13. One can see at a glance the direct connection which exists between the words "disciple" and "discipline": equally close in the Greek is the relation between "children" and "chastening." **Son-training** would be better. It has reference to God's education, nurture and discipline of His children. It is the Father's wise and loving correction which is in view.

It is true that much chastisement is the rod in the hand of the Father correcting His erring child. But it is a serious mistake to confine our thoughts to this one aspect of the subject. Chastisement is by no means always the scourging of His refractive sons. Some of the saintliest of God's people, some of the most obedient of His children, have been and are the greatest sufferers. Ofttimes God's chastenings instead of being retributive are corrective. They are sent to empty us of self-sufficiency and self-righteousness: they are given to discover to us hidden transgressions, and to teach us the plague of our own hearts. Or again, chastisements are sent to strengthen our faith, to raise us to higher levels of experience, to bring us into a condition of usefulness. Still again, Divine chastisement is sent as a preventative, to keep under pride, to save us from being unduly elated over success in God's service. Let us consider, briefly, four entirely different examples.

**David.** In his case the rod was laid upon him for grievous sins, for open wickedness. His fall was occasioned by self-confidence and self-righteousness. If the reader will diligently compare the two Songs of David recorded in 2 Samuel 22 and 23, the one written near the beginning of his life, the other near the end, he will be struck by the great difference of spirit manifested by the writer in each. Read 2 Samuel 22 : 22-25 and you will not be surprised that God suffered him to have such a fall. Then turn to chapter 23, and mark the blessed change. At the beginning of v. 5 there is a heart-broken confession of failure. In vv. 10-12, there is a God-glorifying confession, attributing victory unto the Lord. The severe scourging of David was not in vain.

**Job.** Probably he tasted of every kind of suffering which falls to man's lot: family bereavements, loss of property, grievous bodily afflictions came fast, one on top of another. But God's end in it all was that Job should benefit therefrom and be a greater partaker of His holiness. There was not a little of self-satisfaction and self-righteousness in Job at the beginning. But at the end, when He was brought face to face with the thrice Holy One, he "abhorred **himself**" (42:6). In David's case the chastisement was retributive, in Job's corrective.

**Abraham.** In him we see an illustration of an entirely different aspect of chastening. Most of the trials to which he was subjected were neither because of open sins nor for the correction of inward faults. Rather were they sent for the development of spiritual graces. Abraham was sorely tried in various ways, but it was in order that faith might be strengthened and that patience might have its perfect work in him. Abraham was weaned from the things of this world, that he might enjoy closer fellowship with Jehovah and become the "friend" of God.

**Paul.** "And lest I should be exalted above measure through the abundance of the revelations, there was given to me a thorn in the flesh, the messenger of Satan to buffet me, lest I should be exalted above measure." (2 Cor. 12:7). This "thorn" was sent not because of failure and sin, but as a preventative against pride. Note the "lest" both at the beginning and end of the verse. The result of this "thorn" was that the beloved apostle was made more conscious of his weakness. Thus, chastisement has for one of its main objects the breaking down of self-sufficiency, the bringing us to the end of our selves.

Now in view of these widely different aspects—chastenings which are retributive, corrective, educative, and preventative, how incompetent are we to **diagnose**, and how great is the folly of pronouncing a judgment concerning others! Let us not conclude when we see a fellow-christian under the rod of God that he is necessarily being taken to task for his sins. In our next meditation we shall, D.V., consider **the spirit** in which Divine chastisements are to be received.

ARTHUR W. PINK.

---

Many other advantages there are which men may reap from a **constant reading** of the Scripture; which I therefore reckon as a **general means** of coming to the knowledge of the mind of God therein. By this **reading** of he Scripture I mean the studying of it, to come to a due understanding of it in particular places; for it is about the means of the **solemn interpretation** of the Scripture that we now inquire. Hereunto, I say, the general study of the whole, and in particular the places to be interpreted, is required. It may seem altogether needless and impertinent to give this direction for the understanding of the mind of God in the Scripture, that we should read and study it to that end; for who can imagine how it should be done otherwise? But I wish the practice of many, it may be, of the most, did render this direction unnecessary; for in their design to come to the knowledge of spiritual things, the direct immediate study of the Scripture is that which they least of all apply themselves unto. Other writings they will read and study with diligence; but their reading of the Scripture is for the most part superficial, without that intension of mind and spirit; that use and application of means, which are necessary to the understanding of it, as the event doth manifest. It is the immediate study of the Scripture that I intend. And hereunto I do refer—1. A due consideration **of the analogy of faith** always to be retained; 2. A due examination of the **design and scope of the place;** 3. A diligent observation of **antecedents and consequences;** with all those general rules which are usually given as direction in the interpretation of the Scripture. This, therefore, in the diligent exercise of our minds and reasons, is the first general outward means of knowing the mind of God in the Scripture and the interpretation thereof. (John Owen, 1650).

## GOOD NEWS.

For some time past we have had on our Magazine free-list a Brother in Germany to whom we have sent "Studies in the Scriptures." He has loaned his copies to others there who could read English. One, while reading the issue which contained our exposition of Exodus 12, was unmistakably brought out of darkness into God's marvellous light. Below are quotations from a letter recently received from him:—

"I wish you would praise with me the abundant mercy of the Lord, Who has enlightened me with the light of His Holy Spirit to see that I have a Passover, Christ, who was sacrificed for me. My heart is full of joy and thanks, that I can now recognise Him, I hope you will understand the meaning of what I say: how Israel recognised Him not as the Messiah, because they wished to be saint and just in their own virture; so I have not recognised Him as my Justification. And I was full of fear and anxiety, for I knew (by the testimony of my conscience and the Word) that wrath was upon me, for I did not believe in the name of the Son of God. And now, the merciful God has showed me; that Christ is my Passover, sacrificed for me. He has manifested in me His Son, like He manifested Him in Paul. And God used in His compassion the 'Studies of the Scriptures.'

"I read the Gleanings in Exodus, and the Lord was pleased to enlighten me, when I was reading the word 'About midnight will I go out into the midst of Egypt and all the firstborn in the land of Egypt shall die.' The sentence of death was proclaimed upon the Egyptian and Israelitish firstborns, for all were sinners, like Paul writes in Romans 1 and 2. But the Lord put a difference between the Egyptians and Israel. And you have written there 'Marvellous example was this of the sovereignty of the Divine grace.' Then the Israelite had to kill a lamb and to sprinkle its blood upon the door-posts and lintal of the house wherein the Israelite sheltered that night. They did so and the angel of death passed over. We have also a Passover, Christ, sacrificed for us. I also have put the blood of our Lord Jesus Christ and sprinkled it upon my life, and I was saved from the wrath.

"Next to the Lord I have to thank you, for the Lord has used the 'Gleanings in Exodus' to enlighten me. I know you will praise with me the Lord and give all honor to Him, who be praised for eternity. I hope that the Lord will in His grace, enlighten many souls, that they may see Him as their Passover, sacrificed for them."

Truly this case has the ear-marks of being a genuine work of Divine grace. Note how this babe in Christ acknowledges that he was "full of fear and anxiety," for he knew that "wrath was upon him." The longer we live, the more inclined are we to put a question-mark over against the experience of those who profess to have been saved and yet never felt this fear nor were conscious of God's holy wrath upon them.

Mark how this Brother owns the "**abundant** mercy of the Lord,'' and bows to the statement that "God is absolute sovereign in the exercise of His grace." So too we are fearful of those professing Christians who cavill about and argue against this basic truth of Divine revelation.

Observe how this Spirit-taught "lamb" has been shown the **worthlessness** of his own virtues" and the **preciousness** of the blood of Chrst. These are two things which every truly regenerated soul has impressed upon his understanding and heart.

Finally, admire his "I know you will give all honor to Him." Such is ever the language of sinners saved by grace alone. "Not unto us, O Lord, not unto us, but unto Thy name give glory" (Psa. 115:1) is their daily testimony and ascription of praise.

Surely the above ought to stir us all to more earnest daily prayer that the God of all grace may be pleased to enlarge the present very limited circulation of this Magazine, and that He will deign to use it to His glory in the building up of the converted and the salvation of the unconverted.

ARTHUR W. PINK.

*(Continued from page 193.)*

of spirit is always accompanied by mourning: meekness or lowliness by hungering and thirsting after the righteousness of God: mercifulness toward men is united to purity of heart towards God: and peacemaking is coupled with being persecuted for righteousness' sake. Thus vv. 10, 11 supply us with the key to v. 9.

Thus, approaching the seventh Beatitude from each of three separate viewpoints we arrive at the same conclusion. First, in contrast from the task allotted to the people of God at the beginning of the Legal dispensation, of going forth with the sword to slay the enemies of Jehovah; the service to which the saints are called in this Gospel dispensation, is that of going out as heralds of the Cross, seeking the reconciliation of those who are by nature at enmity against our Master. Second, as supplementing the various graces named in the first six, and in keeping with the fact that this is the **seventh**, the Beatitude which we are now considering gives **completeness**, to our Lord's delineation of Christian character, by showing us that His followers are called to the unspeakable privilege of being sent forth as His ambassadors of peace. Third, as linked with the verses which immediately follow, that speak of persecution, this shows us that the opposition encountered is the result of faithfulness in the service to which we are called, and tells us that the "peacemaking" of our text refers primarily to our being instruments in God's hands of reconciling to Him those who are actively engaged in warfare against Him.

We have dwelt at some length on the reasons which have led us to conclude that the "peacemakers" referred to in our text are those who beseech sinners to be reconciled to God, because most of the commentators are very unsatisfactory in their expositions. They see in this Beatitude nothing more than a blessing pronounced by Christ on those who endeavour to promote unity, heal breaches, and restore those who are estranged. While we fully agree that this is a most blessed exercise, and that the Christian is, by virtue of Christ indwelling him, a lover of peace and concord, yet we do not believe that this is what our Lord had in mind here.

The believer in Christ knows that there is no peace for the wicked, therefore does he earnestly desire, that they should acquaint themselves with God and be at peace( Job 22 : 21). Believers know that peace with God is only "through our Lord Jesus Christ," therefore do they speak of Him to their fellow-men as the Holy Spirit leads them to do so. Their own feet are "shod with the preparation of the Gospel of Peace" (Eph. 6 : 14), therefore will they testify of this to others. Of such it is said, "How beautiful are the feet of them that preach the gospel of peace, and bring glad tidings of good things" (Rom. 10 : 15). All such are pronounced "blessed" by our Lord. They cannot but be blessed. Next to the enjoyment of peace in our own souls, must be the delight of bringing others (by God's grace) to also enter into this peace. In its wider application this word of Christ may also refer to that spirit in His followers which delight to pour oil upon the troubled waters, which aims to right wrongs, which seeks to restore kindly relations, whose amicable feelings have been disturbed, smoothing over difficulties and softening down asperities.

"Blessed are the peacemakers: for they shall be called the children of God." The Word "called" here seems to mean "acknowledge." God shall **own** them as His own children. "He is 'the God o peace' (Heb. 13 : 20), His great object in the wonderful scheme of redemption, is to 'gather together in one all things in Christ,' whether they be 'things in heaven,' or 'things on earth' (Eph. 1 : 10). And all those who, under the influence of Christian truth are peace-makers, show that they are animated, with the same principle of action as God, and as 'obedient children' are co-operating with Him in His benevolent design" (Dr. John Brown). The world may despise them as fanatics, religious professors may regard them as narrow-minded sectarians, and their relatives look upon them as fools, but the great God owns them as His children even now, distinguishing them by tokens of His peculiar regard, and causing His Spirit within to witness to their Divine sonship. But in the Day to come, He will publicly avow His relation to them in the presence of an assembled universe. However humble their present situation in life may be, however despised and misrepresented by their fellowmen, they shall yet " shine forth as the sun in the kingdom of their Father" (Matt. 13 : 43). Then will be the **"manifestation of the sons of God"** (Rom. 8 : 19).

ARTHUR W. PINK.

# VOL. V     OCT., 1926     NO. 10
# STUDIES IN THE SCRIPTURES

"Search the Scriptures" John 5:39.

Copyright in all English-speaking Countries.

Editor: Arthur W. Pink, 22 Parramatta Road, Summer Hill, N.S.W., Australia.
Hon. Agent in U.S.A.: Mr. C. S. Pressel, 559 Dupont Ave., York, Penna.

Price: 10 cents per copy; $1.00 or 5/- per year.

Matt. 5:10-12.

    The Christian life is one that is full of strange paradoxes which are quite insoluable to human reason, but which are easily understood by the spiritual mind. God's saints rejoice with joy unspeakable; yet do they mourn with a lamentation to which the worldling is an utter stranger. The believer in Christ has been brought into contact with a source of vital satisfaction which is capable of meeting every longing, yet does he pant with a yearning like unto that of the thirsty hart. He sings, and makes melody in his heart to the Lord, yet does he groan deeply and daily. His experience is often painful and perplexing, yet would he not part with it for all the gold in the world. These puzzling paradoxes are among the evidences which he possesses that he is indeed blest of God. Such are the thoughts evoked by our present text. Who by mere reasoning would ever conclude that the reviled, the persecuted, the defamed, are "blessed"!

    "It is a strong proof of human depravity that men's curses and Christ's blessings should meet on the same persons. Who would have thought that a man could be persecuted and reviled, and have all manner of evil said of him, for righteousness' sake? And do wicked men really hate justice and love those who defraud and wrong their neighbours? No; they do not dislike righteousness as it respects themselves: it is only that species of it which respects God and religion that excites their hatred. If Christians were content with doing justly and loving mercy, and would cease walking humbly with God, they might go through the world, not only in peace, but with applause: but he that will live godly in Christ Jesus shall suffer persecution (2 Tim. 3: 12). Such a life reproves the ungodliness of men and provokes their resentment" (Andrew Fuller).

    Verses 9 and 10 plainly go together and form the eighth and last Beatitude of this series. It pronounces a double blessing upon a double line of conduct. This at once suggests that it is to be looked at in a twofold way. What we have in verse 10 is to be regarded as an appendix to the whole series, describing the experience which will surely be met with by those whose characters Christ has described in the previous verses. The carnal mind is enmity against God, and the more His children are conformed to His image the more will they bring down upon themselves the spite of His foes. Being "persecuted for righteousness' sake" means being opposed because of right living. Those who perform their Christian duty condemn those who live to please self, and therefore evoke their hatred. This persecution assumes various forms, from annoying and tantalising to oppressing and tormenting.

    Verses 10 to 12 contain a supplementary word to the seventh Beatitude. That which arouses the anger of Satan and most stirs up his children are the efforts of Christians to be peacemakers. The Lord here prepares us to expect that loyalty to Him and His Gospel will result in our own peace being disturbed, introducing us to strife and warfare. Proof of this is found in the "so persecuted they the prophets which were before you": it is service for God which calls forth the fiercest opposition. Necessarily so, for we are living in a world which is hostile to Christ, as His cross once and for all demonstrated.

    Three grades of suffering are here mentioned. "Reviling" is mere verbal abuse: "persecution" involves acts of ill-treatment: "saying all manner of evil

(Continued on page 240)

## IMPORTANT NOTICES

Set of twelve issues for **1922**, unbound, $1.00 or 5/-. Bound $1.65 or 7/-.

1923, 1924, 1925 same as 1922.

Note: We cannot break a set or now supply any **single** 1925 issues.

Subscription—price: **$1.00** or **5/-** per year to any address in the world.

Change of Address: Please notify me promptly of any change of address, and be certain to give both old and new address.

Non-subscribers receiving this Magazine regularly will understand their subscription has been entered by a friend.

Copies lost in the mail duplicated only if we are notified promptly.

## CONTENTS

| | |
|---|---|
| The Gospel of John (John 17: 6-12) | 218 |
| Gleanings in Exodus | 226 |
| Truth and Error | 230 |
| Waiting | 235 |
| Divine Chastisement | 237 |
| Unanswered Prayer | 238 |

## THE GOSPEL OF JOHN

### 58. Christ Interceding Continued:
### John 17: 6-12.

The following is an analysis of the second section of John 17:—
1. What Christ had done for God's elect v. 6.
2. The response of the elect vv. 6, 7.
3. The consequent assurance of the elect v. 8.
4. The elect alone prayed for by the Mediator v. 9.
5. Reasons why Christ prayed for the elect vv. 9-11.
6. Christ praying for their preservation and unity v. 11.
7. Christ's accompanying plea v. 12.

John 17 is the sequel to chapter 13. In each the actions of our great High Priest are in view. But the services are different, both together giving us a full representation of our Advocate on high. "In the 13th chapter He had, as it were, laid one hand on the defiled feet of His saints; here He lays the other hand on the throne of the Father, forming thus a chain of marvellous workmanship reaching from God to sinners. In the 13th chapter His body was girt, and He was stooping down towards our feet; here, His eyes are lifted up (v. 1), and He is looking in the face of the Father. What that is asked for us, by One who fills up the whole distance between the bright throne of God and our defiled feet, can be denied? All must be granted—such an One is heard always. Thus we get the sufficiency and acceptability of the Advocate" (Mr. J. G. Bellett).

The order in which the Saviour here presents His petitions, and the **pleas** by which He urges them, are deserving of the closest notice. The prayer has three main divisions: in vv. 1 to 5 He prays for Himself; in vv. 6 to 19 He prays for the disciples then alive; in vv. 20 to 26 He prays for those who should believe. In praying for Himself, His own glorification, the great end in view is the Father's glory. In v. 1 He says: "Glorify Thy Son, that Thy Son also may glorify Thee," and in v. 5 He adds: "Glorify Thou Me with Thine own self." This, be it noted, is before He asks a single thing for His people. Just as in "The Disciples' Prayer "Our Father which art in Heaven, hallowed be Thy name" was the opening petition, so here in "The Lord's Prayer" the Fathers' interests come first. Inseparably connected are the two things: the Father's glory and the Son's glory. In praying for Himself before His people He shows us that in all things He has the pre-eminence (Col. 1: 18).

In studying the different pleas for His own glorification, we find that they were **seven** in number, and this supplies us with the first of a most striking series of sevens which runs through this prayer. The various pleas were as follows: First, because of His filial relationship with God—"Father," v. 1. Second, because the appointed time for it had arrived—"The hour is come," **v. 1**. Third, because authority over all flesh had been given Him by Divine appointment and promise, v. 2. Fourth, because His bestowal of eternal life on God's elect had also been promised Him, v. 2. Fifth, because in bestowing eternal life on the elect He would be bringing them to a knowledge of the Father, v. 3. Sixth, because He had glorified the Father on the earth, v. 4. Seventh, because He had finished the work which had been given Him to do, v. 4. For these reasons He asks that His request be granted.

Ere passing from the first section of this prayer, attention should be called to the lovely manner in which the Son there kept before Him the glory of the Father. First, He had said: "Father . . . glorify Thy Son" (v. 1), not "the Son": He desired no glory for Himself apart from the Father! Second, "that Thy Son also may glorify Thee" (v. 1): not separately, but in perfect union. Third, "As Thou hast given Him power over all flesh" (v. 2): blessed is it to see the place which He gives the Father. Fourth, "that He should give eternal life to as many as"—He redeems with His blood? No; but—"to as many as Thou hast given Him" (v. 3)! Thus, again, does He refer all to the Father. Fifth, "And this is life eternal that they might know Me"? No; but—"that they might know Thee, and Jesus Christ, whom Thou hast sent" (v. 3). Sixth, "I have finished the work which Thou hast given me to do" (v. 4): nothing was done for self. He ascribes honour to the Father for originating and appointing that work! Finally, when He prays to be glorified, it is touching to see how He puts it: "Glorify Thou Me with Thine own self, with the glory which I had before the world was", No, no; but instead—"with the glory which I had with Thee before the world was": not for a moment would He dissociate His own glory from His Father! Truly is this altogether Lovely One "fairer than the children of men."

We have now completed the first main section of John 17, vv. 1-5, where Christ is seen praying for Himself. In the second section, vv. 6-19, He prays for the living disciples. This second section is also subdivided into two parts, though it is not easy to classify them. In vv. 6 to 12 the fundamental reason is brought out as to why the Saviour prays for His disciples and not for the world—because of their relation to Himself. Out of this grows the petition for their preservation — the essence of all intercession. In vv. 13 to 19 the Lord prays for His disciples as left here in the world, presenting their several needs as growing out of this. We shall confine ourselves now to the first sub-division.

While this prayer resolves itself into three divisions there is a most striking apparent unity about it. The substance of Christ's prayer for Himself is: Place Me in circumstances in which I may glorify Thee in the salvation of men. The substance of His prayer for the disciples is: Fit them for glorifying Thee in promoting the salvation of men, through prosecuting the work to which I have called them as My instrumental agents. The substance of His prayer for the whole company of the redeemed (vv. 20-26) is: Bring them to entire conformity to Thyself in mind, will and enjoyment that Thou mayest be glorified to the uttermost by their being saved to the uttermost. Thus the glory of the Father is the paramount consideration from the beginning to the end. A close study of the details will fully bear this out. But though everything is subordinated by Christ to the Divine glory, yet the blessings asked for the apostles and the whole company of the redeemed are viewed not only in reference to the glory of the Father directly, but to the glory of the Son, in whom and by whom the Father was to be glorified. The plea for blessing them is that "I am glorified in them" (v. 10), and the ultimate design is "that they may behold My glory" (v.24).

"The prayer of our Lord for His apostles, like the prayer for Himself, comprehends both petition and pleading. He asks blessings for them, and He states the grounds on which He asks these blessings for them. The transition at the beginning of the sixth verse is similar to that at the twentieth verse, though not so distinctly defined. There He says, 'I pray not for them alone,' i.e., the apostles (rather the entire company of disciples at that time A.W.P.), 'but for them also which shall believe in Me through their word.' Here He in effect says, 'I pray not for Myself alone, but for the men to whom I have manifested Thy name.'

"The great blessing which our Lord asks for the apostles is that they may be one, as the Father and the Son are; that is, that they may be united with Them as to mind and will, and aim and operation in the great work of glorifying God in the salvation of men. That is the ultimate object of His desire in preference to them; the other petitions are for what is necessary in order to this. The blessings necessary to the obtaining of this blessing are two: First, Conservation—'Keep them through, or in, or in reference to, Thine own name' ; 'Keep them from the evil one or the evil thing that is in the world, that they may be one, as We are.' Then, second, Consecration — 'Sanctify them through, or in reference to. Thine own name'; 'Keep petitions; all the rest is occupied with pleadings—most powerful and appropriate pleadings" (Dr. John Brown).

While it is true that in vv. 6 to 19 the Lord is praying directly and immediately for His apostles, it is clear to us that they are here viewed, as in the preceding chapters, in a **representative** character. Were this not the case, there would be no place at all in this prayer for all the others of His believing disciples at that time, for v. 20 speaks only of those who were to believe at a later date. The careful student will note that Christ was most particular to describe the ones He here intercedes for in terms which are common to all believers. It is with this understanding that we shall now proceed with our exposition.

"I have manifested Thy name unto the men which Thou gavest Me out of the world: Thine they were, and Thou gavest them Me, and they have kept Thy word" (v. 6). Four things are to be carefully noted in this and the following verses: the persons for whom Christ intercedes; the characters in which they are presented; the petitions offered on their behalf; and the particular pleas by which each separate petition is urged. It is to be noted that the Lord did not begin by asking for the blessing of His disciples; rather did He first describe the ones he was about to pray for: in vv. 6 to 10 it is presentation, in vv. 11 and 12 it is supplication. It is beautiful to see that as the Saviour here comes before the Father as intercessor, He presents "His own" along with Himself. It reminds us of His word, spoken long before by the spirit of prophecy, "Behold I and the children whom the Lord hath given Me" (Isa. 8: 18, quoted in Heb. 2: 13). It was the fulfilment of what had been so strikingly foreshadowed by the high priest of Israel: "And Aaron shall bear the names of the children of Israel in the breastplate of judgment upon his heart when he goeth in unto the holy place, for a memorial before the Lord continually." (Ex. 28:29). So here, when our great High Priest entered the presence of the Father, He bore our names on His heart before Him! That which made this possible was His own glorification, consequent upon His "finished work" (vv. 4, 5).

"I have manifested Thy name unto the men which Thou gavest Me out of the world." Here is the first proof that the Lord had more than the eleven apostles in view. He designedly employed language that was strictly applicable to all His believing people at that time. During His earthly life He had made known the Father's name to far more than the Eleven. Cor. 15: 6 speaks of the risen Saviour being seen by "over five hundred brethren at once." So, too, far more than the apostles had been given to Christ out of the world; and, again, a larger company than the apostles had "kept His word." Three things were here mentioned by Christ to recommend to the Father these objects of His petition: they were acquainted with the Father's name; they were the subjects of His distinguishing grace; they were obedient to His will. Thus the Lord Jesus spoke of what He had done, what the Father had done, and what the disciples had done.

"I have manifested Thy name unto the men which Thou gavest Me out of the world." Herein Christ fulfilled that prophecy, "I will declare Thy name unto My brethren: in the midst of the congregation will I praise Thee" (Psa. 22: 22). To make known the Father's name was to reveal Him, manifest His character, display His perfections. As we are told at the beginning of this Gospel, "No man hath seen God at any time; the only begotten Son, which is in the bosom of the Father, He hath declared Him." The Son alone was competent for this. Christ had manifested the Father's perfections in His perfect life, wondrous miracles and sublime teaching. But only those who had been given him by the Father were able to receive this manifestation. Christ has made known the Father to all the elect: "I write unto you, little children, because ye have known the Father" (1 John 2: 13). So perfectly did Christ discharge this office that He could say, "He that hath seen Me hath see the Father" (John 14: 9).

"Thine they were, and Thou gavest them Me." All creatures belong to the Father by creation (Heb. 12: 9), but this is not what is here in view. Christ is speaking of a special company which had been given to Him. The reference, then, is to the sovereign election of God, whereby He chose a definite number to be His "peculiar people"—His in a peculiar or special way. These were eternally His: "Chosen in Christ before the foundation of the world" (Eph. 1: 4); and by the immutability of His purpose of grace (Rom. 11: 29), they are always His. This plea was made by Christ to the Father not only for the urging of the petition which followed, but for the comfort of the disciples. Despised by Israel they might be, hated by men in general, the special objects of Satan's enmity; yet were they the special favourites of God. Again, this plea of Christ's affords us instruction in prayer. The more we discern the Father's interests in us, the greater our confidence when we come to Him in prayer. What assurance would be ours if, when we approached the throne of grace, we realised that the Father's heart had been set upon us from the beginning of all things!

"And Thou gavest them Me." Thine by foreordination; Mine by special donation. "The acts of the three persons of the Trinity are commensurate; of the same sphere and latitude; those whom the Father chooseth, the Son redeemeth and the Spirit quickeneth. The Father loveth none but those which are given to Christ, and Christ taketh charge of none but those that are loved by the Father. Your election will be known by your interest in Christ, and your interest in Christ by the regeneration of the Spirit. All God's flock are put into Christ's hands, and He leaveth them in the care of the Spirit: 'Elect according to the foreknowledge of God the Father, through sanctification of the Spirit, unto obedience and sprinkling of the blood of Jesus Christ' (1 Peter 1: 2). There is a chain of salvation; the beginning is from the Father, the dispensation through the Son, the application by the Spirit; all cometh from the Father, and is conveyed to us through Christ by the Spirit" (Dr. T. Manton).

"Thou gavest them Me." The elect are given to Christ, first by way of reward: "When Thou shalt make His soul an offering for sin, He shall see His seed. . . . He shall see of the travail of His soul, and be satisfied: by His knowledge shall My righteous Servant justify many; for He shall bear their iniquities. Therefore will I divide Him a portion with the great, and He shall divide the spoil with the strong" (Isa. 53: 10-12). "Ask of Me, and I shall give Thee the heathen for Thine inheritance, and the uttermost parts of the earth for Thy possession" (Psa. 2: 8). The elect were given to Christ, secondly, by way of charge. "All that the Father giveth Me shall come to Me, and him that cometh to Me I will in no wise cast out" (reject) . . . And this is the Father's will which hath sent Me. that of all which He hath given Me I should lose nothing, but should raise it up again at the last day" (John 6: 37, 39). The elect were entrusted to Christ to take care of. Thus the faithfulness of Christ to the Father is engaged on our behalf. If a single one of God's elect were to perish, the glory of the perfect Servant would be tarnished for all eternity. How absolute, then, is our security!

"And they have kept Thy Word." The first reference, no doubt, is to God's call, which went forth through Christ. When these disciples heard that word of command, they rose up, left all, and followed Him. Moreover, they had continued with Him. When many "went back and walked no more with Him," the Saviour said unto the Twelve, "Will ye also go away?" Their answer, through Peter, was prompt and unwavering: "To whom shall we go? Thou hast the words of eternal life" (John 6: 66-68); contrast 5: 38. The Lord spoke here absolutely from the standpoint of their faith, no notice being taken of their failures to apprehend that Word. How beautiful, how blessed, to see our great High Priest, notwithstanding the feebleness of their faith and their frequent unbelief, presenting the disciples before the Father according to the perfections of His own love—that love which "imputeth no evil" (1 Cor. 13: 5). They had kept the Father's Word, but O how imperfectly. But love notices not their defects, dwelling only upon their faith, submission and obedience! Satan is an accuser, and ever speaks evil of believers; but Christ, our Advocate, takes our part, and ever speaks well of us. This is the highest commendation Christ could give His people: "They have kept Thy Word."

"Now they have known that all things whatsoever Thou hast given Me are of Thee" (v. 7). The Lord continues to speak in commendatory terms of His disciples. "These are wonderful words when we consider the character of the eleven men to whom they were applied. How weak was their faith! How slender their knowledge! How shallow their spiritual attainments! How faint their hearts in the hour of danger! Yet a very little while after Jesus spoke these words they all forsook Him and fled, and one of them denied Him with an oath. No one, in short, can read the four Gospels with attention and fail to see that never had a great Master such weak servants as Jesus had in the eleven apostles. Yet these very servants were the men of whom the gracious Head of the church speaks here in high and honourable terms. The lesson before us is full of comfort and instruction. It is evident that the Lord sees far more in His believing people than they see in themselves, or than others see in them. The least degree of faith is very precious in His sight. Though it be no larger than a grain of mustard seed, it is a plant of heavenly growth, and makes a boundless difference between the possessors of it and the men of the world. The eleven apostles were weak and unstable as water; but they believed and loved their

Master when millions refused to own Him. And the language of Him who declared that a cup of cold water given in the name of a disciple should not lose its reward, shows plainly that their constancy was not forgotten' (Bishop Ryle).

It is blessed to note the characters in which Christ here presents the disciples to His Father. "It is most comforting to find that all these glorious desires for the saints our Lord grounds simply on this: that they have received the Son's testimony about the Father, and had believed surely in the Father's love. How full of blessing it is to see that we are presented before God simply as believing that love! How surely does it tell us that the pleasure of our God is this: that we should know Him in love, know Him as the Father, know Him according to the words of Him who has come out from His bosom. This is joy and liberty. And it is indeed only as having seen God in love, seen the Father and heard the Father in Jesus, that makes us the family. It is not the graces that adorn us, or the services that we render, but simply that we know the Father. It is this which distinguishes the saint from the world, and gives him his standing, as here, in the presence of the Father." (Mr. J. G. Bellett).

"For I have given unto them the words which Thou gavest Me; and they have received them, and have known surely that I came out from Thee, and they have believed that Thou didst send Me" (v. 8). The "for" which here introduces what follows explains the all things in the previous verse. The disciples had entered, by grace, into that of which the world was completely ignorant, namely, that the Father was the source of all that was given to the Son. Some "wondered" at His words and works; others, in their enmity, blasphemously attributed them to Satan. Not only had the disciples learnt that He came out from the Father, but they had perceived that the means (the "words") of bringing them into such blessing were also of the Father. The Saviour had treated them as "friends, committing to them those intimate communications of grace which the Father gave to Him, and this that they might know the Divine relationship into which His wondrous love had brought them. Nor had this been in vain. Slow of heart they truly were (as, alas! are we), yet they received the truth, and receiving it they knew that He was the Son of the Father's love. Thus does the Saviour explain how souls are brought into such nearness to the Father.

It is instructive to note the order here: "For I have given unto them the words which Thou gavest Me; and they have received them, and have known surely that I came out from Thee, and they have believed that Thou didst send Me." How this makes manifest the fact that "faith cometh by hearing, and hearing by the Word of God" (Rom. 10: 17). How plain is the lesson here taught us! If our faith is to be strengthened, deepened and increased, it can only be by our diligent attention to, prayerful meditation upon, and personal appropriation of the words of God! So, too, knowledge, spiritual knowledge—discernment and understanding—is the fruit of "receiving" God's words. It is to be noted that the initial "receiving" has preceded it. The "believing" comes last here, though the Lord Jesus admits no other faith than that which is based upon an intelligent acquaintance with His person—cf. Rom. 10: 13.

"I pray for them: I pray not for the world; but for them which Thou hast given Me; for they are Thine" (v. 9). The world here is a general name for mankind in their fallen state. There is a "fashion of this world" (1 Cor. 7: 31), a common mould, according to which the characters of men are formed. There is " a course of this world" (Eph. 2: 2), in which all walk, except those who are on the "narrow way" which leadeth unto life. All who have not been "transformed by the renewing of their minds" (Rom. 12: 2) are, as a matter of course "conformed to this world." For the unbelieving, Christ prayed not: "For whom He is the Propitiation, He is an Advocate; and for whom He died, He makes intercession, and for no others in a spiritual saving way." (Dr. Gill).

"I pray not for the world." But how is this to be harmonized with the fact that while He was on the cross the Saviour did pray for His enemies—"Father, forgive them, for they know not what they do?" It is important that we should distinguish between the prayers of Christ as the perfect Man and the prayers of Christ as Mediator. There are several of the Psalms which plainly intimate that the Lord Jesus prayed for His foes, but this was to show us that as a perfect Man, subject to that holy law which required each one to love his neighbour as himself, He harboured no revenge. He prayed for the ungodly in answer to His human duty, but not officially as the Mediator. So He taught His disciples, "Love your enemies, bless them which curse you, do good to them that hate you, and pray for them which despitefully use you, and persecute you" (Matt. 5: 44). But here in John 17 Christ is seen as the great High Priest, therefore He prays only for "His own."

"But for them which Thou hast given Me." How this should bow our hearts in adoring worship! What thanksgivings it calls for! Oh what an inestimable privilege to be one of the objects of Christ's intercession. Millions passed by unprayed for by Him; but those who belong to the "little flock" (Luke 12: 32) held up by Him before the Throne of Grace. One of the disciples asked Him, "Lord, how is it that Thou wilt manifest Thyself unto us, and not unto the world?" (John 14: 32). So may we ask, "How is it that Thou wilt pray for us, and not for the world?" Others more accomplished, with more pleasing dispositions, who daily put us to shame in many ways, left out, and we taken in! The finite mind, yea the renewed mind, can discover no answer. All that we can say is, it was the sovereign grace of the sovereign God who singled us out to be the objects of His distinguishing favors. Let the world call it selfishness in us if they will, but let us express in praise to God our profoundest gratitude, and seek to live as becometh His elect ones. Let us also follow the example of Christ here and manifest our greatest love for those who have been chosen out of the world. "As we have therefore opportunity, let us do good unto all, especially unto them who are of the household of faith" (Gal. 6: 10). But do Christ's words in John 17: 9 forbid us to pray for the wicked? No, indeed. Christ's mediatorial acts as our great High Priest are not our standard of conduct; but in His walk as the perfect Man He has left us "an example." On the cross He prayed for His enemies. So we are commended to pray for our enemies; and it is our duty to pray for all men. See Rom. 10: 1; 1 Tim. 2: 1.

"For they are Thine." In the previous verses the Saviour had described the characters of those for whom He was about to intercede, now He presents the reasons why He prayed for them. The first is, "For they are Thine." Though given to the Mediator by grant—both as a reward and as a charge—they are still the Father's; that is, He has not relinquished His right and property over them. As a father who giveth his daughter in marriage to another does not lose his fatherly propriety, so those given to Christ are still the Father's. "For they (in sharp contrast from "the world") are Thine" fixes the meaning of "Thine they were" in v. 6—"Thine not by creation, but by election. "The world" also belongs to the Father by creation! What a powerful plea was this; the ones for whom Christ was about to pray were the Father's, therefore, for His own glory and because of His affection for that which belonged to Him, He would keep them.

"And all Mine are Thine, and Thine are Mine" (v. 10). Here is the second motive for His request: the interests of the Father and the Son could not be separated; what belonged to the one belonged to the other. Indubitable proof of His absolute Deity; it is because the Saviour is one with the Father that They have rights and interests no less boundless than common. The Holy Spirit is not here mentioned, though He is certainly not to be excluded. As Dr. Manton well said, "They are the Father's children, Christ's members, and the Spirit's temples."

"And I am glorified in them" (v. 10). This was His third plea. Since the Son was the supreme Object of the Father's affections, then this was another reason for Him preserving those in whom the Saviour was glorified. What a place for us! To be the subjects of this mutual affection of the Father and the Son! The world knew Him not, Israel received Him not; but these disciples by their faith, love, and obedience, glorified Him; therefore did He make special intercession for them. And how intensely practical is this for us! The more we glorify Christ, the more confidence shall we have of His intercession for us—"Whosoever therefore shall confess Me before men, him will I confess also before My Father which is in Heaven" (Matt. 10: 32).

"And now I am no more in the world, but these are in the world, and I come to Thee. Holy Father, keep through Thine own name those whom Thou hast given Me, that they may be one, as We" (v. 11). What a touching plea is this! The Saviour reminds the Father that the disciples would be deprived of His personal care as present with them, and this would expose them the more to the world. He had been their Guide, their Guardian, their ever-present and all-sufficient Friend. And how He had borne with their infirmities, upheld them in weakness, protected them from evil! But now He was leaving them, going to the Father, and into His hands He now commits His own charge.

"But these are in the world." God

could take each saint to Heaven the very day be believed (as He did the dying thief) did He so please; but for reasons of His own He leaves them here for a shorter or longer season. He does so for His own wise purposes: "I pray not that Thou shouldest take them out of the world, but that Thou shouldest keep them from the evil" (v. 15). He gets more glory by leaving us here. As a quaint old writer said, "It is more wonderful to maintain a candle in a bucket of water than in a lantern." God's power is made perfect in our weakness (2 Cor. 12: 9). God sent Jacob and his family into Egypt that He might there exhibit before his descendants His mighty power on Pharaoh. We are left here that we might be tried: "Be not slothful, but followers of them who through faith and patience inherit the promises" (Heb. 6: 12). There is a measure of sufferings appointed (1 Thess. 3: 3), and each of us must receive his share. Another reason why we are left in the world is to make us appreciate the more the coming glory. The roughness of our pilgrim path makes us yearn for rest; our present strangership deepens our desire to be at Home.

"Holy Father, keep through Thine own name those whom Thou hast given Me." The term "holy" is here descriptive of character. The root meaning of the word is separation, and as applied to God it signifies that He is far removed from evil. But this is simply negative. God is not only elevated high above all impurity, but He is absolutely, essentially pure in Himself. That God is Holy signifies that He is lifted high above all finite creatures. "Who shall not fear Thee O Lord, and glorify Thy name? For Thou only art holy" (Rev. 15: 4).

The titles of God in Scripture are suited to the requests made of Him: "Now the Lord of peace Himself give you peace" (2 Thess. 3: 16); "Now the God of patience and consolation grant you to be like-minded one toward another" (Rom. 15: 5), where the apostle prays for brotherly forbearance among the saints. The connection in which the Saviour here addresses "the Holy Father" is striking. He was asking for the preservation and unification of His disciples, and He requests the Father to do this for them in strict accord with His holy nature. The Lord would have us know with whom we have to do; He would have us pray for an ever-deepening abhorrence of sin—"Ye that love the Lord, hate evil" (Psa. 97: 10).

"Keep through Thine own name those whom Thou hast given Me." How this brings out the value Christ sets upon us and the deep interest He has in us! About to return to the Father on high, He asks the Father that He will preserve those so dear to His heart, those for whom He bled and died. He hands them over to the care of the very One who had first given them to Him. It was as though He said: I know the Father's heart! He will take good care of them! And why was it, why is it, that we are so highly esteemed by Christ? Clearly not for any excellency which there is, intrinsically, in us. The answer must be, Because we are the Father's love-gift to the Son. It is striking to observe that just seven times in this chapter Christ speaks of those whom the Father had "given" Him—see vv. 2, 6 (twice), 9, 11, 12, 24. In John 3: 16 we learn of the Father's love to us; here in John 17 we behold the Father's love to Christ. God so loved the world as to give his only-begotten Son; and He so loved His Son as to give Him a people who, conformed to His image, shall through all eternity, show forth His praises. Marvellous fact! We are the Father's love-gift to His Son. Who then can estimate the value which Christ puts upon us! The worth of a gift depends upon the one who made it; its intrinsic value may be paltry, but when made by a loved one it is highly prized for his sake. So we, utterly unworthy in ourselves, are ever regarded by Christ in all the inestimable worth of that love of the Father which gave us to Him! Thus does the eye of our great High Priest ever look upon us with affection and delight. How this ought to endear Him to our hearts!

Little wonder then, in view of what has just been before us, that the first thing the Saviour asked for on behalf of those given to Him by the Father was their preservation. He was leaving them in a hostile world: "He asks that they may be kept from evil, from being overcome by temptation, from being crushed by persecution, from every device and assault of the Devil" (Bishop Ryle). But some find a difficulty here: why should Christ pray for their continuance in grace? Was not such a request meaningless, useless? Had He not affirmed that no sheep of His should ever perish! Ah, how futile for the finite mind to reason about spiritual and Divine things! But does Scripture throw any light on this apparently needless petition of Christ? Yes; it shows us, throughout, that God's decrees do not render void the use of means; yea, many of God's decrees are accomplished through the employment of instrumental agencies; and one of these chief means is prayer! It is the old nature, still in the Christian, which makes needful the intercession of Christ!

"That they may be one, as We." This refers not to a manifestation of ecclesiastical oneness; rather is it a oneness of personal knowledge of and fellowship with the Father and the Son, and therefore oneness in spirit, affection, and aim. It is a oneness which is the outcome not of human agreement or effort, but of Divine power, through making each and all "partakers of the Divine nature." Has this request of the Saviour been granted? It has. In Acts 4: 32 we read, "And the multitude of them that believed were of one heart and of one soul." And is it not still true that among the real people of God, despite all their minor differences, there is still a real, a fundamental, and a blessed, underlying unity—they all believe God's Word is inspired, inerrent, of final authority; they all believe in the glorious person and rest upon the all-sufficient sacrifice of the Lord Jesus Christ; they all aim at the glory of God; they all pant for the time when they shall be forever with the Lord. "One as We" shows that the union here prayed for is a Divine, spiritual, intimate, invisible, unbreakable one!

"While I was with them in the world, I kept them in Thy name; those that Thou gavest Me I have kept, and none of them is lost, but the son of perdition; that the Scripture might be fulfilled" (v. 12). "The Lord, then, in committing His own to the Father, whom in that name He was keeping whilst here, speaks of having kept them safe, save that one who was doomed to destruction. Awful lesson! that even the constant presence of Jesus fails to win where the Spirit brings not the truth home to the conscience. Does this enfeeble Scripture? On the contrary, the Scripture was thereby fulfilled. Chapter 13 referred to Judas that none should be stumbled by such an end of his ministry. Here it is rather that none should therefore doubt the Lord's care. He was not one of those given to Christ by the Father, though called to be an apostle; of those so given He had lost none. Judas was an apparent, not a real, exception, as he was not a child of God but the son of perdition. To see the awful end of so heartless a course would only give more force to His works of grace who, if He left the world for the Father, was bringing them into His own associations before the Father" (Bible Treasury).

"While I was with them in the world, I kept them in Thy name; those that Thou gavest Me I have kept." None but a Divine person could "keep" them. He had preserved them from the machinations of the world, the flesh, and the devil. None had apostasized; all had "continued" with Him in the day of His humiliation. (Luke 22: 28).

"And none of them is lost, but the son of perdition." Note carefully, He did not say, "Except the son of perdition," rather, "but the son of perdition." He belonged not to "them," that is, to those who had been given Him by the Father. The disjunctive participle is used here. as frequently in Scripture, to contrast those belonging to two different classes. Compare Matt. 12: 4, Acts 27: 22, Rev. 21: 27. Not one of them given to Christ can or will be lost. "Father, I will that they also, whom Thou hast given Me, be with Me where I am."

"That the Scripture might be fulfilled." The reference is to Psalms 41 and 109. The presence of the traitor among the apostles was one of the many proofs that the Lord Jesus was the promised Messiah. Four reasons may be suggested for Christ referring to Judas here. To show there was no failure in discharging the trust which the Father had committed to Him; to assure the disciples of this, so that their faith might not be staggered; to demonstrate that Christ had not been deceived by Judas; to declare God's hand and counsel in it—"that the Scripture might be fulfilled."

The following questions are to prepare the student for our next lesson:—

1. What is meant by "My joy fulfilled in themselves," v. 13?
2. What is meant by "they are not of the world," v. 14?
3. Why are believers left here in the world," v. 15?
4. Why the repetition of v. 14 in v. 16?
5. What is the "sanctification" of v. 17?
6. What is the meaning of v. 18?
7. How did Christ "sanctify Himself," v. 19?

Arthur W. Pink.

# GLEANINGS IN EXODUS.
### 34. The Tabernacle: Ex. 25: 1-9.

The neglect of typology and the ignorance which prevails to-day concerning the spiritual significance of the Tabernacle is one of the many solemn signs of the times. The pyramids of Egypt and the catacombs of Rome are never-failing objects of interest. The ancient abbeys of England and the temples of heathendom attract thousands every year from the ends of the earth, to admire their architectural designs and to study their historical features. But the Tabernacle of Jehovah, which possesses a charm and a claim unknown to any other building is, like its Antitype, despised and rejected of men. True, it is no longer to be seen on earth in concrete form, yet a Divinely-inspired and detailed account of it has been given to us in the Holy Scriptures. But so widely is the study of typology neglected, comparatively few among the great masses of professing Christians know anything of the Divine wonders and spiritual beauties in which the closing chapters of Exodus abound.

In our day even students of theology leave those fruitful fields to glean elsewhere. Many of them are wasting their time reading through almost countless volumes treating of the authorship of the Pentateuch, instead of poring over the sacred pages themselves. They prefer to wade through the polluted streams which the higher critics have digged, rather than drink from the pure river of the Water of Life. Even where the Divine inspiration of the books of Moses is accepted, comparatively few are occupied with their deeper teachings and blessed foreshadowings. Alas that it is so.

"The typical portions of Scripture are supremely important and as a study vastly interesting. Types are shadows. Shadows imply substance. A type has its lessons. It was the design of Jehovah to express His great thought of redemption to His people Israel in a typical or symbolic manner. By laws, ceremonies, institutions, persons and incidents, He sought to keep alive in Israel's hearts the hope of a coming Redeemer. Christ is therefore the key to Moses' gospel. This then is our advantage, that we can minutely compare type and antitype, and learn thereby the lessons of grace which bringeth salvation" ("Shadow and Substance," by G. Needham).

In our last article we dwelt upon the typical purport of the Tabernacle; here we shall say a few words concerning its doctrinal lessons. One of the chief values which the closing sections of Exodus possesses to the true people of God is that there we have set before us Divine illustrations, concrete representations, vivid pictures of the fundamental verities connected with our "great salvation." God, in His infinite condescension, graciously adapted His instructions to the spiritual intelligence of His children. An abstract statement of truth is much harder to apprehend than a visible representation of it to the eye. Just as in natural things a child is able to grasp the meaning of pictures before it learns to spell and to read, so God has first given us a full description of the Tabernacle and all its contents, setting before the eye that which is found in the N.T. Epistles in the form of doctrinal expositions. Thus by means of material symbols we are assisted to understand the better the riches of God's grace in Christ our Saviour.

The Tabernacle—the materials of which it was composed, the seven pieces of furniture, the priesthood who ministered therein, the offerings and sacrifices—is to be regarded as one great object-lesson, setting forth spiritual truth. For this reason, among others, was it designated "the Tent of the Testimony" (Num. 9: 15). There, witness was borne of "good things to come" (Heb. 10: 1). There, was proclaimed the holiness and majesty of the great Jehovah. There, were set forth the terms of communion with Him. There, was revealed the way of approach by blood-shedding. There, was exhibited the imperative need of a Divinely-appointed Mediator. There, was shown the efficacy of atonement by the sacrifice of an innocent victim in the room of the guilty. There, was established the Mercy-seat, from which God communed with the representative of His people.

Our great difficulty in seeking to interpret the portions of Scripture which now lie before us is the multitude of the revelations contained therein. By means of the Tabernacle Jehovah revealed His character and made known His purpose of redemption. There, devouring holiness and righteous indignation against sin declared the fact that God was just even while He justified. The Tabernacle was the place of sacrifice; its most vivid spectacle was the flowing and sprinkling of blood, pointing forward to the sufferings and death of Christ. It was also the place of cleansing; there was the blood for atonement and also the water for washing away the stains of defilement. So Christ "loved the Church and gave Himself for it, that He might sanctify and cleanse it, with the washing of water by the Word; that He might present it to Himself a glorious Church, not having spot or wrinkle, or any such thing, but that it should be holy and without blemish" (Eph. 5: 25-27). The Tabernacle had inner chambers, setting forth the fullness of those blessings which the believer has in Christ. In them was light, bread, and the altar of prayer—all finding their antetypical fulfilment in our blessed Redeemer.

Probably the outstanding lesson taught us through the Tabernacle was the way in which a sinner might approach God. First of all, he was most forcibly reminded that sin had separated him from God. The Tabernacle was God's dwelling-place, and it was enclosed, being encircled by walls of pure white curtains. This at once taught Israel the holiness of the One who had come to dwell in their midst; they were shut out and He was shut in. Their sinfulness unfitted them to enter His holy presence. O my reader, have you ever pondered the ineffable holiness of God, and realised that your sins have placed you at a guilty distance from Him?

But though the sanctuary of Jehovah was enclosed, there was a door through which the Israelite might enter the outer court, though further he might not advance. There, within the outer court, stood the Tabernacle proper, with its two compartments, surrounded by walls of wooden boards, and only the priests were allowed therein, and they but in the first chamber—the holy place. Beyond, lay the holy of holies, where the Shekinah glory, the visible representation of God's presence, resided between the cherubim on the mercy-seat. Into this compartment none ever entered save Moses the mediator, and Aaron the high priest one day in the year.

Marvellous is the progressive order of teaching in connection with the various objects in the Tabernacle. At the brazen altar sin was judged, and by blood-shedding put away. At the laver purification was effected. In the holy place provision was made for prayer, food and illumination; while in the holy of holies the glory of the enthroned King was displayed. The same principle of progress is also to be seen in the increasing value of the sacred vessels. Those in the outer court were of wood and brass; whereas those in the inner compartments were of wood and gold. So too the various curtains grew richer in design and embellishment, the inner vail being the costliest and most elaborate. Again, the outer court, being open, was illumined by natural light; the holy place was lit up by the light from the golden candlestick; but the holy of holies was radiated by the Shekinah glory of Jehovah. Thus the journey from the outer court into the holy of holies was from sin to purification, and from grace to glory. How blessedly did this illustrate the truth that "the path of the just is as the shining light, that shineth more and more unto the perfect day" (Prov. 4: 18).

The order in which the Tabernacle and its contents are described is most significant. The first thing mentioned is the ark (25: 10) and its covering—the mercy-seat (25: 17), which was Jehovah's throne in Israel's midst. Then comes the table (25: 23) and the candlestick (25: 31), the curtains (26: 1), and boards (26: 15) of the Tabernacle proper, with the separating veil (26: 31). Last comes the brazen altar (27: 1) and the hangings of the court (27: 9). Thus it will be seen that the order is from the interior to the exterior. It is the order of **sovereign grace**, God coming from His throne right to the outer door where the sinner was! How this reminds us of the Incarnation; the sinner in his sins could not go from earth to heaven, so God in the person of His Son came from heaven to earth, and died the Just for the unjust "that He might bring us to God (1 Peter 3: 18). Blessedly was this emphasised by Christ in His teaching— the Shepherd going after the lost sheep (Luke 15: 4), the good Samaritan journeying to where the wounded traveller lay (Luke 10: 33), etc.

"In describing the things that pertain to worship, He commences with the most precious type of all—the breast-plate the high priest wore on his heart (28: 4) and ends with the laver of brass in which Aaron's sons were to wash their hands and feet daily (30: 18). It is thus too in the book that takes up the sacrifices —Leviticus. It commences not with the offerings for sins, but the highest form of all—the burnt offering (Lev. 2: 1). **God's glory must be the first object to be established by the work of Christ, and then our need met** (Lev. 4). But that which we first apprehend is surely that which meets our need in the sin-offering. And the vast difference in the ancient and it is often years before we understand that it is a "sweet savor" sacrifice that met the need of God's heart and established His glory" (Mr. C. H. Bright in "Pictures of Salvation").

It is very striking to note that in the second description of the Tabernacle, where we have the record of its manufacture and erection, there is a notable variation—instead of beginning with the contents of the holy of holies where Jehovah dwelt, we have described the Tabernacle and curtains of the outer court, which the common people saw. Here the order is from without to within —the experimental order, the order in which Divine truth is apprehended by the soul. This same twofold order may be seen in the Epistles to the Romans and Ephesians. In the former, the Holy Spirit begins with man's sinfulness, guiltiness, and ruin; goes on to speak of God's provision in Christ, and then closes the doctrinal section by showing us the redeemed sinner in the presence of God, from whom there is no separation. In Ephesians the Spirit begins with God's eternal counsels, choosing us in Christ before the foundation of the world, and then treats of redemption and regeneration and the consequent privileges and responsibilities flowing therefrom. In Romans it is the sinner going in to God; in Ephesians, God coming out the sinner. Such is the double teaching in the twofold order of the description of the Tabernacle.

Before Jehovah gave instructions to Moses concerning the various articles in the Tabernacle, He first ordered him to require of Israel as an offering, the different materials out of which they were to be made. "And the Lord spake unto Moses, saying, Speak unto the children of Israel that they bring Me an offering: of every man that giveth it willingly with his heart ye shall take My offering" (Ex. 25: 1-2). Very beautiful is this. The materials out of which the Tabernacle was to be made were to be provided by the voluntary offerings of devoted hearts. The great Jehovah who inhabiteth the praises of eternity condescended to take up His abode in a boarded and curtained Tent, erected by those who desired His presence in their midst (see 15: 2).

Historically, we may admire the fruit of God's grace working in the hearts of His redeemed so that they willingly offered the required materials. Their offering was so spontaneous and full (see 35: 21-29) that we are told, "And they spake unto Moses, saying, the people bring much more than enough for the service of the work, which the Lord commanded to make. And Moses gave commandment, and they caused it to be proclaimed throughout the camp, saying, Let neither man nor woman make any more work for the offering of the sanctuary, so the people were restrained from bringing. For the stuff they had was sufficient for all the work to make it, and too much" (36: 5-7). But behind the historical we are to look for the spiritual, and behold here a lovely type of the voluntariness and joy of the Lord Jesus, who freely and gladly became flesh, thus providing God with a perfect Sanctuary as He tabernacled among men!

"And this is the offering which ye shall take of them; gold, and silver and brass; and blue, and purple, and scarlet, and fine linen; and goats, and rams skins dyed red, and badgers skins; and shittim wood; oil for the light, spices for anointing oil, and for sweet incense; onyx stones, and stones to be set in the ephod, and in the breastplate" (v. 3-7). Each of these articles tells forth one of the manifold perfections of Christ. The gold, His Divine glory. The silver, the redemption which He wrought and bought for us. The brass, His capacity to endure the wrath of God against our sins. The blue, His heavenly origin. The purple, His royal majesty. The scarlet, His earthly glory in a coming day. The fine linen, His holiness made manifest by His righteous walk and ways. The goats hair, His atonement. The rams skins, His devotedness to God. The badgers skins, His ability to protect His people. The shittim wood, His incorruptible humanity. The oil for the light, His Divine wisdom. The spices, His fragrance unto God. The precious stones, His priestly perfections. We do not now offer proofs for these definitions nor enlarge upon their blessedness, as, God willing, each one will come before us for fuller consideration in the articles to follow.

With the above verses should be compared Exodus 38: 24-31, where the Holy Spirit has given us the respective weights of the gold, silver and brass. Careful students have estimated there would be fully a ton and a quarter of gold, which at modern value would be worth upwards of one hundred and seventy-five thousand pounds, or eight hundred and sixty thousand dollars, but allowing for present-day purchasing values, worth much more. Of silver there would be fully four tons and a quarter, and worth forty thousand pounds or two hundred thousand dollars. Of brass (more likely, copper) there was also over four tons. In addition, there were the textile fabrics, blue, purple, scarlet and fine twined linen, besides goats' hair, rams and badgers' skins, and large quantities of shittim wood, the amounts of which are not recorded. Last, but not least, were the precious stones for the breastplate of the high priest. All of this indicates the great costliness of the Tabernacle. At modern values its materials would be worth at least a million pounds or five million dollars. How this, in type, told of God's estimate of Christ; how it shows us the Father saying, This is My Beloved Son in whom I am well pleased!

It is noteworthy that there were fifteen separate articles specified in the above verses, the factors of which are three and five—almost every numeral connected with the Tabernacle was a division or multiple of one of these. Now three is the number of **manifestation and therefore of God**—in the three Persons of the Trinity. Five is the number of grace. Putting these together, fifteen signifies, in the language of spiritual arithmetic, God's grace manifested. How eminently suited were these numerals as the predominating ones in that dwelling-place of God which pointed forward to His incarnate Son! It was in Christ, come to earth, that the grace of God was fully made known. How this shows us, again, that there is a deep meaning to the minutest detail of Holy Writ!

"And let them make Me a sanctuary; that I may dwell among them" (v. 8). Here is the leading feature to bear in mind concerning the Tabernacle; it was to be Jehovah's "sanctuary," God's dwelling-place. It is important to observe that it was not until He had redeemed a people unto Himself that God dwelt amid them on the earth. He visited Adam in Eden, He appeared to and communed with the patriarchs, He gave communications to Moses even in Egypt, but not until He had redeemed His people out of the house of bondage, not until they had been separated from their enemies at the Red Sea, not until His government over them had been established at Sinai, did He propose the making of a sanctuary, in which He might dwell among His saints.

The Tabernacle then was the pledge and proof that God had graciously brought His redeemed people into relationship with Himself, yea, into a place of nearness to Himself. So we, who once were (because of sin) far off from Him, have been made nigh by the precious blood of Christ (Eph. 2: 13). The awful distance which once separated is now gone; we have been brought "to God" (1 Peter 3: 18). O the wondrous riches of Divine mercy! First bought by Christ, then sought by the Spirit, and in consequence, brought to the Father; and that not as guilty criminals, but as happy children. Blessedly is this illustrated at the close of that wondrous parable in Luke 15. There we are shown that the one who had wasted his substance in the far country, then convicted of his deep need and brought to repentance, finally welcomed by the Father, fitted for His presence and given a seat at His table.

But as at the marriage-feast in Cana of Galilee, the best wine is reserved for the last. "And I saw a new heaven and a new earth; for the first heaven and the first earth were passed away; and there was no more sin. And I, John, saw the holy city, new Jerusalem, coming down from God out of heaven, prepared as a bride adorned for her husband. And I heard a great voice out of heaven saying, Behold, **the tabernacle of God is with men, and He will dwell with them**, and they shall be His people, and God Himself shall be with them, and be their God" (Rev. 21: 1-3). "Then the counsels of God's heart will be displayed in their consummated perfection, and, inasmuch as the former things, with all the sorrows connected with them through man's sin, will have passed away, there will be nothing to hinder the full, perfect, and blessed enjoyment arising out of the unhindered flow of God's heart to His people, and their hearts to Him, and from His perfect manifestation and their perfect worship and service" (Mr. Ed. Dennett).

"According to all that I show thee, after the pattern of the Tabernacle, and the pattern of all the instruments thereof even so shall you make it" (v. 9). It is to be noted that Moses not only received implicit instructions as to what materials the tabernacle was to be made from, and (as we shall see later) complete details as to the dimensions, plan, and furnishings thereof; but that a pattern or model was set before him, after which it was to be constructed. That this is a point of importance for us to weigh is evident from the number of times it is repeated in the Scriptures. No less than seven times are we informed that Moses was commanded to make the Sanctuary after the pattern of it which was shown him in the Mount—see Exodus 25: 9; 25: 40; 26: 30; 27: 8; Numbers 8: 4; Acts 7: 44; Heb. 8: 5. Nothing was left to man's wisdom, still less to "chance"; everything was to be in exact accordance with the Divine model. Does not this teach us that everything concerning Christ and His people has been wrought out according to the eternal purpose of Him who worketh all things after the counsel of His own will! May Divine grace enable us to rest there in perfect peace and joyous worship.

ARTHUR W. PINK.

## TRUTH AND ERROR
or
### LETTERS TO A FRIEND.

10. The Spirit and the Word (concluded).

"Then opened He their understanding that they might understand the Scriptures."—Luke 24: 45.

"When He the Spirit of Truth is come, He will guide you into all truth."—John 16: 13.

In confirmation of the preceding remarks, let me proceed to quote and examine a few passages of scripture.

1. Luke 11: 12, "When they bring you into the synagogues and unto magistrates and powers, take no thought of how or what things ye shall answer, for the Holy Ghost shall teach you in the same hour what ye ought to say." Here, then, we have the direct and immediate operation of the Spirit upon the soul, suggesting suitable truth for the occasion. Anyone reading the chapter will see that this promise is to all believers, not to the apostles alone. It refers not to what we would call miraculous inspiration, but to the ordinary operation of the Spirit. Oh, it will be said, but He does this by means of the truth. Now, what does this mean but that He suggests truth through the truth; that is, I suppose, He suggests one truth by means of another; in other words, one truth suggests another without His interference at all. But even granting that He suggests one truth by means of another, granting that this is all that is meant by the Spirit teaching, the question naturally occurs, who or what suggested the first of the series? If I stand upon the margin of some lake, and find all of a sudden ripple after ripple beating upon the grass that skirts it, I look around to see the cause of this—what began the rippling. How absurd to say, Oh, it is merely one ripple raising another and forcing it forward to the shore. I am sure it was either the wind that suddenly rose or some stone that had been cast into the water. Some such cause must have begun the series. And so with truth in the case I have referred to. Even granting that the Spirit did suggest one truth by means of another, how will this account for the suggestion of the first? This must have been done in some more direct way and by some more immediate touch. So that the difficulty still remains; only in the one case it is removed a little further back and placed a little more out of sight, as if it was a reluctance to admit the idea of God working directly, as if such an idea were only fitted to alarm and discourage the sinner.

With the daily consciousness of having within me a heart of sin, a hard and ever-rebelling heart, I know not for myself a more blessed, more precious truth than that I am the clay and God is the Potter—that it is His hand that grasps me, compassing me about, and coming in close, direct, warm contact with my naked soul. The thought of nothing but indirect dealing and communication between Him and me is desolate and cold to me beyond conception. And instead of feeling relieved and comforted by being told that the Spirit never works directly upon the soul, but only through the truth, I am cast down indeed, as if bereaved of that which was my chiefest hope, my most precious consolation in the hours of infirmity and conflict, when the flesh within and principalities and powers without assail me till I faint upon the field, and all that bears me up is the felt grasp of an inward hand, the encircling pressure of the everlasting arm.

2 Rom. 8: 26, "Likewise the Spirit also helpeth our infirmities, for we know not what we should pray for as we ought, but the Spirit Himself maketh intercession for us with groanings which cannot be uttered." This is something very distinct in regard to the working of the Holy Spirit. He helpeth our infirmities, or, as it literally implies, He takes hold of our burden, puts His shoulder under it and sustains the weight so as to prevent it crushing us. How He can do all this, simply and only through the truth,

it is hard to discover. What words can more strongly express His direct operation upon the soul? If they do not express this, I know not where words can be found to do so. But the case is far stronger when we consider the expression "groanings which cannot be uttered." How does He awaken those groanings within which cannot be clothed in words? By suggesting truth to the soul? This is absurd. If the Spirit presented truth to the soul, and in that way created these longings, then surely the soul could express these longings. If this had been said merely of the poor unlettered saints, this objection of mine might not be altogether applicable, for I know that oftentimes they cannot find words whereby to express their thoughts; but it is of all saints equally that the apostle is speaking. If in answer to all this it is said that we frequently get a glimpse of truth, natural truth, which awaken in us longings which we cannot express, I admit that such is the case; but if this be all that is affirmed by the apostle here, there was no necessity for introducing the Spirit at all. His statement in that case is most incorrect, and fitted to mislead; for He speaks of the Spirit actually making intercession for us (or in us) with those groanings which cannot be uttered. He is represented as one who has come unto us and taken up His abode in us; as one who thus carries on a work from within by means of a direct though hidden agency; as one who is so identified with us that the apostle speaks of His prayers as ours, His voice as ours, as if they were one. He is represented here as dwelling in us, filling us, using our faculties and organs as instruments for expressing Himself, till, as His operations upon the soul become more close and powerful, faculties, words, voice, give way, and nothing comes forth but the unutterable groan. This, surely, is something very direct. It conveys most plainly the idea that there is no intervention of anything (be it the truth or aught else) between the touch of the Almighty hand and the soul in which He is dwelling. It shows us a workman within, carrying on His operations there, quickening, fashioning, moulding all things to His will—bringing every part of the soul into contact with the truth that is without, by means of the pressure of His hand from within.

3. 1 Cor. 12: 3, **"No man can say that Jesus is the Lord but by the Holy Spirit."** This expression corresponds to many others in the New Testament, such as these: "Flesh and blood hath not revealed it unto thee, but My Father which is in Heaven" (Matt. 16: 17) "God, who commanded the light to shine out of darkness, hath shined in our hearts to give the light of the knowledge of the glory of God in the face of Jesus Christ" (2 Cor. 4: 6). "When it pleased God, who separated me from my mother's womb and called me by His grace, to reveal His Son in me" (Gal. 1: 5). These passages all suggest the same idea—that it is directly through the agency of the Spirit that we are enabled to call Jesus Lord, and that but for this agency we should have remained His enemies. I merely, however, take the first of them (1 Cor. 12: 3) as being the most suitable to the object which I have in view. It occurs in a chapter where the miraculous gifts of the Spirit are discoursed of, and this enables us to fix its meaning with more distinctness. Let me cite a verse or two: "There are diversities of gifts, but the same Spirit; there are diversities of operation, but it is the same God which worketh all in all; to one is given by the spirit the word of wisdom; to another the word of knowledge by the same Spirit; **to another faith by the same Spirit;** to another the gifts of healing by the same Spirit . . . **all these worketh that one and the selfsame Spirit dividing to every man severally as He will."** Such is a brief enumeration of the operations of the Spirit. In these His mode of working is to a certain extent plainly enough declared. It is direct and immediate. How otherwise is it possible that He can confer the gift of tongues, of prophecy, of healing, etc.? No one in his right mind would say that these were conferred through the truth. It must have been the direct and immediate touch of His hand upon the soul. Nothing else could have made them prophesy with tongues. Well, it is just in the midst of this statement of His works, or, rather, as the introduction of them that it is said, "No man can say that Jesus is the Lord but by the Holy Ghost." And what are we to infer from this but that He teaches the soul to own Jesus as his Lord in the same way as He teaches to prophesy. If it is said, but the passage refers to the inspired teachings of the apostles in proclaiming Jesus to others, I answer that this only confirms my argument, for if the direct agency of the Spirit was needed to enable them to declare what they knew, much more is that same agency needed to show us the

things of Christ. Hence the apostle says in another place, "For we have received not the spirit of the world, but the Spirit which is of God, that we might know the things that are freely given to us of God." 1 Cor. 2: 12.

4. Phil. 2: 13, "**It is God that worketh in you both to will and to do of His good pleasure.**" This is one of the plainest statements we could possibly have had. We are told that it is God Who worketh in us. It is an inward operation that is spoken of — an operation which none could perform but He who has access to the inmost recesses of the soul. But this is not all. We are told more particularly in what way He operates upon us—"both to will and to do." The springs of willing and doing must both be operated upon. The hand of the Physician must be laid upon the diseased organ, else there can be no cure. Hence David prayed, "Incline my heart unto Thy testimonies" (Psa. 119: 36).

5. Ezk. 36: 26, "**A new heart also will I give you, and a new spirit will I put within you, and I will take away the stony heart out of your flesh, and I will give you a heart of flesh, and I will put My Spirit within you and cause you to walk in My statutes.**" If this does not denote a direct inward operation upon the soul, removing what is old and imparting what is new, we know not how language can describe it. To twist such expressions and say that they merely refer to the outward means which God uses is to do the most reckless violence to the scripture that can be conceived.

6. Eph. 1: 17, "**The God of our Lord Jesus Christ, the Father of glory, gives unto you the Spirit of wisdom and revelation, in (or in order to) the knowledge of Him; the eyes of your understanding being enlightened that ye may know what is the hope of His calling.**" Here the apostle prays that the Holy Spirit may be given to the Ephesians. And he speaks of Him as the Spirit that imparts wisdom, the Spirit that reveals truth. This Spirit is given for the purpose "of enlightening the eyes of the understanding." Surely the enlightening the eyes of the understanding must be an inward process, a thing accomplished not through the truth, but in order to their understanding the truth. The truth could not be known and felt without this inward enlightening work of the Spirit. I know that in another sense the truth does enlighten; and I would not on any account undervalue the truth. I would rejoice in it as "a lamp unto my feet and a light unto my path." But when I find this kind of enlightenment declared to be all that the Spirit does; when I find His direct work upon the soul denied, then it is time to declare most broadly the whole truth of God. And here I would offer a single remark upon these passages which speak of the Spirit being given "to them that obey Him" (Acts 5: 23), and of His being "received through faith." In these our opponents triumph. They need not. I am quite willing to take scripture plainly and naturally, just as I find it. I admit at once these passages all refer to those blessings which we receive after believing and in consequence of it. I have no doubt about that. It is quite plain that we do receive far more abundantly of the Spirit after believing. But this has nothing at all to do with the question. Admitting that we receive the Spirit after believing, does that prove that we do not receive Him also before believing, and in order to believing? The truth is that there is one class of passages which speak of what God does in us and for us before believing, and another which speak of what He does in us and for us after believing. And both of these declarations must be held fast. Our opponents admit the one, but deny the other.

7. Eph. 3: 16, "**Strengthened with might by His Spirit in the inner man, that Christ may dwell in your hearts by faith.**" Here is another testimony equally explicit to the inward operation of the Holy Spirit. The Spirit is said to "strengthen," and He is said to do this in order "that Christ may dwell in our hearts by faith." What meaning has this language if there be no working of the Spirit but the outward and the indirect, through the medium of the truth alone? I might refer to other passages in this Epistle—1: 19, 3: 20. In these we read of the "exceeding greatness of His power to us-ward, who believe according to the working of His mighty power" and "the power who worketh in us." Surely no simple-minded reader can fail to see in these expressions the assertion of a power working in us, as different from that which the word possesses. It is along with the word, but it is not in the word, but directly in us. In what stronger or more explicit language could this direct power have been stated?

Let these references suffice. I could quote many more equally strong and satisfactory, but there is no need. No simple-minded student of the Word of God can read such passages without being convinced that the Holy Spirit works **by a direct, inward operation upon the soul.**

But perhaps some may here object to much of what has been now adduced in favour of the direct inworking of the Spirit by saying that they do not deny that He works thus in the souls of believers, but that there is no proof that He works thus in the soul of the sinner **before** he believes, and in order to his believing. With regard to this, I submit the following remarks:—

1. It is an objection that can come only from a few of the new sect, for most of them maintain that the Spirit never works directly in any, but always indirectly, whether upon believer or unbeliever.

2. There is no scriptural reason for supposing that there is one kind of operation in the believer and another in the unbeliever—that in the case of the one it is direct, and in the case of the other indirect.

3. If the direct work of the Spirit be needed to carry on the work, much more to begin with. The first step is the most difficult, and if an unbeliever can take that first step without the direct operation of the Spirit, a believer may easily take all the rest. On the other hand, if a believer needs the direct power of the Spirit to carry on the work, much more does the sinner need that power to begin it.

4. There are passages which imply the direct work of the Spirit before believing.

Ezek. 27: 14. **"I will put My Spirit within you, and ye shall live"**—where the living is the effect of God's putting His Spirit within them.

Zech. 12: 10. **"I will pour upon the house of David . . . and they shall look upon Me Whom they have pierced and mourn"**—where the looking to Christ is the effect of God's Spirit being poured out, and where the persons spoken of were evidently unconverted, who had never looked before.

John 16: 8. **"He will convince the world of sin, because they believe not on Me"**—where it is plain that the Spirit's work must be before and in order to believing, for it is to show men the sin of which they are guilty by remaining in unbelief. That is, He comes up to an unbelieving soul and shows its awful guilt, and then convinces it of righteousness, i.e., leads it to Christ, the righteous One.

Acts 5: 31. **"Him hath God exalted with His right hand to be a Prince and a Saviour for to give repentance to Israel, and forgiveness of sins."** Here repentance is said to be the gift of the risen Jesus. It is He Who gives repentance, and He gives it just as directly and decidedly as He gives pardon. It will be said, Yes, Christ gives repentance by sending His messenger to proclaim that truth through which repentance is produced. Now, I have no doubt that He does this, but is this all that He does? Is this all that the above passage implies? Surely to give repentance is something very different from merely sending men to proclaim the truth which has the tendency to produce repentance. To give a man an estate is something very different from sending instructions to a man as to how he can contrive to procure it for himself. To give repentance has reference to something far more efficacious, as well as far more gracious and loving, than merely to preach to men the truth by which repentance may be wrought in them.

Acts 9: 2. **"The hand of the Lord was with them, and a great number believed, and turned to the Lord."** In this statement it is plainly implied that it was the hand or power of the Lord that was the cause of the believing of this great number. Had it not been for this, none would have believed or turned. The first act of believing and turning is thus plainly ascribed to the hand of God—to that mighty power which is here said to have accompanied the preaching of the Word. It is not said that the hand of the Lord was in the Word, but "with them," that is, with the disciples, for they were men full of the Holy Ghost. The words of praying men are blessed for the conversion of sinners. Why? Because their prayers and faith draw down a peculiar blessing which might not otherwise have accompanied the Gospel. This could not be the case if the power were in the Word alone.

Acts 16: 14. **"Whose heart the Lord opened that she attended to the things which were spoken of Paul."** This is very clear. Lydia's heart was shut before, but the Lord opened it. It was so shut that she did not even attend to what was spoken, far less believe them. God opened her closed heart. Then she began to attend to the truth; and after having attended to it she believed it.

In one of a series of lectures upon the leading tenets of the new sect we have the following comment upon this passage:—"He was speaking heart-searching and heart-opening truth; and by this truth which she heard He opened her mind so to attend to what was spoken as to believe it. . . . This gives us no idea of any other opening of the heart than that which takes place by means of the inspired testimony of the Apostles." Where were the faculties of the lecturer wandering to when he penned the above statement? It is singularly absurd and contradictory. Lydia's heart is closed against the truth; and how is this removed? By letting in the truth, says the lecturer! Lydia does not even attend unto the truth. How is this to be overcome? By the truth moving her attention to itself! But how can the truth make her attentive if she will not attend to it? Suppose I wish to enter a house which has been shut against me and secured by two gates, an outer and an inner. I come up to the outer gate, for it is only through it that I can pass to the inner. I knock, but no attention is given to my summons; the dweller is within, but he declines to admit me, even to a conversation at the door. I ask a friend who is nigh what I can do. He very simply tells me that I must go into the house and converse with the inmate and persuade him to open the door to me! In vain I tell him that the doors are closed, and that I cannot get in, even at the outer. He just repeats his advice that, in order to get them opened, I must go in and persuade the owner to unbar them; adding, perhaps, the remark that any other way than this would be an encroachment upon human responsibility. Is it not clear, then, that God's opening of Lydia's heart was in order that she might attend to and receive that truth which otherwise she never would have allowed to enter? Paul preached the same "heart-searching and heart-opening truth" to many others in the same place; and how, let me ask, is it said of Lydia alone that the Lord opened her heart? Surely He did something for her which He did not do for the others? and yet we are told by some that He works equally in all! Why, then, is it not said He opened the hearts of all if He had done the same in regard to all? We are told that He did no more for Lydia than for any other! Yet the passage says He opened her heart, and does not say that He opened the hearts of others. Oh, but it will be said, Lydia yielded, while the rest persisted in unbelief. And what does this amount to but just this, that the expression "The Lord opened the heart of Lydia" means that Lydia opened her own heart, and attended and believed!

1 John 5: 20. "We know that the Son of God is come, and hath given us an understanding that we may know Him that it is true." Here the word translated "understanding" is very explicit. It does not mean knowledge, but the power by which we receive knowledge — the understanding. It is the same word in the original as in Matt. 22: 37, "with all thy soul and with all thy mind"; Eph. 1: 18, "The eyes of your understanding being enlightened"; 4: 18, "Having the understanding darkened"; Heb. 8: 10, "I will put My laws into their mind." These passages show us the true sense of the term. And, taking all these together, how very strong and decided is the apostle's statement, "He hath given us an understanding that we may know Him that is true."

At the same time, while I maintain all this, I am quite aware of the many passages in which the truth is spoken of as the instrument or channel through which the Spirit works. I am far from wishing to deny this or to depreciate the value of the Word. All I wish is to preserve you from running into the most fatal error of the present day that the Spirit is "in the Word," and that He only operates through the Word, and in no other way. This I consider to be not only unscriptural, but thoroughly poisonous to the soul. It is one of Satan's devices in these last days for producing a religion like the real shape and form of godliness that multitudes will be deceived by it, cheating themselves into the belief that they are sure of Heaven when they have never been born again. Such religion has no depth. It is meagre, lean and shallow. It is self-taught, self-produced religion. For where is the indwelling, inworking Spirit in all? Where is the living Saviour Himself? Ah! He has been superseded by an abstract something that men call truth; and, as Israel made their God-given law a substitute for the living Father, so men are now making the Christ-given Gospel a substitute for the living Son!

I shall conclude this long letter with one observation on which I should gladly have dwelt had there been space. It is this. The expression "influences of the Spirit" is not a scriptural one, and ought to be avoided. The Bible always speaks of the working of the Spirit, or the indwelling of the Spirit — not of His mere influences. And there is a most important difference between these two things. In the former case, everything connected with the Spirit's operations would be direct and personal; in the latter there is nothing but a vagueness which may mean anything or nothing at all. The influence of a person is very different from his personal presence and operation. And we ought to be upon our guard against this form of expression, which I am sorry to think extends far beyond the holders of the new theology. It is of an indwelling Spirit that the Bible speaks. It is of an indwelling Spirit that Christ promises "He dwelleth with you, and shall be in you" John 16: 17. We are not certain objects acted upon by some distant influence, as the sea is by the moon; we are the vessels which the Spirit fills; we are temples in which the Spirit dwells. "Know ye not that ye are the temple of God, and that the Spirit of God dwelleth in you?"

### THUS SAITH THE LORD:

"The hand of God was to give them one heart to do the commandments." 2 Chron. 30: 12.

"Create in me a clean heart, O God, and renew a right spirit within me." Psalm 51: 10.

"Quicken us, and we will call on Thy name." Psalm 80: 18.

"Thou sendest forth Thy Spirit; they are created." Psalm 119: 18.

"Give me understanding, that I may learn Thy commandments." Psalm 119: 73.

"Incline not mine heart to any evil thing." Psalm 141: 4.

"I shall put My Spirit in you, and ye shall live." Ezek. 37: 14.

"He dwelleth in you, and shall be in you." John 14: 17.

When He, the Spirit of Truth, is come, He will guide you into all truth." John 16: 13.

"The love of God is shed abroad in our hearts by the Holy Ghost which is given unto us." Rom. 5: 5.

"Stephen, a man full of the Holy Ghost." Acts 6: 5.

"Be filled with the Spirit." Eph. 5: 18.

"The Holy Ghost who dwelleth in us." 2 Tim. 1: 24.

H. Bonar (1851).

## WAITING.

This is the posture in which the Lord delights to find His people. It is hard to maintain it, because our natural impatience and restlessness would hurry us along our chosen paths without delay. But it is well to curb the eagerness and self-confidence that would inevitably lead us into danger, and He seeks to hold us back until we are filled with a sense of entire dependence upon Himself. He is often saying to us, as he said to the first disciples, "Wait for the promise of the Father" when He commanded them to tarry in the city of Jerusalem until endued with power from on high.

Hence we are told to wait on Him for strength. "Wait on the Lord; be of good courage, and He shall strengthen thine heart; wait, I say, on the Lord" (Psalm 27: 14). So it is written, "They that wait upon the Lord shall renew their strength; they shall mount up with wings as eagles; they shall run and not be weary; they shall walk, and not faint" (Isa. 40: 31). But we never get the strength until we reach the end of our own resources. Even the devoted apostle was made to hear His voice, "My grace is sufficient for thee; for My strength is made perfect in weakness. Most gladly, therefore, will I rather glory in my infirmities that the power of Christ may rest (tabernacle) upon me. Therefore, I take pleasure in infirmities, in reproaches, in necessities, in persecutions, in distresses, for Christ's sake; for when I am weak, then am I strong" (2 Cor. 12: 9, 10). Blessed paradox, which the believer well understands!

We must wait upon Him only. "My soul, wait thou only upon God; for my expectation is from Him" (Psalm 62: 5). It is good to be shut up to Him alone, looking nowhere else for needed comfort, or light, or power. There is too much waiting upon men to know what they think before daring to express an opinion, and altogether too much reliance upon an arm of flesh for deliverance and direction. Greater singleness of aim, with the mind and heart entirely and intently fixed upon the Lord, would make the path plain to many who walk in darkness. "Behold, as the eyes of servants look unto the hand of their masters, and as the eyes of a maiden unto the hand of her mistress, so our eyes wait upon the Lord our God" (Psalm 123: 2).

We must wait **patiently**. "Rest in the Lord, and wait patiently for Him" (Psalm 37: 7). Calmness and forbearance and silence become His followers when they remember that as a sheep before her shearers is dumb, so He opened not His mouth. "Say not thou, I will recompense evil, but wait on the Lord, and He shall save thee" (Prov. 20: 22). If tempted to fretfulness and resentment and self-vindication, let us remember the word of the Holy Spirit, "It is good that a man should both hope and quietly wait for the salvation of the Lord" (Lam. 3: 26).

We must wait **prayerfully**. "I waited patiently for the Lord; and He inclined unto me and heard my cry" (Psalm 40: 1). Sometimes we may say with the suffering One, "I am weary of my crying; my throat is dried: mine eyes fail while I wait for my God" (Psalm 69: 3); but we have His unchanging promises, and can therefore add, with the prophet, "I will look unto the Lord; I will wait for the God of my salvation; my God will hear me" (Micah 7: 7). Praying breath was never spent in vain when the supplicant can pour forth the desire of a sincere heart, "O Lord, be gracious unto us; we have waited for Thee"; for His unchanging promise tells us "they shall not be ashamed that wait for Me" (Isa. 33: 2, 49: 23).

We can still wait upon Him in **darkness**. "I will wait upon the Lord that hideth His face from the house of Jacob, and I will look for Him" (Isa. 8: 17). We may not at all understand His dealings with us, but His word comes through the gloom, "Who is among you that feareth the Lord, that obeyeth the voice of His servant, that walketh in darkness and hath no light? Let him trust in the name of the Lord and stay upon his God" (Isa. 1: 10). Thank God, we can say to Him, "the darkness hideth not from Thee; but the night shineth as the day: the darkness and the light are both alike unto Thee" (Psalm 139: 12).

We must wait for the **precious fruit** of toil and suffering. "Behold, the husbandman waiteth for the precious fruit of the earth, and hath long patience for it, until he receive the early and latter rains" (Jas. 5: 7). So must we wait, knowing that in due season we shall reap if we faint not. God knows that His chastening is not joyous, but grievous, for if it were not hard to bear it would not be chastening at all, and yet He tells us to look to the great afterward, when beautiful and immortal fruit will grow on the plant watered with our tears.

So we are to wait for the **coming of the Lord**. The early disciples who turned to God from idols were taught by the Holy Spirit "to wait for His Son from Heaven, whom He raised from the dead, even Jesus, which delivered us from the wrath to come" (1 Thess. 1: 10); and it was the crowning commendation betowed upon another church that they were waiting "for the coming of our Lord Jesus Christ" (1 Cor. 1: 7). It is not death, it is not Heaven, for which we wait, but it is Himself. Well may we heed His word, "Let your loins be girded about, and your lights burning, and ye yourselves like unto men that wait for their lord" (Luke 12: 35, 36).

Thank God the time to wait is not long. No one can read the New Testament without seeing that the Lord Jesus, and the Holy Spirit through the apostles, everywhere represent the second advent as imminent. Nor will anyone with proper respect for the authority of the inspired scriptures try to explain away these plain and positive testimonies. "The Lord is at hand" (Phil. 4: 5). "For yet a little while and He that shall come will come, and will not tarry" (Heb. 10: 37); "For the coming of the Lord draweth nigh" (James 5: 8); "Surely I come quickly" (Rev. 22:20), mean nothing but His personal return. It must be remembered, however, that in the bright home where Jesus and our beloved ones now wait for us a thousand years are as one day; and hence it has not been two days since He ascended from the Mount of Olives.

—DR. J. H. BROOKES.

---

Are you praying daily for God's blessing on this magazine, and for an enlarging of its circulation?

## DIVINE CHASTISEMENT.

"My Son, despise not thou the chastening of the Lord, nor faint when thou art rebuked of Him" (Heb. 12: 5).

Not all chastisement is sanctified to the recipient of it. Some are hardened thereby; others are crushed beneath it. Much depends on the spirit in which afflictions are received. There is no virtue in trials and troubles in themselves: it is only as they are blest by God that the Christian is profited thereby. As Heb. 12: 11 informs us, it is those who are "exercised" under God's rod that bring forth "the peaceable fruit of righteousness." A sensitive conscience and a tender heart are the needed adjuncts.

In our text the Christian is warned against two entirely different dangers: despise not, despair not. These are two extremes against which it is ever necessary to keep a sharp look-out. Just as every truth of scripture has its balancing counterpart, so has every evil its opposite. On the one hand there is a haughty spirit which laughs at the rod, a stubborn will which refuses to be humbled thereby. On the other hand, there is a fainting which utterly sinks beneath it and gives way to despair. Spurgeon said, "The way of righteousness is a difficult pass between two mountains of error, and the great secret of the Christian's life is to wind his way along the narrow valley."

### 1. Despising the Rod.

There are a number of ways in which Christians may "despise" God's chastenings. We mention four of them:

**1. By callousness.** To be stoical is the policy of carnal wisdom—make the best of a bad job. The man of the world knows no better plan than to grit his teeth and brave things out. Having no Divine Comforter, Counsellor or Physician, he has to fall back on his own poor resources. It is inexpressibly sad when we see a child of God conducting himself as does a child of the Devil. For a Christian to defy adversities is to "despise" chastisement. Instead of hardening himself to endure stoically, there should be a melting of the heart.

**2. By complaining.** This is what the Hebrews did in the wilderness; and there are still many murmurers in Israel's camp. A little sickness, and we become so cross that our friends are afraid to come near us. A few days in bed, and we fret and fume like a bullock unaccustomed to the yoke. We peevishly ask, Why this affliction? What have I done to deserve it? We look around with envious eyes, and are discontented because others are carrying a lighter load. Beware, my reader: it goes hard with murmurers. God always chastises twice if we are not humbled by the first. Remind yourself of how much dross there yet is among the gold. View the corruptions of your own heart, and marvel that God has not smitten you twice as severely. "My Son, despise not thou the chastening of the Lord."

**3. By criticisms.** How often we question the usefulness of chastisement. As Christians we seem to have little more spiritual good sense than we had natural wisdom as children. As boys we thought that the rod was the least necessary thing in the home. It is so with the children of God. When things go as we like them, when some unexpected temporal blessing is bestowed, we have no difficulty in ascribing all to a kind Providence. But when our plans are thwarted, when losses are ours, it is very different. Yet, is it not written, "I form the light and create darkness. I make peace and create evil: I the Lord do all these things" (Isa. 45: 7).

How often is the thing formed ready to complain "Why hast thou made me thus?" We say, I cannot see how this can possibly profit my soul. If I had better health I could attend the house of prayer more frequently! If I had been spared those losses in business I would have more money for the Lord's work! What good can possibly come of this calamity? Like Jacob, we exclaim: "All these things are against me." What is this but to "despise" the rod? Shall thy ignorance challenge God's wisdom? Shall thy shortsightedness arraign omniscience?

**4. By carelessness.** So many fail to mend their ways. The exhortation of our text is much needed by all of us. There are many who have "despised" the rod, and in consequence they have not profited thereby. Many a Christian has been corrected by God, but in vain. Sickness, reverses, bereavements have come, but they have not been sanctified by prayerful self-examination. O brethren and sisters, take heed. If God be chastening thee "consider your ways" (Hag. 1: 5), "ponder the path of thy feet" (Prov. 4: 26). Be assured that there is some reason for the chastening. Many a Christian would not have been chastised half so severely had he diligently inquired the cause of it.

### 2. Fainting Under It.

Having been warned against "despising" the rod, now we are admonished not to give way to despair under it. There are at least three ways in which the Christian may "faint" beneath the Lord's rebukes:—

1. **When he gives up all exertion.** This is done when we sink down in despondency. The smitten one concludes that it is more than he can possibly endure. His heart fails him; darkness swallows him up; the sun of hope is eclipsed, and the voice of thanksgiving is silent. To "faint" means rendering ourselves unfit for the discharge of our duties. When a person faints, he is rendered motionless. How many Christians are ready to completely give up the fight when adversity enters their life. How many are rendered quite inert when trouble comes their way. How many, by their attitude, say, God's hand is heavy upon me: I can do nothing. Ah, beloved, "sorrow not, even as others which have no hope" (1 Thess. 4: 13). "Faint not" when thou art rebuked of Him." Go to the Lord about it: recognise His hand in it. Remember thine afflictions are among the "all things" which work together for good.

2. **When he questions his sonship.** There are not a few Christians who, when the rod descends upon them, conclude that they are not sons of God after all. They forget that it is written "Many are the afflictions of the righteous" (Psa. 34: 19)), and that "we must through much tribulation enter the kingdom of God" (Acts 14: 22). One says, "But if I were His child I should not be in this poverty, misery, pain." Listen to verse 8: "But if ye be without chastisement, whereof all are partakers, then are ye bastards, and not sons." Learn, then, to look upon trials as proofs of God's love—purging, pruning, purifying thee. The father of a family does not concern himself much about those on the outside of his household: it is they who are within whom he guards and guides, nurtures and conforms to his will. So it is with God.

3. **When we despair.** Some indulge the fancy that they will never get out of their trouble. One says, I have prayed and prayed, but the clouds have not lifted. Then comfort yourself with this reflection: It is always the darkest hour that precedes the down. Therefore, "faint not" when thou art rebuked of Him. But, says another, I have pleaded His promise, and things are no better. I thought He delivered those who called upon Him; I have called, and He has not answered, and I fear He never will. What, child of God, speak of thy Father thus! You say He will never leave off smiting because He has smitten so long. Rather say He has now smitten so long I must soon be delivered. Despise not: faint not. May divine grace preserve both writer and reader from either sinful extreme.

—ARTHUR W. PINK.

---

N.B.—Several of the leading thoughts of the above we owe to a sermon by the late C. H. Spurgeon.

---

# UNANSWERED PRAYER.

It is well to inquire into the reason why prayer is so often poured out in vain. It may be sincerely offered, and yet the answer, at least in the form and manner in which the petition was presented, is withheld. In such instances many are prone to charge God foolishly, complaining that He is unfaithful to His promises, instead of tracing the cause of their disappointment to their own failure. A little examination of the Scriptures would bring to light some of the clouds that hide the Father's face, some of the barriers that rise between us and hinder the going forth of our supplications to a successful issue at the foot of the throne.

First, a wordly spirit will prevent acceptable prayer. Jericho as a type of the world, stood at the very entrance into Canaan, and was doomed to utter destruction. The ransomed of the Lord were strictly charged to keep themselves from the accursed thing, and to touch nothing that belonged to the city. Yet Achan saw, and coveted, and took a goodly Babylonish garment, and two hundred sheckles of silver and a wedge of gold. The result was defeat and disaster at the town of Ai. Joshua fell upon his face in dismay, and in an agony of entreaty, but the answer came, "Get thee up; wherefore liest thou thus on thy face? Israel hath sinned" (Josh. 7:10). His prayer was not heard, nor did victory perch again upon his banner, until the sin was exposed and punished.

Second, indulged iniquity will shut out all access to the mercy-seat. "If I regard iniquity in my heart, the Lord will not hear me" (Psalm 66:18). "Behold, the Lord's hand is not shortened, that it cannot save; either His ear heavy, that it cannot hear: but your iniquities have separated between you and your God, and your sins have hid His face from you, that He will not hear" (Isa. 59:1-2).

Third, formality in prayer hurls it back unaccepted and unanswered. "Bring no more vain oblations: incense is an abomination unto Me; the new moons and sabbaths, the calling of assemblies, I cannot, away with: it is iniquity, even the solemn meeting. Your new moons and your appointed feasts My soul hateth they are a trouble unto Me; I am weary to bear them. And when ye spread forth your hands, I will hide Mine eyes from you; yea, when ye make many prayers, I will not hear" (Isa. 1:13). The Pharisees were famous for praying, but Jesus said to them, "Ye hypocrits! Well did Isaiah prophesy of you, saying, This people draweth nigh unto Me with their mouth, and honoureth Me with their lips; but their heart is far from Me," (Matt. 15:7, Alas! judged by this rule, who can wonder that the professing Christian body is so powerless in prayer.

Fourth, resistance of the Holy Spirit renders all supplication inoperative. Of Israel, it is said, "they made their hearts as an adamant stone, lest they should hear the law, and the words, which the Lord of hosts hath sent by His Spirit in the former prophets: therefore came a great wrath from the Lord of hosts. Therefore it has come to pass, that as He cried, and they would not hear; so they cried, and I would not hear, saith the Lord of Hosts" (Zechariah 7:12-13). Very weighty in the light of this truth become the admonitions of the New Testament, addressed, be it remembered, only to believers: "Grieve not the Holy Spirit of God, whereby ye are sealed unto the day of redemption" (Eph. 4:30); "Quench not the Spirit" (I Thess. 5:19).

Fifth, disregard of truth revealed in the inspired Scriptures is another insuperable barrier to acceptable prayer. "He that turneth away his ear from hearing the law, even his prayer shall be an abomination" (Prov. 28:9). "When once the Master of the house is risen up, and hath shut too the door, and ye begin to stand without, and to knock at the door, saying, Lord, Lord, open unto us: and He shall answer and say unto you, I know you not whence ye are: then shall ye begin to say, We have eaten and drunk in Thy presence, and Thou hast taught in our streets" (Luke 13:25-23). They will pray, but their prayers will be unanswered because they received not the teaching of our Lord.

Sixth, unbelief drags many a prayer back to earth, that otherwise would go soaring to the skies. "If any of you lack wisdom, let him ask of God, that giveth to all liberally, and upbraideth not: and it shall be given him. But let him ask in faith, nothing wavering. For he that wavereth is like a wave of the sea driven with the wind and is tossed. For let not that man think that he shall receive anything of the Lord." (James 1:5-7). But "all things are possible to him that believeth;" and well may we cry out with the father of the child, that was vexed with a demon, "Lord, I believe; help Thou mine unbelief" (Matt. 9:23-24). Thank God! faith is His gift, and we can go to our Lord with the prayer of the apostles in our hearts, "Increase our faith" (Luke 17:5).

Seventh, perhaps the most common cause of failure in prayer is found in the solemn admonition of the Holy Spirit, "Ye ask, and receive not, because ye ask amiss, that ye may consume it upon your lusts," or "desires," or as the Revised Version has it "that ye may spend it on your pleasures" (James 4:3). What mixed motives we have in prayer. How much of self intrudes even into the presence of the Majesty on high! We may be somewhat under the constraining love of Christ, and aim with some degree of sincerity at His glory as the supreme end; but an honest examination of our hearts in the light of His truth, and under the guidance of His Spirit, would probably reveal much personal ambition, and a desire for our own gratification. The prayers we offer for the conversion of others may minister, if we are not watchful, to our vanity, or spring chiefly from a desire to secure our comfort.

Dr. J. H. Brookes.

*(Continued from page 217.)*

against you" is defamation of character. This last is doubly painful to sensitive temperaments, finding its realisation in the countless calumnies which the Devil is never weary of inventing in order to intensify the sufferings of the children of God. The words "persecuted for righteousness' sake" and "for My sake" caution us to see to it that we are opposed and hated only because we are the followers of the Lord Jesus, and not on account of our own misconduct or injudicious behaviour.

Persecution has ever been the lot of God's people. Cain slew Abel—and why? "Because his own works were evil, and his brother's righteous." 1 John 3: 12.) Joseph was persecuted by his brethren, and down in Egypt he was cast into prison for righteousness' sake. (Gen. 37). Moses was reviled again and again; see Ex. 5: 21; 14: 11; 16: 2; 17: 2, etc. Samuel was rejected; 1 Sam. 8: 5. Elijah was despised (1 Kings 18: 17) and persecuted (1 Kings 19: 2). Miciah was hated (1 Kings 18: 17). Nehemiah was oppressed and defamed (Neh. 4). The Saviour Himself, the Faithful Witness of God, was put to death by the people to whom He ministered. Stephen was stoned, Peter and John cast into prison, James beheaded, while the entire course of the apostle Paul was on long series of bitter and relentless persecutions.

It is true that the persecution of the saints to-day is in a much milder form than it assumed in other ages; nevertheless, it is just as real. Through the goodness of God we have long been protected from legal persecution, but the enmity of the Serpent finds other ways and means of expressing itself. Let persecuted Christians remember that comforting truth, "For unto you it is given in the behalf of Christ, not only to believe on Him, but also to suffer for His sake (Phil. 1: 29). The words of Christ in John 15 have never been repealed: "If ye were of the world, the world would love his own; but because ye are not of the world, but I have chosen you out of the world, therefore the world hateth you. Remember the word that I said unto you: The servant is not greater than his Lord. If they have persecuted Me they will also persecute you; if they have kept my saying, they will keep yours also (vv. 19, 20). The world's hatred manifests itself in derision, reproach, slander, ostracism. May Divine grace enable us to heed that word: "If when ye do well and suffer for it ye take it patiently, this is acceptable to God" (1 Peter 2: 29).

The Lord Jesus here pronounced blessed or happy those who, through devotion to Him, would be called upon to suffer. They are "blessed" because such are given the unspeakable privilege of having fellowship with the sufferings of the Saviour. They are "blessed" because such tribulation worketh patience, and patience experience, and experience hope, and such a hope that will not make hem ashamed. They are "blessed" because they shall be fully recompensed in the Day to come. Here is rich comfort indeed. Let not the soldier of the cross be dismayed because the fiery darts of the Wicked One are hurled against him; rather let him gird on more firmly the divinely-provided armour. Let not the child of God become discouraged because his efforts to please Christ make some of those who call themselves by His name speak evil of him. Let not the Christian imagine that fiery trials are an evidence of God's disapproval.

"Rejoice, and be exceeding glad." Not only are the afflictions which faithfulness to Christ involves, to be patiently endured, but they are to be received with joy and gladness. And this for a threefold reason: they come upon us for Christ's sake—if He suffered so much for us, how we should rejoice if called upon to suffer a little for Him; they bring us into fellowship with a noble company of martyrs—to meet with afflictions associates us with the prophets and apostles, and in such company reproach becomes praise, and dishonour glory; they are promised a 'great reward in Heaven." Verily, we may rejoice, however fierce the present conflict may be. Having deliberately chosen to suffer with Christ rather than enjoy the pleasures of sin for a season, we must also reign with Him, according to His own sure promise (Rom. 8: 17). Remember Peter and John, who "departed from the presence of the council rejoicing that they were counted worthy to suffer shame for His name" (Acts 5: 41). So, too, Paul and Silas, in the Philippian dungeon and with backs bleeding, "sang praises unto God" (Acts 16: 25). So of others we are told that they "took joyfully the spoiling of their goods, knowing in themselves that they had in Heaven a better and an enduring substance" (Heb. 10: 34). May Divine Grace enable all maligned, misunderstood and oppressed saints of God to draw from these precious words of Christ that comfort and strength which they need.

ARTHUR W. PINK.

# STUDIES IN THE SCRIPTURES

VOL. V     NOV., 1926     NO. 11

"Search the Scriptures" John 5:39.

Copyright in all English-speaking Countries.

Editor: Arthur W. Pink, 22 Parramatta Road, Summer Hill, N.S.W., Australia.
Hon. Agent in U.S.A.: Mr. C. S. Pressel, 559 Dupont Ave., York, Penna.

Price: 10 cents per copy; $1.00 or 5/- per year.

## THE BEATITUDES AND CHRIST.

Our meditations upon the Beatitudes would not be complete unless they turned our thoughts to the person of our blessed Lord. As we have endeavoured to show, they describe the character and conduct of a Christian, and as Christian character is nothing more or less than being experimentally conformed to the image of God's Son we must turn to Him for the perfect pattern. In the Lord Jesus Christ we find the brightest manifestations and the highest exemplifications of the different spiritual graces which are found, dimly reflected, in His followers. Not one or two but all of these perfections were displayed by Him, for He is not only "lovely," but "altogether lovely." May the Holy Spirit who is here to glorify Him take now of the things of Christ and show them unto us.

First, "Blessed are the poor in spirit." Most blessed is it to see how the Scriptures speak of Him who was rich becoming poor for our sakes, that we through His poverty might be rich. Great indeed was the poverty into which He entered. Born of parents who were poor in this world's goods, He commenced His earthly life in a manger. During His youth and early manhood, He toiled at the carpenter's bench. After His public ministry had begun He declared that though the foxes had their holes and the birds of the air their nests, the Son of Man had not where to lay His head. If we trace out the Messianic utterances recorded in the Psalms by the Spirit of prophecy, we shall find that again and again He confessed to God His poverty of spirit: "I am poor and sorrowful" (Psa. 69:29); and, "Bow down Thine ear, O Jehovah, for I am poor and needy" (Psa. 86:1); and again, "For I am poor and needy, and My heart is wounded within Me" (Psa. 109:22).

"Blessed are they that mourn." Christ was indeed the chief Mourner. Old Testament prophecy contemplated Him as "the Man of Sorrows and acquainted with grief." See Him "grieved for the hardness of their hearts" (Mark 3:5). Behold Him "sighing" ere He healed the deaf and dumb men (Mark 7:4). Mark Him weeping by the graveside of Lazarus. Hear His lamentation over the beloved city "O Jerusalem, Jerusalem . . . how often have I gathered thy children together" (Matt. 23:37). Draw near and reverently behold Him in the gloom of Gethsemane, pouring out His petitions to the Father "with strong crying and tears" (Heb. 5:7). Bow in worshipful wonderment as you hear Him crying from the cross, "My God, My God, Why hast Thou forsaken Me?" Hearken to His plaintive plea, "Is it nothing to you, all ye that pass by? Behold, and see if there be any sorrow like unto My Sorrow" (Lam. 1:12).

Third, "Blessed are the meek." A score of examples might be drawn from the Gospels illustrating the lovely lowliness of the incarnate Lord of glory. Mark it in the men selected by Him to be His ambassadors: He chose not the wise, the learned, the great, the noble, but poor fisherman for the most part. Witness it in the company which He kept: He sought not the rich and renowned, but was "the Friend of publicans and sinners." See it in the miracles which He wrought: again and again He enjoined the healed to go and tell no man what had been done for them. Behold it in the unobtrusiveness of His service: unlike the hypocrites who sounded a trumpet before them, He

*(Continued on page 264)*

## IMPORTANT NOTICES

Set of twelve issues for **1922**, unbound, $1.00 or 5/-. Bound $1.65 or 7/-.

1923, 1924, 1925 same as 1922.

Note: We cannot break a set or now supply any **single** 1925 issues.

Subscription—price: **$1.00** or **5/-** per year to any address in the world.

Change of Address: Please notify me promptly of any change of address, and be certain to give both old and new address.

Non-subscribers receiving this Magazine regularly will understand their subscription has been entered by a friend.

Copies lost in the mail duplicated only if we are notified promptly.

## CONTENTS

| | |
|---|---|
| The Gospel of John (John 17: 13-19) | 242 |
| Gleanings in Exodus | 249 |
| Truth and Error | 254 |
| Headship | 257 |

## THE GOSPEL OF JOHN

### 59. Christ Interceding Continued: John 17: 13-19.

The following is an Analysis of the passage which is to be before us:—

1. Christ's desire for His disciples' joy v. 13.
2. The disciples hated by the world v. 14.
3. Christ's prayer for their preservation v. 15.
4. The disciples indentified with Christ in separation from the world v. 16.
5. Christ's prayer for their sanctification v. 17.
6. The disciples sent into the world as Christ was v. 18.
7. Christ's provision for their sanctification v. 19.

One chief reason why the Lord Jesus uttered audibly the wonderful prayer recorded in John 17 in the hearing of His apostles was, that they might be instructed and comforted thereby, and not the apostles only, but all His people since then. This is clear from v. 13: "And now come I to Thee; and these things I speak in the world that (in order that) they might have My joy fulfilled in themselves." "He addresses His Father as taking His own place in departing, and giving His disciples theirs (that is, His own), with regard to the Father and to the world, after He had gone away to be glorified with the Father. The whole chapter is essentially putting the disciples in His own place, after laying the ground for it in His own glorifying and work. It is, save the last verses, His place on earth. As He was divinely in heaven, and showed a divine, heavenly character on earth, so (He being glorified as man in heaven) they, united with Him, were in turn to display the same. Hence we have first the place He personally takes, and the Work which entitled them to it." (Mr. J. N. Darby).

The above quotation (rather clumsily worded) will repay careful thought. It is to be noted that the final ground on which the Saviour asked to be glorified was not His own personal perfections not His essential oneness with the Father, but, instead, that **Work** which He completed here below. In this He presented a valid and sure title **for us** to join Him in the same heavenly blessedness, and also laid the foundation for us taking His place here below. Mark how this is emphasised all through: First, "I have given them the words which Thou gavest **Me**" (v. 8). Second, "that they might have My joy fulfilled in themselves" (v. 13). Third, "they are not of the world, even as I am not of the world" (v. 16). Fourth, "As Thou hast sent Me into the world, even so have I sent them into the world" (v. 18). Fifth, "I sanctify **Myself** that they also might be **sanctified**" (v. 19). Sixth, "the glory which Thou gavest Me, I have given them" (v. 22). Seventh, "that the love wherewith Thou hast loved **Me** may be in them" (v. 26). What a place! What a privilege! What an honor! Amazing the grace and the love which bestowed it.

Wondrous is the position we occupy, the place which is ours—the same place of blessing which **Christ** enjoyed when He was here. It is true that we are blest through Christ, but that is not all the truth, nor by any means the most striking part of it: we are also blest **with Him**. The love wherewith the Father had loved the Son, should be in the disciples. They should enter into the consciousness of it, and thus would His joy be fulfilled in them. It is this that we are called to, the enjoyment in this world of the love which Christ knew here below His Father's love. What was His delight? Was it from the world? Surely not. He was in the world, but never of it; His joy was from and in the Father. And He has communicated to us the means which ministers to this joy: "I have given unto them the words which Thou gavest Me" (v. 8).

The above aspect of truth is further developed in John 17 in the sevenfold way in which the Lord Jesus has identified us with Himself. First there is identity in fellowship: "As Thou hast given Him power over all flesh that He should give eternal life (Himself, see 1 John 1:1) to as many as Thou hast given Him" (v. 2). Second, identity of spirit and aim: "that they may be one as We" (v. 11). Third, identity in separation: "they are not of the world even as I am not of the world" (v. 14). Fourth, identity of mission, "as Thou hast sent Me into the world, even so have I sent them into the world" (v. 18). Fifth, identify in fellowship: "As Thou Father art in Me, and I in Thee, that they also may be one in Us" (v. 21). Sixth, identity of imparted glory: "The glory which Thou gavest Me I have given them" (v. 22). Seventh, identity in love: "that the world may know that Thou hast sent Me, and hast loved them, as Thou hast loved Me" (v. 23).

Another thing which it is blessed to behold is that, in this Prayer the Lord Jesus renders an account of His work to the Father, and this in seven particulars: First, He had glorified the Father on earth (v. 4). Second, He had finished the work which had been given Him to do (v. 4). Third, He had manifested the Father's name unto His own (v. 6). Fourth, He had given them them the Father's words (vv. 8, 14). Fifth, He had kept them as a Shepherd keeps his sheep (v. 12). Sixth, He had esnt them forth into the world (v. 18). Seventh, He had given them the glory which the Father had bestowed upon Him (v. 22)—mark the "I have" in each verse. How striking it is to note that in His work among the saints everything was in connection with the Father: it was the Father He had glorified; it was the Father's name He had manifested; etc.

The portion which is now to engage our attention is the second division of the second section of this Prayer. In the first section, vv. 1-5, the Saviour prays for Himself. In the second section, vv. 6-19, He prays for His disciples. From v 6 to v 12, He is principally engaged in presenting to the Father the persons of those for whom He was about to intercede, interspersing two petitions for their preservation and unification. In vv. 13-19, He continues His supplicaions on their behalf, v. 13 being the transitional point between the two sub-divisions.

"And now I come to Thee; and these things I speak in the world, that they may have My joy fulfilled in themselves" (v. 13). Thought it be by no means easy to trace the connection between this verse and those which precede and follow, yet the meaning of its contents is clear and blessed. The Saviour would not only have His people safe in eternity, but He desires them to be happy here and now: He would have them enter into His joy. It was for this reason He had uttered this Prayer while He was here upon earth. How this reveals the affections of our great High Priest! He might have offered this Prayer in silence to the Father, so that we had known nothing of its gracious and comforting details. But that would not have satisfied the heart of the Lord Jesus. He spoke audibly so that the apostles might hear Him, and He has caused it to be written down too, so that we also might know of His deep interest in us. How it behoves us, then, to prayerfully read and re-read and meditate frequently upon what is here recorded for our peace, our edification, our happiness!

"And now come I to Thee." The commentators are divided as to whether these words signify. And now I address Thee in prayer, or, And now I am leaving the earth and returning to Thee. Probably both senses are to be combined. The whole of this Prayer was in view of His almost immediate departure from the world and His ascension on high. But it is more than this. As pointed out in the introductory remarks of our first article on John 17, what we have here is also a pattern, a sample we might almost say, of the intercession which the Mediator is now making at God's right hand. This Prayer was first uttered on earth, therefore the "now I come to Thee" would signify, I supplicate before Thy Throne of Grace. This Prayer is now being repeated in Heaven (whether audibly or not we cannot say), and for that, Christ had to return to the Father, hence "now I come to Thee" would have this additional force.

In the verse before us there is both declaration and supplication. The Saviour is pressing His suit on behalf of those whom the Father had given Him. In view of His own departure, and their condition in the world, he justifies His earnestness in prayer for them. I am leaving them, therefore I must make provision for them. I approach Thee on their behalf; I am speaking aloud for their benefit; I have let them know that I am to be restored to that glory which I had with Thee before the world was; I have given them the assurance that they are the objects of Thy distinguishing favour, and that they are Thy love-gift to Me; I have let them see how deeply concerned I am about their preservation and unification—and all of this that "they might have My joy fulfilled in themselves."

"These things I speak in the world, that they might have My joy fulfilled in themselves." In the immediate application to the apostles, we understand our Lord's reference to be: In view of their deep dejection, I have sought to turn their sorrow into joy, by permitting them to hear Me commending them and their cause, with such cheerful confidence, to My Father and their Father. But this by no means exhausts the scope of His words here. There was a more specific reference in His mind, something which was designed for the instruction and consolation of all His people.

"That they might have **My joy** fulfilled in themselves." **What joy?** The joy that He had at that very time, the joy which had been portion of His heart all through those thirty-three years while He tabernacled among men. It was the joy of **fellowship with the Father**. It was this which He had before Him, when, speaking by the Spirit of prophecy long before, He said: "The Lord is the portion of Mine inheritance and of My cup: Thou maintainest My lot. The lines are fallen unto Me in pleasant places; yea, I have a goodly heritage. I will bless the Lord, who hath given Me counsel: My reins also instruct Me in the night seasons. I have set the Lord always before Me: because He is at My right hand, I shall not be moved. Therefore My heart is glad, and My glory rejoiceth" (Psa. 16:5-9). Though a Man of Sorrows and acquainted with grief, yet 'the joy of the Lord "was His "strength" (Neh. 8:10). It was to this He referred when He said to the disciples. "I have meat to eat" (**a satisfying portion**) that ye know not of" (John 4:32).

That they might have My joy fulfilled in themselves." This was what the heart of the Saviour craved for His people, and for this He had made full provision. In this Prayer, Christ makes it known that we have been brought into the same position before the Father that He had held, and just in proportion as we consciously enter into it, His joy is fulfilled in us. As the result of His finished work every barrier has been removed, the veil has been rent, a "new and living way" has been opened for us, and therefore have we access into "the Holiest of all," and are invited to "draw near with a true heart in full assurance of faith" (Heb. 10:19-22). **His Father is our Father**; His relation to God—that of Son—is now ours; for "because ye are sons, God hath sent forth the Spirit of His Son into your hearts, crying, Abba, Father" (Gal. 4:6). Therefore, does the Holy Spirit tell us, "Truly our fellowship is with the Father, and with His Son Jesus Christ. And these things write we unto you, THAT **your joy may be full**" (1 John 1:3-4).

It is blessed to mark how solicitious the Saviour was over the happiness of His people. When He departed He sent the Holy Spirit to be their Comforter. In His Paschal Discourse He said. "These things have I spoken unto you, that My joy might remain in you, and **your joy** might be full" (15:11). In His instructions He bade them: "Ask and ye shall receive, that **your joy** may be full" (16:24). A miserable Christian is therefore a self-contradiction. A joyless Christian is one who is out of communion with the Father: other objects have engaged his heart, and in consequence he walks not in the light of His countenance. What is the remedy? To confess our sins to God; to put away everything which hinders our communion with Him; to make regular use of the means which He has graciously provided for the maintenance of our joy—the Word, prayer, meditation, the daily occupation of the heart with Christ, dwelling constantly on the glorious future that awaits us, proclaiming to others the unsearchable riches of Christ.

"I have given them Thy word; and the world hath hated them" (v. 14). The connection of this with the previous verse is easy to perceive. In v. 8, the Lord had said, "I have given unto them the **words** which Thou gavest Me": this means more than that He had expounded to them the Old Testament Scriptures. The reference, we believe, is to what we read of in Isaiah 50:4: "The Lord God hath given Me the tongue of the learned, that I should know how to speak a word in season to him that is weary: He wakeneth morning by morning. He wakeneth Mine ear to hear, as the learned." Each morning had the perfect Servant waited upon the Father for **His** message or messages for each day, and those messages had been faithfully delivered. But here He says, "I have given them Thy **word."** It was the testimony of what the Father was—**that** was the source of **His** joy, and now would be of **theirs.** **"And** the world hath hated them": "In proportion as they had their joy in God, would it be realised how far the world was away from Him, and it would hate them as not of it. The light would bring its shadows, and they would be identified with Him in sorrow and joy alike" (Numerical Bible).

"And the world hath hated them, because they are not of the world" (v. 14). The inhabitants of this world are fully under the dominion of its "Prince," and led by him are wholly taken up with the things of time and sense, namely, all that is "not of the Father" (1 John 2:16). Therefore do the men of the world bear an implacable hatred to Christ and His people, because "they are not of the world." Once Christians were "of the world," they followed its "course," and were fully "conformed" to its policy, its principles, its aims. But grace has delivered them from this "present evil world" (Gal. 1:4), so that they now have new affections, new interests, a new Master. They have been separated from the world, and in proportion as they follow Christ their lives **condemn** the world (Heb. 11:7). Therefore does the world hate them: it secretly plots against them, it inwardly curses them, it says all manner of evil against them, it opposes them, it rejoices when any evil befalls them.

"Even as I am not of the world." "The first man is of the earth, earthy: the second man is the Lord from heaven" (1 Cor. 15:47). Christ never was of the world. He was "holy, harmless, undefiled, **separate** from sinners" (Heb. 7:26). So He declared to the Jews:
"Ye are from beneath; I am from above; ye are of this world; I am not of this world" (John 8:23). But **how** is it also true of His people that **they** are "not of the world?" Because, "If any man be in Christ he is a new creation" (2 Cor. 5:17). In consequence of this, he is a "partaker of the heavenly calling" (Heb. 3:1), his "citizenship is in heaven" (Phil. 3:20), he has been begotten unto an heavenly inheritance (1 Peter 1:3-5). In view of this, he is but a "stranger and pilgrim" here, journeying to his Home on High.

"I have given them Thy word; and the world hath hated them, because they are not of the world, even as I am not of the world." This is another argument or plea—their **danger**—by which the Saviour urges His petition for their preservation. They were being left by Him in the midst of an hostile world, therefore were they in sore need of protection. They no longer had anything in common. They could have no fellowship with the world: they could not take part in its worship: they could not further its plans. Therefore would they be despised, boycotted, persecuted. "They also that render evil for good are mine adversaries; **because** I follow the thing that is good" (Psa. 38:20). "For Herod feared John, knowing that he was a **just** man and an **holy"** (Mark 6:20). "Marvel not, my brethren, if the world hate you" (1 John 3:13). The Saviour knowing that the world would not change, therefore besought the Father on behalf of those whom He left here.

"I pray not that Thou shouldest take them out of the world, but that Thou shouldest keep them from the evil" (v. 15). "This also He speaks, most assuredly, for the instruction of the hearers of His prayer. He thus admits that it might be reasonable to ask this: on the one hand, it must appear to the disciples a good and desirable thing, while on the other hand, by declining such a prayer intimates that it would be the reverse . . . . So, also, contrary to the deep desire which all future disciples would feel: a desire which is not to be compared, however, with that of Elijah, oppressed by despondency (1 Kings 19: 4), nor to be regarded as the desire of lethargy, but such as the apostle expressed in Phil. 1:23. In their first conversion and joy almost all more or less feel a desire to be at once with Him above. And often we think concerning others, Well for them now to die, for then would be safe in Heaven! But the Lord knows better, and we should learn a better lesson from His words on this occasion. He asked not for this, then ask it not thyself, either for thyself or for others! Reply to thine own desires to depart, nevertheless, it is better, for it is more needful, to remain in the flesh and in the world. Content thyself with praying for thy preservation, until thou hast fulfilled all thy work" (Stier). Bishop Ryle has pointed out that, Three of the only prayers not granted to saints, recorded in Scripture, are the prayers of Moses, Elijah, Jonah to be 'taken out of the world.'" How very striking!

"I pray not that Thou shouldest take them out of the world, but that Thou shouldest keep them from the evil." In v. 11 Christ had said, "Holy Father, keep through Thine own name those whom Thou hast given Me," here He amplifies for the benefit of His disciples—"keep them from the evil." The Greek word for "evil" may be translated either "Evil One" or "evil things": probably both are included. "Keep them from the Author of evil, and from evil itself; from sin, from the power and snares of the Devil, from destruction, until their course is run. Satan is the author; the world is the bait; sin is the hook. Keep them from the Devil that they may not come under his power; from the world, that they may not be deceived by its allurements" (Dr. Manton). A spiritual victory over it is therefore be ter than a total exemption from it. Thus the Lord, again teaches us here how to pray: not to be delivered from the world, but from its evil. That Christ asked the Father to "keep us" shows that it is not within our power to keep ourselves: "kept by the power of God through faith unto salvation ready to be revealed in the last time" (I Peter 1:5).

God has many ways of keeping us, but they may be reduced to two: by His Spirit or His providence. The one is inward, the other is outward. By the power of the Holy Spirit the evil within us is restrained: "I also withheld thee from sinning against Me" (Gen. 20:6). By the Spirit grace is imparted to us: "I will put My fear in their hearts, that they shall not depart from Me" (Jer. 32:40). By His providences He removes occasions to and objects of sin: "For the rod of the wicked shall not rest upon the lot of the righteous; lest the righteous put forth their hands unto iniquity" (Psa. 125:3). "God is faithful, who will not suffer you to be tempted above that ye are able; but will with the temptation also make a way to escape, that ye may be able to bear it" (1 Cor. 10:13).

The fact that we are unable to keep ourselves should work in us the spirit of dependancy. Our daily confession should be, "O our God, wilt Thou not judge them? For we have no might against this great company that cometh against us; neither know we what to do: but our eyes are upon Thee" (2 Chron. 20:12); our daily prayer should be, "Lead us not into temptation, but deliver us from evil." The fact that God is able and willing to keep us should inspire confidence, deepen assurance, and fill us with praise: "I know whom I have believed, and am persuaded that He is able to keep that which I have committed unto Him against that day." Just as the diver, encased in his watertight suit is surrounded by water, but preserved from it, so the believer, living in this evil world is kept by the mighty power of God, His arm encircling us.

"They are not of the world, even as I am not of the world" (v. 16). The same words are found in v. 14, but in a different connection: there He was stating the chief reason why the world hated them; here He is advancing a reason why He asked the Father to keep them from evil—because "they are not of the world." The truth of this verse applies in a sevenfold way: First, Christians have a different **standing** from those who belong to the world: their standing is in Adam ours in Christ; they are under condemnation, we "accepted in the Beloved." Second, we possess a different **nature**: theirs is born of the flesh, ours "of the Spirit"; theirs is evil and corrupt, ours holy and Divine. Third, we serve a different Master: they are of their father the Devil, and the desires of their father they do; we serve the Lord Christ. Fourth, we have a different **aim**: theirs is to please self, ours to glorify God. Fifth, we have a different **citizenship**: theirs is on earth; ours in heaven. Sixth, we live a different **life**: far below the standard set before us it is true: nevertheless, no Christian (in the general tenor of his conduct) goes to the same excess of sin as does the worldling. Seventh, we have a different **destiny**: theirs is the Lake of Fire, ours is the Father's House on High. The "world" is a system built up away from God, and from it we have been taken delivered.

separated. The Lord grant needed grace to us all that we manifest this in our daily walk.

"They are not of the world, even as I am not of the world." "It is a fact and not an obligation, though the firmest ground of obligation. They are not of the world, not merely they ought not to be; whilst if they are not, it is grievious inconsistency to seem to be of the world. It is false to our relationship for we are the Father's and given to the rejected Son who has done with the world; and if it be said that this is to bring in everlasting and heavenly relationships now, be it so: this is exactly what Christianity means in principle and practice. It is faith possessing Christ who gives the believer His own place of relationship and acceptance on high, as well as of testimony apart from His rejection by the world below; which He has to make good in words and ways, in spirit and conversation, whilst waiting for the Lord . . . That the world improves for Christ or His own is as false as that the flesh can ameliorate. It is the light become darkness! It is the natural man knowing enough to forego what is shameless, and invested with a religious veil; it is the world essentially occupying itself with the things of God in profession, but in reality of the world where commonsense suffices for its services and its worship, and the mind of Christ would be altogether inappliable. What a triumph to the enemy! It is just what we see in Christendom; and nothing irritates so much as the refusal so to walk, worship or serve.

"It does not matter how loudly you denounce or protest: if you join the world, they will not mind your words, and you are faithless to Christ. Nor does it matter how much grace and patience you show: if you keep apart as not of the world, you incur enmity and hatred, and contempt. A disciples is not above his Master; but every one that is perfected shall be as his Master. To act as not of the world is felt to be its strongest condemnation! And no meekness or love can make it palatable. Nor does God intend that it should, for He means it as part of the testimony to His Son.. And as the world neither receives nor understands the Father's Word, so it hates those who have and act on that Word" (Bible Treasury).

"Sanctify them through Thy truth: Thy Word is truth" (v. 17). On no detail in this Prayer, perhaps, has there been wider difference of opinion than on this verse. Those who regard vv. 6-19 as containing our Lord's intercession for the apostles only (among whom is Dr. J. Brown as well as several other eminent expositors), understand this to mean: Consecrate them, (as were Israel's priests of old) to the important mission that lies before them, i.e., by anointing them with the Holy Spirit. But against this view there are, in our judgment, insuperable objections. Not only is it, we think, abundantly clear, that the Saviour was here praying for all His people, but the preposition used in this verse precludes such a thought: it is "Sanctify them **through (by) Thy** truth." Had it been a matter of setting apart unto ministerial duties it would have been "Sanctify them **for (unto) Thy** truth."

The subject of **sanctification** is a deeply important one; one on which much ignorance prevails, and we are tempted to turn aside and discuss it at some length; but this would be beside the scope of our present work; suffice it now if we offer a bare outline. First of all, the word **"sanctify"** (so "holy") has one uniform meaning throughout Scripture, namely, **to set apart**; usually but not always, some one or some thing set apart unto God for His use. The word never has reference to inward cleansing, still less to the eradication of the carnal nature. Take its usage in 17:19: "For their sake I **sanctify Myself.**" This can **only** mean, For their sakes **I** set **Myself apart.**

In Jude 1, we read of those who are "sanctified by God **the Father.**" The reference there is to His eternal predestination of the elect when He set them apart in Christ from our doomed race. In Heb. 10:10 (cf. Heb. 13:12) we read of being sanctified "through the offering of the body **of Jesus Christ,** once for all." The reference there is to our being set apart by ransom from those who are the captives of Satan. In 2 Thess. 2:13 and 1 Peter 1:2, we read of "sanctification **of the Spirit."** The reference there is to the new birth, when He sets us apart from those who are dead in trespasses and sins. Here in John 17:17 sanctification is "by **the Truth,"** that is, by the written Word of God. The sanctification of the Father, of Jesus Christ and of the Spirit, each have to do with that which is **positional** and **absolute,** admitting of no degrees, concerned not with a gradual process, but with what is complete and final. But "sanctification by the Truth" is **practical** and **progressive.** Just so far as I walk according to God's Word shall I be **separated** from evil. Thus we discover a most intimate connection between these two petitions of Christ for His own: "keep them from the evil." (v. 15), "Sanctify them by Thy truth" (v. 17): the former is secured by the latter. So also we may perceive the close relation of v. 17 to v. 16: "They are not of the world, even as I am not of the world"—now "Sanctify them by Thy truth": because they **are not** of the world, cause them to walk in separation from it.

"Thy Word is truth." The written Word is (not "contains") unadulterated truth, because its Author cannot lie. In it there is no error. Because the Word is God's truth it is of final authority. By it every thing is to be tested. By it our thoughts are to be formed and our conduct is to be regulated. Just because God's Word is **truth it sanctifies** those who obey it: "According to the faith of God's elect, and the acknowledging of the truth **which is after godliness**" (Titus 1:1). If then the Word is truth what a high value we should put upon it. If it is by the truth we are sanctified, how dearly we should prize it. How solemn too is the converse: if truth **separates** from evil, error **conducts into** evil. It was so at the beginning: it was believing the Devil's lie which plunged our race into sin and death! Then beware of error: as poison is to the body, so is error to the soul. Shun those who **deny** any part of God's truth as you would a deadly plague: "Take heed **what ye hear**" (Mark 4:24).

"As Thou hast sent Me into the world, even so have I also sent them into the world" (v. 18). Wonderful statement is this, anticipatory of what He says in 20:21: "as My Father hath sent Me, so send I you." How evident that Christ **has** given us **His** place—His place of acceptance on high, His place of witness here below! But those who witness here below have a special character: it is as those belonging to **Heaven** that we are called upon to bear testimony in the world. Christ did not belong to the world, He was the Heavenly One come down to earth; so we, as identified with Him, as partakers of the heavenly calling, are now commissioned to represent Him here below. What a proof that we **are not** "of the world!" It is only as first "chosen out of the world," that we can be "sent into the world!" That this is not limited to the apostles is clear from 1 John 4:17, which is speaking of **all** believers—"as He is, so are we in this world."

"As Thou hast sent Me into the world, even so have I sent them into the world." Christ was sent here to reveal the Father, to show forth His glory so we are sent into the world to show forth Christ's glory, which is to the glory of the Father. Christ was sent here on an errand of mercy, to seek and to save that which was lost; so we are here as His agents, His instruments, to preach His gospel, to tell a world dead in sin of One who is mighty to save. Christ was here "full of grace and truth"; so we are to commend our Master by gracious and faithful lives. Christ was here as the Holy One in the midst of a scene of corruption; so we are to be the salt of the earth." Christ was here as the Light: so we are to shine as lights in this dark place. Christ was furnished with the Spirit, who anointed, filled, and led Him; so we have received the Spirit, to anoint, fill and guide us. Christ was ever about His Father's business, pleasing not Himself but ever making the most of His brief sojourn here below; so we are to redeem the time, to be instant in season and out of season, always abounding in the work of the Lord. It is thus that Christ is "glorified" **in** us (v. 10). What a dignity this gives to our calling!

"As Thou hast sent Me into the world, even so have I also sent them into the world." The connection of this verse to the previous one is most significant. There the Saviour had prayed the Father to sanctify by the Truth those that He was leaving behind; here He adds, I have sent them into the world. This is a plea to support His petition. It was as though He had said: 'Father, Those for whom I am interceding are to be **My** representatives here below, as I have been **Thy** Representative; therefore separate them from the pollutions of this evil world, fill them with the spirit of devotedness, that they may be examples of holy living. It is to be noted that when Christ first sent forth the Twelve, He instructed them: "Go not into the way of the Gentiles, and into any city of the Samaritans enter ye not. But go rather to the lost sheep of the house of Israel" (Matt. 10:5-6). But now He sends them into the "world," to preach the Gospel to every creature.

The chosen Nation does not occupy the place of distinctive blessing during this Dispensation; Christianity bears a witness to Jew and Gentile alike.

"And for their sakes I sanctify Myself, that they also might be sanctified through the truth" (v. 19). "This is the second plea advanced by Christ in support of His petition in v. 17: He had urged their commission, now His own merit. Justice might interpose and say, 'They are unworthy; but Christ saith, 'I sanctify Myself for them.' He dealeth with the Father not only by way of entreaty, but merit; and applieth Himself not only to the goodwill of the Father, as His beloved One, but to His justice, as One that was ready to lay down His life as a satisfaction" (Dr. Manton).

"And for their sakes I sanctify Myself." Just as there is a **double** meaning to the hour" (v. 1), and "I come to Thee" (v. 13) etc., so is there to "I sanctify Myself." Its first and most obvious reference is to **the Cross.** I, the great High Priest, set apart Myself for My people—I devote Myself as the Lamb of God to be slain for them, see Heb. 10:14. In saying He did this that they might be "sanctified by the truth," He affirmed that His own official sanctification was the **meritorious cause** of their being sanctified practically. In declaring that He sanctified Himself, the Lord Jesus called attention to how **freely** and **voluntarily** He entered upon His sacrificial service. There was no necessity or compulsion: He laid down His life of Himself (John 10:18). This He did for **"their** sakes," namely, the whole company of God's elect—another sure proof that **all** His people are in view throughout this Prayer! "Christ also loved the **Church,** and gave Himself for it; that He might **sanctify** and cleanse it" (Eph. 5:25, 26)! "Wherefore Jesus also, that He might sanctify **the people** with His own blood, suffered without the gate" (Heb. 13:12)!

"And for their sakes I sanctify Myself, that they also might be sanctified through the truth." The deeper and ultimate reference of Christ in these words was to His being set apart on High as the glorified Man, the Object of His people's affections, contemplation, and worship. "He set Himself apart as a heavenly man above the heavens, a glorified man in the glory, in order that all truth might shine forth in Him, in His Person, raised up from the dead by the glory of the Father—all that the Father is, being thus displayed in Him; the testimony of divine righteousness, of divine love, of divine power; the perfect model of that which man was according to the counsels of God, and as the expression of His power morally and in glory—the image of the invisible God, the Son, and in glory. Jesus set Himself apart, in this place, in order that the disciples might be sanctified by the communication to them of what He was; for this communication was the truth, and created them in the image of that which it revealed. So that it was the Father's glory revealed by Him on earth, and the glory into which He had ascended as man; for this is the complete result—the illustration in glory of the way in which He had set Himself apart for God, but on behalf of His own. Thus there is not only the forming and governing of the thoughts by the Word, setting us apart morally to God; but the blessed affections flowing from our having this truth in the Person of Christ, our hearts connected with Him in grace" (Mr. J. N. Darby).

The following questions are to prepare the reader for our closing study on John 17:—

1. How many series of sevens can you find in John 17?
2. What is the unity prayed for in v. 21?
3. What is the "glory" of v. 22?
4. What is the unity of v. 23?
5. What is the connection of v. 24?
6. Why "righteous" Father v. 25?
7. What is the meaning of v. 26.

ARTHUR W. PINK.

## GLEANINGS IN EXODUS.

### 35. The Ark: Exodus 25:10-16.

Of the seven pieces of furniture which were found in the Tabernacle the Holy Spirit has described first the ark and the mercy-seat. Though these two are intimately related, so intimately that together they formed one complete whole—the mercy-seat being the cover or lid of the ark—yet are they mentioned, and are therefore to be considered, separately. The ark was a wooden chest, slightly over four feet in length and about two and a half feet broad and high. The wood of which it was made was overlaid with gold, both within and without, so that nothing save gold was visible to the eye.

The great importance of the ark is clear from several considerations. When Jehovah gave instructions to Moses concerning the Tabernacle, He began with the ark. It was first in order because first in importance. Before any details were communicated concerning the sanctuary itself, before a word was told Moses about its court and chambers, its priesthood and ritual, its furniture and garniture, minute directons were given regarding the ark; without the ark the whole service of the Tabernacle had been meaningless and valueless, for it was upon it, as His throne, that God dwelt. The ark was the object to which the brazen altar pointed, the sacrifice of which gave right of access to the worshipper, who came to the ark representatively in the person of the high priest. It was the first of the holy vessels to be made, and made by Moses himself (Deut. 10 : 1-5). It was the place where the tables of the law were preserved. Its pre-eminence above all the other vessels was shown in the days of Solomon, for the ark alone was transferred from the tabernacle to the Temple.

"The ark was a symbol that God was present among His people, that His covenant blessing was resting upon them. It was the most sacred and glorious instrument of the sanctuary; yea, the whole sanctuary was built for no other end, but to be as it were a house, an habitation for the ark (see Exodus 26 : 33). Hence sanctification proceeded unto all the parts of it; for, as Solomon observed, the places were holy whereunto the ark of God came, 2 Chron. 8 : 11" (A. Saphir). We shall consider the ark in seven connections.

### 1. Its Significance.

The ark typified the person of our Lord Jesus Christ. This is so obvious that it is hardly necessary to pause and furnish proof. The other two arks, that of Noah, in which he and his family found shelter from the flood; and that in which the infant Moses was preserved, plainly foreshadowed Christ Himself. The fact that the ark of the covenant was composed of two materials and of two only—the wood and the gold—clearly point to the two natures of our Lord: the human and the Divine. The fact that the two tables of stone were preserved in the ark, and the words of the Saviour, "Thy law is within My heart" (Psa. 40 : 8) supply us with a sure key. The fact that the mercy-seat (where God received the representative of His sinful but blood-cleansed people) rested upon the ark, furnishes additional confirmation.

It is the typical significance of the ark which explains its pre-eminence over the other sacred vessels. Each of them pointed to some aspect of Christ's work, or its effects, but the ark spoke of His person: they of what He has done, this of what HE is. It is the blessed person of Christ which gave value to His work. To-day, in evangelical circles, the emphasis is placed on what the Saviour has done for us, rather than on what He is in Himself. Scripture ever reverses this order. Note how in the typical ritual on the annual day of atonement, the high priest first entered the holy of holies with his hands full of sweet incense (Lev. 16 : 12), before he took in and sprinkled the blood (v. 14)—God would first be reminded of the fragrant perfections of Christ's person, ere that which spoke of His redemptive work was placed before Him! Mark the order in the announcement of the Lord's forerunner "Behold the Lamb of God" (first His person) which taketh away (second, His work) the sin of the world," (John 1 : 29). So with the apostle Paul, "I determined not to know anything among you save Jesus Christ( His person) and Him crucified"—His work" (1 Cor. 2 : 2). So again, in the apocalyptic visions: 'I beheld . . . and in the midst of the elders, stood a Lamb (His person) as it had been slain"—His work (Rev. 5 : 6). Thus it was in this order of the Tabernacle furniture: first the ark which tells of Christ's person, then the mercy-seat, etc., which point to His work.

### 2. Its Materials.

The ark was made of "shittim wood," a species of the acacia, which is said by many to be imperishible. It is a tree which is found in the arid desert. The "shittim wood," grown here on earth, typified the humanity of our Saviour. Isaiah 53 : 2 speaks in the language of this type: "For He shall grow up before Him as a tender plant, and as a root out of a dry ground." "There are three things about this shittim-tree which makes it a peculiarly fitting as a type of this. It is the tree now called the acacia seyal—the only tree that grows to any size in the deserts through which Israel passed. First it is a tree that can thrive in a very dry soil. Second, it has very long, sharp thorns. Third, it is the tree from which is obtained the gum arabic so largely used in medicinal preparations, which is procured simply by piercing the tree at nightfall, and that which oozes out is, without any preparation, the gum-arabic of commerce. To the spiritual 'mind these facts are sweetly suggestive of Him who, in a dry and thirsty land, where surely there was naught to sustain His spirit, was in the constant freshness of communion with God, for other than an earthly stream sustained Him. Though indeed crowned now with glory, a crown of thorns was all this world had for Him. And we remember too, that it was He who was pierced for us in that blackest night of guilt, when the blood flowed forth from His side, to be the only balm for the troubled soul and sin-burdened conscience" (Mr. C. H. Bright).

As the shittim-wood was one that never rotted, it was a most appropriate emblem of the sinless humanity of the Lord Jesus. It is indeed striking to find that in the Septuagint (the first translation ever made of the Old Testament—into Greek) it is always translated "incorrupible wood." Now it is of paramount importance that we should hold fast and testify to the fundamental truth conveyed by the "incorruptible wood," namely, the real but absolute untainted humanity of Christ. That Christ was truly Man is clear from His repeated use of the title "the Son of Man," and from the Holy Spirit's appellation "the Man Christ Jesus" (1 Tim. 2:5). But His humanity was uncorrupt and incorruptible. In Him was no sin (1 John 3:5) for He was the Holy One of God; and therefore disease and death had no claim upon Him, Begotten by the Holy Spirit, and born of a virgin, His immaculate humanity was pronounced "that holy thing which shall be born" (Luke 1:45).

The wood of the ark was overlaid with gold, within and without. This perfigured His **Divine nature.** "While the acacia boards gave **form** and **dimensions** to the ark, the **appearance** was all gold—no wood was visible. Thus our Lord's humanity gives Him the form in which He was and is. Light of light, the Creator and Upholder of all things, He became a Man, and was and is eternally 'the Man Christ Jesus.' But how God guards us from having a single low view of this most lowly One. The gold covers all Look at Him, gaze, as far as finite mind and heart can, upon the the majesty of His being, and all is Divine! The Divine nature is displayed over the 'form' of a servant' and wherever the all-seeing eye of God rests, within that pure and and holy mind, affections and will, as well as without upon that blameless walk, meekness and obedience, He owns Him as His Equal, His co-eternal Son. It is all gold, though the form of the Servant was there, with perfect human faculties and dependence—everything that belongs to man, sin apart. But spread over all this is the gold of His deity. And does not faith see the same?" (Lectures on the Tabernacle by S. Ridout).

Thus, in the wood and the gold together forming the ark we have foreshadowed the great mystery of godliness —God manifest in flesh. Here we see, in symbol the **union** of the two natures in the God-man, a Scriptural conception of whom is so important and vital—important, as God has shown us by making the ark to be the first object of contemplation as we take up the study of the Tabernacle; vital, because sound views of Christ are inseparable from our very salvation: "This is life eternal, that they might **know** Thee the only true God, and Jesus Christ whom Thou hast sent" (John 17:3).

### 3. Its Dimensions.

The ark was two and a half cubits in length, one and a half in breadth, and one and a half in height. The repeated half at once arrests attention. The word "half" in the Hebrew comes from a root which means to cut in two. Another has pointed out that these half cubits suggest that the knowledge of Christ given to us now is only partial: "Now we know in part" ( Cor. 13:9). "Those who have the fullest knowledge of Christ are the first to say, in the language of the Queen of Sheba, 'it was a true report that I heard . . and behold the half was not told me' (1 Kings 10:6-7). So with our all-glorious Lord, the scale is reduced—may we say?— that our finite minds may grasp something of the wondrous fulness of that which passeth knowledge" (Mr. S. Ridout).

Two and a half is half of five, and one and a half is half of three, and both of these numbers have a meaning in Scripture which is deeply significant. Take the latter first. Three is the number of manifestation, that is why it is the number of resurrection, for only in resurrection is life fully manifested; for the same reason three is the number of Deity, for God is fully manifested in the three persons of the Holy Trinity. How significant then that the breadth and height (which both have to do with the display of an object) of the ark, were both half of three. Remembering that the ark speaks of the person of Christ and three is the number of manifestation, do we not find here more than a hint that when Christ came to the earth He would not fully manifest Himself? Nor did He: Had He completely unveiled His glory men had been blinded as was Saul of Tarsus (Acts 9:8), or had fallen at His feet as dead, as did John (Rev. 1:17). But blessed be God we shall yet "see Him as He is," and then shall we eat of "the hidden Manna" (Rev. 2:17). So, too, with the other number. Five stands for grace, and the length of the ark speaks of the span of God's grace in Christ. That span is eternal; but eternity is endless duration both backwards and forwards. Therefore is the five halved for though believers now know of the grace that was given them in Christ before the foundation of the world (2 Tim. 1:9), the endless ages yet to come await its future display (Eph. 2:7).

It is to be noted that the ark measured the same in height as in breadth, which at once points to the perfections and uniqueness of Christ. The "breadth" would speak of Him in His dealings with man, the "height" His relations Godward. How far our spiritual height falls short of our breadth! For example, how much more cautious are we against displeasing our fellows than God! Not so with the Perfect One. In meeting the needs of men, He never lost sight of the claims of His Father: Mark how in responding to the appeal of Lazarus' sisters, the glory of the Father was His only motive and consideration (John 11:4-6).

### 4. Its Contents.

These are described in Heb. 9:4: "The ark of the covenant overlaid round about with gold, wherein was the golden pot that had manna, and Aaron's rod that budded, and the tables of the covenant." Some have seen a contradiction between this verse and 1 Kings 8:9: "There was nothing in the ark save the two tables of stone." But there is no conflict between the two passages, for they are not treating of the same point in time. Hebrews 9:4 is speaking of what was in the ark during the days that it was lodged in the Tabernacle, whereas 1 Kings 8:9 tells us of what comprised its contents after it came to rest in the Temple. Thus we see how quickly disappears one of the stock 'contradiction' arguments of infidels!

The distinction noted above between what was inside the ark during its respective sojourns in the Tabernacle and in the Temple supplies the key to the typical significance of its contents. The three articles specified in Heb. 9:4 point to God's provisions in Christ while they are journeying through the wilderness. This becomes abundantly clear when we consider the first thing named, "the golden pot that had manna." The manna was the food which Jehovah gave to Israel while they were journeying from the house of bondage to the promised inheritance. It foreshadowed Christ as the Bread of life, the food of His pilgrim people. But most blessed is the added word here. In Exodus 16:3, we simply read that Moses said unto Aaron "take a pot and put an omer full of manna therein and lay it up before the testimony, to be kept; whereas in Hebrews 9:4, the Spirit tells us it was "a golden pot." The Old Testament could not give us that, it is reserved for the New Testament to bring it out. The Manna was the grace of God meeting the need of His people in the wilderness. Now while the Old Testament makes it plain that Israel's deepest need would be met through the promised Messiah, yet it was by no means clear that the Messiah would be a member of the Godhead; rather was the emphasis thrown upon the fact that He was to be the seed of Abraham and of David. But with the New Testament before us, we have no difficulty in perceiving that naught but a vessel which was holy and Divine was adequate to hold what God had for needy sinners and that that vessel was no other than His beloved Son incarnate. It is in John's Gospel, particularly, that we get the truth of the "golden pot." There we see the Vessel which was capable of holding the grace of God for His people: **"full** of grace and truth" is found only in John!

There is, no doubt, an additional thought connected with the golden pot," which contained the manna. The amount stored therein was "one omer" which, as we learn from Exodus 16:16, was the quantity for each man. Thus the amount preserved was the measure of a man; but the **golden** pot which contained it tells us that this Man is now **glorified**, the same thought being found in the "crown of gold which was round about the ark." This is confirmed by a comparison of Exodus 25·18 with Heb. 9:5, where the cherubim of "gold" are called the cherubim of "glory." It is, then, in the Man Christ Jesus, now crowned with glory and honour, that God's food for His people is to be found. Just as in another type, when the famine stricken people came to Pharaoh for corn, he referred them to the once humbled, but then exalted Joseph.

The second article within the ark was "Aaron's rod that budded." This takes us back to Numbers 17 where we have the historical account of it. In Numbers 16, we read of a revolt against Moses and Aaron headed by Korah, a revolt occasioned by jealously at the authority God had delegated to His two servants. This revolt was visited by summary judgment from on High, and was followed by a manifest vindication of Aaron. The form that this vindication took is most interesting and instructive. The Lord bade Moses take twelve rods, one for each tribe, writing Aaron's name on the rod for Levi. These rods were laid up before the ark, and the one that should be made to blossom would indicate which had been chosen of God to be the priestly tribe. Next morning it was found that Aaron's rod had "brought forth buds, and blossomed blossoms, and yielded almonds." Afterwards, the Lord ordered Moses to bring Aaron's rod before the testimony "to be kept for a token against the rebels." The spiritual and typical significance of this we shall now endeavour to indicate.

The issue raised by Korah and his company was that of priestly ministry—who had the right to exercise it? In deciding this issue the tribal rods (symbols of **authority**) were laid up before the Lord, to show that the matter was taken entirely out of the hands of man and was to be decided by God alone. Thus the question of the priesthood was determined solely by Jehovah. The manner in which God's mind was made known on this momentous point is very striking. The "rods" were all of them lifeless things, but during the interval that they were laid up before the testimony, unseen by the eye of man, the mighty power of the living God intervened, a miracle was wrought, the dead rod was quickened, and resurrection-life and fruit appeared.

The spiritual eye will have no difficulty in perceiving what all of this pointed forward to. Numbers 16 foreshadowed Israel's rebellion against Him, whom Moses and Aaron jointly prefigured. Moses, the prophet proclaimed the **truth** of God; Aaron, the priest, expressed His **grace**; both were hated without a cause. So He who was full of grace and truth was despised and rejected of men; not only so but put to a shameful death. And what was God's response? He fully vindicated His beloved Son by raising Him from the dead. Moses entering the Tabernacle on the morrow (Num. 17:8) and there beholding the evidences of God's resurrection power, reminds us of the disciples entering the empty sepulchre and beholding the signs that Christ had risen from the dead. Moses bringing out the rods and showing them to the people (v. 9), finds its antitype in the resurrection of Christ established before many witnesses (1 Cor. 15:6). In the rod laid up before the Lord, we have a picture of Christ, now hidden, at the right hand of God.

But it is with the rod in the ark that we now have to do. All that was in the ark speaks of the wondrous provision which God has made for His people in Christ. Now what is before us in Numbers 17, is not God dealing in judgment, but in grace: "And the Lord said unto Moses, Bring Aaron's rod again before the testimony, to be kept for a token against the rebels; and thou shalt quite **take away** their murmurings from Me, **that they die not.**" Thus, the priestly ministry of Aaron was to **preserve** God's people before Him while they were passing through the wilderness. How plain is the type. That which answers to it is found in the ministry of our great High Priest in heaven, who secures our salvation to the uttermost by His constant intercessions for us (Heb. 7:25). Here, then, is God's provision for us in Christ: food to strengthen, priestly grace to sustain.

One other point remains to be considered in connection with Aaron's rod. In Heb 9:4, it is referred to simply as "Aaron's rod that budded," whereas in Numbers 17:8, we are told that it "brought forth buds, and blossomed blossoms, and yielded almonds." We believe that the omission in Heb. 9:11 of the latter part of this statement is most significant. Numbers 17:8 refers to resurrection-life in three stages, all, of course pointing to Christ. We would suggest that the "budding" of the rod found its fulfilment in the resurrection of Christ Himself; that the "blossomed blossoms" will receive its realisation in the resurrection of "them that are Christ's at His coming"; while the "yielded almonds" points forward to the raising of Israel from the dead who shall then fill the earth with fruit. As the "blossoming" and the "yielding almonds" is yet future, the Holy Spirit has most appropriately omitted these in Heb 9:4.

The third thing in the ark was the two tables of stone on which were written the ten commandments. The reader will recall that the Lord gave to Moses on two separate occasions tables of stone engraved by His own finger. The first ones Moses dashed to the ground when he beheld the idolatry of the people (Ex. 32), thereby intimating that fallen man is unable to keep the law. But God's counsels cannot be thwarted, neither will He abate the requirements of His righteousness: "At that time the Lord said unto me, Hew thee two tables of stone like unto the first, and come up unto Me into the Mount, and make thee an ark of wood. And I will write in the tables the words that were in the first tables which thou breakest, and thou shalt put them in the ark" (Deut. 10:1-2).

The second set of tables of stone were deposited in the ark. The careful student will observe a notable omission in the above quotation from Deut. 10:1-2, an omission emphasised by its repetition in the next verse—"And I made an ark of shittim wood, and hewed two tables of stone." Nothing is said of the wood being overlaid with gold, nor of the cherubim of glory on its cover. It is simply said that the two tables of stone were to be placed in "an ark of **wood.**" The law which fallen man had broken was to be preserved intact by the perfect **Man.** It was as "the second Man, the Last Adam" that Christ "magnified the law and made it honourable" (Isa. 42:21). How perfect is every jot and tittle of Scripture, even in its omissions!

The fulfilment of this aspect of our type is given in Psalm 40 where, speaking by the Spirit of prophecy, our glorious Surety exclaimed, "Lo, I come: in the volume of the book it is written of Me, I delight to do Thy will O My God; yea, **Thy law is within My heart**" (vv. 7, 8). The blessed Substitute of God's elect was "made under the law" (Gal. 4:4), and perfectly did He "fulfil" it (Matt. 5:17). Therefore is it written "By the obedience of One shall many be made righteous" (Rom. 5:19), Christ has answered every requirement of God's law for His people. He has fully discharged all their creature responsibilities. In Christ, as our type plainly shows, and in Christ alone, is found that obedience which meets every demand of God's throne. Therefore may each believer joyfully exclaim **"In the Lord** have I righteousness" (Isa. 45:24). Thus can the whole ransomed Church hail its covenant Head as "The Lord our Righteousness" (Jer. 23:6).

In our next paper, God willing, we shall ponder the coverings of the ark, its various names, and its remarkable history. In the meantime may the Holy Spirit occupy both writer and reader, more and more, with Him whom the ark typified.

ARTHUR W. PINK.

# TRUTH AND ERROR
## or
### LETTERS TO A FRIEND.

#### 11. Assurance.

But while such is the gospel, you will perhaps ask me what I think of the doctrine of assurance, as maintained by the holders of the new theology. On this point I have the following remarks to offer.

1. The doctrine of assurance is stated and pressed by many of them in a most arrogant and offensive way; so much so, indeed, that the word has become a suspicious one. They make a god of their assurance, and condemn with utmost flippancy and ease every one who does not come up to their standard of assurance. Just say that you believe, say that you are perfectly assured of your salvation, join the sect, and this will cover many defects which others would not have consented to overlook. I have been often both amazed and shocked at the vain-glorious boastings of assurance, and the contemptuous condemna-

tion of others, which are indulged in. Ah, it is easy to speak of assurance, to boast of it, to despise others for not having it; but it is not so easy to "walk humbly with our God." And I have seen such pride, such unmeekness, such boasting, such sectarianism, such censoriousness, such evil speaking in connection with this pretended assurance, that I could not help coming to the conclusion, that the man who could boast of his assurance while indulging in such tempers was deceiving himself or others most grossly, and had no title to the name of Christian at all. I am not prepared to deny the name of Christian to men, simply because they hold much that I conceive is error; but I am quite prepared to deny such a name to the proud, the censorious, the uncharitable boasters of their assurance.

2. The doctrine of assurance is made wholly to rest upon the doctrine that Christ died for all, in the most universal sense. It is maintained that there can be no assurance if this be not its foundation. "Christ died for me," is that which every sinner is called upon to believe. Yet it is maintained, at the same time, that Christ did not die for any, so as to actually secure salvation for them! And to believe that Christ died so as to make salvation possible to me, is all I need to believe in order to have assurance.

3. The doctrine of assurance sounds very strangely in the lips of men who deny the perseverance of the saints. No man, it is said, can be a Christian who is not assured of his salvation, yet a sinner may fall from grace. Can any thing be more absurd than this? In becoming a Christian I am to be quite sure of being saved, yet I am also to believe that I may fall away and be lost. What is this but telling me that I am to be sure of heaven, and yet I am not to be sure of it? It is plain then, that if the doctrine of the saints' perseverance be denied, there can be no such thing as assurance. It is an absurdity, an impossibility. The doctrine of assurance implies that of perseverance, and that of perseverance implies that of election.

But having made these remarks, I would not leave the matter here. While I say these things, I am not denying assurance. Far from it. I would maintain it most strenuously as a vital and momentous truth. The doctrine of the Reformation, and that which Popery hated so mortally, was, "that a man is justified through faith alone, and that he must know that he is justified." And in truth, HOW CAN THERE BE OTHERWISE PEACE OF CONSCIENCE, OR PEACE WITH GOD? But just in proportion as I would prize and preach the doctrine of "assurance of God's love" and "peace of conscience," in that very proportion would I condemn and warn you against the flippant, boastful assurance of our day. "Peace with God" is the most humbling, solemnising, and sanctifying of all truths. And when I see no such fruits brought forth by those who speak of it so loudly, I would beseech you to be upon your guard, lest the peace into which you may thus be led be the peace of a seared conscience, or the peace of a deceived heart, or the peace of the Devil, or the peace of the fancy of the flesh.

As to the doctrine of assurance, I should like to have spoken at some length. This, however, I cannot do without curtailing other points of much moment to which I am hastening on. To be as brief as possible, and to give greater weight to what I advance, I would quote from that admirable work of Mr. Haldane's, to which I have already referred. He thus writes: "The full assurance of faith in which believers are commanded to draw near to God, stands inseparably connected with having their hearts sprinkled from an evil conscience. An evil conscience accuses a man as guilty, as liable to punishment, and keeps him at a distance from God, regarding Him as an enemy and avenger, so that the natural enmity of the mind is strengthened. On the contrary, a good conscience is a conscience discharged from guilt by the blood of Christ. Conscience tells a man that the wages of sin is death, and that he is liable to it; but when the atonement made by Christ is believed in, it is seen that the punishment due for sin, which is death, has been inflicted on him, the demands of the law have been fulfilled, and its penalty suffered. On this the believer rests, and his conscience is satisfied. It is thus purged from dead works; and this is what is called the answer of a good conscience toward God. (I Peter 3:21). This answer of a good conscience cannot be separated from assurance of our acceptance with Him to whom we draw near, and the degree in which both this assurance and a good conscience are enjoyed will be equal.

"The same is true respecting the grace of hope. This, as well as having a good conscience, purged from dead works (the duty of possessing which, no Christian will deny), stand inseparably connected with the personal assurance of an interest in the Saviour and all of them lie at the foundation of love to God and consequently of acceptable obedience to Him. We love Him when we see that He hath loved us, and that His Son, is the propitiation for our sins. How can there be love without a sense of reconciliation with God, and how can there be fruits of joy and peace brought forth, till the conscience is discharged from guilt? Love proceeds from a pure heart, a pure heart from a good conscience, and a good conscience from true faith.

"In the hope of the promised salvation, they who received the doctrine of the apostles rejoiced as soon as it was announced to them, Acts 2:41; 8:39; 16:34. Their joy then had not its source in reflecting upon or being conscious of their faith, although afterwards so confirmed, but arose from the view they had of the glory and all-sufficiency of the Saviour and His perfect righteousness, made theirs by faith resting on the Divine warrant and promise. Although the assurance of sense be confirmatory of the assurance of faith, it is not so strong as the latter. 'Sanctification,' says Rutherford, 'does not evidence justification as faith does evidence it, with such a sort of clearness as light evidences colours, though it be no sign or evident mark of them, but as smoke evidences fire, and as the morning star in the east evidences that the sun will shortly rise, or as the streams prove there there is a head-spring from whence they issue; so doth sanctification give evidence of justification only as marks, signs, effects give evidence to the cause. But the light of faith, the testimony of the Spirit, will cause us, as it were, to see justification and faith, not by report, but as we see the sun's light.'

"If it be objected, that a man cannot know that he has faith without seeing its effects, it is replied that this is contrary to fact. When a thing is testified or a promise is made to us, we know whether or not we believe it or trust in it. According to this objection, when Philip said, 'If thou believest with all thine heart thou mayest,' the eunuch should have replied, you ask me to tell you a thing I cannot know, but instead of this he answers, 'I believe.' When the Lord asked the blind man, 'Believest thou in the Son of God?" he did not ask a question which it was impossible to answer. 'In this fact of believing,' says Mr. Bell on the Covenants, 'sinners have no evidence of grace in themselves; they feel nothing within but sin; they see a word without them as the sole foundation of faith; and on that alone they build for eternity; this is a point of no small importance to saints and sinners.' Many of the modern builders are at great pains to keep their hearers from all confidence, till they first discern the evidence of grace in their hearts, and having got evidence, then, and not till then can they have any just lawful, or well-grounded confidence; nay, they seem pretty plainly to intimate that a sinner's right to Christ turns on something wrought in him, or done by him, and till he has evidence of this he can claim no interest in Christ, nor assure himself of salvation by Him. According to this, Christ, the tree of life, is forbidden fruit which the sinner must not touch till he has seen inward evidence. I confess that I have not so learned Christ .. The religion of the Church of Rome leaves a man nothing but doubts respecting his salvation. It teaches that a Christian should believe in general the promises of God, while the application to himself of these promises, and the assurance of God's love, it calls presumption. This subject was one of the grand points of discussion between that "church" and the Reformers. But how many Protestants have forsaken the ground which their predecessors here occupied, and have gone over to their opponents? The doctrine of the duty of our personal assurance of salvation, and the persuasion of our interests in Christ, is denied by many, and even doubts concerning this are converted into evidence of faith, although they are directly opposed to it. **Doubts of a personal interest in Christ are evidences either of little faith or no faith."**

Such is the doctrine of assurance, as stated by one whose jealously for every jot and tittle of Divine truth gives peculiar weight to all he wrote. And with this statement I leave the subject. The sentences I have quoted are worthy of being pondered. While they give no countenance to the boastful assurance of the false professor, they equally condemn those who either deny that there can be assurance, or who place it afar off, at the end instead of the beginning of the believer's career; who discountenance the idea of its immediate possession; who actually prefer the doubting to the assured Christian; nay, who make doubts an evidence of faith, darkness an evidence of light!

There is a great danger of making a Saviour of our actings, our feeling or our faith. These may steal the heart away from Christ as effectually as the works of the self-righteous. The search for these, in which many seem to spend their lives, and which makes up the religion of not a few, is often Satan's subtle device for drawing the eye off from the cross of Christ.

There is oftentimes a greater prominence given to what man has to do in order to be saved, than what God has done for his salvation. It is the latter, not the former, that contains the Gospel, for it is the latter that opens up the riches of the grace of God. It is not the sight of what we do or feel, but the sight of what Christ has done and felt that relieves our consciences, removes our burdens, and fills the soul with assured peace. As preachers of the everlasting Gospel, we come to tell the sinner not what he has to do, but WHAT GOD HAS DONE. It is this that is the "Good news," the "glad tidings of great joy" which was freely preached to ALL. "I am come a light unto the world, that whosoever believeth in Me should not walk in darkness."

## HEADSHIP.

Address by Dr. A. W. Pink, at the Particular Baptist Church, Belvoir Street, Sydney, on Sunday Evening, 16/5/1926.

To-night, instead of preaching a textual sermon as usual, I feel led of the Lord to expound a sixteen-verse passage in the first Epistle to the Corinthians. Before we turn to that, however, let me preface what I have to say by a few exegetical remarks.

The first four books of the New Testament give us the historical foundations upon which Christianity is built, namely, the birth, the life, the death, the resurrection and the ascension of Jesus Christ. The fifth book (the Acts) completes that foundation by telling us of the descent of the Holy Spirit and of the extension of God's mercy unto the Gentiles. The sixth book (the Epistle to the Romans) contains an exposition of the gospel of God. It is the great doctrinal treatise of the New Testament. It gives an interpretation and it sets forth the application of what is historically given us in the Gospels and the Acts. Now the distinctive theme of the first Epistle to the Corinthians is that of church order and church government, so notice the order in which the truth of God is given us in the New Testament:—First, the historical foundation, laid in the earthly ministry of the Lord Jesus Christ, followed by the coming of the Holy Spirit during His absence; then the first of the Epistles gives us an exposition of the gospel of God—interpreting and applying those historical principles. That having been done, the next thing the Holy Spirit gives us is a treatise upon church order and government.

Now in the 18th chapter of the Acts we learn how that Paul came to Corinth, and while he was there he preached the gospel; how that the Lord appeared to him and said to the Apostle, "I have much people in this city," and in consequence Paul remained there eighteen months preaching the gospel. God honoured that preaching and through grace many believed, and those believers were baptised, and, being baptised, they were organised into a local church or assembly—the church at Corinth. From Corinth Paul journeyed to Ephesus, which was a city not very far distant, where he remained three years. After the apostle settled in Ephesus, Apollos, a man mighty in the Scriptures, went yonder to the church at Corinth, preached the Word, strengthened their hands, but—O the sad "buts"—but after the apostle's departure, and notwithstanding the help of Apollos, the tares crept in among the wheat and the leaven was introduced into the pure meal, and it was because of that the apostle was moved by the Holy Spirit to write this Epistle to this church at Corinth.

That which first gave rise to the need of it was certain disorders and abuses that had crept in among the saints in the Corinthian church, and it was to remove those abuses and to correct those disorders that the apostle was led to write this Epistle. A party spirit had come in and the sequel was that the saints were divided into cliques—contending and opposing companies—that is dealt with in the first four chapters of the Epistle. Then there was a great laxity to maintain church discipline. So lax were they that even fornication was tolerated in their midst, therefore in the fifth chapter the apostle insists upon the duty of the church to exclude immoral members. In the sixth chapter, the Apostle rebukes the church because brother was going to law against brother—a most reprehensible thing. Then in the seventh chapter we find him discussing various aspects of the marriage relationship. In the eighth chapter he treats of the lawfulness or the unlawfulness of meats which had been previously offered to idols. In the ninth and the tenth he speaks of the exercise of self-denial and the foregoing of our rights for the sake of weaker brethren, and then in the 11th chapter, which we are to look at in a moment, the apostle takes up certain grave abuses that had crept into the public worship of the assembly.

Now before I proceed further let me say that the Scriptures contain nothing that is solely local and ephemeral. Most of the Bible was written in the first instance to meet local needs, but because human nature is the same in all ages and the same all over the world, and because God changes not, the great principles of His Word are of general application and are perpetually binding. I say that because there are some who claim that much in this first epistle to the Corinthians only had to do with local conditions that then existed and does not apply to the churches of God to-day. I emphatically deny it. No part of Scripture is obsolete. All Scripture is needed by us and all Scripture is for us to-day.

Now the passage that I want to take up is found in the 11th chapter of the first Epistle to the Corinthians. The opening verse of this chapter, strictly speaking, belongs to the preceding one, the second verse beginning a new section. "Be ye followers of me, even as I also am of Christ" concludes what the apostle had been saying at the end of chapter 10. The second verse of chapter 11, begins a new section. "Now I praise you brethren, that ye remember me in all things, and keep the ordinances, as I delivered them to you." Interpreters are divided as to the meaning of that second verse—wheher the apostle meant what he said, or whether he was speaking ironically. He says, "I praise you, brethren because ye remember me in all things, and keep the ordinances as I delivered them to you." Personally, I believe that was the language of irony, because I think it is very clear that in this Epistle there is most conclusive proof that they were not keeping the ordinances as they were delivered to them—far from it. It was because they were not, that he had occasion to write this Epistle to them. But be that as it may. Pass on now to the third verse.

"But I would have you know." Here is where the theme of this chapter begins. "I would have you know, that the head of every man is Christ; and the head of the woman is the man; and the head of Christ is God." Now in the verses that follow attention is given to details that many of us may think are insignificant and trifling, dealing with such small matters that one wonders why they ever found a place in the Word of God. It is because God knew that we would think these were trifles that He begins this passage by saying "I would have you know." My friends, there is nothing small or trivial in the things of God. Big doors swing on little hinges. To natural reason it was a very small thing that brought about the downfall of the human race—just the plucking of fruit, yet disobeying the Almighty.

"I would have you know," then says the Holy Spirit through the apostle, "that the head of every man is Christ; and the head of the woman is the man; and the head of Christ is God." Here the apostle takes up the most important, but the well-nigh totally forgotten subject, of headship, and before mentioning the thing which he was about to condemn he states the principle on which that condemnation rested; namely, that order and subordination pervade the entire universe and are necessary to its well-being. Now that third verse tells us the woman is subordinate to and is under the rule of the man: that the man is subordinate to and is under the rule of Christ; and that Christ, in His mediatorial character, is subordinate to and is under the rule of God.

Now then, having stated that fact, having laid down that principle—that of headship or rule pervading the entire universe—in the fourth and fifth verses the apostle says, Since God has established this order both men and women are commanded to act in accordance therewith, and especially so when they enter one of God's churches.

"Every man praying or prophesying,

having his head covered, dishonoureth his head" (v. 4).

Notice it does not say dishonoureth his own head, though that is included; but it says "dishonoureth his head." Who is his head? Who is the head? Who is the head of man? The previous verse has told us: "The head of every man is Christ." Therefore, for any man to enter a church and to pray or prophesy, speaking as God's mouthpiece, with his head covered, dishonours his spiritual head which is Christ, and also dishonours himself—his own head. Let me give you a simple illustration. Suppose that a major or a general should appear at the head of his soldiers in the uniform or the garb of a common soldier, instead of in his official accoutrements; he would both dishonour his king and he would disgrace himself. So any man who enters the church praying or prophesying with his head covered dishonours his spiritual head—Christ—and disgraces himself.

"Every woman that prayeth or prophesieth with her head uncovered dishonoureth her head" (v. 5). That also has a double significance: she dishonors her natural head which is her husband or her father or her eldest brother as the case may be—the head of the household—and she also dishonours her spiritual head, namely, her brethren in Christ who have the rule in the church. She dishonours her head because she refuses to wear the sign and symbol that she is in subjection to another. Go back to the third verse. "The head of every man is Christ; the head (the ruler) of every woman is the man; the head of Christ is God." Now God has appointed that because man is the head, because headship or dominion or rule has been delegated by God into the hands of man, God has ordained that **that** shall be symbolically shown forth when he enters the house of God. His head shall be uncovered; his head shall be revealed; his head shall be manifest, because God has given to him the headship. But because God has not given headship to the woman, because he has placed her in subjection to man, therefore that must be symbolically shown forth by her having head covered, her head concealed, showing that she is not her own head and her own ruler. In other words, dear friends, God has given to woman the place of subjection, and all His ways are in harmony with that.

If you go back to the Old Testament Scriptures you will find God never made provision for a woman to occupy the throne of Israel. Woman had no part in the priestly ministrations in the tabernacle or the temple. God never made a covenant with a woman—never. Never once in the Old Testament do you find the woman offering sacrifices unto God, and when the Lord would make known to Israel the weakness of their own government He likened it unto being ruled by women and children. Turn back to the third of Isaiah and the 12th verse:—"As for my people, children are their oppressors, and women rule over them." That was when the government of Israel had failed, had broken down, when the king was no longer obeying God, when he was no longer administering the law in righteousness. When government had failed, God spoke of that failure in a figurative way by likening to them being ruled by women and children.

But perhaps some of you are saying in your minds, But that is all in the Old Testament; that all belonged to Judaism; things are very different in Christianity. Why, my friends, if you think so you are sadly mistaken, for Christ observed the same principle that woman has been given the place of subjection. Christ never called a single woman to be His apostle. Christ never commissioned a woman to preach His gospel. Christ never appointed a woman to hold office in His churches. The woman is created for the home and has not been called by God to take part in public affairs, still less administer government, and, my friends, the very fact that to-day we find that more and more woman is taking the place of man in public affairs is a moral scandal and is a witness to the decline and corruption of law and order, and is among the solemn signs of the times forecasting that day when the will of God will be finally and openly repudiated.

Now coming back to 1 Corinthians 11, the 5th verse:—"But every woman that prayeth or prophesieth with her head uncovered dishonoureth her head: for that is even all one as if she were shaven." That is to say, she is not only lacking in respect for others, but she has none for herself. Any woman that will come into the house of God without a hat or without a covering for the head, or removes that covering after she enters the house of God, not only has no respect for her brethren in Christ.

but she is without self-respect; for God says it is even all one as if she were shaven."

Now, I make no apology, my friends, for speaking on this subject to-night. It is a part of the whole counsel of God and, as I have already shown you, this passage begins by saying "I would have you know;" therefore it is not without significance, not without importance, and not without value.

"For if the woman be not covered" (If she refuses to wear a head-covering, a hat, or a veil), "let her also be shorn" (have her hair cut). (v. 6.) And in view of that fashion which is becoming increasingly popular among women today, that "also" there is most solemn and searching. My friends, I fully believe that the vast majority of Christian women who have had their hair cut have done so in ignorance of the teaching of God's Word and of the requirements of God. I cannot make myself believe that my sisters in Christ have deliberately defied God: charity requires that I must conclude that they have done it in ignorance of the Scriptures: and it is because of the ignorance that prevails so widely to-day that I feel it laid upon me to give you what God says on this subject to-night.

Now what is so solemn in that sixth verse is the word "also." I want you to notice that the Holy Spirit has there linked two things together. "If the woman be not covered" (have a hat on her head when she enters the church) "let her **also** be shorn" (not shaven, but shorn—have her hair cut). The Holy Spirit has joined the two things together and it is not difficult to see why, because the cutting off of the long hair **exposes** the head: it reveals the size, the shape of it, and the cutting off of the hair places her on the same level before God as those who enter the church without any hat on at all! The two things are inseparably linked together here. "What God hath joined together let not man put asunder." God estimates and regards the cutting off of the hair on the same level as entering His house without any hat on! Look at that sixth verse again please:—"If the woman be not covered, let her **also** be shorn." In other words, God requires a **double** covering. He has given the woman the long hair to cover her head naturally, so that her head is covered when she is **outside** the church, to show that she is not her own ruler, her own head, but in subjection to another; but when she enters the house of God, another covering is required, to show that she is also in subjection to her **spiritual** head—those who have the rule in the house of God.

Now, in that sixth verse, the second half, there is an "if" which may perhaps have puzzled some of you:—"but if it be a shame for a woman to be shorn." The word "shame" there means a disgrace. If it be a disgrace for a woman to be shorn or shaven let her be covered. Now the word "if" there does not raise a doubt. The word "if" there does not open the door for debate: the word "if" there is used—as it so frequently is in the New Testament—in the sense of "since" or "because." "If I go away I will come again." Since I go away, because I go away, and prepare a place for you, I will come again" (John 14:2). "If ye be risen with Christ, seek those things which are above" (Col. 3:1). **Since** ye be risen, because ye be risen with Christ, seek those things which are above. So the "if" in this sixth verse has the same force of "because" or "since." **Since** it be a shame for a woman to be shorn or shaven. Now brethren and sisters there you have the clearly revealed mind of God. God says it is a "shame," a **disgrace** for a woman either to have her head shorn or shaven. If in ignorance of God's mind your head has been shorn, then let it grow again!

In Scripture, the cutting of the hair symbolises one of two things: it is either a mark of lamentation (see Job 1:20), or a sign of degradation (see Jer. 7:29).

Now coming to the seventh verse:—"For a man indeed ought not to cover his head, forasmuch as he is the image and glory of God." The man is "the image and the glory of God." That takes us back to the first chapter of Genesis and the 26th verse. You remember we read there that God created man in His own image and likeness. Those two words do not mean the same thing. "Likeness" means a resemblance; "image" means that which represents. The image on our coins is a representation of the King—his majesty, his dominion, his authority. "Man indeed ought not to cover his head, forasmuch as he is the image"—he **represents** God on this earth. What did God immediately say to Adam in the first chapter of Genesis and the 26th verse after that it was said, "Let us make man in our image"? He said, "Let them have **dominion**." That is the thought. Then man is not only the image, but he is the "glory" of God. In what sense is man the glory of God? How does man glorify God? By his submission and by his obedience. The seventh verse concludes by saying:—"but the woman is the glory of the man"—not the "image" of the man. The woman does not represent the man: rule and headship have not been committed to her, but she is the "glory" of the man. In what sense? How? The woman is the glory of the man in the same way as the man is the glory of God, by submission and by obedience to her head.

To amplify that turn with me now to Ephesians 5.22. Remember, dear friends, that I am reading now from the Word of God: may it come home in power. Ephesians 5:22:—"Wives, submit yourselves unto your own husbands, as unto the Lord. For the husband is the head of the wife." Now turn over to Titus 2, verses 3 to 5. "I will give you the first verse for a certain reason. Titus 2, beginning at verse 1:—"But speak thou the things which become sound doctrine." These were the words of the Holy Spirit through the apostle Paul to the young pastor Titus, and here is what the aged apostle says to him. These were words of counsel to this young man. "Speak thou the things which become sound doctrine." Now notice what he was to speak and what were the things that became "sound doctrine":—"That the aged men be sober, grave, temperate, sound in faith, in charity, in patience. The aged women likewise, that they be in behaviour as becometh holiness, not false accusers, not given to much wine, teachers of good things; that they may teach the young women to be sober, to love their husbands, to love their children, to be discreet, chaste, keepers at home, good, **obedient to their own husbands**" I am not reading now from a Church of England prayer-book. There has been a hard fight for years to expunge that word from the marriage-ceremony there, but if they expunge it from the marriage-ceremony of the Episcopal Church they will never expunge it from God's Word. This is God's Word—"obedient to their own husbands, that the Word of God be not blasphemed"—as it is blasphemed on many sides to-day through the wives' disobedience. Now one other passage in 1 Peter 3, verses 3 to 6:—"Whose adorning let it not be that outward adorning of plaiting the hair" (which by the way presupposes long hair because you cannot "plait" short hair!), "let it not be that outward adorning of plaiting the hair, and of wearing of gold, or of putting on of apparel: But let it be the hidden man of the heart, in that which is not corruptible, even the ornament of a meek and quiet spirit, which is in the sight of God of great price." It may be of great ridicule in the world: it may be scoffed at by your sisters: it may be taken advantage of by an ungodly husband: but it is of "great price" in the sight of God, and He says so. "For after this manner in the old time the holy women also, who trusted in God, adorned themselves, being **in subjection unto** their own husbands; Even as Sara obeyed Abraham, calling him lord: whose daughters ye are, as long as ye do well."

Now come back to 1 Corinthians, 11, verses 8 and 9:—"For the man is not of the woman; but the woman of the man. Neither was the man created for the woman; but the woman for the man." There the apostle appeals to two facts in connection with man's history which bring out the subordination of the woman to the man. First he tells us that the woman was formed out of the man and derived her origin from his. Listen! The man and the woman were not created together; they were not created simultaneously (at the same time); the man and not the woman was created first, and the Holy Spirit here appeals to that fact in connection with their history to support what he is here dealing with—the subordination of the woman to the man. Second, it says in verse 9, that the woman was created on man's account and not man on her account. "Neither was the man created for the woman; but woman for the man." And my friends that is not negatived by what you have in the Epistle to the Galatians where we are told that in Christ there is neither male or female but we are all one in Him. That verse has to do with our **standing** before God and not with our walk here in this world: just as 2 Corinthians 5:17 says "If any man be in Christ, he is a new creature: old things are passed away; behold, all things are become new." That has to do with our **standing** before God; it has no reference to our actual experience and state, as the words "in Christ" plainly show.

Then in the 10th verse the Apostle gives us a further reason why decorum should be observed in the assembly or church:—"For this cause ought the woman to have power on her head (or, as the margin says, "a covering, in sign that she is under the authority of her husband." "For this cause ought the woman to have power on her head because of the angels." That introduces a phase of the subject that is most interesting and that is little understood, but which I am compelled to pass over entirely through lack of time; but it means this, that the sisters in Christ are commanded by God to observe the laws of propriety in His house not only for their own sakes, not only out of respect for their brethren in Christ, but also because the angels are present. The angels are present in this room right now. At every service, unseen by the outward eye, observing our deportment, noting our order, taking knowledge of our reverence or irreverence, the angels are present. The Holy Spirit here indicates that, and it is because of their presence He stresses the importance, the need, an additional reason, why the sister should observe the place God has given them, and why they should wear the symbol of that place. Just because God has placed woman in the position of subordnation her head must be covered.

Now coming to verses 11 and 12:— "Nevertheless neither is the man without the woman, neither the woman without the man, in the Lord." That is to say they are each mutually dependent upon the other. "For as the woman is of the man, even so is the man also by the woman." That is brought in to humble man. That is brought in to prevent the man from getting a swelled head. That is brought in to show the mutual dependence of the man upon the woman. "For as the woman is of the man, even so is the man also by the woman; but all things of God" which is brought in at this point to show that the Holy Spirit is not here discussing the superiority or the inferiority of either the man or the woman, considered in themselves, but what He is dealing with is the position that the Creator of all has assigned unto each. "All things are of God." It is God who has given the man the position of rule: it is God who has delegated authority and dominion to him—not because of any superiority he may or may not possses of himself. As I said a few minutes ago in another connection to-night, the old saying is that comparisons are odious. It is a most invidious distinction to try and draw comparisons between a man and a woman as to which is inferior and which superior. As far as my personal opinion is concerned, I have no hesitation in saying that in many things the woman is the superior of the man: in the finer sensibilities, in the nobler qualities that go to make up character, in patience and powers of endurance, in gentleness, in tenderness, in unselfishness, in ministering to the suffering, in love, the woman is the superior of the man. But that is not what is under discussion here. What is under discussion here is the **position** that God has given unto each and how that position must be **owned** and acknowledged by the symbol that God has appointed. Because the woman has not been given rule and headship her head must be covered, and covered with a double covering: first, the long hair that God has given her by nature, so that even when she is outside the church that covering shall indicate that she is not her own head, but that she is under the dominion of the head of her household: secondly, that when she comes into the house of God there must be the additional cover of the hat because she is also in subjection to her spiritual brethren to whom God has appointed rule.

"Judge in yourselves." The apostle now appeals to their sense of propriety: "Judge in yourselves: is it comely that a woman pray unto God uncovered" with nothing on her head. (v. 13.) Do not even natural proprieties and instincts prompt—"Doth not even nature itself teach you, that, if a man have long hair, it is a shame unto him? But if a woman have long hair it is a glory to her: for her hair is given her for a covering." (vv. 14, 15). That is the opposite of what you have in verse 6. The **short** hair is a "shame;" the long hair is a "glory" to the woman. Now what does that mean? Her "glory" is not to be limited to her physical attractions, but refers to the loveliness of **submission**, and the beauty of **obedience**.

I want you to turn now to John 12, verse 3:—"Then took Mary a pound of ointment of spikenard, very costly, and anointed the feet of Jesus, and wiped His feet with her hair." Now link that up with the verse we have just had in 1 Corinthians 11: her hair is her glory. Mary placed her "glory" at the feet of Christ! Have you? I mean you brothers as well as sisters. Have I? She wiped His feet with the hair of her head.

She placed her "glory" at the feet of Christ. Oh may God give grace unto His daughters here to-night to be lowly and in subjection to Him.

Do you know, my sisters in Christ, that God has given to you a means and a way of imitating and following Christ which is denied to us brethren? He has When Jesus was here He wore long hair as a sign of His complete subjection to God (see Num.: 6:5). "The head of Christ is God," says the apostle, and when He came here He came in the the place of subjection. "He made Himself of no reputation." "It is a shame for a man to have long hair." Oh the marvel of it that the Lord of glory, the Son of God, should so make Himself of no reputation that He voluntarily entered the place of shame as the symbol of His submission and subjection unto God. And I say, sisters in Christ, there is granted unto you a way and a method of imitating and following Him that is denied even to the brethren. It may cause the world to sneer. It may bring down upon you the taunt of "old-fashioned" and so forth, but what matters that, if it brings upon you the approval of God and brings you into the place of following and imitating Christ in a way that even the brethren cannot!

Now coming back for a final word to 1 Corinthians II. The closing verse 16: "But if any man seem to be contentious, we have no such custom, neither the churches of God." And there the apostle closes his discussion of this section. Having presented the various arguments why God requires the woman to be in the place of subjection, "if any seem to be contentious"—if you want to argue about this and debate the matter—"we have no such custom," we (the apostles) nor the churches of God. In other words, if the sisters will not listen to what God says, then it is a waste of time for His servants to argue about it. When God's will is clearly revealed, debate is set at an end for the real Christian. It is either obey or disobey! Submit or defy! If the woman will not bow to God's precepts, they will not heed our reasonings. In such case, we can only leave them with God to suffer either His chastisements or judgments. This chapter says it is a shame for a woman to have her hair short. It also says the long hair is her glory.

Now just one other word on verse 3. I would not be fair if it were to be left out. Verse 3 says "the head of every man is Christ." The woman is not her own head for God has placed her under the dominion of man, but the man is not his own head or his own lord. He also is under dominion to another and that word applies to believing brethren, just as much as it does to believing sisters. Though the Creator has placed rule and dominion in the hands of the man, the man is not to misuse his authority by being a tyrant. He, too, is in subjection to another. "One is our master, even Christ." O brethren in Christ, rule your homes over which God has placed you as the "head"—rule your homes in a way that is pleasing to Him and in the spirit which will glorify Him. Christ said, "My yoke is easy and My burden is light." Then see to it that the yoke and the burden you place on your wife is equally light and is equally easy. O brethren and sisters, the Christian home ought to be a veritable Bethel upon earth —the woman (the wife) in meek, Godfearing subjection to her husband; the husband ruling in the fear of God reflecting the glory of his Head.

ARTHUR W. PINK.

---

hours He was not left in peace, but was persecuted by revilings and scoffings. How unutterable mild in comparison is the persecution we are called on to endure for His sake!

In like manner, each of the promises attached to the Beatitudes find their accomplishment in Christ. Poor in spirit He was, but His, supremely is the kingdom. Mourn He did, yet will He be comforted as He sees of the travail of His soul. Meekness personified, yet shall He sit on a throne of glory. He hungered and thirsted after righteousness, yet now is He filled with satisfaction as He beholds the righteousness He wrought imputed to His people. Pure in heart, He sees God as none other does (Matt. 11:27). As the Peacemaker, He is owned the Son of God by all the blood-bought children. As the persecuted One, great is His reward, having been given the Name above all others. May the Spirit of God occupy us more and more with Him who is fairer than the children of men.

ARTHUR W. PINK.

sought not the limelight, shunned advertising, and distained popularity. When the crowds would make Him their Idol, He avoided them (Mark 1:45; 7:17). When they would come and "Take Him by force to make Him a king, He departed again into a mountain Himself alone" (John 6:15). When His brethren urged "Show Thyself to the world," He declined, and went up to the feast, in secret (John 7). When He, in fulfilment of prophecy, presented Himself to Israel, as their King, He entered Jerusalem "lowly, and riding upon as ass" (Zech. 9:9).

Fourth, "Blessed are they which do hunger and thirst after righteousness." What a summary is this of the inner life of the Man Christ Jesus! Before the Incarnation, the Holy Spirit announced, "Righteousness shall be the girdle of His loins" (Isa. 4:5). When He entered this world, He said, "Lo, I come to do Thy will, O God" (Heb. 10:17). As a Boy of twelve He asked, "Wist ye not that I must be about My Father's business?" (Luke 2:41). At the beginning of His public ministry He declared, "Think not that I am come to destroy the law, or the prophets: I am not come to destroy, but to fulfill" (Matt. 5:17). To His disciples He declared, "My meat is to do the will of Him that sent Me" (John 4:34). Of Him the Holy Spirit has said, "Thou lovest righteousness, and hatest wickedness: therefore God, Thy God, hath anointed Thee with the oil of gladness above Thy fellows" (Psa. 45:7). Well may He be called "The Lord our righteousness."

Fifth, "Blessed are the merciful." In Christ we see mercy personified. It was mercy to poor lost sinners which caused the Son of God to exchange the glory of Heaven for the shame of earth. It was mercy, wondrous and matchless, which took Him to the Cross, there to be made a curse for His people. So it is "not by works of righteousness which we have done, but according to His mercy He saved us" (Titus 3:5). He still exercises mercy to us as our "merciful and faithful High Priest" (Heb. 2:17). So also we are to be "looking for the mercy of our Lord Jesus Christ unto eternal life" (Jude 21), because He will show us mercy in "that Day" (2 Tim. 1:18).

Sixth, "Blessed are the pure in heart." This too was perfectly exemplified in Christ. He was the Lamb "without spot and without blemish. In becoming Man, He was uncontaminated, contracting none of the defilements of sin. His humanity was "holy" (Luke 1:35). He was "holy, harmless, undefiled, separate from sinners" (Heb. 7:26). "In Him was no sin" (I John 3:5), therefore He "did no sin" (1 Peter 2:22) and "knew no sin" (2 Cor. 5:21). "He is pure" (I John 3:3). Because He was absolutely pure in nature, His motives and actions were always pure. "I seek not Mine own glory" (John 8:50) sums up the whole of His earthly career.

Seventh, Blessed are the peacemakers." Supremely true is this of our blessed Saviour. He is the One who "made peace through the blood of His cross" (Col. 1:20). He was appointed to be "a propitation" (Rom. 3:25), that is, the One, who should pacify God's wrath, satisfy every demand of His broken law, glorify His justice and holiness. So, too, has He made peace between the alienated Jew and Gentile: see Eph. 2:14-15. In a coming day He will yet make peace on this sin-cursed and war-stricken earth. When he shall sit upon the throne of His father David, then shall be fulfilled that word, "Of the increase of His government and peace, there shall be no end" (Isa. 9:7). Well may He be called "The Prince of Peace."

Eighth, "Blessed are they which are persecuted for righteousness' sake." None was ever persecuted as was the Righteous One. What a word is that in Rev. 12:4! By the spirit of prophecy He declared, "I am afflicted and ready to die from My youth up" (Psa. 88:15). On His first public appearance we are told they "rose up, and thrust Him out of the city, and led Him unto the brow of the hill whereon their city was built, that they might cast Him down headlong" (Luke 4:29). In the temple precincts they "took up stones to cast at Him" (John 9:59). All through His ministry His steps were dogged by enemies. The religious leaders charged Him with having a demon (John 8:38). Those who sat in the gate spake against Him, and He was the song of the drunkards (Psa. 69:12). At His trial they plucked off His hair (Isa. 50:6), spat in His face, buffeted Him, and smote Him with the palms of their hands (Matt. 26:67). After He was scourged by the soldiers and crowned with thorns, carrying His own cross, He was led to Calvary, where they crucified Him. Even in His dying

(*Continued on page 263*).

# STUDIES IN THE SCRIPTURES

"Search the Scriptures" John 5:39.

Copyright in all English-speaking Countries.

Editor: Arthur W. Pink, 22 Parramatta Road, Summer Hill, N.S.W., Australia.
Hon. Agent in U.S.A. : Mr. C. S. Pressel, 559 Dupont Ave., York, Penna.

Price : 10 cents per copy ; $1.00 or 5/- per year.

### "THANKS BE UNTO GOD."

This issue brings us to the end of another year. As we look back over the past months we see much that evidences the grace and goodness of our ever-faithful God. It has been a time of testing, and we have been kept constantly on our knees—what a blessing! There has been a further decrease in the number of subscriptions, especially in U.S.A. The postal authorities appear to be increasingly careless in their handling of religious publications, for many of our friends in America have failed to receive several copies of the Magazine, both last year and this; which has resulted in not a few ceasing to renew. For this we are very sorry. At this end we have done our utmost to address the wrappers plainly and correctly, and post them out as promptly as we could get the Magazine from the printer. May we remind those who are anxious to preserve the Magazine complete, that we can supply either the 1925 or the 1926 issues in bound form for $2, post-paid. But the falling off in subscriptions has been almost balanced by increased gifts for sending out "Studies" free to God's servants and to "the poor of the flock." We are writing this in September; by the end of December, God willing, we believe there will be no deficit.

There has been a great deal of sickness in these parts, all through this winter especially, from an epidemic of influenza. Though the Editor has not entirely escaped, yet the Lord has granted such health and strength that out of over two hundred and fifty speaking engagements he has been prevented from filling only five of them. This is a great mercy for which we are not sufficiently thankful. Deeply grateful are we to the many loyal friends who have daily held up our hands in prayer. The Bible-classes in the different suburbs have been a constant source of joy. The Lord has brought us into touch with many hungry souls who are getting no spiritual food in the "churches." In two of these Classes the attendances are steadily growing.

There have been an increased number of letters from readers in every part of the world, and we much appreciate their encouraging words. There are many devoted souls labouring in the dark places of the earth, amid much difficulty and discouragement; some of them cut off from all fellowship with other ministering brethren, and who never hear any voice but their own. These are especially grateful for the visits of the Magazine which cheers them in their loneliness, affords food for thought and material for addresses. In England, Germany, Brazil, Mexico and China, brethren are transcribing and translating portions of "Studies" for wider circulation; only "that Day" will declare how many the Lord has been pleased to help through these pages.

The articles from the writings of the late Dr. Bonar and the reported Addresses of the Editor on God's Sovereignty and on Election have been blest to many. The great majority of preachers do not believe these fundamental verities of the Faith, and some who profess to do so are afraid to proclaim them. But many who have never heard them expounded from the pulpit, have derived instruction and joy from reading them. Their faith has been strengthened, their understandings enlightened, and their hearts brought to realise that "salvation is

*(Continued on page 288)*

## IMPORTANT NOTICES

Set of twelve issues for 1922, unbound, $1.00 or 5/-. Bound $1.65 or 7/-.

1923, 1924, 1925 same as 1922.

Note: We cannot break a set or now supply any single 1925 issues.

Subscription—price: $1.00 or 5/- per year to any address in the world.

Change of Address: Please notify me promptly of any change of address, and be certain to give both old and new address.

Non-subscribers receiving this Magazine regularly will understand their subscription has been entered by a friend.

Copies lost in the mail duplicated only if we are notified promptly.

## CONTENTS

| | |
|---|---|
| The Gospel of John (17: 20-26) | 266 |
| Gleanings in Exodus | 273 |
| Truth and Error | 277 |
| Sin of Unbelief | 281 |
| Missionary Address | 284 |

## THE GOSPEL OF JOHN

**60. Christ Interceding Concluded: John 17: 20-26.**

The following is an Analysis of the closing section of John 17:—
1. Christ's heart embracing all the redeemed v. 20.
2. Christ's prayer for their unity v. 21.
3. Christ's imparting to them His glory v. 22.
4. Christ and His saints manifested in glory v. 23.
5. Christ yearning for us to be with Himself v. 24.
6. Christ contrasting the world from His own v. 25.
7. Christ assuring us of the Father's love v. 26.

We have now arrived at the closing section of this wonderful Prayer, a section which supplies a glorious climax to all that has gone before. In it our Lord gives the gracious assurance that He was here praying not for the apostles only, nor simply for the entire company of those who had followed Him while He was here on earth; but for all His people: "Neither pray I for these alone, but for them also which shall believe in Me through their word" (v. 20). It is not that the Saviour now begins to present separate petitions for another company than those prayed for in the preceding verses, but that those who were to believe all through the generations that should follow, are here linked with the first Christians.

Seven things Christ asked the Father for the whole company of His redeemed. First, He prayed for their **preservation**: "Holy Father, keep through Thine own name those whom Thou hast given Me" (v. 11. Second, for their **jubilation**: "that they might have My joy fulfilled in themselves" (v. 13). Third, for their **emancipation** from evil: "that Thou shouldst keep them from the evil" (v. 15). Fourth, for their **sanctification**: "sanctify them by Thy truth" (v. 17). Fifth, for their **unification**: "that they all may be one" (v. 21). Sixth, for their **association** with Himself: "that they also, whom Thou hast given Me, be with Me where I am" (v. 24). Seventh, for their **gratification**: "that they may behold My glory" (v. 24).

A careful analysis of this Prayer reveals the fact that just as the Lord urged the one petition which He made for Himself by seven pleas, so He supported the seven petitions for His people by seven pleas. First, He asked the Father to preserve, sanctify and glorify His people, because they were the Father's love-gift to the Son; see v. 9: this was an appeal to the Father's love for Him. Second, because of the Father's personal interest in them, see vv 9, 10. What a mighty plea was this: "they are Thine"—Thine elect, Thy children; therefore undertake for them! Third, because His own glory was connected with them, v. 10: Mine honour and glory are infinitely dear to Thee, and what glory have I in the world save what comes from My redeemed! These are they who show forth My praises here below! were they to perish, were they to apostatise, where would My honour be? Note how the Saviour presses this again at the end of v. 21 and in v. 23. Fourth, because He was leaving them: He pleads their desolation, and asks the Father to make it up to them in another way. Fifth, because He was leaving them "in the world," see vv. 11, 15: consider, O Father, where I am leaving them: it is a wicked, polluting place—then protect them for My sake. Sixth, the world hated them, see v. 14:

they are surrounded by bitter enemies, and urgently need Thy protection. Seventh, because He set Himself apart (died) for their sakes, see v. 19: therefore, let not My costly sacrifice be in vain!

It is also to be observed that in this Prayer believers are contemplated in a **sevenfold** relation to the world. First, they are given to Christ out of the world, v. 6. Second, they are left in the world, v. 11. Third, they are not of the world, v. 14. Fourth, they are hated by the world, v. 14. Fifth, they are kept from the evil in the world, v 15. Sixth, they are sent into the world, v. 18. Seventh, they will yet be manifested in glorified unity before the world, v. 23.

There are **seven** "gifts" referred to in this chapter: four of which are bestowed upon the Mediator, and three upon His people. First, Christ has been given universal "power" or dominion (v. 2). Second, He was given a "work" to do (v. 4). Third, He was given a "people" to save (v. 6). Fourth, He has been given a richly-merited "glory" (v. 22). Fifth, we have been given "eternal life" (v. 2). Sixth, we have been given the "Father's Word" (v. 8). Seventh, we have been given the "glory" which the Father gave to the Son (v. 22).

Though vv. 20-26 form a clearly-defined separate section of John 17, yet are they so closely connected with the previous sections that the perfect unity of the whole is apparent. That which is **distinctive** about these closing verses is the glorification of Christ's people. The Lord looks forward to the blessed consummation, while tracing the several steps or stages which lead up to it. Just as it was with the Head Himself, so is it with His members: in His own case, His impending **sufferings** merged into His **glorification** (vv. 1, 4), so after speaking of the afflictions which His people would suffer while in the world (vv. 14-19), He turns now to their glorification (vv. 22, 24). Thus did He fill out His "I am glorified in them" (v. 10)—nothing more being said of them entering the kingdom of God through much tribulation.

The position which vv. 20-26 occupy in this Prayer is the key to their interpretation. They are found at the end of it. This of itself is sufficient to indicate the scope of their contents. In the previous sections the Lord Jesus had prayed for His people according to their needs while they were here **in the world**. But now He looks forward to the time when they shall no more be in the world; when, instead, they shall be where He now is. Therefore does He pray that they may be unified, glorified, and satisfied. This will come before us in detail in the course of our exposition.

"Neither pray I for these alone, but for them also which shall believe on Me through their word" (v. 20). Up to this point the Lord had referred specifically only to the body of disciples alive at that time, but now He lets us know that He was here praying for all Christians. The "neither pray I for these alone" takes in all the petitions and pleas contained in vv. 6 to 19; "but for them **also**" intimates that not only does He hereby appropriate to all future disciples what He had just said of and asked for the living disciples of that day, but also that they, as well as we, were included in all that follows. What honour did the Lord here put upon individual believers: their names are in Christ's will or testament; they are bound up in the same bundle of life with the apostles. Just as David, when about to die, prayed not only for Solomon his successor, but also for all the people, so Christ not only prayed for the apostles, to whom was committed the government of the church after His departure, but for all believers unto the end of the age.

"Neither pray I for these alone." How this reveals Christ's love for **us**! He thought of us before we had our being: He provided for us before we were born! As parents provide for their children's children yet unborn, so did the Lord Jesus remember **future** believers, as well as those of the first generation. Christ foresaw that the Gospel would prevail, notwithstanding the world's hatred, and that numbers would yield themselves to the obedience of the faith; therefore, to show that **they** had a place in His heart, He names them in this His testament. It was Esau's complaint, "Hast thou but one blessing, O my father?" when he came too late, and Jacob had already carried away the blessing. But **we** were not born too late to receive the blessing of Christ's prayers. He had regard to us even then; therefore, each born-again soul can say, "He prayed for me"! "Who can reckon up the numbers which have been saved? Who can say how many more will be brought to swell the dimensions of the one flock, ere Christian testimony shall have attained its predestined consummation? Till then the full tale of those for whom the Lord prayed will not be disclosed" (Mr. C. E.

Stuart). As this wondrous Prayer stretches forward into eternity, only in eternity will it be fully understood.

"But for them also which shall believe on Me through their word:" Note three things: the persons prayed for; the mark by which they are identified—faith in Christ; the ground and warrant of their faith—the Word. Once again (cf. v. 9) the Lord makes it known that believers, and believers only, have an interest in His mediatorial intercessions. Christ still confines Himself to the elect! He does not pray for all man, whether they believe or no. "His prayers on earth do but explain the virtue and extent of His sacrifice. He sueth out what He purchased, and His intercession in heaven is but a representation of His merit; both are acts of the same office. Partly because it is not for the honour of Christ that His prayers should fall to the ground: 'I know that Thou hearest Me always' (John 11:42). Shall the Son of God's love plead in vain; and urge His merit and not succeed? Then farewell the sureness and firmness of our comfort. Christ's prayers would fall to the ground if He should pray for them that shall never believe" (Dr. Manton).

The description here given of those who do have an interest in Christ's intercession is their faith in Him. This is the fundamental mark of their identification. He mentions not their love, their obedience, their steadfastness (though these are necessary in their place), but their faith. Wherever our participation of the benefits of Christ's death and resurrection are spoken of, the one thing named is faith. Why? Because this is a grace which compels us to look outside of ourselves to Him! Faith is the great essential, for faith is the mother of obedience and the other graces. But mark it is no vague and undefined faith: "which shall believe on Me." To believe in Christ is to have confidence in and to rely upon Him; it is to trust Him, to rest upon Him.

The ground and warrant of our faith is "their word," that is, the word of the apostles. "Before the apostles fell asleep, they, under the guidance of the Holy Spirit, embodied in the books of the New Testament their doctrine and its evidence, gave an account of what they had taught, and of the miraculous works which had proved that they were taught of God. In these writings they still continue to testify the Son. The apostles alone are 'God's ambassadors' in the strict sense of that word. They alone stand 'in Christ's stead' (2 Cor. 5:20). They had 'the mind of Christ' in a sense peculiar to themselves; and that mind is in their writings. 'Their sound is gone out into all the earth, and their words unto the ends of the world.' Rom. 10:18." (Dr. J. Brown). It is only through the Word that we believe in Christ (Rom 10: 14, 17).

"Neither pray I for these alone, but for them also which shall believe in Me through their word." This is the more blessed if we bear in mind the circumstances under which these words were uttered. The public ministry of Christ was now over, and those who believed on Him, in comparison with those who believed not, were few indeed. And now He was to be put to a criminal's death, and the faith of His disciples, already severely tried, would be made to tremble in the balance. How blessed then to listen to these words of His; He was not discouraged; He knew that the corn of wheat, which was to fall into the ground and die, would bring forth much fruit; like Abraham of old, He "staggered not at the promise of God (that He should have a 'Seed' that would satisfy him) through unbelief, but was strong in faith, giving glory to God." He looked to the future, from things seen to things unseen, and beheld them who were yet to swell the numbers of His "little flock." "This was the 'joy set before Him' (Heb. 12:2), and 'these things He spake in the world,' in the presence of His apostles, 'that they might have His joy fulfilled in themselves' (v. 13). How well fitted was His cheerful confidence to re-assure their failing spirits—to revive their all-but-expiring hopes ! And how must the recollection of this Prayer have delighted them amid their painful yet joyous labors, when He successfully employed them to 'gather to Him His saints; those with whom He had made covenant by sacrifice' Psa. 50:5!" (Dr. J. Brown).

"That they all may be one; as Thou, Father, art in Me, and I in Thee, that they also may be one in Us: that the world may believe that Thou hast sent Me" (v. 21). Upon this verse we write with some reserve, not being at all sure of the nature of the unity here prayed for by Christ. In v. 11 He had asked for the oneness of all His people who were on earth at that time, here He add to them those who were afterwards to believe—"that they all may be one." In v. 11 His request was that His people "may be one as We," here that "they all may be one as Thou, Father, art in Me, and I in Thee, that they also may be one in Us." It seems that a mystical union is in view here. But who is compe to define the manner in which the Father is in the Son and the Son in the Father! No doubt one reason why the Saviour mentioned the unity of His people so frequently in this Prayer (vv. 11, 21, 22, 23) was to intimate that the middle wall of partition which had for so long divided Jews from the Gentiles was on the point of being broken down, and that now He would "make in Himself of twain one new man." (Eph. 2:15).

"That the world may believe that Thou hast sent Me." This is what presents a real difficulty to the writer. The previous part of the verse seems to speak of the mystical union which binds believers together; but the last clause shows that it is one that shall powerfully affect the world. It is clear then the unity here prayed for by the Lord is yet to be manifested upon the earth. But it is equally clear that this manifestation is still future, for Christ is here speaking of those which were to believe on Him (v. 20), and now asks, "that they all may be one." We are therefore strongly inclined to think that the Father's answer to this petition will be exhibited in the Millennium, when the Divine oneness of all the elect shall be displayed before the world.

"That the world may believe that Thou hast sent Me." It is to be carefully noted Christ did not here pray that the result of the manifested unity of His people should be that "the world may believe in Me," but "That the world may believe that Thou hast sent Me." These two things are widely different. By the "world" is here meant, the world of the ungodly. But unregenerate men are never brought to believe in Christ by any external displays of Divine power and goodness—the benevolent miracles wrought by Him clearly prove this. Nothing but the Word applied by the Spirit ever quickened sinners into newness of life. But when the perfect oneness of Christ's redeemed is manifested on earth during the Millennium, then will the world be provided with a conclusive demonstration that the Lord Jesus was sent here by the Father, and that despite the seeming failure of His mission at His first advent, despite His rejection by the world all through this Christian dispensation, despite the painful divisions which have divided His friends, yet there manifested unity will then convince the world that He was "sent" by the Father to give Himself a ransom for many. Then shall it be seen, even by those who have scorned the testimony of the Holy Scriptures, that He was no impostor and His Gospel no fable. Thus we understand "that the world may believe" to mean that the world will then be convinced of the truth of His claims to be the sent One of the Father: cf. 2 Thess. 1:10!

"And the glory which Thou gavest Me I have given them" (v. 22). Christ here speaks of a "glory" which the Father had given to Him. Clearly, this is not His essential glory, which He possessed as the eternal Son, as co-equal with the Father; which glory He never relinquished. Nor is it the visible and external glory which He laid aside when He took the Servent form (Phil. 2:6, 7), when He "who was rich" for our sakes became "poor," which glory He had asked to be restored to Him again (17:5). Rather is it that "glory" which He acquired as the incarnate One, as the reward for His perfect work here on earth. It is to this that Isaiah referred when he said, "Therefore will I divide Him a portion with the great, and He shall divide the spoil with the strong, because He hath poured out His soul unto death" (53:12). An inheritance has been given Him (Heb. 1:2), and this He will share with His own, for, by wondrous grace, we are "joint-heirs" with Christ (Rom. 8:17)

But what is meant by "the glory which Thou gavest Me I have given them"? The Lord is speaking from the standpoint of the Divine decrees, and thus "calleth those things which be not as though they were" (Rom. 4:17). It is parallel with Rom. 8:30: "Whom He justified, them He also glorified"—not "will glorify." So absolutely certain is our future glorification, it is spoken of as a thing already accomplished. But though the actual bestowment of the glory be yet future, it is presented for faith to lay hold of and enjoy even now, for "faith is the substance of things hoped for, the evidence of things not seen" (Heb. 11:1).

"That they may be one, even as We are one" (v. 22). This confirms what we have said above about the unity mentioned in v. 21, namely, a future manifestation on earth of our oneness. V. 22 opens with the word "And," and what follows explains what the Lord had said in the previous verse. The union referred to is the consequence of "glory given" to us—"the glory which Thou gavest Me I have given them; that (in order that) they may be one, even as We are one"! Our spiritual union is begun now, but it only attains its full fruition in the life to come. That this oneness results from Christ's bestowal on us of His acquired glory proves that it is no man-made unity about which we hear so much talk and see so little evidence these days!

"I in them, and Thou in Me, that they may be made perfect in one; and that the world may know that Thou hast sent Me, and hast loved them, as Thou hast loved Me" (v. 23). Here is further evidence that the unity for which our Lord prayed in v. 21 is one that is to be manifested in the future, for vv. 22 and 23 follow without any break. The being "made perfect in one" is to have its realization at the return of Christ for His saints: "Till we all come in the unity of the faith, and of the knowledge of the Son of God, unto a perfect man, unto the measure of the stature of the fullness of Christ." (Eph. 4:13). "God having provided some better things for us (N. T. saints), that they (O. T. saints) without us should not be made perfect." (Heb. 11:40). It is then that Christ will "present it to Himself a glorious Church... holy and without blemish." (Eph. 5:27). Then will there be perfect oneness in faith, knowledge, love, holiness, glory.

"That the world may know that Thou hast sent Me, and hast loved them, as Thou hast loved Me" (v. 23). This furnishes one more proof that these closing petitions of our Lord's prayer are to receive their answer in the Millennium. When God's elect have all been gathered together in one (John 11:52), when the glory which Christ received from the Father has been imparted to them, when they shall have been made perfect in one, then shall the world have such a clear demonstration of God's power, grace and love toward His people they shall know that the One who died to make this glorious union possible was the sent One of the Father, and that they had been loved by the Father as had the Son, for "When Christ, who is our life, shall appear, then shall ye also appear with Him in glory" (Col. 3:4); then "He shall come to be glorified in His saints and admired in all them that believe... in that day" (2 Thess. 1:10).

"And hast loved them, as Thou hast loved Me." As one has rightly said, "This expression is stupendous—God loveth the saints as He loveth Christ." Dr. Manton points out that "The 'as' is a note of casuality as well as similitude. He loveth us because He loved Christ; therefore it is said, 'He hath made us accepted in the Beloved' (Eph. 1:6). The ground of all that love God beareth to us is for Christ's sake. We are chosen in Him as the Head of the elect (Eph. 1:4), pardoned, sanctified, glorified, in and through Him. All these benefits and fruits of God's love are procured by Christ's merit. Three chief ends are accomplished thereby. First, it makes the more for them the freeness of His grace that the reason why He loveth us is to found outside of ourselves. Second, it makes for His own glory: God could not love us with honour to Himself if His wisdom had not found out this way of loving us in Christ: there was a double prejudice against us—our corrupt nature was loathed by His holiness, our transgressions provoked a quarrel with His justice. Third, it makes for our comfort, for if God should love us for our own sakes it would be a very imperfect love, our graces being so weak, and our services so stained."

The particle "as" also signifies a similitude and likeness. First, there is likeness in the grounds of it. The Father loveth Christ as His Son, so He loveth us as His sons—John 3:1. Again; the Father loveth Christ as His Image, He being "the Brightness of His glory and the express Image of His person" (Heb. 1:3); so He loveth the saints, who are by grace renewed after His image (Col. 3:10). Second, there is a likeness in the properties of it. He loves Christ tenderly; so us—"as dear children." (Eph. 5:1). He loves Christ eternally: so us—"I have loved thee with an everlasting love." (Jer. 31:3). He loves Christ unchangeably: so us—"see Mal. 3:6. Third, there is a likeness in the fruits of it. In the intimacies of communion: John 5:30 cf. 15:15. In the bestowal of spiritual gifts: John 3:35 cf. 1 Cor. 3: 22; 23. In reward: Psa. 2:7, 8 cf. Rev. 2:26. What a stay for our poor hearts is this! What comfort when hated by the world, to know that the Father loved us as the Son! What a glorious theme for our daily meditation! What cause for adoring worship!

"Father, I will that they also, whom Thou hast given Me, be with Me where I am; that they may behold My glory, which Thou hast given me." (v. 24). As we have meditated upon the different verses of this profound chapter the words of the Psalmist have occurred to us again and again: "Such knowledge is too wonderful for me; it is high, I cannot attain unto it." (Psa. 139:6). How pertinently do they apply to the lofty point which we have now reached! This 24th verse may well be regarded as the climax of this wonderful Prayer. Once more, the Redeemer says, "Father," for He is sueing for a child's portion for each of His people; it is not simply wages, such as a servant receives from his master, but an inheritance such as children receive from their parents—the inheritance being the Father's House, where the Saviour now is. Here for the first time in this prayer Christ says "I will." It was a word of authority, becoming Him who was God as well as man. He speaks of this as His right, on account of His **purchase** and of the **covenant** transactions between the Father and the Son concerning those given to Him. "I will" comported with the **authority** (v. 2) which the Father has given Him over all flesh and the **glory** into which He has entered (vv. 5, 22). Or again, this "I will," uttered just before His death, may be regarded as His "testament"—this was the legacy which He bequeathed to us: Heaven is ours, an inheritance left us by Christ!

"Father, I will that they also, whom Thou hast given Me, be with Me where I am." What **comfort** is here! What sweeter words for **meditation** than these of Christ? What **assurance** they breathe: not one of the elect shall fail to enter Heaven! What joy is here: "In Thy presence is fullness of joy; at Thy right hand there are pleasures forever more." (Psa. 16:11). The queen of Sheba said, "Happy are thy men, happy are these thy servants, which stand continually before thee, and that hear thy wisdom." (1 Kings 10:8). They that shall stand before the Lord and see His glory are much more happy. How this reveals to us the heart of the Saviour: He will not be satisfied till He has all His blood-bought ones in His presence— "for ever with the Lord." For this He is coming personally to take us to be with Himself: "I will come again, and receive you unto Myself; that where I am, there ye may be also." (John 14:3).

"That they may behold My glory, which Thou hast given Me." "It is not on the one hand that which is personal from everlasting to everlasting, beyond creature ken, that in the Son which I presume none really knows nor can, save the Father who is not said to reveal Him. Neither is it on the other hand the glory given to the blessed Lord which is to be manifested even to the world in that day, in which glory we are to be manifested along with Him. Here it is proper to Himself on high, yet given Him by the Father, as we are in His perfect favour to behold it: a far higher thing than any glory shared along with us, and which the Lord, reckoning on unselfish affections Divinely formed in us, looks for our valuing accordingly as more blessed in beholding Him thus than in aught conferred in ourselves. It is a joy for us alone, wholly outside and above the world, and given because the Father loved Him before its foundation. None but the Eternal could be thus glorified, but it is the secret glory which none but His own are permitted to contemplate—'blest answer to reproach and shame'—not the public glory in which every eye shall see Him. Nothing less than that meets His desire for us. How truly even now our hearts can say that He is worthy!" (Bible Treasury).

"For Thou lovest Me before the foundation of the world" (v. 24). This is mentioned as the reason why the Father had given Him this glory. And how it supplies us with a standard for measurement—the glory which has been conferred upon our blessed Saviour is commensurate with the everlasting love which the Father had for Him! What a glory must it be! And O the privilege, the honour, the bliss of beholding i` How this should make us yearn for the time when we shall gaze upon His resplendent glory!

"O righteous Father, the world hath not known Thee; but I have known Thee" (v. 25). It is not easy to determine the precise relation which the last two verses of John 17 bear to the preceding ones. If their words be attentively considered, they will be seen to express no desire and to ask for no blessing nor do they contain any plea to entorce the previous petitions. With Dr. Manton we are inclined to say, "It is a part of Christ's supplication; He had made His will and testament, and now allegeth the equity of it." Thus we understand the "O **righteous** Father" here to have a double force. First, God is not only merciful, but just, in glorifying the elect; His grace reigns through righteousness (Rom. 5:21). It expressed the Saviour's confidence in the **justice** of the Father that He would do all things well. "He was asking for what **He** was entitled to according to the stipulation of the eternal covenant. Justice required that His requests should be granted." (Dr. J. Brown).

The words "O righteous Father" are also to be connected with what follows— "the world hath not known Thee." This is very solemn. Christ not only left t' world without His intercession, but He turned it over to the justice of the Father. Not only did Divine righteousness bestow heavenly glory on the elect, but Divine righteousness refuses to bestow it on the unbelieving world. "The world hath not known Thee" therein lies their guilt—"Because that which may be known of God is manifest to them; for God hath showed it unto them. For the invisible things of Him from the creation of the world are clearly seen, being understood by the things that are made, even His eternal power and Godhead; so that they are **without excuse.** (Rom. 1:19, 20).

"O righteous Father, the world hath not known Thee; but I have known Thee, and these have known that Thou hast sent Me." "The Lord draws the line definitely between the world and His own, and makes it turn not on rejecting Himself but on ignoring His Father. Here, therefore, it is a question of judgment in result, however grace may tarry and entreat; and therefore He says, 'Righteous Father,' not 'Holy Father,' as in v. 11 where He asks Him to keep those in His name, as He had done whilst with them. Now He sets forth not the lawlessness of the world, not its murderous hatred of Himself or of His disciples, nor yet of the grace and truth revealed in the Gospel, nor of the corruptions of Christianity and the church, which we are sure lay naked and open before His all-seeing eyes, but that on the one side the world knew not the Father, and on the other that the Son did, as the disciples that the Father sent the Son: words simple and briefly said, but how solemn in character and issues!" (Bible Treasury). How blessed to see the Lord here linking us with Himself—"I have known. . . these have known!"

"And I have declared unto them Thy name, and will declare it: that the love wherewith Thou hast loved Me may be in them, and I in them" (v. 26). Here the Lord briefly sums up what He had done and would still do for His disciples—make known the Father unto them. He returns at the end to what He had said at the first, see v. 6. The I "will declare it" is not to be limited; true, Christ is now, by the Spirit, revealing the Father, but He will continue so to do throughout eternity. Then He states why He is the Declarer of the Father's name "**that** (in order that) the love wherewith Thou hast loved Me may be **in** them, and I in them." "Where Christ is known as the Father's sent One, the deepest blessing and the highest privileges are even now given, and not merely what awaits the saints at Christ's coming. If ever there was one capable of estimating another, it was the Son in respect of the Father; and His name, the expression of what He was, with equal competency He made known to us. He had done it on earth to the disciples; He would do so from heaven whither He was going; and this that He might give them and us, the consciousness of the same love of the Father which rested ever on Himself here below. As if to cut off the not unnatural hesitation of the disciples He added the blessed guarantee of His own being in them, their life. For they could understand that, if they lived of His life, and could be somehow as He before the Father, the Father might love them as Him. This is just what He does give and secure by identification with them, or rather as He puts it, 'and I in them.' Christ is all and in all." (Bible Treasury).

"And I have declared unto them Thy name, and will declare it; that the love wherewith Thou hast loved Me may be in them, and I in them." How striking to note that love, not eternal life, or faith, or even glory, is the last word here: "And now abideth faith, hope, love, these three; but **the greatest** of these is **love.**" (1 Cor. 13:13). But let it be particularly observed that the love of the Father dwelleth in us only through the mediation of the Son, hence the final words, "and I in them," cf. v. 23. Again, how blessed the conjunction here: Christ in us, the love of the Father in us, by the power of the **Holy Spirit,** "the love of God is shed abroad in our hearts by **the Holy Spirit.**" (Rom. 5:5)! Suitable close was this. The section began with, "having loved His own which were in the world, He loved them unto the end." (13:1), and it closes with "that **the love** wherewith Thou hast loved Me may be in them, and I in them!" In the genial warmth and glorious radiance of that love shall we bask throughout eternity.

The following questions are to prepare the student for our next lesson:—
1. What type was fulfilled in v. 1?
2. What is suggested by the "garden" v. 1?
3. Why is there no reference here to His agony?
4. What made them fall to the ground v. 6?
5. Why did Christ repeat His question v. 7?
6. In what character did Christ speak at the end of v. 8?
7. What important practical truth is exemplified in v. 11?

—Arthur W. Pink.

## GLEANINGS IN EXODUS.
### 36. The Ark (Continued).

As the Ark is singled out from the seven pieces of furniture in the Tabernacle for special sanctity and prominence, and as so much more is recorded about its history than that of any of the other holy vessels, we felt it needful to devote two articles to its consideration. In the preceding one we pondered its importance; its significance, its materials, its dimensions and its contents. In this we shall deal with its coverings, its varied names or titles, and its remarkable career. May the Holy Spirit, whose office it is to take of the things of Christ and show them to His people, graciously enlighten our sin-darkened understandings and draw out our hearts in adoring worship to Him whom the Ark so strikingly perfigured.

### 5.—Its Coverings.

The actual cover or lid of the Ark was the mercy-seat, but it is not of this we shall now treat, as that will be the object of contemplation in the next article. The coverings of the Ark which we shall here notice are those which protected it as it was borne from place to place during the journeyings of Israel. These are suitably mentioned in Numbers—the Wilderness book. In Numbers 4: 5, 6, we read, "And when the camp setteth forward, Aaron shall come, and his sons, and they shall take down the covering vail, and cover the Ark of testimony with it: And shall put thereon the covering of badgers' skins, and shall spread over it a cloth wholly of blue, and shall put in the staves thereof."

First, the Ark was wrapped in the "covering veil"—the most precious of all the curtains. The veil, as we learn from Heb. 10:20, typified the perfect humanity of Christ, rent for His people by the hand of God. This tells us that when God the Son was here in this wilderness-world His Divine glory was hidden from the eyes of men by His flesh, He who was in the form of God having taken upon Himself the form of a servant.

Second, over the covering veil was placed "the covering of badgers' skins." Unlike the skins of other animals, the lion, tiger,or leopard, the badger's is quite unattractive. In Ezek. 16:10 we read of badgers' skins for making sandals, hence when used symbolically they would speak of lowliness. In our present type the badgers' skins tell of our Lord's humiliation, particularly that aspect of it from which nature turns away, saying, "He hath no form or comeliness, and when we shall see Him there is no beauty that we should desire Him"; but an aspect which those who through sovereign grace are in communion with Him, ever recognise as that which fills them with adoring love.

Third, the external covering of the Ark was "a cloth wholly of blue"—this alone being seen by men as the Ark was carried through the wilderness from place to place. It was this which distinguished the Ark, once more, from the other vessels, for all of them had the badgers' skins for their outer covering. Why, then, was the cloth of blue the external garment of the Ark? Blue is the colour of heaven and is ever employed for the setting forth of celestial things. All heavenly things are not suitable for testimony to the world, but Christ as the God-man is to be borne witness to before all!

### 6. Its Names.

"His name shall be called Wonderful" (Isa. 9:6) was the language of Messianic prophecy, and strikingly was this foreshadowed by the different titles of the Ark. They are seven in number, and are wonderful for their variety, dignity and sublimity.

First, the ark was termed "the ark of the Testimony" (Ex. 25:22). This is the name by which it is most frequently called. It was thus designated because it was there that the "two tables of testimony" (31:18) were deposited for safe keeping. The Ark was given this appellation because it testified to the holiness and grace, the majesty and condescension of Jehovah. It was so denominated because Christ, to whom the Ark pointed, is the Centre of all God's counsels.

Second, the Ark was called "the ark of the covenant" (Num. 10:33). This brings before us a most blessed though much neglected subject, upon which we feign would linger, but must not. Christ is expressly termed the "Surety of a better testament" or covenant" (Heb. 7:23); of which He is also the Mediator (Heb. 9:6). This covenant is one into which He entered before the foundation of the world (Heb. 13:20), a covenant "ordered in all things and sure" (2 Sam. 23:5); a covenant in which Christ agreed to discharge all the obligations and responsibilities of His people.

Third, the Ark was named "the ark of the Lord, the Lord of all the earth" (Josh. 3:15). This title was used just after Israel had crossed the Jordan, when the unconquered land of Canaan lay before them. It was, at that time, filled with enemies. But there was the symbol and word of assurance—the Ark which went before them was the Ark of the Lord of all the earth. The antitypical fulfilment of this is yet future. When Christ returns He will find the inheritance occupied with usurpers. But a short work will He make of them: the enemy will be ejected and His own throne securely established—Zech. 14:9!

Fourth, the Ark was denominated "the Ark of God" (1 Sam. 3:3). This is very striking. God never identified Himself with any of the other vessels of the sanctuary. But how appropriate that He should do so with that which, in a special way, symbolized the person of Christ, How this title of the Ark pointed to the absolute Deity of Him who was made in the likeness of men.

Fifth, the Ark was entitled "the Ark of of the Lord God" (1 Kings 2:26)—in the Hebrew, "Adonai Jehovah." "Adonai" always has reference to headship, and to God's purpose of blessing. "Jehovah" is God in covenant relationship. The connection in which this particular name of the Ark occurs is most interesting and blessed. The first chapter of King's records a conspiracy at the close of David's reign, to prevent Solomon securing the throne. The second chapter tells how the conspirators and their abettors were dealt with after Solomon came to the throne: Adonijah and Joab were slain, but Abiathar, the priest, was spared because he had borne the Ark.

Sixth, the Ark was designated "the holy Ark" (2 Chron. 35:3). It was so spoken of by king Josiah, in whose days there was a blessed revival of true godliness. Preceding his reign there had been a long period of awful declension and apostasy, and the Ark was no longer kept in the Temple, therefore one of the first acts of Josiah was to give orders for the placing of the holy Ark in the House which Solomon had built. How this shows us that the holiness and majesty of Christ's person is only appreciated when God is working in power among His people!

Seventh, the Ark was spoken of as "the Ark of Thy strength" (Psa. 132:8). Lovely title was this. How it reminds us of that word: "I have laid help upon One that is mighty" (Psa. 89:19); and again, "Christ the power of God," "and the wisdom of God" (1 Cor. 1:24). Blessed be His name, there is no feebleness in our Redeemer; all power in heaven and earth is His. He is none other than "the migty God" (Isa. 9:6). O that His dear people may draw more and more from His fullness, proving that His strength is made perfect in their weakness.

### 7. Its Career.

By its career we have particular reference to its journeyings and history. Provision was duly made for the Ark to be carried while the Tabernacle was being borne from one camping place to another. "And thou shalt cast four rings of gold for it, and put them in the four corners thereof; and two rings shall be in the one side of it, and two rings in the other side of it. And thou shalt make staves of shittim wood, and overlay them with gold. And thou shalt put these staves into the rings by the sides of the Ark, that the Ark may be borne with them. The staves shall be in the rings of the Ark: they shall not be taken from it" (Ex. 25: 12-15).

"This shows that God's people were pilgrims in the wilderness, journeying on to the place which God had prepared for them. But the time would come when the inheritance should be possessed, and when the temple, suited in magnificence to the glory of the king of Israel should be built. The staves, which in the desert were not to be taken from the rings of the Ark, should then be withdrawn (2 Chron. 5:9), because the pilgrimage past, the Ark would, with the people, have entered into its rest (Psa. 132:8). The staves in the rings, therefore, speak of Christ with His pilgrim host, as being Himself with them in wilderness circumstances. It is Christ in this world, Christ in all His own perfectness as man—Christ, in a word, in all that He was as the revealer of God: for in truth, He was the perfect presentation of God to man" (Mr. Ed. Dennett).

Before we attempt to trace the actual career of the Ark, there is one other point to be considered concerning its history, namely, that before its journeyings commenced it was anointed. This is recorded in Ex. 30:26, "And thou shalt anoint the Tabernacle of the congregation therewith, and the Ark of the Testimony." The antitype is presented to us in Acts 10:38: "God anointed Jesus of Nazareth with the Holy Spirit and with power: who went about doing good and healing all that were oppressed of the devil." Notice the "anointing" of the Saviour occurred before He "went about doing good," just as the anointing of the Ark preceded its travels. The anointing of our Redeemer with the Holy Spirit took place at His baptism when, at the solemn inauguration of His public ministry, the Spirit came upon Him in the form of a dove (Matt. 3).

(1) "And they departed from the mount of the Lord three days' journey and the Ark of the covenant of the Lord went before them in the three days' journey, to search out a resting place for them" (Num. 10:33). Very blessed and beautiful is this. Lovely type was it of the Good Shepherd going before His sheep (John 10:4), leading them into the green pastures and beside the still waters. But the preciousness of the type here will be lost unless we attend to the context—note the "and" at the beginning of Numbers 10:33!

First, mark Numbers 9:18-20, where we have a notable instance of God's grace, and faithfulness in providing Israel with the cloud to guide them, intimating when they were to move and when to stop. Second, observe the failure of Moses. Forgetful of the Lord's promise to guide them, he desired to lean upon the arm of flesh, and said to his father-in-law, "Leave us not, I pray thee; forasmuch as thou knowest how we are to encamp in the wilderness, and thou mayest be to us instead of eyes" (10:31). Alas, what is man, even the best among men! Third, beautiful is it to see how mercifully the Lord intervened: the Ark was now to go before Israel as their guide—type of Christ as the **Leader** of His pilgrim people. As another has said, "In the path Homeward, the brightest human eyes and the keenest human wisdom are absolutely of no avail." The "three days' journey" intimate that it is on **resurrection-ground** that the Lord directs His people.

(2) "But they presumed to go up unto the hill top: nevertheless the Ark of the covenant of the Lord and Moses departed not out of the camp" (Num. 14:44). The whole of this chapter is very solemn, recording as it does the judgment of God, which would descend upon a people who feared to follow the counsel of Caleb and Joshua. But the people believed not the Divine warning, and next morning, feeling the folly of their timidity on the previous day, determined to go up, and, in their own strength, disposes the enemy. Nevertheless the Ark and Moses departed not out of the camp. Therefore we need not be surprised at what follows: "Then the Amalekites came down, and the Canaanites which dwelt in that hill, and smote them, and discomfited them, even unto Hormah" (v. 45). What a solemn warning is this for us to-day: unless the Lord Himself is leading us, when we act simply in the energy of the flesh, failure and disaster are the sure consequence.

(3) Joshua 3: 5 to 17. This passage is too long for us to quote here, but let the student please turn to it and read it carefully ere he proceeds with our comments. Here we see Israel crossing the Jordan and the Ark going before them to open up a way through its waters. Though Israel's journey across the wilderness was one long record of unbelief, murmuring and rebelling, the Ark still continued to guide them, and now that the promised land was spread before their eyes conducted them into it. Blessed type was this of the marvellous and matchless long-suffering of God, who, notwithstanding all the sins and miserable failures of His people, has promised, "I will **never** leave thee nor forsake thee."

The Jordan is the river of judgment and a figure of death. The Ark of the Lord's presence entering Jordan, dividing its waters for Israel to pass over dryshod, is a type of the Lord Jesus suffering death for His people. "The fact that the Ark of the Lord had passed before them into Jordan and that its waters had dried up before it, was to be proof positive that the Lord would drive out all their enemies before them: the fact that Jesus entered death for us, received its sting, tasted what real death as the wages of sin is, exhausted its bitterness, is also certain proof to us that no enemy can ever prevent our final entrance into and enjoyment of the Heavenly Canaan. And this fact is of fullest blessing. The king of terrors is disarmed for us; he is powerless that had the power of death, and those are delivered who through fear of death were all their lifetime subject to bondage" (Mr. C. H. Bright). In consequence, those for whom Christ died shall never themselves receive the wages of sin. Fall asleep they may, but die they shall not: "If a man keep My saying, he shall never see death" (John 8:52); "Whosoever liveth and believeth on Me shall never die" (John 11:26).

(4). Joshua 6:4 to 20. Once again we would ask the student to read the Scripture before noting our brief remarks thereon. The one thing which we here single out for mention is that the Ark of the covenant **led the way** as Israel marched around the walls of Jericho. How plainly this teaches us that, if the strongholds of Satan are to fall before the people of God, if proud imaginations and every high thing that exalteth itself against the knowledge of God are to be cast down, it can only be under the immediate leadership of the Captain of our salvation. Notice how the "Ark" is mentioned no less than ten times in Joshua 6! The power was not in the trumpets, nor in the marching or shouting of the people, but in the Ark with its blood-sprinkled mercy-seat going before them; and strikingly did God bear witness to its efficacy.

(5). "And all Israel, and their elders, and officers, and their judges, stood on this side of the Ark and on that side before the priests and Levites, which bear the Ark of the covenant of the Lord, as well the stranger, as he that was born among them; half of them over against Mount Gerizim, and half of them over against Mount Ebal; as Moses the servant of the Lord had commanded before, that they should bless the people of Israel" (Josh. 8:33). Here a lovely scene is presented to us. At their first attempt to capture Ai, Israel had failed miserably, due to their pride and self-sufficiency—see 7:3. Deeply exercised in heart Joshua had sought unto Jehovah, who made known to him the sin of Achan. After that had been dealt with, the Lord assured Joshua (8:1) that He had given Ai into his hands. The sequel made this manifest: the city was burned and its king hanged. Then we are told, Joshua built an altar unto the Lord, upon whose stones He wrote the ten commandments, and then summoning all Israel together, read in their ears all the words of the law. But what is so blessed to behold is, that the Ark formed the centre. "And all Israel . . . . stood on this side of the Ark and on that side." Precious figure was this of Christ in the midst of His assembly, and praise being rendered to Him for the victories He has wrought.

(6). "And the children of Israel inquired of the Lord, for the Ark of the covenant of God was there in those days (Judges 20:27). The chapter in which this is found records another of Israel's sad failures into which we must not now enter. The tribe of Benjamin had sinned grieviously and the remaining tribes undertook to punish them. Though vastly superior in numbers, Israel was defeated. Then it was that they wept and fasted before the Lord, and inquired of Him. The reference to the Ark here, typically shows us that the mind of God can only be learned through and in Christ.

(7). 1 Sam 4: This chapter presents to us the sad spectacle of the Ark of God captured by the Philistines (v. 11)—permitted by God because of the apostasy of His people. Typically, this points to the humiliation of that One whom the Ark ever prefigured, and foreshadowed His being delivered into the hands of the Gentiles! Two details here emphasise what we have just said, and exceedingly striking they are. Connected with, yea, synchronising with, the Ark being laid hold of by the Philistines, was **the death of the high priest** (v. 18). According to the eternal counsels of God, the Lord Jesus was delivered into the hands of the Gentiles in order to the death of the great High Priest! Equally noteworthy were the words of Eli's daughter-in-law: "The glory of God is **departed from Israel, because the Ark of God was taken**" (v. 21). So it was with the Antitype. With the delivering up of Christ into the hands of the Gentiles the glory of God departed from Israel!

(8). 1 Sam 5: This chapter traces the history of the Ark while it was away from Israel in the land of the Philistines. First, they took it into the house of Dagon, and set it before this idol. The sequel was startling: "And when they of Ashdod rose early on the morrow, behold Dagon was **fallen upon his face to the earth before the Ark of the Lord.**" How forcibly this reminds us of what is mentioned in John 18: 3-6, when the officers came to arrest Christ they "fell to the ground before Him!" And afterwards God troubled the Philistines so severely they got rid of the Ark by sending it back to Israel. Did not this foreshadow the Gentiles' rejection of Christ, their aspostasy, and the subsequent return of Christ to the Jews!

(9). "And they set the Ark of God upon a new cart and brought it out of the house of Abinadab" (2 Sam. 6:3). In setting the Ark on a new cart (imitating the Philistines—1 Sam 6:7-11) they disregarded the Divine injunction—see Num. 3:27-31. "And when they came to Nachom's threshing floor, Uzzah put forth his hand to the Ark of God, and took hold of it; for the oxen shook it. And the anger of the Lord was kindled against Uzzah: and God smote him there for his rashness; and there he died by the Ark of God" (2 Sam 6: 6, 7). This was God's judgment because of their disobedience to His word. Numbers 4:15 specifically prohibited any from touching the holy things save the Levites, and Num. 1:51 threatened death. "David carried it aside into the house of Obed-edom the Gittite. And the Ark of the Lord continued in the house of Obed-edom three months. And the Lord **blessed** Obed-edom, and all his household" (vv. 10, 11). This gives us the other side of the typical picture—Divine grace flowing out to the Gentiles while Christ is with them (Acts 15:14).

(10). "So David went and fetched up the Ark of God from the house of Obed-edom into the city of David with gladness" (2 Sam. 6:12): with this should be carefully compared 1 Chron. 15, from which we learn that all was now done according to Divine order. "And they brought in the Ark of the Lord, and set it in his place, in the midst of the Tabernacle that David had pitched for it: and David offered burnt offerings and peace offerings before the Lord" (v. 17). It is exceedingly striking that after the Ark left the Tabernacle in the days of Eli, it is not again found in Jerusalem until the king chosen of God, the man after His own heart, had ascended the throne! In the days of Solomon the Ark was deposited in the Temple, indicative of Christ present in Israel's midst during the Millennium.

May the Lord add His own blessing to this little study and make it as refreshing to others as it has been to us.

ARTHUR W. PINK.

## TRUTH AND ERROR
### or
### Letters to a Friend.
### 12. Present State of Religion.

"Clouds without water, carried about of winds."—Jude 12.

"Alas we are a company of worn-out Christians; our moon is on the wane; we are much more black than white; more dark than light; we shine but little; grace, in the most of us, is sore decayed."—Bunyan.

You ask me what I think of the religion of the présent day—its character as well as its progress. I answer, I can hardly tell. Nor am I willing to enter upon a very full or explicit answer to such a question. I am not qualified to judge. Instead, therefore, of attempting any lengthened answer to such a question I would merely point out a few things which lie upon the surface, which may help your own judgment upon this point, and may tend to establish you in the midst of so much instability and conflict.

As to the religion of our day, it has a very mixed sort of complexion. Its nature is rather of an indefinite kind, and its progress is not easily ascertained. Our present state is not a healthy or a natural one. It is doubtful and unsatisfactory. There is much to rejoice in, but much to grieve over. There is bustle, activity, zeal, and liberality; yet all these may exist, and still spiritual life may be low. There may be much blossom and little fruit, and even that little not of the rich mellow kind that, in other days, drew our Beloved into His garden "to eat of His pleasant fruits."

Religion among us lacks the intense vitality of other days. It intermits and fluctuates, and then, not seldom, evaporates. It lacks depth and strength. It lacks natural warmth; and too often seems to make up for a want of it by friction and excitement. Hence it is often wan and pale, relieved by hectic glows which soon depart. It has not the heavenly complexion of more primitive times. And in evidence of this, we find it continually turning in upon itself, feeling its own pulse, watching its various symptoms, a sure sign of disease, for health is unconscious of itself.

It bears about it many marks of man's handiwork. The finger of Jehovah is not visibly impressed upon it, so that one looking at it would be constrained to say, This is the doing of the Lord. There is much that is hollow and superficial. It is too hasty, too easy, too light and frivolous. It is wanting in the freshness, the calmness, the simplicity of primitive times. We desire something more solid and more solemn; peaceful but not stagnant; earnest but not feverish, energetic but not unstable.

On the one hand, we have some zealous for orthodoxy—tenacious of old forms and phrases, and making an idol of their ancestral creed. On the other hand, we have men reckless and headstrong in their innovations; rushing from doctrine to doctrine, in the feverish love of change: rash in judgment, and shallow in intellect, despising creeds, confessions, catechisms, and old divinity of every kind; setting themselves up as those who alone preach or know the Gospel,—the people with whom alone wisdom can be supposed to exist, and with whom it is almost certain to die.

On the one hand, we have men preaching the Gospel, and, at the same time, hedging it about with terms, conditions, restrictions, prerequisites as if afraid of the very freeness which they preach; telling men to come to Christ, yet enjoining humiliation, sorrow for sin, prayer, etc., as qualifications, without which they cannot be received, as if disliking the idea of our having to deal with Christ absolutely and simply as sinners, and as nothing else. On the other hand, we have men, in their zeal for a free Gospel, reducing it to a mere form of words—a current set of phrases, talking of it with flippancy and irreverence, as if the process of receiving it were a mere mechanical one, like the learning of the alphabet.

On the one hand there are those who keep the Gospel in the background, and dwell continuallly on conviction of sin, and repentance, and certain preparatory graces, the depth, and amount, and kind of which are pointed out; as if afraid that men should come to Christ too soon, and have peace. On the other hand, we have men making light of convictions, as if they were but hindrances, disparaging repentance as inconsistent with the peace of the Gospel.

On the one hand, we have some dwelling upon evidences, and experiences, and feelings, continually turning the eye backward and inward, in quest of something there to rest upon. On the other hand, we have men spurning everything of the kind; not merely regarding them as the ground of peace with God, but utterly contemning them as nothing but self-righteousness and pride.

On the one hand, we have some giving no counsel to an anxious soul, but merely to go on praying and waiting; speaking of "the pool of ordinances," at which they instruct the sinner to wait till the troubling of the water, as if he was doing right in continuing in unbelief, and as if they themselves shrunk from proclaiming the commandment of God, that men should immediately believe and turn, and that it is infinite guilt, as well as unutterable peril, to remain one moment longer in unbelief. On the other hand, we have men forbidding such to pray at all, because God has commended them to believe, as if prayer were not oftentimes the first utterance and expression of faith.

On the one hand, we have those who think assurance nothing else than presumption, and the inlet to Antinomian licentiousness; who speak of it only as a thing attainable at the close of a sinner's career—as the result of a summing up of evidences; who make doubts a proof of faith, and a mark of humility, and who look suspiciously upon any who are rejoicing in the Lord. On the other hand, there are those men who make a god of their assurance, and a saviour of their faith, and an idol of their peace; who will hear of no struggle with an evil heart of unbelief; no warfare between the flesh and the spirit; no deep self-loathing and mourning over indwelling corruption, as if all these were but the symptoms of the weakness or the non-existence of faith, instead of their being certain indications of its presence and power. For it is where faith is in its strength, that the conflict is often most desperate.

On the one hand, there are those who make the work of the Spirit in them a resting-place for their soul, and the ground of peace between them and God, instead of singly and steadfastly looking to Christ and His work for them, as the resting-place, the foundation of peace and joy. On the other, we see men ridding themselves of the Spirit's work almost entirely, and in professing to make the Gospel simple and faith easy, explaining away the office and operation of that very Spirit without whom, "gospel" and "faith" are, to the sinner, but empty and unmeaning names.

Thus far I have stated the two opposite extremes. But it is with only one of these that I have at present to do. And it is only of the latter that I would speak in the remainder of this letter.

The individuals referred to are certainly very zealous for the propagation of their opinions, and spare no pains in persuading others to join them. "They compass sea and land to make one proselyte." Wherever an inquiring sinner is heard of, he is immediately searched out, and drawn along with them to attend their meetings and hear their minister. Books and tracts are thrust upon him, and visits are paid him; and the means are plied so preseveringly, that he finds it not very easy to shake himself free. They think it very uncharitable in him to refuse to attend their place of worship, but they do not deem it so never to enter his. They seem to think that every denomination should join them, while they themselves stand aloof from all.

They are very censorious. A great part of their religion appears to consist in judging others, and pretending to determine their spiritual state. They talk flippantly about conversion and seem to have no difficulty in settling who are converted and who are not, by some peculiar tests of their own. Those who have a single doubt, or who shrink from their language of assurance, are pronounced to be on the way to hell. They will have it, that nobody preaches a free gospel but themselves, and that it is scarcely possible to hear the gospel out of their meeting-place, and beyond their sect. Their self-confidence is amazing. They boast much of the progress of their sect, and of all their doings, in advancing their cause. If they have contrived to raise a little excitement in a place, immediately they announce a revival of religion, number up their converts, and proclaim abroad their success.

They are harpers upon one string—what they call the gospel. One would suppose that there was nothing else in the Bible but this. They never seem to get farther than the first principles of the oracles of God. Those passages or chapters out of which they cannot extract this gospel are passed over. Many portions of Scripture are left unread. We have heard of such profane contempt for the Word as omitting in family reading such chapters as the ninth of the Romans, or the first of Ephesians. As for the "sure word of prophecy," they turn from it. None of them seem to know aught about it. The second coming of the Lord is little thought of, little preached upon, as the church's blessed hope. To the millennarian views they have a very strong hostility; for their idea is, that they will ere long be able to convert the world, and thus the thought of Christ's speedy coming, and of the world's waxing worse and worse until He comes, are sad interruptions to their magnificent plans. Hence their antipathy to the subject.

They sit in judgment upon what they hear; not so much caring to be fed, as to criticize and discuss the subject afterwards—to be able to say whether the minister knows the gospel or not—whether he be a converted man or not. They would not scruple to rise and leave the church, if any part of the discourse was not exactly to their taste. "They will not endure sound doctrine: but, after their own lusts, they heap to themselves teachers, having itching ears."

With these things before me, may I not be permitted to question the reality and solidity of much that is called religion in the present-day?

I see careless men taking an easy way of getting to heaven by saying that they believe; and making their confidence their Saviour. No wrestling with flesh and blood, or with principalities and powers, with the rulers of the darkness of this world, with spiritual wickedness in high places! I see troubled souls saying peace to themselves when there is no peace, by resolving to be quite sure that all is well with them, though their hurt is not healed, but only skinned over, and their conscience remains unpurged by the blood of sprinkling. I see men intent upon widening the strait gate and the narrow way, making what they call faith a substitute for everything, superseding conviction, repentance, self-abasement, by their own act of faith. I see men, instead of trembling at the Word, taking it into their lips as they do a song or a proverb, with all the easy flippancy of men who were above being solemnized and over-awed by the majesty of the voice of Jehovah. I see men turning the grace of God into lasciviousness, boastful of their conversion, forward to speak of it, yet living much as others live, and holding it bondage or legality to be strict in Sabbath-observance, or days of fasting, or similar forms and duties;—nay, some are already denying the authority of the Sabbath. I find men holding the doctrine of perfection," (some having attained it, and some not), yet still censorious, proud, uncharitable, sectarian. I see men mistaking indifference to sin and ignorance of their own deceitful hearts for holiness,—making a merit of not mourning for sin, as if that were unsuitable to one who is forgiven,—not seeking pardon, nor confessing sin in their prayers,—thus combining the vileness of Antinomianism with the mock-sanctity of perfectionism. I see some, even, whom I believe to be at heart Christians, running from doctrine to doctrine, from book to book, from church to church, attracted by every novelty in the man or the message. Having lost the glow of their first love, they are seeking it in change and excitement, or the bold asseveration of their assurance. Miserable exchange, indeed, for the loss of their first love! Vain device to recover the fresh life and glow of other days by having recourse to something else than the living Christ Himself! Sad delusion of the false spirit, to which some seem to be given over, in righteous recompense for having rejected the function of the Holy One!

But I shall not prolong the description. I have already said enough to give you some idea of the state of religion among many in our day. I do not say that this description applies to all the holders of the new theology. No; I believe there are some to whom it does not. They are holy, and godly living men, in spite of their system, and in opposition to their theology.

Those to whom it may apply may take offence at what I have written. They may deem me uncharitable and harsh. But I have written strongly because I felt that the evil was great, and that smooth words would have but concealed its magnitude. The words may seem sharp and severe but no hostile feelings towards any individuals whatever mingle with my exposition of their doctrines.

Having myself written much in defence of a free gospel, I felt the more called upon now to write what I have written here, and to write it in the way that I have done. I hold and preach as free a gospel as ever I did; nor shall I be driven from it by the extremes into which some have gone. They have brought reproach upon the freeness of the gospel by the false doctrine with which they encircle it. They have made many suspicious even of the very name gospel. But this is only Satan's old device. He wants to make the gospel odious; and he has to no small extent, succeeded. But shall this hinder us form proclaiming it as before? Shall this lead us to hedge it about and guard it, and affix conditions to it, because of such abuse? No; let us lift up our voices as loudly as ever,—"Ho every one that thirsteth, come ye to the waters."

Let us not limit the gospel, or abate aught of its absolute and unconditional freeness. Let us not cast any stumblingblock in the sinner's way, nor tell him that he is not at liberty to come and be forgiven, just as he stands this very instant. Let us not tell him that he must get quit of his sins, and repent and pray, and wait, and do his best, in order that after all this he may be qualified for coming to the Saviour. Let us not allow him to suppose that there is any one thing required of him before coming, or that he is not welcome to his Father's house and His Father's arms, even now, poor prodigal as he is.

We may be accused of inconsistency and self-contradiction,—one sermon may be contrasted with another,—one statement may be held up as the antagonist of the other. But still let us not be moved away, either from the gospel or its hope.

We belive in a gospel free to all, and we preach it as such,—going up to every man with the message of peace on our lips, and the blessings of salvation in our hands, saying, "Be thou reconciled to God."

Or perhaps we may be accused of an ignorant attachment to antiquated creeds, and of blind veneration for the straitened theology of other days. Now, though wishing to draw direct from the fountainhead, and to call no man master, yet we do confess a liking to those doctrines which, in life and in death, were grasped so strongly by our fathers,—those much-praying, much believing, much-thinking, hard-toiling, sore-suffering men, whose eyes grew early dim; and whose hair grew early gray. We are not ashamed to confess a satisfaction in sitting at the feet of such men, and listening to their solemn teaching, in preference to seeking instructions from men whose shallowness and self-confidence made us feel that instead of teaching others, they have need that one teach them again what be the first principles of the oracles of God.

## THUS SAITH THE LORD.

"They have healed also the hurt of the daughter of My people slightly, saying, Peace, peace, where there is no peace."—Jer. 6:14.

"They are prophets of the deceit of their own hearts." Jer. 23:26.

"I am against the prophet, saith the Lord, that stealeth My words, every man from his neighbour."—Jer. 23:30.

"A voice of a multitude being at ease with her."—Ezek. 23:42.

"Ever learning, and never able to come to the knowledge of the truth"—2 Tim. 3:7.

"Beguiling unstable souls."—2 Peter 2:14.

(H. Bonar, 1851).

N.B. Conditions have not improved any during the last 75 years. Human nature—depraved and dominated by a thoroughly deceitful and desperately wicked heart—is the same in every age. The devices which Satan employs vary but little. The exaltation of man and the denial of the claims of God, which began in Eden, will continue to the end of the age. There is only one hope for this sin-cursed world, and that is, the personal return of the Lord Jesus Christ to take the government upon His shoulder! A. W. P.

# THE SIN OF UNBELIEF.

"He that believeth not God hath made Him a liar; because he believeth not the record that God gave of His Son." 1 John 5:10.

I am afraid that there are very few who realise what a terrible thing unbelief is and see that it is the sin of sins. If continued in, it is a sin which hath never forgiveness. I am afraid that most of the unconverted look upon unbelief as a matter of very small moment, but our text shows us the awfulness of it, for unbelief is to make God a liar, and you surely could scarcely imagine anything worse than that! Oh, I want every sinner here to-night to be awakened by the Holy Spirit to realise the sinfulness, the heinousness, the awfulness of the sin of unbelief.

It is always well that a person should know just where he is. If one were to see a ship that was drifting towards the rocks, it would be an act of mercy to give warning to the captain. If one knew that there was a person asleep in a house afire, it would be a deed of charity to go and arouse that sleeper. The sleeper might growl, and want to go back to sleep again, not realising his danger, but it would be an act of common charity to get hold of him by the shoulder, awaken him, and tell him of his imminent peril. Oh, may the Holy Spirit arouse the unconverted here to-night!

God has spoken, and you do not believe what He has said; you make Him out to be a liar, for our text says, "He that believeth not God hath made Him a liar, because he believeth not the record that God gave of His Son." God tells the sinner that he is guilty, that he is even now under condemnation, that the sword of Divine justice is suspended over his head, and he believes it not! God says there is but a step betwixt thee and death, and after death the judgment, but it all sounds to the sinner as an idle tale. He believes it not. And the awfulness of it is that his unbelief makes God out to be a liar! As to how it does so we shall explain in a few moments.

God says that he that believeth not shall be damned, and the unconverted do not believe it. If they did, they would not continue in their indifference. If they did, they would seek to flee from the wrath to come. If they really believed they were in the danger that God's Word says they are in, if they really believed that they were as near to the Pit as they are, they would be aroused; they would seek the Lord in earnest; they would put the matter of their souls' salvation above everything else; they would let everything else go until they had believed for themselves in the Lord Jesus Christ. But Oh, there are so many who have false and inadequate conceptions of unbelief! I am almost afraid there are some here in this place who have heard so much of human depravity and of man's helplessness, that they have used those very things to console themselves that they cannot help their unbelief, and that really they are to be more pitied than blamed. Oh, may the Spirit of God stir you up to-night!

Now very briefly I want to speak first of the *cause* of your unbelief. I have no doubt there are some here to-night who say, "Well, I **cannot** believe," and they say it to appease their conscience. "I cannot believe" —what a terrible thing to say! I cannot believe **whom?** "I cannot believe in Christ." What? Why, He is the Truth. Do you dare tell me that you cannot believe in Him? Did He ever tell a lie? Is not He worthy of your confidence? What would you think of a child who had been brought up by a noble father and mother—loving, wise, tender—who had done everything possible for him, who were upright and truthful, and who had never told a single lie; and then that child should turn round and say, "I cannot believe my father; I cannot trust my mother"? What a horrible thing to say! Do you mean to tell me that you cannot believe God — you cannot trust in Christ? Is He such a monster, is He so wicked that He is unworthy of your heart's confidence? Oh, my friends, be honest. Say, "I will not belive." That is where Christ puts the emphasis. Your inability to believe consists of the fact that you will not. The Lord Jesus says in John 5:40, "Ye will not come to Me." That is why they did not; it is because they would not. What does He say again in Matthew 23:37, "How often would I have gathered thee ... and ye would not." So they said in Luke 19:12, "We will not have this Man to reign over us." Oh, unconverted sinner, your cannot is a will not, and Christ says so. If you were honest, instead of saying, "I cannot believe," you would say "I won't believe."

Now let me take that unbelief to pieces. Why is it that you cannot believe? The first answer is, because you will not give your serious attention to the matter. Your mind is occupied with other concerns. Your heart is set upon other things, and you treat the matter of your soul's salvation as of secondary importance. You are more occupied with the things of the world—with business or pleasure. Let me give you an illustration. Two young men went down to the beach for a row. An old sailor met them just before they pulled out, and he said, "Boys, I warn you there is a storm coming; you are running into danger —don't go." They went, and in their going — by their action — they made him a liar. They did not call him such in so many words; they did not turn round to the old sailor and tell him to his face, "We do not believe that yarn; we think that is all imagination; you are trying to frighten us." They did not say that in so many words, but by their actions they made him out to be a liar. Oh, unconverted sinner, you do not in so many words stand up and say, "I do not believe God; I do not believe what He says; God is a liar," but by your actions that is what you are making Him out to be. By your continued neglect, by your indifference to your soul's welfare, you are saying that God is not true when He affirms that you are in sore danger. You are saying that salvation is not a matter of such importance as His Word tells you it is. By your actions, your indifference, your carelessness, your procrastination, your unbelief, you are making God a liar!

Let me give you another illustration to press that home, or to make it a little clearer to you. I am not giving it to explain the way of salvation, but to show what it means when it says, "He that believeth not God hath made Him a liar." Here is a man lying very sick in bed, and the doctor comes along and says to him, "I have a medicine that is a cure; it is the only thing known in pharmacy that will relieve your distress. If you take it, in all probability you will recover; if you do not, you will die." But the man just lies there, indifferent, shakes his head and refuses to take the medicine, and dies. What has he done? The doctor told him that he had ministered to many others who were just as sick as he was, who had the same symptoms, and he had given the same medicine to others, and they had recovered. The man by his actions made out that doctor to be a liar. He did not tell him so in so many words, but by his actions, in refusing to take the medicine, in refusing to heed what the doctor had said, he made him out to be a liar.

God says, "He that believeth not shall be damned," and if you really believed that, right here to-night, you would cry out to Him for mercy; but you do not believe it; you do not really believe it in your heart; your actions show it; your carelessness, your indifference, your procrastination, prove that you do not believe what God says, and your actions make Him out to be a liar.

In the second place, your unbelief not only arises from the fact that you are careless, and do not give your serious attention to this matter, but the sinner's inability to believe the Gospel rises out of the fact that the Gospel is true. It is because the Gospel is true that the sinner won't believe it. Oh, you say, nonsense! All right, turn with me now to John 8:45: "And because I tell you the truth ye believe Me not." Those are the words of Christ. That is a strange reason why they would not believe, isn't it? "Because I tell you the truth ye believe Me not." Now turn over to the Second Epistle of Thessalonians, second chapter, verses 10 and 11: "And with all deceivableceivableness of unrighteousness in them that perish; because they received not the love of the the truth, that they might be saved. And for this cause God shall send them strong delusion that they should believe a lie." Oh, my friends, there are millions in this world to-day whose capacity to believe a lie is infinitely greater than their capacity to believe the truth; and the sad thing is, those who believe the truth, are given up by God to believe a lie. It is a most solemn thing, which I have observed for the last ten or fifteen years, that nearly all the false cults of the day, nearly all of the Satanic systems around us, are largely made up of those who were once members of orthodox churches. Three-fourths of the Theosophists, of the Spiritualists, of those who call themselves Christian Scientists, were once members of orthodox churches; but they received not the love of the truth, and God has given them up to believe a lie!

Oh, sinner, what is going to become of you? God's truth has been presented to you faithfully, tenderly, lovingly, again and again, for years past, and you believe it not. Beware, lest God give you up to believe a lie. Things which seemed incredible and absurd to you, once, did so to others. There are lots of people walking this earth to-night who believe that there is no such thing as sin or sickness, or death! There was a time when they would have sneered at such ridiculous statements, but they believe them now. They received not the love of the truth, and God has given them up to believe a lie. Oh, the incredulity of unbelief! My friends, the difficulty to believe the truth lies not in what has to be believed; it is not the nature of the truth that creates the difficulty; it is the state of your own evil heart. It is because it is true that you won't believe it! Men would rather believe a lie! I am very much afraid we are going to witness another demonstration of it in Sydney before long. God grant that it may not be true of any here to-night. But when an impostor, a false teacher comes along, those who are the readiest to flock to his banner and subscribe to his errors, are they who heard the truth and rejected it. There is a false Christ coming to Australia in the near future—unless God hinders. He is on earth to-night, and he is going to come with all deceivableness of unrighteousness and appear as an angel of light; and God is going to permit some who have rejected the truth to believe his lie. Will you be among that number? "He that believeth not God hath made Him a liar," and justice calls aloud for the punishment of such. No punishment can be too severe for the man or woman who tells God to His face that He is a liar.

The time has almost gone. I wanted to deal with some forms of unbelief. It is just possible there may be one here to-night who says, "My sins are so many and so terrible I do not believe I can be saved." My friend, you dare not stand up and tell God that. God says to you to-night, "Come, now, and let us reason together . . . though your sins be . . . red like crimson, they shall be as white as snow." Dare you stand up and say, "Lord, I do not believe that"? Shall your actions say so? Shall your continued refusal to come to Christ say so?

Perhaps someone says, "Well, my trouble is that I doubt if God is willing to save me; I do believe that Christ can save; I do believe that Christ is the Saviour, and the only Saviour, but Oh, I wish I could believe that He was willing to save me." Listen! Christ said, "Him that cometh to me I will in no wise cast out." God's Word says to you to-night, "Believe on the Lord Jesus Christ and **thou** shalt be saved." Three times over in the lesson to-night we had the words "that whosoever believeth"—that includes you, if only you will believe.

Perhaps someone says, "I do not see how that simply 'believing' in Christ can save me." God does not ask you to understand how. He asks you to believe the fact.

Perhaps someone says, "Well, it sounds too good to be true—that I can be saved right now by simply believing in Christ." Yes, God says, "My thoughts are not your thoughts, neither are your ways My ways, saith the Lord. For as the heavens are higher than the earth, so are My ways higher than your ways, and My thoughts than your thoughts."

Now I must give one last word on the doom of the unbeliever. Oh, unbeliever, what is going to happen to you if you continue in this unbelief? I read in the third chapter of Hebrews that 600,000 graves were dug in the wilderness between Egypt and Canaan. Six hundred thousand of those men and women that were delivered from Egypt's plagues, and delivered from Egypt's king at the Red Sea, perished in the wilderness; they never reached Canaan! And God's Word says that they could not enter in **because of unbelief.** That was their doom. They missed the promised land. They missed Canaan, the type of Heaven, because of their unbelief (Heb. 3:19). I read again, in the 11th of Hebrews, and the 31st verse, that those who perished in Jericho did so not because they were heathen, not because they were idolaters, not because they were living immoral lives—for there was one living an immoral life, but God saved her—but they perished because of **their unbelief.** Oh, unbeliever, what is going to become of you? Christ says in John 3:18, "He that believeth not is **condemned already,** because he hath not believed in the name of the only begotten Son of God."

Let this be my last word. Listen! Many of those in Hell to-night are tormented with this thought: I knew the truth, and I believed it not; it has come to pass just as God said it would; God told me that if I believed I should be saved, and God told me that if I believed not I should perish. Oh, I believed not, and now God's word has come true." That is the worm that dieth not—the memory of Gospel sermons that have been heard and despised! The Lord says in that solemn passage in Luke 16 of the man who was asking for a drop of water to cool his tongue, "Son, remember." Oh, the most awful thing that the lost take with them out of this world is a memory that cannot forge the truth of God; that they have heard and refused to believe, and those in Hell will acknowledge this, they will justify God. They will say, "Thou didst declare in Thy Word that he that believeth not God hath made Him a liar; that is what I did; now I am suffering the just punishment because of it."

Oh, sinner, why won't you believe? "He that believeth not shall be damned" (Mark 16:16). May God impress upon each unconverted soul here to-night the awfulness of making Him out to be a liar because of their unbelief.

The above is a digest of a sermon preached in Sydney by the Editor.

## A MISSIONARY ADDRESS.

Delivered by the Editor at the Belvoir Street Particular Baptist Church, Sydney, on June 24, 1926.

You will find the passage that I wish to make the basis of my remarks to-night in the 20th chapter of John's Gospel, particularly the 21st verse, but I will read from the 19th:—

"Then the same day at evening, being the first day of the week, when the doors were shut where the disciples were assembled for fear of the Jews, came Jesus and stood in the midst, and saith unto them, Peace be unto you. And when He had so said, He showed unto them His hands and His side. Then were the disciples glad, when they saw the Lord. Then said Jesus to them again, Peace be unto you; as My Father hath sent Me, even so send I you."

"As my Father hath sent Me, even so send I you." Now my subject to-night is the three-fold need for Christians in **connection with world-wide evangelism,** and without spending any unnecessary time in an introduction I will get right down to business.

The first thing needed by each of us is a missionary mind. One of the greatest deficiencies in the churches of Jesus Christ to-day is the lack of a missionary mind; and by that expression I mean something more than information concerning the work of God in heathen lands. I mean more than being posted with details of what the Lord is doing in the foreign field. There is a vast difference between the possession of knowledge concerning missionary enterprise and the possession of a missionary mind. You would all understand at once what I meant were I to refer to a certain man having a scientific mind. You all know what is meant when you hear of a certain person being a worldly-minded one, and you know something of what is signified when the term is used of a Christian having a spiritual mind. Such expressions as those denote quality. They define the character of the mind. They indicate bent and interest. They stand for fixed attention, sustained interest, enthusiasm, eagerness, and often self-sacrifice. And so, my friends, just as there is such a thing as a scientific mind, a worldly mind, a spiritual mind, so there is a missionary mind; but, sad to say, very few possess it.

Now a missionary mind is based upon enlightened conviction. It rests upon principle rather than upon information. It is begotten by faith rather than by statistics. It is regulated, not by stirring appeals, not by the moving of the emotions, nor by figures; but by the eternal purpose of God in Christ Jesus and our **fellowship** and **co-operation** with that purpose. And yet, my friends, many of God's people to-day are strangely indifferent to the missionary character of Christianity.

The Bible is a missionary book; our gospel is a missionary gospel; our Saviour is a missionary Redeemer; and our God is a missionary God, whose heart, whose compassions, whose love is not confined to any single nation or people, but reaches out unto the ends of the earth. And, O my friends, missions are not an optional task; missions are not a subject for debate; missions are the very essence and the substance of our commission. They are the work to which we have been called; they are that for which the churches exist.

The preaching of the gospel to every creature is not a task that God has given to preachers only, and foreign missions are not a responsibility which God has delegated merely to a missionary circle in the church, but they are that to which He has called **all** His people. The deplorable thing is (I hate to raise a note of criticism on a subject like this and on an occasion like this, but faithfulness demands it), there is much zeal in missionary work today that is not according to knowledge; there is much enthusiasm that is of the flesh, and not kindled by the Spirit; there is much sentimental compassion for perishing sinners rather than loyalty and devotion to Christ.

During my Christian life I have read a great deal of missionary literature, and missionary sermons, and missionary appeals, and most of them have made me very sad. What does the average missionary society do to-day when it is requiring more labourers, when it is needing additional missionaries? What is their appeal usually based upon?—the deep need of perishing humanity. Stirring appeals are made, dreadful pictures are painted of the darkness, and the superstition, and the cruelty that exists in heathendom; or the wonderful opportunities that arise, the doors that are open—whole districts crying out for the Gospel. And because of this, and on **that** foundation, appeals are made for the support of missions. And the sad thing is that so few of God's people see that there is anything wrong in it. My friends, listen! In all our work and witnessing for Christ we must have a "Thus saith the Lord." God has promised to honour those who honour Him, and that which most honours God in connection with missions is that which is most in accord with His written Word! And if our faith is to be maintained it must be rooted in the truth, and if our enthusiasm or our zeal and self-sacrifice are to be sustained it must be **by devotion** unto the Lord Jesus Christ.

Now, to summarise the first point, what I mean is this: I believe that we as a church here, and I believe that every church and company of Christians that is represented here to-night, will never do their full duty in connection with Christian missions until we are made to realise that the sending forth of the Gospel to the ends of the earth is not a matter of expediency, and it is not a matter of passion for souls, but it is a matter of loyalty to our Lord and our Master. We are under marching orders from **Him!** We have His **command** to go forth, and just so long as we interpret "Go" as "Stay at home," "Go ye" as "Go somebody else," "Go into all the world" as "Limit your attentions to Sydney," "Make disciples" as "Coddle Christians," "Preach the Gospel" as simply "Enjoy the Gospel," just so long as we misinterpret the Word of God in that way, we are **traitors** to our mission and **false** to our commission. I say the first thing that we need is a missionary mind that is based upon enlightened conviction; that interest in world-wide evangelisation is not simply an extra, or sideline, or a branch, that we may feel interested in or not as we please, but obedience to Christ and loyalty to our Lord demand that we should heed His final command: "Go ye into all the world and preach the Gospel to every creature" (Matt. 28:19). I say, my friends, that appeal for the support and extension of Christian missions must be based, not upon the piteous condition of our fellow-men abroad, but upon a "Thus saith the Lord." We must come back to **the authority of Scripture!** Oh, I know that arousing demonstrations to the eye (and I have witnessed many, and probably some of you have, too)—people dressed up in native costume and so forth—touching appeals to the emotions—they are just like fireworks; they make a fizz and a splutter, and then they grow dim and die. The only faith in connection with missions that will wear, is a faith that is rooted in the truth; and the only enthusiasm that is created out of devotion to Christ and obedience to our Lord. Oh, may God give us, each of His own people, that is present to-night, a missionary mind, and enlightened conviction that we are under marching orders from the Head of the Church, and that the sending forth of the Gospel is His command, and therefore, whether men will hear or forbear, whether there are cries of demand or not, it is our duty through loyalty to Him to send forth that Gospel.

In the second place (I want to be very brief here) we not only need a missionary mind, but we need a **missionary conscience**. There are those who openly say that they do not believe in missions, and yet they profess to be followers of the Lord Jesus Christ. Such a conviction of unbelief and such a profession of faith cannot be harmonised. A church, to be Christian at all must be a missionary church. If it is not a missionary church it is not entitled to be regarded as a Christian church, for Christianity, in sharp contrast from Judaism, is no parochial, localised religion, but is international in its outlook, world-wide in its scope. "Every creature" is the limits of its parish. Listen, my friends! **Christ's mission is our mission.** Christ took our place on the cross; we are now to take His place in this world. **"As the Father hath sent Me, even so send I you."** What did the Father send Him to do? To preach the glad tidings, to seek out and to save that which was lost, to proclaim deliverance to the captives; **that was His mission.** "As the Father hath sent Me, even so," He declares, "send I you."

Did Christ interpret the purpose of His mission as being world-wide in its scope? Certainly He did. In the Parable of the Sower, where He tells us He Himself is the sower, Christ sowed the seed in **every** section of the field, and the "**field**" **is the world** (Matt. 13:38). In His conversation with Nicodemus, He announced that "God so loved the world that He gave His only begotten Son" (John 3:16). In Matthew 8:11 the Saviour declared there would be many that should come from the east and the west and should sit down with Abraham in the kingdom. To the Pharisees in John 10.16 He said, "**Other sheep I have** which are not of this fold; them also I must bring." Oh, brethren and sisters, our Redeemer is a missionary Redeemer. Over His cross was written, "This is Jesus, the King of the Jews," and that was written in Hebrew, and in Latin and in Greek, the three leading tongues of mankind of that day, to indicate that the Saviour on the cross was to be preached unto the ends of the earth. And, my friends, I repeat it—we need a missionary conscience.

We need to be made to feel that the mission of Christ is now our mission in this world. We are here to represent an absent Saviour. Oh, I know what creatures of extremes we are; I know how easy it is to swing over. Some of you perhaps are saying in your minds, right now, "Is it not the work of the Spirit; is it not the mission of the Holy Spirit to maintain the interests of Christ in this world?" Certainly it is; I would not deny that for a moment; but the Holy Spirit is pleased to use human instrumentality, and the fact that the Holy Spirit is here to maintain the interests of and to glorify an absent Christ is only half the truth; the other half is that the churches of Jesus Christ are here for, are organised for the purpose of maintaining, the interests and bringing glory to the name of our absent Saviour. That is the other side of the truth.

I want you to notice, for a moment, the text. Look at it again. John 20, verse 20, "And when He had so said, He shewed unto them His hands and His side." I want you to notice the order of these statements. First He **showed them** His hands and His side. He first appealed to their love. Second, we are told (in verse 20), "Then were the disciples glad." He kindled their joy. Verse 21: "Then said Jesus to them again, **Peace** be unto you." He **satisfied** their own souls. And then He added, "As the Father hath sent Me, even so send I you." Now that brings me to the third point. I have to speak very rapidly and briefly to-night. We not only need a missionary mind, enlightened convictions, convictions that are based on our relation to Christ, and the task He has allotted His churches; we not only need a missionary conscience, but we need a **missionary heart**. "He shewed unto them His hands and His side," and then He said, "As the Father hath sent Me, even so send I you." Let me try and summarise it all by putting it in this way: "If any man will come after Me, let him deny himself, and take up his cross and follow Me." "He shewed unto them His hands," and His side—the marks of the cross. "If any man will come after Me, let him deny himself and take up his cross." And, do you know, the appalling thing is that in this late age, this twentieth century, that the vast majority of Christians do not begin to understand the simple language of that verse. "Let him take up his cross." Why, I have heard some fritter that away as though it meant nothing more than the minor trials and troubles of life. Some mother has a fractious child that is hard to manage, or a husband that has an awful temper, and she says, "That is 'the cross' I have got to bear." Ah, my friends, that is not the meaning of the verse. The "cross" is definitely defined in Scripture; the cross stands for sacrifice, a life laid down in service for others. That is what "the cross" stands for—a life poured out in self-sacrifice for others. And oh, the Saviour says, "If any man will come after Me, let him deny himself and take up his cross." Let the cross be the badge of Christian discipleship. Is there any blood in your Christian life? Are there the marks of the cross stamped on your soul? He showed unto them His hands and His side, and then He said, "As the Father hath sent Me"—sent Me to endure the cross, sent Me to sacrifice My life for others, even so,—"even so send I you." Not to make an atonement—no, no, no; no human being could do that—but to follow the example that He has left us.

Oh, brethren and sisters, we need a missionary heart, and in order to acquire and obtain a missionary heart we have to be much in the presence of Christ; we have to walk more closely with Him, if ever we are going to have more compassion for poor sinners. If there is going to be more warmth and fervour in our prayers, there has to be more of the cross in our lives. Do you know, while the church—while any church—is largely indifferent to perishing sinners around its own walls you cannot expect it to have much sympathy for and much interest in sinners thousands of miles away, can you? You notice the commission states that. In the 24th Luke the Lord says, "**Beginning** at Jerusalem." You have it again in Acts 1:8. The disciples were to tarry till they were endued with power from on high, then they were to be witnesses of the Lord in Jerusalem, and in Judea, and in Samaria, and unto the uttermost part of the earth. Did you notice the four circles? First, witnesses in Jerusalem. Translate that into modern terms. First, witness for Christ in your own home, witness for Christ in your own workshop, in your own office. Then in Judea. That means in the neighbourhood, the suburb of the city in which your lot is cast. Then in Samaria—the adjoining territory, the whole State. Then unto the uttermost parts of the earth. And so, to sum it all up, beloved friends, I have not time now to expound it further, our threefold need as Christians is, first a missionary mind —our thoughts connected with missions formed by and moulded by the Word of God, not based upon emotionalism, touching appeals and stirring addresses, but rooted and grounded in the truth of God. Second, a missionary conscience, and that is a sense of our loyalty to Christ. Each one of us that has been redeemed by His blood has yet to stand before Him. You have, as I; and you have to give an account of your stewardship; you have to render an account unto Him Who died for you. He has placed His Gospel in our hands; He has not committed the Gospel to the charge of angels, but to His saints, and He has commanded those saints to send it out and take it out and preach it out to every creature; and you have to answer to Him yet! Oh, God give to you and to me a sensitive conscience, a conscience that realises something of our loyalty to Christ. And then may He give us a missionary heart, a love for souls, a compassion for the lost, a travailing for the perishing, and that can only be found at the feet of the Crucified One. May God bless His own Word to-night. "As the Father hath sent Me, even so send I you."

of the Lord," and of Him alone—man contributing nothing whatever to it. They now see that it was discriminating and wondrous grace, which singled them out from Adam's ruined race, and appointed them to be the recipients of the unbought and unsought favours of God.

The grace of God has moved us to institute a change in connection with the publication of the Magazine. A few weeks ago the words "Freely ye have received, freely give" (Matt. 10:8) were applied by the Spirit to our hearts in overwhelming force. Therefore, we no longer feel free to make any charge for "Studies in the Scriptures." Henceforth it will be sent out free. We shall look alone to the Lord for funds to make possible a continuation of its publication. And why not? It is His work. He has said, "The silver is Mine, and the gold is Mine" (Haggai 2:8). If then, He desires this printed testimony to go on, He will supply every need (Phil. 4:19). We shall make no appeals to our fellow Christians, for we believe that is dishonouring to Him in whom we profess is all our confidence.

We do not propose to send out this Magazine to anybody and everybody, for there are, comparatively speaking, very few who will relish its contents. We want to be assured that those who receive it will read it. To all who desire we shall gladly send it as far as the Lord enables—will any who no longer welcome it, or who are too busy to read it, kindly send us a line. We are hoping that this change will result in an increased circulation. If our friends will send in the names and addresses of those whom they have first ascertained will read the Magazine, and whom they believe will enjoy its messages, we shall be very glad to add them to our list.

We have also adopted the same principle in connection with all tracts and booklets of which we are the publishers. The "Three Crosses," the "Manna," the "New Birth," "the Christian's Greatest Need," the "Lost Sheep, Silver and Son of Luke 15," the "Wrath of God," and "Salvation," are now for free distribution —for those who will read them. We reserve the right to look to the Lord for guidance as to how many we send to each one; and none can be sent to those who desire to sell them.

An exception will be made in connection with the bound volumes of "Studies in the Scriptures." It would not be just to the many who have already purchased these to allow others to receive them gratis. So the price of these will be 7/- as hitherto, which is practically what they cost us.

More than ever we shall be cast back upon the Lord. But we have no fear or hesitation. He is faithful, and never disappoints real faith in Himself. "God will provide" can be relied upon. At the same time, we shall value, yea, we seek, the prayers of fellow Christians that He will enlarge the present circulation, that He will bring this Magazine into the hands of an increasing number who are seeking just such a publication, that He will graciously help in the composing of each article, and own and bless them to the glory of His name, the edification of His saints, and the conversion of those who are yet dead in trespasses and sins. "Brethren, pray for us" (1 Thess. 5:25).

With every good wish to all, we remain,

Yours by wondrous grace,

ARTHUR W. PINK.

N.B.—Will U.S.A. friends kindly not that Mr. Pressel will not have any bound volumes of 1926 for sale. Those desiring one, please order direct from the Editor, enclosing International M.O. for $2.00 in an envelope with a five cent. stamp on.

Will Australian subscribers who desire their 1925 or 1926 copies bound, write their name on front page of each month, and mail to us with 2/6, and D.V. we will have them bound and forwarded to you.

VOL. VI.        JAN., 1927        NO. 1

# STUDIES IN THE SCRIPTURES

"Search the Scriptures". John 5:39.

Copyright in all English-speaking Countries.

Editor: Arthur W. Pink, 22 Parramatta Road, Summer Hill, N.S.W., Australia.
Hon. Agent in U.S.A.: Mr. C. S. Pressel, 559 Dupont Ave., York, Penna.

FREE TO ALL WHO WILL READ IT

As we contemplate another year's ministry, our prayer is that while we are left on earth we may ever put the claims and glory of God first and foremost; that we may make everything of Him and nothing of man. Much as we may desire to be used in blessing to our fellows—either in pointing sinners to Christ as the only and all-sufficient Saviour, or the edifying of believers—there is something which must take precedence, namely, the honor and praise of the Lord Himself To magnify Him, to give Him the pre-eminence in all things, is our earnest longing. By His grace we shall seek to delight ourselves in the Lord (Psalm 37:4) and His written Word (Jer. 15:16), leaving Him to supply every need, care for the work which He has entrusted to us, and defend against all enemies.

Our purpose is to "Contend earnestly for the faith" (Jude 3). This does not mean (as so many suppose) attacking error; it signifies, publishing the unsearchable riches of Christ, proclaiming the whole counsel of God, neither adding to nor taking from the Word of truth. Souls are not built up by exposing the sophistries of Satan. There may be times when the servants of God are justified in refuting error, but for our own part we feel that the more excellent way is to expound the Truth. The most effective method of dispelling the darkness is to let in the light. We desire that our ministry should be constructive rather than destructive; positive, and not simply negative. Our business is to feed the sheep, and this is not done by occupying them with poisons. We are called to be witnesses for Christ, to be a scribe bringing forth out of the inexhaustable treasures of Scripture things new and old; and if we are faithful in this, we shall have no time to waste in denouncing heresies.

This year's issues will (D.V.) bring to a conclusion our exposition of John's Gospel. To those who are profiting from the present portions we desire to say that the previous ones are still obtainable, though our stock may soon be exhausted. The "Gleanings in Exodus" will be occupied with the richest section of the typical teachings of that book, and will, we trust, bring out some of the manifold perfections of Him who is "altogether lovely." In addition, we hope to continue publishing digests of some of the sermons we are now preaching in Sydney, so that our congregation will be enlarged by distant friends having them in printed form.

As was announced in the last issue, no charge is any longer being made for this Magazine. It will be sent gladly to all who apply for and promise to read it. We do not wish to waste copies on those who have no relish for it, or who are too busy to read it, or who already have sufficient reading matter in hand. We are most anxious to reach those of the Lord's people who are living in places (and there are many such) where they cannot hear an oral ministry which magnifies Christ and edifies His people. The vast majority of the so-called churches are so full of worldliness that the Spirit of God has long since departed from them. So many of the preachers are themselves unregenerate men (by their fruits they are known) that being blind, they are only capable of leading the blind. Others are so afraid of the denominational heads, or so anxious to retain the goodwill of godless but wealthy men in their congregations, that only too often their mouths are muzzled.

(Continued on page 24)

## BACK NUMBERS

OF THIS MAGAZINE obtainable, 5/- (1 dollar) per year; Bound at 7/- (1 dollar 75.) Each year is yet obtainabl .

ADVISE PROMPTLY of Change of Address.

THIS MAGAZINE is published as a work of faith and labor of love. It is gladly sent to all who would value it.

We want the names and addresses of Christians who would read it.

Christians who feel definitely led to do so many have fellowship with us in this Ministry.

## CONTENTS.

| | |
|---|---|
| The Gospel of John (18: 1-11) | 2 |
| Gleanings in Exodus | 10 |
| Christian Fools | 14 |
| The Jew in History | 21 |
| Justification | 24 |

## THE GOSPEL OF JOHN

**61. Christ in the Garden: John 18: 1-11.**

Below is an Analysis of the passage which is to be before us:—
1. Jesus and His disciples cross the Cedron v. 1.
2. Judas' knowledge of this place of retirement v. 2.
3. Judas conducting the Lord's enemies there v. 3.
4. Christ's challenge and their response vv. 4, 5.
5. Christ's power and their lack of discernment evidenced vv. 6, 7.
6. Christ protecting His own vv. 8, 9.
7. Peter's rashness and Christ's rebuke vv. 10, 11.

The eighteenth chapter begins a new section of our Gospel. Chapter 1 is introductory in its character; 2 to 12 record our Lord's ministry in the world; 13 to 17 show Him alone with His disciples, preparing them for His departure; 18 to 21 is the closing division, giving us that which attended His death and resurrection. Here, too, everything is in perfect accord with the distinctive character of John's delineation of Christ. The note struck here is in quite a different key from the one heard at the end of the Synoptics. That which is prominent in the closing scenes of the Fourth Gospel is not the **sufferings** of the Saviour, but the lofty **dignity** and Divine **glory** of the God-man.

"As the last section (13 to 17) involved His death, it must take place. He has given in His record to Him who sent Him, whose counsels had determined before what was to be done, and whose prophets showed before that Christ should suffer (Acts 2: 23; 3: 18; 4: 28); and now that must be which makes all these assertions true. Without these two chapters (18, 19), therefore, none of the precious things which have thrilled the heart in the previous chapters could be possible; nay more, none of His own assertions as to what He would be and do, of giving eternal life, of having any out of the world, of coming again for them, of sending the Holy Spirit, of preparing a place for them, of having them in the glory with Him, or of having that glory at all; there would be no assembly of God, no restoration of Israel, no gathering of the nations, no millennium, no new heavens and new earth, no adjustment in righteousness of the 'creation of God' of which He is the beginning, no display of grace, no salvation, no revelation of the Father—all these and much more were contingent on His death and resurrection. Without these all things in this book drop out and leave a blank, the blackness of darkness" (Mr. Mal. Taylor).

John 18 opens with an account of the Saviour and His disciples entering the Garden, but in recording what took place there nowhere is the presiding hand of the Holy Spirit more evident. Nothing is said of His taking Peter and James and John into its deeper recesses, that they might "watch with Him." Nothing is said of His there praying to the Father. Nothing is said of His falling upon His face, of His awful agony, of the bloody sweat, of the angel appearing to strengthen Him. Perfectly in place in the other Gospels, they are passed over here as unsuited to the picture which John was inspired to paint. In their place other details are supplied—most appropriate and striking—which are not found in the Synoptics.

"Into that Garden, hallowed by so many associations, the Lord entered, with the Eleven; and there took place the Agony related in the Synoptics, but wholly passed over by John. Yet he was very near the Lord, being one of the three taken apart from the rest by Christ, and asked to watch with Him. The rest were told to sit down a little way off from the Master. If any of the Evangelists then could have written with authority of that solemn time John was the one best fitted to do it. Yet he is the one who omits all reference to it! It might be thought that what the others had written was sufficient. Why, then, did he describe so minutely circumstances connected with the Lord's apprehension! The special line of his Gospel, presenting the Lord as a Divine Person, will alone explain this. As Son of God incarnate he presents Him, and not as the suffering Son of man. We shall learn, then, from him that which none of the others mention, though Matthew was present with Him, how the Lord's personal presence at first over-awed Judas and the company with that traitor" (Mr. C. E. Stuart).

In each of the Synoptics, as the end of His path drew near, we find the Saviour speaking, again and again, of what He was to suffer at the hands of men; how that He would be scourged and spat upon. be shamefully treated by Jew and Gentile alike, ending with His crucifixion, burial and resurrection. But here in John, that which is seen engaging His thoughts in the closing hours was His **return to the Father** (see 13: 1; 14: 2; 16: 5; 17: 5.) And everything is in perfect accord with this. Here in the Garden, instead of Christ falling to the ground before the Father, we behold those who came to arrest the Saviour falling to the ground before Him! Nowhere does the perfect supremacy of the Lord Jesus shine forth more gloriously: even to the band of soldiers He utters a **command**, and the disciples are allowed to go unmolested.

"When Jesus had spoken these words, He went forth with His disciples over the brook Cedron" (v. 1). The "these words" refer to the Paschal Discourse and the High Priestly prayer which have engaged our attention in the previous chapters. Having delivered His **prophetic message**, He now prepares to go forth to His **priestly work**. The "Garden" is the same one mentioned in the other Gospels, though here the Holy Spirit significantly omits its name—Gethsemane. In its place, He mentions the "brook Cedron," identical with "Kidron," its Hebrew name, which means "dark waters"—emblematic of that black stream through which He was about to pass. The Cedron was on the east side of the city, dividing Jerusalem from the Mount of Olives (Josephus). It was on the west side of the city that He was crucified: thus did the Sun of Righteousness complete His atoning circuit!

What, we may ask, were our Lord's design and purpose in entering the "Garden" at this time? First, in accord with the typical teaching of the Day of Atonement. The victim for the sin-offering (unlike the burnt offering) was destroyed "without (outside) the camp" (see Lev. 4: 12, 21; 16: 27); so the Lord Jesus offered Himself as a sacrifice for sin outside of Jerusalem: "Wherefore Jesus also, that He might sanctify the people with His own blood, suffered without the gate" (Heb. 13: 12). Therefore, as His atoning sufferings began here, He sought the Garden, rather than remain in Jerusalem.

Second, in crossing the brook Cedron, accompanied by His disciples, another Old Testament type was most strikingly fulfilled. In 2 Samuel 15: (note particularly vv. 23, 30, 31) we read of David, at the time of his shameful betrayal by his familiar friend Ahitophel, crossing the same brook; crossing it in tears, accompanied by his faithful followers. So David's Son and Lord, crossed the Cedron while Judas was betraying Him to His foes.

Third, His object was to afford His enemies the more free scope to take Him. The leaders of Israel had designed to lay hands on Him for some time past, but they feared the common people; therefore, that this impediment might be removed, the Saviour chose to go out of the City to the Garden, where they might have full opportunity to apprehend Him, and carry Him away in the night, quietly and secretly. In addition to these reasons, we may add, His arrest in the solitude of the Garden made it the easier for His disciples to escape.

The entrance of Christ into the Garden at once reminds us of Eden. The contrasts between them are indeed most striking. In Eden, all was delightful; in Gethsemane, all was terrible. In Eden, Adam and Eve parleyed with Satan; in Gethsemane, the Last Adam sought the face of His Father. In Eden, Adam sinned; in Gethsemane, the Saviour suffered. In Eden, Adam fell; in Gethsemane, the Redeemer conquered. The conflict in Eden took place by day; the conflict in Gethsemane was waged at night. In the one Adam fell before Satan; in the other, the soldiers fell before Christ. In Eden the race was lost; in Gethsemane Christ announced, "Of them which Thou gavest Me have I lost none (John 18: 9). In Eden, Adam took the fruit from Eve's hand; in Gethsemane, Christ received the cup from His Father's hand. In Eden, Adam hid himself; in Gethsemane, Christ boldly showed Himself. In Eden, God sought Adam; in Gethsemane, the last Adam sought God! From Eden Adam was "driven"; from Gethsemane Christ was "led." In Eden the "sword" was drawn (Gen. 3: 24) in Gethsemane the "sword" was sheathed (John 18: 11).

"Where was a garden, into the which He entered and His disciples" (v. 1). Christ did not dismiss the apostles as they left the upper-room in Jerusalem, but took them along with Him to Gethsemane. He would have them witness the fact that He was not seized there as a helpless victim, but that He voluntarily delivered Himself up into the hands of His foes. He would thereby teach them, from His example, that it is a Christian duty to offer no resistance to our enemies, but meekly bow to the will of God. He would also show them His power to protect His own under circumstances of greatest danger.

"And Judas also, which betrayed Him, knew the place" (v. 2). "Our Lord and Saviour knew that He should be taken by Judas, and that this was the place appointed by His Father wherein He should be taken; for the 4th verse tell us 'Jesus therefore, knowing all things that should come upon Him,' etc. He knew that Judas would be there that night, and, therefore, like a valiant champion, He cometh into the field first, afore His enemy. He goeth thither to choose, and singles out this place on purpose" (Dr. Thomas Goodwin).

"For Jesus oftimes resorted thither with His disciples" (v. 2). This was the Saviour's place of prayer during the last week— a quiet spot to which He frequently retired with His apostles. In Luke 21: 37 we read, "And in the daytime He was teaching in the Temple; and at night He went out and abode in the Mount that is called the Mount of Olives." In Luke 22: 39 we read, "And He came out, and went, as He was wont to the Mount of Olives; and His disciples also followed Him." This was Christ's place of devotion, and the place, no doubt, where many precious communications had passed between Him and the disciples; it is mentioned here to show the obduracy of the Traitor's heart—it also aggravated his sin.

The Saviour knew full well that the treacherous apostate was well acquainted with this spot of holy associations, yet did He, nevertheless go there. On previous occasions He had **avoided** His enemies: "Then took they up stones to cast at Him; but Jesus hid himself, and went out of the Temple." (8: 59). "These things spake Jesus, and departed, and did hide Himself from them" (12: 36). But now "the hour" was come; therefore did He make for that very place to which He knew Judas would lead His enemies.

"Judas then, having received a band of men and officers from the chief priests and Pharisees, cometh thither with lanterns and torches and weapons" (v. 3). The "band" which Judas "received" evidently signifies a detachment of Roman soldiers, which Pilate had granted for the occasion; the Greek word means the tenth part of a legion, and therefore consisted of four or five hundred men. Some have questioned this, but the words of Matt. 26: 47, "A great multitude with him"—strongly confirms it. The "officers from the chief priests and Pharisees" refer to the servants of Israel's leaders. Luke 22: 52 shows that the heads of the Nation themselves also swelled the mob— "Then Jesus said unto the chief priests, and captains of the temple, and the elders, which were come to Him, Be ye come out, as against a thief, with swords and staves?" As Christ was to die for sinners, both among the Jews and Gentiles, so God ordered it that **Gentiles** (Roman soldiers) and **Jews** should have a hand both in His arrest and in His crucifixion!

"Cometh thither with lanterns and torches and weapons" (v. 3). What an anomaly! Seeking out the Light of the world with torches and lanterns! Approaching the Good Shepherd with "weapons!" As though He would seek to hide Himself; as though He could be taken with swords and staves! Little did they know of His readiness to be led as a lamb to the slaughter. Significant too is the general principle here symbolically illustrated: attacks upon the Truth were made by artificial lights and carnal weapons! It has been thus ever since. The 'light of reason' is what men depend upon; and where that has failed, resort has been had to brute force, of which the "weapons" speak. How vain these are, when employed against the Son of God, He plainly demonstrated in the sequel.

"Jesus therefore, knowing all things that should come upon Him" (v. 4). With this should be compared 13: 3, which presents a most striking comparison and contrast: "Jesus knowing that the Father had given all things into His hands"; the comparison is between our Lord's omniscience in either reference; the contrast between the subjects of His knowledge there and here. In 13: 3 Christ spoke of "all things" being given into His hands; here in 18: 4 He anticipates the moment when "all things" were to be taken from Him, when He was to be "cut off" and "have nothing" (Dan. 9: 26). His foreknowledge was perfect: for Him there were no surprises. The receiving of "all things" from the Father's hands was not more present to His spirit than the loss of "all things" by His being cut off. In John 13 He contemplates the glory; here the sufferings, and He passed from the one to the other in the unchanging blessedness of absolute perfection.

"Jesus therefore, knowing all things that should come upon Him." These were the "all things" decreed by God, agreed upon by the Son in the eternal convenant of grace, predicted in the Old Testament scriptures, and foretold, again and again, by Himself; namely, all the attendant circumstances of His sufferings and death. "Jesus therefore, knowing all things that should come upon Him, went forth"—not out of the Garden as v. 26 plainly shows, but from its inner recesses, where He had prayed alone. "Went forth," first to awaken the sleeping three (Matt. 26: 46), then to rejoin the eight whom He had left on the outskirts of the Garden (Matt. 26: 36), and now to meet Judas and his company. This "went forth" shows the perfect harmony between John and the Synoptics.

"And said unto them, Whom seek ye?" (v. 4). Our Lord was the first to speak: He did not wait to be challenged. His reason for asking this question is indicated in the "therefore" of the previous clause—"Jesus therefore, knowing all things that should come upon Him, went forth, and said unto them, Whom seek ye?" That which the Holy Spirit has here emphasised is the willingness of Christ to suffer, His readiness to go forth to the cross. He knew full well for what fell purpose these men were there, but He asks the question so that He might solemnly and formally surrender Himself to them. Once, when they wanted to take Him by force and make Him a king. He departed from them (6: 15); but now that He was to be scourged and crucified, He boldly advanced to meet them. This was in sharp contrast from the first Adam in Eden, who, after his sin, hid himself among the trees of the garden. So, too, Christ's act and question here bore witness to the futility and folly of their "lanterns and torches and weapons."

"They answered Him, Jesus of Nazareth. Jesus saith unto them, I am" (v. 5). Why did they not answer, "Thee!"? Jesus of Nazareth stood before them, yet they did not say, "Thou art the one we have come to arrest." It is plain from this circumstance that they did not recognise Him, nor did Judas, who is here expressly said to have "stood with them." Despite their "lanterns and torches" their eyes were holden! Does not this go far to confirm our thought on the closing words of v. 3—the Holy Spirit designedly intimated that something more than the light which nature supplies is needed to discover and discern the person of the God-man! And how this is emphasised by the presence of Judas, who had been in closest contact with the Saviour for three years! How solemn the lesson! How forcibly this illustrates 2 Cor. 4: 3, 4: "But if our gospel be hid, it is hid to them that are lost: in whom the god of this world hath blinded the minds of them which believe not." Even the Traitor failed now to recognise the Lord: he too was stricken with dimness of vision. The natural man is spiritually blind: the Light shone in the darkness, and the darkness comprehended it not (1: 5)! It is only as the light of God shines in our hearts that knowledge is given us to behold the glory of God in the face of Jesus Christ (2 Cor. 4: 6)!

"And Judas also, which betrayed Him, stood with them" (v. 5). Only a few hours previous he had been seated with Christ and the Eleven, now he is found with the Lord's enemies, acting as their guide. Some have argued that there is a discrepancy here between John's account and what we read of in the Synoptics. In the latter we are told Judas had arranged with the soldiers that he would give them a sign, identifying the One they should arrest by kissing Him. This he did, and they laid hands on Him. But here in John 18 he is viewed as failing to recognise the Saviour, yet there is no discrepancy at all. John does not relate what Matthew and the others give us, but instead, supplies details which they were guided to omit. John tells us what took place in the Garden before the Traitor gave his vile sign. If the reader will compare Luke's account he will see that the kiss was given by Judas at a point between what we read of in John 18, vv. 9, 10.

"As soon then as He had said unto them, I am, they went backward, and fell to the ground." (v. 6). Another reason why notice is taken of Judas at the close of the preceding verse is to inform us that he, too, fell to the ground. Observe the words "they went backward." They were there to arrest Him, but instead of advancing to lay hands on Him, they retreated! Among them were five hundred Roman soldiers, yet they retired before His single "I am." They fell back in consternation, not forward in worship! All He said was "I am"; but it was fully sufficient to overawe and overpower them. It was the enunciation of the ineffable Name of God, by which He was revealed to Moses at the burning bush (Ex. 3: 14). It was a display of His Divine majesty. It was a quiet exhibition of His Divine power. It was a signal demonstration that He was "The Word" (1: 1)! He did not strike them with His hand—there was no need to; He simply spoke two monosyllables and they were completely overcome.

But why, we may ask, should our Lord have acted in such a manner on this occasion? First, that it might be clearly shown He was more than "Jesus of Nazareth": He was "God manifest in flesh," and never was this more unmistakably evidenced. Second, that it might appear with absolute clearness that He voluntarily delivered Himself up into their hands—that it was not they who apprehended Him, but He who submitted to them. He was not captured, for He was not to (passively) suffer merely, but to (actively) offer Himself as a sacrifice to God. Here is the ultimate reason why it is recorded that "Judas also, which betrayed Him, stood with them": the Traitor's perfidy was needless and the captor's weapons useless against One who in giving up Himself unto death was soon to give Himself in death. If none had power to take His life from Him (10: 18, 19), none had power to arrest Him. He here showed them, and us, that they were completely at His mercy —helpless on the ground—and not He at theirs. How easy for Him then to have walked quietly away, unmolested! First, they failed to recognise Him; now they were prostrate before Him. What was to hinder Him from leaving them thus? Nothing but His Father's will, and to it He submissively bowed. Thus did the Saviour give proof of His willingness to offer Himself as a sacrifice for sin. In the third place, it left these men without excuse. Every detail in connection with our Lord's passion had been determined by the Divine counsels, yet God did not treat those who had a hand in it as mere machines, but as responsible moral agents. Before Pilate sentenced Christ to death, God first gave him a plain intimation that it was an innocent Man who stood before him, by warning his wife in a dream (Matt. 27: 19). So here with these Roman soldiers, who may never have seen Christ before. They cannot plead in the Day of Judgment that they were ignorant of the glory of His person: they cannot say that they never witnessed His miraculous power, and had no opportunity given them to believe on Him. This exhibition of His majesty, and their laying hands on Him afterwards, makes their condemnation just!

It is very striking to observe that the Lord Jesus had uttered the same words on previous occasions, but with very different effects. To the woman at the well He had said "I am" (4: 26), and she at once recognised Him as the Christ (4: 29). To the disciples on the storm-lashed sea He had said, "I am" (6: 20—see Greek), and we are told "they willingly received Him into the ship." But here there was no conviction wrought of His Messiahship, and no willing reception of Him. Instead, they were terrified, and fell to the ground. What a marvellous demonstration that the same Word is to some "a savour of life unto life," while to others it is "a savour of death unto death"! Observe, too, that His Divine "I am" to the disciples in the ship was accompanied by "Be not afraid" (6: 20); how solemn to mark its omission here!

Vividly does this forewarn sinners of how utterly helpless they will be before the Christ of God in a coming Day! "What shall He do when He comes to judge, who did this when about to be judged? What shall be His might when He comes to reign, who had this might when He was at the point to die?" (Augustine.) What, indeed, will be the effect of that Voice when He speaks in judgment upon the wicked!

"As soon then as He had said unto them, I am, they went backward, and fell to the ground." This was a remarkable fulfilment of an Old Testament prophecy given a thousand years before. It is recorded in the 27th Psalm, the whole of which, most probably, was silently uttered by the Saviour as He journeyed from the upper-room in Jerusalem, across the brook Cedron, into the Garden. "The Lord is My light and My salvation; whom shall I fear? The Lord is the strength of My life; of whom shall I be afraid? When the wicked, even My enemies and My foes, came upon Me to eat up My flesh, **they stumbled and fell**" (vv. 1, 2). Let the reader pause and ponder the remainder of this Psalm: it is blessed to learn **what** comforted and strengthened the Saviour's heart in that trying hour. Psalm 27 gives us the musings of Christ's heart at this time **Godwards**. Psalm 35 recorded His prayers against His enemies, **manwards**: "Let them be confounded and put to shame that seek after My soul: let them be **turned back and brought to confusion** that devise My hurt" (v. 4). Still another Psalm should be read in this connection, the 40th. That this Psalm is a Messianic one we know positively from vv. 7, 8. Verses 11-17 were, we believe, a part of His prayer in Gethsemane, and in it He asked, "Let them be ashamed and confounded together that seek after My soul to destroy it; let them be **driven backward and put to shame** that wish Me evil" (v. 14). Thus was both Messianic prophecy fulfilled and prayer answered in this overwhelming of His enemies.

"Then asked He them again, Whom seek ye?" (v. 7). "This second question carries a mighty conviction, a mighty triumph with it over their conscience as if He had said, I have told you I am; and I have told it you to purpose, have I not? Have you not learned by this who I am, when your hearts are so terrified that you all fell down before Me! They had been taught by woeful experience who He was, when He blew them over, flung them down with His breath; and it might have turned to a blessed experience had God struck their hearts, as He did their outward man" (Dr. Thomas Goodwin).

"And they said, Jesus of Nazareth" (v. 7). They would not own Him as **the Christ**, but continued to speak of Him according to the name of His humiliation —"Jesus of Nazareth." How striking and how solemn is this after what has been before us in v. 6—such an exhibition of Divine majesty and power, yet their hard hearts unmoved! No outward means will soften those who are resolved on wickedness. No miracles, however awesome, will melt men's enmity: **nothing will suffice except God works directly by His Word and Spirit**. Another signal proof of the desperate hardness of men's hearts is the case of those who were appointed to guard the Saviour's sepulchre. While keeping their watch, God sent an earthquake, and then an angel to roll away the stone from the grave's mouth, and so awful were these things to the keepers that they "became as dead men." And yet, when they reported to their masters and were offered a bribe to say His disciples stole the body of Christ while they slept, they were willing parties to such a lie. O the hardness of the human heart: how "desperately wicked"! Even Divine judgments do not subdue it. In a coming day God will pour out on this earth the vials of His wrath, and what will be the response of men? This: "They gnawed their tongues for pain, and **blasphemed** the God of heaven because of their pains and their sores, and **repented not of their deeds**" (Rev. 16: 10, 11). Nothing but a miracle of sovereign grace, the putting forth of omnipotent power, can bring a blaspheming rebel out of darkness into God's marvellous light. Many a soul has been terrified, as were these men in the Garden, and yet continued in their course of alienation from God.

"Jesus answered, I have told you that I am" (v. 8). The dignity and calmness of our Lord are very noticeable here. Knowing full well all the insults and indignities He was about to suffer, He repeats His former declaration, "I am"; then He added, "if therefore ye seek Me, let these go their way." "Christ was about to suffer for them, and therefore it was not just that they should suffer too; nor was it proper that they should suffer with Him, lest their sufferings should be thought to be a part of the price of redemption. These words then may be considered as an emblem and pledge of the acquittal and discharge of God's elect, through the surety-engagements and performances of Christ who drew near to God on their behalf, substituting Himself in their room, and undertaking for them in the counsel and covenant of peace, and laid Himself under obligation to pay their debts. Now, as there was a discharge of them from eternity, a non-imputation of sin to them, and a **secret** letting of them go upon the surety-engagements of Christ; so there was now an open discharge of them all upon the apprehension, sufferings, death and resurrection of Him" (Dr. John Gill).

"If therefore ye seek Me, let these go their way" (v. 8). In 13: 1 we are told of Christ that "having loved His own which were in the world, He loved them unto the end." How blessedly this is seen here. Christ's first thought is not of Himself and what He was about to suffer, but of His disciples. It was the Shepherd protecting His sheep. "The tender sympathy and consideration of our great High Priest for His people come out very beautifully in this place, and would doubtless be remembered by the Eleven long afterwards. They would remember that the very last thought of their Master, before He was made a prisoner, was for them and their safety" (Bishop Ryle). And how the Saviour's majesty here shines forth again! He was about to be taken prisoner, but He acts as no helpless captive, but rather like a king. "Let these go their way" was a command. Here am I, take Me; but I charge you not to meddle with them— touch not Mine anointed! He speaks as Conqueror, and such He was; for He had thrown them to the ground by a word from His lips. They were about to tie His hands, but before doing so He first tied theirs!

"If therefore ye seek Me, let these go their way." There is much for us to learn here. First, it supplied another proof of how easily He could have saved Himself had He so pleased: He that saved others could have saved Himself; He who had authority to command them to let these go, had authority to command them to let Himself go. Second, Christ only was to suffer: in the great work before Him none could follow—"And there shall be no man in the tabernacle of the congregation when he goeth in to make an atonement" (Lev. 16: 17). He was to tread the winepress alone. Third, Christ had other work for them yet to do, and until that work was done their enemies should and must leave them alone. So long as God has something for His servants to do the Devil himself cannot seize them. "Go," said Christ, when warned that Herod would kill Him, "and tell that fox, Behold, I cast out demons, and I do cures to-day and to-morrow" (Luke 13: 30). I will do those things in spite of him; he cannot prevent Me. Fourth, here we see grace, as in the previous verse Divine power, exercised by this One who so perfectly "declared the Father" (v. 18). Fifth, Christ would thus show His disciples how fully competent He was to preserve them amid the greatest dangers. We have no doubt but that these Roman soldiers and Jewish officers intended to seize the apostles as well—Mark 14: 51, 52, strongly indicates this—but the Word of power went forth, "Let these go their way," and they were safe. We doubt not that the coming day will make it manifest that this same word of power went forth many times, though we knew it not, when we were in the place of danger.

"That the saying might be fulfilled, which He spake, Of them which Thou gavest Me have I lost none" (v. 9). This "saying" refers not to an Old Testament prophecy but to that part of His prayer recorded in 17: 12—"While I was with them in the world, I kept them in Thy name: those that Thou gavest Me I have kept, and none of them is lost." Though this has a peculiar respect unto the apostles, it is true of all God's elect, who are given to Christ, and none of them shall be lost, neither their souls nor their bodies; for Christ's charge of them reaches to both: both were given to Him, both are redeemed by Him, and both shall be saved by Him with an everlasting salvation; He saves their souls from eternal death, and will raise their bodies from corporeal death; therefore, that His care of His disciples, with respect to their temporal lives as well as eternal happiness, might be seen, He made this agreement with those who came to take Him, or rather laid this injunction upon them, to dismiss them and which it is very remarkable they did, for they laid hands on none of them, even though Peter drew his sword and struck off the ear of one of them. Thus did Christ give another signal proof of His power over the spirits of men to restrain them; and thus did He again make manifest His Deity.

"Then Simon Peter having a sword drew it, and smote the high priest's servant and cut off his right ear. The servant's name was Malchus" (v. 10). Peter exercised a zeal which was not regulated by knowledge: it was the self-confident energy of the flesh acting in unconsidered haste. It was the inevitable outcome of his failure to heed Christ's word, "Watch and pray, lest ye enter into temptation"—it is failure to pray which so often brings us into temptation! Had Peter observed the ways of his Master and heeded His words, he would have learned that carnal weapons had no place in the fight to which He has called him and us. Had he marked the wonderful grace which He had just displayed in providing for the safety of His own, he would have seen that this was no time for smiting with the sword. What a fearful warning is this to every Christian for the need of walking in the Spirit that we fulfil not the lusts of the flesh! The flesh is still in the believer, and a lasting object-lesson of this is the humbling history of Peter—rash yet courageous when he should have been still; a few hours later, cowardly and base when he ought to have witnessed a good confession for Christ. But though Peter failed to act according to grace, the grace of God was signally manifested towards him. No doubt Peter struck with the intention of slaying Malchus—probably the first to lay hands on the Saviour—but an unseen Power deflected the blow, and instead of the priest's servant being beheaded he lost only an ear, and that was permitted so that a further opportunity might be afforded the Lord Jesus of manifesting both His tender mercy and all-mighty power. We may add that the life of Malchus was safe while Christ was there, for none ever died in His presence!

"Then Simon Peter having a sword drew it, and smote the high priest's servant, and cut off his right ear." The sequel to this is supplied by Luke: "and He touched his ear, and healed him" (22: 51)! Very striking indeed is this; it rendered the more excuseless the act of those who arrested Him, aggravating their sin and deepening their guilt. Christ manifested both His power and His grace before they laid hands on Him. This act of healing Malchus' ear was the last miracle of the Saviour's before He laid down His life. First, He appealed to their consciences, now to their hearts; but once they had seized their prey He left them to their own evil lusts.

"Then said Jesus unto Peter, Put up thy sword into the sheath" (v. 11). This was a rebuke, though mildly administered. Peter had done his best to nullify his Master's orders, "Let these go their way." He had given great provocation to this company armed with swords and staves: he had acted wrongly in resisting authority, in having recourse to force, in imagining that the Son of God needed any assistance from him. "Put up thy sword into the sheath": the only "sword" which the Christian is ever justified in using is the Sword of the Spirit, the Word of God.

"The cup which My Father hath given Me, shall I not drink it?" (v. 11). How blessedly this entire incident brings out the varied glories of Christ: perfect supremacy and perfect subjection. He declared Himself the great "I am," and His enemies fall to the ground; He gives the word of command, and His disciples depart unmolested. Now He bows before the will of the Father, and receives the awful cup of suffering and woe from His hand without a murmur. Never did such perfections meet in any other: Sovereign, yet Servant; the Lion-Lamb!

God's dispensations are frequently expressed as a cup poured out and given to men to drink. There are three "cups" spoken of in Scripture. First, there is the cup of salvation: "I will take the cup of salvation, and call upon the name of the Lord" (Psa. 116: 13). Second, there is the cup of consolation: "Neither shall men tear themselves for them in mourning, to comfort them for the dead; neither shall men give them the cup of consolation to drink for their father or for their mother" (Jer. 16: 7). To this the Psalmist referred: "My cup runneth over" (23: 5). Our Lord Himself used the same figure, previously when He said, "Father, if it be possible let this cup pass from Me" (Matt. 26: 39). It was a dreadful cup which He was to drink of. This third one is the cup of tribulation: "Upon the wicked He shall rain snares, fire and brimstone, and an horrible tempest; this shall be the portion of their cup" (Psa. 11: 6). So the prophet Jeremiah is bidden, "Take the wine cup of this fury at My hand, and cause all the nations, to whom I send thee, to drink it" (25: 15 cf. Psa. 75: 8).

"The cup which My Father hath given Me, shall I not drink it?" "He doth not say, A necessity is laid upon Me to drink this cup. He doth not simply say, My Father hath commanded Me to drink it, but, 'Shall I not drink it?' It is a speech that implies His spirit knew not how to do otherwise than obey His Father, such an instinct that He could not but choose to do it. Even just as Joseph said, 'How then can I do this great wickedness, and sin against God?' (Gen. 39: 9), so Christ here, 'Shall I not drink it?' It implies the highest willingness that can be" (Dr. Thomas Goodwin).

"The cup which My Father hath given Me, shall I not drink it?" What a lesson

Christ here teaches us. The Serpent was about to bruise His heel; the Gentiles were about to mock and scourge Him; the Jews cry, Away with Him. But the Saviour looks beyond all secondary causes direct to Him of whom and through whom and to whom were all things (Rom. 11: 36). Peter's eyes were upon the human adversaries; but no, He saith to Peter, there is a higher Hand in it. Moreover, He did not say, "which the **Judge** of all the earth giveth Me," but "My Father"—the One who dearly loveth Me! How this would sweeten our bitter cups if we would but receive them from the **Father's** hand! It is not until we see **His** hand in all things that the heart is made to rest in perfect peace.

The following questions are to help the student prepare for our next lesson:—

1. What types and doctrinal truths are suggested by "bound" v. 12?
2. Why is v. 14 inserted here?
3. Why has the Holy Spirit given Peter so prominent a place?
4. Why of "His disciples and doctrine" v. 19?
5. Why did Christ say nothing about His disciples v. 20?
6. Why did Christ say v. 21?
7. What is the meaning of v. 24?

ARTHUR W. PINK.

## GLEANINGS IN EXODUS.
### 37. The Mercy-seat: Exodus 25: 17-22.

The Mercy-seat was a solid sheet or slab of pure gold. Though a separate and distinct article in itself, it formed the lid of the Ark, being placed "above upon the Ark"; whose "crown of gold round about" (forming the top of its sides) would support and prevent it from slipping off. The Mercy-seat differed from the Ark in that no wood entered into its composition. There was only one other piece of furniture in the Tabernacle made solely of gold, namely the candlestick, which was smaller in size and weight; therefore th Mercy-seat, according to its intrinsic worth, was **the most valuable** of all the holy vessels. How this tells us of the **preciousness** in the sight of God of that which the Mercy-seat foreshadowed.

The Mercy-seat, or better, the Propitiatory, derived its name from the blood of propitiation which was sprinkled thereon. It was the same length and breadth as the Ark, being two and a half by one cubit and a half. At either end of it was a cherub, not fastened thereto, but beate out of the same one piece of gold of which the Mercy-seat was formed. These symbolic figures had their wings outstretched, thus overshadowing the Mercy-seat, with their faces looking down upon it. Let us now consider:—

### 1. Its Significance.

Concerning the typical meaning of the Mercy-seat there is quite a variety of interpretations offered to us. Some writers have been turned aside from the right track by dwelling upon the etymology of the Hebrew word, instead of seeking a definition from its **usage** in the Scriptures. Others have caused confusion through failing to distinguish between the respective foreshadowings of the brazen altar and the Mercy-seat. The real typical meaning of the Mercy-seat has been Divinely explained to us in Romans 3: 25, though the Authorised Version partly hides this from view: "Being justified freely by His grace through the redemption that is in Christ Jesus: whom God hath set forth to be a Propitiation (better, a "Propitiatory") through faith in His blood, to declare His righteousness for the remission of sins that are past." The Greek word here rendered "propitiation" is the identical one translated "Mercy-seat" in Hebrews 9: 5. Romans 3, then, declares that in the gospel God presents Christ before us as the antitypical Mercy-seat.

It were better, because less ambiguous, if we rendered "Kapporeth" (the Hebrew word) by "Propitiatory" rather than Mercy-seat; the added light from the New Testament not only justifies, but requires this change. Christ is the **Mercy-**seat, but He is so by virtue of the propitiation which He offered to God. In 1 John 2:2 and 4: 10 the Greek (in a **different** form from Romans 3: 25) is rightly rendered "propitiation," for in these verses the reference is to the Lord Jesus as the Sacrifice which pacifies God's offended justice; but the word in Romans 3: 25 is the one which is always employed in the Septuagint as the equivalent of "Kapporeth," and is actually translated "Mercy-seat" in Hebrews 9: 5. The Propitiatory was not the place where propitiation was made, but instead, the place where its abiding value was borne witness to before God. It is failure to mark this distinction which has resulted in so much confusion of thought.

The verb "to propitiate" signifies to appease, to placate, to make satisfaction. When, then, we read in Romans 3: 25 that Christ is now set forth a Propitiatory, the evident meaning is that, through the Gospel, God now bears testimony to His blessed Son as the One by whom He was propitiated, the One by whom His holy wrath against the sins of His people was pacified, the One by whom the righteous demands of His law were satisfied, the One by whom every attribute of Deity was glorified. The type of Christ as "the propitiation for our sins" is the bleeding victim on the altar; the type of Christ as God's resting place or Propitiatory is the Mercy-seat within the veil. Christ has become God's rest, in whom He can now meet poor sinners in all the fulness of His grace because of the propitiation made by Him on the cross.

The great propitiation which Christ made, and the propitiatory which is the result of it, were both borne witness to in the ritual of Israel's annual Day of Atonement. This is described for us in Lev. 16. Into the most interesting and important details of this chapter we cannot here enter; the one point bearing on our present theme being found in v. 14: "And he shall take of the blood of the bullock, and sprinkle it with his finger upon the Mercy-seat eastward, and before the Mercy-seat shall he sprinkle of the blood with his finger seven times." The blood (obtained through the death of the animal—type of propitiation) told of judgment already visited upon the innocent substitute; the blood sprinkled on the Propitiatory announced that God had accepted the victim offered to Him; the blood sprinkled before the propitiatory secured a standing-ground in God's presence. Once was sufficient for the eye of God; seven times grace suffered it to be sprinkled before the propitiatory, to assure us (who are so slow of heart to believe) of the perfectness of the standing-ground which Christ has procured for His people!

2. Its Purpose.

In the Tabernacle there was a table, but no chair for Aaron or any of the priests to sit on, because their work was never finished, needing constant repetition—emblematic of the fact that the one great Sacrifice, which would provide rest and satisfaction, was yet to come. But there was one seat, the Mercy-seat, reserved for Jehovah Himself, who sat there between the cherubim. This Mercy-seat, resting upon the Ark, foreshadowed the grand truth that God would find His rest in that perfect work which His incarnate Son should perform. The Mercy-seat, then, was God's throne here on earth. "And thou shalt put the Mercy-seat above upon the Ark; and in the Ark thou shalt put the testimony that I shall give thee. And there I will meet with thee, and I will commune with thee from above the Mercy-seat, from between the two cherubim which are upon the Ark of the testimony, of all things which I will give thee in commandment unto the children of Israel" (vv. 21, 22).

The fact that the Mercy-seat formed God's throne in the midst of Israel is referred to in quite a number of Old Testament passages. In 1 Sam. 4: 4 we read, "So the people sent to Shiloh, that they might bring from thence the Ark of the covenant of the Lord of hosts, who dwelleth between the cherubim." In 2 Sam. 6: 2 it is said, "And David arose, and went with all the people that were with him from Baale of Judah to bring up from thence the Ark of God, whose name is called by the name of the Lord of hosts that dwelleth between the cherubim." Hezekiah addressed his prayer to Jehovah as "O Lord God of Israel, which dwellest between the cherubim" (2 Kings 19: 15). The Psalmist cried, "Give ear, O Shepherd of Israel, Thou that leadest Joseph like a flock; Thou that dwellest between the cherubim, shine forth." (Psa. 80: 1). In Psalm 99: 1 we are told, "The Lord reigneth; let the people tremble: He sitteth between the cherubim; let the earth be moved."

But now the question arises, How was it possible for the thrice holy God to dwell in the midst of a sinful people? The answer is, On the ground of accepted sacrifice. His throne was a blood-sprinkled one. This is shown us in Lev. 16: 14, already quoted. The blood of the sin-offering was sprinkled upon that Mercy-seat which constituted Jehovah's throne, and there that blood was left under His searching eye, as the abiding witness that the claims of His justice had been met, and that He could righteously dwell in the midst of a people who had broken His law—righteously, because their sin had been put away.

Now it is impossible to over-estimate

the importance of thoroughly-settled views of **God's** satisfaction in Christ. Many Christians never get beyond the fact, though a precious fact it is, that Christ's death has procured and secured their life; and even this, in the case of many, is not maintained. The reason for this is that we listen so often to the dictates of our evil hearts of unbelief, which tell us that **self** must have a hand in the work of salvation, must contribute something to it—if not works, then feelings! But the truth is that God has entirely set aside **ourself**, and acted for **Himself** in saving us. God's glory and our salvation are indissoluably linked together. Accordingly we ought not only to enjoy the assurance of our eternal security, but also enter into a deeper communion with God's revealed thoughts concerning the power of Christ's blood in relation to **His Throne in Heaven!** It is this which the Mercy-seat or Propitiatory particularly and so blessedly typifies.

The Mercy-seat, which formed God's throne in Israel, then, directs our thoughts to the **governmental** aspect of the Atonement. Not only is it true that Christ died for sinners, but it is equally true—though in a different sense—that He died for God: He died **in the stead of** His sinful people, He died **on behalf of** the thrice holy God. Christ lived and died to make it possible for God to take hell-deserving sinners into fellowship with Himself, and that, consistently with His holiness and justice. He died to **vindicate** the character of God before all the intelligences of the universe. He died that God's **throne** might be established: "justice and judgment are the habitation (or "base") of Thy throne" (Psa. 89: 14). God's throne is settled in Christ, because all the claims of God's righteousness have been settled by Christ. The Antitype of this is most gloriously brought before us in Rev. 5: 6: "And I beheld, and, lo, **in the midst of the throne**... stood a Lamb as it had been slain"!!

"Whom God hath set forth a Propitiatory through faith in His blood **to declare His righteousness**" (Rom. 3: 25). To "declare" here signifies to make manifest, to proclaim and exhibit publicly. Divine righteousness requires that His law should be obeyed, and that its penalty should be enforced where its precepts have been broken. Divine mercy could not be exercised at the expense of justice, The character of God as the Ruler of the universe was involved. But the Antitype of the Mercy-seat sets forth the precious fact that God's avenging holiness was fully satisfied by the shedding of the blood of His Son on the cross. Justice, instead of being reduced to the necessity of taking a part from the bankrupt, has received full payment from the bankrupt's Surety and thus his deliverance is guaranteed. Thus Christ by His life of obedience "magnified the law and made it honourable" (Isa. 42: 21), and by His death glorified all the Divine perfections. God's love, grace, and mercy were manifested at Calvary as nowhere else; equally so were His holiness, justice and righteousness. For this reason, then, the Mercy-seat was made solely of **pure gold**—the Divine glory displayed. Propitiation has been made, and God points all to His Son, the Propitiatory, as the proof of it; just as the Mercy-seat with the blood sprinkled thereon attested that propitiation had been typically accomplished.

### 3. Its Dimensions.

It is not without good reason, for there is nothing meaningless or even trivial in **God's** Word, that the Holy Spirit has been pleased to give us the measurements of the Propitiatory. Its length was two and a half cubits and its breadth one cubit and a half. But nothing is told us of its thickness: does not this designed omission suggest what is recorded in Psalm 103: 112, "For as the heaven is high above the earth so great is His mercy toward them that fear Him"! What, then, are we to learn from the measurements which are recorded? This, its length and breadth were precisely the same as those of the Ark. The dimensions speak clearly of the **strict limitations** which God has set to His saving grace. As another has said, "It is all very well to say 'there's a wideness in God's mercy like the wideness of the sea,' but it is much better to understand clearly what is signified by the words 'two cubits and a half shall be the length, thereof, and a cubit and a half the breadth thereof.' God's mercy is, indeed, wide enough to take in every sinner who contritely presents himself at the appointed Mercy-seat, but it ex**tends no further than that.** The limits are Divinely established, and are unalterable."

There are some who count upon the

love of God apart from Christ and His atoning death, which is virtually to devise a Mercy-seat which is wider than the Ark. But this is a vain delusion. God's grace reigns "through righteousness unto eternal life by Jesus Christ our Lord" (Rom. 5 :21). No grace can be shown unto any sinner apart from the redemptive blood of the Lord Jesus. "A just God and a Saviour" (Isa. 45: 21). Saving mercy is extended to none except those for whom Christ met the demands of Divine justice. There is much so-called Evangelism to-day which is condemned by the strictly defined dimensions of the Mercy-seat! Christ died not to make possible the salvation of the whole human race, but to make certain the salvation of God's elect: He made "propitiation for the sins of the people" (Heb. 2: 17. R.V.).

### 4. Its Ornamentation.

This was in the form of two cherubs, one on either end of the Mercy-seat, with wings outstretched over it, thus overshadowing and as it were protecting God's throne. That there is some profound and important significance connected with the figures of the cherubim is clear from the prominent place which they occupy in the Divine description of the Mercy-seat: if the student will re-read Exodus 25: 17-22 he will find that mention is made of them, either in the single or plural number, no less than seven times. Much has been written on the subject, but nothing we have seen is satisfactory.

The first time the "cherubim" are mentioned in Scripture is in Gen. 3: 24, where they are viewed guarding the way to the tree of life, the "flaming sword," seen in connection with them suggesting that they are associated with the administration of God's judicial authority. In Rev. 4: 6-8 (compare Ezekiel 1: 5-10) we find them related to the throne of God. Rev. 5: 11-14 indicates that the cherubim are the highest among the angelic order of creatures. In the Psalms and in Ezekiel the cherubim come before us in connection with judicial acts, with Divine interference in judgment, and this gives a striking significance to their place here on the Mercy-seat: God's righteousness, nay, His wrath against sin, is seen to be of one piece with His mercy! God's attributes do not conflict: light and love are but two sides of His nature!

On the Mercy-seat the two cherubim stood facing each other, attracted by a common object, heads bowed as in adoration. Their number speaks of competent witness. The subject is too vast for us to even outline here, but there is more than one hint in Scripture that the redemption of the Church is an object lesson unto the angels. 1 Cor. 4: 9 declares that the suffering apostles were "made a spectacle (theatre) unto angels." Eph. 3: 10 tells us that "the manifold wisdom of God is now being made known by (through) the Church unto the principalities and powers in the heavenlies." 1 Peter 1: 11, 12 announces that the sufferings of Christ and His glories which were to follow are "things which the angels desire to look into." We take it, then, that the figures of the two cherubim, with their bowed heads over the Mercy-seat, denote the interest of the angelic hierarchies in the unfolding of God's redemptive purpose.

### 5. Its Blessedness.

First, this comes out in the fact that the Mercy-seat completely hid from view the tables of stone which were kept in the Ark. As the cherubim stood there with their faces downward, they saw not those holy statutes which condemned their transgressors; instead, they gazed on that which spoke of the glory of God—Deity magnified by sacrifice. There was blood between the law and its Administrator and His executors!

Suppose an Ark with no Mercy-seat: the Law would then be uncovered: there would be nothing to hush its thunderings, nothing to arrest the execution of its righteous sentence. The law expresses God's righteousness, and demands the death of its violator: "Cursed is everyone that continueth not in all things which are written in the book of the Law to do them" (Gal. 3: 10). Such is the inevitable judgment pronounced on all sinners by the inexorable sentence of the law. The only man who could stand before God on the basis of having kept that law was the Man Christ Jesus. He could have been justified by it, enthroned upon it, and from it have pronounced sentence of just doom on all of Adam's guilty race. But He did not do so. No; blessed be His name, instead of coming to earth as the Executioner of the law, He bared His holy bosom to its righteous sword. The same heart which held the law unbroken (Psalm 40: 8) received the penalty which was due His people for having broken it. The storm of wrath having spent itself upon Him, the law can no longer touch those who have fled to Him for refuge. It is of this that the blood-sprinkled Mercy-seat, covering the tables of stone within the Ark, so blessedly speaks.

A nation of transgressors could never stand before the naked law. An uncovered Ark furnishes naught but a throne of judgment. This supplies the key to a passage in the Old Testament that has puzzled many. When the Philistines sent back the Ark, which Jehovah had suffered to fall into their hands, we are told, "And He smote the men of Beth-shemesh, because they had looked into the Ark of the Lord, even He smote of the people fifty thousand and three score and ten men: and the people lamented, because the Lord had smitten many of the people with a gross slaughter. And the men of Beth-shemesh said, Who is able to stand before this holy Lord God?" (1 Sam. 6: 19-20). The sin which God here punished so severely was Israel's daring to uncover what God had covered. In order to "look into the Ark" the Mercy-seat had to be removed, and in removing it they exposed the Law, and thus severed mercy from judgment, the result of which must ever be, death for the guilty. The thrice holy God can only meet the guilty, polluted sinner, in Him by whom "righteousness and peace have kissed each other" (Psa. 85: 9). No man can draw near unto the Father but by Him.

Second, the Mercy-seat was the place where Jehovah met the sinner in the person of His representative: "And he (Aaron) shall take of the blood of the bullock, and sprinkle it with his finger upon the Mercy-seat eastward and before the Mercy-seat shall he sprinkle of the blood with his finger seven times " (Lev. 16: 14). This tells us that Christ is the one appointed meeting-place between God and His high priestly place where He meets with them not in judgment but in grace. But be it remembered that the typical Mercy-seat was in the holy of holies, hidden from the view of the sinner who desired to approach God. So it is with the Antitype: God's throne of grace is not visible to the eye of sense; it can be approached only by faith. Hence the exhortation of Heb. 10, "Having therefore, brethren, boldness to enter into the holiest by the blood of Jesus, By a new and living way, which He hath newly-made for us, through the veil, that is to say, His flesh; and having an high priest over the house of God; Let us draw near with a true heart in full assurance of faith" (vv. 19-22).

Third, the Mercy-seat is the place of communion: "And there I will meet with thee, and I will commune with Thee from above the Mercy-seat, from between the two cherubim, which are upon the Ark of the testimony" (Ex. 25: 22). A beautiful example of this is furnished in Numbers 7: 89: "And when Moses was gone into the Tabernacle of the congregation to speak with Him, then he heard the voice of One speaking unto him from off the Mercy-seat that was upon the Ark of testimony, from between the two cherubim: and he spake unto Him." Precious indeed is this. It is in the Lord Jesus that Christians have been brought into this place of inestimable blessing. Not only have we been brought nigh to God, but we are permitted to speak to Him and hear Him speaking to us. Having been reconciled to God by the death of His Son, He now says "I will commune with thee." Wondrous grace is this! O that our hearts may enter into and enjoy this blessed privilege. Then "Let us come boldly unto the throne of grace." There is nothing between: no sin, no guilt; and the veil has been rent. We may worship in the Holy of Holies! Then "Let us draw near in full assurance of faith."

ARTHUR W. PINK.

## CHRISTIAN FOOLS

"Then said He unto them of fools and slow of heart to believe all that the prophets have spoken." Luke 24: 25.

Those of you who read the religious announcements in the newspaper of yesterday would see the subject for my sermon this evening is "Christian fools." Possibly some of you thought there was a printer's error and that what I really meant to announce was "Professing Christian fools." The paper gave it quite correctly. My subject to-night is "Christian fools." Probably some of you think that this is a most unsuitable title for a servant of God to give to his sermon, and yet I make no apology whatever for it. It fits exactly my subject for to-night: it expresses accurately what I am going to speak about: and—what is far more to the point—it epitomises our text: "Then He said unto them, O fools, and slow of heart to believe all that the prophets have spoken."

Those words were spoken by Christ on the day of His resurrection: spoken not to worldlings but to Christians. That which occasioned them was this. The disciples to whom He was speaking were lopsided in their theology: they believed a certain part of God's truth and they refused to believe another part of the truth that did not suit them; they believed some Scriptures but they did not believe all that the prophets had spoken, and the reason they did not was because they were unable to harmonise the two different parts of God's truth. They were like some people to-day: when it comes to their theology they walk by reason and by logic rather than by faith.

In the Old Testament there were many prophecies concerning the coming Messiah that spoke of His glory. If there was one thing that Old Testament prediction made plain it was that the Messiah of Israel should be a glorious Messiah. It spoke of His power, His honor, His majesty, His dominion, His triumphs. But, on the other hand, there were many prophecies in the Old Testament that spoke of a suffering Messiah, that portrayed His humiliation, His degradation, His rejection, His death at the hands of wicked men. And these disciples of Christ believed the former set of prophecies, but they would not believe in the second: they could not see how it was possible to harmonise the two. If the coming Messiah was to be a glorious Messiah, possessing power and majesty and dominion: if He would be triumphant, then how could He, at the same time, be a suffering Messiah, despised, humiliated, rejected of men? And because the disciples could not fit the two together, because they were unable to harmonise them, they refused to believe both, and Christ told them to their faces that they were fools. He says "O fools, and slow of heart to believe all that the prophets have spoken."

I suppose some of us have wondered how it was possible for these disciples, these followers of Christ, these men who had been privileged to be with Him during His public ministry, those who had been so intimate with Him, had been instructed by Him, had witnessed His wonderful miracles; how it was possible for such men to err so grievously and to act so foolishly. And yet we need not be surprised; the same thing is happening all around us to-day. Christendom to-night is full of men and women who believe portions of God's truth, but who do not believe all that the prophets have spoken. In other words, my friends, Christendom to-night is full of men and women that the Son of God says are "fools" because of their slowness of heart to believe.

Now very likely my sermon to-night will make some of my hearers angry: probably they are the ones who most need the rebuke of the text. When a servant of God wields the sword of the Spirit, if he does his work faithfully and effectively, then some of his hearers are bound to get cut and wounded: and, my friends, that is always God's way. God always wounds before He heals. And I want to remind you at the outset that this text is no invention of mine. These are the words of One who never wounded unnecessarily, but they are also the words of the True and Faithful Witness who never hesitated to preach the whole truth of God, whether men would receive it or whether they would reject it. I know it is not a pleasant thing to be called a fool, especially if we have a high regard for ourselves and rate our own wisdom and orthodoxy very highly: it wounds our pride. But we need to be wounded, all of us. We need to be humbled; we need to be rebuked; we need to have that word from the lips of Christ which is as a sword, yea, sharper than any two-edged sword.

Now notice, dear friends, that Christ did not upbraid these disciples because they did not understand, but because of their lack of faith. The trouble with them was they reasoned too much. Very likely they misled themselves on their logical mind and said, Well, surely we are not ask to believe impossibilities and absurdities both of these cannot be true; one is true and the other cannot be. Either the Messiah of Israel is going to be a glorious and a triumphant Messiah, or else He is going to be a rejected and a humiliated one they cannot both be true. That is what Christ said to them— not because of their failure to understand, but because of their lack of faith —"O fools, and slow of heart to believe all that the prophets have spoken."

I am afraid that to-day there are many who only believe what they can understand, and if there is something else that they cannot understand, they do not believe it. If they have devised to themselves a systematized theology (or more probably they have adopted someone else's system of theology), and they hear a sermon (no matter how much Scripture there may be in it) which they cannot fit into their little system of theology, they won't have it. They place a higher value on consistency than they do on fidelity. That is just what was the matter with these disciples: they could not see the consistency of the two things and therefore they were only prepared to believe the one.

The same thing, my friends, is true to-day with many preachers. There are multitudes of preachers in Australia to-night whose theology is narrower than the teaching of this Book. Then away to the winds with theology!—I mean human systems of theology which are narrower than Scripture. For example, there are men to-day who read God's Word, and they see that the gospel is to be preached to every creature, and that God commands all who hear that gospel to believe in Christ; then they come across some texts on election, predestination:—"Many are called but few are chosen," and they say, Well, I cannot harmonise this, I cannot see how it is possible to preach, untrammelled, a gospel to every creature, and yet for election to be true. And because they cannot harmonise the two things they neither believe the two nor will they preach both. They cannot harmonise election with a gospel that is to be preached to every creature, and so the Arminians preach the gospel but they leave out election.

Yes, but there are many Calvinists who equally come under the rebuke of our text. They believe in the sovereignty of God, but they refuse to believe in the responsibility of man. I read a book by a hyper-Calvinist only a few weeks ago, by a man whose shoe-latched the present speaker in many things is not fit to stoop down and unloose—a man of God, a faithful servant of His, one from whom I have learned not a little—and yet he had the effrontery to say, that responsibility is the most awful word in the English language, and then went on to tirade against human responsibility. They cannot understand how that it is possible for God to fix the smallest and the greatest events, and yet not to infringe upon man's accountability—men themselves choosing the evil and rejecting the good—and therefore because they cannot see both they will only believe in one.

Listen! If man were nothing more than clay in the hands of the Potter there would be no difficulty. Scripture affirms in Romans 9 that man is clay in the hands of the Potter, but that only gives you one aspect of the truth. That emphasises the absoluteness of God's control over all the works and creatures of His hands; but from other Scriptures we learn that man is something more than lifeless clay. Man has been endowed with understanding; man has been given a will. Yes, I freely admit that his understanding is darkened; I fully allow that his will is in bondage; but they are still there; they have not been destroyed. If man was nothing more than a block of wood or a block of stone, it would be easy to understand how that God could fix the place that he was to occupy and the purpose that he was to fulfil; but, my friends, it is very far from easy to understand how that God can shape and direct all history and yet leave man fully responsible and not infringe upon his accountability.

Now there are some who have devised a very simple but a most unsatisfactory method of getting rid of the difficulty, and that is to deny its existence. There are Arminians who have presented the "free-will" of man in such a way as to virtually dethrone God, and I have no sympathy whatever with their system. On the other hand, there have been some Calvinists who have presented a kind of fatalism (I know not what else to term it) reducing man to nothing more than a block of wood, exonerating him of all blame and excusing him for his unbelief. But they are both equally wrong, and I scarcely know which is the more mischievous of the two. When the Calvinist says, All things happen according to the predestination of God, I heartily say Amen, and I am willing to be called a Calvinist; but if the Arminian says that when a man sins, the sin is his own, and that if he continues sinning he will surely perish, and that if he perishes his blood is on his own head, then I believe the Arminian speaks according to God's truth; though I am not willing to be called an Arminian. The trouble is when we tie ourselves down to a theological system.

Now listen a little more closely still. When the Calvinist says that faith is the gift of God and that no sinner ever does or can believe until God gives him that faith, I heartily say Amen; but when the Arminian says that the gospel commands all who hear it to believe, and that it is the duty of every sinner to believe, I also say Amen. What? you say, You are going to stand up and preach faith-duty—duty-faith? I know that is a bogey to some of you. Now bear with me patiently for a moment and I will try and not shock you too badly. Whose is the gospel? It is God's. Whose voice is it that is heard speaking in the gospel? It is God's. To whom has God commanded the gospel to be preached? To every creature. What does the gospel say to every creature? It says, "Believe on the Lord Jesus Christ." It says "Whosoever believeth in Him should not perish but have everlasting life." It says, The gospel of Christ is the power of God unto salvation to everyone that believeth. God commands, not invites. God commands every man, woman and child that hears that gospel to believe it, for the gospel is true, therefore it is the duty of every man to believe what God has said. Let me given you the alternative. If it is not the duty of every sinner to believe the gospel, then it is his duty not to believe it—one or the other. Do you mean to tell me it is the duty of an unconverted sinner to reject the gospel? I am not talking now about his ability to believe it.

Some of you say, Well how can it be his duty to believe it, when he **cannot** do so? Is it his duty to do an impossibility? Well, listen! Is my duty, is my responsibility measured by my ability, by my power to perform? Here is a man who has ordered a hundred pounds' worth of furniture; he receives it, and he is given thirty days' credit in which to pay for it; but during the next thirty days he squanders his money, and at the end of the month he is practically a bankrupt. When the firm present their bill to him he says, "I am sorry but I am **unable** to pay you." He is speaking the truth. "I am unable, it does not lie within my power to pay you." Would the head of that business house say, "All right, that ends the matter then: sorry to hear that you do not have the power, but evidently we cannot do anything." No, my friends, ability does not measure our responsibility. Man is responsible to do many things that he is not able to do. You that are Christians are responsible to live a sinless life, for God says to you, "Awake to righteousness and sin not," and in the first Epistle of John we read, "These things write I unto you, that ye sin not." God sets before you and me a standard of holy perfection. There is not one of us that is capable of measuring up to it, but that is our responsibility, and that is what we are going to be measured by when we stand before the judgment-seat of Christ.

Now then there are many Arminian preachers who are afraid to preach sermons on certain texts of the Bible. They would be afraid to stand up and preach from John 6: 44—"No man can come to Me, except the Father which hath sent Me draw him." They would be afraid to stand up and preach from Romans 9: 18—"Therefore hath He mercy on whom He will have mercy, and whom He will He hardeneth." Yes, and it is also true that there are many Calvinist preachers who are equally afraid to preach from certain texts of the Scriptures lest their orthodoxy be challenged and lest they be called Freewillers. They are afraid to stand up and preach, for example, on the words of the Lord Jesus: —"How often would I have gathered thy children together, even as a hen gathereth her chickens under her wings, and ye would not!"; on such a verse as this:—"The kingdom of heaven suffereth violence, and the violent take it by force"; or "Strive (agonize) to enter in at the Strait Gate." And to show you that I am not imagining things, I am just going to read you three lines. Listen! "At the meeting at . . . (I will leave out the name) on January 15th last the question was asked to the effect, Had not some of our ministers for the sake of orthodoxy abstained from preaching from certain texts, and the answer was in the affirmative." I am reading now from a Strict Baptist magazine! That was a meeting of Strict Baptist preachers and they were honest enough to admit, themselves, that because they were afraid of their orthodoxy being challenged, and so they were silent on certain texts of Scripture. O may God remove from all of us the fear of man.

Some of you perhaps are thinking right now in your own minds, Well, Dr. Pink, I do not see how you are consistent with yourself. My friends that does not trouble me one iota, and it won't cause one hair in my head to go grey if I am inconsistent with any Calvinistic creed: the only thing that concerns me is to be consistent with the Holy Scriptures and to teach, as the Holy Spirit shall enable, the whole counsel of God; to leave out nothing, to withhold nothing, and to give a proportionate presentation of God's truth. Do you know, I believe that most of the theological errors of the past have grown out of, not so much a denial of God's truth, as a **disproportionate emphasis** of it. Let me give you a simple illustration. The most comely countenance with the most beautiful features would soon become ugly if one feature were to grow while the others remained undeveloped. You can take the most beautiful baby there is in the world tonight and if that baby's nose were to grow while its eyes and its cheeks and its mouth and its ears remained undeveloped, it would soon become unsightly. The same is true with every other member of its face.

Beauty is mainly a matter of proportion and this is true of God's Word. It is only as truth is presented in its proper proportions that the beauty and blessedness to it are maintained in the hearts and lives of God's people. The sad thing is that almost everywhere to-day there is just one feature of truth being disproportionately emphasised. And listen again! If God's truth is to be presented proportionately and effectively then each truth of God's Word must be presented separately. If I am speaking upon the humanity of Christ, if I am seeking to emphasise the reality of His manhood, how that He was made like unto His brethren in all things, how that He was tempted in all points as they were—sin excepted—I would not bring into my sermon a reference to His Godhood; and if you were to hear me preach the next twelve Sunday nights on the manhood of Christ and never referred to His Deity in those sermons, I hope none of you brethren would be so foolish as to draw the conclusion, Oh dear me, Dr. Pink no longer believes in the Godhood of our Saviour.

Again, if I am preaching on the wrath of God, the holy hatred of God for sin and His vengeance upon it, I would not weaken my sermon by bringing in at the close a reference to His tenderness and His mercy and His love, for in my judgment that would be to blunt the point of the special truth I was seeking to press on the unconverted. And, in the same way, if I am pressing on the unconverted their need and their duty and the importance of them seeking the Lord, calling upon Him, coming to Him, believing on Him for themselves, I would not bring in or explain the work of the Holy Spirit in conversion.

Each truth needs to be presented separately that it may have its clear outline presented to the heart and to the mind. And after all, my friends, we are not saved by believing in the Spirit, we are saved by believing in Christ. We are not saved by believing in the work of the Spirit within us (no man was ever saved by believing that); we are saved by trusting in the work of Christ outside of us. O may God help us to maintain the balance of truth. There is something more in this Book, brethren and sisters, beside election and particular redemption and the new birth. They are there, and I would not say one word to weaken or to repudiate them, but that is not all that is in this Book. There is a human side: there is man's responsibility: there is the sinner's repentance: there is the sinner's believing in Christ: there is the pressing of the gospel upon the unsaved; and I want to tell you frankly that if a church does not evangelise it will fossilise: and, if I am not much mistaken, that is what happened to some of the Strict Baptist Churches in Australia. Numbers of them that once had a healthy existence are now no more; and some others are already dead but they are not yet buried; and I believe one of the main reasons for that is this:—they failed at the vital point of evangelism. If a church does not evangelise it will fossilise. That is God's method of perpetuating His work and of maintaining His churches. God uses means and the means that the Holy Spirit uses in His work is the preaching of the gospel to the unconverted, to every creature. True, the preaching will avail nothing without the Spirit's blessing and application. True, no sinner will or can believe until God has quickened him. Yet he *ought* to, and is commanded to.

Now I meant, if time had allowed me, to come back again to the text and give you a few striking examples of where many have failed in holding the balance of God's truth. Take for example the Unitarians. I have met numbers of Unitarians who believe this Book is God's Word, and believe that they can prove their creed from this Book. They appeal to such Scriptures as Deuteronomy 6.4:—"The Lord our God is one Lord." Their creed is the unity of God and they argue that if there be three divine persons there must be three Gods; they cannot harmonise them, they cannot reconcile three persons with one God; so what do they do? Well, they hold fast to the one and they let go the other. They say the two won't mix—either God is one or else He is three. He cannot be both. When they come to the Person of Christ they emphasise such passages as "He grew in wisdom." Well, they say, if He was a divine person how could He grow in wisdom? They emphasise such passages as "He prayed," and they say it is an absurdity to think of God praying to God. They say He died—how could God die? No, He cannot be divine: He is a good man; He is a holy man; He is a perfect man; and because they cannot reconcile the two classes of Scriptures they believe the one and they reject the other. And Christ says to them, Ye are fools because ye are slow of heart to believe all.

Take the Universalists. I have met numbers of Universalists—several here in Sydney. I was going to say that I have less suspicion of the reality of their own salvation than I have of some of yours. At any rate they seem to give such evidence in their daily walk that they commune with Christ that it really makes one wonder where they are. Well now, the Universalists are staggered by the doctrine of eternal punishment. They say "God is love." "The mercy of God endureth forever." God is good: how can a merciful, loving God send any to eternal suffering? The Universalist says they cannot both be true: if there is such a thing as eternal punishment then God can't be love: if God is love, there cannot be such a thing as eternal punishment. You see what they are doing? They are reasoning: they are walking by logic: they have drawn up their own scheme and system of theology and that which they cannot fit exactly into that scheme, somewhere, well, away with it!

But the Unitarians and the Universalists and the Arminians are not the only ones who are guilty of that. I am sorry to say that it is equally true, in some respects, of many Calvinists. They are unsound when it comes to the gospel. They are all at sea when it comes to the matter of believing. I am not going to keep you very much longer, but listen closely now. There are many Calvinists who say, Believing is an evidence of our salvation, but it is not a condition or the cause of salvation. But, my friends, I make so bold as to say that those who so teach take issue with this Book. Now I want you to turn with me to four passages in the New Testament. I am not asking you to take my word for anything. You turn with me now to four passages in God's own Word. First of all Romans 1, 16 and 17:—"For I am not ashamed of the gospel of Christ: for it is the power of God unto salvation to." The power of God unto salvation to whom?—"the power of God unto salvation to everyone that believeth." Now I have no hesitation whatever in saying to every grown-up person in this room to-night, if you had read that verse just now for the first time in your life, and had never read a page of either Calvinistic or Arminian literature; if you read that verse without any bias one way or the other, it would only mean one thing to you.

Now turn to Romans 13, verse 11:— "And that, knowing the time, that now it is high time to awake out of sleep, for now is our **salvation nearer than when we believed.**" The salvation that is spoken of there is the salvation of the body, the glorification of the believer, the final consummation of our redemption: but what I want you to notice is where the Holy Spirit Himself puts the starting-point. "Now is our salvation nearer than when we believed." That is when it begins, so far as our actual experience is concerned.

Now turn to Hebrews 10.39, and you have one there that is plainer still—that is outside the realm of debate—that has no ambiguity about it. Hebrews 10.39: "But we are not of them who draw back unto perdition; but of them that **believe to the saving of the soul.**" You cannot get around that if you live to be a thousand years old. "Them that believe to the saving of the soul." The sinner's believing does have something to do with his salvation: God says so! If you deny it you are taking issue with God. "Believe to the saving of the soul."

Now turn back to the 7th Luke and the 50th verse:—"And he said to the woman, **Thy faith hath saved thee.**" He did not say thy faith is an evidence that you have been saved. "Thy faith hath saved thee." Now in the light of those last two verses I make this assertion, that believing in Christ is **the cause** of the sinner's salvation. But listen closely to this qualification. It is neither the meritorious cause nor is it the effectual cause! You must put these three things together to get the complete thing. The blood of Christ is the meritorious cause of salvation: the regenerating work of the Spirit is the effective cause of salvation; but the sinner's own believing is the **instrumental** cause of his salvation. We believe to the saving of the soul. I repeat that. The blood of Christ is the meritorious cause: without that all the believing in the world could never have saved anyone. The regenerating work of the Spirit is the effectual cause: without the regenerating work of the Spirit no sinner would come or will believe with the heart. But the believing of the sinner in Christ is the instrumental cause—that which extends the empty hand to receive the gift that the gospel presents to him—and where there is no personal trust in Christ there is no salvation—I did not say "quickening."

Now I want to make this very plain and I am going to weigh my words. If instead of you trusting in the sacrificial blood of Christ, you are trusting in something that you believe the Spirit has done in you, you are building your house upon the sand and in the day of testing it is going to fall to the ground.

"On Christ the solid rock I stand,
All other ground is sinking sand."

If you are building your hope for eternity on what you think or feel that the Spirit of God has done in you, instead of putting your trust in what Christ did for sinners, you are building your house on the sand. And that may apply to some church-members here to-night. O my friends, the gospel of God does not invite you to look inside and pin your faith to what you think the Holy Spirit has done in you; the gospel of God commands you to look outside of yourself, away from all your feelings and frames, to what the Lord Jesus Christ did on the cross for sinners as sinners.

Now my last word of all is to the unconverted, for my text also applies directly to them. Last Sunday evening I said a good deal about the necessity of being quiet, of standing still, of waiting upon God; but I want to supplement those remarks in concluding to-night by saying that those are all admonitions that are given to the converted, and that the Holy Scriptures speak in very different terms to those of you who are unconverted. The Bible does not bid you to sit still and to wait and be quiet; the Bible commands you to flee from the wrath to come. It bids you to strive to enter in at the strait gate. I am quoting Scripture now. It bids you seek the Lord. It bids you come unto Him. It bids you believe in Him, and if you do not you will be damned, whoever you are.

I am very much afraid that there are some here to-night who entertain the notion that all they have to do is just to sit still and wait until God comes and saves you. My friends, I do not know of a single promise in all this Book that God will do so. I do not know of a single line in this Book that encourages you to continue in your sinful inactivity. I am going to speak very plainly now. The devil will tell you there is no cause for you to be concerned: there is not a bit of need for you to worry: if your name is in the Lamb's Book of Life you will be saved, whether you believe or no. That is the devil's lie! It is not God's truth. The devil will tell you that if you have been elected to salvation there is not a bit of need for you to be alarmed and disturbed and exercised; no need at all for you to seek and search after the Lord; that when God's good time comes He is going to do it all for you: not a bit of good for you to read the Bible and cry out to Him: and if He has not elected you, well, there is still less any need, for it is useless.

Yes, the devil will speak in those tones and terms and he will come quoting Scripture to you. But there is no salvation for the sinner apart from his believing in Christ. I close with this quotation:—II Thessalonians 2, 13:—"God hath from the beginning chosen you to salvation through"—Through what?—"Sanctification of the Spirit and belief of the truth." That is how God saves. That is how God carries out His purpose—by the sanctification of the Spirit and by your belief of the truth. And my friends, I have not limited God. God could, if He so chose, make the fields to grow crops without the farmer plowing them and sowing the seed, but that is not His way; that is not the method He selects. God could keep you and me in health and strength without our taking any food at all or wasting time in sleeping if He so chose, but that is not His way. And God could save every sinner on earth to-night without them believing if He wanted to, but it is not His way! I am not limiting God, I am describing to you the plan and method that God Himself has set forth in His Word, and if you would be saved, sinner, you have got to believe in the Lord Jesus Christ for youself. I say it reverently: the Holy Spirit won't believe for you. The Holy Spirit may put it into your heart and give you the desire to believe. If you have the desire it is because He has put it there, but He won't believe for you: believing is a human act. It is the sinner himself, in all his wretchedness and need, coming to Christ, as a drowning man clutches a straw, and as the old hymn says:—

"Just as I am without one plea,
But that Thy blood was shed for me."

O sinner, Christ is saying to you to-night, "O fools and slow of heart to believe all." You do believe much as you sit there. There are some of you who be-believe that Jesus is the Son of God. There are some of you who believe that

He is the only Saviour who can save any sinner. You believe that all right, then why not believe all? Why not believe in Him for yourself? Why not trust His precious blood for yourself; and why not to-night? Why not to-night my friend? God is ready, God is ready to save you now if you believe on Him. The blood has been shed, the sacrifice has been offered, the atonement has been made, the feast has been spread. The call goes out to you to-night, "Come, for all things are now ready." And I say again, the devil will tell you as you are sitting there, "There is no need for me to come to-night; I will just wait till God gets ready to come and save me." How do you know that while you are waiting death may not come and smite you down. "Boast not thyself of to-morrow for thou knowest not what a day may bring forth." The Holy Spirit saith, "To-day if ye will hear His voice harden not your hearts." Yes, man can "harden" his heart: God says so; and God calls to you, "Harden not your heart." That is something you do yourself—not the devil—you do it. God is speaking to you through His Word to-night. O may His grace forbid that He shall say our text to any of you after you have left this room—O God forbid that you should be among those "fools" who believe not all. You do believe that Christ is God's appointed Saviour for sinners, why not your Saviour? O may the Spirit draw you by the cords of love to that One who has said, "Him that cometh to Me I will in no wise cast out."

The above is a sermon preached by the Editor in Sydney.

## THE JEW IN HISTORY.

**Hosea 3:4.**

To the man of affairs the Jews present an interesting problem, for they are the greatest paradox of the ages. No nation has been so highly favoured of God, and none has ever been so severely chastised by Him. The Jews are the only people to whom God ever gave a land, and they are the only people who for two thousand years have been without one. In all the annals of the world there is nothing which can for a moment compare with the history of this peculiar and mysterious people. They are beloved of God, yet hated by the world. They are the people who for many centuries eagerly awaited the advent of the Christ, yet they are the ones who delivered Him up to death. They are the only nation to whom God ever gave a king, and yet the only people who for two thousand years have been without a ruler or head. To no other nation are the saints so greatly indebted, yet none have been so wickedly neglected by Christians than have the poor Jews. Their immediate future is dark indeed, but beyond it stretches that morning without clouds.

The Jews are the outstanding miracle of history. They are the only nation whose experiences were written beforehand—forecast hundreds of years in advance. Scattered throughout the earth, they are yet a unit. Taxed and plundered as none others have been, yet are they the wealthiest of all peoples? Persecuted as no other nation, yet miraculously preserved from annihilation. Dispersed among the Gentiles, yet not assimilated by them; they will no more mix than will oil and water. The Jews are not wanted anywhere; yet, because of their financial strength, needed everywhere. All through the "Dark Ages" they were without a friend, and are still without a national home, yet to-day they are more numerous than they were in the time of Moses or Joshua.

The history of the Jews supplies us with the most conclusive of all proofs for the Divine Inspiration of the Bible. It was forecast many centuries before it was acted out on the stage of this world. The Lord has placed in our hands a weapon against which no infidel or atheist can possibly stand. The history of the Jews furnishes us with an argument which it is impossible for unbelief to refute. Yet most of God's people have been deplorably slow in making use of it. I am now going to bring before you quite a number of scriptures in which, many centuries before they became actual history, the experiences of the Jews during the last two thousand years were definitely foretold. I am going to show that the agreement between prediction and fulfilment is so exact, and that the number of details given are so many, as to make it abundantly clear that only He who knows the end from the beginning could possibly be the Author of them.

1. The Babylonian Captivity was foretold: see Deut. 28: 36. This was over eight hundred years before Nebuchadnezzar was born! It was given through Moses before Israel ever entered Canaan. It was accurately and literally fulfilled.

2. The duration of the Babylonian captivity was made known beforehand. See Jer. 29: 10. Here the exact length of time that Israel was to spend in Babylon was revealed before the captivity began! The fulfilment of this prophecy may be seen by comparing Dan. 9: 1,2 and 2 Chron. 36; 21-23.

3. The rejection of the Messiah by Israel was predicted. See Psa. 118: 22 and note the word "refused"; also Isa. 53: 2-3. How utterly unlikely this seemed! that One for whom the Jews waited so long and so eagerly, should nevertheless be rejected by them! Yet how accurately and how tragically were these prophecies realized!

4. The conquest by the Romans was announced long beforehand. See Deut. 28: 49-53. One has but to read Josephus' account of the siege of Jerusalem by Titus, to see how accurately this scripture was fulfilled.

5. The world-wide dispersion of the Jews was revealed centuries in advance. See Lev. 26: 33; Deut. 28: 64.

6. The restless migrating of the Jews was anticipated before their dispersion. See Deut. 28: 65. So literally has this been fulfilled that "the wandering Jew" has become a proverbial expression.

7. The wasteness of the land during their absence was described. See Lev. 26: 34,35. It was to remain "desolate" while they were away from it. In view of Numbers 13: 27 how unlikely this appeared—that a land so exceedingly fertile should become a waste! But remarkably has this prediction been fulfilled. Since the Roman devastation, Palestine has always remained more or less desolate. The Turks, lacking the enterprise of most Europeans, never developed nor cultivated it.

8. The taunts universally cast upon them were announced. See Deut. 28: 37; Jer. 24: 39. Who has not heard the expression "as greedy as a Jew"! When one man gets the better of another by means of tricky dealings it has become the custom, throughout the English-speaking world, to say "he Jew'd me." Literally has he become a "proverb and a byword."

9. The success and financial strength of the Jews was promised of old. See Deut. 28: 12. How remarkably this has been verified needs not to be illustrated.

10. The severe punishment of the Jews and their survival notwithstanding it was assured. See Jer. 30: 11.

11. The preservation of the Jew in spite of their dispersion and oppression was prophetically announced. See Lev. 26: 44. At short intervals throughout their long exile they have been plundered and outraged, tortured and slain; sometimes by the decrees of kings and princes, sometimes by the license of infuriated mobs, often at the instigation of ecclesiastical authorities. They were the sport of the brutal crusaders; they were taxed by kings and barons to pay fines beyond their means, under pain of death: they have been charged with crimes of horror which they never committed, and became the prey of frenzied rabbles, hounded on by merciless priests. Every effort which malice and wickedness could devise have been employed, again and again, for their total extermination. But they could no more be annihilated by persecution than Nebuchadnezzer could destroy the three Hebrews by casting them into the fiery furnace.

12. The preservation of their national distinctness was declared thousands of years ago. See Num. 23: 9. Though scattered, among all nations, they still subsist as a distinct people by themselves. There is nothing comparable to this in the histories of the other nations. No other people have remained "alone" as have the Jews. The Gauls went forth in great hordes to seek their fortunes in foreign parts, but to-day no traces of them now remain. In Spain it is almost impossible to distinguish between the original Spaniards, the Goths and Moors. So in England there are few indeed who can say whether his family has descended from the original Britons, the Romans, Saxons, Danes, or Normans. But no matter where the Jew has gone he preserves his national distinction as clearly to-day as ever.

From the above we draw four conclusions which are clear and irrefutable:—First, the striking fulfilment of the above prophecies furnishes a most conclusive proof for the Divine Inspiration of the Bible. These predictions, which are verified before our eyes, were all given hundreds of years before Christ came to this earth. They were given not in the form of vague generalizations, but with a precision and minuteness which only Omniscience can account for.

Second, they furnish us with a most conclusive proof of God's rule over this earth and its inhabitants. Nothing but a supernatural power, operating directly in human affairs, could have preserved the scattered Jews all through these centuries. Prophecy and Providence are twin sisters; the one announcing things to come, the other securing the actual accomplishing of them. There is no grander thought in the Bible than this: that back of all the seemingly capricious, conflicting and accidental changes in human history, there is an infinite God, whose omniscience and omnipresence forbid that anything should escape His knowledge or evade His power. Prophecy, outlining events beforehand, shows that God is behind the curtain, shaping history, controlling nations, deciding destiny.

Third, herein is furnished a sure key to interpret all prophecy, which is yet unfulfilled. Those forecasts which have been realized, were accomplished to the very letter, showing us that those predictions which concern the future are also to be taken at their face value and understood literally.

Fourth, the above supplies a clear indication that God has miraculously preserved the Jews with some definite object in view, for some future destiny. God does not work miracles for the mere sake of performing them, but ever has a wise and good end in view. The preservation of the Jews agues their future restoration to God's favour and to their land.

The above is a digest of a sermon preached by the Editor in Sydney.

## EXPECTING TOO MUCH OF FELLOW-SAINTS.

This needs to be put before the people of God, and their attention called to it. It is strange, but we are always looking for a sort of perfection in our fellow-believers. The word of God, while providing for a life of faithfulness, shows us the failures of the most illustrious saints and reminds us that "in many things we all offend"; and yet we are so surprised and disappointed when failure comes. It would save us all a great deal of disappointment if we would not expect so much from our brethren, if we were prepared for things to turn out very differently from what we expected, and from what we think is the right way. We need to remember that our way may not be God's way, that whatever the failure on man's part or on His people's part, He cannot fail.

Too often we are so taken up with the failures of others that we forget the faithfulness of our God. We think so much of what is being done down here, that our hearts and eyes get off from what He is up there. Our God never fails, never changes. His Word and truth are always the same. We can turn away from all here below and should do so often, and fix our hearts on the things up there, where Christ is seated at the right hand of God.

It makes a great difference whether we are in communion with the Lord about the failures of fellow-Christians. To dwell on them apart from communion with Him is great loss to the soul. Many are thereby ensnared and their peace destroyed, their usefulness hindered or ruined entirely. Satan likes nothing better than to get saints thinking of the failures of others, occupied with them so as to forget the power, grace, and love of God. From this comes much of the back-biting, gossip, whisperings, which so often grieve the Holy Spirit of God.

—Help and Food, 1900.

Are you praying for an increased circulation? Do you speak of this Magazine to other Christians? Remember it is free for all who would like to read it!

The above has not been written in any censorious spirit. Scores of letters to hand from all parts of this Country and from many foreign lands testify to the fearful conditions which now prevail throughout Christendom. Spiritual churches, whose members are walking humbly before God, are few and far between; pastors after God's own heart seem almost as scarce to-day as in the time of Ezekiel. The shades of a starless night are gathering swiftly, and there seems to be every indication that it will not be long ere "darkness covers the earth, and gross darkness the people" (Isa. 60: 2). But as the shadows deepen, there is the more reason for true Christians to heed the injunction of their Master, and hide not their light under a bushel. To spread the light should be our chief business.

There seem to be many intimations that the present Dispensation has almost run its course. In every realm—the religious, the social, the industrial, the political and that of international diplomacy—things are at the breaking-point. Singly and collectively, they announce that "the coming of the Lord draweth nigh." But God is not willing that any of His own people should perish, therefore is He "longsuffering to usward." A few more brands remain to be plucked from the burning; a few more stones to be quarried and added to the spiritual temple. Then shall the Lord Jesus come and receive us unto Himself. In the meantime, we are to "occupy." The hour calls for increased diligence, the Night is far spent; the Day is at hand.

We trust that Christian readers will "strive together" with us in their prayers (Rom. 15: 30). None can say how much is done by God in direct answer to the earnest and believing cries of His people. To philosophise about prayer borders on the impious. One thing we know, both from Scripture and experience, that our God works mightily in response to the united supplications of His children. We are anxious for the circulation of this Magazine to be not only doubled, but multiplied. We long to reach thousands of Christ's starved sheep. We desire the help and co-operation of our readers to this end: be constantly looking out for Christians who will value it, and send us their names and addresses if you are sure they will read it. Pray daily for the Editor and his wife that health and strength may be given to enable them to cope with the increased demands upon them. Above all, pray that Christ may become more real and precious to His blood-bought ones, and that they may manifest more obedience and devotion to Him in return. With loving greetings, we remain.

Yours by Sovereign Grace,

A. W. and V. E. PINK.

We are thankful to report that we closed 1926 with a small balance in hand.

"He is faithful that promised." So we have proven these five years past.

## THE JUSTIFICATION OF GOD'S ELECT.

### Sovereignly by God:

"Who shall lay anything to the charge of God's elect? It is God that justifieth." (Rom. 8:33).

### Freely by His Grace:

"Being justified freely by His grace, through the redemption that is in Christ Jesus." (Rom. 3:24.)

### Meritoriously by Jesus' Blood:

"Much more then being now justified by His blood, we shall be saved from wrath through Him." (Rom. 5:9).

### Imputatively by His Obedience:

"By the obedience of One shall many be made righteous (Rom. 5:19).

### Authoritatively by His Resurrection:

"Who was raised again for our justification." (Rom. 4:25).

### Efficaciously by His Spirit:

"Justified in the name of the Lord Jesus, and by the Spirit of our God." (1 Cor. 6:11).

### Experimentally by His Faith:

"Knowing that a man is not justified by the works of the law, but by the faith of Jesus Christ." (Gal. 2:16.)

### Evidentially by His Works:

"Ye see then, how that by works a man is justified, and not by faith only." (James 2:24).

—Thos. Bradbury.

# STUDIES IN THE SCRIPTURES

"Search the Scriptures" John 5:39.

Copyright in all English-speaking Countries.

Editor: Arthur W. Pink, 22 Parramatta Road, Summer Hill, N.S.W., Australia.
Hon. Agent in U.S.A.: Mr. C. S. Pressel, 559 Dupont Ave., York, Penna.

FREE TO ALL WHO WILL READ IT

"For whom the Lord loveth He chasteneth, and scourgeth every son whom He receiveth." (Heb. 12: 6).

This life is but a schooling. In saying this we are uttering a platitude, yet is it a truth of which all Christians need to be constantly reminded. This is the period of our childhood and minority. Now in childhood everything has, or should have, the character of education and discipline. Parents and teachers are constantly directing, warning, rebuking; the whole of the child's life is under rule, restraint and guidance. But the only object is the child himself—his good, his character, his future; and the only motive is love. Now as childhood is to the rest of our life, so is the whole of our earthly sojourn to our future and heavenly life. Therefore let us seek to cultivate the spirit of childhood. Let us regard it as natural that we should be daily rebuked and corrected. Let us believe with the docility and meekness of children, with their trustful and sweet assurance, that love is behind all our chastenings, that we are in the tender hands of our Father.

There is something very striking and unusual about our present text in that it is found, in slightly varied form, in no less than five different books of the Bible. Let the reader look up Job 5: 17, Psalm 94: 12, Prov. 3: 12, Rev. 3: 19. Probably there is a twofold reason for this reiteration. First, it hints at the importance and blessedness of this truth. God repeats it so frequently lest we should forget, and thus lose the comfort and cheer of realising that Divine chastisement proceeds from love. This must be a precious word if God thought it well to say it five times over! Second, such repetition also implies our slowness to believe it. By nature our evil hearts are inclined in the opposite direction. Though our text affirms so emphatically that the Christian's chastisements proceed from God's love, we are ever ready to attribute them to His hardness. It is really very humbling that the Holy Spirit should deem it necessary to repeat this statement so often!

It will be noted that our text supplies a reason to enforce the exhortation of the previous verse. In v. 5 there is an admonition concerning the spirit in which chastisement should be received. First, it must not be "despised"; second, we must not "faint" beneath it. Here in v. 6 a reason is given why we should not act thus—"for," because. The reason is this: the chastisement which descends on the Christian is the consequence of God's love. Therefore it is wicked for us to "despise" it, and foolish to "faint" under it. Consider now three things:—

1. The Christian's chastisements flow from God's love. Not from His anger or hardness, nor from arbitrary dealings, but from God's heart do our afflictions come. It is love which regulates all the ways of God in dealing with His own. It was love which elected them. The heart is not warmed when our election is traced back merely to God's sovereign will. But our affections are stirred when we read "in love having pre-destinated us" (Eph. 1: 4, 5). It was love which redeemed us. We do not reach the center of the Atonement when we see nothing more in the Cross than a vindication of the Law and a satisfaction of Justice: "God so loved the world that He gave His only begotten Son" (John 3: 16).

So it is love which ordained our trials and orders our chastisements. O

*(Continued on page 4)*

## BACK NUMBERS

OF THIS MAGAZINE obtainable, 5/- (1 dollar) per year; Bound at 7/- (1 dollar 75.) Each year is yet obtainable.

ADVISE PROMPTLY of Change of Address.

THIS MAGAZINE is published as a work of faith and labor of love. It is gladly sent to all who would value it.

We want the names and addresses of Christians who would read it.

Christians who feel definitely led to do so may have fellowship with us in this Ministry.

## CONTENTS.

| | |
|---|---|
| The Gospel of John (18: 12-27 | 26 |
| Gleanings in Exodus | 34 |
| Homegoing of a Saint | 39 |
| Divine Chastisement | 44 |

## THE GOSPEL OF JOHN

**62. Christ before Annas: John 18: 12-27.**

Below is an Analysis of the second section of John 18:—

1. Christ bound and led to Annas vv. 12-14.
2. Peter follows and is admitted to the palace vv. 15, 16.
3. Peter's first denial of Christ vv. 17, 18.
4. Annas questions Christ, and His reply vv. 19-21.
5. Christ smitten and His remonstrance vv. 22, 23.
6. Annas sends Christ to Caiaphas v. 24.
7. Peter's second and third denials vv. 25-27.

In the passage before us John again supplies details which are not given by the other Evangelists. The Synoptics describe our Lord's appearing before Caiaphas: in the Fourth Gospel this is passed over, and in its place we have His arraignment before Annas. As in the Garden, so in the high priest's palace, two of the Saviour's perfections are prominently displayed: His lowliness and dignity: His immeasurable superiority over all who surrounded Him, friends or foes, and His complete submission before those in the seat of human authority. As the Son of God we see Him exposing the wickedness of all with whom He comes into contact; as the Son of man He carried Himself meekly before those who acted more like fiends than humans.

The structure of our present passage is quite complex. From Christ being led away to Annas the Holy Spirit pauses to notice Peter following and then entering the high priest's house. After recording Peter's first denial, he is left warming himself at the fire, and then a brief account is given of what passed between Annas and Christ. Following the announcement that Annas sent Jesus bound to Caiaphas, the Spirit returns again to Peter and describes the second and third denials. The central thing is plainly Christ's appearing before Annas and afterwards before Pilate, but the narrative is interrupted again and yet again to tell of the apostle's awful fall. Most vividly does this point a solemn lesson. God is not the author of confusion: it is sin which produces disorder and hinders the Spirit from taking the things of Christ and showing them unto us! It is this which is written large across John 18 if attention be paid to its structure and order of narrative.

But why is it that the Holy Spirit has made so prominent the sin of Simon in this portion of Scripture? Why has He broken into His account of what befell the Saviour, by mentioning the threefold denial? Why, especially, after having previously recorded the same in each of the Synoptics? Ah, is it not to emphasise the **need** of Christ's atoning death, by showing us the **character** of those for whom He died! Was it not His design to show how fearfully sin had "abounded" before He portrayed the super-abounding **of grace!** Was it not suitable that He should first paint a **dark** background, so that the **perfections** of the Holy One might be brought into sharper relief! What comes out so plainly all through John—never more so than in these closing incidents—is Christ glorifying the Father in a scene where the ruin of sin was **complete** and **universal.**

"Then the band and the captain and the officers of the Jews took Jesus, and bound Him" (v. 12). Behold here the amazing hardness of unconverted men. The company of those who arrested the Saviour was made up of men of marked differences; it was composed of Gentiles and Jews, soldiers and servants of the priests and Pharisees, heathen and those who belonged to the covenant people of Jehovah. But in one respect they were all alike—they were blind to the glories of Him whom they apprehended. Both parties had witnessed a signal exhibition of His power, when by a word from His lips He had thrown them all to the ground. Both parties had witnessed His tender mercy, when they saw Him heal the torn ear of the first to lay rough hands on Him. Yet, both remained insensible and unmoved, and now proceeded to coolly carry out their odious business of binding the incarnate Son of God. Terrible indeed is the state of the natural man. Let us not wonder, then, at the unbelief and hardness of heart which we see on every side to-day; these things were manifested in the presence of the Saviour, and will continue until He returns in judgment.

"Behold also the amazing **condescension** of our Lord Jesus Christ. We see the Son of God taken prisoner and led away bound like a malefactor—arraigned before wicked and unjust judges—insulted and treated with contempt. And yet, this unresisting Prisoner had only to will His deliverance, and He would at once have been free. He had only to command the confusion of His enemies, and they would at once have been confounded. Above all, He was One who knew full well that Annas and Caiaphas, and all their companions, would one day stand before His judgment seat and receive an eternal sentence. He knew all these things and yet condescended to be treated as a malefactor without resisting. One thing at any rate is very clear: the love of Christ to sinners is 'a love that passeth knowledge.' To suffer for those who are in some sense worthy of our affection, is suffering that we can understand. To submit to ill-treatment quietly, when we have no power to resist is submission that is both graceful and wise. But to suffer voluntarily, when we have the power to prevent it, and to suffer for a world of unbelieving and ungodly sinners, unasked and unthanked—this is a line of conduct which passes man's understanding. Never let us forget that this is the peculiar beauty of Christ's sufferings when we read the wonderful story of His cross and passion. He was led away captive, and dragged before the high priest's bar, not because He could not help Himself, but because He had set His heart on saving sinners—by bearing their sins, by being treated as a sinner, and by being punished in their stead" (Bishop Ryle).

"Then the band and the captain and the officers of the Jews took Jesus, and bound Him." The first word ought to be translated "Therefore," not "Then:" the words of the previous verse explaining its force: "Then said Jesus unto Peter, Put up thy sword into the sheath: the cup which My Father hath given Me, shall I not drink it?" Having rebuked Peter for offering resistance, He bowed to the Father's will. "**Therefore**" they "took Jesus and bound Him"—like savage beasts they sprang upon their prey. We believe it was to this the Saviour referred when, speaking by the Spirit of prophecy, He declared, "Many bulls have compassed Me: strong bulls of Bashan have beset Me round. They gaped upon Me with their mouths, as a ravening and a roaring lion. . . dogs have compassed Me, the assembly of the wicked have enclosed Me." We doubt not that they bound Him with heavy chains, for of him who furnishes, perhaps, the fullest type of Christ it is written, "Joseph was sold for a servant: whose feet they hurt with fetters he was laid in iron" (Psa. 105: 17, 18). Is not the anti-type of this more than hinted at in Isa. 53: 5, where we are told not only that He was "wounded for our transgressions" but "bruised for our iniquities"!—was it not when they "bound" His wrists and ankles with handcuffs and fetters!

Why did they "bind" Him? For historical reasons we may give: because Judas had bidden them hold Him fast (Matt. 26: 48), this because he remembered what is recorded in Luke 4: 29, 30; John 8: 59, etc.; because they would heap shame upon Him, treating Him as a lawless character; because they deemed Him worthy of death, thereby prejudicing His sentence. But behind these we may see a typical reason: God over-ruling for the fulfilment of it. All that befell Christ was to fulfil the types and prophecies that went before of Him. The most eminent type of Christ in His sufferings was Isaac, and the first thing that Abraham did to him, when about to offer him up as a sacrifice, was to **take and bind him** (Gen. 22: 9)! So it was with the animals which were offered: bind the sacrifice with cords, unto the horns of the altar (Psa. 118: 27). But deeper still, there was a **mystical** significance to this binding of the Saviour: we were Sin's captives, therefore was He theirs! Our sins were the **cause** of His binding, therefore did He, as our Substitute, cry, innumerable evils have taken hold upon Me; Mine iniquities (ours, made His) have compassed me about (Psa. 40: 12)! He was bound that we might be set free. "It is a certain rule that what should have been done to us, something correspondent was done to Christ; and the virtue of His person was such, though it was done to His body, it brought us freedom from the like due to our souls; and by Him being thus bound and led, He Himself afterward, when He ascended, led captivity captive" (Dr. Thomas Goodwin). How ready, then, should we be to be bound for Christ (in Heb. 13: 3 afflictions for His sake are called "bonds"!); and how little ought we to be moved by the vileness of those who persecute us, when we remember Him!

"And led Him away to Annas first" (v. 13). The Saviour was neither "driven" nor "dragged," but led: thereby the Holy Spirit informs us, once more, of His willing submission. He offered no resistance. With infinitely greater ease than Samson of old, could He have burst His bonds "as a thread when it toucheth the fire"; but as prophecy had announced, "He was led as a lamb to the slaughter"—gentle and tractable. Here also He fulfilled not only prophecy but type: each animal that was to be offered in sacrifice was first led to the priest (Lev. 17: 5), so Christ was first brought to Annas. The road followed from the Garden to the house of the high priest was also significant. Gethsemane was at the foot of Olivet, on the east side of Jerusalem, beyond the brook Cedron. In journeying from there to the City, the gate through which they would pass was "the sheep gate" (Neh. 3: 1, 32; 12: 39; John 5:2 and see our notes on the last). The "sheep gate" was nigh unto the Temple, and through it the sacrificial animals passed (first having been fed in the meadows adjoining the Cedron); so also went the true Lamb on this occasion! Note a striking contrast here: Adam was driven out of the Garden (Gen. 3: 24); Christ was led!

"And led Him away to Annas first; for he was father-in-law to Caiaphas, which was the high priest that same year" (v. 13). John is the only one who tells of the Saviour being brought before Annas; the Synoptics describe His appearance before Caiaphas. Both Annas and Caiaphas are called "high priests." The fact that there were two high priests shows the confusion which prevailed at that time. Much has been written on the subject that provides neither information nor edification. So far as our own limited light goes, we take it that the Roman rule over Palestine supplies the key. In view of 11: 49 it seems that the Romans elected a high priest for Israel each year (compare Acts 4: 6, which mentions no less than four, all living, who had filled that office), but in the light of Luke 3: 1 it is clear that sometimes they were re-elected. According to the Law of God the high priest retained his office till death (Ex. 40: 15; Num. 35: 25, etc.), therefore in the eyes of the Jews Annas, not Caiaphas, was the real high priest: Caiaphas was formally acknowledged in a civic way, but Annas took precedence over him in ecclesiastical matters. This, we believe, explains why the Saviour was brought first before Annas.

"Now Caiaphas was he, which gave counsel to the Jews, that it was expedient that one man should die for the people" (v. 14). The reference here is to what is recorded in 11: 49-52. Caiaphas apparently, was the first man to make the motion that Christ be put to death. The reason he advanced being a political one, with the evident intention of currying favour with the Romans. The callous selfishness of the man comes out plainly in his "consider that it is expedient for us that one man should die for the people" (11: 50). He was addressing the Sanhedrin, the Supreme Court of Judaism, and in saying "for us," rather than "for them" he shows that he cared more for his office than for his nation.

"Now Caiaphas was he, which gave counsel to the Jews, that it was expedient that one man should die for the people." Why is this mentioned here? To show on what ground (from the human side) our Saviour was crucified: it was out of political considerations, and those imaginary at best—lest perchance "the Romans take away our place and nation." The Holy Spirit has premised all the other sufferings of Christ thus, in order to show us that no equity is to be expected from all their proceedings against Him. They had resolved, before they took Him, to put Him to death, and that for State considerations, therefore they would be sure to keep to their resolutions whether He were innocent or no, whether they could convict Him or not. The judge had given his verdict and determined the sentence before the trial took place! Here then is one of the Spirit's reasons for introducing this reference to the words of Caiaphas—to show us that in what follows we must not expect to find any favour shown to the Lord Jesus, nor must we be surprised if His trial was simply a farce, a glaring travesty of justice. In addition to this, we believe that God saw to it that there should be a plain testimony from the legal head of the Nation as to the purpose and character of His Son's death: He was dying "FOR the people"!

"And Simon Peter followed Jesus" (v. 15). Matthew tells us that he "followed afar off" (26: 58). In following Christ at all on this occasion Peter was clearly acting in the energy of the flesh, for Christ's will as to His disciples had been plainly expressed in the "Let these go their way" (v. 8). "Lovingly anxious to see what was done to Him, yet not bold enough to keep near Him like a disciple. Anyone can see that the unhappy Peter was under the influence of very mixed feelings—love made him ashamed to run away and hide himself; cowardice made him ashamed to show his colours, and stick by his Lord's side. Hence he chose a middle course, the worst, as it happened, that he could have followed" (Bishop Ryle).

"And Simon Peter followed Jesus, and so did another disciple: that disciple was known unto the high priest, and went in with Jesus into the palace of the high priest" (v. 15). There has been much discussion and speculation as to who this "other disciple" was. A few of the old commentators and most of the modern believe that he was the writer of this Gospel; but whoever he may have been, it is almost certain that he was not John. In the first place, John was a poor fisherman of Galilee—far removed from Jerusalem—therefore it is most unlikely that he was on sufficiently intimate terms with the high priest as to enter his house and have authority over the door-keeper so as to order her to admit Peter. In the second place, John, being a Galilean, would have been recognised and challenged as was Peter (Matt. 26: 69, 73). In the third place, whenever John refers to himself in this Gospel it is always as "the disciple whom Jesus loved" (13: 23; 19: 26; 20: 2; 21: 7, 20). Finally, Acts 4: 13 makes it very plain that the high priest was not personally acquainted with either Peter or John! Who, then, was this "other disciple"? The answer is, We do not know. It may have been Nicodemus or Joseph of Arimathaea, but we cannot be sure.

"But Peter stood at the door without" (v. 16). How significant and suggestive is this little detail—the door was shut! Was it not by God's providence that the door was now closed? Happy for Peter had he remained on the outside. The Lord had plainly warned him to "watch and pray lest he enter into temptation." But Peter disregards His admonition, and knocks for admission—why else should the other disciple have gone out? There is a practical lesson for us right here: God in His mercy put an impediment in Peter's way, stopped him from going on to that which should be the occasion of his sin; so does He, ofttimes, with us. Therefore, when we find God, in His providence, placing some barrier in our path, it behooves us to pause, and examine well our grounds for going further along the same path we are in. If our way is warranted by the Word and our conscience is clear as to a certain line of duty, then obstacles are to be regarded only as testings of faith and patience; but otherwise they are warnings from God.

"Then went out that other disciple, which was known unto the high priest, and spoke unto her that kept the door, and brought in Peter" (v. 16). Ah, says the reader, does not this conflict with what has just been said on the first part of the verse? Would not the coming forth of the other disciple, his speaking to the door-keeper (unasked by Peter), and his bringing him in, indicate that God's providences were working in favor of Peter entering the palace? Did it not look as though God were calling Peter to enter? The difficulty seems real, yet it is capable of a simple solution. Peter had disregarded the warning of God—the shut door; he had persisted in having his own way—knocking for entrance; now God removes His providential barrier. How solemnly this speaks to us; may the Lord grant to each the hearing ear. When we disregard both the Word and warning providence of God, we must not be surprised if He then sets a snare for us. When we insist in having our own way we must be prepared if God gives us up to our own heart's lust (Psa. 81: 12). Jonah chafed against God's word, therefore when he fled from going to Nineveh and set his heart on Tarshish, he found a ship all ready for him to sail in! Here, then, is another most important practical lesson pointed out for us: the outward providences of God must not be taken for our guide when we have refused His Word and His warnings!

"Then saith the damsel that kept the door unto Peter, Art not thou also one of this man's disciples? He saith, I am not" (v. 17). That the door-keeper was a maid rather than a man was obviously overruled by the providence of God: He would humble the pride of Peter in this way, that his weakness might stand out as a lasting warning against self-confidence. It was neither by one of the Roman soldiers nor one of the Jewish officers that the apostle was first challenged, but by a young woman! Why she should ask him the question she did, we are not told; whether she was moved by idle curiosity, or detected that he was a Galilean, or whether his countenance bore marks of agitation and fear, or whether—as is more likely—she concluded from Peter being a friend of the "other disciple" that he "also" was a follower of Christ, we cannot be sure. Note how mildly she framed her question: not, Are you a follower of this Insurrectionist, this Enemy of Judaism, this Blasphemer against God, but simply, "This Man"! Yet, notwithstanding the sex of his questioner, and the mild form of her question, Peter told a downright lie. He said, "I am not." "The betrayal by Judas, though more dreadful, is almost less startling than the denial by Peter. We are less prepared for the cowardice of the one, than for the covetousness of the other. That the one should turn timid seems less natural, so to say—was less to be expected—than that the other should prove a traitor. 'Wherefore let him that thinketh he standeth take heed lest he fall'" (Dr. G. Brown).

"And the servants and officers stood there, who had made a fire of coal, for it was cold: and they warmed themselves: and Peter stood with them, and warmed himself" (v. 18). What we have here is introductory to the second and third denials, recorded in vv. 25-27. Peter was cold. How profoundly and solemnly significant! The Christian who follows Christ "afar off" will soon be chilled and grow cold spiritually; then will recourse be had to fleshly stimulants for warmth and comfort. And the enemies of Christ —the world, the flesh, and the Devil— will provide their "fire"—their places and means of cheer!

"And Peter stood with them." Ominous words are these. Of the Traitor it was said "And Judas also, which betrayed Him, stood with them"; now we find Simon in the same evil company! "The apostle stood among the crowd of his Master's enemies, and warmed himself like one of them, as if he had nothing to think of but his bodily comfort; while his beloved Master stood in a distant part of the hall, cold, and a prisoner. Who can doubt that Peter, in his miserable cowardice, wished to appear one of the party who hated Christ, and sought to conceal his real character by doing as they did? And who can doubt that while he warmed his hands he felt cold, wretched, and comfortless in his own soul?" (Bishop Ryle). How true it is that "The backslider in heart shall be filled with his own ways" (Pro. 14: 14)! Some have pointed out that the Holy Spirit has here told us "it was cold" in order to impress us the more with the bloody sweat of Christ only a short while before!

"The high priest then asked Jesus of His disciples, and of His doctrine" (v. 19). The gross injustice of such a mode of procedure is glaringly apparent. Instead of preferring a charge against the Saviour, and then summoning witnesses to prove it, Annas acted after the manner of the Inquisition, asking questions so as to ensnare the One before him. And this was the religious head of Israel, acting altogether against and without law, no indictment having been drawn up, no evidence brought forward to support it; nothing but a cowardly attempt to overawe the Prisoner by brow-beating Him, so that he could obtain something which might be used against Him.

"The high priest then asked Jesus of His disciples, and of His doctrine." The fact that Annas referred here to our Lord's "disciples" at once indicates the malevolent character of his questioning: it was an ironical reference to those who had forsaken Him and fled! The high priest "asked Jesus of His disciples"— With what design did you gather them round you? Where are they? How many have you in reality now? He asked of them; he did not call for them: none were allowed to testify on His behalf! "And of His doctrine"—not for edification, but to see if it were a new teaching of His own, so that they might have wherewith to accuse Him. It is plain that at this stage they were at a loss for a charge. "The disciples are mentioned as His dependents, His followers, His party, His sworn confidents; the doctrine is inquired into as novelty, heresy, dangerous misleading error; both together pointing to the two charges which afterwards were urged—Insurrection against the Roman power, error or blasphemy against the Jewish" (Stier).

"Jesus answered him, I spake openly to the world" (v. 20). Not before, but to, the world." Why did He not say "to the multitudes"? why "to the world"? It was the first hint of the universality of His message—note how the "Jews" are referred to separately later in the verse! "I spake openly to the world": truth is bold and fears not the light. It is the emissaries of Satan who hide the leaven in the meal (Matt. 13: 33); it is the servants of the Prince of Darkness who haunt the "secret chambers" (Matt. 24: 26). In saying that He spake openly to the world the Lord was indirectly rebuking Annas and his co-conspirators for their injustice of refusing Him a trial in open court.

"I ever taught in the synagogue, and in the temple, whither the Jews always resort" (v. 20)—there is no article before "synagogue." In affirming that He taught in the established places of public worship, the Lord gave proof that He was no lawless separatist, clandestinely proselytising, but honoring the institutions of God and acting as became His Prophet. "Whither the Jews always resort." "He describes His cause and doctrine as properly national, for all the Jews. There is in the background of both question and answer, though the Lord put it directly not in words, the meaning that the main point in His teaching was the testimony to Himself as the Messiah:—thus where all the Jews as Jews are assembled in their national religion to worship God, there have I testified that which applies to all the Jews, that they all should be 'My disciples' and ought to acknowledge and join themselves to Me!" (Stier).

"And in secret have I said nothing" (v. 20). This does not mean that He had never instructed His disciples in private. The Lord was giving a general description of His public ministry. Moreover, His confidential communications to His own were but explanations or amplifications of what he had taught in the open. He had not two doctrines, one exoteric for the multitudes, and another esoteric for His intimate friends. In secret He had said nothing. In like manner, the badge by which His messengers may always be identified is described in 2 Cor. 4: 2: "Not walking in craftiness, not handling the Word of God deceitfully but by manifestation of the Truth commending ourselves to every man's conscience in the sight of God." In saying "in secret have I said nothing" the Saviour unhesitatingly appropriated to Himself the identical declaration of Jehovah of old—"I have not spoken in secret, in a dark place of the earth: I said not unto the seed of Jacob, Seek ye Me in vain: I the Lord speak righteousness, I declare things that are right" (Isa. 45: 19). It is also blessed to observe that while Christ here gave a full, if brief, answer, to Annas concerning His "doctrine," not a word did He say about His "disciples." As the Shepherd He protected His sheep! He alone was to suffer, therefore He alone assumed all responsibility!

"Why askest thou Me?" (v. 21). Mark the quiet dignity of Christ. So far from being cowed He turned and challenges the judge: Why, or better, "Wherefore askest thou Me?" It was one of those questions of the Lord which never failed to pierce the heart. Why, do you, the high priest, pretend to be ignorant of what is common knowledge among the people! You have had many opportunities to hear Me yourself! You have expelled from the synagogue those who believe in Me; what meanest thou, then, by this questioning! It was the Light exposing the "hidden things of dishonesty." It was the Holy One condemning the high priest for attempting to make a prisoner incriminate himself and supply evidence to be used against him.

"Ask them which heard Me what I have said unto them: behold, they know what I said" (v. 21). By thus appealing to those who had heard Him, the Lord still further rebuked the malicious secrecy which had induced them. through fear of the people, to take Him by night. The direction in which Christ pointed Annas is very striking. He did not say, Summon the deaf, the lame, the blind, the lepers I have healed. He did not say, Send for Lazarus of Bethany and question him! But, "Ask them which heard Me." It was "the Word" challenging them! "Survey the dignity, the clearness, the gentleness, the supremely measured rightness and wisdom of this answer! In the full and perfect consciousness that He was no founder of a sect, deserving inquisition, He began with I openly, continued with I, and closed with profound feeling who He was, yet not expressing it with 'what I have said.' But, with the most proper discretion of one arrested and charged, more righteous than Annas and his foolish questioning:—I may not and will not now, My life and doctrine lying before you, testify for Myself, or defend Myself—let all be investigated! Let the testimony of all bear witness!" (Stier).

"And when He had thus spoken, one of the officers which stood by, struck Jesus with the palm of his hand (margin "with a rod"), saying, Answerest Thou the high priest so?" (v. 22). How fearfully does this exhibit the enmity of the natural man against God, here manifest in the flesh! Meekly and mildly had our Lord replied to questions which deserved no answer, and all that He received in return was a cruel and cowardly blow. There is no hint of any remonstrance from Annas, nor have we any reason to suppose that he made any. And what shall be thought of a judge who allowed a bound prisoner to be treated in this fashion! Unable to meet the convicting and condemning truth, resource was had to force. It was might attempting to crush the right. This was the first blow which the sacred body of our Saviour received from the hands of sinners, and this came not from one of the Roman soldiers, but from a Jew! The Greek word signifies "gave a blow on the face," whether with his hand or with a stick is not determined; personally, we believe it was with the latter, and thus fulfilled Micah 5: 1—"They shall smite the Judge of Israel with a rod upon the cheek."

"Jesus answered him, If I have spoken evil, bear witness of the evil: but if well, why smitest thou Me?" (v. 23). There was no hot surging of the flesh here, no angry retort, no spirit of resentment. Under all circumstances the Lord Jesus manifested His perfections. But He only was "without sin": contrast the apostle Paul in Acts 23. When the high priest Ananias commanded them that stood by him to strike their prisoner in the mouth, Paul said, "God shall smite thee thou whited wall." Yet it is beautiful to see how grace in him triumphed over the flesh: as soon as they asked him, "Revilest thou God's high priest?" he answered "I wist not, brethren, that he was the high priest, for it is written, Thou shalt not speak evil of the ruler of thy people" (vv. 2-5). But He who is fairer than the children of men never had to retract a single word! O that we may learn of Him who was meek and lowly in heart.

"But if well, why smitest thou Me?" The Saviour still acted as became the Son of God: He questioned His questioner! He judged the one who had so unrighteously condemned Him. If the smiter had any sense of justice he must have felt keenly our Lord's calm rebuke.

"Now Annas had sent Him bound unto Caiaphas, the high priest" (v. 24). The word "had" here is misleading and is not warranted by the Greek. It was following what we read of in vv. 19-23 that Christ was turned over to Caiaphas. Annas had heard sufficient. He saw that to prolong the uneven contest would damage himself rather than his Prisoner; so, ignoring Christ's piercing question, the blow of the officer and our Lord's rebuke, he sends Him bound to his son-in-law, that the specious judgment might proceed as prudently as possible, but with the "If I have spoken (not "done"!) evil, bear witness of the evil" ringing in his ears.

"And Simon Peter stood and warmed himself. They said therefore unto him, art not thou also one of His disciples? He denied it, and said, I am not (v. 25). The first clause here is repeated from v. 18 so as to connect the history. The "therefore" informs us why it was that these men should challenge Peter. He was standing "with them" (v. 18), as one of them, and no doubt it was the flames from their "fire" which lit up his face and caused them to recognise him. He was warming himself—more concerned about his body than his soul. He was listening to their blasphemous talk about his Master, too timid to speak up and witness for Him. And it is written "Be not deceived, evil communications corrupt good manners" (1 Cor. 15: 33). So it proved here, for when these men asked the apostle if he were one of Christ's disciples he denied it. This gives additional force to the "therefore": Peter's being in the company of these enemies of the Lord was the occasion of his being challenged, and that became the occasion of his greater sinning! What a solemn warning for us to avoid the company of the ungodly! How urgently we need to heed the command? "Be ye not unequally yoked together with unbelievers"! But note it carefully that Peter did not deny that Jesus was the Christ, the Son of God, or the Saviour of sinners—which, we think, none indwelt by the Holy Spirit ever did—but only that he was one of His "disciples"!

"One of the servants of the high priest, being his kinsman whose ear Peter cut off, said Did not I see thee in the Garden with Him?" (v. 26). What a rebuke was this! Peter was standing "with them" (v. 18), and now one reminds him that, only a little while before, he had stood "with Him." How this should have searched his conscience; how it ought to have opened his eyes to the place he now occupied. But poor Peter had boasted, "Although all shall be offended yet will not I... I will not deny Thee in any wise" (Mark 14: 29, 31); and so God left him to stand alone, to show him and us that except omnipotent grace upholds us we are certain to fall. Alas, what is man. What is our boasted strength but weakness, and when we are left to ourselves how our most solemn resolutions melt like snow before the sun!

"Peter then denied again: and immediately the cock crew" (v. 27). "If any of his companions had been asked at what point of Peter's character the vulnerable spot would be found, not one of them would have said, He will fall through cowardice. Besides, Peter had a few hours before been so emphatically warned against denying Christ that he might have been expected to stand firm this night at least. Perhaps it was this very warning which betrayed Peter. When he struck the blow in the garden, he may have thought he had falsified his Lord's prediction, and when he found himself the only one who had courage to follow to the palace, his besetting self-confidence returned and led him into circumstances for which he was too weak. He was equal to the test of his courage which he was **expecting**, but when another kind of test was applied in circumstances and from a quarter he had not anticipated his courage failed him utterly.

"Peter probably thought he might be brought bound with his Master before the high priest, and had he done so he would probably have stood faithful. But the Devil who was sifting him had a much finer sieve than that to run him through. He brought him to no formal trial, where he could gird himself for a special effort. The whole trial was over before he knew he was being tried. So do most of our real trials come; in a business transaction that turns up with others in the day's work, in the few minutes' talk or the evening's intercourse with friends, it is discovered whether we are so truly Christ's friends that we cannot forget Him or disguise the fact that we are His. In these battles which we must all encounter, we receive no formal challenge that gives us time to choose our ground and our weapons; but a sudden blow is dealt us, from which we can be saved only by habitually wearing a coat of mail sufficient to turn it, and which we can carry into all companies" (Dr. M. Dods).

Many are the lessons which we ought to learn from this sad fall of Peter. First, in himself the believer is as weak as water. Only two hours before, Peter had partaken of the Lord's Supper, had heard the most touching Address and Prayer that ever fell on mortal ears, and had received the plainest possible warning—yet he fell!! Second, it shows us the danger of self-confidence. "It is a beacon mercifully set up in Scripture, to prevent others making shipwreck." Third, it warns us of the consequences of prayerlessness: had Peter watched and prayed when the Lord bade him, he would have found grace to help in time of need. Fourth, it reveals to us the perils of companioning with the wicked. Fifth, it shows us the disastrous influence of the fear of man—"the fear of man bringeth a snare" (Pro. 29: 25), making us more afraid of the face of those we can see than the eye of God whom we cannot see. Sixth, it should prepare us against surprise when our familiar friends fail us in the crucial hour—God often permits this to cast us back the more on Himself! Seventh, did not God permit Peter to sin more grievously than any of the Eleven because He foreknew the extravagant regard which should afterwards be paid to him and his self-styled "successors"!

"After all let us leave the passage with the comfortable reflection that we have a merciful and faithful High Priest, who can be touched with the feeling of our infirmities, and will not break the bruised reed. Peter no doubt felt shamefully, and only rose again after heartfelt repentance and bitter tears. But he **did** rise again; he was not cast off forevermore. The same pitiful Hand that saved him from drowning, when his faith failed him on the waters, was once more stretched out to raise him when he fell in the high priest's hall. Can we doubt that he rose a wiser and better man? If Peter's fall has made Christians see more clearly their own great weakness and Christ's great compassion, then Peter's fall has not been recorded in vain" (Bishop Ryle).

The following questions are to help the student on the closing section of John 18:—
1. Compare the Synoptics for what happened ere Christ appeared before Pilate.
2. What does v. 30 prove?
3. What does the second half of v. 31 go to show?
4. What did Christ mean by v. 36?
5. What is the force of the last clause of v. 37?
6. Why did God cause Pilate to say v. 39?
7. What is the deeper significance of v. 40?

Arthur W. Pink.

---

# GLEANINGS IN EXODUS.

### 38. The Table: Exodus 25: 23-30.

Having described the contents of the innermost chamber of the Tabernacle, the Holy Spirit now conducts us into the Holy-place. In the former the high priest ministered on the annual day of atonement, in the latter the Levites served daily. In this second chamber stood three pieces of furniture: the table, the candlestick, and the altar of incense. The order in which these are brought before us in the sacred narrative is most suggestive, and the very reverse of what would have occurred to us. We had surely put the golden altar of incense first, then the seven-branched candlestick, and last, the table. But God's thoughts and ways are ever the opposite of ours. When we see what the table stood for, perhaps we shall the better appreciate the Divine arrangement.

As it was in the innermost shrine, so it is in the holy place—nought but gold met the eye of him who had entered: it was therefore a scene displaying the Divine glory. Silence reigned in the sacred apartment. No prayers were offered, no songs of praise were sung. The voice of man was still, but the voice of the golden vessels therein mutely, yet eloquently, spoke of Christ; for the light of the knowledge of the glory of God shines "in the face of Jesus Christ" (2 Cor. 4: 6). None but the priestly family ever penetrated this sacred precinct, telling us that only those who, by wondrous grace, are "an holy priesthood," those who by sovereign mercy are "a chosen generation, a royal priesthood" (1 Peter 2: 5, 9), can enter into the spiritual significance of its symbolic contents. Coming now to the Table, let us consider:—

### 1. Its Meaning.

In seeking to ascertain the spiritual purport of the Table the first thing which arrests our attention in the Divine description of it is the word "also" in Exodus 25: 23—found only once more in connection with the holy vessels and furnishings of the Tabernacle, see 30: 18. The "also" at the beginning of our present passage suggests a close link of connection with what has gone before. In the preceding verse we read, "And there will I meet with thee, and I will commune with thee from above the Mercy-seat," and then following right after this, "Thou shalt also make a Table." Thus God has graciously hung the key right over the entrance, and told us that the Table has to do with communion. This is in full accord with other scriptures where the "table" is mentioned.

A lovely picture of that blessedness of which the "table" speaks is found in 2 Sam. 9. There we find David asking "Is there yet any that is left of the house of Saul, that I may show him kindness for Jonathan's sake?" (v. 1). A beautiful illustration is this of the wondrous grace of God, showing kindness to those who belong to the house of His enemies, and that for the sake of His Beloved One. There was one, even Mephibosheth, lame on his feet; him David "sent and fetched" unto himself. And then to show that he was fully reconciled to this descendant of his arch-enemy, David said, "Mephibosheth shall eat bread always at my table" (v. 10); showing that he had been brought into the place of most intimate fellowship.

In 1 Cor. 10 we are also taught that the "table" is inseparably connected with communion: "But I say, that the things which the Gentiles sacrifice, they sacrifice to demons, and not to God: and I would not that you should have fellowship with demons. Ye cannot drink the cup of the Lord, and the cup of demons: ye cannot be partakers of the Lord's table, and of the table of demons" (vv. 20, 21). The "Lord's table" is the symbol of fellowship with Christ, in separation from all that owns not His authority and denies His claims and rights.

Returning now to the "also" with which our passage opens and noting its relation to the immediate context, we learn that the blood-sprinkled Mercy-seat speaks of Christ as the **basis** of our fellowship with God, while the Table points to Christ as the **substance** of that fellowship. What we have here is the person of Christ as the Food of God and the One in whom He has communion with His people. The Table sets forth Jehovah's feast of love for His saints and for Himself in fellowship with them. This will be still more evident when we ponder the Contents of the Table, meanwhile let us turn to:—

### 2. Its Composition.

Like the Ark, the table was made of shittim wood (v. 23), overlaid with pure gold. Both typified the union of Deity and humanity in the person of Christ. It is indeed striking to observe, and important to note, the several points of oneness between the ark and the table. They were both of the same height—the only pieces of furniture that were so. They were both ornamented with a crown of gold. They were both provided with rings and staves. They both had something placed upon them: the one, the Mercy-seat; the other, the twelve cakes of bread. These points of likeness emphasise the truth that it is the person of the God-man which is the basis of all communion with God.

"The natural suggestion of a "table" is a place for food, and the food upon it. 'Thou preparest a table before me in the presence of mine enemies' (Psa. 23: 5). We will find this thought of food linked with our Lord's **person** in the sixth chapter of John: 'Verily, verily, I say unto you, Moses gave you not that bread from heaven; but My Father giveth you the true bread from heaven. For the bread of God is He which cometh down from heaven, and giveth life unto the world (John 6: 32, 33). The One who 'came down from heaven' reminds us of the deity of our Lord; this is the gold.

"'I am the living bread which came down from heaven: if any man eat of this bread, he shall live forever; and the bread that I will give is My flesh, which I will give for the life of the world. The Jews therefore strove among themselves, saying, How can this man give us His flesh to eat? Then Jesus said unto them, Verily, verily, I say unto you, except ye eat the flesh of the Son of man, and drink His blood, ye have no life in you.' (John 6: 51, 52). Evidently our Lord here is speaking of His death. But His death presupposes His incarnation. He must become man that He may die. We have in this way the twofold truth of our Lord's deity and His humanity linked together, and put before us in this chapter, where He is presented as the Bread of life. We have thus the gold and the acacia wood which form the table" (Mr. S. Ridout). Let us turn next to:—

### 3. Its Dimensions.

"Thou shalt also make a table of shittim wood: two cubits shall be the length thereof, and a cubit the breadth thereof, and a cubit and a half the height thereof" (Ex. 25: 23). Thus the Table was the same height as the Ark, though it fell short of its length and breadth. This intimates that though our communion with God rises to the level of our apprehension of the two natures in the person of His beloved Son, yet there is a breadth or fulness of perfection in Him which we fail to realize and enjoy. The length of the Table was two cubits, which supplies an additional hint to the meaning of this piece of furniture, for one of the significations of two is that of communion—"How can two walk together except they **be agreed?**" (Amos. 3: 3). In breadth the Table was one cubit, which speaks of unity, for there can be no fellowship where there is discord.

### 4. Its Contents.

"And thou shalt set upon the table shewbread before Me alway" (v. 30). This shewbread consisted of twelve loaves or cakes, made of fine flour; baked, and placed in two rows upon the Table, on which was sprinkled pure frankincense for a memorial. Here they remained before the Lord for seven days, when they were removed and eaten by Aaron and his sons, in the holy place—see Lev. 24: 5-9.

There is much difference of opinion as to the precise typical purport of these twelve loaves. One class of commentators see in them a figure of the twelve tribes of Israel presented before the Lord, but these offer no satisfactory interpretation of this bread being eaten afterwards by the priestly family. Others see in the loaves a foreshadowing of Christ as the Food of God and His children, but they are far from clear as to why there should be twelve loaves and why these were placed in two rows of six. Personally we believe there is a measure of truth in each view, but great care needs to be taken in seeking accurate expression.

It is clear that the thoughts suggested by the Table and by the bread placed upon it are intimately related, for later on we find the Table taking its name from the loaves thereon: in Numbers 4: 7 it is called the "Table of Shewbread." But though they are closely connected Heb. 9: 2 teaches us they have a distinctive significance and are to be considered separately. A close parallel to this is found in 1 Cor. 10 and 11: in the former we read of "the Lord's table" (v. 21), in the latter of "the Lord's supper" (v. 20): the one speaking of the **character** of our fellowship, the other of what forms the **substance** of our fellowship. This, we believe, supplies the key to the distinction in our type: the Table pointing to the person of Christ as the **Sustainer** of fellowship between God and His saints, the bread directing our thoughts to Christ as the **substance** of it.

The bread on the Table points first, as does everything in the Tabernacle, to Christ Himself. The name by which it is called clearly indicates this—"**shewbread**" is, literally, "bread of faces." faces being put by a figure for **presence** —pointing to the Divine presence in which the bread stood: "shewbread before Me alway." The fact that the bread was before the face of God always, told of its acceptableness to Him, and foreshadowed the person of Christ as the One in whom the Father has ever found His delight. In Lev. 24: 5 the bread on the Table is described as "twelve cakes," and Young's Concordance gives as the meaning of challoth "**perforated**" cakes. How solemnly significant! This bread which spoke of Christ had been **pierced**! The fine flour in the form of cakes, which had therefore been **baked**, points to the Lord Jesus as having been exposed to the fires of God's holy wrath, when on the cross He was made sin for His people.

But why **twelve** pierced cakes? Clearly this number has specially to do with Israel and suggests the different tribes being here **represented** before God. But representation implies a representative, and it is at this point that so many have missed the lesson. That which is here so blessedly symbolized is the Lord Jesus **identifying Himself** with God's covenant people. There is a striking passage in the New Testament which brings out—under this figure of bread —the identification of the Lord with His people and they with Him, "The cup of blessing which we bless, is it not the **communion of the blood of Christ?** The bread which we brake, is it not the **communion of the body of Christ?** For **we being many are one bread**, and one body: for we are all partakers of that one bread" (1 Cor. 10: 16, 17).

The twelve loaves then speak of Christ in immediate connection with His people. "The marvellous fact that Jehovah condescends to receive into fellowship with himself the people of His choice, is mirrored on every feature of the Tabernacle ritual. They were always before Him on the priestly mitre, breastplate, and shoulder-stones, and on the shewbread table. And surely this Old Testament symbolism finds its prophetic complement in New Testament fact, for by its revelation believers are said to be presented faultless in the presence of His glory, unreproveable and unrebukable in His sight—Col. 1: 22" (Mr. G. Needham).

The cakes were all of the same quality, size and weight, showing that the smallest tribe was represented equally with the greatest. In spreading them out in two rows, instead of piling them up in a heap, each one would be **seen** equally as much as another. Our acceptance in Christ and our representation by Him admits of no degrees. All of God's covenant people have an **equal** standing before Him, and an **equal** nearness to Him.

The cakes were made of "fine flour" (Lev. 25: 5) in which was no grit or unevenness, foreshadowing the moral perfections of the Word as He tabernacled among men. "Pure frankinscence" was placed upon them, emblematic of the **active** graces of Christ, and assuring us that those who are in Christ are ever before God according to the value and fragrance of His blessed Son. Every Sabbath these cakes were renewed, so that they were "before the Lord continually" (Lev. 24: 8); never was the Table unsupplied. "The loaves being placed on the Table every **Sabbath** day may accord with the fact that it was when the spiritual sabbath, the rest for our souls, obtained by Christ's atonement, was gained, that He took His place in the presence of God for us" (Mr. C. H. Bright). Each cake contained **two** "tenth deals" or omers of flour (Lev. 24: 5). This is indeed precious. A **double portion** is the thought suggested (contrast Exodus 16: 16, 36), foreshadowing the truth that Christ is the Food or delight of **both** God and His people. In Lev. 21: 21 it is expressly called "The bread of his (the priest's) God.

"And it shall be Aaron's and his sons; and they shall **eat** it in the holy place" (Lev. 25: 9). This bread which had been before Jehovah seven days, was now enjoyed by the priestly family. It speaks of Christ as the One who delights both the heart of the Father and His beloved people. "Eating" indicates **identification and communion** with what we feed upon: compare again 1 Cor. 10: 16, 17. The twelve cakes on the Table speak of Christ identified with His covenant people—not simply Israel after the flesh, for note **"everlasting covenant"** in Lev. 24: 8; the cakes eaten by the priestly family, His people identifying themselves (by faith's appropriation) with Christ! But this eating must be in "the holy place": we can only really feed upon Christ as we are in communion with God. The eating of the twelve cakes on "the Sabbath day" prophetically hints at the literal Israel's appropriation of Christ in the great dispensational Sabbath, the millennium.

### 5. Its Ornamentation.

"And thou shalt overlay it with pure gold, and make thereto a crown of gold round about. And thou shalt make unto it a border of an hand-breadth round about, and thou shalt make a golden crown to the border thereof round about" (vv. 24, 25). The "crown" speaks of Christ glorified—"a **crown** of **glory**" (1 Peter 5: 4)—now at the right hand of God for us, "crowned with glory and honour" (Heb. 2: 9). The crowned border on the top of the Table was for the purpose of protection, guarding whatever was placed upon it. The bread was not removed from the Table even when Israel was on the march (Numbers 4: 7), and the raised border would hold the cakes in place, preventing them from slipping off. This tells of the absolute security of that people with whom the incarnate Son has identified Himself.

First, the Table itself was encircled with "a crown of gold" (v. 24). "It is 'the **glory** of His **grace**' (Eph. 1: 6) that is suggested by the loaves of bread held in their place by the crown. It is a glorified Christ who maintains His own, according to all that He is" (S. Ridout). Beautifully is this brought out here in the measurement that is given "a border of an **handbreadth** round about," which is the more striking because all the other dimensions in the Tabernacle are cubits or half cubits. How blessedly does this border of the handbreadth round about point to that which guarantees the eternal preservation of all Christ's redeemed: "Neither shall any pluck them **out of My hand**" (John 10: 28)!

Everything here about the ornamentation speaks of the security of the cakes and of those whom they typified. The Hebrew word "border" means **"enclosing,"** and in 2 Sam. 22: 46 it is rendered "close places." Again, observe that this border of an hand-breadth was, in turn, protected by "a golden crown" (v. 25). This announces that the very glory of God is concerned in the preservation of His people: His honour is at stake:—"He leadeth me in the paths of righteousness for **His name's sake**" (Psalm 23: 3). How often Moses fell back upon this: see Exodus 32: 11-13; Numbers 14: 13-19, etc.!

The same thought is emphasised and reiterated by the second "crown," for the "border" had one as well as the Table— vv. 24, 25. "Again we are confronted with the precious grace that each believer, all believers, are secured by God. The highest revealed blessings are theirs, and these cannot be alienated, nor the believer removed from the position given him. Christ, the Table, maintains him before God; Christ, the border, **secures** him there. The border too has a crown as well as the Table. There is a certain glory attaching to our maintenance, and **further** a glory attaching to our security. If a believer could be lost, if anything could impair his security, if the border could be damaged, the crown must share it, and the very glory of Christ be sullied. Impossible! 'Neither shall any pluck them out of my hand' (John 10: 28)." (Foreshadowments by E. C. Pressland).

There is one other detail which perhaps falls under this present division of our subject. In v. 29 we read, "and thou shalt make the dishes thereof, and spoons thereof, and covers thereof, and bowls thereof, to cover withal: of pure gold shalt thou make them" (v. 29). The "dishes" would no doubt be used when the bread was removed from the Table and eaten by the priestly family. The "spoons" and the "cover" would be employed in connection with the frankinscence. The "bowls thereof to cover withal" should be rendered "the cups to pour out withal"—see margin of Authorised Version. These "cups" were used in connection with the "drink offerings" which were poured out before the Lord "in the holy place" (Num. 28: 7). The "drink-offerings" expressed **thanksgiving.** The fact that the "cups," used in connection with the drink-offerings, were placed upon the Table, tells us that communion is the basis of thanksgiving!

### 6. Its Rings and Staves.

These are described in Exodus 25: 26-28 and tell of provision made for journeying. "The children of Israel were pilgrims in the wilderness and hence the Tabernacle and all its furniture were made for them in this character, and accompanied them in all their wanderings" (Mr. E. Dennett). Thus the particular detail in the type now before us speaks of the provision which God has made for His people in Christ while they pass through this world. That provision is feeding upon Christ Himself in communion with God. Wherever Jehovah led the Hebrews, His Table accompanied them! So wherever the Christian's lot may be cast, even though it be for years in jail like Bunyan, there is ever a precious Christ to feed upon and commune with!

### 7. Its Coverings.

These are described in Numbers 4: 7, 8. They were three in number. First a cloth of blue draped the Table, its bread and its utensils; over this was spread a cloth of scarlet, and on the outside of all was cast a covering of badger's skins. These were only used while Israel was on the march. The Table standing in the holy place speaks of Christ now on high as God's bread and ours. The Table accompanying Israel in their journeyings, with its threefold covering, reminds us of the varied perfections manifested by Christ as He passed through this wilderness scene, the contemplation of which is an essential part of our food.

First, came the cloth of blue, which points to Christ as the Bread from Heaven. Seven times over in John 6 did our Lord thus announce Himself. If Christ be not recognised and enjoyed as wholly above and beyond all that this earth can yield, there will be no true devotion nor any scriptural testimony to Him. But let Him be known as the heavenly portion of the soul and these are secured. It is most significant to note that this first covering was seen only by the eyes of the priestly family.

Second, came the cloth of scarlet. According to its scriptural usage "scarlet" is the emblem of **earthly glory,** as may be seen by a reference to its various occurrences. This colour was so called because it was obtained from a worm, in fact was named after it, the same Hebrew word being variously translated "scarlet" or "worm" as the connection requires. There is something most appropriate in this, for truly the glory of man is that of a perishing worm. How then are these two thoughts, so dissimilar, to be combined, in connection with Christ? Does not Psalm 22: 6— the cross-Psalm—tell us? There we find the Saviour saying "I am a **worm** (same word as "scarlet") and no man." Thus the "scarlet" reminds us of the glory of the cross (Gal. 6: 14). The Lord Jesus, by becoming a "worm," by His cross brought forth the true glory. Another glory shall be manifested by Him (Col. 3: 3) when He returns to the earth. This second covering also was seen only by the priests!

Third, the external covering was one of badgers' skins, and met the eyes of all as the Table was borne through the wilderness. This typified our Lord's **humiliation.** This covering was provided to protect the Table and its inner coverings from the defiling dust and atmosphere of the wilderness. We are thus reminded not only of the unattractiveness to men's eyes of the servant-form which our Saviour took, but also of His personal holiness, repelling all the unholy influences of this defiling world. No speck or stain ever fouled the Holy One of God—He touched the leper without being polluted; nothing of earth could in anywise tarnish His ineffable glory.

It is thus that the Spirit of God would have the saints contemplate Him who is their appointed Food: as the One who is heavenly in His nature and character, as the One who came down to this earth and glorified Himself and the Father by His obedience unto death, and as the One who through His holy vigilance repelled all evil and kept Himself from the path of the Destroyer. Thus contemplated our meditation of Him will be "sweet."

ARTHUR W. PINK.

# THE HOME-GOING OF A SAINT.

"For me to live is Christ, and to die is gain" (Phil. 1: 21).

---

This world is called the land of the living: in reality it is the land of the dying. The lamb that skips in the fields is only waiting for the knife. The ox that lows in the meadow is simply being fattened for the slaughter. The trees that grow on the mountain-side are awaiting the axe. The broad-arrow of death is stamped upon everything below. "Change and decay in all around I see" sums it up; and O, how brief, how short, is the distance between birth and death! Our pilgrimage on earth is but a journey to the tomb, and the very pulse that preserves our being beats out our death-march! To-day we see our friends in health and strength: to-morrow we hear of their decease. To-night we sit here in comfort in this church: ere long, unless the Lord come first, we shall be journeying in the hearse! But thank God there is one blessed country where death never comes: one blessed land where graves are never digged, where the sombre black is never worn, where tears are never shed—that land that is fairer than day, that lies beyond the skies. And O beloved, if God's own people would more frequently make a prayerful and believing study of what His Word teaches concerning the departure of His people from this world, and their Homegoing, death would lose most, if not all, of its terrors for them: but the sad thing is that, instead of resting on and meditating upon the truths and the teaching of God concerning the Home-going of His people, we let our imaginations run riot: we give way to carnal fears and we walk by sight.

To-night I want to dwell upon three things:—First death itself as it affects the saint; second the accompaniments of the saint's death; and third some of the things which immediately follow the Home-going of the Lord's people.

Now in the New Testament there are three different words that are used, figures of speech, that are most suggestive in setting forth spiritual realities in connection with the death of God's people. First, death is likened unto a sleep. The Lord Jesus said in John 11: 11, I go to awaken our friend Lazarus out of his sleep. In Acts 7, 59 and 60 we are told concerning Stephen that he knelt down and cried with a loud voice, "Lord, lay not this sin to their charge. And when he had said this, he fell asleep." Amid the curses of his enemies, amid the stones that they were flinging at him, he "fell asleep." Could anything be more blessed than that? And so also the Holy Spirit says through the apostle Paul concerning the departed saints, "They sleep in Jesus." I do not think the reference there is exclusively to the body, and I think we miss the point altogether if we turn our thoughts to the idea of unconsciousness. The figure of sleep is a very full and a very suggestive one. Let me try and open it up to you briefly.

First of all, sleep in this natural state brings welcome relief from cares and anxieties. However worried we may be during our waking state, sleep brings welcome relief. Then we are oblivious to the problems and the perplexities that harrass us during our waking hours. And that is what death is to the saint of God—release, deliverance from all the cares and all the things that worried him while down here. Those in heaven are for ever emancipated from that which caused them to groan while here on earth.

Again, death brings deliverance from toils and burdens. The work of the day is exchanged for sweet repose, and so Revelation 14. 13 tells us that the Christian rests from his labors. "Blessed are the dead which die in the Lord. . . Yea, saith the Spirit, that they may rest from their labours." The fight has been fought; the race has been run; now comes rest.

Again, sleep is a season of preparation and recuperation. During sleep the body is fitted for the toils of another day. When the sleeper arises he has been refreshed and reinvigorated and prepared for new duties. And, my friends, I believe that at death the souls of God's people are being prepared for new service for the Lord in the future.

Again, sleep brings welcome relief from pain and suffering. O what a merciful provision sleep is! No matter how pain-wracked the body may have been during the waking hours, sleep brings gracious deliverance, and so those who have passed through the portals of death are oblivious to the sufferings of earth.

Again, sleep is of brief duration. We lie down to sleep and then we rise again: a few hours of repose and we are wakened to a new day. And so in Scripture death is likened unto a sleep, and resurrection unto an arousing, an awakening unto the eternal day.

The most important point that "sleep" suggests to my mind is this: when Christ likened death to a sleep it was to tell His people of its complete harmlessness. What is there about sleep to dread? Is sleep an object of horror? Is sleeping a terrifying experience? And yet God's Word likens the death of His people to a sleep—to show us that there is an analogy between the two experiences, to comfort us with the knowledge that there is nothing more to be dreaded in the article of death for His own people than there is in lying down on your bed to slumber.

One other reason I would suggest. I think the Lord likened death to a sleep to intimate how easily He will quicken our mortal bodies. To raise the dead, incredible though that appears to the infidel, will be to Christ just as easy as rousing a sleeper. It is a striking thing that, normally, a sleeping person responds to the human voice quicker than anything! I have observed that in numbers of people; doubtless you have too. It may thunder and they take no notice. The dogs may bark just outside and it has no effect, but you just speak to them in a low tone of voice and address them personally and they are awake at once. So will it be in connection with the great miracle of the resurrection. They that are in the graves shall hear His voice. And I believe He likens death to a sleep, among other reasons, for the purpose of showing us what a simple matter resurrection will be to Him—just rousing the sleeper, that is all.

Now, in the second place, Scripture likens the death of the believer not only to a sleep but to an exodus. In II. Peter 1. 15, the apostle there says, "After my decease." The Greek word there is exodus, spelled that very way, e-x-o-d-u-s. "After my decease"; literally, "after my exodus." And I believe the Holy Spirit caused the apostle Peter to use that expression there with a definite reference to what took place in the history of Israel as they came forth from Egypt. There is a striking analogy and correspondence between the death of the Christian and Israel's exodus from Egypt.

First, death for the Christian is an emancipation. That is to say, it is deliverance from cruel taskmasters. O my friends, our life down here at best is little more than a bondage, but death is deliverance from that bondage. Death for the Christian is a snapping of his fetters, an escape from the bands which held him and the going forth to a life of freedom. Again, the exodus of Israel from Egypt was a leaving behind of all their enemies. That is what death is to the Christian: the flesh (his worst enemy), the world, the devil, his fears, everything that opposes God—all his enemies left behind at death. Again, the exodus of Israel was a crossing over unto the other shore, and therefore the Holy Spirit uses that word here in connection with the death of His people. First He likens it unto a sleep. Second He likens it unto an exodus.

There is a third word that is used in II. Timothy 4.6, where the apostle Paul says, "the time of my departure is at hand." The Greek word there for "departure" is a nautical term and refers to a ship being loosed from its moorings. And again the figure is most suggestive. Who that has set out on a long voyage will ever forget the first moments of departure? I think there are few things more impressive than the starting-out of a great ocean liner. For hours everything has been stir and bustle and activity in making the preparations, and then five minutes before the appointed time there is a sudden stillness. Those who are not sailing have left the vessel. The officers come up the gangway with their final papers; the captain is on the bridge; the men stand ready with the ropes; and then when the finger of the clock reaches the appointed time the signal is given, the siren sounds, the ropes are released, the handkerchiefs are waved, and gently the great boat glides down the river into the almost infinite reaches of the ocean beyond. That is what death is to the child of God—a loosening of the moorings that hold us to the land, a gliding out into the larger, greater, life of freedom.

Now in the second place I want to speak of the accompaniments of death. Turn with me now to Luke 16.22:—"And it came to pass, that the beggar died, and was carried by the angels into Abraham's bosom." I for one am simple enough to believe that that means just what it says. I understand that literally. He was carried by the angels. Ah, my friends, angelic ministry occupies a much more extensive place in our lives than any of us realise. "Are they not all ministering spirits, sent forth to minister for them who shall be heirs of salvation?" I believe this 16th of Luke and the 22nd verse indicates that the angels are our escort as we leave this earth and pass out into the unknown territory. I believe the angels are a guard of honor around the redeemed soul as the Lord conducts it into His Father's House. So that the first accompaniment of death is that the angels take immediate charge of the soul as it leaves the body, and, under the superintending presence of the Lord, as a guard of honor, conduct that soul from its earthly house to its heavenly abode.

I think the second accompaniment of death is, that the Lord is with that soul in a very special sense. Psalm 116, verse 15:—"Precious in the sight of the Lord is the death of his saints." I believe that those words signify that a dying saint is an object of special notice unto the Lord. I freely confess that I am dealing now with something that is beyond my reach of understanding. While it is true that the eyes of the Lord are ever upon us, for He never slumbers nor sleeps; while it is true that each one of us can say at all times, "Thou Lord seest me," yet I believe that Scripture justifies me in saying that there are times and occasions when the Lord notices and when the Lord is with His people in a special manner. "God is our refuge and strength, a very present help in trouble." That is what I mean by a special manner. "When thou passest through the waters I will be with thee." O I know that it is true in one sense that He is always with us—blessed be His Name for that—but I believe there is a special sense in which the Lord is with His own when they come to pass through death. I think the 23rd Psalm bears that out:—". . . though I walk through the valley of the shadow of death, I will fear no evil: for Thou art with me."

I want you to turn for a moment to that 23rd Psalm, familiar though it may be: the Lord has recently given me new light upon one little point therein. Have you ever noticed the change of person in the pronouns in this Psalm? I am going to give you a little lesson in grammar now, but it is a very blessed one— the grammar of Scripture repays careful and prayerful study. Have you ever noticed the change in person of the pronouns in this Psalm? "The Lord is my shepherd; I shall not want. He maketh me to lie down in green pastures: He leadeth me." Verse 3:—"He restoreth my soul: He leadeth me." But when you come to the fourth verse there is a change, a change from the second to the third person:—"Yea, though I walk through the valley of the shadow of death, I will fear no evil: for He is with me"? Not at all. "For **Thou** art with me; **Thy** rod (not "His" rod) and **Thy** staff they comfort me. **Thou** preparest a table before me. . . **Thou** anointest my head." Why that change? Do you think it has no meaning? Do you think it has no message? O how carelessly we read the Word of God! Probably the most familiar portion in the whole Bible, and yet I doubt if more than a handful here to-night had ever noticed that change. Now what is the difference? O it is most blessed, it is most precious! While we are here in this world we speak of the Lord. "**He** leadeth me. . He restoreth," but when we come to the valley of shadows we speak to the Lord: He is with us there. It is no longer a speaking of Him: He is there present: we are speaking to Him. "Thou art with me." Yes, my friends, the grammar of Scripture is worth studying. Just a little change in the person of the pronoun, but how precious!

Now let me give you another thought from that same Psalm, under the present head of the sermon, the accompaniments of death. First, the angels as a guard of honor; second, the Lord with us in an especial sense: third; the Lord Himself preparing us for His immediate presence. Now I am going to submit a thought to you that I have never seen in print or heard from another. I submit it to your prayerful attention. Psalm 23.4: —". . . though I walk through the valley of the shadow of death, I will fear no evil: for Thou art with me: Thy rod and Thy staff they comfort me. Thou preparest a table." The "table" always speaks of fellowship, and in Scripture, of closest intimacy. "Thou preparest a table before me in the presence of mine enemies." I have not time to take that up to-night. "Thou anointest my head." Why are we told that in this connection? And what does it signify? "Thou anointest my head with oil." Listen! Moses anointed the heads of the priests just before they entered upon their tabernacle-privileges and duties. The last thing that Moses did ere the priests went into the presence of God was to anoint them. And I believe that, like everything else in the Mosaic ritual, that that had a spiritual significance; and I believe the reference here means this, that just as we are leaving this body of sin, this depraved body of death, as we are on the point of leaving it, and are about to enter the thrice-holy presence of God, the Lord Jesus Himself places upon that soul the sweet fragrance, the blessed perfume, that only He Himself can give, to fit that soul for the presence of God. It is not a matter of putting away sin: that was all done at the cross: but it is a matter of fitting the soul as it passes out of this sinful body for the presence of the thrice-holy God. "Thou anointest." It comes right after the passing through the valley of the shadow. I believe that that means the Lord by communicating His own fragrancy to the soul fits it for the presence of the true Sanctuary above. Just as Moses anointed the priests before they went into the tabernacle, so the Lord Himself anoints those souls that are about to enter the true Sanctuary above.

Now, in the third place, and rather briefly, **What happens** immediately after death? First of all the angels convey the soul, not simply to heaven in a general sense, but to his own people. Did you ever think that when you should die (I speak now to Christians) that the moment you are taken to Heaven you would almost be lost amidst the whole crowd of redeemed up there? Did that thought ever enter your mind? I do not know whether my mind is a queer one or not. That thought bothered me for some time, that I would almost be lost in the crowd up there: I wouldn't know who was who. Now I want you to turn first of all to Genesis 49.33. I dare not indulge in speculation on this holy subject: I want to keep closely to Scripture: but I think there is more in Scripture than any of us are aware along the lines of comfort for God's bereaved people.

Genesis 49.33:—"And when Jacob had made an end of commanding his sons, he gathered up his feet into the bed, and yielded up the ghost, and was gathered **unto his people.**" Where was Jacob when he died? Why, he was down in Egypt, wasn't he, and this verse says that when he died he was gathered "unto his people." Why, my friends, **where** were "his people"? Why, the bodies of Abraham and Isaac were hundreds of miles away. It certainly does not mean that his body was placed alongside of theirs, and it does not simply say he was gathered to God's people, but he was gathered to **his** people.

Now I believe that means, when one of the Lord's people dies the angels not only conduct the soul to Heaven, but take that soul to the immediate circle where his own people are. Why not? Who would give them a greater welcome? Who would be more glad to see them? I think that is the significance of that word of Christ—when the beggar died the angels took him to **Abraham's** bosom. He was a **Jew**, therefore they took him to "Abraham's" bosom. The word "bosom" there signifies the place of endearment, affection, fellowship. If I should die before the Lord comes, I do not expect to be lost in Heaven among a crowd of Old Testament saints that I never met and know very little about and could not have very much fellowship with (except those that are mentioned in Scripture), but I believe that I shall be gathered to my own people, the redeemed of the Lord that have gone on before.

Now I will give you a further Scripture to support that theory, and show you that I am not indulging in imagination. The 16th chapter of Luke and the 9th verse:—"And I say unto you, Make to yourselves friends of the mammon of unrighteousness." The word "of" there means "by means of." It is called the mammon of unrighteousness because it is referring to lucre—filthy lucre—money, the money of this world. Use the money that the Lord gives you. It does not mean that money that has been unrighteously obtained, but it is contrasted with the true riches. Now then, "Make to yourselves friends of the mammon of unrighteousness; that, when ye fail (that is, when ye die, when ye pass out of this world) they may receive you into everlasting habitations." Now who are the ones that are going to receive us into the everlasting habitations? You may not agree with my interpretation of the first half of the verse: that makes no difference; the last half of the verse says that it is going to be our "friends" that will "receive" us into the "everlasting habitations"; which confirms the previous thought that, when the soul reaches Heaven it is taken promptly to that circle, that immediate circle, of its "own people"; and it is our "friends" who receive us into those everlasting habitations!

Now then, in the third place, and what is most blessed of all, the 17th chapter of John, the 24th verse, the words of the Lord Jesus Christ in the great highpriestly prayer:—"Father, I will that they also, whom Thou hast given Me, be with Me where I am; that they may behold My glory." And that is something that I am incapable of interpreting. I haven't been up there to behold His glory. I have attempted to visualise it. I have tried to picture it, so have you; but the reality, the blissful occupation itself, defies description in human language. "That they may behold My glory." That is the blessed portion of the soul after it has been carried by the angels to heaven, after it has joined its own immediate circle of its own people. Absent from the body it is then present with the Lord, and present with Him for the purpose of "beholding His glory."

Now, one other point. I believe that while the soul is there in Heaven, in Paradise (for Paradise is only another name for Heaven, as the 12th chapter of II. Corinthians indicates) I believe that the soul in Paradise **makes progress in knowledge.** If you turn to II. Corinthians 12, verses 1 to 7:—"It is not expedient for me doubtless to glory. I will come to visions and revelations of the Lord. I knew a man in Christ above fourteen years ago (whether in the body, I cannot tell: or whether out of the body, I cannot tell: God knoweth;) such an one caught up to the third heaven. And I knew such a man (whether in the body, or out of the body, I cannot tell: God knoweth); How that he was caught up into Paradise, and heard unspeakable words." Verse 7, "And lest I should be exalted above measure through the abundance of the revelations, there was given to me a thorn in the flesh." Now what I want you to notice from that first to the seventh verse is this, that Paradise or Heaven is a place of "visions" and "revelations" to those who are removed from earth and are permitted to be there. While the apostle Paul was in Paradise he saw and heard visions and revelations. Much that we knew in this world will be forgotten. Thank God it will not even so much as come into remembrance, but that will be more than compensated for by the fact that we shall then have imparted to us a knowledge that is suited to that time and that place; and personally I am strongly inclined to think that much of these revelations will be given us by the saints who have already gone on before. I do not think that they will be given directly by Christ at that time because He is engaged with something else—"He ever liveth to make intercession." We shall be beholding His glory. But now, for example's sake, how much would I be able to learn if I could be in the presence of the apostle Paul for a few hours up there in Paradise! They have not yet entered the perfect state because they are yet without bodies. It is a state of waiting, of resting. They are beholding the glory of the Lord but I do not believe they are passive, doing nothing; I believe they are sharing with each other the light and the revelations which God gave to them by His Spirit through the Word—inter-communicating. Paradise then is a place of visions and revelations.

Now dear friends, let me just in a few moments try and make a practical application of what has been before us. Fellow-Christian, how profoundly thankful we ought to be to God for this precious Book. If we had not this Book what would we know of what lies beyond the portals of the tomb? God's Word not only reveals to us the way of salvation, not only makes clear to us the path of duty in which we should now walk, but its blessed light illumines the valley of shadows and lifts a corner of the veil and shows us the glories beyond. And O my friends we only appreciate that at its proper value when we contrast it with the theorisings and reasonings of men. O, as you sit there to-night, many of you comforted and rejoicing in the things that you have been hearing, there are tens of thousands of your fellow-creatures who believe that there is no sickness and there is no death—that they are simply images of a diseased mind. What comfort is there in such an absurdity as that? There are hundreds of thousands of your fellow-creatures who believe that when the souls of God's own people pass out of this world they go at once to "purgatory" to enter a place of suffering, and that there is no release from it until the priest has paid them out of it. What comfort is there in that? There are many others, yes, right here in Sydney, who say that the death of a human being is just the same as the death of a dog, that consciousness ceases and that there is extinction of being and that man is dead in the absolute sense of the word. What comfort is there in that? There are countless thousands of others who say, Well, we don't know, we cannot be sure, no one has ever come back to tell us. O beloved brethren and sisters in Christ, how thankful we should be for this precious revelation from God that casts its light on the glorious future that awaits the people of God!

In the second place, what abundant praise is due to our blessed Saviour! He is the One who has robbed death of its terrors for us. He is the One who has removed its sting. Because He endured the outpoured flood of God's judgment, we pass through Jordan dry-shod. O brethren and sisters, forget not at this hour it is because your Saviour endured the cross that death is "gain" to His people. Then let us say with the apostle Paul, "Thanks be to God, which giveth us the victory through our Lord Jesus Christ"!

What shall I say to the unconverted? O how different would it be for you if death should seize you in your present condition! Scripture says "the righteous hath hope in his death but the wicked are driven away." Christ said to those who despised and rejected Him, "Ye shall die in your sins and whither I go, ye cannot come." O unsaved friend, death for the non-Christian, death for the unbeliever, means passing out into the blackness of darkness for ever—the world of eternal suffering and woe. And every funeral is a call to those that are left behind. None can tell in this congregation whose turn may come next. Three Sunday nights ago three people were seated in this church: one now lies at home, seriously ill; another is in the hospital; the body of the third is in the cemetery! What a solemn call to you! O what need has every sinner to flee to Christ for refuge! How shall we escape if we neglect so great salvation? I believe that by the grace of God there are some present here to-night who have been seeking the Lord, but they have been seeking Him in a half-hearted way, and they have not yet found Him. Now listen while I read just one verse from Scripture:—"Ye shall seek Me and find, when ye shall search for Me with all your heart." That is God's own Word. "Ye shall seek Me and find, when ye shall search for Me with all your heart." Does not that reveal the reason why some of you have not found Him? You have not been seeking Him with all your heart. You have been half-hearted in the matter. You never will find Him until you seek Him with all your heart. "Ye shall seek Me and find when ye shall search for Me with all your heart"—Jeremiah 29.13. May the Lord have mercy upon you, and bring you to Himself.

The above is a sermon preached in Sydney by the Editor.

## DIVINE CHASTISEMENT.

### Heb. 12: 7, 8.

These verses enumerate a principle which is so simple and plain that really no words are needed by way of explanation. When Christians meet with affliction, trouble, and trial, they should not draw the conclusion that because of these they are not the objects of God's favor; rather should they infer that such afflictions are the evidence, the proof, of their Divine sonship. There is no natural child who is without the need of chatisement in some form or in some degree, and there is no father who is worthy of the name that withholds chastisement when it is needed, and when it is for the good of his child. So with us who, by the wondrous grace of God, sustain the relationship of children to Him who is our Father; He, in His infinite wisdom, faithfulness and love, withholds not that chastisement which is for His glory and which is for our growth and good.

In verse 8 we have the negative side given of what is positively affirmed in verse 7. Not only is it true that afflictions are no proof that we are not the children of God, but the absence of affliction would be ground to doubt whether we are His sons at all. "If ye be without chastisement, whereof all are partakers, then are ye bastards, and not sons. And I suppose it is a tragic fact of observation that illegitimate children rarely are cared for by their fathers—though I believe that such is a crime. What a solemn voice this verse has for Sinless Perfectionists! There are those who say that God never chastises them, for they never do anything that deserves chastisement. There are those who claim that because the sinful nature has been eradicated from them they are never disobedient, and therefore God's rod never descends upon them. God says that such are "bastards" and not sons at all! It is a very solemn thing to me that some of the severest indictments of the New Testament are reserved for Sinless Perfectionists. Here is one: God calls them bastards: and in 1 John 1.8 He calls them "liars." You could not have two harder words, could you?

Now this morning I want to confine myself to the first clause of the 7th verse and concentrate upon a single word in it. I take it that what we have here in v. 7 is the supplement to what we have in v. 5. Both vv. 5 and 7 speak of the spirit in which chastisement is to be received. Verse 5 gives us the negative side: we must not despise it, we must not faint under it. Verse 7 gives us the positive side:—"If ye endure chastisement." I need hardly say that the word "endure" here is used not in its lowest and carnal sense like men of the world use it to-day. You know there is an old adage that what can't be cured must be endured. That means you have got to make the best of a bad job—just summon all the fortitude you can and grit your teeth and bear it. But not so is the word "endure" used in Scripture. The word "endure" here is used in its highest and noblest sense.

"If ye endure chastening whereof all are partakers, God dealeth with you as with children." In vv. 2, 3 of this same chapter we have that word "endure" used twice in connection with our Saviour. In v. 2 we are told that He "endured," endured the cross, endured the acutest form of affliction, endured the most painful and agonising species of suffering; but He "endured" it in the highest sense of the word—meekly and heroically. He stood steadfast under it. So again in the third verse He "endured" the contradiction of sinners against Himself. He never fretted, He never murmured, He never faltered; He stood like a rock. He steadfastly bore with patience and meekness. Now in this 7th verse Christians are told that they are to "endure" chastening, and this morning we come to the most practical side of our subject. How are we to "endure."

First, we should always endure chastening inquiringly. While it is true that all chastisement is not the direct consequence of personal sins or wicked conduct, much of our chastisement does come from that source; therefore it is the part of wisdom for us to seek the why and the wherefore of it. There is a cause for every effect: God does not act capriciously, therefore whenever the chastening hand of the Lord is laid upon us it is the part of wisdom to examine ourselves, to take heed to our ways, to ponder the path of our feet, to daily seek and search out the reason for that chastening. There is a very solemn warning given us on this point in the II. Chronicles, chapter 16, verses 12 and 13. "And Asa in the thirty and ninth year of his reign was diseased in his feet, until his disease was exceeding great: yet in his disease he sought not to the Lord, but to the physicians. And Asa slept with his fathers, and died." And there are multitudes of professing Christians to-day, doing exactly the same as Asa. As soon as some painful sickness or serious disease comes upon their bodies, the first thought is not that this sickness may be sanctified to their spiritual good, that it may be improved to the profit of their souls, but that they may get relief from, or get rid of it. Just the same as with the man of the world—that is his first thought! Did you say, That is natural? Yes, I know it is "natural"; that is the sad part of it. It is carnal, it is not spiritual. Now, beloved friends, I do not go so far as some do and say that we ought never to call in the physician, because all doctors are of the devil. There are some who say that. I do not believe that our blessed Lord would have said when He was here upon earth, "They that are whole need not a physician but they that are sick," nor do I believe that the Holy Spirit would have spoken of Luke as the "beloved physician," if all physicians were of Satan. There is a happy medium even here, a middle course between two sinful extremes—the fanaticism which says I will never call in a physician; and, on the other hand, whenever a serious sickness or painful affliction comes our way, having recourse to the physician first of all. Heed the warning of Asa. "If ye endure chastening," and the first way in which chastening should be endured is inquiringly. Instead of rushing off to the doctor our first duty is to earnestly seek the face of God, and enquire of Him what is the cause. Ask Him what is the lesson that He would have us learn from it; examine our ways and seek to discover the why of it.

Secondly, how are we to "endure" chastening? Prayerfully. That follows logically from our first point. If our enquiry as to the cause of the chastening is to be prosecuted successfully, then we certainly need the Lord's help. If we lean unto our own understandings we shall most certainly err. We need Divine assistance even to diagnose our own spiritual state and to ascertain what it is in our lives that the Lord is laying His finger upon. If we rely on our own judgment we shall make a mistake. In other words we need to get alone with God, and to say with Job "shew me wherefore Thou contendest with me" (Job 10: 2). "Wherefore": that is the question that Job asked God. He asked God to reveal to him the cause of it. "Wherefore?" And at the end of the book you will find that his prayer was answered. He discovered the wherefore of it. In other words, earnestly ask the Lord to reveal to you what there is in your life, in your ways, in your walk, that is displeasing to Him. Say with the Psalmist, "Search me, O God, and know my heart: try me, and know my thoughts: and see if there be any wicked way in me, and lead me in the way everlasting." Ask the Lord to sanctify the chastening to you, and for grace to bear it.

Third, endure chastening humbly. After the Lord has answered your prayer, after God has been pleased to show you the cause why His chastening rod has fallen upon you, then see to it that you do not quarrel with Him about it. In other words, instead of feeling that your chastisement is far more severe than your conduct calls for, just remind yourself, dear friend, of how much worldliness and of how much waywardness there still is in your heart and life, therefor how much sorer chastisement your sins really call. Ah, beloved, it remains true of each one of us, "He hath not dealt with us after our sins, nor rewarded us according to our iniquities." Instead of God being unduly severe, and chastening us more frequently and more heavily than our sins call for, the truth is, His chastisements are very mild and very gentle. Then when they do come, let us be humble and meek before Him. O beloved take not issue with the Most High, or He will make you smart the sorer for your pains. Heed that word of Peter's, "Humble yourselves therefore under the mighty hand of God." That was the one chief reason why God chastened Job so severely, and that was the one thing poor Job was so slow to do—humble himself under the mighty hand of God.

In the fourth place, we should endure patiently. Probably that is the main thought here in our text, for that is what "endurance" is. Endurance is patience under fire. Endurance is steadfast, persevering fortitude. In order to help you on this point, remember your blessed Saviour. He was led as a lamb to the slaughter, and when He came before His shearers He was "dumb"! And He has left us an example that we should follow His steps. But in order for that we need the help of God's Spirit. Notice in the 11th verse of Hebrews 12: there is a very important word for us on enduring God's chastisement patiently: "Now no chastening for the present seemeth to be joyous, but grievous:" The Holy Spirit concedes that much: chastisement is not pleasant, we are not expected to rejoice over it. If the chastening were pleasant it would cease to be chastening. The very fact that it is chastening makes it "grievous." But now notice:—"No chastening for the present seemeth to be joyous, but grievous: nevertheless afterward." "Afterward," there is where the call for patience comes in. I have no doubt some of you here—many of you—have had the same experience as me: Again and again in the past, when I have been under the chastening rod of God, I scrutinised my own spiritual character and graces, and sought hard to see if I could find where the chastening was doing its work—whether it really was developing more patience and more meekness; and I tell you frankly, my friends, while the chastening was on, I could not see one particle of improvement. I could not see that it was doing one bit of good spiritually. No, and God does not say it should. It is "afterward" that it yieldeth the peaceable fruit of righteousness unto them which are exercised thereby. Therefore endure chastening with patience.

In the fifth place, endure it believingly. I mean by that, exercise faith. To make that simple let me give you the opposite. How often in our afflictions and trials we see nothing more than the malice of man, the cruelty of the world or the enmity of Satan. How often when things go wrong in the details of our lives and friction comes instead of things running smoothly, we manifest our unbelief. For example, the stove goes wrong when you have the least time for it to do so; or the grocer fails to deliver his goods just when you are most needing them, and you haven't much time to wait to get the meal ready. And you fret and fume, and if you do not call the grocer names, you feel like doing so. Now listen! That all goes to show that you are walking by sight. That proves your eye is on man instead of God. Don't you believe that God is over-ruling the actions of your grocer? O yes I know that I need the word just as badly as any of you. Sometimes when the train is held up outside Redfern and I know I am going to get to church about ten minutes late, I often forget the Lord is regulating the signals and His hand is on the throttle. But beloved friends, let us seek help from on high to endure chastenings—and remember that word includes something more than the extreme trials of life. The little frictions, the little irritations, the little unpleasant things, the little disappointments, in your business life, **they** are "chastenings" from the Lord! Then learn to endure them believingly.

I mean by that, look behind your fellow-men that are the instrumental cause; look behind the devil who is stirring them up perhaps. There is no peace for the heart, there is no rest for the mind, until you learn to rest in **God.** Some of you are travelling-men. You go out at the beginning of the day or the week, and you ask the Lord to give you that measure of prosperity and success that is good in His sight. All right, so far so good! You get up on Monday morning and it is a wet day: you cannot get around as much as you wanted to do: and you go out on Tuesday and you find your customers are depressed with the weather. O, you say, I wish the weather would change! Ah, beloved friends, you are walking by sight. Look beyond the instrumental causes and walk by faith. Turn to the 27th Psalm for a moment, v. 13, "I had fainted unless" (Now some of you are going to discover why you did "faint"), "I had fainted unless I had believed to see the goodness of the Lord." You know the old proverb of the world is, "Seeing is believing." Well the very opposite is true in God's order, in connection with spiritual things; you have to believe in order to see. "I had fainted unless I had believed **to** see." What is it that you desire to see? Why, the "goodness of the Lord": and unless we **believe to see that,** then we shall surely faint. Very well, then, faith brings God into the scene. If we endure chastening in unbelief we shall faint with despair; but if we exercise 'faith, like Job did—"The Lord gave and the Lord hath taken away" —then we shall bring God into the scene. Faith recognises that all these disappointments and irritations and troubles proceed from **God's** love, that they are all directed by **God's** wisdom, and they are all among those things that "work together for **our** good"!

Sixthly, how are we to endure chastening. Spiritually? I was almost on the point of saying "philosophically," but that is such a carnal word; it savors too much of the flesh for the Christian to use. When I say that chastenings should be endured "spiritually," I mean that we should exercise our spiritual discernment and see the gracious design of God in them. Let us remember that the ground has to be plowed—yes, and harrowed too —before it will yield a crop; the gold has to be cast into the furnace for the dross to be removed; the tree must be pruned if it is to bear much fruit. Let us look upon chastisement with spiritual eyes and see the beneficent purpose of God within it. Turn for a moment to Psalm 119, verse 71: "It is good for me that I have been afflicted." I hope that every afflicted soul can say Amen to that as you look back. "It is good for me that I have been afflicted; that I might learn Thy statutes." That means that we might learn them experimentally. We knew them intellectually before, but after we have been afflicted, we learn them in a new way, with a new preciousness. David says, "It is good for me that I have been afflicted." He was "enduring," or he had "endured," chastening spiritually. He had seen the beneficial purpose, the gracious design of his loving Father in them.

Now, lastly, how is chastening to be endured? **Thankfully.** We ought to be grateful to our Heavenly Father that He cares so much for such worms of the earth. His chastisement is an evidence of His care, and how thankful we should be for that, that He does so care for us, that He is at so much pains to promote our spiritual education! Then again, what ground we have for gratitude when our text reminds us that these chastisements are among the evidences of our Divine sonship. There are some of the Lord's people who are all the time searching for evidences of their acceptance in Christ. Well, one of the best evidences of God's favor is, as our text says, "If ye endure chastening, then are ye children —God dealeth with you as with sons." How thankful we should be, then, for His tender care. Did you ever notice in 1 Corinthians 11.32, "We are chastened of the Lord," (that is, now) "that we should not be condemned with the world" (that is, in the day to come)? Then how thankful we should be that our suffering is in the present. Our chastisement is now: their condemnation will be for eternity. Finally, we should be thankful because of the precious fruit that will yet be yielded: see Heb. 12: 11!

May divine grace enable both speaker and hearer to heed these words of counsel, to endure chastening inquiringly, prayerfully, believingly, humbly, patiently, spiritually, and thankfully!

N.B.—The above is the substance of a sermon preached by the Editor.

Christian never doubt the love of God. A quaint old Quaker, who was a farmer, had a weather-vane on the roof of his barn, from which stood out in clear-cut letters "God is love." One day a preacher was being driven to the Quaker's home. His host called attention to the vane and its text. The preacher turned and said, "I don't like that at all. It misrepresents the Divine character. God's love is not variable like the weather." Said the Quaker, "You have misinterpreted its significance. That text on the weather-vane is to remind me that no matter which way the wind is blowing, no matter from which direction the storm may come, still God is love." "Whom the Lord loveth He chasteneth." All our chastisements flow from His love."

2. The Christian's chastisements **express God's love**. Oftentimes we do not think so. As God's children we think and act very much as we did when children naturally. When we were little and our parents insisted that we should perform a certain duty we failed to appreciate the love which had respect to our future well-being. Or, when our parents denied us something on which we had set our hearts, we felt we were very hardly dealt with. Yet was it love which said "No" to us. So it is spiritually. The love of God not only gives, but also withholds. I believe this explains some of our unanswered prayers. God loves us too much to give what would not really be for our profit. "Whom the Lord loveth He chasteneth." The duties insisted upon, the things withheld, are **expressions of His faithful love**.

3. The Christian's chastisements **magnify God's love**. Our very trials make manifest the fulness and reveal the perfections of God's love. What a word is that in Lam. 3: 33: "He doth not afflict willingly"! If God consulted only His own pleasure, He would not afflict us at all: it is for our profit that He "scourges." Ever remember that the great High Priest Himself is "touched with the feeling of our infirmities"; yet, notwithstanding, He employs the rod! God is love, and nothing is so sensitive as love. Concerning the trials and tribulations of Israel of old, it is written, "In all their afflictions He was afflicted" (Isa. 63: 9); yet out of love He chastened. How this manifests and magnifies the unselfishness of God's love!

Notice how our text supplies the Christian with an effective shield to turn aside the fiery darts of the Wicked one. Satan ever seeks to take advantage of our trials. Like the fiend that he is, he makes his fiercest assaults when we are most cast down. Thus it was that he attacked Job—"Curse God and die." And thus some of us have found it. Did he not, in the hour of suffering and sorrow seek to persuade you that when you had become increasingly diligent in seeking to please and glorify God, the dark clouds of adversity came and with them came the devil, saying, How unjust God is! What a misersble reward for your devotion and zeal! Here is your recourse, fellow-Christian, say to the Devil, it is written, "Whom the Lord loveth He chasteneth."

Again; if Satan cannot succeed in traducing the character of God and cause you to doubt his goodness and question His love, then he will assail your assurance. The devil is most persevering. If a frontal attack fails, then will he make one from the rear. He will assault your assurance of sonship. He will whisper "You are no child of His. Look at your condition; consider your circumstances. Contrast those of other Christians! You cannot be an object of His favour. You are deceiving yourself; your profession is an empty one. If you were His child God would treat you very differently. Such privations, such losses, such pain show that you cannot be one of His. But say to him, It is written, "Whom the Lord loveth He chasteneth."

Let our final thought be upon the last word of our text: "For whom the Lord loveth He chasteneth, and scourgeth every son whom He receiveth." The one whom God scourges is not rejected, but "received"—welcomed in His House above, received up into glory. First the cross, then the crown, is God's unchanging order. This was vividly illustrated in the history of the Children of Israel. God "chose them in the furnace of affliction," and many and bitter were their trials ere they reached the Promised Land. So it is with us. First the Wilderness, then Canaan. First the scourging, and then the "receiving." May we keep ourselves more and more in the love of God.

Arthur W. Pink

VOL. VI.          MARCH 1927          NO. 3

# STUDIES IN THE SCRIPTURES
"Search the Scriptures" John 5:39.

Copyright in all English-speaking Countries.

Editor: Arthur W. Pink, 22 Parramatta Road, Summer Hill, N.S.W., Australia.
Hon. Agent in U.S.A.: Mr. C. S. Pressel, 559 Dupont Ave., York, Penna.

FREE TO ALL WHO WILL READ IT

## THE FAITHFUL REMEMBERER

"Who remembered us in our low estate: for His mercy endureth for ever." (Psalm 136:23).

"Who remembered us." This is in striking and blessed contrast from our forgettings of Him. Like every other faculty of our beings, the memory has been affected by the Fall and bears on it the marks of depravity. This is seen from its power to retain what is worthless and the difficulty encountered to hold fast that which is good. A foolish nursery-rhyme or song heard in youth, is carried with us to the grave; a helpful sermon is forgotten within twenty-four hours! But most tragic and solemn of all is the ease with which we forget God and His countless mercies. But, blessed be His name, God never forgets us. He is the faithful Rememberer.

We were very much impressed when, on consulting the concordance, we found that the first five times the word "remember" is used in Scripture, in each case it is connected with God. 'And God remembered Noah, and every living thing, and all the cattle that was with him in the ark" (Gen. 8:1). "And the bow shall be in the cloud; and I will look upon it, that I may remember the everlasting covenant between God and every living creature of all flesh that is upon the earth" (Gen. 9:16). "And it came to pass, when God destroyed the cities of the plain, that God remembered Abraham, and sent Lot out of the midst of the overthrow, when He overthrew the cities in which the Lord dwelt" (Gen. 19:29), etc. The first time it is used of man we read, "Yet did not the chief butler remember Joseph, but forgat him" (Gen. 40:23)!

The historical reference here is to the children of Israel, when they were toiling amid the brick-kilns of Egypt. Truly they were in a "low estate": a nation of slaves, groaning beneath the lash of merciless task-masters, oppressed by a godless and heartless king. But when there was none other eye to pity, Jehovah looked upon them and heard their cries of distress. He "remembered" them in their low estate. And why? Exodus 2:24, 25 tells us: "And God heard their groaning, and God remembered His covenant with Abraham, with Isaac, and with Jacob. And God looked upon the children of Israel, and God had respect unto it."

And history is to repeat itself. Israel's lowest estate has not yet been reached. Fearful as have been their experiences during the last nineteen centuries, the blackest hour of their dark night is yet before them. After the present Dispensation of Grace is ended, yet sorer judgments will descend on the Jews than those which their fathers suffered in the house of bondage. The "great tribulation" will be the time when their acutest sufferings will be experienced. But even then God will "remember" them. As it is written, "Alas! for that day is great, so that none is like it: it is even the time of Jacob's trouble; but he shall be saved out of it" (Jer. 30:7). He will "remember" His covenant with their ancestors (Lev. 24:42, 44, etc.).

(Continued on page 72.)

## BACK NUMBERS

OF THIS MAGAZINE obtainable, 5/- (1 dollar) per year; Bound at 7/- (1 dollar 75.) Each year is yet obtainabl .

ADVISE PROMPTLY of Change of Address.

THIS MAGAZINE is published as a work of faith and labor of love. It is gladly sent to all who would value it.

We want the names and addresses of Christians who would read it.

Christians who feel definitely led to do so may have fellowship with us in this Ministry.

## CONTENTS.

| | |
|---|---|
| The Gospel of John (18:28-40) | 50 |
| Gleanings in Exodus | 57 |
| The Greatest Miracle | 62 |
| Abiding in Christ | 66 |
| The Jew in Prophecy | 69 |

## THE GOSPEL OF JOHN.

**63. Christ before Pilate: John 18: 28-40.**

The following is an Analysis of the closing section of John 18:—

1. Christ brought to Pilate's court v. 28.
2. Pilate demanding a formal charge vv. 29, 30.
3. Pilate seeking to shelve his responsibility vv. 31, 32.
4. Pilate examining Christ vv. 33-37.
5. Pilate affirms Christ's innocence v. 38.
6. Pilate's attempt at compromise v. 39.
7. Pilate's attempt fails v. 39.

In our last article we contemplated the Lord Jesus in the presence of Annas, the real high priest of Israel: in the portion of Scripture which is for our present consideration we behold the Saviour arraigned before Pilate. Much that occurred between these two things is omitted by John. In 18: 24 we read, "Now Annas sent him bound unto Caiaphas the high priest," and following the account of Peter's second and third denials we are told, "Then led they Jesus from Caiaphas unto the hall of judgment" (v. 28). This Fourth Gospel tells us nothing about what transpired when our Lord appeared before Caiaphas, the legal high priest (by Roman appointment), of Israel. For this we have to compare Matt. 26: 57-68; 27: 1,2; Mark 14: 53 to 15: 2; Luke 23: 54 to 24: 1. Let us briefly summarise the contents of these passages.

As was pointed out in our last, sentence of death had been passed upon Christ before He was brought to trial at all (18:14); the examination before Caiaphas was, therefore, nothing more than a horrible farce. The Saviour was tried before what ought to have been the holiest judicature on earth, but was condemned by the most fearful perversion of justice and abuse of its forms that is recorded anywhere in history. The amazing contrasts presented are intensely affecting. The Friend of sinners was shackled by handcuffs and leg-irons. The Judge of all the earth was arraigned before a fallen son of Adam. The Lord of glory was treated with the foulest scorn. The Holy One was condemned as a blasphemer. Liars bore witness against the Truth. He who is the Resurrection and the Life was doomed to die.

With Caiaphas were assembled the "scribes and elders" (Matt. 26:57): in addition to these were the "chief priests and all the Council" (Matt. 26:59). At this decisive crisis, when Israel's rejection of their Messiah took its final and official form, all the leaders of the Nation were solemnly convened. Their first act was to summon witnesses against the Lord, and the unprincipled character of the Sanhedrin, their utter unrighteousness, is glaringly apparent in that they "SOUGHT false witnesses against Jesus" (Matt. 26:59). The Sanhedrin had not the power to execute the death-penalty, therefore, some charge must be preferred against Him when they brought Him before Pilate—hence the seeking of the false witnesses. There were thousands who could have testified to the genuineness of His miracles; their own agents had acknowledged that never did man speak as He did; but such testimony as this was not what they wanted. Something must be devised which would give a semblance of justice in clamoring for His execution.

For a time their iniquitous quest was fruitless: "though many false witnesses came, yet found they none"—none who could supply what they wanted. But "at the last came two false witnesses"—the minimum number required by the Mosaic law, just as Jezebel obtained two false witnesses to testify against Naboth (1 Kings 18:10). They affirmed that Christ had said, "I am able to destroy the temple of God, and to build it in three days." In obedient submission to His Father's Word, the Saviour had stood by in silence while these children of the father of lies had perjured themselves. Evidently dissatisfied at the flimsiness of such a charge, and uneasy at Christ's calm dignity, the high priest arose "and said unto Him, Answerest Thou nothing? What is it which these witness against Thee?" But Jesus held His peace. Alarmed, most probably at the dignified demeanor of his Prisoner, and fearful perhaps that His bearing might move the hearts of some in the Council, Caiaphas said, "I adjure Thee by the living God, that Thou tell us whether Thou be the Christ, the Son of God" (Matt. 26.63)." "This was the method among the Israelites of proffering and accepting the oath; the appeal to God (and the formula of curse as the penalty of lying—which, however, was not ventured on now) was made on the one side, and the answer made thereupon was received, without any repetition of the oath being regarded as necessary on the part of the respondent. I adjure Thee by the living God (in whose office I stand, under whose power we all are, before whom Thou also standest, who knowest the truth, and judgeth between us and Thee) that Thou tell us, this holy Sanhedrin now here as before God, the truth. Thus does he avow, bearing testimony against himself in this most awful abuse of the name of God that he knows this God as a living God who will not be mocked! He testifies of His truth, even while he is aiming to get the victory by a lie; of His power and majesty, while he is pushing his opposition to the uttermost!" (Stier).

Now, for the first time, Christ spoke before Caiaphas. He penetrates the meaning of His questioner, recognizes all the consequences of His affirmation, but hesitates not to answer. As an obedient Israelite, it was His duty to respond to the adjuration of the ruling power (Lev. 5:1; 1 Kings 22:16). Made "under the law" (Gal. 4:4), He was submissive to the last, even when it was perverted against Him. The Saviour not only replied to His judge, but, maintaining His dignity to the last, added, "Hereafter shall ye see the Son of man sitting on the right hand of power, and coming in the clouds of heaven" (Matt. 36:64):—"Sitting" in contrast from Me now standing before you, while you sit in judgment upon Me; "power" in contrast from His then weakness (i.e., refusing to exercise His might); "coming in the clouds of heaven" in contrast from going to the cross! Caiaphas' response was to rend his official robes—instead of putting them off before the majesty of the great High Priest. In this act Caiaphas did, unknown to himself, but intimate that God had rent asunder the Aaronic priesthood!—a garment is only torn to pieces by its owner when he has no more use for it.

Following the rending of his robes, Caiaphas said, "What further need have we of witnesses? Behold, now ye have heard His blasphemy. What think ye?" He was the blasphemer. "What further need have we of witnesses?" betrayed his uneasy conscience, "Behold, now ye have heard Him" was the signal that the mock trial was over. The answer he wanted was promptly given: "He is guilty of death." Elated at their fancied triumph, "then did they spit in His face, and buffeted Him; and others smote with the palms of their hands, saying, Prophesy unto us thou Christ, who is he that smote Thee?" Thus did Israel condemn their Messiah, rebellious man his God.

"When the morning was come, all the chief priests and elders of the people took counsel against Jesus to put Him to death: And when they had bound Him, they led Him away, and delivered Him to Pontius Pilate the governor" (Matt. 27:1, 2), thus fulfilling our Lord's prediction, "The Son of man shall be delivered unto the chief priests, and unto the scribes; and they shall condemn Him to death, and shall deliver Him to the Gentiles: And they shall mock Him, and shall scourge Him, and shall spit upon Him" (Mark 10:33, 34). This brings us to the first point touched upon by John, whose narrative we shall now follow.

"Then led they Jesus from Caiaphas unto the hall of judgment: and it was early" (v. 28). "Then," following the decision of the Council, recorded in Matt. 27:1; "led they"; still unresisting, He went as a lamb to the slaughter, Mark tells us (15:1) they "bound" Him; "unto the hall of judgment," Pilate's courtroom. "And it was early": the disciples could not watch with Him one hour; His enemies had acted against Him all through that night! Alas, man has more zeal and energy, because more heart, for that which is evil than for that which is good. The same people who will listen, untired, half a day to a political discussion, or sit three hours through an opera, complain that the preacher is long-winded if he spends the whole hour in expounding the Word of God! "It was early": their one object now was to obtain from Pilate, as swiftly as possible, his confirmation of the death-sentence.

"And they themselves went not into the judgment-hall, lest they should be defiled; but that they might eat the passover" (v. 28). The judgment-hall was Gentile property and to have entered it the Jews would be ceremonially defiled, and from that there was not time to be cleansed ere the Passover-feast arrived. Anxious to partake of the Passover, they therefore went no further than the entrance to the praetorium. They would not enter Pilate's hall, though they were ready to use him to further their own wickedness! What a proof was this of the worthlessness of religion where it has failed to influence the heart. Fully did they merit those awful words of Christ: "Woe unto you, scribes and Pharisees, hypocrites! for ye are like unto whited sepulchres, which indeed appear beautiful outward, but are within full of dead bones, and of all uncleanness. Even so ye also outwardly appear righteous unto men, but within ye are full of hypocrisy and iniquity" (Matt. 23, 27, 28).

These very men were here engaged in the vilest act ever perpetrated on earth, and yet they spoke of being "defiled"! They hesitated not to deliver their Messiah to the Gentiles, yet were scrupulous lest they be disqualified from eating the passover. So to-day there are some who are more concerned about the right form of baptism than they are of a Scriptural walk; more punctilious about observing the Lord's supper than to bring forth fruit to the glory of the Father. Let us beware lest we also strain at a gnat and swallow a camel. "These 'rulers of the Jews' and the multitude that followed them were thorough Ritualists. It was their ritualism that urged them on to crucify the Son of God. Christ and ritualism are opposed to each other as light is to darkness. The true cross in which Paul gloried and the cross in which modern ceremonialists glory, have no resemblance to each other. The cross and the crucifix cannot agree. Either ritualism will banish Christ or Christ will banish ritualism." (Dr. H. Bonar.)

"Pilate then went out unto them" (v. 29). That the whole Sanhedrin (Mark 15:1, 2), accompanied by a large crowd (Luke 23:1), should visit him at such a time (the passover feast), was sufficient to convince Pilate that some important matter required his attention; therefore, early morning though it were, he went out to them. That he was not taken by surprise we know, for only the previous night they had secured a cohort of Roman soldiers, which could not have been obtained without his permission. It was clear to him, then, that here was some culprit whom the Jews wished executed before the Feast began.

"And said, What accusation bring ye against this man?" (v. 29). Pilate's question here confirms what we have just said above. He did not ask them what was the object of their visit, but simply inquired what charge they preferred against their prisoner. This was in accord with the Roman law which required three things: the making of a specific indictment, the bringing of the accusers before the accused, and the liberty granted to the latter to answer for himself (Acts 25: 16). Pilate therefore acted honorably in demanding to know the nature of the crime charged against the Lord Jesus. God saw to it that out of their own mouths they should be condemned.

"They answered and said unto him, If He were not a malefactor, we would not have delivered Him up unto thee" (v. 30). The Jews were piqued at Pilate's question. They were not anxious to prefer a charge, knowing full well that they had no evidence by which they could establish it. It is clear that they hoped that Pilate would take their word for it —especially as they had obtained the soldiers from him so easily—and condemn their Prisoner unheard. With characteristic hypocrisy they now assumed an injured air: they posed as righteous men; they would have Pilate believe that they would never have arrested an innocent man. Their "if He were not a malefactor, we would not have delivered Him up unto thee" was tantamount to saying: "See who is before you—we are none other than the sacred Sanhedrin: we have already tried the case, and our judgment is beyond question: we only ask you now to give the necessary Roman sanction that He may be put to death." Their hands were forced by Pilate, for Luke tells us "they began to accuse Him, saying, We found this fellow perverting the nation, and forbidding to give tribute to Caesar, saying that He Himself is Christ a King" (23: 2).

"Then said Pilate unto them, Take ye Him, and judge Him, according to your law" (v. 31). The whole responsibility now rested on Pilate. He was too well acquainted with the Jews' expectations to suppose that the Sanhedrin would hate and persecute one who would free them from the Roman yoke. Their simulation of good citizenship was too shallow to deceive him. But he did not relish the task before him, and sought to evade it. The real character of the man comes out plainly here—timid, vacillating, temporising, unprincipled. Pilate wished to have nothing to do with the case; he was anxious for the Jews to shoulder the full onus of Christ's death. What cared he for justice, so long as he could get out of an unpleasant situation! He was anxious not to displease the Jews, therefore did he say, "judge Him (sentence Him to death) according to your law."

"The Jews therefore said unto him, It is not lawful for us to put any man to death" (v. 31). This reply completely thwarted the wretched Pilate's attempt to avoid the necessity of judging our Lord. They pressed upon the Roman governor that the legal power of passing the death sentence was no longer in their hands, therefore it was impossible for them to do as he desired. They here warned Pilate that nothing but the execution of Christ would satisfy them. But a Higher Power was overruling: "Of a truth against Thy Holy servant Jesus, whom Thou hast anointed, both Herod and Pontius Pilate with the Gentiles, and the people of Israel, were gathered together, for to do whatsoever Thy hand and Thy counsel determined before to be done" (Acts 4: 27, 28).

"The Jews therefore said unto him, It is not lawful for us to put any man to death." Though they were unaware of it, this was a remarkable confession. It was their own acknowledgment that Gen. 49: 10 was now fulfilled—"The sceptre shall not depart from Judah, nor a lawgiver from between his feet, until Shiloh come." The heads of Israel here owned that they were no longer the rulers of their own nation, but were under the dominion of a foreign power. He that has the right to condemn a prisoner to death is the governor of a country. "It is not lawful" they said; you, the Roman governor, alone can do it. By their consent they no longer had a law-administrator of their own stock, therefore the "sceptre" had departed, and this was proof positive that Shiloh (the Messiah) had come! How unaware wicked men are when they fulfil prophecy!

"That the saying of Jesus might be fulfilled, which He spake, signifying what death He should die" (v. 32). Here again prediction was being fulfilled, all unconsciously by themselves. The refusal of Israel to take matters into their own hands, when Pilate put it there, only worked for the accomplishment of Christ's own words: "and shall deliver Him to the Gentiles to mock, and to scourge, and to crucify" (Matt. 20: 19). Moreover, had the Jews still possessed the power of inflicting capital punishment for such crimes as they alleged against the Lord Jesus, the mode of execution would have been by stoning. By delivering Him to Pilate this ensured the Roman form of punishment, crucifixion, and thus did the saying of Christ come to pass: "As Moses lifted up the serpent in the wilderness, even so must the Son of man be lifted up" (John 3: 14); and again, "I, if I be lifted up from the earth, will draw all unto Me." This He said, signifying what death He should die" (12: 32, 33).

"Then Pilate entered into the judgment hall again, and called Jesus, and said unto Him, Art Thou the King of the Jews?" (v. 33). Here we have another glaring example of the gross injustice which was meted out to the Saviour. First Annas, then Caiaphas, now Pilate, displayed the fearful enmity of the carnal mind against God—here manifest in flesh. Roman law required that the accused and the accusers should be brought face to face, and that the former should have an opportunity of replying to the charge laid against him" (Acts 23: 28), but this Pilate denied Christ. But what was far worse, Pilate examined Christ as the enemy of Caesar and the Jews were His only accusers! If the Lord Jesus were really opposing the authority and rights of the Emperor, why had not the Roman power taken the initiative? Where were the Gentile witnesses against Him? Were all the Roman officers indifferent to their master's interests? Pilate knew that it was for envy (Matt. 27: 18). the Sanhedrin had delivered Him up. He knew full well that the Saviour was no malefactor: he could not have been ignorant of His public life—His deeds of mercy, His words of grace and truth; yet did he refuse Him a fair trial. The fact that Pilate's objection (v. 31) was so easily silenced, revealed the pitiable weakness of his character. Sent to be the Governor of these Jews, they, nevertheless, compelled him to be their slave, the executioner of their wrath.

"Then Pilate entered into the judgment hall again, and called Jesus, and said unto Him, Art Thou the King of the Jews?" What lay behind this question? what was the state of Pilate's mind when he asked it? With Bishop Ryle we are inclined to say, "On the whole, the question seems a mixture of curiosity and contempt." The humble attire and lowly appearance of our Lord cannot fail to have struck the Governor. The entire absence of any signs which the world associates with One possessing a kingdom must have puzzled him. Yet tidings of His "triumphal entrance" into Jerusalem only a few days before had doubtless reached his ears. Who, then, was this strange Character who attracted the multitudes, but was hated by their leaders? who had power to heal the sick, yet had not where to lay His head? who was able to raise the dead, yet here stood bound before him?

"Jesus answered him, Sayest thou this thing of thyself, or did others tell it thee of Me?" (v. 34). Our Lord was addressing Himself to Pilate's conscience. Do you really desire to act justly? Is it information you are in quest of? or are you going to be the tool of those who delivered Me to thee? He would point out to him the injustice of any suspicions he might entertain. If you have reason to think I am a "King" in the sense in which you employ the term, then where are the Roman witnesses? If you are influenced only by what you have heard from the Sanhedrin, beware of heeding the word of those who are plainly My enemies. Christ was pressing upon him his individual responsibility of coming to some definite conviction concerning Himself. But why not have answered with a plain Yes or No? Because that, under the circumstances, were impossible? Pilate used the word "King" as a rival of Caesar, as a rebel against Rome. To have replied Yes, would have misled Pilate; to have said No, without qualification, would have been to deny "the hope of Israel." The Lord therefore presses Pilate for a definition of this ambiguous term. Admire His consummate wisdom.

"Sayest thou this of thyself, or did others tell it thee of Me?" "Our Lord, by this, would learn whether His claims to be king of the Jews was challenged by Pilate as protector of the Emperor's rights in Judea, or merely upon a charge of the Jews. Upon this hung, I may say, everything in the present juncture; and the wisdom and purpose of the Lord in giving the inquiry this direction are manifest. Should Pilate say that he had become apprehensive of the Roman interests, the Lord could at once have referred him to the whole course of His life and ministry, to prove that, touching the king, innocency had been found in Him. He had taught the rendering to Caesar the things that are Caesar's. He had withdrawn Himself, departing into a mountain alone, when He perceived that the multitude would have taken Him by force to make Him a king (6: 15). His controversy was not with Rome... and Pilate would have had His answer according to all this had the challenge proceeded from himself as representative of the Roman power. But it did not" (Mr. J. G. Bellett).

"Pilate answered, Am I a Jew? Thine own nation and the chief priests have delivered Thee unto me: what hast Thou done?" (v. 35). Here Pilate betrayed his insincerity. He evaded Christ's penetrating question. He denied any personal interest in the matter. I am no Jew—I am not concerned about points of religious controversy. "What hast Thou done?"—let us deal with practical matters. We doubt not that Pilate uttered his first question sneeringly—Am I a Jew! You forget that I, a noble Roman, can have no patience with visions and dreams. It was the haughty and contemptuous language of a prominent man of affairs. "Thine own nation and the chief priests" are the ones who are interested in ceremonial rites and recondite prophecies, and they have "delivered Thee to me"! What is it that they have against You? Here he speaks as the judge: let us come to the business in hand.

"Pilate answered, Am I a Jew? Thine own nation and the chief priests have delivered Thee unto me: what hast Thou done?" "This answer of Pilate conveyed the full proof of the guilt of Israel. In the mouth of him who represented the power of the world at that time, the thing was established, that Israel had disclaimed their King and sold themselves into the hand of another. This, for the present, was everything with Jesus—This at once carried Him beyond the earth, and out of the world. Israel had rejected Him, and His kingdom was, therefore, not from hence: for Zion is the appointed place for the King of the whole earth to sit and rule; and the unbelief of the daughter of Zion must keep the king of the earth away. The Lord, then, as the rejected King, listening to this testimony from the lips of the Roman, could only recognize the present loss of His throne" (Mr. Bellett). Hence Christ's next words.

"Jesus answered, My kingdom is not of this world" (v. 36). This sentence has been sadly perverted by some. It has been used by those who deny that the Lord Jesus will ever have an earthly kingdom, that He will yet occupy the throne of David (Luke 1: 32, 33), and reign as King in Jerusalem (Matt. 5: 35, etc). It has been interpreted to mean that the only kingdom over which Christ will rule is an invisible, spiritual one, in the hearts of His people. But such an interpretation is manifestly false, for it is refuted by a score of plain predictions and promises that the Saviour will set up a visible kingdom here on earth and reign as King for a thousand years. Such an interpretation falsifies our Lord's own words in Matt. 16: 28; 25; 31; Luke 19: 12 and other passages which might be referred to. Such an interpretation contradicts the 20th chapter of the Revelation. That such a verse as John 18: 36 should be made the sheet-anchor of postmillenialism only shows how untenable is their whole case.

"My Kingdom is not of this world." If our Lord did not mean by this, The only one I shall ever have is invisible and spiritual, what did He mean? First, observe that He did not say "My kingdom is not in this world," but "My kingdom is not of this world." Believers are not "of" this world (17: 16), yet they are "in it"! Second, observe His own qualifying and yet amplifying words at the close of the verse: "but now is My kingdom not from hence." The "now" is explained by Pilate's declaration in the previous verse —re-read Mr. Bellett's comments thereon. This was not said by Christ until after His final and official rejection by Israel! Third, observe His explanatory "If My kingdom were of this world, then would My servants fight"—to deliver their King. Our Lord was graciously explaining to Pilate the character of that kingdom over which He will yet preside. Unlike all the kingdoms which have preceded it, My kingdom will not originate with man, but be received from God (Dan. 7: 13, 14; Luke 19: 12); unlike the kingdoms of man, which have been dependent upon the powers of the world, Mine will be an absolute theocracy; unlike theirs, which have been propagated by the world's arms, Mine will be regulated by heavenly principles; unlike theirs, which have been characterised by injustice and tyranny, Mine will be marked by righteousness and peace. Though the Lord acknowledged His then loss through Israel's rejection of Him, He maintained His title to it; when the Jews repent, His throne shall be set upon the earth.

In answering Pilate as He did we cannot but admire the wondrous grace and patience of our blessed Lord. The contemptuous "Am I a Jew?" of Pilate annulled his right to any further notice; his "what hast Thou done?" gave the One before him the full right to maintain silence. But ignoring the insult, Christ continued to address Himself to his conscience. "My kingdom is not of this world," warned Pilate that there was another world, to which He belonged! "My kingdom," which will not be brought in by "fighting," was to assure him there was a Power superior to the boasted might of Rome, which then dominated the earth. "Now is My kingdom not from thence intimated that His kingdom would be far otherwise than those in which violence and injustice had ever held sway, and where, after all, there was nothing obtained but the semblance of right and truth. Thus instead of furnishing a positive reply to Pilate's "What hast Thou done?" He gave a negative answer which, however, plainly showed that He was guilty of no political evil and had done nothing against Caesar.

Some have wondered why Christ did not appeal to His wondrous and benevolent works of mercy when Pilate asked Him, "What hast Thou done?" These were a part of His Messianic credentials (Matt. 11: 3-5, etc), and therefore only for Israel. Others have wondered why Pilate did not refer to the smiting of Malchus in the garden, when the Lord affirmed "then would My servants fight." Why had not the Sanhedrin informed Pilate of Peter's temerity? Malchus was a servant of the high priest and nothing was more natural than that he should clamor for redress. The seeming difficulty is at once removed by a reference to Luke 22: 51, where we are told that the Saviour "touched his ear and healed him." "The miracle satisfactorily explains the suppression of the charge— to have advanced it would have naturally led to an investigation that would have more than frustrated the malicious purpose it was meant to serve. It would have proved too much. It would have manifested His own compassionate nature, His submission to the law, and His extraordinary powers" (Dr. J. Blount).

"Pilate therefore said unto Him, Art Thou a king then?" (v. 37). The Governor was puzzled. The quiet and dignified bearing of the One before him, the threefold reference to His kingdom, the declaration that it was not of this world, the calm assertion that though in bonds He was possessed of "servants", plus a strong hint that His dominion would yet be firmly established, though not by the sword, was more than Pilate could grasp. Pilate's change from "Art Thou the King of the Jews?" in v. 33 to "Art Thou a king then?" intimated he was satisfied there was nothing to fear politically, yet that Christ had made a claim which was incomprehensible to his mind. We believe that he had dropt his scornful tone and asked this last question half earnestly, half curiously. That He was "King" our Lord would not deny, but boldly acknowledged "to this end was I born," knowing full well what would be the cost of His affirmation. It is to this the Holy Spirit refers, "who before Pontius Pilate witnessed a good confession" (1. Tim. 6:13). Though Israel received Him not, yet He was their King (Matt. 2: 2). Though the husbandmen were casting Him out, yet He was the Heir of the vineyard. Though His citizens were saying they would not have Him to reign over them, yet He had been anointed to the throne in Zion.

"To this end was I born, and for this cause came I into the world, that I should bear witness unto the truth" (v. 37). Note how the Saviour here linked together His Kingdom and His bearing witness unto the truth. Truth is authoritative, imperial, majestic. This was a further word for Pilate's conscience, if only his heart were open to receive it. Christ informs him that He possessed a higher glory than His title to David's throne, even that of Deity, for it was as the Only-begotten of the Father that He was "full of grace and truth," and His "came I into the world"—distinguished from His being "born" in the previous clause—was a direct hint that He was from Heaven! Moreover, the Lord would have it known that there had been no failure in His mission. The great design before Him at His first advent was not to wield the royal sceptre, but to bear witness unto the truth; that He had faithfully done, yea, was doing, at that very moment. This was His answer to Pilate's "What hast Thou done?" (v. 35)—I have witnessed unto, not simply "truth" but, The Truth; it was as "The Word" He again spoke!

"Every one that is of the truth heareth My voice" (v. 37). He that is "of the truth" means, first, he that is true, honest and sincere; in its deeper meaning, he who is of God: compare 8: 47. It is only the one who has a heart for the truth who really hears Christ's voice, for the Author of the truth is also the Teacher, the Interpreter of it. What a word was this for Pilate's conscience. If you are really seeking the Truth, which I came into the world to bear witness unto, you will listen unto Me! "Would any one ask how he can know that he is 'of the truth'? The Sacred Word supplies a direct answer, leaving none in doubt. 'Let us not love in word, neither in tongue; but in deed and in truth. And hereby we know that we are of the truth' (1 John 3: 18, 19). Whoever shows himself to be a partaker of the Divine nature, evidenced by loving in deed and in truth, is of the truth, hears Christ's voice, and will be found in His train among the armies of heaven, when He comes forth to deal with the apostate power on earth" (Mr. C. E. Stuart).

"Pilate saith unto Him, What is truth? And when he had said this, he went out" (v. 38). There has been wide difference of opinion as to the spirit in which he asked this question. Clearly it was not that of an earnest inquirer, his at once leaving Christ without waiting for an answer shows that—only an awakened conscience is really desirous of knowing what is Truth. Many have thought it was more a wail of despair: What is truth?: "I have investigated many a system, examined various philosophers, but have found no satisfaction in them." But apart from the fact that everything revealed about his character conflicts with an earnest, persevering quest after light, would he not rather have said, "Truth! there is no truth!" had that been his state of mind? Personally, we regard Pilate's words here as an expression of scorn, ending them not with a question mark but an exclamation, the emphasis on the final word—"What is truth!" It was the Light now manifesting the darkness. This expressed the settled conviction of a conscienceless politician. "Truth"!—is it for that you are sacrificing your life? We think his words in v. 39 bear this out.

"And when he had said this, he went out again unto the Jews, and saith unto them, I find in Him no fault" (v. 38). Pilate was uneasy. The words of Christ had impressed him more deeply than he would care to admit. That He was innocent was clear; that Pilate was now guilty of the grossest injustice is equally patent. If the Roman governor found "no fault" in Christ he ought to have promptly released Him. But instead of yielding to the voice of conscience he proceeded to confer with those who thirsted for the Saviour's blood. Much is omitted by John at this point which is found in the Synoptics—the chief priest's remonstrance (Mark 15: 3-12); Pilate sending Him to Herod; and the brutal treatment which He received at the hands of his soldiers, followed by Herod sending Him back to Pilate (Luke 23: 5-18).

"But ye have a custom, that I should release unto you one at the Passover: will ye therefore that I release unto you the King of the Jews?" (v. 39). The nature of such a proposal at once reveals the unscrupulous character of him who made it. Pilate feared to offend the Jews (feared because an uprising at that time would have brought him into disfavour with Caesar, who had his hands full elsewhere) and so sought an expedient which he hoped would please them, and yet enable him to discharge the Lord Jesus. Remembering the custom which obtained at the Passover of releasing a prisoner—a most striking custom it was, grace, deliverance, connected with the Passover!—he suggests that Christ be the one to go free. It was as though he said, Let us suppose that Jesus is guilty; I am willing to declare Him a criminal worthy of death, providing He be freed —Luke tells us that he went so far as to offer to "chastise" Christ before he released Him (23: 16). Little did he recognise the type of men he was dealing with, still less the One above who was directing all things.

"Then cried they all again, saying, Not this man, but Barabbas. Now Barabbas was a robber" (v. 40). The Jews revealed themselves as worse than Pilate and demanded what he least expected. Thirsting for the blood of their victim, impatient for him to yield up to them their prey, they all "cried (the Greek signifies "shouted") not this man, but Barabbas." Pilate's compromise not only showed plainly that he was not "of the truth" but only drew out the extent of their enmity. "Barabbas was a robber," better "bandit"—one who used force; Luke says he was a murderer. How very striking: the Jews chose Barabbas, and plunderers and blood-shedders have ruled over them ever since!! In this their history is without a parallel.

"We have noticed elsewhere how strangely yet significantly this name Barabbas, 'son of the father,' comes in here. It was the Son of the Father—just as that—whom they were refusing now; but of what father was this lawless one the son? A shadow it is, surely, of the awful apostasy to come, when they will receive him who comes in his own name (the Antichrist A. W. P.), true child of the rebel and 'murderer from the beginning.' Yet there is a Gospel side to this also. How good to see that here it is the question, Shall the Saviour or the sinner suffer? and to remember that under the law, the unclean animal might be redeemed with a lamb (Ex. 13), but the lamb could not be redeemed. Impossible for the Saviour to be released in this way. But the sinner may" (Mr. F. W. Grant).

The following questions are to aid the student on John 19: 1-11.:—

1. Why did God allow Christ to wear "a crown of thorns" v. 2?

2. Why "a purple robe" v. 2?

3. How many times in the four Gospels "I find no fault" v. 4?

4. What was Pilate's aim in "behold the Man!" v. 5?

5. What is the meaning of v. 6 in the light of 18: 31?

6. What made Pilate "the more afraid" v. 8?

7. Why did Jesus make no answer v. 9?

—Arthur W. Pink.

## GLEANINGS IN EXODUS.

### 39. The Lampstand: Ex. 25: 31-40.

The particular piece of the Tabernacle's furniture which is now to engage our attention, is, in our English Bibles termed the "Candlestick," but we believe that this is a very faulty rendition of the Hebrew word. Why term it a "Candlestick" when no candles were burned thereon? It strikes the writer that such a translation is a relic of Romish perversion. "M'nourah" means "lightbearer" or "lampstand," and thus we shall refer to it throughout this article. The fact that it had "seven lamps" (Ex. 25: 25, 37) and that these were fed with "oil" (Lev. 24: 2, 4) is more than sufficient to warrant this correction.

The Lampstand was in the Holy Place. This was the chamber entered by none save the priestly family, and was the place where these favoured servants of Jehovah ministered before Him. It was therefore the place of communion. In keeping with this, each of the three vessels that stood therein spoke of fellowship. The Table, with its twelve loaves, pointed to Christ as the Substance of our fellowship, the One on whom we feed. The Lampstand foreshadowed Christ as the power for fellowship, as supplying the light necessary to it. The Incense-altar, prefigured Christ as maintaining our fellowship, by His intercession securing our continued acceptance before the Father.

The fact that the Lampstand stood within the Holy Place at once shows us that it is not Christ as "the Light of the world" which is typified. It is strange that some of the commentators have erred here. The words of Christ on this point were clear enough: "As long as I am in the world, I am the Light of the world" (John 9: 5)—then only was He manifested here as such. So again in John 12: 35, 36 He said to the people, "Yet a little while is the Light with you . . . while ye have light, believe in the light, that ye may be the children of light." But they loved darkness rather than light. The world rejected the Light, and so far as they were concerned extinguished it. Since He was put to death by wicked hands, the world has never again gazed on the Light. He is now hidden from their eyes.

But He who was put to death by the world, rose again, and then ascended on High. It is there in the Holy Place, in God's presence, the Light now dwells. And while there—O marvellous privilege —the saints have access to Him. For them the veil is rent, and thus the Holy Place and the Holy of Holies are no longer two separate compartments, but one; and, the substance of all that was shadowed forth by the sacred vessels in each is now the wondrous portion of those who, by grace, are "built up a spiritual house, an holy priesthood, to offer up spiritual sacrifices acceptable to God by Jesus Christ" (1 Peter 2: 5).

Black shadows rest upon the world which has cast out the Light of Life: "the way of the wicked is as darkness" (Prov. 4: 19). It is now night-time because the "Dayspring from on High" is absent. The Lampstand tells of the gracious provision which God has made for His own beloved people during the interval of darkness, before the Sun of righteousness shall rise once more and usher in for this earth that morning without clouds. The Lampstand is for the night season! Therefore the illuminating Lampstand speaks of Christ neither in the days of His first advent nor of the time of His second advent, but of the interval between, when those who have access into the true sanctuary walk in the light as He is in the light (1 John 1: 7). Let us now consider:—

### 1. Its Composition.

"And thou shalt make a Lampstand of pure gold: of beaten work shall the lampstand be made" (v. 31). Unlike the ark and the table of shewbread, no wood entered into the composition of the Lampstand. It was of solid gold. But there is one word here which has been overlooked by almost all the commentators, and by losing sight of it their interpretations have quite missed the mark. The Lampstand, though made of pure gold, was "of beaten work," that is to say, the talent of gold from which it was made was wrought upon by the hammers of skilled workmen until it was shaped into a beautiful and symmetrical form. Only by Divinely-given wisdom could they evolve from a solid talent of gold this richly ornamented vessel with base, shaft and branches, in consistent proportions (Ex. 31: 6).

What is before us now in our present type is the more noteworthy in that the Lampstand was the only vessel or portion of the Tabernacle which was made of "beaten work." It is in striking contrast from the "golden calf" which Aaron made, for that was cast in a mould (Ex. 32: 4). What is idolatrous or according to man's mind, can be quickly and easily cast into shape; but that which has most of all glorified God and secured the redemption of His people was wrought at great cost. Clearly, the "beaten gold" here speaks of a suffering Christ glorified, glorified as the reward of His perfect but painful Work.

That the "pure gold" speaks of the divine side of things is obvious, for the One that is here prefigured was none other than the God-man. It was His deity which sustained His humanity. Had Christ been merely a creature He had completely succumbed to the storm of judgment which burst upon Him. It was His deity which enabled Him to suffer within the compass of a brief span what otherwise would have been the eternal portion of all His people. But after all, the primary thought in the "gold" is glory as Heb. 9: 5 teaches us, and the beaten gold plainly foreshadowed the glorification of Him who was beaten with many stripes on our behalf.

"Of a talent of pure gold shall he make it" (v. 39). This would be worth more than five thousand pounds, upwards of twenty-five thousand dollars. A "talent" was one hundred and twenty lbs., so that sufficient gold was provided to ensure the

Lampstand being of a goodly size. Most probably it stood higher than the Table or the Incense-altar, for by its light the priests were enabled to attend to the one and minister at the other. Thus was foreshadowed not only the **preciousness** of the person of our Redeemer, but also His **sufficiency** to make manifest the perfections of the Godhead.

### 2. Its Construction.

The pattern of the Lampstand is described in Ex. 25: 31-36. It consisted of one central stem, with three lateral branches springing from either side. Each branch was adorned with knops, flowers and bowls. The "knops" seem to have been buds, probably of the almond; the "bowls" were for holding the oil which fed the lights. Upon the end of each branch was the bowl or lamp. All was of one piece, beaten out by workmen endowed with divine skill.

The seven lamps while an intrinsic part of the Lampstand itself, may also be contemplated separately. This seems clear from the fact that in Numbers 8: 2 we read, "When thou lightest the lamps, the seven lamps shall give light over against the Lampstand." The accuracy of the type here is most impressive. The sevenfold radiance of the Lampstand speaks of Christ as the "brightness of God's glory" (Heb. 1: 3). It tells of His **perfections** as the Light. It is worthy of note that when the white light is broken into its varied parts we have just seven colors, as seen in the rainbow. But it is equally clear that the seven "lamps" also symbolise the Holy Spirit in the plenitude of His power and perfections—the "seven Spirits which are before His throne" (Rev. 1: 4). That the type appears to overlap at this point, or rather, has a double application, only shows its marvellous and minute accuracy, for in His ministry toward and in believers, the Spirit works as "the Spirit of Christ" (Rom. 8: 9; 1 Peter 1: 11).

The fact that the seven lamps were supported by the Lampstand foreshadowed the fact that the Spirit, given to us, has come from our glorified Redeemer. There are several scriptures which prove this. The Lord Jesus said to His apostles, "When the Comforter is come, whom I will send from the Father" (John 15: 26). On the day of Pentecost, when explaining the outpouring of the Spirit's gifts, Peter distinctly attributed them to the ascended Christ: "Therefore being by the right hand of God exalted, and having received of the Father the promise of the Spirit He hath shed forth this, which ye now see and hear" (Acts 2: 36). So also in Rev. 3: 1 Christ is spoken of as "He that hath the seven Spirits of God."

### 3. Its Ornamentation.

"And six branches shall come out of the sides of it; three branches of the Lampstand out of the one side, and three branches of the Lampstand out of the other side: Three bowls made like unto almonds, a knop and a flower in one branch; and three bowls made like almonds in the other branch, a knop and a flower; so in the six branches that come out of the Lampstand." (vv. 32, 33). Mr. S. Ridout has offered an illuminating suggestion that the "knop" might portray the rounded unopened bud, so that the central stem and each of its branches would be ornamented with that which set forth the three stages of the almond—the bud, the flower and the ripened fruit. He has also pointed out how that this suggestion receives confirmation in what is recorded of Aaron's rod in Numbers 17: "Behold, the rod of Aaron for the house of Levi was budded, and brought forth buds, and blossomed blossoms and yielded almonds" (v. 8). Thus the three stages of life were also seen on the branches of the Lampstand—bud, flower, fruit.

The prominence of the "almond" on the Lampstand supplies an important key to its interpretation. It corresponds closely, though it is not exactly parallel in thought with what is foreshadowed in the "acacia (shittim) wood" in the other vessels. The "wood" speaks of the incorruptible humanity of Christ. The "almond" is the emblem of resurrection, here the resurrection of the Lord Jesus, which, of course, presupposes His incarnation. It is not so much the holiness of His humanity which is here foreshadowed, as it is the glory of the Risen One—the "almonds of gold"!

The "almond" is the first of all trees in Palestine to bud, manifesting the new life of spring as early as January. The Hebrew word for "almond" means "vigilent," and is used with this significance in Jer. 1: 11, 12: "And I said, I see a rod of an almond tree. And Jehovah said unto me, Thou hast well seen; for I am **watchful** over My word to perform it." God has seen to it that His every promise has been vindicated and substantiated in a risen Christ. That the "almond" is the emblem of resurrection is further established in Numbers 17. The twelve rods, cut off from the trees on which they grew, were lifeless things. The budding of Aaron's rod manifested a re-impartation of life—the work of God. Aaron's rod not only exhibited the signs of life, but produced the full results of it, in bud and flower and fruit—and that of the "almond"! So, too, our Saviour was, according to the flesh, "a rod out the stem of Jesse" (Isa. 11: 1) and was "cut off" (Dan. 9: 26) out of the land of the living. But on the third day He rose again from the dead. Mr. Ridout has strikingly pointed out that just as there was first the bud, then the flower, and then the almond fruit on Aaron's rod, and on each branch of the Lampstand so was there a manifest gradation in the evidences of Christ's resurrection!

"The stone rolled away, the empty tomb, the linen clothes lying in quiet order and the napkin lying by itself—no sign of a struggle, but the witness that the Prince of life had risen from His sleep of death; these may be called the 'buds,' the first signs of His resurrection. The angel who rolled away the stone and sat on it (Matt. 28: 2), the 'young man sitting on the right side' of the tomb (Mark 16: 5, 6), the 'vision of angels' seen by the women which came early to the sepulchre (Luke 24: 23); the two angels in white sitting, the one at the head, the other at the feet, where the body of Jesus had lain (John 20: 12)—these may be called the 'flowers'—the more advanced witnesses of His resurrection. Lastly, His own personal manifestations to Mary Magdalene, to Peter, to the women, to the two disciples at Emmaus, to the gathered disciples in the upper room, to them again when Thomas was present; again at the Sea of Tiberius, and at a mountain in Galilee—these and other 'infallible proofs' might be called the full almond fruit. The empty tomb might have been a precious boon to faith, and was enough for John (John 20: 8); the testimony of the angels would have been stronger testimony; but the crown of all was to behold Him, to hear Him, to see Him eat, hear Him speak, this was indeed the full fruit."

### 4. Its Position.

As we have already seen, the Lampstand was one of the three pieces of furniture which were in the holy place. But there is a word in Ex. 40: 24 which defined its location still more precisely, "And He put the lampstand in the tent of the congregation over against the table, on the side of the Tabernacle southward."

Like everything else in Scripture the points of the compass are referred to with a moral and spiritual significance. Briefly, we may say that the "west" is the quarter of prosperity and blessing: see Ex. 10: 19; Deut. 33: 23; Josh. 8: 12; Isa. 59: 19. The "east," the opposite quarter, tells of sharp distress and Divine judgment: see Gen. 3: 24, 13: 11, 41: 6; Ex. 10: 13, 14: 21; Isa. 46: 11. The "north"—the Hebrew word means "obscure, dark"—is the direction from which evil comes: see Jer. 1: 14, 4: 6, etc. The sunny "south," the opposite quarter from the north, tells of warmth light, and blessing: see Job 37: 17; Psa. 126: 4; Luke 12: 55; Deut. 33: 3; Acts 27: 13. It is most significant then that the Lampstand was placed on the south side of the Tabernacle, the more so when we discover that the Hebrew word for "south" means "bright, radiant"!

### 5. Its Significance.

There are a number of details which enable us to fix the typical meaning of the Lampstand. First, the fact that it was made of beaten gold and was ornamented with almonds shows that it is the suffering Christ now risen and glorified which is here foreshadowed. Second, its being set in the Holy Place intimates that it is Christ hidden from the world, enjoyed only by the priestly family. Third, its seven lamps of oil tell of the sufficiency of the Spirit as Christ's gift to His people. Fourth, the time when the Lampstand was used furnishes another sure key to its interpretation. It was for use in the Holy Place during the night: "Aaron and his sons shall order it from evening to morning before the Lord (Ex. 27: 21). It thus typified the maintenance of light within the true Sanctuary during the time that our Lord was absent from the earth, that is, while the nation of Israel is no longer God's witness here below.

That which was most prominent in connection with the Lampstand was its seven branches, supporting the lighted "lamps." These, as we have seen, foreshadowed the person and ministry of the Holy Spirit. It is this which brings out the distinctive aspect of our present type. It is the Spirit as the gift of Christ —the result of His death and resurrection—the "beaten work" and the "almonds" to His people. It is the Spirit shining in their hearts to give them "the light of the knowledge of the glory of God in the face of Jesus Christ" (2 Cor. 4: 6). It is the Spirit within the Sanctuary, glorifying Christ, taking of the things of Christ and showing them to His people. It is the operations of the Spirit directed by the glorified Son of God. The several purposes which were served by the seven lighted lamps portray the leading aspects of the Spirit's ministry to Christ's people.

First, the lighted lamps revealed the beautiful workmanship of the Lampstand itself: "And thou shalt make the seven lamps thereof: and they shall light the lamps thereof, that they may give light over against the face of it" (v. 37) cf. Numbers 8: 2. This tells us of the principal design of the Spirit's ministry toward and in the saints. As the Saviour promised, "He shall glorify Me: for He shall receive of Mine, and shall show it unto you" (John 16: 14). This He does by revealing to us the perfections of Christ, by making Him real to us, by endearing Him to our hearts. It is only by the Spirit that we are enabled to behold and enjoy the excellencies of Him who is "fairer than the children of men." It is in His light alone that we "see light" (Psa. 36: 9).

Second, the Lampstand was placed opposite the Table, so as to cast its light upon its contents: "And he put the Lampstand in the tent of the congregation over against the Table" (Ex. 40: 24). The shewbread remained on the Table seven days, when it became the food of Aaron and his sons, who were bidden to "eat in the Holy Place" (Lev. 24: 8,9). There they refreshed themselves with that which had delighted the eye of God. Can we think of them sitting down and enjoying such a feast in darkness? Impossible. Light was a necessity: without it all would have been confusion and disorder. This teaches us that it is only by the ministry and power of the Spirit that Christians can perceive Christ as the Bread of God to sustain His people. It is only by the Spirit we are enabled to feed on Christ and draw from His fulness, that the new man may be nourished and strengthened.

Third, the Lampstand is mentioned in connection with the burning of incense on the Golden-altar: "And Aaron shall burn thereon sweet incense every morning: when he dresseth the lamps, he shall burn incense on it. And when Aaron lighteth the lamps at even, he shall burn incense upon it" (Ex. 30: 7, 8). Apart from the light furnished by the Lampstand the priests could not have seen the golden altar and would have been unable to minister thereat. This altar speaks both of worship and supplication. Here too the aid of the Spirit is indispensible. Apart from Him we can neither praise nor petition Christ as we ought.

Fourth, the Lampstand is said to shed its light "before the Lord" (Ex. 40: 25). The antitype of this is specially brought before us by the Spirit in the closing book of Scripture. There we see Christ vindicating the government of God. There the "seven lamps" which are "the seven Spirits of God" are expressly said to be "burning before the Throne" (Rev. 4: 5), while in Rev. 5: 6 they are seen in connection with the Lamb as He rises to administer judgment. The Lampstand shining "before the Lord" will find its accomplishment when Christ overthrows the foes of God and reigns till He hath put all enemies under His feet. This will be during the Millennium when Christ, in the fulness of the Spirit's power, shall be manifested as the "Sun of righteousness" (Mal. 4: 2).

There is a very remarkable Scripture in Isa. 11 which gives us the final antitypical fulfilment of the sevenfold radiance of the Lampstand. There we read, "there shall come forth a rod out of the stem of Jesse, and a Branch shall grow out of his roots: And the Spirit of the Lord shall rest upon Him: The Spirit of wisdom and understanding, the Spirit of counsel and might, the Spirit of knowledge and of the fear of the Lord" (vv. 1, 2). There is here a sevenfold reference of the relation of the Holy Spirit to Christ during His Millennial reign, note v. 4. But observe carefully the arrangement here. Mark the absence of any "and" between "Him" and "the Spirit of wisdom," and so between the second and third and between the third and fourth mentionings of the Spirit. The order corresponds exactly with the construction of the seven - branched Lampstand "The Spirit of the Lord shall rest upon Him:" this is separated from the other six by the absence of a connecting "and" to what follows, reminding us of the one central stem. The next six references are arranged in three pairs (as the "ands" show), like the three pairs of branches growing out of the central stem!

### 6. Its Covering.

"And they shall take a cloth of blue, and cover the Lampstand of the light, and his lamps, and his tongs, etc., and they shall put it and all the vessels thereof within a covering of badgers' skins" (Num. 4: 9, 10). This point needs not to be developed at length as the typical significance of these coverings has been dealt with in previous articles. In the "cloth of blue" we have emphasised the Divine glory of Christ, and are reminded that only saints in priestly communion can recognize and enjoy the Light of life as the Holy One. As we see the "blue" folded and concealed in the "badgers' skins" we have a solemn portrayal of the fact that the ungodly are without any knowledge of the true Light: "The way of the wicked is as darkness" (Prov. 4: 19).

### 7. Its History.

Only twice is the Lampstand referred to after the Pentateuch is passed, but in each case the connection is a most striking one. First, in 1 Sam. 3 the Spirit has informed us that Jehovah revealed Himself to young Samuel in the Temple or Tabernacle "ere the lamp of God went out" (v. 3), and a most solemn communication did He give him. The Lord announced that He would do a thing in Israel "at which both the ears of every one that heareth it shall tingle." This "thing" was the sore judgment which fell upon the degenerate sons of Eli. The prophetic and dispensational application of this is obvious. Ere the long Night of Israel's unbelief is ended, God will bring upon them the Great Tribulation and judge them for their sins.

The second reference is in Dan. 5. Here again a night scene is presented to our view. Belshazzar, attended by his debauched courtiers and concubines, in the midst of a drunken revelry, gave orders that the "golden vessels" which had been taken from the Temple when his grandfather captured Jerusalem, should be brought in and drunk out of. Heaven's response was prompt: "In the same hour came forth fingers of a man's hand and wrote over against the Lampstand upon the plaister of the wall" (v. 5). This time it was a message of woe pronounced upon the Babylonians, pointing forward to the end of the times of the Gentiles, when the vials of God's wrath shall be poured out upon this Christ-rejecting world.

The appropriateness of these two messages of judgment being linked with the Lampstand is evident. God is light and in Him is no darkness at all (1 John 1: 5). "God is light" means, He is ineffably holy, and therefore must punish sin: it brings before us the other side of the truth. Light exposes and burns as well as warms and illumines! For believers the Light is the Light of life; but for unbelievers it will yet blind and overwhelm: that is why the Judgment-seat in the great Assize is a "great white Throne. How thankful should every Christian reader be that we are "children of light." Christ is the Light to His people—Prov. 4: 18, 2 Cor. 4: 6; in His people—Eph. 1: 18, 5: 13, 14; through His people—Matt. 5: 14-16.

—ARTHUR W. PINK.

## THE GREATEST MIRACLE.

We have two short texts for to-night. The first is found in Psalm 136, the first part of the 4th verse: the second I will announce, God willing, a little later.

"To Him who alone doeth great wonders." The God of Scripture, unlike the lifeless and useless idols of men is a wonder-working God. He that sitteth in the heavens performs great marvels. There have been many professing Christians who were seriously exercised over the subject of miracles. It is one of the points in our faith that is commonly assaulted by the enemies of God. Much that has been written against miracles by infidels has shaken the faith of not a few. I am thankful to say that by the mercy of God the writings of such men as Voltaire and Ingersoll and, more recently, Charles Bradlaugh and Robert Blatchford, have never shaken my own faith a particle. It seems to me that if you predicate an Almighty God, that miracles are inevitable. They are the natural and the necessary consequences.

Now the question we are to take up tonight is, What is the greatest miracle that God has ever wrought? Undoubtedly it is a difficult matter for the finite mind to attempt comparisons between things which are supernatural. I rather doubt whether we are fully capable of measuring the difference between one miracle and another, and no doubt for that reason our opinions vary considerably. Some, no doubt, would point to the many miracles recorded in the Old Testament Scriptures such as the plagues of God upon Egypt: —the turning of the water into blood; the miracle that He performed at the Red Sea, when by the breath of His nostrils the waters stood up in solid walls and His people passed through dry-shod, and then when at His command the wind came and caused those walls to collapse and overthrew the enemies of His people;

the wonderful miracle of the capture of Jericho when, without a shot being fired or a blow being struck, that mighty stronghold of the Canaanites fell before them; the miracle of the sun standing still in the days of Joshua; the miracle of Elijah being taken up to heaven without seeing death; the miracle of the three Hebrews yonder in the fiery furnace in Babylon and yet being unharmed or unhurt; the miraculous preservation of Jonah and his being cast forth on to the dry land after three days and nights inside of a marine monster. Yes, He alone doeth great wonders.

Before I pass on to the others, let me just seek to make a brief practical application of that, for I am not speaking here just to instruct your minds or hold your attention, but by the grace of God give out that which will help your spiritual lives. Our God is a wonder-working God: then why do not we trust Him more? Our God is One with whom all things are possible: then why have we so little confidence in Him? O beloved brethren and sisters, He is able: everything is at His command: then doubt Him not but ask great things of Him and expect great things from Him.

No doubt there are others who would appeal to the wonders that were performed by the Lord Jesus Christ in the days of His public ministry as recorded in the four gospels: His walking upon the waters, the turning of the water into wine, the feeding of the multitudes with a few loaves and fishes, the healing of most desperate cases of sickness, the giving of sight to the blind, the cleansing of the leper, the raising of the dead. Yes, those too were great marvels. "He alone doeth great wonders."

And again let me pause for a moment and make application. Of old it was written, "His name shall be called Wonderful"—and a most appropriate designation. O my friends, the Saviour that God has provided for sinners is no feeble one. As His own Word tells us in Isaiah 63:1, He is "mighty to save." No case ever yet baffled the Great Physician: none was too far gone in sin for His long and strong arm to reach down to deliver. O let no poor sinner here to-night listen to one of the favourite lies of the devil, that you have sinned beyond the hope of mercy. The blood of Jesus Christ, God's Son, cleanseth from all sin. Put Him to the test for yourself. Christ never yet turned away one sinner that ever sought Him with all the heart.

But what is the greatest miracle that God ever wrought? I suppose some would appeal to the miracle of creation, when God by the mere fiat of His lips called this vast and stupendous universe into existence—formed it all out of nothing. Yes, indeed, that is a wonder, and a great wonder. "Through faith we understand that the worlds were framed by the word of God, so that things which are seen were not made of things which do appear," therefore we bow in wonderment and awe before our wonder-working God. And yet I believe there are still greater wonders than those that I have just mentioned. There are some who feel that the greatest miracle that God ever wrought is in the realm of the new creation when He puts forth His hand and delivers from death and saves a hell-deserving sinner. That is indeed a wonder of wonders. First of all it is a wonder of divine wisdom for nothing short of divine omniscience could ever have devised a way whereby justice and mercy might be reconciled. None but God Himself could possibly have solved the problem that the salvation of sinners presented: as to how His righteous law could be enforced, its penalty insisted upon, the demands of His justice maintained, and yet the guilty dealt with in mercy. That was indeed a miracle of wisdom that devised a way whereby all the attributes of God could be glorified. Not only so, but it was a miracle of grace that the Just should suffer for the unjust, that God's people should receive everything for nothing, without money, without price. Truly that is a miracle of grace, and not only a miracle of wisdom and a miracle of grace, but truly a miracle of power. What but divine power could transform enmity and hatred into love? What but divine power could turn our wayward stubborn wills, melt our stony hearts, and free us from the bondage of sin and Satan? Truly that is a great miracle, for He alone doeth great wonders.

Then I suppose there are others (and I think they are right) who would say the greatest miracles that God ever performed were in connection with the person of His own beloved Son. Take first of all the miracle of the incarnation. O what a stupendous wonder was that when God became man; that the Ancient of Days became a little infant; that the Lord of Glory nestled in a woman's arms; that the Word was made flesh; O what a wonder! And more wonderful still that He should become the Son of Man and yet not be begotten by a man; that He should partake of human nature and be man in the real and full sense of the word; that He should be made in all things like unto His brethren and yet have no actual human father. True, that was a miracle, a miracle that altogether transcends the grasp of the finite mind, and before it we can only bow in adoring worship. Still greater is that miracle when we bear in mind the fact that the incarnate Son of God was made in the likeness of sinful flesh without partaking of the slightest degree of sin. We are shapen in iniquity; not so with Him. He entered the Virgin's womb and yet contracted no defilement. I sometimes liken that miracle to a parable from nature. You have seen a stagnant pool of water and the pure glorious rays of the sun shining, not only upon it, but into it, and yet those pure rays of the sun being undefiled and unsullied by the mud and mire of the water. And so He became the Seed of Abraham and the Seed of David and yet escaped all contamination and corruption that sin had brought into human nature. Very well, that too was a miracle.

There are others who think that the resurrection of the Lord Jesus Christ was a greater miracle still; that after dying the death that He died, that after being in the grave for three days He should suddenly and by His own inherent power burst asunder the trappings of death and come forth triumphant from the tomb. The greatness of that miracle is increased when we think of the efforts men made to retain Him—in the sealing of the tomb and the setting of the watch: increased still more as we think (and I believe we are justified in so doing) of the concentrated and determined efforts that the enemy, Satan, made to hold Him captive in the sepulchre. But He is greater and stronger than the strong man and destroyed him that had the power of death—on the third day demonstrated that He is indeed the Resurrection and the Life.

And yet, dear friends, I believe there is one miracle that I have not yet mentioned that is greater than all those others—wondrous and stupendous though they be. I grant you that the wonderment of it is not so apparent, nor are we as familiar with that aspect of the subject. I refer to the death of the incarnate Son of God. Much has been written upon the atoning sufficiency and the divine value and the wonderment of that death, and yet little or nothing seems to have been written upon the miracle of His death. I suppose the very word "miracle" as linked with the death of Christ has a strange sound upon some of your ears, and yet, my friends, it was a miracle, and, in my judgment, the miracle of miracles. Before I endeavor to present to you some of the proofs and the evidence that demonstrate it to be the greatest miracle, let me, if time allows, just speak of one or two other aspects concerning that death; and that brings me to our second text in Romans 5.6:—"Christ died for the ungodly."

Now I am not going to take up the death of Christ to-night in its doctrinal significance (if the Lord permits, ere long I hope to take up that important subject) nor am I going to speak of its atoning significance: but I just want to speak tonight on the fact and the act of Christ's death: and I think there are four words that sum it all up. His death was natural, His death was unnatural, His death was preternatural, and His death was supernatural. Now let me just briefly say a few words upon each point.

When I say that His death was natural, I simply mean that it was a real death. There are those who deny that, but with their denials I shall not be concerned this evening. It is because we are so familiar with the fact itself that the very statement of it seems commonplace and trivial. But when we remember that the One who died upon the cross was Jehovah's Fellow, the incarnate Son of God, the question at once arises, How was it possible for Jehovah's Fellow to die? He was God—God the Son. How could God the Son die? The answer is, by becoming incarnate, by taking upon Himself flesh, by being made man. He who was in the form of God thought it not robbery to be equal with God; but made Himself of no reputation and took upon Him the form of a servant, and was made in the likeness of men: and being found in fashion as a man He humbled Himself and became obedient unto death, even the death of the cross. It was by becoming incarnate that He became capable of dying, and that He did actually die, the Scriptures affirm again and again. I do not know what your thoughts have been concerning it, but it seems to me that one reason at least why God permitted that Roman soldier to thrust his spear into the side of the Saviour was to furnish us with unequivocal evidence that He actually died. I believe it was for the same reason God permitted His Son to remain in the grave for three days and nights, viz., to furnish conclusive proof that, as the Scriptures state in I. Corinthians 15, He died according to the Scriptures and was buried and rose again the third day according to the Scriptures. In the first place, the death of Christ was natural inasmuch as it was a real and an actual death.

But now in the second place the death of Christ was altogether **unnatural.** By that I mean this, that death itself had no legitimate claim upon Him. His death was **abnormal.** It is true that in becoming man He became capable of dying, but death had no legitimate claim upon Him. Death is the wages of sin and He was the sinless One. Therefore I repeat it. Death had no claim upon Him. Christ is the only Man who has ever walked this earth since the days of Adam who had no debt of nature to pay. Galatians 4: 4 tells us that He was made under the law. What were the terms of the law? He that doeth these things shall live. And He did do them: He kept the law perfectly, constantly. The law was unable to find any cause in Him whatsoever so far as His own person was concerned to pass sentence of death upon Him. Even Pilate, His judge, announced, "I find no fault in Him," and the very sentence that he passed was an outrage against human law and justice. So that I say in the second place the death of Christ was altogether unnatural, abnormal, outside the realm of the ordinary, inasmuch as death being the wages of sin and Christ being the Sinless One, and inasmuch as the One who kept the law was entitled to live—and He kept it—therefore for Him to die was unnatural.

In the third place (I am being very brief in the first three points) the death of Christ was **preternatural.** I mean by that that the death of Christ was appointed and ordered for Him by God beforehand. Christ was the Lamb that was slain from the foundation of the world. Before Adam was created the fall was anticipated. Before sin entered this world God made full provision in His own purpose for the salvation of His sinning people. In the eternal counsels of Deity it was decreed that Christ as a Saviour for sinners should die, the Just for the unjust. It was in view of the coming death of Christ we are told in Romans 3: 25 that God passed over the sins of His people in Old Testament times. Let us just turn to that verse for a moment because there are few who understand it. Romans 3, verse 25:—"Whom God hath set forth to be a propitiation through faith in His blood, to declare His righteousness for the remission of sins that are past"—"remission of sins that are past." Now there are many who take that verse and teach from it that all that Christ did on the cross was to die for those sins that we commit up to the time of conversion—our past sins —and that if we sin after conversion we have to ask forgiveness to obtain it, and if we fail to, then our sins are upon our own heads and we shall eternally perish: and this is one of the verses that those who teach such a horrible error appeal to for support. Now the sins that are past refer not to the sins of our past lives, but to the sins that God's people committed before Christ came here. **We** are saved to-day by a faith that looks back to the blood that was shed at Calvary: the saints of the Old Testament dispensation were saved by a faith that looked **forward** to the blood that was to be shed at Calvary: and just as God now remits sins (puts away our sins) to-day because of the blood that was shed there, so God passed over the sins of His Old Testament people on the credit of the blood that was to be shed at the cross.

Now in the fourth place, and this is what I am specially anxious in the closing few minutes to make clear to you, the death of Christ was not only natural, real; and unnatural, abnormal, in the nature of things; and preternatural, because God had appointed it from the foundation of the world, but the death of Christ was **supernatural.** It was a stupendous marvel that Christ should die, for His death was altogether unique. His holy Person is different from all others. He was born in a manner different from anyone else; His life was different from all other lives; and His death was unique, for in all things He has the preeminence. Now the first point, and the main point is this: Every member of Adam's race that has ever died was entirely **passive** in death: it could not be otherwise. When the King of Terrors lays his clammy hands upon us, man has no power whatever to resist. Neither will-power, nor wealth, the skill of science, nor the ministrations of loved ones can cope with death. When death comes man is passive, helpless, impotent. But it was far otherwise with Christ when He died. In death itself **He was active,** not passive—the victor, not the victim. Scripture says that He **offered** Himself a sacrifice unto God. He **gave** Himself for the Church, He **poured out** His soul unto death. No one else ever did that: in every other instance their souls were taken from them. He poured out His soul unto death. He dismissed His spirit as a king dismissing a servant. "Into Thy hands I commit My spirit."

Herein lies the uniqueness of Christ's death and the glory of the Cross. O, brothers and sisters, the Cross was the place of a glorious victory; not the empty sepulchre, the cross was the place of a glorious victory, the triumph of weak but sinless flesh over the worst that men and Satan could inflict. Listen, my friends, Christ did not die from a broken heart. Christ did not die from the thrust of the Roman spear. Christ did not die from the attack of the Serpent. No man took His life from Him. He laid it down of Himself, and it required a miracle for Him so to do. To me it is far more wonderful that Emmanuel should die than that He should rise again from the dead. The second chapter of Acts says it was not possible that He should be holden of death, but O what a wonder of wonders that He ever entered the portals of death! He could only do so by an act of His own volition, by an act of His own power, by a direct miracle. It was the Prince of Life that died, the fountain, the source of life, and in the nature of the case man could not take His life from Him; He laid it down of Himself. And therefore I say that the death of Christ was a supernatural death and, in my personal judgment, the miracle of miracles.

Have you ever noticed in the first Epistle to Corinthians and the first chapter, verses 23 and 24, that we are there told that Christ crucified, not Christ risen, is the power of God! And nowhere was the power of God more vividly demonstrated and more gloriously manifested than when the Prince of Life died. Have you ever noticed in the Book of Revelation that all heaven is moved to its profoundest praise, not when the King of Kings comes forth crowned with many diadems, but when it sees the Lamb standing as it had been slain! And whether or not the Spirit of God grips your souls as He has mine with the amazing marvel, the miracle of the Prince of Life dying, when we enter the glory I believe that will be the source of our greatest wonderment, the Lamb that was slain.

Now just a closing word of application. For whom did He die? And the text, our second text, answers. "Christ died for the ungodly." Not for the righteous, for there are none: not for the good, for in ourselves, judged by the perfect standard of God, there is not one on all the earth. "Christ died for the ungodly." O what a blessed gospel! And my closing word is this:—What does the death of Christ mean to you? Have you a personal and a saving interest in it? Are you able to say by the grace and Spirit of God, "Who His own self bare my sins in His own body on the tree"? The 3rd of Romans and the 25th verse says, He is a propitiation **through faith in His** blood. Is your faith in His blood? Are you resting alone, are you relying on the precious blood of God's Lamb as the only ground of your acceptance with God? "Whom God hath set forth to be a propitiation." (That means an atonement) "through faith in His blood." O, friends are you trusting in the blood of Christ? Have you renounced all your own works, all your own efforts, to win the esteem of God? Is your faith in the crucified Lamb? O, if it is not, look away from self and behold to-night the Lamb of God who alone taketh away the sin of the world. "Not by works of righteousness which we have done, but according to His mercy He hath saved us" is the testimony of God's redeemed. "For by grace (unmerited favor) are ye saved through faith; and that not of yourselves, it is the gift of God; not of works, lest any man should boast." O, dear friends, if God has drawn into this place to-night a sin-sick soul, someone who is weary with what this world has to offer, someone who feels his own misery and wretchedness, his own unfitness to stand before a holy God, his own unpreparedness to die, and if that one is asking from his heart, What must I do? O, what is the remedy for such as I? Listen, "Come unto Me, all ye that labor and are heavy laden," says Christ, "and I will give you rest." Then come! O may the Spirit of God put forth His divine drawing power and bring some one here to-night to the feet of Christ and He shall have all the praise.

A Sermon preached by the Editor in Sydney.

## ABIDING IN CHRIST.

The complaints which supplant the songs of love and joy that ought to dwell on the tongues of the redeemed even, here, are, alas! not groundless; and we would not have them attempt to conceal or forget their actual condition in these evil times, by feigned songs. Yet we ask, Why should there be such complaints among those who are called to rejoice in the Lord always? Why should there be such coldness of love, such feebleness in testimony, such failure in service, such joylessness of worship, so little of the power of prayer, so many doubts and fears and tormenting cares, such unrest, darkness, barrenness, and poverty to be wailed, when the strength and fulness of God is the supply provided for us, when the peace and joy of Christ remain for us, and when it can still be said to us. "All things are yours; and ye are Christ's, and Christ is God's"?

There are many proximate causes which might be enumerated, and these should not be overlooked. It behoves us to search ourselves thoroughly, and judge ourselves unsparingly before the Lord. But in this place we would at once reach out to the ultimate reason, and in doing so we reach the remedy also. The remedy is found in the Lord's loving charge, "Abide in Me, and I in you;" and it is evident that the ultimate reason of the lamentable condition of things among us must be found in the neglect of this charge, for the Lord says: "He that abideth in Me and I in him, the same bringeth forth much fruit; for without Me ye can do nothing."

A correspondent asks: "What is the precise meaning of Abide in Christ?" We might answer by asking first of all: What is the precise meaning of "coming to Christ"? The Lord in one place makes it equivalent to believing in Him: "He that cometh to Me shall never hunger, and he that believeth on Me shall never thirst." It implies the abandonment of every other rest, and refuge, help and hope, for CHRIST; the severance of all other alliances and dependences for CHRIST—for a confiding rest in Him, union with Him, and appropriation of Him, in all His fulness; and abiding in Him is continuing there and thus. For we do not come to receive pardon, righteousness, strength, healing, and eternal life as blessings from Christ, which, having received, we can use and enjoy independently of Him. The truth in the case is illustrated by His beautiful simile: "I am the vine, ye are the branches." It is not as though a dead branch we are touched by Him into life, and planted to flourish as an independent vine. It is rather grafted on the true vine and incorporated with it; so that the life and fertility of the vine are manifested in the verdure which adorns the branch, and the rich cluster which it bears. So the believer is admonished, "as the branch cannot bear fruit of itself, except it abide in the vine, no more can ye except ye abide in Me." And this figure also illustrates the two-fold aspect of the relation, "Abide in Me and I in you," the branch in the vine, the life and fertility of the vine in the branch.

We need scarcely say that the fruit borne by the believer as a branch of the true vine, is one and the same thing with what is elsewhere styled the fruit of the Spirit; for, practically, in both aspects of the relation—our abiding in Him and His abiding in us, is by the Spirit, "For by one Spirit we are all baptized into one body;" and as the branches in the vine make one vine, so the members in the body in union with the Head make one Christ; and "Hereby we know that He abideth in us, by the Spirit that He hath given us." In speaking of the office of the Spirit, the Lord said: "He shall testify of Me; He shall glorify Me: for He shall receive of Mine and show it unto you." And the fruit of the Spirit is but the manifestation of Christ in us. The charge, "Abide in Me, and I in you," is not an announcement of the abstract doctrine of our oneness with Christ which we are formally to acknowledge; but it implies a cherished consciousness of the fact; the occupation of the soul not with benefits derived from Him, but with Christ Himself as containing them all; a living trust and dependence—walking in fellowship with Him, leaning our helplessness on His ability to save to the uttermost, bringing our emptiness to Him in whom it pleased the Father that all fulness should dwell. Believer, "all things are yours;" but you can use and enjoy them only as you live and move and have your being IN HIM.

Abide in Him as your righteousness. He does not communicate to believers certain qualities and qualifications in virtue of which they are justified and accepted by themselves. It is not as though a ruined bankrupt were, by the counsels of a wise friend, put in the way of paying his own debts and amassing a fortune: but rather as though a princely bridegroom should discharge the obligations of his bankrupt bride, and should then endow her with all his goods, invest her with all his honour, make her the partner of all that he is and has. The twain are one; but all that she is and has is in him. Christ has put away sin by the sacrifice of Himself, and He is our righteousness; to us in Him there is no condemnation; we are accepted in the Beloved; we are made the righteousness of God in Him. "The Lord," says Bunyan, "led me into the knowledge of the mystery of the union with Christ—that I was joined to Him—that I was bone of His bone, and flesh of His flesh. By this also my faith in Him as my righteousness was the more confirmed; for if He and I were one, then His righteousness was mine,

His merits mine, His victory also mine. Now could I see myself in heaven and on earth at once, in heaven by my Christ, my risen head, my righteousness and life, though on earth by my body or person."

Abide in Christ as your wisdom. He is not like one of the masters of the schools who has bequeathed to their disciples a system of philosophy or theology, or who had embodied their wisdom and experience in practical maxims to be studied and learned. He is a living fountain of wisdom, and we are called to abide in Him and to let His words abide in us; like Mary sitting still at His feet to learn of Him; not dead learning, to load the memory or engage the intellect, but living truth to sanctify, mould, and guide the heart. Thus abiding in Him and being thus taught by Him, we shall mourn the failure of our testimony and service. There will be an unction from the Holy One in all which will make itself owned as the power of God.

Thus abiding in Him we will never lose sight of His footprints, "as He has left us an example that we should follow His steps." Such a following will not be an affected mimicry of His acts. "He that saith he abideth in Him ought himself also so to walk even as He walked." Such a walk will be holy as well as wise, and it will be lowly and loving. It will be seen that the same mind is in us as was also in Christ Jesus. It will be seen that we live, yet not we, but Christ liveth in us. Believer walk with Him, hand in hand, in loving fellowship. Live in the conscious nearness of the Lord as your living and loving friend. Go nowhere and into no society if, in order to go, you must part company with Christ. And yet you may go anywhere, in fellowship with Him who was reproached as "the friend of sinners," when you go upon the errand of "the Saviour of sinners." Abide in Him, and that will be far aloof from the world, or rather it will be far above the world, in conscious oneness with Him who is at God's right hand, your life, your strength, your all.

Abide in Him as your rest and peace. We are taught every day that we must cease from man—even from redeemed man. If we lean upon the creature, we find only disappointment and sorrow. But we can cast not only our burdens but ourselves upon Him. How blessed it is to know practically that the Good Shepherd, when He hath found that which had gone astray, "laying it upon His shoulders rejoicing." If we consciously abide there, and He carries both us and our burdens, there can be no more complaints of our feebleness—of the toil of the journey—of the roughness and steepness of the mountain-path that leads homeward. There is rest in His might and His peace keeps the heart.

These two are inseparable—our abiding in Christ and His abiding in us. The soul never says exultingly, "My Beloved is mine," without adding lovingly, "and I am His." We never appropriate Christ without acknowledging that we are not our own, but bought with a price. As we live in Him we live not unto ourselves, but unto Him who died for us and rose again. And this does not mean merely that you are occupied with His service, doing His will, and aiming at His glory, but also that you are simply an instrument in His hand, glorying in your infirmity, that the power of Christ may rest upon you—in yourself no more than an axe or a hammer without a hand to wield it.

Abide in Him, and you will not only have a title to the fulness there is in Him, but you will have the use and enjoyment of it all, as having nothing, yet possessing all things. Yes, believer, "all things are yours;" yet it often seems as though these treasures had been locked up and the key were lost. Here is the key that unlocks them—or rather they stand open, and here is the opening of your hand to receive them: "If ye abide in Me and My words abide in you, ye shall ask what ye will, and it shall be done unto you." Could Divine bounty go farther in opening up to you a Divine fulness?

To exhaust this subject would be to exhaust the fulness of God; which is just to say that, at the best, we can only dip our shallow vessel into the ripple along the shore of this infinite. We therefore only add, as we break off an unfinished and unending meditation: Abide in Him, and you will dwell in love and joy; and thus you will not only anticipate heaven in your own soul, but reflect something of its radiance on the darkness of the earth. When we speak of dwelling in love, we refer to the exceeding great love wherewith He loved us. Many are both torturing and chilling their hearts in vain attempts to analyze their own feelings and affections. A child in years who had learned in another school, when asked if he loved Jesus, answered: "I believe I do love Jesus, but Jesus loves me; that is what I think most of." Oh! how blessed to continue in His love, and to know that His intercession prevails with the Father, "that the love wherewith Thou lovest Me may be in them, and I in them!" Then gazing on the Divine glories and perfections without fear in that embrace the heart glows with adoring love, and can be satisfied with nothing short of the vision of His unveiled glory, the cup of His unhindered love. Dwelling in love, you will love. The heart in its native selfishness is an iceberg locked up in itself and blighting all around it; but in this love, like the iceberg in the summer sun, the heart thaws and dissolves and flows out as the waters of Siloah that go softly, to murmur His praise and refresh the souls of those whom we recognise as the representatives of Him whom we love unseen. Need we say how the will of all who dwell there must become identified with His, and how holy and unblamable a life in Christ must be? "Whosoever abideth in Him sinneth not."

"And now little children, abide in Him; that when He shall appear, we may have confidence, and not be ashamed before Him at His coming."

—Waymarks in the Wilderness, 1865.

## THE JEW IN PROPHECY.

#### Hosea 3: 4, 5.

In seeking the text for my sermons for this morning and evening I desired to select one which would present a real difficulty to those who are so anxious to "spiritualize" (as they call it) those scriptures in the O.T. where Israel is mentioned: I mean those who imagine that "Israel" is only another name for the Christian Church. Really, the word "spiritualize," in such a connection, is quite out of place; "allegorise" would be better, "vapourise" would be more accurate—for such a process evacuates many a passage of its real signification; "burglarise" would be truer still, for those who adopt this method are very dishonest. When they come across some precious promise which Jehovah made to Israel of old, they say, "That belongs to us: it is the spiritual Israel who is there in view. But when they meet with some woe, judgment, or curse pronounced upon Israel—often in the same chapter as the promises—they are not willing to appropriate such, and apply it to the literal or carnal Israel. Not content with the exceeding great and precious promises recorded in the N.T., Christians go to the O.T. and often pilfer those which are the peculiar property of the Jews, so that "burglarizing" more accurately describes this method which has been wrongly termed "spiritualising."

Now in our text there are some statements which will severely tax the ingenuity of the "spiritualisers." The first part of it contains solemn threatenings of judgment: hence I suppose that all present will allow it is the literal Israel that is there in view. Most assuredly its language could not apply to the Christian Church, for it has not abode many days "without a King," nor has it been many days "without a Sacrifice." But the literal Israel has!

This morning I called attention to twelve lines of prophecy which have already been fulfilled in the history of the Jews. Centuries before those events came to pass, it was expressly foretold that the Jews would reject their Messiah, be conquered by the Romans, be dispersed abroad, be wanderers throughout the earth, be severely oppressed and persecuted, become a proverb and a byword. It was predicted that while they were exiles from their own land that God would preserve them in the lands of their enemies (Ezek. 11: 16); and that they should not be amalgamated with or assimilated by the Gentiles (Num. 23: 9). From this I pointed out the inevitable inference to be drawn is, that God has miraculously preserved the Jews for some special purpose, for some future destiny.

God does not work miracles for the mere sake of performing them: He always has a wise and good end in view. That the preservation of Israel all through the centuries is a Divine miracle —an unparalleled and perpetual miracle ——scarcely needs arguing. On no other ground can their survival as a distinct people be accounted for. Every weapon that their enemies could forge has been used against them. Every engine of destruction that Satan could devise for the extermination of them from the earth has been employed. The hatred they have experienced, the oppressions they have endured, the persecutions they have suffered—not occasionally but repeatedly; not here and there, but everywhere they have gone—is without any parallel in all history. And yet they have survived!

Now the same scriptures which foretold God's past and present judgments on the Jews, also announce His future mercy and grace toward them. Just as definitely and clearly as their Dispersion was predicted, so their Restoration is promised. Just as accurately and literally as the former prophecies have been fulfilled, so will be the latter. Just as surely as they have "abode many days without a king, or sacrifice," so shall they "seek the Lord their God, and David their king, and shall fear the Lord and His goodness in the latter days." Before turning to these prophecies, let me say that two attempts have been made to neutralise their force:

First, there are those who have affirmed that all the prophecies which announced the restoration of the Jews to Palestine were fulfilled at their return from the Babylonian captivity in the days of Ezra and Nehemiah. But this was not the case. There were many prophecies concerning Israel's restoration which were not then fulfilled. Turn to Isa. 11: 11-16 and read the same carefully. There are at least five details in it which found no fulfilment in the days of Ezra and Nehemiah. First, the context plainly shows, see especially verses 4 and 10, that the reference is to a period long after Ezra and Nehemiah, namely, the advent of Christ. Second, the words "the second time" conclusively show that a later restoration is here in view. Third, the regathering here predicted is a general one and not a local—from Babylon only. Fourth, the restoration foretold in this passage includes both the House of Israel and the House of Judah: that of Nehemiah's did not, for the Ten Tribes were not then delivered. Fifth, note the words of verses 14 to 16: nothing like this occurred in the days of Ezra and Nehemiah.

The second attempt to neutralise those prophecies which announced the literal restoration of Israel, has been by a process of "spiritualizing" (?) and applying them to the spiritual prosperity of the Christian Church. Such have been guilty of the very sin with which Christ charged the Pharisees—they have made void the Word of God by their "traditions." I shall now refer to many passages in both Old and New Testaments and must leave you to judge whether they view the Christian Church or whether they contemplate the lineal descendants of Abraham. May the Spirit of God grant you discernment.

Lev. 26: 44-46. Deut. 30: 1-9. Isa. 14: 1-3. Jer. 16: 14-16. Jer. 23: 7-8. Jer. 31: 27-40. Look again at v. 28: who are they over whom the Lord has watched to "pluck up and to break down"? The very same people to whom He here promises that He will "build and plant"—the literal Israel. Look at v. 32; with whose "fathers" did Jehovah make a covenant when He took them by the hand out of Egypt? With the identical people to whom He here promises to make a new covenant! Look at vv. 38 and 39: how can the "tower of Hananeel" and the "hill Gareb" be spiritualised? And what mystical meaning can be attached to the "horse gate" in v. 40? If it is not the literal and actual Jerusalem which is here in view, what language could give expression to it? See further Jer. 32: 37-44. Ezek. 11: 16-18. Dan. 12: 1. Hosea 3: 5. Joel 3: 16-21. Amos 9: 11-15. Obad. 17. Micah 7: 18-20. Nah. 1: 15. Zeph. 3: 16-20. Hag. 2: 6-9. Zech. 2: 10-13.

The same restoration of the Jews to Palestine and to Jehovah's favour is just as clearly taught in the New Testament. See Matt. 23: 37-39. The same One who here declared "your house is left unto you desolate" affirmed that they should see Him again when they said "Blessed is He that cometh in the name of the Lord": and most surely none will use such language as this at the end of time, when the Day of Judgment has dawned. Luke 21: 24: why use the qualifying word "until" if Jerusalem is to be trodden down forever?

Acts 3: 17-21: note that these words were said (see v. 12) to "men of Israel." Here the apostle assured the Jews that upon their repentance, God would send Jesus Christ to them and that times of refreshing would come from His presence. Acts 15: 14-17. What could be plainer than this? First, a people is being taken out from the Gentiles: this refers to God's work of grace in the present dispensation. Second, after this people has been taken out, the Lord returns and restores Israel. Romans 11: 25-29: these words are so plain they call for no comment. 2 Cor. 3: 13-16: here we have the Divine promise that the veil which is now over Israel's heart, "shall be taken away." Finally, in Rev. 7: 1-4 we have a record of God's first act of mercy when He once more resumes His dealings with Israel.

There are unmistakable evidences that the restoration of the Jews to Palestine has already begun and is even now well on its way. In 1897 the great Zionist Movement was inaugurated, supported by leading Jews all over the world. At their first Congress in Basle, Switzerland, on Aug. 28 of that year, the Jews solemnly proclaimed to the world that they are a nation and that: "The aim of Zionism is to create for the Jewish people a publicly recognised and legally secured home in Palestine upon a national basis of its own." No such previous organised effort had been made. Since then tens of thousands of Jews have settled in Palestine.

In November, 1917, God made it clear to those who have intelligence in the Signs of the Times what was His leading design in the great war. Then it was that Jerusalem was freed by General Allanby from the hand of the Turk in a way that was truly startling. In consequence, Palestine to-day enjoys the protection of Great Britain. As a result, there are more Jews in Jerusalem to-day than there have ever been during the past nineteen hundred years. During the last seven years eighty thousand Jews have entered Palestine, which makes their present population there almost two hundred thousand.

In 1923 there was another most striking providential interposition on the part of God in behalf of His ancient people. One of the principal methods by which Jehovah rules in the kingdoms of men, is by opening and shutting. In Rev. 3: 7 God is presented as "He that openeth and none shutteth, and shutteth and none openeth." In 1917 God opened the door into Palestine for the Jew; but many of them in Russia and other European countries availed not themselves of it: moved by greed of gold they preferred going to America. But in 1923 the U.S.A. imposed most stringent restrictions on the immigration laws. Little did that government realize the Hand of God guiding them and His purpose in it. Their idea was to restrict and curtail the incoming of all nations; but God was closing the door against the Jews! The result has been that, while in the preceding ten years one hundred thousand Jews annually entered the U.S.A., their quota is now limited to nine thousand per year! The Jew is the key to international politics and more and more is coming into his own. In the meantime let Christians give the Gospel to this neglected people and pray for the peace of Jerusalem—Isa. 62: 6, 7.

N.B.—The above is a digest of a sermon preached by the Editor in Sydney.

## Jude 11.

This verse describes three of the marks found on the apostates of these last days. The "Way of Cain" is that of seeking acceptance before God on the ground of our own doings: it is ignoring the blood of the Lamb. The "error of Baalam" is the love of money: it is hiring out as the servants of men. The "gainsaying of Korah" is open rebellion against the revealed will of God—see Num. 16. The verbs here are very solemn. Into the way of Cain, the apostates have "gone"; into the error of Baalam, they "ran greedily"; in the gainsaying of Korah, they shall "perish". Cain acknowledged that God's punishment was greater than he could bear. God visited the error of Baalam with a fearful and destroying plague. Unto Korah and his company the earth opened her mouth, and they went down alive into the pit!

---

We shall value the daily prayers of all Christian readers that the Lord may endow the Editor with all-needed wisdom, grace and guidance in the preparation of each issue of this Magazine, and that He will greatly increase its circulation.

But our text is not to be limited to the literal seed of Abraham: it has reference to the whole "Israel of God" (Gal. 6: 16). The saints of this present Day of Salvation also unite in saying, "Who remembered us in our low estate." How "low" was our "estate" by nature! As fallen creatures we lay in our misery and wretchedness, unable to deliver or help ourselves. But, in wondrous grace, God took pity on us. His strong arm reached down and rescued us. He came to where we lay, saw us, and had compassion on us (Luke 10: 33). Therefore can each Christian say, "He brought me up also out of an horrible pit, out of the miry clay, and set my feet upon a rock, and established my goings" (Psa. 40: 2).

And why did He "remember" us? The very word "remember" tells of previous thoughts of love and mercy towards us. As it was with the children of Israel in Egypt, so it was with us in our ruined condition by nature. He "remembered" His covenant, that covenant into which He had entered with our Surety from everlasting. As we read in Titus 1: 2 of eternal life "which God, that cannot lie, promised before the world was." Promised to Christ, that He would give that eternal life to those for whom our covenant Head should transact. Yes, God "remembered" that He had "chosen us in Him before the foundation of the world" (Eph. 1: 4), therefore did He, in due time, bring us from death unto life.

Yet this blessed word goes beyond our initial experience of God's saving grace. Historically, our text refers not only to God remembering His people while they were in Egypt, but also, as the context shows, while they were in the Wilderness, on their way to the Promised Land. Israel's experiences in the desert but foreshadow the saints' walk through this hostile world. And Jehovah's "remembrance" of them, manifested in the daily supply of their every need, adumbrated the rich provisions of His grace for us while we journey to our Home on High. Our present estate, here on earth, is but a lowly one, for we do not now reign as kings. Yet, is our God ever mindful of us, and hourly does He minister to us.

"Who remembered us in our low estate." Not always are we permitted to dwell upon the mount. As in the natural world, so in our experiences. Bright and sunny days give place to dark and cloudy ones: summer is followed by winter. Disappointments, losses, afflictions, bereavements came our way, and we were brought low. And ofttimes just when we seemed to most need the comfort of friends, they failed us. Those we counted on to help, forgot us. But, even then, there was One "who remembered us" and showed Himself to be "the same yesterday and to-day and forever," and then did we prove afresh that "His mercy endureth forever."

"Who remembered us in our low estate." There are some who may read these lines that will think of another application of these words: namely, the time when you left your first love, when your heart grew cold, and your life became worldly. When you were in a sadly backslidden state. Then, indeed, was your estate "a low" one; yet even then did our faithful God "remember" thee. Yes, each of us has cause to say with the Psalmist "He restoreth my soul; He leadeth me in the paths of righteousness for His name's sake" (23: 3).

"Who remembered us in our low estate." Still another application of these words may be made, namely, to the last great crisis of the saint, as he passes out of this world. As the vital spark of the body grows dim and nature fails, then too is our "estate" low. But then also the Lord remembereth us, for "His mercy endureth for ever." Man's extremity is but God's opportunity. His strength is made perfect in our weakness. It is then that he "remembers" us by making good His comforting promise, "Fear thou not, for I am with thee; be not dismayed, for I am thy God; I will strengthen thee, yea, I will help thee; yea, I will uphold thee with the right hand of My righteousness" (Isa. 41: 10).

"Who remembered us in our low estate." Surely this text will furnish us with suitable words to express our thanksgiving when we are at Home, present with the Lord. How we shall then praise Him for His covenant faithfulness, His matchless grace, and His loving kindness, for having "remembered us in our low estate"! Then shall we know, even as we are known. Our very memories will be renewed, perfected, and we shall "remember all the way the Lord our God hath led us" (Deut. 8:2), recalling with gratitude and joy His faithful remembrances, acknowledging with adoration that "His mercy endureth for ever."

—ARTHUR W. PINK.

VOL. VI.        APRIL, 1927        NO. 4

# STUDIES IN THE SCRIPTURES
"Search the Scriptures" John 5:39.

Copyright in all English-speaking Countries.

Editor: Arthur W. Pink, 22 Parramatta Road, Summer Hill, N.S.W., Australia.
Hon. Agent in U.S.A.: Mr. C. S. Pressel, 559 Dupont Ave., York, Penna.

FREE TO ALL WHO WILL READ IT

## PRECIOUS DEATH.

"Precious in the sight of the Lord is the death of His saints" (Psalm 116: 15). This is one of the many comforting and blessed statements in Holy Scripture concerning that great event from which the flesh so much shrinks. If the Lord's people would more frequently make a prayerful and believing study of what the Word says upon their departure out of this world, death would lose much, if not all, of its terrors for them. But alas, instead of doing so, they let their imagination run riot, they give way to carnal fears, they walk by sight instead of by faith. Looking to the Holy Spirit for guidance, let us endeavor to dispel, by the light of Divine revelation, some of the gloom which unbelief casts around even the death of a Christian.

"Precious in the sight of the Lord is the death of His saints." These words intimate that a dying saint is an object of special notice unto the Lord, for mark the words "in the sight of." It is true that the eyes of the Lord are ever upon us, for He never slumbers nor sleeps. It is true that we may say at all times "Thou God seest me." But it appears from Scripture that there are occasions when He notices and cares for us in a special manner. "God is our refuge and strength, a very present help in trouble" (Psalm 46: 1). "When thou passest through the waters, I will be with thee" (Isaiah 43: 2).

"Precious in the sight of the Lord is the death of His saints." This brings before us an aspect of death which is rarely considered by believers. It gives us what may be termed the Godward side of the subject. Only too often, we contemplate death, like most other things, from our side. The text tells us that from the viewpoint of Heaven the death of a saint is neither hideous nor horrible, tragic or terrible, but "precious." This raises the question, Why is the death of His people precious in the sight of the Lord? What is there in the last great crisis which is so dear unto Him? Without attempting an exhaustive reply, let us suggest one or two possible answers:—

First, their persons are precious to the Lord.

They ever were and always will be dear to Him. His saints! They were the ones on whom His love was set before the earth was formed or the heavens made. These are they for whose sakes He left His Home on high and whom He bought with His precious blood, cheerfully laying down His life for them. These are they whose names are borne on our great High Priest's breast and engraven on the palms of His hands. They are His Father's love-gift to Him, His children, members of His body; therefore, everything that concerns them is precious in His sight. The Lord loves His people so intensely that the very hairs of their heads are numbered: the angels are sent forth to minister unto them; and because their persons are precious unto the Lord so also are their deaths.

Second, because death terminates the saint's sorrows and sufferings.

There is a needs-be for our sufferings, for through much tribulation we **must**

*(Continued on page 96)*

## BACK NUMBERS

OF THIS MAGAZINE obtainable, 5/- (1 dollar) per year; Bound at 7/- (1 dollar 75.) Each year is yet obtainabl .

ADVISE PROMPTLY of Change of Address.

THIS MAGAZINE is published as a work of faith and labor of love. It is gladly sent to all who would value it.

We want the names and addresses of Christians who would read it.

Christians who feel definitely led to do so may have fellowship with us in this Ministry.

## CONTENTS.

The Gospel of John .................. 74
Gleanings in Exodus ............... 81
Acceptable Gifts ................... 86
Tithing ........................... 90

## THE GOSPEL OF JOHN.

### 64. Christ before Pilate Concluded: John 19: 1-11.

Below is an Analysis of the passage which is to be before us:—

1. Christ scourged and mocked vv. 1-3.
2. Pilate re-affirms His innocency v. 4.
3. Pilate appeals to the Jews' sympathies v. 5.
4. The Jews' response vv. 6, 7.
5. Pilate's fear vv. 8, 9.
6. Pilate's beast v. 10.
7. Christ's reprimand v. 11.

Nowhere in Scripture, perhaps, is there a more striking and vivid demonstration of the sovereignty of God than Pilate's treatment of the Lord Jesus. First, Pilate was assured of His innocency, acknowledging, no less than seven times, "I find no fault in Him." Second, Pilate desired to release Him! "Pilate therefore willing to release Jesus" Luke 23: 20, "I will let him go" (Luke 23: 22); "Pilate sought to release Him" (John 19: 12); "Pilate was determined to let Him go" (Acts 3: 13), all prove that unmistakably. Third, Pilate was urged, most earnestly by none other than his own wife, not to sentence Him (Matt. 27: 19). Fourth, he actually endeavored to bring about His acquittal: he bade the Jews themselves judge Christ (18: 31); he sent Him to Herod, only for Christ to be returned (Luke 23: 7); he sought to induce the Jews to have him convict Barabbas in His stead (19: 39). Yet in spite of all Pilate did give sentence that Christ should be crucified!

What does man's will amount to when it runs counter to the will of God? Absolutely nothing. Here was Pilate, the Roman Governor of Judea, determined to release the Saviour, yet prevented from doing so. From all eternity God had decreed that Pilate should sentence His Son to death, and all earth and hell combined cannot thwart the purpose of the Almighty—He would not be all-mighty if they could! Christ was "delivered up (Greek) by the determinate counsel and foreknowledge of God" (Acts 2: 23). As God's servant fearlessly announced, "Both Herod and Pontius Pilate, with the Gentiles, and the people of Israel, were gathered together for to do whatsoever Thy hand and Thy counsel determined before to be done" (Acts 4: 27, 28). This is not simply "Calvinism," it is the explicit declaration of Holy Writ, and, woe be unto the one who dares to deny it. Christ had to be sentenced by Pilate because the eternal counsels of Deity had foreordained it. Moreover, Christ was dying for sinners both of the Jews and of the Gentiles, therefore Divine wisdom deemed it fitting that both Jews and Gentiles should have a direct hand in His death.

But, it will at once be objected, this reduces Pilate to a mere machine! Our first answer is, What of that?—better far to reduce him to a non-entity than to deny the Word of the living God! Away with the deductions of reason; our initial and never-ceasing duty is to bow in absolute submission to the teaching of the Holy Scriptures. Our second answer is, The deduction drawn by the objector is manifestly erroneous. An honest mind is forced to acknowledge that the Gospel records present Pilate to us as a responsible agent. Christ addressed Himself to Pilate's conscience: "Everyone that is of the truth heareth My voice" (18: 37); God faithfully warned him that Christ was a just Man and to have nothing to do with Him (Matt. 27: 19). Should it be asked, How could God consistently warn him when He had decreed that he should sentence Christ to death? Our reply is, His decree was a part of His own sovereign counsels; whereas the warning was addressed to Pilate's responsibility, and he will be justly held accountable for disregarding it. Christ announced that Peter would deny Him, yet a few minutes later said to him, "Watch and pray, that ye enter not into temptation"! Finally, the Saviour Himself told Pilate that He was sinning in holding Him: "he that delivered Me unto thee hath the greater sin" (19: 11)—therefore it follows that Pilate's failure to release Him was a great sin!

"Then Pilate therefore took Jesus, and scourged Him" (v. 1). We believe that the real explanation of this awful act of the Roman Governor is intimated in v. 4— "Pilate therefore went forth again, and saith unto them, Behold, I bring Him forth to you, that ye may know that I find no fault in Him." It was a desperate move, made against his better judgment, and, also made, we fully believe, against the strivings of his conscience. It was his third and last effort at a compromise. First, he had asked the Jews to judge Christ for themselves (18: 31). Second, he had pitted against Him a notable outlaw, Barabbas, and made them take their choice. That having failed, he made a final effort to escape from that which he feared to do. He hesitated to speak the irrevocable word, and so scourged the Lord Jesus instead, and suffered the soldiers to brutally mistreat Him. We believe Pilate hoped that when he should present to the gaze of the Jews their suffering and bleeding King, their rage would be appeased. Luke 23: 16 bears this out: "I will chastise Him and release Him." How entirely this wretched devise failed we shall see by and by.

"Then Pilate therefore took Jesus, and scourged Him." "The cruel injury inflicted on our Lord's body, in this verse, was probably far more severe than an English reader might suppose. It was a punishment which among the Romans generally preceded crucifixion, and was sometimes so painful that the sufferer died under it. It was often a scourging with rods, and not always with cords, as painters and sculptors represent. Josephus, the Jewish historian, in his 'Antiquities,' particularly mentions that malefactors were scourged and tormented in every way before they were put to death. Smith's Dictionary of the Bible says that under the Roman mode of scourging, 'The culprit was stripped, stretched with cords or thongs on a frame, and beaten with rods'" (Bishop Ryle).

"And the soldiers plaited a crown of thorns, and put it on His head, and they put on Him a purple robe, and said, Hail, King of the Jews! and they smote Him with their hands" (vv. 2, 3). 'One question springs from the heart on reading this—How could it be! Where is the lauded Roman justice in this scourging of a bound prisoner of whom the judge says, 'I find no fault in Him!' Why is an uncondemned one given into the rude hands of Roman soldiers for them to mock and smite at their pleasure? Where is the cool judgment of Pilate, that a little while ago refused to take action lest injustice be done? Why is Jesus treated in a way wholly unparalleled so far as we know? What is the secret of it all?" (Mr. Mal. Taylor). Difficult as it would be, impossible perhaps, for unaided reason to answer these questions, the light which Scripture throws on them removes all difficulty.

First, who was this One so brutally, so unrighteously treated? He was Immanuel, "God manifest in flesh," and fallen man hates God. "The heart is deceitful above all things, and desperately wicked" (Jer. 17: 9). "The carnal mind is enmity against God" (Rom. 8: 7). "Their throat is an open sepulchre; with their tongues they have used deceit; the poison of asps is under their lips. Whose mouth is full of cursing and bitterness: Their feet are swift to shed blood: destruction and misery are in their ways" (Rom. 3: 13-16). Never before or since did these awful facts receive such exemplification. Never were the desperate wickedness of the human heart, the fearfull enmity of the carnal mind, and the unspeakable vileness of sin's ways, so unmistakably evidenced as when the Son of God was "delivered into the hands of men" (Mark 9: 31). All Divine restraint was withdrawn, and human depravity was allowed to show itself in all its naked hideousness.

Second, this was Satan's hour. Said the Saviour to those who came to arrest Him in the Garden, "This is your hour, and the power of Darkness" (Luke 22: 53). On the day when sin entered the world, Jehovah announced that He would put enmity between the Serpent and the woman, and between his seed and her seed (Gen. 3: 15). That enmity was manifested when Christ became incarnate, for we are told, "And the Dragon stood before the woman which was ready to be delivered, for to devour her Child as soon as it was born" (Rev. 12: 4), and he it was who moved Herod to slay all the young children in Bethlehem. But God interposed and the Dragon was foiled. But now God hindered no longer. The hour had arrived when the Serpent was to bruise the Saviour's heel, and fully did he now avail himself of his opportunity. Jews and Gentiles alike were "of their father, the Devil," and his lusts (desires) they now carried out with a will.

Third, Christ was on the point of making atonement for sin, therefore sin must be revealed in all its enormity. Sin is **lawlessness**, therefore did Pilate scourge the Innocent One. Sin is **transgression**, therefore did Pilate set aside all the principles and statutes of Roman jurisprudence. Sin is **iniquity** (injustice), therefore did these soldiers smite that One who had never harmed a living creature. Sin is **rebellion** against God, therefore did Jew and Gentile alike maltreat the Son of God. Sin is an **offence**, therefore did they outrage every dictate of conscience and propriety. Sin is **coming short of the glory of God**, therefore did they heap ignominy upon His Son. Sin is **defilement**, uncleanness, therefore did they cover His face with their vile spittle.

Fourth, Christ was to die in the stead of sinners, therefore must it be shown what was righteously due them. The Law required "an eye for an eye and a tooth for a tooth," a quid pro quo. All sin is a revolt against God, a treating of Him with contumacy, a virtual smiting of Him; therefore was Christ **scourged** by sinners. Again, when man became a sinner the righteous curse of the thrice holy God fell upon him, hence Christ will yet say to the wicked "Depart from Me ye **cursed**"! Unto Adam God declared, "Cursed is the ground for thy sake .. thorns also and thistles shall it bring forth to thee" (Gen. 3: 17, 18); therefore the last Adam, as the Head of those He came to deliver from the curse, was **crowned with thorns!** Again, by nature and practice we are defiled: our iniquities cover us from head to foot—sins which are "scarlet" and "crimson" (Isa. 1: 18); therefore was the Saviour enveloped in "a purple robe"—Matthew actually terms it "a **scarlet robe**" (27: 28), and Mark says "they clothed Him with **purple**" (15: 17). Finally, they mocked Him as "King of the Jews," for "sin hath **reigned** unto death" (Rom. 5: 21). Here then is the Gospel of our salvation: the Saviour was scourged, that we might go free; He was crowned with thorns, that we might be crowned with blessing and glory; He was clothed with a robe of contempt, that we might receive the robe of righteousness; He was rejected as King, that we might be made kings and priests unto God.

"Pilate therefore went forth again, and saith unto them, behold, I bring Him forth to you that ye may know that I find no fault in Him" (v. 4). The private interview which Pilate had had with Christ at least convinced him that He had done nothing worthy of death; he therefore returned to the Jews and re-affirmed His innocence. The "therefore" points back to what is recorded in vv. 1-3: he had gone as far as he meant to. "I bring Him forth to you": there is nothing more that I intend to do. "I find no fault in Him": how striking that the very one who shortly after sentenced Him to death, should give this repeated witness that the Lamb was "without blemish!" More striking still is it to observe that at the very time the Lord Jesus was apprehended and crucified as a criminal, God raised up one after another to testify of His guiltlessness. Of old the prophet had asked, "And who shall declare His generation? for He was cut off out of the land of the living" (Isa. 53: 8). A sevenfold answer is supplied in the Gospels. First, Judas declared "I have sinned in that I have betrayed the innocent blood (Matt. 27: 4). Second, Pilate declared, "I find no fault in Him" (John 18: 4). Third, of Herod Pilate said "No, nor yet Herod: for I sent you to him; and, lo, nothing worthy of death is done unto Him." Fourth, Pilate's wife entreated, "Have thou nothing to do with that just Man: for I have suffered many things this day in a dream because of Him." (Matt. 27: 19). Fifth, the dying thief affirmed, "We receive the due reward of our deeds: but this Man hath done nothing amiss" (Luke 23: 41). Sixth, the Roman centurion who glorified God, said, "Certainly this was a righteous Man" (Luke 23: 47) Seventh, those who stood with the Centurion acknowledged, "Truly this was the Son of God" (Matt. 27: 54)!

"Then came Jesus forth, wearing the crown of thorns, and the purple robe" (v. 5). "That our blessed Lord, the eternal Word, should have meekly submitted to be led out after this fashion, as a gazing-stock and an object of scorn, with an old purple robe on His shoulders, a crown of thorns on His head, His back bleeding from scourging, and His head from thorns, to feast the eyes of a taunting, howling, blood-thirsty crowd, is indeed a wondrous thought! Truly such love 'passeth knowledge' " (Bishop Ryle).

"And Pilate saith unto them, 'Behold the Man'!" (v. 5). We fully believe that Pilate was here appealing to the Jews' pity. See, saith he, what He has already suffered! He had no need to say more. The shame, the bleeding wounds, were tongues sufficiently moving if only they had ears to hear. Pilate hoped that their wrath would now be appeased. Is He not already punished enough! It is surely striking that the Governor said not "Behold this Man," but "Behold the Man." It was the ungrudging testimony of an unprejudiced witness. Never before had any other who had stood before his bar carried himself as this One. Never before had Pilate seen such quiet dignity, intrepid courage, noble majesty. He was deeply impressed, and avowed the Lord's uniqueness.

"When the chief priests therefore and officers saw Him, they cried out, saying, Crucify, crucify" (v. 6). Pilate's scheming failed here as completely as had his previous attempts to avoid condemning our Lord; nothing short of His death would satisfy the Jews. The pitiful sight of the bleeding Saviour softened them not a whit. Like beasts of prey who have tasted blood, they thirsted for more. The humiliating figure of their Messiah crowned with thorns by these heathen, instead of humbling, only infuriated them. They were "past feeling." Solemn it is to observe that the **chief priests** were to the fore in demanding His crucifixion—the "officers" were the personal followers and servants of the priests, and would naturally take up the cry of their masters; the word for "cried out" signifies a boisterous shout. It is a painful fact that all through this dispensation the most cruel, relentless, and bloodthirsty persecutors of God's saints have been the religious leaders—in a hundred different instances the "bishops" (?) and "cardinals" of Rome. Nor is it otherwise to-day. The form of persecution may have changed, yet is the opposition which comes from those who profess to be the servants of Christ the most relentless and cruel which God's children have to endure. It is to be noted that the cry was not "Crucify Him," but "Crucify, crucify"—**refusing** Him the "**the Man**" of Pilate! It was Israel, all through, who hounded Him to His death: how wondrous then that God shall yet have mercy upon them.

"Pilate saith unto them, Take ye Him, and crucify: for I find no fault in Him" (v. 6) Pilate was disgusted at their lawless clamor, indignant at their challenging his decision, angry at their insistence. "Take **ye** Him," if you want; "and crucify" if you dare. They had had the affrontery to appeal against the findings of his court, now he mocks them in regard to the impotency of their court, for according to their own admission, they were powerless (18: 31). The Jews were insisting that Pilate should commit a judicial murder, now he challenges them to defy the Roman law. His **"For I find no fault in Him"** was his challenge for them to continue opposing Caesar's authority.

"The Jews answered him, We have a law, and by our law He ought to die, because He made Himself the Son of God" (v. 7). Their words here show plainly that they discerned the satire in Pilate's offer: had he really given them permission to crucify Christ, they would have acted promptly. They knew that he had not spoken seriously; they felt his biting irony, and stung by his sarcasm they now attempted some defence of their outrageous conduct. "We **have a law**" they insisted, much as you scorn us for wanting to act lawlessly. **We** have a law as well as **you!** "By our law He ought to die, because He made Himself the Son of God"—their reference was to Lev. 24: 16. Instead of retreating before Pilate's outburst of indignation, they continued to press their demands upon him. We charge your Prisoner with having broken our law, the punishment for which is death. Their aim was to make out Christ to be a dangerous imposter as well as a seditious person, opposed both to Jewish religion and Roman law. Pilate had challenged them; now they challenge him. You have dared us to defy the Roman law; we now dare you to refuse to maintain the Jewish law.

"We have a law, and by our law He ought to die, because He made Himself the Son of God." It is indeed remarkable that as soon as Pilate said "Behold the **Man**," they proceeded to charge Him with "making Himself the Son of God"! **Their** motive was an evil one, but how evident that a Higher power was overruling!. Finding the charge of sedition had broken down, and that Pilate could not be induced to sentence Him to death on that score, they now accused Christ of blasphemy. But how their hypocrisy was manifested: they appealed to their own "law," yet had no respect for it, for their law called for stoning not crucifixion, as the penalty for blasphemy! A careful comparison of the Gospel records reveals the fact that the Jews preferred just seven indictments against Christ. First, they charged Him with threatening to destroy the Temple (Matt. 26: 61); second, with being a "malefactor" (John 18: 30); third, with "perverting the nation" (Luke 23: 2); fourth, with "forbidding to give tribute to Caesar" (Luke 23: 2); fifth, with stirring up all the people (Luke 23: 5); sixth, with being "a King" (Luke 23: 2); seventh, with making Himself the Son of God (John 19: 7). This sevenfold indictment witnessed to the completeness of their rejection of Him!

"When Pilate therefore heard that saying, he was the more afraid" (v. 8). The meaning of this is evident, yet, strange to say, many of the commentators have missed it. Some have supposed that fear of the Jews is what is intended; others, that Pilate was fearful lest it should now prove impossible to save Christ; others, lest he should take a false step. But the "therefore" is sufficient to show the error of these views: it was the declaration that Christ "made Himself the Son of God" which alarmed the Roman Governor. Moreover, the "he was the more afraid" shows it was not an emotion which he now felt for the first time. The person of the Lord Jesus was what occasioned his fear. We believe that from the beginning there was a conscious uneasiness in his soul, deepened by an awe which the bearing and words of Christ had inspired. He had seem many malefactors, some guilty, some innocent, but never one like this. His "Ecce Homo" (v. 5) witnesses to his estimate of Christ. The warning which he had received from his wife must also have impressed him deeply; and now that he is reminded his Prisoner called Himself the Son of God, he was the more afraid.

"And went again into the judgment hall, and saith unto Jesus, Whence art Thou? But Jesus gave him no answer" (v. 9). This was the sixth question Pilate asked Christ, and it is deeply interesting to follow his changing moods as he put them. First, he asked "Art Thou the King of the Jews?" (18: 33)—asked, most probably, in the spirit of sarcasm. Second, "Am I a Jew?" (18: 35)—asked in the spirit of haughty contempt. Third, "What hast Thou done?" (18: 35)—a pompous display of his authority. Fourth, "Art Thou a king then?" (18: 37)—indicating his growing perplexity. Fifth, "What is truth?" (18: 38)—asked out of contemptuous pity. Sixth, "Whence art Thou?" In what spirit did he ask this question? Much turns upon the right answer, for otherwise we shall be at a loss to understand our Lord's refusal to reply.

"Whence art Thou? Not "Whom art Thou?" nor, "Art Thou the Son of God then?" but "Whence art Thou?" Yet it is clear that Pilate was not asking about His human origin, for he had already sent Christ as a "Galilean" to Herod (Luke 23: 6) Was it then simply a question of idle curiosity? No, the "more afraid" of the previous verse shows otherwise. Was it that Pilate was now deeply exercised and anxiously seeking for light? No, for his outburst of scornful pride in the verse that follows conflicts with such a view. What, then? First, we think that Pilate was genuinely puzzled and perplexed. A Man altogether unique he clearly perceived Christ to be. But was He more than man? The deepening fear of his conscience made him uneasy. Suppose that after all, this One were from Heaven! That such a thought crossed his mind at this stage we fully believe, and this leads to the second motive which prompted his question:—Pilate hoped that here was a way out of his difficulty. If Christ were really from Heaven, then obviously he could not think of crucifying Him. He therefore has Christ led back again into the judgment hall, and says, Tell me privately Your real origin and history so that I may know what line to take up with Thine enemies. "We may well believe that Pilate caught at this secret hope that Jesus might tell him something about Himself which would enable him to make a firm stand and deliver Him from the Jews. In this hope, again, the Roman Governor was destined to be disappointed" (Bishop Ryle).

"But Jesus gave him no answer." Ominous "but"; perplexing silence. Hitherto He had replied to Pilate's questions; now He declined to speak. At first our Lord's silence surprises and puzzles us, but reflection shows that He could not have acted otherwise. First, the fact that in v. 11 we do find Christ speaking to Pilate, shows that His silence here in v. 9 was no arbitrary determination to say no more. "With us, when we would patiently suffer in silence, there may be some such arbitrary purpose of our own; or, to put a better construction upon it, we cannot actually speak and at the same time suffer in patience, for we have inwardly too much to do with our own spirits, in order to maintain our proper posture of mind. But Christ is in His profoundest humanity elevated above this human imperfection; in His lips (as we shall hear from the cross) the Word of God is never bound" (Stier). Second, Christ's silence here makes evident the spirit in which Pilate had put his question: it was not the cry of an earnest soul, honestly seeking light, for our Lord never closed the door against any such! Third, Pilate was not entitled to a reply. He had acted in grossest injustice when he refused to release One whom he declared was innocent; he had despised God's warning through his wife; he had declined to wait for an answer to his "What is truth?"; he had, against his own conscience, scourged the Saviour and suffered his soldiers to mock and maltreat Him. Why then should Christ reveal to him the mystery of His person!

"Pilate had forfeited his right to any further revelation about his Prisoner. He had been told plainly the nature of our Lord's kingdom, and the purpose of our Lord's coming into the world, and been obliged to confess publicly His innocence. And yet, with all this light and knowledge, he had treated our Lord with flagrant injustice, scourged Him, allowed Him to be treated with the vilest indignities by his soldiers, knowing in his own mind all the time that He was a guiltless person. He had, in short, sinned away his opportunities, forsaken his own mercies, and turned a deaf ear to the cries of his own conscience.

" 'He gave him no answer.' Most men, like Pilate, have a day of grace, and an open door put before them. If they refuse to enter in, and choose their own sinful way, the door is often shut, and never opened again. There is such a thing as a 'day of visitation,' when Christ speaks to men. If they will not hear His voice, and open the door of their hearts, they are often let alone, given over to a reprobate mind, and left to reap the fruit of their own sins. It was so with Pharaoh, and Saul, and Ahab; and Pilate's case was like theirs. He had his opportunity, and did not choose to use it, but preferred to please the Jews at the expense of his conscience, and to do what he knew was wrong. We see the consequence— 'Jesus gave him no answer' " (Bishop Ryle)

In addition to what has been pointed out above, may we not say, that as it had been Divinely appointed Christ should suffer for the sins of His people, He declined to say anything which was calculated to hinder it! True, Pilate was morally incapable of receiving the truth: to make him a definite answer would simply have been casting pearls before swine, and this the Saviour refused to do. Moreover, had He affirmed His Deity, it would have afforded Pilate the very handle he sought for releasing Him. Thus we may say with Bishop Ryle, "Our Lord's silence was just and well merited, but it was also part of God's counsels about man's salvation." Finally, let us learn from Christ's example here that there is "a time to be silent," as well as "a time to speak" (Ecc. 3: 7)!

"Then saith Pilate unto Him, speakest Thou not unto me? knowest Thou not that I have power to crucify Thee, and have power to release Thee?" (v. 10). Here the haughty, fierce, and imperious spirit of the Roman was manifested; the authoritative I asserting itself. We doubt not that all the emphasis was thrown upon the personal pronouns—Thou mayest keep silence before the Jews, the soldiers and before Herod; but me also? What lack of respect is this! It was the proud authority of an official politician displaying itself. Knowest Thou not in whose presence Thou standest! You are no longer before Annas and Caiaphas— mere figure-heads. I am the Governor of Judea, the representative of Caesar Augustus. "Speakest Thou not unto me?" It was his seventh and last question to our Lord, asked in the spirit of sarcasm and resentment combined. Accustomed to seeing prisoners cringing before him, willing to do anything to obtain his favor, he could not understand our Lord's silence. He was both perplexed and angered: his official pride was mortified.

"Knowest Thou not that I have power to crucify Thee, and have power to release Thee!" How he condemned himself. How he revealed his true character. Here was one on the bench talking about his power to commit a judicial murder! Here was one who had, over and over again, affirmed the innocency of his Prisoner, now owning his power to release Him, and yet shortly after condemned Him to death. And this from a man holding high office, who belonged to that Nation which prided itself in its impartial justice! Mark also his consummate folly. Here was a worm of the earth so puffed up with a sense of his own importance, so obsessed with the idea of his own absolute freewill that he has the effrontery to say that the Son of the Highest was entirely at his disposal! Mark too his utter inconsistency. He was boasting of his legal authority: but if the Lord were innocent he had no judicial power to "crucify" Him; if He were guilty, he had no judicial power to "release" Him! Out of his own mouth he stands condemned. Carefully analysed his words can only mean—I am above the law: innocent or guilty, I can do with You as I please.

"This high-handed claim to absolute power is one which ungodly great men are fond of making. It is written of Nebuchadnezzar, "Whom he would he slew; and whom he would he kept alive; and whom he would he set up; and whom he would he put down" (Dan. 5: 19). Yet even when such men boast of power, they are often, like Pilate, mere slaves, and afraid of resisting popular opinion. Pilate talked of 'power to release,' but he knew in his own mind that he was afraid, and so unable to exercise it" (Bishop Ryle).

"Jesus answered, Thou couldest have no power at all against Me, except it were given thee from above" (v. 11). For His Father's honor and as a rebuke to Pilate, the Lord once more spake, giving His last official testimony before He was crucified. Blessed it is to mark carefully the words of grace and truth which now proceeded from His lips. How easy for Him to have given the lie to Pilate's boast by paralyzing the tongue which had just uttered such blasphemy! How easy for Him to have made a display of His power before this haughty heathen similar to what He had done in the Garden! But, instead, He returns a calm and measured answer, equally expressive of His glory, though in another way. A careful study of His words here will reveal both His voluntary lowliness and His Divine majesty—how wonderful that both should be combined in one brief sentence!

"Jesus answered, Thou couldest have no power at all against Me except it were given thee from above." The Lord acknowledged that Pilate did have "power" but of quite a different kind, from quite a different source, and under different restrictions from what he supposed. Pilate had boasted of an arbitrary discretion, of a sovereign choice of his own, of a lawless right to do as he pleased. Christ referred him to a power which came from above, delegated to men, limited according to the pleasure of the One who bestowed it. Thus Christ, first, denied that Pilate had the "power" to do with Him as he pleased. Second, He maintained His Father's honor by insisting that He alone is absolute Sovereign. Even so temperate a writer as Bishop Ryle says on this verse: "Thou talkest of power: thou dost not know that both thou and the Jews are only tools in the hands of a higher Being: you are both, unconsciously, mere instruments in the hands of God"!

"Jesus answered, Thou couldest have no power at all against Me, except it were given thee from above: therefore he that delivereth Me unto thee hath the greater sin." Our Lord conceded that Pilate did have power: He acknowledged the authority of the human courts. To the very last Christ respected law, nor did He dispute the power of the Romans over the Jews. But He insisted that Pilate's power came from above, for, "There is no power but of God: the powers that be are ordained of God" (Rom. 13: 1) and compare Pro. 8: 15, 16. Christ acknowledged that Pilate's power extended over Himself—"No power against Me except," etc.—so thoroughly had He made Himself of no reputation. But it was because Pilate's "power," both personal and official, was "from above," that the Saviour bowed to it. In His "he that delivered Me unto thee hath the greater sin," the Lord, as in Luke 22: 22, shows us that God's counsels do not abolish the guilt of the men who execute them. And mark here, for it is most striking, that the same One who meekly bows to Pilate's (God-given) authority, manifests Himself as the Judge of men, apportioning the comparative guilt of Pilate and the Jews. Thus did He maintained His Divine dignity to the end. This, then, was our Lord's reply to Pilate's "Knowest Thou not?" I know, first, that all the power you have is from above; second, I know the precise measure both of your guilt and of him who delivered Me to thee! This, we take it, is the force of the rather difficult "therefore." Mark how, out of respect for Pilate's official personage, the Lord did not actually say "he that delivered Me unto thee hath greater sin than thee"!—though plainly that was implied. Here, as in Luke 12: 47, 48 Christ teaches **degrees** of sin and guilt, and therefore degrees of future punishment. The "**he** who delivered Me up" refers not to Judas (his was the "**greatest** sin") but Caiaphas, acting as the representative of the Nation. Finally observe that the **last** word which Pilate heard from the lips of Christ was "**sin**"!—the next, in all probability, will be the sentence of his eternal doom.

Below are the questions for our next study:—

1. Why did the "chief priests" take the lead v. 15?
2. Why was Christ "delivered to them" v. 16?
3. Why "in the Hebrew" v. 17?
4. Why were two others crucified with Him v. 18?
5. Why the inscription v. 19?
6. Why in three languages v. 20?
7. What is the meaning of v. 23?

—Arthur W. Pink.

## GLEANINGS IN EXODUS.

### 40. The Curtained Ceiling: Ex. 26: 1-14.

Having described the contents of the inner chambers of the Tabernacle, excepting the Golden-altar which is mentioned later in another connection, the Holy Spirit now informs us of what comprised the roof of Jehovah's dwelling-place. This consisted of a number of linen curtains, elaborately embroidered, and joined together; over these was a set of goats' hair curtains; over these was a covering of rams' skins dyed red, and on the outside of all was a covering of badgers' skins. It is noteworthy that the curtained ceiling, which we are now to contemplate, is described before the boards, which formed the framework or sides of the holy structure. Man would naturally have begun with a description of the framework, then the roof, and then the furniture placed within the finished building. But here, as elsewhere, God's thoughts and ways are the opposite of ours.

In this article we shall confine ourselves to the inner ceiling. This was composed of ten white curtains, richly ornamented. each twenty-eight cubits (forty-two feet) in length, and four cubits (six feet) in width. These were coupled together in fives, breadth to breadth, thus giving a total length of forty-two feet and a breadth of sixty feet, which would not only reach across the Tabernacle, which was fifteen feet in width, but would overlap its sides. The two sets of five white curtains were linked together by fifty loops of blue in each, which were fastened with fifty taches or clasps of gold, thus firmly uniting the whole together in one solid piece. There are seven things about these Curtains which we shall now consider:—

### 1. Their Material.

"Thou shalt make the Tabernacle of ten curtains of fine twined linen" (v. 1). It is striking to note that in 26: 15 we read, "Thou shalt make boards for the Tabernacle": whereas the Curtains were themselves called "the Tabernacle." Thus what we have before us here is Christ incarnate providing a dwelling-place on earth for God. These spotless Curtains pointed to the person of the Lord Jesus Christ and exhibited the holiness of His nature. "The priests were on this account clothed with it (Ex. 28: 39-43); and on the great day of atonement Aaron was dressed in this material (Lev. 16: 4) that he might typify the absolute purity of the nature of the One of whom he was the shadow" (Mr. Ed. Dennett).

The Curtains were made of "fine linen" —not linen merely, but **fine** linen, linen of peculiar excellency. In Rev. 19: 8 we have the Holy Spirit's definition of the significance of this figure, for there the fine linen, "clean and white," is declared to be **"the righteousnesses of the saints."** (R. V.). Thus the leading thoughts are unsullied purity and manifested righteousness. This concept may be the more clearly grasped by noting the contrast presented in Isa. 64:6, "But we are all as unclean, and all our righteousnesses are as filthy rags." This will be the confession of the Jews in a day to come, when they are convicted of their sins and made to mourn before their revealed Messiah. It is also the confession of God's saints to-day. Viewed in ourselves,• measured by the standard of Divine holiness, the best efforts of the Christian are comparable only to "filthy rags." The fine white linen, then, typified the **manifested** holiness and righteousness of Christ.

It is in the four Gospels which record the earthly life of our Lord, that the antitypical Curtains are displayed. See Him as a Boy of twelve. He had been taken to Jerusalem. Joseph and Mary lost sight of Him for three days. Where did they find Him? In the Temple, and in reply to His mother's question, He said, "Wist ye not that I must be about My Father's business?" (Luke 2: 49). His concern was to be occupied with the things of God. Pertinently has one asked, "Was there ever a child like that, to whom God was Father in such a way that He absorbed His soul?" Behold Him as He went down to Nazareth and was subject to His parents, owning the place of earthly responsibility and manifesting His perfection in this relationship. So, too, we read of Him, in those early days, "Jesus increased in wisdom and stature, and in favour with God and men." "There was the fabric of spotless linen being woven before the eye of God." (Mr. S. Ridout). Follow Him into the wilderness, where for forty days He was tempted of the devil: utterly vain were the efforts of Satan to foul His white robes. Thus may we trace Him all through the inspired record. He eats with publicans and sinners, yet is unsullied by the most polluting atmosphere. He lays His hand on the leper, but instead of contracting defilement, His fingers healed. He touches the bier, but instead of becoming ceremonially unclean, the dead is restored to life.

"Coming to His death, we see the spotless white shining in all its purity. The world puts Him between two thieves. "Ah," says Satan, "I will at least besmirch His whiteness; I will associate Him with malefactors and turn loose the rabble upon Him, railing and casting dust into the air. I will see what will become of His spotlessness! Yes, let us see what will become of His spotlessness. God only brings it out into clearer relief amidst the blackness of human and satanic wickedness. The very thief at His side is constrained to own His sinlessness (Luke 23: 40, 41). The Centurion, too, who presided at the crucifixion, declared Him a righteous Man" (Mr. S. Ridout). The white Curtains, then, foreshadowed the sinless ways and righteous acts of the Holy One of God.

### 2. Their Colours.

"Of fine twined linen, and blue, and purple, and scarlet" (v. 1). These were used for embroidering the cherubim upon the white Curtains. Each of the colours brings out a separate perfection in the Person of our blessed Redeemer, and was manifested by Him as He passed through this world of sin. "Blue" is the celestial colour—"as it were the body of heaven in its clearness" (Ex. 24: 11). The "blue" upon the white background tells us that He who came down into fathomless depths of humiliation was "the Lord from heaven" (1 Cor. 15: 47).

It is most blessed to go through the Gospels with the object of looking for the "blue" as it was revealed in connection with the second Man. First, we see it at His birth. How carefully God saw to it that testimony should be borne to the heavenly source of that One who then lay in the manger. The angels were sent to announce Him as "Christ the Lord" (Luke 2:11). Later, the wise men from the east came and worshipped the young Child—how beautifully this manifested the "blue"! Those who heard Him asking and answering the questions of the doctors in the Temple, when twelve years of age, were "astonished at His understanding" (Luke 2: 47)—here again we may perceive the heavenly colour. In His words to Nicodemus He spoke of Himself as "The Son of man which is in heaven" (John 3: 13)—as one has said "the One whose whole life here breathed the air of heaven." "Though He was 'very man,' yet He ever walked in the uninterrupted consciousness of His proper dignity, as a heavenly Stranger. He never once forgot whence He had come, where He was, or whither He was going. The spring of all His joys was on High. Earth could neither make Him richer nor poorer. He found this world to be 'a dry and thirsty land, where no water is,' and hence His spirit could only find its refreshment above" (C.H.M.).

"Purple" is emblematic of royalty. This is established by a reference to John 19. When the Roman soldiers expressed their scorn for Israel's Ruler by going through the form of a mock coronation, they placed upon His brow a crown of thorns, and then "put on Him a purple robe" (v. 2). It is in Matthew's Gospel that this second colour comes out most conspicuously. First, the "purple" is seen in the record of the royal genealogy of the Son of David. Next we behold it in the question of the magi, "Where is He that is born King of the Jews?" (Matt. 2: 2). Then we see it in the proclamation of His forerunner, "The kingdom of heaven is at hand" (3: 2)—"at hand," because the King Himself was in their midst. The royal "purple" is plainly evident in the "Sermon" recorded in chapters 5, 6, 7, prefaced by the statement, "He went up into a mountain, and when He was seated . . . He said " etc.—symbolically, it was the King taking His place upon His throne, enunciating the laws of His kingdom. Still more vividly did the "purple" shine when He made His triumphal entry into Jerusalem (21: 1-11). Over His cross was placed the royal banner, "This is Jesus, the King of the Jews" (27: 37).

"Scarlet" is a colour which is used in Scripture with a variety of emblematic significations. From these we select two which seem to bear most closely upon our present type. First, "scarlet," the colour of blood, vividly suggests the sufferings of Christ. This is borne out by the fact that the complete Hebrew word for "scarlet" is "tolaath shani," meaning scarlet-worm. Mr. Ridout has pointed out, "It is the 'cocus cacti,' the cochineal, from which the scarlet dye is obtained. In the 22nd Psalm our holy Lord, in the midst of His anguish as a sin-offering on the cross, says 'I am a worm and no man' (v. 6). This is the word which is used in connection with scarlet. Thus our Lord, 'who knew no sin,' was 'made sin' for us (2 Cor. 5: 21), taking the place which we deserved. He took the place of being a worm, went down into death, crushed under the wrath and judgment of God, His precious blood shed to put away our scarlet sins."

Thus the "scarlet" speaks first of the sufferings of Christ. Side by side with His purity, His heavenly character, and His royal majesty, the Gospel records bring before us the afflictions of the Saviour. We may discern the "scarlet" in the manger-cradle. This colour was also evidenced when Satan assailed Him, for "He suffered, being tempted (Heb. 2: 18). He "sighed deeply in His spirit" (Mark 8: 12), "groaning in Himself" (John 11: 38), "weeping over Jerusalem" (Luke 19: 41) are further examples. How tragically the "scarlet" may be seen in Gethsemane, when "His sweat was as it were great drops of blood falling down to the ground" (Luke 22: 44)!

But "scarlet" is also the emblem of glory. The woman seated upon the scarlet-coloured beast in Rev. 17 symbolizes that satanic system which, under Antichrist, will yet ape the millennial glory of Christ. By His sufferings the Saviour has won the place of highest honor and glory. In the coming Age, this world will be the scene of His splendour. The scarlet mantle will then be upon Him whose right it is. It is striking that in the 22nd Psalm—the first part of which describes the Saviour's sufferings—its closing verses depict His royal authority and coming glory: "All the ends of the world shall remember and turn unto the Lord: and all the kindreds of the nations shall worship before Thee," etc. (v. 27). A bright glimpse of the "scarlet" was afforded to the sight of the favoured apostles upon the Mount of Transfiguration.

### 3. Its Ornamentation.

"With cherubim of cunning work shalt thou make them" (v. 1). The pure white linen was the material on which the various colours were displayed and with which were embroidered the cherubim. Thus, as the priests ministered in the Holy Place and gazed upward, there above their heads were the mystic forms of these highest of all God's creatures— their outstretched wings forming a firmament of feathers upon the ceiling. We believe that reference is made to this sheltering canopy in the following scriptures: "I will abide in Thy Tabernacle forever; I will trust in the covert of Thy wings" (Psa. 61: 4); "He shall cover thee with His feathers; and under His wings shalt thou trust" (Psa. 91: 4); "Hide me under the shadow of Thy wings" (Psa. 17: 8), etc.

As the "cherubim" will come before us again, a brief word thereon must here suffice. They speak of judicial authority, as the first mention of them in the Bible clearly shows: (Gen. 3: 24). A glimpse of what these symbolic figures portrayed in connection with Christ was given by Him when He affirmed, "For the Father judgeth no man, but hath committed all judgment unto the Son. . . and hath given Him authority to execute judgment also because He is the Son of man" (John 5: 22, 27).

### 4. Their Dimensions.

"The length of one curtain shall be eight and twenty cubits, and the breadth of one curtain four cubits; and every one of the curtains shall have one measure" (v. 2). "Seven is the perfect number, being absolutely indivisible except by itself, and the highest prime number; and four is that of completeness on earth— as seen for example, in the four corners of the earth, four square, four gospels, etc. The dimensions of the Curtains will then betoken perfection displayed in completeness on earth; and such a meaning could only be applied to the life of our blessed Lord. The Curtains of the Tabernacle, consequently, speak of the complete unfolding of His perfections as Man when passing through this scene" (Mr. E. Dennett).

### 5. Their Meaning.

This has been brought out, more or

less, in what has been already before us. The spotless white Curtains, with the beautifully tinted cherubim worked upon them, typified, distinctively, neither the Deity nor the humanity of our Lord, but the person of the God-man and the varied glories manifested by Him while He tabernacled among men. It should be noted that in every other instance where we have the four colours mentioned, the blue is first and the white is last. But here the order is reversed. There, it is the Spirit emphasising the heavenly origin of the One who came down to earth; here, it is drawing our attention to the sinlessness and righteousness of the Man who sits now at God's right hand.

The fact that these Curtains formed the inside ceiling of the holy places and were seen, therefore, only by the priestly family, intimates that none but those that had access to God were able to appreciate the perfections of His Son as they were manifested by Him during His earthly sojourn. The rank and file of the Jews saw in Him no beauty that they should desire Him. His moral loveliness was lost upon them; yea, it only served to condemn their moral ugliness, and thus aroused their enmity. But the favoured few, who were the objects of distinguishing grace, exclaimed, "We beheld His glory, the glory as of the only begotten of the Father full of grace and truth" (John 1: 14).

It is the same to-day. Christ is still despised and rejected of men. The unregenerate have no capacity to discern His excellencies. A good Man, the best of men, He is acknowledged to be; but as the Holy One of God (the "white"), the Lord from heaven (the "blue"), the King of kings (the "purple"), and the One who because of His sufferings will yet come back to this earth and reign over it in power and glory (the "scarlet"), He is unknown. But notwithstanding there is even now a company that is "an holy priesthood" (1 Peter 2: 5), and they, having received "an unction," a divine anointing (1 John 2: 20, 27), recognise Him as the altogether Lovely One.

The fact that the Curtains formed the inner ceiling of the Tabernacle suggests that they set before us the One who humbled Himself and became obedient unto death, but who is now exalted and glorified on High. Whenever the worshipper looked up he would see nought but that spotless linen with its rich ornamentations. Does not this announce to us, in accents too plain to be misunderstood, that as God's worshippers enter, in spirit, the heavenly Sanctuary, they are to be occupied with the person and perfections of Him whom, by faith, we now see "crowned with glory and honour" (Heb. 2: 9)! In worship we are occupied not with ourselves—either our failures or our attainments, our needs or our blessings—but with the Father and His blessed Son. It is only as our hearts are absorbed with that which the Curtains and their lovely colours prefigured, that we present to God that which is acceptable in His sight.

### 6. Their Loops.

Before we take up the distinctive significance of these, let us first consider their use. They were appointed for the joining of the Curtains together. Thus the ten Curtains were arranged in two sets of five each: "The five curtains shall be coupled together one to another; and other five curtains shall be coupled one to another" (v. 3). Now, in Scripture, one of the meanings of "ten" is that of human responsibility. Hence after ten plagues upon Egypt had measured and demonstrated the failure of their responsibility, Pharaoh and his hosts were destroyed at the Red Sea. When Gentile dominion reaches its final form, it will consist of ten kingdoms, and then will be fully manifested the breakdown of its responsibility. When at Sinai God gave a summary of man's duty it was in the form of ten commandments. But these were written upon two tables of stone, or in two sets of fives, similarly to the Curtains here. The first five commandments— joined together by the words "The Lord thy God," which is not found in any of the last five—define our responsibility Godwards; the last five, our responsibility manwards. The ten Curtains, grouped together in two sets of fives, speak of Christ, as the Representative of His people, meeting the whole of their obligations both Godwards and manwards. He loved God with all His heart, and His neighbour as Himself; He was the only one by whom these responsibilities were fully and perfectly discharged.

By this "coupling" of the Curtains together, both their length and breadth would be the better exhibited. "'Length' is the extension, and may well stand for the whole course of life. It is used this way in Scripture—'length of days' is a familiar expression. 'Breadth' is from a root meaning 'spacious, roomy.' It has a metaphorical use with which we are familiar. King Solomon had great largeness (breadth) of heart (1 Kings, 4: 29). 'Breadth' thus suggests the character of the life and its attendant circumstances. In speaking then of our Lord's life, 'length' would suggest its whole course, and 'breadth' its character and the circumstances in which this was displayed" (Mr. Ridout). How blessed then to behold that each of these ten Curtains was 28 or 7 x 4 cubits long, and 4 broad, telling us that in the discharge of our responsibiliites He manifested nought but perfection here on earth!

"Fifty loops shalt thou make in the one curtain, and fifty loops shalt thou make in the edge of the curtain that is in the coupling of the second; that the loops may take hold one of another" (v. 5) "The loops were blue—the colour of Heaven. Thus the fact that He was from Heaven, lived in Heaven, and was to return to Heaven characterised His whole life of obedience. The mark of Heaven was upon it all. Upon that which spoke of His perfect love and obedience to God were loops of blue, to show that love and obedience were to be united to a life upon earth in which its responsibilities were to be made one with His obedience to God. So the blue loops upon the second set of Curtains show that all was of one with His devotedness to God.

"No life ever was so perfectly given up to God as was His: heart, soul, mind and strength were all and always for God. Yet this devotedness did not make of Him a recluse. There is not the slightest thought of that selfish monasticism with which human self-righteousness has linked the name of Christianity. He loved His Father perfectly, but that was the pledge of His perfect life to man. No hands or heart were ever so filled with love and labour for men; but there was nothing of the sentimental nor merely philanthropic in this. The loops of blue were on all, linking all with His Father's will. He wrought many miracles. . . but we cannot think of these works of love ending there. He was manifesting the works which the Father gave Him to do; 'I must work the works of Him that sent Me'—John 9: 4" (Mr. Ridout).

### 7. Their Couplings.

"And thou shalt make fifty taches of gold, and couple the curtains together with the taches: and it shall be one Tabernacle" (v. 6). The word "taches" means "couplings": passed through the loops of blue they united the Curtains together. The "loops of blue" and these "hooks of gold" might seem very unimportant, but, without them, there would have been no unity. The beautiful Curtains would have hung apart one from another, and thus one main feature of their manifestation would have been lost.

Significantly were these "couplings" of gold. They tell us that it was the heavenly and Divine character of our Lord which secured the perfect adjustment of His twofold responsibility as Man towards God and His neighbour. These "couplings" fastened the whole of the ten Curtains together so that they were "one Tabernacle." Thus they pointed to that blessed unity and uniformity of the character and life of Christ. "We have here displayed to us in the 'loops of blue' and 'taches of gold' that heavenly grace and divine energy in Christ which enabled Him to combine and perfectly adjust the claims of God and man, so that in responding to both the one and the other He never, for a moment, marred the unity of His character. When crafty and hypocritical men tempted Him with the inquiry, 'Is it lawful to give tribute to Caesar or not?' His wise reply was, 'Render to Caesar the things that are Caesar's, and to God the things that are God's.' Nor was it merely Caesar's, but man in every relation, that had all his claims perfectly met in Christ. As He united in His perfect person the nature of God and man, so He met in His perfect ways the claims of God and man." (C.H.M.).

In the life of the blessed Lord Jesus, and in all the scenes and circumstances of that life, we not only see each distinct phase and feature perfect in itself, but also a perfect combination of all those phases and features by the power of that which was heavenly and divine in Him. The perfect ways and works of our Lord were not only beautiful in themselves, but they were beautifully combined, exquisitely linked together. But it is only those who have been, in some measure, instructed in the holy mysteries of the true Sanctuary who can discern and appreciate these "loops of blue" and "taches of gold" Study the record of His life with this thought in mind. Mark His inflexible righteousness and then His exceeding tenderness; His uncompromising faithfulness in denouncing hypocrisy and then the wondrous compassion for poor sinners; His stern denunciation of error and human traditions, and then the tender patience toward the ignorant and those that were out of the way. Side by side we may see the dignity and majesty of His Godhead and the meekness and lowliness of His Manhood—blessedly united and consistently combined into one, like His robe "without seam"! May the Spirit of truth enable the reader to look for the "loops of blue" and the "taches of gold" as he studies the antitypical Curtains in the New Testament.

—Arthur W. Pink.

## ACCEPTABLE GIFTS.

"To offer up spiritual sacrifices, acceptable to God by Jesus Christ" (1 Pet. 2: 5).

Our subject is "Acceptable Gifts," but before I seek to develop that theme let me first review the ground which we covered last Lord's Day morning. First of all, I sought to show from Scripture that God refuses to accept anything from anyone who is not a believer in the Lord Jesus Christ. I appealed to the case of Cain. He brought an offering to the Lord, and the Lord rejected it. Why? Because it was a bloodless one. He brought as an offering "of the fruit of the ground." I have no doubt that to the outward eye, it was a very attractive and beautiful offering—the most luscious fruits and the most fragrant flowers that he could select and combine together, but it was unacceptable to God, because "without shedding of blood there is no remission." And, as God changes not, He will not receive any bloodless offering from anybody today. That is to say, unless (to use the language of Romans 3, 25) we have "faith in His blood." Unless we come before God pleading the blood of Christ as the ground of our acceptance, He will neither own our worship, answer our prayers, nor receive our gifts. As Watts said in one of his hymns, "As Jesus appears in your view"—in your view, not in God's, mind you,

"As Jesus appears in your view,
   As He is beloved or not,
So God is disposed to you,
   And mercy or wrath is your lot."

While you are rejecting His Son, God will reject everything you present to Him. The second reason why God did not receive the offering of Cain was, because there was no faith behind it. And God will neither receive our gifts nor hearken to our prayers while we remain in a state of unbelief. There are many sinners who look upon unbelief as more or less a misfortune, or an infirmity, rather than the sin of sins. And, my friends, the ungodly are likely to continue looking upon unbelief as a very light matter; if we encourage them to foster the idea that God will receive their worship and accept their gifts while they are in a state of unbelief!

Next, I called attention to seven passages which describe the awful condition and position of the ungodly; showing from Scripture that the unbeliever is under condemnation, that He is an enemy of God, that he is a child of wrath; that he is alienated by wicked works; that he is living in this world without God, and without hope. My purpose in appealing to these Scriptures was, mainly, this: to show how impossible it is for God to receive anything at the hands of such. Will God receive something from His enemies? Will God accept offerings from those under condemnation?

Then, in the third place, I appealed to three Scriptures in further support of the first proposition. Proverbs 15: 8, "The sacrifice of the wicked is an abomination to the Lord"—the word "sacrifice" there meaning offering or gift. The sacrifice of the wicked is an abomination. Now you can puzzle your brains the rest of your lives and you will never be able to make "abomination" mean acceptable! The sacrifice of the wicked is an abomination unto the Lord. There is no honest way of evading those plain words. Then in Mark 9: 41 our Lord Himself tells us that it is the cup of water which is given "in His name" which receives a reward, and that is something that no rejector of Him can do—to offer anything in "the name of Christ." Then I appealed again to our text, 1 Peter 2: 5, that spiritual sacrifices which are acceptable to God by "Jesus Christ"; which clearly presupposes that they are not acceptable to Him apart from Jesus Christ. Now, my friends, if that does not establish from Scripture the proposition that I started out with, I know not how to establish anything from Scripture.

Next I want to read you three lines from one of the decrees of the Council of Trent, which are the authoritative standard of the Church of Rome. The Decrees of Trent were drawn up by the fiat of the Pope, to counter the teaching of the Reformers, and each one of the decrees of that Council was in direct opposition to what Luther and his contemporaries were teaching: so that when you read the decrees of the Council of Trent you may know for sure what the Reformers did teach. Now one of the decrees of the Council of Trent is as follows:—"If anyone shall affirm that all works done before justification, in what way soever they are done, are properly sins, and deserve the displeasure of God, let such an one be accursed." Well the man standing before you this morning is anathematised by Rome, for that is exactly what he does teach. I boldly affirm with the Reformers that all the religious works of the sinner before his justification by faith, are sins in the sight of heaven and provoke the displeasure of the thrice-holy God. And those of you who believe otherwise link yourselves with Rome! Rome teaches that the sinner before he is converted can do that which is acceptable to God. Now there is the issue drawn. Scripture teaches that God will not receive anything at the hands of anyone while they are dishonoring His Son by refusing to give Him His rightful place in their lives.

Now in my second proposition, I sought to show that God prohibits His people from receiving gifts at the hands of the ungodly. God's people, in their individual lives, should not be beholden to worldlings, and should receive no favors at their hands. In other words, there is a holy independency which Christians should maintain and manifest in their walk through this world, exemplified by the conduct of God's faithful ones in the past—Abraham refusing to be enriched at the hands of the king of Sodom (Gen. 14: 23); David refusing to be enriched by Arunah (2 Sam. 24: 18-24); Daniel declining to receive the emoluments of king Belshazzar; Ezra ashamed to ask for assistance from Cyrus (Ezra 8: 21-23)—all of them setting before us an example to maintain a holy independency of receiving any help or favors from worldlings. The third Epistle of John and the seventh verse contains a sentence that clearly clinches the point and closes all argument for those who are submissive to God's Word:—"Taking nothing of the Gentiles."

Now through lack of time I was unable last Lord's Day morning to make the practical application from those points that I desired. Let me do so briefly now. Our duty is to maintain the line of separation which God has drawn. Our duty is to press upon the unconverted the awfulness of their condition and position before God: that it is such that He cannot and will not receive anything at their hands, while they continue to reject His Son. By our attitude and by our actions we ought to make it clear that the privileges of God's believing people cannot be shared with and enjoyed by unbelievers. Failure here is to make the unconverted comfortable in their sins, and tends to encourage their false hopes. O I know that the horse begins to chafe when the reins are tightened, but the reins need tightening to-day, for everything is sadly lax.

Do you know, my friends, that many of the faithful men who occupied our pulpits of old went so far as to exhort their unbelieving hearers to refrain from so much as singing the hymns that belong to God's people? Yes, the lines were drawn then! Some of you remember that hymn, "Marching to Zion." Well there is a verse in that which says, "Let those refuse to sing who never knew our God, But children of the Heavenly King must tell their joys abroad." And if you search our own hymn book you will find several that bear out the same thought. I believe it is positively injurious to unconverted souls to stand up and sing, "On Christ the Solid Rock I stand," for they are singing a lie, and we are encouraging hypocrisy. O, how far we have departed from the methods and ways of our forefathers!

Now I know there are those, and I have a deep respect for them, who feel that if we draw the lines so strictly, we are going to cast a stumbling-block before some of God's little ones; but, my friends, that ought not to be our first concern. Our first concern should ever be the glory of God. There are many who conscientiously believe that we are casting a stumbling-block before many if we preach the doctrine of election, and they are honest and conscientious in so believing. But this must not deter us from proclaiming all the counsel of God. God's Word is a sharp and a piercing one; and, my friends, if I understand God's Word at all, God Himself has erected a wall around Zion and it is not for us to break that wall down. To call attention to that wall may annoy the ungodly, but I had a thousand times rather annoy them, than grieve the Holy Spirit. Giving is an act of worship, and while it is true that the unconverted may go through the outward form of the act of worship, they cannot worship in spirit and in truth; and while the unconverted may place their offerings in that box God will not receive them and own them.

Now I want to turn to the positive side of the subject, and show, as the Spirit shall enable, that in order for gifts to be acceptable to God these three things must precede. First, acceptable gifts must be presented to the true and living God. There are multitudes of our fellow-men and women who make offerings, some of them at the point of self-sacrifice; and yet they are not offered to the true God. The heathen make sacrifices and offerings to their idols. Romanists make offerings to Mary and the priests, not to the living, true God. Now it needs no argument from me to show that such gifts are not accepted by Heaven, and yet I would remind you that many of those very people believe that they are acceptable, and they would be hurt if you told them they were not. They are quite sincere in their motive.

But now, coming a little nearer home. Listen! It is not quite such an easy and a simple matter as many think to present an offering to the true God, for sin has separated man from his Maker. By nature and by practice the natural man is far from Him. Yes, and it is just that which the ungodly hate to be reminded of. It makes them very uncomfortable to be told that they are at an awful guilty distance from God; but nevertheless it needs to be pressed upon them.

How can one who is sinful approach unto Him who is holy? But it is just at this point that God has revealed Himself as the God of all grace. He has mercifully provided a **Mediator**—one who is both God and Man; one who has bridged the whole distance between the Throne of God in Heaven and the poor sinner here on earth. Now that brings me to the second point.

Second, in order for an offering to be acceptable to God, it must not only be offered to the true God Himself, but it must be offered to Him **through the appointed Mediator**. That was impressively taught under the Old Testament economy. There is not time now for me to read the passages in Leviticus. In the second chapter and in the fifth chapter you will find quite a number of verses which teach that when an Israelite desired to bring an offering to God, it was only by means of the appointed priest that the blood of that offering was carried in and presented before Jehovah, typifying, in that dispensation of shadows, that even the Israelites did not have direct access to God. They could not approach unto God themselves—it was only by means of a Mediator they had access unto Jehovah.

The Lord Jesus Christ Himself emphatically taught the same thing when He said, "No man cometh unto the Father but by Me." No sinner can even approach to God, let alone give God something; no sinner can even approach to God, except and only as he comes through the Mediator, our Lord Jesus Christ. Listen! To argue that God will receive offerings from those who are rejecting His Son is to repudiate and deny the Mediator. O brethren and sisters, with all the earnestness of which I am capable, I beseech you weigh carefully that solemn consequence. If the sinner in his sins can worship God acceptably, if God will receive an offering from the hands of one who is rejecting His Son, then a Mediator is no longer needful! And, brethren and sisters, to deny the Mediatorship of Christ is a million times more serious than casting a stumbling-block before worms of the earth!

Now let me give you a few scriptures from the New Testament which emphasise and reiterate the fact that our only access to God, and the only ground of anything being acceptable to God is in and by and through the Lord Jesus Christ. Take first of all our text. "Spiritual sacrifices acceptable to God by Jesus Christ." A spiritual sacrifice presupposes a spiritual offerer: a carnal person cannot bring a spiritual sacrifice. A spiritual sacrifice necessarily implies a spiritual sacrificer; and the first evidence and mark of a spiritual sacrificer or of a spiritual person, is faith in our Lord Jesus Christ. And that brings me to the third prerequisite.

In order for an offering to be acceptable it must be presented to the true God. It must be presented to the true God through the appointed Mediator, and it must be **offered in faith**. What are we told in Hebrews 11.6? "Without faith it is impossible to please God." Now that is simple; that needs no deep theologian to explain it to you; that defines the issue. There is only one other alternative; a thing is either pleasing or it is displeasing to God; it is either acceptable or it is abominable. Some have asked the question, Do you believe that the gifts of So-and-so would be an abomination unto God? Answer your own question in the light of this verse. Answer it honestly for yourself. Without faith it is impossible to please God. Well, perhaps some reply, but Dr. Pink, how do we know whether a certain person has faith or not? My answer to that is, I don't know. I do not profess to have any gift to read people's hearts; I am simply making the affirmation that if there is no faith then their gifts are unacceptable to God. If there is faith, even though it be as a grain of mustard, their gifts are acceptable. But, mark you, not a mere notional faith in the existence of God, not simply an intellectual faith in the doctrines of grace, but a saving faith that has laid hold of the Lord Jesus Christ. It was the presence of such faith which made Abel's offering acceptable unto the Lord, as it was the absence of such faith that caused Cain to be rejected. In 2 Cor. 8, where the subject of "Giving" is developed at length, we read in v.5: they "first gave their own selves to the Lord." All true "giving" begins there—first faith in Christ, then the consecration of ourselves unto Him, and then giving to the support of His cause.

What are we told in Romans 8.8? "They that are in the flesh cannot please God." No matter how you try, no matter what you do, while you are out of Christ, nothing that you do, or try to do, is pleasing or acceptable to God. Now listen! Do you mean to tell me that God will accept something that is displeasing to Him? "They that are in the flesh cannot please God." Do you mean to tell me that God is going to accept what is displeasing to Him? and whatever is presented by a man in the flesh—a man out of Christ—is displeasing.

Now turn to Ephesians 5.20. "Giving thanks always for all things unto God and the Father in the name of our Lord Jesus Christ." We cannot give thanks unto God, in the scriptural sense of the term, except it be "in the name of our Lord Jesus Christ." You have the same thing again in Romans 1, verse 8. I want you to see how specifically and carefully the Holy Spirit has qualified the apostle's statement there. "First, I thank my God . . . for you all, that your faith is spoken of throughout the whole world." Yes, but notice the qualifying clause that I omitted! Notice the importance of it! "I thank my God **through Jesus Christ.**" You cannot thank God while you are rejecting Jesus Christ: it is a piece of mummery and mockery to attempt it. Listen again to Hebrews 13, verse 15:—"By Him therefore let us offer the sacrifice of praise to God." By Him! **By Him!** You cannot offer the sacrifice of praise to God while you are rejecting Him. Now, once again, in the first Epistle of Peter, chapter 4, verse 11: this is the last I will give you now, and a most important verse it is for all of us:—"If any man speak, let him speak as the oracles of God; if any man minister, let him do it as of the ability which God giveth: that God in all **things** may be glorified **through Jesus Christ.**" The word "glorified", there, means owned and acknowledged.

Now let me close with these two words of practical application. First, to my brothers and sisters in Christ. How profoundly thankful we ought to be that God, in His mercy, **has** provided a Mediator; that we—miserable, ignorant, sinful, unworthy, unprofitable creatures, —can offer that which is acceptable to the great and holy God! How thankful we should be that, in spite of the weakness of our faith, the poverty of our love, the utter inadequacy of our gifts; nevertheless, if we place them in the hand of Christ by simple faith, He will present them to the Father **acceptable** in His sight! O brothers and sisters, that is the ground of our comfort, that is the ground of our confidence. I would not dare approach the thrice holy God without a Mediator. I dare not enter this pulpit and preach the most carefully-prepared sermon without first asking God to help in the delivery of it, and to bless the message **for the sake of** His blessed Son. That is the ground of the believer's confidence and the believer's comfort; that in spite of our failings, in spite of the poorness and the inadequacy of our efforts, our prayers, our service and our worship; yet, nevertheless, they **are** acceptable to the Almighty God; because they are presented to Him, accompanied by the merits and the virtues of our blessed Mediator! O brethren, take that away, take that away as Rome does, and tell me that by my **own** efforts and by my own merits, apart from Christ, I can come to God, and that I can offer to Him that which He will receive and—speaking for myself—the foundation is gone; and "If the foundations be destroyed, what can the righteous do?" saith the Psalmist.

Now my last word is to the unconverted. Dear friends, you have been reminded once more of the awfulness of your condition and position before God—that it is such that God cannot and will not receive aught at your hands while you are rejecting Christ. Does that make some of you say, Well then, I might just as well stop trying to please God? O dear friend, that is the very point I want to bring you to. By the Holy Spirit's help that is the very corner I want to drive you into; that you may cease from your own efforts to please God, for they are worthless, and useless. You cannot do one single thing that is acceptable to God while you reject His beloved Son! I have reminded you that God has erected a wall around Zion; but, O dear friends, there is a door into that wall. The Saviour said, "I am the door: by Me if any man enter in, he shall be saved." Through that Door you may enter, you may have access to God, and you may join the company of God's favored people, join with them in their happy privileges; join with them in rendering to God that which is acceptable to Him through Jesus Christ.

I have tried to put the issue before you plainly this morning that there are certain privileges which belong to God's believing people alone. If you don't enjoy them it is your own fault, not the fault of the church. If you want to present an offering in that box which is acceptable to God, you may do so. How? By throwing down the weapons of your warfare and by kissing the Son lest He be angry. And, my friends, that door stands wide open this morning—not ajar but wide open. "By Me if any man enter he shall be saved." O, if there is an unconverted soul exercised over this very subject (and I firmly believe God is using the subject to exercise some), may the Holy Spirit use the message to make clear to you your need of a Mediator. It is only as your gifts are placed in His hands that God will receive them. May God bless you for Christ's sake!

Sermon by the Editor at Belvoir Street, Sydney, Particular Baptist Church, on Sunday Morning, 29/8/'26.

## TITHING (No. 1)

Our text is found in the 14th chapter of Genesis and the last sentence of the 20th verse:—"And he gave him tithes of all."

There are few subjects on which the Lord's own people are more astray than the subject of Giving. They profess to take the Bible only as their rule of faith and practice, and yet in the matter of Christian finance, the vast majority have utterly ignored its plain teachings and have tried every substitute the carnal mind could devise; therefore there is no wonder that the majority of Christian enterprises in the world to-day are handicapped and are crippled through lack of funds. Is our giving to be regulated by sentiment and impulse or by principle and conscience? That is only another way of asking, Does God leave us to the spirit of gratitude and generosity or has He definitely specified His own mind and particularised what portion of His gifts to us are due to Him in return? Surely God has not left this important matter without fully making known His will! The Bible is given to be a lamp unto our feet and therefore He cannot have left us in darkness on any obligation or privilege in our dealings with Him or His with us.

Now this morning I am only going to attempt to bring before you an outline of what the Scriptures teach on the subject of tithing. If the Lord permits, next Sabbath morning I shall go more deeply into the significance or the meaning of the Scriptures that will come before us.

Now first of all I want to take up tithing in the Old Testament. At a very early date in the history of our race God made it known that a definite proportion of the saint's income should be devoted to Him who is the giver of all. There was a period of twenty-five centuries from Adam until the time that God gave the law to Israel at Sinai, but it is a great mistake to suppose that the saints of God in those early centuries were left without a definite revelation, without a knowledge of God's will of their obligations to Him, and of the great blessings which resulted from a faithful performance of their duties. As we study carefully the Book of Genesis there are clear traces there of a primitive revelation, an indication of God's mind to His people long before the system of legislation that was given at Sinai; and that primal revelation seems to have centred about three things:—First, the offering of sacrifices to God; second, the observance of the sabbath; and third, the giving of tithes.

Now follow me closely at this stage. While it is perfectly true that to-day we are unable to take up the Bible and place our finger upon any positive enactment or commandment from God that His people in those early days should either offer sacrifices to Him or keep the Sabbath or give the tithe (there is no definite "Thus saith the Lord" recorded concerning any one of those three), nevertheless, from what is recorded we are compelled to assume that there must have been such a commandment given.

Take first of all the presenting of sacrifices to God. Is it thinkable that man would ever have presented blood to Deity if he had never first received a command so to do? Do you think it would ever have occurred to the human mind itself to have brought a bleeding animal unto the great Creator? And yet we find in the very earliest times that Abel, that Noah, that Abraham, presented bleeding offerings unto Jehovah—clearly presupposing that God had already made it known that such was His will for His creatures; that the Most High required just such an offering.

Take again the Sabbath. There is nothing in the early pages of Scripture to show us that God Himself appointed one day in seven and that He made it a law that all of His creatures should so observe it; and yet there are clear indications that such must have been the case, or otherwise we cannot explain what follows. When God gave the ten commandments to Israel at Sinai, in the fourth commandment He did not tell Israel to keep the Sabbath; He commanded them to remember the Sabbath day, which clearly implies two things: that at an earlier date the mind of God concerning the Sabbath had been revealed, but, that their forefathers had forgotten. The Book of Ezekiel clearly establishes that.

The same is true in connection with the tithe. At this day we are unable to go back to the earliest pages of Scripture and put our finger upon a "Thus saith the Lord," a definite commandment where Jehovah specified His will and demanded that His people should render a tenth of all their increase unto Him; and yet as we take up the Book of Genesis we cannot account for what is there unless we presuppose a previous revelation of God's mind and a manifestation of His will upon the point.

Now first of all in our text we are told that Abraham gave tithes unto Melchisedec. We are not told why he did so. We are not told in the previous chapters that God had told him to do so. I repeat it, that there is no "Thus saith the Lord" preceding this action, any more than there was a "Thus saith the Lord" that required the patriarchs to bring an offering to Him, but the fact that he did so, implies that he was acting in accordance with God's will and that he was carrying out His revealed mind.

Now take again the 28th chapter of Genesis and the 22nd verse. Perhaps I had better begin at verse 19 and give you the context:—"And he called the name of that place Bethel." (You remember the circumstances. This was the night when Jacob was fleeing from Esau, a fugitive from home, starting out to Laban's, and that night while he was asleep he had the vision). "And Jacob vowed a vow, saying, If God will be with me, and will keep me in this way that I go, and will give me bread to eat, and raiment to put on, so that I come again to my father's house in peace; then shall the Lord be my God; and this stone, which I have set for a pillar, shall be God's house: and of all that Thou shalt give me, I will surely give the tenth unto Thee." There again you have the tithe. Jacob vowed that in return for the Lord's temporal blessings upon him, he would render a tenth in return to the Lord. We are not told why he selected that percentage; we are not told why he should give a tenth; but the fact that he did determine so to do indicates that there had previously been a revelation of God's mind to His creatures, and particularly to His people, that one-tenth of their income should be devoted to the Giver of all.

Now when we come to the Mosaic law we find that the tithe was definitely and clearly incorporated into it. The 27th of Leviticus and the 30th verse, "And all the tithe of the land, whether of the seed of the land, or of the fruit of the tree, is the Lord's: it is holy unto the Lord. And if a man will at all redeem ought of his tithes, he shall add thereto the fifth part thereof. And concerning the tithe of the herd, or of the flock, even of whatsoever passeth under the rod, the tenth shall be holy unto the Lord." Now what I want you to notice in that is the twice-repeated expression concerning the tithe, that it was "holy unto the Lord." That is to say, God reserves to Himself, as His exclusive right, as His own, one tenth of that which He has given us. It is "holy" unto the Lord. Now that anticipates a point that may have been engaging some of your minds. When we say that one-tenth of our gross income belongs to the Lord I suppose some are inclined to say, Well, all of our income belongs to the Lord: everything that we have has been given us by God: nothing is our own in the full sense of the word, it is all His. Perfectly true in one sense, but not so in another sense. In one sense it is true that all of our time belongs unto God, that it is not ours; and we shall yet have to give an account of every idle moment; but in another real sense it is also true that God has set apart one-seventh of our time as being holy unto Him. That is to say, it has been set apart for a sacred use: it is not ours to do as we please with. The sabbath is not a day for doing our own pleasure, it is a day that has been appointed and singled out by God as being peculiarly His—holy unto Him —one-seventh of our time spent in His service. Now then, here in Leviticus 27, 30-32, we are told that the tithe is holy unto the Lord. That is to say that one-tenth is not our own personal property at all: it does not belong to us in the slightest; we have no say-so about it whatsoever: it is set apart unto a holy use: it is the Lord's and His alone.

Now proceeding. In the 18th chapter of Numbers, verse 26:—"Thus speak unto the Levites, and say unto them, When ye take of the children of Israel the tithes which I have given you from them for your inheritance, then ye shall offer up an heave-offering of it for the Lord, even a tenth part of the tithe." Let me read that again; I don't think I emphasised that correctly. Beginning at the 25th verse (Numbers 18, verse 25):—"And the Lord spake unto Moses, saying, Thus speak unto the Levites, and say unto them, When ye take of the children of Israel the tithes which I have given you from them for your inheritance, then ye shall offer up an heave offering of it for the Lord, even a tenth part of the tithe." Now that shows us that the support of the priestly family in Old Testament times was not left to the whims of the people or as to how they felt led to give. God did not leave it for them to determine. The support of the priestly family was definitely specified. The priestly family was to derive their support out of one-tenth of all that the other tribes received from their annual increase, and the priests themselves were required to take one-tenth of all out of their portion and present it to the Lord. They were no exceptions to the rule. No, and it is very significant to notice in going through the balance of the Old Testament (What I have just read you has been from Leviticus and from the Book of Numbers which contain the laws which the Lord gave to Moses in the wilderness before Israel settled down in the land of Canaan). Well now, those of you who have read through the historical books of Scripture know full well what a miserable failure Israel made of it under the law after they had settled down in the land, how that almost every fundamental precept and statute of the legislation that Jehovah gave to Moses was disregarded by them. But what is very significant is this, that in each great revival of godliness that Jehovah sent unto Israel the tithing is one of the things that is mentioned as being renewed and restored among them. Now first of all turn to the second Book of Chronicles and the 30th chapter. This records a great revival that took place in the days of Hezekiah. There had been a fearful time of declension in the reigns of the preceding kings, but in the days of Hezekiah God graciously gave a blessed revival and in II. Chronicles 30, verse 1, we read:—"And Hezekiah sent to all Israel and Judah, and wrote letters also to Ephraim and Manasseh, that they should come to the house of the Lord at Jerusalem, to keep the passover unto the Lord God of Israel." Things had got in such an awful state that they had not even kept the passover for several centuries! But when God works a revival one of its most prominent features is to cause His people to return to the written Word. Do you get that? A heaven-sent revival consists not so much of happy feelings and spasmodical enthusiasm and fleshly displays and great crowds of people in attendance —those are not the marks of a heaven-sent revival—but when God renews His work of grace in His churches one of the first things that He does in connection with that is to cause His people to return to that written Word from which they have departed in their ways and in their practices. Now then, that was what happened in the days of Hezekiah. We read that he wrote letters to Ephraim and Manasseh that they should come to the house of the Lord at Jerusalem, to keep the passover unto the Lord God of Israel. Think of them needing letters! It is like the Secretary of this Church having to send out letters to its members informing them that on the first Sabbath of the month the Lord's Supper is going to be commemorated! You see what that would imply? Well now that is what you have here. Now if you will read on to chapter 31, verses 4, 5 and 6, you will find the tithes mentioned. Verse 4:—"Moreover he commanded the people that dwelt in Jerusalem to give the portion of the priests and the Levites, that they might be encouraged in the law of the Lord. And as soon as the commandment came abroad, the children of Israel brought in abundance the first fruits of corn, wine, and oil, and honey, and of all the increase of the field; and the tithe of all things brought they in abundantly. And concerning the children of Israel and Judah, that dwelt in the cities of Judah, they also brought in the tithe of oxen and sheep, and the tithe of holy things which were consecrated unto the Lord their God, and laid them by heaps." That is what I wanted to call attention to, that following the great revival in the 30th chapter where the passover was restored we find that the Israelites brought in their tithes.

Now the same thing is true again in the 10th chapter of Nehemiah. You remember the Book of Nehemiah brings you to a later point in the history of Israel. Nehemiah records a return of a small remnant of the people after the nation had been carried away into captivity after the seventy years' captivity in Babylon was over and God raised up Cyrus to make a decree permitting those who desired to go back to their own land. In the Book of Nehemiah, the 10th chapter, we find that in the revival of his day the tithe is also mentioned. Nehemiah 10, beginning at verse 34:— "And we cast the lots among the priests, the Levites, and the people, for the wood offering, to bring it into the house of our God, after the houses of our fathers, at times appointed year by year, to burn upon the altar of the Lord our God, as it is written in the law: And to bring the firstfruits of our ground, and the firstfruits of all fruit of all trees, year by year, unto the house of the Lord: Also the firstborn of our sons, and of our cattle, as it is written in the law, and the firstlings of our herds and of our flocks, to bring to the house of our God, unto the priests that minister in the house of our God: And that we should bring the first fruits of our dough, and our offerings, and the fruit of all manner of trees, of wine and of oil, unto the priests, to the chambers of the house of our God; and the tithes of our ground unto the Levites, that the same Levites might have the tithes in all the cities of our tillage," and so on. So that one of the things that is specified in connection with the revival in the days of the returned remnant from captivity was that the tithe was restored in connection with the maintenance of the house of the servants of God.

Now if you will turn to the last Book of the Old Testament, Malachi 3. Malachi brings us to a point still later and shows us how the remnant that had returned in the days of Nehemiah had also degenerated and deteriorated and had departed from the word of the law of the Lord, and, among other things, what are the charges that God brings against Israel in verses 7 and 8? "Even from the days of your fathers ye are gone away from mine ordinances, and have not kept them. Return unto me, and I will return unto you, saith the Lord of hosts. But ye said, Wherein shall we return? Will a man rob God? Yet ye have robbed me. But ye say, Wherein have we robbed thee? In tithes and offerings." How solemn to notice that in the last chapter of the Old Testament that makes mention of the tithe we are there taught that those who withheld the tithe from Jehovah are charged with having robbed God! How solemn!

Now coming to the New Testament, the first thing I want to say here is this. Only God has the right to say how much of our income shall be set aside and set apart unto Him. God has so said clearly, repeatedly, in the Old Testament Scriptures, and there is nothing in the New that introduces any change or that sets aside the teaching of the Old.

Now first I want to show you that Christ Himself has placed His approval and set His imprimatur upon the tithe. Matthew 23, verse 23:—"Woe unto you, scribes and Pharisees, hypocrites! for ye pay tithe of mint and anise and cummin, and have omitted the weightier matters of the law, judgment, mercy, and faith: these ought ye to have done, and not to leave the other undone." Now in that verse Christ is rebuking the scribes and the Pharisees because of their hypocrisy. They had been very strict and punctilious in tithing the herbs, but on the other hand they had neglected the weightier matters such as judgment or justice and mercy. But while Christ acknowledged that the observance of justice and mercy is more important than tithing—it is a "weightier matter"—while, He says, these ye ought to have done, nevertheless, He says, these ye ought not to have left undone. He does not set aside the tithe. He places justice and mercy as being more weighty, but He places His authority upon the practice of tithing by saying "These ought ye to have done, and not to leave the other undone." It is well for us if we by the grace of God have not omitted justice and mercy and faith: it is well if by the grace of God those things have found a place in our midst: but the tithing ought not to have been left undone. Do you see the point? The justice, the mercy, and the faith are weightier matters than tithing, and these ye ought to have done, but the tithing ought not to be left undone, and Christ Himself says so.

Now the second passage I would have you turn to is in I. Corinthians 9, verses 13 and 14:—"Do ye not know that they which minister about holy things live of the things of the temple? and they which wait at the altar are partakers with the altar? Even so hath the Lord ordained that they which preach the gospel should live of the gospel." Now the emphatic words there are "even so," the beginning of the 14th verse. The word "tithe" is not found in these two verses but it is most clearly implied. In the 13th verse the Holy Spirit reminds the New Testament saints that under the Mosaic economy God had made provision for the maintenance of those who ministered in the temple. Now then, He says, in this New Testament dispensation (verse 14) "Even so"—the same means and the same method should be used in the support and maintaining of the gospel as was used in supporting the temple and its services of old. "Even so." It was the tithe that supported God's servants in the Old Testament dispensation: even so God has ordained, God has appointed that His servants in the New Testament dispensation shall be provided for.

Now take the 16th chapter of I. Corinthians, verses 1 and 2. Here again the word "tithe" does not actually occur, and yet once more it is plainly implied. The principle of it is there surely enough. "Now concerning the collection for the saints, as I have given order to the churches of Galatia, even so do ye. Upon the first day of the week let every one of you lay by him." Now what does "laying by" imply? Certainly it implies a definite pre-determined act, rather than a spontaneous impulse and just acting on the spur of the moment—as you feel led. Now secondly, look at it again. Verse 2:—"Upon the first day of the week let every one of you lay by him in store." Why are we told that? Why is it put that way? Why use such an expression, "Lay by in store"? Clearly that language points us back to Malachi 3, 10:—"Bring ye your tithes into the——" Where? The "storehouse"! That is where the tithes were to be brought. "Bring ye your tithes into the storehouse." Now what does God say here in Corinthians? "Upon the first day of the week let every one of you lay by him in store." There is a clear reference back to the terms of Malachi 3, but that is not all. Look at it again. "Let every one of you lay by him in store, as God hath prospered him." That signifies a definite proportion of the income." Not let every one of you lay by him as he feels led: it does not say that: it does not say let everyone lay by him as he feels moved by the Spirit: no, Sir, it does not say anything of the kind. It says, "Let every one . . . lay by him. . . as God hath prospered him": in a proportionate way: according to a percentage basis. Now listen! If my income to-day is double what is was a year ago and I am not giving any more to the Lord's cause than I gave then, then I am not giving "as the Lord hath prospered": I am not giving proportionately. But now the question arises, what proportion? What is the proportion that is according to the will of God? "As He hath prospered him." Can one man bring one proportion and another man bring another proportion and yet both of them obey this precept? Must not all bring the same proportion in order to meet the requirements of this passage? Turn for a moment to 2 Corinthians 8. 14:—"But by an equality, that now at this time your abundance may be a supply for their want, that their abundance also may be a supply for your want: that there may be **equality.**" Now that verse occurs in the middle of a chapter that is devoted to the subject of giving, and what I want you to observe is that at the beginning of that 14th verse and at the end of it you have repeated the word "equality," which means that God's people are all to give the same proportion of their means, and the only proportion that God has specified anywhere in His Word is that of the tenth.

Now there is only one other passage I want you to look at now and that is in Hebrews 7, verse 5:—"And verily they that are of the sons of Levi, who receive the office of the priesthood, have a commandment to take tithes of the people according to the law, that is, of their brethren, though they come out of the loins of Abraham: But he whose descent is not counted from them received tithes of Abraham, and blessed him" (Notice the order:—"received tithes of Abraham, and blessed him that had the promises. And without all contradiction the less is blessed of the better." Now in that 7th chapter of Hebrews the Holy Spirit through the apostle Paul is arguing the superiority of Christ's priesthood over the order of priesthood of the Levites, and one of the proofs by which he establishes the transcendency of the Melchisedec order of the priesthood of Christ was that Abraham, the very father of the chosen people, acknowledged the greatness of Melchisedec by rendering tithes to him. Now then the reference here in Hebrews 7 is to what we have recorded in the 14th chapter of Genesis, where we have two typical characters brought before us—Melchisedec, a type of Christ in three ways: first, in his person combining the kingly and the priestly offices; second, a type of Christ in his names, combining righteousness and peace, for "Melchisedec" itself means "King of righteousness" and "Salem" means "peace"; and third, a type of Christ in that he pronounced blessing on Abraham and brought forth bread and wine—the memorials of his death.

But not only was Melchisedec there a type of Christ, but Abraham was also a typical character, a representative character, seen there as the father of the faithful, and we find that he acknowledged the priesthood of Melchisedec by giving to him a tenth of the spoils that the Lord had enabled him to secure in vanquishing those kings, and as that is referred to in Hebrews, where the priesthood of Christ and our blessings from our relations to it and our obligations to it are set forth, the fact that Abraham paid tithes to Melchisedec as mentioned there indicates that as Abraham is the father of the faithful so he left an example for his children to follow—in rendering tithes unto Him of whom Melchisedec was the type. And the beautiful thing to me in connection with this Scripture is that the last time the tithe is mentioned in the Bible (here in Hebrews 7) it links the tithe directly with Christ Himself. All intermediaries are removed. In the Old Testament the tithes were brought to the priests, then carried into the storehouse, but in the final reference in Scripture the tithe is linked directly with **Christ,** showing us that our obligations in the matter are concerned directly with the great Head of the Church.

Now this morning, beloved, I have only just had time and strength to introduce the Scriptures to you that present God's mind on the matter. Next Sabbath morning, if the Lord permits, I hope to deal with the subject in an expository and in an argumentative way. This morning I have just presented an outline of Scripture without attempting to give you any inferences and conclusions.

One evil ever leads to another. God's appointed method for the financing of the work which He has been pleased to place in our hands, is that of Tithing—the strict setting aside of one tenth of all we receive, to be devoted to His cause. Where the Lord's people faithfully do this, there is never any shortage or going into debt. Where Tithing is ignored there is almost always a deficit, and then the ungodly are asked to help or worldly methods are employed to raise money. If we sow the wind, we must not be surprised if we reap the whirlwind.

A. W. P.

enter into the kingdom of God. (Acts 14: 22). Nevertheless, the Lord does not "afflict willingly" (Lamentations 3: 33). God is neither unmindful of nor indifferent to our trials and troubles. Concerning His people of old it is written "In all their affliction He was afflicted" (Isaiah 63: 9). "Like as a father pitieth his children, so the Lord pitieth them that fear Him" (Psalm 103: 13). So also are we told that our great High Priest is "touched with the feeling of our infirmities" (Heb. 4: 15). Here, then, may be another reason why the death of a saint is precious in the sight of the Lord—because it marks the termination of his sorrows and sufferings.

Third, because death affords the Lord an opportunity to display His sufficiency.

Love is never so happy as when ministering to the needs of its cherished object, and never is the Christian so needy and so helpless as in the hour of death. But man's extremity is God's opportunity. It is then that the Father says to His trembling child, "Fear thou not; for I am with thee: be not dismayed, for I am thy God: I will strengthen thee; yea, I will help thee; yea, I will uphold thee with the right hand of My righteousness" (Isaiah 41: 10). It is because of this that the believer may confidently reply, "Yea, though I walk through the valley of the shadow of death, I will fear no evil: for Thou art with me; Thy rod and Thy staff they comfort me." Our very weakness appeals to His strength, our emergency to His sufficiency. Most blessedly is this principle illustrated in the well-known words "He shall gather the lambs (the helpless ones) with His arm, and carry them in His bosom (Isaiah 40: 11). Yes, His strength is made perfect in our weakness. Therefore is the death of the saints "precious" in His sight because it affords the Lord a blessed occasion for His love, grace and power to minister unto and undertake for His helpless people.

Fourth, because at death the saint goes direct to the Lord.

The Lord delights in having His people with Himself. Blessedly was this evidenced all through His earthly ministry. Wherever He went, the Lord took His disciples along with Him. Whether it was to the marriage at Cana, to the holy Feasts in Jerusalem, to the house of Jairus when his daughter lay dead, or to the Mount of Transfiguration, they ever accompanied Him. How blessed is that word in Mark 3: 14, "He ordained twelve, that they should be with Him." And He is "the same yesterday and to-day and for ever." Therefore has He assured us "If I go and prepare a place for you, I will come again, and receive you unto Myself, that where I am, there ye may be also" (John 14: 3). Precious then is the death of the saints in His sight, because absent from the body, we are "present with the Lord" (2 Cor. 5: 8).

While we are sorrowing over the removal of a saint, Christ is rejoicing. His prayer was "Father, I will that they also, whom Thou hast given Me, be with Me where I am; that they may behold My glory" (John 17:24), and in the entrance into Heaven of each one of His own people, He sees an answer to that prayer and is glad. He beholds in each one that is freed from "this body of death" another portion of the reward for His travail of soul, and He is satisfied with it. Therefore the death of His saints is precious to the Lord, for it occasions Him ground for rejoicing.

It is most interesting and instructive to trace out the fulness of the Hebrew word here translated "precious." It is also rendered "excellent." "How excellent is Thy loving kindness, O God! (Psalm 36: 7). "A man of understanding is of an excellent spirit" (Prov. 17: 27). However worthily or unworthily he may live, the death of a saint is excellent in the sight of the Lord.

The same Hebrew word is also rendered "honourable." "Kings' daughters were among thy honourable women" (Psa. 45: 9). So Ahasuerus asked of Haman "What shall be done unto the man whom the king delighteth to honour?" (Esther 6: 6). Yes, the exchange of heaven for earth is truly honourable, and "This honour have all His saints. Praise ye the Lord."

This Hebrew word is also rendered "brightness." "If I beheld the sun when it shined, or the moon walking in brightness" (Job 31: 26). Dark and gloomy though death may be unto those whom the Christian leaves behind, it is brightness "in the sight of the Lord:" "at evening time it shall be light" (Zech. 14: 7). Precious, excellent, honourable brightness in the sight of the Lord is the death of His saints. May the Lord make this little meditation precious unto His saints.

—ARTHUR W. PINK.

… VOL. VI.     MAY, 1927     NO. 5

# STUDIES IN THE SCRIPTURES

"Search the Scriptures" John 5:39.

Copyright in all English-speaking Countries.

Editor: Arthur W. Pink, 15 Hurlstone Avenue, Summer Hill, N.S.W., Australia.
Hon. Agent in U.S.A.: Mr. C. S. Pressel, 559 Dupont Ave., York, Penna.

FREE TO ALL WHO WILL READ IT

Numbers of old friends in various parts of the world desire us to give them, every once in a while, a little news about ourselves. With one or two exceptions we have refrained from using the pages of the magazine for this purpose, mainly because it seemed out of keeping with the central design for which "Studies in the Scriptures" are published—we have steadily endeavoured to remain true to the title. But trusting it will be for God's glory and the good of His people, we shall recount some of the Lord's dealings with us.

By the time this issue is in print, the editor and his wife will have spent upwards of two years in Australia. The Lord has mercifully granted us both a goodly measure of health and strength. The magazine requires much time and attention, and were it not for the labors of Mrs. Pink we could not very well continue. She types out all the articles, helps with the correspondence and other items of the office work. For about two months in the year the weather is very trying. Heat temperatures varying from 85 to 105 during January and February, and sometimes March, and are accompanied by heavy humidity, often from 70 to 95. But usually after three or four hot days, God mercifully sends relief in the form of a "southerly." This is a wind blowing at a velocity of from 30 to 45 miles an hour and lasting from twelve to forty-eight hours, gradually reducing in strength. The thermometer drops from 10 to 25 degrees in an hour and the cool breezes at once act as a tonic. This braces us and prepares for the next hot spell. "As thy days so shall thy strength be" is God's never-failing promise.

In the editorial of December, 1925, we announced that Bible-study classes had been organized in three different centers, one night a week being given to each of them. By the goodness of God, these are still going on, with an average total attendance of over two hundred. Almost all who come bring their Bibles and have settled down to real systematic study, and many are the testimonies of help and blessing received. Interest is well maintained. In April, 1926, we started a fourth class in a distant suburb and continued same till the end of the year, closing down then for three months till the hot weather was over. In this last mentioned one, God was pleased to unmistakably bring two precious souls out of darkness into His own marvelous light.

In the May, 1926, issue, of "Studies" (in "Regions Beyond"), we mentioned that the editor and his wife had united with the Strict and Particular Baptist Church, Sydney. Here we have enjoyed the Lord's continuous blessing, receiving many tokens of His gracious favor. Several changes have been introduced which we believe are in accord with God's Word, and therefore honoring to Him whom we serve. First, we are now using the unleavened bread at the Lord's table. In Scripture "leaven" is uniformly employed as the figure of evil, and was expressly prohibited in the Passover-feast, which foreshadowed the Saviour's death (2 Cor. 5:7). If, then, God forbade leavened bread in the type which pointed to Christ's death, by what right may we now use leavened bread as one of the emblems to "show" that death? "As often as ye eat," not bread, but "this bread" (1 Cor. 11:26) —i.e., the same kind of bread used by the Saviour Himself when He instituted the supper—is decisive.

(*Continued on page 120*).

## BACK NUMBERS

OF THIS MAGAZINE obtainable, 5/- (1 dollar) per year; Bound at 7/- (1 dollar 75.) Each year is yet obtainable.

ADVISE PROMPTLY of Change of Address

THIS MAGAZINE is published as a work of faith and labor of love. It is gladly sent to all who would value it.

We want the names and addresses of Christians who would read it.

Christians who feel definitely led to do so may have fellowship with us in this Ministry.

## CONTENTS.

| | |
|---|---|
| The Gospel of John (19:12-24) | 98 |
| Gleanings in Exodus | 105 |
| Tithing (No. 2) | 109 |
| Experimental Salvation | 114 |
| Perfected for Ever | 118 |

## THE GOSPEL OF JOHN.

### 65. Christ Condemned to Death: John 19:12-24.

The following is an Analysis of the passage which is to be before us:—

1. Pilate's effort foiled: v. 12.
2. Pilate on the Bench: v. 12.
3. The Jews' rejection of their Messiah: v. 15.
4. Christ delivered to the Jews: v. 16.
5. Christ crucified: vv. 17-18.
6. The inscription of the Cross: vv. 19-22.
7. The soldiers and Christ's garments: vv. 23-24.

The death of Christ may be viewed from five main viewpoints. From the standpoint of God the Cross was a propitiation (Rom. 3:25-26), where full satisfaction was made to His holiness and justice. From the standpoint of the Saviour, it was a sacrifice (Eph. 5:2), an offering (Heb. 9:14), an act of obedience (Phil. 2:8). From the standpoint of believers, it was a substitution, the Just suffering for the unjust (1 Peter 3:18). From the standpoint of Satan it was a triumph and a defeat: a triumph, in that he bruised the heel of the woman's Seed (Gen. 3:15); a defeat, in that through His death Christ destroyed him that had the power of death, that is, the Devil (Heb. 2:14). From the standpoint of the world it was a brutal murder (Acts 3:15). It is with this last-mentioned aspect of the death of Christ that our present passage principally treats.

The ones who (from the human side) took the initiative in the slaying of the Lamb of God, were the Jews; the one who was judicially responsible was Pilate. In the introduction to our last article we pointed out two things: first, that God had ordained Pilate should pass sentence upon His Son; second, that Pilate was, nevertheless, morally guilty in so doing. We shall not review the ground already covered, but would supplement our previous remarks by a few words upon Pilate's final actions.

From the very first move made by the Jews for Pilate to sentence their Messiah, it is evident that he had no relish for the part which they wished and urged him to play; and the more he saw of Christ for himself, the more his reluctance increased. This is apparent from his restless journeying back and forth from the judgment-hall; evidenced by his repeated protestations of Christ's innocence; evidenced by the compromises he offered them; evidenced by the appeals he made to them. If, then, he was unwilling to pass the death-sentence, how comes it that he, the Roman Governor, was finally prevailed upon to do so? In seeking to answer this question we shall now confine ourselves to the human side of things.

In the first place, the Jews had charged Christ with perverting the Nation, stirring up the people, teaching them to refuse to pay tribute, and claiming Himself to be the King of the Jews (Luke 23:2-5). These were charges which Pilate could not afford to ignore. It is true the preferring of such charges was one thing, and the proving of them quite another; but the Governor was too much of a politician not to know how easy it was to manufacture evidence and to hire false witnesses. In the second place, Pilate had himself incurred the hatred of the Jews by mingling the blood of certain Galileans with their sacrifices (Luke 13:1)—a thing not only morally wrong, but legally reprehensible. In the third place, when Pilate showed signs of weakening, the Jews told him that if he did let Jesus go, he was no friend of Caesar (John 18: 12). Pilate was quick to perceive that if he released his Prisoner, complaint would at once be made to the Emperor, and under a charge of conspiracy and treason, he was likely not only to lose the governorship, but his head as well.

Here, then, was the issue which Pilate had to pass on: on the one hand he knew that Christ was innocent, that He was a unique Man, possibly more than man; on the other hand, he was threatened by the Sanhedrin with exposure before Caesar. In its final analysis, Pilate had to choose between Christ and the world. When the issue was clearly defined, he did not hesitate; he decided to please the people and win their applause, rather than intensify their already fierce hatred against him and condemn him to Caesar. "Here is the anticipative result of Pilate's vacillation. When a man begins to temporise with his conscience, to trifle with sin—be it the love of applause, the fear of man, or whatsoever thing is contrary to sound doctrine and plain morality—it is easy to predict what is sure to follow. Sin is at the first like a tiny spark. Tread it out at once—that is your duty. But indulge, foster, toy with it, and it will kindle and spread, and lay waste in a fearful conflagration the very temple of the soul. So here with this unhappy Pilate, trying to join together what God hath forever put asunder —his carnal inclination and his duty; hoping all in vain to harmonise equity and injustice; to comply with the voice of wicked men without, and yet not offend the voice of God within him; thinking to serve two masters—God and mammon. Miserable, impossible compromise (Dr. G. Brown).

"And from thenceforth Pilate sought to release Him" (v.12). The time-mark here is significant. Following the Jews' accusation that Christ had "made Himself the Son of God" (v.7), Pilate, thoroughly uneasy, had retired within the judgment-hall, and asked the Saviour, "Whence art Thou?" (v.9). But the Lord returned him no answer. Thereupon Pilate said, "Speakest Thou not unto me? knowest Thou not that I have power to crucify Thee, and have power to release Thee?" To this Christ made reply, "Thou couldest have no power against Me, except it were given thee from above: therefore he that delivered Me unto thee hath the greater sin." That Pilate was deeply impressed, both by his Prisoner's demeanor and words, we cannot doubt. Previously unwilling to condemn an innocent Man, he now resolves to make a real effort to save Him. Leaving Christ behind in the judgment-hall, Pilate returned once more to the Jews. What he now said to them John has not told us: all we know is that he must have made an earnest appeal to the Saviour's enemies, which they as decisively rejected.

"But the Jews cried out, saying, If thou let this Man go, thou art not Caesar's friend: whosoever maketh himself a king speaketh against Caesar" (v.12). The Jews knew their man, for hypocrites are usually the quickest to detect hypocrisy in others. They had reserved their strongest card for the last: with diabolic cunning they insinuated that no matter what the Governor's personal feelings might be, no matter how unwilling he was to please them, he could not afford to displease the Emperor. For him this was a clinching argument. From this moment his hopes of escaping from his unhappy situation were dashed to the ground. It is hard to decide which was the more despicable: the duplicity of the Jews in feigning to care for Caesar's interests, or the cowardice and wickedness of Pilate in conniving at a foul murder. On the one hand we see the descendents of Abraham, the most favoured of all people, professing to be eagerly awaiting the appearing of the promised Messiah, now clamouring for His crucifixion. On the other hand, we behold a judge of one of the high courts of Rome, defying conscience and trampling upon justice. Never did human nature make such a contemptible exhibition. Never was sin more heinously displayed.

"When Pilate, therefore, heard that saying, he brought Jesus forth, and sat down in the judgment seat in a place that is called the Pavement, but in the Hebrew, Gabbatha." (v.13). "'Pilate's playing with the situation,' observes Lange, 'is now passed; now the situation plays with him. First he said, not asked, What is truth! Now his frightened heart, to which the Emperor's favor is the supreme law of life, says, What is justice! He takes his place on the judgment-seat, therefore, and with what seems something between a taunt and a faint, final plea, says to the Jews, 'Behold your King!'" (Numerical Bible.) Pilate dared no longer oppose the bloody demands of the Jews. There remained nothing now but for him to take his seat publicly on the bench and pronounce sentence. It is striking to note that the trial of Christ before Pilate was in **seven** stages. This is seen by noting carefully the following scriptures, which speak of the Governor passing in and out of the judgment-hall. The first stage was on the outside: 18:28-32. The second on the inside: 18: 33-37. Third, on the outside: 18: 38-40. Fourth, inside: 19: 1-3. Fifth outside: 19:4-7. Sixth inside: 19: 8-11. Seventh, outside: 19:12-16.

"When Pilate, therefore, heard that saying, he brought Jesus forth, and sat down in the judgment-seat in a place that is called the Pavement, but in the Hebrew, Gabbatha." Here, as everywhere in Scripture, if only we have eyes to see, there is a deep significance to the proper noun. The word for 'Pavement' is found nowhere else in the New Testament, but its Hebrew equivalent occurs just once in the Old Testament, and it is evident that the Holy Spirit would have us link the two passages together. In 2 Kings 16:17 we read, "King Ahaz cut off the borders of the bases, and removed the laver from off them; and took down the sea from off the brazen oxen that were under it, and put it upon a pavement of stones." In Ahaz's case, his act was the conclusive token of his surrender to abject apostasy. So here of Pilate coming down to the level of the apostate Jews. In the former case it was a Jewish ruler dominated by a Gentile idolator; in the latter, a Gentile idolator dominated by Jews who had rejected their Messiah!

"And it was the preparation of the passover" (v.14.) There has been an almost endless controversy concerning this. The Lord and His disciples had eaten the passover together on the previous night (Luke 22: 15), and yet we read here of the "**preparation of the passover.**" Sir R. Anderson wrote much that was illuminating on the point. We can only give a brief selection: "These writers one and all confound the Passover-supper with the feast which followed it, and to which it lent its name. The supper was a memorial of the redemption of the firstborn of Israel on the night before the Exodus; the feast was the anniversary of their actual deliverance from the house of bondage. The supper was not a part of the feast; it was morally the basis on which the feast was founded, just as the Feast of Tabernacles was based on the great sin-offering of the Day of Expiation which preceded it. But in the same way that the Feast of Weeks can now be commonly designated Pentecost, so the Feast of Unleavened Bread was popularly called the Passover. (Luke 22:1.) **That** title was common to the supper **and** the feast, including both; but the intelligent Jew never confounded the two. No words can possibly express more clearly this distinction than those afforded by the Pentateuch in the final promulgation of the Law: 'In the fourteenth day of the first month is the Passover of the Lord, and in the fifteenth day of this same month is the Feast.' (Num. 28:16-17.)"

But to what does "the **preparation of** the Passover" refer? "Among the Jews 'the preparation' was the common name for the day before **the sabbath**, and it is so used by all the Evangelists. Bearing this in mind, let the reader compare with John 19:14 vv. 31-42, and he will have no difficulty in rendering the words in question, 'it was **Passover Friday.**'" (Sir Robert Anderson.) Let the reader also compare Mark 15:42, which is even more conclusive.

"And about the sixth hour." (v. 14.) This expression has also occasioned much difficulty to many. It is supposed to conflict with Mark 15:25, "and it was the **third** hour, and they crucified Him." But there is no discrepancy here whatsoever. Mark gives the hour when our Lord was crucified; John is speaking of the Passover Friday, i.e., the day when preparations were made for the sabbath (which began at Friday sunset) preparing food, etc., so that none would have to be cooked on the sabbath. It was about the sixth hour after this "preparation" had commenced. This is the view which was taken by Augustine and Dr. Lightfoot. We believe the Holy Spirit has recorded this detail for the purpose of pointing a comparison and a contrast. For six hours the Jews had been working in preparation for the approaching sabbath; during the **next** "six hours" (compare Mark 15:25, 33-37), Christ finished His great work, which brings His people into that eternal rest of which the sabbath was the emblem! "And he saith unto the Jews, Behold your King!" (v. 14). This was evidently spoken in irony and contempt.

"But they cried out, Away with Him; away with Him, crucify Him." (v. 15). As on the previous occasions of Pilate's private appeals, so now this final and public appeal of his had no effect upon the Jews. Once more they raised their fierce, relentless cry, demanding the Prisoner's death by crucifixion. Nothing but His blood would satisfy them. He must die: so had God decreed; so they demanded. The decree of the One was from love; the insistence of the other, was from hatred. The design of the One, was mercy unto poor sinners; the aim of the others, barbarous cruelty to Him who was sinless. This rejection of their Messiah by Israel fulfilled two prophecies: "We hid as it were our faces from Him; He was despised, and we esteemed Him not " (Isa. 53:3); "Thus saith the Lord, the Redeemer of Israel, and His Holy One. to Him whom man despiseth, to Him whom the nation abhorreth" (Isa. 49:7).

"Pilate saith unto them, "Shall I crucify your King?" (v. 15). As one has said, "Pilate speaks here with a mixture of compassionate feeling and mockery." For the last time the Roman Governor put the decisive question to the Jews, giving them a final chance to relent, throwing the emphasis, we believe, on the word 'crucify.' It was a frightful mode of execution, reserved for slaves and the most abandoned criminals.

"The chief priests answered, We have no king but Caesar" (v. 15). "They are entirely infidel, throwing off all alleigence to any but Caesar, and cry that they had no other king. It is purely of the Jews, the whole transaction, for they consign to the most cruel death Him whom the Roman Governor would have let go. This is man's religion, and it will, in the end, enthrone 'the Wilful One' and bow to his image. (Rev. 13)." (Mr. Mal. Taylor.)

"The chief priests answered, We have no king but Caesar." God took them at their word: they have been under their own verdict ever since. History repeated itself, though with a tragic addition. In the days of Samuel, Israel said, "Make us a king to judge us like all nations" (1 Sam. 8:5), and Jehovah's response was, "Hearken unto the voice of the people in all that they say unto thee: for they have not rejected thee, but they have rejected Me, that I should not reign over them." So it was here with their rebellious descendants, when they rejected Christ the King. In consequence of their fatal decision, Israel have abode "many days without a king, and without a prince, and without a sacrifice." (Hosea 3:4.) Bitter indeed have been the consequences. Jotham's parable has received its tragic fulfilment: "And the bramble said unto the trees, If in truth ye anoint me king over you, then come put your trust in my shadow; and if not, let fire come out of the bramble and devour the cedars of Lebanon." (Judges 9:15, and see vv. 7-16).

"The chief priests answered, We have no king but Caesar." "It was not the verdict of the Jews alone, and they have not suffered alone. The whole world has been lying under the yoke which they have preferred to the easy yoke of Christ. They have got very tired of Caesar—true; and, as we see by their fitful movements every now and then, would feign be rid of him. They are always crying, 'Give us better government'; but all they can do is, with doubtful betterment, to divide him up into many little Caesars; better as they think, because weaker, and with divided interests, so that the balance of power may secure the even weights of justice. That is still an experiment some think; but this chronic war is never peace, nor can be; and the reason is, men have refused the Prince of Peace. Modify it, rename it, disguise it as you please, the reign of Caesar is the only alternative." (Numerical Bible.)

"Then delivered he Him therefore unto them to be crucified" (v. 16). Between vv.15 and 16 comes in what is recorded in Matthew 27: 24-25. Seeing that the Jews would not be turned from their purpose, and afraid to defy them, he took water and washed his hands before them (cf. Deut. 21:1-6; Psa. 26:6), saying, "I am innocent of the blood of this Just Person, see ye to it." Thus did this cowardly, world-loving Roman betray his trust. Never was a name more justly handed down to the world's scorn than Pilate's. By his act he sought to cast the entire onus upon the Jews. Their terrible response was, "His blood be on us, and on our children." Then, we are told, "Pilate gave sentence that it should be as they required. . . He delivered Jesus to their will." (Luke 23:24-25.) Thus the Lord's execution was now in Jewish hands (Acts 2:23), the Centurion and his quarternion of soldiers merely carrying out the decision of the chief priests.

"Then delivered he Him therefore unto them to be crucified." Our Lord's own estimate of Pilate's act is recorded by the Spirit of prophecy through the Psalmist: "Shall the throne of iniquity have fellowship with that which frameth mischief by a law? They gather themselves together against the soul of the Righteous, and condemn the innocent blood" (Psa. 94:20, 21)! Let us not forget, however, that behind the governor of Judea, who delivered the Lord Jesus unto the Jews, was the Governor of the Universe, who "spared not His own Son, but delivered Him up for us all." (Rom. 8:32.) And why? Because He was "delivered for our offences" (Rom. 4:25.). Christ was delivered to death, that we might be delivered from death.

"And they took Jesus and led Him away." (v. 16.) Observe the word "led" again. How often has the Holy Spirit repeated it! Christ was neither driven nor dragged, for He made no resistance. As prophecy had foretold long before, "He was led as a lamb to the slaughter." (Isa. 53:7.)

"And He, bearing His cross, went forth into a place called the place of a skull, which is called in the Hebrew Golgotha." (v. 17.) The Jews lost no time: Christ was taken straight from Gabbatha to Golgotha; from judgment to execution. The Saviour "bearing His cross," had been marvellously foreshadowed of old when Abraham took the wood of the burnt offering, and laid it upon Isaac his son." (Gen. 22:6.) "He, bearing His Cross, went forth." That is, out of Jerusalem, or as Heb. 13:12 puts it, "Jesus also, that He might sanctify the people with His own blood, suffered without (outside) the gate." This, too, fulfilled an Old Testament type—every detail of the Passion fulfilled some prophecy or type. In Lev. 16:27 we read, "And the bullock for the sin-offering, and the goat for the sin-offering; whose blood was brought in to make atonement in the holy place shall one carry forth without the camp." "Little did the blinded Jews imagine that when they madly hounded on the Romans to crucify Jesus outside the gates, that they were unconsciously perfecting the mightiest sin-offering of all!" (Bishop Ryle.)

At this point the other Gospels supply a detail which John, for some reason, was guided to omit. In Matt. 27:32 we are told, "As they came out, they found a man of Cyrene, Simon by name; him they compelled to bear His cross." Almost all of the commentators, both ancient and modern, draw the conclusion that Simon was compelled to bear the Saviour's cross because He was staggering and sinking beneath its weight. But there is not a word in the New Testament to support such a conjecture, and everything recorded about Christ after He was nailed to the tree decidedly conflicts with it. That Simon was "compelled" to bear His cross, shows there was not one in all that crowd with sufficient compassion and courage to volunteer to carry it for Him!

"Went forth into a place called the place of a skull, which is called in the Hebrew Golgotha." "The place of a skull—the place of the kingdom of death. This is plainly what the world is, because of sin—death being the stamp of the government of God upon it. For this the Lord sought it; here His love to men brought Him; only He could lift this burden from them, and for this He must come under it." (Numerical Bible.)

"Which is called in the Hebrew, Golgotha." This expression—used twice in connection with the Saviour's crucifixion (vv. 13, 17)—is found elsewhere only in John 5:2: "Now there is at Jerusalem by the sheep-gate a pool, which is called in the Hebrew tongue Bethesda." What a contrast; there at Bethesda, we see His mercy; here at Golgotha, their brutality! Luke gives us the Gentile name, "Calvary" (23:33); John the Hebrew, "Golgotha," of the place where our Saviour was crucified. Compare the same double name of the place of Pilate's judgment-seat (v. 13.) "May it be that in these instances of double meaning that God is giving His in the words which He used with His people, and man is giving his in the language of the world? Moreover, this Death was for both Jews and Gentiles! There is a reason for every word which the Holy Spirit records." (Mr. Mal. Taylor.)

"Where they crucified Him, and two others with Him, on either side one, and Jesus in the midst" (v. 18.). This one verse records the fulfilment of at least three Old Testament prophecies. First, the manner in which the Saviour was to die had been clearly foretold. A thousand years before this He had cried, by the Spirit of prophecy, "they pierced My hands and My feet." (Psa. 22:16); this is indeed most striking. The Jewish form of capital punishment was stoning. But no word of God can fall to the ground, therefore did Pilate give orders that Christ should be crucified, which was the Roman form of execution, reserved only for the vilest criminals. Second, Isaiah had declared, "He was numbered with the transgressors" (53:12). The Jews' object was to add a final indignity and insult to the Lord; it was a public declaration that He was counted no better than the scum of the earth. Little did they realise that this expression of their malice was but a means for the carrying out of Messianic prediction! Third, it had been written that He should be **"with the wicked** at His death." (Isa. 53:7—literal translation). But why did God permit His Beloved to be so outrageously treated? To show us the place which His Son had taken. It was the place which was **due us** because of our sins—the place of shame, condemnation, punishment. Moreover, the Lord crucified between the two malefactors, gave Him the opportunity to work one more miracle ere He laid down His life—a miracle of sovereign grace. (Let the reader at this point carefully ponder Luke 23:39-43, and there he will find that the One on the central cross clearly demonstrated that He **was** the Redeemer by snatching a brand from the burning, and translating from the brink of the Pit into Paradise, one of these very thieves as the first trophy of His all-sufficient sacrifice.

"And Pilate wrote a title, and put it on the cross. And the writing was, **Jesus of Nazareth, the King of the Jews**" (v. 19.) "He comes thus into death as King—'King of the Jews,' indeed, but which in its full rendering implies so much. It faces the Jew, the Greek, the Roman, affirming to each in his own language, with a positiveness which His enemies vainly strive to set aside, a meaning for each one. Here is indeed God's King—King in death as in life—here in a peculiar way affirmed; His cross henceforth to be the very sign of His power, the scepter under which they bow, in adoring homage." (Numerical Bible.) Pilate's reason for placing such a description of our Lord over His cross is not easy to determine; probably it was so worded in anger, and with the aim of annoying and insulting the Jews. Whatever his motive, it was clearly overruled by God. It is well known that the words of the four Evangelists vary in their several descriptions of this title. Enemies of the truth have pointed to this as a "contradiction." But all difficulty is removed if we bear in mind that we are told Pilate wrote the inscription in three different languages—most probably not wording them alike. The Holy Spirit moved Matthew to translate one( most likely the Hebrew )and Luke another (most likely the Greek); Mark only quoting a part of what John has given us—most likely from the Latin. There is, therefore, no discrepancy at all, and nothing for an impartial reader to stumble over.

"This title then read many of the Jews; for the place where Jesus was crucified was nigh to the city." (v. 20.) No one could fail to see who it was that hung upon the central cross. Even in death God saw to the guarding of His Son's glory. Before He was born, the angel announced to Mary His "kingdom." (Luke 1:32, 33.) In His infancy, wise men from the East heralded Him as "King." (Matt. 2:2.) At the beginning of the Passion week, the multitudes had cried "Blessed is the King of Israel." (John 12:13.) Before Pilate, He Himself bore witness to His "kingdom." (18:36-37.) And now His royal title was affixed to His very gibbet. As King He will yet return to the earth, and reign over it for a thousand years. In the interval of His rejection, may we, His subjects loyally acknowledge His scepter and bow to His sovereign will.

"And it was written in Hebrew, and Greek, and Latin." (v. 20.) Note that the Holy Spirit has placed "Hebrew" first! Hebrew was the language of the Jews; Greek of the educated world; Latin of the Romans; hence all who were gathered around the cross could read the title in his own language. Remember that the **confusion of tongues** was the sign of Babel's curse. (Gen. 11), significantly are we reminded of this here, when Christ was being made a curse for us! Hebrew was the language of **religion;** Greek of **science, culture and philosophy;** Latin of law. In each of these realms Christ is "King." In the religious, He is the final revelation of the true God. (Heb. 1:2; John 14:9.) In science He is the Force behind all things. "By Him all things consist." (Col. 1:17). "Upholding all things by the word of His power." (Heb. 1:3); so, too, in Him are hid "all the treasures of wisdom and knowledge." (Col. 2:3.) In jurisprudence He is supreme; the Law-giver and Law-administrator. (1 Cor. 9:21.)

"Then said the chief priests of the Jews to Pilate, Write not, The King of the Jews; but that He said, I am King of the Jews." (v. 21.) It is noteworthy that this is the first and only time that they are termed **"the chief priests of the Jews,"** the Holy Spirit thereby intimating that **God** no longer owned them as **His** priests; having rejected their Messiah, Judaism was set aside, and therefore its official leaders are regarded as serving the Jews, but not Jehovah. The words of the priests here show that they resented Pilate's insult. It was most humbling to their pride that this crucified criminal should be publicly designated their "king." They desired the Governor to alter the wording of the inscription so that it might appear Christ was nothing more than an empty-boasting impostor.

"Pilate answered, What I have written, I have written" (v. 22.). Pilate could be firm when it suited him. The haughty, imperious character of the Roman comes out plainly here. His decisive reply evidences his contempt for the Jews: Trouble me no further; what I have written must stand; I shall not alter it to please you. "It, therefore, stands written forever. Caiaphas, as representative of the Jews proclaimed the Lord as Saviour of the world; Pilate fastens upon the Jews the hated name of the Nazarene as their King." (Companion Bible.) The truth is that God would not allow Pilate to change what he had written. Unknown to himself he was the amanuensis of Heaven. This was part of the Word of God—the Scriptures, the Writings, and not a jot of it shall ever pass away. And wondrously was it manifested that very day that what Pilate had written was the Word of God. This was the text used by the Spirit of Truth to bring about the regeneration and conversion of the repentant thief. His "Lord remember me when Thou comest into Thy kingdom," shows that his faith rested on that which the Roman Governor had written and placed on the cross, and which his Spirit-opened eyes read and believed!

"Then the soldiers, when they had crucified Jesus, took His garments and made four parts, to every soldier a part." (v. 23.) "The soldiers having now finished their bloody work, having nailed our Lord to the cross, put the title over His head, and reared the cross on end, proceeded to do what they probably always did—to divide the clothes of the criminal among themselves. In most countries the clothes of a person put to death by the law are the perquisite of the executioner. So it was with our Lord's clothes. They had most likely stripped our Lord naked before nailing His hands and feet to the cross, and had laid His clothes on one side till after they had finished their work. (They now turned to the clothes, and, as they had done many a time on such occasions, proceeded to divide them." (Bishop Ryle.) There were four soldiers; some think this emblemizes the four quarters of the Gentiles' world. It seems clear that they ripped His several garments to pieces, so as to divide them in equal parts. How this, once more, makes manifest the depths of humiliation into which the Son of God descended!

"And also His coat; now the coat was without seam, woven from the top throughout. They said therefore among themselves, Let us not rend it, but cast lots for it, whose it shall be" (vv. 23,24). The deeper significance of this is not difficult to perceive. Garments in Scripture, speak of **conduct**, as a display of **character**—cf. Psa. 109:18; 1 Peter 5:5, etc. Now, the Saviour's "coat," His outer garment, was of one piece—intimating the unity, the unbroken perfection of His ways. Unlike our "garments," which are, at best, so much patchwork, His robe was "without seam." Moreover, it was "woven from the top throughout"— the mind of Him above controlled His every action! This "coat" or "robe" was a costly one, so owned even by the soldiers, for they declined to tear it to pieces. It spoke of the righteousness of Christ, the "**robe of righteousness**." (Isa. 61:10), the "best robe" (Luke 15) with which the Father clothes each prodigal son. For this "robe" the soldiers cast lots, and we are told in Pro. 16:33 that "The lot is cast into the lap, but the whole disposing thereof is of the Lord." Thus the action of these soldiers declares that the "best robe" is not left to the caprice of man's will, but the Lord Himself has determined whose it shall be! Note another contrast; the sinful first Adam was clothed by God; the sinless last Adam was unclothed by wicked men.

"That the scripture might be fulfilled, which saith, They parted My raiment among them, and for My vesture they did cast lots. These things therefore the soldiers did" (v. 24.). Three things come out plainly: First, that God Himself was master of this whole situation, directing every detail of it to the out-working of His eternal counsels. Second, that no word of God's can fail. A thousand years beforehand it had been predicted that these soldiers should both divide the Saviour's raiment among them, and also cast lots for His vesture or coat. Literally was this fulfilled to the very letter. Third, that the One who hung there on the Tree was, beyond a shadow of doubt, the **Messiah of Israel**, the One of whom all the prophets had written.

Below are the questions on the closing section of John 19:—

1. Why "woman," v. 26?

2. What perfections of Christ are seen in v. 28?

3. What was "finished," v. 30?

5. What is the spiritual meaning of "blood and water," v. 34?

4. Why "bowed His head" v. 30?

6. What prophecy was accomplished in v. 38?

7. What type was fulfilled in vv. 41, 42?

Arthur W. Pink.

## GLEANINGS IN EXODUS.
### 41. The Coverings: Ex. 26:7-14.

As was pointed out at the beginning of our last article, the Tabernacle had four separate Coverings, one over another. The first and innermost was the ten white curtains. These curtains have already been before us. It should be carefully noted that they are themselves designated "the tabernacle," see vv. 1, 6. Over these were placed eleven "curtains of goats' hair," and these are called "the tent," vv. 11, 12. Above these were spread "rams' skins dyed red" and "badgers' skins," v. 14, which are simply called "coverings." That a distinction is drawn between the "Tabernacle" and the "Tent" is clear from several scriptures For example, Numbers 3:25: "The Tabernacle and the Tent." This intimates they are to be contemplated separately.

The above distinction is clearly established in the Hebrew, where two distinct words are employed—"Mishkan" for Tabernacle, "ohel" for Tent. The former signifies "dwelling-place"; the latter, simply "tent." The one refers to the abode of Jehovah, the other to the meeting-place for His people. It is to be regretted that the translators of our English Bible have failed to preserve the difference which is noted in the original. In the A.V. we find the expression "Tabernacle of the congregation" constantly occurring, but in almost every instance the Hebrew has "Tent of the congregation." This holy building was their place of assembly, but it was Jehovah's place of abode: they visited it, He remained there! Looking now, first, at the eleven goats' hair curtains let us note:—

#### 1.—Their Materials.

"And thou shalt make curtains of goats' hair to be a covering upon the Tabernacle" (v. 7). The word for 'curtains' is yerioth, from a root meaning to tremble or waive, as suspended curtains do. A similar root with a similar primary meaning is the word for 'fear.' How suggestively do these thoughts describe the Lord Jesus as He was here. He was the dependent One, not relying upon His own inherent strength, but cleaving ever to His Father. He was perfectly obedient, because perfectly dependent upon the will of God. Thus the true 'fear' of the Lord characterized Him. He was ever moved by the slightest breath of the Spirit. There was thus in the eyes of men entire weakness, for He had no will apart from perfect subjection unto God; therefore the whole character of God with reference to sin, the world and Satan, was manifested. So also He gave fullest expression to God's thoughts and ways of mercy over judgment with reference to man.

"The word 'curtain' is a feminine one, and in speaking of them being joined together 'one to another,' it is 'a woman to her sister.' This, too, is in keeping with the holy place of dependence and subjection taken and kept by our Lord" (Mr. S. Ridout). As though emphasizing this same thought, the Holy Spirit has been careful to tell us that these goats' hair curtains were spun by the women (Ex. 35:26). We may add that this same material was used for making their own tents, and was of a dark colour, as a reference to Song of Sol. 1:5; 6:5 shows.

It is to be noted that the word "hair" in Ex. 26:7 is in italics, which denotes it has been supplied by the translators, and we believe in this case, rightly so. It is not found in the Hebrew of Ex. 35:26, yet the word "spun" clearly implies it. The reason why the word "hair" is omitted from Ex. 26:7 is to direct our attention more particularly to the goats themselves—i.e., to what they typically signified.

#### 2.—Their Number.

"Eleven curtains shalt thou make" (v. 7). As though God anticipated we should experience difficulty with this number, He has Himself here supplied the very help we need. He has told us that these Curtains were divided into two groups: "Thou shalt couple five curtains by themselves, and six curtains by themselves" (v. 9). Thus in order to discover the spiritual significance of this number eleven, we are thus shown that we are not to consider it by itself as a whole, but as made up of five and six. This simplifies things very much. Five, as we have before had occasion to remark, stands for grace, while six is the number of man. It was on the sixth day that man was created (Gen. 1:26, 31). Six days are the span of man's weekly labour (Ex. 20:9). It is striking how prominent is this numeral in the measures which man uses in connection with his labours: each of the following is a multiple of six. There are twelve inches to the foot; eighteen to the cubit; thirty-six to the yard. It is thus with man's divisions of time. The day has twenty-four hours, each of these is made up of sixty minutes, and these of sixty seconds. It is remarkable there are just six separate words in the Bible for "man"—four in the Hebrew and two in the Greek. How fitting that He who took the place of sinful man was crucified at the sixth hour (John 19:14)! In the indignities man heaped upon the suffering Saviour this same number was stamped upon his vile handiwork: (1) scourging His back; (2) smiting His face with the palms of their hands; (3) spitting upon Him; (4) placing the thorns on His brow; (5) driving the nails into His hands and His feet; (6) plunging the spear into His side. In the light of these examples it is not difficult to trace the significance of the five and the six in the goats' hair Curtains.

### 3.—Their Dimensions.

"The length of one curtain shall be thirty cubits, and the breadth of one curtain four cubits: and the eleven curtains shall be all of one measure" (v. 8). The width of the Curtains was the same as those which formed the innermost Covering, namely, four cubits—the number which speaks of the earth. But the length of the goats' hair Curtains exceeded those of the white ones: these were thirty cubits, they but twenty-eight. The significance of these larger numbers is always ascertained by the spiritual meaning of their factors. The factors of thirty are either three and ten, or five and six. Three is the number of full manifestation, ten of responsibility. But in view of the fact that the Curtains were divided into two groups of five and six, we probably have there the key to the interpretation of their length. This will come before us more fully when we take up their meaning.

### 4.—Their Arrangement.

This is by no means obvious at first glance. In v. 9 we are told, "Thou shalt couple five curtains by themselves, and six curtains by themselves and shalt double the sixth curtain in the forefront of the Tabernacle." Then in vv. 12, 13 we read, "And the remnant that remaineth of the curtains of the Tent, the half curtain that remaineth, shall hang over the backside of the Tabernacle. And a cubit on the one side, and a cubit on the other side of that which remaineth in the length of the curtains of the Tent, it shall hang over the sides of the Tabernacle on this side and on that side, to cover it." Now the Tabernacle itself was thirty cubits long, ten cubits broad, and ten cubits high. Thus by taking these Curtains lengthwise and throwing them over the width of the Tabernacle, its two sides and top would be completely covered, for they were just thirty cubits in length. In breadth, joined side by side, they would be forty-four cubits, and thus long enough to cover the rear, stretch right across the length of the top and then over-lap four feet in front. This balance of four cubits in the front was turned back or "doubled" so as to leave eight cubits clear for the entrance.

### 5.—Their Meaning.

The material of which they were made, supplies the first key to this. The "goat" was pre-eminently the animal used in the sin offerings, in fact, in connection with Israel's great feasts under the law, when the people were collectively represented before God, it was the only one used in their sacrifices for sins. Israel's year began with a commemoration of the Passover. Inseparably connected with this was the ordinance of the feast of unleavened bread: in Luke 22:1 they are identified. During the seven days of this feast, besides other sacrifices, a "goat" was slain for a sin offering (Num. 28:17, 22). The next feast was that of "weeks" or "Pentecost": in this, too, a goat as a sin offering for an atonement was commanded (Lev. 23:15, 19). Then came the feast of Trumpets, and here also the goat for a sin-offering was used (Num. 29:1, 5). Following this was the most solemn of them all, namely, the annual Day of Atonement, when a special sin-offering was appointed. This consisted of two goats: the one being slain, the other having the sins and iniquities of all Israel confessed upon it, then being led away into a land not inhabited (Lev. 16). Finally came the feast of Tabernacles, the feast of ingathering, when Israel rested from their toil and rejoiced in the blessing of God upon their labours. This feast lasted for eight days, and on each one a "goat" was slain as a sin-offering (Num. 29).

In addition to the national convocations when the "goats" alone was used for making atonement, we may observe the prominence of this animal in other sin-offerings. When a ruler sinned, the appointed sacrifice was "a kid of the goats" (Lev. 4:23); so, if one of the common people sinned (Lev. 4:27, 28). At the consecration of the priesthood a "kid of the goats for a sin-offering" was required (Lev. 9:2, 3). At the dedication of the altar each of the "princes" offered "one kid of the goats for a sin-offering" (Num. 7:16). For the sin of ignorance a "kid of the goats" made atonement (Num. 15: 24, 27). At the beginning of each month a special sin-offering was appointed, and this also consisted of "a kid of the goats" (Num. 28: 11, 15). This completes the list where the "goat" was exclusively appointed as the sin-offering. Surely it is more than a coincidence that they are precisely eleven in number—corresponding exactly with the eleven Curtains in our type!

It is also very striking to find that where the "goat" is not used in sacrifice, yet is it generally found in an evil connection. Rebekah placed "skins of the kids of the goats" upon Jacob's hands and neck for the purpose of deceiving Isaac (Gen. 27:16). So the brethren of Joseph "killed a kid of the goats" and dipped his coat in it to aid their deception upon their father (Gen. 37:31). In the trick which Michal imposed upon Saul, a pillow of "goats' hair" was employed (1 Sam. 19:13). So in contrast from the "sheep" (His own people) the Lord likens the wicked unto "goats" (Matt. 25:33).

In the light of what has just been before us it is unmistakably plain that the "goats' hair" Curtains pointed to Christ as the great sin-offering for the iniquities of his people. He who knew no sin, was "made sin for us" (2 Cor. 5:21). Of old it was announced "Thou shalt make His soul an offering for sin" (Isa. 53:10), and thus was the fulfilment recorded—"He hath poured out His soul unto death" (Isa. 53:12). In this connection it is remarkable to note the words of Lev. 4:25: "The priests shall . . . pour out his blood at the bottom of the altar." This was only said of the blood of the "sin-offering": of the blood of the burnt-offering we read that it was "sprinkled" only (Lev. 1:5).

The numerals connected with these Curtains confirm our interpretation: they were six, five, and four. Thus we learn that it was the **Manhood** of our blessed Redeemer, in wondrous **grace**, suffering for the sin of His people here on **earth**. But it is the **six** which is doubly prominent, the eleventh Curtain being expressly termed "the sixth" (v. 9), and the thirty cubits in length, has for its factors five and six. Thus, by this emphasis, the Holy Spirit has most graciously pointed out the direction which our thoughts should take. The fact that the "women" spun these goats' hair Curtains still further emphasises the truth that in our present type it is distinctively Christ as the "woman's" Seed (Gen. 3:15)., who is before us. It is true that the God-man suffered and died, and it is true that His two natures are inseparably united; yet, it was His **humanity** which made possible the great sacrifice, for Deity cannot suffer.

Underneath these goats' hair Curtains was the gorgeous tapestry of the cherubim-embroidered white Curtains. But these were seen only by those **inside** the Holy Place, telling us that it is not until we have personally appropriated Christ, by a God-given faith, as our Sin-offering, that we can delight ourselves by being occupied with His personal perfections. Thus, how deeply and how solemnly significant, was the doubled-over curtain, right over the entrance into the Tabernacle. Just above its beautiful gate hung that which would remind the worshipper of the great cost paid by Another to procure entrance for him.

### 6.—Their Loops and Taches.

"And thou shalt make fifty loops on the edge of the one curtain that is outmost in the coupling, and fifty loops in the edge of the curtain which coupleth the second. And thou shalt make fifty taches of brass, and put the taches into the loops, and couple the Tent together, that it may be one" (vv. 10, 11). Some excellent commentators have insisted that the goats' hair Curtains speak primarily of Christ in His earthly life, and that they pointed to Him as the perfect

Prophet. We think this is a mistake. It is true that "hairy" garments are found connected with false prophets (Heb.. of Zech. 13:5), but no "goats' hair." In the case of John the Baptist we are explicitly told that his raiment was of "camel's hair" (Matt. 3.4).

It will be noted that while the white Curtains were linked together with "gold" taches, the ones now before us were united by "brass" clasps. This important detail both reveals the mistake of others and confirms the interpretation which we have given above. "Brass" in scripture is the symbol of Divine judgment—as this will come before us again in connection with the "Brazen-altar we shall not now adduce the proofs. Now in His prophetic office Christ's ministry was the very reverse of the exercise of judgment—throughout it was marked by grace: John 1: 17; 3; 17. But regarding the goats' hair Curtains as foreshadowing Christ "made sin" for His people, the taches of "brass" are most significant, for they tell us that, while on the Cross, the Saviour suffered the outpoured judgment of God (Isa. 53: 10; Zech. 13:7).

It should also be observed that two little words in connection with the "loops" are here most significantly omitted. The ten white Curtains were linked together through "loops of blue" (26:4); but of the eleven goats' hair Curtains we read, three times over in 26:10, 11, simply of "loops." Had these second Curtains been designed of God to portray Christ in His prophetic office the "blue" had surely been mentioned, for His heavenly Character shone out ceaselessly during His earthly ministry. But when "made sin for us" His heavenly glory was hidden, as the three hours of darkness testified. The minute and wondrous perfection of our type is thus evidenced by the omission of "loops of blue"!

### 7.—Their Purpose.

These goats' hair Curtains were designed not only as a protection for the white Curtains beneath, but also to cover the golden boards of its sides and rear. These, the under Curtains failed to completely drape. It was a distance of thirty cubits from the ground on the one side, over the roof, to the ground on the other side. The white Curtains were only twenty-eight cubits in length, leaving one cubit of the golden boards exposed at the bottom on either side. And most fittingly so. As we have seen, the white Curtains, with their lovely colours embroidered upon them, foreshadowed the perfections of Christ's person as He tabernacled among men. During His walk through this world, He did not conceal, but revealed, the glory of God, therefore was there one cubit (one is the number of unity, and thus of God in His essential nature) of the golden boards left uncovered by the white Curtains on either side of the Tabernacle!

But these goats' hair Curtains were thirty cubits long, and thus of sufficient length not only to overlap the white Curtains, but also to completely cover the golden boards on the side of the Tabernacle. By this God intimated the great truth that He could have no tabernacle among men, and could not manifest His beauty and glory in their midst, except as His dwelling-place proclaimed, in every part of it, the fact that sin had been fully met and put away by the sacrifice of His Son!

It remains for us now to offer a brief remark on the outermost Coverings. "And thou shalt make a covering for the tent of rams' skins dyed red, and a covering above of badgers' skins" (v. 14). In a word, these external Coverings, on the outside of the goats' hair Curtains, give us a twofold view of Christ enduring the judgment due the sins of His people: they show how He then appeared to the eye of God and to the eyes of men. The rams' skins presented the Godward aspect first. The "ram" was the victim used at the consecration of the priests (Ex. 29:26), when they were separated unto the service of Jehovah. It spoke, therefore, of devotedness to God. In beautiful accord with this we find that it was a "ram" (Gen. 22:13) which took the place of Isaac when Abraham, in his devotion and obedience to God, had bound him to the altar! "The ram, being the head of the flock, tells of strength and dignity, hence the figurative significance of Psalm 114:3. The skipping and the leaping of the mighty mountains shows the Divine majesty of God, before whom the strongest and mightiest must quail" (Mr. Ridout).

The rams' skins Covering was "dyed red," which plainly expressed devotion unto death. Thus, in the first of these Coverings we have foreshadowed Christ as the Head of His sheep, the Mighty One, living only for God, and manifesting His perfect devotion to the Father by being "obedient unto death, even the death of the cross."

The rams' skins Covering, then, foreshadowed Christ as the Head of His people (the "sheep") perfectly consecrated to God. As a Child it was the Father's business which occupied Him (Luke 2:49). The key-note to His ministry was "I must work the works of Him that sent Me" (John 9:4). Zeal for the Father's honour consumed Him (John 2:17). But the rams' skins were "dyed red," which pointed to bloodshedding. Not only did Christ live entirely for God, but He also laid down His life in obedience to the Father's command (John 10:18). All the varied excellencies of Christ were covered by devotedness to God. At Calvary, men saw only the execution of a condemned criminal, but Heaven looked down upon the unreserved and unparalleled consecration of the Son to the Father.

Over the rams' skins were placed badgers' skins, and this was the outer Covering of all. This alone would be seen by the eyes of men as Israel were in the wilderness. It, therefore, brings before us Christ as He appeared to men. It specially portrays the fact that He "made Himself of no reputation" (Phil. 2:7). Born in a manger; brought up in despised Nazareth; working at the carpenter's bench, were examples of what the rough and unsightly badgers' skins foreshadowed. To such a degree did Christ humble Himself, the glories of His Divine person were hidden from the eyes of sinful creatures. "Is not this the carpenter?" (Mark 6:3), shows their estimation of Him. They could see none of the spiritual grace, the heavenly beauty, or even the moral perfections, which lay beneath the outward form of the despised Jesus of Nazareth. "As for this fellow, we know not from whence He is" (John 9: 29) reveals the fact that they saw only the badger's skins.

As it was with Him during His life, so also was it at His death. Just as the desert tribes through whose territory Israel passed while journeying to Canaan, saw not the lovely Curtains underneath, so the morbid throngs which congregated at Calvary, discerned not the precious significance of what was there transpiring. Many were astonished at Christ because "His visage was more marred than any man's, and His form than the sons of man" (Isa. 52:14). He was regarded as smitten by a curse from God because of blasphemy (Isa. 53:4). They deemed Him utterly helpless, unable to come down from the cross. Thus the rough and unsightly badgers' skins over all, spoke of the shame and humiliation of our precious Saviour before men.

It is most blessed and solemn to observe that, in sharp contrast from the ten white Curtains and the eleven goats' hair Curtains, beneath, **no dimensions** are given of the two outer Coverings. Does not this intimate that that which these Coverings foreshadowed was beyond our power to measure! There was a depth and a height both in our Saviour's devotedness to God and in His humiliation before men which it is utterly impossible for us to gauge.

—Arthur W. Pink.

## TITHING (No. 2).

"Bring ye all the tithes into the storehouse, that there may be meat in Mine house, and prove Me now herewith, saith the Lord of hosts, if I will not open you the windows of heaven, and pour you out a blessing, that there shall not be room enough to receive it" (Malachi 3:10).

I believe that deep down in the heart of every Christian there is a conviction that he ought to tithe. There is an uneasy feeling that this is a duty that has been neglected or, if you prefer it, a privilege that has not been appropriated. It is correct both ways. Possibly there are some who soothe themselves by saying, Well, other Christians don't tithe. And maybe there are others who say, But if tithing be obligatory in this present dispensation why are the preachers silent upon the subject? My friends, they are silent on a whole lot of subjects to-day; that does not prove anything.

Now in the sermon last Lord's Day morning I attempted to show three things: first, that tithing existed among the people of God long before the law was given at Sinai, and that in the brief record we have of that early history we learn that Abraham, the father of the faithful, gave tithes unto Melchisedec, the priest of the Most High God, and that Jacob, when he had that revelation from the Lord on his way out to Padan-aram, promised to give a tenth unto God. Second, we saw that when the law was given the tithe was clearly and definitely incorporated in it, but—and like almost everything else in that law—Israel neglected it, until, in the days of Malachi, we find Jehovah expressly telling His people that they had robbed Him. Then I tried to show in the third place that in the New Testament itself we have both hints and plain teaching that God requires His people to tithe even now, for tithing is not a part of the ceremonial law, it is a part of the moral law. It is not something that has a dispensational limitation, but is something that is binding on God's people in all ages.

Now let me go a step farther. Tithing is even more obligatory on the saints of the New Testament than it was upon God's people in Old Testament days—not equally binding, but more binding, and that for two reasons:—first, on the principle of "unto whom much is given shall much be required." The obligations of God's saints to-day are much greater than the obligations of saints in Old Testament times, because our privileges and our blessings are greater. As grace is more potent than law, as love is more constraining than fear, as the Holy Spirit is more powerful than the flesh, so our obligations to tithe are greater, for we have a deeper incentive to do that which is pleasing to God. Listen! The Christian should tithe for the very same reason that he keeps all the other commandments of God, and for the same reason that he keeps the laws of his country—not because he must do so, but because he desires to do so. As a citizen in the kingdom of God he desires to maintain the government of God and do that which is pleasing in His sight.

Again, in proportion as the priesthood of Christ is superior to the priesthood of Aaron so are our obligations to render tithes to Him. The Aaronic priesthood was recognised and was owned by Israel through their payments of a tithe to them. Now in the 7th chapter of Hebrews the Holy Spirit has argued the superiority of the priesthood of Christ—which is after the order of Melchisedec—on the fact, or on the basis of the fact rather, that Melchisedec himself received tithes from Abraham. That is the very argument the Holy Spirit uses there to establish the superiority of the Melchisedec order of Christ's priesthood. He appeals to the fact as recorded in Genesis 14, that Melchisedec, who was the type of Christ, received tithes from Abraham, and argues from that that inasmuch as Levi was in the loins of Abraham, therefore the Melchisedec priesthood of Christ is greater than that of Aaron because Abraham himself paid tithes to Melchisedec, who is a type of Christ. Therefore, I say that in proportion to the greater blessings and privileges that we enjoy, we are under deeper obligations to God, and in proportion as Christ's priesthood is superior to that of the Levites, so is our obligation the greater to render tithes unto the Lord to-day than that under which His people in the Old Testament times lived.

Now in the next place let me just suggest a few reasons why God has appointed tithing. In the first place, as a constant recognition of the Creator's rights. As our Maker He desires that we should honor Him, and honor Him by giving Him one-seventh of our time and one-tenth of our income. In other words, the tenth is the recognition of His temporal mercies and the owning that He is the Giver of them. It is the acknowledgement that temporal blessings come from Him and are held in trust for Him.

Again. I believe that God has appointed tithing as an antidote against the spirit of covetousness, for by nature we are full of covetousness. That is why in the ten commandments God incorporates this one, "Thou shalt not covet." That is why Christ said to His disciples, "Beware of coveteousness." And tithing has been appointed by God to deliver us from the spirit of greed, to counteract our innate selfishness; therefore, it has been designed for our blessing for, like all of His commandments, none of them is grievous, but appointed for our good.

Again. I believe that God has appointed tithing as the solution of every financial problem that can arise in connection with His work. While the Children of Israel practised tithing there was no difficulty in maintaining the system of worship that God had appointed. And, my friends, if God's people to-day practised tithing there would be an end of all financial straits that are crippling so many Christian enterprises. No church could possibly be embarassed financially where its members tithed. And I believe that that is the solution of rural church work in thinly populated districts. Yes, and in connection with the mission fields. Wherever you have ten male Christians you have quite sufficient to organise a church and support a pastor or a permanent worker in their midst, for no pastor should desire any greater remuneration than the average income of his members. Therefore, if you have ten male Christians giving one-tenth of their income—no matter what it may be—it is sufficient to sustain them—you have sufficient to maintain and sustain a regular worker in their midst. That is God's solution to the missionary problem. Wherever you have ten average male Chinese you have a situation where they ought to be independent and no longer leaning upon the help of God's people at home here. It is a scandal and a shame to see churches in India and in China to-day that have been in existence fifty years still looking to God's people in Australia and England and America for their financial support. And why is it? Because the teachings of this Book have been neglected. It is because they have never been taught the foundation of Christian finance. No wonder the missionary world is calling out to-day that they are crippled for lack of funds! They need to be taught scriptural finance. That is why God appointed tithing. It is the solution of all financial problems in connection with His work. Where tithing is practised there will never be any going into debt.

Now then in the fourth place, God has appointed tithing as a test of our faith, and for the nourishing and developing of our faith—especially of the young Christians. Here is a young man who has just started housekeeping. He professes to trust God with the enormous matter of his eternal future. He professes to have confidently left his immortal interests in the hands of God. Well now, dare he trust God with one-tenth of his income for a year, and see if at the end of that year the Lord has permitted him to be a loser? My friends, tithing develops in young Christians the spirit of trusting the Lord in their temporal affairs. I will have more to say on that yet.

Now before I come to the next point let me just anticipate two objections. When the subject of tithing is brought before the Lord's people, there are usually a few who are ready to say, Well, I think it is a man's duty to provide for his own household, for his own family. Yes, so do I. Scripture says so. There is nothing wrong in that. I go further. I believe it is perfectly proper for a young Christian man to desire and to seek after an increasing income with which to properly support his growing family, but if he is not a tither he has no guarantee from God that his present income will even be maintained, let alone enlarged. But the tither has that guarantee from God as we shall yet see, unless our eyes are shut.

And then perhaps there are some who say, I cannot afford to tithe, for I have made some investments which have turned out very badly. Yes, and you are likely to meet with some worse ones if you continue to rob God! My friends, you need divine guidance in the matter of investing, and God won't give that guidance while you are walking contrary to His revealed will in the matter of church finance. I am fully persuaded that in the vast majority of cases, if not all (This may sound harsh: God's Word is piercing and condemning and rebuking and humbling) that where you have children of God in middle life or in old age, who are in financial straits, it is because they robbed God in their earlier years. Be not deceived: God is not mocked. If they did not handle to His glory and use according to His Word the money He did give them, then they must not be surprised if He withholds from them now. There is a cause for every effect. There is an explanation to all things right here in this Book, too.

Now I want to come at closer grips with the text itself. There are three things I wish you to notice carefully. Verse 10, Malachi 3:—"Bring ye all the tithes into the storehouse, that there may be meat in Mine house, and **prove Me now herewith**, saith the Lord of hosts." My friends, that is a startling expression. It is a remarkable expression. God says, "Prove Me." Those words mean this:— Place the Almighty on trial; and it would be sin, it would be positively wicked, for any creature so to do, unless he was definitely commanded to. "Prove Me now herewith"—with a tithe. In other words, our text tells us to put God to the proof, to test Him out and see what He will do. We are bidden to give to Him one-tenth of our income and then to see whether He will let us be the loser or no. "Prove Me now herewith." O I tell you, my friends, my soul is overwhelmed by the amazing condescension of the Most High to place Himself in such a position. God allows Himself to be placed on trial by us, and tithing is a process of proof. Tithing is a means whereby we can demonstrate in the material realm the existence of God and the fact of His governorship over all temporal affairs. If you have any shadow of doubt in your mind and heart as to whether or no God exists or as to whether or no He controls all temporal affairs, you can have that doubt removed and you can have an absolute demonstration of the actuality of God's existence and of His control over temporal affairs. How? By regularly, faithfully, systematically giving to Him one-tenth of your gross income, and then seeing whether He will let you be the loser or not: **proving** whether He **does** honor those who honor Him: proving whether He will allow Himself to be any man's debtor. He says, "Prove Me, prove Me, put Me to the test." You trembling, fearful saints, never mind if your income is only £1 a week and you have to scheme and scratch and strain to make both ends meet out of 20/- Take two of them away and devote them to the Lord, and then see if He will remain your debtor. "Prove Me now herewith," He says, Try Me out and see whether I am worthy of your confidence; put Me to the test and see whether I will disappoint your faith. As I said a few minutes ago, God has appointed tithing as a test of faith, for the development of it; and if the young Christian would only start by proving God in the material realm, testing Him out in God's own appointed way, what a confirmation it would be! How it would enable him to trust God in temporal things—which is one of the hardest things that the average Christian finds to do.

Now coming again to the text. Notice the expression, "Prove Me now herewith, saith the Lord of hosts, if I will not open you the windows of heaven." What does He mean by that? "And see if I will not open the windows of heaven." What does He mean? Now Scripture always interprets Scripture. If you go back to the 7th chapter of Genesis, verses 11 and 12, you will find that identical expression used there, and it explains the force of it here in Malachi 3. Genesis 7.11:—"In the six hundreth year of Noah's life, in the second month, the seventeenth day of the month, the same day were all the fountains of the great deep broken up, and the windows of heaven were opened. And the rain was upon the earth forty days and forty nights." Now the same expression that is used in Genesis 7 in connection with the Deluge is used here in Malachi 3 in connection with the return, the response, the blessings that God has promised to give those who honor Him with their substance, by devoting a tithe to His service. In other words, that expression "Open the windows of heaven" signifies **an abundant outpouring.** Now listen! That does not mean an abundant spiritual blessing. It does not mean that at all, for spiritual blessings cannot be purchased. You ask, Can temporal? In one sense ,yes. Certainly they can, in the sense that God has promised that we shall reap what we have sown; in the sense that He has promised to honor those who honor Him; in the sense that He has promised a bountiful return to a bountiful giver. Certainly! Just in the same way that He has promised length of days to those who honor their parents when they are children. That is a blessing that is purchased! Now then, listen! When God has promised to open the windows of heaven and pour out a blessing, it is not a spiritual one, it is a temporal one. He promises an increase in your income. Of course He does. Do you suppose Almighty God would be **your** debtor? Do you suppose the Most High will allow you to be the loser because you are faithful to His Word and obedient to His will and give Him a tenth out of your income? Why, of course not. And I say again, the great reason why so many of God's people are poor is because they have been unfaithful with the money that God gave them. They robbed God. No wonder they have suffered adversities and misfortunes. No wonder! Some of you need to re-read your Bibles on the subject of the principles and conditions of temporal prosperity. Some of you need to learn that the God of the New Testament is the God of the Old Testament and that He changes not. God changes not. God does not vary the principles of His government. The God who gave bountiful crops to a people in the Old Testament times who honored Him and kept His Word is the same God who is on the throne to-day, and the same God gives bountiful crops and prosperity in business to them who honor Him. But those who meet with financial adversities and financial misfortunes—there is a reason for it; of course there is. The world calls it "bad luck"; they know no better; though we ought to!

Now, in closing (I am going to keep you a little late this morning), did you notice the perplexity of the translators in the text? The translators did not know what to do with this text. That is very obvious if you notice the words they have put in italics. It made me smile when I was studying this text. Now look at it as it reads: the last verse:—"I will open the windows of heaven and pour you out a blessing, that" (now leave out the words in italics )"that not enough." The words in italics are not in the original. They have been supplied by the translators and they had to supply more words in the last clause than were actually there, which shows they did not know what to do with it. The Hebrew as nearly as I can get it in the original means, "there shall be enough and more than enough." That does not vary very much from the translation that the translators have given us. In other words it means, "The liberal soul shall be made fat." Turn for a moment to II Chronicles 31. We looked at the beginning of this last Lord's Day morning, but I want you to notice now the 10th verse:—"And Azariah the chief priest of the house of Zadok answered him, and said, Since the people began to bring the offerings into the house of the Lord, we have had enough to eat, and have left plenty; for the Lord hath blessed His people; and that which is left is this great store." Now if you read the preceding verses you will find it was when the tithe was restored in that revival in the days of Hezekiah; and here we are told that since the people brought their offerings (their tithes) into the Lord's house there was not only enough, but there was more than enough; there was a great store left over! It is ever thus when we faithfully honor God with our substance.

Now in closing I want to give you a few practical suggestions. They are very important and they are very simple. In the matter of tithing, Christian friends. be just as strict and careful and systematic as you are in business matters— in fact, even more so, for it is not the world's money and it is not your own, but it is the Lord's money which is involved. Now do not trust to memory. There are some Christians who say, Well I have never bothererd to keep any records, but I am quite sure that if I had done so I should find that I had given at least a tenth to the Lord. Some of you might be surprised to find—if you did keep a record and looked it up—how much short of a tenth you had given!

Now in the first place I would suggest this. Form the habit of taking out one-tenth from all the moneys that you receive either as wages or gifts. Subtract one-tenth and put it into a separate bag or box or purse. That is what it means when it says in Corinthians, "laying by in store." And that box or purse is the Lord's, not yours. It is holy unto Him. Form the habit of taking out a tenth from all you receive and putting it into a separate compartment belonging to the Lord.

In the second place, get a small book— a cheap notebook—and on one page put down all your receipts (it will not take some of you very long—one entry, I suppose, at the end of the week) and on the other page put down the disbursements.

And then in the third place make it a matter of definite prayer to God to guide you in the disbursement as to where He would have you use that money that belongs to Him. It is not yours; it is His; for remember you have not even begun to give at all until you have first paid your tithe. Giving comes in afterwards. The tithe is the Lord's. That is His. That is not yours to give at all; that belongs to the Creator. You have not begun to give until you have done your tithing.

Now in the last place I just want to read to you a number of extracts that I clipped from a religious magazine published in England called "The Life of Faith." In that magazine there has been going on for some time a correspondence —a number of letters—and the subject has been the unemployment in England among the Lord's people. Now here is the testimony of one who has written to that paper:—

"Twenty-five years ago, being influenced by reading the life of George Muller, I was led to give a tenth of my income to the Lord. I think I was earning 6/- a week at the time. The first few years I found it sometimes a sacrifice. One shilling out of ten seemed a lot. But it became such a habit with me to divide at once and put away the Lord's tenth, that for years it has been no sacrifice. Now what is the result? This: I have proved the truth that "Him that honoreth Me I will honor." All through the War, and since, I have experienced no poverty. Though a shop assistant and now over forty (and it is a woman that is writing) I have been away ill only one week in twenty-five years. What makes it even more wonderful is that after twenty I become slightly deaf and this has increased (and they do not want deaf assistants to wait on people in a shop, do they?) and yet, praise the Lord, I am still holding my situation. When I read of so many other sad cases of unemployment I praise the Lord for His mercy to me."

One testimony like that is worth twenty arguments. And, my friends, I want to bear my own witness that after seventeen years' experience and observation I have proven the truth of our text that God **does** open the windows of heaven and that He **does** give more than enough in response to simple obedience to Him.

Now, I do not know whether I will be likely to occupy this pulpit twelve months from now—that is known to God—but if I am here twelve months hence, the Lord willing, I am going to invite the men present this morning and who will be alive then, to give me a brief statement as to how they have found this plan work out, for I know there are some of you (I am not hopeful enough to believe that all of you will) who are going to carry out God's Word. You are going to start right away dividing and devoting one-tenth of your income to the Lord. And my friends I am not one bit afraid to put God to the test and make public the result. If I am here twelve months hence I am going to read out and announce the statements of the brothers that tried this during the year, and we will then see whether or not God has allowed them to be the losers for having given Him a tenth. "Prove Me now herewith." That is God's challenge to you. God dares you to test Him out in the financial realm. You profess to have faith in Him, to trust your soul into His keeping; now He challenges you to see whether you have faith enough to just trust Him with one-tenth of your income for a year, for mind you, in the case of the children of Israel it was a matter of waiting for very nearly twelve months for any returns. They were farmers. You test the Lord out for twelve months. You wait a reasonable length of time, and then see whether He lets you be the loser or not. Prove Me now herewith." That is God's challenge to your faith. O brethren and sisters do so and see if He will not open you the windows of heaven, and pour you out a blessing that there shall be enough and more than enough."

Substance of a sermon preached by the Editor.

## EXPERIMENTAL SALVATION.

Salvation may be viewed from many angles and contemplated under various aspects, but from whatever side we look at it we must ever remember that "Salvation is of the Lord." Salvation was planned by the Father for His elect before the foundation of the world. It was purchased for them by the holy life and vicarious death of His incarnate Son. It is applied to and wrought in them by His Holy Spirit. It is known and enjoyed through the study of the Scriptures, through the exercise of faith, and through communion with the triune Jehovah.

Now it is greatly to be feared that there are multitudes in Christendom who verily imagine and sincerely believe that **they** are among the saved, yet who are total strangers to a work of Divine grace in their hearts. It is one thing to have clear intellectual conceptions of God's truth, it is quite another matter to have a personal, real, heart acquaintance with it. It is one thing to believe that sin is the awful thing that the Bible says it is, but it is quite another matter to have a holy horror and hatred of it in the soul. It is one thing to know that God requires repentance, it is quite another matter to experimentally mourn and groan over our vileness. It is one thing to believe that Christ is the only Saviour for sinners, it is quite another matter to really trust Him from the heart. It is one thing to believe that Christ is the Sum of all excellency, it is quite another matter to love Him above all others. It is one thing to believe that God is the great and holy One, it is quite another matter to truly reverence and fear Him. It is one thing to believe that salvation is of the Lord, it is quite another matter to become an actual partaker of it through His gracious inworkings.

While it is true that Holy Scripture insists on man's responsibility, and that all through the piece God deals with the sinner as an accountable being, yet it is also true that the Bible plainly and constantly shows that no son of Adam has ever measured up to his responsibility, that every one has miserably failed to discharge his accountability. It is this which constitutes the deep need for GOD to work in the sinner and do for him what he is unable to do for himself. "They that are in the flesh **cannot** please God" (Rom. 8:8). The sinner is "**without strength**" (Rom. 5:6). Apart from the Lord, we "can do **nothing**" (John 15:5).

While it is true that the Gospel issues a Call and a Command to all who hear it, it is also true that all disregard that call and disobey that command. "They all with one consent began to make excuse" (Luke 14:18). This is where the sinner commits his greatest sin and most manifests his awful enmity against God and His Christ: that when a Saviour, suited to his needs, is presented to him, he "despises and rejects" Him (Isa. 53:3). This is where the sinner shows what an incorrigible rebel he is, and demonstrates that he is deserving only of eternal torments. But it is just at this point that God manifests His sovereign and wondrous grace. He not only planned and provided salvation, but He actually bestows it upon those whom He has chosen.

Now this bestowal of salvation is far more than a mere proclamation that salvation is to be found in the Lord Jesus: it is very much more than an invitation for sinners to receive Christ as their Saviour. It is God actually saving His people. It is His own sovereign and all-powerful work of grace toward and in those who are entirely destitute of merit, and who are so depraved in themselves that they will not and cannot take one step to the obtaining of salvation. Those who have been actually saved owe far more to Divine grace than most of them realize. It is not only that Christ died to put away their sins, but also the Holy Spirit has wrought a work in them—a work which applies to them the virtues of Christ's atoning death.

It is just at this point that so many preachers fail in their exposition of the Truth. While many of them affirm that Christ is the only Saviour for sinners, they also teach that He actually becomes ours only by our consent. While they allow that conviction of sin is the Holy Spirit's work and that He alone shows us our lost condition and need of Christ, yet they also insist that the decisive factor in salvation is man's own will. But the Holy Scriptures teach that "Salvation is of the Lord" (Jonah 2:9), and that nothing of the creature enters into it at any point. Only that can satisfy God which has been produced by God Himself. Though it be true that salvation does not become the personal portion of the sinner until he has, from the heart, believed in the Lord Jesus Christ, yet is that very believing wrought in him by the Holy Spirit: "By grace are ye saved through faith, and that not of yourselves; it is the gift of God." (Eph. 2:8).

It is exceedingly solemn to discover that there is a "believing" on Christ by the natural man, which is not a believing unto salvation. Just as the Buddhists believe in Buddha, so in Christendom there are multitudes who believe in Christ. And, this "believing" is something more than an intellectual one. Often there is much feeling connected with it—the emotions may be deeply stirred. Christ taught in the Parable of the Sower that there is a class of people who hear the Word and with joy receive it, yet have they no root in themselves (Matt. 13:20, 21). This is fearfully solemn, for it is still occurring daily. Scripture also tells us that "Herod heard John gladly." Thus, the mere fact that the reader of these pages enjoys listening to some sound Gospel preacher is no proof at all that he is a regenerated soul. The Lord Jesus said to the Pharisees concerning John the Baptist, "Ye were willing for a season to rejoice in his light," yet the sequel shows clearly that no real work of grace had been wrought in them. And these things are recorded in Scripture as solemn warnings!

It is striking and solemn to mark the exact wording in the last two scriptures referred to. Note the repeated personal pronoun in Mark 6:20: "For Herod heard John (not 'God'!), knowing that he was a just man and an holy, and observed him and when he heard him he did many things and heard him gladly." It was the personality of John which attracted Herod. How often is this the case to-day! People are charmed by the personality of the preacher: they are carried away by his style and won by his earnestness for souls. But if there is nothing more than this, there will one day be a rude awakening for them. That which is vital is a "love for the Truth," not for the one who presents it. It is this which distinguishes the true people of God from the "mixt multitude" who ever associate with them.

So in John 5:35 Christ said to the Pharisees concerning His forerunner: "Ye were willing for a season to rejoice in his light," not " in the light!" In like manner, there are many to-day who listen to one whom God enables to open up some of the mysteries and wonders of His Word, and they rejoice "in his light" while in the dark themselves, never having personally received "an unction from the Holy One." Those who do "love the truth" (2 Thess. 2:10) are they in whom a Divine work of grace has been wrought. They have something more than a clear intellectual understanding of the Scripture: it is the food of their souls, the joy of their hearts (Jer. 15:16). They love the Truth, and because they do so, they hate error and shun it as deadly poison. They are jealous for the glory of the Author of the Word, and will not sit under a minister whose teaching dishonors Him; they will not listen to preaching which exalts man into the place of supremacy, so that he is the decider of his own destiny.

"Lord, Thou wilt ordain peace for us, for Thou also hast wrought all our works in us" (Isa. 26:12). Here is the hearty and unqualified confession of the true people of God. Note the preposition: "Thou also hast wrought all our works in us." This speaks of a Divine work of grace wrought in the heart of the saint. Nor is this text alone. Weigh carefully the following: "It pleased God, who separated me from my mother's womb, and called me by His grace, to reveal His Son in me" (Gal. 1:15, 16). "Unto Him that is able to do exceeding abundantly above all that we ask or think according to the power that worketh in us." (Eph. 3:20.) "Being confident of this very thing, that He which hath begun a good work in you will finish it" (Phil. 1:6). "It is God which worketh in you both to will and to do of His good pleasure" (Phil. 2:13). "I will put my laws into their hearts and in their minds will I write them" (Heb. 10:16). "Now the God of peace . . . make you perfect in every good work to do His will, working in you that which is well-pleasing in His sight" (Heb. 13:20, 21). Here are seven passages which speak of the inward workings of God's grace; or in other words of experimental salvation.

"Lord, Thou wilt ordain peace for us, for Thou also hast wrought all our works in us" (Isa. 26:2). Is there an echoing response in your heart to this, my reader? Is your repentance something deeper than the remorse and tears of the natural man? Does it have its root in a Divine work of grace which the Holy Spirit hath wrought in your soul? Is your believing in Christ something more than an intellectual one? Is your relation to Him something more vital than what some act of yours has brought about—having been made one with Him by the power and operation of the Spirit? Is your love for Christ something more than a pious sentiment, like that of the Romanist who sings of the "gentle" and "sweet" Jesus? Does your love for Him proceed from an altogether new nature, which God has created within you? Can you really say with the Psalmist "Whom have I in heaven but Thee? and there is none upon earth that I desire beside Thee"? Is your profession accompanied by true meekness and lowliness of heart? It is easy to call yourself names, and say "I am an unworthy and unprofitable creature." But do you realise yourself to be such? Do you feel yourself to be "less than the least of all saints"? Paul did! If you do not; if instead, you deem yourself superior to the rank and file of Christians—who bemoan their failures, confess their weakness, and cry "O wretched man that I am"—there is grave reason to conclude that you are a stranger to God!

That which distinguishes genuine godliness from human religiousness is this: the one is external, the other internal. Christ complained of the Pharisees, "Ye make clean the outside of the cup and platter, but within ye are full of extortion and excess." (Matt. 23:25). A carnal religion is all on the surface. It is at the heart God looks and with the heart God deals. Concerning His people He says: "I will put My laws into their hearts, and in their minds will I write them." (Heb. 10:16.)

"Lord, Thou wilt ordain peace for us, for Thou also hast wrought all our works in us." How humbling is this to the pride of man! It makes everything of God, and nothing of the creature! The tendency of human nature, the world over, is to be self-sufficient and self-satisfied; to say with the Laodiceans, "I am rich, and increased with goods, and have need of nothing" (Rev. 3:17). But here is something to humble us, and empty us of pride. Since God has wrought all our works in us, then we have no ground for boasting. "What hast thou that thou didst not receive? Now if thou didst receive it, why dost thou glory, as if thou hast not received it?" (1 Cor. 4:7).

And who are the ones in whom God thus works? From the Divine side: His favoured, chosen, redeemed people. From the human side: those who, in themselves, have no claim whatever on His notice; who are destitute of any merit; who have everything in them to provoke

His holy wrath; those who are miserable failures in their lives, and utterly depraved and corrupt in their persons. But where sin abounded, grace did much more abound, and did for them and in them what they would not and could not do for themselves.

And what is it God "works" in His people? **ALL** their works. First, He **quickens** them: "it is the Spirit that quickeneth; the flesh profiteth nothing" (John 6:63). "Of His own will begat He us with the word of truth" (James 1:18). Second, He bestows **repentance**: "Him hath God exalted with His right hand to be a Prince and a Saviour, for to **give** repentance to Israel" (Acts 5:31). "Then hath God also to the Gentiles **granted repentance** unto life" (Acts 11:18 and compare 2 Tim. 2:25). Third, He gives **faith:** "for by grace are ye saved through faith; and that **not of yourselves: it is the gift of God**" (Eph. 2:8). "Ye are risen with Him through the faith of the **operation of God**" (Col. 2:12). Fourth, He grants a spiritual **understanding**: "and we know the Son of God is come, and hath **given** us an understanding, **that we may know Him that is true**" (1 John 5:20). Fifth, He effectuates our service: "I laboured more abundantly than them all: yet not I, but the grace of God which was with me" (1 Cor. 15:10). Sixth, He secures our **perseverance**: "who are kept by the power **of God** through faith unto salvation" (1 Pet. 1:5). Seventh, He produces our fruit: **"from Me is thy fruit found"** (Hos. 14:8). "The fruit of the **Spirit"** (Gal. 5:22). Yes, **He** has wrought all our works in us.

Why has God thus "wrought all our works in us"? First, because unless He had done so, all had eternally perished (Rom. 9:29). We were "without strength," unable to meet God's righteous demands. Therefore, in sovereign grace, He did for us what we ought but could not do for ourselves. Second, that all the glory might be His. God is a jealous God. He says so. His honour He will not share with another. By this means, He secures all the praise, and we have no ground for boasting. Third, that our salvation might be effectually and securely accomplished. Were any part of our salvation left to us it would be neither effectual nor secure. Whatever man touches he spoils: failure is written across everything he attempts. But what God does is perfect and lasts forever: "I know that whatsoever God doeth, it shall be forever: nothing can be put to it, nor anything taken from it: and God doeth it, that men should fear before Him" (Eccl. 3:14).

But how may I be sure that my works have been "wrought in me" by God? Mainly by their effects. If you have been born again, you have a new nature within. This new nature is spiritual and contrary to the flesh—contrary in its desires and aspirations. Because the old and new natures are contrary to each other, there is a continual war between them. Are you **conscious** of this inward conflict?

If your repentance be a God-wrought one, then you abhor yourself. If your repentance be a genuine and spiritual one, then you marvel that God did not long ago cast you into Hell. If your repentance be the gift of Christ, then you daily mourn the wretched return which you make to God's wondrous grace; you hate sin, you sorrow in secret before God for your manifold transgressions. Not simply you did so at conversion, but daily do so now.

If your faith be a God-communicated one, it is evidenced by your turning away from all creature confidence, by a renunciation of your own self-righteousness, by a repudiation of all your own works. If your faith be "the faith of God's elect" (Titus 1:1), then you are resting alone on Christ as the ground of your acceptance before God. If your faith be the result of "the operation of God," then you implicitly believe His Word, you receive it with meekness, you crucify reason, and accept all that He has said with childlike simplicity.

If your love for Christ be the fruit of the Spirit (Gal. 5:22), then it evidences itself by constantly seeking to please Him and by abstaining from what you know is displeasing to Him: in a word, by an obedient walk. If your love for Christ be the love of "the new man," then you pant after Him, you yearn for communion with Him above everything else. If your love for Christ be the same in kind (though not in degree) as His love for you, then you are eagerly looking forward to His glorious appearing, when He shall come again to receive His people unto Himself, that they may be forever with the Lord. May the grace of spiritual discernment be given the reader to see whether his Christian profession be real or a sham, whether his hope is built upon the Rock of Ages or the quicksands of human resolutions, efforts, decisions, or feelings; whether, in short, his salvation is "of the Lord" or the vain imagination of his own deceitful heart.

—Arthur W. Pink.

## PERFECTED FOR EVER.

In the tenth chapter of Hebrews we see the glorious perfection of the work of God for sinners, not only in having justified them from all things, but also in having appointed them as sanctified priests to stand with confidence before Him in His holiest place. We must see that this is God's word concerning us who believe; and contrary to all our sense of unfitness for such glory and blessing, we must receive it as our own because He, in grace, has so ordained. While we rejoice in it, we must be forever humbled by the remembrance that it is all of grace and gift, and that we have no part in it save as objects of His love and recipients of His blessing. When we turn from communing with God in His Word, to contemplate our daily walk, whether we look at our failures in the polluted paths of this world, or at the sins even of our holy things, we must be tempted to exclaim, Can this blessed position be ours?

Our Lord knew this, and among His last lessons to His beloved disciples there is one that meets all these difficulties: "He riseth from supper and laid aside His garments; and took a towel and girded Himself. After that He poured water into a basin and began to wash His disciples' feet, and to wipe them with the towel wherewith He was girded. . . . . Jesus saith unto him (Peter) he that is washed (bathed) needeth not save to wash his feet, but is clean every whit; and ye are clean." He thus taught them what the Holy Spirit afterward more fully unfolded, that faith in Him brings a cleanness that is never lost again. The believer can never be regarded as having lost his perfection in Christ and become exposed to wrath and final condemnation, though the consciousness and the joy of his position may be obscured; for let it be observed it was Peter who was so soon to fall into the grievous sin of denying his Lord with oaths and curses, to whom Jesus first addressed this lesson of the need of having his feet washed.

The figure derives its significance from the Eastern custom of going to a bath and being completely bathed, while, in returning from the bath in sandals, the feet would inevitably be soiled by the dust or mire of the road, and thus need to be "washed." The defilements of the way are not regarded as casting the person who has bathed back to his old condition of complete uncleanness, but as stains that have come upon one who as to the totality of his condition continues clean. He is clean, but his soiled feet need to be washed. The believer knows that he is represented before God by a High Priest, not as guilty and unreconciled, but as cleansed for ever by the efficacy of the one offering. Yet he knows that he does not escape defilement as he treads the path of life—that he is not like his Master, "spotless." "In many things we all offend" (James 3). Yet he no longer cries with the publican, "God be merciful to me a sinner," but: "If we confess our sins He is faithful and just to forgive us our sins, and to cleanse us from all unrighteousness." In this confession we recognise the existence of a stain, but not a stain imputed unto condemnation, for grace has delivered him from the place of a criminal and brought him into a relation of everlasting favour and love. Our Lord made "reconciliation for the sins of His people," and in confessing our sins it is our happy privilege to realize in present peace of conscience that He hath made us "clean every whit."

When a child of disobedience becomes a believer, nothing is seen but the blood of atonement covering his sin; but too often those who belong to "the household of God" recognise nothing in relation to **trespass** (mis-step) beyond their former positions as aliens and enemies. Yet surely God now "dealeth with us as with sons," an entirely new relation. The needed cleansing has reference to our ways and walk rather than to our persons, which are already redeemed. A sovereign in the government of his family proceeds on different principles from those on which he deals with outlaws and rebels. Having delivered us from condemnation and wrath and placed us under grace, Christ is made a great

High Priest for the family of God, supplying all their need, faithful where they fail, pure though they be defiled; the same yesterday and to-day and forever, however they may change; the perpetual Advocate and Propitiation. "For if, when we were enemies, we were reconciled to God by the death of His Son, much more being reconciled we shall be saved by His life." Christ has imparted to us His own eternal life, and henceforth maintains His death-bought people in continual acceptance before God. Our High Priest, if we may say, continually points to the blood which purchased us, and cleanses us from all defilement of the way. This is surely the meaning of 1 John 1:9: when we confess our sins, He is faithful to forgive us, in that He hath promised; just in that He will not again punish a sin once dealt with at the Cross. When, therefore, the believer confesses his sins, he becomes happily conscious of our Lord's blessed offices in washing his feet from all the defilements of the way.

How needful this is every hour for the maintenance of our cleanness, is seen directly in looking at our sins, even of ignorance. Did one of the holy angels step where we walk, what innumerable defilements would he see in the path where our blunted vision can discern no pollution, nor see aught but pure service! Who, beside Christ, could ever say in presence of the holiness of God, concerning the best of our lives, "Search me, O God, and know my heart; try me and know my thoughts, and see if there be any wicked way in me"; or "As for me, I will walk in my integrity"? Again, even in our best service, there is "the iniquity of the holy things in all our holy gifts" (see Exodus 38:38), which must needs be borne by the high priest. We cannot see the full meaning of those things, beloved reader, till we walk in the light. It is blessed that God does not show us the full measure of the depth of our ruin all at once, or we should sink in despair. It is only revealed to us as the perfection of the work of Christ in all its bearings—bathing the person, then washing the feet—is discovered; so that in the measure in which we grow in the knowledge of the Lord and in practical holiness of life, so do we grow in the knowledge of our sinfulness, "rejoicing in Christ Jesus and having no confidence in the flesh." This seems to be the meaning of Paul when he adjudged himself chief among sinners. He walked in more light than others, and therefore saw more of indwelling sin, yet, through all, rejoiced in the exceeding abundant grace bestowed, "with faith and love which is in Christ Jesus."

Beloved Christian reader, in these pages on the words of the Holy Spirit through Paul "PERFECTED FOR EVER" we have sought to lead thy heart into happy, abiding rest in the finished work of Jesus Christ. Many a saint sees it all clearly at the end of life, and passes away in rapture as he recognises the fulness of his redemption; but we would have thee to live in the joy and power of these truths as well as to die in them.

"Have you a glimpse of glory now?" asked a friend as he stood by the bedside of a departing saint in Scotland. "I'll ha'e nane of your glimpses now that I am dying," was the reply, "since **I've had a full look at Christ these forty years past!**"

In closing, let me remind you that the same blessed cross which separates you from your sins should also separate you from your worldliness. In taking to you the benefits of Christ's death, you declare that you are a dead and risen man; as one has happily said, not so much an earthly man looking up to heaven, as one seated by faith with Christ in heavenly places, and looking down upon the earth. We are not of those who say, "Shall we continue in sin that grace may abound?"—whose damnation is just. We should not profess to enjoy the blessing of Christ's work for us, without dying in spirit to that world which crucified the Lord, and which now hates the doctrine of the Cross, where ever preached in purity and power.

"I thirst—but not as once I did,
　The vain delights of earth to share;
Thy wounds, Immanuel, all forbid
　That I should set my treasures there.

It was the sight of Thy dear cross,
　First weaned my soul from earthly things;
And taught me to esteem as dross,
　The mirth of fools and pomp of kings.

I want that grace that springs from Thee,
　That quickens all things where it flows,
And make a wretched thorn like me
　Bloom as the myrtle or the rose."

—Waymarks in the Wilderness, 1865.

Second, we have abolished passing around the collection-plates. Because there is no scripture to justify such a practice; because—in the midst of the service—it interrupts and detracts from the spirit of worship; because it encourages the ungodly to contribute to the maintenance of the Lord's work, and because it gives the appearance of making a charge for the Gospel. A box has been placed at the rear of the church, where the Lord's people are free to put in their offerings as led of the Spirit—every few weeks the unconverted being told that their contributions are not acceptable to the Lord (Prov. 15:8). No appeals whatever are made. The Lord has honored this change, as we knew He would, by a marked increase in the offerings. The Sabbath-school and the Sisters' Dorcas Society have also ceased taking up any collections.

Third, we have made it a hard and fast rule that none but a member of our own church or one of like faith and order shall be a teacher in our Sabbath-school. There is much laxity along this line to-day. The Word of God is plain enough on it. Of old Jehovah said to His people, "Thou shalt not plow with an ox and an ass together" (Deut. 22:10), that is, with a clean and an unclean animal. "Unto the wicked (all who are not righteous) God saith, What hast thou to do to declare My statutes?" (Psa. 50:16). When the adversaries of Judah and Benjamin heard that those who had returned to Palestine from Babylon "builded the temple unto the Lord," they came and said, "Let us build with you." But we read that Zerubbabel and the chief of the fathers replied, "Ye have nothing to do with us to build an house unto our God" (Ezra 4:1-3). O that we had more Zerubbabels to-day, who would refuse to compromise and in order to please men, dishonour God.

Connected with our church is a Dorcas Society, which meets every second Thursday evening. The Sisters come together to make garments for the poor children with whom our Missionaries in India come into contact. When these are sent out, they are supplemented by other little gifts, such as toys, and soaps, stationery, etc., for the missionaries. Each member of the Society pays sixpence (twelve cents a month), and a box is placed on a table to receive gifts. From this, materials are purchased and then made up. Their bi-weekly meetings are of a spiritual nature; in addition to praying and singing, one of the Sisters gives a short address or reads something of interest connected with missionary work. The Lord has given them a most capable president, is adding to their numbers, and is blessing their labours.

General religious conditions here are very similar to those which obtain in the U.S.A. The vast majority of the churches are in a sorry state. Those that are out and out worldly are at their wits' end to invent new devices for drawing a crowd. Others which still preserve an outward form of godliness provide nothing substantial for the soul; there is little ministering of Christ to the heart and little preaching of "sound doctrine," without which souls cannot be built up and established in the faith. The great majority of the "pastors" summon to their aid some professional "evangelist," who, for two to four weeks, puts on a high-pressure campaign and secures sufficient new "converts" to take the place of those who have "lapsed" since he was last with them. What a farce it all is! What an acknowledgement of their own failure! Imagine C. H. Spurgeon needing some evangelist to preach the Gospel for him for a month each year! Why do not these well-paid "pastors" heed 2 Tim. 4:5 and themselves "do the work of an evangelist," and thus "make full proof of their ministry"?

The great need of Australia to-day is for God-sent and God-anointed men, who will shun not to declare all the counsel of God; men in whom the Word of Christ dwells richly, so that they can say with the apostle, "Woe is me if I preach not the Gospel"; men on whom rests the fear of God, so that they are delivered from the fear of man. Will Christian readers in distant lands join us in daily prayer that the Lord of the harvest will raise up and thrust forth more of His laborers into this portion of His Vineyard.

Assuring our many friends throughout the U.S.A. that they are not forgotten, but often thought of and prayed for, and with loving greetings and every good wish to them will remain,

Yours by Divine Grace,

A. W. and V. E. Pink.

# STUDIES IN THE SCRIPTURES
"Search the Scriptures" John 5:39.

Copyright in all English-speaking Countries.

Editor: Arthur W. Pink, 15 Hurlstone Avenue, Summer Hill, N.S.W., Australia.
Hon. Agent in U.S.A.: Mr. C. S. Pressel, 559 Dupont Ave., York, Penna.

FREE TO ALL WHO WILL READ IT

"Oh how love I Thy law! it is my meditation all the day." (Psa. 119:97).

This was more than a mere affirmation of the Psalmist's love for God's Word. It is an exclamation, full of feeling: "Oh how love I Thy law." It expresses strong affection. It were as though he said, My love for Thy law is more than I can express in words.

Now where there is a renewed heart there is a love for the Word. Said the apostle Paul, "I delight in the law of God after the inward man" (Rom. 7:22). Just as a babe cries for its mother's breast, so the young Christian longs for the pure milk of the Word, and the more he feeds upon it the more will he love it. Physically, it is when we are sick that we lose our appetites and no longer relish our food. So it is spiritually. One sure test of the believer's state, his present spirituality, is his measure of love for the Word. If his hunger for it be gone, that is a sure proof that he is out of communion with the Lord; in other words, he is in a backslidden state.

The Holy Scriptures **deserve** our love. First, because of their **Author.** The Bible is not the product of the O.T. prophets and N.T. apostles. If it were nothing more, it would still be entitled to our highest respect. Nor is the Bible a revelation from the holy angels. If it were nothing higher than that, it would merit our veneration and esteem. But it is the Word of God.

You know how it is in the human realm. You see some books advertised by a certain author who is a stranger to you: you are not interested, so do not purchase. But you meet the author, and learn to know and to love him. Then you desire his books. So it should be with the Bible. By grace, the Christian has learned to know and love God; then he should love His Word, too. It is a communication from the Father who loves His children, and who has their highest interests at heart. Therefore, we should welcome it, prize it, and delight in constantly reading it.

Again, God's Word deserves our love because of its **intrinsic excellencies.** It is true, yea, truth itself. It is truth without any admixture of error. It is **pure.** Said the Psalmist: "Thy Word is very pure, therefore Thy servant loveth it" (Psa. 119:140). Because it is pure, it purifies (119:140). It is good (Heb. 6:5). Is water "good" when we are thirsty? Is food "good" when we are hungry? So the Word of God is "good" because suited to every need of our souls. It is a **sure** Word (Psa. 19:7; 2 Pet. 1:19). It contains not the guesses of fallible men, nor the sayings of wise men; it is given by the inspiration of the infallible God. Its history is dependable; its prophecies are reliable; its promises may be counted on. For these reasons the Word of God should command our esteem and win our hearts.

Once more, God's Word deserves our love because of its **bestowments.** It is able to make wise unto salvation (2 Tim. 3:15) and converts the soul (Psalm 19:7). It purifies (Psa. 119:9) and sanctifies (John 17:17). It conveys an increased knowledge of God. Said Moses, "Show me Thy glory" (Ex. 33:18)—he would fain know more of the excellencies of God. This is still the longing of His saints, and it can be satisfied only by a better acquaintance with His Word. It brings

(Continued on page 144).

## BACK NUMBERS

OF THIS MAGAZINE obtainable, 5/- (1 dollar) per year; Bound at 7/- (1 dollar 75.) Each year is yet obtainable.

ADVISE PROMPTLY of Change of Address

THIS MAGAZINE is published as a work of faith and labor of love. It is gladly sent to all who would value it.

We want the names and addresses of Christians who would read it.

Christians who feel definitely led to do so may have fellowship with us in this Ministry.

## CONTENTS.

| | |
|---|---|
| The Gospel of John (19:25-42) | 122 |
| Gleanings in Exodus | 130 |
| Midnight at Midday | 135 |
| Assurance | 139 |

## THE GOSPEL OF JOHN.

**66. Christ laying down His life: John 19:25-42.**

Below is an Analysis of John 19:25-42:

1. The mother of Jesus and the beloved disciple vv. 25-27.
2. The Saviour's thirst vv. 28, 29.
3. The Saviour's victorious death v. 30.
4. God guarding the Saviour's body vv. 31-33.
5. The piercing of the Saviour's side vv. 34-37.
6. The boldness of Joseph and Nicodemus vv. 38, 39.
7. The Saviour's burial vv. 40-42.

Each of the Evangelists treats of our Lord's death with more or less fulness of detail. The birth, the baptism, and the temptation of Christ are described in only two of the Gospels; several of His miracles and discourses are found only in one; but the Saviour's Passion is recorded in all four, which at once denotes its supreme importance. But though each Evangelist devotes not a little space to the events of the last hours of Christ, there is a striking variation about their several narratives. Nowhere is the Hand of the Spirit more evident than in what He guided each Gospel-writer to insert and omit. Each of them was manifestly moved by Him to bring in only that which was strictly pertinent to the distinctive design before him.

The four Gospels are not four biographies of Christ, nor do the four together supply one. A harmony of the four Gospels reveals great blanks, altogether incompatible with the theory that they supply us with a "Life of Christ." Only the briefest mention is made of His birth and infancy, and then nothing more is told us about Him till He had reached the age of twelve. After the few words relating to His boyhood, we see Christ no more till He was about thirty. Even His public ministry is not given us with anything approaching completeness: a journey, a miracle, a discourse, here and there, and that is about all. What, then, are the four Gospels, and what was the principle of selection which determined what should have a place in each of them?

The four Gospels give us delineations of the Lord Jesus in four distinct characters: the principle of selection is, that only that which serves to illustrate and exemplify each of these characters was included. Matthew presents Christ as the Son of David, the King of Israel, and everything in his Gospel contributes to this theme. Mark portrays Him as God's Workman, and everything in his Gospel bears directly upon the Servant and His service. Luke depicts Him as the Son of man, hence it is His human perfections, sympathies, and relations which he dwells upon. John reveals Him as the Son of God incarnate, the Word become flesh, tabernacling among men; hence it is His Divine glories, the dignity and majesty of His person, which are most prominent here. Strikingly is this evidenced in what he has related and what he has omitted concerning the Redeemer's sufferings.

John says nothing about the Saviour's agony in Gethsemane, but he and he only does mention the falling backward to the ground of those who came to arrest Him. John omits all details of what took place when our Lord appeared before Caiaphas, but he describes the trial before Annas. The fourth Gospel, and it alone, records our Lord's words to Pilate about His kingdom (18:36), of His coming into this world to bear witness unto the truth (18:37), of his having no power to crucify Him except what God gave (19:11). John alone makes mention of His seamless robe (19:23), His legs not being broken (19:33), and the blood and water which came from His pierced side. John omits altogether the awful cry, "Why hast Thou forsaken Me?" and in its place gives His triumphant "It is finished." John says nothing of His being numbered with the transgressors, but does tell us of Him being with the rich in His death. John alone mentions the costly spices which Nicodemus brought for the anointing of the Saviour's dead body. Clearer proofs of the verbal inspiration of the Scriptures we could not ask for.

Seven times the Saviour spoke while He was upon the cross, thus exhibiting His perfections as the Word, in death, as in life. The first, the word of forgiveness, for His enemies (Luke 23-34). The second, the word of salvation, to the dying thief (Luke 23:42, 43). The third, the word of affection, to and for His mother (John 19:25, 26). The fourth, the word of anguish, to God (Matt. 27:46). The fifth, the word of suffering, to the spectators (John 19:28). The sixth, the word of victory, to His people (John 19:30). The seventh, the word of contentment, to the Father (Luke 23:46). The third, fifth and sixth of these Cross-utterances are recorded by John, and will come before us in our present study.

"Now there stood by the cross of Jesus His mother, and His mother's sister, Mary the wife of Cleophas, and Mary Magdalene" (v. 25). The Jews were present at the crucifixion to satisfy their fiendish craving for His death; the Roman soldiers were there from duty; but here is a group noticed by the Spirit who had been drawn there by affectionate devotion for the central Sufferer. They were not looking on from a distance, nor mingling with the morbid crowds in attendance. They stood "by the Cross." A pitiably small company, five in all; yet a deeply significant number, for five is the number of grace, and in contrast from the crowds which evidenced man's depravity and enmity, these were the trophies of Divine favour. This little company comprised four women and one man. The first was Mary, the Saviour's mother, who now realised the full force of that prophetic word spoken by the aged Simeon more than thirty years before: "Yea, a sword shall pierce through thine own soul also" (Luke 2:35). The second was Mary the wife of Cleophas, of whom we read but little, yet in that little what a wealth of love!—here at the cross, in Matt. 28:1 at the sepulchre; called here "His mother's sister"—evidently her sister-in-law, sister of Joseph, for it is most unlikely that she was a full-blood sister with the same name as herself. The third was Mary of Magdala, out of whom Christ had cast seven demons, and to whom He appeared first when He was risen from the dead. How significant that each of them was named "Mary," which means bitterness! What anguish of spirit was theirs as they beheld the dying Lamb! Equally significant is the absence of another Mary—the sister of Lazarus! A fourth woman was there—Matt. 27:56—the mother of John, though she is not mentioned here. The fifth one was "the disciple whom Jesus loved"—so far as we know, the only one of the eleven apostles which was present.

"Now there stood by the cross of Jesus His mother." "Neither her own danger, nor the sadness of the spectacle, nor the insults of the crowd, could restrain her from performing the last office of duty and tenderness to her Divine Son on the cross" (Dr. Doddridge). After the days of His infancy and childhood, we see and hear little of Mary. During His public ministry her life was lived in the background. But now, when strikes the supreme hour of her Son's agony, when the world has cast out the Child of her womb, she stands there by the cross! Baffled, perhaps, at the unprecedented scene, paralysed at His sufferings, yet bound by the golden chain of love to the Dying One, there she stands. His disciples may desert Him, His friends may forsake Him, His nation may despise Him; but His mother is there, where all might see her—near Him in death as in birth. Who can fully appreciate the mother-heart!

Marvellous fortitude was Mary's. Hers was no hysterical or demonstrative sorrow. There was no show of feminine weakness; no wild outcry of uncontrolable anguish; no falling to the ground in a swoon. Not a word that fell from her lips on this occasion has been recorded by any of the four Evangelists: apparently she suffered in unbroken silence. The crowds were mocking, the thieves taunting, the soldiers callously occupied with His garments, the Saviour was bleeding—and there was His mother beholding it all! What wonder if she had turned away from such a spectacle! What wonder if she had fled from such a scene! But no! She did not crouch away nor fall in a faint. She stood by the cross. What tremendous courage! What love! What reverence for the Saviour!

"When Jesus therefore saw His mother, and the disciple standing by, whom He loved, He saith unto His mother, Woman, behold thy son!" (v. 26). Occupied with the most stupendous work ever done, not only on earth but in the entire universe; under a burden which no mere creature could possibly have sustained; the Object of Satan's fiercest malignity; about to drain the awful cup which meant separation from God Himself for three hours; nevertheless, even at such a time, the Lord Jesus did not deem natural ties as unworthy of recognition. To the very end He showed Himself both perfect Son of God and perfect Son of man. In boyhood He had "honored" His parents (Luke 2:52), so does He now on the cross. About to leave this world, He first provides a home for His widowed mother. First He had prayed for His enemies; then He had spoken the words of salvation and assurance to the repentent thief; now He addresses His mother.

"He saith unto His mother, Woman, behold thy son!" Twice do we find our Lord addressing Mary as "Woman": at the Cana marriage-feast (2:4), and here. It is noteworthy that both of these references are found in John's Gospel, the Gospel which treats specifically of His Diety. The Synoptics present Him in human relationships, but John portrays Him as the Son of God—above all; hence the perfect propriety of Christ here addressing His mother as "Woman." That this term is neither harsh nor discourteous is clear from a comparison with 20: 13. But there was another reason why He would do longer call her "mother"— as, doubtless, He had addressed her many a time. The death on the cross made an end of all His natural ties: "Henceforth know we no man after the flesh: yea, though we have known Christ after the flesh, yet now henceforth know we no more" (2 Cor. 5:16)! From now on, believers would be linked to Christ by a closer bond, by a spiritual relationship, and this is what the Saviour would now teach both His mother and His beloved apostle. "Behold thy son!" I am thy "Son" no longer. It is a striking confirmation of this that Mary is not mentioned at all in connection with Christ's resurrection: the only other time she is referred to in the New Testament is in Acts 1:14, where we see her taking her place among (not over) believers at a prayer-meeting.

"Here it is that our Lord lays aside His human affections. He sees His mother and His beloved disciple near the cross, but it is only to commend them the one to the other, and thus to **separate Himself** from the place which He had once filled among them. Sweet, indeed, it is, to see how faithfully He owned the affection up to the last moment that He could listen to it; no sorrow of His own could make Him forget it! But He was not always to know it. The 'children of the resurrection' neither marry, nor are given in marriage. He must now form their knowledge of Him by other thoughts, for they are henceforth to be joined to Him as 'one spirit'; for such are His blessed ways. If He takes His distance from us, as not knowing us in 'the flesh,' it is only that we may be united to Him in nearer affections and closer interests" (Mr. J. G. Bellett).

"Then saith He to the disciple" (v. 27) —the one standing by "whom He loved." In Matt. 26:56 we read concerning the Eleven, "They all forsook Him and fled." This was the accomplishment of His own sad prediction, "all ye shall be **offended** because of Me this night" (Matt. 26: 31)—the Greek signifying "scandalized." They were ashamed to be found in His company. But it is blessed to know that one returned to His side ere He died. And which one was it? Who of the little band shall manifest the superiority of his love? Even though the Sacred Narrative had concealed his identity, it would not have been difficult for us to name him. But the fact that Scripture informs us that it was the writer of this fourth Gospel, supplies one of the many silent but indubitable proofs of the Divine inspiration of the Bible.

"Woman behold thy son! Then saith He to the disciple. Behold thy mother!" (v. 27). First, to His mother, Behold now this one who cares for you, who has taken his place by your side, who would not allow you to stand here alone. Second, to John, Behold thy mother!—regard her henceforth with the tenderest affection: she is My living legacy to you! Thus did the Redeemer give to the apostle who had leaned on His breast, the one on whose breast He had once rested! Thus did He give to John the place which He had filled—a higher place than that which He gave to Peter! The order is indeed striking: Christ bade Mary look to John, **before** He commended him to care for her—John was to be the stay of Mary, not Mary of John!

"And from that hour that disciple took her unto his own home" (v. 27). First, the Saviour's act has forever set an example for children to honor their parents—to the end, not only while they are minors. Second, it marked His tender compassion: He would graciously spare His mother the worst, and therefore made arrangements that she would not witness the awful darkness, hear His cry of agony, or be present when He died. Third, it showed Him Son of God, the Protector and Provider of His people: it was the pledge of His equal care for all He leaves behind on earth—while we are here in the world He will supply our "every need." Fourth, He here confirmed the law of love, under the shadow of the cross. He united together those who loved Him and whom He loved. There was no command, for love needs none; love will respond to a gesture, a glance. The beloved disciple at once understood His Lord's mind. Fifth, He intimated that in providing for His people, He would do so by means of His people: it was John who was to provide hospitality for Mary. Christ is still saying to us: "Behold thy son! . . . Behold thy mother!"—compare Matt. 25:40. How marvellously are the Divine and human perfections of Christ blended here: as Man honoring His mother; as God, the Head of the Family, making arrangements for the childen!

"From that hour that disciple took her unto his own home." Of old it had been predicted that the Lord Jesus should act discreetly: "Behold, My Servant shall deal prudently" (Isa. 52:13). In commending His mother to the care of His beloved apostle, the Saviour evidenced His wisdom by the choice of her future guardian. Perhaps there was none who understood Him so well as His mother, and it is almost certain that none had apprehended His love so deeply as had John. We see, therefore, how they would be most suited companions for each other, the intimate bond of spiritual love uniting them together and to Christ. None so well fitted to take care of Mary; none whose company she would find so congenial; none whose fellowship either would more appreciate.

"From that hour that disciple took her unto his own home." Here, as ever, the Roman Catholics err—"not knowing the Scriptures, nor the power of God." From this verse they argue that Mary could have had no other children, otherwise Christ had never committed her, a widow, to John. But the Word of God plainly declares that she did have other children—"Is not His mother called Mary? and His brethren, James and Joses, and Simon, and Judas? and His sisters are they not all with us?" (Matt. 13:55, 56). The same Word of God also shows us that they were, at that time, ill-fitted to be Mary's companions and guardians—"I am become a stranger unto My brethren, and an alien unto My mother's children" (Psa. 69:8), were the Saviour's own words. How, then, could they take the Saviour's place, and be unto Mary what He had been! "We surely need no stronger proof than we have here, that Mary, the mother of Jesus, was never meant to be honored as Divine, or to be prayed to, worshipped and trusted in, as the friend and partoness of sinners. Common sense points out that she who needed the care and protection of another, was never likely to help men and women to heaven, or to be in any sense a mediator between God and man!" (Bishop Ryle.) How this incident also illustrates, once more, that spiritual bonds have the preference over natural ties! Moreover, what a heart-piercing rebuke to His unbelieving "brethren" (John 7:5) were His words here to Mary and John.

"After this, Jesus knowing that all things were now accomplished, that the scriptures might be fulfilled, saith, I thirst" (v. 28). What a sight is this—the Maker of heaven and earth with parched lips! the Lord of glory in need of a drink! the Beloved of the Father crying, "I thirst!" First, it evidenced His humanity. The Lord Jesus was not a Divine man, nor a humanized God; He was the God-man. Forever God, and now forever man. When the eternal Word became incarnate, He did not cease to be God, nor did He lay aside any of His Divine attributes; but He did become flesh; being made in all things like unto His brethren". He "increased in wisdom and stature" (Luke 2:52); He "wearied" in body (John 4:6); He was "an hungered" (Matt. 4:2); He "slept" (Mark 4:38); He "marvelled" (Mark 6:6); He "wept" (John 1::35); He "prayed" (Mark 1:35); He "rejoiced" (Luke 10:31); He "groaned" (John 11:23); and here, He "thirsted." God does not thirst; there is no hint (so far as we are aware) that the angels ever do; we shall not in the Glory (Rev. 7:16). But Christ did, as Man, in the depths of His humiliation.

This fifth cross-utterance of the Saviour, "I thirst," followed right after the three hours of darkness, during which the light of God's countenance had been withdrawn from the Sin-Bearer. It was then that the blessed Saviour endured the fierceness of the outpoured wrath of a holy God. It was this which made Him exclaim, "My moisture is turned into the drought of summer" (Psa. 32:4). This cry, then, tells of the intensity of what He had suffered, the awful severity of the conflict through which He had just passed. "He hath made Me desolate and faint" He cried (Lam. 1:13).

But unparalleled as had been His sufferings, great as was His thirst, it was not desire for the relief of His body that now opened His lips. Far different, far higher, was the motive which prompted Him. This comes out clearly in the first part of v. 28. Carefully has the Holy Spirit guarded the Saviour's glory, with delight has He brought before us His unique perfections. First, the very fact that He did now "thirst" evidences His perfect submission. He that had caused water to flow from the smitten rock for the refreshment of Israel in the wilderness, had the same infinite resources at His disposal now that He was on the cross. He who turned the water into wine by a word from His lips, could have spoken the same word of power here, and instantly met His own need. Why, then, did He hang there with parched lips? Because, in the volume of that Book which expressed the will of God, it was written that He should thirst! He came here to do God's will, and ever did He perfectly perform it.

In death, as in life, Scripture was for the Lord Jesus the authoritative Word of the living God. In the temptation He had refused to minister to His own need apart from that Word by which He lived; so now He makes known His need, not that it might be relieved, but that "the scriptures might be fulfilled"! Observe that He did not Himself seek to fulfill it —God can be trusted to take care of that; but He gives utterance to His distress so as to provide occasion for the fulfilment. "The terrible thirst of crucifixion is upon Him, but that is not enough to force those parched lips to speak; but it is written, 'In My thirst they gave Me vinegar to drink'—this opens them" (Mr. F. W. Grant). Here, then, as ever, He shows Himself in active obedience to the will of God, which He came to accomplish. He simply says, "I thirst," the vinegar is tendered and the prophecy is fulfilled. What perfect absorption in the Father's will!

But mark how His **Divine** perfections come out here: "Jesus knowing that all things were now accomplished." How completely self-possessed the Saviour was! He had hung on that cross for six hours, and had passed through suffering unparalleled: nevertheless His mind was perfectly clear and His memory entirely unimpared. He had before Him, with perfect distinctness, the whole Truth of God. He reviewed in a moment the entire scope of Messianic prediction. He remembered there was one prophetic scripture yet unaccomplished. He overlooked nothing. What a proof was this that He was Divinely superior to all circumstances! Finally, mark the wondrous grace here: He thirsted on the cross, that we might drink the water of life and thirst no more forever!

"Now there was set a vessel full of vinegar; and they filled a sponge with vinegar, and put it upon hyssop, and put it to His mouth" (v. 29). The act recorded here must be carefully distinguished from that mentioned in Matthew 27, 34, being the same as that found in Matt. 27:48. The first drink of vinegar and gall, commonly given to criminals to deaden their pains, the Lord refused; the drink of vinegar or sour wine, He here accepted—in obedience to His Father's will. The ones who tendered the sponge were, most probably, the Roman soldiers, who carried out the details of the crucifixion. Little did they think that they were executing the counsels of God! In view of the context in Matt. 27 we believe that these Romans had been deeply impressed by the Saviour's words from the cross, and especially by that mysterious darkness for three hours, and that they now acted either out of compassion or reverence.

"When Jesus therefore had received the vinegar, He said, It is finished" (v. 30.) "It is finished"—a single word in the original. It was the briefest and yet the fullest of His seven cross-utterances. Eternity will be needed to make manifest all that it contains. All things had been done which the law of God required; all things established which prophecy predicted; all things brought to pass which the types foreshadowed; all things accomplished which the Father had given Him to do; all things performed which were needed for our redemption. Nothing was left wanting. The costly ransom was given, the great conflict had been endured, sin's wages had been paid, Divine justice satisfied. True, there was the committal of His spirit into the hands of the Father, which immediately followed His word here; there was His resurrection, ascension, and session on High, but these are the fruit and reward of that Work which He completed. Nothing more remained for Him to do; nothing more awaited its fulfilment; His work on earth was consummated.

"It is finished." This was not the despairing cry of a helpless martyr. It was not an expression of satisfaction that the end of His sufferings was now reached. It was not the last gasp of a worn-out life. No, it was the declaration on the part of the Divine Redeemer that all for which He came from heaven to earth to do, was now done; that all which was needful to reveal the glorious character of God had now been accomplished; that everything necessary for the putting away of the sins of His people, providing for them a perfect standing before God, securing for them an eternal inheritance and fitting them for it, had all been done.

"It is finished." The root Greek word here, "teleo," is variously translated in the New Testament. A reference to some of its alternative renditions in other passages will enable us the better to discern the fullness and finality of the term here used by the Saviour. In Matt. 11:1 "teleo" is translated as follows, "When Jesus had made an end of commanding His twelve disciples." In Matt. 17:24 it is rendered, "They that received tribute money came to Peter, and said, Doth not your Master pay tribute." In Luke 2:39 it is translated, "And when they had performed all things according to the law of the Lord." In Luke 18:31 it is rendered, "All things that are written by the prophets concerning the Son of man shall be accomplished." Putting these together we learn the scope of Christ's sixth cross-utterance. "It is finished." He cried—it is "made an end of," it is "paid," it is "performed," it is "accomplished." What was "made an end of"?—our sins, our guilt! What was "paid"?—the price of our redemption! What was "performed"?—the utmost requirements of God's law. What was "accomplished"?—the work which the Father had given Him to do! What was "finished"?—the making of atonement!

"And He bowed His head, and gave up the spirit" (v. 30). The order of these two actions strikingly evidences the Saviour's uniqueness: with us the spirit departs, and then the head is bowed; with Him it was the opposite! So, too, each of these actions manifested His Deity. First, He "bowed His head"; the plain intimation is that, up to this point, His head had been held erect. It was no impotent sufferer who hung there in a swoon. Had that been the case, His head had lolled helplessly on His chest, and He would have had no occasion to "bow" it. Weigh well the verb here: it is not that His head "fell forward," but He consciously, calmly, reverently, bowed His head. How sublime was His carriage even on the Tree! What superb composure did He evidence! Was it not His majestic bearing on the cross that, among other things, caused the centurion to cry, "Truly this was the Son of God" (Matt. 27:54)!

"And gave up (delivered up) the spirit." None else ever did this or died thus. How remarkably do these words exemplify His own declaration in 10:17, 18: "I lay down My life, that I might take it again. No man taketh it from Me, but I lay it down of Myself. I have power to lay it down, and I have power to take it again"! The uniqueness of Christ's action here may also be seen by comparing His words with those of Stephen's. As the first Christian martyr was dying, he prayed, "Lord Jesus receive my spirit" (Acts 7:59). In sharp contrast from Stephen, Christ "gave up the spirit"; Stephen's was taken from him, not so the Saviour's.

"The Jews therefore, because it was the preparation, that the bodies should not remain upon the cross on the Sabbath day (for that sabbath day was an high day), besought Pilate that their legs might be broken, and that they might be taken away" (v.31). The day on which the Saviour was crucified was "an high day": it was on the eve of the regular weekly sabbath and also of the first day of the Feast of Unleavened-bread, from which the Jews reckoned the seven weeks to Pentecost; the same day was also the one appointed for the presentation and offering of the sheaf of new corn, so that it possessed a treble solemnity. Hence the Jews' urgency here—the breaking of the legs would serve the double purpose of hastening and ensuring death. Behind this motive and act of "the Jews," zealous for the Law (Deut. 21:22, 23), we may behold, again, the over-ruling Hand of God. Seemingly, Pilate would have allowed the body of Christ to remain on the cross, perhaps for several days, after He was dead. But the Lord Jesus had declared He would be "buried" and that He would be in the grave three days. For the fulfilment of this He must be buried the same day that He died; therefore did God see to it that no word of His failed! Once again were the Lord's enemies unconsciously executing the Divine counsels.

"Then came the soldiers, and break the legs of the first, and of the other which was crucified with Him" (v. 32). Why did the soldiers first give their attention to the two thieves? We cannot be certain, but most likely because they perceived that Christ was dead already. The Greek word for "break" here signifies to "shiver to pieces." A heavy mallett or iron bar was used for this. On this verse Bishop Ryle says, "It is noteworthy that the penitent thief, even after His conversion, had more suffering to go through before he entered into Paradise. The grace of God and the pardon of sin did not deliver him from the agony of having his legs broken. When Christ undertakes to save our souls, He does not undertake to deliver from bodily pains and conflict with the last enemy. Penitence, as well as impenitence, must taste death (unless the Saviour returns first A.W.P.)" Yet it is blessed to know that these Roman soldiers were also the unwitting agents for fulfilling Christ's promise "To-day shalt thou be with Me in Paradise"!

"But when they came to Jesus, and saw that He was dead already, they break not His legs" (v.33). This affords further evidence of the uniqueness of Christ's death. The Lord Jesus and the two thieves had been crucified together. They had been on their respective crosses the same length of time. But now, at the close of the day, the two thieves were still alive; for, as it is well known, execution by crucifixion, though exceedingly painful, was usually a slow death. No vital member of the body was directly affected, and often the sufferer lingered on for two or three days, before being finally overcome with exhaustion. It was not natural, therefore, that Christ should be dead after but six hours on the cross—observe how that "Pilate marvelled if He were already dead (Mark 15:44). The request of the Jews to Pilate shows that they were not expecting the three to die unless death were hastened. In the fact that the Saviour was "dead already" when the soldiers came to Him, though the two thieves still lived, we have a further demonstration that His life was not "taken from Him," but that He "laid it down of Himself"!

"But when they came to Jesus, and saw that He was dead already, they break not His legs." This was the first proof that the Son of God had really died. Trained executioners as these Roman soldiers were, it is quite unthinkable that they would make any mistake in a matter like this. Pilate had given orders for the legs of the three to be broken, and they would not dare to disobey unless they were absolutely sure that Christ were "dead already." Infidels expose themselves to the charge of utter absurdity if they claim that Christ never died, and was only in a swoon. The Roman soldiers are witnesses against them!

"But one of the soldiers with a spear pierced His side, and forthwith came there out blood and water" (v. 34). That blood should flow from one now dead, that blood and water should issue together, yet separated, was clearly a miracle. "The water and the blood came forth to bear witness, that God has given to us eternal life, and that this life is in His Son (1 John 5:8-12). "We have not here the centurion's confession, 'truly this was the Son of God'; we have not Pilate's wife, nor the convicted lips of Judas, bearing Him witness; Jesus does not here receive witness from men, but from God. The water and the blood are God's witnesses to His Son, and to the life that sinners may find in Him. It was sin that pierced Him. The action of the soldier was a sample of man's enmity. It was the sullen shot of the defeated foe after the battle; the more loudly telling out the deep-seated hatred that there is in man's heart to God and His Christ. But it only sets off the riches of that grace which met it, and abounded over it; for it was answered by the love of God. The point of the soldier's spear was touched by the blood! The crimson flow came forth to roll away the crimson sin" (Mr. Bellett).

"But one of the soldiers with a spear pierced His side, and forthwith came there out blood and water." Here was the second proof that our Lord really died. One of the soldiers determined to make sure work and leave nothing uncertain—in all probability directing his spear at the Saviour's heart. He was singled out from the others even while dead between the dying thieves. "He has a place even here that belonged to Him alone!" (Mr. W. Kelly). "Behold now the sleeping last Adam, and out of His side formed the evangelical Eve. Behold the Rock which was smitten, and the waters of life gushed forth. Behold the Fountain that is opened for sin and uncleanness" (Augustine). "The blood and water signified the two great benefits which all believers partake of through Christ—justification and sanctification. Blood stands for remission, water for regeneration; blood for atonement, water for purification. The two must always go together." (Dr. Matthew Henry).

"And he that saw it bear record, and his record is true: and he knoweth that he saith true, that ye might believe" (v. 35). The reference is to what is recorded in the previous verse: John vouches as an eye-witness for the flowing of the blood and water from the Saviour's pierced side. It is evident that he had returned to the cross after conducting Mary to his own home, and it is equally evident that he must have remained there to the end. John's solemn asservation here plainly intimates that what is recorded in the previous verse is a notable miracle. We believe that the "record" of John includes both what he has written here and that which he says in his 1st Epistle: "This is He that came by (i.e., was manifest by means of) water and blood" (1 John 5:6). In the Gospel the blood is mentioned first, as satisfying God; then comes the "water" as applied to us. In the Epistle the order is the **experimental** one: we have to be regenerated **before** we have faith in the blood!

"For these things were done, that the scripture should be fulfilled. A bone of Him shall not be broken" (v. 36). The Holy Spirit here quotes Psa. 34:20: "**He** keepeth all His bones: not one of them is broken." Marvellously had this been fulfilled. God had kept all the bones of His incarnate Son. Notwithstanding Pilate's order, the soldiers broke not **His** legs. All the legions of Caesar could not have broken a single bone: they, too, had "no power" except what was given them from above! The preservation of Christ's bones was the fulfilment of an ancient type; "Neither shall ye break a bone thereof" (Ex. 12:46), i.e., of the paschal lamb. For fifteen hundred years Israel had punctilliously observed this item in the Passover-observance, and none of them (so far as we know) had any idea of its meaning. Now the Holy Spirit explains it.

"And again another scripture saith, They shall look on Him whom they pierced" (v. 37). In a most striking way the piercing of the Saviour's side demonstrated the **sovereignty** of God—His absolute control over all His creatures and their every act. The soldier had received instructions to break the legs of Christ, but this he **did not**: had he done so, Scripture had been broken! The soldier **had not** received orders to pierce the Saviour's side, yet this he **did**: had he not, prophecy had failed of its accomplishment! The quotation is from Zech. 12:10 and the reference is to a coming day, when Israel shall look upon Him whom they pierced—**they** pierced Him, though the act was performed by a Roman. Observe here the minute accuracy of Scripture: in v. 36 the word "**fulfilled**" is suitably used; but here in v. 37 it is significantly absent. And why? Because the **complete** "fulfilment" of Zech. 12:10 is yet future, hence the "another scripture **saith**."

"After this Joseph of Arimathaea, being a disciple of Jesus, but secretly for fear of the Jews, besought Pilate that he might take away the body of Jesus: and Pilate gave him leave. He came therefore and took the body of Jesus" (v. 38). This, too, was in fulfilment of prophecy: "Men appointed His grave with the wicked, but He was with the rich in His death" (Isa. 53:9, corrected translation). It is blessed to see the Holy Spirit here bringing Joseph to light in connection with the last offices of love to the precious body of the Lord; he was allowed a privileged part in the accomplishment of Isaiah's prediction. How true it is that man proposes, but God disposes! Wicked men had prepared three graves for the occupants of the three crosses, but one of them was destined to remain unoccupied that day. Just as God would not suffer Christ's bones to be broken, so He would not allow His body to be placed in a malefactor's tomb; but instead, in a sepulchre prepared by one who loved Him. Hitherto, Joseph had, through fear of the Jews, been a secret disciple; but though afraid to own the Saviour while He lived, now that He was dead, he went in "boldly" (Mark 15:43) and craved His body. What a witness was this to the power of the Redeemer's death!

"And there came also Nicodemus, which at the first came to Jesus by night, and brought a mixture of myrrh and aloes, about a hundred pound weight" (v. 39). This also witnessed to the power of Christ's death. Like Joseph, Nicodemus came out into the light but slowly. Timid by nature, yet grace overcoming, here is Nicodemus the only one, apparently, who dared to help Joseph in the holy work of burying the Lord. How great the contrast between his conduct in John 3, when he crept into the Lord's place of lodging under cover of night, and here, where he is not ashamed to openly show himself as one who loved the crucified Saviour! The value of his gift testifies to the greatness of his love. "Joseph and Nicodemus had done what they could. That service done for Christ has never been forgotten. The names of these two are embalmed in the volume of inspiration, and the amount in weight of the spices that Nicodemus brought is likewise recorded. Service done to Christ, or in His name, is never by God forgotten" (Mr. C. E. Stuart).

Mr. M. Taylor has pointed out that there is a deep though hidden dispensational significance to these acts of devotion by Joseph and Nicodemus. "May there not, in the fact that having been hidden, are now by the death revealed, the one 'Joseph of Arimathaea' (meaning 'the added one on high'), and the other Nicodemus (the peoples' ruler), tell of how Israel, looking on him who died for that nation, shall at once emerge into that eminence among the nations which from the beginning Jehovah meant for them?" We may add, that just as Joseph and Nicodemus were the last on the scene here, so Israel will be the last to believe.

"Then took they the body of Jesus, and wound it in linen clothes with the spices, as the manner of the Jews is to bury" (v.40). "They wrapped that incorruptible body in spices, for it is to be fragrant for evermore to all His people as the death like which there is no other" (Mr. F. W. Grant). Here, too, a beautiful type was fulfilled. In 2 Chron. 16:14 we read, "And they buried him in his own sepulchre, which he had made for himself in the city of David, and laid him in the bed which was filled with sweet odours and divers kinds of spices."

"Now in the place where He was crucified there was a garden; and in the garden a new sepulchre, wherein was never man yet laid" (v. 41). Beautifully suggestive is the reference to the "garden." It was in a "garden" that the first Adam sowed the seed which issued in death; so here, in a "garden" was sown the Seed which was to bear much fruit in immortal life. In the "new" sepulchre "wherein was never yet man laid" we have the fulfilment of still another type: "And a man that is clean shall gather up the ashes of the Heifer (previously slain) and lay them up without the camp in a clean place" (Num. 19:9).

"There laid they Jesus therefore because of the Jews' preparation; for the sepulchre was nigh at hand" (v. 42). Here was the third conclusive proof that the Lord Jesus actually died—He was buried. He who had been born of a virgin mother, was laid in a virgin grave; there to remain for three days when He came forth as the mighty Victor.

The following questions are to prepare for our next study:—
1. Why was the "stone" removed v. 1?
2. What is shown by Mary's words v. 2?
3. Why seek the two she did v. 2?
4. Why went not John in v. 5?
5. What is the significance of v 7?
6. What was it he "saw" that made him "believe" v. 8?
7. Why did they go "home" v. 10?

—Arthur W. Pink.

## GLEANINGS IN EXODUS.
### 42. The Boards: Ex. 26:15-30.

That which is now to occupy us is the framework and foundation of the Tabernacle proper. The sides of the Tabernacle were comprised of boards of acacia wood, fitly framed together, standing upon a base of silver sockets. The Tabernacle stood on the west side of the Court, facing the gate. Its solid framework was made up of forty-eight boards, twenty being used on the north side, twenty on the south, six on the west, with a corner-board at each end; the eastern or front side being the entrance, having five pillars between which was suspended an "hanging for the door," which will come before us for separate consideration in a later article (D.V.). Each of the boards was overlaid with gold.

"The north and south sides of the Tabernacle were each composed of twenty boards. Thus the length of the holy building would be thirty cubits (forty-five feet), the boards being a cubit and a half in breadth. Its height was ten cubits (fifteen feet), its width was exactly the same, namely, ten cubits (fifteen feet). Each board was maintained in its place by two tenons, or hands, which again were grasped by two sockets of silver. Then in order to bind the whole in one compact body of strength and security, five bars of shittim wood with gold—same as the boards—ran along the two sides, and also along the end at the west; fifteen bars in all being inserted in rings of gold attached to the boards. The third, or middle bar, stretched across the whole length of the building—forty-five feet; of the length of the other cross-bars we are not informed. The corner-boards at the extreme end — north and south — were coupled together at top and bottom by rings of gold, in addition to the tenons and silver sockets at the base. These corner-boards then would knit the ends so firmly by their fastening of rings, tenons, and sockets, or blocks of silver, that a breakdown was impossible, while the sides were equally upheld and maintained by the bars. Here then we have the Rock of Ages embodied in the Tabernacle." (Mr. W. Scott.)

There has been much confusion on the part of the commentators concerning the typical import of the Boards and that which secured them together. Many who have seen Christ displayed in the Curtains and in the different Vessels, depart from this primary interpretation when they come to the Boards, and regard them as portraying believers in their individual and corporate relationships. That much connected with the Tabernacle may have a secondary application to the saints we do not deny, but that everything in it points first and foremost to our Saviour we are fully assured, and it is with Him that our hearts need most to be engaged; so with the primary signficance of our type we shall now proceed. There are seven things connected with the Boards that claim our careful attention:—

### 1.—Their Materials.

"And thou shalt make Boards for the tabernacle of shittim wood. . . . . And thou shalt overlay the boards with gold" (vv. 15, 29). As we have had occasion before to remark, the acacia wood foreshadowed our Lord's humanity, particularly the incorruptibility of it, the Greek version of the O.T. actually translating it "incorruptible wood." It is of paramount importance that we should hold fast to and testify of the fundamental truth conveyed in this typical wood—the real and the untainted Manhood of the Lord Jesus. Error here is most serious and solemn, affecting as it would our estimate of the Saviour's person. There are those who, in their zeal to maintain His absolute Deity, entertain an inadequate conception of His humanity. But His Manhood was just as real as His Godhood. It was not simply that He assumed a human body, but that He became Man in the full sense of the term, having a human spirit and soul and body. "In all things it behoved Him to be made like unto His brethren" (Heb. 2:17). "Forasmuch then as the children are partakers of flesh and blood, He also Himself likewise took part of the same" (Heb. 2:14). Therefore is He called "the Man Christ Jesus" (1 Tim. 2:5).

But in becoming Man, the Lord of glory took unto Himself a spotless and perfect humanity, expressly designated "that Holy Thing" (Luke 1:35). The Son of man "did no sin" (1 Pet. 2:22) and that because "He knew no sin" (2 Cor. 5:21). and that because "in Him was no sin" (1 John 3:5). He ever was and always remained "the Holy One of God." To question this is to cast dishonour both on the Father and on the Son, and undermines the very foundation on which the Christian's peace is based. Some carelessly, or profanely, talk of "Jesus assuming our sinful and our mortal nature," but such could never be, or He had Himself needed a Saviour. Not only did Christ commit no sin, but He was entirely incapable of sinning. Nor were the seeds of death in His Manhood: He did not die from pain and weakness, but laid down His life of Himself (John 10:18), and in death He saw "no corruption" (Acts 2:27). The Virgin-birth and the immaculate nature of the Saviour lie at the very foundation of the Gospel message: without them there would be and could be no announcement of good news for poor sinners.

Inseparable from His humanity is the glorious truth of our Redeemer's Deity. This also is a fundamental part of our faith and underlies all true evangelical testimony. "Unto you is born . . .

a Saviour, which is Christ the Lord" (Luke 2:11). None but a Divine Saviour could meet the deep need of fallen creatures: the endurance of God's curse was wholly beyond the resources of human weakness—His Deity alone could sustain the weight of redemption. If the acacia wood foreshadowed the humanity of Christ, the gold spoke of His Divine nature and glory. In the two conjoined we have set before us God manifest in flesh. "The Word was God. . . the Word became flesh" (John 1:1, 14). A profound mystery we grant, yet a blessed truth on which the faith of God's elect rests with unquestioning confidence.

### 2.—Their Dimensions.

"Ten cubits shall be the length of a board, and a cubit and a half shall be the breadth of one board" (v. 16). "In all structures if there is to be symmetry, there must be accuracy of measurements, and for this there must be a standard. In Scripture it was the cubit, or ammah, from a word meaning 'mother.' It was the length of the 'mother-arm,' the forearm, as the chief and prominent part of the arm, from the elbow to the tip of the finger: that which is used in all work. It was thus a standard taken from man, not above him. God's requirements are absolutely reasonable and righteous, not going beyond human capacity. And yet how true it is that not one of the fallen sons of Adam could measure up to that perfect human standard: 'all have sinned and come short of the glory of God.' But God delighted in man, and even the measurement of the heavenly city is by the human standard (Rev. 21:17). If God is to be in any measure apprehended by His creatures, it must be, not in that unutterable glory and infinity which no one knoweth but the Son, but rather in the One who humbled Himself and was found in fashion as a man. How amazing! God is manifested in the flesh, and we are invited to appropriate the standard of measurement (which is in our hands and by which we have been condemned )to Him, and to see how perfectly He has measured up to the fullest requirements of God" (Mr. Ridout).

How profoundly suggestive and significant that in the very unit of measurement which Jehovah ordered Moses to employ, we are reminded of our Lord's incarnation, and that more than a hint is given of His Virgin birth—the word "cubit" being of the feminine gender, not masculine! He was and is God, but He became flesh. So the length of the Boards reiterates and emphasises the same truth. Ten, as we have seen previously, is the number which speaks of the Divine measure of human responsibility. What is here so blessedly foreshadowed, then, is the Son of God become Man, perfectly glorifying His Father in the place of human accountability. Beautiful is it to ponder in this connection the closing words of v. 15: "And thou shalt make boards for the Tabernacle of shittim wood standing up." What a contrast this points! We are all fallen creatures; not so the perfect Man, who was "separate from sinners" (Heb. 7:26). He was upright in all His ways. Ten cubits was the height of every board. Each part of Christ's life was of an unvarying standard. Nothing was out of proportion. Looking at each of the ten commandments we cannot say that Christ kept one more perfectly than the others. Each was fully, constantly, and consistently obeyed by Him.

"A cubit and a half shall be the breadth of each board." This is not the first time that we have had this particular measurement: the Ark was, too, a cubit and a half in breadth and a cubit and a half in height (Ex. 25:10); the Mercyseat was also a cubit and a half in breadth (25:17). Both the Ark and the Mercyseat portray the Lord Jesus in the combined glory of His person as the God-man. Thus the breadth—that which gives form and character to a thing— reminds us that while these Boards prefigure our Saviour in the place of human responsibility, they also tell us that it was One who was more than Man who honored and magnified the Law.

### 3.—Their Sockets.

"And thou shalt make forty sockets of silver under the twenty boards; two sockets under one board for his two tenons and two sockets under another board for his two tenons" (v. 19). These forty sockets of silver were for the twenty boards on the south side; in vv. 20, 21 we find that the same provision was made for the twenty boards on the north side; while in v. 25 we learn that the eight boards at the western rear had also two sockets each. Thus there were ninety-six in all. Each board was maintained in its place by the two tenons or "hands" which fitted into and were grasped by the silver sockets.

The ninety-six silver "sockets" formed the foundation, and upon them rested the whole fabric of the tabernacle. This tells us, in language too plain to be misunderstood, that **redemption** is the basis on which Christ has become the meeting-place between the ineffably holy God and His inherently sinful people. It was only through redemption that the perfect humanity and Divine glory of Christ could avail us. Had He not "given Himself a ransom for us," He must have forever remained alone (John 12:24). He was in Himself the "true" and "perfect" Tabernacle, but only by the gift and sacrifice of Himself could He bring us nigh to God. It is because in the Gospel He is set before our eyes "crucified" (Gal. 3:1), that Christians have confidence before God. Reconciliation rests upon redemption by ransom.

It was the **preciousness of redemption** which was typically expressed in the "sockets of silver." This is definitely established by the fact that all the silver used in connection with the Tabernacle was derived from "the atonement money" (Ex. 30:16). As we hope to deal with this more fully when we come to Ex. 30, a brief summary must here suffice. In Ex. 30:12 we learn that when Moses took the sum of the number of Israel that every man was required to give a ransom for his soul. This ransom consisted of half a shekel (by comparing Ex. 30:13 with Lev. 27:3 it will be found that this was a **silver** coin, in value about 2/6 or 62 cents: the rich might not give more, nor the poor less (v. 15). Concerning this atonement-money God ordered Moses to "appoint it for the service of the Tabernacle (v. 16)—a part of this "service" being to make the silver sockets for its foundations.

It was elsewhere taught Israel that it was the blood "that maketh an atonement for the soul" (Lev. 17:11)—typified by the blood of animals. The blood of their sacrifices came nearest to exhibiting the **mode** of atonement; but in Ex. 30 the silver "atonement-money" proclaimed the **preciousness** of Christ's atonement. The significance of both types may be seen by noting how the Holy Spirit has set each aside, because the Reality has been manifested. Just as we are told in the presence of the **one** "sacrifice for sins" that it was not possible "that the blood of bulls and goats should take away sins" (Heb. 10:4), so we appreciate the design of the atonement-silver when, beholding Him in whom is treasured up all redemption wealth, we read, "Ye were not redeemed with corruptible things as silver and gold" (1 Peter. 1:18).

We must not further enlarge on this fascinating topic, but ere passing from it attention must be called to two most remarkable statements in the Psalms which plainly anticipated the replacing of the shadows by the Substance. In Psa. 49 the costliness of redemption is emphasised by affirming that it lies far beyond the resources of human riches: "They that trust in their wealth, and boast themselves in the multitude of their riches; none of them can by any means redeem his brother, nor give to God a ransom for him: For the redemption of their soul is precious, and it (the type) ceaseth forever" (vv. 6-8). This finds its sequel in 1 Peter 1:18, 19. In Psa. 50 we find Jehovah saying "I will take no bullock out of thy house, nor he-goats out of thy folds," which finds its sequel in Heb. 10:4. Thus Psa. 49 disallows the silver and gold which once pointed to the precious ransom, while Psa. 50 disallows the sacrificing of bulls and goats which once foreshadowed the precious blood.

### 4.—Their Meaning.

The relation of the Boards to the Tabernacle, to its holy vessels, and to the ministrations of the priests therein, supplies the key to their distinctive significance. Without these Boards there had been no tabernacle to house its furniture and no place for the priests to serve in. Moreover, without them the beautiful Curtains could not have been displayed. Upon the golden Boards, held together by the golden bars, resting in their silver sockets, were sustained all the weight of the Curtains and Coverings. So on the God-man was hung all the weight of the Divine government and all the glories of His Father's house. In Him has been completely realised what was typified by Eliakim—read carefully Isa. 22:20-25. It is this which brings out the meaning of the other numerals here. There were forty-eight boards in all and ninty-six sockets: thus we have 6x8 or 4x12 and 12x8. Six is the number of man and eight that of a new order or a fresh beginning. This would point to Christ as "the Second Man" (1 Cor. 15:47), the Head of the new race, the "new man" (Eph. 2:15). Four is the number of earth, and twelve of governmental perfection: so that 4x12 and 8x12 would suggest the governmental claims of God vindicated on earth by the Head of the Church, the "New Man."

That which is foreshadowed in the Boards is the Person of Christ as what sustained His work. The massive framework of the golden Boards was to the Curtains and Coverings, suspended from them, what the poles are to a tent. "They upheld and sustained the glorious display of the blue, purple, scarlet, and fine linen cherubim, as also the goats' hair curtains. Thus what the Lord Jesus Himself was, and is, viz., Son of God, Son of Man, that He has made manifest in His life, and above all, in His death on the cross: and His blessed work there, derives all of its unspeakable value and eternal efficacy from Himself. It is faith in Him that is salvation: 'He that believeth on the Son hath life.' May there not be a tendency to separate too much the work of the Lord Jesus from His person? to preach the death of the blessed Lord without sufficiently preaching also the Lord Himself?

"The boards and bars have the same relation to the Tabernacle itself, as the truth contained in the first two chapters of the Epistle to the Hebrews has to the rest of the Epistle. In the first two chapters, the great foundations of faith are laid. The Lord Jesus Christ is presented to us as the Son; the brightness of God's glory, and the express image of His person; God, the Creator—the Sustainer of all things. He is also presented to us as the Son of Man, partaker of flesh and blood in order to die; the Firstborn from the dead; all things put under Him; anointed above His fellows; not ashamed to call them brethren. On these great truths respecting Christ, depend all the other great verities connected with the value of His sacrifice; the glory and power of His priesthood; the eternal salvation, the eternal redemption, and the eternal inheritance which are obtained for us by His blood" (Mr. G. Soltau).

### 5.—Their Distribution.

Twenty of the acacia Boards, overlaid with gold, were used for the south side of the Tabernacle (v.18), twenty were used on the north side (v. 20), two boards were used for the corners of the two sides at the rear; and six more completed the back (v. 25). Thus the numeral which is most prominent here is two, one of the scriptural meanings of which is testimony or witness: "in the mouth of two or three witnesses the truth shall be established." So also when Christ sent forth the disciples to bear testimony unto Him it was by two and two. Therefore is the second person of the Godhead called "the faithful and true Witness" (Rev. 3:14). Thus have we another hint here of the distinctive significance of our present type—it is the person of the Lord Jesus with His two natures, Divine and human.

Separate consideration should be given to the two "corner boards" see vv. 23, 24. It was these which gave increased stability to the whole structure. "Our thoughts naturally turn to the two occasions on which the Lord is spoken of in Scripture with reference to the corner; 'Behold, I lay in Zion, for a foundation, a Stone, a tried Stone, a precious corner Stone, a sure foundation' (Isa. 28:16). 'The Stone, which the builders refused, is become the Head-stone of the corner.' (Psa. 118:22). Here we have presented to us, a corner-stone as foundation, and a corner-stone crowning the building: the beginning and the end. The whole strength of the edifice depending on the firmness of the foundation corner-stone; and the whole compactness, and knitting together of the building as one depending on the head-stone of the corner. God laid the foundation in the death of His Son; He completed the building in His resurrection. The walls of living stones rest securely on this Rock of Ages, and are bound everlastingly together on the top-stone. The corner-boards of the Tabernacle may have some reference to these blessed truths." (Mr. G. Soltau).

### 6.—Their Couplings.

"Two tenons shall there be on one board, set in order one against another: thus shalt thou make for all the boards of the Tabernacle" (v. 17). As the margin informs us, the Hebrew word rendered "tenons" is literally "hands," and it is to be regretted that the translators did not use this word in the text itself. These "hands" grasped the Boards and held them securely in place. Most beautifully did they prefigure the God-man in His voluntary humiliation, dependent upon and in subjection to the Father. As the perfect Servant He was upheld and sustained by the hands of God the Father from above, the Spirit below ministering to Him. Of old the Spirit of prophecy cried "Let Thy hand be upon the Man of Thy right hand, upon the Son of Man whom Thou madest strong for Thyself" (Psa. 80:17). So in one of the Messianic Psalms (see v. 5) we find the dependent One saying, "My times are in Thy hand" (Psa. 31:15). Beautiful is it to hear Him crying from the cross, "Father, into Thy hands I commend My spirit" (Luke 23:46). But how blessed to know that He is now seated on "the right hand of the Majesty on high" (Heb. 1:3)! Thus we see, once more, there is a spiritual significance to the minutest detail in these Tabernacle types.

### 7.—Their Bars.

These are described in much detail in vv. 26-29, to which we would ask the reader to turn. The "bars" were employed to unite the Boards together firmly and solidly. "Each of the boards terminated, as to the lower extremity, in two tenons, which were inserted into mortises in two sockets of silver. The boards were also sustained in their upright position and linked together by five bars of shittim wood, overlaid with gold, which ran through rings or staples of gold inserted in the boards. The middle bar of the five ran the whole length of the Tabernacle, uniting all the twenty boards together; the other four bars, of which two were placed above, and two below the middle bar, are not described as running all the length, but perhaps only extended half the distance, namely, fifteen cubits each. A similiar number of bars coupled the boards composing the north side, and also the west end of the Tabernacle. On the whole therefore there were forty-eight boards and fifteen bars" (Mr. Soltau).

The typical meaning of these "bars" is not difficult to perceive, though they point to that which lies altogether beyond our finite grasp. They served to give unity to the structure by securely linking the Boards together. The wooden Boards, overlaid with gold, portrayed the two natures in Christ: the "bars" pointed to the perfect union between them. Though very God of very God, and also very Man of very Man, yet is our Saviour not two persons, but one—the God-man. Though totally distinct, yet are His two natures perfectly and forever joined together, though none of us can say where nor understand how they meet. How significant, then, that these very "bars" which united the boards were themselves made of wood overlaid with gold! May the Spirit of God continue to unfold to us the glories of our Divine Saviour.

—Arthur W. Pink.

## MIDNIGHT AT MIDDAY.

"Now from the sixth hour there was darkness over all the land unto the ninth hour." (Matt. 27:45).

Calvary is the greatest paradox in all history, for its brow became the meeting-place of conflicting forces and antagonistic agents. If we may say so, there we see God at His best and Satan at his worst. There we have displayed a matchless love and an unparalleled hate. There we see sin in all its hideousness, and there we see the Ransom for sinners in all its blessedness. In keeping with this paradox, there shines from Calvary a glory which time and eternity can never dim; yet was there a darkness which could be felt, a darkness unrelieved and which could not be pierced.

The Cross was both a terrible tragedy and a glorious triumph. It was a tragedy because wicked hands had nailed to it One who was "fairer than the children of men." It was a tragedy, because there we behold One who though entirely innocent was condemned to die the death of a criminal. It was a tragedy, because man was slaying his greatest Benefactor: the wicked were putting to death the Friend of sinners. But the Cross was also a glorious triumph. It was a triumph, because it bore witness to the fact that the vile outpourings of human hatred could not quench the love of Christ for poor sinners. It was a glorious triumph, because in receiving the wages of sin, Christ put away sin; in dying, He made an end of death for His people. It was a glorious triumph, because the convict's gibbet became the Conqueror's throne, and on it Grace sits triumphant.

In like manner, the Cross stirs up the most conflicting emotions within the breast of the Christian. As he contemplates Calvary, he is moved to godly sorrow and grief, for he knows that it was his sins which drove the nails into the Saviour's body. As he contemplates Calvary, he is moved to deep humiliation —how fearful must his state be, by nature and by practice, if nothing but the blood of Immanuel could wash away stains so foul! As he contemplates Calvary, he is moved to true contrition—asking God to create in him a deeper hatred of that dread monster called sin. But there are other emotions which looking at the Cross stirs within us. As faith is called into exercise, the Christian is moved to deep gratitude and thanksgiving, for there he beholds a Sacrifice all-sufficient, there he sees the Fountain in which the foulest may be cleansed. As he beholds Calvary, his heart is warmed, and his affections stirred: the realization of the Saviour's love begets love in return for Him. Such a contemplation stirs up the spirit of consecration, for at Calvary we are taught that we are "not our own, but bought with a price," therefore must we seek to "glorify God in our spirits and bodies."

Everything connected with the Cross partakes of this same strange element of paradox, this co-mingling of opposites, this meeting together of conflicting forces. In Luke's Gospel we read, "And it was about the sixth hour, and there was a darkness over all the earth, until the ninth hour. And the sun was darkened, and the veil of the temple was rent in the midst" (23:44, 45). How remarkable that the Holy Spirit should here have linked these two things together: the "darkness" tells of shutting out from God, the "rending of the veil" speaks of giving access to God! This same feature of paradox is also true of that detail to which our text calls attention. The "darkness" was mysterious, solemn and sad; yet was there a silver lining to this blackest of all clouds. There are precious lessons to be learned even from this sombre phenomenon. Why was there this three hours' darkness? What was the meaning of this black pall? May the Holy Spirit grant us heavenly light as we seek to interpret the three hours of darkness which enveloped Calvary.

1. **This darkness was the physical symbol of the spiritual state of the sinner.** To show that this is something more than a flight of the preacher's imagination, let me remind you that on the Cross Christ took the sinner's place. There it was the Saviour was paid the full wages of sin. There He was "made sin" for His people. Therefore did God cause to be solemnly and unmistakably exhibited what is the state in which the sinner, by nature, lies.

Turn to Prov. 4:19. There we are told, "The way of the wicked is as darkness: they know not at what they stumble." They have no light on their path, no light in their souls, no light in the hour of perplexing gloom and sorrow. The sinner is in the dark. That is why he is blind to his awful peril. The Pit yawns before him, Hell is ready to receive him; but the awfulness of his state, the greatness of his danger, the fearfulness of the judgment awaiting—these things are not real to him. And why? He **cannot see** them. And why? Because he is in the dark!

"Having the understanding darkened, being alienated from the life of God through the ignorance that is in them, because of the **blindness of their heart**" (Eph. 4:18). This expresses the same solemn fact. No matter how faithfully, or how simply, or how clearly, the preacher presents the Gospel of Christ, the poor sinner perceives not its application to himself, its suitability to his own case. His heart is blinded; he is in the dark. This, then, is the first meaning of the Darkness at Calvary; it made known the state in which the sinner lies, for on the Cross Christ was in the place of sinners.

2. **The darkness was a warning to the Jews.** God does not smite without first warning: ere the stroke of His judgment descends, He gives plain intimation beforehand. As the Jews witnessed that three hours of Darkness which enshrouded Golgotha, their minds ought at once to have gone back to the ten plagues which the Lord sent upon Egypt—which were so many **warnings** unto Pharaoh and his subjects. Time after time God gave the Egyptians space for repentance; but they availed not themselves of it. The ninth plague, and the last before the actual slaying of the firstborn, was a "thick darkness in all the land of Egypt for three days" (Ex. 10:1, 22). Yet solemn as was this Divine sign, the Egyptians heeded not, but continued rushing headlong to destruction.

Now here at Calvary, God also sent three hours of "darkness." It was a solemn intimation that the Jews had committed a horrible work of wickedness, a dark crime on which the sun refused to shine, and because of which (unless they owned their sin before God), death and destruction would as surely come upon them as they had upon the Egyptians. It was a call from heaven for Israel to repent, but they heeded it not, and therefore did wrath come upon them, "to the uttermost" (1 Thess. 2:16).

Oh sinner, how often hath God sent thee warnings, and thou hast not profited by them. How often hath He given thee opportunities to repent, and you have only hardened your heart! But, "be not deceived; God is not mocked; for whatsoever a man soweth, that shall he also reap" (Gal. 6:7). There are limits to God's forbearance with thee, as there was to His patience with Pharaoh and with the unbelieving Jews. Therefore, "Because there is wrath, beware lest He take thee away with His stroke: then a great ransom cannot deliver thee" (Job. 36:18).

**3. The Darkness attested the uniqueness of the Saviour's death.** That Christ's death was no ordinary one was indicated by the supernatural phenomena which attended it. The beginning of His life on earth was marked by miracles—the virgin birth, the angels' announcement, the star in the heavens. So, too, was His death accompanied by miracles—the three hours' darkness, the rending of the veil, the great earthquake, the rending of the rocks (Matt. 27:51). Each of these signified the supernatural character of His death, and each of them had a profound meaning. This "darkness" was no ordinary one. Midday suddenly became midnight, for the darkness began at noon and lasted till three p.m. Nor was it caused by an eclipse of the sun, for the moon was then at its farthest distance from it! Christ died at the time of the Passover, and at this Feast the moon was always at the full. The "darkness," then, was supernatural and attested the supernatural character of Christ's death.

This mysterious "darkness" was typified of old: "And when the sun was going down, a deep sleep fell upon Abraham; and, lo, an horror of great darkness fell upon him. . . And it came to pass, that, when the sun went down, and it was dark, behold a smoking furnace, and a burning lamp that passed between those pieces (i.e., of the sacrifice). In **the same day** the Lord made a covenant with Abraham" (Gen. 15: 12, 17, 18). So, too, this "darkness" was the subject of Old Testament prophecy: "I form the light and **create** darkness:" (Isa. 45: 7). We believe that in the light of what immediately follows this quotation, the reference here (though not exclusively) is to what took place at Calvary, and that the "darkness" there was a Divinely created one. The words which follow are, "**I make peace,** and create evil: I the Lord do all these things. Drop down, ye heavens, from above, and let the skies pour down **righteousness** (i.e., the justice of God smiting the Sinbearer); let the earth open, and let the earth bring forth salvation (i.e., the raising of Christ from the dead), and let righteousness spring up together; I the Lord have created it."

**4. The darkness intimated that a mystery in the Divine counsels was then being wrought out.** This "darkness" was God's veil over the holy scene. For three hours the spectators had gazed upon the Crucified One: some in amazement, some with malicious satisfaction, some in profoundest grief. But now the time had arrived when none should be permitted to behold what took place. It was too sacred, too solemn, too incomprehensible for finite creatures to witness. Lev. 16:17 was the type of this: "And there shall be **no man** in the tabernacle of the congregation when he goeth in to make an atonement." During those three hours there took place a transaction between the Father and the Son which no creature-eyes might behold. This "darkness" intimated that a mystery too profound for us to comprehend was being wrought out.

The Bible is not written to satisfy an idle curiosity. Many questions occur to our minds to which no complete answer is forthcoming. We are staggered before the Problem of Evil and all the untold sufferings which its introduction has involved. Why did the ineffably holy God permit the entrance of evil into His universe? We may reason and speculate, but we soon find that we are out of our depths. But on reaching Calvary the mystery is still further increased. When we see the Beloved of the Father nailed hand and foot to the Cross of shame, when we listen to His cry of agony, "My God, My God, why hast Thou forsaken Me?" we ask, **Why** was it necessary for Him to die such a death in order for atonement to be made? Here is a depth which no finite mind can fathom. "The secret things belong unto the Lord our God" (Deut. 29:29). This is what "the darkness" tells us, for the darkness hides. When night spreads her black wings the beauties of the landscape are blotted out. So, at Calvary, there took place that which is hidden from man. This "darkness" intimated a mystery too profound for us to fully comprehend.

**5. The Darkness denoted the presence of Satan at the Cross.** Here, too, we encounter that which lies beyond our ken. The Arch-enemy of God and man is a mysterious being about whom we know nothing save what Scripture tells us. And there are some things said about him in the Bible which are "hard to be understood." For example, in Heb. 2:14 we are told that the devil "had the power of death." It seems that when he encompassed the downfall of our first parents that God permitted the devil to acquire some right or authority in connection with death, which authority Christ took from him when He died. But that which is specially pertinent to our present theme is the fact that Satan and "darkness" are repeatedly linked together.

Just as God is called the "Father of lights" (James 1:17), so Satan is the father of gloom and darkness. The lieutenants of Satan are called, in Eph. 6:12, "the rulers of the darkness of this world." In Acts 26:18 we learn that Paul's commission was to "turn men from darkness to light and the power of Satan unto God." In Col. 1:17 the saints are said to be "delivered from the power of darkness and translated into the kingdom of God's dear Son."

That the Prince of Darkness was present at Calvary there can be no doubt; that he was permitted to assault our Saviour the Scriptures make clear. In Luke 22:52, 53 we find the Saviour saying, "Be ye come out as against a thief, with swords and staves? . . . but this is your hour and the Power of Darkness." Of old God said to the Serpent, "I will put enmity between thee and the woman, and between thy seed and her Seed; it shall bruise thy head, and thou shalt bruise His heel" (Gen. 3: 15), and at Calvary Satan did bruise Christ's heel. Therefore, among other things, the three hours' "darkness" intimated that the Father of Darkness was assaulting the Light of Life, hence His cry from the Cross "Save Me from the lion's mouth" (Psa. 22:21).

6. **The Darkness was the outward proof that Christ was abandoned of God.** In 1 John 1:5 we read that God is **"light,"** hence the "darkness" at Calvary was the natural sign of His having turned away. Thus the darkness revealed as well as concealed: it revealed the solemn fact that the ineffably holy God had withdrawn from that scene. Christ in the darkness was the evidence that He was there bearing the sins of His people. His cry of desertion interpreted it. As said the prophet of old, "Thou art of purer eyes than to behold evil, and canst not look on iniquity" (Hab. 1:13).

A deeper darkness had fallen upon the Saviour's soul than ever overspread this earth. It was the darkness of separation from God. He who had, from all eternity, enjoyed unhindered and unbroken fellowship with the Father, was now cut off from Him. The Blessed One was there "made a curse for us" (Gal. 3:13). Into those three hours was compressed an equivalent of what otherwise the elect of God had suffered through the endless ages of the future. He became poor that we might be made rich. He died that we might live. He suffered the Darkness that we might be brought into God's marvellous light and enjoy it forever.

7. **The Darkness was a solemn forecast of what awaits all who shall die in their sins.** On the Cross Christ suffered in the stead of all who believe on Him. That which He endured was the portion which their sins deserved. Hence, what He suffered, they who reject Him shall yet experience. The awful darkness which He felt for three hours, and caused Him to cry out in agony, will yet be the eternal portion of those who die without Him.

"Then said the King to the servants, Bind him (the one without a weddinggarment) hand and foot, and take him away, and cast Him into **outer darkness;** there shall be weeping and gnashing of teeth" (Matt. 22: 13). "Cast ye the unprofitable servant into **outer darkness"** (Matt. 25:30). Concerning apostates it is written, "to whom is reserved the **blackness of darkness** forever" (Jude 13). Eternal banishment from Him who is light will be the portion of the lost. Nor will this be unjust, for the wicked "love darkness" (John 3:19). Oh may not this be the portion of any reader of these lines. It will not be if you cast yourself at the feet of Christ, who has been given "a Light to lighten the Gentiles," and who declares "he that followeth Me shall not walk in darkness, but shall have the light of life" (John 8:12).

The above is a sermon preached by the Editor in Sydney.

## ASSURANCE.

### Rom. 8:16.

Like every other subject that is treated of in the Holy Scriptures, that of Christian assurance is capable of being grossly perverted. As creatures of extremes we are in grave danger of erring on either side. On the one hand, we may under-estimate the blessedness of assurance: we may regard it so lightly that we make little real effort to obtain that blessing. On the other hand, we may over-estimate its importance: our thoughts may be engaged to such an extent upon the subject of assurance that everything else may be excluded from our hearts and minds. Again; on the one hand, we may be so unduly occupied with the human side of the subject that we overlook, as many do, the absolute necessity for the Holy Spirit's power and operation to communicate this blessing to the heart. On the other hand, we may dwell so much on assurance being a gift and a blessing from the Spirit that we altogether fail to bestir ourselves and employ the means which He uses in communicating the blessing.

In like manner, there are two dangers to be guarded against. First, there are those who deny that real, solid, settled assurance is possible to anybody, while we remain in these mortal bodies. That is one of the errors of Rome, for, in her declarations of faith she says, "No man as long as he liveth in this mortal life ought so far to presume concerning the hidden mystery of pre-destination as positively to conclude that he is actually in the number of the predestined." In other words, Rome teaches that while we are down here, cumbered with this sinful flesh, that full assurance is an impossible attainment, and that those who claim to have it are wickedly presumptuous and fall beneath her anathema.

And the sad thing is that to-day there are a goodly number of so-called Protestants who believe just about the same thing; who suppose that the full assurance of faith is either a species of fanatical enthusiasm or else is to be attributed to an unholy presumption. Such people are only happy when they are miserable. Such people make a god of their doubts. Such people feed on their own experiences. I am referring now to those who take their spiritual temperature every night and morning and only feel happy when they find it varying as much as the weather. Such people count their spiritual pulse a dozen times every day and it makes them feel glad if they find their heart is missing a beat or two. They look upon their carnal fears as the fruits of the Spirit. And the truth of the matter is their feelings supplant Christ. They are occupied more with their own hearts than they are with His precious blood. They are more frequently contemplating and analysing their own faith instead of being occupied with the great Object of faith, and consequently they know little or nothing of a real settled peace, and they imagine that no one else ought to enjoy it either! That is one danger on one extreme, the denial of such an experience as the full assurance of faith while we are still down here.

On the other hand, there is another danger, equally real and equally detestable and equally injurious, and that is a spurious assurance; for, my friends, the Devil counterfeits even this spiritual grace. I fully believe that there are many in Sydney to-night who have not a single doubt about their own salvation, who make a loud boast of their full assurance, but who are not entitled to the name of Christian at all, for their walk and conversation repudiate their profession. I am thinking of men who are filled with the spirit of pride, and who look down with contempt and condemnation upon all who cannot pronounce their Shibboleths. I mean those who have in their possession a mechanical counterfeit for that assurance that is conveyed by the Holy Spirit of God. I have with my own ears, numbers of times, heard some of these men speaking to exercised souls, and they act something like this:—"Now here in God's Word: it says "he that believeth on Him is not condemned," and "he that believeth on the Son hath everlasting life. That is what God says: do you believe it?"—"Er, yes." "You do not believe that God would put in His Word what was not true? Well, here is what God says, He that believeth on the Son hath life. Now say that you believe that?" "Yes, I believe that." Well, now say you have assurance; that ends the matter." That ends the matter. Yes, I am afraid it does with some of them. My friends, it is one thing to say we have assurance; it is one thing to talk about assurance; it is one thing to boast of assurance; but it is altogether another thing to walk humbly with our God, and assurance and humility of spirit always go together. There are two experiences that are never separated—a love for Christ and a loathing of self; a deep sense of my own utter unworthiness and the realisation that Christ is sufficient to meet my desperate need.

Now, having spoken briefly in regard to the dangers to be guarded against, let me come at closer grips with the subject. The first point I want to bring out of our text is this:—Assurance is a grace that is imparted by the Spirit of God. I mean by that, the converted soul can no more obtain assurance by his own efforts than the unconverted can believe by their own efforts. The regenerated soul can no more work himself up into a state of assurance than the unregenerate can believe in the Lord Jesus Christ. And that is one of the things that is most generally overlooked and ignored in Christendom to-night on this subject. There are many who say, Now here are the promises of God: rest upon them and settled peace is yours. Quite true, but it is not such a simple and an easy matter to rest on the promises of God as some imagine. To use the language of Romans 7, there are many whose experience is described in these words:—"To will is present with me" (they have the desire) "but how to perform that which is good I find not."

The trouble with Arminians (and it is Arminians that I have particularly in mind in this sermon to-night: I am preaching it specially for the benefit of some of our visiting brethren and sisters who have been brought up more or less under a freewill ministry)—the trouble with Arminians is, that they imagine that believing in Christ is an act of the will, and an exercise of the mind. It is neither. Believing in Christ is an act of the heart; and God only has access to and can move the heart. The fundamental error of Arminians is, that they utterly fail to give the Holy Spirit of God His true place in their system or scheme. If it lies in my power to believe in Jesus whenever I get ready, well, of course, the Holy Spirit is not needed. But it is just because it does not lie within my power, or in any other man's power, to believe in Christ when he wants or decides to. It does not lie within his power because he is too depraved and too sinful and corrupt. It does not lie within his power because the heart cannot at the same time love darkness and love light. You cannot love what you naturally hate, and the natural man is born with a heart that hates spiritual things and therefore if ever a sinner is to believe, the intervention and the operation of the Holy Spirit of God are absolute, imperative necessities. And just as the operation of the Holy Spirit is a necessity for the unconverted to believe, it is equally imperative for the Holy Spirit to operate before the converted can have any spiritual assurance.

Now in proof of this first point, I ask you to turn with me to seven passages in the New Testament which predicate assurance as the result of the Holy Spirit's working. First of all Romans 5, verse 5:—"And hope maketh not ashamed; because the love of God is shed abroad in our hearts by the Holy Spirit." Now what could be plainer than that? The love of God does not enter our hearts in response to an act of our will; the love of God is not shed abroad in our hearts in return for our love; the love of God is shed abroad in our hearts by the Holy Spirit which is given unto us. The 8th chapter and the 16th verse, which is our text:—"The Spirit Himself beareth witness with our spirit, that we are the children of God." Those words are so plain, so simple, they call for no explanation; they simply say what they mean and mean what they say. Now pass on to the 15th chapter of Romans, the 13th verse:—"Now the God of hope fill you with all joy and peace in believing, that ye may abound in hope, through the power of the Holy Spirit." Now I want you to notice how emphatically it is stated in that verse. It is repeated at the beginning of the verse and at the end of it. First it is the God of hope who fills us with all joy and peace in believing; second, that we may abound in hope through the power of the Holy Spirit.

Now turn to 1 Corinthians 12:3:— "Wherefore I give you to understand, that no man speaking by the Spirit of God calleth Jesus accursed: and that no man can say that Jesus is the Lord, but by the Holy Spirit." It is the last clause I want you to observe. "No man can say that Jesus is the Lord, but by the Holy Spirit." That means, so far as I understand it, no man can say in the real sense of the word that he is a follower of the Lord Jesus Christ; no man can own his Lordship; no man can know and enjoy Him as Lord, but by the Holy Spirit.

Probably what I am saying so emphatically to-night is most simple and obvious to many of the members of this church: well, it won't do you any harm to hear it again. But there are those who have been brought up under preaching where the Holy Spirit is nothing more than an empty, meaningless title, and where He has not been given His true place in the plan and scheme of God and His salvation. I repeat it. It is utterly impossible for any Christian to obtain or attain unto assurance without the direct working and witness of the Spirit of God. No man can actually, truthfully, experimentally say that Jesus is the Lord, no man can own Him as Lord, no man can acknowledge Him as Lord, but by the Holy Spirit.

Again, in Ephesians 1, verses 16 to 18, the apostle says, "I . . . cease not to give thanks for you, making mention of you in my prayers; that the God of our Lord Jesus Christ, the Father of glory, may give unto you the Spirit of wisdom and revelation in the knowledge of Him; the eyes of your understanding being enlightened; that ye may know." A knowledge of God and the enlightening of the understanding come, alone, through the working and witness of the Holy Spirit. First Epistle of Thessalonians, the first chapter and the fifth verse:—"For our gospel came not unto you in word only, but also in power, and in the Holy Ghost, and in much assurance." There again you have the two things inseparably united together—the Holy Spirit and much assurance. Now one other verse, the first epistle of John, chapter 5, verse 20:—"And we know that the Son of God is come, and hath given us an understanding, that we may know Him that is true." And whatever the Son does and gives us to-day is by and through the Holy Spirit. Now I want you to notice how emphatic this verse is. "We know that the Son of God is come, and hath given us an understanding." Understanding is more than knowledge—understanding is the power or the capacity by which knowledge is obtained. It is only by this understanding "given" us that we can know Christ.

Now then, in the next place, assurance is not only a gift that is communicated by the Holy Spirit, but assurance is a blessing which God desires that all His children should enjoy. The hyper-Calvinist would put a question-mark against that. The hyper-Calvinist would argue in this way: If God desired that all His people should enjoy assurance, then all would do so: but all of His children do not enjoy assurance, therefore it cannot be God's desire that they all should. Now as a matter of cold logic that reasoning is correct and flawless, but it is repudiated; by Scripture! If any Christian is not enjoying assurance, the fault is his own, and is not to be attributed to any reluctance on God's part to communicate it. Now if you do not agree with that statement, follow me with double attention. Do you think that it is the desire of Him who died for them, that any of His beloved people should be wretched and miserable? A thousand times no! Has He not said, "Let not your heart be troubled, neither let it be afraid" (John 14:27)? What could more plainly reveal the desires of the Saviour's heart for His own than that? Do you think it is the desire of our Heavenly Father that any of His children, in whose hearts He has shed abroad His love, should spend their days in doubt and gloom, wondering whether they are His or no? A thousand times no! "If ye then, being evil, know how to give good gifts unto your children, how much more shall your Father which is in heaven give good things to them that ask Him." Do you think it is the desire of the Holy Spirit that those whom He indwells should spend all their lifetime in bondage, unassured whether they have been accepted in the Beloved or not? A thousand times no! The Spirit has been sent here to bear witness with our spirit that we are the children of God. Then banish from your minds such God-dishonoring thoughts as to entertain the conception that our gracious, loving, Triune Jehovah desires not that any of His children should enjoy perfect peace and lasting assurance and holy confidence.

I repeat it. If there is a Christian here to-night who is lacking in assurance, the fault is his or hers, and if you think that God is unwilling to bestow assurance you greatly err, not knowing the Scriptures. Now turn with me to first John one and the fourth verse:—"And these things write we unto you, that your joy may be full." There is the revealed will of God concerning His children: could anything be plainer than that? These things write we unto you that your joy may be full. How that verse reveals to us the heart of God!—desiring the happiness of all those who are dear to Him. Now turn again to the fifth chapter of the same Epistle and the 13th verse:—"These things have I written unto you that believe on the Son of God; that ye may know that ye have eternal life." There we are expressly told that God has written an entire Epistle for the very purpose of establishing His own people in the full assurance of faith. Then in the light of that, in the light of these Scriptures, how can anyone say that God is not willing to give you assurance? O my friend, place the blame where it belongs—on yourself.

Now, in the third place, assurance is a blessing that is communicated by the Holy Spirit, but it is altogether erroneous to conclude from that fact that therefore there is nothing left for us to do. I fear there are some who think that they ought to remain submissively inert, quietly waiting until the Spirit's time comes to give them assurance. They seem to feel that that is very honoring to the Spirit of God, that they should just wait until His time arrives to grant this precious blessing to them. But it is contrary to the Scriptures, for, my friends, the Holy Spirit does not place a premium on slothfulness. The Spirit of God does not encourage idleness and lethargy. In the first Epistle of Timothy, chapter 4, verse 14, we are told that Timothy had received a gift from the Spirit, and yet the apostle Paul wrote and told him to "**neglect not** the gift that is in thee." And in the 2nd Epistle of Timothy, the first chapter and the sixth verse he wrote and told him to "stir up" that gift. Now listen, beloved, if it were the will of God that each of His people should just sit still and quietly wait until the Holy Spirit was pleased to communicate assurance, the apostle Peter would never have been moved to write unto God's people, "Give diligence to make your calling and election sure." No, God would never tell His people to make their calling and election sure if it were His will that they should just sit down and do nothing until His time came to make it sure for them.

Assurance is a gift from the Spirit; assurance is a blessing that God desires all His people to enjoy; and though assurance is communicated alone by the Spirit, that does not imply that we are to sit still and just wait until He gives it. In the last place, the Spirit communicates the blessing of assurance when God's people make a diligent use of the means that He has provided to that end. The Holy Spirit ever works in and through and by means of the written Word of God. It is by that Word that He quickens; it is by that Word He enlightens and instructs; and it is also by that same Word that He communicates His witness and bestows assurance. "The Spirit Himself beareth witness with our spirit, that we are the children of God." Yes, but someone says, He has not borne that witness to my spirit: I do not have that witness! Then the fault is yours.

There may be one of a number of things, beloved, which are acting as hindering causes why the Spirit of God is not witnessing with yours. The Spirit of God is very sensitive. The Spirit of God is easily grieved, and there are many things which act as hindering causes why the Spirit will not bear witness with our spirit. Sometimes it is a defective preaching ministry. If you are accustomed to sit week by week and month by month under preaching that does not exalt Christ, that does not make everything of Him, you are not likely to receive any real witness from the Spirit. On the other hand, if you sit under a ministry that is too introspective, a preaching that is all the time encouraging you to examine yourself and look within (which has its proper place, but is not to be unduly emphasised and disproportionately pressed); a preaching that is subjective rather than objective, and causing you to look within at self instead of without at Christ—you cannot expect to have the witness of the Spirit. Sometimes, I say, it is a deficient ministry that is responsible for it.

At other times an "idol" may be the hindering cause. Listen! The last verse of this very Epistle of John, that was written to establish God's people in assurance, gives us warning, "Keep yourselves from idols." God is a jealous God, and if you are loving this world more than you are loving Christ, if there is a secret sin in your life that you cherish more highly than you do Christ, the Holy Spirit will not grant assurance to you while you are in that state. Again; a very serious and real cause of hindrance to the Holy Spirit's giving assurance is to get into a state of backsliding and to fall into open sin that is grieving and dishonoring to God. That is the state that David was in in the 51st Psalm when he said, "Restore unto me the joy of Thy salvation." He had lost that joy; why? Because he had dishonored God, because he had become a backslider and because he had fallen into open sin, and that sin had to be confessed: it had to be put right between his own soul and God before there was any assurance again.

And that may be true of some in this congregation to-night: you may be lacking in assurance because your heart is not right in the sight of God: there is something that is being hidden from Him, that is not being brought out into the open and spread before and confessed to Him. And while that is true the Spirit of God will withhold His witness from your spirit. Again, there are many who are lacking in assurance because they are waiting for something that God has not promised. They are expecting something that God's Word does not warrant. They are hoping to receive some vision or to hear some mysterious voice or to experience some particular feeling. In other words, I very much fear there are one or two present to-night who are expecting God to give them a flood of joy in their heart before they get assurance. My friends, that is to get things upside down: the flood of joy follows assurance. It is "peace and joy in believing," and if you are waiting to experience that joy before you will really rest on the promise of God, that may be the reason why the Spirit is withholding His witness—failure to trust in the bare Word of God. The Holy Spirit will not honor doubtings. The Holy Spirit will not reward unbelief. Peter said in John 6:69, "We believe and are sure." There must first be a simple childlike resting upon the Word of God and then assurance is given.

Now my closing word, very briefly, is to any exercised soul here to-night who is anxious for peace of heart and rest of soul. O beloved friend, cease being occupied with yourself. Cease looking within to find out whether you have faith or not. Look away to Christ. Behold Him upon the cross and see there the very One that such a sinner as you needs: the very One who just meets that need. Do not look within for the evidence of faith. The surest evidence of faith within is looking without and seeing in Christ just the Saviour that such a poor lost sinner like me needs. It is Christ who is the Prince of Peace. It is Christ who has made peace by the blood of His cross, and we have peace with God through our Lord Jesus Christ. Dear friends, if you are truly anxious for peace and rest, then spend much of your time in reading God's Word, for it is in the Scriptures that the person and the glories of Christ are set forth. It is there that God has revealed Him. They are they which testify of Him. To be more definite still, go home and read slowly, carefully and prayerfully through the first Epistle of John, which has been written by God for the express purpose that His own people might have joy and might know that they have eternal life.

---

wonder if it would be possible for me to make out the raised characters with my tongue, which seems to be sensitive?'

"He called for his teacher, and together they worked over those characters, until in a short time he was able to read the Lord's prayer with his tongue. It was not long till he was able to read the New Testament. He said, 'I had an awful time for a while, for both my lips and my tongue would bleed from the roughness of the paper; but I stuck at it, until after a while they became hardened to it, and now I can read for hours and it does not bother me. With great gratitude he said, 'I have read the whole Bible through four times, and many of the books of the Bible over and over again.

"Do you love God's Word like that? Would it break your heart if you had to lose the privilege of reading your Bible—no, not good books or newspapers, but your Bible? Have you and I fully appreciated the marvellous gift of His Word?

"Then the blind man took down from the rack one of the books of the Bible with just those stumps of arms, and showed us how he could read. He placed the book on an easel which a kind friend had made for him and then began to read to us, stopping between words and sentences and repeating what he had read with his tongue.

"As I left that home I said to myself: 'What a man; and what a God!' Yes, His grace was sufficient for the great unusual physical and spiritual needs of my Scotch friend. Is anything too hard for God? No, there is no circumstance too much for Him."

May the reading of the above bring many to their knees, confessing to God their shameful sin of neglecting His Word, and asking Him to implant in their hearts a deeper love for it.

Arthur W. Pink.

comfort to the distressed: "Great peace have they which love Thy law; and nothing shall offend them" (Psa. 119:165). It establishes and builds up in the faith (Acts 20:38). Thus, we ought to love the Word.

Greater love for the Word is one of our deepest needs. More prayerful study of it, more daily meditation on it, will wean us from worldly and fleshly delights. Either sin will kill our love for the Word, or occupation with the Word will kill our love for sin! Closer acquaintance with the Word will deepen our assurance; "Remember the word unto Thy servants upon which Thou hast caused me to hope (Psa. 119:49). The Word is the foundation of all true hope: hopes built on anything else are worthless. A more faithful application of ourselves to the Word will bring a deeper insight into the mysteries of God. It is by comparing scripture with scripture and by prayerful contemplation of its statements that we obtain clearer views of the Truth.

How may our love for the Word be deepened? First, by bearing in mind the fact that to neglect the Word is to slight its Author. And God feels this slight. Of old He said of Israel, "I have written to him the great things of My law, but they were counted as a strange thing" (Hos. 8:12). Second, by daily reminding ourselves how much we lose through our careless and sinful neglect. Absence of a continual renewing of our strength, light on our path, comfort in sorrow, deliverances from the snares of Satan, are the inevitable losses. Third, by earnest prayer for more light. David prayed "incline my heart unto Thy testimonies, and not to covetousness" (Psa. 119:36).

In closing we would refer to an example of most unusual devotion to God's Word which will put all of us to shame. It is recorded in a Fellowship Magazine sent to us by a brother in England.

A servant of God was invited to visit a godly Christian man in Kansas City, U.S.A. He states, "As I entered that home I realised I was in the presence of one who knew God in a real way. After we had been singing and enjoying Christian fellowship for a while, my friend asked this Christian Brother if he would tell the story of what God had done for him. He gladly assented, for he welcomed this new opportunity to praise his all-sufficient Christ.

"Then he told us the story of how, about a year or so after his conversion, while at work one day doing some blasting, he was about to put a charge of dynamite in place, when there was a premature explosion and the charge went off in his hand. 'You see,' he said, 'it took off both my hands,' for they were gone at the wrists, 'and my whole face and body was terribly torn by the explosion.

"The doctor did a wonderful piece of work in replacing the flesh upon his face. After he had been in the hospital for several weeks, his head completely covered with bandages, one day he called the nurse and said to her: 'Nurse, I must have these bandages removed from my eyes; I simply cannot stand this darkness any longer.' Then he learned for the first time that he would never see again, and he raised his dark glasses to show us that his eyes were entirely gone.

"He was then thrown utterly upon the mercy and grace of God, but his heart was broken as he realized that because his sight was gone he would never again be able to read God's wonderful Word, which had become a part of his life. Many kind friends were ready to read the Word to him, but he said, 'It did not seem the same to have some one who did not know my Lord as I knew Him read the Scriptures to me; and O how I longed and prayed that I might read that precious Word for myself. But there seemed to be no possible hope that this could be. Then one day, in a meeting, I heard the story of a woman in England who had learned to read with her lips when she lost the use of her fingers and was kissing her precious raised-letter Bible good-bye. He said the mention of this fact went to his very soul as he thought of the possibility of being able to read with his lips, too.

Some friends kindly sent for the Moon raised-letter type system for him, and he could hardly wait until the books arrived. However, the poor man was doomed to disappointment, for he had not taken into consideration the fact that in the explosion his face had been so terribly blown away that the nerves of his lips were gone and there was no sense of touch there. He wept over his Bible in great agony as he realised that he could not learn to read it as that young woman in England had learned to do, and then—a wonderful thing happened. His tongue touched and rested on one of the raised letters. At once he said to himself: 'I

(Continued on page 143).

# STUDIES IN THE SCRIPTURES

"Search the Scriptures" John 5:39.

Copyright in all English-speaking Countries.

Editor: Arthur W. Pink, 15 Hurlstone Avenue, Summer Hill, N.S.W., Australia.
Hon. Agent in U.S.A.: Mr. C. S. Pressel, 559 Dupont Ave., York, Penna.

FREE TO ALL WHO WILL READ IT

### DIVINE CHASTISEMENT.
### Heb. 12:9.

The word "furthermore" signifies that an additional reason is now advanced why Christians should expect and endure chastenings. First, the apostle had reminded the saints of the teachings of Scripture—vv. 5, 6: how significant that he began with this! Second, he had comforted them with the assurance that chastisement proceeds from God's heart and is regulated by His love: v. 6. Third, he affirms that God chastens all His children, there being no exceptions, reverence." They had the authority to chastise us because of their relationship. We have had natural parents, and they corrected us; and we "gave them reverence." They had the authority to chastise us because of their relationship and we submitted. Now if it was right and meet for us to submit to their chastening, much more should we be in subjection to our Heavenly Parent.

Ere passing from this point it should be noted that there is at least a fourfold contrast between the chastisements of our earthly parents and our Heavenly Father. The one came from our fathers according to the flesh; the other comes from the Father of spirits, i.e. the Creator of both our natural and spiritual lives. The one was for a brief period, while we were children; the other extends through our whole early life. The one was from much imperfect knowledge, "after their own pleasure" or will; the other proceeds from unerring wisdom and love. The one was aimed at our temporal good; the other has in view our spiritual blessing. Yet, imperfect as was our earthly parent's discipline we gave it "reverence," as was right—according to God's will and for our safety. Then how "much rather should we be in subjection to the Father of spirits"!

This word "furthermore" is very humbling and searching. One would think sufficient had been said in the previous verses to make us submissive under and thankful for the tender chastenings of our God. Is it not enough to be told that the scriptures teach us to expect chastisements, and exhort us not to "despise" them? Is it not sufficient to be assured that they all flow from and express the love of God? No, a "furthermore" is needed! The Holy Spirit deigns to give us still further reasons. I believe the explanation of this is that we are so slow to submit to the rod, and because the older we get the more need is there for it.

One thing which has much impressed me of late, both in my study of the Word and in the observation of fellow-Christians, is, that God uses the rod very little and very lightly on the babes and younger members of His family, but more frequently and more severely on the more mature Christians. I have often heard older saints warning the younger brethren and sisters of their great danger. But let me remind you there is not a single instance in Scripture of a young saint disgracing his profession. Ponder the histories of young Joseph, the Hebrew maid in Naaman's household, the youth David and Goliath, Daniel as a young man, the three Hebrews in Babylon. But on the other hand there are numbers of instances where men of middle age and grey hairs grievously dishonoured the Lord.

I allow that young Christians are feeblest, and with rare exceptions they know it; and therefore does God manifest His grace and power by upholding

(Continued on page 168).

## BACK NUMBERS

OF THIS MAGAZINE obtainable, 5/- (1 dollar) per year; Bound at 7/- (1 dollar 75.) Each year is yet obtainable.

ADVISE PROMPTLY of Change of Address

THIS MAGAZINE is published as a work of faith and labor of love. It is gladly sent to all who would value it.

We want the names and addresses of Christians who would read it.

Christians who feel definitely led to do so may have fellowship with us in this Ministry.

## CONTENTS.

| | |
|---|---|
| The Gospel of John (20:1-10) | 146 |
| Gleanings in Exodus | 153 |
| Crossbearing | 158 |
| Blind Bartimaeus | 162 |
| Fellowship | 167 |

## THE GOSPEL OF JOHN.

### 67. Christ risen from the dead: John 20:1-10.

Below is an Analysis of the first section of John 20:—

1. The stone removed from the sepulchre, v. 1.
2. Mary Magdalene's appeal to the two disciples, v. 2.
3. Love's race to the sepulchre, vv. 3, 4.
4. John's hesitation and Peter's boldness, vv. 5, 6.
5. The grave-clothes and John's conclusion, vv., 7, 8.
6. The disciples' slowness of heart, v. 9.
7. Their return home, v. 10.

The resurrection of Christ was more than hinted at in the first Divine promise and prophecy (Gen. 3:15): if Christ was to bruise the Serpent's head after His own heel had been bruised by the Enemy, then must He rise from the dead. The passing of the ark through the waters of judgment on to the cleansed earth, foreshadowed this same great event (I. Peter, 3:21). The deliverance of Isaac from the altar, after he had been given up to death three days before (see Gen. 22:4), is interpreted by the Holy Spirit as a receiving of him back, in figure, from the dead (Heb. 11:19). The crossing of the Red Sea by Israel on dry ground, three days after the slaying of the Paschal lamb, was a type of Christians being raised together with Christ. The emergence of Jonah after three days and nights in the whale's belly forecast the Saviour's deliverance from the tomb on the third day. Prophecy was equally explicit: "Therefore My heart is glad, and My glory rejoiceth: My flesh also shall rest in hope. For Thou wilt not leave My soul in hades; neither wilt Thou suffer Thine Holy One to see corruption. Thou wilt show Me the path of life" (Psa. 16: 9-11).

We cannot make too much of the death of Christ, but we can make too little of His resurrection. Our hearts and minds cannot meditate too frequently upon the Cross, but in pondering the sufferings of the Saviour, let us not forget the glories which followed. Calvary does not exhaust the Gospel message. The Christian Evangel is not only that Christ died for our sins, but also that He rose again the third day according to the Scriptures (I. Cor. 15:1-4). He was delivered for our offences and raised again for our justification (Rom. 4:25). Had Christ remained in the sepulchre it had been the grave of all our hopes; "If Christ be not raised," said the apostle, "then is our preaching vain, and your faith is also vain" (I. Cor. 15:14). To be a witness of His resurrection was a fundamental qualification for an apostle (Acts 1:22). That God raised up the One whom the Jews had crucified, was the central truth pressed by Peter in his Pentecostal sermon (Acts 2:24-36). The same fact was urged again by the apostles in Solomon's porch (Acts 3:15), and before the Sanhedrin (Acts 4:10; 5:30). This foundation-truth was proclaimed also to the Gentiles (Acts 10.40; 13:34). Its prominence in the Epistles is too well-known to require quotations.

The 20th chapter of John records the appearances which the Saviour made to some of His own after He was risen from the dead—we say "after," for none of them witnessed the actual resurrection itself. "As no eye beheld what was deepest in the cross, so only God looked on the Lord rising from among the dead. This was as it should be. Darkness veiled Him giving Himself for us in atonement. Man saw not that infinite work in His death; yet was it not only to glorify God thereby, but that our sins might be borne away righteously. We have seen the action of the world, and especially of the

Jews, in crucifying Him; high and low, religious and profane, all played their part; even an apostle denied Him, as another betrayed Him to the murderous priests and elders. But Jehovah laid on Him the iniquities of us all; Jehovah bruised and put Him to grief; Jehovah made His soul an offering for sin; and as this was Godward, so was it invisible to human eyes, and God alone could rightly bear witness, by whom He would, of the eternal redemption there obtained, which left Divine love free to act even in a lost and ungodly world.

"So with the resurrection of Christ. He was raised up from the dead by the glory of the Father; God raised up Jesus whom the Jews slew and hanged on a tree; He had laid down His life that He might take it again, in three days raising the temple of His body which they destroyed. But if no man was given to see the act of His rising from the dead, it was to be testified in all the world, as well as His atoning death. Assuredly he who withholds His resurrection maims the glad tidings of its triumphant proof and character, and compromises the believer's liberty and introduction into the new creation, as he immensely clouds the Lord's glory; even as the denial of resurrection virtually charges God's witnesses with falsehood and makes faith vain." (Bible Treasury.)

The resurrection of Christ was brought about by the joint-action of the three Persons of the Trinity. Just as they co-operated in connection with His incarnation (Heb. 10.5 for the Father; Phil 2:7 for the Son; Luke 1:35 for the Spirit), just as They had Each been active in connection with the atonement (Isa. 53:6, 10 for the Father; Eph. 5:2 for the Son; Heb. 9:14 for the Spirit), so the whole Godhood was engaged on the resurrection-morning. "Christ was raised up from the dead by the glory of the **Father**" (Rom. 6:4): "I lay down My life, that I might take it again" (John 10:17): "But if the Spirit of Him that raised up Jesus from the dead dwell in you," etc. (Rom. 8:11).

"The first of the week" (v. 1). All the ways of God express His perfect wisdom, and everything recorded of them in Scripture is written for our learning. Most fitting was it that the Lord Jesus, as Head of the new creation, should rise from the dead on the first day of the week—intimating that a new beginning had been inaugurated. The full requirements of the moral law had been met; the shadows of the ceremonial law had all been fulfilled; the old system, connected with man in the flesh, was ended; a new and spiritual dispensation had begun. It was this "first of the week" which the Spirit of prophecy had in mind when He moved the Psalmist to write, "The Stone which the builders refused is become the Head of the corner. This is the Lord's doing; it is marvelous in our eyes. This is the day which the Lord hath made (appointed); we will rejoice and be glad in it" (Psa. 22:24). Here is the reason why the Lord's people are under obligations to keep Sunday as their day of rest and worship. During Old Testament times the Sabbath was the memorial of God's finished work in the old creation (Gen: 2:3; Ex. 20:11); in New Testament times the Sabbath is the memorial of Christ's finished work from which issues the new creation.

"The first of the week cometh Mary Magdalene early, when it was yet dark, unto the sepulchre" (v.1). Mark tells us that Mary Magdalene was accompanied to the grave by Mary the mother of James, and Salome (16:1, 2); but John mentions them not. It is characteristic of this fourth Gospel to present individual souls to our notice; Nicodemus alone with Christ, the woman at the well, the blind beggar in chapter 9 being well-known examples. Another thing which is prominent in John is the heart's affection, the soul finding a satisfying Object: the two disciples who abode with the Lord, on their very first meeting with Him (1:39); the bringing of others to the Saviour, that they also might bask in His presence (1:41, 45); the words of Peter (6:68), the appeal of the sisters (11:3), and the devotion of Mary (12:3), are so many illustrations. It is this which Mary of Magdala so vividly exemplifies. To whom much is forgiven, the same loveth much (Luke 7:47), and abundant cause had this woman to love the Saviour, for out of her He had cast seven demons (Luke 8:2).

It was "very early in the morning" (Mark 16:2) that Mary came to the sepulchre; as John tells us "when it was yet dark." But though she had reason for expecting to find the Roman soldiers on guard there (Matt. 27:66), though there had just been "a great earthquake" (Matt. 28:2), though there were no male disciples accompanying her, though this was the midst of the Feast, when thousands of strangers were most probably sleeping under any slight shelter near the walls of Jerusalem, love drew Mary to the place where the Saviour's body had been laid. How this devotion of hers puts to shame many of us, who perhaps have greater intelligence in spiritual things, but who manifest far less love for Christ! Few were as deeply attached to the Redeemer as was this woman. Few had received as much at His gracious hands, and her gratitude knew no bounds. How this explains the listlessness and half-heartedness among us! Where there is little sense of our indebtedness to Christ, there will be little affection for Him. Where light views of our sinfulness, our depravity, our utter unworthiness, are entertained, there will be little expression of gratitude and praise. It is those who have had the clearest sight of their deservingness of hell, whose hearts are most moved at the amazing grace which snatched them as brands from the burning, that are the most devoted among Christ's people. Let us pray daily, then, that it may please God to grant us a deeper realization of our sinfulness and a deeper apprehension of the surpassing worthiness of His Son, so that we may serve and glorify Him with increasing zeal and faithfulness.

"And seeth the stone taken away from the sepulchre" (v. 1). Matthew tells us that, "Behold, there was a great earthquake: for the angel of the Lord descended from heaven, and came and rolled back the stone from the door, and sat upon it" (28:2): Upon this Dr. J. Gill has said, "This stone was removed by an angel, for though Christ Himself could easily have done it, it was proper that it should be done by a messenger from Heaven, by the order of Divine justice, which had lain Him a prisoner there." The stone was rolled away from Lazarus' sepulchre by human hands (11:39), the stone from Christ's tomb by angelic—in all things He has the pre-eminence! We believe that God's principal design in sending His angel to remove the stone was that these believers might see for themselves that the sepulchre was now tenantless. The angel seated on the stone (later, inside the sepulchre) would demonstrate that God Himself had intervened. Apparently Mary was the first to perceive that the entrance to the grave was now open.

"Then she runneth, and cometh to Simon Peter, and to the other disciple whom Jesus loved, and saith unto them, They have taken away the Lord out of the sepulchre, and we know not where they have laid Him" (v. 2). There is no difficulty in reconciling this statement with the record of Matthew if the following points be kept in mind: First, either Mary was in front of the other women as they journeyed to the sepulchre, or else her vision was keener than theirs; at any rate, she appears to have been the first to perceive that the stone had been removed. Second, she was so excited over this that, instead of going right up to the sepulchre with her companions, she at once rushed off to acquaint the apostles—hence she missed seeing the angel. Third, after Mary's hurried departure, the rest of the little party drew near the grave, hardly knowing what to conclude or what to expect. Fourth, Mary was, most probably, a long way on the road to John's dwelling before the other women left the tomb.

Various reasons have been advanced as to why Mary sought out Peter and John. These two seem to have been nearer the Saviour than the other apostles. They were among the highly favoured three who witnessed His transfiguration, and whom He also took with Him further into the Garden than the others (Matt. 26:37). These two had also stuck more closely to Him after His arrest, following to and entering the high priest's residence. Moreover, as another has said, "John alone of all the apostles, had witnessed Peter's sad fall and observed his bitter weeping afterwards. Can we not understand that from Friday night to Sunday morning John would be lovingly employed in binding up the broken heart of his brother, and telling him of our Lord's last words? Can we doubt that they were absorbed and occupied in converse about their Master on this very morning, when Mary Magdalene suddenly ran in with her wonderful news." Mary, then, sought Peter and John because she knew that among the disciples they would be most likely to respond (at that early hour) to the anxious inquiry that filled her own soul. It is indeed beautiful to see these two disciples now together: "The love and tender nature of John's character come out most blessedly in his affection for Peter, even after his denial of Christ....John clings to him, and has him under his own roof, wherever that was. When Judas fell, he had no friend to raise and cheer him. When Peter fell, there was 'a brother born for adversity' who did not despise him!" (Bishop Ryle).

"And saith unto them, They have taken away the Lord out of the sepulchre and we know not where they have laid Him." How this shows us that love needs to be regulated by faith. Mary's affection for the Saviour cannot be doubted, and most blessed it was; but her faith certainly was not in exercise. She had judged by the sight of her eyes. The stone had been removed, and she at once jumped to the conclusion that some one had been and "taken away" the Saviour's body. The thought that He was now alive had evidently not entered her mind. She supposed that He was yet under the power of death. His own repeated declaration that He would rise again on the third day had made no impression. "Alas, how little of Christ's teaching the best of us take in! How much we let fall!" What a strange mingling of spiritual intelligence and spiritual ignorance we behold here. "They have taken away the Lord"! How often we see the same confusion in ourselves and in others! Observe her "We know not where they have laid Him"—agreeing with Matthew's account that other women had accompanied her on the journey to the sepulchre.

"Peter therefore went forth, and that other disciple, and came to the sepulchre" (v. 3). The announcement which Mary had made to them was so startling that the two disciples arose at once, setting forth to ascertain what this removal of the stone from the sepulchre really meant: It is most likely that they would first ask Mary, Are you sure the body is gone? But all she could tell them was that the stone was no longer in its place. Finding that Mary had not actually looked in the sepulchre, they deemed it best to go and inspect it for themselves. Strikingly may we behold here the over-ruling providence of God. According to the Mosaic law a woman was not eligible to bear witness (note no mention of them is made in I. Cor. 15!), and the truth could not be established by less than two men. Here then we have the needed two in Peter and John, as eye-witnesses of the empty grave and the orderliness of the clothes which the Saviour had left behind!

"So they ran both together: and the other disciple did outrun Peter, and came first to the sepulchre" (v. 4). Their running evidences that they were both excited and anxious. "We can well suppose that Mary's sudden announcement completely overwhelmed them, so that they knew not what to think. Who can tell what thoughts did not come into their minds, as they ran, about our Lord's oft-repeated predictions of His resurrection? Could it really be true? Could it possibly prove that all their deep sorrow was going to turn to joy? These are all conjectures, no doubt. Yet a vast amount of thoughts may run through a mind, at a great crisis, in a very few minutes." (Bishop Ryle).

As to the physical reason of John's outdistancing Peter we cannot be certain, but the popular idea that John was the younger of the two is most likely correct, for he lived at least sixty years afterwards. As to the spiritual reason, we think they err who attribute to Peter a guilty conscience, which made him fearful of a possible meeting with the Saviour. Had this been the case, he had hardly set out for the sepulchre at all, still less would he have gone there on the run! Moreover, the promptness with which he entered the tomb argues against the common view. Yet we cannot doubt that there is a moral significance to this detail which the Spirit has recorded for our learning. Peter had not yet been restored to fellowship with the Saviour. John, too, was the one of all the Eleven who was on most intimate terms with the Lord. This is sufficient to account for his winning love's race to the sepulchre.

"And he stooping down, saw the linen clothes lying; yet went he not in" (v. 5). Here again we are left to conjecture. The simple fact is recorded; why John entered not in we are not told. Some say, to prevent himself being ceremonially defiled; but that seems very far-fetched. Others think it was out of reverence for the place where the Saviour had lain; this, while being more plausible, seems negatived by the fact that only a short while after he did enter the sepulchre (v. 8). It appears to us more likely that, after looking in and seeing the sepulchre was empty, he waited for Peter to come up and take the lead—John being the younger of the two, this would be the more gracious thing for him to do. Whatever the motive which guided him, certainly we can see, again, the over-ruling Hand of God—two must be present to witness the condition of the grave so as to establish the truth!

"And he stooping down, saw the linen clothes lying." What is the moral significance of John's act here? Surely it is this: John would never see the risen Christ while he was "stooping down" and looking within the sepulchre! How many there are to-day who conduct themselves as John did! They wish to ascertain whether or not they are real Christians. And what is the method they pursue? How do they prosecute their inquiry? By self-examination, by introspection, by looking within! They attempt to find in their own hearts that which will give them confidence towards God. But this is like seeking to make fast a ship by casting the anchor within its own hold. The anchor must be thrown outside of the ship, so that, lost to sight beneath the waves, it pierces through the mud or sand of the ocean's bed, and grips the rock itself. The surest way to discover whether or not I am trusting in Christ is not to peer within to see if I have faith, but to **exercise** faith, by looking away to its Object—faith is the eye of the soul, and the eye does not look at itself. If I look within, most likely I shall see only what John saw—the tokens of **death**! "Looking off **unto Jesus**" is what the Word says.

"Then cometh Simon Peter following him, and went into the sepulchre" (v. 6). "How this illustrates that there are widely different temperaments among believers! Both ran to the sepulchre. John, of the two, the more gentle, quiet, reserved, deep-feeling, stooped down, but went no further. Peter, more hot and zealous, impulsive, fervent and forward, cannot be content without going into the sepulchre, and actually seeing with his own eyes. Both, we may be sure, were deeply attached to our Lord. The hearts of both, at this critical juncture, were full of hopes and fears, anxieties and expectations, all tangled together. Yet each acts in his own characteristic fashion! Let us learn from this to make allowance for wide varieties in the individual character of believers. To do so will save us much trouble in the journey of life, and prevent many an uncharitable thought. Let us not judge brethren harshly, and set them down in a low place, because they do not see or feel things as we see and feel. The flowers in the Lord's garden are not all of one colour and one scent, though they are all planted by the One Spirit. The subjects of Christ's kingdom are not all exactly of one tone or temperament, though they all love the same Saviour, and are written in the same book of life. The Church has some in its ranks who are like Peter, and some who are like John, but a place for all, and a work for all to do. Let us love all who love Christ in sincerity, and thank God that they love Him at all" (Bishop Ryle).

"And seeth the linen clothes lie, and the napkin, that was about His head, not lying with the linen clothes, but wrapped together in a place by itself" (vv. 6, 7). In the Greek the word for "seeth" is different from that for "saw" in the preceding verse: the word used in connection with John signifies to take a glance; the one used of Peter means that he beheld intently, scrutinised. The design of the Holy Spirit in this verse is obvious: He informs us that Peter found in the empty tomb the clearest evidences of a deliberate and composed transaction. There were no signs of haste or fear. What had taken place had been done "decently and in order," not by a thief, and scarcely by a friend. "There they beheld, not their Object, but the trophies of His victory over the power of death. There they see the gates of brass and the bars of iron cut in sunder. The linen clothes and the napkin which had been wrapped around the Lord's head, as though He were death's prisoner, were seen strewing the ground like the spoils of the vanquished, as under the hand of death's Conqueror. The very armor of the strong man was made a show of in his own house; this telling loudly that He, who is the plague of death, and hell's destruction, had been in that place doing His glorious work." (Mr. J. G. Bellett.)

"Then went in also that other disciple, which came first to the sepulchre, and he saw, and believed" (v. 8). There is wide difference of opinion as to the meaning of this verse. **What** was it that John "saw and believed"? Many say that John saw the grave was **tenantless** and believed what Mary had said,—"they have taken away the Lord." But John had already looked into the grave and seen the linen clothes (v. 5); what is said here in v. 8 is clearly something different. But what alternative is left us? Only this, that John now believed that Christ had risen from the dead. But if this be the reference here, how are we to understand the next verse—"For as yet they knew not the Scripture, that He must rise again from the dead"? Does not this bar out the thought that John now believed that Christ was alive? We do not think so; the contrast pointed between vv. 8 and 9 is not between believing and not believing, but between the **grounds** on which faith rested!

We believe that the key to the meaning of this verse lies in the word "saw." In the Greek it is a different one from that which is used either in v. 5 or v. 6; the word here in v. 8 has the force of "perceived with the understanding." But **what was** it that John now "saw"? In v. 5, when he looked into the sepulchre from the outside, he saw (by a glance) "the linen clothes lying"; but now, on the inside, he saw also "the napkin that was about His head, not lying with the linen clothes, but wrapped together in a place by itself" (v. 7). On this the late Dr. Pierson wrote: "'Wrapped together,' fails to convey the true significance. The original means **rolled up**, and suggests that these clothes were lying in their original convolutions, as they had been tightly rolled up around our Lord's dead body. In 19:40 it is recorded how they tightly wound—bound about—that body in the linen clothes; how tightly and rigidly may be inferred from the necessity of loosing Lazarus, even after miraculous power had raised up the dead body and given it life (11:44). This explains v. 8: 'And he (John) saw and believed.' There was nothing in the mere fact of an empty tomb to compel belief in a miraculous resurrection; but, when John saw, on the floor of the sepulchre, the long linen wrappings that had been so tightly wound about the body and the head, lying there undisturbed, in their original convolutions, he knew that nothing but a miracle could have made it possible."

John "saw and believed" or understood: it was a logical conclusion, an irresistible one, drawn from the evidence before him. The body was gone from the sepulchre; the clothes were left behind, and the condition of them indicated that Christ had passed out of them without their being un-wrapped. If friends had removed the body, would they not have taken the clothes with it, still covering the honored corpse? If foes had removed the body, first stripping it, would they have been so careful to dispose of the clothes and napkin in the orderly manner in which John now beheld them? Everything pointed to deliberation and design, and the apostle could draw only one conclusion—Christ had risen. Our blessed Lord had left the grave-clothes just as they had rested upon Him. He had simply risen out of them by His Divine power. We believe that this shows there is a deeper significance than is generally perceived in the angel's word to the women, "Come see the place where the Lord lay" (Matt. 28.6). The clothes themselves marked His resting-place, somewhat as one would leave the impression of his form upon the bed on which he had been lying—body, arms, head. Here then we have the first proof that the mighty Victor had risen from the sleep of death.

In leaving behind His grave-clothes an Old Testament type was strikingly fulfilled. Joseph, through no fault of his own, was cast into prison—the place of condemnation. While in prison he was numbered with transgressors—two, as Christ was crucified between the two thieves; to the one he was the means of blessing, to the other he was the pronouncer of judgment. All of this is so clear it needs no comment. But Joseph did not remain forever in the prison-house, any more than Christ continued in the tomb. Joseph's place of shame and suffering was exchanged for one of dignity and glory. But before he left the dungeon "he shaved himself, and changed his raiment" (Gen. 41: 14). So the Saviour left behind Him the habiliments of death, coming forth clothed in immortality and glory. This was the pledge that at Christ's second coming His people will also be rid forever of everything connected with the old creation— "Who shall change our vile body, that it may be fashioned like unto His glorious body" (Phil. 3:21).

"For as yet they knew not the Scripture, that He must rise again from the dead" (v.9). Very searching and humbling is this. For three years these two leading apostles had heard our Lord speak of his resurrection, yet had they not understood Him. Again and again had He told them that He would rise again on the third day, yet had they never taken in His meaning. His enemies had remembered what He said, (See Matt. 27:63), but His friends had forgotten! What a piercing rebuke was that of the angel's—"He is risen, as He said" (Matt. 28:6)! And again, "Why seek ye the living among the dead? He is not here, but is risen: remember how He spake unto you when He was yet in Galilee, saying, The Son of man must be delivered into the hands of sinful men, and be crucified, and the third day rise again" (Luke 24:5-7)!! But these words of Christ had fallen on unheeding ears. Moreover, the apostles had had the Old Testament scriptures in their hands from the beginning, and such passages as Psa. 16:9-11, etc., ought to have prepared them for His resurrection. But wrong teaching in childhood, traditions imbibed in their youth (John 12:34), had prejudiced them and made void the Word of God. This statement of John's here brings out, once more, his trustworthiness as a witness. "Hereby it appears that they were not only honest men, who would not deceive others, but cautious men, who would not themselves be imposed upon" (Matthew Henry).

"For as yet they knew not the scripture that He must rise again from the dead." The Holy Spirit here contrasts a faith which rests on the Word of God, with an intellectual assurance which proceeds from mere external evidence. Much has been made by Christian Apologists of the value of "evidences," but it has been greatly over-rated. Creation demonstrates a Creator, but the outward proofs of His hand do not move the heart, nor bring the soul into communion with Him —the written word, applied by the Spirit, alone does that! "Facts are of high interest and real importance; and as the Israelite could point to them as the basis of his religion, to the call of Abram by God, and the deliverance of the chosen people from Egypt and through the desert and into Canaan, so can the Christian to the incomparably deeper and more enduring ones of the incarnation, death, resurrection, and ascension of the Son of God, with the consequent presence of the Holy Spirit sent down from Heaven. But faith to have moral value, to deal with the conscience, to purify the heart, is not the pure and simple acceptance of facts on reasonable grounds, but the heart's welcoming God's testimony in His Word. This tests the soul beyond all else, as spiritual intelligence consists in the growing up to Christ in an increasing perception and enjoyment of all that God's Word has revealed, which separates the saint practically to Himself and His will in judgment of self and the world.

"To 'see and believe' therefore is wholly short of what the operation of God gives us; as traditional faith or evidence answers to it now in Christendom. It is human, and leaves the conscience unpurged and the heart without communion. It may be found in him who is in no way born of God (John 2:23-25), but also in the believer as here; if so, it is not what the Spirit seals and in no way delivers from present things. And this it seems to be the Divine object to let us know in the account before us. Faith, to be of value and have power, rests not on sight or inference, but on Scripture. And as the disciples show the most treacherous memory as to the words of the Lord till He was raised up from the dead (2:22), so were they insensible to the force and application of the written Word: after that they believed both, they entered into abiding and enlarging blessing from above. This, as Peter tells us in his first Epistle (1:8), is characteristically the faith of a Christian, who, having not seen Christ, loves Him; and on whom, though not now seeing Him but believing he exults with joy unspeakable and full of glory. The faith that is founded on evidences may strengthen against Deism, Pantheism, or Atheism, but it never gave remission of sins, never led one to cry Abba Father, never filled the heart with His grace and glory who is the Object of God's everlasting satisfaction and delight" (The Bible Treasury).

"Then the disciples went away again unto their own home" (v. 10). "Here also we have the further and marked testimony of its powerlessness (John's 'believing' A.W.P.). The fact was known on grounds indisputable to their minds, but not yet appreciated in God's sight as revealed in His Word, and hence they return to their own unbroken association" (Bible Treasury). Doubtless this is one reason why the Holy Spirit recorded this detail, but are we not meant to link it up with 19:27 as well—"From that hour that disciple took her unto his own home." Did not Peter and John now hasten to tell the Saviour's mother that He was now risen from the dead!

It only remains for us to call attention to the dispensational significance of the passage which has been before us. That we have here another of those wondrous typical pictures in which John's Gospel abounds is fairly evident on the surface, and though (through the feebleness of our spiritual vision) some of its details may seem blurred, the general outline of it is unmistakable. What we have here— —right after the crucifixion of the Messiah—is the condition of Israel when God again resumes His dealings with them. It is not the Nation as such, but the godly Remnant which is in view. Observe the following details:—

1. We have marked here a new beginning: "the first of the week" (v. 1). The present dispensation of the Spirit is over. 2. "It was yet dark": the time referred to, being that, when "darkness shall cover the earth, and gross darkness the people" (Isa. 60:2). 3. The heart-condition of the Remnant is hinted at in the name of the woman here: "Mary" (v. 1), which means bitterness. 4. The Remnant will be characterised by devotion to the Lord mixed with spiritual ignorance, for they will not then have the Spirit—c.f. Mary's words in v. 2. 5. The type passes from Mary to Peter and John, and in their anxiety to reach the sepulchre we have a hint of the deep exercise of soul of the Remnant after Christ, ere the testimony of His glory shines forth. 6. Though exercised in heart, yet the Remnant is, as yet, walking by sight, not faith—hence the "saw" v. 5 "seeth" and "saw" v. 8. 7.

At first coming to it (v. 4) the Remnant ultimately, enter the place of death (vv. 6, 8). 8. When the Remnant "believe" (v. 8) it is a seeing faith, as Israel's has ever been: note how in Heb. 11 the only acts of faith recorded of the Nation as a whole were their passing through the Red Sea and the falling down of Jericho's walls, both of which were visible to sight. So in the Tribulation period, it will be the outward "signs" on which the Remnant's faith will rest—note "When ye therefore shall **see**" (Matt. 24:15)!! 9. As yet the Remnant will not know the power of Christ's resurrection, nor have intelligence in the Scriptures (v. 9). 10. In the interval before Christ's appearing to the Remnant they will have a home prepared for them by God (v. 10). cf Rev. 12:6.

The following questions are to aid the student for our next lesson:—

1. What is the typical picture in vv. 11-23?
2. Why did not Mary recognise Him in v. 15?
3. Why did she recognise Him in v. 16?
4. Why "touch Me not" v. 17?
5. Why refer to the ascension here v. 17?
6. What do the last words of v. 19 prove?
7. Why the repetition in v. 21 from v. 19?

Arthur W. Pink.

## GLEANINGS IN EXODUS.

### 43. The Veil: Ex. 26:31-33.

In our last article we had before us the framework of the Tabernacle proper. i.e, the holy place and the most holy. Outside of this, as we shall yet see, D.V., was the court of the Tabernacle, completing its threefold division. Thus there was really a Tabernacle within a tabernacle. Inside the framework of the golden-covered boards, ceiled by the lovely curtains and their coverings, were the two inner rooms. These were separated by another curtain, called "the Veil." It was this which divided the holy place from the holy of holies. The first compartment would thus be thirty feet by fifteen, and the innermost, a separate apartment of fifteen feet by fifteen. In this innermost chamber was Jehovah's throne upon the ark, where the Shekinah-glory dwelt between the two cherubim.

In the verses which form the basis of our present study, we find Jehovah giving instructions to Moses concerning the Veil. He is told of what material it must be made, the manner of its workmanship, and where and how to hang it. Its presence before the holy of holies invested it with a peculiar sanctity and the light from the lampstand shining upon it would reveal its varied beauties. There it hung for five hundred years before the eyes of Israel's priests as they ministered at the table and the golden altar. It announced, in the language of symbolry, that the way of approach to God was not then made known. But inasmuch as it was a curtain and not a wall of stone or metal, there was more than a hint given of its temporary nature, and that ultimately a way of access would be revealed. Seven things will now engage our attention:—

#### 1. Its Material.

"And thou shalt make a veil of blue, and purple, and scarlet, and fine twined linen of cunning work" (v. 31). Like the ten white curtains which formed the inner ceiling of the Tabernacle, the Veil was made of linen, on which the beautiful colours were wrought. But it was not merely linen, but of "fine twined linen," pointing to the moral excellency of Him who was foreshadowed. The same thought is given in the **"fine flour"** (Lev. 2:1), and in the **"refined gold"** (1 Chron. 28:18) and **"refined silver"** (1 Chron. 29:4), which was used in the Temple.

The whiteness of the pure linen used in the Veil pointed to the sinless purity of "the Man Christ Jesus" both in His inward thoughts and desires and in His outward ways and works. The eye of God, who is light, could rest upon that Holy One, and find every ray of His own perfect Being reflected in this lowly but lovely Son of man. "The fine linen of the Veil seems, then, especially to present to us 'the Righteous One,' who in His life of toil and sorrow, and most especially in His death of shame and suffering, manifested that unsullied purity, that perfect obedience, and that delight in accomplishing the will of His Father, whereby He has earned for Himself a name, which is above every name, the name of Jesus; 'Who was made sin for us, that we might be made the righteousness of God in Him'" (Mr. Soltau).

Attention should be called to the words "fine twined linen of **cunning work**," an expression used in connection with the Tabernacle only in the "linen" and the "breastplate." As there is nothing meaningless in Scripture we are assured there is a profound spiritual significance in this detail too. It tells us that this fabric was skilfully wrought: literally, the Hebrew is: "the work of a devisor." Divine wisdom was given for its manufacture and it was copied from a heavenly pattern: its equal never again being found on earth. As this "fine twined linen" foreshadowed the humanity of our Saviour, would not the "cunning work" point to the Divine omniscience in devising for Christ a human nature that was **sinless**? "A body hast **Thou** prepared Me" (Heb. 10:5) would give us the antitype. Gabriel's words to Mary betokened the **wonder** of Immanuel's birth—see Luke 1: 28-35.

### 2. Its Colours.

"And thou shalt make a veil of blue, and purple, and scarlet, and fine twined linen of cunning work." There is one little variation here from what was before us in 26:1. In connection with the Curtains, the ground-work of "fine twined linen" was mentioned first, ere the colours are specified; but here in the directions for the making of the Veil the colours are referred to first. This seems to intimate that our attention now is to be concentrated more on what was prefigured by the blue and purple and scarlet rather than on what was foreshadowed by the linen itself. The colours told of Heaven, the Cross and the Throne. Probably the colours were used so freely that little of the white linen would be visible.

### 3. Its Meaning.

This is specifically defined for us by the Holy Spirit in Hebrews 10:19, 20: "Having therefore, brethren, boldness to enter into the holiest by the blood of Jesus, by a new and living way, which He hath newly-made for us, through the veil, that is to say, **His flesh**." The Veil, then, spoke of the humanity of Christ, of the Son of God **incarnate**. The one side of it was seen by human eyes, as the Levites ministered in the Sanctuary; the other side was beheld only by Jehovah. The Veil, therefore, was a fitting type that Christ incarnate was perfect God and perfect Man. The colours which were embroidered upon it told of the perfections of His person. Its purpose was to shut out the priests of Israel from the holy of holies, where Jehovah had His earthly throne. The object of a veil is to hide. "Come not" (Lev. 16:2) was the warning which it consistently gave forth. Thus the Veil foreshadowed the moral glories of the Saviour, but at the same time showed, by the very display of such heavenliness of character, how far fallen man was away from God.

The perfect Manhood of Christ exhibited the only humanity which can approach unto God, which can live in His presence, which can dwell in the blazing light of His manifested glory. The perfections of the God-man only served to emphasise the imperfections of fallen man. The flawless life of Christ made the more evident the awful distance between the thrice holy God and depraved and guilty sinners. "The Incarnation of Christ, while it proclaimed God, shuts out man. Men might admire the beauty of the Veil; as men may to-day admire the human character of Christ after the flesh, and the teaching of His earthly life. But the more perfect we find that humanity, the greater the evidence that it is totally distinct from man's. The Incarnation by itself (apart from the **redemption** which was the purpose and object of it) neither brings man to God, nor God to men. True, it was 'God with us' just as the Tabernacle was with men: but, when the symbol of God's presence was with men, man could not have access to it. The beautiful Veil was an effectual bar, and its one and only voice was 'Come not.' The life of Christ on earth was an unceasing proclamation of the fact that only **His** humanity was shone upon by and dwelt in the glory of God. The proclamation of His life ever was: 'Except ye be holy, sinless, spotless, perfect, as I am, ye cannot enter into the presence of God. It was not the object of the Veil to give access to God; for it was that which prevented it. Even so it was not the perfection of Christ's life on earth that brings us into the presence of God" (Dr. E. W. Bullinger).

Typically, the Veil, in O.T. times, announced that the way in to God's presence was not then made manifest. It did not suggest that there **was** no way, but simply that the way was not then revealed. Subsequently, we find that Jehovah gave instructions as to how Israel's high priests **might** pass within the Veil, and that was, by the blood of sacrifice (Lev. 16:19). This, too, foreshadowed the coming Substance, yet also bore testimony to the temporary nature of that dispensation. It announced that the way for sinful man to go to God was by sacrifice, yet the one Aaron offered was not that which opened up the real way to God. The Veil unrent signified that the way into the Holiest was not yet revealed. The sacrifice by which Aaron went in once a year foreshadowed the perfect Sacrifice, and his admittance typified the entrance of our Great High Priest into the Heavenly Sanctuary.

"The Veil still unrent declared that if the way in was by sacrifice, the true Sacrifice—the one which really opened up the actual way to the presence of God—had not yet been provided. But if the unrent Veil signified that the true way was not yet made known, it also implied it would be made known. Faith, then, using what was a figure for the time then present, and what had been imposed on Israel until the time of reformation looked forward to the time of the revelation of the true Sacrifice and the manifestation of the true way of approach to God. Turning now to the N.T., we find that when Christ died as a Sacrifice the Veil of the Temple was rent from the top to the bottom. This rending of the Veil declared that the true way to God had been made known. The sacrifice of Christ is the true ground of approach to God. His death, His blood, has opened up the way to His presence. The rending of the Veil of the Temple when Christ died, was the sign that the way to God which faith had been taught to look forward to had been opened up. The Sacrifice which the yearly sacrifice of Lev. 16 had pointed forward to had been made, and the way to God, of which the Veil was a witness, while declaring it to be unmanifested, was now revealed" (Mr. C. Crain).

### 4. Its Cherubim.

"With cherubim shall it be made" (v. 31). The typical significance of the cherubim here is a double one, accordingly as we view the Veil itself in its twofold aspect. First, the Veil sets forth the excellencies of Christ's person as the incarnate Son of God. In this connection the cherubim would intimate that no matter whether the Lord Jesus be contemplated as the Man from Heaven (1 Cor. 15:47), yet in it (John 3:13), even when on earth (the "blue"); or on the Cross as an expiatory sacrifice (the "scarlet"); or on the Throne (the "purple"), He carries in His own person the judicial authority of the eternal God. Second, the Veil unrent signified that the perfections of Christ only served to emphasise the truth that sinful man had no access to God. This solemn fact would be the more impressively set forth by the cherubim wrought upon it. As the priests gazed on the Veil and saw the mystic figures standing out in vivid colours, would not their thoughts turn at once to what is recorded in Gen. 3:24? When God banished His rebellious creatures from Eden, He placed cherubim at the entrance to the Garden, with flaming sword which turned every way. Here on the Veil these cherubim taught the same lesson: sinful man, as such, cannot approach the ineffably holy God!

### 5. Its Position.

"And thou shalt hang up the Veil under the taches . . . and the veil shall divide unto you between the holy place and the most holy" (v. 33). The Veil was placed right over the entrance of the holy of holies and thus effectually shut out those who ministered in the holy place. God dwelt behind the Veil. Its very location, then, furnished the key to its significance. As the Veil sets forth the "flesh" of Christ, we are specifically taught that His humanity was the veil of the Godhead. God was enveiled, as well as unveiled, by the Lord Jesus. "God was in Christ reconciling the world unto Himself" (2 Cor. 5:19). And most effectively did the unsullied person of the Son of man bar the sinner's way unto God. This is self evident. If the humanity of Christ is the standard humanity, if it is the humanity in which alone God will dwell, if it is the only humanity which can enter the Glory, then the humanity of Christ is a barrier to the fallen sons of men. So long as Christ walked this earth He witnessed to the separation of the natural man from God.

"He stood forth, as the perfect Man, who alone was fit to appear before God; the standard weight of the sanctuary. Any one, weighed against Him, was found wanting. His perfect righteousness placed in dark shade the uncleanness of all men. The measure of His stature declared the utter insignficance of all human attainments. His fulness proved man's emptiness. The white and glistening purity of His character, exceeding white as snow, put to shame the filthiness of all that was born of woman. Thus, the very display of the Perfect One on earth, showed the impossibility of any approach to God, unless some way could be devised whereby the sinner could draw near, clothed in garments unsullied. Man, both Jew and Gentile, had made it plain that he was by nature a sinner, and had come short of the glory of God; and the presence amongst men, of One who was fit for that glory, only rendered the melancholy fact the more apparent. The Veil, as it hung on its golden pillars, precluded entrance into the holiest: the ark and the mercy-seat were hidden, instead of being laid open to public gaze" (Mr. G. Soltau).

### 6. Its Supports.

"And thou shalt hang it on four pillars of shittim wood overlaid with gold: their hooks shall be of gold, upon the four sockets of silver" (v. 32). The "pillars" of wood and gold, symbolized once more, the two natures in the God-man. They intimated that everything in redemption depended upon the **person** of Christ. Unless He had become Man, it had been impossible for Him to die; unless He had been more than Man, His sacrifice could not have availed. But being both God and Man He was fully competent to make propitation for the sins of His people. The whole value of His work accrues from the peerless excellency of His person. That these "pillars" were four in number, shows it is Christ on earth which was contemplated. It is to be carefully noted that these "four pillars" were without the "fillets" and "chapiters" which adorned the five pillars at the door of the Tabernacle (36:38): thus they lacked the architectural completeness of a pillar. Their abrupt termination pointed to the Saviour "cut off" in the midst of His days" (Isa. 53:8; Psa. 102: 23, 24).

But the **"four** pillars" were for another purpose: they served to display the **Veil** in all its beauty. Between them the Veil was stretched out. Without them, the Veil had hung in folds, and the loveliness of its embroidered designs would not have appeared. The Veil spoke of God the Son **incarnate.** Now the antitype of this is clearly before us in the opening books of the N.T. It is in the **four Gos**pels that the glories of the God-man are revealed to our eyes. They accomplish exactly the same design as did the "four pillars." In them we have spread out, as it were, the lovely antitypical Veil. There, too, we behold the "cunning work" of the Divine Designer, blending together the varied perfections of our blessed Lord, yet severally presenting Him as the Son of David, the flawless Servant, the Son of man, and the Son of God.

"Their hooks shall be of gold": not wooden hooks overlaid, but of solid gold. This is very beautiful. In connection with the ephod of the high priest we are told, "He made the ephod of gold, blue and purple, and scarlet, and fine twined linen. And they did beat the gold into thin plates, and cut it into wires, to work it in the blue, and in the purple, and in the scarlet, and in the fine linen" (39:2, 3). And, as we shall yet see, D.V., goldenstrands were also woven into other articles. But there were none in the fabric of the Veil. No wires of gold were mingled with the fine linen, which formed the basis of its structure. This could not be. for their presence would have implied that His humanity was commingled with His Deity, which was not the case. Though Deity and humanity were perfectly united in one Person, yet they are not confounded. Nevertheless, the Veil **was** held by "golden hooks" **from above,** thus signifying the Son of man was, throughout His earthly course, sustained and supported from on High!

"Upon the four sockets of silver." It was in them that the "four pillars" securely rested. As we saw in our last article, the "silver" was provided by the "atonement-money." How significant then is this detail of our type! The "sockets" conduct us to the foundation, and point to the redemptive-work of Christ on the cross. In perfect accord with this we may note that in Heb. 10:19, 20 the "blood of Jesus" and "the Veil" are brought together. God will never have it forgotten that the Cross is the basis of all blessing.

### 7. Its Rending.

The Veil unrent shut man out from God. It spoke of separation from Him because of sin. Between the priests and Jehovah stood this Veil. Between the ordinary worshipper in the outer court and Jehovah was a double partition, for he had no access into the holy place; while between the one outside the court was a threefold barrier between him and Jehovah! The whole ritual of Israel's worship emphasised the **distance** between God and the creature. Bounds were set about Sinai, so that not even a beast must touch it. One Tribe alone was permitted to encamp, immediately, around the Tabernacle: one family alone of that Tribe was singled out and allowed to enter the holy place: and one man alone of that family had access into the holiest, and that, only once a year, and with such awe-inspiring preparations and ceremonies as must have filled him with fear lest he should incur the judgment of the Most High. Yet, as previously intimated, God did, even then, give a hint, that a way would be made for sinners to approach Him. In Lev. 4:6 we learn that the priest was commanded to take of the blood of the sin-offering and sprinkle it seven times before the Lord, before the Veil of the sanctuary"! Clearer still was what was foreshadowed by the ritual of the Day of Atonement, when the high priest passed within the Veil (Lev. 16: 15). The antitype of this is found in Heb. 4:14; 6:19; 9:12. Christ has passed into Heaven itself, and what is more, He has opened up a way for us to enter too —Heb. 10:19, 20. But this was consequent upon His death.

"It was not the beauty of the veil which made entrance possible, but the sprinkling of atoning blood before it! That beauty might be admired by the worshipper: he might sing hymns in its praise, and give all sorts of sentimental and endearing names to it. He might use all kinds of poetical language in describing it; he might even copy it, and produce similiar patterns of embroidery, or schemes of colours; but there was only one way of passing to the other side of it, and of standing alive in the presence of God's glory; and that was by sprinkling the blood before it, and taking the blood of the victim beyond it. This blood told of substitution, and acknowledged that he who entered did so as a sinner, who had died, and suffered the wages of sin. By no other means could he stand on the other side of that veil and live.

"The great antitypical lesson for us all is, that it is not by the beautiful life of Christ that we can enter into the presence of God. It is not by any 'imitation of Christ,' not by the observance of any Rules for Daily Living, not by leading a religious and devout life, that we can pass beyond that veil. To attempt it is to confess our ignorance of the very first letter of the Christian's alphabet; and it is to own that we are destitute of the first fundamental lesson of the Christian's life. It is only when the precious blood of that perfect humanity of Christ had been shed that it avails us as our title to enter God's presence. This is why, in 1 John 1:7, when speaking of our entrance into the light of God's presence, and walking therein, that we are at once reminded of that Blood, which alone gives us our title to enter, and preserves us alive when we have entered into that Presence. 'God is light....If we walk in the light as He is in the light, we have fellowship one with another, and the blood of Jesus Christ His Son cleanseth us from all sin!' It is here, in this connection, that the cleansing-power of the blood is mentioned; not in connection with our sin or sinning.

"When it is a case of sin, then it is that we are reminded, not of the atoning blood of Christ, but of our Advocate with the Father! Then it is that we are simply assured of two facts:—(1) that relationship is not broken; God is still our Father; and (2) that Christ is our all-sufficient propitiation (1 John 2:1). But it is in connection with approaching to and walking in the light of God's presence within the veil that we are reminded of the blood which must first be sprinkled before we can have either admission to Him, or preservation when there (1 John 1:7). Hence it is not the life which Christ lived in His spotless humanity (still less our own imperfect copy of it) that gives us liberty to enter, but only when that humanity had been stained by His own blood of atonement. Then it is that we have 'boldness to enter into the Holiest, by the blood of Jesus, by a newly-slain and living way, which He hath newly-made (or opened) for us, through the veil, that is to say, His flesh' Heb. 10:19, 20" (Dr. B. W. Bullinger).

The historical reference to what is referred to in Heb. 10 is given us in the Gospels. There we learn that simultaneous with the death of Christ the veil was rent. (Matt. 27: 45-52.) There are some remarkable resemblances between the shadow and the Substance. First, the veil was rent while hanging between heaven and earth: so Christ was smitten while suspended from the Cross. Second, the veil was rent in twain from the top, this showed it was down by the same Hand as had fallen so heavily on the suffering Substitute—see Psa. 38:2; 42: 7; 88:6, 7; Isa. 53:10; Zech. 13:7. This is the only type where God Himself represented by His own act that it was His hand which smote the Lord Jesus! Third, it was rent "from the top to the bottom" —not an inch of it was left untorn: so the atoning work of Calvary was a complete one, nothing being left for the sinner to do or add. Fourth, it was rent "in the midst" (Luke 23:45), and thus the Mercy-seat in the centre of the holy of holies would be fully revealed: so the believing sinner is not asked to approach God in any roundabout way, or through a side entrance, but has direct access to the Father through the Son. The rending of the veil in the midst, would be such that all within the temple would see it: so the death of Christ was not in a corner, but public and before many eye-witnesses. Fifth, the veil was rent the moment that Christ died (Matt. 27:50), showing that the barrier between God and the contrite sinner was gone. Sixth, as soon as the veil was rent it was changed from a barrier to a gateway: the moment Christ died a "newly-slain and living way" was opened for sinners to God. Seventh, it is deeply significant that the Holy Spirit has linked together the rending of the veil with the opening of the graves (Matt. 27:51, 52), though in time the latter did not occur till after Christ's resurrection. Does not this tell us that, full atonement having been made by Him, a way has been made from the deepest depths into which sin had plunged us, into the highest heaven where grace has placed us!

The purpose of God has now been accomplished. The Corn of wheat, having fallen into the ground and died, now bringeth forth much fruit (John 12:24). The Blood has been shed, the Sacrifice has been offered, the Veil has been rent; and Christ, as the Forerunner of His people, has passed into the Holiest. We then may draw near. Because Christ received the wages of sin which were due us, we share the reward which was due Him. We may boldly enter in. By faith we have unhindered access into the Heavenly Sanctuary. Every barrier having been removed, the believing worshipper may, with perfect liberty, draw near to the Throne of Grace. Then "**let us draw near**, with a true heart, in full assurance of faith, having our hearts sprinkled from an evil conscience" (Heb. 10:22).

Arthur W. Pink.

## CROSS-BEARING.

**"Then said Jesus unto His disciples, If any man come after Me, let him deny himself, and take up his cross, and follow Me." (Matt. 16: 24).**

"Then said Jesus unto His disciples, if any man will"—the word "will" here means "desire to" just as in that verse, "If any will live godly." It signifies "determine to." "If any man will or desires to come after Me, let him deny himself and take up his cross (not a cross, but his cross) and follow Me." Then in Luke 14.27 Christ declared, "And whosoever doth not bear his cross, and come after Me, cannot be My disciple." So it is not optional. The Christian life is far more than subscribing to a system of truth or adopting a code of conduct, or of submitting to religious ordinances. Preeminently the Christian life is a personal experience of fellowship with the Lord Jesus, and just in proportion as your life is lived in communion with Christ, to that extent are you living the **Christian** life, and to that extent only.

The Christian life is a life that consists of following Jesus. "If any man will come after Me, let him deny himself, and take up his cross, and **follow Me**." O that you and I may gain distinction for the closeness of our walk to Christ, and then shall we be "close communionists" indeed. There is a class described in Scripture of whom it is said, "These are they which follow the Lamb whithersoever He goeth": but sad to say, there is another class, and a large class, who seem to follow the Lord fitfully, spasmodically, half-heartedly, occasionally, distantly. There is much of the world and much of self in their lives, and so little of Christ. Thrice happy shall he be who like Caleb followeth the Lord fully.

Now, beloved, our chief business and aim is to follow Christ, but there are difficulties in the way. There are obstacles in the path, and it is to them that the first part of our text refers. You notice that the words "follow Me" come at the end. Self, **self** stands in the way, and **the world** with its ten thousand attractions and distractions is an obstacle; and therefore Christ says, "If any man will come after Me—(first) let him deny himself, (second) take up his cross, (third) and follow Me." And **there** we learn the reason why so few professing Christians **are** following Him closely, manifestly, consistently.

The first step toward a daily following of Christ is the denying of self. There is a vast difference, brethren and sisters, between denying self and so-called self-denial. The popular idea that obtains both in the world and among Christians is that of giving up things which we like. There is a great diversity of opinion as to what should be given up. There are some who would restrict it to that which is characteristically worldly, such as theatregoing, dancing, and the racecourse. There are others who would restrict it to a certain season when amusements and other things which are followed during the remainder of the year are rigidly eschewed at that time. But such methods as those only foster spiritual pride, for surely I deserve some credit if I give up so much! Ah, my friends, what Christ speaks of in our text (and O may the Spirit of God apply it to our souls this morning) as the first step toward following Him, is, the denial of self itself, not simply some of the things that are pleasing to self, not some of the things after which self hankers, but the denying of self itself. What does that mean—"If any man will come after Me, let him deny himself"? It means in the first place, abandoning his own righteousness; but it means far more than that. That is only its first meaning. It means refusing to rest upon my own wisdom. It means far more than that. It means ceasing to insist upon my own rights. It means repudiating self itself. It means ceasing to consider our own comforts, our own ease, our own pleasure, our own aggrandisement, our own benefits. It means being done with self. It means, beloved, saying with the apostle, For me to live is, not self, but Christ. For me to live is to obey Christ, to serve Christ, to honor Christ, to spend myself for Him. That is what it means. And "if any man will come after Me," says our Master, "let him deny himself," let self be repudiated, be done with. In other words it is what you have in Romans 12:1, "Present your bodies a living sacrifice unto Him."

Now the second step toward following Christ is the taking up of the cross. "If any man will come after Me, let him deny himself, and take up his cross." Ah, my friends, to live out the Christian life is something more than a passive luxury; it is a serious undertaking. It is a life that has to be disciplined in sacrifice. The life of discipleship begins with self-renunciation and it continues by self-mortification. In other words, our text refers to the cross not simply as an object of faith, but as a principle of life, as the badge of discipleship, as an experience in the soul. And, listen! Just as it was true that the only way to the Father's throne for Jesus of Nazareth was by the cross, so the only way for a life of communion with God and the crown at the end for the Christian is via the cross. The legal benefits of Christ's sacrifice are secured by faith, when the guilt of sin is cancelled; but the cross only becomes efficacious over the power of indwelling sin as it is realised in our daily lives. .

I want to call your attention to the context. Turn with me for a moment to Matthew 16, verse 21:—"From that time forth began Jesus to show unto His disciples, how that He must go unto Jerusalem, and suffer many things of the elders and chief priests and scribes, and be killed, and be raised again the third day. Then Peter took Him, and began to rebuke Him." He was staggered and said, "Pity Thyself, Lord." That expressed the policy of the world. That is the sum of the world's philosophy— self-shielding and self-seeking; but that which Christ preached was not "spare" but "sacrifice." The Lord Jesus saw in Peter's suggestion a temptation from Satan and He flung it from Him. Then He turned to His disciples and said, "If any man will come after Me, let him deny himself, and take up his cross, and follow Me." In other words what Christ said was this: I am going up to Jerusalem to the cross: if anyone would be My follower there is a cross for him. And, as Luke 14 says, "Whosoever doth not bear his cross cannot be My disciple." Not only must Jesus go up to Jerusalem and be killed, but everyone who comes after Him must take up his cross. The "must" is as imperative in the one case as in the other. Mediatorially the cross of Christ stands alone, but experimentally it is shared by all who enter into life.

Now then, what does "the cross" stand for? What did Christ mean when He said that except a man take up his cross? My friends, it is deplorable that at this late date such a question needs to be asked, and it is more deplorable still that the vast majority of God's own people have such unscriptural conceptions of what the "cross" stands for. The average Christian seems to regard the cross in this text as any trial or trouble that may be laid upon him. Whatever comes up that disturbs our peace, that is unpleasing to the flesh, that irritates our temper, is looked upon as a cross. One says, "Well, that is my cross," and another says, "Well, this is my cross," and someone else says something else is their cross. My friends, the word is never so used in the New Testament. The word "cross" is never found in the plural number, nor is it ever found with the indefinite article before it—"a cross." Note also that in our text the cross is linked to a verb in the active voice and not the passive. It is not a cross that is laid upon us, but a cross which must be "taken up"! The cross stands for definite realities which embody and express the leading characteristics of Christ's agony.

Others understand the "cross" to refer to disagreeable duties which they reluctantly discharge, or to fleshly habits which they grudgingly deny. They imagine that they are cross-bearing when, prodded at the point of conscience, they abstain from things earnestly desired. Such people invariably turn their cross into a weapon with which to assail other people. They parade their self-denial and go around insisting that others should follow them. Such conceptions of the cross are as Pharisaical as false, and as michievous as they are erroneous.

Now, as the Lord enables me, let me point out three things that the cross stands for. First, **the cross is the expression of the world's hatred.** The world hated the Christ of God and its hatred was ultimately manifested by crucifying Him. In the 15th chapter of John, seven times over, Christ refers there to the hatred of the world against Himself and against His people; and just in proportion as you and I are following Christ, just in proportion as our lives are being lived as His life was lived, just in proportion as we have come out from the world and are in fellowship with Him, so will the world **hate us.**

We read in the Gospels that one man came and presented himself to Christ for discipleship, and he requested that he might first go and bury his father—a very natural request, a very praiseworthy one surely (?)—and the Lord's reply is almost staggering. He said to that man, "Follow Me; and let the dead bury their dead." What would have happened to that young man if he had obeyed Christ? I do not know whether he did or not, but if he did, what would happen? What would his kinsfolk and his neighbours think of him? Would they be able to appreciate the motive, the devotion that caused him to follow Christ and neglect what the world would call a filial duty? Ah, my friends, if you are following Christ the world will think you are mad, and some natures and dispositions find it very hard to bear reflections on their sanity. Yes, there are some who find the reproaches of the living a harder trial than the loss of the dead.

Another young man presented himself to Christ for discipleship and he requested the Lord that he might first be allowed to go home and say farewell to his friends—a very natural request, surely—and the Lord presented to him the cross: "No man, having put his hand to the plough, and looking back, is fit for the kingdom of God"! Affectionate natures find the wrench of home-ties hard to bear; harder still are the suspicions of loved ones and friends for having been slighted. Yes, the reproach of the world becomes very real if we are following Christ closely. No man can keep in with the world and follow Him.

Another young man came and presented himself to Christ and fell at His feet and worshipped Him, and said, "Master, what good thing shall I do?" And the Lord presented to him the cross. "Sell all that thou hast and give to the poor ....and come and follow Me." And the young man went away sorrowful. And Christ is still saying to you and to me this morning, "Whosoever doth not bear his cross, and come after Me, cannot be My disciple." The cross stands for the reproach and the hatred of the world. But as the cross was **voluntary** for Christ, so it is for His disciple. It can either be avoided or accepted; ignored or "taken up"!

But secondly, **the cross stands for a life that is voluntarily surrendered to the will of God.** From the standpoint of the world the death of Christ was a brutal murder, but from the standpoint of Christ Himself His death was a voluntary sacrifice. Turn for a moment to the 10th of John, beginning at the 17th verse:— "Therefore doth My Father love Me, because I lay down My life, that I might take it again. No man taketh it from Me, but I lay it down of Myself. I have power to lay it down, and I have power to take it again." Why did He thus lay down His life? Look at the closing sentence of verse 18: "This commandment have I received of My Father." The cross was the last demand of God upon the obedience of His Son. That is why we read in Phillippians 2 that, He "being in the form of God, thought it not robbery to be equal with God: but made Himself of no reputation, and took upon Him the form of a servant, and was made in the likeness of men: and being found in fashion as a man, He humbled Himself, and became **obedient unto death**" (that was the climax, that was the end of the path of obedience)—"even the death of the cross."

Christ has left us an example that we should follow His steps. The obedience of Christ should be the obedience of the Christian—voluntary, not compulsory—voluntary, continuous, faithful, without any reserve, unto death. The cross then stands for obedience, consecration, surrender, a life placed at the disposal of God. "If any man will come after Me, let him take up his cross and follow Me" and "Whosoever doth not bear his cross and come after Me, cannot be My disciple." In other words, dear friends, the cross stands for the principle of discipleship, our life being actuated by the same principle that Christ's was. He came here and He pleased not Himself: no more must I. He made Himself of no reputation: so must I. He went about doing good: so should I. He came not to be ministered unto but to minister: so should we. He became obedient unto death, even the death of the cross. That is what the cross stands for: first, the reproach of the world—because we have antagonised it, raised its ire by separating ourselves from it, and are walking on a different plane, and through being actuated by different principles from those by which it walks. Second, a life sacrificed unto God—laid down in devotion unto Him.

In the third place, the cross stands for **vicarious sacrifice and suffering.** Turn to the first Epistle of John, the third chapter, verse 16: "Hereby perceive we the love of God, because He laid down His life for us: and we ought to lay down our lives." That is the logic of Calvary. We are called unto fellowship with Christ, our lives to be lived by the same principles that His was lived by—obedience to God, sacrifice for others. He died that we might live; and, my friends, we have to die that we may live. Look at the 25th verse of Matthew 16: "For whosoever will save his life shall lose it": that means every Christian, for Christ was speaking there to disciples. Every Christian who has lived a self-centred life, considering his own comforts, his own peace of mind, his own welfare, his own advantages and benefits, that "life" is going to be lost for ever—all wasted so far as eternity is concerned; wood, hay and stubble, that will go up in smoke. But "whosoever will lose his life for My sake," that is, whosoever has not lived his life considering his own well-being, his own interests, his own profit, his own advancement, but has sacrificed that life, has spent it in the service of others for Christ's sake; he shall find—"find" what? —he shall find it, not something else: it, not another: he shall find it. That life has been immortalised, perpetuated, it has been built of imperishable materials that will survive the testing-fire in the day to come. He shall find "it." He died that we might live, and we have to die if we are to live! Whosoever will lose his life for My sake shall find it."

Again, in the 20th chapter of John, Christ said to His disciples, "As the Father hath sent Me, even so send I you." What was Christ sent here to do? To glorify the Father; to express God's love; to manifest God's grace; to weep over Jerusalem; to have compassion on the ignorant and those that are out of the way; to toil so assiduously that He had no leisure so much as to eat; to live a life of such self-sacrifice that even His kinsfolk said, "He is beside Himself." And, "as the Father hath sent Me, even so," says Christ, "send I you." In other words, I send you back into the world out of which I have saved you. I send you back into the world to live with the cross stamped upon you. O brethren and sisters, how little "blood" there is in our lives! How little is there the bearing of the dying of Jesus in our bodies (II. Cor. 4:10).

Have we begun to "take up the cross" at all? Is there any wonder that we are following Him at such a distance? Is there any wonder that we have such little victory over the power of indwelling sin? There is a reason for that. Mediatorially the cross of Christ stands alone, but experimentally the cross is to be shared by all His disciples. Legally the cross of Calvary annulled and put away our guilt, the guilt of our sins; but, my friends, I am perfectly convinced that the only way of getting deliverance from the power of sin in our lives and obtaining mastery over the old man within us, is by the cross becoming a part of the experience of our souls. It was at the cross sin was dealt with legally and judicially: it is only as the cross is "taken up" by the disciple that it becomes an experience—slaying the power and defilement of sin within us. And Christ says, "Whosoever doth not bear his cross, cannot be My disciple." O what need has each Christian here this morning to get alone with the Master and consecrate Himself to His service.

---

Sermon preached by the Editor in Sydney.

## BLIND BARTIMAEUS.

"And they came to Jericho: and as He went out of Jericho with His disciples and a great number of people, blind Bartimaeus, the son of Timaeus, sat by the highway side begging. And when he heard that it was Jesus of Nazareth, he began to cry out and say, Jesus, thou Son of David, have mercy on me, And many charged him that he should hold his peace: but he cried the more a great deal, Thou Son of David, have mercy on me. And Jesus stood still, and commanded him to be called." (Mark 10: 46-49).

In the verses I have just read the Spirit of God has drawn a picture that most strikingly and accurately depicts the condition, the conduct and the success of a sinner who sought Christ. The case of Bartimaeus is full of important instruction to any who are really exercised about their spiritual state and are anxious to rejoice in God's salvation. It has been recorded for the encouragement of such, and my earnest prayer to God is that He may be pleased to use our exposition of this passage to the liberation of some who may now be in bondage. In this picture there are at least ten distinct lines and each one of them, separately, might profitably engage our attention for the whole hour, but as our time will not permit me to dwell at length upon each, I will just briefly notice some and comment at greater length on the others.

The first thing I want you to notice in this seeker after Christ—Bartimaeus—was his condition. Two words sum up his state: he was blind, and he was a beggar. As such he accurately portrays the state of the natural man, for all of Adam's fallen race are born into this world in a state of spiritual darkness, and they are in the dark because they are blind. As Ephesians 4, 17 and 18 says, "Walk not as other Gentiles walk, in the vanity of their mind, having the understanding darkened, being alienated from the life of God through the ignorance that is in them, because of the blindness of their heart." Because the sinner is blind he sees not the awfulness of his own condition. Because he is blind he perceives not the imminency of his danger, the urgency and desperateness of his case; and, furthermore, recognises not the only One who can deliver him. So that just as Bartimaeus was blind, so the sinner is spiritually.

Furthermore, we are told that he was a beggar. That is to say he was poor— so poor that he was dependent upon charity. He had only that which was gratuitously given to him. And that also is true of the sinner. Spiritually the unconverted are bankrupts: they have nothing whatever to their credit before God. Scripture says there is none that doeth good, no, not one. Hence the sinner is unable to purchase his salvation, for he has nothing with which to buy it. But that is something about which all sinners are ignorant until the Holy Spirit of God reveals it to them. The attitude and the sentiment of the natural mind is that of the Laodiceans, who boasted that they were rich and increased in goods and had need of nothing, and knew not that they were blind and poor and miserable and wretched and naked. But it is a hopeful sign when the sinner has come to the place where he recognises that he is spiritually blind, and longs for that spiritual sight which only Christ can give. It is a happy omen when he is made to realise and feel his spiritual poverty, and desires the true riches—the riches of God's grace. Such an one is not far from the kingdom of God.

In the second place, I want you to notice attentively the conduct of this man while he was seeking sight. By the mercy of God, Bartimaeus acted in such a manner that he may be held up as an example to all those who are seeking the light of life. Bartimaeus was a very notable character. There is a clear-cut individuality about him which at once raises him above the level of the commonplace, for he was a man who thought and acted for himself. He was not quickly daunted, and he was not easily swayed. I suppose that as poor Bartimaeus sat there by the wayside, in his darkness, day after day, he had meditated much. Probably his thoughts had turned to the Old Testament prophecies that announced the coming of the Messiah, which foretold that when He did come He would open the eyes of the blind and would preach the Gospel to the poor. And then I doubt not that as he had sat there he had heard the reports which were being circulated all over the land that a great physician was now in their midst, ministering to the needy, healing the sick, cleansing the leper; and I have no doubt that Bartimaeus had compared those reports with the prophecies that he knew concerning the Messiah in the Holy Scriptures, and he had discovered that they were identical—that the reports concerning Jesus of Nazareth accurately corresponded with the prophecies concerning the Messiah, and he realised that Jesus of Nazareth must be none other than the Son of David. He concluded that the claims which were being made by Jesus of Nazareth harmonised with what was recorded concerning the promised Messiah. Have you, my friend, ever pondered carefully the claims of Christ? He has said, "I am the Door: by Me if any man enter in, he shall be saved." That is His claim. Have you pondered it? He says, "He that cometh to Me shall never hunger and he that believeth on Me shall never thirst." Have you put Him to the test? Satisfied that Jesus of Nazareth was the true Messiah, I doubt not that Bartimaeus had formed the resolution that if He ever came his way he would seek sight at His hands and cast himself on the mercy of this Friend of sinners.

Now notice the 47th verse: I want you to keep your Bibles open at this passage —"And when he heard that it was Jesus of Nazareth, he began to cry out." First of all let me emphasise the fact that Bartimaeus, this seeker after the Saviour, used the faculties that he did have. In some quarters there is so much said about the inability of the natural man to perform acts of grace, there is such a disproportionate emphasis laid upon the helplessness of the creature, that a most deplorable and a tragic lethargy has been fostered and encouraged. And I am afraid there are some present to-night who are so obsessed with this do-nothing-ism that they sadly need to be shaken up and aroused to a sense of their responsibility. Now what I want to point out particularly is this: though Bartimaeus was unable to see, he could hear and he could shout. And I want to press upon the unconverted here to-night that it will be time enough for you to talk about what you cannot do, when you have done what you can do.

I am afraid some of my brethren are saying in themselves, What, are we going to hear about the ability of the natural man? Yes, you are. I am quite sure there are some things that the natural man can do, which some of you have not done; and it is a species of hypocrisy and dishonesty for you to shelter behind your inability when you have not used the strength that God has already given you. Now listen. Some of you can attend the services of God's house and hear the Gospel more frequently than you do. That is something you can do. Some of you can read God's Word more often and more diligently than you do. And what is more, you can cry to God for mercy. You have the same vocal organs to cry unto God with as you have to speak to your fellow-man with, and I say it is a species of hypocrisy for you to shelter behind your inability when you have not done what you can do. Now listen. It is true that Bartimaeus could not see: he was blind: but he could hear with the outward ear and he could cry for mercy with the outward mouth; and he did, and in consequence he received a blessing. Yes, my friends, there will be plenty of time for you to think about and talk about what you cannot do, when you have done what you can do. As a matter of fact your very inability is simply a species of perversity and obstinacy. You cannot, because you will not!

Now I want you to notice the circumstances of this case. Come back again to verse 46:—"And they came to Jericho: and as He went out of Jericho with His disciples and a great number of people, blind Bartimaeus, the son of Timaeus, sat by the highway side begging." What I want to point out there is this. No human being prompted him. No sympathetic friend whispered in his ear, "Jesus of Nazareth is passing by, now is your opportunity; cast yourself upon His pity." No, he sat there alone: the crowd was around Jesus as He was walking along. It is just possible there may be a soul here to-night who can say, "No one careth for my soul." Apparently none cared for poor Bartimaeus, but O, with the majority of you, the conditions and the situation are far different! How often you have been entreated; how often people have manifested an interest in your soul! O how this man Bartimaeus should put you to shame! There was no sympathetic friend that spoke to him. There was no one inviting him to avail himself of the presence of Jesus, and yet, notwithstanding that, without any encouragements, he cried out, "Son of David have mercy on me."

In the third place I want us to follow his experiences—the experiences of this soul seeking after the Saviour. Verse 48: "And many charged him that he should hold his peace." That is all he got at first for his pains. He was tested!— did he really mean what he said; was he truly in earnest? He lifted up his voice and cried unto Jesus for mercy and the spectators told him to shut up. Notice the word "charged": They did not just suggest to him in a mild way that he had better be still, but they spoke authoritatively—they charged him: Be still will you! They thought it was very infra dig. They considered it was a matter of impropriety that he should shout out in that vulgar manner. They charged him that he should hold his peace. I greatly fear that there are many congregations to-day who would act in a similar manner, were some convicted sinner present to audibly cry to God for mercy. Never having groaned themselves under the intolerable burden of a convicted conscience, they would not understand the conduct of one who did.

But what are we told? Verse 48: "He cried the more a great deal." Yes, he was in earnest. He was not to be silenced! The more they snubbed him the more he cried out. It was like pouring oil on a fire. Yes, and when a sinner is determined to find Christ at all costs, the more the Devil opposes him and the more the Devil's agents seek to hinder him, the greater efforts he puts forth. He is more determined still to overcome every difficulty and opposition until he actually obtains that which he is seeking. This man was blind, mind you, and he realised that Jesus was passing by. Now was his opportunity and he was not going to let people prevent him from availing himself of it. He was not going to be silenced by them. He did not mind what the critics thought; he was determined to shout all the louder, "Son of David have mercy on me." Ah, my friends, how many there are who are intimidated and who were hindered from seeking Christ because of the frowns and sneers of the world? He cried out the more. Are you going to let the scoffs of the ungodly cause you to miss heaven? O you must expect rebuffs, but what matters the sneers of the world if you have the smile of Christ?

I want you to notice that he had another discouragement. "And many charged him that he should hold his peace: but he cried the more a great deal, Thou Son of David, have mercy on me. And Jesus stood still" (vv. 48, 49). Jesus did not stand still the first time he called. Apparently Jesus paid no attention to him at his first supplication for mercy. It was not until he had cried out "a great deal more" that Jesus stood still. And yet even that did not deter Bartimaeus, for he cried out the louder. Apparently the Great Physician was passing by unheeding, failing to grant this poor blind beggar his desire and give him sight. Yes, my friends, the Lord loves earnestness and importunity. There may be one here who has cried for mercy and apparently the Lord has not answered. Be not discouraged, beloved. He may be testing you. He may be seeing whether you really mean what you say, whether you are really in earnest or not. Follow the example of this blind beggar and cry out the more a great deal.

Verse 49: "And Jesus stood still and commanded him to be called." Yes, and Jesus calls for thee! Perhaps someone says, I wish I could be sure of that: O I wish I could be sure that Jesus is calling for me! Well, He is: He is calling for you! The Gospel is to be preached to every creature. You are a "creature," are you not? Then it is for you! The terms of the Gospel are, "Whosoever believeth," and I refuse to narrow them. The Gospel is as free as the air you breathe. What is the Gospel but a presentation of Christ, a Saviour sufficient for the chief of sinners? What is the Gospel but Christ calling to the sinner, "Come unto Me"? And the Gospel is for every creature, therefore it is for you. Never mind about election. Do not confuse your mind by bringing in other subjects now. Think only of Christ.

"And Jesus commanded that he should be called." Yes, called even while he was yet blind. You do not have to be enlightened to qualify you for coming to Jesus. Some of you have got to learn yet what the real Gospel is and the first principles of it. The Gospel is for someone else besides enlightened souls. Do you get that? Jesus called Bartimaeus while he was yet blind. And He is calling for you, my friend, you who are spiritually blind. There is a welcome for you if you will come, I care not who you are, what your record may be, how many or how great your sins. There is a Saviour for you if you will come. He calleth for thee! O may He give you grace to respond. The Master is come and calleth for thee.

"And Jesus stood still, and commanded him to be called. And they call the blind man, saying unto him, Be of good comfort." Yes, the very people who had been rebuffing him, the very people who had told him to hold his peace, the very people who had been discouraging him, now encouraged him. Human nature is very fickle isn't it? I was very much amused: it was ludicrous to read through the commentators' explanations. I won't waste your time by repeating them, but it seems to me the key is right in the passage. Evidently this crowd when they saw Jesus stand still were anxious to see

Him perform a miracle. They were sensationalists, curiosity-mongers, who loved to see wonders performed. As soon as they saw Jesus arrest His steps they said, "Be of good comfort, rise; He calleth thee." And so I would endeavour by the Lord's help to speak a word of comfort, a word of cheer, to any seeking, burdened, distressed sinner to-night. "He calleth for thee." And again I say, no matter who you may be, no matter what your history may be, no matter how many vows and resolutions you have broken, no matter how many times you have turned a deaf ear to the voice of God's Word, He is still calling for thee. See Prov. 8:4!

Now in the last place I want you to notice his salvation. Verse 50: "And he, casting away his garment." In the first place observe that this man did not rest in these words of comfort that he had received from the people, but arose and cast off his garment. He had heard a word of comfort but he did not rest in it. He had received a word of encouragement but he did not allow that to make him continue in a passive condition. The word of comfort had no more deterring effect upon him than the rebukes had. And so I want to say to those here to-night who are unsaved, you may often have heard words of comfort—yes, and some of them very unwise words too—for there are still false comforters, like Job's comforters of old; I mean those who would seek to speak words of peace to you who are still in unbelief, and encourage a state of passivity, do-nothing-ism. "O you have nothing very much to fear, you are the child of many prayers; I am sure that God is going to save you when His good time comes"—encouraging you in your unbelief. O unsaved friends, pay no attention to such wretched counsel, any more than blind Bartimaeus did. Follow his example and seek Christ for yourself, for I am going to tell you plainly God's time to pardon never will come until you believe in Christ for yourself. There is no more spiritual sight to be given to you than there was physical sight given to Bartimaeus while you remain away from Christ. Bartimaeus had to come to Christ for himself, and so have you, if ever your eyes are going to be opened. "And he, casting away his garment." I have no doubt that that referred to the outer cloak. It is in the singular number. And that garment had been very precious to him as he had sat there all weathers, day after day, by the wayside. But precious or not, he was willing to lose anything, if only he could gain his sight. Anything that impeded him he cast away as worthless. O young man or young woman, if ungodly companions are an impediment in your path, stand in your way of seeking after Christ, cast them away as Bartimaeus did his cloak. (A friend has since suggested that the "garment" typified the sinner's filthy rags of self-righteousness, which have to be abandoned before Christ saves.)

Now notice again in verse 50: "And he, casting away his garment, rose," or, as the Greek is, "leapt to his feet." He was no laggard. He evidently was not a believer in this do-nothing-ism. He knew that now was his opportunity, and he determined to make the most of it. Jesus was passing by. Yes, and He never came that way any more. That was the last time that He ever passed through Jericho! And Bartimaeus seized his opportunity. O that you too might seek the Lord while He is to be found. "Strive to enter in at the straight gate: for many, I say unto you, will seek to enter in, and shall not be able, when once the Master of the house is risen up, and hath shut to the door."

Again notice in verse 50: "And he casting away his garment, rose, and came to"—Peter? No, he did not stop half way. He did not stop short at the apostles, he came to Jesus Himself. How often an anxious sinner comes to the poor preacher. Ah, my friend, your need lies deeper than any human hand can reach down to. No preacher on earth can help you, my friend: you are only wasting your time to seek out these professional evangelists and preachers. They cannot help you. Some of you have tried them, haven't you? And poor physicians you found them. O heed the example of Bartimaeus. He cast away his garment, he rose, and he came to Jesus.

Now verse 51:—"And Jesus answered and said unto him, What wilt thou that I should do unto thee?" Well, didn't He know? Wasn't Christ omniscient? Wasn't He fully aware of all the details of this case and the desires of this man's heart? Why ask him such a question? "What wilt thou that I should do unto thee?" Jesus requires a full confession, a pouring out of the heart to Him. Jesus requires that you should get alone with Him and unbosom yourself to Him. "What wilt thou that I should do unto thee?" Tell Him your case; describe the details of it to Him. O do not tell Him that you have not got suitable language.

My friends, what He wants is sincerity. Tell Him that you are a Hell-deserving wretch, and will perish unless His grace rescues you. Tell Him that you are a sinner undone and that only He can save you. "What wilt thou that I should do unto thee?" Tell Him what you want, sinner! The mere hearing of sermons isn't going to save you. You can come to church every Sunday for the rest of your life, even if you live to be as old as Methuselah, but merely sitting still in the pews listening to the preacher won't save you. O go home and get alone in your own chamber; kneel down and frankly tell Him your case; hide nothing; out with it; be honest before Him; tell Him what a wicked lost sinner you are, and cast yourself on His mercy. Or, better still, do it where you are sitting even now, for your life might be taken from you before you get home.

"What wilt thou that I should do unto thee?" The blind man said, "Lord, that I might receive my sight. And Jesus said unto him, Go thy way; thy faith hath made thee whole. And immediately he received his sight." Yes, and so shall you, to-night, now, this moment, if you will come to Him as Bartimaeus came, without reserve, conscious of your blindness, realising your need. He will give you sight immediately. Put Him to the test and see. He never turned away one soul yet. He never will. No case ever baffled Him. No case was too desperate for Him to heal. He is mighty to save! You may be a mighty big sinner: I am sure you are—bigger than you realise even now; but He is a mighty Saviour. O put Him to the proof, my friend. Why delay any longer? He calleth for thee.

Now one last word. The closing line in the picture here is very beautiful. "And Jesus said unto him, Go thy way: thy faith hath made thee whole. And immediately he received his sight, and followed Jesus in the way." It is pitiable beyond words to see the miserable explanations of almost all of the commentators on that verse. Jesus said, "Go thy way" and most of them tell us that he disobeyed Him, but that it was a commendable disobedience. What rubbish! How could disobedience ever be commendable? Notice carefully that Jesus did not say "Go away," but He said, "Go thy way." And, my friends, he obeyed; he did not disobey. Look at the balance of the verse, the last sentence: "And immediately he received his sight, and followed Jesus in the way." He says, Lord, that is my way! When Jesus said "Go thy way" it was a word of testing; and Bartimaeus says, Well, this is my way—to follow Thee: Thy way is now my way! He followed Jesus in the way.

"Go thy way" was a word to test him out. Ah, my friends, did not Bartimaeus make a good use of his sight? There was no fairer object to gaze upon than the Son of David, and now he enlisted under His banner and became one of His followers. he followed Jesus. Do you know whither he followed Him? I wonder how many of you have ever thought that over. This occurred less than one week before the crucifixion. He followed Jesus up to Jerusalem, where, in a few days, his newly-found Saviour was spat upon and scourged and crucified. He followed a rejected and a hated Christ; but he followed Him! "Go thy way" said the Saviour to him. Well here is my choice, Lord; this is my preference: I am going Your way. He followed Jesus in the way. Is not that a beautiful closing line in the picture?

O dear friends, do not tell me that God has given you sight, unless you are following Him in the way. Do not make profession that your eyes have been opened unless you are following Jesus. That is the closing line in the picture. O beloved, follow Him, follow Him in His own ordained way through the waters of baptism. Follow Him in the way. Ah, what the cause of Christ needs to-day is soldiers—brave men and women. We have too many of those half-hearted people who turn timorous when the world shrugs its shoulders at them. This is a generation that calls for Daniels and Esthers. May God give you holy boldness to follow Jesus in the way, to cast in your lot with a despised Saviour and to take your place with those who are seeking to honor Him. What would become of the churches and what would become of the preaching of the Gospel and what would become of the ministry of the Word if everyone did as you do? I mean those of you who profess to be Christians and are on the outside? Supposing everyone followed your course—well there would be no churches. And, my friends, if there had been no church here I would not be in Sydney to-night. Had there been no Belvoir Street Church, I would not have been in Sydney this length of time. It is only by the grace of God that there was an open door and the people here that stood for the whole counsel of God. O may God cause this closing word to sink into your hearts.

After Jesus had opened the eyes of this seeker he used his sight to follow Jesus in the way, and, my friends, the first step in following Jesus is to emulate the example that He has left us. And do you know where His "example" began? His example began at Jordan; that is where His public ministry commenced. And you are not following Jesus scripturally until you begin where He began. And listen again! The ministry of Jesus began at Jordan by going down into the water that spoke of death; it began with Jesus indentifying Himself with His poor people, for He said to the Baptist when John demurred at baptising Him—What did the Saviour say? "Thus it becometh Me to fulfil all righteousness? He said nothing of the kind. He said, "Thus it becometh us." Why did He use the plural number? It was Jesus at the place of baptism. It was there that He first identified Himself with His people. And He has left us an example that we should follow His steps! O believing brethren and sisters, begin where He began, and as Bartimaeus used his sight to follow Jesus in the way, follow Him through the waters of baptism into His own ordained and organized church, and cast in your lot with His own people who are seeking, by God's grace to keep unfurled the banner of His gospel.

Sermon preached by the Editor in Sydney.

## FINANCIAL FELLOWSHIP.

Though this Magazine is gladly sent forth free of charge to all who desire to read it, yet it may be as well to remind our readers that we do not get it printed gratis. It will cost us this year over two hundred pounds (over one thousand dollars) to pay printing and postage bills. We feel the more free to mention this, inasmuch as neither the editor nor his wife will receive a penny's remuneration for their services. Nor do they desire any. Whatever balance may be left on hand at the end of the year, will, D.V., be used for the printing of tracts and booklets for free distribution.

Our purpose in saying what we have above is to remind our Christian readers of their responsibility. Many need no reminding, but it seems that a few do. Probably it has not occurred to them that heavy expenses are incurred in publishing and circulating this Magazine, and that if they are receiving spiritual blessing from its contents it is both their duty and privilege to share in its financial support. It is not that we want them to feel that they are paying for what they are getting, for spiritual mercies cannot be bought or paid for in money; but that they may have fellowship with us in sending forth these Studies in the Scriptures.

In this self-seeking and self-centred age, God's people need reminding that there is such a thing as laying up for themselves "treasures in heaven." (Matt. 6:20). Diffident as we certainly feel in mentioning these things, we are impressed that it is our duty to speak plainly thereon. Some have sent in a list of names of those they felt sure would value the Magazine. We have replied thanking them and saying they have been duly entered on our mailing list. They have sent in a second list, and then a third, and no monetary gift accompanying. This has made us wonder whether they realized they had a responsibility towards the maintenance of this publication. Are they taking advantage of its now being free? We believe not. Rather do we attribute it to thoughtlessness on their part. Hence this word. This does not mean that names to the Magazine are un-welcome when not accompanied by a gift; but that we desire all to seek God's guidance as to how far He would have them be "workers together" with us (2 Cor. 6:1).

We know that numbers who are receiving this Magazine are quite unable to send in pounds, or perhaps even shillings. But surely there are none unable to send in a few pence, in postage stamps. Remember the widow's "mite" was more acceptable to the Lord than the larger gifts of the rich; and He is still the same! Let it not be thought that we are hard pressed financially—we are not. Nor do we wish this to be construed as an appeal for funds; it is not. Instead, our earnest desire is that "fruit" may abound "to your account" (Phil. 4:17). May God enlarge all our hearts and give us to prove that "the liberal soul shall be made fat" Prov. 11:25).—A.W.P.

them — it is the "lambs" which He carries in His arms! But some older Christians seem far less conscious of their danger, and so God often suffers them to have a fall, that He may stain the pride of their self-glory and that others may see that it is nothing in the flesh — standing, rank, age, or attainments — which ensures our safety; but that He upholds the humble and casts down the proud. David did not fall into his great sin till he had at least reached the prime of life. Lot did not transgress most grossly till he was an old man. Isaac seems to have become a glutton in his old age, and was as a vessel no longer "meet for the Master's use," which rusted out rather than wore out. It was after a life of walking with God, and building the ark, that Noah disgraced himself. The worst sin of Moses was committed not at the beginning but at the end of the wilderness journey. Hezekiah became puffed up with pride near the sunset of his life. What warnings are these!

God thus shows us there is no protection in years. Yea, added years seems to call for increased chastenings. Often there is more grumbling and complaining among the aged pilgrims than the younger ones. I know that their nerves can stand less, but God's grace is sufficient for worn-out nerves. Oftentimes there is more occupation with self and circumstances among the fathers and mothers in Israel, a less talking of Christ and His wondrous love, than there is among the babes. Yes, there is much need for all of us to heed this "furthermore" of our text. Every physician will tell you that there are some diseases which become most troublesome in middle life, and others which are incident to old age. The same is true of different forms of sinning. If we are more liable to certain sins in our youth, we are in greater danger of others in advanced years. Of this I am fully convinced, the older we get the more need there is to heed this "furthermore" which prefaces the call of our being in subjection to the Father of spirits. If we do not need more grace, certain it is that we need as much grace, when we are grown old as when we are growing up.

The aged meet with as many temptations as do young Christians. They are tempted to live in the past, rather than in the future. They are tempted to take things easier, spiritually as well as temporally, so that it has to be said of some "ye did run well." O to be like Paul "the aged," who was in full harness to the end. They are tempted to be unduly occupied with their increasing infirmities; yet is it not written "the Spirit also helpeth our infirmities"! Yet because this is affirmed, we must not think there is no longer need to earnestly seek His help. This comforting word is given in order that we should fervently and confidently pray for this very thing. If it were not recorded, we might doubt His readiness to do so, and wonder if we were asking "according to His will." Because it is recorded, when feeling your "infirmities" press most heavily upon you, cry, "O Holy Spirit of God do as Thou hast said, and help me."

In this connection I want to remind you of a verse which long puzzled me, but on which I would now throw out a simple hint as to its probable meaning: "Who satisfieth thy mouth with good things: so that thy youth is renewed like the eagle's" (Psa. 103:5). As you know, the "eagle" is a bird renowned for its longevity, often living to be more than a hundred years old. The "eagle" is also the high-soaring bird, of lofty flight, building its nest on the mountain summit. Now how is the eagle's "youth renewed"? By a new crop of feathers, by the rejuvenation of its wings. And that is precisely what some middle-aged and elderly Christians need: the rejuvenation of their spiritual wings—the wings of faith, of hope, of zeal, of love for souls, of devotedness to Christ. So many leave their first love, losing the joy of their espousals, and instead of setting before younger Christians a bright example of trustfulness and cheerfulness, they often discourage by gloominess and slothfulness. Thus God's chastenings increase in severity and frequency! Instead of saying, The days of my usefulness are over, say rather, The night cometh when no man can work: I must make the most of my opportunities while it is yet called day.

The most active worker in the last church of which I was pastor, was seventy-seven years old when I went there, and during my stay of three and a half years she did more for the Lord, and was a greater stimulus to me, than any other member of that Church. She lived another eight years, and they were, to the very end, filled with devoted service to Christ. I believe that the Lord will yet say of her, as of another woman, "She hath done what she could." O brethren and sisters, especially you who feel the weight of years, remember that word, "Let us not grow weary in well doing, for in due season we shall reap, if we faint not." (Gal. 6:9).

—Sermon preached by the Editor in Sydney.

VOL. VI.       AUGUST, 1927       NO.

# STUDIES IN THE SCRIPTURES
"Search the Scriptures" John 5:39.

Copyright in all English-speaking Countries.

Editor: Arthur W. Pink, 15 Hurlstone Avenue, Summer Hill, N.S.W., Australia.
Hon. Agent in U.S.A.: Mr. C. S. Pressel, 559 Dupont Ave., York, Penna.

FREE TO ALL WHO WILL READ IT

### SUBJECTION UNDER CHASTISEMENT.
### Heb. 12:9.

By nature we are not in subjection. We are born into this world filled with the spirit of insubordination. As the descendants of our rebellious first parents we inherit their evil nature. "Man is born like a wild ass's colt" (Job 11:12). This is very unpalatable and humbling, but nevertheless it is true. As Isa. 53:6 tells us, "we have turned every one to his own way" and that way is opposition to the revealed will of God. Even at conversion this wild and rebellious nature is not eradicated. A new nature is given, but the old one lusts against it. It is because of this that discipline and chastisement are needed by us, and the great design of these is to bring us into subjection to the Father of spirits. We shall now attempt two things: explain the meaning of this expression "be in subjection unto the Father," enforce this with reasons presented in our text.

#### 1.—The Subjection Designed.

To be "in subjection unto the Father" is a phrase of extensive import, and it is well that we should understand its various significations.

**1. It denotes an acquiescence in God's sovereign right to do with us as He pleases.** Turn to Psa. 39:9: "I was dumb, I opened not my mouth; because Thou didst it." It is the duty of saints to be mute under the rod and silent beneath the sharpest afflictions. But this is only possible as we see the hand of God in them. If God's hand be not seen in the trial, the heart will do nothing but fret and fume. Read 2 Sam. 16:10, 11, "And the king said, What have I to do with you, ye sons of Zeruiah? so let him curse, because the Lord hath said unto him, Curse David. Who shall then say Wherefore hast thou done so? And David said to Abishai, and to all his servants, Behold, my son, which came forth of my bowels, seeketh my life: How much more now may this Benjamite do it? let him alone, and let him curse for the Lord hath bidden him." What an example of complete submission to the sovereign will of the Most High was this! David knew that Shimei could not curse him without God's permission.

"This will set my heart at rest,
What My God appoints is best."

But with rare exceptions many chastenings are needed to bring us to this place, and to keep us there.

**2. It implies a renunciation of Self-will.**
To be in subjection unto the Father presupposes a surrendering and resigning of ourselves to Him. A blessed illustration of this is found in Lev. 10: 1-3, "And Nadab and Abihu, the sons of Aaron, took either of them his censer, and put fire therein, and put incense thereon, and offered strange fire before the Lord, which He commanded them not. And there went out fire from the Lord, and devoured them, and they died before the Lord. Then Moses said unto Aaron, This is it that the Lord spake, saying I will be sanctified in them that come nigh Me, and before all the people I will be glorified. And Aaron held his peace." Consider the circumstances. Aaron's two sons, most probably intoxicated at the time, were suddenly cut off by Divine judgment. Their father had no warning to prepare him for this trial; yet he "held his peace"! O quarrel not against Jehovah. Be

(Continued on page 192).

## BACK NUMBERS

OF THIS MAGAZINE obtainable, 5/- (1 dollar) per year; Bound at 7/- (1 dollar 75.) Each year is yet obtainable.

ADVISE PROMPTLY of Change of Address

THIS MAGAZINE is published as a work of faith and labor of love. It is gladly sent to all who would value it.

We want the names and addresses of Christians who would read it.

Christians who feel definitely led to do so may have fellowship with us in this Ministry.

## CONTENTS.

| | |
|---|---|
| The Gospel of John (20:11-23) | 170 |
| Gleanings in Exodus | 180 |
| Songs in the Night | 185 |
| Distinguishing Grace | 186 |
| Security | 191 |

## THE GOSPEL OF JOHN.

### 68. Christ appearing to His own: John 20:11-23.

Below is an Analysis of our present passage:—

1. Mary at the sepulchre vv. 11-13.
2. Christ revealing Himself to Mary vv. 14-16.
3. Christ commissioning Mary vv. 17-18.
4. The apostles in the upper room v. 19.
5. Christ revealing Himself to the apostles v. 20.
6. Christ commissioning the apostles v. 21.
7. Christ enduing the apostles vv. 22, 23.

Our Lord had triumphed o'er the grave, "as He said." Before the sun of this world had risen upon the third day since the crucifixion, the Son of Righteousness had already risen; the Bridegroom had gone forth from His chamber (Psa. 19). The One whose heel was bruised by the Serpent had, through death, become the Destroyer of him who had the power of death. The eye of no earthly watcher had beheld the actual resurrection of the body, the rising, and the going forth. That He had risen was evident by the stone rolled away, the empty sepulchre, and the condition of the grave-clothes which He had left behind; corroborated, too, by the witness of the angels. But now He was to appear in person unto His own: the manner in which He did so is very striking. "Although the impulse of His love urged Him at once to the company of His own upon earth, who are still in the sorrow of death; yet He does not overwhelm them with sudden surprise at His glorious reappearance, but restrains Himself, yields Himself to their view by degrees, regulated by the highest wisdom of love. Their minds are gradually prepared, each one according to its temperament and need" (Stier).

So far as our present light reveals, the Saviour made **eleven** appearances between His resurrection and ascension. First, to Mary Magdalene alone (John 20:14). Second, to certain women returning from the sepulchre (Matt. 28:9, 10). Third, to Simon Peter (Luke 24:34). Fourth, to the two disciples going to Emmaus (Luke 24:13). Fifth, to the ten apostles in the upper-room (John 20:19). Sixth, to the eleven apostles in the upper-room (John 20:26-29). Seventh, to seven disciples fishing at the sea of Tiberias (John 21). Eighth, to the eleven apostles and possibly other disciples with them (Matt. 28:16). Ninth, to above five hundred brethren at once (1 Cor. 15:7). Tenth, to James (1 Cor. 15:7). Eleventh, to the eleven apostles, and possibly other disciples on the mount of Olives at His ascension (Acts 1). His twelfth appearance, after His ascension, was to Stephen (Acts 7). His thirteenth, to Saul on the way to Damascus (Acts 9). His fourteenth, to John on Patmos (Rev. 1). And this was the last—how profoundly significant. The final appearing was His **fourteenth**! The factors of fourteen are seven and two, seven being the number of **perfection**, and two of **witness.** Thus we have His own **perfect witness** to His triumph over the tomb!! His next appearing will be unto His blood-bought saints all together, when He shall descend into the air with a shout, and catch us up to be with Himself for evermore (1 Thess. 4:16). **This will be His fifteenth** appearance. The factors of fifteen are three and five, three being the number of **full manifestation**, and five of **grace.** Thus, at His coming for us, His grace, His wondrous grace, will be **fully manifested**!!

It is with the first and the fifth of

these appearings of the risen Saviour that our present lesson is concerned. And here, too, the significance of these numerals holds good. One is the number of God in the unity of His essence. It speaks of His absolute sovereignty. The sovereignty of God comes out here most vividly and blessedly in the character of the one selected to have the high honor of being the first to gaze upon the triumphant Redeemer. It was not to the Eleven, not even to John, that Christ first showed Himself; it was to a woman, and she the one out of whom He had cast seven demons—one who had been the complete slave of Satan. And to her He revealed Himself as God the Son (see v. 17). And to whom was His fifth appearance made. To His mother? No. To Joseph of Arimathaea and Nicodemus? No. It was to the unbelieving apostles, to those who had regarded as idle tales the testimony of the women who had seen Him. His fifth appearance was made to those who had least reason to expect Him, whose faith was the weakest. Wondrous grace indeed was this!

"But Mary stood without at the sepulchre weeping" (v. 11). This is the sequel to what was before us in the last lesson. At the beginning of the 20th chapter, we read, "The first of the week cometh Mary Magdalene early, when it was yet dark, unto the sepulchre, and seeth the stone taken away from the sepulchre. Then she runneth, and cometh to Simon Peter, and to the other disciple whom Jesus loved, and saith unto them. They have taken away the Lord, out of the sepulchre, and we know not where they have laid Him." In the interval, the two apostles had been to the sepulchre, inspected the clothes within, and then returned to their home, to acquaint the Saviour's mother that He was risen from the dead. Meanwhile Mary, not knowing of this, had returned to the sepulchre, desolate and sorrowful. But soon her grief was to be turned into gladness: in but a little while the One who had taken captive her heart and who now occupied her every thought would be manifested to her. Strikingly does this illustrate Proverbs 8:17: "I love them that love Me; and those that seek Me early shall find Me." Mary, and the other women, were the first to seek the sepulchre on the resurrection morning, and they were the first to whom the Victor of death showed Himself (Matt. 28:9). Alas that so many put off the seeking of Christ till the last hour of life, and then never find Him!

"But Mary stood without at the sepulchre weeping." Here, once more, the Holy Spirit shows us that love needs to be regulated by faith. It was love for Christ that caused her to weep: she was weeping because the sepulchre was empty, yet in fact that was the very thing which should have made her rejoice. Had the Lord's body been still there, she might have wept indeed, for then His promise had failed, His Work on the cross had been in vain, and she (and all others) yet in her sins. The weeping manifested her affection, but it also showed her unbelief. "How often are the fears and sorrows of saints quite needless! Mary stood at the sepulchre weeping, and wept as if nothing could comfort her. She wept when the angels spoke to her: 'Woman,' they said, 'why weepest thou'? She was weeping still when our Lord spoke to her: 'Woman,' He said, 'why weepest thou?' And the burden of her complaint was always the same: 'They have taken away my Lord, and I know not where they have laid Him'! Yet all this time her risen Master was close to her! Her tears were needless. Like Hagar in the wilderness (Gen. 21:19), she had a well of water by her side, but she had not eyes to see it!

"What thoughtful Christian can fail to see that we have here a faithful picture of many a believer's experience? How often we mourn over the absence of things which in reality are within our grasp, and even at our right hand! Two-thirds of the things we fear in life never happen at all, and two-thirds of the tears we shed are thrown away, and shed in vain. Let us pray for more faith and patience, and allow more time for the development of God's purposes: Let us believe that things are often working together for our peace and joy, which seem at one time to contain nothing but bitterness and sorrow. Old Jacob said at one time in his life 'all these things are against me' (Gen. 42:36), yet he lived to see Joseph again, rich and prosperous, and to thank God for all that had happened." (Bishop Ryle.)

"And as she wept, she stooped down, and looked into the sepulchre" (v. 11). Such is ever the effect of uncontrolled grief. When we sorrow, even as others who have no hope, when we walk by sight instead of faith, when we are moved by the flesh instead of the spirit, we stoop down, and are occupied with things below. "Unto Thee lift I mine eyes, O Thou that dwellest in the heavens" (Psa. 123:1) should ever be the believer's attitude. Mary points a timely warning for us. We are living in days when "men's hearts are failing them for fear, and for looking after those things which are coming on the earth" (Luke 21:26), and the more we are occupied with the evil around us, the more will our hearts fail. Heed then the Saviour's admonition, "When these things begin to come to pass, then look up and lift up your heads; for your redemption draweth nigh" (Luke 21:28). Let us, instead of looking down like Mary, say with the Psalmist, "I will lift up mine eyes unto the hills. From whence cometh my help? My help cometh from the Lord, which made heaven and earth" (Psa. 121:1, 2).

"And seeth two angels in white sitting, the one at the head and the other at the feet, where the body of Jesus had lain" (v. 12). How long-suffering is our God! How patiently He deals with our dulness! Where the heart is really engaged with Christ, even though faith be weak and intelligence small, God will bear with us. Here were two messengers from Heaven ready to re-assure Mary! Their presence in the sepulchre was proof positive that God had not suffered it to be rifled by wicked hands. Their very posture signified that all was well. Their number indicated a testimony from on High, if only this sorrowing woman had eyes to see and ears to hear.

"And seeth two angels in white sitting." The sepulchre was not so deserted as it seemed. Luke tells us of two angels appearing to the other women a little earlier, and it is instructive to note the several points of difference. "And it came to pass, as they were much perplexed thereabout, behold, two men stood by them in shining garments." (24:4). Luke calls them "two men"—from their appearance, we suppose. John is more explicit: "Two angels." When these other women saw the two angels, they were on the outside of the sepulchre; but when Mary looked down they were now within. In Luke 24 the angels were "standing," here in John 20 they are "seated'! Nowhere are we told the names of the two angels, but some have thought that they were Michael and Gabriel, arguing that the supreme importance of our Lord's resurrection would call for the presence of the highest angels. Probably the same two appeared to the disciples at Christ's ascension (Acts 1:10).

"And seeth two angels in white sitting, the one at the head, and the other at the feet." This is the only place in Scripture where we see angels sitting. The fact that they were sitting in the place where "the body of Jesus had lain" was God's witness unto the rest which was secured by and proceeds from the finished Work of the Lord Jesus. It is in striking accord with the character of this Fourth Gospel that it was reserved for John to mention this beautiful incident. Who can doubt that the Holy Spirit would have us link up this verse with Exodus 25:17-19—"And thou shalt make a mercy-seat of pure gold . . . and thou shalt make two cherubims of gold, of beaten work shalt thou make them, in the two ends of the mercy-seat." More remarkable still is the final word which Jehovah spake unto Moses concerning the mercy-seat: "And there I will meet with thee, and I will commune with thee from above the mercy-seat from between the two cherubims (Ex. 25.22). Here, then, in John's Gospel, do we learn once more that Christ is the true Meeting-place between God and man!

The question has often been asked, Why did not Peter and John see these two angels when they entered the sepulchre? It seems clear that they must have been there, though invisible. In view of Psalm 91:11 we are satisfied that they had been about that sepulchre from the first moment that the sacred body was deposited there; "For He shall give His angels charge over Thee, to keep Thee in all Thy ways"—this was God's promise to Christ. From the general teaching of the Scripture we learn that the angels of God are visible and invisible, appear and disappear, instantaneously and supernaturally, according as God commissions them. Most probably they are near to each believer every moment of his existance (Heb. 1:14). though we are unaware of their presence. Yet, while they are of a higher order of beings than humans, not the smallest particle of worship is to be given them; for, like ourselves, they are but the creatures of God.

That the angels were "in white" denotes purity and freedom from defilement, which is the character of all the inhabitants of heaven. White was the color of our Lord's raiment in the transfiguration; it is the color in which the angels ever appeared; it will be the color of our garments in glory (Rev. 3:4). The late Bishop Andrews drew a timely moral from the positions occupied by the two angels in the sepulchre. "We learn that between the angels there was no striving for places. He that sat at the feet was as well content with his place, as he that sat at the head. We should learn from their example. With us, both angels would have been at the head, and never a one at the feet! With us, none would be at the feet; we must be head-angels all!"

"And they say unto her, Woman, why weepest thou"? (v. 13). We have no reason for supposing that the angels were ignorant of the occasion of Mary's lamentation, therefore, we understand their words here as a gentle inquiry, made for the purpose of stirring her mind. Why weepest thou? Have you any just cause for those tears? Search your heart! Does not the fact that Christ is not here afford ground for rejoicing! It is to be noted that the angels used precisely the same language as the Saviour does in v. 15, thereby intimating that their words are ever spoken by the command of God. Observe that their words to the disciples at the ascension of Christ also began with a "Why?" No doubt our unbelief, our fears, our repinings, our lack of obedience and zeal, afford much ground of surprise to these unfallen beings.

"She saith unto them, Because they have taken away my Lord, and I know not where they have laid Him" (v. 13). Before the angels had time to add the comforting assurance, "He is not here; He is risen, as He said," Mary interrupts by explaining why she was so heart-broken—How can I do anything else but weep, when He is not here, and I know not where they have taken His body! A strange mingling of faith and unbelief, of intelligence and ignorance, of affection and fear, was hers. "Lord," she owned Jesus of Nazareth to be, and yet imagined that some one had taken Him away! It is indeed striking that she replied so promptly and naturally to the angels: instead of being awe-struck at their presence, she answered as though they were nothing more than men. She was so swallowed up with her grief, so occupied with her thoughts about Christ, that she paused not to gaze upon these Heavenly visitors. Mark the change of her language here: to Peter and John she had appropriately said, "They have taken away the Lord"; but to the angels she (now alone) says "My Lord," thus expressing the depths of her affections. And how blessed that each individual believer may speak of Him as "my Lord." "The Lord is my Shepherd" said David (Psa. 23, 1). "My Beloved is mine, and I am His" (Song of S. 2:16). "Who loved me, and gave Himself for me" (Gal. 2:20) said the apostle Paul.

"And when she had thus said she turned herself back" (v. 14). Very, very, striking is this. Christ meant so much to her that she turned her back on the angels to seek His body! He was the One her affections were set upon, and therefore, even these angels held no attraction for her! How searching is this: if Christ really occupied the throne of our hearts, the poor things of this world would make no appeal to us. It is because we are so little absorbed with Him, and therefore so little acquainted with His soul-satisfying perfections, that the things of time and sense are so highly esteemed. O that writer and reader may be able to say with the Psalmist, and say with ever-increasing fervor and reality, "Whom have I in heaven but Thee? and there is none upon earth that I desire beside Thee."

"And when she had thus said she turned herself back and saw Jesus standing" (v. 14). Such devotion as Mary's could not pass unrewarded: to her who loved Him so deeply does the Saviour first appear. "Those who love Christ most diligently and perseveringly, are those who receive most privileges at His hands. It is a touching fact, and one to be carefully noted, that Mary would not leave the sepulchre, even when Peter and John had gone to their own home. Love to her gracious Master would not let her leave the place where He had lain. Where He was now she did not know, but love made her linger about the empty tomb; love made her honor the last place where His precious body had been seen by mortal eyes. And here love reaped a rich reward. She saw the angels whom Peter and John had not observed. She heard them speak. She was the first to see our Lord after He had risen from the dead, the first to hear His voice. Can any one doubt that this was written for our learing? Wherever the Gospel is preached throughout the world, this little incident testifies that those who honor Christ will be honored by Christ" (Bishop Ryle). "And saw Jesus standing." Very blessed is this. Why was the Saviour standing there, beside His own sepulchre? Ah, was it not the **response** of His heart to one who loved Him! He was there for the purpose of meeting and comforting this sorely-wounded soul!

"And saw Jesus standing, and knew not that it was Jesus" (v. 14). It is strange how many of the commentators have erred on this point. The popular idea is that Mary failed to recognise Christ because her eyes were dimmed with tears. But how comes it, we ask, that when she looked into the sepulchre she **saw** the two angels and the respective positions which they occupied? No; we believe there is far more reason for us to conclude that her eyes were "holden" supernaturally, like the two disciples walking to Emmaus, so that she did not distinguish the figure before her to be that of our Lord. The condition of His resurrection-body was very different from that of His body before the crucifixion. Moreover, He was to be known no more "after the flesh" (2 Cor. 5:16), but, as the Head of the new creation. Yet, as others have pointed out, this incident was a striking emblem of the spiritual experience of many Christians. "I will never leave thee nor forsake thee" is His promise; yet how often are we un-conscious of His presence with us!

"Jesus saith unto her, Woman, why weepest thou? whom seekest thou?" (v. 15). These were the first words of our risen Saviour, and how like Him! He came here to bind up the broken-hearted (Isa. 61:1), and in the end He will wipe away tears from off the faces of all His people (Isa. 25:8; Rev. 21:4). This was His evident design here: He would arouse Mary from the stupefying effects of her sorrow. His first question was a gentle reproof: Ought you not to be rejoicing, instead of repining? His second question was still more searching; Who is it you are seeking among the dead? Hast thou forgotten that the crucified One is the Lord of Life, the Resurrection and the Life, the One who laid down His life that He might take it again! Devoted and affectionate as she was, had she not forgotten those words of His which had so often been spoken in her hearing! "Whom seekest thou?—it was only in really finding Him that the ever-flowing fountain of her grief could be stayed.

"She, supposing Him to be the gardener, saith unto Him, Sir, if thou have borne Him hence, tell me where thou hast laid Him, and I will take Him away" (v. 15). Notice, first, her artless simplicity. Three times over in these few words did Mary speak of "Him" without stopping to define or mention His name. She was so wholly absorbed with Christ that she supposed every one would know whom she sought—like the Shulamite crying to the watchman, "Saw ye Him whom my soul loveth?" (Song of S. 3:3). Note also her, "I will take Him away." He was all **her own**; what depth of affection! What a sense of her **title** to Him! But mark how there may be much ignorance even in a devoted believer—she supposed Him to be the "gardener"! And yet, as one has said, "Devout Mary, thou art not much mistaken. As it was the trade of the first Adam to dress the Garden of Eden, so is it the trade of the last Adam to tend the Garden of His Church: He digs up the soil by seasonable affliction; He sows in it the seeds of grace; He waters it with His Word;" (Bishop Hall).

"Jesus saith unto her, Mary" (v. 16). This was the second utterance of the risen Christ to this devoted soul, and it is important to note that it **was** the second. **Before** He addressed her by name, He first called her "woman"! In addressing her as "Woman" He spoke as **God** to His creature; in calling her "Mary" He spoke as **Saviour** to one of His redeemed. The former gave her to know that He was exalted high above every human relationship; the latter intimated His love for one of His own. "I know thee by name, and thou hast found grace in My sight" (Ex. 33:12) said Jehovah in the Mount. So here, Jehovah, now incarnate, knows this woman by name, for she, too, had "found grace" in His sight. In Christ addressing Mary by name we have a beautiful illustration of His own words in John 10:3, "And He calleth His own sheep **by name**." It was the **seal of redemption**: "But now thus saith the Lord that created thee, O Jacob, and He that formed thee, O Israel, Fear not: for I have **redeemed** thee, I have called thee by thy **name**; thou art **Mine**" (Isa. 43:1)!

"She turned herself, and saith unto Him, Rabboni; which is to say, Master" (v. 16). This shows that Mary now recognised Him. "The sheep follow Him, for they know His voice." (John 10:4), and here was one of the sheep responding to the call of the Good Shepherd. One word only did He utter, "Mary"! But that was sufficient to transform the weeper into a worshipper. It shows us, once more, the power **of the Word**! "Rabboni," she exclaimed, as she fell at His feet— a Hebrew term signifying "my Master."

Here was the rich reward for her devotion, her faithfulness, her perseverance. The one who had before cast the demons from her, now addressed Himself to her heart. She knew now that the Fairest among ten thousand to her soul had triumphed over the tomb: her sorrow was ended, her cup of joy overflowing. There is one little detail in the picture here, most lovely, which is usually overlooked. As soon as Christ addressed her by name, she "turned herself," and saith unto Him, "Rabboni." After His first word, when she supposed Him to be the gardener, she had turned away from Him, her attitude still toward the tomb; but now that He called her by name, she turns her back on the tomb and falls at His feet—it is only as He is known that we are delivered, experimentally, from the power of death!

"Jesus saith unto her, Touch Me not; for I am not yet ascended to My Father" (v. 17.) We believe that these words have a double significance and application. First the "Touch Me not," in its direct force, is clearly explained by Christ Himself—"for I am not yet ascended." Mary had, we think, fallen at His feet, and was on the point of embracing them—remembering, perhaps, the words of the Shulamite, "I found Him whom my soul loveth: I held Him, and would not let Him go" (Song of S. 3:4). But the Lord instantly checked her: "Touch Me not, for I am not yet ascended." "On this very day, the morrow after the Sabbath, the high priest waved the sheaf of the first fruits before the Lord while He, the First-fruits from the dead (1 Cor. 15:23), would be fulfilling the type by presenting Himself before the Father" (Companion Bible). This we are satisfied supplies the key to the primary meaning of our Lord's words to Mary, for He who was so jealous of the types would not neglect this one in Lev. 23:10, 11. Yet, we do not think that this exhausts the scope of what Christ said here. Everywhere in this Gospel there is a fullness about the Lord's utterances which it is impossible for us to fathom; and beyond their force to those immediately addressed, is ever a wider application. So here.

"Touch Me not." These words are not found in the Synoptics and therein lies the key to their deeper meaning and wider application. In Matt. 28:9 we read "As they went to tell His disciples, behold, Jesus met them, saying, All hail. And they came and held Him by the feet." How sharp the contrast here, yet how perfectly in keeping with the particular scope of each Gospel! Matthew presents Christ as the Son of David, in Jewish relationships, and Israel will know Him "after the flesh," when He appears, corporeally, on the earth. But John portrays Him as the Son of God, connected with the sons, as Head of the new creation, the members of which know Him not "after the flesh" (2 Cor. 5:16). Therefore in His "Touch Me not" to Mary, the Lord was giving plain intimation that the Christian would know Him only in spirit, as the One with the Father on High; hence His "for I am not yet ascended"! It was the first hint—abundantly amplified in the sequel of the new relationship into which the resurrection of Christ has brought us, linking us with Himself as the Son of God in the Father's House! How significant that this was His third word to Mary—the number which speaks of resurrection!

"But go to My brethren, and say unto them, I ascend (the proper present "I am ascending") unto My Father, and your Father; and to My God, and your God" (v. 17). Mary was to be the first witness of Christ's resurrection. This illustrates a truth of great practical importance. A woman—more devoted, perhaps, than any of the Twelve—had anointed Him for His burial (John 12), and now a woman is the first to whom Christ revealed Himself in resurrection glory. How this tells us that the heart leads the mind in the apprehension of God's truth. The men were quicker to grasp, intellectually, the meaning of the empty tomb, but Mary was the more devoted, and this Christ rewarded. Mary exemplifies the case of those whose hearts seek Christ, but whose minds are ill-informed. It is the heart God ever looks at. We may know much truth intellectually, but unless the heart is absorbed with Christ, He will not reveal Himself to such an one in the intimacies of love and communion.

"Go to My brethren, and say unto them I ascend." This is the first time that the Lord Jesus addressed the disciples as "brethren." How blessed! It is on resurrection-ground that we are thus related to Christ. "Except the corn of wheat fell into the ground and died, it had abode alone" (12:24), but now that He has emerged from the grave, He is "the Firstborn among many brethren" (Rom. 8:29). Of old had the Spirit of prophecy expressed the language of the Messiah thus: "I will declare Thy name unto My brethren" (Psa. 22:22). Like Joseph after he was delivered from the prison and raised to a position of dignity and honor (Gen. 45:16), so Christ "is not ashamed to call us brethren" (Heb. 2:11). The blessedness of this comes out in the closing words of v. 17: "I ascend unto My Father, **and your Father; and to My God, and your God."** Believers are, by amazing grace, brought into the **same** position with Himself before God His Father. It was in view of **this** that the Lord said to Mary **"Touch** (Greek "cling to") **Me not**"—we are **detached** from Him by all earthly contact, and instead commune with Him by faith, in spirit, on High.

"Go to My brethren and say unto them, I ascend unto My Father, and your Father; and My God and your God." The terms of this message to His brethren deserve the closest notice. He did not bid Mary say to them "I have **risen,"** but **"I ascend."** True, the one necessarily presupposed the other, but it is clear He would have them understand that His resurrection was only a step toward His return unto the Father. That which the Saviour would impress upon His beloved disciples was the fact that He had not left the grave simply to **remain** with them here on earth, but in order to enter Heaven as their Representative and Forerunner. In saying "I ascend unto **My Father and your Father, and My God, and your God,"** He was conveying a message of real comfort. He is **your** Father and God, as well as Mine; all that He is to Me, the Head, He is also to you, the members. But mark His precision: He did not say "Our Father, and our God." He still maintains His pre-eminency, His uniqueness, for God is His Father and God in a singular and incommunicable manner. Finally, note the contrast between Mary's commission here and the one given to the other women in Matt. 28:10: there the message was for the disciples to meet Him in **Galilee,** and accordingly they did so; here, He names no place on earth, but simply tells them that He is going to Heaven, there in spirit to meet them before the Father.

"Mary Magdalene came and told the disciples that she had seen the Lord and that He had spoken these things unto her" (v. 18). "As by a woman came the first message of death, so by a woman came also the first notice of the resurrection from the dead. And the place also fits well, for in a garden they came, both" (Bishop Andrews). Observe that Mary told the disciples that she had "**seen the Lord,**" not simply "Jesus"! Mark records the immediate effect of her message: "She went and told them that she had been with Him, as they mourned and wept; and they, when they had heard that He was alive, and had been seen by her, believed not." (16:10, 11). What a tragic forecast of the general reception which the Christian evangelist meets with! How few he finds that promptly receive the glad tidings of which He is the bearer! Often the ones he deems most likely to welcome the good news, are the very ones whose unbelief will be the most outspoken.

"Then the same day at evening, being the first of the week, when the doors were shut where the disciples were assembled for fear of the Jews, came Jesus and stood in the midst" (v. 19). Observe in the first place how the Holy Spirit here emphasises the fact that what follows is a **first-day** scene. On this first Christian Sabbath the "disciples were **assembled"** in separation from the world, and from this point on to the end of the N.T. the first day of the week is stamped with this characteristic: Sunday, not Saturday, was henceforth to be the day set apart for rest from the work and concerns of the world, and for occupation with the things of God. Note in the next place, that from the beginning non-Christians have manifested their opposition and hatred against these holy exercises. Observe that those gathered together are here called "disciples," not "apostles." It is striking that never once are they termed "apostles" in John's Gospel. The reason for this is not far distant: the word "apostle" means "one sent forth"; but here, where it is the family which is in view, they are always seen with Christ!

"Then the same day at evening, being the first of the week, when the doors were shut where the disciples were assembled for fear of the Jews, came Jesus and stood in the midst and saith unto them, Peace be unto you" (v. 19). Very striking is this. John is the only one who mentions the doors being "shut" (Greek signifies **"barred").** But no closed doors could keep out the Conqueror of death. There was no need for Him to knock for admission, nor for an angel to open to Him as for Peter (Acts 12:10); nor do we consider that a miracle was wrought, in the ordinary meaning of that term. Our resurrection-body will not be subject to the limitations of the mortal body: sown in weakness it will be raised in **power** (I. Cor. 15:43).

Most blessed is it to ponder our Lord's

greeting to the Ten—Thomas was absent. Very touching and humbling was the Lord's gracious salutation. Peter had denied Him, and the others had forsaken Him. How, then, does He approach them? Does He demand an explanation of their conduct? Does He tell them that all is now over, that henceforth He will have no more to do with such unfaithful followers? No; indeed. Well might He have said, "**Shame** upon you!" But, instead He says, "**Peace** be unto you." He would remove from their hearts all fear which His sudden and unannounced appearance might have occasioned. He would quieten each uneasy conscience. Having put away their sins He could now remove their fears. Be not afraid: I come not as Judge, to reckon with your perfidy and unbelief; nor do I enter as One who has been injured by you, to utter reproaches. No; I bring from My sepulchre something very different from upbraidings: "Peace be unto **you**" was the blessed greeting of the Prince of Peace, and none but He **can** speak peace to any. "Peace" was the subject of the angel's carol in the night of the Lord's nativity; so "peace" is the first word He pronounced in the ears of His disciples now that He is risen from the dead. So will it be when we meet Him face to face—we, with all our miserable failures, both individual and corporate; we with all our sins of omission and commission; we, with all our bitter controversies, and deplorable divisions. Not "Shame! Shame!" but "Peace! Peace!" will be His greeting. How do we **know** this? Because He is "The **same** yesterday and to-day and forever." Almost his last words to the disciples on the "Yesterday" were "these things have I spoken unto you, that in Me ye might have **peace**" (John 16:33); so here His first word to them in the "To-day" was **peace**; and **this** is the pledge that "Peace" will be His word **to us** at the beginning of the great "Forever."

"And when He had so said, He showed unto them His hands and His side" (v. 20). This was, first, to assure the astonished disciples that it was really their Saviour who stood before them. He bade them see with their own eyes that He had a real material body, that it was no ghost now appearing to them. He would have them recognise that He was indeed the **same** person whom they had known before the crucifixion, that He had risen in His incorruptible humanity. Significant is the omission here: Luke tells us that He said, "Behold My hands and My feet, that it is I Myself: **handle Me,** and see" (24:39). It was most appropriate that **this** word should be recorded in the Third Gospel, which portrays Him as the Son of man; and it was most suitable to omit this detail in the Gospel which speaks of His Divine dignity and glory. Observe here, "He showed unto them His hands and His **side."** Luke says "His hands and His **feet."** This variation is also significant. Here His word in John would presuppose His "feet," for they, in common with His hands, bore the imprint of the nails. But there was a special reason for mentioning His "side" here—see 19:34: through His pierced side a way was opened to His **heart,** the seat of the affections! In John we see Him as the Son of God, and God is love.

"And when He had so said, He showed unto them His hands and His side." The "so" indicates there is a close connection between this **act of** Christ's and His words at the end of the preceding verse. The marks in His hands and side were shown to the disciples not only to establish His identity, not only as the trophies of His victorious fight, but principally to teach them, and us, that the **basis** of the "peace" He has made, and which He gives, is His death upon the cross. In saying "Peace be unto you" He announced that enmity had been removed, God placated, reconciliation effected; in pointing to the signs of His crucifixion, He showed what had accomplished these. These marks are still upon His holy body —Rev. 5:6. These marks our great High Priest shows to God as He intercedes. In a coming day the sight of them will bring Israel to repentance—Zech. 12:10. In the Day of Judgment they will confront and condemn His enemies.

"Then were the disciples glad, when they saw the Lord" (v. 20). What must have been their feelings! Their fears all gone; their hopes fulfilled; their hearts satisfied. Now indeed had the Lord made good His promise: "And ye now therefore have sorrow: but I will see you again, and your hearts shall **rejoice** (16:22). But observe an important distinction here: First, Christ said, "**Peace** be unto you, and when He had **so** said, He **showed** unto them His hands and His side." Second: "Then were the disciples **glad** when they saw **the Lord."** Peace comes through His perfect **work;** joy is the result of being occupied with His blessed **person.** This is a precious secret for our hearts. There are many Christians who suppose that they **cannot** rejoice while they remain in circumstances of sorrow. What a mistake! Observe here that Christ did not change the circumstances of these disciples; they were still "shut in for fear of the Jews," but He drew out their hearts unto Himself, and thus raised them above their circumstances! We see the same principle exemplified in 1 Peter 1. There we read of saints of God enduring a great fight of afflictions: they were persecuted, scattered abroad, homeless. But what of their spiritual condition? This —"Wherein ye greatly **rejoice**, though now for a season if need be, ye are in heaviness through manifold temptations. And then, having mentioned the person of the Saviour, he at once adds, "**Whom having not seen**, ye love, in whom though now ye see Him not, yet believing, ye **rejoice** with joy unspeakable" (v. 8). Their circumstances had not been changed, but their hearts were lifted above them. This then is the great secret of joy—occupation and fellowship with Christ.

"Then said Jesus to them again, Peace be unto you: as My Father hath sent Me, even so send I you" (v. 21). This was no mere repetition. Just as the first "Peace be unto you" is interpreted by the Lord's act which at once followed, so this second "Peace" is explained by the next words. The first peace was for the **conscience**; the second for the **heart**. The first had to do with their **position** before God; the second with their **condition** in the world. The first was "peace with God" (Rom. 5:1); the second was "the peace of God" (Phil. 4:7). The first is the consequence of the atonement; the second is that which issues from communion. These disciples were not going to Heaven with Christ, but were to remain behind in a hostile world, in a world which provides no peace. He therefore communicates to them the secret of His peace, which was that of communion with the Father in separation from the world.

"As My Father hath sent Me, even so send I you." He now does formally what He contemplated in that wondrous address to the Father: "As Thou hast sent Me into the world, even so have I also sent them into the world" (17:18). Let it be remembered that it was in immediate connection with this that He said "Neither pray I for these alone, but for them also which shall believe on Me through their word" (17:20). The mission He announced there was not peculiar to the company He then addressed: it defined the mission of all His people in that world which has rejected Him. And what a marvellous mission it is—to represent our Lord here below, as He represented the Father. What a wondrous dignity to show in our life and by our words how He would speak and walk. This is the standard of practical holiness —nothing lower, "He that saith he abideth in Him ought himself also so to walk, **even as He walked**" (1 John 2:6). But how unspeakably blessed to observe that the Lord first said "Peace be unto you" before "I send you." We are constantly disposed to look for peace as the earned reward of service: what a travesty! and how worthless! Such "Peace" is but a transient self-complacency which connot deceive any one but the self-deluded hypocrite. The truth is that peace is the **preparation** for service: "the joy of the Lord is your strength" (Neh. 8-10). The order in John 20:21 is most significant: "Peace ....I sent you." "The sons of peace are not to retain it for themselves; its possession makes them also **messengers of peace**" (Stier). Note the **Son** is a "Sender" in equal authority with the Father. "As My Father hath sent Me, **even so send I you**." Christ was sent to manifest the Father, and with a message of grace to this sinful world; we are sent to manifest the Son, and with a similar message. Yet observe how carefully He guarded His glory: two different words are here used for "send" —Christ was God, we men; He came to atone, we to proclaim His atonement: He did his work perfectly, we very imperfectly!

"And when He had said this, He breathed on them, **and** saith unto them, receive ye the Holy Spirit" (v. 22). The first key to the Receive ye the Spirit, lies in the "**And** when he had said this"— "even so send I you." Christ had entered upon His ministry as One anointed by the Holy Spirit, so should His beloved apostles. This was the final analogy pointed by the "as....so." The second key is found in the "He **breathed** on them **and** saith, Receive ye the Holy Spirit": the Greek word here used is employed nowhere else in the N.T., but is the very one used by the Septuagint translators of Gen. 2:7: "And the Lord God formed man of the dust of the ground, and **breathed** into his nostrils the breath of life; and man became a living soul." There, man's original creation was completed by this act of God; who, then, can fail to see that here in John 20, on the day of the Saviour's resurrection, the new creation had begun, begun by the Head of the new creation, the last Adam acting as "a quickening Spirit" (1 Cor. 15:45)! The impartation of the Holy Spirit to the disciples was the "first-fruits" of the resurrection, as well as a proof that the Spirit proceeds from the Son as well as the Father—wonderful demonstration of the Saviour's Godhead! In Gen. 2:7 we have Jehovah "breathing" into Adam; in John 20:22 the Saviour "breathing" upon the apostles; in Ezek. 37:9 the Spirit "breathing" upon Israel. Finally, it is solemn to contrast Isa. 11:4: "With the breath of His lips shall He slay the wicked"——the Antichrist.

"Receive ye the Holy Spirit." This was supplementary to "Go tell My brethren." They were, before this, born from above; but the heir, as long as he is a child, differeth nothing from a servant, though he be lord of all. But the time appointed by the Father had now come. He who came to redeem them that were under the law, that they might receive the adoption of sons, had accomplished His undertaking. They were no more servants but sons; yet it was only by the Spirit of adoption that they could be made conscious of it or enter into the joy of it. From this moment the Spirit dwelt within them. We have been accustomed to look upon the change which is so apparent in the apostles as dating from the day of Pentecost, but the great change had occurred before then. Read the closing chapter of each Gospel and the first of Acts, and the proofs of this are conclusive. Their irresolution, their unbelief, their misapprehensions, were all gone. When the cloud finally received the Saviour from their sight, instead of being dispersed in consternation "they worshipped Him" and "returned to Jerusalem with great joy" (Luke 24.52)—this was "joy in the Holy Spirit" (Rom. 14.17). Moreover, they continued "with one accord in prayer and supplication" (Acts 1:14)—this was "the unity of the Spirit in the bond of peace" (Eph. 4:3). Peter has a clear understanding of O.T. prophecy (Acts 1:20)—this was the Spirit guiding into the truth (John 16:13). And these things were before Pentecost. What happened at Pentecost was the baptism of power, not the coming of the Spirit to indwell them!

"Whose soever sins ye remit, they are remitted unto them; and whose soever sins ye retain, they are retained" (v. 23). upon this controverted verse we cannot do better than quote from the excellent remarks of the late Bishop Ryle: "In this verse our Lord continues and concludes the commission for the office of ministers, which He now gives to the Apostles after rising from the dead. His work as a public teacher was ended: the Apostles henceforth were to carry it on. The words which formed this commission are very peculiar and demand close attention. The meaning of these words, I believe, may be paraphrased thus: 'I confer on you the power of declaring and pronouncing authoritatively whose sins are forgiven, and whose sins are not forgiven. I bestow on you the office of pronouncing who are pardoned, and who are not, just as the Jewish high priest pronounced who were clean and who were unclean in cases of leprosy. I believe that nothing more than this authority to declare can be got out of the words, and I entirely repudiate and reject the strange notion maintained by some that our Lord meant to depute to the Apostles, or any others, the power of absolutely pardoning or not pardoning, absolving, or not absolving, any one's soul.

"(a) The power of forgiving sins, in Scripture, is always spoken of as the special prerogative of God. The Jews themselves admitted this when they said, 'Who can forgive sins but God only?' (Mark 2:7). It is monstrous to suppose that our Lord meant to overthrow and alter this great principle when He commissioned His disciples.

"(b) The language of the O.T. shows conclusively that the Prophets were said to do certain things when they declared them to be done. Thus Jeremiah's commission runs in these words, 'I have this day set thee over the nation and over the kingdom, to root out, and to pull down, and to destroy, and to throw down, to build, and to plant' (1:10). This can only mean to declare the rooting out and pulling down, etc. So also Ezekiel says 'I came to destroy the city' (4:33).

"(c) There is not a single instance in the Acts or Epistles of an Apostle taking on himself to absolve, or pardon, any one. When Peter said to Cornelius: "Whosoever believeth in Him shall receive remission of sins' (Acts 10:43); when Paul said, 'Through this Man is preached unto you the forgiveness of sins' (Acts 13:38), they pointed to Christ alone as the Remitter."

So Calvin: "When Christ enjoins the apostles to forgive sins, He does not convey to them what is peculiar to Himself. It belongs to Him to forgive sins —He only enjoins them, in His name, to proclaim the forgiveness of sins."

Add to these the fact that Peter and John were sent down to Samaria to inspect and authorise the work done through Philip (Acts 8:14), that Peter said to Simon Magus, "I perceive that thou art in the gall of bitterness, and the bond of iniquity" (Acts 8:23), and that Paul wrote "To whom ye forgive anything, I also: for if I forgave anything, to whom I forgave it, for your sakes forgave I it **in the person of Christ**" (2 Cor. 10), we have clear evidence of the unique authority and power of the apostles.

The question has been asked, Was this ministerial office and commission conferred on the apostles by Christ transferred by them to others? Again we quote Bishop Ryle. "I answer, without hesitation, that in the strictest sense the commission of the apostles **was not** transmitted, but was confined to them and St. Paul. I challenge any one to deny that the Apostles possessed certain ministerial qualifications which were quite peculiar to them, and which they could not, and did not, transmit to others. (1) They had the gift of declaring the Gospel without error, and with infallible accuracy, to an extent that no one after them did. (2) **They confirmed their teaching by miracles.** (3) They had the power of discerning spirits. In the strictest sense there is no such thing as apostolic succession."

In closing let us admire together the lovely typical picture which our passage contains. Here we have a wondrous portrayal of the essential features of **Christianity, in the present Dispensation.** 1. Christ is known in a **new way,** no longer "after the flesh," but in spirit, on High. "Touch Me not"....ascended (v. 17). 2. Believers are given a **new title**—"Brethren" (v. 17). 3. Believers are told of a **new position**—Christ's position before the Father (v. 17). 4. Believers occupy a **new place**—apart from the world (v. 19). 5. Believers are assured of a **new blessing**—"peace" made and imparted (vv. 19, 21). 6. Believers are given a **new privilege**—the Lord Jesus in their midst (v. 19). 7. Believers have a **new joy**—through a vision of the risen Lord (v. 20). 8. Believers receive a **new commission**—sent into the world by the Son as He was sent by the Father (v. 21). 9. Believers are a **new creation**—indicated by the "breathing" (v. 22). 10. Believers have a **new Indweller**—even the Holy Spirit (v. 22). How Divinely meet that all this was on the "first of the week"—indication of a **new beginning,** i.e., Christianity supplanting Judaism!!

The following questions are to aid the student on the closing section of John 20:—

1. What is the Dispensational picture here?

2. What does the absence of Thomas teach us, v. 24?

3. What do his words in v. 25 prove?

4. What is the difference between the "Peace" of v. 26 and vv. 19, 21?

5. Why the great similarity between vv. 19 and 26?

6. What practical lesson does v. 23 teach?

7. What is the meaning of v. 29?

ARTHUR W. PINK.

## GLEANINGS IN EXODUS.

### 44. The Tabernacle Door: Ex. 26:36-37.

One important principle which must be observed if the Word of God is to be intelligently studied, is noting carefully the **order** in which truth is there presented to us. God is a God of order, and infallible wisdom marks all His handiwork; yet His order is often different from ours. In the Scriptures the Holy Spirit frequently ignores the sequence of events and places side by side things which did not immediately follow each other in time. The books of the Bible are not always placed in their historical order: Job takes us back to a period long before the Israelites settled in Canaan. The Psalms and the Proverbs were written centuries before the events described in Nehemiah and Esther. So it is with many of the smaller details in the different books. Take the following as examples. The opening of the graves and the coming forth of many of the saints is mentioned right after the Saviour's death and rending of the Temple's veil (Matt. 27:51-52), yet, as a matter of fact, these occurred **after** the resurrection of Christ. So in Luke 23.45 the rending of the veil is recorded **before** the Lord committed His spirit into the hands of the Father.

The arrangement followed by the Holy Spirit varied according to His several designs. Sometimes the chronological order is departed from for a dispensational reason: sometimes details are arranged so as to present a climax: sometimes the order is a moral one: at others, things are placed in juxtaposition to show the relation between cause and effect.

Notably is that the case in Matt. 27:51-53: the opening of the graves there attested the efficacy of the Saviour's death and shows it is the ground of the saints' walk in newness of life. Sometimes the design of the Spirit is to point a contrast: such is the case in Luke 23:45. There He has linked together the three hours of darkness and the rending of the Veil: in the former we have Christ shut out from God, in the latter the way is now opened for us into the presence of Him who is Light!

The student of Scripture loses much when he fails to diligently bear in mind this principle. Strikingly is it exemplified in connection with the Tabernacle. It is not always easy to discern the Divine plan, and much prayerful meditation is required to discover the perfections of every detail. That which we are now to contemplate is the Entrance into the Tabernacle, and what we would here particularly take notice of is that this "Door" is mentioned immediately after the description of the Veil. Doubtless there is more than one reason for this; but that which is almost apparent on the surface is that the one points a striking contrast from the other, and the details connected with each bear this out. The Veil had "cherubim" embroidered upon it, the Door had not: the Veil was suspended from four pillars, the hanging for the Door from five: the former had no "chapiters," the latter had; the sockets of the former were made of silver, the latter were of brass. But the outstanding difference between them was this: the Veil was to shut out, whereas the Door was to give admittance: the Veil barred the way into the Holiest, the "hanging" was for the constant entrance of the priests into the Holy Place. Let us now consider:—

### 1. Its Location.

The Door into God's dwelling-place was no narrow one, but stretched right across the whole of its length, and was ten cubits (fifteen feet) in height. Some of the commentators are in error here through confounding the Door of the Tabernacle (26.36) with the Gate of the Court (27:16). It is important that the student should clearly distinguish between them, for they typically set forth two entirely different lines of truth.

The Door into the Tabernacle spanned the whole of the eastern side. Most significant and most fitting was this, for the east is the quarter of the sun-rising. It is in the east that we discover the evidences of the ending of night and the dawning of another day. Thus a further contrast is here presented. In Gen. 3:24 we read that the Lord God "drove out the man, and he placed at the east of the garden of Eden cherubim, and a flaming sword which turned every way, to keep the way of the tree of life." There, through his sin, man was in the darkness, and in consequence, banished from that place where God had communed with him; and at the east was stationed a flaming barrier. But here, where sin had been typically put away, the priestly family walking in the light, found a door on the eastern side of the Tabernacle which admitted them into Jehovah's dwelling-place!

### 2. Its Material.

"And thou shalt make an hanging for the door of the tent, of blue, and purple, and scarlet, and fine twined linen, wrought with needlework" (v. 36). The fabric of this hanging for the Door was of the same goods and of the same fine quality that composed the Curtains and the Veil. Fine twined linen formed its basis. It was only as the Son of God became incarnate that the true dwelling-place for Deity on earth was provided. But, as shown in the last article, the Incarnation, though bringing God down to men, did not of itself give men access to God—for that the Veil must be rent, death must come in. Here, too, in the entrance to the Tabernacle, we are shown that it is only through the Man Christ Jesus that God could be approached unto.

There is one added word here in connection with the fine twined linen which claims our notice: it was "wrought with needlework." This was not said in connection with the Curtains or Veil, and is only mentioned elsewhere in the description of the Gate in the outer Court (v. 27:16) and the Girdle of the high priest (v. 28:39). We may add that the Hebrew word here for "needlework" is, in Ex. 35:35, rendered "the work of the embroiderer," in 1 Chron. 29:2 and Ezek. 17:3, "divers colours," and in Psalm 139:15 "curiously wrought." Combining these slightly varied meanings, the term would denote **minutely variegated**. Thus, it appears, that the Holy Spirit here intimates that attention should be fixed upon the manner in which the different colours were wrought into and interwoven with the fine linen.

### 3. Its Colours.

The "blue" points to Christ as the Heavenly One, the Son of God; the "scarlet" refers to Him as the Son of man—suffering in the past, glorified on earth in a coming day. The "purple" speaks, distinctively, of the kingship of Christ, but also points to the wonderful union between His Deity and His humanity. The mention of the "blue, and purple, and scarlet," is repeated no less than twenty-four times in connection with the Tabernacle's accessories and priesthood, yet never once is the order varied. This suggests an important truth and lesson in connection with their arrangement. So beautifully has this been brought out by another in a book long-since out of print, we transcribe freely from its most helpful interpretation:—

"If we are to place the blue and the scarlet side by side, without the intervention of some other colour, the eye would be offended with the violent contrast; for, though each is beautiful in itself, and suitable to its own sphere, yet there is such a distinction, we might almost say opposition, in their hues, as to render them inharmonious if seen in immediate contact. The purple interposing remedies this unpleasing effect: the eye passes with ease from the blue to the scarlet, and vice versa, by the aid of this blended colour, the purple. The blue gradually shades off into its opposite, the scarlet; and the gorgeousness of the latter is softened by imperceptible degrees into the blue. The purple is a new colour formed by mingling the two: it owes its peculiar beauty alike to both; and were the due proportion of either absent, its especial character would be lost.,

"The scarlet and the blue are never placed in juxtaposition throughout the fabrics of the Tabernacle. Does not this intimate a truth of an important character? Would the Spirit of God have so constantly adhered to this arrangement had there not been some significant reason for it? Are we not hereby taught a very precious fact respecting the Lord Jesus? He is God and Man; and we can trace in the Gospels all the fulness of the Godhead, as well as the dignity and sympathy of the perfect Man. But besides this, in His thoughts, feelings, ways, words, and actions, there is an invariable blending of the two. . . . In contemplating Christ it is well to remember that the first syllable of His name, as given in Isa. 9:6 is 'Wonderful'; and part of this marvel is, that in Him are combined the deep thoughts and counsels of God, with the feelings and affections of man.

"Three instances are recorded in the Gospels of the dead being raised to life by Christ: Jairus's daughter, the widow of Nain's son, and Lazarus of Bethany. Together they afford us a complete display of His mighty power: for, in the first case, death had only just seized its victim; in the second, the sorrowing mother was on her way to commit the body of her only son to the grave; in the third, the corpse had already been deposited sometime, and had become corrupt in the tomb. In each of these scenes the three colours may be traced. We can have no hesitation in recognizing the blue in the manifestation of the love of God, when His blessed Son at the entreaty of the sorrowful father, went to the house to heal the dying child. On the way, the message came, 'Thy daughter is dead, why troublest thou the Master any further?' Little did they, who spoke these words, understand who the Master was: or the depths of trouble in which He would be overwhelmed, in order that the dead might live. They knew not that God was present with them, manifest in the flesh: but He at once stilled the fear of the damsel's father; thus doing what none but God could do—commanding peace into his bosom in the very presence of death! Again, the voice of the Mighty God sounds forth to hush the boisterous grief of those who have no hope, saying, 'Weep not: the damsel is not dead, but sleepeth'. But they perceived not who it was that thus spoke. Death was to them a familiar sight; they knew its palor; but they laughed Christ to scorn; ought not the believer to exactly reverse this? In the presence of the Lord, he may well laugh death to scorn. Lastly; were not the power and the grace of the One from Heaven now known, when He spake those words—'Damsel, I say unto thee, arise'!

"Let us now turn to the scarlet in this beautiful picture. Who but the Son of man would have pursued the path of kindness and sympathy, notwithstanding the rude scoffs with which His ready love was met? and who but One that knew what hunger and exhaustion were, would have added to this mighty miracle the command, 'Give her something to eat'? And does not this also exhibit to us the purple? With sympathy and love for the child, deeper than the mother's, and yet presented in the scene as one who was Lord in it and above it; He can call the dead to life and at the same moment enter into the minutest want of the little maid. The mere human beings who were present, even the very parents, were so over-powered with what they had witnessed, and with the joy of receiving the dead one back to life, that their human sympathies failed. None but God could thus have abolished death; and none but He who was God and Man, could have so combined power, majesty, grace, sympathy and tenderest care!

"The next instance, already alluded to, depicts in few but full sentences, the same lovely colours. Unsolicited, the Son of God went to the city where He knew the stroke of death had fallen, and had inflicted another wound upon another heart already stricken with grief. He timed His visit so as to meet, at the gate, the mournful procession, bearing to the grave the only son of a widowed mother. If any hope of God's intervention had at one time cheered her, whilst she watched her dying child, all such hope must now have fled. A little interval only remained and the earth would close over her lost son. But attracted by the very extremity of the case, He, who declared the Father (John 1:18), drew nigh. With the authority of God, He touched the bier, and arrested the bearers in their progress to the tomb. Struck by a sudden consciousness that they were in the presence of One who had a right to stop them on their way, they stood still. They did not, like the attendants on the dead in former case, laugh Him to scorn; and, therefore, they had the blessing of witnessing His mighty act. He commanded the young man to arise from the bier, as He ordered the child to rise from her bed; and in like manner, He was obeyed: 'He that was dead sat up, and began to speak.' Here, then, the **heavenly** colour was evident, so that even they that looked on said, 'God hath visited His people'. But the heart of Christ was occupied with the mother as well as the child. As the voice of the risen youth reached His ear, He knew how the widow felt, as she heard it. Himself undisturbed by the exercise of His life-giving power, yet fully occupied in sympathy and grace with the yearning of the mother to embrace her son, and thus to assure herself of the reality, which even the evidence of her eyes and ears could scarcely credit, He gave completeness to the scene by **delivering him to his mother**. Here was the perfection of human sensibility, such as no man could have exhibited in such circumstances, unless that man were also God.

"But perhaps the most complete manifestation of 'the Word made flesh,' is to be found in John 11, if we except, as we always must do, the Cross, where all was marvellously concentrated. It seemed to the sisters as if the Lord had strangely disregarded their urgent message: for He still abode at a distance, and allowed not only death to bereave them of their brother, but the grave to close upon his remains, His very reply to their announcement ('Lord, he whom Thou lovest, is sick') contained in it a paradox which they were unable to comprehend, and which the subsequent circumstances apparently falsified; for, His answer was 'This sickness is not unto death, but for the glory of God, that the Son of God might be glorified thereby.' And yet He tarried till death had, for four days, retained its victim. Thus, love and truth in Him who is Love, and who is the Truth, for a while appeared to have failed; but in reality the glory of God was the more to shine forth in His Beloved.

"What mingled feelings occupied the heart of Christ, when, seeing the grief of Mary, and of those around, He groaned in the spirit, and was troubled! He grieved over their unbelief and ignorance of Himself; and yet He wept in sympathy with them, and sorrowed for the very sorrow which His presence might have prevented. Who could have shed tears in such circumstances but Christ? Had a mere man been gifted by God with the power to raise the dead, he would be so eager to exhibit that mighty power, and thereby still the mourners' grief, that he would be unable to weep whilst on the way to the grave. He must be more than man who could display what man in perfection is. The tears of Jesus are precious, because they are those of true human feeling: but they are most precious because they flow from the heart of Him who is the Mighty God. And, when those tears plenteously fell from His eyes, all questions as to His love were at an end; and even the Jews exclaimed, 'Behold, how He loved him!'

"As with authority He had touched the bier, so now He commanded that the stone should be removed. But Martha interposed her objection and though she owned Christ as Lord, and had heard from His lips the wondrous words, 'I am the Resurrection and the Life,' yet she believed not that there could be a remedy for one who had already seen corruption. It was then that Jesus reminded her of the message He had returned when they sent to inform Him of Lazarus's sickness—that it should not be unto death, by answering, 'Said I not unto thee, that, if thou wouldst believe, thou shalt see the glory of God?' God's glory was ever His object: and to accomplish that He had been content to bear the questioning of those near to Him, who could not understand why He had not at once come to their aid.

"The sepulchre was now laid open; and

Jesus lifted up His eyes from that receptacle of death to the Heaven above, resting His spirit in the bosom of His Father, and audibly expressing His dependence on Him, before He cried with a voice of almighty power, 'Lazarus, come forth'. What a wondrous **blending** was here of subjection and authority, of obedience and command, of 'the open ear,' and of the great 'I am'! The dead, hearing the voice of the Son of God, came forth. The corrupt corpse stepped out in life. What a moment of astonishment and delight must that have been to the sisters, as well as to their brother! But here again the Lord alone entered into the minutest details of this astonishing act of power. He saw, or rather felt (for He loved Lazarus), that His friend was still encumbered with the relics of the grave; and he left it not till others awoke from their surprises, to perceive the clothes that bound and troubled the risen one, but gave another command, 'Loose him, and let him go.' " (Mr. G. Soltau.)

### 4. Its Meaning.

The "hanging for the door" shut off the court of the Tabernacle from the holy place, yet also formed the entrance to it. It was that which gave the priests access to accomplish their service within. It spoke, then, of the Christian's worship and works being acceptable to God **through the Lord Jesus Christ.** Apart from the Mediator even the saints can offer nothing which the great and holy God will receive. We give thanks unto the Father "in the name of our Lord Jesus Christ" (Eph. 5:20). It is "by Him" we are to continually offer to God a sacrifice of praise (Heb. 13:15). Our spiritual sacrifices are acceptable to God only "by Jesus Christ" (1 Peter 2:12). In our ministry, God is to be glorified in all things, "through Jesus Christ" (1 Peter 4:11). It is striking to note that the "cherubim" are **absent** from the Door-hanging. They view the Son of man in His judicial character. Whereas, in the "hanging" He is presented in grace to those that were without, as the Way into the privileges of priests.

### 5. Its Pillars.

"And thou shalt make for the hanging five pillars of shittim wood, and overlay them with gold" (v. 37). The number of the "pillars" confirms what has just been said above respecting the significant omission of the "cherubim" from the "hanging": for **five** is the number of grace. These pillars served to support the "hanging" and also to display its beautiful colours. Their materials intimate that it is the God-man, in wondrous grace through whom entrance is given into the sphere of priestly privileges. And where is it, in Scripture, that we have these distinctively set forth? Not in the Prophets, nor in the Gospels, but in the N.T. Epistles. And is it not something more than a curious coincidence that the Epistle-writers were just five in number? Just as the Veil was stretched between four pillars, corresponding to the four Gospels; so the Entrance-curtain into the place of worship hung between five pillars, anticipating the ministry of Paul and Peter, James, John and Jude—note how this very term "pillars" is expressly applied to them in Gal. 2:9!

### 6. Its Chapiters.

"And the five pillars of it with their hooks: and he overlaid their chapiters and their fillets with gold" (36:38). This was in striking contrast from the "pillars" which supported the Veil, for they had none—foreshadowing Christ as the One "cut off" in the midst of His days. But here, as giving access to the antitypical priestly family into the place of worship and service, Christ is pointed to as the One who is "crowned with glory and honour"! And this is the very viewpoint taken in all the Epistles: their writers proceed on the basis of Christ being at the right hand of God!

### 7. Its Sockets.

"And thou shalt cast five sockets of brass for them" (v. 37). These formed the foundation for the "pillars" and speak therefore, of redemption. "Brass," when used symbolically, always prefigures the capability of the Saviour to **"endure the cross."** Thus is the worshipper reminded once more, that Christ is the Door by reason of **His sufferings in death.** May the Spirit of God ever keep before us the tremendous price which was paid to enable the redeeemd to come before God with sacrifices of praise and thanksgiving.

—Arthur W. Pink.

## SONGS IN THE NIGHT.

While visiting a friend recently, there suddenly stole into our conversation about Christ, the softest and sweetest strain of music. It was not the ordinary whistle of a bird, meaningless except as it expresses the longing of suffering creation, but it was a connected and most melodious snatch from one of the masters of song. The first thought was that a music box had in some mysterious manner become sprung, and was pouring forth these exquisite notes; but a glance around the room revealed a cage containing a beautiful bullfinch; and then it was discovered that the delightful harmony proceeded from the throat of the little warbler.

In answer to an expression of surprise and admiration, the lady of the house explained that the bird had been taught to sing in the night. It had been found necessary to exclude it from the light, and all objects that might divert its attention, and then when the teacher sat near it in the darkness, and played over and over the same tune, at last the bird was able to catch the notes, and to repeat them in perfect unison with the mind of the composer and the hand of the performer.

Of course the words of Elihu, that marvellous type of Christ, instantly came into remembrance: "Where is God my Maker, who giveth songs in the night?" (Job 35:10). It may be that He can teach some of His people to sing only in the night; and it is certain that their sweetest songs are learned when darkness closes about them. What would David have been to the saints of all subsequent ages, if he had not been compelled to say "Deep calleth unto deep at the noise of Thy waterspouts: all Thy waves and billows are gone over me?" And then he could add, "In the night His song is with me, and my prayer unto the God of my life" (Psa. 42:7-8). In another place he says "In the day of my trouble I sought the Lord: my sore ran in the night and ceased not (or as Dr. De Witt renders it, 'My hand is stretched forth in the night, and is not withdrawn'): my soul refused to be comforted." But then he adds, "I call to remembrance my song in the night" (Psa. 77:2-6).

First, he could sing in the night, because he had **faith** in God's Word; as he says of the fathers, "then believed they His words; they sang His praise" (Psa. 106:12). So he says for himself, "Thy statutes have been my songs in the house of my pilgrimage" (Psa. 119:54); and in a day yet future, "All the kings of the earth shall praise Thee, O Lord, when they hear the words of Thy mouth. Yea, they shall sing in the ways of the Lord." (Psa. 138:4, 5). God's Word remains even in the darkest hour of affliction, and for this we sing.

Second, he could sing for **mercy**. "I will sing aloud of Thy mercy in the morning;" and again, "I will sing of the mercies of the Lord forever" (Psa. 59:16; 89:1). Yet, there is mercy in the night, mercy in the stroke that lays us low, and mercy to crown sorrow, when the Lord teaches in the dark the song He wishes us to learn. "Behold, we count them happy which endure. Ye have heard of the patience of Job, and have seen the end of the Lord; that the Lord is very pitiful, and of tender mercy" (James 5:11). It was a very dark night, when the prophet could say, "Though He cause grief, yet will He have compassion according to the multitude of His mercies. For He doth not afflict willingly, nor grieve the children of men" (Lam. 3:32, 33).

Third, he could sing of **redemption**. "My lips shall greatly rejoice when I sing unto Thee; and my soul, which Thou hast redeemed." (Psa. 71:23). This not only gives us occasion to sing in the night of our Lord's absence from earth, and in the darkness of bereavement, but it will tune the voices of the saved in heaven, for we read, "They sung a new song, saying, Thou are worthy to take the book and open the seals thereof; for Thou wast slain, and hast redeemed us to God by Thy blood, out of every kindred, and tongue, and nation; and hast made us unto God kings and priests: and we shall reign upon the earth" (Rev. 5: 9, 10).

Fourth, he could sing of God's **righteousness**. "My tongue shall sing aloud of Thy righteousness" (Psa. 51.14); and "they shall abundantly utter the memory of Thy great goodness, and shall sing of Thy righteousness" (Psa. 145:7). That God made Him, who knew no sin, to be sin for us, that we might be constituted the righteousness of God in Him, is surely enough to wake the songs of gratitude and of praise even in the gloomiest night. As Christ is, so are we, though still in sorrow.

Fifth, he could sing of **deliverance**. "I waited patiently for the Lord! and He inclined unto me, and heard my cry. He brought me up also out of an horrible pit, out of the miry clay, and set my feet upon a rock, and established my goings. And He put a new song into my mouth, even praise unto our God: many shall see it, and fear, and shall trust in the Lord" (Psa. 40:1-3). Of course this refers primarily to our Lord Jesus Christ; but it is true in a measure of every believer, to whom God is saying, "Call upon Me in the day of trouble; I will deliver thee and thou shalt glorify Me" (Psa. 50:15).

Sixth, we can sing to the anticipation of Israel's joy. "In that day shall this song be sung in the land of Judah" (Isa. 27:1). For other passages which plainly tell of Israel's song, when that now scattered people shall be put back into their own land, and look upon the face of their now rejected Messiah, see Isa. 30: 29, 39; 52: 8; 54: 1-3; Hosea 2: 15; Rev. 15: 3.

Seventh, no matter how dark the night, blessed be the Lord, we can sing of resurrection. "Awake and sing, ye that dwell in the dust; for thy dew is as the dew of herbs, and the earth shall cast out the dead (Isa. 26: 19). Nothing else may be left to us; but in view of this certain resurrection, we may still sing through the gloom. "At midnight Paul and Silas prayed, and sang praises unto God." We know that "the night is far spent, the day is at hand" (Rom. 13: 12); and oh, how we shall sing when we are caught up together with our loved ones to meet the Lord in the air.

—Dr. J. H. Brookes.

The night of trial, of suffering, of sorrow, ought not to silence the songs of God's children. David said, "I will bless the Lord at all times; His praise shall continually be in my mouth" (Ps. 34: 1). A psalm was sung as the Saviour and His apostles were about to leave the upper room for Gethsemane (Matt. 26:30). At midnight Paul and Silas "sang praises unto God" (Acts 16:25) in the Philippian dungeon! And many of the Protestant martyrs sang psalms and hymns while burning at the stake! How these examples should rebuke our silence and gloominess! O brethren and sisters, take down your harps from the willows (Psa. 137:2) and make melody unto the Lord. Ponder God's promises, His mercy, His redemption, His deliverances, and before you know it your heart will burst into song.

—A.W.P.

## DISTINGUISHING GRACE.
### 2 Tim. 1:9.

This is one of the many verses in the Bible which treats of and sets forth the distinguishing grace of God in the salvation of His elect people. By distinguishing grace I mean discriminating grace, grace which makes distinctions, grace which singles out certain ones to be the objects of His favor but which passes by others and leaves them to suffer the due reward of their iniquities. It was distinguishing grace that singled out Abraham from his heathenish surroundings and from his idolatrous neighbours and kinsmen. It was distinguishing grace which, in the days of our Lord Jesus upon earth, singled out and saved publicans and harlots and passed by self-righteous, moral religionists. It was distinguishing grace that laid hold of Saul of Tarsus when persecuting the church of God, and blaspheming against the name of the Saviour.

But distinguishing grace is something that the natural man does not like to hear about, and when it is pressed upon his attention it riles him. It brings into evidence the enmity of the carnal mind. A worm of the earth dares to call into question the justice of the Almighty. The clay rises up against the Potter, and says, "Why hast Thou made me thus?" In fact, the idea of the natural man is that all sinners ought to have an equal chance of salvation, and they object that unless God does give all men an equal chance of salvation, then He is acting unjustly. Let me just try and reason with you for a moment, or rather let me point out how such an objection overlooks two vital elements in the case—I mean now the one who cries out against distinguishing, discriminating, sovereign grace, and calls it "Injustice!" This overlooks two vital elements in the case.

First, the objector loses sight of the condition of those whom he imagines are wronged. If it be true that all men ought to have a fair and equal opportunity of salvation, and if it were true that God was unjust because He did not so give it, then it would necessarily follow that salvation was something to which every man was entitled. If a man is wronged in not having salvation fairly offered to him, then salvation must be his right. If salvation is not his right, then he is not wronged if it is not presented to him. If he is wronged because it is not offered to him, then salvation must be his right. In other words, to put it plainly, heaven is something to which he is entitled. Is that so? Is that true? Is it not rather true that "all have sinned and come short of the glory of God"?—that everyone has, again and again, broken His righteous laws and therefore stands before the thrice-holy God as a guilty transgressor and a condemned criminal. Do you mean to tell me that a company of condemned criminals have the right to say how the judge shall deal with them? That is preposterous on the face of it. That is turning things upside down with a vengeance. But that is precisely the position the objector takes when he insists that all ought to have an equal chance of salvation. He is only saying in other words that the condemned criminals themselves have the right to say what the judge shall do to them.

Secondly, the objector not only loses sight of the condition of those he imagines are wronged, but he also utterly ignores the character of grace. What is grace? What do you understand by the term "grace"? Listen! Instead of grace being a blessing to which all are entitled, grace is something that none can claim. Why, my dear friends, if grace could be won or bought or earned it would case to be grace. The very meaning of the term itself shows that. The word "grace" signifies unmerited, undeserved favor. Then if it be un-deserved, certainly none are entitled to it! In other words, dear friends, grace is like charity, it is gratuitously bestowed upon beggars. Well, can a beggar demand charity as his right? No more can sinners demand grace as that to which they are entitled.

Now, just because grace is unmerited, something which we do not deserve and to which we are not entitled, it must be exercised and shown in a sovereign manner. Let me repeat that. I am anxious for you to get hold of that. The very nature of grace, the very character of grace requires that it should be exercised in a discriminating way. Let us suppose the opposite for a moment. If God were to bestow grace upon all members of the human race without an exception, if God were to give His saving grace to every descendant of fallen Adam, then His grace would not be appreciated. Are the temporal blessings which He does bestow upon all, appreciated? I go farther than that. If God were to bestow His saving grace upon all sinners without exception, the pride and self-righteousness of man would at once conclude that God was obliged to do so, as a sort of compensation for allowing the race to fall into sin. But God is under no obligations to fallen men. Man forfeited every claim upon the notice of God when he, in the person of his representative, rebelled against Him in Eden.

My friends, as a matter of fact, grace is our only hope. Desert we have none; spirituality we have none; righteousness we have none. But distinguishing grace steps in and snatches from Hell a chosen number who have neither fitness nor title to Heaven. Grace is our only hope, and if God is pleased in His sovereignty to bestow that grace upon a limited chosen number, who is wronged? Listen! Eternal life is a gift. If eternal life be a gift, not only is it impossible to earn it, but we have no claim upon it. We cannot demand it as a right. And because it is a gift, God reserves to Himself the sovereign right to bestow it upon whom He pleases, and therefore He says "I will have mercy on whom I will have mercy." Let none murmur against this, if bare justice be enforced then all would necessarily be damned. It is not that God refuses eternal life to any. Every sinner who truly, penitently and believingly seeks salvation at His hands shall surely be saved. But if out of a world of impenitent and unbelieving God is determined to exercise His sovereign rights by choosing a certain number unto salvation, who is wronged? Is God obliged to force His gifts on those who do not value them? Is He obliged to save those who desire and are determined to go their own way?

Now, coming closer to our text. We have set before us, first, the Author of to the power of God—Who hath saved us." The opening word is a pronoun that obliges us to go back to the preceding verse for the antecedent. The last sentence of verse 8 is:—" . . . according to the power of God—Who hath saved us." Wherever you get that Divine title used without any qualifying clause it always embraces the three Persons of the Godhead. It does so here. "Who hath saved us": God hath saved us—Father, Son, and Holy Spirit. First of all, the Father hath saved us (His people). Take 1 John 3.1:—"Behold, what manner of love the Father has bestowed upon us, that we should be called the children of God." It was the Father who first purposed to honor and glorify His Son by giving Him a people to show forth His praises. It was the Father who planned our salvation, and it was the Father who chose the objects that should be saved. "Blessed be the God and Father of our Lord Jesus Christ, who hath blessed us with all spiritual blessings in the heavenlies in Christ: according as He (the Father) hath chosen us in Him before the foundation of the world" (Ephesians 1: 3, 4). But now that does not exclude the honor and the glory of the Son. The Father hath saved us because the plan of salvation originated with Him. He is the great Initiator, but salvation flows to us through the Son. "No man cometh unto the Father but by (through) Me." (John 14:6). "Who hath saved us." God hath: the Father hath; the Son hath through His redemptive work, because it is on the basis of His redemptive work that we are accepted by the Father. But we must not exclude the Holy Spirit. The Holy Spirit has His part, His place, His honor and glory in connection with the salvation of God's elect. It is the Holy Spirit who quickens them from death into life, who convicts them of their sins, who shows them their need of a Saviour, who breaks down their stubborn wills, who draws them to the feet of Christ. (John 6.63). The flesh profiteth nothing. It is the Spirit that quickens us. So first of all in the text you have the **Author** of salvation,. **God**—Father, Son and Holy Spirit.

Second, we have revealed here the **method** of the Christian's salvation. Notice carefully the tense of the verb: "Who **hath** saved us," not who will save us when we come to die; not Who has put us on probation for salvation; but "Who **hath** saved us." Ah, my friends, salvation is something more than a deathbed blessing that we are going to sing about in the future state: salvation is something that the children of God rejoice in even now. Who hath saved us from the wrath to come, from the everlasting burnings, from the guilt and the penalty of sin, saved us gratuitously, perfectly, eternally.

"Who hath saved us **and** called us." The order here is very striking. It is something that no Arminian knows what to do with, in fact some of them are so wicked as to say that there was a little slip of the apostle's pen. I could mention one Arminian commentator of considerable eminence and prominence who says that the words there should be transposed, that what Paul really meant was, "Who hath called us and saved us." And thus they would try to fit Scripture to their theology instead of their theology to the Scriptures. "Who hath saved us and called us." Now I want you to notice carefully the order here. "Salvation" comes **before** the "calling"! What? Do you mean to say that we are saved before He calls us from death unto life? Well, it looks very much like it, doesn't it? If this text means what it says, and Scripture always means what it says and it always says what it means. But is it true that we are saved **before** we are called? In the sense of our experience, No; in the sense of the Holy Spirit's application to our consciences and hearts, no; but in the sense of God's eternal, invincible purpose, yes; in the sense of God's elect having been eternally united to the Covenant Head, yes. Listen! You were lost before you were born, lost before you were born into this world I mean, lost before you committed a single sin yourself, lost when the first Adam fell, for my Bible says, "In Adam all died." In the same way God's elect were saved before they were born, by virtue of their union to their Covenant Head. But that is not all.

I am going to labor this point because some of you need it very much. Saved before we were called in this sense also, in the sense that the redemptive work of Christ was finished, the ransom-price was paid, and God accepted it and all that it had been paid to accomplish had been performed. Let me give you a simple illustration. Here is a man who has been imprisoned for debt and a friend comes along and pays his debt and obtains a receipt and thereby secures his release; and yet the ransomed debtor **is** still in prison, and knows nothing of what has been done. But that does not alter the fact that the moment his friend paid his debt and obtained his receipt, that moment he **was** released. The prison held him legally no longer. He did not know it, but that does not alter the fact. When the advice came to him of what his benefactor had done, when he learned that his debt had been discharged, why he just leapt for joy and walked out a free man. Do I need to apply the illustration? The Lord Jesus on the cross purchased His people, ransomed them from the grave, and sin and Satan lost their legal hold upon them. They are still—some of them, as you sit there to-night, and **you** may be among the number—they are still, experimentally speaking, sitting in the prison-house, and it has not yet been brought home to their hearts what has been done for them. That does not alter the fact that they **have been** legally released, that their debt has been paid. Once they learn it, once the fact comes home to their heart in the power of God the Spirit, they will rejoice, they will walk forth free. So that is the reason, beloved, why in the order of our text we read, "Who hath saved us **and** called us."

Now notice again what follows that:— ". . . called us with an holy calling." In other words, called us **unto** holiness, called us to be separated from sin and conformed to Christ. It seems to me that the Holy Spirit moved the apostle to bring in this clause in order to refute the error of those who say that God elected certain ones to be saved because He foresaw their holiness—which is taught very commonly in certain quarters. But our text plainly repudiates this God-dishonouring and grace-denying sophistry. Saved and called, not because they were holy, but unto holiness. Open your Bibles at Ephesians 1.4. What do you read there? "According as He hath chosen us in Him before the foundation of the world, because we were holy"? No, no, no! Look at it and see how it reads in your Bible—Ephesians 1.4:—"According as He hath chosen us in Him before the foundation of the world that we should be holy." The choice was the cause; holiness is the effect—not chosen us because of some holiness there was in us either actual or foreseen.

"Who hath saved us, and called us with an holy calling, not according to our works." That completes the statement of the process of our salvation. "Not according to our works." The world says, Live a good life, do all the good you can, be upright and moral and then God will save you. The Gospel says, You are a lost sinner and all you will get if justice be demanded, if you are to receive what you are entitled to, will be eternal punishment. But God in His mercy has blotted out our sins, accepted us in the Beloved, and saved us with an everlasting salvation; and this, not according to our works—as Eph. 2:9 says, "Not of works, lest any man should boast." And, my friends, that includes not according to our willingness, not according to our anything. There are lots of churches today which profess to believe that God saves, that Christ is the only Saviour for sinners, and yet in almost the next breath they will make the sinner his own saviour by telling him that "Christ has done all that He can; it is now left for you to decide whether His blood shall be shed in vain or no." If that is true, then we are saved by our own works. If some action of my will is the final factor, the deciding element, then I have a hand in it.

Third, our text defines the Origin of the Christian's salvation: "and hath called us with an holy calling, not according to our works, but according to His own purpose." In the past, when I have stressed that point, when I have sought to emphasise and make clear the meaning of that (I do not want to raise a smile) there was always a few in the congregation who reminded me of fishes squirming on a hook. They could not bear to hear about **God** having a "purpose." Oh, of course it is all right for **me** to have a purpose, a plan, and I am willing for other men to have a purpose; I am willing for them to make their plans; but the Almighty, forsooth, He must not have one! His hands must be tied, and tied by us, too. O, do you see the awfulness, the wickedness, the sinfulness of the clay dictating to the Potter, the creature prescribing for the Creator? A child of a few years wishing to dictate the policy of the Ancient of Days? Ah, my friends, it stands written here, and you cannot get rid of it, that God has a purpose, and we are saved "according to" His purpose. And notice how strongly it is put! It not only says, "According to His purpose," but it says, "According to His **own** purpose."

But again I must pass on. Fourth, we have here, the Antiquity of our salvation: ". . . . according to His own purpose and grace which was given us in Christ Jesus" when we **believed**? O did I make a slip? When we **yielded ourselves** to Christ. Is that **when** His grace was "given" to us? **That** is the belief of nine-tenths of Christendom to-night. That is the teaching of those who are looked upon as the soundest of our evangelists to-day—that God's grace is given to the sinner when he believes. What does our text say? O may God give you grace to bow to His Word no matter how much of your theology it upsets. "According to His own purpose and grace, which was given us in Christ Jesus **before the world began**"! I would like you to tell me how much we had to do with that. Why, we were not even in existence then! And yet this text distinctly says that the grace of God was given to His own people before the world began! How that absolutely and completely closes the door against man having any part or place in his own salvation. Behold, then, the sovereign, distinguishing, eternal grace of God consulting with none; acting freely, according to His own good pleasure!

Fifth, the **Mediator** of our salvation is here specified. In our text the Holy Spirit has been careful to state the Channel through which this salvation of God comes to His people, for every word in the text here has a meaning and a message and a value. "According to His own purpose and grace, which was **given us in Christ Jesus**." I want to pass on to you just one sentence that I culled this last week from one of the old Puritans. I thought it was such an apt and striking and beautiful way of summing up this part of the truth. "Not only is the **well** of salvation provided by the grace of God, but God does not ask us to furnish our own buckets to bring it up to the surface. **Christ is the channel through which the water of life flows to our parched and needy souls.**"

No, my friends, this church does not believe in a gospel where sinners are asked to bring their buckets with them and provide their own means. By grace, we believe in a God and we proclaim a Gospel where **everything** has been done for the sinner who has been chosen by God unto salvation. "Who hath saved us, and called us with an holy calling, not according to our works, but acording to His own purpose and grace, which was given us in Christ Jesus before the world began."

Now my closing word is this. What a message of **comfort** is there in this truth of God's sovereign grace to poor, needy sinners. I am rather afraid that the doctrine of election has been presented by some preachers as though it were a high wall with a lot of spikes on the top to keep poor sinners from coming to Christ. I am rather afraid that the doctrine of predestination in the hands of some—unwittingly no doubt—has been handled like a sharp spear that has been thrust at some poor sinner that was crying to God for mercy. O beloved, where would any of us be to-night were it not for the distinguishing grace of God? I want, if the Lord will help me, in two or three more moments to apply that to any burdened, anxious soul that may be present to-night. "Grace" means undeserved and unmerited favor, shown to those who are entitled to nothing but Hell. Does not that open the door wide to you? Does not that afford you some encouragement, sinner? Suppose we were to tell you that salvation was on any other principle but grace; suppose we were to tell you that it was only the good and the moral and the upright and the spiritual who were going to Heaven; then where would **you** be? Yes, where would any of us be? Grace, God's electing grace, has singled out some of the blackest, vilest, foulest sinners that have ever walked this earth, then why may not **you** be included in the number? O I wonder is there one who feels himself or herself to be too black, too foul, too vile, to ever have the slightest prospect of entering that fair land of holiness. I wonder if Satan has told you that you are such a sinner that it is useless for you to cry for mercy. Why, my friends, if I have read my New Testament aright, I believe I find there how that the distinguishing grace of God laid its saving hand upon some of those that spat in the Saviour's face and nailed Him to the cross of shame and suffering: certainly I can single out one who was a murderer and a persecutor of the Church of God. Why, if the electing grace of God did not pass by a Saul of Tarsus, surely there is some hope for **you**, my friend, black though you be, sinful though you are. O surely this blessed doctrine of salvation by grace alone is one of real encouragement to those who feel themselves to be too sinful to ever enter Heaven.

My friends, it is because it is an encouraging doctrine that I preach it. May God in His grace apply His Word to some convicted, burdened, anxious sinner here to-night. "This Man," says the Gospel of Luke, referring to the Saviour, the Lord Jesus, "this Man receiveth **sinners.**" He Himself declared, "I came not to call the righteous, but **sinners** to repentence." "This is a faithful saying, and worthy of all acceptation, that Christ Jesus came into the world to save sinners." Why not **you**? Why should not you be included among that number? Come to Him just as you are in all your blackness, in all your wretchedness and sinfulness, and put Him to the proof. He can but turn you away, but He is never known to have done that yet. He is never known to have turned away one poor convicted, needy sinner who casts himself upon His mercy. O put Him to the proof yourself. "This Man receiveth sinners and eateth with them." If you have been made to feel your need of Christ, if you have been made to realise your awful sinfulness and your deservingness of Hell, if you have been made to wonder "Is it possible that such a wretch as I can ever enter Heaven" then that is evidence that the Spirit of God has been showing to you your need of a mighty Saviour. O may He draw you to Him to-night. Come unto Him and He will in no wise cast you out.

---

The above is a sermon that was preached by the Editor in the Strict and Particular Baptist Church, Sydney, March 20th, 1927.

## SECURITY.

#### "He laid down His life for us" (John 3:16)

Did my Saviour lay down His life for me? Then, how safe am I! We who know the Gospel, see in the fact of the death of Christ a reason that no strength of logic can ever shape, and no power of unbelief can remove, while we should be saved. There may be men with minds so distorted that they can conceive it possible that Christ should die for a man who afterwards is lost; I say, there may be such. I am sorry to say that there are still to be found some such persons, whose brains have been so addled in their childhood, they cannot see that what they hold is both a preposterous falsehood and a blasphemous libel. Christ died for a man, and then God punishes that man again; Christ suffers in a sinner's stead, and then God condemns that sinner after all! Why, my friends, I feel quite shocked in only mentioning such an awful error; and were it not so current as it is, I should certainly pass it over with the contempt that it deserves.

The doctrine of Holy Scripture is this: that Christ died in the stead of His people, and that, as God is just, He will never punish one solitary soul of Adam's race for whom the Saviour did thus shed His blood. No, my soul, how shalt thou be punished if thy Lord endured thy punishment for thee? Did He die for thee? O, my soul, if Jesus was not thy Substitute, and did not die in thy very stead, then He is no Saviour for thee! But if He was thy Substitute, if He suffered as thy Surety, then, Who is he that condemneth? Christ hath died, yea, rather, hath risen again, and sitteth at the right-hand of God, and maketh intercession for us. There stands the master-argument: Christ "laid down His life for us," and "if, when we were enemies, we were reconciled to God, by the death of His Son, much more, being reconciled, we shall be saved by His life." If the agonies of the Saviour put our sins away, the everlasting life of the Saviour, with the merits of His death added thereunto, must preserve His people unto the end.

This much I know,—ye may hear men stammer when they say it,—but what I preach is the old Lutheran, Calvinistic, Augustinian, Pauline, Christian truth,— there is not one sin in the Book of God, against any one that believeth. Our sins were numbered on the Scapegoat's head, and there is not one sin, that even a believer could commit that hath any power to damn him, for Christ hath taken the damning power out of sin, by allowing it (to speak by a bold metaphor) to damn Himself, for sin did condemn Him; and, inasmuch as sin condemned Him, sin cannot condemn us. O believer, this is thy security, that all thy sin and guilt, all thy transgressions and iniquities have been atoned for, and were atoned for before they were committed; so that thou mayest come with boldness, though red with all crimes and black with every lust, and lay thine hand on that Scapegoat's head, and when thou hast put thine hand there, and seen that Scapegoat driven into the wilderness, thou mayest clap thine hands for joy, and say, "It is finished, sin is pardoned."

"Here's pardon for transgressions past,
It matters not how black their cast;
And oh, my soul, with wonder view,
For sins to come here's pardon too."

This is all I want to know; did the Saviour die for me? Then I will not continue in sin that grace may abound; but nothing shall stop me of thus glorying, in all the churches of the Lord Jesus, that my sins are entirely removed from me; and, in God's sight I say sing, as Hart did sing,

"With Christ's spotless vesture on,
Holy as the Holy One."

O marvellous death of Christ, how securely doest thou set the feet of God's people on the rock of eternal love; and how securely dost Thou keep them there!

—C. H. Spurgeon.

Will all friends in the U.S.A. when forwarding money to us please send International Money Orders on Summer Hill P.O.

clay in the hands of the Potter. Take Christ's yoke upon you and learn of Him who was "meek and lowly in heart."

**3. It signifies an acknowledgment of God's righteousness and wisdom in all His dealings with us.**

We must vindicate God. This is what the Psalmist did. "I know, O Lord, that Thy judgments are right, and that Thou in faithfulness hast afflicted me" (119:75). Let us see to it that Wisdom is ever justified by her children. Let our confession of her be "righteous art Thou, O Lord, and upright are Thy judgments" (Psa. 119:137). Whatever is sent, we must vindicate the Sender of all things. The Judge of all the earth cannot do wrong.

The Babylonish captivity was the severest affliction which God ever brought upon His earthly people during Old Testament times. Yet even then a renewed heart acknowledged God's righteousness in it: "Now therefore, our God, the great, the mighty and the terrible God, who keepest covenant and mercy, let not all the trouble seem little before Thee, that hath come upon us, on our kings, on our princes, and on our priests, and on our prophets, and on our fathers, and on all Thy people, since the time of the kings of Assyria unto this day. Howbeit Thou art just in all that is brought upon us; for Thou hast done right, but we have done wickedly." (Neh. 9:32, 33). God's enemies may talk of His injustice; let His children proclaim His righteousness. Because God is good, He can do nothing but what is right and good.

**4. It includes a recognition of His care and a sense of His love.** There is a sulking submission and there is a cheerful submission. There is a fatalistic submission which takes this attitude—this is inevitable, so I must bow to it; and there is a thankful submission, receiving with gratitude whatever God may be pleased to send us. "It is good for me that I have been afflicted; that I might learn Thy statutes" (Psa. 119:71). The Psalmist viewed his chastisements with the eye of faith, and doing so he perceived the love behind them. Remember that when God brings His people into the wilderness it is that they may learn more of His sufficiency, when He casts them into the furnace it is that they may enjoy His presence.

**5. It involves an active performance of His will**

Submission to the "Father of spirits" is something more than a passive thing. The other meanings to this expression which we have already considered are more or less of a negative character. But there is also a positive and an active side to it as well. To be "in subjection" also means to walk in His precepts and run in the way of His commandments. It means being submissive to His Word, our thoughts being formed and our ways being regulated by it. There is a doing as well as a suffering of God's will. God requires obedience from His children, a performance of duties. When we pray "Thy will be done" something more is meant than a pious acquiescence in the will of the Almighty; it also signifies, May Thy will be performed by me. Subjection unto the Father of spirits, then, is the practical owing of His Lordship.

**II.—Reasons for this Subjection.**

**1. Because He is our Father.** It is but right and meet that children should be in subjection to their father. How much more so when we have such a Father! There is nothing tyrannical about Him; His commandments "are not grievous," but are designed for our good. How profoundly thankful we should be that the great God now stands revealed as our "Father"! This is one of the distinctive revelations of the N.T. I very much doubt if Aaron or Eli, Job or David knew God in this relationship; yet they "submitted"! How much more ought we! May grace ever enable us to say with the Saviour, "the cup which My Father hath given Me, shall I not drink it!" (John 19:11).

**2. Because this is the secret of true happiness.** I believe that the force of the last two words in our text are "and be happy." The word "live" or "life" is used in this sense in Deut. 5.23—note "prolong your days" is in addition. Such is its force in Psalms 69:42; 119:116. It is the fretful the murmuring and rebellious. who are miserable and wretched. Making the will of God our haven is the true resting-place for our hearts. Our lives conformed to His will is the secret of contentment and joy. "Take My yoke upon you . . . and ye shall find rest unto your souls," declared the Saviour. In keeping God's commandments there is great reward. "Great peace have they that love Thy law," said the Psalmist. May the Spirit of God work in all of us the true spirit of subjection, even though it take severe chastisement to effect it.

—Sermon preached by the Editor in Sydney.

# STUDIES IN THE SCRIPTURES

"Search the Scriptures" John 5:39

Copyright in all English-speaking Countries.

Editor: Arthur W. Pink, 15 Hurlstone Avenue, Summer Hill, N.S.W., Australia.
Hon. Agent in U.S.A.: Mr. C. S. Pressel, 559 Dupont Avenue, York, Penna.

FREE TO ALL WHO WILL READ IT

## DIVINE CHASTISEMENT.
(Heb. 12:10.)

This morning we are to consider the *benefits* of chastisement. I suppose that when it was announced there would be a whole series of sermons on this subject some of you wished that another theme had been chosen in its stead. The word "chastisement" has an unpleasant sound in many ears. But as we have proceeded to ponder the various aspects of this blessed truth, I trust that many of us have caught some of the sweet melodies sounded out in Heb. 12. First, we have seen that chastisement is not punishment: instead of being judicial, it is parental; instead of being retributive, it is corrective. Second, we have seen that our chastenings proceed from no unkind God, but from our tender Father; that they are not the scourgings of anger, but that the rod is wielded by love. Third, that so far from justifying doubts in the Christian as to his acceptance, they are among the evidences of his Divine sonship.

A Christian is one who is seldom long at ease, for it is "through much tribulation" that we must enter into the kingdom of God (Acts 14:22). Read through the inspired history of the saints of Old and New Testament times, and see how long any of them went before trials came upon them. The Christian may ask, Why should this be? If the Father really loves me, why does He deal so hardly with me? Our present text gives answer: it is "for our profit." Here is the silver lining to the dark cloud: here is comfort and encouragement. O may God give us faith to lay hold on this precious truth.

A little child needs coaxing so as to take its medicine. It may be very ill, and mother may assure the child that the medicine will effect a cure. But it answers, "I can't take it; it is so bitter." But *men* need not to be persuaded thus: the bitterness is nothing to them. They think of the health it will bring, and so take it without wincing. Now, if Christians are spiritually but little children, and do not call to remembrance the fruit which afflictions bear, they may cry and murmur; but if they have grown to be men in Christ and are assured that "all things work together for good to them" they will take the cup willingly and thank God for it. Why should I dread to enter the shaft of affliction if it leads to the gold-mines of spiritual experience? The Hebrews entered Egypt very poor, but following their trials and groanings they came out with jewels of silver and jewels of gold.

We are now to consider some of the advantages conferred and the blessings produced through and by means of God's chastenings. This comes out in our text in the clause, "but He for our profit," which means for the development of character, for growth in grace, for the enrichment of our spiritual lives, for greater conformity to the image of God's Son. Our Heavenly Father never chastises His children *except* for "their profit." His object is uniformly their blessing. Whatever the form, degree, or duration of their afflictions, all is ordered by infinite wisdom so as best to secure this object.

1. *It weans us from the world.* One would think that after the soul has once seen the King in His beauty it would henceforth discover no attractions elsewhere. One would suppose that once we had quenched our thirst at the Fountain of living waters we should no more want to drink from the unsatisfying cisterns of this earth. Surely

(Continued on page 216)

# IMPORTANT NOTICES

## BACK NUMBERS

OF THIS MAGAZINE may yet be secured for 5/- (1 dollar 25.) per year; Bound, at 7/- (1 dollar 75.). Each year is yet obtainable. Soon out of print.

ADVISE PROMPTLY of Change of Address.

THIS MAGAZINE is published as a work of faith and labour of love. It is gladly sent to all who would value it.

We want the names and addresses of Christians who would read it.

Christians who feel definitely led to do so may have fellowship with us in supporting this Ministry.

## CONTENTS.

| | |
|---|---|
| The Gospel of John (20:24-31) | 194 |
| Gleanings in Exodus | 200 |
| Parables of Matt. 13 | 205 |
| The Lawgiver | 208 |
| Forbidden Mixtures | 211 |
| Triumphant Faith | 214 |

## THE GOSPEL OF JOHN.

*69. Christ and Thomas: John 20:24-31.*

Below is an Analysis of our present passage:—
1. The absence of Thomas v. 24.
2. The scepticism of Thomas v. 25.
3. Christ appears to Thomas vv. 26, 27.
4. The confession of Thomas v. 28.
5. Christ's last beatitude v. 29.
6. The signs of Jesus v. 30.
7. The purpose of this Gospel v. 31.

In our last article we were occupied with the appearing of the Lord unto the apostles as they were assembled together in some room, probably the "upper-room" in which the Lord's Supper was instituted. But on this occasion one of the Eleven, Thomas, was absent. We are not expressly told *why* he was not present with his brethren, but from what we learn of him in other passages, from his words to the Ten when they told him of their having seen the Lord, and from Christ's own words to Thomas when He appeared unto the Eleven, it is almost impossible to avoid the conclusion that *unbelief* was the cause of his absence. In three different passages Thomas is mentioned in this Gospel, and on each occasion he evidenced a gloomy disposition. He was a man who looked on the darker side of things: he took despondent views both of the present and the future. Yet was he not lacking in courage, nor in loyalty and devotion to the Saviour?

The first time Thomas comes before us is in chapter 11. At the close of 10 we read how the enemies of Christ "sought again to take Him; but He escaped out of their hand, and went away again beyond Jordan." While there, the sisters of Lazarus sent unto Him, acquainting Him with the sickness of their brother. After waiting two days, the Saviour said unto His disciples, "Let us go into Judea." The disciples at once reminded Him that it was there the Jews had, only lately, sought to stone Him; so they ask, "Goest Thou thither again?" At the end of His colliloquy with them, He said, "Let us go." And then we are told, "Thomas, which is called Didymus, said unto his fellow-disciples, Let us also go, that we may die with Him" (11:16). These words throw not a little light on the character of him who uttered them. First, they reveal Thomas as a man of morbid feeling—*death* was the object which filled his vision. Second, they indicate he had an energetic disposition, "Let us *go*." Third, they exhibit his courage—he was ready *to go* even to death. Fourth, they manifest his affection for Christ—"Let us *also* go, that we may die *with Him*."

The next time Thomas is brought to our notice is in chapter 14. The Lord had announced to the apostles that in a little while He would leave them, and whither He was going, they could not come. In consequence, they were filled with sadness. In view of their grief, the Lord said, "Let not your heart be troubled," supporting this with the comforting assurances that He was going to the Father's House, going there to prepare a place for them, and from which He would come and receive them unto Himself: ending with "Whither I go ye know, and the way ye know." Thomas was the first to reply, and his doleful response was, "Lord, we know not whither Thou goest; and how can we know the way?" (14:5). Ignoring the precious promises of the Saviour, Thomas saw in His departure only the extinction of hope. Thus we behold, once more, His gloomy nature, and, in addition, his sceptical turn of mind. He reminds us very much of John Bunyan's "Fearing," "Despondency," and "Much Afraid." In his Pilgrims' Progress —types of a large class of Christians who are successors of doubting Thomas.

The third and last time that Thomas occupies any prominence in this Gospel is in the 20th chapter. Here the first thing noted about him is that he was not with the other disciples when the Lord appeared unto them. In view of what has been before us above, this is scarcely to be wondered at. "If the bare possibility of his Lord's death had plunged this loving yet gloomy heart into despondency, what dark despair must have preyed on it when that death was actually accomplished! How the figure of his dead Master had burnt itself into his soul, is seen from the manner in which his mind dwells on the prints of the nails, the wound in His side. It is by these only, and not by well-known features or peculiarity of form, he will recognise and identify his Lord. His heart was with the lifeless body on the cross, and he could not bear to see the friends of Jesus or speak with those who had shared his hopes, but buries his disappointment and desolation in solitude and silence. Thus it was that, like many melancholy persons, he missed the opportunity of seeing what would effectually have scattered his doubts!" (Dr. Dods).

"But Thomas, one of the Twelve, called Didymus, was not with them when Jesus came" (v. 24). The "But" is ominous and at once exposes the folly of the inventions which have been made to excuse Thomas. The disciples convened in the evening of that first day of the week under most unusual circumstances. John, at least, was satisfied that the Saviour had risen; of the others, some were sceptical, for they believed not the report of the women who had seen Him that very morning. No doubt the apostles assembled with mingled feelings of suspense and excitement. That Thomas was absent can only be accounted for, we believe, by what the other passages reveal of his gloomy and sceptical disposition. Note how the Holy Spirit was here added "Thomas called Didymus," which is evidently designed as a connecting link cf. 11:16. On the resurrection day he least of all believed the tidings of the women, isolating himself in the sorrow of death in wilful unbelief—the wilfulness of it is seen in the next verse.

The state of Thomas' soul coincided with his absence on that memorable evening. He resisted the blessedness of the resurrection, and therefore did not join his brethren, and thus share the joy of the Master's presence in their midst. Slow of heart to believe, he remained for a whole week in darkness and gloom. One important lesson we may learn from this is, how much we lose by our failure to cultivate the fellowship of Christian brethren. "*Not* forsaking the assembling of ourselves together, as the manner of some is (Heb. 10:25), is the word of Scripture. Two warnings against disobeying this were furnished in connection with Christ's resurrection. In Luke 24:13 we read, "And *behold*, two of them went that same day to a village called Emmaus, which was *from Jerusalem* about three score furlongs": mark the words in italics. These two disciples had turned their backs on their brethren in Jerusalem. Little wonder, then, that when the Lord Himself drew near to them "their eyes were holden that they should not know Him" (Luke 24:16). Yet even to them the Lord manifested His long-suffering grace by making Himself known (v. 31)! And what was the effect upon them? This: "They rose up the same hour, and *returned to Jerusalem* and found the Eleven" (v. 33)! When Christians are in fellowship with Christ, they desire and seek the fellowship of His people; conversely, when they are out of fellowship with the Lord they have little or no desire for communion with believers. It was thus with Thomas. Out of fellowship with Christ, through unbelief, he forsook the assembly. And how much he lost! God's blessing, Christ's presence, the Holy Spirit's power, joy of heart, and in addition, a whole week spent in despondency. What a warning for us!

"The other disciples therefore said unto him, We have seen the Lord" (v. 25). This is most blessed. The Ten were not callously indifferent to the welfare of their erring brother. They did not say, "O, well, there is no need for us to be troubled; *he* is the loser; if he had been in his proper place, he, too, would have seen the Saviour, heard His blessing of 'Peace be unto you,' and received the Holy Spirit; but he was *not* here, and it only serves him right that he should suffer for his negligence; let us leave him alone." O, no. The selfish world may reason and act thus; but not so those who are truly constrained by the love of Christ. The more we love Him, the more shall we love His people. So it was here. As soon as the Ten had been favoured with this gracious visit from the risen Redeemer, they *sought out Thomas* and communicated to him the glad tidings. How this rebukes some of us! If we were more in fellowship with Christ, we should have more heart for His wayward and wandering sheep. It is those who are "spiritual" that are exhorted to restore the one "overtaken in a fault" (Gal. 6:1)!

"But he said unto them, Except I shall see in His hands the print of the nails, and put my finger into the print of the nails, and thrust my hand into His side, I will not believe" (v. 26). This illustrates the same principle so sadly exemplified in v. 18. Those who know Christ will bear testimony of Him to others, but they must be prepared for the unbelief of those whom they address. The Ten spoke to Thomas, but he believed them not. This also shows how that the best of men are subject to unbelief. Thomas had witnessed the resurrection of Lazarus, he had heard the Lord's promises that He *would* rise again on the third day, yet believed not now that He *was* risen. What point this gives to the admonition in Heb. 12:1, where we are exhorted to lay aside "*the* sin (unbelief) which doth so easily beset us!" Thomas refused to accredit the testimony of ten competent witnesses who had seen Christ with their own eyes, men who were his friends and brethren, and who could have no object in deceiving him. But he obstinately declares that he *will not* believe, unless he himself sees and touches the Lord's body. He presumes to prescribe the conditions which must be met before he is ready to receive the glad tidings. Thomas was still sceptical. Perhaps he asked his brethren, Why did not Christ remain with you? Where is He now? Why did He not show Himself to *me?* He implied, though he did say it directly, that they were labouring under a delusion. And were *they* altogether blameless? They told Thomas "We have *seen* the Lord," but apparently they said nothing of the gracious and wonderous *words* which they had *heard* from His lips! Is there not a lesson, a warning, here for us? It is not *our experiences* which we are to proclaim, but *His words!*

"Except I shall see in His hands the print of the nails, and put my finger into the print of the nails, and thrust my hand into His side, I will not believe." This is the only place in the New Testament where the "nails" which pierced the Saviour's hands and feet are actually mentioned. The Romans did not always use nails when crucifying criminals. Sometimes they bound the victims hands and feet to the cross by strong cords. The fact that "nails" *were* used in connection with the Saviour, and the express mention of them here by Thomas, witnesses to the actual and literal fulfilment of Psa. 22:16: "they *pierced* My hands and My feet."

"And after eight days again, His disciples were within, and Thomas with them: then came Jesus, the doors being shut, and stood in the midst, and said, Peace be unto you" (v. 26). "After eight days" signifies, according to the Jewish manner of reckoning time (who counted any part of a day as a whole one), after a week. It was, therefore, on the second Christian Sabbath that the Eleven assembled together, this time Thomas being present. Observe that the Holy Spirit mentions the fact that again the doors were shut, for He would emphasise once more the supernatural character of the resurrection-body. The close similarity between this and v. 19 makes it plain that *this* visit of the Saviour was for the special benefit of Thomas. But mark a significant omission here: nothing is *now* said of their "fear of the Jews!" His "Peace be unto you" (v. 19) had calmed their hearts and taken away their fear of men. It is one more witness to the power of the Word.

"And Thomas was with them: then came Jesus, the doors being shut, and stood in the midst and said, Peace be unto you." Marvellous grace was this. As we have said, this second manifestation of Christ unto the apostles was expressly made for the special benefit of Thomas. The Saviour made the same mysterious entrance through the closed doors came with the same comforting salutation. There is much for us to learn from this. How patient and tender is the Lord with *dull* and *slow* believers! Forcefully does this come out here. Christ did not excommunicate His unbelieving disciple, but addressed to him the same word of "Peace" as He had previously saluted the Ten. O, how graciously does He bear with the waywardness and infirmities of His people. Timely are the admonitions of Bishop Ryle: "Let us take care that we drink into our Lord's spirit and copy His example. Let us never set down men in a low place, as graceless and godless, because their faith is feeble and their love is cold. Let us remember the case of Thomas, and be very pitiful and of tender mercy. Our Lord has many weak children in His family, many dull pupils in His school, many raw soldiers in His army, many lame sheep in His flock. Yet He bears with them all, and casts none away. Happy is that Christian who has learned to deal likewise with his brethren. There are many in the Family, who, like Thomas, are dull and slow, but for all that, like Thomas, are real and true believers."

"And said, Peace be unto you." This is the third time that we find this precious word on the lips of the Saviour in this chapter, and on each occasion it was used with a *different* design. The first (v. 19), tells of the glorious *consequences of His atoning work*: peace has been made with God, peace is now imparted to those whose sins have been put away. The second (v. 21), is His *provision for service*, using that word in its largest scope. It is this which supplies power for our walk, and it is only to the extent that the peace of God *is* ruling our hearts that we are able to rise above the hindrances of our path and the opposition of the flesh. But the third "Peace" is the *means of recovery*. This comes out most strikingly in the next verse. "*Then* saith He to Thomas, Reach hither thy finger, and behold *My hands.*" —compare the "*when* He had *so* said ('Peace be unto you' v. 19) He showed unto them His hands and His side" (v. 20).

"Then saith He to Thomas, Reach hither thy finger, and behold My hands; and reach hither thy hands, and thrust it into My side, and be not faithless but believing" v. 27). Thus the Lord did for Thomas what He had done for the Ten—He pointed out that which memorialised the *ground* on which true "peace" rests. The Lord went back to first principles with this erring disciple. Thomas needed to be re-established in the truths taught by the pierced hands and side of the Saviour, and therefore he got just what was required to restore his wandering soul. What a lesson for us! When we have gone astray, what is it that recalls us? Not occupation with the intricacies of prophecy or the finer points of doctrine (important and valuable as these are in their place), but the great foundation-truth of the Atonement. It was the sight of the Saviour's *wounds* which scattered all Thomas' doubts, overcame his self-will, and brought him to the the feet of Christ as an adoring worshipper. So it is with us. Have we grown cold and worldly; are we out of communion with the Lord Jesus—He recalls us to Himself by the same precious truth which first won our hearts. This is what breaks us down:—

"And yet to find Thee still the same—
'Tis this that humbles us with shame."

Was it not for this reason the Lord appointed the loaf and the cup for the Feast of Remembrance! It is the emblems of His broken-body and poured-out blood which move the heart, quicken the spirit, thrill the soul, and rekindle the joy which we tasted when we first looked by faith upon His hands and side. This, then, we believe, is the force of the *connection* between v. 27 and what immediately precedes. What a lesson for us; the most effective way of dealing with backsliders is to tenderly remind them of the dying love of the Lord Jesus!

"Then saith He to Thomas, Reach hither thy finger, and behold My hands; and reach hither thy hand and thrust it into My side: and be not faithless but believing." While the link between this and the verse before is unspeakably blessed, yet the actual contents of it are most searching and solemn. The language which the Saviour here employed affords positive proof that He had heard the petulent and sceptical words of Thomas to his fellow-apostles—cf. v. 25. No one had seen the Lord as visibly present when Thomas gave utterance to his unbelief. None had reported his words to Christ. Yet was He fully acquainted with them! He had listened to the outburst of His disciple, and now makes Thomas aware of it. Wonderous proof was this of His omniscience! Searching warning is it for us! The One who died on Calvary's cross was "*God* manifest in flesh," and being God, he not only sees every deed we perform, but also hears every word that we utter. O that we might be more conscious, hour by hour, that the Eye of Divine holiness is ever upon us, that the Ear of the omnipresent One is ever open to all that we say, that He still stands in the midst of the seven golden candlesticks! To realise *this* is to walk "in the fear of God."

"Reach hither thy hand and thrust it into My side." What solemn light this casts upon what we read in 19:34. It must have been a *large wound* for the Lord to tell Thomas to thrust in his *hand!* What indignites the Saviour suffered for our sakes! Again, do not these wounds of Christ throw light upon the character of the resurrection-body? Do they not argue strongly that our personal identity will survive the great transformation? It needs to be borne in mind that the bodies of those who sleep in the dust of the earth are not going to be re-created, but resurrected! And grand and glorious as will be the change from our present mortal bodies, yet it seems clear from several scriptures that our personal identity will be so preserved that recognition will not only be possibile but certain.

"Be not faithless, but believing." "This is a rebuke and an exhortation at the same time. It is not merely a reproof to Thomas for his scepticism on this particular occasion, but an urgent counsel to be of a more believing turn of mind for the time to come. 'Shake off this habit of doubting, questioning, and discrediting every one. Give up thine unbelieving disposition. Become more willing to believe and trust.' No doubt the primary object of the sentence was to correct and chastise Thomas for his sceptical declaration to his brethren. But I believe our Lord had in view the further object of correcting Thomas' whole character, and directing his attention to his besetting sin. How many there are among us who ought to take to themselves our Lord's words! How faithless *we* often are, and how slow to believe!" (Bishop Ryle).

"And Thomas answered and said unto Him, my Lord and my God" (v. 28). How blessed! In a moment the doubter was transformed into a worshipper. Like Paul (Acts 21:19), Thomas "was not disobedient to the heavenly vision." There was no room for scepticism now, no occasion for him to put his finger "into the print of the nails," and thrust his hand "into His side" (v. 25). The language of Christ in the next verse—"Because thou hast *seen* Me, thou hast believed"—makes it clear that Thomas *did not do* as he had boasted. There was no need for him to handle Christ now: his *intellectual* doubts had vanished because his *heart* was satisfied! The words of Thomas on this occasion gave evidence of his faith *in* Christ, his subjection *to* Him, and his affection *for* Him.

"And Thomas answered and said unto Him, My Lord and my God." This is the only time in the Gospels that anyone owned Christ as "*God.*" And what was it that evoked this blessed testimony? The context tells us. The fact that Christ knew the very words which he had used, satisfied Thomas that Immanuel stood before him; hence his worshipful confession. And when *we* meet Him in the air, see the glory streaming through His pierced hands and side ("He had bright beams out of His *side!*" Hab. 3:4), when we hear His "Peace be unto you," when we perceive that He knows all about us, *we* too shall cry "My Lord and my God."

How marvellous are the ways of Divine grace. Doubting Thomas was the one who gave the strongest and most conclusive testimony to the absolute Deity of the Saviour which ever came from the lips of a man! Just as the railing thief became the one to own Christ's Lordship from the cross, just as timid Joseph and Nicodemus were the ones who honoured the dead body of the Saviour, just as the women were the boldest at the sepulchre, just as unfaithful Peter was the one whom Christ bade "Feed My sheep," just as the prime persecutor of the early church became the apostle to the Gentiles, so the sceptical and materialistic Thomas was the one to say "My Lord and my God." Where sin abounded, grace *did* much more abound!

"And Thomas answered and said unto Him, My Lord and my God." Mark the word "said unto Him." it was no mere ejaculation. Thomas was not here speaking to the Father nor of the Father, but to and of the Son. The fact that Thomas addressed Him as "my *Lord*" evidences that he too had now "received the Holy Spirit" (cf. v. 22), for "no man can say that Jesus is the Lord, but by the Holy Spirit" (1 Cor. 12:3). It is very striking to contrast what we read of in 1 Kings 18:39. When Elijah met the prophets of Baal on Mount Carmel, and in response to his faith and prayer, Jehovah was pleased to manifest Himself by sending fire from heaven to consume the sacrifice and lick up the water; the people exclaimed, "The Lord, He is the God, the Lord, He is the God." But Thomas here did far more than this: he not only acknowledged that Jesus of Nazareth was Lord and God, but he confessed Him as "*my* Lord and *my* God." And how striking that *this* is recorded in connection with the *third* notice of Thomas, and the third appearance of the resurrected Christ in this Gospel—it is only as risen from the dead the Lord Jesus could be *our* Lord and God!

"And Thomas answered and said unto Him, My Lord and my God." "This noble confession of Thomas admits of only one meaning: it was a blessed testimony to our Lord's Deity. It was a clear, unmistakeable declaration that Thomas believed Him, when he saw Him that day, to be not only man, but God. And, above all, it was a testimony which our Lord received and did not prohibit and a declaration which He did not say one word to rebuke. When Cornelius fell down at the feet of Peter and would have worshipped him, the apostle refused such honour at once: 'Stand up; I myself am a man' (Acts 10:26). When the people of Lystra would have done sacrifice to Paul and Barnabas, 'they rent their clothes and ran in among the people, saying, Sirs, why do ye these things? We are men of like passions with you,' Acts 14:15. (When John fell down to worship before the feet of the angel. he said unto him, 'See thou do it not': Rev. 22:8, 9.—A.W.P.). But when Thomas said to Jesus, 'My Lord and my God,' the words do not elicit a syllable of reproof from our holy and truth-loving Master. Can we doubt that these things were written for our learning?

"Let us settle it firmly in our minds that the Deity of Christ is one of the grand foundation truths of Christianity, and let us be willing to go to the stake rather than deny it. Unless our Lord Jesus is very God of very God, there is an end of

His mediation, His atonement, His priesthood, His whole work of redemption. These doctrines are useless blasphemies unless Christ is God. Forever let us bless God that the Deity of our Lord is taught everywhere in the Scriptures, and stands on evidence that can never be overthrown. Above all, let us daily repose our sinful selves on Christ with undoubting confidence, as one that is perfect God as well as perfect man. He is man, and therefore can be touched with the feeling of our infirmities. He is God, and therefore 'is able to save unto the uttermost them that come unto God by Him.' That Christian has no cause to fear who can look to Jesus by faith and say with Thomas, 'My Lord and my God.'" (Bishop Ryle).

"Jesus saith unto him, Thomas, because thou hast seen Me, thou hast believed: blessed are they that have not seen, and yet have believed" (v. 29). Christ accepted Thomas' confession, but reminded him that it was occasioned by outward signs, the appeal to his sight. What a warning against the modern craving for "signs"— a tendency upon which Satan is now trading in many directions. And how it condemns those materialists who say they will not believe in anything which they cannot examine with their physical senses! Thomas had insisted upon *seeing* the risen Christ, and the Lord graciously granted his request. The result was he believed. But the Lord pointed out to His disciple that there is a greater blessedness resting on those who have never seen Him in the flesh, yet who have believed—an expression which looked back to the Old Testament saints as well as forwards to us! This was the last of our Lord's beatitudes.

"Blessed are they that have not seen, and yet have believed." What a precious word is this for *our* hearts. *We* have never seen Him in the flesh. Here, then, is a promise for us. Should it be asked: How do you *know* that the rejected One is now in the glory? the answer would be, Because of His own word that when He went there He would send down to His people the Holy Spirit. Therefore, every joy in God which we now have, every longing for Christ, manifests His Spirit's presence in our souls, and this is a precious testimony to the fact that Christ is now on High. These manifestations of the Spirit *here* are the proofs that Christ is *there*. They are the antitype of the "bells" on the robe of the high priest when he went unto the holy of holies on the Day of Atonement (see Lev. 28:33-35). As the people listened on the outside, they *heard* the unseen movements of their representative within; so we are conscious of the presence of *our* High Priest in the Holiest by the *tongues* of the "bells"—the sweet testimony now borne to us by the Holy Spirit. And *why* is there a greater blessedness pronounced on us than upon those who saw Christ during the days when He tabernacled among men? Because *we* own Him during the Day of His Rejection, and therefore *He* is more honoured by such faith! It is *faith* in Himself, faith which rests alone on the Word, which Christ pronounces "blessed."

"And many other signs truly did Jesus in the presence of His disciples, which are not written in this book" (v. 30). This and the following verse comes in parenthetically. The whole of chapter 20 is occupied with a recountal of the appearances of the risen Christ unto His own, and this is continued in chapter 21 as the very first verse shows. We take it that the "many other signs" refer not to what the Lord had done through the whole course of His public ministry, but to the proofs which the risen Christ had furnished His apostles. This is confirmed by the words "Many other signs truly did Jesus *in the presence of His disciples,*" whereas, most of His ministerial signs were performed before the general public. There *were* other signs which the Saviour gave to the Eleven which proved that He had risen from the dead, but the Holy Spirit did not move *John* to record them. Some of them are discribed in the Synoptics. For example, His appearing to the two disciples on the way to Emmaus (Luke 24:15). His eating in the presence of the Eleven (Luke 24:43). His opening their understandings to understand the Scriptures (Luke 24: 45). His appearing to them in Galilee (Mat. 28:16), His declaration that all power was given unto Him in heaven and earth (Matt. 28:18). His commissioning them to make disciples of all nations, baptising them in the name of the Triune God (Matt. 28:19, 20). Others of these "signs" are recorded in Acts 1, 1 Cor. 15, etc. When John says that these "other signs" which Jesus did are not written in *this* book (the Fourth Gospel), he implies that they *are* in some other book or books. On this, one has quaintly said, "St. John generously recognises the existence of other books beside his own, and disclaims the idea of his Gospel being the only one which Christians ought to read. Happy is that author which can humbly say 'my book does not contain everything about the subject it handles. There are others books about it. Read them.'"

"But these are written, that ye might believe that Jesus is the Christ, the Son of God; and that believing ye might have life through His name" (v. 31). Here the Holy Spirit tells why the resurrection-signs of Christ mentioned by John *are* recorded in this Gospel. They are written not merely to furnish us with historical information about the Lord Jesus, but that we might *believe* on Him! They are written that we might believe on Him *as* "the Christ," the Messiah, the anointed One—Him to whom the Old Testament prophets pointed. They are written that we might believe on Jesus *as* "the Son of God," the second Person of the Godhead incarnate, the One whose Divine glories are unfolded more particularly in the New Testament. And they are written that we might believe on Him thus in order that we might have "life through His name." It is *faith* in the *written* revelation which God has given of His Son which brings "life" and all that is included in that word—salvation, immortality, eternal glory. Reader, hast *thou* "believed"? Not *about* Christ, but *in* Him? Have you received Him as your own *personal Saviour?* If so, the blessing of Heaven rests upon you. If not, you are, even now, "under condemnation," and if you remain in your wicked unbelief there awaits you nought but "the blackness of darkness forever."

Once again the Holy Spirit has favoured us with a lovely typical picture. Just as the first section of John 20 views the godly Remnant in the Tribulation, just as the second section contemplates this present interval of Christianity—how striking that this comes in here *parenthetically*—so this third section looks forward to the time when the Saviour will be revealed to the nation of Israel. Observe the following details:—

1. Note that a whole week—a *complete period*—elapses between what is recorded in vv. 19 to 23, and what we have in vv. 24 to 29! 2. Observe that this section is an *eighth*-day scene (v. 26)—the number of *a new beginning!* 3. Mark that Thomas was not with those to whom Christ first revealed Himself (v. 24); so Israel is away from God during this time that we enjoy fellowship with Christ in spirit. 4. Note that those who were acquainted with the risen Lord bore witness to Thomas, but he believed them not (v. 25); so Israel rejects the Gospel preached to them by Christians. 5. Note that during the whole of this intervening week Thomas remained in unbelief (v. 25): so Israel! 6. Note the Lord's salutation to Thomas—"Peace" (v. 26)—so will He yet manifest His grace to the Nation. 7. Note that it was the *sight* of Christ's wounds which removed Thomas' doubts v. 27): so will it be with Israel: Zech. 12:10. 8. Note that Thomas owns Christ as "Lord" and "God" (v. 28). so will Israel when they see him: Isa. 25:9. 9. Note that his name is given in two languages: "Thomas" (Hebrew) "the Jew first," and "Didymus" (Greek): each meaning "a twin"—intimating that a *twin company*—saved Gentiles and saved Israel—will yet enjoy the blessings of Christ's death and resurrection! 10. Note that the final word of Christ to Thomas (v. 29) intimates that blessed as will be Israel's millennial portion, it will be *inferior* to that occupied by the Church! Verily, none but God could have drawn such a picture!

The following questions are to help the student on John 21:1-14.
1. What is the typical picture here?
2. Why did not the disciples recognise Christ v. 4?
3. Why did Christ ask the question in v. 5?
4. What does Peter's act denote v. 7?
5. Why mention the "fire of coals" v. 9?
6. Why was not the net broken v. 11?
7. What is the spiritual significance of vv. 12, 13?

*Arthur W. Pink.*

## GLEANINGS IN EXODUS.

### 45. *The Brazen Altar: Ex. 27:1-8.*

In Ex. 25 and 26 we have had before us the vessels that occupied and the materials which composed the Holy of Holies and the Holy Place. Here in chapter 27, we are conducted to the Outer Court. But there is one notable omission: the golden or incense altar, which stood in the Holy Place, has not been mentioned, nor is it referred to till the thirtieth chapter is reached. The reason for this we shall, D.V., endeavor to indicate when we come to that chapter. Suffice it now to say that the golden altar "is not spoken of until there is a priest to burn incense thereon, for Jehovah showed Moses the patterns of things in the heavens according to the order in which these things are apprehended by faith" (C.H.M.).

The Brazen-altar, which we are now to contemplate, was the biggest of the Tabernacle's seven pieces of furniture. It was almost large enough to hold all the other vessels. Its size indicated its importance. It was placed "before the door" (Ex. 49:6), just inside the Outer Court (40:33), and would thus be the first object to meet the eye of the worshipper as he entered the Tent of the congregation. It is designated "the brazen altar" (38:30), to distinguish it from the golden altar. It was also called "the altar of burnt offering" (30:28).

The Brazen-altar was the basis of the Levitical system. To it the sinner came with his Divinely-appointed victim. There was a fire continually burning upon it (Lev. 6:13), and the daily sacrifice was renewed each morning. There it stood: ever smoking, ever blood-stained, ever open to any guilty Hebrew that might wish to approach it. The sinner, having forfeited his life by sin, another life—an innocent one—must be given in his stead. When the Israelite brought his offering, before killing it he laid his hand on the animal's head, thus becoming identified with it, and thereby the acceptableness of the flawless victim passed to him, while his sin is transferred to it. So, too, this Altar stood in the path of the priests, as they went in to minister within the Holy Place. At this Altar the high priest officiated on the great day of atonement (Lev. 16). Seven things concerning it will now engage our attention:—

1. *Its Position.*

The Brazen-altar was not placed outside the Gate, but just within the Court (40:33): thus it would be the first object encountered as the Israelite entered the sacred precincts. Herein we may admire the accuracy of the type, and, too, discover in this detail a refutation of much which now passes for sound Gospel-preaching. The New Testament does not teach universal salvation, nor does it represent the sacrifice of Christ as offered for all mankind; rather was it designed for those who believe. The Old Testament types are in perfect accord with this. No lamb was provided for the Egyptians on that night when the angel of death smote the firstborn. On the day of atonement the high priest confessed over the head of the scapegoat only the sins of Israel (Lev. 16:21). So in our present type: the Altar was provided for none save the Chosen People. Had it been designed for the wilderness-tribes also, it had been placed *outside* the Tabernacle's court; but it was not!

Within the Court, the Altar was placed facing the Door into the Tabernacle proper. It was there that Jehovah met with His people (Ex. 29:11; 33:9; Lev. 15:14). As a matter of fact the Laver stood between the Altar and the Door, yet so vital is the connection of that which spoke of Divine judgment with that which gave entrance into the Divine presence, that in several scriptures nothing is said of the Laver coming in between the two (see 40:6, etc.). How forcibly this tells us of the intimate relation between sacrifice and access to God! The Tabernacle could not be entered till one had first passed the Altar. Blood-shedding is the basis of approach to God.

2. *Its Materials.*

"And thou shalt make an altar of shittim wood . . . and thou shalt overlay it with brass" (vv. 1, 2). Excepting the "taches" for the Curtains (26:11), and the "sockets" for the "pillars" of the Door (26:36), this is the first time we have had "brass" before us. In the former cases the "brass" would be invisible. Those who entered within the inner compartments would see nothing but a dazzling display of gold, and the lovely tints of the inner Curtains, and the Veil. But here in the Outer Court naught but brass met the eye. There is some doubt as to the precise nature of this metal. So far as we can now ascertain, the ancients had no knowledge of "brass" (which is a mixture of copper and zinc), the Romans being the first to use it. Therefore some students prefer to render the Hebrew word "copper," others think it may have been bronze that was used (a mixture of copper and tin). However, we shall continue speaking of it as "brass."

The symbolical import of "brass" in Scripture is as definitely defined as is that of gold and silver. As gold speaks of *glory* and silver of *redemption*, so brass signifies *judgment*. This may be gathered from the connections in which it is found. The serpent (reminder of the one who was responsible for the bringing in of the "curse") which Moses was ordered to make and affix to the pole, was made of *brass* (Num. 21:9). When Jehovah made known the sore judgments which would come upon Israel for their disobedience (see the whole of Deut. 28), among other things He threatened, "and thy heaven that is above thy head shall be *brass* (v. 23). When describing the millennial blessedness of Israel, following their long alienation from God, the promise given is "for brass I will bring gold" (Isaiah 60:17), i.e., judgment shall give place to glory. When Christ appears in judicial character, inspecting His churches, pronouncing sentence upon them, we read that "His feet (were) like unto *fine brass* as if they burned in a furnace" (Rev. 1:15).

Many are the references to "brass" in

the Old Testament, but it is invariably found in an evil association. The first time that it is mentioned is in connection with the descendants of *Cain* (Gen. 4:22)! Samson was *bound* with "fetters of brass" (Judges 16:21); so, too, was Zedekiah (2 Kings 5:27). Goliath's helmet and armour were of "brass" (1 Sam. 17:5, 6). Saul's armour was of the same material, but David disdained it (1 Sam. 17:38). In delivering His people from the prison-house in which sin had placed them, the Lord says, "He hath broken the gates of brass and cut the bars of iron in sunder" (Psalm 107:16). When remonstrating with His wayward and rebellious people, God said, "I know that thou art obstinate, and thy neck is an iron sinew, and thy brow brass" (Isa. 48:4).

"The acacia wood, of which it was made, need occupy us but briefly, as we have already learned its meaning. It speaks of the incorruptible, sinless humanity of our Lord, and therefore not subject to death. How fitting, then, that it should be connected with the constant witness of death —the altar. Our Lord *need not* die, therefore He could 'lay down' His life! On all others, judgment had a claim; none, therefore, could make atonement even for themselves, much less for others. We see then our Lord as 'the Altar that sanctifieth the gift' (Matt. 23:19). But how necessary was this humanity if there was to be an atonement. The very word for altar is connected with 'slaughter'—the shedding of blood. Therefore the one who was to be the true altar must be capable of dying, and at the same time One upon whom death had no claim" (Mr. S. Ridout).

The wooden boards, overlaid with brass, tell us that the Altar points to the capability of the Sin-bearer to endure the judgment of God. The incarnate Son was no feeble Saviour: "I have laid help upon One that is *mighty*" (Psalm 89:19) was Jehovah's witness of old. The shittim wood spoke of the humanity of the Redeemer; the brass of which it was overlaid told of His power to "endure the Cross."

### 3. *Its Meaning.*

This is the easiest to interpret of all the holy vessels. Being the place where sacrifice was offered to God, it spoke, unmistakably, of the Cross of Christ. It pointed to the most solemn aspect of Calvary. The Lord Jesus was the Antitype of both the altar and its sacrifice, as also of the priests who there officiated. That which is distinct in our present type is what is set forth by the brass. This is the hardest of all metals, possessing a greater resistance to fire than gold or silver: in Deut. 33:25 and in Jer. 1:18 "brass" is used as the symbol of ability to endure. Our Saviour was the true Brazen-altar, possessed of that power of enduring, in its awful intensity, the fires of God's holiness. He only could *endure* the Cross. He only could stand, unconsumed, under the storm of Divine judgment. As the brass plates on the Altar protected it from the fervent heat and prevented it from being burnt up, so Christ passed through the fires of God's wrath without being consumed. He is mighty to save, because He was mighty to endure.

As we have shown above, "brass" in Scripture symbolises judgment. Hence we see the solemn propriety of Moses being instructed to make "a serpent of *brass*" to place upon the pole. Many have wondered how it was possible for the Holy One of God to be represented by a "serpent"—surely *that* was the last of all objects suited to portray Him who is fairer than the children of men! But no mistake was made. As a fact, the "serpent" was the only similitude of all created things which could suitably picture that particular aspect of the Redeemer's death which was there foreshadowed. The "serpent" was the reminder of the "curse" (Gen. 3), and in Gal. 3:13 we are expressly told that Christ was "made a *curse*" for His people. It was because that uplifted object, presented to the eyes of the bitten Israelites, pointed forward to the Lord Jesus as "made a curse," that it was designed in the form of a serpent. For the same reason, that serpent was made not of silver or gold, but of *brass*. As made a curse for us, the *judgment* of God descended upon Christ, and the sword of Divine justice smote Him (Zech. 13:7).

It was at the Brazen-altar that the holiness and righteousness of God were displayed: His hatred of sin, and His justice in punishing it. Have you ever considered the *holiness* of God, dear reader, and how that your *sins* have unfitted you to come before Him? When Isaiah, the best man in all Israel of his day, was brought into God's presence, and saw the unsullied purity of His person, and beheld the seraphim (who had never come into contact with defilement of any kind) veil their faces with their wings and cry, "Holy, holy, holy is the Lord of hosts," there was wrung from his heart that word, "Woe is me! for I am undone; because I am a man of unclean lips, and I dwell in the midst of a people of unclean lips"

(Isa. 6:5). When he saw the holiness of God, the righteousness of His throne, the profound reverence of the heavenly intelligences, on the one hand; and on the other, his own sinfulness and the iniquities of the people among whom he lived; he saw also the awful distance there was between his soul and God, and he cried, "Woe is me!"

As another has pointed out, "In the preceding chapter Isaiah had pronounced six woes on six different classes in Israel; but when brought into the Lord's presence, he pronounced the seventh upon *himself*. His neighbour's sin troubled him no more, but his own did. These must be attended to at once; and, thank God, they were, but not by Isaiah. How could *he* put them away by the power of his hand? or wash them away by his tears? or have them removed by any efforts of his own? Ah, no; but thank God, if a sight of God and His throne, and a sight of his own unfitness for the presence of One so holy, led him to pass judgment upon himself and take his place in the dust, it also brought him low enough to see another thing, and that was *the altar*, and the provision of the altar. The live coal had done its work; the sacrifice had been consumed; and nothing remained but 'the live coal'; this was applied to Isaiah's lips, and the sweet and blessed assurance given, 'thine iniquity is taken away, and thy sin is purged" (Isa. 6:7). The look of anguish passes from his face, and there comes instead the light of holy joy as he believes what is said to him" (Gospel Add. on the Tab., by A.H.).

Does the reader understand what is portrayed in Isa. 6? The "altar" is Christ: the sacrifice consumed on it by the live coal speaks of His work on the cross for poor sinners. The "live coal" is a figure of God's holiness consuming that which offends Him. When Christ was "made sin" (2 Cor. 5:21) for all who shall believe on Him, it pleased Jehovah to "bruise" Him, to "put Him to grief," to "make His soul an offering for sin" (Isa. 53). It was then that the "live coal" reached Him, and He exclaimed, "My heart is like wax; it is melted in the midst of My bowels" (Psalm 22:14). Yes, the coal had done its work, its "strange work" (Isa. 28:21); a sacrifice had been presented—all had gone up to God. And that "live coal" (figure of God's holiness) lies now upon the Altar, waiting for the sinner to take the place Isaiah took, and pass judgment on himself, as he did; and the moment he does so his iniquity is taken away and his sin is purged.

The Brazen-altar, inside the Court, faced the door into the Tabernacle proper, and it was at this place Jehovah met with His people: "*There* will I meet with the children of Israel" (Ex. 29:42, 43). So the Cross is now the meeting-place between God and the sinner. "It is on the foundation of what was accomplished there that He can be just and the Justifier of everyone that believeth in Jesus. There is no other ground on which He can bring the sinner into His presence. If the Israelite rejected the brazen altar, he shut himself out for ever from the mercy of God, and, in like manner, whoever rejects the cross of Christ, shuts himself out for ever from the hope of salvation" (E. Dennett). Inexpressibly blessed are the words of Ex. 29:37, "everything that toucheth the altar shall be holy": so every sinner who, by faith, lays hold of Christ is cleansed—cf. Mark 5:27-29.

It is very striking to observe that of the different vessels in the Tabernacle the two "altars" alone are spoken of as being "most holy." The other pieces of furniture are called "holy," but the golden altar (30:10) once, and the brazen altar twice, is termed "most holy" (39:37; 40:10). The reason for this is not far to seek: it was at Calvary, pre-eminently, that the holiness of God was so signally and solemnly manifested. So holy is God that He would not spare His beloved Son (Rom. 8:32) when the sins of His people were laid upon Him.

Though the Altar had no "steps" up to it (Ex. 20:26), yet it is clear from Lev. 9:22 that it stood on elevated ground, for there we read of Aaron ministering at the Altar, and then he "came down." Most probably the ground in the Outer Court was made to slope upwards, and on the top of this ascent stood the Altar. How this reminds us of the "lifted up" Saviour upon that Hill called Golgotha!

### 4. *Its Dimensions.*

"Thou shalt make an altar of shittim wood, five cubits long, and five cubits broad; the altar shall be foursquare: and the height thereof shall be three cubits" (v. 1). The measurements here are very striking and blessed. Five, as we have shown before, is the number that tells of *grace*, and this was stamped both on the length and breadth of the Altar. Nowhere was the wondrous grace of God to poor sinners so clearly displayed as it was at the Cross. What could we possibly do which would call for such a costly Sacrifice on our behalf? A ransom so precious was utterly unmerited. It was provided by the pure benignity of God. Nor was it a sudden impulse on the part of the Father to bestow favours on those who had no claims on Him. As we are told in 1 Peter 1:20, the Lamb was "foreordained before the foundation of the world." So in 2 Tim. 1:9 we read, "Who hath saved us, and called us with an holy calling, not according to our works, but according to His own purpose *and grace*, which was given us in Christ Jesus before the world began." Here then is the *length*: grace appointed the antitypical Altar long ere time began. The *breadth* is also measured by grace. "I will have mercy on whom I will have mercy, and I will have compassion on whom I will have compassion" (Rom. 9:15) expressed this truth. Its height—*three* cubits—speaks of *manifestation*. At the Cross, God, man, sin, Satan, holiness, righteousness, grace and love were exhibited as nowhere else.

"The altar shall be foursquare." Thus it faced each point of the compass, telling of the *world-wide* aspect and application of the Cross. Christ's death was not only for the Israelitish nation, but also for the children of God "scattered abroad" (John 11:51, 52). He is a propitiation for the sins of "the whole world" (1 John 2:2), which does not mean all mankind, but that it was not restricted to Israel, but was also designed for favoured sinners among the Gentiles too.

### 5. Its Horns.

"And thou shalt make the horns of it upon the four corners thereof, his horns shall be of the same" (v. 2). These horns were for the binding of the sacrifice to the Altar: see Psalm 118:27. In Scripture the "horn" is the symbol of power or strength (see Hab. 3:4). Typically, the "horns" on the Altar pointed to the unfaltering purpose of the Saviour, and the strength of His love. It was not the nails which held Him to the Cross. Christ was bound to the Altar by the constraint of His devotedness to the Father (John 10:19; Phil. 2:9). While on the Cross, His enemies challenged Him to come down; His refusal to do so evidenced the cords which bound Him to its "horns."

### 6. Its Utensils.

"And thou shalt make his pans to receive his ashes, and his shovels, and his basins, and his fleshhooks, and his firepans: all the vessels thereof thou shalt make of brass" (v. 3). The "pans" were used in receiving the ashes of offering and removing them to their appointed place (Lev. 6:10, 11). The "ashes" testified to the thoroughness of the fire's work in having wholly consumed the offering. They also witnessed to the acceptance of the sacrifice on behalf of the offerer, and so they were to him a token that his sins were gone. The words of Christ from the Cross express the fulfilment of this detail of our type: "It is finished" announced that the Sacrifice had been offered, accepted, and gone up to God as a sweet savor.

The "shovels" were no doubt employed about the fire, collecting the dead embers. The "basins" were receptacles for the blood, in order to convey it to each place of sprinkling. The "fleshhooks" would be for arranging the different parts of the sacrifice on the fire of the Altar. The "firepans" are identical with the "censers," which formed the necessary link between the two Altars (Lev. 16:12, 13). "The utensils speak of all that was necessary in order that the offerings might be presented and dealt with in a suitable manner. We can understand in the case of Christ how perfect it all was: it was 'by the eternal Spirit' that He 'offered Himself without spot to God.' Every detail connected with the offering up of Christ has been provided and arranged and carried out according to God's mind and glory. The Scriptures have been fulfilled in every detail" (C. A. Coates). Each utensil had its own distinctive typical significance, which becomes apparent through prayer, meditation, and comparing scripture with scripture. That all were made of "brass" emphasises, again, the prominent and dominant truth associated with this Altar—the unsparing *judgment* of God upon the believing sinner's Substitute.

"And thou shalt make for it a grate of network of brass; and upon the net thou shalt make four brazen rings in the four corners thereof. And thou shalt put it under the compass of the altar beneath, that the net may be even to the midst of the altar" (vv. 4,5). The Brazen-altar was hollow within, and in its midst was fixed a "grate" on which the fire was built and where the severed parts of the offering were laid. This brings before us the most solemn aspect of all in this type. It tells of the inward sufferings of the Saviour as He endured the wrath of God.

"Our Lord did not bear the fire of Divine judgment in any external, superficial way. It is but a feeble and a partial view of those sufferings which would enlarge upon the persecution of ungodly men, or even the malice of Satan who urged them on. These might explain the bodily anguish to which our holy Lord permitted Himself to be subjected, but the fire of Divine holiness, the heart-searching judgment against sin, went down into the utmost centre of His being. Reverently may we tread upon such holy ground. Sin is not an external thing, though it mars the outward man. Its source is in the heart, the centre of man's being; and therefore in the sinless Substitute the flame searched down into His holy soul. Atoning suffering, like the sin of man, was in the heart. The piercing of the nails, the crown of thorns, the jeers of the people, the spear-thrusts, did not set forth the deep essence of His sufferings. God only, who searcheth the heart, knew what it meant. "The Son, who bore the judgment, knows the intensity of that fire which burned down into His soul when made an offering for sin" (Mr. Ridout). In wondrous accord with this fire being *within* the altar, is the fact that its grate was "even in the midst" (v. 5). The Saviour suffered on the Cross for six hours, and they, too, were divided *in the midst*: the first three He suffered at the hands of men; the last three (when darkness overspread the earth) He suffered at the hands of God!

### 7. Its Covering.

The details recorded in Ex. 27:6, 7 show us that provision was made for its carrying about when Israel were on the march. In Num. 4:13, 14 we are told how it was then covered: "And they shall take away the ashes from the altar, and spread a purple cloth thereon . . . and they shall spread upon it a covering of badgers' skins." This was the *only* piece of the Tabernacle's furniture which was wrapped in purple—the royal colour. Was not this to denote how closely connected were Christ's "sufferings" with the "glory which was to follow"? (Luke 21:26; 1 Peter 1:1). Over the purple cloth was spread the badgers' skins; once more telling us of the world's incapacity to discern the preciousness and the value of the Death Divine. The repentant thief discerned the royal purple over the Altar—the Cross—as his words "Lord, remember me, when Thou comest into Thy *kingdom*" clearly denote. His wicked and scoffing companion saw naught but the rough badgers' skins!

Let us summarise. The Brazen-altar was the place where sin was judged and its wages paid. If the Veil told of separation because of sin, the Altar says, *death* is the consequences of sin. But the Altar also speaks of sin remitted. Nature knows nothing of this: break her laws, and you must suffer the consequences; repent, but she knows no mercy and shows no pity. Science is equally powerless: it endeavours to relieve the effects entailed, but has no remedy for the disease itself. Divine revelation alone makes known an adequate provision—the Cross of Christ. There the uncompromising judgment of God dealt with sin; not by punishing the sinner, but by smiting the sinner's Substitute—"Who His own self bear our sins in His own body on the tree, that we (believers), being (legally) dead to sin, should live unto righteousness, by whose stripes we are healed" (1 Peter 2:24). Thanks be unto God for His unspeakable Gift.

—*Arthur W. Pink.*

## THE PROPHETIC PARABLES OF MATTHEW 13.

### 1. Foreword.

There is little room for wonder, though there is much for humiliation, at the widespread ignorance and error that now obtains among the people of God on many of the leading subjects of Prophecy. For almost fourteen centuries, as "Church-history" clearly shows, prophecy was neglected. Those known as the "Church fathers," with only one or two exceptions, like Origen, devoted their time to wrangling over doctrines and the ordinances; while prophecy was ignored. In view of 2 Peter 1:19—"We have also a more sure word of prophecy, whereunto that ye do well that ye take heed, as unto *a light that shineth* in a dark place"—and the general neglect of prophecy for fourteen hundred years, those centuries have very aptly been termed "The Dark Ages"—dark because the light from the lamp of prophecy did not illumine them.

Nor was it much better when the Reformers came on the scene. God forbid that we should utter one word of criticism against those honoured men of God, but *their* hands were more than full in preaching the Gospel to a people who were utterly ignorant of it, in translating the Scriptures into their own mother-tongues, and in expounding the great fundamentals of the Christian faith. So busily occupied were they in those good works, they had little or no time to give to the real study of prophecy itself. As a matter of fact, practically all that the Reformers saw in the prophetical portions of Scripture was the foretold judgment of God upon the Satanic system of the Papacy, out of which they had been mercifully delivered.

Those who have any knowledge at all of human nature can readily understand how it would be with men who had been cradled in Romanism and who later had, by the grace of God, been enabled to see its blasphemous errors. When they came to the prophecies of Scripture, their thinking was coloured by Romanism, and consequently when they met with an object which was the predicted subject of God's judgment, they viewed it through coloured glasses. "Babylon" was the Papacy; the "Man of Sin" was the Pope; the "Beast" was Rome, and so on. The sad thing is, that most of those who have *followed* the Reformers, instead of studying the prophecies of God's Word for themselves, have done little more than echo what the Reformers before them said. In consequence, little or no advance has been made, and God's people at large to-day have very little more light upon prophecy than had their forefathers of three hundred years ago.

There is, therefore, pressing need for all Christians to give at least part of the time they spend in reading the Scriptures to studying its predictions. We purpose giving a series of studies on the thirteenth chapter of Matthew, which, in the writer's judgment, is, from the standpoint of prophecy, the most important chapter in all the New Testament. There is much in God's prophetic programme which must necessarily remain dark until the parables of this chapter are thoroughly mastered. At present they are much misunderstood and misinterpreted.

It will be found that in Matthew 13:10, 11 the Lord Jesus has designated these seven parables "mysteries of the kingdom of heaven." This expression "the kingdom of heaven" comprehends in a brief form the contents of the whole chapter. This will be seen by a reference to vv. 24, 31, 33, etc., where it will be found that each of the last six parables begin with "the kingdom of heaven is like unto." What is meant by this expression? There is perhaps no term in Scripture used so extensively, but which is so little understood. Though it is found in Matthew's Gospel only, yet it occurs there no less than thirty-two times. Thus our interpretation of this expression affects a great deal of Scripture, and a correct definition of it supplies the first key to the understanding of Matthew 13; for it should be obvious to all that none can begin to understand its seven parables until they have obtained a right definition of that term.

There is the utmost confusion to-day and a fearful amount of misunderstanding concerning the Scriptural purport of this expression, "the kingdom of heaven." There are some who think that it refers to Heaven itself. There are others who understand it refers to that Church of which Christ is the Head. But there is one Scripture in the New Testament which conclusively refutes both of those definitions. In Matt. 16:19 we find the Saviour saying to Peter, "I will give unto thee the keys of the kingdom of heaven." Most assuredly Christ *did not* give to Peter the keys of the Church; still less did He give to him the keys of Heaven itself. Then of *what* did He give Peter the keys? What does the reader understand by "the keys of the kingdom of heaven?" Could you give a simple and satisfactory explanation of this verse to a Romanist who came to you desiring help upon it? We have raised this point in order to show what a need there is for a careful inquiry and a close study of what this particular expression does not connote and what it does signify.

It is because the great majority of Christians, including most of their leaders and teachers, have no right understanding of this term—the "kingdom of heaven"—they encounter so much in Matthew's Gospel that is perplexing and puzzling to them. Let us refer to one other passage where this expression occurs so as to make more manifest the prevailing ignorance. In the opening verse of Matt. 22 we read, "And Jesus answered and spake unto them again by parables, and said, The kingdom of heaven is like unto a certain king which made a marriage for his son," etc. Now go down to v. 11: "and when the king came in to see the guests he saw there (at the banquet itself) a man which had not on a wedding garment: and He saith unto him, Friend, how camest thou in hither, not having a wedding garment? And he was speechless. Then said the king, Bind him hand and foot," etc. How many of our readers are really satisfied with the explanations which they have heard or read of this passage? Our only object in calling attention to it now is to point out that it is part of one of the parables relating to "the kingdom of heaven," and to show that until we obtain a correct definition of this expression there is not a little in Scripture that we shall never begin to understand.

Before we are ready to take up in detail

the subject of "the kingdom of heaven" we need first to weigh the wider expression of "the kingdom of God," and in considering this we must begin where Scripture begins, and that is in the Old Testament. In the remainder of this article we shall attempt nothing more than an outline of "the kingdom of God" in the Old Testament.

In contemplating "the kingdom of God" in the O.T. Scriptures great care must be taken to distinguish between two *aspects* of it. First, Scripture speaks of an *unlimited* kingdom of God, namely, the sovereign rule of the Most High over all His vast dominions. Such Scriptures as Daniel 4:34, 35 refer to *this* aspect of His kingdom: "And I blessed the Most High, and I praised and honoured Him that liveth forever, whose dominion is an everlasting dominion, and His kingdom is from generation to generation. And all the inhabitants of the earth are reputed as nothing: and He doeth according to His will in the army of heaven, and among the inhabitants of the earth, and none can stay His hand, or say unto Him, What doest Thou?" This rule of God over all His creatures is universal, absolute, and eternal. But Scripture also speaks of a *limited* kingdom, which is restricted both in its scope and time, which is neither eternal nor universal; and it is not until we learn to distinguish between these two separate aspects of the kingdom of God that we rightly divide the Word of truth and secure the key which unlocks quite a little of the Old Testament.

This second aspect of God's kingdom is what may be termed the *dispensational* one: it is localised and temporal. This is God's kingdom *on earth*, where His rule is publicly *manifested* over and is *owned* by men. It was first established among the children of Israel, when the Lord Himself was in their midst, when He made the mercyseat upon the ark His *throne*, and dwelt between the cherubim. That was God's "kingdom" on earth. In Joshua 3: 11, 13—a passage which takes us back to a point not long after Jehovah took up His dwelling in Israel's midst—occurs a striking expression: "Behold the ark of the covenant of *the Lord of all the earth* passeth over before you into Jordan . . . . and it shall come to pass, as soon as the soles of the feet of the priests that bear the ark of the Lord, *the Lord of all the earth*, shall rest in the waters of Jordan, that the waters of Jordan shall be cut off from the waters that come down from above; and they shall stand upon an heap." It is to be carefully noted that here is the *first* time in Scripture that God assumed *this* title, and that here it was connected with the ark, and was assumed on the occasion of Israel's passing through the Jordan: it was Jehovah *formally taking possession* of that land which He had given to His people. Had Israel remained in subjection to their King and obeyed His laws, not only would He have continued in their midst, but through them He would have governed the whole earth—as He will yet do in the Millennium. Proof of this is found in the fact that during the brief seasons they remained obedient, He overthrew their enemies and subdued the surrounding Gentiles.

But Israel waxed disobedient and rebelled against Jehovah their King. "And the Lord said unto Samuel, 'Hearken unto the voice of the people in all that they say unto thee: for they have not rejected thee, but they have rejected Me, that I should not *reign* over them'" (1 Sam. 8:7). For centuries after this the long suffering of God continued to bear with them, but in the days of Ezekiel the Shekinah-glory—His manifested Presence in their midst—departed. This is referred to in Ezek. 10:18, "Then the glory of the Lord departed from off the threshold of the house, and stood over the cherubim"; and 11:23, "and the glory of the Lord went up from the midst of the city, and stood upon the mountain which is on the east side of the city." First the Shekinah-glory left the ark in the holy place, then gradually receding, it left the temple, then going farther away it stood over the Mount of Olives, until it vanished from their sight. God had *forsaken* His earthly throne and dwelling-place!

Now at this point, God, in a *dispensational* way, assumed a *new* title. In 2 Chron. 36:23 we read, "Thus saith Cyrus, king of Persia, all the kingdoms of the earth hath *the Lord God of heaven* given me." So in the opening verses of Ezra we are told that this same Cyrus made a proclamation saying, "*The Lord God of heaven* hath given me all the kingdoms of the earth, and He hath charged me to build Him an house at Jerusalem." These are the first occurrences of this Divine title in Scripture. It is no mere casual expression, but the employment of it marked a great crisis and denoted a radical change in God's dealings with the earth. It will be found that this is a characteristic title of God in those books which treat of the *captivity* of Israel. It emphasised the fact that, while His *eternal* throne can never be given up, God's *dispensational* throne upon earth had been forsaken.

In the stead of His visible throne in Israel's midst, God set up another throne on earth, a throne which He *delegated* to men, and which was to continue throughout the times of the Gentiles—an expression which concerns the interval during which the Gentiles have dominion over Jerusalem. This is the theme and subject which is developed in the book of Daniel. In its second chapter, where we have recorded Nebuchadnezzar's dream and the divine interpretation thereof, we find that the prophetic significance of the great image furnished an outline of the history of the times of the Gentiles and the character of their *rule* over this earth (see vv. 37-39).

The prophetic dream of Nebuchadnezzar looked forward not only to the end of the four Gentile world-empires, but also beyond them, contemplating another and future empire which would be totally different in character. In v. 44 we are told, "And in the days of these kings (the "*kingdoms*" before referred to) shall the God of heaven set up a kingdom, which shall never be destroyed: and the kingdom shall not be left to other people, but it shall break in pieces and consume all the kingdoms, and it shall stand forever." This was the fifth kingdom, the promised kingdom of Messiah. Further details concerning it are given in Dan. 7:13, 14, "I saw in the night visions, and, behold, one like the Son of Man came with the clouds of heaven, and came to the Ancient of days, and they brought Him near before Him. And there was given Him dominion, and glory, and a kingdom, that all people, nations, and languages, should serve Him; His dominion is an everlasting dominion, which shall not pass away, and His kingdom that which shall not be destroyed"—compare Luke 19:12, 15.

After Daniel, the voice of prophecy was soon silenced, and for four hundred years the people of Israel remained in a state of eager expectation, waiting for God to fulfil His promises. Next appeared John the Baptist, who took up the *kingdom* message just where the O.T. prophets had dropt it. In Matt. 3:1, 2, we read, "In those days came John the Baptist, preaching in the wilderness of Judea, and saying, Repent ye: for *the kingdom of heaven* is at hand"—it was "at hand," because the King Himself was about to appear in the midst of the Jews. When John said, "The *kingdom of heaven* is at hand," what do you suppose his Jewish hearers understood by that expression? They had the whole of the Old Testament in their hands, but *that* is *all* which they then had. Obviously, their thoughts would naturally turn to that kingdom which the Son of Man was to receive *in heaven* at the hands of the Ancient of days.

It is to be noted that the Baptist's preaching was "in the wilderness of Judea." The *position* occupied by the Messiah's forerunner was a sad portend of the outcome of his mission. John appeared outside the temple, away from Jerusalem. And his message, "Repent ye," bore witness to Israel's sad spiritual condition—I do not need to say "Repent ye" to a people who are walking in communion with God. "Repent ye" was a word for those who were *away from God*.

Then appeared the One whom John heralded. The King Himself once more drew near to Israel on earth. He who had of old vacated His earthly throne and who had in the days of Ezekiel retired to heaven, and who from that time onwards became known as "The Lord God of heaven," had in matchless grace incarnated Himself in human form, and because He was now once more upon earth, because the King Himself was present in Israel's midst, the Kingdom was "at hand." Therefore, we are told in Matt. 4:17, "From that time Jesus began to preach, and to say, Repent: for the kingdom of heaven is at hand." Both the "signs" (Matt. 11:4; 16:3) and the "powers" (Heb. 2:3; 6:5) of the kingdom—the Messianic, earthly one—were displayed by Christ. Humanly speaking, everything was ready for the establishment of that which had been promised by Daniel. Nothing was wanting but this —*loyal hearts* to welcome and receive the Divine-King. But, alas! this was lacking: "He came unto His own, and His own received Him not" (John 1:11).

The steps of the Messiah's rejection are traced in Matthew 12, which we shall take up in our next article. Because Israel rejected their King, He temporarily rejected them, and therefore the setting up of His Messianic kingdom on this earth was postponed. The King would depart from this world and be absent for a lengthy season, before He returned again and set up His kingdom—see Luke 19:12, 15. In the interval of His absence the "kingdom" takes another form. It is now His kingdom among the Gentiles, and is found wherever His authority is publicly owned; it is the sphere of Christian profession: in a word, Christendom.

## THE LAWGIVER.

*"Thou hast commanded us to keep Thy precepts diligently"* (Psa. 119:4).

One of the surest tests of the spirituality of a Christian is his respect for the *authority* of God. If he is fonder of the prophecies of Scripture than he is of its commandments, or if he loves the Divine promises more than the Divine precepts, his heart is not right with God. This is very searching, is it not? No doubt it condemns many of the readers, as alas, it does the writer.

The first question asked by Saul of Tarsus when the Saviour apprehended him was, "Lord, what wilt Thou have me to do?" This should be the daily desire of the Christian: to please God, to respect His authority, to do His bidding. *Obedience* is one of the best "evidences" that a work of grace has begun in our hearts, for "to obey is better than sacrifice, and to hearken than the fat of rams" (1 Sam. 15:22).

Now God has told us what He *would* have us do; told us in the statutes, precepts, commandments of His Word. His mind regarding us *has been made* known; His will is clearly revealed. If we are ignorant of it, it is because of our sloth, because we have been too lazy to search and see what He has said to us. But if we seek His glory, and desire our own spiritual good, we *shall* seek His will and conform to His arrangements. In our text three things are said about the Divine Lawgiver:—

### 1. His Authority.

This comes out in the opening words: "*Thou* hast *commanded.*" In these days of lawlessness, when both Divine and human authority are being more and more flouted, we need to be reminded that the precepts of Scripture are not so much good advice which people may heed or ignore at their pleasure, but instead, they are the authoritative fiats of the Most High, the commandments of the Almighty, which men despise at their peril. They are not only wise counsels, but mandates from the throne of Jehovah.

I believe that of late God has been deepening our assurance of the Divine Authorship of the Bible, strengthening our faith in its Divine inspiration. Evidence has been brought before us that no man or men *could* have written *such* a Book. Some of its wonders have been opened to us, convincing us that a higher wisdom than man's must have written it. Such strengthening of faith is no small mercy, and is much to be thankful for. But there is something else we need and should prayerfully seek, namely, that we may be more deeply impressed with the Divine *authority* of Scripture, that our hearts may be *awed* and our lives brought into fuller subjection to its precepts. To help us:

Think first of *Who* it is that commands us! It is not a fellow-mortal, nor is it an angel, but the Lord God Himself, the One before whom the highest angels veil their faces in awe. It is Him upon whom we are dependent for every breath we draw. It is One whose power is without limit. So that He cannot be defied with impunity, nor rebelled against successfully.

Think secondly of His *right* to command us! He *made* us; *He* gave us being. Therefore none has such absolute dominion over us as He has. He is the *Lord*, we His subjects and servants, so that it is for Him to regulate our ways. If we are Christians, He is our *Father,* and we His children, and it is right for a Father to command His sons. He is our *Redeemer*, we are His purchased property: "Ye are not your own, but bought with a price"; therefore we are entirely at His disposal.

Think, thirdly, of His *power to enforce* His commandments! He is able to execute His threatenings against disobedience and to bestow rewards upon the obedient. Listen to the words of Christ, spoken not to the unbelieving multitude, but to His own disciples: "Fear not them which kill the body, but are not able to kill the soul: but rather fear Him which is able to destroy both soul and body in Hell" (Matt. 10:28). *Man* may threaten us with fines, floggings, imprisonments. But *God* with a Pit without bottom, with fire that shall never be quenched, with torments that shall never cease! *This is the Person* spoken of in our text: "*Thou* hast commanded us."

### 2. The Exercise of His Authority.

God not only has the *right* of authority, but He has exerted it; He actually *commands* us. The precepts of Scripture proceed not only from the love of God, and so are for our good; they not only proceed from the wisdom of God, and therefore are "holy and just"; but they proceed from His *authority,* and therefore are binding and imperative. Compliance with them is not optional, but obligatory.

God may command what He pleases, for He is absolute. *His* will is the only reason for all things. Again and again in Scripture we find Him asserting His sovereignty: you *shall* do this, or you *shall not* do that. Why? "I am the Lord," *that* is the only reason given. To command is God's part; to obey is ours. And God is neither ignorant of nor indifferent to our disobedience: "The eyes of the Lord are in every place, *beholding* the evil and the good" (Prov. 15:3).

God *urges* the *authority* of His "precepts." What did He say to Israel through Hosea? This: "I have written to him the great things of My law, but they were counted as a strange thing" (8:12). Mark you the "great things" of His law, *not* "trivial," not details of little moment, which we may ignore. Every jot and tittle of God's law is "great" because invested with the infinite authority of the Almighty.

Because of this, God's servants are called on to *charge* you in His name to *bow* to that authority and *heed* His precepts, which "charge" you will have to answer in the Day to come. Unless you mean to defy the sovereign majesty of God and break out in open rebellion against Him, you *must* do what He has commanded you. Timothy was told to *charge* (not "advise" or "recommend") them that are rich in this world, that they be not high-minded nor trust in uncertain riches. To Titus God said, "These things speak and exhort, and rebuke *with all authority*. Let no man despise thee" (2:15). God *will* have the creature know that He requires submission from men. God can, and surely will punish disobedience: "There is one Lawgiver, who is able to save and to destroy" (James 4:12). How this should awe and curb us!

3. *The Requirement of His Authority.*

This is, that we must keep His precepts diligently! What is meant by this? To observe the whole rule of faith; to do *all* that God has commanded us: to "live by *every* word of God." O my brethren, if the awe of God's authority *were* on our hearts, what kind of people would we be at all times, in all places, in all companies! What a curb would it be on our proud thoughts, self-will, angry speech! How carefully we should order our walk, had we serious thoughts of God's authority *forbidding* these things in His Word! Let me suggest three reasons why we need to *consider* the authority of God behind His precepts:—

First, because otherwise we shall have little respect for them. God has bidden us "redeem the time," then shall I have no conscience as to how I waste my precious hours? God has ordered us to "search our ways," then shall I live in constant neglect of this duty? God has commanded us to "owe no man anything," then is it a matter of little moment whether I run into debt or no? God has said, "Son, go work to-day in My vineyard," then does it matter little whether I heed Him or no? O my brethren, obedience to God's precepts is a debt which we owe, and which we *must* pay, or answer at our peril in the Day of accounts. These things are not commended, but commanded. But it is only the awe of God's authority which will prompt diligent obedience.

Second, because we cannot be so bold and venturesome in sinning when the authority of God awes us. Ah, we profess to believe in the *sovereignty* of God; intellectually we do, no doubt. But what effect does it have on our hearts and lives? If the Divine authority really weighed with us, when tempted to do anything that *He* has forbidden we should promptly say, I *dare not*, I am afraid to defy *Him!* This was what restrained Joseph. When tempted to do evil he said, "How can I do this great wickedness and sin *against God?*" The heart is not right before Him till it really bows before His throne and acknowledges His authority. What a word is that in Jude 9, "Michael, the archangel, when contending with the Devil . . . durst *not* bring against him a railing accusation"—dare not because a commandment of God stood in his way. O that the Divine prohibition may be as terrible to us as an angel with a flaming sword!

Third, because otherwise we shall be more occupied with the *outcome* of obedience, than with the obedience itself. How many are fearful to do their duty because of wondering of what would come from it! How many think if they were to conduct their business, in everything, according to the principles of Scripture, they would soon be bankrupted! Yes, and how many think that if the Church, and all its departments, were run according to the precepts of God's Word, the unconverted would be stumbled or driven away! Such an attitude and such reasonings betray a heart that is *not* in subjection to God's authority. When *He* commands, it is not for us to reason why, nor for us to make reply; our duty is to *comply*. Remember the case of Peter who, when bidden to "let down the nets for a draught," and this after toiling all night and taking nothing, said, "Nevertheless *at Thy word I* will let down the nets" (Luke 5:5). *This* is ever sufficient for a heart that is right with God. If He has signified *His* will, then no matter how it may fall contrary to my thoughts, desires, or interests, I *must* obey.

Now God not only requires obedience but *diligent* obedience. God not only takes note of what we do, but *how* we do it, for "the Lord weigheth the spirits" (Prov. 16:2). He not only requires to be loved, but loved with *all* the heart. When writing to the Corinthians about the incorruptible crown, the apostle not only enjoined them to "run," but said, "*so run that ye may obtain.*" Half-hearted obedience is an offence to God: "*fervent* in spirit, serving the Lord" (Rom. 12:11). Whatsoever thy hand findeth to do, do it with *thy might*. So, in our text, we are commanded to keep God's precepts *diligently*.

"Thou hast commanded us *to* keep Thy precepts diligently." All of us are apt to put God off with anything; therefore we need to rouse ourselves to serve Him "with diligence." Serving the Lord is something very different from what the worldling imagines. Mark the solemn words of Joshua to the disobedient Israelites: "Ye *cannot* serve the Lord: *for* He is an holy God, He is a jealous God" (24:19). He is jealous of His honour and majesty, and therefore hates the least failure.

God has severely punished men for doing what the world deems very *little* things. To us it may seem a *small* matter for Adam and Eve to eat of the forbidden fruit; but behold the awfulness of their punishment! "Remember Lot's wife," said our Lord: she was suddenly turned into a pillar of salt. For what? Cursing God? No; just for turning her head and looking back at her burning home! Zachariah, the father of John the Baptist, was struck dumb for one moment's unbelief. Moses, for a few rash words, was debarred from entering Canaan. In the book of Numbers we read of a man being stoned to death for "gathering sticks" on the Sabbath. Uzziah was stricken down by Divine judgment for failing in one minor detail—just steadying with his hand the shaking ark! David, for his proud conceit in numbering the people, lost seventy thousand from a pestilence sent from heaven. These examples show us *how* God regards the slighting of His precepts. Remember that His Word says, "Rebellion is as the sin of witchcraft, and stubbornness as iniquity and idolatry" (1 Sam. 15:23). Again, I say, the "precepts" of Scripture are not the counsels of men who wish us well and advise for the best, but the commandments of God, which *must* be obeyed.

How great then is our need for diligently *searching the Scriptures!* The Bible must be studied not merely to obtain food for our souls, or comfort for our sorrows, but first and foremost to *learn God's will*. Shall He have gone to the trouble of making known His mind, of pointing out the path I should follow, the manner in which I should conduct myself, the things *He* would have me avoid, the duties which *He* would have me perform; and shall I be too dilatory to take the trouble to find out about these things? Do *we* respect His authority? Do we *desire* to "keep His precepts diligently"? Then the first thing is for us to study His Word, and find out what they are! Search the Scriptures for His "precepts" concerning the home, the church, and the State, and then *keep* them "diligently"!

In conclusion, let me remind you of the blessed and perfect example left us by our Saviour and Master. For *Him* the "precepts" of Scripture were binding duties, authoritative decrees. Does the law of God bid children "honour thy father and mother"? then see Him as a Boy of twelve going down to Nazareth and being "subject unto them" (Luke 2:51)! Behold Him walking sixty miles to be baptised of John! Why? "For thus it becometh us *to fulfil* all righteousness" (Matt. 3:15)! Mark His conduct in the Temptation: not parleying or even arguing with Satan, but "living by every word that proceeded out of the mouth of God" (Matt. 4). Witness His action after the cleansing of the leper —"go thy way, show thyself to the priest, and offer the gift that Moses *commanded*," and this "for a testimony unto them" (Matt. 8:4)—a "testimony" of *His* subjection to the law! Bow in wonderment and worship, as the Scripture shows Him, on the very eve of His death, "keeping the passover" with His disciples. Why? Because the "precepts" of God's Word so required. O that we might realise more the binding *authority* of God's "precepts," which He has *commanded* us to keep diligently.

The above is a sermon preached by the Editor in Sydney.

## FORBIDDEN MIXTURES.

*Deut. 22:9-11.*

God abhors mixtures. At the beginning, He divided the light from the darkness. When His grace stooped down and laid hold on Abraham, he was called on to forsake his heathen surroundings and become a stranger and pilgrim in Canaan. In His dealings with the children of Israel Jehovah separated them from the Gentiles and built a wall around them. Even within the Camp of Israel, the Tribe of Levi was separated from the others, and only its sons were permitted to engage in the service of the Lord's House.

Mixtures are of the Devil. He, and not God, is the author of confusion. It was the Devil who sowed his tares among the wheat, as it was the Devil who moved the woman to place her evil leaven within the pure meal. And he is still engaged in the same work, seeking to cause confusion and striving to break down God's order of *no* mixtures.

In our text we find the Lord making known His abhorrence of mixed principles and prohibiting His people of old from indulging in them. "Thou shalt not sow thy vineyard with divers seeds: lest the fruit of thy seed which thou hast sown, and the fruit of they vineyard be defiled. Thou shalt not plow with an ox and an ass together. Thou shalt not wear a garment of divers sorts, of woollen and linen together." I need hardly say that while these words had first a *literal* application to the Hebrews, they have also a *spiritual* application to Christians to-day. As 2 Tim. 3:16 tells us, "*All* scripture is profitable for doctrine, for reproof, for correction, for instruction in righteousness."

Now if we allow Scripture to interpret Scripture there is no difficulty in ascertaining and defining the exact spiritual meaning and application of the terms of the text unto ourselves. Three things are therein forbidden: mixed teaching, mixed service, mixed conduct. Let us now briefly consider each separately.

### 1. *Mixed Teaching.*

"Thou shalt not sow thy vineyard with divers seeds." "Seed" is one of the Divinely-chosen figures for the Word itself. "Being born again not of corruptible seed, but of incorruptible, by the Word of God, which liveth and abideth for ever" (1 Peter 1:23). In the parable of the Sower Christ said, "the seed is the Word of God" (Luke 8:11). Here it was the Word of God *as taught to others,* for under the figure of the "Sower" Christ was referring to His own earthly ministry as He went about teaching the people.

The example of Christ is that which His servants must follow, and *He* sowed *only one* kind of "seed," namely, God's Word. If we turn to that wondrous 17th of John, where Christ is seen rendering an account to His Father of His stewardship, among other things we find Him declaring, "I have given unto them the word which Thou gavest Me" (v. 8). O that His servants may be able to say this. Again and again God's order to them is: "Preach the Word," in its purity, in its entirety.

How different would Christendom be to-day if this first precept of our text had been heeded! Sad to say it has been almost universally disregarded. "Divers seeds" *have been* sown. Man has attempted to mix Scripture and science, Scripture and art, Scripture and politics; and in consequence the pulpit has lost its power; the Spirit has been "quenched." It is a tragedy of tragedies to behold a man who professes to speak in the name of God descending from the high level of Divine revelation to the topics of the newspaper.

"Thou *shalt not* sow thy vineyard with divers seeds." The man who occupies the pulpit should be a man of one book—the Holy Scriptures; of one theme—Christ; of one sword—that of the Spirit. But alas, where are such men to be found to-day? That prophecy through Amos is now almost completely realised: "Behold, the days come, saith the Lord God, that I will send *a famine* in the land, not a famine of bread, nor a thirst for water, but of *hearing the words of the Lord*. And they shall wander from sea to sea, and from the north even to the east, they shall run to and fro, to seek the Word of the Lord, and shall not find it" (8:11, 12). How little of the pure, unadulterated Word is being sown to-day!

### 2. *Mixed Service.*

"Thou shalt not plow with an ox and an ass together." Plowing is work, and, in Scripture, the "ox" is the symbol of *service*. Proof of this is found in 1 Cor. 9:9, 10: "Thou shalt not muzzle the mouth of the ox which treadeth out the corn. Doth God take care for *oxen*? Or saith He it altogether for our sakes? For *our* sakes, no doubt, this is written: that *he that ploweth* should plow in hope; and that he that thresheth in hope should be partaker of his hope." The "ass" represents the *natural man*. Job 11:12 says: "Man is born like a wild *ass's* colt."

"Thou shalt not plow with an ox and an ass together." What could be plainer? Under the Law the "ox" was a clean animal, and the "ass" an unclean one. Thus, one who has been cleansed by the precious blood of Christ is forbidden to engage in His service with one who has not been cleansed. Does someone ask, Why? The all-sufficient answer is, Because *God* has so *commanded*. It is not for us to question *His* arrangements, but to promptly fall into line. It is not for us to quibble over *His* commands, but to obey. "Thou hast commanded us to keep Thy precepts diligently" (Psa. 119:4), and *this* is one of His "precepts."

"Thou shalt not plow with an ox and an ass together." As another has said, "Not only are God's furrows to be sown with nothing but God's Seed, His plow must be drawn only by His own oxen." Our text expressly forbids an "ox" being yoked with an "ass." The New Testament as plainly teaches the same thing: "Be ye not *unequally yoked* together with unbelievers: for what fellowship hath righteousness with unrighteousness? and what communion hath light with darkness?" (2 Cor. 6:14).

Under the preceding head we pointed out how that the first precept in our text is to-day almost universally disregarded. So obvious is this that it was unnecessary for us to enlarge. But this second prohibition is now just as widely disobeyed, and the deplorable thing is that so many professing Christians not only see nothing wrong in it, but argue in favour of and cling tenaciously to their disobedience.

Christian friends, if our service is to be acceptable to God then it *must be* regulated by His Word, and His Word says, "Thou shalt *not* plow with an ox and an ass together"; "Be not *unequally yoked* together with unbelievers." This applies to all Christian activities—Sunday School work, and the Sisters' work in the Church, etc. And it is for us to comply, to conform *all* of our service to the requirements of God's holy and authoritative Word.

If we saw *how hideous* the "ass" is in *God's* sight we should not want him *to* "plow" with us. There dwelleth *no* "good thing" in him. From the crown of his head to the sole of his feet there is *no* soundness in him. *Every* thought of the imagination of his heart is *only* evil continually. What then have the regenerate and unregenerate in common? Nothing. The one believes in and loves the Lord Jesus; the other "despises and rejects" Him. And there is no third class: "he that is not for Me, is *against* Me," said Christ.

"The *plowing* of the wicked (that is, unbelievers) is sin" (Prov. 21:4). Here is what *God* says of the service of the ungodly. Then shall *we* encourage them to add sin to all their iniquities? Of old God said to Pharaoh, "Let My people go, *that* they may serve Me" (Ex. 9:1). Israel could not serve Jehovah in Egypt: they must first be separated from unbelievers!

The only acceptable *motive* in service is seeking to promote the *glory* of God: does, can, an unbeliever do that? The only *impulse* of all true service is *gratitude*, the love of Christ constraining; does an unbeliever have that? No; and because he does not, God says, "Thou shalt not plow with an ox and an ass together."

3. *Mixed Conduct..*

"Thou shalt not wear a garment of divers sorts, of woollen and linen together." *Conduct* expresses a man's character as his suit reveals the outline of his body. Hence, in Scripture, "garments" are frequently used as a figure of conduct. "Thou hast a few names even in Sardis which have not *defiled* their garments" (Rev. 3:4), which means, they had kept themselves unspotted from the world. So, too, in Rev. 19:8 R.V. we read, "The fine linen is the righteous *acts* of the saints."

"And it shall come to pass, that when they enter in at the gates of the inner court, they (the priests) shall be clothed with linen garments and *no* wool shall come upon them" (Ezek. 44:17). Woollen garments make us perspire, and therefore speak of the heat and energy of the flesh. In Jude 23 we are told to "hate even the garment spotted by the flesh," that is, conduct which is stained or defiled by the heat or filth of the flesh. Thus woollen garments are in contrast from the "fine linen," which speaks of those righteous acts which are produced by the Holy Spirit.

"Thou shalt not wear a garment of divers sorts, of woollen and linen together." The conduct of the Christian is not to consist of holy principles adroitly mingled with worldly maxims and compromising ways. It is to be a godly fabric *throughout*. I must not be a regular attender at and dutiful in the Church, and then indulge in shady practices in my business. I must not have a family altar in my home, and then be ambitious that my children should shine in society and make a name for themselves in the world. At all times, in all places, in all companies, the Christian's motto should ever be, "For me to live is *Christ*" to please, serve, honour and glorify Him.

"Thou shalt not wear a garment of divers sorts, of woollen and linen together." Proverbs 3:6 is parallel with this: "In all thy ways acknowledge Him, and He shall direct thy paths." Not in some of your ways, but in *all* of them. How significant, in this connection, is it that we are told the coat of the Lord Jesus was "without seam, woven from the top throughout" (John 19:23)!

May the Lord in His grace keep both writer and reader from *mixed* teaching. *mixed* service, and *mixed* conduct, and make us like Caleb of whom the Lord said, he "hath followed Me *fully*" (Num. 14:24).

—*Arthur W. Pink.*

N.B.—For several thoughts in this sermon we are indebted to an article by Mr. D. M. Panton.

## TRIUMPHANT FAITH.

The story of Charlie Coulson's last days, as told by Dr. Rossvally, the surgeon who attended him in his last hours, is full of interest and deeply pathetic. Charlie, a young lad of 17 years, had joined the Northern Army during the American Civil War as a drummer-boy. He was severely wounded at the Battle of Gettysburg, and was among those who required the army surgeon's attention at once. On the assistant-surgeon and steward approaching him to get him in readiness for the surgeon, he refused the chloroform that was about to be administered, and the brandy that was afterwards offered as a stimulant. He told the surgeon that he had put his trust in Jesus, and added: "I know I can trust Him now. He is my strength; He will support me while you amputate my arm and leg." The surgeon, who was a Jew, tells that at this time he hated Jesus, but he could not help respecting the boy's loyalty to his Saviour, and he says: "When I saw how he loved and trusted Him to the last, there was something that touched my heart, and I did for that boy what I had never done for any other soldier—I asked him if he wished to see his chaplain." The chaplain was sent for at Charlie's request, and the wounded youth indicated that he was not long to be in this world. "Chaplain," he then said, "please put your hand under my pillow and take my little Bible; in it you will find my mother's address. Please send it to her, and write a letter and tell her that since the day I left home I have never let a day pass without reading a portion of God's Word, and daily praying that God would bless my dear mother—no matter whether on the march, on the battlefield, or in the hospital." After giving some other instructions he turned to the surgeon and said, "Now, doctor, I am ready, and I promise you that I will not even groan while you take off my arm and leg, if you will not offer me chloroform." The ordeal was telling more on the surgeon than on the patient, for he writes: "I had not the courage to take the knife in my hand to perform the operation without first going into the next room and taking a little stimulant to nerve myself to perform the duty." When the surgeon was cutting through the flesh no groan escaped Charlie's lips, but when he saw the surgeon taking the saw to sever the bone, the young lad took the corner of the pillow in his mouth, and the surgeon heard him utter the words :"O Jesus, blessed Jesus, stand by me now!"

That night no sleep came to the surgeon's eyes; wherever his eyes turned they seemed to be met by Charlie's soft, blue eyes, while the words of his prayer—"O Jesus, blessed Jesus, stand by me now"—kept ringing in his ears. Between twelve and one o'clock in the early morning the surgeon rose and was informed that twenty-six of the hopeless cases had died. "How is Charlie Coulson?" he asked. "He is sleeping sweetly as a lamb, sir," was the answer. Five days after the amputation, Charlie sent for the surgeon. "Doctor," he said, "my time has come: I do not expect to see another sun rise, but, thank God, I am ready to go, and before I die I desire to thank you with all my heart for your kindness to me. Doctor, you are a Jew: you do not believe in Jesus; will you please stand here and see me die, trusting in my Saviour to the last moment of my life?" "I tried to stay," says the surgeon, "but I had not the courage to stand by and see a Christian boy die rejoicing in the love of Jesus whom I had been taught to hate, so I hurriedly left the room." About twenty minutes after this one of the stewards came with the message: "Doctor, Charlie Coulson wishes to see you." "I have just seen him," said the surgeon, "and I cannot see him again." "But, Doctor, he says he must see you before he dies." The surgeon, in obedience to the urgent request, hastened to his bedside, but determined to steal himself against anything that would change his mind towards the Redeemer. He purposed to say an endearing word to the dying boy and leave him. When he entered the room he saw that Charlie was sinking fast. He sat down by his bedside, and the dying boy asked him to take hold of his hand, and then addressed him thus: "Doctor, I love you because you are a Jew; the best friend I have found in this world was a Jew." "Who was that?" asked the surgeon. "Jesus Christ, to whom I want to introduce you before I die; and will you promise me, doctor, that what I am about to say to you, you will never forget." On the doctor promising, Charlie said: "Five days ago, while you amputated my arm and leg, I prayed to the Lord Jesus Christ to convert your soul." "These words," said the doctor, "went deep into my heart. I could not understand how, when I was causing him the most intense pain, he could forget all about himself and think of nothing but his Saviour and my unconverted soul." All I could say to him was "well, my dear boy, you will soon be alright." With these words I left him, and twelve minutes later he fell asleep, safe in the arms of Jesus." "Hundreds of soldiers," he adds, "died in my hospital during the war, but I only followed one to the grave, and that one was Charlie Coulson, the drummer-boy, and I rode three miles to see him buried. I had him dressed in a new uniform and placed in an officer's coffin, with the United States flag over it. That dear boy's dying words made a deep impression on me. I was rich all that time, so far as money is concerned, but I would have given every penny I possessed if I could have felt towards Christ as Charlie did: but that feeling cannot be bought with money. Alas! I soon forgot all about my Christian soldier's little sermon, but I could not forget the boy himself. I now know that at that time I was under deep conviction of sin, but I fought against Christ with all the hatred of an orthodox Jew for nearly ten years, until, finally the boy's prayer was answered and God converted my soul."

Eighteen months after the surgeon's conversion he was quite unexpectedly brought into touch with Charlie's mother. It was a happy meeting, and the converted man joyfully announced to the dead lad's mother, "Your boy's prayer has been heard and answered. I am the Jewish doctor for whom your Charlie prayed, and His Saviour is now my Saviour."

What an examplification is this of those words, "My grace *is* sufficient for thee!" And what an illustration is it of the power of prayer.—A.W.P.

---

hundred men. The promises of resurrection mean little till some of our loved ones are removed by death!

"When thou passest through the waters, I will be with thee; and through the rivers, they shall not overflow thee: when thou walkest through the fire, thou shalt not be burned" (Isa. 43:2) means far more to afflicted souls than to those who are not under the rod. So, too, the many "fear not" promises are most valued when our own strength fails us and we are ready to sink under despair. As the late C. H. Spurgeon was wont to say, "There are some verses written, as it were, in a secret ink, which must be held before the fire of adversity before they become visible.

Only a few days ago I was looking through an old Bible of mine, and there discovered certain dates which I had put in the margin opposite some precious promises. There are many passages in Job, the Psalms, and the Lamentations of Jeremiah which do not appeal to one while the sun is shining; but which, in times of adversity, are like the welcome beams of the moon on a dark night. It was his painful thorn in the flesh which taught Paul the blessedness of that text, "My grace is sufficient for thee: for My strength is made perfect in weakness" (2 Cor. 10:12).

4. *It qualifies us to sympathise with others.* If we have never trod the vale of sorrow and affliction we are really unable to "weep with those that weep." There are some surgeons who would be more tender if they had suffered from broken bones themselves. If we have never known much trouble, we make poor comforters to others. Even of our Saviour it is written, "For in that He Himself hath *suffered* being tempted, He *is able* to succour them that are tempted" (Heb. 2:18). Bunyan could never have written the book which he did, unless God had permitted the Devil to tempt and buffet him severely for so many years. How clearly is all this brought out in 2 Cor. 1:4: "Who comforteth us in all our tribulations, *that we* may be able to comfort them which are in any trouble, *by* the comfort wherewith we ourselves are comforted of God."

Here, then, are some of the benefits of afflictions when sanctified by God to the heart: they wean us from the world, they cast us back the more upon God, they make His promises more precious to us, they qualify us to sympathise with others. If, then, chastisement issues in such precious blessings, such peaceful fruits, let us be thankful for them; yea, let us welcome them.

(Substance of a sermon preached by the Editor.)

now that we have experienced a taste and foretaste of heaven, we shall be repelled and nauseated by the world. But, alas! the "old man" is still in us, unchanged; and though Divine grace subdues his activities, still he is very much alive. It is because of this that we are called on to "crucify the flesh with its affections and lusts." And this is not only an unpalatable, but a very hard, task. Therefore does God in His mercy help us—help us by chastenings which serve to loosen the roots of our soul downwards and tighten the anchor-hold of our hearts heavenwards.

This, God does in various ways. Sometimes He causes us to lose our confidence in and draw us away from fellowship with worldlings by receiving cruel treatment at their hands. "Come out from among them, and be ye separate" is the Lord's word to His people. But they are slow to heed; oftentimes they must be *driven out!* So with worldly pleasures. God often makes the grapes of earthly joys bitter to our taste, so that we should no longer seek after them. It is earthly disappointments and worldly disillusionments which make us sigh for our Heavenly Home. While the Hebrews enjoyed the land of Goshen they were content: hard and cruel bondage was needed to make them ready to leave for the promised land!

One of the greatest surprises of my Christian life in connection with fellow-saints, has not been their ignorance, nor even their inconsistencies; but their *earthliness,* their reluctance to leave this world. As "strangers and pilgrims" we should be longing and yearning for our Heavenly Home. As those who are away from Him whom they love best, we should desire to *"depart* and be with Him" (Phil. 1:23). Paul did. Christ has promised to return for His people, yet how few of them are daily crying, "Even so, come Lord Jesus." How rarely we hear them saying, in the language of the mother of Sisera, "Why is His chariot so long in coming? Why tarry the wheels of His chariot?" Without being dogmatic, I am inclined to believe this is one reason why so many of God's people are undergoing fiery trials.

"And all the trials here we see
Should make us long to reign with Thee."

Scripture speaks of this world as a "dry and thirsty land, where no water is" (Psa. 63:1). And God intends for us to *prove* this in our experiences. His Word also affirms that it is a "dark place" (2 Peter 1:19). And He means for us to learn that this *is* so.

2. *It casts us back the more upon God.* By nature we are filled with a spirit of independency. The fallen sons of Adam are like wild asses' colts. Chastisement is designed to empty us of our self-sufficiency, to make us feel our weakness and helplessness. Afflictions cast us back upon God, and surely *this* is for our "profit." Trials and troubles often drive us to our knees: sickness and sorrow make us seek unto the Lord. Have you noticed in the four Gospels how very rarely men and women that were in health and strength sought out Christ? It was trouble and illness which brought them to the great Physician! A nobleman came to Christ—why? Because his son was at the point of death. Jairus sought out the Master—why? Because his little daughter was so low. The Canaanitish woman interviewed the Lord Jesus—why? On behalf of her tormented daughter. The sisters of Lazarus sent a message to the absent Saviour—why? Because their brother was sick.

Afflictions may be very bitter, but they are a fine tonic for the soul, and are a medicine which God often uses on us. Most vividly is this illustrated in Psa. 107—read carefully vv. 11 to 28. Note that it is when men are "brought down," when they are "afflicted," when they are "at their wits' end" that they "*cry* unto the Lord in their trouble." Yes, it is "trouble" which makes us turn unto the Lord, not in a mechanical and formal way, but in deep earnestness. Remember that it is the "effectual *fervent* prayer of a righteous man that availeth much." When you observe that the fire in your room is getting dull, you do not always put on more coal, but simply *stir* with the poker; so God often uses the black poker of adversity in order that the flames of devotion may burn more brightly.

3. *It makes the Promises of God more precious to us.* Trouble often acts on us as a sharp knife which opens the truth of God to us and our hearts to the Truth. Experience unlocks passages which were otherwise closed. There is many a text in the Bible which no commentator can helpfully expound to you: it must be interpreted by experience. Paul wrote his profoundest Epistles while in prison; John was "in tribulation" on Patmos when he received the Revelation. If you go down into a deep well or mine in the day-time you will then see the shining of stars which were not visible from the earth's surface: so God often brings us low in order that we may see the shining beauty of some of His comforting assurances. Note how Jacob, in Gen. 32, pleaded God's promises when he heard that Esau was approaching with four

(Continued on page 215)

# STUDIES IN THE SCRIPTURES

"Search the Scriptures" John 5: 39

Copyright in all English-speaking Countries.

Editor: Arthur W. Pink, 15 Hurlstone Avenue, Summer Hill, N.S.W., Australia.
Hon. Agent in U.S.A.: Mr. C. S. Pressel, 559 Dupont Avenue, York, Penna.

FREE TO ALL WHO WILL READ IT

## DIVINE CHASTISEMENT.
### Heb. 12:10.

I feel led to continue the sermon of last Lord's day morning (when we considered some of the *benefits* of Divine chastisement), and that for two reasons: to help our unbelief, and to deepen our gratitude. The Christian's heart is very sceptical and takes much convincing. You have heard a person say to someone who claims he has done or can do some unusual thing, "You must *show* me before I will believe you." Most of us are very much like that in connection with spiritual things. Though the Scriptures assure us, again and again, that chastisement proceeds from our Father's love, and is for our good, yet we are slow, very slow, to really believe it. Therefore would I seek, by the Spirit's help, to *show* you that it *is* so, by making mention of and describing some of the blessings which issue from the Father's rod, and this that your faith may be established.

My second reason for prolonging this series of sermons and continuing the one of last week is, that we may be more grateful and increasingly thankful for the merciful discipline of our Father. We are on a low plain of spiritual experience if we do nothing more than simply bow to God's hand. Scripture says, "Giving *thanks* always *for all things* unto God and the Father in the name of our Lord Jesus Christ" (Eph. 3:20); and again it declares, *"Rejoice* in the Lord alway" (Phil. 4:4). We are to "glory in tribulations" (Rom. 5:3), and *we shall* when we perceive more clearly and fully what blessed fruits are brought forth under God's pruning knife.

Last week I pointed out how that our heavenly Father never chastens *except* for "our profit": that His object is uniformly our blessing; that whatever the form, degree, or duration of our afflictions, all are ordered by infinite Wisdom so as best to secure this object. We saw, first, chastisement is sent to wean us from the world: to loosen the roots of our soul downwards and to tighten the anchor-hold of our heart heavenwards. I was once familiar with a Christian who had formed the habit of meeting each worldly disappointment or trial to the flesh by saying, "That is another nail in my coffin." Now that is a very gloomy way of viewing things. Rather should the child of God say after each loss or affliction, "That severs another strand in the rope that binds me to this world, and makes me long all the more for Heaven." Second, chastisement is sent to cast us back the more upon God. We delight in being made to lie down in the "green pastures" and being led beside the "still waters," but at those times there is a real danger of us becoming occupied more with His blessings rather than with the Blesser Himself. Oftentimes the sheep have to be brought into the dry and desolate wilderness that they may learn the sufficiency of the Shepherd Himself. Third, chastisement makes the promises of God more precious to us. Fourth, chastisement qualifies us to minister to others. I shall now mention three other blessings:—

5. *It demonstrates to us the blessedness and sufficiency of Divine grace.* "My grace is sufficient for thee: for My strength is made perfect in weakness" (2 Cor. 12:9). But in order to *prove* this we have to be brought into the place of severe testing and trial, and made to feel our own incompetency and nothingness. Brethren, if you have prospered in business all your lives and have always had an easy time financially, then you do not know much about God's strength being perfected in your weakness. If

Continued on page 240

# IMPORTANT NOTICES

## BACK NUMBERS

OF THIS MAGAZINE may yet be secured for 5/- (1 dollar 25.) per year; Bound, at 7/- (1 dollar 75.). Each year is yet obtainable. Soon out of print.

ADVISE PROMPTLY of Change of Address.

THIS MAGAZINE is published as a work of faith and labour of love. It is gladly sent to all who would value it.

We want the names and addresses of Christians who would read it.

Christians who feel definitely led to do so may have fellowship with us in supporting this Ministry.

## CONTENTS.

| | |
|---|---|
| The Gospel of John (21:1-14) | 218 |
| Gleanings in Exodus | 225 |
| Parables of Matt. 13 | 229 |
| A Live Coal | 232 |
| A Testimony | 236 |
| Things to Come | 238 |

## THE GOSPEL OF JOHN.

70. *Christ by the Sea of Tiberias: John 21:1-14.*

The following is an Analysis of our present passage:—

1. Christ's third appearing to the apostles vv. 1, 14.
2. The seven on the sea vv. 2, 3.
3. Their dulness and emptiness vv. 4, 5.
4. The miracle of the fishes v. 6.
5. John's recognition and Peter's response v. 7.
6. The landing of the six vv. 8, 9.
7. Christ's welcome vv. 10-13.

The opening verses of this Gospel are in the nature of a Prologue, so the closing chapter is more or less an Epilogue. In the former, the Holy Spirit has set forth what Christ was *before* He came forth from the Father; in the latter He has shown, in mystical guise, how He now rules the world *after* His return to the Father. "The prologue is intended to exhibit the eternal life of Christ as it preceded His manifestation in the world; the epilogue appears to have for its scope, to exhibit His spiritual sway in the world as it would continue after He had left it" (Lange). All here has a profound significance. The disciples are on the sea; the Lord, no longer with them, directs from the shore, manifesting His power by working with them in their seemingly lonesome toil, and exhibiting His love in providing food for them. Then the charge is left to "feed His sheep." His final word was a reference to His coming again.

The varied details of chapter 21 supply a most instructive and marvellously complete lesson on *service*. In the previous chapter we have seen the Saviour establishing the hearts of the apostles by His word of "Peace," enduing them with the Holy Spirit, and then commissioning them to proclaim remission of sins. Here we have, in symbolic form, the apostles engaged in active ministry. The *order* is most suggestive. What we receive from the Lord Jesus is to be used for the good of others. Freely we have received, freely we are now to give. The key to the practical significance of the scene here portrayed lies in the almost identical circumstances when the apostles received their first ministerial call—Luke 5.

The chapter as a whole falls into *seven* parts as we analyse it from the viewpoint of its teaching on *service*. First, we see men serving in the energy of the flesh (vv. 2, 3). Peter says, "I go a fishing." He had received no call from God to do so. His action illustrates self-will, and the response of the other six men acting under human leadership. Second, we are shown the barrenness of such efforts (vv. 3-5). They toiled all night, but caught nothing, and when the Lord asked if they had any meat, they had to answer, No. Third, the Lord now directs their energies, telling them where to work (v. 6): the result was that the net was filled with fishes. Fourth, we learn of the Lord's gracious provision for His servants (vv. 12, 13): He had provided for them, and invites them to eat. Fifth, we are taught what is the only acceptable motive for service—love to Christ (vv. 15, 17). Sixth, the Lord makes known how that *He* appoints the time and manner of the death of those of His servants who die (vv. 18, 19). Seventh, the Lord concludes by leaving with them the prospect of His return; not *for* death, but *for* Himself they should look (vv. 20-24).

The miracle in John 21 stands alone: it is the only recorded one which Christ wrought after His resurrection, and most fittingly is it the last narrated in this Gospel. Its striking resemblance to the first miracle which some of these disciples had witnessed (Luke 5:1-11) must have brought to their remembrance the very similar circumstances under which they had been called by Christ to leave their occupation as fishermen and become fishers of men. Thus they would be led to interpret this present "sign" by the past one, and see in it a *renewed summons* to their work of catching men, and a renewed assurance that their labour in the Lord would not be in vain. Suitably was it the *last* miracle which they witnessed at the hands of their Master, for it supplied a symbol which would continually animate them to and in their service for Him. It was designed to assure them that just as He had prospered their efforts while He was with them in the flesh, so they could count on His guidance, power, and blessing when He was absent from them.

This *final* miracle of the Saviour was performed in Galilee, so also was His *first* (i.e., the turning of the water into wine), and it seems clear that the Holy Spirit would have us use the "law of comparison and contrast" again. The author of "The Companion Bible" has called attention to quite a number of striking correspondences between the two miracles: we mention a few, leaving the interested reader to work out the others for himself. In both miracles there is a striking background: in the one we have the confession of Nathaniel (1:49); in the other, the confession of Thomas (20:28). The first miracle was on "the third day" (2:1); the latter was "the third time" the Lord showed Himself to the apostles (21:14). The one was occasioned by them having "no wine" (2:3); the other, by them having "no fish" (21:3, 5). In both the Lord uttered a command: "Fill the waterpots" (2:7); "Cast the net" (21:6). In both Christ furnished a bountiful supply: the waterpots were "filled to the brim" (2:7); "the net *full* of great fishes" (21:11). In both a number is mentioned: "six waterpots" (2:6); "one hundred and fifty and three fishes" (21:11). In both Christ manifested His Deity (2:11; 21:12, 14). How much we lose by not carefully *comparing* Scripture with Scripture!

"After these things Jesus showed Himself again to the disciples at the sea of Tiberias; and on this wise showed He" (v. 1). "After these things" always marks off a distinct section in John's writings. The earlier appearances of the risen Saviour were in view of the then condition and need of the apostles to establish their faith and assure their hearts. But here, what the Lord did and said, had a prophetic significance, anticipating and picturing His future relations to them.

"Jesus showed Himself," not presented Himself, but *manifested* His presence, power, and glory. It was not simply that the disciples *saw* Him, but that He *revealed* Himself. "His body after the resurrection was only visible by a distinct act of His will. From that time the disciples did not, as before, *see* Jesus, but He *appeared* unto them. It is not for nothing that the language is changed. Henceforth, He was to be recognised not by the flesh, but by the spirit; not by human faculties, but by Divine perceptions: His disciples were to walk by faith, and not by sight" (Chrysostom). When we are told in Acts 1:3 that the Lord Jesus was "seen of them forty days," it does not mean that the Lord was corporately present with them throughout this period, nor that He was seen by them each day. He was visible and invisible, appeared in one form or another, according to His own pleasure.

"At the sea of Tiberias." In 6:1 we read, "The sea of Galilee, which is the sea of Tiberias," the latter being its Roman name. In Matt. 28:10 we learn that the risen Saviour had said to the women at the sepulchre, "Go tell My brethren that they go into Galilee, and *there* shall they see Me." This, then, explains the presence of the seven disciples here in Galilee. Where the other four were, and why they had not yet arrived, we do not know. But it seems clear that these seven had no business there at the sea, for Matt. 28:16 distinctly says, "The Eleven disciples went away into Galilee, into *a mountain* where Jesus had *appointed* them." It looks very much as though Peter was restless, and while waiting the coming of the other apostles he said, "I go a fishing"—to the last we see his energetic nature at work. Others have suggested that the reason they went a fishing was in order that they might obtain food for a meal, and possibly this did supply an additional motive—cf. v. 12.

"There were together Simon Peter, and Thomas called Didymus, and Nathanael of Cana in Galilee, and the sons of Zebedee, and two other of His disciples" (v. 2). Peter being mentioned first intimates that the enumeration here is the order of *grace*. "Thomas" occupying the second place in the list is a further indication of this. The removal of his doubts had restored the Eleven to unity of faith, and prepared them for mutual fellowship again. "There were *together* Simon Peter *and* Thomas," which is a beautiful contrast from 20:24—"But Thomas was *not with* them!" Thomas is named next to Peter, as if he now kept closer to the meetings of the apostles than ever. "It is well if losses by our neglect make us more careful afterwards not to let opportunities slip" (Matthew Henry). Of "Nathanael" we read elsewhere only in 1:45-51: probably he is the "Bartholemew" of Matt. 10:3. Next come the "sons of Zebedee," emphasising their *fishermen*-character. This is the only place where John *does not* refer to himself as "the disciple whom Jesus loved": the absence of this expression here being in full accord with the fact that it is the order of *grace* which is before us. Who the other two disciples were we are not told.

"Simon Peter saith unto them, I go a fishing. They say unto him, We also go with thee. They went forth and entered into a ship immediately; and that night they caught nothing" (v. 3). That Peter is here seen taking the lead is in full accord with what we read elsewhere of his impulsive and impetuous nature. Most of the commentators consider that the disciples were fully justified in acting as they did on this occasion. But the Lord had not given them orders to fish for any but *men*. It seems to us, therefore, that they were acting according to the promptings of nature. The fact that it was *night-time* also suggests that they were not walking as children of light. Nor did the Lord appear to them during that night: they were left to themselves! The further fact that they "caught nothing" is at least a warning hint that servants of the Lord cannot count on His blessing when *they* choose the time and place of their labours, and when they "run, unsent." These beloved disciples had to be taught in their own experience, as we all have to be, the truth which the Lord had enunciated just before His death— "Without Me, ye can do nothing" (15:5); not, a little, but *nothing!* The further fact that we are told, "*They* went forth, and intered into a ship *immediately*" as soon as Peter had said, "I go a fishing," instead of first looking to God for guidance, or weighing what Peter had said, supplies further evidence that the whole company was acting in the energy of the flesh—a solemn warning for each of God's servants to wait on the Lord for their instructions instead of taking them from a human leader!

"But when the morning was now come. Jesus stood on the shore; but the disciples knew not that it was Jesus" (v. 4). The "but" here adds further confirmation to what we have said above on v. 3. That these disciples now failed to recognise the Saviour indicates that their *spiritual* faculties were not then in exercise. It seems evident that they were not expecting Him. And how often He draws near to us and we know it not! And how often our acting in the energy of the flesh and following the example of human leaders is the cause of this! In the Greek, the closing words of this verse are identical with those found at the end of 20:14: "And (Mary) knew not that it was Jesus." She was immersed in sorrow, occupied with death, and she recognised not the Saviour. These men had returned to their worldly calling, and were occupied with their bodily needs and recognised Him not. Surely these things are written for *our* learning!

"Then Jesus saith unto them, Children, have ye any meat? They answered Him, No" (v.5). Our Lord's form of address here is also searchingly suggestive. He did not use the term of endearment, employed in 13:33, "Little children," but employed the more general form of salutation, which the margin renders "Sirs." He spoke not according to the intimacies of love, but as from a distance—a further hint from the Spirit as to how we are to interpret (vv. 2, 3). But why did He ask: "Have ye any meat?" He knew, of course, that they had none; what, then, was the purpose of His enquiry? Was it not designed to draw from them a confession of their failure, ere He met their need? And is not this ever His way with His own? Before He furnishes the abundant supply, we must first be made conscious of our emptiness. Before He gives strength, we must be made to feel our weakness. Slow, painfully slow, are we to learn this lesson; and slower still to *own* our nothingness and take the place of helplessness before the Mighty One. The disciples on the sea picture *us*, here in this world: the Saviour on the shore (whither we are bound) Christ in Heaven. How blessed, then, to behold Him occupied with us below, and *speaking* to us from "the shore!" It was not the disciples who addressed the Lord, but He who spoke to them!

"And He said unto them, Cast the net on the right side of the ship, and ye shall find" (v. 6). How this evidences the Deity of the One here speaking to these disciples! *He* knew on which side of the ship the net should be cast. But more, did it not show them, and us, that He is sovereign of the sea? These men had fished all their lives, yet had they toiled throughout that night and taken nothing. But here was the Lord telling them to cast their net but once, and assuring them they *should* find. Was it not He, by His invisible power, that *drew* the fishes into their net! And what a striking line is this in this picture of Christian *service*. How He tells the servants that success in their ministry is due not to their eloquence, their power of persuasion, or *their* any thing, but due alone to *His* sovereign drawing-power. A most blessed foreshadowment did the Saviour here give the apostles of the Divine blessing which should rest upon their labours for Him. In full and striking accord with this was the fact that the Lord bade them "Cast the net on the *right* side of the ship"—cf. Matthew 25:34: "Then shall the King say unto them on His *right* hand, come, ye blessed of My Father, inherit the kingdom prepared for you *from the foundation of the world!*"

"They cast, therefore, and now they were not able to draw it for the multitude of fishes" (v. 6). This is very striking. The Lord was a hundred yards away from them (v. 8), yet they heard plainly what He said. Again: He was, so far as their recognition of Him at the moment, an entire stranger to them. Moreover, notwithstanding the fact that they had fished all night and caught nothing, and had already drawn up the net into the boat, as being useless to prolong their efforts; nevertheless, they now promptly cast it into the sea again. How strikingly this demonstrated once more the power of *the Word*—in making them hear His voice, in overcoming whatever scruples they may have had, in moving their hearts to prompt obedience. Verily, "all power in heaven and in earth *is* His." In the abundant intake the disciples were taught that in "keeping His commandments there is great reward" (Psa. 19:11). And what a lesson for those who seek to serve: *His* it is to issue orders, *ours* to obey—unmurmuringly, unquestioningly, promptly.

"Therefore that disciple whom Jesus loved saith unto Peter, It is the Lord" (v. 7). This is in perfect keeping with what we read elsewhere about John—the most devoted of the apostles, *he* possessed the most spiritual discernment. He was the one who leaned on the Master's breast at the Supper, and to whom the Lord communicated the secret of the Betrayer's identity (13:23-26). He was the one that was nearest to the cross, and to whose care the Saviour committed His mother (19:26, 27). He it was who was the first of the Eleven to perceive that the Lord had risen from the dead (20:8). So here, he was the first of the seven to identify the One on the shore. How perfectly harmonious are the Scriptures! "The tenderest love has the first and surest instincts of the object beloved" (Stier). And, what a lesson is here again for the Lord's servants:

when He grants success to our labours, when the Gospel-net in our hands gathers fishes, let us not forget to own "It is the *Lord!*" To how much more may and should this principle be applied. As we admire the beauties of nature, as we observe the orderliness of her laws, as we receive countless mercies and blessings every day, let *us* say "It is the *Lord!*" So, too, when our plans go awry, when disappointment, affliction, persecution comes our way, still let us own "It is *the Lord!*" It is not blind chance which rules our lives, but the One who died for us on the cross.

"Now when Simon Peter heard that it was the Lord, he girt his fisher's coat unto him (for he was naked) and did cast himself into the sea" (v. 7). This was in full keeping with Peter's character: if John was the first to recognise Christ, Peter was the first to act! Nor do we believe that it was mere impulsiveness which prompted him—his collectedness in first girding himself with the outer garment makes decisively against such a superficial conclusion. Peter, too, was devoted to Christ, deeply so, and it was *love* which here made him impatient to reach Christ. Peter's action makes us recall that night on the stormy sea when the Saviour walked on the waves toward the ship in which the disciples were. Peter it was, then, who said unto the Lord, "Bid me come unto Thee on the water" (Matt. 14:28), for he could not wait for his Beloved to reach him. Beautiful is it now to observe that there was *no reserve* about Peter. In the interval between Matt. 14 and John 21, he had basely denied his Master; but in the interval, too, and after the denial, he had heard His "Peace be unto you," and, plainly, this re-assuring word had been treasured up in his heart. Observe that Peter left the net full of fishes for Christ, like the Samaritan woman who left her waterpot. The "girding" of himself evidences the deep reverence in which he held the Saviour!

"And the other disciples came in a little ship (for they were not far from the land, but as it were two hundred cubits) dragging the net with fishes" (v. 8). Love does not act uniformly; it expresses itself differently, through various temperaments. John did not jump out of the ship, though he was equally devoted as Peter, nor did the other five. The six remained in the skiff or punt which usually accompanied the large fishing vessels, so as to draw the net full of fishes safely to land; illustrating the fact that faithful evangelists will not desert those who have been saved under their preaching, but will labour with them, care for them, and do all in their power to ensure their safely reaching the shore. The parenthetical remark seems to be brought in here to emphasise the miraculous character of this catch of fish, and to teach us that sometimes converts to Christ will be found in the most *unlikely* places—the net was cast *close in* to the shore!

"As soon then as they were come to land, they saw a fire of coals there, and fish laid thereon, and bread" (v. 9). This is most blessed. It illustrates once more the precious truth that Jesus Christ is "the same yesterday, and to-day and forever." Even in His resurrection-glory He was not unmindful of their physical needs. Ever thoughtful, ever compassionate for His own, the Saviour here showed His toiling disciples that He cared for their bodies as well as their souls: "For He knoweth our frame; He *remembereth* that we are dust" (Psa. 103:14). We doubt not that this provision of His was miraculously produced: the fire, the fish on it, and the bread by its side, were the creations of Him who has but to will a thing and it is done. It is surely significant that the food which Christ here provided for the disciples was of the same variety as that with which He had fed the hungry multitude close by the same sea. The *fish* and the *bread* would doubtless recall the earlier miracle to the minds of the apostles.

"They saw a fire of coals there, and fish laid thereon, and bread." What is the deeper significance of this? First, it tells us of the Lord's care for His servants, and is the concrete pledge that He *will* supply all their need. Second, the Lord has left us an example to follow: if the Son of God condescended to spread this table for His children after their night of toil, let us not think it beneath us to take loving forethought whenever we have the opportunity of ministering to the physical comfort of His servants: even a cup of water given in His name will yet be rewarded. Third, it signifies that in the midst of labouring for others, *our own* souls need warming and feeding—a lesson which many a servant of God has failed to heed. Fourth, the fact that there were fish already on the fires *before* the disciples drew their full net to land, intimates that the Lord is not *restricted* to the labours of His servants, but that He can and does save souls altogether apart from human instrumentality—another thing we need to take to heart these days when *man* is so much magnified. Finally, does not this gracious provision of Christ forecast the refreshment and satisfaction which will be ours when our toiling on the troublous sea of this world shall be ended, and we are safely landed on the Heavenly shore!

"Jesus saith unto them, bring of the fish which ye have now caught" (v. 10). "In this verse our Lord calls on the disciples to bring proof that, in casting the net at His command, they had not laboured in vain. It was the second word that He spake to them, we must remember, on this occasion. The first saying was, 'Cast the net on the right side of the ship, and ye shall find.' The second saying was, 'Bring of the fish which ye have now caught,' with a strong emphasis on the word 'now.' I believe our Lord's object was to show the disciples that the secret of success was to work at His command, and to act with implicit obedience to His word. It is as though He had said, 'Draw up the net, and see for yourselves how profitable it is to do what I tell you.' Fish for food they did not want now, for it was provided for them. Proof of the power of Christ's blessing, and the importance of working under Him was the lesson to be taught, and as they drew up the net they would learn it" (Bishop Ryle). This also is in full accord with the fact that the *practical* teaching of this chapter is instruction upon *service*.

"Bring of the fish which ye have now caught." Is there not also a *spiritual* hint in this verse? The "fish" symbolise the souls which the Lord enables His servants to gather in. In bidding them bring of the fish *to Him*, He intimated they would have fellowship together, not only in labouring, but also in enjoying the fruits of it! It reminds us of His words in 4:36: "He that reapeth receiveth wages, and gathereth fruit unto life eternal: that both he that soweth and he that reapeth may *rejoice together*." The Lord delights in *sharing* His joy with us. Beautifully is this brought out again in Luke 15:6: "When He cometh home, He calleth together His friends and neighbours, saying unto them, Rejoice *with Me;* for I have found My sheep which was lost." How marvellous the grace which here said to the disciples: "Bring of the fish which ye have now caught!"

"Simon Peter went up and drew the net to land full of great fishes, an hundred and fifty and three; and for all there were so many, yet was not the net broken" (v. 11). Peter drew the net to land: how remarkable is this in view of what is said in v. 6: "*They* were not able to draw it for the multitude of fishes." Surely this points another important lesson in connection with *service*. What six men had been unable to do in their own strength, one man now did when he went to his work from the feet of Christ! Peter was weaker than gossamer thread when he followed his Lord afar off; but in His presence, a sevenfold power came upon him! A similar example is found in Judges 6:14: "The Lord looked upon him (Gideon) and said, Go *in this* thy might." The place of strength is still at the feet of the Saviour, and strength will be imparted exactly in proportion as we are in conscious fellowship with Him and drawing from His infinite fullness. *"He* giveth power to the faint; and to them that have no might He increaseth strength. Even the youths shall faint and be weary, and the young men shall utterly fail; but they that wait upon the Lord shall renew their strength; they shall mount up with wings as eagles; they shall run, and not be weary; and they shall walk, and not faint" (Isa. 40:29-31). How much each of us need to heed that word, "Wait on the Lord, be of good courage, and He shall strengthen thine heart; wait, I say, on the Lord" (Psa. 27:14). How lamentable, and how humbling, that we are so slow to avail ourselves of the unfailing strength which is to be found in Him; found for the feeblest who will wait on Him in simple faith and earnest entreaty.

"Simon Peter went up, and drew the net to land full of great fishes, an hundred and fifty and three: and for all there were so many, yet was not the net broken." There are two details here upon which the ingenuity of many have been freely exercised: the number of the fish, and the not breaking of the net. There is little room to doubt that Peter would recall the miraculous draught of fishes on a former occasion, when the net *did* break (Luke 5). On that occasion the miracle was followed by the Lord saying unto Simon, "From henceforth thou shalt catch *men."* There it is the work of the *evangelist* which is in view, and therefore there is *no* numbering, for it is impossible for him to count up those who are saved under his Gospel message. Following this second miraculous draught, the Lord said unto Simon, "Feed My *sheep."* Here it is the work of the *pastor* or *teacher* which is in view, and hence there *is* numbering, for he ought to be able to determine which are sheep and which are goats. In the former the net breaks, for though many profess to believe the Gospel, yet few really do so to the saving of their souls. In the latter, the net breaks not, for none of the *elect* (the "right" side of the ship) shall perish. As for the *spiritual* meaning of the numbering of the fish here, observe that they were not counted *till the end,* not in v. 6, but in v. 11; not while in the ship, but *after* "the land" is reached! Not till we come to Heaven shall we know the number of God's elect!

"Jesus saith unto them, Come and dine" (v. 12). How beautifully this evidenced the fact that He was still the same loving, gracious, condescending One as in the days of His humiliation! The disciples were not kept at a distance. They were invited to draw near, and partake of the provision which His own compassion had supplied. So He still says to the one who responds to His knocking, "I will come in to him and sup with him, and he with Me" (Rev. 3:20). Here for the last time we hear His blessed and familiar "Come." "Come" not "Go." He did not send them away, but invited them to Himself.

"And none of the disciples durst ask Him, Who art Thou? knowing that it was the Lord" (v. 12). "This statement is by no means to be understood as implying any doubt, but on the contrary a full persuasion that it was Christ Himself. Yet may we infer from it the change which had passed upon *Him,* and the awe which possessed *them,* after His resurrection. He was the same, and yet not the same. There was so much of His former appearance as to preclude doubtfulness; there was so much of change as to prevent all curious and carnal questioning. They sat down to the meal in silence, wondering at, while at the same time they well knew, Him Who was thus their Host" (Dr. G. Brown). It was reverence for Him which suppressed their inquiries.

"Jesus then cometh, and taketh bread, and giveth them, and fish likewise" (v. 13). As Master of the feast, as Head of the family he now dispensed His mercies. But we may observe that no longer does the Lord give thanks before meat with His guests, as formerly He did (6:11). Then, it was as the perfect Man, the Servant ministering, that He gave thanks to God, with and for and before them all, for what God had given them; but now, as God, He Himself gives, and requires them to recognise Him as the Lord. There, it was His humanity which was the more prominent; here, His Deity. Yet how unspeakably blessed to observe that this One who is now "crowned with glory and honour" was still *their* Minister, caring for them! Not only was this the emblem of that spiritual fellowship which it is our unspeakable privilege to enjoy with Christ even now, but also the pledge of the future relations which will exist. Even in a coming day He will "gird" Himself, and make them to sit down to meat, and will come forth and *serve* them" (Luke 12:37). He will yet give us to "eat of the tree of life" (Rev. 2:7), and of the "hidden manna" (Rev. 2:17).

"This is now the third time that Jesus showed Himself to His disciples, after that He was risen from the dead" (v. 14). This does not mean that the Lord made but three appearances in all, but the third that John was led to record: the other two he mentions, are found in chapter 20. It should be remembered that during the "forty days" of Acts 1, which intervened between His resurrection and ascension, Christ did not consort with His disciples as before, but only showed Himself to them occasionally.

It is deeply interesting to compare the record found in Luke 5 of the earlier miraculous draught of fishes: there are a number of comparisons and contrasts. Both took place at the sea of Galilee; both were preceded by a night of fruitless toil; both evidenced the supernatural power of Christ; both were followed by a commission to Peter. But in the former, the Lord was in the ship; here, on the shore: in the one the net broke, in the other it did not: the one was at the beginning of Christ's public ministry; the latter, after His resurrection: in the former, Peter's commission was to fish for "men"; in the latter, to feed Christ's "sheep"; in the one the number of fishes is not given; in the latter it is.

The dispensational picture found in our present passage is very striking. In chapter 20 we had a typical view of the essential features of Christianity during this age, and then followed a symbolic portrayal of the salvation of Israel. Here we naturally look for a forecast of millennial activities, nor are our expectations disappointed. Both the bold outlines of the scene here described and the details with which it is filled in, alike point to the conditions which will obtain during the Kingdom age. Observe the following particulars:—

1. That a new dispensation is here in view is intimated by the opening words: "After these things" (v. 1), i.e., the things recorded in 20; that is, after the present age is over and Israel has been restored to God's favour. 2. The Lord manifests Himself by the sea of Tiberias, or Galilee (v. 1), which at once reminds us of "Galilee of the *Gentiles*" (Matt. 4:15). 3. Peter, the "Apostle to the Circumcision," is the representative of *Israel*—the one who for so long has denied the Messiah, but who shall yet confess Him—and his announcement "I go a fishing" hints at the future mission of Israel to the Gentiles, of which the *sea* is ever the figure. Blessedly has this been foretold by Israel's prophets:

"He shall cause them that come of Jacob to take root: Israel shall blossom and bud, and fill the face of the world with fruit" (Isa. 27:6). "And the remnant of Jacob shall be in the midst of many people as a dew from the Lord as the showers upon the grass" (Micah 5:7). 4. That there were *seven* disciples here fishing on the sea at once brings to mind the Millennium, the *seventh* dispensation. 5. The names of the other Apostles which are here given besides Peter's, supplies additional evidence that it is *Israel* evangelising the nations that is in view; for "Thomas" represents the unbelieving Nation convinced by a sight of Christ, while "Nathanael" speaks of the believing Remnant who owned Christ as King of Israel during the days of His rejection (1:49); while James and John, here termed "the sons of Zebedee," which means *gift*, emphasises the *grace*-aspect of Israel's future mission. 6. The standing of Jesus "on the shore" in the "morning" (v. 4), tells of His presence again on earth after the long night of Israel's apostasy has ended. 7. The miraculous draught of fish (v. 6), after the fruitless toil of the previous night, contrasts Israel's future fruitfulness from their lengthy season of barrenness: cf. Ezek. 47:8-10. 8. The hastening of Peter to the Lord's side (v. 7), tells of the happy relations which will then obtain between Christ and the Redeemed Nation. 9. The fact that the Lord had already provided fish *before* their miraculous draught (v. 9), points to those who will have been saved prior to the Millennium. 10. The word of Christ, "*Bring* of the fish which ye have *now* taken" (v. 10) tells of the unity and fellowship which will finally obtain between and among *all* the saints. 11. The fact that the net was not broken (v. 11) is the pledge that there will be no failure in the work of Christ's servants during the Millennium. 12. The number here seems to find its interpretation in its *dispensational* setting: These figures "certainly contain the sum of three, *God's* own number, and twelve, *Israel's* as well as the number of *governmental completeness* on the earth, and these *squared* before being added—9 plus 144, equals 153" (Mal. Taylor). 13. The Lord serving them with bread and fish (v. 13) tells of Israel entering into *His* joy, fellowship with Him, and being refreshed by Him. 14. The final word "This is now the *third* time that Jesus *showed Himself* to them" announces that it will be in the Millennium that Christ's glory is fully manifested (Matt. 25:31). What marvellous depths there are in this wondrous Word of God! What joy will be ours in eternity as its inexhaustible fulness shall then be unfolded to us!

The following questions are to aid the student on our final section:—
1. Why after "they had dined" did Christ speak v. 15?
2. Why did Christ ask Peter v. 15?
3. What is the difference between Peter's three commissions vv. 15, 16, 17?
4. What is meant by "grieved" v. 17?
5. Why did Peter turn around v. 20?
6. What should Christ's rebuke teach us v. 22?
7. What is the force of v. 25?

Arthur W. Pink.

## GLEANINGS IN EXODUS.

### 46. *The Outer Court: Ex. 27:9-19.*

The Tabernacle proper, which has already been before us, stood in an open space of ground, an hundred cubits long, by fifty cubits broad, and was enclosed by hangings of fine twined linen. These linen curtains were suspended from sixty pillars, twenty of which stood on the south side, twenty on the north, ten on the west, and ten on the east. The Scriptures do not expressly state of what these pillars were made, but there is good reason to conclude they were of shittim wood. This open space, in which the priestly compartments and the dwelling-place of Jehovah stood, formed the third division of the Tabernacle as a whole, and was designated "the Court." The Court was in form a parallelogram, or double square, being twice the length of its breadth. On its eastern side was a gate or entrance, which was also made of fine linen, but rendered attractive by the same beautiful colours which were wrought into the Veil.

It is striking to note that neither the Court nor the Holy Places were paved. The Tabernacle rested upon the bare sand of the desert. This was in significant contrast from its golden-sheeted sides and beautiful inner ceiling. Thus, more than a hint was given for the priests to *look up*, where all was glorious and gorgeous, and tells us that there is nothing down here to satisfy the heart. In striking contrast from the Tabernacle we read of Solomon's Temple that "the floor of the House he overlaid with gold, without and within" 1 Kings 6:30), foreshadowing the blessed fact that in the Millennium this world will no longer be a wilderness to God's people; for when Christ is present in it again, then shall be fulfilled that word, "As truly as I live, all the earth shall be filled with the *glory* of the Lord" (Num. 14:21).

Immediately around the Court of the Tabernacle were the tents of the Levites; beyond, but encircling them, were grouped the twelve Tribes, three on either side; thus forming a square of vast extent. Consequently, even the Court itself was thoroughly screened from the eyes of the wilderness nomads. The Tabernacle therefore formed the centre of Israel's camp. Outside the Tent, a fire was kept constantly burning, on which the bodies of the sin-offerings were consumed, and where the refuse was destroyed. In contemplating the Court, let us notice:

### 1. *Its Hangings.*

"And thou shalt make the court of the tabernacle: for the south side southward there shall be hangings for the court of fine twined linen of a hundred cubits long for one side" (v. 9). As we have before pointed out, the "fine linen" is the emblem of *righteousnesses* (Rev. 19:8). The spotless white walls which surrounded the Tabernacle on every side were a standing witness to the holiness of Him whose dwelling it was. This was in striking contrast from the unholiness of those who inhabited the surrounding tents, which were made, most probably, from goats' hair, of a very dark colour. There is a reference to this in Song of Sol., 1:5: "I am black, but comely, O ye daughters of Jerusalem; *as* the *tents* of Kedar, as the curtains of Solomon": black as the tents of Kedar, comely as the curtains of Solomon. The dark-coloured cloth woven from goats' hair is commonly used for making tents in the East to this day. There would be, then, a most vivid contrast between the white linen surrounding Jehovah's dwelling-place and the dark fabric of the Israelites tents.

The white walls of the Tabernacle's Court served both as a barrier and a protection. To those without, the holiness, of which it spoke, was an exclusion to all who would approach the Divine Courts otherwise than as God Himself had ordered. To those within, it served as a shield, a shelter, an adornment, a glory, a defence. It was the thought of these spotless curtains around the sacred precincts, in which stood the atoning altar and the cleansing laver, which moved David to sing, "How amiable are Thy tabernacles, O Lord of Hosts! My soul longeth, yea, even fainteth, for the courts of the Lord" (Psa. 84:1, 2).

### 2. *Its Pillars.*

These were sixty in number, placed at intervals of five cubits all around the Court.

The material from which they were made is not expressly stated. The words of v. 10, "and the twenty pillars thereof (i.e., of the south side) and their twenty sockets shall be of brass," have led some to conclude that the pillars themselves were made of brass; but it is to be noted that the words "shall be" are supplied by the translators, there being no verb in the original—the modifying clause "of brass" referring only to the "sockets." That the columns themselves were *not* made of brass seems clear from their omission in Ex. 38:29-31. Nor were they made of silver, for that metal was only used in the foundations and in the upper ornamental parts; whilst gold was employed in covering boards in the Tabernacle and in the construction of certain vessels inside, but was not found at all in the Court.

We believe that these "pillars" were made of shittim wood, and that, for three reasons. First, the other "pillars," i.e., those used for the door and for the support of the Veil (26:32, 37) were of wood, therefore in the absence of any word to the contrary here, we naturally conclude that these also were made of the same material. Second, because from a careful comparison of the twenty-nine talents of gold (Ex. 38:24), the hundred talents of silver (Ex. 38:25, 27), and the seventy talents of brass (Ex. 38:29 with the sizes of the different vessels and the amount of metals required for them, it seems clear that they would not leave sufficient to make sixty pillars for the Court out of the remainder. Third, the typical meaning of the Court requires "wood" rather than one of the metals.

A "pillar" speaks of support and strength. The sixty which were stationed around the sides of the Court sustained the white curtains. There is a word in Song of Sol. 3:6, 7 which seems to borrow its imagery from our present type: "Who is this that cometh out of the wilderness like pillars of smoke, perfumed with myrrh and frankincense, with all powders of the merchants? Behold his bed, which is Solomon's; three score valiant men are about it, of the valiant of Israel." Note first the allusion to "the wilderness!" There a procession is seen: a palanquin or curtained-litter (for this is the literal meaning of the Hebrew word here rendered "bed") is seen, surrounded by all the marks of royalty and majesty; *sixty* mighty ones are about it. The "litter" was the *temporary* resting-place of the king. So the Tabernacle was God's resting-place, in the midst of Israel, during their wilderness wanderings. The "ark" was the symbol of His presence, and as 2 Sam. 7:2 tells us "the ark of God dwelleth *within curtains*," while in Numbers 10:33, 35 a "resting-place" is also mentioned in connection with it. Around the ark in the Holy of Holies, were these sixty pillars of the Court, like the "sixty valiant men" about the wilderness resting-place of Solomon. The typical significance of this will appear in our next division.

### 3. *Its Meaning.*

Like everything else connected with this first dwelling-place of God on earth, the antitypical significance of the Court is found in the person of the Lord Jesus Christ and in Him alone. It is really pitiful to witness the attempts that have been made to refer the curtains and the pillars to the saints of this New Testament dispensation. Neither individually nor in their corporate capacity are they here in view. The Court is called the "Tent of the Congregation" (Ex. 39:40); it was the appointed place of assembly, where the Israelites came together and worshipped Jehovah, and where He met with them (Ex. 29:42, 43). Now it is in Christ, and in Him alone, that God and His people meet together. The Court, then, spoke of Christ as the Meeting-place between God and His people.

The Court foreshadowed Christ on earth tabernacling among men, accessible to all who sought Him, but His glory beheld only by those who drew near in faith (John 1:14). In the opening paragraphs we have pointed out that the Court was *unpaved*, the Tabernacle resting upon the bare earth of the desert. This pointed to Christ as "a Root out of a dry ground"—Israel (Isa. 53:2). But although the floor of the Court was the dust of the wilderness, yet was it a sacred enclosure, so that he who entered it stood on holy ground; from Lev. 16:6, 16 we learn that even the Court itself was termed "the *holy* place." This tells us that Christ, though "a Root out of a dry ground," was none other than "the Holy One of God." We may add, these linen hangings were suspended from pillars seven and a half feet in height, so that all on the outside would be prevented from seeing what was done on the inside; thus making it a truly separated and holy place.

The distinctive spiritual significance of the Court is intimated by its order of mention in Ex. 27. First there is a description of the brazen altar (vv. 1-8), and then follow the details concerning the Court. This is very striking. The natural order would be to have told of the Court first, and then of the altar which stood within it. But here again God's thoughts are different from ours. As we have seen, the altar speaks of the place where sin was dealt with: the consequence of this is, that entrance is afforded into the place where God meets with His people. Thus, that which the altar typified was the *basis* of the privileges foreshadowed by the Court. As soon as the Israelite entered the sacred precincts, the first object to meet his eyes was the standing witness to both the justice and the grace of God. The altar testified that his sins had been put away through the sacrifice offered thereon. It was there God showed, typically, that He is just and the Justifier of the believing sinner (Rom. 3: 26).

It is to be carefully noted that the Court was for an elect and redeemed people. There are several references in the Psalms to this: "Blessed is the man whom Thou choosest, and causest to approach unto Thee, that he may dwell in Thy Courts" (Psalm 65:4); "Enter into His gates with thanksgiving, and into His Court with praise: be thankful unto Him, and bless His name" (Psa. 100:4). But most blessed is it to note that in the Old Testament types of the Court there was a definite hint and foreshadowing of *Gentiles* also entering into and partaking of God's grace (Lev. 17:8, 22:18; Num. 15:14-16). The "stranger" had the same liberty of approach to the altar as had an Israelite. Thus, at that early date, it was intimated "there is no difference between the Jew and the Greek: for the same Lord over all is rich unto all that call upon Him. For whosoever shall call upon the name of the Lord shall be saved" (Rom. 10:12, 13).

The sixty pillars around the Court told of the strength and sufficiency of that Refuge into which the believing sinner was fled: "The name of the Lord is a strong tower: the righteous runneth into it and is safe" (Prov. 18:10). That the pillars were made of "wood" was in harmony with the promise, "And a *Man* shall be as an hiding-place from the wind, and a covert from the tempest" (Isa. 32:2). That these pillars were sixty in number (5 x 12 or grace and perfect *government*), tell us it is the grace which *reigns* in righteousness by Christ Jesus that is our defence. This, like the sixty valiant men about Solomon's litter, is a guard of honour around us, so that none can lay anything to our charge. That there was an interval of five cubits between each pillar, intimates that no matter which aspect of our salvation we contemplate, all is of *grace* alone. The spotless white hangings suspended from them, depicted the fitness of the Lord our Righteousness to be the One in whom His God and our God could meet with us.

4. *Its Dimensions.*

In contemplating this we must first consider the measurements of the linen hangings which surrounded the Court, and then the space enclosed by them. From v. 9 we learn that the linen hangings were a hundred cubits long on the south side, ditto on the north side (v. 11), fifty on the west side (v. 12), and thirty on the east side (vv. 14, 15)—the other twenty there being accounted for by the "gate," which differed from the curtains on either side of it, in that it was of "blue and purple and scarlet" (v. 16). Thus there was a total length of these white hangings of two hundred and eighty cubits. The factors of this total would be 7 x 4 x 10, which speak of *perfection on earth*, seen in human *responsibility* fully discharged.

It is striking to note that the length of the white hangings surrounding the Court was identical with the length of the curtains which were spread over the inner Tabernacle. "The curtains of the Tabernacle present Christ, Christ in His nature and character, and Christ in His future glories and judicial authority; but as so presented He was for the eye of God, and for the eye of the priest. As such He could not be seen from without, only within. The fine twined linen hangings (of the Court) present Christ also, but not so much to those within as to those without. *They* could be seen by all in the camp. It is therefore the presentation of Christ to the world, Christ in the purity of His nature. He could thus challenge His adversaries to convict Him of sin. Pilate had to confess again and again that there was no fault in Him; and the Jewish authorities, though they sought with eagle-eyed malice, failed to establish, or even produce, a single proof of failure. Not a single speck could be detected upon the fine twined linen of His holy life, His life of practical righteousness which flowed from the purity of His being" (Mr. E. Dennett). Thus, the linen hangings of the Court being of equal length with the Curtains of the inner tabernacle tell us that Christ manifested on earth *the same* holiness as He had and does before God in heaven!

The linen hangings which formed the walls of the Court were divided by "pillars," which were erected at intervals of five cubits; note in vv. 9, 10 there were "twenty" pillars for the "hundred cubits" of linen on either length. The white linen spoke of righteousness, five is the number of grace; thus, these measurements pronounced that the grace of God to poor sinners is not bestowed at the expense of justice, but, as Rom. 5:21 declares, "As sin hath reigned unto death, even so might grace reign *through righteousness*, unto eternal life by Jesus Christ our Lord." Five is, again, the dominating number in the measurements of the enclosure: as v. 18 tells us, "the length of the court shall be an hundred cubits, and the breadth fifty everywhere, and the height five cubits." How *small* was the Court in comparison with the camp! Hebrews 13:13, read in the light of that whole Epistle, indicates that the "Camp" refers to the religious world, Christendom—the sphere of nominal Christian profession. The smallness of the Court in contrast from the vastness of the Camp (for how *few* was accommodation provided!) contains more than a hint of the *fewness* of those, from among the crowds of professing Christians, that really enter God's presence! God's "flock" is only a "LITTLE one" (Luke 12:32); only the "few" are in the *Narrow* Way (Matt. 7: 14). Are *you* one of the favoured "few"?

5. *Its Sockets.*

"And their sockets of brass" (v. 18). This detail needs no lengthy comment. The "sockets" formed the foundation for the pillars. The "brass" of which they were composed speaks of endurance, capacity to bear the action of fire: type of Christ suffering, but not being consumed by the outpoured judgment of God upon the sinner's Substitute. Thus, once more, are the saints reminded of that upon which all their blessings are based.

6. *Its Hooks and Fillets.*

"The hooks of the pillars and their fillets of silver" (v. 11). These "fillets" were connecting-rods from pillar to pillar, and the hooks would link the linen hangings to the fillets. They bring out a most important detail in our present type. As we pointed out in an earlier article, "silver" is the symbol of *redemption*, and it was through the redemption which is in Christ Jesus that Divine righteousness and Divine grace were united. There is an inseparable connection between Christ our Righteousness and Christ our Redeemer: these two must never be separated. Righteousness could never have been imputed to us unless the Lord Jesus had ransomed us by His blood. The worshipping Israelite would see that the boards of the Tabernacle owed their stability to the fact that the atonement-money had been paid, for they rested on silver sockets. He would also perceive that the fine linen curtains of the Court hung securely from silver chapiters and rings, made from the same ransom-money. Beautifully has this been commented upon by one writing of the blessedness of those who had entered the court:—

"While outside, the wall shut *off*, now that he is inside, it shuts him *in*. Instead of being opposed by 'righteousness,' he is now *surrounded* by it. God is just, and as long as the sinner is rejecting Christ He must be against him; but once the latter has come to Him through Christ all is reversed; He is 'just, and the *Justifier* of him which believeth in Jesus (Rom. 3: 26). But how can this be? It can be in the way set forth in this fine linen wall; the linen ("righteousness") was *not* suspended to the brass ("judgment"), but was connected with it by means of silver rods that joined pillar to pillar. . . . Thus, typically we have the truth as it is plainly stated in Rom. 3:24, 'Being justified freely by His grace, *through the redemption* that is in Christ Jesus'" (Mr. C. H. Bright).

Thus, the redeemed Israelite who entered the Court was shut in by walls of righteousness upheld by the tokens of redemption. This is the blessed portion of every sinner who has fled to Christ for refuge. Because Christ was made sin for him, he has been made "the righteousness of God in Him" (2 Cor. 5:21). "For as by one man's disobedience many were made sinners, so by the obedience of One shall many be made righteous" (Rom. 5:19). The Christian is vested with that which meets every requirement of God's holiness. What cause, then, has each believing reader to join with the writer in saying, "I will greatly rejoice in the Lord, my soul shall be joyful in my God; for He hath clothed me with the garments of salvation, He hath covered me with the robe of righteousness" (Isa. 61: 10).

7. *Its Gate.*

"And for the gate of the Court shall be an hanging of twenty cubits, of blue, and purple, and scarlet, and fine twined linen, wrought with needlework: and their pillars shall be four, and their sockets four" (v. 16). This "hanging" which formed the entrance to the Court is closely connected in thought with the Veil and the Gate of the Tabernacle. Each of them served as a door, hiding the interior from one approaching from the outside. All were made of the same materials, and the colours are mentioned in the same order; the dimensions of all were alike, each measuring one hundred square cubits. The same truth was embodied in each of these typical curtains: there could be no access to God of any kind—whether of comparatively distant worship, or of closer intimacy—except by Him who said "I am the Way." The Israelite who came to the brazen altar with his offering must pass through this gate of the Court; the priest who placed incense on the golden altar must enter by the door of the Tabernacle; the high priest who entered the Holy of Holies on the day of atonement must do so through the Veil, thus realising the thrice repeated proof of the only way of access to God.

The antitypical teaching of the Gate is brought before us in John 10:9, where Christ says, "I am the Door, by Me if any man enter in he shall be saved." But as another has observed, "It is not thinking about the Door, or believing that He *is* the Door, but *entering* the Door, that saves. Many need help right on this point. There are (figuratively speaking) crowds of *semi-believers* around the Gate. They believe it is the Gate, and the only one, but they *do not take the step*. They are always saying, '*Let* me hide myself in Thee.' instead of hiding in Him once for all. Oh! why not dare to trust Him now, at once and forever? You say that you do not feel that He accepts you. . . . How *can* you, as long as you remain outside? Jesus makes no promise to the one who does not enter, but to the one who does. Enter in, and then, feeling or not, you may know that you are saved, *because He says so*. The Altar was inside the Gate, not outside! How, then, can you know that you are saved until you enter? Come, just as you are, in all your sinfulness, with *no* feeling, with no consciousness of any 'marks of grace,' and *as a sinner* believe in the sinner's Saviour."

*Arthur W. Pink.*

## THE PROPHETIC PARABLES OF MATTHEW 13.

### 2. *Introduction.*

The thirteenth chapter of Matthew opens with these words "The *same day* went Jesus out of the house, and sat by the seaside." This statement clearly looks back to the preceding chapter, where the Holy Spirit has traced for us the various steps in Israel's rejection of their King. At the beginning of Matt. 12 we find the Pharisees challenging the disciples of Christ because they had plucked the ears of corn on the Sabbath day, which is followed by the Lord's vindication of them. Next we are told, "*Then* the Pharisees went out, and held a council against Him, how they might destroy Him" (v. 14). This is the *first* time that we read of anything like this in Matthew's Gospel.

Next in vv. 22-24 we are told, "*Then* was brought unto Him one possessed with a demon, blind, and dumb: and He healed Him, insomuch that the blind and dumb both spake and saw." Up to that point this was the most remarkable miracle that the Lord Jesus had performed, in fact, it was three miracles in one. Such an impression was produced upon those who witnessed it that we are told, "and all the people were amazed, and said, Is not this the Son of David?"—not "is not this the Son of God?" but "the Son of David," i.e., the Messiah Himself. Following this we are told, "*But* when the Pharisees heard it, they said, This fellow doth not cast out demons, but by Beelzebub the prince of the demons"—there they committed the sin for which there was no forgiveness.

Following our Lord's sentence upon the Pharisees for their unpardonable blasphemy, we are next told. "*Then* certain of the scribes and the Pharisees answered, Master, we would see a sign from Thee" (v. 38). His response was that the only sign which should be given to that evil and unfaithful generation should be that of "the sign of the prophet Jonah"—i.e., that after three days in the place of death the Servant of God should come forth and go *unto the Gentiles*. Following this, the Lord solemnly pronounced the coming judgment of Heaven upon that wicked generation, so that their last state should be worse than the first (vv. 43-45).

The chapter closes by telling us that while Christ yet talked to the people one said unto Him, "Behold, Thy mother and Thy brethren stand without, desiring to speak with Thee." In reply, He asked, "Who is My mother? and who are My brethren?" Then He stretched forth His hand toward His *disciples* and said, "Behold My mother and My brethren! For whosoever shall do the will of My Father which is in Heaven, the same is My brother and sister, and mother" (vv. 46-50). This was a *severing* of fleshly ties: it denoted the Saviour's break with Israel: it announced that henceforth He would only own as *His* kinsmen those who did the will of His Father which was in Heaven.

It will thus be seen that the opening words of Matt. 13 supply the first key to the interpretation of what follows. The parables of this chapter were spoken by Christ "the *same* day" as when the Pharisees had taken council together to destroy Him, as when they had committed the unpardonable sin, as when He had pronounced solemn judgment upon the Nation, and as when He had severed the fleshly ties which united Him to the Jews and had intimated that henceforth there should be a people united to Him by spiritual bonds. Thus the relation between Matt. 12 and Matt. 13 is that of cause to effect; in other words, Matt. 12 makes known the cause which led up to Christ's acting as He did in the thirteenth chapter: that cause was Israel's *rejection* of their King and His rejection of them. His action in 13:1 was indicative of a great *dispensational crisis*, it was an anticipation of what is found developed at length in the books of Acts—God, temporarily, turning away from the Jews and turning unto the Gentiles.

"The same day went Jesus *out of the house*, and sat by the *seaside*." The "house" is the place of ordered relationship and natural ties. This was now *left*, Jesus "went out" of it! Symbolically, it was a *confirmation* of His own words at the close of Matt. 12: the link which had bound Him to the Jews was now severed. Christ's next act was to take His place by the seaside. This also had a deep symbolical significance for those who had eyes to see. The "sea" speaks of fallen man in the restlessness and barrenness of nature, of man apart from God, and thus of the Gentiles (F.W.G.). If the reader will turn to Dan. 7:1, 2; Rev. 17:15, etc., he will there find this figure defined.

"And He spake many things unto them *in parables*" (13:3). This marked a new departure in Christ's method of teaching. The first twelve chapters of this Gospel will be searched in vain for any parables. Hitherto Christ had instructed the people in plain language, using simple terms of speech; but now His message was veiled and His meaning hidden. This explains what we are told in the tenth verse: "And the disciples came, and said unto Him, *Why* speakest Thou unto them *in parables?*" The disciples were surprised: not being accustomed to *this* form of teaching, they were at a loss to account for it here. The Lord's answer to their question confirmed what we have said on v. 1. His answer is recorded in vv. 11-15: our Lord's quotation there of the solemn words from Isa. 6 supplied further proof that the Nation had rejected their King. In consequence of this rejection He had taken a place of distance from them, as this new form of teaching plainly evidenced. It is a principle exemplified all through the Scriptures that, wherever parables or symbolic utterances were employed they are addressed to a people *estranged* from God—hence the absence of them in the Epistles.

Turning once more to Matt. 13:11, we find here the second important key which unlocks the contents of our present chapter. The Lord Himself there designates the seven parables "mysteries of the kingdom of heaven." But before we proceed further let it be pointed out that the word "kingdom" does not primarily refer to *territory*. Webster's first meaning of this word is "royal authority, sovereign power, rule, dominion." The term "kingdom" refers, directly, not to territory but authority, not to a locality but to sovereignty. Let us borrow a simple illustration. France was once a "kingdom," but to-day it is a "republic." Yet there has been *no territorial change*: the country is the same, and it is inhabited by the same race of people. It is no longer a "kingdom" for the simple reason that it no longer acknowledges the sovereign authority of any king; instead, it is governed by the public, and is therefore a "republic." The public are the rulers, authority being vested in those whom they elect to office. Thus it will be seen from this simple illustration that the term "kingdom" looks not to a localised sphere of territory, but refers to the *form* of its government and speaks of the *sovereignty* of its ruler. Therefore the "kingdom of heaven" is not heaven itself, but a people who *own* the sovereign authority of heaven.

Further proof of what has been said above will be found in the Saviour's words to Peter as recorded in Matt. 16:19: "And I will give unto thee the keys of the kingdom of heaven." "Keys" speak of two things: they are the symbol of authority and they are for the purpose of opening something and giving admission and access. When I give to some person the key to my house, he has the right of authority to enter it. In Rev. 1:18 Christ is spoken of as having "the keys of death and hades," which means that He has complete authority over them. Now to Peter were "given" the keys of the kingdom of heaven, a *delegated* authority being in view. In the book of Acts the meaning of the Lord's words to Peter are made plain.

In the second chapter of the Acts we find Peter using those "keys" on the day of Pentecost—opening the door of the kingdom to *the Jews*. In Acts 10 we find Peter using those "keys" again—giving admission to *the Gentiles* into the kingdom. It is very striking to weigh the details in the last mentioned: the particular Gentiles referred to were Cornelius and his household. Now in Acts 9 we read of the conversion of Saul of Tarsus, and, as we know, *he* was the apostle to the Gentiles. Yet, when the Lord appeared to Cornelius and told him to send for one of His servants, it was not Paul but Peter that was invited, for it was the latter and not the former who held the "keys"! That which Peter gave admission into was *not* heaven nor was it the Church, but the sphere of *Christian profession.* Thus the language of 13:11 assures us that the parables which follow have respect unto Christendom, i.e., that sphere where the authority of heaven and the sovereignty of Christ are professedly owned. Before leaving Matt. 16:19, we may add that a successional and vested right in "St. Peter's keys" is a manifest absurdity; for this reason: Peter left the door of the kingdom *wide open!*

The eleventh verse of Matt. 13 supplies yet another key, in the word *"mysteries* of the kingdom of heaven." In Scripture the term "mystery" signifies a Divine *secret* made known by the Holy Spirit. This is confirmed by what is told us in verse 35. namely, that Christ was here uttering "things which have been kept secret from the foundation of the world." Thus, in these parables, Christ was making known that which was *outside* the scope of O.T. prediction, something which God had *not* made known to Israel through the prophets. This needs to be carefully noted, for it refutes the popular interpretation of these parables.

There are many who regard the parables of Matt. 13 as containing predictions of the ushering in of the Millennium: those of the Mustard-tree and the Leaven are regarded as being parallel with the promise that "the knowledge of the glory of the Lord shall cover the earth as the waters cover the sea." But *that* statement is found in Isa. 11:9: *that* was no "secret" in O.T. times! Therefore, none of the parables in Matt. 13 can be treating of the same subject as Isa. 11:9, or what is stated in v. 35 would not be true. No; Matt. 13 deals with something *nowhere* revealed in the O.T.; it is an entirely new revelation.

The *number* of parables here, seven intimates that they furnish a *complete* outline or setting forth of something, and that something is *the History of Christendom.* What is in view in the first four parables is the sphere of human responsibility, and hence it is a picture of *failure* that is presented to us. In the first, only one out of the four castings of the good Seed yields any fruit. In the second, the crop as a whole is spoiled by the mingling of the tares among the wheat. In the third, the little mustard-seed develops into a great tree, whose branches afford shelter for the agents of Satan. In the fourth, the three measures of meal are, ultimately, completely corrupted by means of the leaven surreptitiously introduced into them.

Look where you will in Scripture, and it is the same: whenever God has committed anything to man as a responsible creature, he has failed. God placed Adam in Eden on the ground of human responsibility and he fell. God gave to Noah the sword of magisterial authority and he failed to govern himself. God gave to Israel the law, and they broke it: before Moses came down from the mount they were worshipping the golden calf. God instituted priesthood in Israel, and Aaron and his sons were duly consecrated to their office; but on the very first day, two of them offered strange fire and judgment fell upon them. God instituted kingship in Israel and failure was written large upon this. God endowed Nebuchadnesser with power, but he became so bloated with self-importance that he made an image to himself and demanded that all should worship it. Nor has the Christian profession proven any exception. "Grievous wolves shall enter the flock after my departure," said the apostle Paul (Acts 20), and they did. The evil introduced by Satan at the beginning of this dispensation has never been eradicated, nor will it be till the harvest-time. Instead of things getting better, they will get worse—until Christ spues out (Rev. 3:16) the whole system which bears His name. But, blessed be His name, there is no failure *with God.* In spite of man's failure and Satan's opposition. He has been slowly but surely working out His eternal purpose. Acts 15:18 declares, "Known unto God are all His works from the beginning of the world," and a clear proof of this is given us in the unmistakable fulfilment of the prophetical parables of Matt. 13.

The seven parables of Matt. 13 divide into four and three, which is the usual division of a septenary series. The first four were spoken to the multitude on the seashore, the last three to the disciples inside the house. Hence, the first four give us the *external* view in the history of Christendom, while the last three portray that which is more *internal* and spiritual. The first four are arranged in two pairs: the first—the wheat and the tares—giving us *individual* aspects; the second pair—the mustard-tree and the corrupted meal—set forth the *corporate* view. Again: the first parable shows us a sowing, while the fifth and sixth show the resultant crop. The second parable also shows us a sowing, while the third and fourth give us the resultant crop. If it be asked, Why is the "crop" of the second sowing given *before* the harvest from the first? the answer is, It is ever the order of Scripture to give us first that which is natural, then that which is spiritual. In our next article we shall take up the parable of the Sower.

*Arthur W. Pink.*

N.B.—For not a little in this article we are indebted to the writings of the late F. W. Grant.

## A LIVE COAL.

(*Isaiah* 6:6, 7.)

It is the eternal purpose of God to gather around Himself a people who shall delight in Himself, a people who shall be on terms of nearness and intimacy to Him; and again and again in His Word God has given intimations and foreshadowings of this. At the very beginning we find man in communication with his Maker—God and Adam together on most intimate terms, just as we are told in Genesis 2:19 that the Lord did bring the animals to Adam that he might name them. And even after the fall, when sin had come in and man had been driven out of Eden, we still have case after case recorded where men were brought into intimate fellowship with Jehovah; how that God in His condescending grace walked for three hundred years with Enoch. Did you notice the way I put that, how that God for three hundred years walked with Enoch. And I could imagine some of you saying: Why, I think it says that Enoch walked with God. Yes, beloved, that is what Genesis 5:24 declares, but if Enoch walked with God, God must have been walking with Enoch! So, too, we are told that when wickedness and violence was on the earth in the days of the Antediluvians, God said unto Noah, after he had builded the ark, "Come thou and all thy house into the ark." Why did not God say, "Go thou"? Why didn't He say, "Go into the ark." Because, beloved, God Himself was present in that ark, and He desired that there should be *with* Him that one who had found grace in His sight. And so again we read in connection with the patriarchs, how that Abraham walked and talked with God. Yea, how that the Lord came and ate with him and was on such familiar terms that Abraham is spoken of as "the friend of God."

So also after the Lord had brought forth His people out of the land of Egypt, again He made known and illustrated His eternal purpose to have around Himself a people on intimate terms of fellowship with Him. While Israel was crossing through the wilderness and in their pilgrim character were living in tents, O think of it! the mighty God says, "I will be a pilgrim, too, with thee; make Me a tent that I may dwell in your midst." O what amazing condescension! The fact is familiar to us; the words we have often read; but I wonder if our hearts have been moved by them. The mighty God saying, "Make Me *a tent*," the One whom the heaven of heavens cannot contain! What a beautiful and blessed foreshadowing of the purpose that God had formed in His heart before time began, to have a people around Himself on intimate terms of communion. So after He had conducted them across the wilderness and over the Jordan and had brought them into the Promised Land, and we are told they dwelt in ceiled houses, then the Lord said, "Build Me a house." And they built Him a house and His glory filled it, and He abode in their midst—a foreshadowing of what we have in the 21st of Revelation and the 3rd verse, where after this heaven and earth have passed away and the new heaven and the new earth have been created, we read, "Behold, the tabernacle of God is with men, and He will dwell with them, and they shall be His people, and God Himself"—I like that word "Himself," it is the Holy Spirit emphasising, as it were, the amazing wonder of such a fact —"God Himself shall be with them."

But now what I want to speak upon this evening, particularly, as the Holy Spirit may be pleased to enable, is that which gives the sinner fitness *to dwell* with the great and holy God. By nature and by practice we are sinners, breakers of His righteous law, condemned by that law. How is it possible then for us to be taken into a place of nearness to Himself? for sin separates. Now, in order to answer that question in what I trust will be a simple and a vivid manner, turn with me to the 6th chapter of the prophet Isaiah. I want you to look at this Scripture and keep the Bible open at this passage throughout the remainder of the sermon.

Isaiah 6; "In the year that king Uzziah died I saw (the speaker is Isaiah himself) —I saw also the Lord sitting upon a throne, high and lifted up, and His train filled the temple. Above it stood the seraphim: each one had six wings; with twain he covered his face, and with twain he covered his feet, and with twain he did fly. And one cried unto another, and said, Holy, holy, holy, is the Lord of Hosts: the whole earth is full of His glory. And the posts of the door moved at the voice of him that cried, and the house was filled with smoke. Then said I, Woe is me! for I am undone." Isaiah was probably the best man there was in all Israel at this time, and he was given a sight (how, we are not told, and speculation would be irreverent), but he was given a sight of the Lord in His heavenly temple seated upon His throne. And, dear friends, it is a solemn and a soul-subduing experience for a sinful creature to be brought face to face with the thrice-holy God. That was the experience that Isaiah the prophet here had. He found himself standing before the throne of the Lord, and himself unable to meet the claims of that throne; in the light of that throne Isaiah saw his true condition.

Now, what is so unspeakably solemn is what you have in the second verse: "Above it stood the seraphim: each one had six wings; with twain he covered his face." So far as my own study of God's Word has gone, I believe that the seraphim are the highest of all created beings. They are above the angels, for they are in immediate attendance upon God. They are round about and above His very throne. But what is so arresting here is this, that these exalted seraphim, sinless in their beings, creatures that have never come into contact with defilement, yet their faces are veiled! They cannot gaze into the face of God. The highest of God's creatures, at the head of the heavenly hierarchies, sinless in their beings, never having come into contact with defilement, and yet their faces are veiled as they are before the throne of heaven! O dear sinful friend, unconverted one, if the seraphim cannot stand before God and gaze into His face, how shall you ever be able to do so? How shall you, with all your sins, ever hope to dwell in His presence?—in the presence of that One before whom the seraphim cry, Holy, holy, holy, and veil their faces.

Now look again, "Then said I, Woe is me! for I am undone" (v. 5). And, mark you, the one who said that was no thief; he was not what the world would call a wicked man; he was a servant of God; he was one who had been faithfully performing his duty, and yet when he is brought into the heavenly temple and has a sight of that exalted throne and the Holy One seated upon it; and the seraphim with veiled faces before it, he is completely overcome and he says, "Woe is me! for I am undone." Now notice, dear friends, he did not blame himself for what he had done. It was not his sinful actions that he was occupied with. He did not say, "Woe is me! for I have failed in my duty," "Woe is me! for I have not lived up to the light that I had," "Woe is me! for I have not always done my best," "Woe is me! because I have often-times sinned." It was not his deeds, it was not his actions that he was now occupied with. It went deeper than that. He saw what he was in *himself*. He says, "Woe is me; for *I* am undone." This was the utterance of one whose heart had been pierced to its centre, by a light which made manifest its desperate wickedness. He felt himself to be a *lost man!* And, my friends, that is the experience and that is the confession of every sinner that is brought face to face with the holiness and the righteousness of the mighty God. O that the Spirit of Truth may by His blessed operations bring some sinner here to-night face to face with God and give him such a vision of His holiness that he may see how impossible it will be for any of us to ever stand before Him in our own righteousness or on the basis of anything that we have done.

"Woe is me!" It is a very striking thing (if you turn back to the previous chapter for a moment) that six times over in Isaiah 5 we find the prophet pronouncing woe on six different classes of people. Notice (verse 8 of chapter 5) "Woe unto them that join house to house," and so on. Verse 11: "Woe unto them that rise up early in the morning, that they may follow strong drink." Verse 18: "Woe unto them that draw iniquity with cords of vanity." Verse 20: "Woe unto them that call evil good, and good evil." Verse 21: "Woe unto them that are wise in their own eyes." Verse 22: "Woe unto them that are mighty to drink wine." Six times over in Isaiah 5 we find the prophet pronouncing a woe upon the sinners and transgressors that were in Israel in his day. But when he is brought face to face with God he forgets all about his neighbours, he forgets all about the crimes of his fellow-sinners, the seventh woe is pronounced *on himself!* "Woe is me! for *I* am undone."

Ah! dear, friend, unsaved friend, up to this hour you may not have felt that you have been guilty of any great sins; you may not realise that you have much to repent of; you may feel that you are a very respectable, upright member of society and citizen of this country. Measured by your fellow-men, you may be; but here was Isaiah, and I repeat it, he was the best man in Israel at this time, but now he measures himself by a standard that he had never measured himself by before; he weighs himself in a balance that he had never weighed himself in before. He sees himself now in the white light of God's unsullied and ineffable holiness, and as he saw himself there, he *condemned himself*. He said, "Woe is me! for I am undone." And I say again, dear friends, if the Spirit of God, and O the Spirit of God alone can do this for you; no preacher can, no evangelist can, no Sunday School teacher can, it is only the Spirit of God that can give you a sight of the holiness of God, and you are either going to see it now in this life or you are going to see it revealed in all its terrifying power in the day of judgment. O may the Holy Spirit in His grace show you yourself to-night in the light of God's holiness, that in His light you may see light.

But now let us notice the blessed and glorious sequel. Verse 5: "Then said I, Woe is me! for I am undone; because I am a man of unclean lips, and I dwell in the midst of a people of unclean lips: for mine eyes have seen the King, the Lord of Hosts." Then (then, without any delay, without any interval, at once, *then*), "then flew one of the seraphim unto me, having a live coal in his hand, which he had taken with the tongs from off the altar." Notice the two central objects in this solemn and yet blessed vision. In the first verse Isaiah saw a "throne." Now in the sixth verse, the end of it, he sees an "altar." The *throne* speaks of God's righteousness; the *altar* tells of His mercy. But notice he did not see the altar first. Aparently he did not notice it at all. He was occupied with the throne, holy and mighty and lifted up, and the attendant seraphim around it, but as soon as he took his place in the dust before God as an acknowledged and self-condemned sinner (with no excuses, with no extenuations but a 'Woe is me!"), then he had got down low enough to *see* the altar! Ah, beloved, we must first of all be abased before we may be exalted. We have first of all got to have a realisation of our own sinfulness and of our own condemnation before God, ere we are ready to receive and appreciate the provisions of His redeeming mercy.

But now just briefly I want to interpret, expound, the terms of this sixth verse—Isaiah 6: It is speaking, I believe, in the symbolism borrowed from the altar that stood in the tabernacle of old. Turn back for a moment to the sixth chapter of Leviticus, verse 12: "And the fire upon the altar shall be burning in it; it shall not be put out: and the priest shall burn wood on it every morning, and lay the burnt offering in order upon it; and he shall burn thereon the fat of the peace offerings. The fire shall *ever* be burning upon the altar; it shall never go out." The fire on the altar was to consume the sacrifice that was upon it. Now "the altar" foreshadowed, of course, the person of Christ—that altar that sanctifieth the gift—that altar that is referred to in Hebrews 13:10: "We have an altar, whereof they have no right to eat which serve the tabernacle." The fire upon it was the symbol of God's holiness consuming everything that was antagonistic to His nature. The offering that was laid upon that altar typified the sacrifice of Christ that was offered to God upon the Cross, and the live coal that remained upon the altar was the witness to the sacrifice having been offered *and accepted* by God. There was the altar; there was the fire; there was the sacrifice laid upon the altar over the fire. The fire consumed it, until only the embers of the sacrifice that had gone up in smoke to God remained. So that the "live coal" was the witness to the sacrifice having been offered to and accepted by God. The "fire" spoke of God's judgment upon sin: the "live coal" of His holiness satisfied.

Now, then, here in Isaiah 6, and the 6th verse: "Then flew one of the seraphim unto me, having a live coal in his hand, which he had taken with the tongs from off the altar." It was the *memorial* of the sacrifice, it was the *value* of it now being *applied* to him. And I want you to notice carefully the word "flew" there. Then *"flew"* one of the seraphim with this live coal. O how that little word lets us into the blessed secrets of the very bosom of Deity! You know, my friends, it makes a great deal of difference *how* a thing is done. A man may do me a good turn, and yet he may do it in such a way that all the value of it is lost upon me. Much depends upon *how* a thing is done. Now here in this verse we have brought out *how* God pardons or bestows pardon upon those who take their place in the dust before Him as acknowledged sinners. "Then flew." How it links up at once with what you have in the parable of the Prodigal Son. When the Prodigal Son had left the far country and was on his way home, the Father *ran* to meet Him! And just here, when Isaiah had condemned himself and said, "Woe is me!" *then* "flew" one of the seraphim with a live coal from off the altar. How that shows us—may I say it reverently; I believe I can; I hope it will not offend any of your ears; but does not that make manifest the very *eagerness* of God—not only the readiness, but the very eagerness of God—to bind up the brokenhearted, to speak words of peace to the distressed soul, to pour in the balm of Gilead into the wounds that His own Spirit has made; the readiness of God to bestow pardon on any sinner who is truly seeking it. "Woe is me! . . . *Then flew.*" How that brings out, I say, not only the readiness, but the very desire of God to communicate pardon and peace to the poor burdened, awakened, convicted sinner. I want to press that upon any sinner who may be here to-night—any poor sin-burdened soul—and I believe there is at least one present, one who has been seeking the Lord earnestly. O may the Holy Spirit be pleased to use this word to-night to speak peace and comfort, to bind up the broken-hearted, to give deliverance to the captive. "Then flew."

Now notice, in closing, verse 7: "And he laid it upon my mouth, and said, Lo, this hath touched thy lips: and thine iniquity is taken away, and thy sin purged." What beautiful completeness that gives to the typical picture that is here set before us. Isaiah was brought into *personal contact* with the sacrifice which had been offered and accepted, and the immediate effect was perfect cleansing. He now stood in the light of that throne unabashed. The same light which had revealed his uncleanness now made manifest the efficacy of the atoning blood! Nor would God allow this self-confessed sinner to leave His presence until the word of assurance had been spoken.

O, my friends, there is something sadly defective in our theology if we imagine that it is according to the desire of God that a poor sinner who has cried unto Him for mercy should be kept in suspense waiting for assurance. God did not allow *this* poor sinner, who had condemned himself, to depart from His presence until the word of peace and assurance had been spoken. The seraphim said to him, "Thine iniquity *is* taken away, and thy sin purged." How did Isaiah know it? Because God said so through the seraphim. What more did he want? What more could he desire? And O I want to say again in closing, to the seeking sinner, if there is one here to-night who is conscious of his or her lost condition before God, and who is weighted down with a load of conscious guilt, and there is that desire in your heart for peace and pardon, "through this Man is preached unto *you*," and I care not who you may be, while God gives me breath and strength I will not tie down the proclamation of His truth and narrow it within bounds that are narrower than those the apostle preached in. The apostle Paul standing before a miscellaneous audience (search your Bibles and see—Acts 13:38. Look up the context and see to whom he was speaking) said, "Through this Man is preached *unto you* the forgiveness of sins." And on the authority of God's truth, without any shackles on my hands or lips, I say to any sinner in this church to-night, every sinner in this church: "Through this Man" —the Man at God's right hand—"is preached unto you the forgiveness of sins: and by Him all that believe are justified from all things." O sinner, look unto Him and be ye saved. Look away from self. Look away from broken vows and resolutions. Look away from your good works (if you think you have any), and from your evil works, and look alone to "the Lamb of God, which taketh away the sin of the world." "And by Him all that believe are justified from all things." O take the position before God that Isaiah took. Bow before Him in the dust as an acknowledged, guilty, ruined, lost sinner, and "believe on the Lord Jesus Christ." Then shall *you* also receive the assurance from God, "Thine iniquity is taken away, and thy sin purged."

## TESTIMONY OF LELAND WANG.

(*Psa.* 66:16; *Gal.* 2:20; 1 *Tim.* 1:15.)

I praise God for His Son Jesus Christ who is made unto me Wisdom, and Righteousness, and Sanctification, and Redemption. Glory to the Lamb of God who loves me and gave Himself up for me. I was born in a heathen home in Foochow, China, and studied in the Chefoo Naval College when I was sixteen years old. In 1917 I married a Christian girl who, through the ministry of Miss R. Paxton, became a Christian after she was engaged to me. I read her Bible, and she and some others prayed for me. She also asked Miss Wallace to help me in the Bible study. At first I despised the Bible, and did not enjoy it, but gradually I began to like its teachings. I thought Jesus was a very good man, and His influence is wonderful. But, praise God, I did not stop there. I remember the first prayer I made was, "God, make me believe." God has convinced me that I was a lost sinner, and Christ died and shed His blood on the Cross for my sins. So by grace I am saved through faith. Before my conversion I used to gamble, drink, steal things, tell lies, etc., yet still I thought I was much better than others. I was a miserable sinner living in this world without Hope, Joy, Peace. Now I praise Him for Christ in me, the hope of glory, and the blessed hope, and the unspeakable joy, and the peace of God which passeth understanding. He brought me out of an horrible pit, out of mirey clay, and set my feet upon a rock. I know the most precious Jesus through the Bible, the written Word testifies of the Living Word. When I was very young someone gave my father a nice New Testament. My father did not care to read it, and I asked him to give it to me. I thought it was a useless Book, and I pasted old post-stamps on it. I made the Holy Book a post-stamps album. O what a sin! Now I put my heart and sometimes my tears on the Bible. Now I preach the Book which once I destroyed (Gal. 1:23). Now I preach this Jesus whom once I hated. I used to think Jesus was a foreigner. Now He is my all-in-all.

> "If ask'd what of Jesus I think?
> Though still my best thoughts are but poor,
> I say He's my meat and my drink,
> My life and my strength and my store;
> My Shepherd, my Husband, my Friend,
> My Saviour from sin and from thrall,
> My hope from beginning to end,
> My Portion, my Lord, and my All."

In November, 1918, the Lord worked mightily in me. I thought; I have been a church member more than one year, though I have given up gambling and drinking yet my heart is not pure, and my love toward Him is cold. I had no assurance of salvation. I did not read my Bible daily, and often left my Bible alone for many days. I, by the grace of God, decided to read the Bible every day (Acts 17:11). I found out the great hindrance to my Bible reading was my late rising in the morning. I often got up at 7 or 8 o'clock—of course no time for the morning watch. When the day was over I found myself tired, and had no taste for the Bible. One day I read Proverbs 19:15, "Slothfulness casteth into a deep sleep; and an idle soul shall suffer hunger." Also Proverbs 6:9-11. "How long wilt thou sleep? O sluggard! when wilt thou arise out of thy sleep? Yet a little sleep, a little slumber, a little folding of the hands to sleep: So shall thy poverty come as one that travelleth, and thy want as an armed man." These two verses spoke to my heart and woke me up. I decided to get up at 5.30 in the morning to study the Bible and pray. (Now five o'clock is the usual time for me to get up.) I realise that early morning is the best time for Bible study. "No Bible no breakfast" is my daily rule. "Awake. . . . and Christ shall give thee light." (Eph. 5:14.)

My plan of Bible study: to read seven chapters of the Word, namely: two from the Psalms and Proverbs, two from the other books of the O.T., three from the N.T.; thus, reading through the N.T. four times a year, Psalms and Proverbs four times a year, and the remainder of the O.T. once a year.

The Lord hath graciously revealed Himself to me by the Word of the Lord (1 Sam. 3:21). He showed me the way of baptism is by immersion only (Rom. 6:4; Col. 2:12). So I gladly obeyed Him, and was baptised in January 19, 1920, in the sea of Amoy.

In 1921 one question came to my heart; whether I ought to stay in the Navy, or leave the Navy and preach the Gospel (Acts 6:4). I could not decide for myself, so brought it to the Lord in definite prayer. One day the Lord spoke to me through Isa. 52:11-12. At first it seemed hard, to me to take this step, because I have been in the Navy nine years, a sudden change of position would cause one to worry about his future. But as I considered the dying love of our dear Lord Jesus, I could not but forsake the Navy and follow Him. His love constraineth me indeed. This hymn helped me a great deal before I made the definite decision.

> 1. "How shall I follow Him I serve?
> How shall I copy Him I love?
> Nor from those blessed footsteps swerve,
> Which lead me to His seat above?
>
> 2. Lord, should my path through suffering lie?
> Forbid it I should ere repine,
> Still, let me turn to Calvary,
> Tor heed my griefs, remembering Thine.

3. O let me think how Thou didst leave,
   Untasted every pure delight,
   To fast, to faint, to watch, to grieve,
   The toilsome day, the homeless night.

4. To faint, to grieve, to die for me,
   Thou camest not Thyself to please,
   And dear as earthly comforts be,
   Shall I not love Thee more than these?

5. Yes, I would count them all but loss,
   To gain the notice of Thine eye,
   Flesh shrinks and trembles at the Cross,
   But Thou canst give the victory."

My father did not like me to leave the Navy. I told him that I had heard the call of God, and I must obey at any cost. Some of his friends supposed I was mad. Some of my schoolmates came and advised me to stay in the Navy. I thank God that my wife agreed with me in making this decision. I praise God that I left the Navy in April, 1921.

As soon as I decided to leave the Navy I received some invitations to work in some missions. I told the Lord in prayer, and He told me to refuse all and lean on Him, only to trust only in Him, to be free in His hands. One day my friend told me that when the Israelites had corn the Manna stops. He meant to encourage me to be a free worker living on Manna. Meanwhile I received a little pamphlet from my friend, "A proof of Phil. 4:19," by Gibbud. After I read that book I got another book, "The Life of George Muller." My faith was strengthened. I said to myself if my God is a dead God, then all is in vain, but glory and honour to His Name, my God is a living and true God, who changeth not in hearing and answering the prayers of His children; then why should I fear and doubt? So I started out in this path of faith, which is the safest way to those who know God and dare to trust Him at all times. Many times my faith was deeply tried; sometimes we did not have one cent in our home for several days, but this gave us greater joy when the Lord proved His faithfulness to us. One day my father came to see us; he was very sorry for us about the financial problem. I told him we have a safest bank in Phil. 4:19. My brother was not converted that time; he said "It is dangerous." I told him if the heaven falls down or the earth sinks what a danger it would be, but Jesus said, "Heaven and earth shall pass away: but My words shall not pass away" (Luke 21:33). O it is safer to stand on His promises. May we have more faith in our God.

Praise the Lord for His unspeakable gift. Glory to His Name. Please pray for us that we may stand perfect and complete in all the Will of God, and whatsoever we do, do all to the glory of God. Pray also for my father and father-in-law that they may be saved. Please pray also for the Foochow Church (local church). Worthy is the Lamb that was slain to receive power and riches and wisdom and strength and honour and glory and blessing. Amen.

Will the reader now ask himself or herself the following questions: Do missions to the heathen pay? Is money spent in supporting servants of God in foreign lands wasted? Is it worth-while to give up a few personal home comforts to carry the Light to those who are in darkness? Does not the testimony of this Chinese Christian put many English-speaking believers to shame—believers who have enjoyed spiritual opportunities and privileges for many more years than has Brother Leland Wang? Do *you* act on the principle, "No Bible, no breakfast"? Do *you* "seek *first* the Kingdom of God and His righteousness"? Are *you* trusting "*only* in God" for the supply of every temporal need? Finally, dare you turn a deaf ear to His earnest appeal for prayer? Will you not now say daily, "Lord, bless the Foochow Church"?

—A.W.P.

## THE PATH OF FAITH.

This is most blessedly described in Heb. 11. In vv. 4-7 the Holy Spirit has epitomised the three essential characteristics of walking by faith. First, Abel submitted to the righteousness of God which is ever the initial step in the path of faith. He bowed to the judgment of God: by his act confessing that his own life was forfeited, therefore, did he bring a lamb as a substitute—putting blood between God and his sins. And God accepted his offering and gave witness that "he was righteous."

Of Enoch we read that "he walked with God." This is communion. Enoch received a better testimony than Abel, namely, that "he pleased God." This is more than being owned as righteous. There is only one other who received such a testimony from God—the Lord

Jesus. But note here, as ever, how He has "the pre-eminence." The voice from heaven not only said that Christ pleased God, but that "This is my Beloved Son in whom I am *well pleased*"—pleased to the uttermost.

Of Noah it is written that he "became heir of the righteousness which is by faith." It is striking to note how that in Gen. the same things mentioned about Abel and Enoch are here repeated in connection with Noah. First, he "found grace in the eyes of the Lord." Second, he was "a just man." Third, he "walked with God" (Gen. 6:8,9). But more than that, he entered into a goodly inheritance. Dominion was given to him—see Gen. 9:2,3.

Thus we have the initial act of faith—reposing on the Blood of the Lamb; the privilege of faith—walking with God; the crowning of faith—entering into the Inheritance. Blessedly suggestive are the words of Gen. 9:3, "I have given you all things." They are ours to enjoy by faith now.—A.W.P.

---

## THINGS TO COME.

Passing on a little further in the Word of God we have certain dark hints as to the grand events of the future, which concern the church and the world. I must confess myself to be, in the presence of the writtings of Ezekiel and Jeremiah and John of Patmos, as a little child wandering through the museum, marvelling at the Egyptian heiroglyphs and the Assyrian cunieform characters, but quite unable to spell them out; fancying, sometimes, that I have the key of the mysteries, and, anon, discovering some new form of Divine symbology which quite confuses me, and makes me confess that I am but as yesterday, and know nothing. Yet does it appear that we are to expect the overturning of many things which now we regard as permanent.

The rule of the ages is to "overturn, overturn," till He shall come whose right it is to reign. Heavings and convulsions there will be till all things which can be shaken will be removed in the general conflagration; when the earth also, and all the works that are therein, shall be burned up, and the elements shall melt with fervent heat. I am not putting these events in order, for I do not even know their order, and am neither a prophet nor an expounder of prophecy. But it is clear we are to look for the establishment of the Jews in their own land, the conversion of Israel with the fulness of the nations. We are to expect the literal advent of Jesus Christ, for He Himself, by His angel, told us, "This same Jesus which is taken up from you into heaven shall so come *in like manner* as ye have seen Him go into heaven," which must mean literally and in person. We expect a reigning Christ on earth; that seems to us to be very plain, and to be put so literally that we dare not spiritualise. We anticipate a first and second resurrection: a first resurrection of the righteous, and a second resurrection of the ungodly, who shall be judged, condemned, and punished forever by the sentence of the great King.

We foresee from the Word, despite its obscurity, that strange and wonderful things will happen, such as are depicted by vials, and warriors with avenging swords, and falling stars, and a shrivelled sky, and reeling earth, and I know not what beside; but when we have put all together and have been sore amazed at the visions that flit before us like dreams of the night, we rejoice to learn at the end of them all, "All these things are ours, whatever they may be." In the present political crisis there is much alarm and trepidation felt by some as to what may become of a movement which is very dear to most of us, and to accomplish which we would almost be prepared to die; but

I foresee in the distance no adversary who can long withstand us, and the brief opposition which may be offered will increase the ultimate victory. All things that shall happen, be they ever so cross to your thoughts and counter to your views, will, nevertheless, come up, like Blucher at Waterloo, at the exact moment when they shall help on the grand old cause.

Justice must reign; the church of God must be freed from her adulterous connection with the State. God ordereth everything in providence; neither the good by excess of zeal, nor the bad by their malice, shall mar His work. Through the thick darkness I hear the tramp of another host marching to battle, and though. I cannot see their plumes, yet am I assured that whether friend or foe, they must, ere the battle is over, have yielded no mean service to our holy cause. Homage must be done even by the powers of darkness to the great King, the Lord of hosts. Therefore, by the cross and by the crown of Jesus, ye lovers of truth and justice, ye children of a free church and a just God, charge home against the foes of God and man; who under pretence of religion would continue to oppress the sister isle. Ye that love the Lord hate evil, abhor the doing of evil, that good may come; believe in the true and the just, but have no faith in wrong. Jesus, your Lord, would not worship Satan though all kingdoms were offered as a bribe, neither must we be guilty of injustice though we anticipated from it the happiest results. Let right be done, come what may. Consequences are with God; duty alone is ours. Sever the church from the state; let it cost what it may. Even if for the moment advantage should seem to be given to the enemies of our faith, it is but so in appearance, or if it were real we can afford to give it them and yet defeat them.

We can hurl down this day the gauntlet of our God and of His Christ, in the presence of earth and hell, and let those take it up who dare; for with all the deadliest odds against us we shall triumph yet, for the Lord is in the midst of His church, and therefore is she invincible. We will give Goliath his greaves of brass, his spear, his armour, and his shield, for what are these? The Lord's power, and a stone from His servant's sling, shall lay the monster in the dust. Let every Christian, then, look forward to future events, on the largest scale, with complete composure. Let empires shake, let crowns fall from heads anointed, let the great ones of the earth put their hands upon their loins like women in travail, let those that were full hire themselves out for bread, and let the rulers be astonished; but as surely as God is God, the day cometh when the Lord will maintain the right and avenge the oppressed, and set up His throne, from which He will "judge the poor" and "save the children of the needy," and "break in pieces the oppresser." So be it, good Lord, and we will bless Thy name.

—C. H. SPURGEON, 1869.

When men's hearts are "failing them for fear, and for looking after those things which are coming on the earth," God's word to His people is, "Lift up your heads, for your redemption draweth nigh" (Luke 21:28).—A.W.P.

---

felt when Peter denied Him. As we, in some small measure, obtain an experimental acquaintance with such trials, it makes Christ increasingly precious to us, and enables us to appreciate the more all that He went through on our behalf. In a coming day we are going to share His throne, now we are privileged to taste His cross. Sanctified afflictions bring us more closely into fellowship with the sufferings of the Lord Jesus.

If, then, trials and tribulations, under God, produce such delightful fruits, then *welcome* chastisements, that are for "our profit." Let the rains of disappointment come if they thus water the plants of spiritual graces. Let the winds of adversity blow if they serve to root more securely in grace the trees of the Lord's planting. Let the sun of prosperity be eclipsed if this brings us into closer communion with the Light of life. O brethren and sisters, however distasteful they are to the flesh, chastisements are not to be dreaded, but welcomed, for they are designed to make us "partakers of God's holiness."

Substance of a sermon by the Editor.

you have been healthy all your lives and have never suffered much weakness and pain, then you know little about the strength of God. If you have never been visited with trying situations which bring you to your wits' end, or by heart-rending bereavements, you have discovered little of the sufficiency of Divine grace. You may have *read* about it in books, or *heard* others speak of it, but you have little *experimental* acquaintance of it for yourself. It is much tribulation which brings out the sufficiency of God's strength to support under the heaviest trials and demonstrates that His grace can sustain the heart under the heaviest losses.

It is in the stormiest weather that the captain gives most heed to the steering of his ship; so it is in seasons of stress and grief that Christians most heed the exhortation of Heb. 4:16—"Let us therefore come boldly unto the Throne of Grace, that we may obtain mercy and find grace to help in time of need." If Israel had journeyed direct from Egypt to Canaan, they had missed the tender care of Jehovah in the Wilderness. If Lazarus had not died, Martha and Mary would not have received such a demonstration of Christ as the Resurrection and the Life. And if *you*, my brother, my sister, had not been cast into the furnace of affliction, you would not have known the nearness and preciousness of His presence with you there. Yes, God intends us to *prove* the reality and sufficiency of His grace.

6. *It develops our spiritual graces.* This is clearly set forth in that familiar passage Rom. 5:3:5. "We glory in tribulations also: knowing that tribulation worketh patience; and patience, experience; and experience, hope: and hope maketh not ashamed." This "rejoicing" is not in tribulations considered in themselves, but because the Christian knows they are appointed by his Father, and because of their beneficial effects. Three of these effects or spiritual graces thus developed are here mentioned.

Tribulation worketh patience. Patience never thrives except under buffetings and disappointments: it is not even called into exercise while things are going smoothly and pleasantly. Sanctified tribulations call into activity that strength and fortitude which is evidenced by a submissive endurance of suffering. The "patience" here referred to signifies deliverance from murmuring, refusing to take things into our own hands (which only causes additional trouble), a contented waiting for God's time of deliverance.

Patience worketh experience, that is, a *vital* experience of the reality of what we profess; a personal acquaintance with that which before we knew only theoretically and intellectually. An experience of the sufficiency of Divine grace to support and to sustain. An experience of God's faithfulness, that He *is* "a very present help in trouble." An experience of the preciousness of Christ, such as the three Hebrews had in the furnace. The Greek word for "experience" also means *the obtaining of proof.* The patient submission which tribulation works in the saint *proves* both to him and to his brethren the *reality* of his trust in God: it makes manifest the fact that the faith which he professes is genuine. Instead of his faith being overcome, it triumphs. The test of a ship is to weather the storm; so it is with faith. Real faith ever says, "Though He slay me, yet will I trust in Him."

Experience worketh hope. As I have so often told you, Hope looks forward, it anticipates the future. While circumstances are as we like them, our outlook is mainly confined to the present: but sorrows and trials make us long for the future bliss. "*As an eagle stirreth up her nest . . . . so* the Lord led Israel" (Deut. 33:11). God removes us from our comfortable nests, for the purpose of teaching us to use the wings of hope. A man was seated in the backyard of a farm. Suddenly he was startled by seeing a cow poke its head over the wall. Turning to his host he said, *Why* is that cow looking over the wall? The farmer quaintly answered, "Because it cannot look through it!" The illustration may be crude, but it is pointed. It is thus with our tribulations. Though unable to see through them, we should ever look beyond and above.

7. *It brings us into fellowship with the sufferings of Christ.* The cross is the symbol of Christian discipleship and sufferings. Like the scars which the wounded soldier prizes above all other distinctions, so our sufferings are the proofs of our oneness with Christ (Rom. 8:17). Not only so, they make us appreciate the more what He endured for us. While we have plenty, we cannot properly appreciate nor estimate the poverty which our Saviour endured. While we enjoy a comfortable bed we cannot truly sympathise with Him who "had not where to lay His head." It is not till some familiar friend, on whom we counted, has basely betrayed our trust, that we can enter into something of what the Saviour suffered through the perfidy of Judas. It is only when some brother has denied you, that you begin to understand what Christ

Continued on page 239

# STUDIES IN THE SCRIPTURES

"Search the Scriptures" John 5: 39

Copyright in all English-speaking Countries.

Editor: Arthur W. Pink, 15 Hurlstone Avenue, Summer Hill, N.S.W., Australia.
Hon. Agent in U.S.A.: Mr. C. S. Pressel, 559 Dupont Avenue, York, Penna.

FREE TO ALL WHO WILL READ IT

## DIVINE CHASTISEMENT.
### Heb. 12:11.

This verse is added to what has been said in the previous ones for the purpose of anticipating and removing an objection. After all the comforting and encouraging statements given, namely, that chastisements proceed not from an enemy but from our Father, that they are sent not in anger but in love, that they are designed not to crush but "for our profit"; carnal sense and natural reason interposes an objection. "But we find no joy under our afflictions, but much sorrow. We do not *feel* that they are for our profit; we cannot *see* how they can be so; therefore, we are much inclined to doubt what you have said."

The apostle grants the force of the objection: that for the present chastening *does* "seem to be grievous and not joyous." But he brings in a double limitation or qualification: in reference to outward sense, it only "seems" so; in reference to time, this is only for "the present." Having made this concession, the apostle turns to the objector and says, "Nevertheless." He reminds him that, first, there is an "afterward" beyond the present moment, to be borne in mind; second, he presses on him the need of being "exercised thereby"; third, he assures him that if he is so exercised "peaceable fruit" will be the happy issue. This morning we shall confine ourself to the objection of carnal sense and the apostle's reply. There are four things told us in the text about Chastisement as it is viewed by human reason.

*1. All that carnal reason can perceive in our chastenings is BUT SEEMING.* All that flesh and blood can discover about the nature and quality of Divine afflictions is but their outward and superficial appearance. The eye of reason is utterly incapable of discovering the virtue and value of sanctified trials.

How often we are deceived by mere "seeming!" This is true in the natural sphere; appearances are proverbially deceptive. There are many optical illusions. Have you not noticed some nights when the sun is sinking in the west that he is much bigger than at his zenith? Yet he is not so in reality, he only "seems" to be so. Have you stood on the deck of a ship in mid ocean, and, while gazing at the horizon, have suddenly been startled by a sight of land? The outline of the coast, with the rising hills in the background, were clearly defined. Yet after all it was but "seeming"; it was nothing but clouds. In like manner you have read of a mirage seen by travellers in the desert. Away over the sands, they see in the distance green trees and a shimmering pool of water. But this is only an optical delusion, reflected in some way by the atmosphere.

Now, if this be so in connection with natural things, the "seeming" *not* being the actual, the apparent *not* being the reality, how much more is it true of the things of God! Afflictions are *not* what they "seem" to be. They appear to work for our ill, and not for our good, so that we are inclined to say, "An enemy hath done this." They seem to be for our injury, rather than our "profit," so that we murmur and are cast down. So often *fear* distorts our vision. So often *unbelief* brings scales over our eyes, and we exaggerate the dimensions of trials in the dark and dim light. So often we are selfish, fond of our fleshly ease; and therefore spiritual discernment

Continued on page 264

# IMPORTANT NOTICES

Back numbers of each year of the magazine are yet obtainable at 5/- (1.25) per year. Bound at 7/6 (1.75) post paid. They will soon be out of print. Those in U.S.A. wanting them, please purchase from Mr. Pressel (see front cover page).

Advise promptly of change of address. This Magazine is published as a work of faith and labour of love. The Editor gladly gives his services. It is freely sent to all who will read it. No charge is made for it.

Christians who feel definitely led to do so, may have fellowship with us in this Ministry. Send only *Inter-National M.O.*

## CONTENTS.

| | |
|---|---|
| The Gosepl of John (21:15-25) | 242 |
| Gleanings in Exodus | 249 |
| Parables of Matt. 13 | 253 |
| Gospel Responsibilty | 256 |
| Glorifying God | 261 |

## THE GOSPEL OF JOHN.

The following is an Analysis of our final section:—

*71. Christ and Peter: John 21:15-25.*

1. The threefold question vv. 15, 17.
2. The threefold reply vv. 15, 17.
3. The threefold commission vv. 15, 17.
4. Christ's prophecy concerning Peter's death vv. 18, 19.
5. Peter's question concerning John vv. 20, 21.
6. Christ's reply vv. 22, 23.
7. John's final testimony vv. 24, 25.

The final section of this truly wondrous and most blessed Gospel contains teaching greatly needed by our fickle and feeble hearts. The central figures are the Lord and Simon Peter, and what we have here is the sequel to what was before us in chapter thirteen, the Lord washing the feet of His disciples. There, too, Peter was to the fore, and that because he occupies the position of a representative believer; that is, his fall and the cause of it, his restoration and the means employed for it, illustrate the experiences of the Christian and the provisions which Divine grace has made for him. Before we take this up in detail let us add that, just as in the first part of John 21 we have, in symbol, the confirmation of the calling of the Apostles to be fishers of men, so in this second section we have the final establishment of the one to whom the keys of the kingdom were entrusted.

The first thing recorded in connection with Peter's fall is our Lord's words to him before it took place: "Simon, Simon, behold, Satan hath desired to have you, that he may sift you as wheat. But I have prayed for thee, that thy faith fail not: and when thou art converted, strengthen thy brethren" (Luke 22:31, 32). This is very solemn and very blessed. Solemn is it to observe that the Lord prayed not to keep Peter from falling. In suffering His apostle *to* fall, the Lord's mercy comes out most signally, for that fall was necessary in order to reveal to Peter the condition of his heart, to show him the worthlessness of self-confidence, and to humble his proud spirit. The need for Satan's "sifting" was at once made manifest by the Apostle's reply, "And he said unto Him, Lord, I am ready to go with Thee, both into prison, and to death" (Luke 22:33). "This is a condition which not only exposes one to a fall, but from which the fall itself may be the only remedy. We have to learn that when we are weak only are we strong; and that Christ's strength is made perfect in our weakness. Peter's case is a typical one; and thus it is so valuable for us.

"The Lord Himself, in such a case as this, cannot pray ("cannot" *morally* do so —A.W.P.) that Peter may not fall, but that he may be 'converted' by it, turned from that dangerous self-confidence to consciousness of his inability to trust himself, even for a moment. Here Satan is foiled and made to serve the purpose of that grace which he hates and resists. He can overpower this self-sufficient Peter; but only to fling him for relief upon his omnipotent Lord. Just as the 'messenger of Satan to buffet' Paul (2 Cor. 12), only works for what he in nowise desires, to repress the pride so ready to spring up in us, and which the lifting up to the third heaven might tend to foster. Here there had been no fall, and all was over-ruled for fullest blessing; in Peter's case, on the other hand, Satan's effort would be to assail the fallen disciple in suggestions of a sin too great to be forgiven—or, at least, for restoration to that eminent place from which it would be torture to remember he had fallen. What he needed to meet this with was *faith;* and this, therefore, the Lord prays, might not fail him.

"How careful is He to revive and strengthen in the humbled man the practical confidence so needful! The knowledge of it all given him *before-hand*—of the prayer made for him—of the exhortation addressed to him when restored, to 'strengthen his brethren'—all this would be balm indeed for his wounded soul; but even this was not enough for his compassionate Lord. The first message of His resurrection had to be addressed specially 'to Peter' (Mark 16:7), and to 'Cephas' himself He appears, before the Twelve (1 Cor. 15:5). Thus He will not shrink back when they are all seen together. When we find him at the sea of Tiberias, it is easy to realise that all this has done its work. Told that it is the Lord who is there on the shore, he girds on his outer garment, and casts himself into the sea, impatient to meet his Lord. But now he is ready, and only now, for that so necessary dealing with his conscience, when his heart is fully assured" (Numerical Bible).

When the Saviour washed the feet of Peter, He said, "What I do thou knowest not now, but thou shalt know hereafter" (13:7). This cleansing, as we saw, has to do with the *maintenance* of a "part *with*" Christ (13:8). It tells of the Lord's gracious work in restoring a soul which has become defiled and out of communion with Him; the "water" figuring the means which He uses, the Word. Now, at that time Peter had not fallen, and therefore he perceived not the significance of the Saviour's (anticipatory) act. But now he is to learn in his conscience the holy requirements of Christ, and experience the purifying power of the Word and the recovering grace of our great High Priest.

In 21:9 we learn that the first thing which confronted the Apostle when he joined the Lord on the shore was "a *fire* of coals," an expression found again in John's Gospel only in 18:18. There we read of "a *fire* of coals" in the priest's palace, and that Peter stood by its side with Christ's enemies "warming himself." It was *there* that he had denied his Master. How this "fire of coals" by the sea of Tiberias would prick his conscience: a silent preacher, but a powerful one, nevertheless! Christ did not point to it, nor say anything about it; that was unnecessary. Next we read of the seven disciples partaking of the food which the Saviour had provided, showing that the Lord's attitude toward Peter had not changed. The meal being over, He now turned and addressed Simon. It was there by the side of this "fire of coals" that the Lord entered into this colloquy with him, the purpose of which was to bring the Apostle to *judge* himself, for "fire" ever speaks of judgment.

"So when they had dined, Jesus saith to Simon Peter, Simon, son of Jonas, lovest thou Me more than these?" (v. 15). Mark carefully how the Lord began: not with a reproach, still less a word of condemnation, nor even with a "*Why* did you deny Me?" but "*Lovest* thou Me more than these?" Yet, observe that the Lord did not now address him as "Peter," but "Simon son of Jonas." This is not without its significance. "Simon" was his original name, and stands in contrast from the new name which the Lord had given him: "And when Jesus beheld him, He said, Thou art Simon the son of Jonas: thou shalt be called Cephas (Peter), which is by interpretation, A stone" (1:42). The way in which the Lord now addressed His disciple intentionally called into question the "Peter." Mark how that in Luke 22:31 the Lord said, "*Simon, Simon,* behold Satan hath desired to have you, that he may sift as wheat." Christ would here remind him of his entire past as *a natural man*, and especially that his fall had originated in "Simon" and not "Peter!" On only one other occasion did the Lord address him as "Simon son of Jonah," and that was in Matt. 16:17, "Jesus answered and said unto him, Blessed art thou, Simon son of Jonah: for flesh and blood hath not revealed it unto thee, but My Father which is in heaven." But note that the Lord is quick to add, "And I say *also* unto thee, that *thou art Peter*, and upon this rock I will build My church: and the gates of hell shall not prevail against it. And I will give unto *thee* the keys of the kingdom." Thus this first word of the Lord to His disciple in John 21:15 was designed to pointedly remind him of his glorious *confession*, which would serve to make him the more sensitive of his late and awful *denial*.

"Lovest thou Me more than these?" This was still more searching than the name by which Christ had addressed His Apostle. He would not heal Peter's wound slightly, but would work a perfect cure; therefore, does He, as it were, open it afresh. The Saviour would not have him lose the lesson of his fall, nor in the forgiveness forget his sin. Consequently He now delicately retraces for him the sad history of his denial, or rather by His awakening question brings it before his conscience. Peter had boasted, "Though *all* shall be offended, yet will not *I*": he not only trusted in his own loyalty, but congratulated himself that *his* love to Christ surpassed that of the other Apostles. Therefore did the Lord now ask, "Lovest thou Me *more* than these?" i.e., more than these apostles love Me?

"He said unto Him, Yea Lord; Thou knowest that I love Thee" (v. 15). And opportunity had graciously been given Peter to retract his former boast, and gladly did he now avail himself of it. First, he began with a frank and heartfelt confession—"*Thou* knowest." He leaves it to the Searcher of hearts to determine. He could not appeal to his ways, for they had reflected upon his love; he would not trust his own heart any longer; so he appeals to Christ Himself to decide. Yet observe, he did not say "Thou knowest *if* (or *whether*) I love Thee," but "Thou knowest *that* I love Thee"—he rested on the Lord's knowledge *of* his love; thus there was both humility and confidence united. "It was as though he said, 'Thou hast known me from the beginning as son of Jonah; drawn me to Thee, hast kindled love in my soul, hast called me Peter; Thou didst warn of my blindness, and pray for my faith, and hast since forgiven me; Thou hast looked, both before and since Thy death, into my heart, with eyes of grace, so *Thou* knowest all! What *I* feel concerning my love is this, that I am far from loving Thee as I ought and as Thou art worthy of being loved; but Thou, O Lord, knowest that in spite of my awful failure, and notwithstanding my present weakness and deficiency, I *do* love Thee'" (Stier).

"He saith unto him, Feed My lambs" (v. 15). What marvellous grace was this! Not only does the Lord accept Peter's appeal to His omniscience, but He gives here a blessed commission. Christ was so well satisfied with Peter's reply that He does not even confirm it with, "Verily, I *do* know it." Instead, He responds by honouring and rewarding his love. Christ was about to leave this world, so He now appoints others to minister to His people. "Feed My lambs." The change of figure here from fishing to shepherding is striking: the one suggests the evangelist, the other the pastor and teacher. The order is most instructive. Those who have been saved need shepherding—caring for, feeding, defending. And those whom Christ first commends to Peter were not the "sheep" but the "lambs"—the weak and feeble of the flock; and these are the ones who have the first claim on us! Note Christ calls them *"My* lambs," denoting His authority to appoint the under-shepherds.

"He saith to him again the second time, Simon, son of Jonas, lovest thou Me?" (v. 16). The Lord now drops the comparative "more than these" and confines Himself to love itself. This question is one which He is still asking of each of those who profess to believe in Him. "'Lovest thou Me?' is, in reality, a very searching question. We may know much, and do much, and talk much, and give much, and go through much, and make much show in our religion, and yet be dead before God for want of love, and at last go down to the Pit. Do we *love* Christ? That is the great question. Without this there is no vitality about our Christianity. We are no better than painted wax-figures: there is no life where there is no love" (Bishop Ryle).

"He saith unto Him, Yea, Lord; Thou knowest that I love Thee" (v. 16). In this passage there are two distinct words in the Greek which are translated by the one English word "love," and it is most instructive to follow their occurrences here. The one is a much stronger term than the other. To preserve the distinction the one might be rendered "love" and the other "affection" or "attachment." When the Lord asked Peter, *"Lovest* thou Me?" He used, both in vv. 15 and 16, the stronger word. But when Peter answered, what he really said, each time, was "Thou knowest that I *have affection for* Thee." So far was he now from boasting of the superiority of his love, he would not own it as the deepest kind of love at all! Once more the response of Divine grace is what Peter receives: "He saith unto him, Feed My sheep" (v. 16). The word for "feed" here is more comprehensive than the one which the Lord had used in the previous verse, referring primarily to rule and discipline. Observe the Lord again calls them *"My* sheep," not *"thy* sheep"—thus anticipating and refuting the pretensions of the Pope!

"He saith unto him the third time, Simon, son of Jonas, lovest thou Me?" (v. 17). Here the Lord Himself uses the weaker term—"Hast thou *affection* for Me?" "Grace reigns *through righteousness*" (Rom. 5:21). Three times had Peter *denied* his Master; three times, then, did the Lord *challenge* his love. This was according to "righteousness." But in thus challenging Peter, the Lord gave him the opportunity of now thrice *confessing* Him. This was according to "grace." In His first question the Lord challenged the *superiority* of Peter's love. In His second question the Lord challenged whether Peter had *any love* at all. Here, in His third question the Lord now challenges even his *affection!* Most searching was this! But it had the desired effect. The Lord wounds only that He may heal.

"Peter was grieved because He said unto him the third time, Lovest thou Me?" (v. 17). Here we are shown once more the power of *the Word.* This was indeed the sequel to John 13. That Peter was "grieved" does not mean that he was offended at the Lord because He repeated His question, but it signifies that he was touched to the quick, was deeply sorrowful, as he recalled his *threefold* denial. It is parallel with his "weeping *bitterly*" in (Luke 22:62). This being "grieved" evidenced his perfect *contrition!* But if it was grievous for the disciple to be thus probed and have called to remembrance his sad fall, how much more grievous must it have been to the Master Himself to be denied?

"And he said unto Him, Lord, Thou knowest all things; Thou knowest that I love Thee" (v. 17). Beautiful is it to behold here the transforming effects of Divine grace. He would not now boast that *his love* was superior to that of others; he would not even allow that he had *any love;* nay more, he is at last brought to the place where he now declines to avow even his affection. He therefore casts himself on Christ's omniscience. "Lord," he says, "*Thou* knowest *all* things." *Men* could see no signs of any love or affection when I denied Thee; but *Thou* canst read my very heart; I appeal therefore to Thine all-seeing eye. That Christ knew *all* things comforted this disciple, as it should us. Peter realised that the Lord knew the *depths* as well as the *surfaces* of things, and therefore, that He saw what was in his poor servant's *heart,* though his *lips* had so transgressed. Thus did he once more own the absolute Deity of the Saviour. Thus, too, did he rebuke those who would now talk and sing of *their* love for Christ! "His self-judgment is complete. Searched out under the Divine eye, he is found and owns himself, not better but worse than others; so self-emptied that he cannot claim *quality* for his love at all. The needed point is reached: the strong man converted to weakness is now fit to strengthen his brethren; and, as Peter descends step by step the ladder of humiliation, step by step the Lord follows him with assurance of the work for which he is destined" (Numerical Bible).

"Jesus saith unto him, Feed My sheep" (v. 17). Does this, after all, warrant, or even favour, the pretensions of the Pope? No, indeed. "The Evangelist relates in what manner Peter was restored to that rank of honour from which he had fallen. The treacherous denial, which had been formerly described, had undoubtedly rendered him unworthy of the Apostleship; for how could he be capable of instructing others in the faith, who had basely revolted from it? He had been made an Apostle, but from the time that he had acted the part of a coward, he had been deprived of the honour of Apostleship. Now, therefore, the liberty, as well as the authority of teaching, is restored to him, both of which he had lost through his own fault. That the disgrace of his apostasy might not stand in the way, Christ blots it out and fully restores the erring one. Such a restoration was needed both for Peter and his hearers; for Peter, that he might the more boldly exercise himself, being assured of the calling with which Christ had again invested him; for his hearers, that the stain which attached to him might not be the occasion of despising the Gospel" (John Calvin). We may add that this searching conversation between Christ and Peter took place in the presence of six of the other Apostles: his sin was a public one, so also must be his repudiation of it! Note that in Acts 20:28 *all* the "elders" are exhorted to feed the flock!

"Jesus saith unto him, Feed My sheep." If you love Me, *here* is the way to manifest it. It is only those who truly *love* Christ that are fitted to minister to His flock! The work is so laborious, the appreciation is often so small, the response so discouraging, the criticisms so harsh, the attacks of Satan so fierce, that only the "love of Christ"—His for us and ours for Him—can "constrain" to such work. "Hirelings" will feed the *goats,* but only those who love Christ can feed His *sheep.* Unto this work the Lord now calls Peter. Not only had Christ restored the disciple's *soul* (Psa. 23:3), but also his official *ministry;* another was not to take *his* bishopric—contrast Judas (Acts 1:20)!

"Jesus saith unto him, Feed My sheep." Marvellous grace was this. Not only is Peter freely forgiven, not only is he fully restored to his apostleship, but the Lord commends to him (though not to him alone) that which was dearest to Him on earth—*His sheep!* There is nothing in all this world nearer the heart of Christ than those for whom He shed His precious blood, and therefore He could not give to Peter a more affecting proof of His confidence than by committing to his care the dearest objects of His wondrous love! It is to be noted that the Lord here returns to the same word for "feed" which He had used in v. 15. Whatever may be necessary in the way of rule and discipline (the force of "feed" in v. 16), yet, the first (v. 15) and the last (v. 17) duty of the under-shepherd is to *feed* the flock—nothing else can take the place of ministering spiritual nourishment to Christ's people!

It is striking to observe that in connection with Peter's restoration he received a threefold commission which exactly corresponds with our Lord's threefold "Peace be unto you" with which He saluted the disciples in the previous chapter. "Feed My lambs" (v. 15) answers to the first benediction in 20:19: it is Gospel-exposition needed by the young believer to establish him in the foundation truth of redemption. "Shepherd" or "discipline" My sheep (v. 16) answers to the second "Peace be unto you" in 20:21, which relates to service and walk. "Feed My sheep" (v. 17) answers to the third "Peace be unto you" in 20:26, spoken for the special benefit of Thomas, and has to do with the work of restoring those who have gone astray. Compare also the threefold written ministry of the Apostle John: unto the "fathers," "young men," and "little children" (1 John 2:13).

"Verily, verily I say unto thee, When thou wast young, thou girdest thyself, and walkest whither thou wouldest: but when thou shalt be old thou shalt stretch forth thy hands, and another shall gird thee, and carry thee whither thou wouldest not" (v. 18). Here, too, the grace of Christ shines forth most blessedly. Not only had Peter been forgiven, restored, commissioned, but now the Lord takes him back to the fervent declaration which he had made in the energy of the flesh: "Lord, I am ready to go with Thee, both into prison, and to death" (Luke 22:33), and assures him that this highest honour of all *shall* be granted him. "Peter might still feel the sorrow of having missed such an opportunity of confessing Christ at the critical moment. Jesus assures him now that if he had failed in doing that of his own will, he should be allowed to do it by the will of God: it should be given him to die for the Lord, as he had formerly declared himself ready to do in his own strength" (Mr. J. N. Darby).

"Verily, verily, I say unto thee, When thou wast young, thou girdest thyself and walkest whither thou wouldest: but when thou shalt be old, thou shalt stretch forth thy hands and another shall gird thee, and carry thee whither thou wouldest not" (v. 18). The connection between this verse and those preceding is as follows: the Lord here warns Peter that his love to Him would be sorely tested, that caring for His sheep would ultimately involve a martyr's death—for thus do we understand His words here. A more direct link is found in that Peter had just said, "Lord, Thou knowest *all* things": Christ now gave proof that He *did* indeed, for He speaks positively and in minute detail of that which was yet future, and could be known only to God. The beloved disciple again would be placed in such a position that he would have to choose between denying and confessing Christ. As the reward for his good confession here, and to supply an encouragement for the future, the Lord assures him that he *shall* confess Him even to death.

"This spake He, signifying by what death he should glorify God" (v. 19). This is a parenthetic remark by John, made for the purpose of supplying a key to the meaning of the Lord's words in the previous verse. When Christ said, "When thou was young, thou girdest thyself, and walkest whither thou wouldest," He signified that during his earlier days Peter had enjoyed his natural freedom. When he said, "But when thou shalt be old thou shalt stretch forth thy hands," He meant that Peter would do this at the command of another. When He added, "And another shall gird thee," He meant that Peter should be bound as a prisoner with cords—cf. Acts 21:11 where Agabus took Paul's girdle and bound his own hands and feet, to symbolise the fact that the Apostle would be "delivered into the hands of the Gentiles." In His final words, "and carry thee whither thou wouldest not," the Lord did not mean that Peter would resist or murmur ("what death he should *glorify* God" proves that), but that the death he should die would be contrary to nature, disagreeable to the flesh. Peter was to die a death of violence, by crucifixion. In the "thou wouldest not" the Lord further intimated that He does not expect His people to *enjoy* bodily pains, though we are to endure them without murmuring. "But the Pope (to whom Peter says in vain, Follow me, as I follow Christ! is the reverse: the older he grows the more arbitrarily will he gird and lead others whither *he* will" (Stier).

"This spake he, signifying by what death he should glorify God." It is not only by acting, but chiefly by suffering, that the saints glorify God. Note how the Lord says to Ananias concerning Saul, "I will show him how great things he shall *suffer* (not "do") for My name's sake" (Acts 9:16)! Note how that when the Apostle would strengthen the wavering Hebrews, instead of reminding them of their works,

He said, 'Call to remembrance the former days, in which, after ye were illumined, ye *endured* a great fight of afflictions" (Heb. 10:32). But what sweet consolation to realise that our whole future has been forearranged by Christ—by Him who is too wise to err and too loving to be unkind.

"This spake He, signifying by what death he should glorify God." What a lesson is there here for us. True, it is the Lord's return, not death, for which we are to look and wait. Nevertheless, all who have gone before us have died, and we may do so before the Saviour comes. Let us remember, then, that should this be the case, we may "glorify" God in *death* as well as in life. We may be patient sufferers as well as active workers. Like Samson, we may do more for God in our death than we did in our lives. The death of the mayrtrs had more effect on men than the lives they had lived. "We may glorify God in death by being ready for it when it comes . . . by patiently enduring its pains . . . . by testifying to others of the comfort and support which we find in the grace of Christ" (Bishop Ryle). It is a blessed thing when a mortal man can say with David, "Yea, though I walk through the valley of the shadow of death, I will fear no evil: for Thou art with me" (Psa. 23:4).

"And when He had spoken this, He saith unto him, Follow Me" (v. 19). Here was the final word of grace to the fallen, now recovered disciple. Now that Peter had discovered his weakness, now that he had judged the root from which his failure had proceeded, now that he had been fully restored in heart, conscience, and commission, the Lord says, "Follow Me." This was what he had pretended to do (18:15), when the Lord had told him he could not (Luke 22:33, 34). But now Christ says, You may, you can, you shall. To "follow" Christ means to "deny self" and "take up the cross." In other words, it means to be "conformed to His death." This, *in spirit;* with Peter, in bodily experience, too. This word of Christ supplies one more link with what is found in chapter thirteen. There the Saviour said to Peter, "Whither I go, thou canst not follow Me now; but thou shalt follow Me aferwards" (v. 26). This is the sequel: "It was a call on him to follow the Lord, through death, up to the Father's House. And upon saying these words to him, the Lord rises from the place where they had been eating, and Peter, thus bidden, rises to follow Him" (Mr. Bellett). The Lord evidently accompanied this final word with a symbolic movement of going on before.

"Then Peter, turning about, seeth the disciple whom Jesus loved following, which also leaned on His breast at supper, and said, Lord, which is he that betrayeth Thee?" (v. 20). What a line in the picture is this, and how true to life! How humbling! Here was a believer, fully restored to communion, there in the presence of Christ, bidden to follow Him; yet here we find him taking his eye off Christ, and turning round to look at John! There is only one explanation possible—*the flesh* still remains in the believer, and *ever* lusts against the spirit! Though fully restored, the old Simon still remained. Christ had told him to "follow," not look around. Stier suggests that there was here "a sideglance once more of comparison with others," hardly that we think, rather the old tendency of taking his eye off Christ was manifested. In beautiful contrast from the fleshly turning of Peter, is the spiritual "following" of John. Christ had not commanded him to do so, nor had He even directly addressed him; but true love was ever occupied with its object, and here the Apostle of love could do no other than follow Christ. Blessed is it to mark how the Holy Spirit now refers to him, not only as "the disciple whom Jesus loved," but also as the one who "leaned on His breast at the Supper." At the beginning of this Gospel (1:18) *Christ* is seen in the bosom of the Father, here at the end, a redeemed sinner is referred to as one who leaned on the bosom of the Saviour!

"Peter seeing him saith to Jesus, Lord, and what shall this man do?" (v. 21). This too, evidenced the flesh in Peter. Christ had announced what awaited him, now the apostle is anxious to know how John—the one with whom he was most intimate and between whom there was a very close bond —should fare. The same curiosity which made him beckon to John that he should "*ask* who it should be" that would betray Christ (13:24), now causes him to say, "what (of) this man?" "Peter seems more concerned for another than for himself. So apt are we to be busy in other men's matters, but negligent in the concerns of our own souls—quick-sighted abroad, but dim-sighted at home—judging others and prognosticating what they will do, when we have enough to mind our own business. Peter seems more concerned about events than duties" (Matthew Henry).

"Jesus saith unto him, If I will that he tarry till I come, what is that to thee? follow thou Me" (v. 22). The Lord rebukes Peter's curiosity about John, and presses upon him his own duty. There is an old saying, Charity begins at home, and there is not a little truth in it. We are naturally creatures of extremes, and it is a hard matter to preserve the balance. On the one side is uncharitable selfishness, which makes us indifferent to the interests of others; on the other side is altruism carried to such an extent that we neglect the cultivation of our own souls. Both are wrong. Let us not be weary in well doing to others, but let us also heed that word of Paul's to Timothy, "Take heed *unto thyself*" (1 Tim. 4:16). Unhappily there are not a few who have reason to say, "They made me the keeper of the vineyards; but *mine own* vineyard have I not kept" (Song of S. 1:6). It was to correct this tendency in Peter that the Lord spoke. His business was to attend to his own duty, fulfil his own course, and leave the future of others in the hands of God—cf. Luke 13:23, 24. What good would it do Peter to know whether John was to live a long life or a short one, to die a violent death or a natural one?—cf. Dan. 12:8, 9. A warning is this to us not to be curious about the decrees of God concerning others—cf. Deut. 29:29. "Follow Me" is also his word *to us*: we are to follow Him as Leader of His people, as Shepherd of His flock, as Exemplar for His saints, as Lord of all.

"Then went this saying abroad among the brethren, that that disciple should not die: yet Jesus said not unto him, He shall not die; but, If I will that he tarry till I come, what is that to thee?" (v. 23). What plain proof does this afford that the Lord's coming does not refer to the decease of His people. How strange that any should have supposed that it did! Death is the believer going to be with Christ, the Lord's return is His coming to be with us. Yet how curious, that even from the beginning, the Lord's word "I come again" in connection with John, was misunderstood and wrested. Another thing which these words of Christ made evident was that His return is an *imminent* event, that is, one which *may* occur at any time, and one which we should be constantly expecting. Note the "If *I* will": a majestic declaration was this that *Christ* is now the Disposer of men's lives: He did not say, if God, or if the Father, wills, but if *I* will. Mark how this verse furnishes us with a warning against following *human traditions*, even though they come from "the brethren": how blessed to have the unerring standard of God's written Word!

"If I will that he tarry till I come." What was the deeper meaning in this word of Christ's? First, are we not intended to see in Peter and John *representatives* of the Church in the early and latter days of this dispensation? Peter, who died a death of violence, points to the first centuries, when martyrdom was almost the common experience of believers. John, who is given the hope that he may (though not the promise that he *shall*) live on till the Lord's return, points to this last century, when the truth of the Lord's coming has been so widely made known among His people! But this is not all. The *ministry* of John actually goes on to the end, for in the Revelation he treats at length of those things which are to usher in the Lord's return to the earth, aye, and beyond the end of the Millennium, to the new heaven and the new earth!

It is most blessed to observe that there is no account given in this Gospel of the Lord's *ascension*, and this is in most perfect keeping with the Spirit's design here. The departure of Christ left the disciples behind on earth. But here it is the family, in which—now in spirit, soon in the body—there are to be *no* separations. The last sight we have of the Saviour in John's Gospel, the sons are *with* Him! So shall we be "forever with the Lord."

"This is the disciple which testifieth of these things, and wrote these things: and we know that his testimony is true. And there are also many other things which Jesus did, the which, if they should be written every one, I suppose that even the world itself could not contain the books that should be written. Amen" (vv. 24, 25). These verses call for little comment. The Gospel closes with the personal seal and attestation of its writer. John, without mentioning his name, vouches for the veracity of what he had recorded, and then adds an hyperbole (cf. Matt. 11:23; Heb. 11:12; for others) to emphasise the fact that it was not possible for him to fully tell out the infinite glories of that One who is the central figure of his Gospel. The final "Amen" —found at the end of each Gospel—is the Holy Spirit's imprimatur.

"The Apostle closes his Gospel with another reminder of the inadequacy of all human words to tell out His glory, of whom he has been speaking. If it were attempted to tell out all the world would be unable to contain the books that would be written. It would be an impracticable load to lift, rather than a help to clearer apprehension. How thankful we may be for the moderation that has compressed what would be really blessing to us into such a moderate compass! which yet, as we all must know, develops into whatever largeness we may have capacity for. Our Bibles are thus the same, and quite manageable by any. On the other hand, are we burning to know more? We may go on without any limit, except that which our little faith or heart may impose. May God awaken our hearts to test for themselves the expansive power of Scripture, and whether we can find a limit anywhere! Like the inconceivable immensity of the heavens, ever increasing as the power of vision is lengthened, we go on to find that the further we go only the more does the thought of infinity rise upon us; but this infinity is filled with an Infinite Presence; in every leaf-blade, in every atom, yet transcending all His works; and 'to us there is but one God, the Father, of whom are all things, and we for Him; and one Lord, Jesus Christ, by whom are all things, and we by Him'" (Numerical Bible).

*Arthur W. Pink.*

## GLEANINGS IN EXODUS.

47. *The Priesthood: Ex. 27:20-28:2.*

Once more we would direct the reader's attention to the *order* of Jehovah's instructions to Moses concerning the Tabernacle and all that was connected with it. At first glance the contents of Exodus 28 and 29 seem to depart from the logical sequence and to introduce confusion. Instead of completing the description of the Tabernacle and its furniture, the priesthood is introduced, and then in chapter 30 the last of the holy vessel is described. But fully assured that God is not the Author of confusion, the prayerful student should diligently seek the mind of the Spirit for an explanation of this perplexity. A new subdivision of Exodus begins with the 28th chapter, or more correctly, at 27:20.

Many years ago it was pointed out by Mr. Darby that everything mentioned in Ex. 25:10 to 27:19 foreshadowed God's coming forth unto His people: each article there mentioned was a symbol of *display,* that is, a manifestation of God in Christ. But from 27:20 to the end of chapter 30 the order is reversed, everything there pointing to the provisions of grace which enable us to go in to God: that is to·say, the priesthood and the vessels referred to in Ex. 30 have to do with *approach.* But before the laver and the incense altar (the vessels needed for access to God) are brought before us, we are shown the appointment and consecration of the priesthood. Thus we may discern Divine order in the seeming confusion, for there must be designated persons for approach, before the vessels could be used. "God has come out in type and figure to His people; then He indicates those who are to be set apart for His service in the sanctuary—those who are to enjoy the special privilege of access to Himself; and lastly, the vessels, etc., are given, which they would need in their holy employment in the house of God" (Mr. E. Dennett).

The blessed *unity,* amid diversity, of the whole of Jehovah's instructions to Moses in this section of Exodus has been dealt with so helpfully by the late Mr. Soltau that we quote from him at length: "The Tabernacle and its vessels, the Priesthood and the various ministrations connected therewith, form but one subject; although divided for the sake of more distinctly contemplating each portion. The Tabernacle would have been useless without its vessels: and the Tabernacle with its vessels would have been of no service but for a living family of priests, constantly engaged in various active ministrations within the holy places, and about the various holy vessels.

"So closely connected is each part of this subject with the other, that in the directions contained in Exodus, there is no break; but the command for making the holy garments and consecrating the priesthood (Ex. 28 and 29), comes betweeen the enumeration of some of the holy vessels and the various parts of the Tabernacle. Indeed, properly speaking, the 27th chapter should end at v. 19, where 'thou shalt command the children of Israel' begins a new subject, viz.: directions concerning the oil for the light of the sanctuary. The 28th chapter continues with ordering the sacrifices for the day of priestly consecration. The 30th carries on the subject connected with the priesthood, by giving the description of the incense altar; and the whole closes with the Sabbath, at the end of the 31st chapter.

"Again; when all the various parts of the work have been completed, ending with the garments of the priesthood (chapters 36-39:31) the following verse is added: 'Thus was all the work of the tabernacle of the Tent of the Congregation finished; and the children of Israel did according to all that the Lord commanded Moses, so did they'. Here, therefore, the priestly garments were considered part of the work of the Tabernacle! And if we turn to Heb. 8 we find that 'the priests, that offered gifts according to the law, served unto the example and shadow of heavenly things, as Moses was admonished of God, when he was about to make the Tabernacle itself; see, saith He, that thou shalt make all things according to the pattern showed to thee in the mount' (vv. 4, 5).

"The service of the priests in offering gifts and sacrifices was connected with the commandments given to Moses in the mount respecting the making of the Tabernacle. The words 'See, that thou make all things according to the pattern showed thee in the mount', as recorded in Exodus, were spoken to Moses respecting the holy vessels (Ex. 25:40), but are in Heb. 8 quoted to prove that the priests and their ministrations were examples and shadows of heavenly things. The whole subject is therefore much blended."

Still observing the *order* of truth presented to us in our present section, it is most striking to find we have in 27:20, 21 that which is obviously the *connecting link* between the two central lines of thought—God coming out to His people, they going in to Him. "And thou shalt command the children of Israel, that they bring thee pure oil olive beaten for the light, to cause the lamp to burn always. In the tabernacle of the congregation without the vail, which is before the testimony, Aaron and his sons shall order it from evening to morning before the Lord: it shall be a statute forever unto their generations on behalf of the children of Israel." Two things are here brought before us: provision for the maintenance of the light and the ministration of the priesthood. These verses are very rich in their typical teaching and must be carefully weighed as a preparation for what follows. Strictly, they begin the section and are the key to the contents of chapters 28 and 29.

Before a description is given of the garments and consecration of the priests, provision is made for perpetual light in the sanctuary. This takes the precedence. As v. 21 tells us the light was to shine "before the Lord." Priestly ministry was for the benefit of the people; but the claims of God must first be met. This was the order in Gen. 1: the *first* thing there, was "Let there be light." This, before a single creature was brought into existence. So here in Exodus. In figure it tells that Christ had first to meet all the demands of God's holiness, ere He could minister for us as our great High Priest: the Cross first, then His intercession on High.

It was at the Cross that God was fully manifested as the Light (1 John 1:5); that is, in His ineffable holiness—His very nature as eternally antagonistic to sin. And in the typical order of God's revelation of Himself through the vessels of the Tabernacle, beginning with that which was in the Holiest (the ark and the mercy-seat), the movement was ever *outward*, past the table and the lampstand in the holy place, to the brazen altar in the outer Court (27:1), which foreshadowed the Cross: the altar marking the *terminal* of the coming out of God in manifestation. Thus provision having been made through Christ's atonement for "the lamp to burn alway," i.e. for the unsullied holiness of God to act without compromise in His gracious dealing with poor sinners, the way was then clear to make known the provisions which Divine mercy had made for reconciled sinners to draw near to God within the veil.

But as we showed in a previous paper, the Lampstand speaks not only of Christ, but also of the Holy Spirit as His gift to the saints. This explains the fact that in v. 20 it is "the people" who were to supply the "pure oil olive beaten for the light." As was the case in connection with all the other materials (see 25:2, etc.), so that which speaks of the Holy Spirit given us by Christ, was also provided by "the people" themselves. The Tabernacle and its services were not only for Jehovah, but for Israel too: thus their providing the materials for it, witnessed to *their* personal interest in it. In keeping with this we may note that 27:21 mentions, for the first time, "the Tabernacle (Tent) *of the congregation!*"

But further: does not this initial mention of the "Tent of the Congregation," in the present connection, supply more than a hint of the formation of that Church which is the Body of Christ—consequent upon His having satisfied the requirements of God's holiness and the descent of the Holy Spirit? In Matthew 16:18 our Lord employed the future tense, not the present—"I *will* build My Church," not "I am building." Ephesians 1:20-23 also plainly teaches that Christ was not given to be the Head over all things to His Church until after His resurrection and ascension. Thus the Church is only seen (typically) *after* the claims of Divine holiness had been met, the throne of God eternally established, and the Holy Spirit sent down as the witness of this: cf. Acts 2:33.

Again; it is in Exodus 27:21 that, for the *first* time, mention is made of "Aaron and his sons." This also has a double significance. Coming right after mention of "the people" in v. 20, it tells us on whose behalf the Priesthood was instituted. "Aaron and his sons" are mentioned twenty-four times in the book of Exodus, but they are not seen until after instructions were given for the children of Israel to furnish the oil for the light. How plainly this foreshadowed the fact that the priestly ministry of Christ is essential to maintaining the gracious working of the Spirit through His people! Up to this point, nothing whatever had been said of any human agents or ministers appointed to officiate in the tabernacle service and to delight themselves in the dwellingplace of God among men, amidst the heaven-given shadows and emblems of the eternal verities which we have previously contemplated. But in God's light we see light (Psalm 36:9). The light makes manifest—here the divinely-chosen ministers of the sanctuary. This introduces to us the subject of Israel's priesthood—one abounding in precious instruction for us; but to which, alas, the vast majority of the saints are total strangers.

Sixty years ago a servant of God wrote, "To a large portion of those who would be regarded as intelligent Christians, and who are something more than mere routine readers of the Bible, the types of the Tabernacle, with its priesthood, service, and offerings, are barren of comfort and edification. Yet it is generally acknowledged that they are pictures by which God, in His condescension, would teach His children things otherwise all but incomprehensible. It is generally admitted, also, that the key to unlock these treasures of spiritual truth lies ready to the hand of every student in the New Testament. Without inquiring particularly why these treasures have fallen into such general neglect in our day, the following suggestion is worthy of the consideration of the earnest among us: 'The real secret of the neglect of the types,' says one who is entitled to be heard on this point, 'I cannot but think may, in part, be traced to this—that they require more spiritual intelligence than many Christians can bring to them. To apprehend them requires a certain measure of spiritual capacity, and *habitual exercise in the things of God*, which all do not possess, for want of abiding fellowship with Jesus. The mere superficial gaze upon the Word in these parts, brings no corresponding idea to the mind of the reader. The types are, indeed, pictures, but to understand the picture, we should know something of the reality. The most perfect representation of a steam-engine to a South Sea savage would be wholly and hopelessly unintelligible, simply because the reality, the outline of which was presented to him, was something hitherto unknown.'

"Paul arrests himself in speaking of Christ as a priest forever after the order of Melchizedek (Heb. 5:11, etc.), by the reflection that those whom he addressed were incapable of receiving instruction on account of their spiritual childhood. A child of a king is unconscious of the dignity and the inheritance to which he is born; but it is none the less a king's child: and so there are many true children of God who seem to remain babes, content, apparently, that they have life and are children; and so they need milk. This accounts for the spiritual feebleness and inactivity of the Church in our day. Babes, indeed, must be fed on milk, but it is not necessary that Christians should continue babes. May we not, therefore, exhort them, in the words of the apostle, 'To leave the principles of the doctrine of Christ and go on to perfection' (Feb. 6:1)—to manhood—to the condition of those who, 'by reason *of use,* have their senses exercised to discern both good and evil'?" (Waymarks in the Wilderness).

Since then, conditions have not improved. There appear to be as many "babes" among Christians as ever. The greater part of the Bible seems a sealed book to them. "*All* scripture is given by inspiration of God and is profitable," and it is to our irreparable loss if we neglect any portion thereof. "*Whatsoever* things were written beforetime, were written for *our* learning" (Rom. 15:4), and if we fail to give proper attention to the types our souls will be the poorer. Notably is this the case with the subject before us. What hazy and inadequate ideas concerning priesthood are entertained by the average believer. That the Lord Jesus *is* the great High Priest of His people, he knows, but as to the place of Christ's priesthood, the nature of its activities, its relation to other truths, especially to redemption; the design accomplished by it, the blessings secured from it, the portion which the saint enjoys by virtue of it, are most indefinitely defined in the minds of most.

On the Cross the Saviour said, "It *is* finished": all that was needed to satisfy the requirements of God and reconcile to Him His alienated people, was accomplished. Then, wherein lies the necessity for the present ministry of our great High Priest? If His blood fully atoned for all our sins, why should He now be making intercession on our behalf? This is a difficulty which has been felt by many. But the same problem is presented in the book of Exodus. Here we see a (typically) redeemed people, protected from judgment by the sprinkled blood of the lamb, brought out from the house of bondage, separated unto Jehovah, He dwelling in their midst. Yet, a priesthood was appointed to act on their behalf! Why? The same book of Exodus reveals the solution. The priesthood was for the *maintaining*, not securing, their relationship with Jehovah. They were still a people compassed with infirmity, subject to temptation, and alas, frequently failing. The holy God dwelling in their midst could not tolerate that which was unclean. Therefore the same grace which had brought them nigh to Himself, now made provision for the keeping of them nigh.

Priesthood has to do with *fellowship*. Its need arises from the fact that the sinful nature remains in those who have been bought with a price. It is to meet the failures of a people who when they would do good evil is present with them: this evil which causes them to offend in "many things" (James 3:2), makes the priestly ministry of Christ so essential. This was what was foreshadowed in Exodus and Leviticus. The application of these types to Christians to-day calls for a wisdom which only the Holy Spirit can supply, for in the light of the Hebrews' Epistle it is clear that the Levitical shadows present contrasts as well as comparisons, and though containing much which finds its antitypical fulfilment in the spiritual blessings of the Church, there is also not a little which will only be made good to Israel in a coming day. The immediate linking together of the Lampstand and the Priesthood in Ex. 27:21 plainly intimates that only in the light of God can the latter be discerned and understood.

First, let us mark and admire the lovely *grace* of God which is brought out in the type before us. This is seen in the choice that He made. "Take thou unto thee Aaron thy brother, and his sons with him, from among the children of Israel, that he may minister unto Me in the priest's office" (28:1). Not Moses, but Aaron, the inferior brother, was the one selected for this great favour. Moreover, the tribe to which he belonged was one of the least honourable of the twelve; yea, it was under the curse, because of Levi's cruelty—see Gen. 49: 5-7. Not Reuben the firstborn, nor Judah whom his brethren should praise (Gen. 49:8), nor Joseph the fruitful bough, but Levi, was to be the priestly tribe. How this exhibited the sovereignity of Divine grace! Finally, the matchless and wondrous grace of God in appointing Aaron to be the high priest is seen in the fact that at the very time His choice was made known to Moses, his brother was taking the lead in the idolatrous worship of the golden calf! Nor do these details mar the accuracy of the type; instead, they strikingly illustrate the fact that our great High Priest was the gift of God's marvellous *grace*.

Second, let us now consider the significance of his name. "Aaron" means "very high." He stood supreme as the high priest, exalted not only above his own house, but also above all the people. Thus was he a type of the Lord Jesus, whom God has exalted with His right hand to be a Priest and a Saviour (Acts 5.31). But as if to magnify the high priesthood of Christ above that of all others, the Holy Spirit has added the word "great"—our "great High Priest" (Heb. 4.14), an adjective used of none other, not even Melchizedek.

We may note that in Ex. 28:1 the names of Aaron's sons are also given, and each of them was most appropriate and striking. Nadab means "willing"; Abihu, "my Father is He"; Eleazer, "help of God"; Ithamar, "land of palm." As another has pointed out, "these four words afford a little prophetic intimation of characteristics attaching to the House of which the Son of God is the Head: deriving its life from God the Father, and all its power and help from Him; following in the footsteps also of its blessed Master, in yielding willing and not constrained service to God; and like the palm trees, lofty in righteousness, and ever bringing forth fruit (Psa. 92: 12-14). The palm-tree is one of the ornaments of the future temple described by Ezekiel, and was also one of the embellishments of Solomon's temple. It is peculiarly the tree of the desert, flourishing where no other could exist; ever marking out to the weary traveller the spot. amidst surrounding desolation, where a grateful shade and a spring of living water were to be found; and remarkable for longevity and ceaseless fruitfulness. Thus it was an apt emblem of the heavenly priesthood" (G. Soltau).

Third, let us dwell upon the significance of the singular pronoun in 28:1: "Take unto thee Aaron, and his sons with him, that *he* may minister." This is very striking and most blessed. Aaron and his sons formed together one priesthood, and Aaron's appointment to his office was inseparable from theirs. What a wondrous foreshadowment was this of the *union* between our great High Priest and His House, and what an intimation that His ministry before God concerned His House, and them alone!

And here we must stop. To write at length upon the Priesthood of Christ would necessitate us expounding almost the entire Epistle of the Hebrews, where this blessed theme is developed by the Spirit of God. To that important New Testament book we would refer the interested student. There, the divine Instructor has pointed out both the comparisons and the contrasts between the type and the Antitype. The Aaronic priesthood furnished much that was the *pattern* of Christ's priesthood, but the *order* of it is vastly superior, being that of Melchidezek—the royal priest. God willing, other aspects of the subject will come before us in future papers.

*Arthur W. Pink.*

## THE PROPHETIC PARABLES OF MATTHEW 13.

### 3. The Parable of the Sower.

"And He spake many things unto them in parables, saying, Behold, a sower went forth to sow." The careful reader will notice an *omission* here, namely, that this parable does not begin with the words "the kingdom of heaven is like unto." This cannot be without some good reason, for that which is omitted from Holy Writ is oftentimes as meaningful as what is recorded. Each of the six parables which follow *do* begin with this clause. The reason why it is left out at the beginning of the first is not difficult to account for. As we have shown in a previous article, "the kingdom of heaven" is an expression which, in the present dispensation, has reference to Christendom—the sphere of Christian profession, that circle where the sovereignty of Christ is publicly owned. But the "kingdom of heaven" did not assume this form until after Christ had returned to the Father. Thus, because this first parable contemplates the period of time covered by our Lord's earthly ministry these words are appropriately omitted. The first parable forms an introduction to those which follow: it describes the work of Christ preparatory to the establishment of His kingdom among the Gentiles.

"*Behold*, a sower went forth to sow." In Mark 4:3 we find that this same parable is introduced by the words, "*Hearken*, behold, there went out a sower to sow."

This word "hearken" indicated that the Saviour was about to communicate something of unusual importance. The figure He was using was so simple as to be almost unimpressive, so that there was a danger of His hearers regarding it as of little account; therefore the "hearken!" "Behold" was also designed to arrest attention; it was a word bidding us to carefully ponder what follows.

The action of Christ at the beginning of this parable was both tragic and blessed. Speaking from the human side, it ought to have been, "A Reaper went forth to reap," or "An Husbandman went forth to gather fruit." For fifteen hundred years there had been a liberal sowing of the Seed in Israel, by Moses, David, the prophets and last of all John the Baptist. But harvest for Jehovah there was not. Touchingly is this brought out in Isa. 5: "My wellbeloved hath a vineyard in a very fruitful hill: And He fenced it, and gathered out the stones thereof, and planted it with the choicest vine and built a tower in the midst of it, and also made a winepress therein: and He looked that it should bring forth grapes, and it brought forth wild grapes" vv. 1, 2.

The *blessedness* of Christ's action here is to be seen in His wondrous condescension and grace in stooping so low as to take the humble place of a "Sower," hence the "behold." The words "*went forth* to sow," or as Mark's Gospel puts it "*went out*" were indicative of the great dispensational change which was soon to be introduced. There was no longer to be a planting of vines or fig-trees in Israel, but a going out of the mercy of God unto the Gentiles; therefore what we have here is the *broadcast* sowing of the Seed in the field at large, for as v. 38 tells us "the field is *the world.*"

One great design of this opening parable is to teach us the measure of success which the Gospel would receive among the Gentiles. In other words, we are shown what the results of this broadcast sowing of the Seed would be. First of all, most of the ground upon which it fell would prove unfavourable: the hard, shallow, and thorny soils were uncongenial to productiveness. Second, external opposition would be encountered: the birds of the air would come and catch it away. Third, the sun would scorch, and that which was lacking in moisture at its roots would wither away. Only a *fractional* part of the Seed sown would yield any increase, and thus all expectations for the ultimate *universal* triumph of the Gospel were removed.

The plain teaching of our present parable should at once dissipate the optimistic but vain dreams of post-millennarians. It answers clearly and conclusively the following questions: What is to be the result of the broadcast sowing of the seed? Will all the world receive it and every part of the field produce fruit? Will the seed spring up and bear a universal harvest, so that not a single grain of it is lost? Our Saviour explicitly tells us that the greater part of the seed produces *no* fruit, so that no world-wide conquests by the Gospel, in the Christianising of the race, are to be looked for. Nor was there any hint that, as the age progressed, there would be any change, and that later sowers would meet with greater success, so that the wayside, stony, and thorny ground hearers would cease to exist or would rarely be found. Instead of that, the Lord Himself has plainly warned us that instead of the fruitage from the Gospel showing an increase, there would be a marked decrease; for when speaking of the fruit borne He said, "which also beareth fruit, and bringeth forth, some an hundred-fold, some sixty, some thirty" (v. 23). These words are too plain to be misunderstood. We believe that the "hundred fold" had reference to the yield borne in the days of the apostles; the "sixty" at the time of the Reformation; the "thirty" the days in which we are now living. The history of the last nineteen centuries has witnessed the fulfilment of Christ's prediction: only a fractional percentage in any land, city or village has responded to the Gospel!

Most of the *details* of this parable are concerned not with the Sower or the Seed, but with the various *soils* in which the Seed fell. In His interpretation the Lord Jesus explained the different soils as representing various classes of those who hear the Word. They are four in number, and may be classified as hard-hearted, shallow-hearted, half-hearted, and whole-hearted. It is important to see that in the parable Christ is speaking not from the standpoint of the divine counsels—for there can be no failure there—but from that of human accountability. What we have here is the Word of the kingdom addressed to man's responsibility, the effect it has on him, and his response. Let us now look briefly at each class separately:

1. The wayside hearers. "And when He sowed, some fell by the wayside, and the fowls came and devoured them up. . . . when any one heareth the word of the kingdom and understandeth it not, then cometh the wicked one, and catcheth away that which was sown in his heart. This is he which received Seed by the wayside" (vv. 4, 19). Here, the heart which receives the Seed is unreceptive and unresponsive. It is like the public highway, hardened by the constant traffic of the world. Though the Word is said to be "sown in his heart" it finds no real lodgment in it, and this is what makes it so solemn. The *"engrafted* word" is that which is received *"with meekness,"* and for this there must be a laying aside of "all filthiness and superfluity of naughtiness" (James 1:21). It is at *this* point that the individual's accountability comes in, the responsibility of the one who hears the Word.

It is to be noted that it is *"when* anyone heareth the word of the kingdom and understandeth it not, *then* cometh the wicked one and catcheth away that which was sown in his heart." Those who hear the Word are *responsible* to "understand" it. It is true that the natural man receiveth not the things of the Spirit of God, but he *ought* to; and that they are "foolishness unto him," but it ought not so to be. As we are told in 1 Cor. 8:2, "if any man think that he knoweth anything, he knoweth nothing yet *as he ought to know."* Understanding of the Word is obtained from God alone, and it is the responsibility of all who hear and read His Word to cry unto Him, "That which I see not, teach Thou me" (Job 34:32). His promise is "the meek *will* He teach His way" (Psa. 25:9). But if there is no humbling of the heart before God, no seeking wisdom from above, then will there be no "understanding" of the Word; and the Devil will "catch away" that which we have heard or read: but we shall have only *ourselves* to blame!

2. The stony-ground hearers. "Some fell upon stony places, where they had not much earth: and forthwith they sprung up, because they had no deepness of earth: And when the sun was up, they were scorched; and because they had no root, they withered away. . . . He that received the seed into stony places, the same is he which heareth the Word, and anon with joy receiveth it; yet hath he not root in himself, but dureth for awhile: for when tribulation or persecution ariseth because of the Word, by and by he is offended" (vv. 5, 6, 20, 21). The type of ground that is here referred to, is that where the bed is of rock, with only a thin layer of earth over it. In this shallow soil the seed is received, but the growth is but superficial. Our Lord's interpretation at once *identifies* the particular class of hearers which are here in view. At first they promise well, but later prove very disappointing. What we have here is *lack of depth*. The emotions have been moved, but the conscience has not been searched; there is a *natural* "joy" but no deep conviction or true repentence. When a Divine work of grace is wrought in a soul, the first effects of the Word upon it are not to produce peace and joy, but contrition, humility and sorrow.

The sad thing is, that to-day almost every thing connected with modern evangelistic (?) effort is calculated to produce just this very type of hearer. The "bright singing," the sentimentality of the hymns (?), the preacher's appeals to the emotions, the demand of the churches for visible and *quick* "results," produce nothing but superficial returns. Sinners are urged to make a prompt "decision," are rushed to the "penitent form," and then assured that all is well with them; and the poor deluded soul leaves with a false and evanescent "joy." And the deplorable thing is that many of the Lord's own people are supporting and fellowshipping this Christ-dishonouring and soul-deceiving burlesque of true Gospel ministry.

"But dureth for awhile." "This is the flesh at its fairest; capable of coming so near to the kingdom of God, and all the more manifesting its hopeless nature. There is the unbroken rock behind that never *yields* to the Word, and gives it no lodgment; and the class of hearers pictured here are born of the flesh only. Let things be outwardly favourable to profession, it is plain that the number of these may multiply largely, and may stick like dead leaves to a tree that has had no rough blast to shake them off. But life is none the more in them" (The Numerical Bible).

3. The thorny-ground hearers. "And some fell among thorns; and the thorns sprung up, and choked them. . . He also that received seed among the thorns is he that heareth the Word; and the care of this world, and the deceitfulness of riches, choke the Word, and he becometh unfruitful" (v. 7, 22). In Mark 4:9 the "lusts of other things entering in" and in Luke 8:14 the "pleasures of this life" are named as additional hindrances represented by the "thorns." Here it is not so much inward causes as it is external snares that render the third class of hearers unfruitful.

Thus the Lord has here made known what it is that, from the human side, makes so much of the Seed sown, unproductive. The reasons why the preaching of the Word does not produce a spiritual harvest in all who hear it are, first, the natural hardness of man's heart and the resultant opposition of Satan; second, the superficiality of the flesh; third, the attractions and distractions of the world. These are the things which produce barrenness, and they are recorded for the Christian's learning and warning. Thus too are the servants of Christ instructed what to expect, and informed what it is which will oppose their labours—the Devil, the flesh and the world.

4. The good-ground hearers. "But other fell into good ground and brought forth fruit. . . He that received seed into the good ground is he that heareth the Word, and understandeth it; which also beareth fruit, and bringeth forth, some an hundred fold, some sixty, some thirty" (vv. 8, 23). It is to be carefully noted that when He was defining the good-ground hearer, Christ did not say "this is he in whom a Divine work of grace hath been wrought," or "whose heart has been made receptive by the operations of the Holy Spirit." True it is that *this* must precede any sinner's receiving the Word so that he becomes fruitful, yet, *this* is not the particular aspect of the Truth with which Christ is here dealing. As already stated, He is speaking here *not* of the accomplishment of God's counsels, but from the

standpoint of *human responsibility.*

What the Lord is here making known is, that which the hearer of the Word must *himself* seek grace to do, if he is to be fruitful. The supplementary accounts given of this parable by Mark and Luke must be carefully compared. In Luke 8:15 we are told, first, that that Word must be received "in an *honest* and good heart." Second, that they "keep it." And third, "bring forth fruit *with patience*." Such are the conditions of fruitfulness: an unprejudiced mind and an open heart; understanding the Word received; holding it fast, perseverance.

In closing let us call attention to one or two practical lessons inculcated by this parable.

First, the *preciousness* of the Seed. If there were only one grain of wheat left in the world to-day, and it was lost, all the efforts of man could not reproduce it. Thus it is with the Word: were it taken from us all the wit and wisdom of man could not replace it. Then let us value, love, and study it more.

Second, the *inconspicuousness* of the Sower. Scarcely anything at all is told us in the parable about Him, beyond the simple fact that He actually sowed the Seed. The emphasis is upon the Seed, the various kinds of soil and the obstacles to and conditions of fruitfulness. Why is this? Because the personality of the sower and the method of sowing are of secondary importance. A little child may drop a seed as effectively as a man; the wind may carry it, and accomplish as much as though an angel had planted it! *All* —not merely preachers only—may be "sowers."

Third, the *conditions* of fruitfulness. There is much "rocky ground" in the garden of each of our souls: then despise not God's hammer and ploughshare. There are many "thorns" in each of our lives which must be plucked up if there is to be more room for fruit! Finally, there needs to be much prayer for "understanding," "patience," and hiding of the Word in our hearts so that we shall "keep" it.

Fourth, the *fulness* of the parable. There are some who decry the idea that we should seek for a meaning to every *detail* in our Lord's parables, and tell us we should be content with discovering its *general* significance. But such a loose conception is manifestly condemned by Christ's own example. In His interpretation *He* gave a meaning to *every* detail; not only so, but by comparing the three accounts of this parable, we learn that the "thorns" represent at least *four* distinct things! How this shows us the need of carefully studying and prayerfully meditating upon every jot and title of Holy Writ!

*Arthur W. Pink.*

## GOSPEL RESPONSIBILITY.

*"In flaming fire taking vengeance on them that know not God, and that obey not the Gospel of our Lord Jesus Christ"* (2 Thess. 1:8).

Many of our readers will be surprised to hear there are those who *deny* that there is such a thing as "Gospel Responsibility." Yet such is the case. The remarkable thing is that these deniers profess to be Christians, "earnestly contending for the faith," yet, they insist that *they* are the only ones who are preserving the faith intact. They regard all who differ from them as being in nature's darkness, or, at any rate, blest by far less Divine light than they are favoured with. Consequently, it is very difficult to secure the attention of such and ask them to weigh any thing attentively in the light of Holy Writ. Their ultimate court of appeal seems to be their "Articles of Faith" rather than the Word of God.

The fact of the matter is that those referred to above believe only a part of the faith once delivered to the saints; a vital and fundamental part, we readily grant, but *only* a "part" nevertheless. There is much in the Bible that these people have no place for in their denominational creed; much upon which their preachers are totally silent; and which when other preachers expound, they turn away from, even though those other preachers base every thing they say on a clear and positive "thus saith the Lord."

An essential and most important part of the faith once delivered to the saints is the preaching of the Gospel to every creature. But on this point those referred to above have sadly failed. To the writer it appears they have so over-emphasised sovereign election, particular redemption and effectual calling, that they have lost the balance of truth. Alas, "in many things we all offend" (James 3:2); how long-suffering is God with us! Oh that He may give both writer and reader willingness to be shown our faults and grace to acknowledge them.

We need to be reminded that the truth of God is one perfect whole. Scripture does not speak of "truths" as we are often apt to do, but of "the truth." Now, as another has said, "We are ever in danger of laying hold on God's truth partially; that is, in accord with some ill-guided conception of our own as to the relative value of different parts of truth. Those to which, from any particular cause, we have been led to pay much attention, naturally assume a large proportion to the eye; just as an object which is near often excludes from the vision a far larger object that is at a greater distance. Hence the mischief that accrues to those who take their views of God's truth from the narrow and contracted views of any man, or any body of men, who, occupying a standpoint of their own, can only present truth accordingly.

"It is a matter of great regret that generally persons who read at all, confine their reading so much to the writings of those with whom they agree. Thereby their views are contracted, and the result is too often a bigotry and a one-sidedness all the greater because it is obtained second-hand. Disciples, rather than original teachers, are the real bigots."

In the past, when faithful servants of God have called upon the unconverted to repent and believe the Gospel (which was what Christ Himself did, Mark 1:5), some have dubbed them duty-repentance, and duty-faith preachers; which, in certain circles, is to be ranked as heretics. Arguing from the premise that because the natural man is dead in trespasses and sins and, in consequence, incapable of repenting and believing, they have drawn the conclusion:—therefore it is an absurdity to call upon him so to do. As a matter of pure logic, the conclusion is unanswerable; but —it will not stand the test of Scripture!

Again; arguing from the premise that repentance and faith are the gifts of God (which we also emphatically maintain), they have drawn the conclusion:—therefore it is useless to bid men repent and believe, when God has not previously bestowed these graces upon them. From the standpoint of reason this, too, is flawless: but —again we say, it breaks down before the Word of God!

Still others say, to call upon sinners, promiscuously, to repent and believe, implies and gives them the impression that they have, in and of themselves, the power to comply; and as this denies the total depravity of man and repudiates the fact that "salvation is of the Lord," therefore we must refrain from such exhortations. To this it is sufficient to reply: God's servants are not responsible for what inferences their hearers may or may not draw: their business is to preach the Word, the whole of it, and leave results entirely with God.

If a preacher repeatedly affirms that in the flesh there dwelleth no good thing; that they that are in the flesh cannot please God; that apart from the drawing power of the Father none can come to Christ; that it is the Spirit that quickeneth, the flesh profiteth nothing; yet, nevertheless (because Scripture requires him so to do), preaches an unfettered Gospel: publicly announces that there is a Saviour for every sinner out of hell who renounces his own righteousness, confesses his lost and undone condition before God, and rests by faith on the shed blood of Christ; and further, exhorts and bids sinners to repent of their sins and come to Christ for salvation, then no one has any right or Scriptural cause for saying that he is a "Yea and Nay" preacher.

Perhaps some reader says, But I cannot see how the two things are harmonisible. Suppose you cannot, does that prove one of them to be untrue? Is your proud reason to sit in judgment upon the eternal truth of the Most High? Beware; that truth is yet going to judge you! The one question for you to decide is not, Is the central proposition of a sermon or article reasonable, or harmonisible with another part of God's truth; but, Is it according to the Scriptures? If it is, then humbly bow to it. Believe it, whether you can understand it or no. God says, "prove all things, hold fast that which is good" (1 Thess. 5:21). This is what we ask you to do with that which follows. Never mind whether it is different from what you may have been taught by other men, or whether it agrees or does not agree with your "Articles of Faith"; search and see for yourself whether it is or is not based on Holy Writ. Do the Scriptures teach that God requires every man who hears His Gospel to believe it—not merely assent to its veracity, but believe and obey it? If so, is it not the bounden duty, the personal responsibility of every one of us, so to do?

Coming back to our opening text, notice two things plainly taught in it: first, the

Gospel is something which calls for *obedience* on the part of those who hear. Second, disobedience is to be *punished* by the Lord Jesus. Let us now consider each of these propositions separately.

First, the Gospel is not an Invitation, though it contains invitations to those who humble themselves before it. Further, though the Gospel is a Proclamation, it is something more than that. From the human side, that is, as it falls upon the ears of men, it is a Publication of good news, a declaration to sinners that Christ died for the ungodly. But from the Divine side (and, as usual, *this* has been largely lost sight of both by Calvinists and Arminians), that is, as it comes to us from God, the Gospel is a *Mandate* or Statute; hence, it is called "the Holy Commandment" (2 Peter 2:21). The demand or requirement of the Gospel is stated in Psalm 2:12: "Kiss the Son, lest He be angry and ye perish from the way." Now whatever God commands, it must be the duty of those commanded to render—their inability to comply does not and cannot nullify the obligation.

Second, the Gospel is therefore a Call from God, and as such, it *tests* all who receive it. If the Word of Truth is to be "rightly divided" (2 Tim. 2:15) on this subject, we must distinguish carefully and sharply between two distinct "calls" from God spoken of in the Scriptures. There is an effectual Call, which is given to the elect only. This we heartily and thankfully believe in. There is also a Call which God makes to a much wider circle of men, namely, to all coming under the sound of His Gospel. As to why He gives a "call" to those who are spiritually dead, is His business. The fact that He *does* give such a call is clearly taught in both Testaments: "Unto you, O men, I call; and My voice is to the sons of man" (Prov. 8:4). "For many be called, but few chosen" (Matt. 20:16). Now that which is pertinent to our present discussion is this: all who receive this general call from God are *responsible* to respond to it. To deny this is to repudiate the rights and claims of God. Furthermore, those who do not respond to this general call from God will be punished for their non-compliance, see Prov. 1:24-28!

Third, the Gospel presents to all who hear it a Saviour for sinners. Notice, please, we say "presents," we do not say "offers." Now all who hear God's Gospel are obliged to do one of two things with the Saviour it presents, i.e., brings before them, namely, receive or reject Him. Which ought they to do? We do not say, which *can* they, but which *should* they do? To despise and reject the Son of God is sin, and sin of the deepest dye. It is sin which will be punished: "But those Mine enemies, which would not that I should reign over them, bring hither, and slay before Me" (Luke 19:27).

Fourth, to hear the Gospel is a great privilege. For a sinful worm of the earth to be addressed at all by the Lord God is a high honour. To be told by Him that His grace has provided an all-sufficient Saviour for all who shall believe on Him, is an unspeakable mercy. No such good news has been sent to the fallen angels. Yet such glad tidings are sent to the fallen descendents of Adam. But every privilege carries with it a corresponding obligation: "Unto whomsoever much is given, of him shall be much required" (Luke 12:48).

In support of what we have said above, our appeal shall be not to the writings of honoured servants of God in the past, though many such might be quoted; nor to Catechisms and Articles of Faith, though these too might be cited in substantiation. Instead, we will turn to the Law and to the Testimony. What saith the Scriptures? This:

"How beautiful are the feet of them that preach the gospel of peace and bring glad tidings of good things! But they have not all *obeyed* the Gospel" (Rom. 10:15, 16). Do not these words show clearly that the Gospel is something more than a "proclamation"? Do they not teach plainly that the Gospel is "the holy commandment" of God, to which all who hear it are responsible to submit?

"Now to him that is of power to stablish you according to my gospel, and the preaching of Jesus Christ according to the revelation of the mystery, which was kept secret since the world began, but now is made manifest, and by the Scriptures of the prophets according to the commandment of the everlasting God, made known to all nations for the obedience of faith" (Rom. 16:25, 26). Could anything be more explicit than this? Does not the Holy Spirit here positively affirm that the Gospel is made known for "the obedience of faith"? Then is not "faith" a *duty*, i.e., something *due to* God on the part of His sinful creature, a ceasing of his rebellion, a submission to the Son?

If it be not the duty of the unconverted to believe the Gospel and receive the Saviour it presents to them, would God *punish* them for not doing so? Can righteousness punish where there is no obligation? Should it be replied, This is merely reasoning! We answer, Very well, we will appeal once more to the Scripture of Truth. Follow closely:—

"He that believeth on Him is not condemned: but he that believeth not is condemned already, *because* he hath not believed in the name of the only begotten Son of God" (John 3:18). Here we are told that the rejector of Christ is "condemned." He is condemned not only on account of Adam's transgression, and not only because of his own tresspasses of the moral law of God, but also and specifically because 'he hath not *believed* in the name of the only begotten Son of God." What will those who ridicule and decry "duty-faith" do with this verse?

"He that rejecteth Me, and receiveth not My words, hath one that judgeth him: the words that I have spoken, the same shall judge him in the last day" (John 12:48). Plainly then, there *are* those who "reject" Christ. Nor is this a guiltless act because they could do nothing else, for such will be "judged" by the *same* "word," i.e., the Gospel, which they neglected.

"In flaming fire taking vengeance on them that know not God, and that obey not the Gospel of our Lord Jesus Christ" (2 Thess. 1-8). Here we are told that in a coming day the Son of God is coming in judgment to take vengeance upon those who have despised His Gospel. Does not this afford proof, positive and incontrovertible, that these *ought* to have obeyed the Gospel? otherwise, how could they be justly "punished" for not doing so? Then is it not the bounden duty of Christ's servants to-day to exhort every man to repent and believe the Gospel, and to warn their hearers of the awful judgment awaiting those who obey it not? Are the preacher's skirts clear till he *has* done this? Until he has, can he say with Paul, "I am pure from the blood of all" (Acts 20:26)?

"For the time is come that judgment must begin at the house of God: and if it first begin at us, what shall the end be of them that obey not the Gospel of God" (1 Peter 4:17). Is it not striking to see how many verses there are in the New Testament which speak of *obeying* the Gospel, and which warn of the dire consequences which will attend continued disobedience to it? In view of this, is it not unspeakably solemn to find those who profess to be ministers of that Gospel decrying the idea that the Gospel is addressed to man's responsibility, and denouncing as heretics those who are, by grace, seeking to press upon all men their *duty* of obeying the Gospel? If the Spirit of God needs to remind Christians that "This is His *commandment* that we should *believe* on the name of His Son Jesus Christ" (1 John 3:23), how much more do non-Christians need to have it pressed upon them!

We might well conclude at this point, submitting what has been said for each reader to weigh prayerfully and carefully in the light of the Word as a whole and in part. But we know from experience how difficult it is (humanly speaking) for any of us to receive the Truth till our minds have first been purged of error. Therefore we shall now take up the leading objection which may be made against the above, and endeavour to show how it completely falls to the ground when tested by the Scriptures.

Let us state the objection in its strongest form. The unregenerate sinner is dead in tresspasses and sins: being dead, he is spiritually powerless; being powerless, he cannot have any responsibility in connection with spiritual things. There are several errors in this statement:

First, there is a wrong conception of the nature or character of the sinner's Inability. "They hated him, and *could not* speak peaceably unto him" (Gen. 37:4). Why could not Joseph's brethren "speak peaceably" unto him? What was the nature of their inability? It was because they "hated" him so much. But did such inability *excuse* them? Certainly not: it only aggravated their sin.

"Having eyes full of adultery, and that *cannot* cease from sin" (2 Peter 2:14). Here again we have spiritual inability; but was it excusable? Nay, verily; in that very thing consisted the greatness of their sin.

"No man can come to Me, except the Father which has sent Me draw him" (John 6:44). This does not mean that if the sinner desired to come, he is unable to carry out that desire; instead, it signifies that his inability to come to Christ consists of lack of desire, and this because his heart is so wedded to other objects. Let me try and show of what this "no man can come" consists. It is not the "cannot" which pertains to a stock of stone, but of a rational and accountable being. It is a moral "cannot." It refers not to the absence of the necessary faculties, but to the pervertion of those which the sinner does have.

How can one who prides himself on his morality and religiousness own himself to be lost and undone? How can one who sees so little amiss in himself, who knows not that he is a spiritual leper, earnestly seek the great Physician? How can one who has a high regard for himself acknowledge that all his righteousnesses are filthy rags? How can one who loves the darkness desire the Light? But the fact that he "loves" the darkness does not excuse him for hating the light. Thus, the inability of the sinner is a moral and spiritual one: "How can ye believe, which receive honor one of another, and seek not the honor that cometh from God only?" (John 5:44).

It needs to be pointed out that when Adam, and all whom he represented, "died" in Eden, that *no* spiritual faculty was lost. In Scripture "death" means not annihilation, but separation. Take the case of the prodigal son: of him the Father said, "This My son was dead, and is alive again." The simple meaning of which is, that he had been away from Him in the "far country." So, being "dead in tresspasses and sins" is clearly enough defined in Eph. 4:18 as "Having the understanding darkened, being *alienated from* the life of God." We have called attention to this because there are some who say, The unregenerate are dead, and *that* ends the matter—they *cannot* have any responsibility. But this is manifestly erroneous. From the same premise we might argue. Because the sinner is "dead," therefore he cannot *refuse* Christ, for a dead man cannot do anything. But he does so do, and is punished for that very thing.

The hyper-calvinist is fond of asking, "Would any sensible man go to the cemetery and bid those in their graves come forth! Why, then, ask one who is dead in sins to come to Christ, when he is equally incapable of responding?" Such a question only betrays the ignorance of the one who puts it. A corpse in the cemetery is no suitable analogy of the natural man. A corpse in the cemetery is incapable of performing evil! A corpse cannot "despise and reject" Christ (Isa. 53:3), cannot "resist the Holy Spirit" (Acts 7:51), cannot disobey the Gospel (2 Thess. 1:8); but the natural man *can* and *does* do these things!!

We have said above that the form of the question "betrays the ignorance of the one who puts it." It evidences that his conception of the *spiritual* "deadness" of the natural man is based upon the supposed analogy of *physical* "death," rather than on the Word of God. What saith the Scriptures? This: "You hath He quickened, who were dead in tresspasses and sins; *wherein* in time past ye *walked*" (Eph. 2:1, 2). Thus, the spiritual deadness of the unregenerate sinner is a state of *active* opposition against God, a state for which *He* is responsible; the guilt and enormity of which the preacher should ever press upon him. If it be asked, "Why speak of a state of *active* opposition against God as a being *dead* in sins?" The answer is, Because in Scripture "death" does not mean cessation of being, but a condition of "alienation" (not merely "separation") from God—Eph. 4:18). "The carnal mind is enmity against God," and "enmity" is not passive (like a corpse in a cemetery) but active!

The fact is that the sinner's inability is a voluntary one, and that is why he is accountable for it. There was a vast difference between the blindness of Bartimeus, who ardently desired his sight, and that of the Jews of whom it is said, "This people's heart is waxed gross, and their ears are dull of hearing, and their eyes *they* have closed" (Matt. 13:15). In this latter case the closing of their eyes was voluntary and criminal. The inability of Scripture (in contrast from much Calvinistic Theology) is aversion of heart and stubbornness of will. As said Stephen Charnock, "No man is an unbeliever, but because he will be so; and every man is not an unbeliever, because the grace of God conquers, changeth their wills, and bends them to Christ" (Discourses, Vol. 7, Page 473). The Word says, "To-day if ye will hear His voice, harden not your hearts." Thus the reason why men *do not* hear is not because they have no ears, but because they harden their hearts! Have they no responsibility in this?

Second. God has not lost His right to demand, even though man has his power to comply. God is *entitled* to the reverence and obedience, the confidence and love of all His creatures. God is the sum of excellence, therefore men ought to love Him, and love Him with all their hearts. God is Sovereign Most High, therefore sinners ought to obey Him. God's Word is true from the beginning, therefore they ought to believe it.

To say the unregenerate is *unable* to do these things, though true, furnishes no excuse for him; instead it deepens his guilt. A creditor does not lose his right to sue, because his debtor has squandered his substance in riotous living. A master does not lose his right to demand compliance with his wishes because his servant is in a drunken stupor. The law does not lose its right to send to prison a man who, because he gave way to stealing and become an inveterate thief, *could not* live honestly. So God has not lost His right to command all men to repent of their sins and believe the Gospel, even though sinners have become so depraved they lack the power to comply. Therefore it is the duty of God's servants to *insist* on *God's* rights, and to demand the sinner's repentance and faith. Christ called upon unregenerate sinners to believe (John 12:36, etc.). And the Holy Spirit through Paul condemns men for not loving Christ (1 Cor. 16:22)!

Third, the plea of inability as cancelling responsibility proves too much. There is no good thing whatever performed in this world, either natural or spiritual, apart from the enabling grace of God. If, then, nothing be the *duty* of men except that which the grace of God actually secures, then it is not the "duty" of sinners to do *anything* good whatsoever!

"Let the wicked forsake his way and the unrighteousness man his thoughts" (Isa. 55:7). *Can* the "wicked" and "unrighteousness" do so? Certainly not. Yet they are *commanded* to, nevertheless! "Repent ye, therefore, and be converted, that your sins may be blotted out" (Acts 3:19). *Could* they "repent" *before* their sins were "blotted out"? Could they, of themselves, "repent" at all? Assuredly not. Yet the apostle bade them do so! Thus Peter was a "duty-repentance" preacher!!

Fourth, the plea of inability to excuse non-responsibility is ruled out of court by Scripture itself. "Hear ye deaf; and look, ye blind, that ye may see" (Isa. 42:18). Here is further proof that God demands of men what they are *unable* to render Him. We may not understand it, but there it is! Let proud reasonings go to the winds; bow to the teaching of God's Word. God Himself calls upon the blind to look, and this, in order that they "may see." Again, God said, to the house of Israel, "Repent, and turn from all your transgressions; so iniquity shall not be your ruin. Cast away from you all your transgressions whereby ye have transgressed; and make you a new heart and new spirit" (Ezek. 18:30, 31). Without insisting upon the particular meaning of the terms in this passage, we simply ask the reader, Did those to whom it was first addressed have the power in themselves to obey? We answer, no; but their very inability was criminal. Let us try and simplify the point still further:

Here is an able-bodied man who has no relish and will for work: is that lack of desire excusable? Is his absence of will to work a valid reason for his doing nothing? Here is a wealthy miser who has no heart for the poor, no compassion for those in need; does this lack annull his responsibility to help them? Here is a man who has so given way to the tendency of speaking untruthfully, so become a slave to the habit of falsifying, that he is now such an inveterate liar he *cannot* speak truthfully. Does that excuse him? So, here is a sinner, so wedded to his lusts, so depraved in heart, so the willing slave of Satan, that he has no desire for Christ. But does that *excuse* him? Does his absence of heart for Christ cancel his responsibility to believe on, love, and serve Him? Most assuredly not.

Let us now summarize: The Gospel contains a Call and Command from God for all to whom it comes to obey it (Rom. 6:25, 26). Those who believe not the Gospel, those who obey not its call, shall be judged by the Gospel (Rom. 2:16). They shall be punished *because* they obeyed it not (John 3:18; 2 Thess. 1:8).

A final word: In view of his total inability *wherein* lies man's responsibility? A separate article is needed to properly answer this question. Suffice it now to say, the responsibility of every man is to cry from his heart to God: "That which Thou requirest of me, work in and through me." Our responsibility is to honestly confess to God our vile and voluntary inability—not to make an excuse of it, and shelter behind it. Our responsibility is to cry to Him for enablement. Since it be true that no man can come to Christ except the Father draw him, then it is the duty of every sinner to implore Him for Christ's sake *to* "draw" him. May God use to the glory of His name and the enlightenment of His people that in this article which is according to His Holy Word.

—*Arthur W. Pink.*

## ON GLORIFYING GOD.

*"My thoughts are not your thoughts"*—Isa. 55:8.

The estimate of God and of Christians generally on this subject are very different: God estimates our glorifying of Him by our *obedience;* Christians, almost universally, by *results*. The preachers of the Gospel, or ministers in churches, who have the greatest names and the most widely spread fame on account of the visible good which they have done in the conversion of souls or the edification of their congregations, may usually be selected as those whom believers generally consider as having in the greatest degree brought glory to their Master. Now, this criterion, specious as it is, and though it *may* perhaps in a few cases lead to results not utterly opposed to truth, is altogether unsound: since, firstly, it is arguing from the end to the means; and, secondly, it introduces int› the comparison the faulty element of man's ideas respecting what is good and what is evil, in effects of which he can necessarily see only the surface or exterior.

That the end does not justify the means, is a string of words in the mouth of almost everyone: yet the same persons will commonly be found upholding their system or their favourite preacher (their Paul or their Apollos) by such statements as, that they could not suppose that God would so bless the system of the man if there were anything in either *greatly* opposed to His will. The maxim, therefore, which they so readily admit, they contradict perhaps as often as they quote. On the other hand, it is in loving consideration for us, and from perfect knowledge of our infirmities, that our heavenly Father has marked out a path for us to walk in, and simply stated the *means* which we should use to glorify Him, without making it necessary for us in the least degree to exercise our own understanding, as we are so prone to do in deciding, first, what *results* are really according to the mind of God, and afterwards, what means or line of conduct is best calculated to bring about these *results*. If our duty were to be determined only by such circuitous reasoning, we could have little hope of distinguishing right from wrong; for if our corrupted judgment should chance now and then to view results as God views them, and thus correctly determine the first part of the process, it would be against all probabilities that we should correctly apply this discovery to the second. In this matter, therefore, as in all others, if we understood our responsibilities and our infirmities, we should cleave in conscious helplessness to the way which a Father's love and wisdom have pointed out. We should go directly to that which is revealed, to *His* estimate, and not our own; of the spirit, the acts, the conduct, by which we shall glorify Him; and we should praise Him that He has been pleased to disconnect our duty from consideration of results, since the latter are far beyond our comprehension and appreciation.

Should it appear to anyone that a trivial subject has been treated too gravely, I fear that the actual evil into which the children of God are led, both as concerns themselves personally and their influence on others, by leaving their own path of *obedience*, and entering on ground which God has reserved for Himself, is of the gravest character; and (if I have been led to see the mind of God in any degree on the subject) the effect of this error has been nothing less than the inversion of good and bad. A *result* which is *considered* good has been arrived at by means which the Word of God does not sanction, and it is set down as good from appearances; on the other hand, the will of God has been here and there faithfully observed, and, no *apparent* good having followed, it is too frequently forgotten that God has been glorified at all, not to say far more than in the preceding case. All this shows a walking as though sight instead of faith were our guide, and a forgetfulness that it will be only as an exception, and not as a rule, that true obedience will be followed by those visible effects which man would expect: were it otherwise, we might with propriety walk by sight here.

What shall we say if it should be found that such men as Chalmers, or Bickersteth, or others, who have been the means of blessing hundreds or perhaps thousands—who have been the instruments of converting souls and of building up the people of God—have in their mode of doing this left *more or less* the way of God's appointment, and set up one of their own; while in some neglected corner of their parishes, some poor unheard-of child of God, laid perhaps for years on a bed of sickness, and known only to two or three whom the ties of natural affection bring near him, has humbly and unswervingly, but with no apparent result, carried out his Master's will in every point in which he was permitted? Shall we say that the world, and with them the people of God, have judged rightly in the different estimates which they form of two such characters? Shall we say that because God has seen fit to make the one the means of much visible good, and to give no such results to the other, the first has greatly glorified Him, and the other less or not at all? Or shall we not rather say that, as *results* are God's, and only dutiful obedience to Him is ours, results (though God will always bring to pass such as *He* sees good) should necessarily enter in no way into our estimate, and that the despised pauper who did his Lord's will glorified Him far more than the gifted reacher who mixed up much of *man's* systems with an obedience which ought to have been unqualified.

To take another instance: if it be a transgression of the revealed will of God for Christians to join with the world (2 Cor. 6:14) in spiritual things (not to mention other objections), it at once, and necessarily, becomes possible—though consequences will be startling to the preconceived notions of most Christians—that the whole Bible Society, or any other society so constituted, is not so much glorifying God, as some solitary Christian, who from obedience to his Lord in the particular alluded to, or some other, can have no connection with them. It is not a matter of doubt with me how far the Lord Jesus Himself, were He in humiliation to revisit this world to-morrow, would be considered to glorify His Father by standing aloof from and testifying against much that man calls right. As He could not pass through a university course or be ordained, the majority of Christian denominations would call Him disorderly and schismatic, were He to be anything but a listener; and with other denominations He would, for other reasons, be equally out of place. This subject cannot be followed out: what has been said may show that it could not be mentioned now, as formerly as a criterion of good respecting any one, that his praise is in "all churches." Neither can the effects of these erroneous estimates be now adequately traced. I know from experience, and from intercourse with other Christians, that looking after results keeps numbers from the truth. If they simply *followed the Word of God,* and leaned not on their own understanding, the path of duty would be plain; but they begin at the wrong end, and either cannot see how God's plain Word can be carried out, or come to the conclusion that something else works as well or better, and that they have authority to make the change. Others, again, judge from effects on themselves; they countenance or attach themselves to this or that, not because it is their bounden duty as *obedient* children to do so, and to neglect doing so would be to *disobey* their Lord, but because they get much benefit to their souls by acting thus; or for some similar reason based on consideration of self and virtual disregard of the glory of God. If *duty* were the rule with such, it would lead them first to see that they are acting in obedience to God, and then to take care that they obtained the benefit which it was the will of God to give them. They would then find that any apparent profit, gained by departure in the least degree from their Father's appointment, was but a dangerous and unsatisfying substitute of the real profit (less showy perhaps and less esteemed by men) which can never be disconnected from obedience to His will. The mind of Him with whom we have to do has been revealed with a clearness which should have prevented error:—"Hath the Lord as great delight in burnt offerings and sacrifices as in obeying the voice of the Lord?" and He must be allowed to choose the mode in which He will be glorified, if we look for His approval at the end of our endeavours. The water of Abana and Pharpar, rivers of Damascus (2 Kings 5:12) may have been to all appearances similar to that of Jordan or even better, as Naaman concluded: yet the water of Jordan only could cleanse him from his leprosy; and the child of God, if he will walk obediently, will be called on to separate from and testify against a multitude of man's appointments, which may appear, perhaps, to be very near approaches to, or good substitutes for, His Father's ordinances.

Christian Testimony, 1863.

---

using me most in His service? Why this removal of a Sunday School teacher, just when he was most needed? Why was my husband called away, when the children most required him? Yes; such afflictions are indeed grievous to the flesh.

But let me add in conclusion, these reasonings are *only* "seeming." The Christian, by grace, triumphs eventually. Faith looks up at the cloud (though it is often very late in doing so) and says: The chastisement was not as severe as it might have been; certainly it was not as severe as I deserved; and truly it was nothing in comparison to what the Saviour suffered for me. O let faith expel carnal reason, and say, "For our light affliction, which is but for a moment, worketh for us a far more exceeding and eternal weight of glory." But note carefully that this is only *"while* we look not at the things which are seen, but at the things which are not seen!" (2 Cor. 4:18, 19)

The above is the substance of a sermon preached by the Editor, in which he acknowledges his indebtedness to one by C. H. Spurgeon on the same text.

drops to a low ebb. No, chastenings for the present do not *seem* to be joyous, but grievous; but that is because we view them through our natural senses and in the light of carnal reason.

2. *Carnal reason judges afflictions in the light of the PRESENT.* The tendency with all of us is to estimate things in the light of the *now*. The ungodly are ever ready to sacrifice their future interests for present gratification. One of their favourite mottos is, "A bird in the hand is worth two in the bush": it may be to the slothful, but the enterprising and diligent would rather be put to a little trouble and secure the two. Man is a very short-sighted creature, and even the Christian is often dominated by the same sentiments that regulate the wicked.

The light of the now is generally the worst in which to form a true estimate of things. We are too close to them to obtain a right perspective and view things in their proper proportions. To view an oil painting to the best advantage, we need to step back a few feet from it. The same principle applies to our lives. Proof of this is found as we now look back upon that which is past. To-day the Christian discovers a meaning, a needs-be, a preciousness in many a past experience, and even disappointment, which he could not discern at the time.

The case of Jacob is much to the point, and should guard us against following his foolish example. After Joseph had been removed from his doting father, and when he thought he had lost Simeon too, viewing things in the light of "the present," he petulently said, "All these things are against me" (Gen. 42:36). Such is often the mournful plaint which issues from our short-sighted unbelief. But later Jacob discovered his mistake, and found that all those things had been working together for good to himself and his loved ones. Alas, we are so impatient and impetuous, so occupied with the present; we fail to look forward and by faith anticipate the happy sequel. Then, too, the effects which afflictions have upon the old man, *disqualify* us to estimate them aright. If my heart is palpitating, if my mind is agitated, and my soul is cast down, then I am in no fit state to judge the quality and blessedness of Divine afflictions. No, chastenings *for the present* do *not* "seem to be joyous, but grievous"; but that is because we take such a short-sighted view of them and fail to look forward with the eyes of faith.

3. *To carnal reason afflictions never seem joyous.* This logically follows from what has been before as under the first two points. Because carnal reason sees *only* the "seeming" of things, and because it estimates them *only* in the light of "the present," afflictions are not joyous. Nor does God intend that, in themselves, they should be. If afflictions *did* "seem" to be joyous, would they be chastisements at all? It would be of little use for an earthly parent to whip his child in such a way as to produce only joy and smiles. Such would be only a make-belief. No smart, no benefit. Solomon said, "It is the blueness of the wound which maketh the heart better"; so if Divine chastisements are not painful to the flesh and extort a groan and cry, what good end would they serve? If God sent us trials such as *we* wished they would not be chastenings at all. No, afflictions do not "seem" to be joyous.

They are not joyous *in the form* they assume. When the Lord smites He does so in a tender place, that we may feel the smart of it. They are not joyous in the *force* of them. Oftentimes we are inclined to say, If the trial had not been quite so severe, or the disappointment had not been so great, I could have endured it. God puts just so much bitter herbs into our cup as to make the draught unpleasant. They are not joyous in the *time* of them. We always think they come at the wrong season. If it were left to our choosing, they would never come; but if we *must* have them, we would choose the time when they are the least grievous; and thus miss their blessing. Nor are they joyous in the *instruments* used. "If it were an enemy, then I could have borne it," said David. That is what we all think. O if my trial were not just *that!* Poverty I could endure, but not reproach and slander. To have lost my health would have been a hard blow, but I could have borne it; but that dear child, the light of my eyes, how can I ever rejoice again? Have you not heard brethren speak thus?

4. *To carnal reason afflictions ever seem to be grievous.* Probably the most grievous part to the true Christian is that he cannot *see* how such a loss or trial can possibly *benefit* him. If he could thus see, he *would* rejoice. Even here we must walk by faith and not by sight. But this is easier said than done; yea, it can only be done by God's enabling. Usually, the Christian altogether fails to see why such a trouble is sent upon *him*: it seems to work harm and not good. Why this financial loss, when I was giving more to the Lord's work? Why this breakdown in health, when He was

Continued on page 263

# STUDIES IN THE SCRIPTURES

VOL. VI.     DECEMBER, 1927     No. 12

"Search the Scriptures" John 5: 39

Copyright in all English speaking Countries.

Editor: Arthur W. Pink, 15 Hurlstone Avenue, Summer Hill, N.S.W., Australia.
Hon. Agent in U.S.A.: Mr. C. S. Pressel, 559 Dupont Avenue, York, Penna.

FREE TO ALL WHO WILL READ IT

"Bless the Lord, O my soul; and all that is within me, bless His holy name." Psa. 103:1.

As we take up our pencil to compose the closing Editorial for 1927 the words of a hymn come to mind, and suitably express the feeling of our heart:—

"When all Thy mercies, O my God,
My wondering soul surveys,
Transported with the view, I'm lost
In wonder, love, and praise."

This has been the best year that God has given us in connection with "Studies in the Scriptures," and once more we have had occasion to prove the verity of that promise, "Them that honour Me, I *will* honour" (1 Sam. 2:30). Toward the close of 1926 God showed that He would have us remove the subscription price from this Magazine, and act on the principle, "Freely ye have received, freely give" (Matt. 10:8), looking only to Him for the supply of all our need. By His grace we have been enabled to do this, nor has He disappointed our confidence in Him. Instead, He has given us "good measure, pressed down, and shaken together, and running over" (Luke 6:38).

Our circulation during 1927 has exceeded that of any previous year, and thus our expenses have increased, too. Moreover, we have been obliged to change printers, at a rise of over twenty per cent. per thousand copies. Yet, the Lord, in His faithfulness and grace, has so moved His stewards to have fellowship with us that, without any appeals, they have sent in such gifts, we have on hand a larger balance this year than in any preceding one—the whole of which is to be used, God willing, in the sending forth of more free literature.

During this year we have also received a greater number of letters, telling of help and blessing received, under God, from the reading of this Magazine. The Good Shepherd has given us the unspeakable privilege and joy of reaching an increasing number of His scattered and starved sheep, many of whom are quite cut off from Christian fellowship and oral ministry. A few extracts given below are samples of many scores which might be quoted:—

"I appreciate very highly your gift of the Studies. Of course, I will gladly read them," Nazareth, Palestine! "Please accept my best thanks for your valuable Magazine sent to me. I appreciate them very much," Salisbury, England. "I happen to get from a friend a sample copy of your monthly magazine, which on being read I found very interesting, as it contains wholesome matter which is not commonly found now-a-

Continued on page 288

## IMPORTANT NOTICES

Back numbers of each year of the magazine are yet obtainable at 5/- (1.25) per year. Bound at 7/6 (1.75) post paid. They will soon be out of print. Those in U.S.A. wanting them, please purchase from Mr. Pressel (see front cover page).

Advise promptly of change of address. This Magazine is published as a work of faith and labour of love. The Editor gladly gives his services. It is freely sent to all who will read it. No charge is made for it.

Christians who feel definitely led to do so, may have fellowship with us in this Ministry. Send only *Inter-National M.O.*

## CONTENTS.

| | |
|---|---|
| John's Gospel: Appendix | 266 |
| Gleanings in Exodus | 269 |
| Parables of Matt. 13 | 273 |
| The Churches of God | 277 |
| Divine Chastisement | 281 |
| Joy in Election | 284 |
| Cloven Tongues | 286 |

## JOHN'S GOSPEL.

### 72. Conclusion.

Our happy task is finished, and it is with a real sense of regret that we take up our pen to add an appendix. Before he commenced this commentary the author devoted ten years of special study to John's Gospel, having gone through it three times in the course of as many pastorates, and since then he has taught it in different Bible classes. For six years more we have laboured hard in preparing a chapter each month. Over forty commentaries and expositions have been read through and their interpretations of each verse carefully weighed, and the endeavour has been made to supplement our own searchings by culling from them what struck us as being most helpful.

Amid many labours and calls upon our time, our gracious God has enabled us to continue and complete this Exposition of John's Gospel, and it is with fervent thanksgiving to Him that we begin these concluding paragraphs. The instruction, the help and blessing which we have received personally, while preparing each chapter, has been a rich compensation for the time, prayer, and work we have put into them. Our own faith in the inerrancy and perfection of the Scriptures has been strengthened, and the conviction we had at the outset, that every verse contains a mine of spiritual wealth, has been confirmed again and again. That our production is very far from being perfect we are fully aware; but such as it is, we lay it before the Lord, and humbly entreat Him to use, own, and bless it to many of His dear people.

One of our aims in prosecuting this work has been to stimulate others to the personal *study* of the Word. The Bible is not only a book to be read devotionally, but it is also a mine of spiritual riches to be worked (Pro. 2:1-5), and the more diligently we seek after its hidden treasures, the greater will be our reward. God does not place a premium on laziness. His call is, "*Study* to show thyself approved unto God, a *workman* that needeth not to be ashamed, rightly dividing the Word of Truth" (2 Tim. 2:15). Alas! most of His people have never been taught *how* to study. In this work we have sought to suggest one method which we have personally found to be very beneficial—the *interrogative* method: asking the Bible questions, drawing up a list on each passage as a preliminary to its careful examination.

The point at which so many readers of the Bible fail the worst is that of *concentration*. Their energies are scattered too much. Suppose a man inherited a thousand acres of arable land, and that he found it impossible to hire labourers. It would be useless for him attempting to farm the whole piece. But if he fenced off, say, five acres, devoted himself to this small section, and went in for *intensive* farming, he would be far more likely to succeed. It is thus with the Bible. While every Christian ought to read three or four chapters daily, and thus go through it once each year; it is impossible to really *study* the whole of it within the brief span of a lifetime. In addition to extensive reading, there should be *intensive study*. Pray for guidance in your selection and then concentrate on a single book or chapter. If the Christian reader would spend fifteen minutes each day for a whole year on a single chapter—say, Exodus 12, Matt. 13, John 17, Rom. 8, or Eph. 1—he would, probably, be surprised at the fruitful results. The necessity and the importance of *concentration* and its invaluable returns are realised by but few.

If sixty-six Spirit-taught Bible expositors would each of them concentrate on one book in the Bible, devoting the whole of their special studies to it for ten years, at the end of that time (should the Lord not return before) the people of God at large would be enriched immeasurably. No one man is competent to write on *all* the books of Scripture; that is why the condensed commentaries on the Bible as a whole are so disappointing and comparatively worthless. Do not be too ambitious, dear friend. Aim at quality rather than quantity. One chapter thoroughly *studied* will yield more to your soul than a hundred chapters which are read but not studied.

Again, other students of Scripture fail through their lack of *perseverance*. Because a passage does not open up to them at the first or second examination of it, they become discouraged. God often tests our earnestness. It is not the dilatory, but the *diligent* soul that is made fat (Prov. 13:4). "Rest in the Lord, and *wait patiently* for Him" (Psa. 37:7) applies as much to Bible-study as it does to prayer. Regular, persistent stick-to-itiveness (to use a word of Spurgeon's) is what counts. Note how one of the marks of the good-ground hearers is that they "bring forth fruit *with patience*" (Luke 8:15). If at first you don't succeed, try, try again.

When Jehovah gave food to His people Israel in the wilderness, He did not furnish them with loaves ready made. Instead, He sent them manna as "a *small* round thing" (Ex. 16:14). Much time and labour were required to gather a sufficient quantity for a day's supply. After the gathering, it had to be "ground" and then "baked." This was a parable in action. It has a voice for us to-day. The way in which most of us learn is "precept upon precept, precept upon precept; line upon line, line upon line; here *a little*, and there *a little*" (Isa. 28:10). Be not disheartened, then, if you appear to get small returns from your Scriptural labours. No time spent in the prayerful study of the Word is ever really lost. To familiarise yourself with the letter of it counts for something, and later (if you keep at it) you *will* reap the benefit.

Oftentimes Christians are almost discouraged when the Spirit of God enables a well-instructed scribe to bring out of his treasures things new and old. They say, "*I* have read that passage again and again, but never saw such beauties in it as *he* has pointed out, or such wonders as he has brought forth." Ah, you may not realise that, probably, he has given that passage special study for years past, that he has prayed over it scores of times, that he examined it again and again and saw no more in it than you did till, ultimately, God rewarded his patience, and now he rejoices as one that "findeth great spoil" (Psa. 119:162).

But something more is needed than concentration and perseverance. We may focalise our attention, be very diligent and patient, but unless the Holy Spirit illumines our understanding, the wonders and beauties of the Word will remain hidden from us. The Bible is addressed not so much to the intellect as it is to the heart. *Prayer* is an essential prerequisite. Before we open the Bible we need, every time, to get down on our knees and humbly beseech God, for Christ's sake, to "open Thou mine eyes that I may behold wondrous things out of Thy law" (Psa. 119:18). Mysteries of grace which are hidden from the wise and prudent are revealed to "babes," i.e., the simple, humble, dependent ones. It is written, "The meek will He guide in judgment: and the *meek* will He teach His way" (Psa. 25:9). Have no confidence in your own powers; remember that "a man can receive nothing, except it be given him from heaven" (John 3:27). Yet God is ever ready *to* give to those who ask in faith.

When the chapter for your *study* has been selected, begin by asking, What is there here *for my own soul?*—what warnings, what encouragements, what exhortations, what promises? Examine it first of all from the *practical standpoint*, with a view to your own personal needs. Ask God to make the passage speak unto your own soul, and to grant you the hearing ear. Next, and closely related to the former, in fact seeking God's answer to your first question, ask, What is there here *about Christ?* What is there that I can learn about Him, what example has He here left me, what perfections of His are portrayed, what typical picture of Him can I discover? From this, pass on to its *evangelical* message, its gospel bearing. Ask, What does this chapter teach me about sin, about the depravity of man, about the grace of God, about the way of salvation, about the blessedness of the redeemed? Every chapter in the Bible leads, ultimately, to Calvary. Then you may ponder its *doctrinal* bearings, its theological instruction. This will require you to look up marginal references from parallel passages. Ask, What is there here about the sovereignty of God, or the responsibility of man? What of the important truths of justification, sanctification, propitiation, preservation, glorification? This will require you to note the setting of the chapter which you are studying—its relation to those which precede and which follow; its bearing on the other chapters in the Epistle.

Finally, study its *dispensational* teachings and *prophetic* intimations.

These are but hints, yet if heeded, Bible-study will cease to be an irksome duty and become a profitable delight. It is from these angles that the writer has endeavoured to examine each chapter in the Gospel of John, and these are the methods which, under God, he has found yield the best results. In addition to the general principles of study named above, we have also sought to give attention to some of the laws which regulate the interpretation of the Scriptures. God is a God of order, and the God of creation and the God of written revelation are one and the same. Just as we may discern "laws of Nature," so are there "laws of the Bible." Some of these have been pointed out during the course of our exposition: the laws of first mention, of progressive unfolding, of comparison and contrast, of parallelism, of numerics, etc.

In connection with the spiritual arithmetic of the Bible we have been deeply impressed with the constantly recurring *seven* in the Gospel of John, and it is surely not without significance that there are twenty-one chapters or 3x7, in it. It is true that the chapter divisions are of human origin, and that man does nothing perfect, yet we believe that in the providence of Him who has "magnified His Word above all His name" (Psa. 138:1, 2), that He has not only superintended the placing of the different books in the Canon of Scripture, but has also guided, or at least over-ruled, many or most of its chapter divisions. Obviously is this so, we are fully assured, in connection with the Gospels.

Matthew has twenty-eight chapters, 7x4. Now, four is the number of the earth and seven of perfection. How appropriate that the Gospel which most directly concerns God's earthly people and the earthly kingdom of Christ, *should be* thus divided; for no perfection on earth will be witnessed until the Son of Man returns and sets up His throne upon it. Mark has sixteen chapters, 2x8. Two is the number of witness and eight of a new beginning. Most suitably are those numbers here, for in this second Gospel Christ is portrayed as the faithful and true Witness, the perfect Servant of God, laying the foundations of the new creation. Luke has twenty-four chapters, 6x4, or 2x12. Whichever way we divide the twenty-four, the result is in striking accord with the subject of this third Gospel. In Luke Christ is presented as the Son of man, the last Adam. Thus 6x4 would speak of *man* connected with the *earth;* or, 12x2 would tell of that *perfect government* which awaits the return to this earth of the "second Man" (1 Cor. 15:47). John has twenty-one chapters, 7x3. How striking this is! For seven speaks of *perfection* and three is the number of *Deity.* Thus, the very number of chapters in this fourth Gospel intimates that here we have revealed *the perfections of God!* These are what have occupied us as we have gone through it chapter by chapter.

Everything in Scripture, down to the minutest detail, has a profound significance. Of course it has, for its Author is Divine. The same God who has expended so much care over the formation and adaptation of every member of our physical bodies—e.g., the eye or the hand—has not devoted less to that Word which is to endure forever. In the Bible God has written a Book *worthy of Himself.* If this fact be firmly grasped, the devout student will *expect* to find in every passage depths, wonders, beauties, such as only the Allwise could produce. But let it not be forgotten that the Inspirer of Holy Writ alone can interpret it to us.

To the reader who has, under God, been helped and blest by this Exposition, we would say, Do everything in your power to make this work known to others. You owe it to your fellow-Christians so to do. Why should not many of them be instructed and gladdened, too? These books are not published as a commercial venture. The demand for this class of literature is tragically small. It takes from three to five years to sell sufficient for the publisher to get back the bare costs of printing and binding. Nor is advertising of much avail. It is the *personal* word that counts. If you can do so conscientiously, earnestly recommend these volumes both by word of mouth and by letters, to your Christian friends, to your Pastor, to Sunday School teachers and other Christian workers. Bear them in mind when making a present to a friend. Another good way of interesting others is to *loan* your own copies, thus others may be induced to purchase for themselves.

And now, dear reader, my work in composing this commentary and yours in going through it (the first time, at least) is now finished; but there remains *the improvement* which ought to be made of it, and *the account* which must yet be given to God, for He "requireth that which is past" (Ecc. 3:15). It is by attending to the former that we shall be prepared for the latter. I have not written for the sake of providing mere religious entertainment, and we trust that you have read with some higher motive than simply to fill in a few spare hours. Unless each of our hearts has been drawn out in warmer love, deeper devotion, and purer worship unto Him whose manifold glories give lustre to every page of Holy Writ; unless the result of our studies of John's Gospel leads both writer and reader to clearer visions of and more whole-hearted obedience unto the Word made flesh, our labours have been in vain.

*Arthur W. Pink.*

## GLEANINGS IN EXODUS.

*48. Aaron's Garments: Ex. 28.*

In the preceding article we pointed out how that the interpretation and application of the typical teachings found in the Pentateuch concerning Israel's priesthood calls for heavenly wisdom and guidance. In the light of the Epistle to the Hebrews it is clear that there are many points of contrast as well as comparison. But that which it is most important to see is, that when commenting there, on the types of Exodus and Leviticus, the Holy Spirit has expressly declared that the entire ritual of the Tabernacle was "a figure for the time then present" (Heb. 9:9), that it was "a shadow of good things to come, and *not* the very image of the things" (10:1). They were not given to Israel as a model for Christians to imitate, but as a foreshadowing of spiritual things which find their fulfilment in Christ Himself. The holy places made with hands were "figures of the true," that is of "Heaven itself" (Heb. 9:24). A true apprehension of this is our only safeguard against the sacerdotalism and ritualism which the flesh so much delights in. After the advent, death, resurrection, and ascension of Christ, the shadows must vanish before the substance. As one has well said, "To imitate a revival of that which God Himself has set aside by a fulfilment perfect and glorious, is audacious, and full of peril to the souls of men. It is not even the shadow of a substance; but the unauthorised shadow of a departed shade." It is failure to observe this which has wrought such confusion and havoc in Christendom, resulting in the denial of that which lies at the very foundation of Christianity.

Under the Mosaic economy, the priests were a special class appointed to minister unto God on behalf of the people. They enjoyed privileges which were not shared by others. Theirs was a nearness to Jehovah peculiar to themselves. They were vested with an authority and were permitted to do that which was not given to those whom they represented. But at the Cross a radical change was brought about. The old order ended, and a new one was inaugurated. Judaism ceased, and Christianity was introduced. Two symbolic actions gave plain intimation of this. First, in Matt. 26:65 we are told, "the high priest rent his clothes," which was expressly forbidden by the law, see Lev. 21:10. God permitted this to show that Israel's priesthood was ended—clothes are only torn to pieces when there is no further use for them. Second, the rending of the vail (Matt. 27:51): the barrier into God's presence no longer existed for His people.

In Heb. 5 and 7 the Holy Spirit has carefully called attention to a number of contrasts between the priesthood of Aaron and that of Christ. One of the things which qualified Israel's high priest to officiate in that office was that he could have compassion on them that were ignorant or out of the way, because he himself was compassed with infirmity (5:2); but the Christian's High Priest is "Holy, harmless, undefiled, separate from sinners" (7:26). Again, in Heb. 5:3 it is pointed out that Israel's high priest needed to offer sacrifice for his own sins: but Christ was "the Holy One of God," and "knew no sin." Again, the priests of the house of Levi were made "without an oath" (7:21), and in consequence, some of them were cut off from the priesthood, as in the case of Nadab and Abihu, and Eli's line; but Christ was made Priest with an oath, "by Him that said unto Him, The Lord swear and will not repent, Thou art a priest forever after the order of Melchizedek" (7:21). Finally, Aaron was made a priest after the law of a carnal commandment (i.e., that which pertained to mortality), but Christ "after the power of an endless life" (7:16).

In view of these differences, and of the exalted superiority of Christ's priesthood over the Aaronic, we are told, "for the priesthood being changed, there is made of necessity a change also of the law" (Heb. 7:12); that is, in its narrower sense, a "change" in the law pertaining to the priesthood; in its wider sense, a "change" concerning the ceremonial law. It is important to note that no part of the ceremonial law was given to Israel till *after* the priesthood was established. Thus, this "change of the law" signified a change of dispensation and everything that pertained to the priesthood.

Now, it is this "change" in the law pertaining to priesthood which the Papacy, and all who are infected by its sacerdotal spirit, sets aside. Romanism is largely a revival of Judaism, plus the corruptions of Paganism. It is a deliberate and pernicious repudiation of what is distinctive in Christianity. It is a wicked denial of the perpetual efficacy of the one offering of the Lord Jesus. Rome perpetuates the Levitical order, claiming that her priests, like Aaron and his sons, are specially authorised and qualified to go to God on behalf of their fellow-men. But 1 Peter 2:5, 9 affirms that *all* believers are now "priests," and that *all* of God's people alike enjoy liberty of access into the Holiest (Heb. 10:19, 22). As another has truly said, "The feeblest member of the household of faith is as much a priest as the apostle Peter himself. He is a spiritual priest—he worships in a spiritual temple, he stands at a spiritual altar, he offers a spiritual sacrifice, he is clad in spiritual vestments." That spiritual temple is Heaven itself, which he enters in spirit through the rent vail; that spiritual altar (Heb. 13:10) is Christ Himself—the altar which "sanctifieth the gift" (Matt. 23:19); that spiritual sacrifice is praise unto God (Heb. 13:15).

Coming now to the robes of Israel's high priest we would call attention once more to the *order* of Jehovah's instructions to Moses. In Ex. 29 we have an account of the *consecration* of Aaron and his sons to their holy office. But before this is given, in Ex. 28, a description is furnished of the various *garments* they were to wear. First, the vestments of the high priest are detailed, and then those of Aaron's sons. The anointed eye may easily discern the propriety of and the reason for this. Typically, the garments foreshadowed the manifold glories of Christ, the great High Priest, which glories and perfections manifested His fitness for that office. The holy garments of Aaron were "for glory and beauty": they gave dignity to his person, being suitable apparel for his position. In figure they pointed to Christ in all His perfections with the Father *before* He was "consecrated" to His work for us.

"And thou shalt make holy garments for Aaron thy brother for glory and for beauty" (v. 2). With this should be compared Lev. 16:4, "He shall put on the holy linen coat, and he shall have the linen breeches upon his flesh, and shall be girded with a linen girdle, and with the linen mitre shall he be attired: these are holy garments." There were two sets of clothing provided for Israel's high priest: the one mentioned in Lev. 16 was what he wore on the annual Day of Atonement. Then he was robed only in spotless white, foreshadowing the personal righteousness and holiness of the Lord Jesus, which fitted Him to undertake the stupendous work of putting away the sins of His people.

It is worthy of note that the garments of Aaron which were "for glory and for beauty" were just *seven* in number. "And these are the garments which they shall make: a breastplate, and an ephod, and a robe, and a broidered coat, a mitre, and a girdle: and they shall make holy garments for Aaron thy brother, and his sons, that he may minister unto Me in the priest's office" (28:4). In addition to the six articles mentioned here, is the "plate of pure gold" on which was engraved the words "Holiness to the Lord" (v. 36). This, as Lev. 8:9 tells us, was "the holy crown." Observe that in the enumeration given in 28:4 the "breastplate" comes before the others, but in the details which follow the order is changed: there it is the ephod, the girdle, the two stones, set upon the shoulders of the ephod, and then the breastplate. The "breastplate" was the chief and most costly of the vestments, the other garments being, as it were, a foundation and background for it—this central article pointing to the very *heart* of Christ Himself.

"And they shall make the ephod of gold, of blue, and of purple, of scarlet, and fine twined linen, with cunning work. It shall have the two shoulder-pieces thereof joined at the two edges thereof; and so it shall be joined together" (vv. 6, 7). The "ephod" is the first garment described in detail. This was the outer robe of the high priest. It was made of two parts, one covering his back and the other his front; these being joined together at the shoulders by golden clasps, which formed the setting for the onyx stones. The ephod served to support the breastplate. The materials of which it was made were "gold," and "fine twined linen"—the blue, purple, and scarlet being emblasoned upon the latter. The mode by which the gold was interlaced with the linen is described in Ex. 39:3: "And they did beat the gold into thin plates, and cut it into wires, to work it in the blue," etc. Thus the strength and sheen of the gold was intimately blended with every part of the ephod, giving firmness as well as brilliancy to the whole fabric.

The spotless linen spoke of the holy humanity of Christ; the gold, of His divine glory; the colours, of the varied perfections of His character. "Christ acts for us as Priest in all that He is as Divine and human, the God-man. The whole value of His person enters into the exercise of His office. . . . The apostle combines these two things in the Epistle to the Hebrews: 'Seeing then that we have a Great High Priest, that is passed into the heavens, Jesus, the Son of God.' He is Jesus, and He is the Son of God. It is this most precious truth that is displayed in type in the materials of the ephod. How it enlarges our conceptions of the value of His work for us as Priest to remember what He is in Himself, and that we are thus upheld in His intercession by all that He is as Jesus, and as the Son of God" (Mr. E. Dennett).

"And the curious girdle of the ephod, which is upon it, shall be of the same, according to the work thereof: gold, blue, and purple, and scarlet, and fine twined linen" (v. 8). In v. 39 we learn that this girdle was made of "needlework." The "girdle" speaks of preparedness for *service*. Beautifully is this brought out in Luke 12:37: "Blessed are those servants, whom the Lord, when He cometh, shall find watching: verily I say unto you, that He shall *gird Himself*, and make them sit down to meat, and will come forth and *serve* them." In the days of His flesh "He took a towel and girded Himself, and then He washed the disciple's feet" (John 13). To-day He stands in the midst of His churches, girt about the breasts with a golden girdle (Rev. 1:13), ready to serve His people on earth. In the millennium it will be said, "And righteousness shall be the girdle of His loins, and faithfulness the girdle of His reins" (Isa. 11:5).

It is most blessed to note that in Jehovah's instructions to Moses He said, "It shall be of the same, according to the work thereof." The girdle of the high priest was of the same materials and beautified with the same lovely colours as the ephod itself. How this tells us that the present gracious activities of Christ's priestly service on our behalf are according to the perfections of His own person and character as the God-man! Though glorified, He is a Servant still, He is gone into heaven to appear in the presence of God for us (Heb. 9:24), and there He "ever liveth to make intercession for us" (Heb. 7:25).

We come next to the two onyx stones—read carefully Ex. 28:9-13. Scholars tell us that the Hebrew word translated "onyx" is derived from an unused root, signifying "to shine with the lustre of fire." They were very different from the "onyx" of modern times, which is neither a costly nor brilliant stone. Job 28:16 speaks of "the *precious* onyx!" Upon these stones were engraved the names of the children of Israel. They were enclosed in "ouches," or, as the Hebrew word denotes, "settings." These, in turn, were secured by "two chains of pure gold" (v. 14), and securely fastened to the shoulders of the ephod. They were borne before the Lord by Aaron "for a memorial." In its typical application to the saints to-day, this tells of their perfect *security*. The "shoulder" (cf. Luke 15:5) is the place of *strength* (Isa. 9:6), and tells us that the omnipotence of Christ is engaged on the behalf of His people. It is not our strength, but His—"Kept by the power of God" (1 Peter 1:5). It is not our perseverance, but His—"*He* is able to keep that which I have committed unto Him" (2 Tim. 1:12). "The shoulder which sustains the universe (Heb. 1:3), upholds the feeblest and most obscure member of the blood-bought congregation" (C.H.M.). The *order* in which the names of Israel's tribes were engraved upon the two shoulder-stones was "according to their *birth*": spiritually this signifies their equality, for as born of God, all the saints have the same nature, the same moral features, the same acceptance to Christ.

Next comes the "breastplate," which we pass by now; as we purpose devoting a separate article to its consideration.

"And thou shalt make the robe of the ephod all of blue. And there shall be an hole in the top of it, in the midst thereof; it shall have a binding of woven work round about the hole of it, as it were the hole of an habergeon, that it be not rent" (vv. 31:32). This robe was worn over the fine linen coat, but underneath the ephod. It was a long loose garment, of woven work, complete in one piece, with openings for head and arms. This is the first time that the word "robe" is found in Scripture. How striking that the "robe" is never seen until the high priest comes before us! The various connections in which this word is found in later passages indicates that this robe of the ephod was a garment of dignity, one of office, one which gave priestly character to Aaron—see 1 Sam. 24:4, 1 Chron. 15:27. Job 29:14, Ezek. 26:16. This robe embodied the colour of the heavens; it was all of blue. It portrayed the heavenly character of our great High Priest, and also pointed to the place where He is now ministering on our behalf. This is most important, for it defines the essential nature of Christianity as contradistinguished from Judaism. The whole system takes its character from the Priest. Because Christ is a *heavenly* Priest, His people are partakers of a heavenly calling (Heb. 3:1), their citizenship is in heaven (Phil. 3:20), their inheritance is there (1 Peter 1). Being worn beneath the ephod itself, this "robe" announces that the official character of Christ is sustained by what He is personally as the Heavenly One (1 Cor. 15:47).

Upon the hem of this "robe of the ephod" were coloured tassels in the form of "pomegranetes," and between each of these was a "golden bell," vv. 33:34. Pomegranate is a fruit, whose seeds float in a crimson liquid; the bell, with its tongue, tells of musical speech. Every step that Aaron took as he went about his sacred duties would cause the golden bells to sound and the variegated pomegranates to be seen. So the activities of our great High Priest cause His voice to be heard in intercession within the heavenly sanctuary, and this results in His fruit being seen through "bringing many sons unto glory" and by the graces which adorn their lives.

The words "his sound shall be heard when he goeth into the holy place before the Lord, and when he cometh out" (v. 35) has a dispensational significance. It was at His ascension that our great High Priest passed into the heavenly sanctuary, and consequent upon this, on the day of Pentecost, His "sound" was heard in the testimony to Himself which was borne by the apostles as the result of the Holy Spirit being poured out from on high. The "fruit" was seen in the multitude that was then saved. Even more glorious will be His sound and fruit when "he cometh out" again, and returns to this earth and redeems His people Israel. The linking of the two together may be seen by a reference to Acts 2:16, 17, where we find Peter quoting from the prophecy of Joel—a prophecy which is to receive its fulfilment in the Millennium: but a sample of which was given on the day of Pentecost.

We next have the "plate of pure gold," upon which was engraved "holiness to the Lord." This was attached to a background of "blue lace" and fastened upon the forefront of the mitre (vv. 36, 37). "The inscription, 'Holiness to the Lord,' signified that the high priest was devoted to, dedicated exclusively to, Jehovah; the golden plate upon which it was engraved sets forth that He who is the One thus truly dedicated to God, 'holy, harmless, undefiled and separate from sinners,' is Divine, the very Son of God; the blue lace upon which it was placed, His heavenliness of character. Thus conspicuous upon Aaron's forehead, it gave its meaning to the whole of his garments and of his office—he was sacred to the Lord, and, as such, interceded for Israel, representing them, and in himself hallowing the gifts of the people" (Mr. C. H. Bright).

"And it shall be upon Aaron's forehead, that Aaron may bear the iniquity of the holy things, which the children of Israel shall hallow in all their holy gifts" (v. 38). "This is the gracious provision which God has made for the imperfections and defilements of our services and worship. He can only accept that which is suited to His own nature. Everything offered to Him, therefore, must be stamped with holiness. This being so, notwithstanding that *we* are cleansed and brought into relation with Him, and have a title to approach, our *offerings* never could be accepted. But He has met our need. Christ, as Priest, bears the iniquity of our holy things; and He is holiness to the Lord, so that our worship, as presented through Him, is acceptable to God. Blessed consolation, for without this provision we were shut out from God's presence! Hence the apostle speaks not only of the blood and the rent veil, but also of the High Priest over the house of God (Heb. 10)." (Mr. E. Dennett)—cf. Rev. 8:3!

Beautiful are the closing words of v. 38: "And it shall be always upon *his* forehead, that *they* may be accepted before the Lord." This golden-plate was the symbol of the essential holiness of the Lord Jesus. The saints are represented by Him and accepted in Him. Because of their legal and vital union with Him, His holiness is theirs. O Christian reader, look away from yourself, with your ten thousand failures, and fix your eye on that golden plate. Behold in the perfections of your great High Priest the measure of thine eternal acceptance with God. Christ is our sanctification as well as our righteousness!

"And thou shalt embroider the coat of fine linen" (v. 39). Apparently the word "embroider" here is explained by what we are told in 39:27: "They made coats of fine linen of *woven* work for Aaron and his sons." This fine linen "coat" was the inner garment, and was supplemented with linen "breeches" or pants (v. 42). These may be called the high priest's *personal* raiment, even as the more beautiful external garments were his *official* vestments. As we have shown previously, "fine linen" was the emblem of purity. There is a verse in the Psalms which confirms this: "Let thy priests be clothed with *righteousness*" (132:9). Typically, these undergarments spoke of the personal righteousness of Christ, over which (so to speak) all His other perfections and glories were displayed. It reminds us of that blessed word in 1 John 2:1, "If any one sin, we have an Advocate with the Father, Jesus Christ *the Righteous*."

"And thou shalt make the mitre of fine linen" (v. 39). This was the head-dress of Aaron, and distinguished him from the ordinary priests, who wore "bonnets" (v. 40). The Hebrew word is derived from a verb which means "to roll, or wind around." This may denote that the high priest's mitre was wound around his head, like a tiara. In 1 Cor. 11:3-10, where we have Divine instruction for the covering of the women's heads in the assembly of the saints, we learn that this symbolises *subjection*. Thus the head-dress of the high priest intimated his subordination to God, his obedience to God's commands and submission to His will. The fine linen of which it was made, tells of the personal righteousness which must be found in the one who stands in the presence of God on behalf of others.

It is most solemn to discover that the only other time "mitznepheth" occurs in Scripture is in Ezek. 21:25, 27, where the Antichrist is in view. There the Hebrew word is translated "diadem," but should have been rendered "mitre" as in Ex. 28. This remarkable prophecy shows that the Man of Sin, who is yet to be revealed, will not only wear the crown of royalty, but will also assume the high priest's mitre. He will not only be the supreme civil head, but the ecclesiastical pontiff as well. This "profane and wicked prince of Israel" will arrogantly and blasphemously wield both regal and priestly power, in Satanic parody of the true Priest and King, the Lord Jesus. This age will close with Satan's son ruling over men, both in the political and religious worlds. Because men have received not the love of the truth that they might be saved, God shall send them strong delusion that they should believe the Lie (2 Thess. 2:3-12).

How profoundly thankful should each Christian reader be for that wondrous grace which has enabled him to flee from the wrath to come and to lay hold of eternal life! What praise is due to God for the great High Priest which His mercy has provided for His feeble and failing people: a Priest who is fully qualified, through His personal perfections, not only to supply our every need, but also to meet every requirement of a holy and righteous God! The last four verses of Ex. 28 will be considered, D.V., when we take up the Consecration of the Priests.

*Arthur W. Pink.*

## THE PROPHETIC PARABLES OF MATTHEW 13.

### 4. *The Parable of the Tares.*

This parable forms the second of the series, and its substance corresponds with the meaning of this numeral. One is the number of *unity*, for it stands alone, excluding all difference. But with two there *is* a difference, another. This other may be either for good or evil. In its evil sense two stands for difference, contrast, and so, enmity. Two is the first number which may be divided, and hence it stands for division, conflict. If we refer back to the opening chapter of Scripture we find that it was on the *second* day's work that God "divided the light from the darkness, and the waters under the firmament from the waters above it." The second in any number of things generally has evil and enmity stamped upon it. Take the second statement in the Bible: the first one is "in the beginning God created the heavens and the earth," but the second statement tells us "and the earth became without form and void." Thus it is with the seven parables in Matt. 13: the first one describes the work of Christ; the second the work of Satan!

The parable of the Tares supplies an explanation of Christendom as it has existed all through these nineteen centuries, and as it is to-day: a *mixed* state of affairs; the true and the false side by side; Rome and her daughters masquerading under the guise of Christianity. The "field" represents the religious world, in which the wheat and the tares "grow *together*." This mixed state of affairs has resulted from the work of the Enemy at the beginning of this dispensation, the effects of which are with us till this day.

This parable, like the former, also supplies a most conclusive refutation of the unscriptural dreams of post-millennarians. They believe that, through the preaching of the Gospel (under the blessing of God), the cause of Christ will extend, until the whole earth is filled with the knowledge of the glory of the Lord as the waters cover the sea. But Christ here explicitly declared that the wheat and the tares should "grow together *until the harvest*," which He defined as 'the end of the age." He gave no hint that the "tares" would gradually die out, or that they would decrease in numbers; but announced that, at the end, they would be found in such quantity as to need binding "in bundles."

The *connection between* this parable and the former one is most marked. The Sower of the good seed is the same, "the Son of Man"; the "field" is the same, "the world" (v. 38), i.e., the religious world. But there is one thing said about the "seed" here which is very striking. In v. 19 it is called "the *word* of the kingdom," while in v. 38 we read "the good seed are the *children* of the kingdom." Like produces like: the word of the kingdom produces sons of the kingdom: the fruit is according to the Seed!

The prominent thing in this second parable of the series is the Enemy and his work. Let us consider:

*1. The Time when he worked.*

This was "while men slept" (v. 25); that is, at *night-time*. In other words, it was under cover of the *darkness* that the Devil sowed his tares! This is characteristic of Satan, for he hates the light: secrecy, stealth, dishonesty, are his favourite tactics. But mark you, the Sower Himself did not sleep: He slumbers not, neither is weary. Nor does Satan. He is ever on the alert, going about, "seeking whom he may devour." He is the personification of perpetual motion.

"While men slept." The reference is to the unwatchful condition which soon developed among the Lord's people. The presence of the "tares" among the wheat was evidenced at a very early date. To the Thessalonians the apostle declared, "The mystery of iniquity doth *already* work" (2 Thess. 2:18). John had to say, "Ye have heard that Antichrist shall come, *even now* are there many antichrists" (1 John 2:18). Jude wrote, "There are certain men crept in unawares, who were before of old ordained to this condemnation, ungodly men, turning the grace of our God into lasciviousness" (v. 4). To the church at Pergamos Christ said, "I have a few things against thee, because thou hast there them that hold the doctrine of Balaam. . . . so hast thou also them that hold the doctrine of the Nicolaians which thing I hate" (Rev. 2:14, 15).

*2. The Method he employed.*

First, we are told that the Son of Man sowed good seed in His field (vv. 24, 37). Then we are informed that the Devil turned farmer (v. 25). Satan is no originating genius, but is ever an imitator. He produces counterfeits of the works of God. It is important for Christians to know this, so that they may be on their guard. If we study Scripture we shall not be ignorant of his devices (2 Cor. 2:11). It is to be carefully noted that as the Enemy mimicked Christ he sowed neither thorns nor thistles—had he done so his work had been easily detected, and there had been no difficulty in distinguishing the false from the true. No, he sowed "tares," or better, "darnel." This is a degenerate wheat, and so closely resembles the genuine article that the one cannot be distinguished from the other until harvest-time. That the "servants of the householder" recognised the tares as soon as they sprang up does not conflict with our last statement, for it is the *apostles* who are here in view, and *they* were specially endowed with the Holy Spirit, and so had a greater measure of discernment than any since.

These "tares" are spurious Christians. When the "servants" first discovered what the enemy had done, they wanted to root out the tares (v. 28). But the Master forbade them, saying, "Nay; lest while ye gather up the tares, ye root up also the wheat with them" (v. 29). It is only when they are both *fully ripe* that the farmer can with safety separate them, for it is not till then that it is seen there is *no grain* in the ears of the tares. Until the harvest-time the tares present a fair picture to the eye. As these imitation blades, green and nourishing, grow side by side with the real wheat, there is every prospect of a bountiful yield. But appearances are deceptive, and much of the product will prove only a disappointment and mockery to those who have spent so much time and labour on their cultivation. All is not gold that glitters. At the Harvest-time there is going to be a great disillusionment. *Then* will it appear that Christ's flock *is* a "little" one!

This parable, then, gives a remarkable expose of the *methods* employed by Satan. He seeks to destroy God's testimony on earth by introducing a spurious Christianity, a clever imitation of the real thing. And this parable reveals that he works from within: he sowed the "tares" *among* the wheat! ¶Satan has an *imitation Gospel*. This is clearly implied in the solemn warning given in Gal. 1:7-9. It is more plainly intimated in 2 Cor. 11, where we are told of "false apostles, deceitful workers, transforming themselves into the apostles of Christ. And no marvel; for Satan himself is transformed into an angel of light. Therefore, it is no great thing if *his ministers* also be transformed as the ministers *of righteousness*" (vv. 13-15). The principal agents of Satan are to be found not in the drinking-houses or race-courses, etc., but in our seminaries and in the pulpits! These are not advocating lawlessness, but are preaching "righteousness": but "being ignorant of *God's* righteousness," they are "going about to establish *their own* righteousness" (Rom. 10:3). It is a mingling of Law and Gospel, and multitudes are deceived thereby.

Satan makes *an imitation Church*. Christ is now building His Church, a Church which will include all the saved of this present dispensation, and none who are not members thereof will be saved. The Devil has caricatured this also. Romanism professes itself to be the "spouse of Christ," and her ministers insist that there is no salvation to be found outside of their pale. They profess the name of Christ, and hold some of the great fundamentals of His teaching. But artfully mingled with these are the deadly errors of Paganism. But so clever is the imitation, so subtly are the Scriptures appealed to in support of their pretensions, that millions are deluded by this soul-destroying system. "There is a way that seemeth right unto a man, but the end thereof are the ways of death" (Pro. 14:12).

Satan will yet be permitted to bring forth *an imitation Christ*. This will be his masterpiece. Much is said in Scripture concerning him. He is the great *antichrist*. He will have power to work miracles; he will at first claim to be the true Christ come back to earth. Multitudes will be deceived by him so that all the world will wander after him (Rev. 13:4). Yes, the Devil sows "tares," imitation wheat—*not* thorns and thistles.

*3. The Enemy's Success.*

It is to be observed that in *this* parable we do not read of any opposition or hindrances to the growth of the tares, like we did in the first parable concerning the wheat. No mention is made here of any soil *un*-congenial to the Devil's seed. There is no "wayside" ground, too hard for them to penetrate. There are no "thorns" to choke them, for they will thrive anywhere. There is no mention made of "fowls of the air" coming to catch them away. All external conditions and circumstances are favourable to the growth of *this* seed. No cultivation is needed; they will thrive anywhere.

The enemy's success is plainly intimated by the *prominence* given to the "tares" in this parable. This comes out very clearly and most solemnly in v. 36. When Jesus had sent the multitude away, and had gone into the house with His disciples, they said, "Declare unto us the parable *of the tares* of the field," not "the parable of the good Seed *and* the tares" (see vv. 24, 25). It is the tares and not the wheat which predominate and occupy the larger portion of the field. The mention of *"bundles"* in v. 30 bears out the same thought.

The Owner of the field *forbade* any interference with the tares. This is a point which has perplexed many. *Why* did the Lord permit the Enemy to sow his "tares?" And why has He permitted them, *for so long*, to occupy the principal part of the field? In other words, *Why* has God allowed the Devil such long-continued freedom? This is not so difficult to answer as many may suppose. They overlook the fact that the leaders of this world rejected its rightful Sovereign: that the Jews preferred Barabbas. Having chosen a murderer in preference to the Lord of Life, both Jews and Gentiles have *reaped what they sowed*. The Devil "was a murderer from the beginning" (John 8:14), and having refused the Saviour, this great soul-destroyer has ruled over them ever since!

The *time* for this is said to be "the end of the world" (v. 39). There is no difficulty in this expression if we bear in mind that there is a world of time, as well as a world of matter. But if we understand it to signify the "end of the earth" or "world-system," then it is manifestly erroneous. Personally, we much prefer the marginal rendering of the R.V.—"consummation of the age." The Greek word is *not* "kosmos," as in John 1:10, but "aion." To show that we are not altering the translation in order to suit our own views, turn to Heb. 9:26: "But now once in the *end of the world* hath He appeared to put away sin by the sacrifice of Himself." What can be made of that? If by "world" be understood the earth, or the world-system, then it is a manifest absurdity, for *that* certainly did not "end" at the crucifixion of Christ. But if "aion" be rendered "*age*," there is no difficulty. Thus Matt. 13:39 should read, "The harvest is the end of the age"; there is another Age to follow this, namely, the Millennium. Further proof that the "Harvest" referred to in Matt. 13:39 takes place at the end of *this* age, rather than at the end of time, is found in Rev. 14:14, 15, which synchronises. *After* Rev. 14 is fulfilled comes Rev. 20:1-6, which treats of the Millennium.

Let us note now the *order* of its procedure. "In the time of harvest I will say to the reapers, Gather ye together first the tares, and bind them in bundles to burn them: but gather the wheat into My barn" (v. 30). The tares are gathered into "bundles" *before* the wheat is actually garnered. In spite of their promising and attractive appearance, everything which has not sprung from the Seed sown by the Son of man is ultimately to be consigned to the everlasting burnings: as He Himself declared, "Every plant which My heavenly Father hath not planted, shall be rooted up" (Matt. 15:13). But what we would particularly direct attention to is the "gathering together" of the tares *into bundles*. There is no actual casting of them into the fire at this preliminary stage, no removal of them from the field. It is the separation of the tares *in* the field, so as to leave the "wheat" distinct, and ready for garnering. The wheat is gathered into the Barn *before* the tares are "burned"—sure proof of the removal of the saints from this scene *prior to* the descent of God's judgment on the world. The gathering of the wheat corresponds with 1 Thess. 4:16, 17.

As we survey current events in the light of Matt. 13:30 it is abundantly clear that the process of binding the tares into bundles is proceeding in various directions, and proceeding with amazing rapidity. In fact it is one of the most prominent of the "signs of the times."

Take the *commercial* world. The individual is fast becoming almost a nonentity, as most business men know to their sorrow. Co-operation, organisation, amalgamation, are the order of the day. Trusts, combines, syndicates, unions, are the "bundles" into which the interests of industry are now being bound. "Gather the tares into bundles": the Divine command has *already* gone forth!

Take the *social* world. Clubs, guilds, fraternities, are multiplied on every side. "Class distinctions" are more and more resented by the masses. Social barriers which have existed for centuries are rapidly being broken down; whilst in many countries, socialism and bolshevism—which aim at the destruction of *individual* enterprise—are seeking to gather all into one great State "bundle." Yes, the word "gather" the tares into bundles *has* already gone forth!

In the *ecclesiastical* sphere the same thing is equally noticeable and prominent. Interdenominational efforts and movements are multiplying. Only last week, in this city, on what is known as "good Friday," members and preachers from churches of four or five denominations met together, and held what they term the celebration of "the Lord's Supper"—and this in a church whose pastor is a pronounced modernist. What a farce! If some noted Evangelist comes to the city a "combined" meeting must be held. The unification of Christendom is the ideal of many, and the goal for which her leaders are aiming. Protestantism is virtually a spent force, and the hindrances and obstacles against the Papacy yet gathering all Christendom under her wings are rapidly disappearing. Those who understand prophesy know well that it will not be long ere she attains that ambition for which she has so long worked, and that one huge ecclesiastical "bundle" will be formed. Yes, the command to "gather" the tares *has* gone forth!

The same principle is more and more regulating the *diplomatic* affairs of the earth. The leading "Powers" are working increasingly in conjunction and co-operation. Witness the demands for concerted action in connection with the ultimatum to China. The League of Nations is another movement in the direction of forming one more great "bundle." Yes, my readers, unless we are blind—and blind we certainly are, if we *cannot* see it—the binding of the tares into "bundles" is already going on before our very eyes; it has not only commenced, but is far advanced. Prophecy is daily becoming history. The next thing will be the *removal of the* wheat!

Let us now draw a few practical conclusions from this parable. First, see here the *worthlessness* of "reform" efforts and movements. It is an idle dream that we can improve the world by gathering out noxious weeds—banish drunkenness and immorality, purify politics, etc. Men might as well attempt to purify the waters of the Dead Sea! The Lord has said, "*Let* both grow together till the harvest." Then do not waste your time on the cultivation of the tares. "Preach the Gospel!" are *our* marching orders!

Second, what a solemn warning is here against *unwatchfulness!* It was "while men slept" that the Enemy came and sowed his tares. Beware of sloth and the relaxation of vigilance. Remember the words of Christ to His disciples, "what I say unto you, I say unto all, *watch*" (Mark 13:37). Heed the warning of Rom. 13:11, 12—it is high time to awake out of sleep!

Third, mark Christ's *love* for His own. When forbidding the servants to root up the tares, He said "Nay, lest while ye gather up the tares, ye root up also the wheat with them" (v. 29). How much *He* must think of the "wheat": He had rather the "tares" grow, than that a single blade of the "wheat" be injured!

Fourth, how terrible is our Lord's description of the ultimate *doom of the wicked!* "And shall cast them into the furnace of fire: there shall be wailing and gnashing of teeth" (v. 42). The "Furnace of Fire" is no mere superstition of the "dark ages," but a dread reality, as multitudes now living will yet discover to their eternal misery. It is the *certain* portion of *all* who continue to reject the Lord Jesus Christ. It is unspeakably solemn to note that the most awe-inspiring descriptions of Hell, to be found anywhere in the Bible, came from the lips of Love incarnate! It is to be carefully noted that whilst Christ interpreted every *figure* in this parable, see vv. 38-40, the "fire" He did not explain. *It* is *literal!* O My reader, if you have not already done so, "Flee from the wrath to come" ere it be too late. Flee to Christ for refuge.

*Arthur W. Pink.*

N.B.—The writer has been helped on this parable by a booklet from the pen of Mr. P. Mauro.

## "THE CHURCHES OF GOD."

(1 *Thess.* 2:14.)

The ignorance which prevails in Christendom to-day concerning the truth about the Churches of God is deeper and more general than error on any other Scriptural subject. Many who are quite sound evangelically and are well taught on what we call the great fundamentals of the faith, are most unsound ecclesiastically. Mark the fearful confusion that abounds respecting the term itself. There are few words in the English language with a greater variety of meanings than "church." The man in the street understands by "church" the building in which people congregate for public worship. Those who know better, apply the term to the members in spiritual fellowship who meet in that building. Others use it in a denominational way and speak of "the Methodist Church" or "the Presbyterian Church." Again, it is employed nationally of the state-religious institution as "the Church of England" or "the Church of Scotland." With Papists the word "church" is practically synonymous with "salvatiion," for they are taught that all outside the pale of "Holy Mother Church" are eternally lost.

Many of the Lord's own people seem to be strangely indifferent concerning God's mind on this important subject. One from whose teachings on the church we differ widely has well said, "Sad it is to hear men devoted in the Gospel, clear expounders of the Word of God, telling us that they do not trouble themselves about church doctrine; that salvation is the all-important theme; and the establishing of Christians in the fundamentals all that is necessary. We see men giving chapter and verse for every statement, and dwelling upon the infallible authority of the Word of God, quietly closing their eyes to its teachings upon the church, probably connected with that for which they can give no Scriptural authority, and apparently contented to bring others into the same relationship."

*What constitutes* a New Testament church? That multitudes of professing Christians treat this question as one of trifling importance is plain. Their actions show it. They take little or no trouble to find out. Some are content to remain outside of any earthly church. Others join some church out of sentimental considerations, because their parents or partner in marriage belonged to it. Others join a church from lower motives still, such as business or political considerations. But this ought not to be. If the reader is an Anglican, he should be so, because he is fully persuaded that his is the most Scriptural church. If he is a Presbyterian, he should be so, from conviction that his "church" is most in accord with God's Word. So, if he is a Baptist or Methodist, etc.

There are many others who have little hope of arriving at a satisfactory answer to the question, What constitutes a New Testament church? The fearful confusion which now obtains in Christendom, the numerous sects and denominations differing so widely both as to doctrine and church-order and government, has discouraged them. They have not the time to carefully examine the rival claims of the various denominations. Most Christians are busy people who have to work for a living, and hence they do not have the leisure necessary to properly investigate the Scriptural merits of the different ecclesiastical systems. Consequently, they dismiss the matter from their minds as being one too difficult and complex for them to hope of arriving at a satisfactory and conclusive solution. But this ought not to be. Instead of these differences of opinion disheartening us, they should stimulate to greater exertion for arriving at the mind of God. We are told to "buy the truth," which implies that effort and personal sacrifice are required We are bidden to "prove *all* things."

Now, it should be obvious to all that there must be a more excellent way than examining the creeds and articles of faith of all the Denominations. The only wise and satisfactory method of discovering the Divine answer to our question, What constitutes a New Testament church? is to turn to the New Testament itself and carefully study *its* teachings about the "church." Not some godly man's views; not accepting the creed of the church to which my parents belonged; but "proving all things" for myself! God's people have no right to organise a church on different lines from those which governed the churches in New Testament times. An institution whose teachings or government are *contrary* to the New Testament is certainly *not* a New Testament "church."

Now if God has deemed it of sufficient importance to place on record upon the pages of Inspiration what a New Testament church *is*, then surely it should be of sufficient importance for every redeemed man or woman to study that record, and not only so but to *bow* to its authority and conform their conduct thereto. We shall thus appeal to the New Testament only and seek God's answer to our question.

1. *A New Testament church is a local body of believers.* Much confusion has been caused by the employment of adjectives which are not to be met with in the N.T. Were you to ask some Christians, To what church do you belong? they would answer, The great *invisible* church of Christ—a church which is as intangible as it is invisible. How many recite the so-called Apostles' Creed, "I believe in the holy *catholic* Church," which most certainly was *not* an article in the *Apostles'* "creed." Others speak of "the Church *militant*" and "the Church *triumphant*," but neither are these terms found in Scripture, and to employ them is only to create difficulty and confusion. The moment we cease to "hold fast the *form* of sound words" (II Tim. 1.13) and employ *un*scriptural terms, we only befog ourselves and others. We cannot improve upon the language of Holy Writ. There is no need to invent extra terms; to do so is to cast reflection on the vocabulary of the Holy Spirit. When people talk of "the *universal* Church of Christ" they employ another unscriptural and antiscriptural expression. What they really mean is "the Family of God." This latter appellation includes the whole company of God's elect; but "Church" does not.

Now the kind of church which is emphasised in the N.T. is neither invisible nor universal; but instead, visible and local. The Greek word for "church" is "ecclesia," and those who know anything of that language are agreed that the word signifies "An Assembly." Now an "asembly" is a company of people who *actually assemble*. If they *never* "assemble," then it is a misuse of language to call them "an Assembly." Therefore, as all of God's people *never have yet* assembled together, there is to-day no "universal Church" or "Assembly." *That* "Church" is yet future; as yet it has no concrete or corporate existence.

In proof of what has been said above, let us examine those passages where the term was used by our Lord Himself during the days of His flesh. Only twice in the four Gospels do we find Christ speaking of the "church." The first is in Matt. 16:18 where He said unto Peter, "Upon this Rock I will build My church, and the gates of hell shall not prevail against it." *What kind* of a "church" was the Saviour here referring to? The vast majority of Christians have understood it as, the great invisible, mystical, and universal Church, which comprises *all* His redeemed. But they are certainly wrong. Had *this* been His meaning He had necessarily said, "Upon this Rock *I am building* My church." Instead, He used the future tense, "I *will build*," which shows clearly that at the time He spoke, His "church" hod no existence, save in the purpose of God. The "church" to which Christ referred in Matt. 16:18 could *not* be a *universal* one, that is, a church which included *all* the saints of God, for the tense of the verb used by Him on this occasion manifestly *excluded* the O.T. saints! Thus, the *first* time that the word "church" occurs in the N.T. it has no reference to a general or universal one. Further, our

Lord could not be referring to the Church *in glory*, for *it* will be in no danger of "the gates of hell"! His declaration that, "the gates of hell shall not *prevail* against it," makes it clear beyond all doubt that Christ was referring to His church upon *earth*, and thus, to a visible and local church.

The only other record we have of our Lord speaking about the "church" while He was on earth, is found in Matt. 18:17, "If he shall neglect to hear them, tell it unto the church: but if he neglect to hear the church let him be unto thee as an heathen man and a publican." Now the *only* kind of a "church" to which a brother could relate his "fault" is a visible and local one. So obvious is this, there is no need to further enlarge upon it.

In the final book of the N.T. we find our Saviour again using this term. First in Rev. 1:11 He says to John, "What thou seest write in a book and send it unto the seven churches which are in Asia." Here again it is plain that the Lord was speaking of *local* churches. Following this, we find the word "church" is upon His lips nineteen more times in the Revelation, and in *every* passage the reference was to *local* churches. Seven times over He says, "He that hath an ear, let him hear what the Spirit saith unto the churches," *not* "what the Spirit saith unto *the Church*"—which is what *would* have been said had the popular view been correct. The last reference is in Rev. 22:16, "I Jesus have sent Mine angel to testify unto you these things in the churches." The reason for this being, that as yet, the Church of Christ has no tangible and corporate existence, either in glory or upon earth; all that He now has here is His local "churches."

In further proof that the kind of "church" which is emphasised in the N.T. is a local and visible one we appeal to other facts of Scripture. We read of "The church which was at Jerusalem" (Acts 8:1), "The church that was at Antioch" (Acts 13:1), "The church of God which is at Corinth" (1 Cor. 1:2)—note carefully that though this church is linked with, yet is it definitely distinguished from "all that in every place call upon the name of Jesus Christ our Lord"! Again; we read of "churches" in the *plural* number: "Then had the churches rest throughout all Judea, and Galilee, and Samaria" (Acts 9:31), "The churches of Christ salute you" (Rom. 16:16), "Unto the churches of Galatia" (Gal. 1:2). Thus it is seen that, that which was prominent and dominant in N.T. times was local and visible churches.

2. *A New Testament church is a local body of baptized believers.* By "baptized believers" we mean Christians who have been *immersed in water*. Throughout the N.T. there is not a single case recorded of any one becoming a member of a church of Jesus Christ without his first being baptized; but there are many cases in point, many indications and proofs, that those who belonged to the churches in the days of the apostles *were* baptized Christians.

Let us turn first to the last clause of Acts 2:47: "And the Lord added to the church daily such as should be (the V.R. correctly gives it *"were"*) saved." Note carefully it does not say that "God," or "the Holy Spirit," or "Christ," but *"The Lord* added." The reason for this is as follows: "The Lord" brings in the thought of *authority*, and those whom He "added to the church" had *submitted* to His lordship. The way in which they had "submitted" is told us in vv. 41, 42: "Then they that gladly received his word were *baptized;* and the same day there were *added* about three thousand souls," etc. Thus, in the earliest days of this dispensation, "the Lord added" to His church saved people who were baptized.

Take the first of the Epistles. Romans 12:4, 5 shows that the saints at Rome were a local church. Turn back now to Rom. 6:4, 5 where we find the apostle saying to and of these church-members at Rome, "Therefore *we* are buried with Him *by baptism* into death; that like as Christ was raised up from the dead by the glory of the Father, even so we also should walk in newness of life. For if we have been *planted together* in the likeness of His death, we shall be also in the likeness of His resurrection." Thus, the saints in the local church at Rome were baptized believers.

Take the church at Corinth. In Acts 18:8 we read, "Many of the Corinthians hearing believed, and were *baptized.*" Further proof that the Corinthian saints were baptized believers is found in 1 Cor. 1:13, 14; 10:2, 6. 1 Cor. 12:13 rightly translated and punctuated (we hope to deal with this passage separately in a future article) expressly affirms that entrance into the local assembly is by water baptism.

Ere passing to the next point let it be said that a church made up of baptized believers is obviously and necessarily a *"Baptist church"*—what else could it be termed? *This* is the name which *God* gave to the first man whom He called and commissioned to do any baptizing. *He* named him "John *the Baptist*." Hence *real* "Baptists" have no reason to be ashamed of or to apologise for the scriptural name they bear. If someone asks, Why did not the Holy Spirit speak of the "*Baptist* church at Corinth" or "The *Baptist* churches of Galatia"? We answer, for this reason: there was, at that time, no need for this *distinguishing* adjective; there were no other kind of churches in the days of the apostles but *Baptist* churches. They were *all* "Baptist churches" then; that is to say, they were all composed of scripturally-baptized believers. It is *men* who have invented all other "churches" (?) and church-names now in existence.

3. *A New Testament church is a local body of baptized believers in organised relationship.* This is necessarily implied in the term itself. An "Assembly is a company of people met together in organised relationship, otherwise there would be nothing to distinguish it from a crowd or mob. Clear proof of this is found in Acts 19:39, "But if ye inquire anything concerning other matters, it shall be determined in a *lawful assembly*." These words were spoken by the "town clerk" to the Ephesian multitude which was disturbing the peace. Having "appeased the people," and having affirmed that the apostles were neither robbers of churches nor blasphemers of their goddess, he reminded Demetrius and his fellows that "the law is open, and there are deputies," and bade them "implead one another." The Greek word for "assembly" in this passage is "ecclesia," and the reference was to the Roman court, i.e., an organisation governed by law.

Again, the *figures* used by the Holy Spirit in connection with the "church" are pertinent only to a local organisation. In Rom. 12 and in 1 Cor. 12 He employs the *human* "body" as an anology or illustration. Nothing could be more unsuitable to portray some "invisible" and "universal" church whose members are scattered far and wide. The reader scarcely needs to be reminded that there is not a more perfect organism on this earth than the human body—each member in its appointed place, each to fulfil its own office and perform its distinctive function. Again, in 1 Tim. 3:15 the church is called the "*house* of God." The "house" speaks of *ordered relationships*: each resident having his own room, the furniture being suitably placed, etc.

Further proof that a New Testament "church" is a local company of baptised believers in organised relationship is found in Acts 7:38, where the Holy Spirit applies the term "ecclesia" to the children of Israel—"the church in the wilderness." Now the children of Israel in the wilderness were a redeemed, separated, baptized, organised "Assembly." Some may be surprised at the assertion that they were baptized. But the Word of God is very explicit on this point. Moreover, brethren, I would not that ye should be ignorant, how that all our fathers were under the cloud, and all passed through the sea; and were all *baptized* unto Moses in the cloud and in the sea" (1 Cor. 10:1, 2). So, too, they were *organised;* they had their "princes" (Num. 7:2) and "priests," their "elders" (Ex. 24:1) and "officers" (Deut. 1:15). Therefore, we may see the propriety of applying the term "ecclesia" to Israel in the wilderness, and discover how its application *to them* enables us to *define* its exact meaning. It thus shows us that a New Testament "church" has its *officers*, its "elders" (which is the same as "bishops"), "deacons" (1 Tim. 3:1, 12), "treasurer" (John 12:6; 2 Cor. 8:19), and "clerk"—the "number of *names*" (Acts 1:15) clearly implies a register.

4. A New Testament church is a local body of baptized believers in organised relaionship, *publicly and corporately worshipping God in the ways of His appointment.* To fully amplify this heading would necessitate us quoting a goodly portion of the N.T. Let the reader go carefully through the book of Acts and the Epistles, with an unprejudiced mind, and he will find abundant confirmation. Attempting the briefest possible summary of it, we would say: First, by maintaining "the apostles' doctrine and fellowship" (Acts 2:42). Second, by preserving and perpetuating Scriptural baptism and the Lord's Supper: "keep the ordinances" as they were delivered to the church (1 Cor. 11:2). Third, by maintaining a holy discipline: Heb. 13:17; 1 Tim. 5:20, 21, etc. Fourth, by going into all the world and preaching the Gospel to every creature (Mark 16:15).

5. *A New Testament church is independent of all but God.* Each local church is entirely independent of any others. A church in one city has no authority over a church in another. Nor can a number of local churches scripturally elect a "board," "presbytery," or "pope" to lord it over the members of those churches. Each church is self-governed, compare 1 Cor. 16:3; 2 Cor. 8:19. By church-government we mean that its work is administrative and *not* legislative.

A N.T. church is to do all things "decently and in order" (1 Cor. 14:30), and its only authoritative guide *for* "order" is the Holy Scriptures. Its one unerring standard, its final court of appeal, by which all issues of faith, doctrine, and Christian living are to be measured and settled, is the Bible, and nothing but the Bible. Its only Head is Christ: He is its Legislator, Resourse, and Lord.

The local church is to be governed by what "the Spirit saith unto the churches." Hence it necessarily follows that it is altogether separate from the State, and must refuse any support from it. While its members are enjoined by Scripture to be "subject unto the higher powers that be" (Rom. 13:1), they must not permit any dictation from the State in matters of faith or practice.

The administration of the government of a N.T. church resides in its own membership, and *not* in any special body or order of men, either within or without it. A *majority* of its members decide the actions of the church. This is clear from the Greek of 2 Cor. 2:6, "Sufficient to such a man (a disorderly brother who had been disciplined) is this punishment, which was inflicted of many." The Greek for the last two words is "hupo ton pleionon." "Pleionon" is an adjective, in the comparative degree, and literally rendered the clause signifies *"by the majority,"* and is so rendered by Dr. Charles Hodge, than whom there have been few more spiritual and competent Greek scholars. Bagster's Interlinear renders it "by the greater portion," and the margin of the R.V. gives "Greek *the more."* The *definite article* obliges us to render it "by the more" or "by the majority."

To sum up. Unless you have a company of regenerated and believing people, scripturally baptised, organised on N.T. lines, worshipping God in the ways of His appointing—particularly in having fellowship with the apostles' doctrine and fellowship, maintaining the ordinances, preserving strict discipline, active in evangelistic endeavour—it is *not* a "New Testament church," whatever it may or may not call itself. But a church possessing these characteristics is *the only institution* on this earth ordained, built, and approved of by the Lord Jesus Christ. Hence, next to being saved, the writer deems it his greatest privilege of all to belong to one of *His* "churches." May Divine grace increasingly enable him to walk as becometh a member of it.

*Arthur W. Pink.*

N.B.—We have not attempted to be exhaustive, but simply to name what we believe the N.T. teaches as being the things which are fundamental in the constitution of "the churches of God." D.V., further articles will follow.

## DIVINE CHASTISEMENT.

### Heb. 11:11.

In the two sermons I preached on verse 10 we dwelt upon the comforting side of our subject, pointing out the advantages which chastenings are designed to confer and the blessings which they are calculated to produce. This morning the most searching aspect of our theme is before us. The word "afterward" should pierce and test each one of us. Have we not all passed through sorrow? Can we look back on the past without recalling seasons of deep and heavy affliction? Has no sword pierced our soul? no painful sacrifice been demanded of us? But do these experiences belong to the *past* in every sense? Have they gone, disappeared, without leaving any effects behind them? No! We are either the better or the worse because of them.

*What* fruit have they produced? Not all Christians improve their chastenings. Some are hardened, and others are soured thereby—they view life more bitterly, the lines of their mouths betray them. But with others, pride has been subdued, hearts have been melted, patience developed. O brethren and sisters, let each of us honestly face the question, *How* have afflictions and chastisements left us? *What* does the "afterward" reveal? After a season in the wilderness, after some financial loss, or some deep family trouble, are you still as worldly, proud, revengeful; are you still seeking refreshment from the broken cisterns of this world instead of from the true Fountain? There are three things in our text which we shall now ponder:

1. *The nature of chastisement.* From the standpoint of flesh and blood they are "grievous." The apostle acknowledges the very nature of afflictions to be painful and sorrowful, that is, "for the present"—while they continue, during the time we feel the smart of them. They produce painful and not pleasant emotions. They are intended to so do. They cannot serve the purpose for which they are sent without doing so. Read 1 Peter 1:6 and note that there is

not only a "needs be" for manifold trials, but *also* for "heaviness" therein! The reason for this is stated in our text: it is that the Christian may be "exercised" thereby. They are sent to shake us up from lethargy and sloth. God does not intend that we should *stoically* endure them. He makes our sufferings "grievous" so as to disturb our rest and drive us to our knees.

2. *The characters benefited.* Not all men are the gainers by afflictions; nor are all Christians. Many seek to flee from trials and troubles instead of being "exercised" thereby. Others are callous and do not yield: as v. 5 says, they "despise the chastenings of the Lord." There are some who imagine that, when visited with affliction, it is a display of courage if they refuse to be affected. They count it weakness to mourn over losses and weep over sorrows. But such an attitude is altogether un-Christian. Christ wept, and again and again we are told that He "groaned." Such an attitude is also foolish to the last degree, for it is calculated to counteract the very design of afflictions, and only calls for severer ones to break our proud spirits. It is no mark of weakness to acknowledge that we *feel* the strokes of an *Almighty* arm. It is the truest wisdom to humble ourselves beneath "the mighty hand of God." If we are among His people, He will mercifully compel us to acknowledge that His chastenings are not to be despised and made light of. He will—and O how easily He *can* do it—continue or increase our afflictions, until He *tames* our wild spirits, and brings us like obedient children into subjection to Himself. What a warning is found in Isa. 9:9, 10, "And all the people shall know, even Ephraim and the inhabitants of Samaria, that say in the pride and stoutness of heart, The bricks are fallen down, *but we will* build with hewn stones: the sycamores are cut down, *but we will* change them into cedars. *Therefore* the Lord shall set up the adversaries of Rezin against him, and join his enemies together." This means that because the people had hardened themselves under the chastening hand of God, instead of being "exercised" thereby, that He sent sorer afflictions upon them.

Now to be "exercised" means more than passive submissiveness. Mere resignation is not sufficient. Micah 6:9 says, "*Hear ye the rod.*" The "rod" *speaks* if we are willing to hear and attentive to listen. It tells us not to be occupied with the trials themselves, but to seek from their Sender the meaning and message of them; to look not at the rod, but at the Hand that wields it. To be truly "exercised" means to humble ourselves before God, for the conscience to be active in His presence. It means to diligently inquire of Him, with Job of old, "*Show me wherefore* Thou contendest with me?" (10:2). Ask, "What is there, Lord, in my life that Thou wouldest have me correct? Wherein have I grieved Thy Holy Spirit?" It involves an honest self-examination, a diligent scrutiny of our ways, and a condemning of those which are wrong. Careful investigation will often show that much of our supposed godly zeal and service is but the result of habit, or the imitating of some eminent saint, instead of really being rendered "unto the Lord." It means praying as in Psalm 139:23, 24.

The Greek word for "exercised" was borrowed from the gymnastic games. It had reference to the athlete *stripping* himself of his outer clothing. Thus, this word in our text is almost parallel with the "laying aside of every weight" in v. 1. If afflictions cause us *to be* stripped of pride, sloth, selfishness, a revengeful spirit, then "fruit" *will be* produced. It is only as we "improve" our chastenings that we are the gainers. The natural effects of affliction on an unsanctified soul is either to irritate or depress, which produces rebellion or sinking in despair. This is the result of hardness of heart and unbelief. Even with regard to the Christian it is true that only as he views them as proceeding from his Father in order to bring him into subjection, and as he is "exercised thereby," that he is truly profited.

Rightly viewed, afflictions are calculated to impress on us the evil of sin generally, and our own depravity particularly; and to show us the vanity of the world, the value of a good conscience, and the blessedness of God's peace ruling the heart. In times of ease and prosperity our tendency is to be careless and thoughtless. The reality and worth of spiritual things are in measure forgotten, and the enjoyment of temporal blessings takes the place of that happiness which comes alone from communion with God. But afflictions should make us see things as they really are: should prevent us saying "Peace, peace" where none is; and should make us fix our affection on heavenly things. Even the Christian is in daily danger of being more occupied with His gifts than with the Giver, of over-estimating the value of temporal mercies and under-rating our trials. Afflictions make us feel our frailty, and cause us to look away from the things seen, "which are temporal," to the things unseen, "which are eternal."

To be "exercised", then, means a searching of ourselves and our ways before God, and a resultant stripping off of sins and "weights." Remember there may be melting in the fire *without* the dross being removed. Even after a severe illness I may go right back again to the same sin or failure which brought it upon me. After a heavy loss in business, perhaps sent by God because I was too much engrossed therein, I may say, "I must work harder now to make it up." Thus, trials in themselves are not enough. We must *take to heart* our Father's lessons in them, so that there may be not only melting, but also a removal of that which He has shown us is dishonouring and grievous to Him. Of what have *you* been "stripped?" What have you seen that you must gladly give up?

I have already pointed out that the Greek word for "exercise" is taken from the gymnasium. Now, in the Greek gymnasium the training-master would challenge the youths to meet him in combat. He knew how to strike, how to wrestle. Many severe blows did these young combatants receive from him, but this was part of their education, preparing them for public appearances later on in the great national contests. The youth whose athletic frame was prepared for future contests, was he who stepped forward boldly to be *exercised* by his master. But he who shirked the task and declined to encounter the trainer received no good from him. So the Christian who sits still sulking, repining, fretting over his trials, brings forth *no* "peaceable fruit of righteousness." But if his attitude be, "Now is my time of trial: I will play the man, I will stir up my faith, lay hold on God and seek His strength," then "fruit" *will* result. Read 1 Tim. 4:7 and note that we are to exercise ourselves "unto godliness." It is only by such exercise that any of us will escape the snares mentioned in Heb. 12:5. To "despise" means to make light of, to grit our teeth and "get over it" as soon as possible, or to be comforted the way the worldling is. To "faint" means to sink under, which is the result of *not* being "exercised."

3. *The fruit produced.* "Nevertheless" is a contrastive word. It is used here to show that this fruit-bearing is not the natural or spontaneous effect of affliction. When metal is plunged into the furnace in order to be refined, the first thing that happens is that a *scum* comes to the surface. That is the *natural* effect of chastenings: they bring out the worst that is in us. It is not natural to love God *for* chastening me. To kiss the Hand that smites is more than natural, it is the product of grace. *This* is why the apostle says "nevertheless."

"Afterward." The fruit is not instantaneous. Many of us are grieved because we have to wait so long for the fruit to become visible. And, hope deferred maketh the heart sick. But "let patience have her perfect work." Remember how it is in the natural world: developed fruit does not appear on the trees within a few days of their being pruned. Then allow time for the "afterward" in the spiritual realm.

What is meant by "the peaceable fruit of righteousness?" If we took this expression by itself, it would signify the *effects of* righteousness, the fruit which righteousness itself brings forth. But in our text it is chastenings or afflictions which are specifically mentioned as producing this fruit. It is the Spirit's tranquilising and purifying of the heart, the commencement of heavenly blessings. I understand the phrase to be parallel with "the *first-fruits* of the Spirit" in Rom. 8:23—note the context there refers to suffering. "Righteousness" is parallel with "partakers of His holiness" in v. 10. It is called the "*peaceable* fruit" because it issues in the taming of our wild spirits, the quieting of our restless hearts, the more firmly anchoring of our souls. But this only comes when we truly realise that it is the Father's *love* which has afflicted us. May the Spirit of God grant us all "exercised" hearts so that we shall daily search ourselves, examine our ways and be stripped of all that is displeasing to Him.

Substance of a sermon preached by the Editor.

*Reader, do you not know of some fellow-Christians who would welcome this Magazine did they but know of it? If so, send us their names and addresses. Pray over this matter.*

## REJOICING OVER ELECTION.

*"Rejoice because your names are written in heaven"* (Luke 10:20).

The reference in our text is to the Lamb's book of life, in which is recorded the names of God's chosen and favoured people. This at once brings before us the glorious subject of Divine election, and tells us that it is a ground of the saints' joy. This is a truth of which we have no reason to be ashamed, and for which the true servants of God offer no apology.

There are those who say that Election is a *dangerous* doctrine, and that it is the part of wisdom for the pulpit to be silent thereon. But this is to impugn the wisdom of the Most High, and implies that He made a mistake in saying so much about it in His holy Word. In reality, it is a species of Romanism, which would withhold the Bible from the common people on the ground of its being a dangerous book.

There are others who say that we had better remain silent upon this doctrine because it stirs up contention and creates divisions. They tell us that if it be preached, it will drive some people away. I grant you that it does, and I for one am glad that it is so. The preaching of God's sovereign electing-grace acts as a flail to divide the wheat from the chaff. It is a great battering-ram against human pride, and therefore it raises the ire of the self-righteous. It is part of the children's bread upon which the "dogs" will not and cannot feed. God often uses its proclamation to bring to light the hidden things of darkness. It increases the love of the sheep for the Shepherd; but it angers and drives away the goats.

The doctrine of election is to be preached for many reasons. First, because it honours and glorifies God, giving Him His true place, and proving that He *is* the Giver "of every good and every perfect gift." Second, because it stirs up the hearts of the regenerate to fervently praise their God: "Praise the Lord; for the Lord is good: sing praises unto His name; for it is pleasant" (Psa. 135:3). Why? *"For* the Lord hath *chosen* Jacob unto Himself, Israel, for His peculiar treasure" (v. 4)! So in our text: saints are bidden to *rejoice* because their names are "written in heaven." So again, in 2 Thess. 2:13, we read, "But we are bound to *give thanks* alway to God for you, brethren beloved of the Lord, *because* God hath from the beginning *chosen you* to salvation, through sanctification of the Spirit and belief of the truth." Third, that the Lord's people may be brought to renounce all confidence in the flesh. Divine election leaves no room either for the religion or irreligion of the flesh. If we have confidence in the flesh Christ profits us nothing. The man who thinks he can be saved *apart from* God's election must have some confidence in the flesh, no matter how strenuously he may deny it in words. Shut out God's election and you must bring in the doings of the creature, and thus make salvation contingent upon man, and then it is *not* of grace alone. Let us now consider:

1. *The Blessedness of Election.*

This cannot be appreciated till we receive and believe what Scripture affirms concerning the lost condition of the natural man. Most, if not all, of the difficulties which people have in connection with God's election arise from their ignorance about or disbelief of the lost estate and total depravity of the sinner. Many seem to think that all which happened to Adam when he fell was to bruise his knee or break his little finger; instead of *killing* himself. As the result of their sin, our first parents *died spiritually,* and in consequence of this, each of their descendants was born into this world "alienated from the life of God" (Eph. 4:18).

Many who claim *to* believe in the total depravity of man really believe nothing of the kind. They allow that man is depraved, but not completely so, for they contend that his *will* has escaped the effects of the Fall. They do not believe with the apostle Paul that in the flesh "dwelleth *no* good thing" (Rom. 7:18), for they insist that there *is* something in the natural man which is capable of co-operating with God, capable of *responding* to His overtures of mercy, capable of "improving" the help of His Spirit. But a *dead* man is incapable of responding to anything, and Scripture repeatedly affirms that the sinner is spiritually "dead." But it is just *this* which so few really believe to-day. If they *did,* they would cease speaking of man's power to do what is good. If they did, they would pray more earnestly for God to do for sinners what they are *unable* to do for themselves. What a dead man needs is not "help," but *life,* and only God can bring forth from the grave of sin and death.

God's Word teaches that *all men* are by nature depraved and corrupt (Rom. 3:12). It teaches that there is *no* soundness in them (Isa. 1:6). It affirms that their very righteousnesses are but filthy rags (Isa. 64:6). It declares that they are destitute of even a spark of spiritual life (John 3:

3). Therefore do they love darkness rather than light (John 3:19). Therefore are their minds "enmity against God" (Rom. 8:7). Therefore are their hearts "deceitful above all things and desperately wicked" (Jer. 17:9). And, *all* men would *continue* thus until the end of time, did not all-mighty power and invincible grace intervene.

Election, then, is God's most merciful provision in view of an otherwise hopeless situation: "Except the Lord of Hosts had left us a seed, we had been as Sodom, and been made like unto Gomorrah" (Rom. 9:29). Had not God's electing love intervened *none* had been saved. In and of themselves none desire to be saved; instead, they wish to be left to go their own way. Scripture declares, "There is none that seeketh after God" (Rom. 3:11). That is final. If, then, there came a time when *you* were convicted of your need, found a desire in your heart for Christ, and earnestly sought Him, this was because God had wrought in you what He has not in others. Then give *Him* the glory for it.

2. *The Nature of Election.*

*It was from eternity.* "According as He hath chosen us in Him before the foundation of the world, that we should be holy and without blame before Him" (Eph. 1:4). I would press this point because there are some to-day that insist God does not elect till after we believe on His Son. But the Scriptures clearly and plainly teach otherwise. In Jer. 31:3 we find Jehovah saying, "I have loved thee with an everlasting love: therefore with loving kindness have I drawn thee." Again, in 2 Tim. 1:9 we read, "Who hath saved us, and called with a holy calling, not according to our works, but according to His own purpose and grace, which was given us in Christ Jesus before the world began."

*It was unto salvation.* As we are told in 1 Thess. 5:9, "For God hath not appointed us to wrath, but to obtain salvation by our Lord Jesus Christ." This also is denied by many. They say that God only elects unto temporal blessings, as in the case of the children of Israel; or unto official honours, as in the case of the apostles. But Scripture is very emphatic and explicit on this point also. In Acts 13:48 we read, "As many as were ordained to eternal life believed." And again, in 2 Thess. 2:13, "We are bound to give thanks unto God alway for you, brethren beloved of the Lord, because God hath from the beginning chosen you to salvation."

*It is of God's sovereign choice.* In Rom. 9:15 we are told that God has affirmed, "I will have mercy on whom I will have mercy, and I will have compassion on whom I will have compassion." There are those silly enough to say that we elect ourselves, but the whole tenor and teaching of Scripture is directly against them. As the Lord said unto His disciples, "Ye have not chosen Me, but I have chosen you" (John 15:16). God is ever the Chooser: see 1 Cor. 1:27-29. In this selection He is guided by nothing but His own imperial will: "Jesus answered and said, I thank Thee, O Father, Lord of heaven and earth, because Thou hast hid these things from the wise and prudent, and hast revealed them unto babes. Even so, Father: for so it seemed good in Thy sight" (Matt. 11:25, 26).

*It is of grace alone.* "Even so then at this present time also there is a remnant according to the election of grace" (Rom. 11:5). Therefore, if it be of grace, it could not be because of anything good which God had foreseen in the creature. Many say that God chose whom He did because He "foresaw" that they would believe. But here, again, Scripture definitely refutes the sophistries of men. "The children being not yet born, neither having done any good or evil, that the purpose of God according to election might stand, not of works, but of Him that calleth, it was said unto her, The elder shall serve the younger" (Rom. 9:11, 12). Even our believing is "through grace" (Acts 18:27)!

3. *The Justice of Election.*

There is a secret thought in the minds of many that God has not given the human race a square deal unless He provided salvation for every member of it. But how can this be? To what are guilty criminals *entitled?* If salvation be a just due which God *owes* to all His fallen creatures, then salvation would not be of "grace," nor could we really praise Him for it.

What salvation did God provide for the angels of Satan when they fell? None. Why not? Because it did not please God so to do. Did God treat them unjustly in not providing salvation for them? Certainly not. As rebels against Him, they had forfeited every claim upon their Maker. What, then, has any fallen son of Adam done which lays the Almighty under obligations of providing salvation for Him? *Wherein* will God be unjust in declining to so provide? If you complain that *you* were not a party to what Adam did, then repudiate his sin by honouring and serving

God: cease quarrelling with and rebelling against Him.

That the election of some *is* just, is proven by the fact that God *has* elected a remnant; for, whatsoever *He* does, is just. "Shall not the Judge of all the earth do right?" None has any right to say to Him, "What doest Thou?" To any who are so presumptuous as to challenge Him, the Most High says, "Nay but, O man, who art thou that repliest against God? Shall the thing formed, say to Him that formed, Why hast Thou made me thus? Hath not the Potter power over the clay, of the same lump, to make one vessel unto honour and another to dishonour?" (Rom. 9:20, 21). Certainly He has. We are but His creatures; *He* gave us being, therefore He has the indubitable right to dispose of each and all as He pleases.

Returning now to our opening text. "Rejoice, because your names are written in heaven," let us note how these words clearly imply that God's elect are privileged *to know* their election of Him; otherwise, how could they "rejoice" over it?

But *how* are they to thus "know?" First, by coming to Christ and receiving Him as the sinner's Saviour. This is clear from His own words in John 6:37: "All that the Father giveth Me, shall come to Me; and him that cometh to Me I will in no wise cast out." Thus each elect sinner obtains evidence of the Father's predestinating love by personally coming to His Son.

Second, by believing God's Word. This is brought out plainly in 2 Thess. 2:13, "God hath from the beginning chosen you to salvation, *through* sanctification of the Spirit *and* belief of the truth." The first part of this quotation declares the Divine end in view, the remainder makes known the appointed means by which this end is reached. This means is twofold. First, there is the "sanctification of the Spirit." The word "sanctification" signifies "setting apart." That which is here referred to is the sovereign action and all-mighty operation of the third Person in the Trinity, whereby He regenerates the heart and thus separates that individual from his fellow-creatures who are "dead in trespasses and sins." Second, by this regenerated individual's own "belief of the truth." Having been given a new heart, he now loves God's Word, he bows to its authority, he rests in simple faith upon its veracity, he believes it; not a part of it, but the whole of it. And thus he "sets to his seal that God is true" (John 3:33).

Third, by daily prayer. This is brought out in Luke 18:7, "Shall not God avenge His own elect which cry day and night unto Him?" God's children have many needs, and the Spirit within, who makes them conscious of these, causes them to make known their requests with thanksgiving. There are no dumb children in God's family: His own elect "cry unto Him day and night." Therefore is it said, in Rev. 8:3, that Christ, in His Angel-of-the-covenant character, adds His own fragrant merits and offers them with "the prayers of all saints upon the golden altar which was upon the throne." Thus a praying soul learns from the infallible Word of God that he is an elect soul. Let those who possess these evidences give heed to the text, and "*Rejoice* because your names are written in heaven."

Arthur W. Pink.

## CLOVEN TONGUES.
### Acts 2:1-11.

It will greatly enhance the grace of this lovely passage of Scripture to bear in mind what it was that rendered the cloven tongues necessary. In the eleventh chapter of Genesis we have the inspired record of the first grand effort of the children of men to establish themselves in the earth—to form a great association, and make themselves a name. And all this, be it remembered, without God. His name is never mentioned. He was not to form any part of this proud and popular scheme. He was entirely shut out. It was not a dwelling-place for God that was to be erected on the plains of Shinar. It was a city for man—a centre round which men were to gather.

Such was the object of the children of men, as they stood on the plain of Shinar. It was not, as some have imagined, to escape another deluge. There is not a shadow of foundation in the passage for any such idea. Here are their words: "And they said, Go to, let us build us a city and a tower, whose top may reach unto heaven: *and let us make us a name*, lest we be scattered abroad upon the face of the whole earth." There is no thought here of escaping another flood. It is sheer imagination, without any Scripture basis. The object is as plain as possible. It is precisely similar to all those great confederacies, associations, or masses of flesh, that have been formed on the earth, from that day to this. The Shinar Association could vie with any association of modern times, both in its principles and object.

But it proved to be a Babel. Jehovah wrote confusion upon it. He divided their tongues and scattered them abroad, whether they would or not; in a word, divided tongues were sent as the expression of Divine judgment upon this first great human association. This is a solemn and weighty fact. An association without God, no matter what its object, is really nothing but a mass of flesh, based on pride, and ending in hopeless confusion. "Associate yourselves, O ye people, and ye shall be broken in pieces" (Isa. 8:9). So much for all human associations. May we learn to keep clear of them! May we adhere to that one Divine Association, namely, the Church of the living God, of which a risen Christ in glory is the living Head, the Holy Spirit the living Guide, and the Word of God the living Charter.

It was to gather this blessed assembly that the cloven tongues were sent, in grace, on the day of Pentecost. No sooner had the Lord Jesus Christ taken His seat at the right hand of power, amid the brightness of heaven's majesty, than He sent down the Holy Spirit to publish the glad tidings of salvation in the ears of His very murderers. And, inasmuch as that message of pardon and peace was intended for men of various tongues, so the Divine Messenger came down prepared to address each "In his own tongue wherein he was born." The God of all grace made it plain—so plain that it cannot be mistaken—that He desired to make His way to each heart, with the sweet story of grace. Man on the plain of Shinar did not want God; but God, on the day of Pentecost, proved that He wanted man. Blessed forever be His holy name! God had sent His Son, and man had just murdered Him; and now He sends the Holy Spirit to tell man that there is pardon through that very blood which he had shed, for his guilt in shedding it. Matchless, marvellous, overwhelming grace! Oh! that it may subdue our hearts and bind us to Him who is, at once, its source, its channel, and the power of enjoyment! The grace of God has far outtopped all the enmity of man. It has proved itself victorious over all the opposition of the human heart, and all the rage of hell.

Thus, then, in Gen. 11 divided tongues were sent in *judgment*. In Acts 2 divided tongues were sent in *grace*. The blessed God of all grace would cause each one to hear of full salvation, and hear of it in those very accents in which his infant ears had hearkened to the earliest whisperings of a mother's love: "his own tongue wherein he was born." It mattered not whether the tongue were soft or harsh, refined or barbarous, the Holy Spirit would use it as the vehicle for conveying the precious message of salvation right home to the poor heart. If divided tongues had once been given to scatter in judgment, they were again given to gather in grace; not now round an earthly tower, but round a heavenly Christ; not for the exaltation of man, but for the glory of God.

In conclusion, we might add that Gen. 11, Acts 2, and Rev. 7:9-17 form a very lovely group of Scriptures. In the first, we see divided tongues sent in *judgment;* in the second, divided tongues given in *grace;* and in the third, divided tongues gathered in *glory*. Well may we say: "Thy testimonies are wonderful, therefore doth my soul love them."

*Waymarks in the Wilderness.*

---

*Numbers who have had "Studies in the Scriptures" during 1926 and 1927 will not receive them in 1928 unless they send us a line asking for them. All who want the Magazine are more than welcome to it.*

days in church literature," Isle of Harris, Scotland. "It has been my privilege to read and study your monthly Magazine with definite profit for nearly three years," China. "It is with joy and rejoicing that I write to you, thanking you for ever sending me your precious Magazine," Preacher in the U.S.A.

A Missionary in Spain writing to have his name added to our mailing list, says: "I have seen numbers 11 and 12 of your Studies in the Scriptures and find them very helpful." A Missionary in India says, "Permit me to thank you for sending me your monthly Magazine. I have been reading them with increasing pleasure and profit." A Missionary in Morocco writes, "Your Magazine means much to me here in my loneliness." A Missionary in Mexico says, "I get great help from your Magazine for my Class-work in the Seminary." A Missionary in Honduras writes, "Much in the Studies I am passing on to my Girls here." "Many thanks for your precious Magazine," an Armenian in Syria. "Studies have greatly helped me to grasp the blessed truth of God's Sovereignty," a Native of the Brit. W. Indies.

As more and more of the pulpits are "giving heed to seducing spirits and doctrines of demons" (1 Tim. 4:1), there is a rapidly growing need to reach God's starved people with the printed page. Subject to the will of God, we are most desirous of reaching thousands more of those who are asking for bread and getting naught but a stone—something which contains no nourishment, and which the children of God cannot digest. We are praying that the Lord will burden the hearts of our readers to share our yearning: that each one will prayerfully consider if there are not other Christians known to them whom they feel sure would enjoy this Magazine. If so, send us the names and addresses of such. Loan out your copies to likely ones. Tell them there is *no* charge for it. All of God's people are more than welcome to it.

Pray also for the Editor that the Holy Spirit may so teach him that he may be fitted to teach others. As the circulation increases, so does our responsibility. To mislead one soul is solemn and serious; to mislead thousands, unspeakably so. Supplicate the Throne of Grace daily that God will mercifully preserve us from all error, and guide us into all truth; above all, that He will use us to glorify Him and edify His people. Pray, too, that the Editor's wife may be given the needed strength for typing, etc., in addition to her household and church duties.

As we do not want to waste copies, we are anxious to know which of our readers desire this Magazine to be sent to them during 1928, D.V. Many to whom it has been sent during 1927 are strangers to us. If they wish to go on receiving it, will they kindly drop us a line to that effect: please note that letters from all countries outside the British Empire require a five cent stamp (2½d.). If we do not hear, we shall conclude that you do not want it. Will readers please note that this does not apply to those who received *before* 1926.

Will those in Australia who desire their 1927 copies to be bound, please take out the clips from each issue, write their names on every copy just below the month, and post to us with a money order for 2/6. About a month later, D.V., we will forward them back to you in bound form. Those who desire the earlier years, bound at 7/6 or $1.75 each, had better send for them at once, as they will soon be out of print. Will friends abroad kindly note that when sending us money they are to use *only* International money orders.

Beginning with the January issue of 1928 we shall start a series of expositions on the Epistle to the Hebrews, similar in style to those just concluded upon John's Gospel. The "Gleanings in Exodus" will be continued and, D.V., completed. In addition, we shall continue publishing summaries of the most important of the sermons we are preaching here in Sydney. Again we say, "Brethren, pray for." Again we ask that each interested reader will co-operate with us in enlarging our present very limited circulation. The Magazine is being sent to upwards of one hundred pastors, scattered through Australia, England, and the U.S.A.: pray that their ministry may be enriched through the instrumentality of this Magazine. "Studies" is also being sent to Missionaries in almost fifty foreign lands: they, too, need our prayers.

Thanking all the Brethren and Sisters for the financial and prayerful fellowship they have given us during another year, and with hearty Christian greetings, we remain,

Yours by God's Wondrous Grace,

V. E. and A. W. PINK.

www.ingramcontent.com/pod-product-compliance
Lightning Source LLC
Chambersburg PA
CBHW072019240426
43667CB00044B/1477